THE NEW CAMBRIDGE HISTORY OF

ISLAM

*

VOLUME I

The Formation of the Islamic World Sixth to Eleventh Centuries

Since the 1970s, the study of early Islamic history has been transformed by new methods and sources. Volume 1 of *The New Cambridge History of Islam*, which surveys the political and cultural history of Islam from its Late Antique origins until the eleventh century, brings together contributions from leading scholars in the field. The book is divided into four parts. The first provides an overview of physical and political geography of the Late Antique Middle East. The second charts the rise of Islam and the emergence of the Islamic political order under the Umayyad and the Abbasid caliphs of the seventh, eighth and ninth centuries, followed by the dissolution of the empire in the tenth and eleventh. 'Regionalism', the overlapping histories of the empire's provinces, is the focus of part three, while part four provides a fully up-to-date discussion of the sources and controversies of early Islamic history, including a survey of numismatics, archaeology and material culture.

CHASE F. ROBINSON, formerly Professor of Islamic History at the Faculty of Oriental Studies, University of Oxford, is currently Distinguished Professor of History and Provost at the Graduate Centre, the City University of New York. He is the author of *The Legacy of the Prophet: The Middle East and Islam, 600–1300* (forthcoming), *Islamic Historiography* (2003) and *Empire and Elites after the Muslim Conquest: The Transformation of Northern Mesopotamia* (2000).

THE NEW CAMBRIDGE HISTORY OF

ISLAM

The New Cambridge History of Islam offers a comprehensive history of Islamic civilisation, tracing its development from its beginnings in seventh-century Arabia to its wide and varied presence in the globalised world of today. Under the leadership of the Prophet Muḥammad, the Muslim community coalesced from a scattered, desert population and, following his death, emerged from Arabia to conquer an empire which, by the early eighth century, stretched from India in the east to Spain in the west. By the eighteenth century, despite political fragmentation, the Muslim world extended from West Africa to South-East Asia. Today, Muslims are also found in significant numbers in Europe and the Americas, and make up about one-fifth of the world's population.

To reflect this geographical distribution and the cultural, social and religious diversity of the peoples of the Muslim world, *The New Cambridge History of Islam* is divided into six volumes. Four cover historical developments, and two are devoted to themes that cut across geographical and chronological divisions – themes ranging from social, political and economic relations to the arts, literature and learning. Each volume begins with a panoramic introduction setting the scene for the ensuing chapters and examining relationships with adjacent civilisations. Two of the volumes – one historical, the other thematic – are dedicated to the developments of the last two centuries, and show how Muslims, united for so many years in their allegiance to an overarching and distinct tradition, have sought to come to terms with the emergence of Western hegemony and the transition to modernity.

The time is right for this new synthesis reflecting developments in scholarship over the last generation. *The New Cambridge History of Islam* is an ambitious enterprise directed and written by a team combining established authorities and innovative younger scholars. It will be the standard reference for students, scholars and all those with enquiring minds for years to come.

General editor

MICHAEL COOK, CLASS OF 1943 UNIVERSITY PROFESSOR OF NEAR EASTERN STUDIES, PRINCETON UNIVERSITY

VOLUME 1
The Formation of the Islamic World
Sixth to Eleventh Centuries
EDITED BY CHASE F. ROBINSON

VOLUME 2
The Western Islamic World
Eleventh to Eighteenth Centuries
EDITED BY MARIBEL FIERRO

VOLUME 3
The Eastern Islamic World
Eleventh to Eighteenth Centuries
EDITED BY DAVID O. MORGAN AND ANTHONY REID

VOLUME 4
Islamic Cultures and Societies to the End of the Eighteenth Century
EDITED BY ROBERT IRWIN

VOLUME 5
The Islamic World in the Age of Western Dominance
EDITED BY FRANCIS ROBINSON

VOLUME 6
Muslims and Modernity
Culture and Society since 1800
EDITED BY ROBERT W. HEFNER

Grants made from an award to the General Editor by the Andrew W. Mellon Foundation, and from the National Endowment for the Humanities RZ-50616-06, contributed to the development of *The New Cambridge History of Islam*. In particular the grants funded the salary of William M. Blair, who served as Editorial Assistant from 2004 to 2008.

THE NEW CAMBRIDGE HISTORY OF ISLAM

*

VOLUME I

The Formation of the Islamic World Sixth to Eleventh Centuries

*

Edited by

CHASE F. ROBINSON

CAMBRIDGE
UNIVERSITY PRESS

CAMBRIDGE
UNIVERSITY PRESS

University Printing House, Cambridge CB2 8BS, United Kingdom

One Liberty Plaza, 20th Floor, New York, NY 10006, USA

477 Williamstown Road, Port Melbourne, VIC 3207, Australia

314-321, 3rd Floor, Plot 3, Splendor Forum, Jasola District Centre, New Delhi-110025, India

79 Anson Road, #06-04/06, Singapore 079906

Cambridge University Press is part of the University of Cambridge.

It furthers the University's mission by disseminating knowledge in the pursuit of education, learning and research at the highest international levels of excellence.

www.cambridge.org
Information on this title: www.cambridge.org/9780521838238

First published 2010
6th printing 2016

A catalogue record for this publication is available from the British Library

Library of Congress Cataloging in Publication data
The new Cambridge history of Islam / general editor, Michael Cook.
p. cm.
Includes bibliographical references.
Contents : v. 1. The formation of the Islamic world, sixth to eleventh centuries / edited by Chase F. Robinson – v. 2. The western Islamic world, eleventh to eighteenth centuries / edited by Maribel Fierro – v. 3. The eastern Islamic world, eleventh to eighteenth centuries / edited by David Morgan and Anthony Reid – v. 4. Islamic cultures and societies to the end of the eighteenth century / edited by Robert Irwin with William Blair – v. 5. The Islamic world in the age of Western dominance / edited by Francis Robinson – v. 6. Muslims and modernity: culture and society since 1800 / edited by Robert Hefner.
ISBN 978-0-521-83823-8
1. Islamic countries – History. 2. Islamic civilization. I. Cook, M. A. II. Title.
DS35.6.C3 2008
909′.09767–dc22
2010002830

ISBN 978-0-521-83823-8 Volume 1 Hardback
ISBN 978-0-521-51536-8 Set of 6 Hardback Volumes
ISBN 978-1-107-45694-5 Paperback

Contents

PART IV
THE HISTORIOGRAPHY OF EARLY ISLAMIC HISTORY *623*

Illustrations

Plates

The plates are to be found between pages 658 and 659

Figures

Maps

Genealogies

Contributors

MICHAEL BONNER is Professor of Medieval Islamic History in the Department of Near Eastern Studies at the University of Michigan. His publications on *jihād* and the medieval Islamic frontiers include *Aristocratic violence and holy war: Studies on the jihad and the Arab–Byzantine frontier* (New Haven, 1996) and *Jihad in Islamic history: Doctrines and practice* (Princeton, 2006). His work on social and economic issues in the medieval Near East has resulted in several publications including *Poverty and charity in Middle Eastern contexts* (co-edited with Amy Singer and Mine Ener) (Albany, 2003).

MICHAEL BRETT is Emeritus Reader in the History of North Africa at the School of Oriental and African Studies, London. He is the author (with Werner Forman) of *The Moors: Islam in the West* (London, 1980); (with Elizabeth Fentress) *The Berbers* (Oxford, 1996); *Ibn Khaldun and the medieval Maghrib* (Aldershot, 1999); and *The rise of the Fatimids: The world of the Mediterranean and the Middle East in the fourth century of the hijra, tenth century CE* (Leiden, 2001).

PAUL M. COBB is Associate Professor of Islamic History at the University of Pennsylvania. He is the author of *White banners: Contention in ʿAbbasid Syria, 750–880* (Albany, 2001) and *Usama ibn Munqidh: Warrior-poet of the age of Crusades* (Oxford, 2005).

ELTON L. DANIEL is Professor in the Department of History, University of Hawaii at Manoa. His publications include *The political and social history of Khurasan under Abbasid rule 747–820* (Minneapolis, 1979) and *The history of Iran* (London, 2001). He has written several articles on ʿAbbāsid history and the *History* of al-Ṭabarī, among which are 'The "Ahl al-Taqaddum" and the Problem of the Constituency of the Abbasid Revolution in the Merv Oasis' (1996) and 'Manuscripts and editions of Bal'ami's *Tarjamah-yi Tarikh-i Tabari*' (1990).

FRED M. DONNER is Professor of Near Eastern History in the Oriental Institute and Department of Near Eastern Languages and Civilizations at the University of Chicago. He is the author of *The early Islamic conquests* (Princeton, 1981), *Narratives of Islamic origins* (Princeton, 1997) and *Muḥammad and the believers: At the origins of Islam* (Cambridge, MA, 2010). He has published a translation of a section of al-Ṭabarī's *History*, *The conquest of Arabia* (Albany, 1992), and numerous articles on early Islamic history.

TAYEB EL-HIBRI is Associate Professor in the Department of Near Eastern Studies at the University of Massachusetts, Amherst. His book *Reinterpreting Islamic historiography: Harun al-Rashid and the narrative of the Abbasid caliphate* (Cambridge, 1999) was awarded an Albert Hourani Book Award Honorable Mention at the 2000 Middle East Studies Association of North America Annual Meeting.

JOHN HALDON is Professor of History at Princeton University and a Senior Fellow at the Dumbarton Oaks Center for Byzantine Studies in Washington, DC. His publications include *Byzantium in the seventh century* (Cambridge, 1990), *Three treatises on Byzantine imperial military expeditions* (Vienna, 1990), *The state and the tributary mode of production* (London, 1993), *Warfare, state and society in Byzantium* (London, 1999), *Byzantium: A history* (Stroud, 2000) and *The Palgrave atlas of Byzantine history* (New York, 2006).

STEFAN HEIDEMANN is Hochschuldozent at the Institute for Languages and Cultures of the Middle East, Jena University. His publications include *Das Aleppiner Kalifat (AD 1261)* (Leiden, 1994) and *Die Renaissance der Städte* (Leiden, 2002). He has edited or co-edited *Raqqa II: Die islamische Stadt* (Mainz, 2003), *Sylloge der Münzen des Kaukasus und Osteuropas im Orientalischen Münzkabinett Jena* (Wiesbaden, 2005) and *Islamische Numismatik in Deutschland* (Wiesbaden, 2000).

R. STEPHEN HUMPHREYS is Professor of History and Islamic Studies at the University of California, Santa Barbara. His previous books include *From Saladin to the Mongols* (Albany, 1977), *Islamic history: A framework for inquiry* (Princeton, 1991), *Between memory and desire: The Middle East in a troubled age* (Berkeley, 1999) and *Muʿawiya Ibn Abi Sufyan: From Arabia to empire* (Oxford, 2006), along with numerous articles and essays on the history of medieval Syria and Egypt, Arabic historiography, and a variety of other topics.

HUGH KENNEDY is Professor of Arabic at the School of Oriental and African Studies, University of London. He is the author of numerous books on Islamic history, including *The Prophet and the age of the caliphates* (London, 1986; new edn Harlow, 2004), *The court of the caliphs* (London, 2004) and *The great Arab conquests* (London, 2007).

ELLA LANDAU-TASSERON is Professor at the Institute for Asian and African Studies at the Hebrew University. She translated and annotated al-Ṭabarī's *Dhayl al-mudhayyal, Biographies of companions and their successors* (Albany, 1998), and has also written on Islamic historiography, *ḥadīth*, Arabian tribal society and Islamic warfare.

MICHAEL LECKER is Professor at the Institute of Asian and African Studies at the Hebrew University. His publications include *Jews and Arabs in pre- and early Islamic Arabia* (Aldershot, 1998), *'The Constitution of Medina': Muhammad's first legal document* (Princeton, 2004) and *People, tribes and society in Arabia around the time of Muhammad* (Aldershot, 2005).

EDUARDO MANZANO MORENO is Research Professor at the Instituto de Historia of the Centro de Ciencias Humanas y Sociales (CSIC-Madrid). He is the author of *Conquistadores, emires y califas: Los Omeyas y la formación de al-Andalus* (Barcelona, 2006), *Historia de las sociedades musumanas en la Edad Media* (Madrid, 1993) and *La frontera de al-Andalus en época de los Omeyas* (Madrid, 1991).

MARCUS MILWRIGHT is Associate Professor of Islamic Art and Archaeology in the Department of History in Art at the University of Victoria, Canada. He is the author of *The fortress of the raven: Karak in the middle Islamic period (1100–1650)* (Leiden, 2008) and *An introduction to Islamic archaeology* (Edinburgh, forthcoming).

CHASE F. ROBINSON is Distinguished Professor of History and Provost of the Graduate Center, The City University of New York. He is the author of *Abd al-Malik* (Oxford, 2005), *Islamic historiography* (Cambridge, 2003) and *Empire and elites after the Muslim conquest: The transformation of northern Mesopotamia* (Cambridge, 2000), amongst other edited volumes and articles on early Islamic history.

MARK WHITTOW is University Lecturer in Bytantine Studies at the University of Oxford, and a Fellow of Corpus Christi College, Oxford. His publications on the history and archaeology of the Late Antique and medieval world include *The making of orthodox Byzantium, 600–1025* (Basingstoke, 1996), 'Recent research on the Late Antique city in Asia Minor: The second half of the 6th c. revisited' (2001) and 'Ruling the late Roman and early Byzantine city: A continuous history' (1990). He has carried out field work in Turkey and Jordan.

JOSEF WIESEHÖFER is Professor of Ancient History at the University of Kiel and director of its Department of Classics. His publications on early Persian history include *Das antike Persien von 550 v.Chr. bis 651 n.Chr.* (Zurich and Munich, 1994; 4th edn 2005, trans. as *Ancient Persia: From 550 BC to 650 AD* (London, 1996; 2nd edn 2001)), *Das frühe Persien* (3rd edn, Munich, 2006), (ed.) *Das Partherreich und seine Zeugnisse – The Arsacid Empire: Sources and documentation* (Stuttgart, 1998), *Iraniens, Grecs et Romains* (Paris, 2005) and (ed.), *Ērān und Anērān: Studien zu den Beziehungen zwischen dem Sasanidenreich und der Mittelmeerwelt* (Stuttgart, 2006).

A note on transliteration and pronunciation

Since many of the languages used by Muslims are written in the Arabic or other non-Latin scripts, these languages appear in transliteration. The transliteration of Arabic and Persian is based upon the conventions used by *The encyclopaedia of Islam*, second edition, with the following modifications. For the fifth letter of the Arabic alphabet (*jīm*), *j* is used (not *dj*), as in *jumla*. For the twenty-first letter (*qāf*), *q* is used (not *ḳ*), as in *qāḍī*. Digraphs such as *th*, *dh*, *gh*, *kh* and *sh* are not underlined. For terms and names in other languages, the individual chapter contributors employ systems of transliteration that are standard for those languages. Where there are well-accepted Anglicised versions of proper nouns or terms (e.g. Baghdad, Mecca), these are used instead of strict transliterations.

As far as the pronunciation of Arabic is concerned, some letters can be represented by single English letters that are pronounced much as they are in English (*b*, *j*, *f*, etc.); one exception is *q*, which is a 'k' sound produced at the very back of the throat, and another is the 'r', which is the 'flap' of the Spanish 'r'. Others are represented by more than one letter. Some of these are straightforward (*th*, *sh*), but others are not (*kh* is pronounced like 'j' in Spanish, *gh* is similar to the uvular 'r' of most French speakers, and *dh* is 'th' of 'the', rather than of 'thing'). There are also pairs of letters that are distinguished by a dot placed underneath one of them: thus *t*, *s*, *d*, *z* and their 'emphatic' counterparts *ṭ*, *ṣ*, *ḍ*, and *ẓ*, and which give the surrounding vowels a thicker, duller sound (thus *s* 'sad', but *ṣ* 'sun'); *ẓ* may also be pronounced as *dh*.

The ʾ is the *hamza*, the glottal stop, as in the Cockney 'bu'er' ('butter'); the ʿ is the *ʿayn*, a voiced pharyngeal fricative that can be left unpronounced, which is what many non-Arab speakers do when it occurs in Arabic loan-words; and the *ḥ* a voiceless pharyngeal fricative that can be pronounced as an 'h' in all positions, just as non-Arabs do in Arabic loanwords. Doubled consonants are lengthened, as in the English 'hot tub'.

The vowels are written as *a*, *i*, and *u*, with *ā*, *ī* and *ū* signifying longer versions; thus *bit* and *beat*. *W* and *y* can function as either consonants or, when preceded by a short vowel, as part of a diphthong.

Persian uses the same alphabet as Arabic, with four extra letters: *p*, *ch*, *zh* (as in 'pleasure') and *g* (always hard, as in 'get').

A note on dating

The Islamic calendar is lunar, and divided into twelve months of twenty-nine or thirty days each: Muḥarram, Ṣafar, Rabīʿ I, Rabīʿ II, Jumādā I, Jumādā II, Rajab, Shaʿbān, Ramaḍān (the month of the fast), Shawwāl, Dhū al-Qaʿda, and Dhū al-Ḥijja (the month of the Pilgrimage). Years are numbered from the *hijra* ('emigration') of the Prophet Muḥammad from Mecca to Yathrib (Medina), conventionally dated to 16 July 622 of the Common (or Christian) Era; this dating is known as *hijrī*, and marked by 'AH'. As the lunar year is normally eleven days shorter than the solar year, the Islamic months move in relation to the solar calendar, and *hijrī* years do not correspond consistently with Western ones; AH 1429, for example, both started and finished within 2008 CE (so indicated as '1429/2008'), but this is exceptional, and most overlap with two Common Era years, and so '460/1067f.'.

Chronology

224	Defeat of the Parthian king Artabanus V by Ardashīr I; Sasanian dynasty takes power in Iran
260	Shāpūr I's victory at Edessa; capture of the Roman emperor Valerian
284–301	Reign of Emperor Diocletian; Roman army is enlarged and administration reformed
298	'Peace of disgrace' concluded between Romans and Sasanians
306–37	Emperor Constantine I; conversion of the Roman empire to Christianity
363	Emperor Julian's Persian expedition
378	Catastrophic Roman defeat by the Goths at Adrianople
387	Partition of Armenia
410	Rome is sacked by the Goths, led by Alaric
439	Vandals conquer Carthage
484	Shāh Fīrūz is defeated by the Hepthalites
527–65	Reign of Justinian; administrative reforms and military victories
528–9	al-Ḥārith ibn Jabala made supreme phylarch by Justinian
531–79	Reign of Shāh Khusrau I; social, economic and administrative reforms undertaken
540	'Eternal peace' between Romans and Sasanians, agreed in 532, is broken by Khusrau
572	Sasanian advance into southern Arabia
c. 575	Birth of Muḥammad in Mecca
602	Assassination of the last Lakhmid ruler Nuʿmān III

603–28	Last great war between Romans and Sasanians, the latter occupying Syria and Egypt
610–41	Reign of Emperor Heraclius
c. 610	Muḥammad delivers first revelations in Mecca
1/622	The 'Emigration' (*hijra*) of Muḥammad and his followers from Mecca to Medina
628	The Sasanian shah Khusrau is murdered; civil war in Ctesiphon ensues
630	Emperor Heraclius restores True Cross to Jerusalem
11/632	Death of Muḥammad in Medina
11–13/632–4	Reign of first caliph, Abū Bakr; the 'wars of apostasy' break out
13–23/634–44	Reign of second caliph, ʿUmar ibn al-Khaṭṭāb: conquest of north-east Africa, the Fertile Crescent and the Iranian Plateau
23–35/644–56	Reign of third caliph, ʿUthmān
31/651	Assassination of the last Sasanian king, Yazdegerd III, at Marw
35/656	First civil war (*fitna*) begins, triggered by the assassination of ʿUthmān; the battle of the Camel
35–40/656–61	Reign of ʿAlī ibn Abī Ṭālib, which ends with his assassination
41–60/661–80	Reign of the (Sufyānid) Umayyad Muʿāwiya ibn Abī Sufyān
61/680	Killing of al-Ḥusayn, the Prophet's grandson, at Karbalāʾ by Umayyad forces
64–73/683–92	Second civil war: the Sufyānids fall, Ibn al-Zubayr rules the caliphate from Mecca and the Marwānid Umayyads come to power
73–86/692–705	Reign of ʿAbd al-Malik ibn Marwān
79/698	Conquest of Carthage
86–96/705–15	Reign of al-Walīd, first of four sons of ʿAbd al-Malik to rule; Qutayba ibn Muslim leads conquests in Transoxania and Central Asia
92/711	Ṭāriq ibn Ziyād crosses the Strait of Gibraltar, and Iberia soon falls to Muslims
98–9/716–17	Failed siege of Constantinople

99–101/717–20	Reign of ʿUmar II, later considered the fifth of the 'rightly guided' caliphs
101–2/720	Revolt of Yazīd ibn al-Muhallab
104/723	Muslim campaigns beyond the Indus
106/724	Muslim defeat in Transoxania on the 'Day of Thirst'; Muslims now on defensive in the east
114/732	Muslim army defeated near Poitiers by Charles Martel
122/740	Berber revolt; Umayyad authority dissolves in North Africa and Spain; revolt led by Zayd ibn ʿAlī, a grandson of al-Ḥusayn
127–32/744–50	Reign of Marwān II, last Umayyad caliph
129/747	Abū Muslim leads the Hāshimiyya in rebellion, conquering Marw in early 130/748
132/749	The ʿAbbāsid Abū al-ʿAbbās acclaimed as caliph in Kūfa
132/750	Umayyad caliphate falls to ʿAbbāsid–Hāshimī armies; Marwān killed in Egypt
132–7/750–4	Umayyad counter-revolts in Syria and al-Jazīra
136–58/756–75	Reign of al-Manṣūr; Abū Muslim is murdered
137/754	Revolt of ʿAbd Allāh ibn ʿAlī, ʿAbbāsid governor of Syria
145/762	Rebellion of the ʿAlid Muḥammad, 'the Pure Soul'; construction of Baghdad begins
170–93/786–809	Reign of Hārūn al-Rashīd
170–80/786–96	'Decade of the Barmakids'; vizieral family dominate ʿAbbāsid administration and culture
180–92/796–808	Hārūn al-Rashīd makes al-Raqqa his capital
193–8/809–13	Civil war between Hārūn's two sons, al-Amīn and al-Maʾmūn; Baghdad besieged
198–218/813–33	Reign of al-Maʾmūn; large numbers of Turkish slave-soldiers are introduced into the army from the 820s
206/821	Appointment of Ṭāhir ibn al-Ḥusayn as governor of Khurāsān; beginning of Ṭāhirid rule
218–27/833–42	Reign of al-Muʿtaṣim; caliphal court is moved to Sāmarrāʾ, where it remains until 892
218–37/833–52	The *miḥna*: the caliphs impose the doctrine of the 'createdness' of the Qurʾān

232/847	Turkish commanders participate in council to decide caliphal succession
232–47/847–61	Reign of al-Mutawakkil: intensive building in Sāmarrā', struggles with the Turkish commanders
247/861	Al-Mutawakkil is murdered in Sāmarrā'
251/865	Civil war in Iraq between al-Musta'īn and al-Mu'tazz
254/868	Ibn Ṭūlūn arrives in Egypt and begins to establish his rule there
255/869	Outbreak of Zanj revolt in southern Iraq
262/876	Ya'qūb the Coppersmith is defeated near Baghdad
270/883	Defeat of the Zanj in the swamps of southern Iraq
295/908	Accession of al-Muqtadir to the caliphate, followed by the revolt of Ibn al-Mu'tazz
297/909	The Fāṭimid 'Abd Allāh the *mahdī* is declared caliph in North Africa
309/922	Execution of the mystic al-Ḥallāj
317/930	The Qarāmiṭa attack Mecca and seize the Black Stone
320/932	Death of al-Muqtadir
323/935	Death of Mardāvīj ibn Ziyār, warlord of northern Iran
324/936	Ibn Rā'iq becomes *amīr al-umarā'* in Baghdad
334/946	Aḥmad ibn Būya Mu'izz al-Dawla enters Baghdad; end of the independent 'Abbāsid caliphate
350/961	'Alī ibn Mazyad al-Asadī establishes Mazyadid rule in Ḥilla and central Iraq
366/977	Sebüktegin seizes power in Ghazna
367–72/978–83	Rule of the Būyid 'Aḍud al-Dawla in Iraq
380/990	al-Ḥasan ibn Marwān establishes Marwānid rule in Mayyāfāriqīn and Amida
381–422/991–1031	Reign of al-Qādir, resurgence of 'Abbāsid authority
389/999	Ghaznavids secure power in Khurāsān
420/1029	Issuing of the 'Qādirī creed' by the caliph al-Qādir; Maḥmūd of Ghazna takes Rayy and ends Būyid rule there
421/1030	Death of Maḥmūd of Ghazna
440/1048	End of Būyid rule in Baghdad
442/1050	Death of Qirwāsh ibn Muqallad al-'Uqaylī

Abbreviations

BAR	British Archaeological Reports
BASOR	*Bulletin of the American Schools of Oriental Research*
BGA	Bibliotheca Geographorum Arabicorum
BSOAS	*Bulletin of the School of Oriental and African Studies*
CII	Corpus Inscriptionum Iranicarum
CSCO	Corpus Scriptorum Christianorum Orientalium
EI2	*Encyclopaedia of Islam*, 2nd edn, 12 vols., Leiden, 1960–2004
EIr	*Encyclopaedia Iranica*, London and Boston, 1982–
IJMES	*International Journal of Middle East Studies*
JA	*Journal Asiatique*
JAOS	*Journal of the American Oriental Society*
JESHO	*Journal of the Economic and Social History of the Orient*
JNES	*Journal of Near Eastern Studies*
JRAS	*Journal of the Royal Asiatic Society*
JSAI	*Jerusalem Studies in Arabic and Islam*
JSS	*Journal of Semitic Studies*
MW	*Muslim World*
OrOcc	Oriens et Occidens
REI	*Revue des études islamiques*
RSO	*Rivista degli Studi Orientali*
SI	*Studia Islamica*
ZDMG	*Zeitschrift der Deutschen Morgenländischen Gesellschaft*

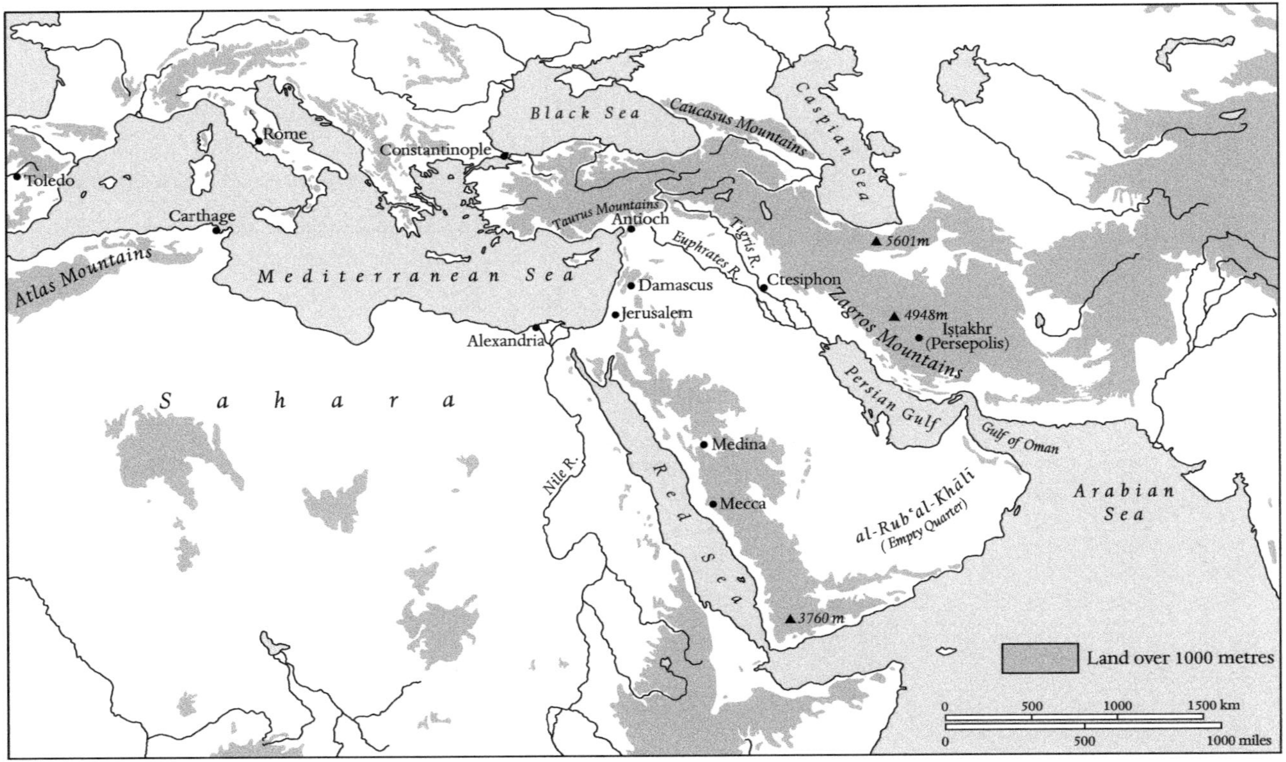

1. The physical geography of the Mediterranean and Near Eastern world

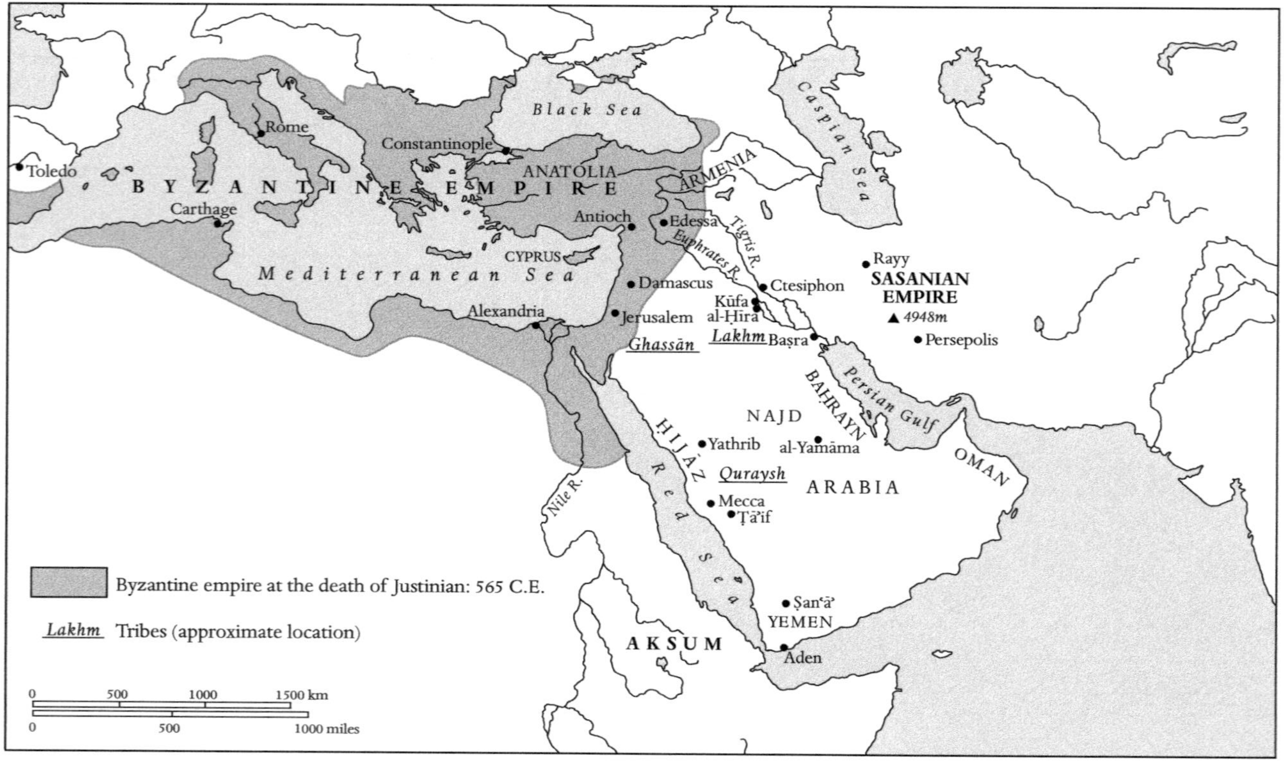

2. The political geography of the Mediterranean and Near Eastern world, *c.* 575

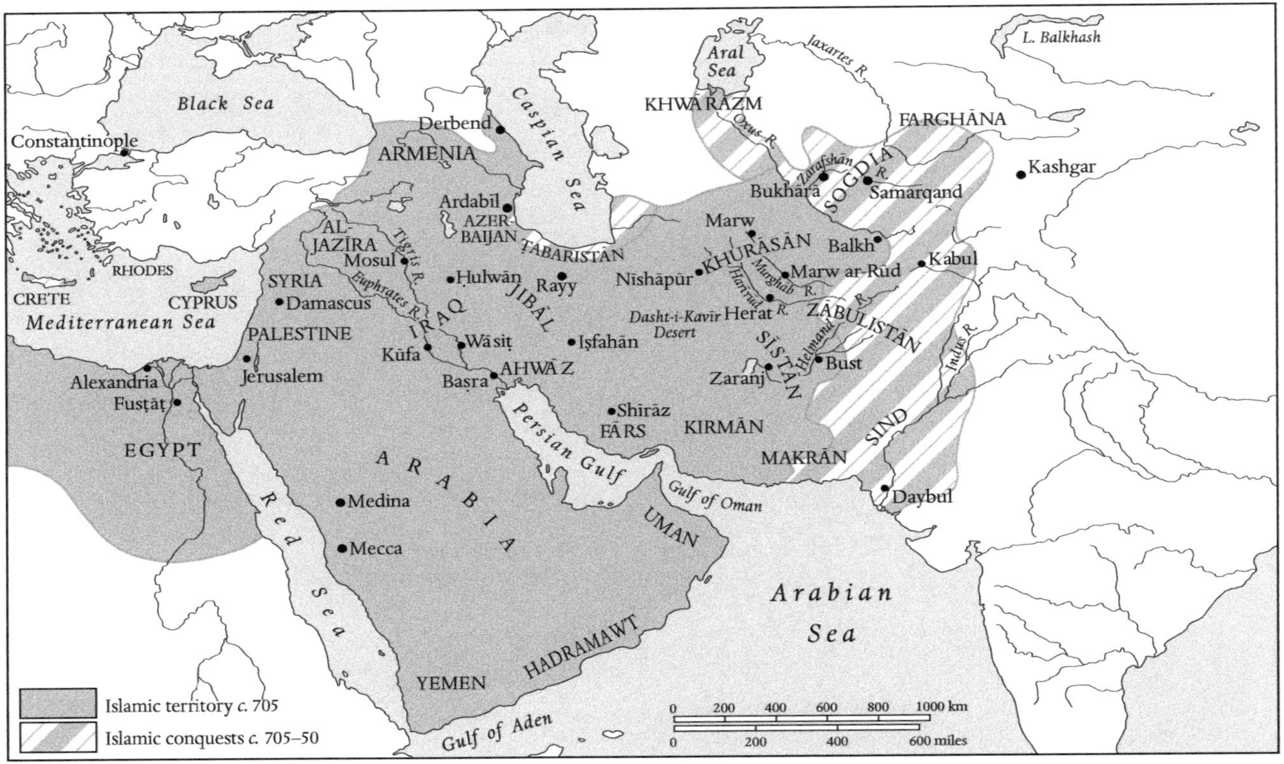

3. The expansion of Islam in the east

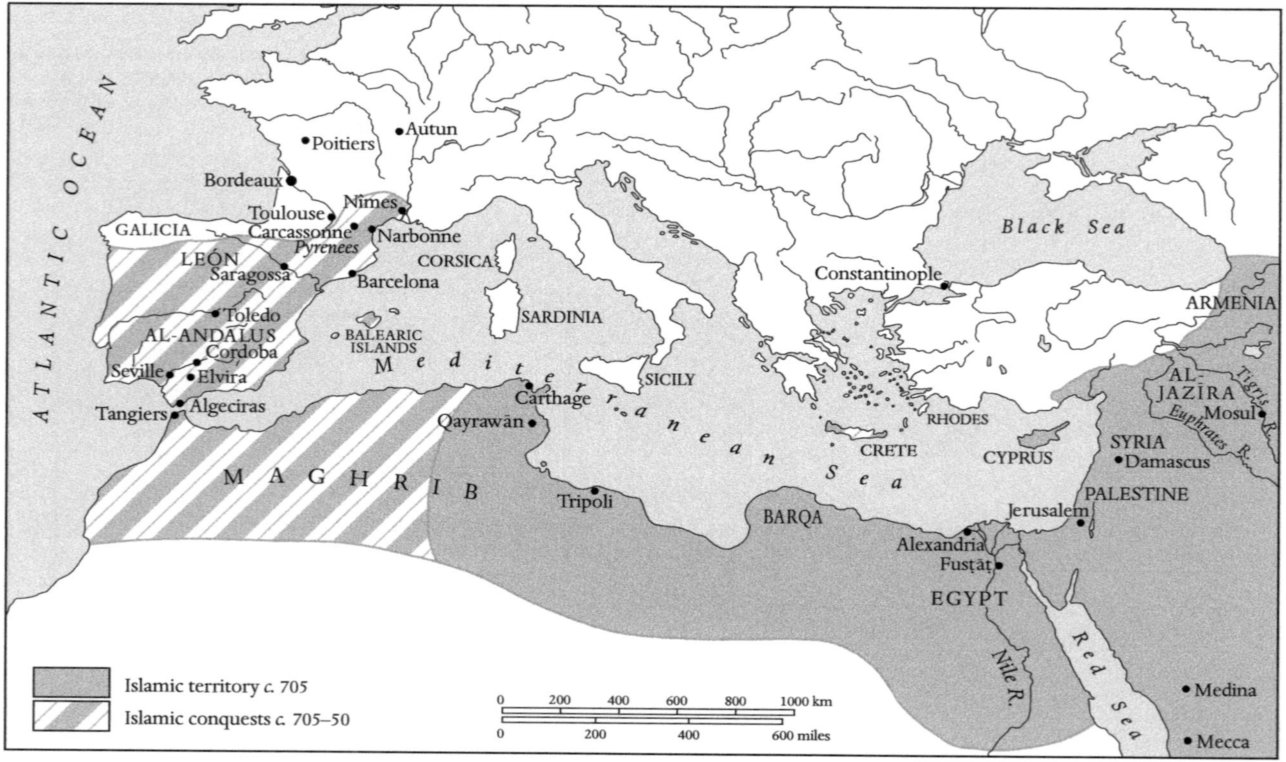

4. The expansion of Islam in the west

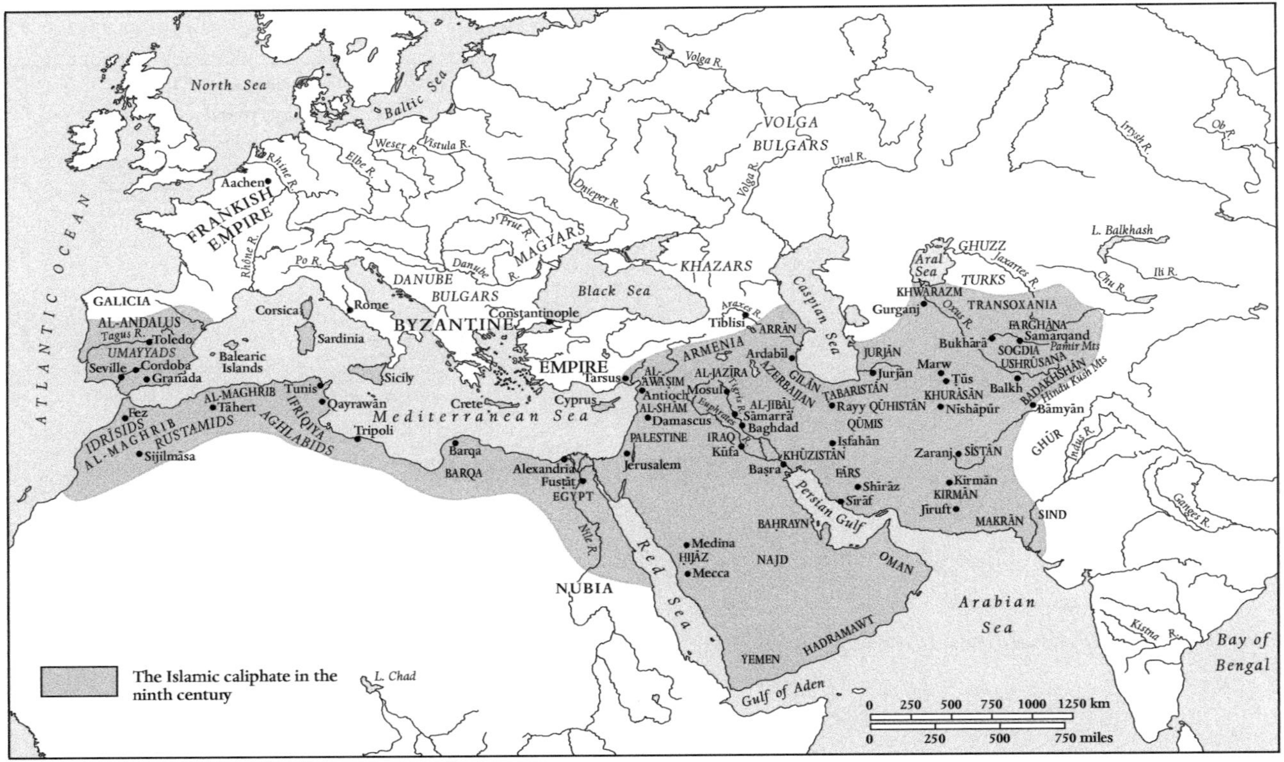

5. The ʿAbbāsid empire in *c.* 800

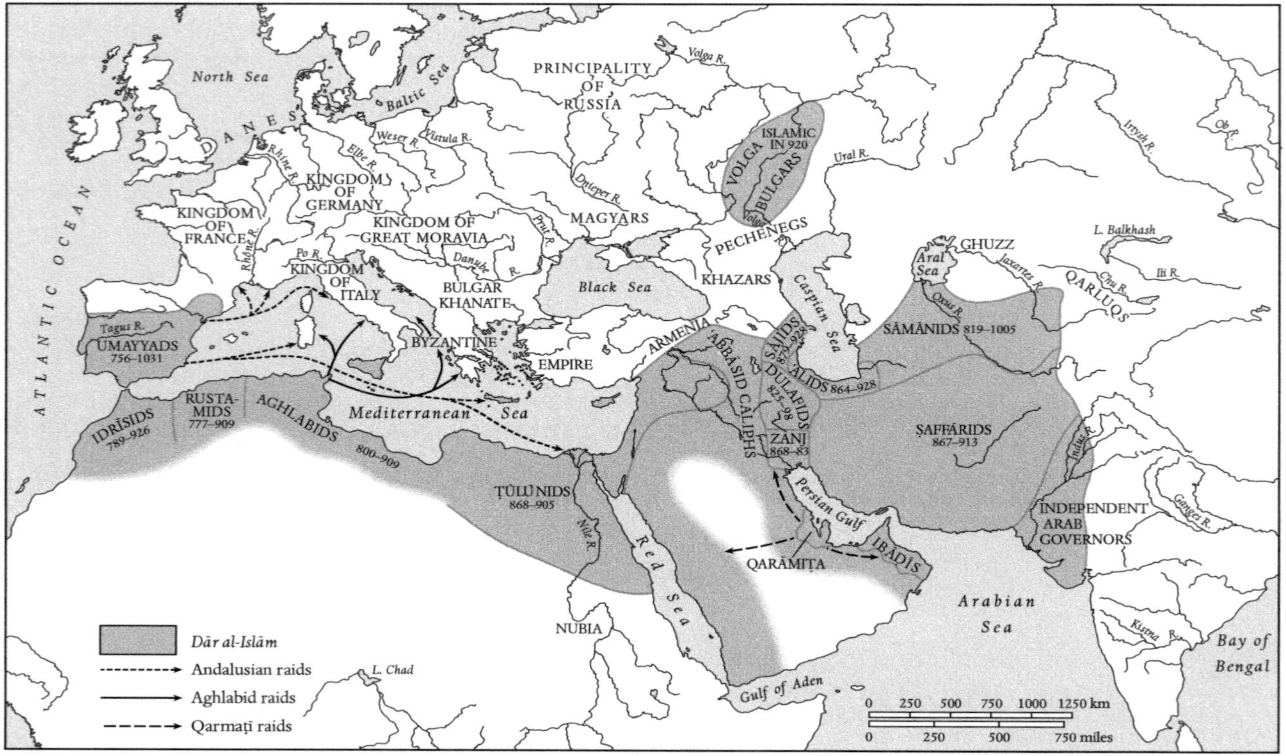

6. The Islamic world in *c.* 950

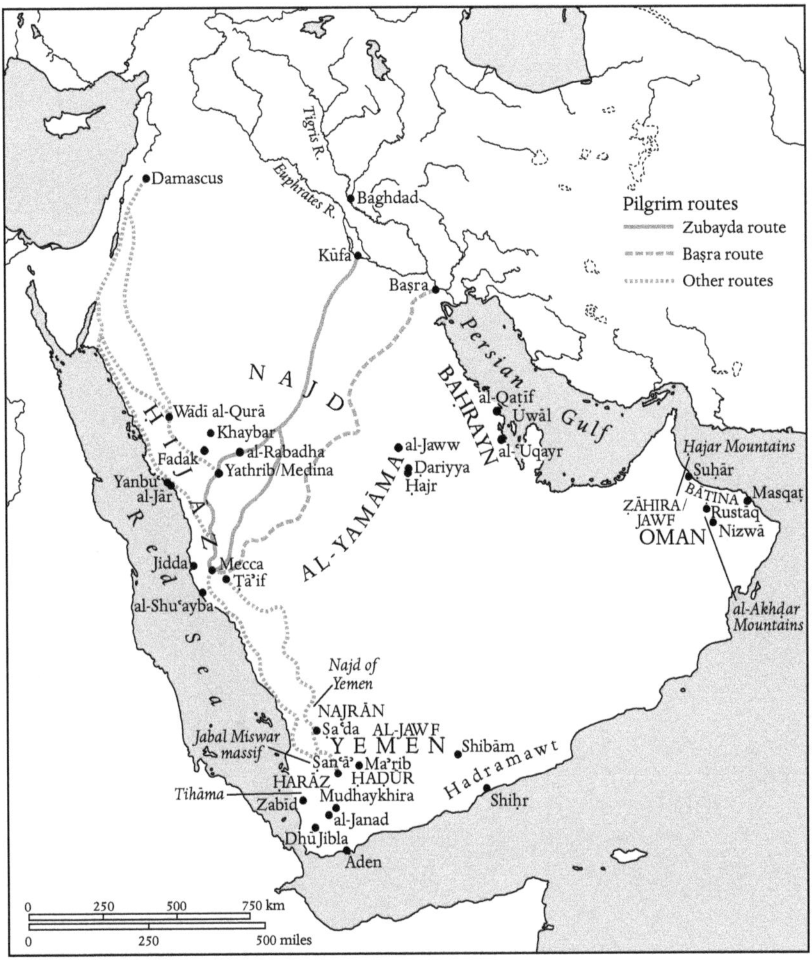

Tigris R.
Euphrates R.
Damascus
Baghdad
Kūfa
Baṣra
Pilgrim routes
Zubayda route
Baṣra route
Other routes
Persian Gulf
NAJD
BAḤRAYN
al-Qaṭīf
Uwāl
al-ʿUqayr
ḤIJĀZ
Wādī al-Qurā
Khaybar
al-Rabadha
Fadak
Yathrib/Medina
Yanbuʿ
al-Jār
al-Jaww
Ḍariyya
Ḥajr
AL-YAMĀMA
Hajar Mountains
Ṣuḥār
BĀṬINA
Masqaṭ
ẒĀHIRA/
JAWF
Rustāq
Nizwā
OMAN
Jidda
Mecca
Ṭāʾif
al-Shuʿayba
Red Sea
al-Akhḍar
Mountains
Najd of
Yemen
NAJRĀN
Ṣaʿda
AL-JAWF
YEMEN
Shibām
Jabal Miswar
massif
Ṣanʿāʾ
Maʾrib
ḤARĀZ
ḤAḌŪR
Tihāma
Zabīd
Mudhaykhira
al-Janad
Dhū Jibla
Aden
Hadramawt
Shiḥr
0 250 500 750 km
0 250 500 miles

7. Arabia

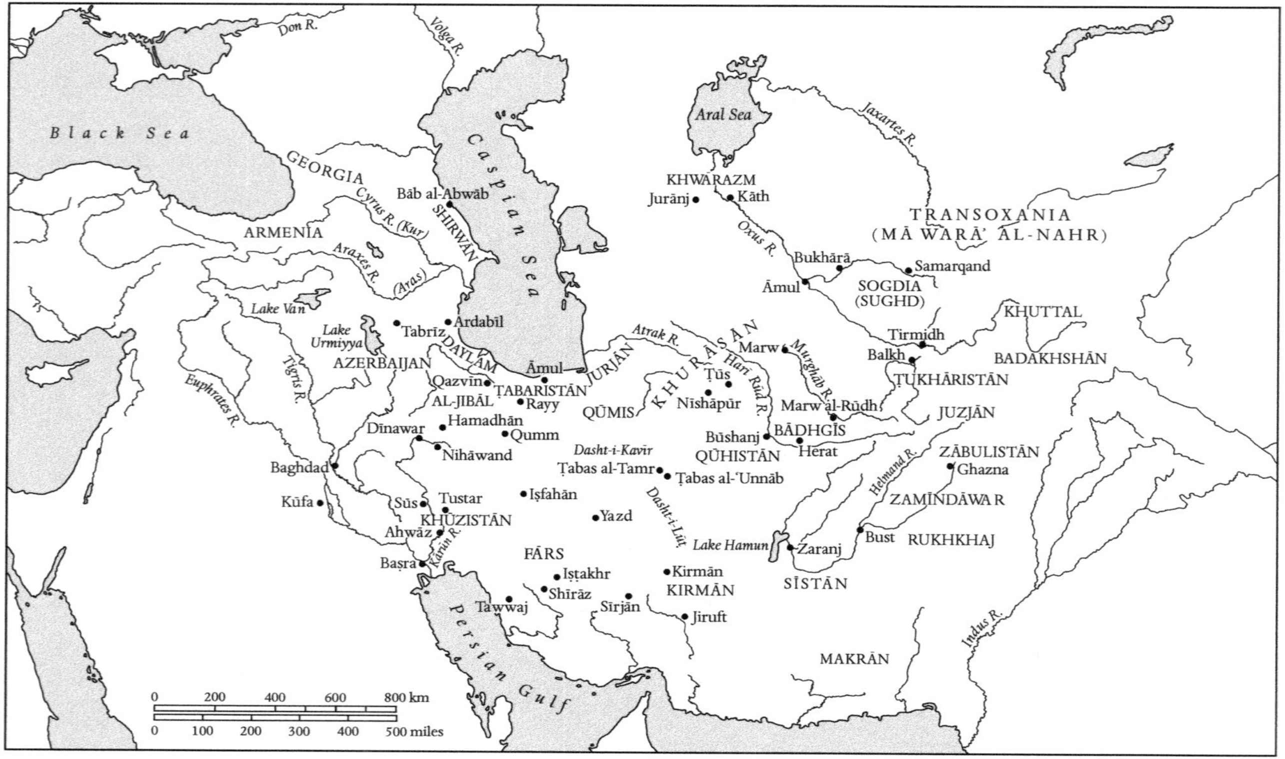

8. The Islamic east

BYZANTINE EMPIRE
Kamkh
Malaṭya
Zibaṭra
Ḥiṣn Manṣūr
Euphrates R.
Amida
Ṭuwāna
AL-THUGHŪR
Ḥiṣn al-Ṣaqāliba
Sayḥān R.
Mar'ash
Kaysūm
Sumaysāṭ
Hārūniyya
Dulūk
Ruhā
Adana
Tarsus
'Ayn Zarba
al-Maṣṣīṣa
Sarūj
Ḥarrān
Qūrus
Jabal al-Lukkām
Dābiq
AL-'AWĀṢIM
Manbij
al-Balīkh R.
Diyār Muḍar
Alexandretta
Antioch
Aleppo
Ḥiṣn Maslama
al-Suwaydiyya
Qinnasrīn
Bālis
al-Raqqa/al-Rāfiqa
Orontes R.
al-Khunāṣira
Ma'arrat al-Nu'mān
al-Ruṣāfa
al-Lādhiqiyya
Apamea
QINNASRĪN
Jabala
CYPRUS
Shayzar
Hama
Qasṭal
Anṭarṭūs
Salamiyya
HOMṢ
Rahba
Ḥomṣ
Tripoli
'Arqa
Palmyra
Jabal Lubnān
al-Bakrā'
al-Qaryatayn
Ba'albaak
Beirut
DAMASCUS
Sidon
'Ayn al-Jar
Damascus
Bāniyās
al-Bathaniyya
Acre
AL-URDUNN
Jābiya
Tiberias
Fīq
al-Ḥawrān
Caesarea
Adhri'āt
Baysān
Fiḥl
Buṣrā
Jerash
Nābulus
Jaffa
al-Ramla
Jericho
'Ammān
'Asqalān
FILASṬĪN
Jerusalem
Gaza
al-Khalīl
al-Balqa
Dead Sea
Ma'āb
al-'Arīsh
Ṣughar
'Arandal
Adhruḥ
Ma'ān
al-Ḥumayma
0 50 100 150 200 250 300 km
0 50 100 150 200 miles

9. Syria

0 200 400 600 800 km
0 100 200 300 400 500 miles
Land over 1000 metres
Nile cataract
Trade routes
Barca
CYRENAICA
(BARCA)
Mean annual rainfall less than 125mm south of this line
Rosetta
Alexandria
Damietta
Cairo
Suez
Siwa Oasis
Al Fayyum
EGYPT
Libyan Desert
Asyut
Nile R.
Qusayr
Thebes
Qus
Luxor
Kharga Oasis
ARABIA
Red Sea
Yanbu
Medina
Aswan
Berenice
NOBATIA OR NUBA
W. al-Allaqi
Aidhab
Begrash
(Faras)
Ibrim
(Prim)
Derheib
BEJA (BLEMMYES)
Selima Oasis
Halfa
Jidda
Mecca
Sai I.
Du (Adu)
NUBIA
Suakin
Khandag
Napata
Old Dongola
ZAGHAWA
MAKURIA OR MUKURRA
Meroë
Uri
Atbara R.
Dahlak Is.
Mean annual rainfall less than 125mm north of this line
Soba
Massawa
Adulis
ALODIA OR ALWA
YEMEN
GEZIRA
Axum
Sennar
KORDOFAN
Aden
Roha
(Lalibela)
DARFUR
White Nile
B. al Abyad
B. al Azrak
Blue Nile
L. Tana
Zeila
ETHIOPIA
Abay R.
Bahr al Ghazal
Sudd

10. Egypt

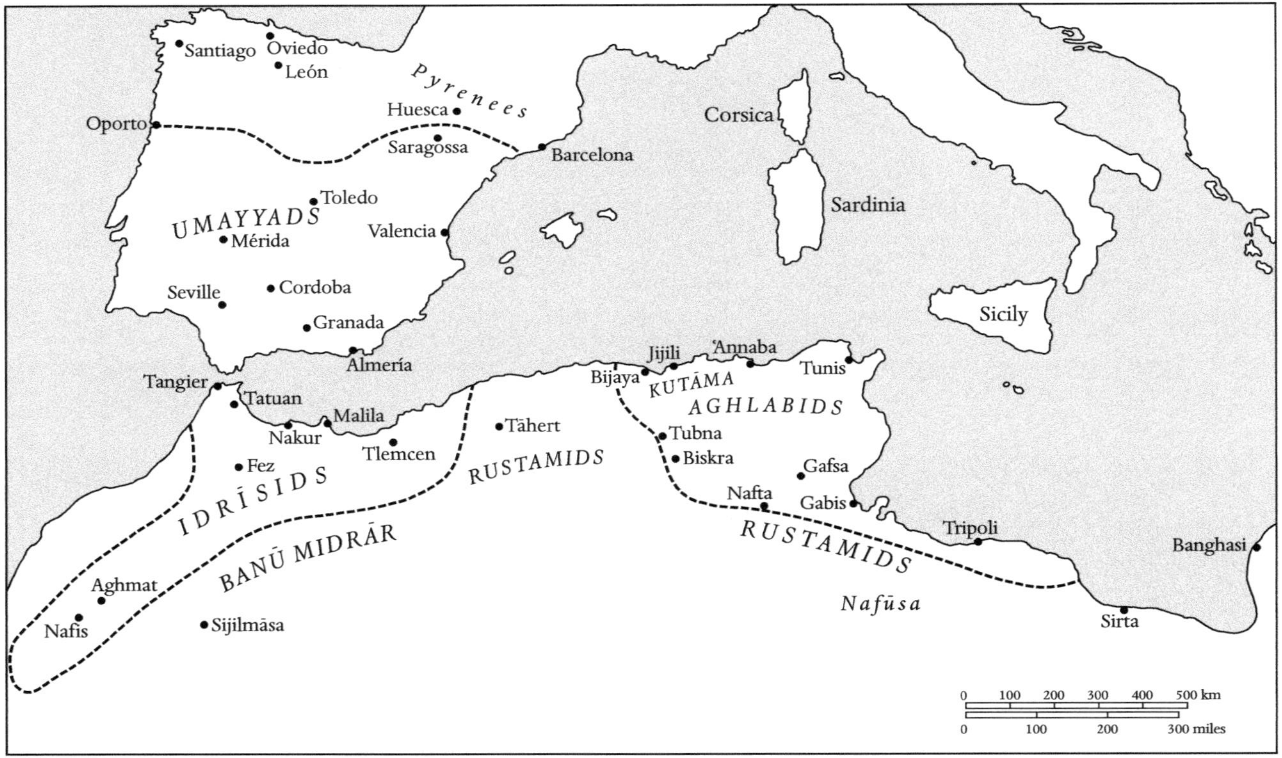

11. Spain and North Africa

Introduction

CHASE F. ROBINSON

The following story, which appears in the *History* of Abū Jaʿfar al-Ṭabarī (d. 310/923), is one of many that describe how the ʿAbbāsid caliph Abū Jaʿfar al-Manṣūr (r. 136–58/754–75) chose the site for his new city of Baghdad. The event is said to have taken place in year 763 of the Common Era, some thirteen years after the revolution that brought the ʿAbbāsids to power.

> It was reported on the authority of Muḥammad b. Ṣāliḥ b. al-Naṭṭāḥ, on the authority of Muḥammad b. Jābir and his father, who said: When Abū Jaʿfar decided to build the city of Baghdad, he saw a monk, to whom he called out. When he responded, he asked him, 'Do you find in your books [a prediction] that a city will be built here?' 'Yes', said the monk, 'Miqlāṣ will build it.' Abū Jaʿfar exclaimed, 'I was called Miqlāṣ when I was young!', to which the monk said, 'Then you must be the one to build it!'
>
> He [the narrator] then continued: Likewise, when Abū Jaʿfar decided to build the city of al-Rāfiqa, which is in territory that once belonged to the Byzantines, the people of [the nearby city of] al-Raqqa objected and resolved to fight him, saying, 'You will ruin our markets, take away our livelihoods and reduce our houses.' Abū Jaʿfar was determined to take them on, and wrote to a monk in the [nearby] monastery, asking: 'Do you know anything about a city that will be built here?' The monk replied, 'I have heard that a man called Miqlāṣ will build it,' so Abu Jaʿfar said, 'I am Miqlāṣ!' So he built it on the model of Baghdad, except for the walls, the iron gates and the single ditch.[1]

The double anecdote, which sits near the middle of the chronological range of this first volume of the *New Cambridge history of Islam*, anticipates many of the themes and issues of this and succeeding volumes in the series, such as state (and city) building, the role of non-Muslims in Muslim societies, the role

1 I translate loosely from Abū Jaʿfar Muḥammad ibn Jarīr al-Ṭabarī, *Taʾrīkh al-rusul wa'l-mulūk*, ed. M. J. de Goeje et al., 15 vols. in 3 series (Leiden, 1879–1901), series III, p. 276.

of caliphs and dynastic politics. Three themes are especially significant, however, and these may profitably be put here in question form.

How do we know what we know of early Islam?

The alert reader will have noticed that while al-Manṣūr's building plans are said to date from 763, the *History* in which we read of these plans was written by a historian who died in 923, about 160 years after the accounts he relates (I leave aside the question of our historian's informants, many of whom lived considerably earlier). The same reader might wonder if there was anything earlier to read, or if al-Ṭabarī's description of Baghdad and al-Rāfiqa can be corroborated by archaeological evidence. The unfortunate fact is that although we do happen to possess some excellent archaeology for al-Rāfiqa (which lay on the Euphrates in present-day Syria),[2] one cannot do better than al-Ṭabarī for the founding of Baghdad; no earlier source has more to say about the foundation of this or any other early Islamic city. Meanwhile, we have no archaeological evidence from Baghdad with which to confirm his description: civil wars, economic decline, Mongols and modernity have conspired to obliterate and seal eighth- and ninth-century layers of the settlement.

Does this matter? After all, one might reasonably base a history of the French Revolution of 1789 upon Georges Lefebvre's *The coming of the French Revolution*, which was published in 1949. The difficulty for us is caused not merely by the passing of time. It lies more in questions of method, purpose, perspective and scope. For all that he was a great historian, al-Ṭabarī was no Georges Lefebvre; he was a great historian by the standards of the day, which, being considerably lower than the Annales school of post-war France, made ample room for myths, legends, stereotypes, distortions and polemics. It is hard to believe that al-Manṣūr conversed with a local monk about his plans for Baghdad, and this for several reasons, one of which is that other Islamic cities are outfitted with similar foundation stories. Surely the nature and date of our sources *must* matter; as the editor of an earlier Cambridge *History* put it: 'It is by solidity of criticism more than by the plenitude of erudition, that the study of history strengthens, and straightens, and extends the mind.' 'For the critic', continued Lord Acton, 'is one who, when he lights on an interesting statement, begins by suspecting it.'[3]

2 On al-Raqqa and al-Rāfiqa, see S. Heidemann and A. Becker (eds.), *Raqqa II: Die islamische Stadt* (Mainz am Rhein, 2003).

3 J. E. E. D. A. (Lord) Acton, *Lectures on modern history*, ed. J. N. Figgis and R. V. Laurence (London, 1906), p. 15.

And suspicious we have become. This – the realisation that what we know about early Islam is less certain than what we thought we knew, and that writing history in this period and region requires altogether more sophisticated and resourceful approaches – is one of a handful of notable advances made in Islamic studies since the original *Cambridge history of Islam* was published in 1970. Now it is true that Islamic studies has long tolerated and occasionally cultivated a critical spirit; Ignaz Goldziher, arguably the greatest Islamicist of all, had published his revolutionarily critical work on early Islam some five years before Lord Acton's Inaugural Lecture.[4] The two scholars were breathing the same air. Still, these and other critical approaches to Islamic history were marginalised for much of the twentieth century, giving way to a less subtle and more credulous positivism; to Acton's dismay, 'the weighing of testimony' was *not* held 'more meritorious than the potential discovery of new matter'.[5] It was only in the last quarter of that century that things changed, as Orientalist positivism fell into disrepute, and historical criticism was put at the heart of understanding early Islam. To some extent, this more critical attitude towards our written source reflects broader academic trends in the 1960s and early 1970s, when adjacent fields, such as the academic study of Rabbinic Judaism, raised their standards of evidence. This said, Orientalism in general and Islamic studies in particular have been relatively insular fields, and the revisionism developed from within, especially through the publication of a small handful of books, which all appeared between 1973 and 1980, and, to lesser and greater degrees, all threw into question the very possibility of reconstructing the first two centuries of Islamic history.[6] Although relatively tame by the standards of more highly developed fields (such as scholarship on the Hebrew Bible and Christian origins), these books sparked off a great deal of controversy, and although their approaches and conclusions remain controversial, it can scarcely be doubted that they served to rouse Islamic studies from something of a post-war slumber.

4 I. Goldziher, *Muhammedanische Studien* (Halle, 1889–90), trans. S. M. Stern and C. R. Barber as *Muslim Studies* (London, 1967–71).

5 Acton, *Lectures*, p. 16.

6 A. Noth, *Quellenkritische Studien zu Themen, Formen und Tendenzen frühislamischer Geschichtsüberlieferung* (Bonn, 1973), trans., rev. and expanded by A. Noth and L. I. Conrad as *The early Arabic historical tradition: A source critical study* (Princeton, 1994); P. Crone and M. Cook, *Hagarism: The making of the Islamic world* (Cambridge, 1977); J. Wansbrough, *Quranic studies: Sources and methods of scriptural interpretation* (Oxford, 1977); J. Wansbrough, *The sectarian milieu: Content and composition of Islamic salvation history* (Oxford, 1978); P. Crone, *Slaves on horses: The evolution of the Islamic polity* (Cambridge, 1980); see also P. Crone, *Meccan trade and the rise of Islam* (Princeton, 1987; repr. Piscataway, NJ, 2004).

So if it was once good enough to offer cursory comments on the principal genres of the Islamic historical tradition (as did the original *Cambridge history of Islam*, whose sedate and authoritative tone gives little indication that the post-war consensus was about to fracture), it is no longer good enough. This is why the reader of this volume will find not only a very different approach to the first two centuries of Islam, but no fewer than three chapters (15, 16 and 17) devoted to a myriad of problems of evidence and interpretation, some of which are solved, but many of which remain very controversial. Few – if any – of the controversies will be settled here; the volume editor sees it as his responsibility to ensure only that the volume reflects the state of the field in the early twenty-first century. Although this means that gaps in our knowledge have to be filled by further research and that scholars continue to disagree on both major and minor matters, the reader can still take solace in knowing that the field of early Islamic history is as exciting as any other. Recorded history scarcely knows a period more creative of religious, cultural and political traditions than the seventh, eighth and ninth centuries. The editor will regard this volume a success if its readers come to share some of this excitement.

What, in broad strokes, is the quality of our evidence for the period covered by this volume? It is mixed. On the one hand, sixth-century Byzantium enjoys some respectable coverage, thanks to a handful of high-quality and contemporary histories that cover war and politics relatively well, including events in the east, especially the Byzantine–Persian wars that dominate the century. Written, as they generally were, in Constantinople, these Greek sources are complemented by another handful of works, these written by the Christians of Syria and Iraq in Syriac, which provide a local perspective on the *histoire événementielle*. There are, of course, problems of interpretation and perspective, but the fact remains that at least some politics and warfare can be described in some detail.[7] Meanwhile, long-term processes of economic exchange and settlement, which were conventionally ignored by historians of earlier generations, can be reconstructed to some degree by the numismatic record and the burgeoning field of Mediterranean archaeology. There are real gaps, of course, but all this contrasts sharply with the situation further east. While late Roman and early Byzantine studies prosper, bringing new texts to bear on old problems and new interpretations and methods to old texts,

7 For an example of some detailed coverage of war, see G. Greatrex, *Rome and Persia at war, 502–535*, ARCA Classical and Medieval Texts, Papers and Monographs 37 (Leeds, 1998); for some sense of the archaeology on offer, see C. Wickham, *Framing the early Middle Ages: Europe and the Mediterranean, 400–800* (Oxford, 2005).

Sasanian studies do not, at least aside from the relatively narrow sub-fields of sigillography and numismatics. Very little indigenous historical writing survives; and this, combined with the fact that archaeology there lags considerably behind its Mediterranean analogue, severely handicaps all attempts to write detailed Sasanian history. (For all that it has contributed to a boom in the academic study of Islam, the Iranian Revolution of 1979 has done little to advance the study of pre-Islamic Iran.) It is an unfortunate and remarkable thing that we must rely so heavily upon ninth- and tenth-century Muslim authors writing in Arabic to provide us with a narrative history of the sixth- and seventh-century Sasanian state, in which Middle Persian and Aramaic were the principal literary and administrative languages, and Zoroastrianism and Nestorian Christianity its privileged religious traditions. Not entirely dissimilar things can be said of pre-Islamic Arabia, which produced virtually no narrative worthy of the name, and which is currently even more innocent of serious archaeology, especially in the west.[8] Although the epigraphic evidence is now accumulating, what we know of the pre-Islamic Ḥijāz derives in very large measure from what later Muslims, who were usually writing at something of a chronological, geographical and cultural distance, believed, and chose to have their readers believe.

If the sixth-century historiographic state of affairs is mixed, that of the seventh century is worse: the flow of contemporaneous sources slows to a trickle, and even the Byzantine historical tradition falters.[9] The Arabic sources pose as many questions as they answer, and although the attack made in the 1970s and 1980s against their reliability has been met with resistance in some quarters,[10] a consensus about how to use them for reconstructing detailed history remains remote. What this means, then, is that the period most productive of spectacular history – of prophecy and revelation within Arabia, and sweeping conquest outside it, of state and empire formation in Syria – proved spectacularly unproductive of durable historiography. Lacking primary sources from within the Islamic tradition, we must perilously rely either on non-Islamic testimony, which, though earlier, is frequently given to problems of perspective and bias,[11] or on

8 Whereas things are looking up in the east: see D. Kennet, 'The decline of eastern Arabia in the Sasanian period', *Arabian Archaeology and Epigraphy*, 18 (2007).

9 See, however, J. F. Haldon, *Byzantium in the seventh century: The transformation of a culture*, rev. edn (Cambridge, 1997), pp. xxiff.

10 See below, chapter 15.

11 See R. Hoyland, *Seeing Islam as others saw it: A survey and evaluation of Christian, Jewish and Zoroastrian writings on early Islam* (Princeton, 1997).

relatively late Islamic ones, which rely on a mix of accounts, some orally transmitted, others textually transmitted, some both. Al-Ṭabarī's history is the most important of these. It can reasonably be called one of the greatest monuments of pre-modern historiography in any language, and it is our best single source for the rise and disintegration of the unified state. And because the early history that it narrates was both deeply controversial and monumentally significant – what could be of greater moment than Muḥammad's prophecy and the political events it set into motion? – it freely mixes prescription and description, polemics and facts, myth, legend and stereotype. Put more broadly, in writing his massive and universal *History*, al-Ṭabarī was both recording and interpreting the rise and disintegration of the unified state. The ʿAbbāsid family continued to supply caliphs during and for centuries after al-Ṭabarī's day, but they were now usually ineffectual, and within a generation of his death, Baghdad would be occupied by Iranian mercenaries. Baghdad survived, but al-Manṣūr's foundation had been abandoned, and much of the city lay in ruins after two civil wars (al-Rāfiqa had long been eclipsed by al-Raqqa). Filled as it is with caliphal *Kaiserkritik*, al-Ṭabarī's work can be read as both triumphalist anthem and nostalgic dirge.

For the history of the ninth, tenth and eleventh centuries, our evidence improves. There are several reasons why. For one thing, the range and quality of the written sources improve: we now have a variety of genres of historical writing, in addition to belles-lettres and poetry, and the yawning chronological, cultural and political gap between event and record narrows; much history is either contemporary or nearly so, and some of it was written by those in a position to know this history well, such as administrators and bureaucrats. For another thing, official and unofficial documents begin to survive in some numbers, even if it is true that many are embedded in historical and literary texts. Finally, the lean material evidence of the seventh and eighth centuries gives way to a somewhat more generous spread of art-historical and archaeological sources. For example, much of the urban fabric of Sāmarrāʾ, which served as capital during the period 221–79 / 836–93, still survives; although Fāṭimid Cairo may be altogether harder to discern than Mamlūk Cairo, some of it *is* still there. ʿAbbāsid Baghdad is not.

The quality of our evidence thus improves with the passing of time, and the tenth century is far less obscure than the seventh. But what is the historian to make of this evidence? What model is he to use? Is disinterested, 'scientific' history even possible? To judge from the vigorous anti-Orientalist literature that appeared in the 1960s and flourished in the 1970s,[12] one might have thought the ground prepared for repudiating altogether the project of reconstructing the past. In the event, the study of Islamic history has remained relatively conservative, with positivism – of a modified sort – continuing to enjoy pride of place. This takes us to a second important change of perspective.

What is Islamic history, and how does Islam relate to Late Antiquity?

Al-Manṣūr designed and built his city as caliph (Ar. *khalīfa*), God's 'deputy' or 'representative', who exercised His authority on earth. Just as God's authority was indivisible, so in al-Manṣūr's day was the caliph's: he possessed both spiritual and temporal authority, which in practice meant everything from leading the prayers to leading his armies into battle. To judge from the evidence, he was considered, *inter alia*, 'God's rope' and the pivot around which the world moved, an idea that was given architectural expression in the very design of his city, a design which would have been so familiar to al-Ṭabarī's reader that a simple allusion would do: the 'model of Baghdad' meant a circular city plan. *Madīnat al-Manṣūr* (al-Manṣūr's city) thus consisted of an elaborately arcaded ring, which, perforated by four gates leading to the principal cities of the empire in the north-west, south-west, south-east and north-east, housed the state's administrative and bureaucratic agencies, and at its very centre stood the congregational mosque and caliphal palace. God's single and universal rule on earth, delegated to His caliphs, was thus given symbolic form.[13]

Much of this first volume can be construed as an attempt to understand the forces that first created and later dissolved this enormously powerful and persuasive idea. In ways made abundantly clear by the Islamic historical tradition, its inspiration lay in part in the career and ideas of Muḥammad himself, who operated in a cultural milieu (north-west Arabia) that was relatively naive of the main currents of Late Antiquity; it was he, the tradition maintains, who put in place the patterns by which his successors (the caliphs) would (or should) model themselves. There is much truth to this: the early

12 See, for example, E. Said, *Orientalism* (New York, 1978); A. L. Macfie, *Orientalism: A reader* (New York, 2000); and R. Irwin, *For lust of knowing: The Orientalists and their enemies* (London, 2006).

13 For the pre-Islamic antecedents, see C. Wendell, 'Baghdad: Imago Mundi and other foundation lore', *IJMES*, 2 (1971).

caliphate can hardly be understood without reference to Muḥammad's legacy of prophecy, social engineering and conquest, not to mention Arabian styles of politics. But it is also the case that in attenuated and largely untraceable ways, some of the creative forces for al-Manṣūr's idea lay much further afield, such as in fourth-century Byzantium, when Constantine and his successors married monotheism to empire building; this was a vision that was refined during the fifth, sixth and seventh centuries, in part as a result of internal divisions and in part as a result of Byzantium's rivalry with the Sasanian state of Iraq and Iran, where Zoroastrianism generally prevailed. Such as it was, the Sasanians' embrace of monotheism came later and remained very mixed, but they, too, eventually had a formative influence upon the Islamic imperial tradition: as early as the first decades of the eighth century, Iraqi styles had filtered into Syria, and the floodgates opened after the ʿAbbāsid revolution, when the seat of the caliphate was moved from Syria to Iraq. In fact, al-Manṣūr's Round City was an easy ride from the last Sasanian capital of Ctesiphon (al-Madāʾin), and its circular design harks back to Sasanian city plans. Umayyad rule in formerly Byzantine Syria, ʿAbbāsid rule in formerly Sasanian Iraq – the cultural ambidexterity that resulted is one of the most striking features of the early Islamic tradition.

Early Islamic history, it follows, cannot be properly understood unless it is made part of the religious and political world of the Late Antique Near East. When al-Manṣūr is given to ask local monks for their views on his building plans, we are reminded of precisely that: Muslims and non-Muslims lived in the same world, their experiences intersecting and their traditions intertwining. (Christian books contain prophecies that Muslims fulfil, the legendary 'Miqlāṣ' of al-Ṭabarī's account probably alluding to an eighth-century Manichaean figure from the area near Baghdad-to-be.) This idea – that although early Muslims did break away from the pre-Islamic world, they also accelerated patterns of change already in process within it – is the second of the field's notable advances of the last thirty-five years. Important exceptions aside,[14] the study of Late Antiquity remains fairly closely related to the study of late Roman and early Byzantine Christian societies (especially their

14 In addition to P. Brown, *The world of Late Antiquity* (London, 1971), see S. A. Harvey, *Asceticism and society in crisis: John of Ephesus and the* Lives of the Eastern Saints (Berkeley, 1990); G. Fowden, *Empire to commonwealth: Consequences of monotheism in Late Antiquity* (Princeton, 1994); E. K. Fowden, *The barbarian plain: Saint Sergius between Rome and Iran* (Berkeley and Los Angeles, 1999); A. H. Becker, *Fear of God and the beginning of wisdom: The School of Nisibis and the development of scholastic culture in Late Antique Mesopotamia* (Philadelphia, 2006); and J. Walker, *The legend of Mar Qardagh: Narrative and Christian heroism in Late Antique Iraq* (Berkeley and Los Angeles, 2006).

cities),[15] so whereas the transition from Byzantine to Islamic rule in Egypt and Syria–Palestine is becoming considerably clearer,[16] that of the lands east of the Euphrates remains more poorly understood. This said, that early Islam 'belongs' to Late Antiquity has become nearly axiomatic among serious scholars.

Here, then, there is another contrast with the original *Cambridge history of Islam*, which was conceived and executed shortly before 'Late Antiquity' had been framed as a distinct cultural and political phase of history.[17] Although earlier scholarship was deeply familiar with the Byzantine and Sasanian (or, in geographical terms, the Syrian and Iraqi / Iranian) influences that would shape Islamic history, an implicit 'Islamic exceptionalism' prevailed, and the volume accordingly began with a single chapter on 'pre-Islamic Arabia'. The *New Cambridge history of Islam* reflects a generation's progress. Just as the concluding volume of the *Cambridge ancient history* integrates the rise of Islam into a more inclusive vision of historical change,[18] so this volume begins with four chapters that lay out the cultural and political history of Late Antiquity in detail; subsequent chapters, which address how Islamic history was made in the empire's provinces, also give some sense of the diverse cultural geography that early Muslims walked. As the birthplace of Muḥammad and Islam, western Arabia naturally deserves special treatment, and so it has it in part I. But it has become increasingly clear that western Arabia was less sheltered from the prevailing winds of Late Antiquity than previously thought: Muḥammad was part of Heraclius' and Yazdegerd's world. What is more, as soon as the conquests had decelerated, Muslims would abandon Arabia as their political capital for Syria and Iraq, and the articulation of much early Islamic doctrine and ritual is a phenomenon of the Fertile Crescent rather than the Arabian Peninsula.

Writing early Islamic history thus means in some measure tracking one distinctive monotheist trajectory among several others (Frankish–Papal, Byzantine and Eastern Christian) in western Eurasia.[19] What does this mean

15 On models of 'transformation', see J. H. W. G. Liebeschuetz, 'Late Antiquity and the concept of decline', *Nottingham Medieval Studies*, 45 (2001); see also R. Martin, 'Qu'est-ce que l'antiquité tardive?' in R. Chevallier (ed.), *Aiôn: Le temps chez les romains* (Paris, 1976).

16 And this in no small measure due to a series of collections and monographs published as Studies in Late Antiquity and Early Islam (Princeton, 1992–).

17 Brown, *The world of Late Antiquity*; the most recent conspectus is G. W. Bowersock, P. Brown and O. Grabar (eds.), *Late Antiquity: A guide to the post-classical world* (Cambridge, MA, 1999).

18 A. Cameron, B. Ward-Perkins and M. Whitby (eds.), *The Cambridge ancient history*, vol. XIV: *Late Antiquity: Empire and successors, AD 425–600* (Cambridge, 2000), chap. 22.

19 See J. Herrin, *The formation of Christendom* (Princeton, 1987).

for this volume? One thing should be made clear: 'Islamic history' is much more than the history of a religious tradition, and those religious ideas, practices or institutions that were without clear and important social or political dimensions will figure here only marginally. Put another way, understanding the development of Muslim societies at least in part turns on an appreciation for the Sunnī–Shīʿite divide and how it came about, but not on a detailed understanding of how Shīʿite law or ritual differs from Sunnī analogues, much less on precisely how Twelver Shīʿa differ from Ismāʿīlī Shīʿa in those matters. The religious and cultural traditions that took root under Islamic rule require separate study, and so they are discussed in volume 5. For the purposes of this volume, Islamic history is the social, religious and cultural history that Muslims made, chiefly (but not exclusively) as rulers of what remained throughout almost all of this early period a predominantly non-Muslim world. As chapters in a subsequent volume make clear,[20] conversion is a poorly understood process, but it seems that Muslims remained in the numerical minority in many if not most of the empire's lands through the ninth century. Early Muslims were political imperialists, but only seldom religious missionaries.

Of course calling the history that Muslims made 'Islamic history' is not to suggest that their history was necessarily any less conditioned by environmental, economic, social or military factors than the history made by non-Muslims. It clearly was conditioned by these variables, and the contributions that follow will frequently measure them, at least as far as they can be measured; one can scarcely understand many of the problems of empire building in south-west Asia without understanding its geography and topography. That is why the geography of the southern and eastern Mediterranean and Middle Eastern lands is carefully described in chapter 1. Nor is it to say that Muslims were necessarily any more committed to religious ideas than were contemporaneous Jews, Christians or Zoroastrians, to name only the leading traditions; indeed, many Muslim rulers were frequently taken to task by their opponents and critics for having failed to discharge fully their religious obligations, whatever these may have been. But it certainly *is* to say that Muslims understood themselves to have made history in exclusively religious terms. This is not simply because religious systems in Late Antiquity were generally as hegemonic as bourgeois liberalism and market capitalism currently are in the developed West, but because this value was given compelling paradigmatic authority in the eighth- and ninth-century construction of the

20 See volume 3, chapter 15 (Bulliet) and volume 4, chapter 5 (Wasserstein).

Prophet's experience: the model of Muḥammad's prophecy and community not only gave birth to the conquest movements that eventually overran much of the Near East, but also shape to the polity that would rule it. Christianity was born on the margins of an empire, which it colonised only fitfully; in Islam, belief and empire fused in quick succession.

How did Muslims of this period build states and empires?

The Abū Jaʿfar al-Manṣūr of our account was the second caliph of the ʿAbbāsid family, which, after the Ottomans, was the longest-lived major ruling dynasty of the Islamic world. Having come to power by overthrowing the Umayyads in 749–750 CE, the ʿAbbāsids would provide an unbroken succession of caliphs until 1258, when the last was executed during the Mongol sack of Baghdad – some 500 years of dynastic rule, which is an impressive achievement by European (if not Japanese) standards. The ʿAbbāsids' success in keeping their dynastic rule intact should not be confused with success in keeping their empire together, however. Already by the time of al-Ṭabarī, who died during the reign of al-Muqtadir (908–32), al-Manṣūr's Round City was in near ruins (the historian himself lived in one of its extramural quarters), and the unified state as envisioned by late Umayyads and early ʿAbbāsids was a distant memory. If al-Ṭabarī had travelled in the year 900 CE from his home in Baghdad to the furthest western reach of the Islamic world (present-day Morocco), he would have left the area under direct ʿAbbāsid control in a matter of days, and travelled through regions ruled by no fewer than four more-or-less independent dynasties, the Ṭūlūnids, Aghlabids, Rustamids and Idrīsids.

The main trajectory of early Islamic history therefore follows two successive phases in politics and society. The first is charted here in chapters 5, 6 and 7, and the second in chapters 8 and 9. Since these processes transcended dynastic change, so do our chapters; we thus break from the dynastic and implicitly ethnic organisation of the original *Cambridge history of Islam*, which directly and indirectly reflected nineteenth-century nationalist narratives as well as the conventional narratives of the tradition itself. And since regional variation in economic, social and political history was considerable, Arabia, the Islamic east (greater Iran), Syria, Egypt and the Iberian Peninsula and North Africa are each treated in separate chapters in part III. This – a clearer sense of regional differentiation that characterises Islamic history – is a third area of research that has greatly advanced since the publication of the original

Cambridge history of Islam.[21] So while part II can be said to chart Islamic history from the viewpoint of the caliphs, part III describes it from the provincials' points of view.

The first phase of Islamic history is the rise and consolidation of a unitary state from its murky origins in the post-conquest polity of the mid-seventh century to its eighth-century transformation under the Umayyads and early ʿAbbāsids into the last and perhaps greatest land-based, bureaucratic empire of Antiquity. By the late seventh century, Muslim rule extended as far west as present-day Tunisia, as far north as the Syrian–Turkish border and as far east as Turkmenistan, and by the early eighth, it had stretched into Spain, Transoxania and the Sind valley in present-day Pakistan. The whole fell under the notional sovereignty of the Arab-Muslim caliph and those delegated by him, the caliph ruling initially from Arabia, then peripatetically in Syria, and then spectacularly in the great Iraqi cities of Baghdad (at this point perhaps the world's largest) and Sāmarrāʾ. What resulted was not merely a robust political order, but a hugely creative cultural moment. Empire building unleashed several processes, particularly a measure of political, social and economic integration, which resulted from a military-administrative system that siphoned rural surpluses into large cities that possessed both state and mercantile elites; complemented by profits from international trade carried across the waves of the Indian Ocean and the steppes of Central Asia, this led to the production of high culture on a massive scale. Baghdad was not only one of the world's largest cities, but one of its most literate and learned ones.

I shall leave the difficult task of explaining a process of empire building as complex as this to the appropriate chapters; the enormous cultural achievements are surveyed in volume 5. Here it is enough to identify two factors that explain the process. The first was the resilience and resourcefulness of the ruling elite, which drew upon not only its own evolving and adaptive ideology of rule, but also upon indigenous traditions of state building that had survived the dislocations of the seventh-century conquests. The second – and one that is

21 For examples from the period covered by this volume, see R. Bulliet, *The patricians of Nishapur: A study in medieval Islamic social history* (Cambridge, MA, 1972); E. Daniel, *The political and social history of Khurasan under Abbasid rule, 747–820* (Minneapolis, 1979); M. Morony, *Iraq after the Muslim conquest* (Princeton, 1984); M. Gil, *A history of Palestine, 634–1099* (Cambridge, 1992); R. Bulliet, *Islam: The view from the edge* (New York, 1994); P. Chalmeta, *Invasión e islamización: La sumisión de Hispania y la formación de al-Andalus* (Madrid, 1994); C. F. Robinson, *Empire and elites after the Muslim conquest: The transformation of northern Mesopotamia* (Cambridge, 2000); P. Cobb, *White banners: Contention in ʿAbbasid Syria, 750–880* (Albany, 2001); E. Manzano Moreno, *Conquistadores, emires y califas: Los omeyas y la formación de al-Andalus* (Barcelona, 2006).

altogether more difficult to measure – was the economy of the eastern Mediterranean, Fertile Crescent and Persian Gulf. Here, too, the contributors can profitably draw from recent advances in our understanding of the material culture of the seventh, eighth and ninth centuries, which decisively reject earlier views that had made agricultural decline and Islamic rule nearly synonymous. Matters are complicated by differing regional profiles and inconclusive evidence, but we now know enough to say that far from ending the economic boom of the eastern Mediterranean, in at least some areas early Islamic rule can be associated to some degree with continuing (and perhaps even increasing) patterns of trade and settlement. The material evidence being so important and generally so inaccessible, it is discussed in a separate chapter (17).

The second phase is the disintegration of this unified state, which begins in the middle of the ninth century and accelerates during the tenth. For reasons already explained, our evidence is better for this period, although much remains very unclear; here, too, economy seems to play a dynamic (and perhaps even dialectic) role with elite politics, as do cultural factors, such as the ninth-century militarisation of politics. On the other hand, explaining this direction of change is somewhat easier on the historian, since, put in terms of the *longue durée* imposed by geography and pre-modern technology, it may be understood as the natural reversion away from the extraordinarily resource-intensive work of state building and state maintaining across huge distances – especially assembling and feeding large armies, along with training and paying the legions of bureaucrats needed to raise, measure and distribute the taxes required to maintain the army – and towards regionalism and some measure of particularism. The Roman and early Byzantine empires had the benefit of the Mediterranean Sea, across which men and cargoes could be moved relatively cheaply and quickly; Baghdad certainly benefited from its position on the Tigris, while Baṣra served as an entrepôt for goods going to and from the Indian Ocean and beyond, but the empire as a whole was too far flung and too geographically heterogeneous to remain whole in the long term.

The late ninth- and tenth-century disintegration of the unified state should not be confused with dissolution of a political order; nor should it be thought that high culture suffered as a result. The pattern of states and polities that emerged in the tenth century and stabilised in the eleventh is sometimes described as a commonwealth of more-or-less independent dynasties that shared the use of Arabic (or an Arabised language, such as Persian),[22]

22 My use of the term 'commonwealth' is altogether different from Fowden's above (note 14).

a repertoire of political thought that centred on the ruling offices of imamate (in the Shīʿite cases) and caliphate (in the Sunnī ones), patterns of military recruitment (notably the employment of non-Muslims of servile origins), and a commitment to the ordering of religious life, especially through the crystallisation of schools of law, the patronage of religious institutions and, in time, the Sufi brotherhoods. Put another way, if a degree of regionalism emerges in the tenth century, it was a regionalism of a particular sort, since disintegration came only after processes of conversion in particular and acculturation in general were already well advanced. To indulge in some counterfactual history: had the state fragmented after the first civil war (Ar. *fitna*) of the 650s, the second civil war of the 680s or perhaps even after the ʿAbbāsid revolution, one presumes that the result would have been some sort of return to the *status quo ante*: a Christian or Christianising world that remained politically and in some measure culturally divided by frontiers that lay along the Tigris and Euphrates rivers. As it happened, disintegration came some 250 years after that first civil war, by which time Arabic had established itself as the prestige language of culture and administration, and although Islam may not have yet been the majority's faith, it had long monopolised the language of politics. (Even well before the turn of the tenth century, movements of rebellion, revolution and secession had been almost invariably expressed and understood in exclusively Islamic terms – even among non-Arabs, Islam provided the repertoire of political action – and movements to revive pre-Islamic religious are conspicuously rare.)

So had al-Ṭabarī made his journey from Baghdad to Idrīsid Morocco, he would have crossed what amounts to political frontiers, but throughout his travels he would have been at home culturally. The idea of commonwealth should not be taken to mean that these so-called 'successor' states lived in peaceful and harmonious synchrony or symbiosis. Far from it, at least at times; dynasts were always Muslim and usually Sunnī, but their ambitions differed, sometimes even radically, from one to the next, some imperial in design, others nothing more than home-rulers. Much depended on distance from Baghdad. Moreover, the tenth-century rise of the Fāṭimid Ismāʿīlīs in North Africa and Egypt, which can be figured as the last large-scale revolutionary movement of early Islam, challenged ideologically and militarily the Sunnī–Twelver Shīʿite coalition of commanders, caliphs and learned men (the *ʿulamāʾ*) that was taking hold in Iraq and the East. In the event, however, the Fāṭimids failed to dislodge the coalition of Easterners: Baghdad survived, the quietist Imāmī Shīʿism that it patronised would flourish, and charismatic Ismāʿīlism, routinised in the Egyptian state, never gained much of a foothold in the central Islamic lands. Aside from the periphery (especially in North Africa, along the Caspian coast and in Yemen), the future lay with Sunnī states of varying size and ambition, legitimised by history, caliphs, the law and, finally, the patronage of high culture. Although the political and economic integration of early Islam is often characterised as a 'golden age', it is incontrovertible that much of what we now reckon to be the greatest achievements of pre-modern Islamic learning – in literature, art, the exact and inexact sciences – were produced in this subsequent period. For all that there was a measure of economic decline in the east, the tenth and eleventh centuries were not about decline, but rather about a rebalancing of political life after a relatively short and hugely spectacular experiment in empire building, and a flourishing of cultural and intellectual life in a polyfocal world of competitive courts and assertive local elites.

PART I

*

THE LATE ANTIQUE CONTEXT

I

The resources of Late Antiquity

JOHN HALDON

The physical and strategic environment

Landscape

The late ancient world in the lands that were to be conquered by the first Muslim armies included a number of disparate regions, each offering a particular environment: Asia Minor or Anatolia, very roughly modern Turkey; the Levant or Middle Eastern regions down to and including Egypt; Mesopotamia and the Iranian plateau to the east; North Africa, from Egypt westwards to the Atlantic; and the Balkans.[1] The Mediterranean and Black Seas united the westernmost of these very different regions, while riverine systems on the one hand and plateaux and desert on the other served both to differentiate and to connect those in the east. Climate determined the patterns of agricultural and pastoral exploitation within these zones, but it also constrained and determined in many respects the nature of state and private surplus-extracting activities.

The limited but fertile agricultural lands of Palestine and western Syria have always been relatively wealthy, in contrast to the more mountainous lands to the north and the deserts to the south and east. Greater Syria, including Palestine and the Lebanon, incorporates a number of very different landscapes, the terrain alternating from rugged highlands, through the fertile plains of northern Syria or central Palestine, the hilly uplands around Jerusalem to the desert steppe of central Syria. These landscapes had stimulated the development of very different communities, and the artificial unity imposed by the Roman state and, later, the early caliphate, should not disguise these stark contrasts. South of Palestine lay the deserts of the Sinai peninsula, leading then into the fertile Nile Valley and Delta regions – an area of fundamentally different

1 Further literature on this section can be found in the chapter bibliography. I am especially grateful to Patricia Crone, Don Whitcomb, Jairus Banaji and Michael Morony for valuable criticism, comments and suggestions; any weaknesses or gaps in the argument are, of course, the author's responsibility alone.

character, heavily dependent on the annual flooding of the great river and the irrigation agriculture which it supported. Westwards from Egypt stretched the provinces of North Africa – desert through the eastern sector of Cyrenaica and Tripolitania in modern Libya, with very limited fertile coastal stretches and inland plateaux. These graduate into the coastal plains of Tunisia and modern Algeria, delineated by the plateaux and sandy desert regions in the south-east, including the al-Jifāra plain (and beyond them, the great desert), by the Aurès range in the centre, and the Saharan Atlas.

The Arabian Peninsula was and is marked out by the contrast between the relatively fertile and more densely settled coastal regions of the south (Yemen) and east (Baḥrayn), on the one hand, and the vast empty centre and north, traversed by the nomadic Bedouin and with no major urban centres and, with the exception of a relatively dense group of oases in the central region (north and south of modern Riyadh), relatively few oasis or valley settlements, on the other. The oasis town of Medina was a partial exception, situated on the western edge of the interior and on the so-called 'spice route' from the southern port of Aden and other coastal settlements further east. Mecca – frequently assumed to have been on the same route – was in fact some 100 miles off to the east, a point which raises some difficulties for traditional assumptions about the origins of Islam and the merchant activities of the Quraysh.[2] The deserts were not entirely devoid of habitation – in the northern Ḥijāz a number of fertile oases offered possibilities, where settlements such as Fadak, Taymā, Wādī al-Qurā, al-Khaybar and Dedan (mod. al-ʿOla) flourished and formed points in a peninsular network of local and long-distance commerce. But relative to Iraq, Syria and Egypt, the Arabian Peninsula remained a marginal zone, impoverished and politically unstable, during the fifth, sixth and early seventh centuries – partly, of course, a reflection of the frequent interventions of the neighbouring powers.

To the east of Syria the desert separates the fertile and semi-fertile zone of greater Syria from Iraq or Mesopotamia, the land between the rivers, historically one of the great centres of early settled agriculture and urban development. The wealth of the Sasanian empire depended largely on the agriculture of Iraq and more especially of the region later known as the Sawād, the 'black land', a great expanse of alluvial and irrigated territory extending from south of Ctesiphon and, later, Baghdad, to the sea, and watered by the two great

2 See P. Crone, *Meccan trade and the rise of Islam* (Princeton, 1987; repr. Piscataway, NJ, 2004), p. 7 with earlier literature.

rivers, Tigris and Euphrates.[3] Since the earliest historical times the region had been the focus of human agriculture and husbandry, with a network of irrigation canals connecting the two rivers. To the east lie the mountains of Media and the great barrier of the Zagros range. In their northern foothills, pushing up towards Azerbaijan, the Diyālā valley extends the fertile zone, and to the south and east of the Sawād the plain of Khūzistān again offers rich agricultural and pastoral possibilities. The successive ridges of the Zagros separate Mesopotamia from the Iranian plateau, running down from the highlands of Kurdistan in the north to east of coastal Khūzistān and Fārs in the south, intersected by many small fertile plains and valleys. The plateau itself is sparsely populated, with settlement confined largely to the valleys formed by the rivers flowing from the eastern ridges of the Zagros, or to oases from which irrigation networks can be fed. To the east the plateau is bounded by a number of larger and smaller arid salt depressions and rocky or sandy deserts, bordered on the eastern and southern edges by further highlands. Its south-central and southern fringes are characterised by arid plains where settlement depended on oases or carefully maintained irrigation, with long stretches of waterless semi-desert extending along the coast into Makrān and Sind and thus into India. In the north, Media is bounded by the Elburz mountains which separate its cooler, steppe-like plains from the near-tropical and forested Caspian littoral. Westwards lie the Talish mountains and then the high steppe of Azerbaijan; eastwards the Elburz give way to the highlands of Ṭabaristān and the steppe of Jurjān and western Khurāsān, with the plateau of Turkistan stretching east and north into Transoxania, through the Karakum and then Kizilkum steppe, past the Aral Sea into Central Asia. To the east and across the central sector of mountain ridges and tracts of desert, intersected by more fertile river valleys, the plain extends along the valley of the Oxus between the western outliers of the Pamirs to the north and the Hindu Kush to the south.

Asia Minor can be divided into three zones: the central plateau; the coastal plains; and the mountain ranges that separate them. The plateau rises from about 3,500 feet in the west to over 6,000 feet in the east, and is typified by extremes of temperature. To the north the Pontic Alps follow the line of the

3 According to Sasanian evidence preserved in the later Arabic tradition, the annual revenues from the Sawād under Khusrau I amounted to 150 million silver drachms, as much as the combined revenues from Fārs, Kirmān and Khūzistān: see the evidence discussed in J. Banaji, 'Precious metal coinages and monetary expansion in Late Antiquity', in *Dal* Denarius *al* Dinar: *L'oriente e la moneta romana. Atti del'incontro di studio, Roma 16–18 sett. 2004* (Rome, 2006), pp. 274–6.

southern shore of the Black Sea; to the south the Taurus and Anti-Taurus ranges extend along the Mediterranean coast and across northern Syria, curving north-eastwards into the Caucasus region. All the mountain zones, but particularly the southern and eastern regions, are characterised by smaller plateaux dissected by crater lakes, lava flows and depressions. Finally, the Balkan peninsula is dominated by mountains which, while not especially high, cover some two-thirds of its area, the main formations being the Dinaric Alps (which run through the western Balkan region in a south-easterly direction) and the associated Pindos range. Extensions and spurs of these mountains dominate southern Greece and the Peloponnese. The Balkan chain itself lies north of Greece, extending eastwards from the Morava river for about 550 kilometres as far as the Black Sea coast, with the Rhodope range forming an arc extending southwards from this range through Macedonia towards the plain of Thrace. River and coastal plains are relatively limited in extent. There are thus very distinct climatic variations between the coastal, Mediterranean-type conditions and the continental-type conditions of the inland and highland regions.

Climate and the problem of climate change

Climate has remained, within certain margins, relatively constant across the late ancient and medieval periods, yet there are a number of fluctuations that need to be borne in mind and which, in conjunction with natural events such as earthquakes, man-made phenomena such as warfare, and catastrophes such as pandemic disease, could have dramatic short- to medium-term results for the human populations of the region, and thus for patterns of settlement, land use, the extraction, distribution and consumption of resources, and political systems.[4] The climate throughout much of the late Hellenistic and Roman imperial periods was relatively warmer and milder than in the period that preceded it, and constituted a 'climatic optimum' which favoured the expansion of agriculture. This expansion is reflected in the so-called Beyşehir

4 Further literature can be found in the bibliography. There is a vast literature on climate change and its impact, especially in respect of societal collapse (see J. Diamond, *Collapse: How societies choose to fail or succeed* (New York, 2005); H. Nüzhet Dalfes, George Kukla and Harvey Weiss (eds.), *Third millennium BC climate change and old world collapse* (New York, 1997)), although 'environmental determinism' is an obvious danger and a major focus for debate (see A. Rosen, 'Determinist or not determinist?: Climate, environment, and archaeological explanation in the Levant', in S. Wolff (ed.), *Studies in the archaeology of Israel and neighboring lands in memory of Douglas L. Esse* (Chicago, 2001), pp. 535–54; A. Rosen, 'Environmental change and human adaptational failure at the end of the Early Bronze Age in the Southern Levant', in Dalfes, Kukla and Weiss (eds.), *Third millennium BC climate change and old world collapse*, pp. 25–38).

Occupation Phase in the southern Balkans and south-western Turkey, for example.[5] Datable by palynological and other paleoenvironmental evidence to begin in about 1250 BCE and to last through to the seventh century CE, this term has been adopted to refer to a period of human activity marked by a dramatic increase in cultivated trees and cereals, clear evidence of a major human impact on the environment which contrasts starkly with the foregoing period. Not all the sites that provide pollen evidence of this shift in vegetation patterns show exactly the same plant profile, but there is a uniform increase in the pollens of domesticated flora, including in particular vines, olives, chestnut and other fruit trees and a range of cereals. At the same time the species of coniferous *pinus* associated with non-cultivated contexts show a marked retreat, whereas species of oak and various herbaceous plants, the latter associated with pastoral activities, increase. While there are a number of sub-zones within the areas affected by the BO Phase, some evidencing less human activity than others, the Phase is a generally recognised phenomenon.

By about 500 CE the climatic situation was changing, with colder and wetter conditions persisting up to the mid-ninth century. But within this broad pattern certain micro-climatic shifts have also been noted: palynological and, more reliably, stable isotope analysis from lake beds in the Levant and Asia Minor, for example, suggest that the climate from about 300 CE until the mid-fifth century was in fact slightly drier and warmer than the preceding centuries (and tree-ring analysis suggests that drought was frequent between the 420s and 480s in several regions of the Levant[6]), but that some time during the later fifth century it became cooler and wetter, until a period of very gradual warming and desiccation began in the seventh century. Precipitation levels declined, affecting highland zones in particular. At the same time the evidence suggests that during the fifth century the level of the Mediterranean began to rise, although the impact of this, which reflects a global phenomenon, remains unclear. Nevertheless, it is very important to note that the characteristic evidence for human activity associated with the BO Phase ends

5 Named for the site at which it was first identified, Beyşehir Gölü, in south-west Turkey: see S. Bottema, H. Woldring and B. Aytug, 'Palynological investigations on the relations between prehistoric man and vegetation in Turkey: The Beyşehir Occupation Phase', *Proceedings of the 5th Optima Congress, September 1986* (Istanbul, 1986), pp. 315–28; W. J. Eastwood, N. Roberts and H. F. Lamb, 'Palaeoecological and archaeological evidence for human occupance in southwest Turkey: The Beyşehir Occupation Phase', *Anatolian Studies*, 48 (1998), pp. 69–86.

6 S. Lev-Yadun, N. Lipschitz and Y. Waisel, 'Annual rings in trees as an index to climate changes intensity in our region in the past', *Rotem*, 22 (1987).

only in the later seventh century. This clearly suggests that climatic stimuli were *not* the major cause of shifts in patterns of human activity.[7]

These micro-climatic fluctuations are important, because climate change does not affect all areas in the same way. Indeed, both the textual evidence assembled for the Late Antique period and the palaeoclimatological evidence suggest marked regional variations across quite short periods of fifty or one hundred years, with droughts alternating with extremely cold and wet conditions, bringing serious difficulties for irrigated lands, on the one hand, and for marginal dry-farming zones, on the other. In those regions, such as the Mediterranean coastal plains, dominated by westerlies, a warmer climate brings less rainfall and desertification of desert marginal regions, whereas in more continental zones such as the Iranian plateau and the drainage areas of the Caspian, rainfall increases. A colder climate brings more rainfall in the former regions – thus exerting pressure on hydrological systems in general – whereas in the continental zones – such as the Anatolian or Iranian plateaux – it brings less precipitation and thus desiccation. Evidence from the Susiana plain suggests that the period around 500–650 CE was relatively dry, for example.[8] Intermediate zones – such as the Mesopotamian lowlands – will be affected according to their position in relation to prevailing winds, rain- and highland-shadow and distance from the sea. Climate change tends to show up first in marginal zones, and temperate or humid regions later. Even if we are not yet in a position anywhere to judge the impact of these shifts on either land use or the social and economic history of the regions concerned, it is nevertheless apparent that they will have played a role and cannot be written out of the causal relationships that determined the pattern of historical change in the late ancient world.

7 M. D. Jones, C. Neil Roberts, M. J. Leng and M. Türkeş, 'A high-resolution late Holocene lake isotope record from Turkey and links to North Atlantic and monsoon climate', *Geology*, 34 (May 2006). For the anthropogenic factors leading to the end of the BO Phase, see J. F. Haldon, '"Cappadocia will be given over to ruin and become a desert": Environmental evidence for historically-attested events in the 7th–10th centuries', in K. Belke, E. Kislinger, A. Külzer and M. Stassinopoulou (eds.), *Byzantina Mediterranea: Festschrift für Johannes Koder zum 65. Geburtstag* (Vienna, 2007); and A. England, W. J. Eastwood, C. N. Roberts, R. Turner and J. F. Haldon, 'Historical landscape change in Cappadocia (central Turkey): A paleoecological investigation of annually-laminated sediments from Nar Lake', *The Holocene*, 18, 8 (2008), pp. 1229–45.

8 R. J. Wenke, 'Imperial investments and agricultural development in Parthian and Sasanian Khūzistān: 150 BC to AD 640', *Mesopotamia*, 10–11 (1975/6), p. 82; H. M. Cullen and P. B. de Menocal, 'North Atlantic influence on Tigris–Euphrates stream-flow', *International Journal of Climatology*, 20 (2000); Jones *et al.*, 'A high-resolution late Holocene lake isotope record from Turkey'.

In any event, the shifts described above will have rendered the human environment of the later fifth to seventh centuries more challenging and the economy of existence more fragile. Combined with the great plague of the middle of the sixth century this established a short but vicious cycle which impacted upon the population and thus upon settlement patterns and density of many regions, although with very varied degrees of intensity. Although generalisations are dangerous, after a period of demographic expansion and intensification of agriculture lasting into the sixth century, a slow decline and retrenchment seems to set in from some time around the middle of the sixth century.[9] In certain provinces of the eastern Roman empire in Asia Minor, for example, some marginal lands were abandoned, soil erosion increased where agriculture receded, and the colder climate generated increasing water volume in rivers and watercourses, contributing to a rapid alluviation accompanied by lowland flooding in many more exposed areas. And while there is some support for an overall reduction in agrarian activity around the early 540s, as reflected in the carbon dioxide content of polar ice-cores, the sources of this change cannot be geographically fixed, and the pattern does not seem to be repeated in Syria and Palestine – the settlement at Nessana in the Negev, for example, flourished well into the later seventh century on the basis of its irrigation agriculture.[10] In other regions an overall reduction in population and thus in the rate of exploitation of natural resources such as forest is shown by an increased variation in woodland flora over the same period. It is important to bear in mind the very different effects such shifts had on different regions, and we must not assume that similar outcomes were exhibited in Anatolia, the Balkans, the Iranian plateau, Mesopotamia, or the northern Syrian uplands; each was subject to its own particular micro-climatic system.[11]

9 Much ink has been expended on the question of the effects of the 'Justinianic' plague. For a reasoned comment on its potential but regionally varied effects, see C. J. Wickham, *Framing the early Middle Ages: Europe and the Mediterranean, 400–800* (Oxford, 2005), pp. 548f. But historians have, on the whole, not yet taken into account the biological and epidemiological evidence associated with the plague, which has shown it to be an especially virulent pathogen: see I. Weichmann and G. Grupe, 'Detection of Yersinia pestis in two early medieval skeletal finds from Aschheim (Upper Bavaria, 6th century AD)', *American Journal of Physical Anthropology*, 126 (2005); and the contributions in L. K. Little (ed.), *Plague and the end of Antiquity: The pandemic of 541–750* (Cambridge, 2006).

10 See Y. Hirschfeld, 'Farms and villages in Byzantine Palestine', *Dumbarton Oaks Papers*, 51 (1997), pp. 50ff.; and in general J. Shereshevski, *Byzantine urban settlements in the Negev desert* (Beer-Sheva, 1991). For the evidence of ice-cores, the levels of carbon dioxide in which have been related to the degree and intensity of agricultural and pastoral production, see W. F. Ruddiman, 'The anthropogenic greenhouse era began thousands of years ago', at courses.eas.ualberta.ca/eas457/Ruddiman2003.pdf.

11 See the relevant discussion in T. J. Wilkinson, *Archaeological landscapes of the Near East* (Tucson, 2003); and the summary in M. G. Morony, 'Economic boundaries? Late

Roads and routes

Communications depended on landscape and climatic conditions, of course, but a series of major strategic routes connected these different cultural and geographical zones. The eastern Roman empire benefited from the creation of military roads, constructed largely in the period 100 BCE – 100 CE by the Roman army, a network that also aided non-military communications – the movement of goods, people and information. But the regular maintenance of roads, which was a state burden upon towns and which was administered and regulated at the local level, seems during the later Roman period to have suffered somewhat. Outside the boundaries of the Roman state road maintenance depended largely on local administration, although the Sasanian state certainly provided for the upkeep of certain key strategic roads through al-Jazīra towards Roman territory, or to the Caucasus and along the western Caspian littoral, as well as eastwards into Khurāsān and down to Fārs and major cities such as Iṣṭakhr. Indeed, there is some evidence to suggest that road building and bridge building were on several occasions carried out using the skills of Roman captives during the third and fourth centuries.[12] The royal court certainly invested in major strategic projects, therefore, although the complex network of military roads maintained in the Roman world was not repeated in Iran or Mesopotamia. And it has been reasonably assumed, albeit on very little actual evidence other than later Islamic tradition, that a postal service and state transport system similar to the Roman *cursus publicus* was maintained by the Sasanian state.[13]

Transport by water was generally much faster and certainly far cheaper than by land, although ought not to be overstated. Long-distance movement of bulk goods such as grain was generally prohibitively expensive – the cost of feeding draught-oxen, maintaining drovers and carters and paying local tolls, combined with the extremely slow rate of movement of ox-carts, multiplied

Antiquity and early Islam', *JESHO*, 47 (2004), pp. 172–5; and the comparative description in Wickham, *Framing the early Middle Ages*, pp. 17–31, and esp. 609ff., on the regionalised urban economies of the eastern provinces and their development

12 See, for example, S. N. C. Lieu, 'Captives, refugees and exiles', in P. Freeman and D. Kennedy (eds.), *The defence of the Roman and Byzantine East*, 2 vols. (Oxford, 1986), vol. II, pp. 476–83; and M. Morony, 'Population transfers between Sasanian Iran and the Byzantine empire', in *La Persia e Bisanzio: Atti dei convegni Lincei 201* (Rome, 2004). Further literature can be found in the bibliography. And see chapter 2 below.

13 An account of various acts of Khusrau I, transmitted through the later Arabic tradition by Miskawayh, gives a very clear picture of a centralised state with an effective and centrally supervised road system. See M. Grignaschi, 'Quelques specimens de la littérature sassanide conservés dans les bibliothèques d'Istanbul', *JA*, 254 (1966), pp. 1–142 (Fr. trans., pp. 16–28; notes, p. 45). See p. 20 with n. 40.

the price of the goods being transported beyond the means of anyone who would otherwise have bought them. Sogdian merchants employed Bactrian camels, and the introduction of the pack-saddle for camels did make the movement of bulk goods more economical. Although the bulk transport of goods over long distances did sometimes happen, it was really only the state, with some activity funded by wealthy private individuals, that could pay for this, except where the luxury value of the goods concerned made the enterprise worthwhile, as with the great silk caravans across the southern steppe zone from China and into Iran, or when conditions made a premium price possible (as with the Quraysh trade in leather in the sixth century: see below). The cost-effectiveness of shipping, entailing the carriage of large quantities of goods in a single vessel handled by a small crew, also gave coastal settlements a great advantage with regard to their access to the wider world. In the case of the Roman world, and in spite of the short-term disruption caused by the Vandals in the mid-fifth century, the Mediterranean and Black Seas offered enormous opportunities for the movement of goods of all sorts, and the archaeological pattern of distribution of a range of products, from pottery to oil, wine, grain and minerals illustrates this very clearly. Similarly, for the Persians the Persian Gulf and the Indian Ocean offered comparable potential for a long-distance commerce and movement of goods and ideas which belie the apparently westward-facing aspect of Sasanian culture and politics presented by many of the sources.[14]

Syria and Palestine were traversed by several major routes connecting the inland regions to the coast, and by a series of major roads stretching from north to south and on down towards Sinai or around the coast through Gaza to Egypt. Travel eastwards from Syria to Mesopotamia was confined largely to the northern corridor across the plains of northern Syria and al-Jazīra, from Amida down the Euphrates, or from Edessa, via Dara and Nisibis, or the Euphrates crossings at Callinicum, towards Nineveh; and although *in extremis* crossings of the Great Syrian Desert could be made (as in the expedition of Khālid ibn al-Walīd in 634/5),[15] this northern corridor was the only practical route for large forces and was thus the key element in the strategic geography of the whole region, determining also local economic activity and the location of fortresses and fortifications. Other routes led north and north-west across what would become the Byzantine frontier during the second half of the seventh century – from al-Raqqa (Callinicum) to Ḥarrān or Edessa, then on to

14 See in general R. W. Bulliet, *The camel and the wheel* (Cambridge, MA, 1975).
15 See F. M. Donner, *The early Islamic conquests* (Princeton, 1981), pp. 119–28.

cross the Euphrates at Samosata, from which Melitene, Germanikeia and Adata could be reached. In northern Syria it was Chalkis (Qinnasrīn) and Beroea (Aleppo) that served as the foci for communications, with routes west to Antioch, north-west into Cilicia and towns such as Tarsus and Adana, and south towards Apamea, Emesa, Damascus, the coast and the cities of Palestine and Arabia (Transjordan). To the south from the Roman provinces of Palestine III or Arabia a number of well-established caravan routes passed along the wadis into the Ḥijāz and on to the coast or inland; and on the opposite side of the Arabian Peninsula a similar network of routes led up parallel to or along the coast into southern Iraq. From northern Syria also a series of key routes led across the Cilician plain and thence through the passes – in particular through the so-called Cilician Gates – northwards onto the Anatolian plateau. From Mesopotamia and northern al-Jazīra further routes led across the steppe-like highlands of Azerbaijan into the southern Caucasus region, or down through the mountains of Daylam into the Caspian littoral and hence north towards Darband and a series of heavily fortified strategic passes giving access from the steppes to the north into the Caucasus and beyond. Routes eastwards from Mesopotamia were constrained primarily by the Zagros, through whose few passes access was had to Media and the Iranian plateau. The major southern road runs from Ahwāz via the so-called Persian Gates across the mountains to Shīrāz. From here further routes radiate south to the coast of the Indian Ocean and the Gulf, north north-east to Yazd or Iṣfahān, across the plateau and desert to the oasis of Kirmān, and then on to Makrān and Sind. From Hamadhān the northern route leads into the Ṭabaristān highlands, and on to the city of Rayy. From there another route crosses the mountains into the coastal plain of the southern Caspian, from where the road east to Jurjān runs along the costal plain; while the eastward road continues across south of the mountains to Nīshāpūr in western Khurāsān. From here radiate routes north-west into the Jurjān region, east and then north-east through Khurasān towards Marw and Transoxania, or south towards Herat and then east on to Balkh, each supported by the agricultural output of its own river basin hinterland. From these cities roads led south into Sīstān and cities such as Zaranj and Kandahar. Eastwards the road continued to Kabul; southwards into the province of Sind and the port of Daybul on the Indian Ocean.

Asia Minor was traversed by a series of major strategic routes which crossed the Taurus and Anti-Taurus via the passes already mentioned and led across the plateau, either to the northern coast and the great entrepôt of Trebizond, or to the north-western and western coastal plains and cities such as

Constantinople, Nicaea and Ephesus. The Balkans likewise were characterised by the important military roads radiating out from Constantinople through Thrace, either north towards the Danube frontier, north and west towards the Adriatic, the most famous in the latter case being the Via Egnatia, of course, which crossed the mountains to Dyrrhachion (mod. Dürres), and the so-called 'military road' from Constantinople up to the Danube.

Land use and exploitation of resources

The exploitation of natural resources and the ways in which human populations employ the land, flora and fauna at their disposal are closely determined by the geophysical and climatic framework described above, and can be grouped under four basic headings: – arable farming; pastoral farming; the exploitation of woodland and scrubland; and the extraction and working of mineral resources. Agriculture can in turn be divided into dry – rainfall-dependent – and wet – irrigation-dependent – cultivation, while the type of pastoral activity depends on a range of variables, in particular height, degree of aridity, type of vegetation and grass cover, and so forth. The extent of agricultural activity, of the exploitation of natural resources such as woodlands, and of particular crops such as cereals or grapes, is reflected also in the climatic fluctuations and shifts that took place across the period in question. Yet even in apparently adverse and hostile conditions human activity produced a thriving agriculture – along the desert fringes of Syria and Palestine, for example, substantial populations were served by extensive and efficient irrigation systems in late Roman times and thereafter. Egypt was the bread basket of the late Roman and early Byzantine state, just as Mesopotamia was by far the most productive and wealthiest region of the Sasanian kingdom. But cereal production was also an important feature of the limited but fertile coastal and riverine plains of central and northern Syria and parts of Palestine, alongside the equally important production of olive oil and a range of fruits and vegetables. Grain production was likewise a major feature of the Sawād and of most of the fertile river valleys and watered uplands of Iran, Anatolia and the Balkans, and rice was also cultivated in parts of Syria and Khūzistān, as well as in Bactria.[16] Considerable regional variations in the types of fruits and vegetables and the different emphasis on oleoculture and viticulture

16 C. Brunner, 'Geographical and administrative divisions: Settlements and economy', in E. Yarshater (ed.), *The Cambridge history of Iran*, vol. III: *The Seleucid, Parthian and Sasanian periods* (Cambridge, 1983), p. 754. For an overview of the Mediterranean in this respect, see P. Horden and N. Purcell, *The corrupting sea: A study of Mediterranean history* (Oxford, 2000), pp. 175–224.

reflected long-term cultural and economic tradition as well, with the Mediterranean lands concentrating on olives and vines in contrast to the production of nuts and a wide range of other fruits in Iraq and Iran. Apart from wheat, barley and rice, for example, al-Ṭabarī lists vines, dates, alfalfa and olives as products which the Sasanian kings taxed; other sources suggest that vegetables, cotton, sesame and cucumbers were untaxed.[17] Between the zones of agricultural production were substantial districts in which a pastoral economy dominated. The marginal regions between the two were the site of mixed economic activity with accordingly differently articulated social relations from those typical of the arable heartlands or the nomadic or transhumant societies of the mountains and plateaux, as in the foothills of the Zagros, for example, where sheep raising was a major aspect of the local economy but where there were small gardens and where limited cereal production was also carried on, or in the Ḥijāz and in southern Arabia. But such economies depended on an accommodation with the systems around them, and both pastoralists and more strictly agricultural economies likewise depend for the most part on a symbiotic relationship with one another, with animal husbandry generally playing an important role in most agrarian cultures. Along the Zagros chain itself and throughout the mountainous steppe of Media and Azerbaijan different groups of nomads maintained their sheep, goats and horses. Horse and cattle farming were typical of the middle and south-eastern plateaux regions of Asia Minor, southern Iran and Khurāsān, and southern Azerbaijan, shared with and giving way to sheep and goats on the middle and higher ground; a transhumant economy characterised the northern face of the Pontic Alps along the southern shore of the Black Sea and much of the central and western Balkan zone, as well as the divide between the Iranian plateau and the surrounding non-arid lowlands. In North Africa the semi-arid zones along the Mediterranean coast in Cyrenaica and Egypt as well as in the foothills of the Atlas and related highlands supported a nomadic or semi-nomadic economy based on camels, sheep and goats.

The early Islamic period saw a considerable number of changes in this traditional pattern, which had itself not been static, since state demands, on the one hand, and market demands, on the other, encouraged shifts in the patterns of production – government demands for wheat for armies impacted on both Roman and Sasanian agriculture as private landlords and taxpayers responded to market and price fluctuations. Production of cash crops for specific markets,

17 T. Nöldeke, *Geschichte der Perser und Araber zur Zeit der Sasaniden* (Leiden, 1879), p. 245.

and in the context of a highly monetised economy, directly affected the organisation of labour on the land and the ways in which it might be taxed in the late Roman empire, most notably in Egypt but almost certainly elsewhere too, as in late Sasanian Iraq.[18] Warfare, natural disaster and demographic changes appear to have adversely affected irrigation systems in Iraq and the Negev, or the production of olive oil in northern Syria, during the later sixth century; although by the same token many districts continued to flourish and to maintain their agricultural and irrigation infrastructure. During the seventh and especially the eighth centuries, however, a number of new crops appear which were to transform the picture of agrarian production, making possible the development of local economic subsystems producing for local and long-distance markets as well as the rapid growth of urban populations and thus taxable resources. Such developments also affected dietary and culinary traditions – as well as ceramic forms, of course. And while changes such as these must in all probability have been stimulated by expanding urban demand following the conquest, the role of the new Arab-Islamic elite as well as their own traditions of estate management and exploitation also played a role; and this in turn affected patterns of political power and control of resources, so that the political history of the early Islamic world cannot adequately be understood in all its complexity without reference to the history of agrarian and urban production and the distribution and pattern of consumption of resources. Some idea of the relative wealth of the different parts of the Islamic world can be gauged by comparing the very different contributions made by different provinces to late Roman and, much later, to Ottoman revenues, in which it becomes clear that Iraq, on the one hand, and Syria and Egypt, on the other, were by far the biggest contributors to government tax income in comparison with most other provinces under their respective rulers.[19] What is important to note, however, is that the arrival of Islam and the rise in importance of cash crops such as sugar and cotton, as well as the introduction of many new crops, stimulated some fairly dramatic changes in this picture.[20]

18 P. Sarris, 'The origins of the manorial economy: New insights from late Antiquity', *English Historical Review*, 119 (2004); P. Sarris, 'Rehabilitating the great estate: Aristocratic property and economic growth in the Late Antique east', in W. Bowden, L. Lavan and C. Machado (eds.), *Recent research on the Late Antique countryside* (Leiden, 2004); Morony, 'Economic boundaries?', pp. 168–72; J. Banaji, *Agrarian change in Late Antiquity: Gold, labour and aristocratic dominance* (Oxford 2001), pp. 16–18, 36ff., 100ff., 214–19.

19 See M. F. Hendy, *Studies in the Byzantine monetary economy, c. 300–1450* (Cambridge, 1985), pp. 613–18.

20 A. M. Watson, 'A medieval green revolution: New crops and farming techniques in the early Islamic world', in A. L. Udovitch (ed.), *The Islamic Middle East, 700–1900: Studies in*

Rice (from which rice flour was ground) was cultivated in southern Iraq, and bread (whether of rice flour or wheat flour) was the basic food of all the populations of the Mediterranean and Iranian worlds. Cereals were therefore the dominant crop grown by the majority of rural producers. Egypt, with the rich alluvial soils of the Nile Valley and watered by extensive local irrigation systems, probably produced by far the greatest quantity per head of the producing population; but the plains of northern Syria, the coastal regions of Asia Minor, Thrace and Thessaly, the North African provinces, the Sawād and Khūzistān floodplains also produced substantial quantities of cereals. The oasis centres of the Iranian plateau and of Khurāsān likewise provided for themselves and for a certain amount of commercial activity in respect of grain production, as well as a range of fruits and vegetables. As well as wheat, a substantial element in the grain production of the empire was barley, with smaller amounts of millet in certain zones (southern Arabia, sub-Saharan Africa) – regarded generally as inappropriate for human consumption. Probably from the fourth century on (although the dating is problematic) hard wheats – with a greater proportion of protein per volume – were gradually replacing the soft wheats that had hitherto dominated Mediterranean cereal agriculture (with certain exceptions, for example, in Egypt, where the introduction of hard wheats appears to have pre-dated its appearance elsewhere in the Roman world), with important consequences for both diet and cereal production in general in the centuries to follow.[21] In Iraq and the oases of Iran and Khurāsān, dates, nuts and fruits were also produced, often in substantial quantities sufficient for export well beyond the centres of production. Vegetables, pulses (beans etc.) and root crops were also cultivated wherever cereals were also grown, usually on the basis of household garden plots rather than extensively, so that villages and towns were for the most part supplied with all the essentials of life – food, drink, clothing, the materials for housing and the livestock for transport – from their immediate hinterlands.

Self-sufficiency was never absolute: villages were also part of a wider world of exchange consisting of many communities within a particular region, from which the inhabitants could obtain goods and services they did not produce themselves, and through which they might also attract commerce from very much further afield. At the same time the organisation of production varied

economic and social history (Princeton, 1981); A. M. Watson, *Agricultural innovation in the early Islamic world: The diffusion of crops and farming techniques*, Cambridge Studies in Islamic Civilization (Cambridge, 1983).

21 R. S. Bagnall, *Egypt in Late Antiquity* (Princeton, 1993); C. Morrisson and J.-P. Sodini, 'The sixth-century economy', in A. Laiou *et al.* (eds.), *The economic history of Byzantium from the seventh through the fifteenth century* (Washington DC, 2002), p. 196.

regionally and offered a multifaceted picture: rural communities of mixed ownership marketing their own produce or that of a landlord, large estates with highly commercialised enterprises worked through wage labour, mixed estates depending less on commercial markets and more on state purchasing for the army, diversified self-sufficient estates, for example, and so forth.[22] Only the largest cities, and then mostly those with access to ports and the sea, had the resources to import goods from further away than their own locality on a regular basis, and these were mostly luxuries for those who could pay for them. Rome and Constantinople imported bulk goods – chiefly grain and oil – on a large scale; but they were notable exceptions, with unusually large urban populations and substantial governmental and ecclesiastical bureaucracies. Madāʾin/Ctesiphon and its Islamic successors were supplied from their immediate hinterland and from further afield by river and canal. But dependence on distant centres of production was possible only because it was paid for by states or governments, or because supply by river and canal was practical. Inland towns were generally entirely dependent on what was produced locally, and this was strongly inflected in terms of variety and availability by seasonal and regional fluctuations.

This was especially the case in those areas where irrigation systems were essential. Particularly significant in this respect were the *qanāt*s of northern Syria, Iraq, Iran and Khurāsān, underground water channels which needed careful maintenance and upon which many major settlements depended for their survival. Irrigation systems had a long history in these areas, but in certain parts of the Sasanian world saw a very considerable expansion as a result of state investment during the fourth and fifth centuries. Under Shāpūr I (r. 241–72 CE), for example, there seems to have taken place a substantial restructuring of the irrigation system in Khūzistān, with new canals and extended *qanāt*s being constructed and connected by a series of reservoirs and sluices, a programme that impacted on both newly irrigated marginal lands and traditionally irrigated areas, and which made possible the substantial

22 See Banaji, *Agrarian change in Late Antiquity*, pp. 6–22, for example, with literature. Village settlements were often of very mixed structure, comprising freeholding cultivators, tenants of local or urban landlords (of varying scale and situation), simple labourers, artisans who also possessed and farmed land, either directly or through the use of hired labour, and so forth. Indeed, recent work has tended to emphasise the interpenetration of large-scale and small-scale landholding and exploitation in both villages and estates. See, e.g., C. Zuckerman, *Du village à l'empire: Autour du registre fiscal d'Aphroditô (525/526)* (Paris, 2004), and note Wickham, *Framing the early Middle Ages*, p. 243.

growth in population and urbanism that took place over this period.[23] In Mesopotamia itself a huge investment in the northern district, probably during the later third and early fourth centuries, linked the Tigris to the Euphrates by a canal from which a network of lesser waterways irrigated the areas to the south, while further south new networks of waterways and irrigation canals were constructed, investments which further stimulated both levels of production and urbanism.[24] The largest and most impressive of these works, however, was carried out through the construction of the system which linked the Tigris and the Diyālā basin, vastly extending the areas already irrigated by works undertaken by the earlier Parthian kings in the region.[25]

Sowing, harvesting and the pattern of seasonal activities depended on location. For those regions dominated by a Mediterranean climate vegetables were harvested in June, cereals in July and vines and olives in the autumn, after which the land not given over to arboriculture was normally opened to livestock for pasturage and manuring. Ploughing and tilling generally took place in October and November, and planting/sowing followed immediately thereafter in order to take advantage of the winter rains and the seasonal humidity of the soil. But the cycle might be different in more arid regions: in Syria and on the Iranian plateau harvesting also took place in November, with ploughing and planting in July and August, for example. In those areas in which agricultural activity was supported by systems of irrigation, as in the Nile Valley, or drier regions with very low annual rainfall, the pattern was

23 See R. M. Adams and D. P. Hansen, 'Archaeological reconnaissance and soundings in Jundi Shapur', *Ars Islamica*, 7 (1968). The dating of the *qanāts* is, however, problematic, by association usually with physically proximate sites, rarely by internal evidence, so that some doubts remain as to whether or not they pre-date or post-date the arrival of Islam.

24 R. M. Adams, *Heartland of cities: Surveys of ancient settlement and land use on the central floodplain of the Euphrates* (Chicago, 1981), pp. 179–83, 208–11; M. Gibson, *The city and area of Kish* (Miami, 1972); R. M. Adams and H. J. Nissen, *The Uruk countryside: The natural setting of urban societies* (Chicago, 1972), pp. 59–63.

25 R. M. Adams, *The land behind Baghdad: A history of settlement on the Diyala plains* (Chicago and London, 1965), pp. 61–80, 104–5; P. Christensen, *The decline of Iranshahr: Irrigation and environments in the history of the Middle East, 500 BC to AD 1500* (Copenhagen, 1993), pp. 107–12, 227, 234; M. Morony, 'The late Sasanian economic impact on the Arabian Peninsula', *Nāme-ye-Irān-e Bāstān*, 1, 2 (2001/2), pp. 30–1 (for similar systems in sixth-century Sasanian-ruled Oman); J. D. Howard-Johnston, 'The two great powers in Late Antiquity: A comparison', in A. Cameron (ed.), *The Byzantine and early Islamic Near East*, vol. III: *States, resources and armies*, Studies in Late Antiquity and Early Islam 1 (Princeton, 1995), pp. 199–203 (now repr. in J. Howard-Johnston, *East Rome, Sasanian Persia and the end of antiquity* (Aldershot, 2006), vol. I).

different again. Returns on planting similarly varied: the highest average returns in fertile regions appear to have been of the order of 7:1 or 8:1, with variations in either direction. Lower returns in drier or less well-watered districts have been calculated at some 5:1, but might be considerably lower; and all these figures varied slightly across each district, according to the type of crop, seasonal climatic fluctuations and whether or not irrigation systems were employed.

Livestock – sheep, goats, cattle, horses and pigs – were a feature of most rural communities, but certain areas concentrated on stock raising more than on other spheres of production. The raising of mules and horses was an essential for the state, for the public postal and transport system as well as for the army. Substantial stud farms were maintained in parts of Asia Minor, but are also known from North Africa, Italy and Syria, as well as Fārs and Khurāsān. The Anatolian plateau was dominated by stock farming, often on large, ranch-like estates, and while agriculture played an essential role in the maintenance of the population, the richest landlords of the region seem generally to have based their wealth on this type of production. But stock farming played an important role throughout the east Roman and Sasanian worlds, and sheep and goats, along with pigs, formed an important element in the productive capacity of many rural communities, sharing with cereal production the attentions of the peasant farmer. Livestock was the source of many essential items – not just meat, skins or milk, but also hides, leather, wool, felt, glues and horn, as well as bone and gut for both decorative and practical purposes.[26]

Land was exploited not just by agriculture and animal husbandry, but also for timber and its derivatives – oils, bark, resins and so forth – and for minerals. Whereas the former has not been studied in any depth, with a few exceptions,[27] the extraction of minerals has been the subject of a good deal of research, and a reasonably accurate picture of what mineral resources were extracted from which regions of the late ancient world can now be drawn. Of the ores mined or collected, iron was probably the most important, needed for weapons and tools. Centres of iron mining included north-eastern Anatolia and the central southern Black Sea coastal regions, central Syria, the Taurus mountains and the south Balkans, Oman and the Arabian

26 For patterns of agricultural production and the seasons, see M. Kaplan, *Les hommes et la terre à Byzance du VIe au XIe siècles* (Paris, 1992), esp. pp. 25–87.

27 A. W. Dunn, 'The exploitation and control of woodland and scrubland in the Byzantine world', *Byzantine and Modern Greek Sudies*, 16 (1992).

Peninsula, and especially in the Elburz range and southern Azerbaijan highlands, as well as parts of the Zagros and, on the Iranian plateau, in the Kirmān region. Tin, generally alloyed with copper to make bronze, was mined in the Taurus and the Arabian Peninsula, but was also imported to the eastern Mediterranean from the south-western parts of Britain; bronze was extremely commonly used – both for low-value coins and for a huge range of household utensils and tools, and ornamental objects. Copper, which could be alloyed with zinc to make brass, was extracted from the Caucasus and southern Pontic regions, northern Syria, Oman, the Zagros and the Iranian plateau, and the central Balkans and Spain. Crucial to the economy of the Roman world was gold, of course, obtained from the Caucasus, from Armenia, which had rich deposits, as did also the Arabian Peninsula, and to a lesser extent from the Balkans, although the location of Roman and Byzantine gold workings remains largely unclear.[28] The Sasanians competed with Rome over Caucasian sources, although limited workings in the western Elburz, as well as further afield in Oman, Nubia and Abyssinia, also provided supplies. The Arabian Peninsula appears to have been far more important as a source of precious metals than has generally been recognised, and this may provide additional reasons for the urgency of Byzantine and Sasanian interest in the area.[29] There were sources of silver, particularly important to the Sasanians in respect of their coinage, in the Elburz, the Iranian plateau and southern Caucasus, Oman, Arabia and also Khurāsān; as well as from the Taurus, the central Pontic Alps and Armenia, and the central Balkans. In the case of both these precious metals governments tried as hard as possible to control both their import and export. Control over stocks of precious metals was achieved partly through recycling, although this could not ensure a constant supply.[30]

28 See in particular G. W. Heck, 'Gold mining in Arabia and the rise of the Islamic state', *JESHO*, 42 (1999); and A. H. M. Jones, *The later Roman empire 284–602: A social and administrative study* (Oxford, 1964), pp. 834–9; O. Davies, *Roman mines in Europe* (Oxford, 1935); K. Greene, *The archaeology of the Roman economy* (Berkeley, 1986), pp. 142–8; J. C. Edmondson, 'Mining in the later Roman Empire and beyond', *Journal of Roman Studies*, 79 (1989); and the brief treatment in M. McCormick, *Origins of the European economy: Communications and commerce, AD 300–900* (Cambridge, 2001), pp. 42–53.

29 See Heck, 'Gold mining in Arabia and the rise of the Islamic state', pp. 368–72.

30 For Iran see J. V. Harrison, 'Minerals', in W. B. Fisher (ed.), *The Cambridge history of Iran*, vol. I: *The land of Iran* (Cambridge, 1968); Morony, 'The late Sasanian economic impact on the Arabian Peninsula', pp. 29, 32–3, 35; and esp. D. M. Dunlop, 'Sources of gold and silver according to al-Hamdānī', *Studia Islamica*, 8 (1957) (repr. in M. G. Morony (ed.), *Production and the exploitation of resources*, The Formation of the Classical Islamic World II (Princeton, 2002), chap. 1).

The social environment

Population, cities and villages in the late ancient world

Discussion of the economic relationships and structures of Late Antiquity has expanded enormously over the last twenty years, a result of two tendencies – to see 'Late Antiquity' as a period stretching from the fourth or even third century CE to the eighth, and to extend its geographical coverage to encompass a much wider world than the territories of the Roman empire. Sasanian Iran, parts of Central Asia and India and the Far East are now, quite reasonably, brought into the picture, as historians and archaeologists recognise the need to see Rome or Persia as parts of a much greater and more complex whole. And although there remain some important disagreements about specific regional differences in the pace and degree of development, recent work has made it possible to offer a fairly coherent account of the nature of the late ancient economy. It has become clear, in addition, that the 'economy' of the late ancient world has to be conceived of as consisting in fact of several economic sub-systems, overlapping and interpenetrating at different points. At the same time, the concept of the 'economy' is complicated by the role of the state, in its Roman and Sasanian forms, in so far as government or court demands for resources in various guises, whether money, produce, services or skills, directly impacted upon the ways in which local society operated.[31] The arrangements and institutional structures through which resources were appropriated and the legal forms that justified this process were affected by notions of property and rights but at the same time directly determined the

31 Such work has taken its cue in particular from the work of Brown and Mazzarino; see e.g. P. R. L. Brown, *The world of Late Antiquity: From Marcus Aurelius to Muhammed* (London, 1971); G. W. Bowersock, Peter Brown and Oleg Grabar (eds.), *Interpreting Late Antiquity: Essays on the postclassical world* (Cambridge, MA, 1999); S. Mazzarino, *La fine del mondo antico* (Milan, 1988). There are now a number of succinct summaries of the material, which provide useful syntheses of the evidence, the literature and current interpretations. See in particular M. Whittow, 'Decline and fall? Studying long-term change in the east', in L. Lavan and W. Bowden (eds.), *Theory and practice in late Antique archaeology* (Leiden, 2003), pp. 404–18; Morrisson and Sodini, 'The sixth-century economy'; B. Ward-Perkins, 'Specialised production and exchange', in A. Cameron, B. Ward-Perkins and M. Whitby (eds.), *The Cambridge ancient history*, vol. XIV: *Late Antiquity: Empire and successors, AD 425–600* (Cambridge, 2000); B. Ward-Perkins, 'Land, labour and settlement', in Cameron *et al.* (eds.), *Late Antiquity*; C. J. Wickham, review of A. Giardina (ed.), *Società romana e impero tardoantico, III: Le merci. Gli insediamenti* (Rome-Bari, 1986), in *Journal of Roman Studies*, 78 (1988); and A. Chavarría and T. Lewit, 'Archaeological research on the late antique countryside: A bibliographic essay', in Bowden, Lavan and Machado (eds.), *Recent research*. Quite apart from these, the substantial volumes of McCormick, *Origins of the European economy*, and Wickham, *Framing the early Middle Ages*, are situated in precisely this milieu.

ways in which political power and authority were expressed and exercised. The first Muslim conquerors thus inherited an exceedingly complex set of economic and political structures and relationships, and it is in consequence hardly surprising that early Islamic institutions and state systems were heavily determined by the framework within which they now had to function, the more so since that framework and its constituent elements were themselves evolving, and continued to evolve, but in an increasingly Islamised context. To speak of 'the economy of the late ancient world' is, therefore, to do this complex and multifaceted set of relationships and social practices a very considerable injustice, yet we cannot escape some degree of generalisation if we are to try to encapsulate the key features of the socio-economic landscape in which Islam was to implant itself from the early 630s CE on. We may thus attempt to summarise the most significant developments under a series of headings, beginning with population and moving on to cities, urbanism and settlement, the state and fiscal systems, and commerce.

Given the geographical constraints described already, it is apparent that the pattern of settlement, and in particular its density, will reflect this environment very closely. A comparison of the areas of settlement density and locations of villages, towns or cities in the late Roman and early Byzantine world with modern demographic patterns demonstrates a remarkable continuity in all the regions with which this volume is concerned. Such a comparison says little about absolute numbers or about the fluctuations across time (seasonally or even on a day-to-day basis) in density and extent of settlement, as marginal lands were brought into, or fell out of, cultivation or as irrigation systems were neglected or maintained or extended; but it does point to the relationship between human populations and the ability of the land to support them. A comparison of the demographic map of Turkey before the Second World War (representing the mid-1930s) with a map showing the density of Roman cities and Byzantine episcopal sees, for example, highlights the fact that it is more or less the same areas that could maintain substantial populations in ancient and medieval times, that saw the densest concentration of urban centres, and that may thus be taken to have remained the most productive and heavily settled regions of the Byzantine period after the transformation of the late ancient city network after the seventh century. A similar pattern emerges from a comparison of Roman and medieval population centres with modern demographic concentrations in the Balkans.

Estimating pre-modern population numbers and densities is notoriously difficult and fraught with dangers, methodological and factual, so while the distribution of settlement can, up to a point, be represented reasonably accurately, the numbers suggested for mean population levels must be taken with a considerable degree of caution, however credible they may appear to be. The climatic and geographical features that determined land use likewise determined where populations were concentrated and how many people the land could support. The degree of continuity from medieval to modern times is, in this respect, considerable. But there were within our period very considerable fluctuations, both in respect of the relationship between the populations of urban and rural regions and in terms of their density. Broadly speaking, it has been assumed that there was a long downward curve in population in the Roman empire during the late ancient period, although with very marked regional variations, which continued into the later seventh and eighth centuries in what was left of the empire after the first Islamic conquests, followed by a slow recovery into the later ninth and tenth centuries, with a fairly dramatic rise in the twelfth century. In fact, archaeological data would now suggest a marked regional upturn during the fifth and sixth centuries in this pattern for much of Syria, Palestine and Egypt, and for Mesopotamia and southern Iraq, with the downturn continuing slowly in North Africa and the western parts of the Roman world at the same time. The evidence for central and eastern Iran is too sparse yet to generate such generalisations. It has been estimated that the population of Roman Europe was in the order of approximately 67–70 million at the end of the second century CE, falling to around 27–30 million by the early eighth century (but rising again by 1300 to some 73 million, with a particularly noticeable rise about 1200 CE). The most recent estimates for the late Roman and Byzantine areas proposes a population for the empire's eastern provinces of some 19–20 million just before the middle of the sixth century (before the plague of the 540s), with a further 7 million in the west; of 17 million in the early seventh century, with a reduction to about 7 million by the middle of the eighth century. But there is no real way of knowing how accurate these actually are.[32]

Some evidence suggests a similar curve in the Near Eastern world, yet it should also be emphasised that there were marked regional variations. Thus in the Sasanian lands, especially Mesopotamia, the Diyālā basin and Khūzistān, population expansion based upon the evidence of expanding irrigation systems and urbanisation has been argued for the period from the

32 Banaji, *Agrarian change in Late Antiquity*, pp. 16–18, 214–19; T. J. Wilkinson, *Town and country in southeastern Anatolia*, 2 vols. (Chicago, 1990), vol. I, pp. 117–28; Ward-Perkins, 'Land, labour and settlement', pp. 320–7 (but emphasising the chronological and regional fluctuations and inflections); C. Foss, 'Syria in transition, AD 550–750: An archaeological approach', *Dumbarton Oaks Papers*, 51 (1997), pp. 259–61; Morrisson and Sodini, 'The sixth-century economy', pp. 174–6.

later third century CE. While it has been argued that on Roman territory this expansion in the eastern provinces may well have drawn to a close around the middle of the sixth and into the first half of the seventh century, beginning in northern Syria and its coastal towns earlier than in the south, a reconsideration of the archaeological material suggests a very much later onset of change – well after the Islamic conquests, in fact;[33] and in the Sasanian world a similar slowing down and possibly an ensuing contraction is proposed, purportedly as a result of the failure of the central government to maintain the expanded irrigation networks in Mesopotamia, perhaps datable to the early seventh century. At the same time, however, the three areas where this expansion and contraction have been highlighted are also the only areas for which substantial survey material is available,[34] and this inevitably renders the general pattern in the Sasanian kingdom somewhat ambiguous, especially in the light of the reassessment of the eastern Roman material from Syria and Palestine. By the same token, it has been argued that demographic change throughout these regions was in fact very gradual, and the dramatic shifts of the middle and later Sasanian period reflect merely the movement of an otherwise stable population from dispersed rural habitats to more concentrated urban centres. Indeed, the expansion may itself reflect an overdevelopment that was not sustainable, so that later 'contraction' is in fact to be seen as a return to a 'normal', or at least sustainable, regime.[35] But while there is some disagreement about the specific demographic pattern in the different regions mentioned above, and while one can point to a number of exceptions, quite apart from a differential rate of change from east to west (including important regional and local variations), the overall pattern – a long-term decline punctuated by marked regional anomalies – seems now generally agreed.[36]

33 For the tailing off of expansion, and subsequent contraction in the later sixth century, see H. Kennedy, 'From *polis* to *madina*', *Past and Present*, 106 (1985); H. Kennedy, 'The last century of Byzantine Syria', *Byzantinische Forschungen*, 10 (1985). The tendency currently is to push these changes into the later sixth and seventh centuries, or beyond, depending upon region. See for example J. Magness, *The archaeology of the early Islamic settlements in Palestine* (Winona Lake, IN, 2003), esp. 195ff.; and J. Magness, 'Redating the forts at Ein Boqeq, Upper Zohar, and other sites in SE Judaea, and the implications for the nature of the *Limes Palaestinae*', in J. H. Humphrey (ed.), *The Roman and Byzantine Near East*, vol. II: *Some recent archaeological research*, JRA Supplementary Series 31 (Portsmouth, RI, 1999).

34 K. Abdi, 'Archaeological research in the Islamabad plain, central western Zagros mountains: Preliminary results from the first season, summer 1998', *Iran*, 37 (1999); K. M. Trinkaus, 'Pre-Islamic settlement and land-use in Dāmghān, north-east Iran', *Iranica Antiqua*, 18 (1983).

35 R. J. Wenke, 'Western Iran in the Partho-Sasanian period: The imperial transformation', in F. Hole (ed.), *The archaeology of western Iran* (Washington, DC, and London, 1987), pp. 252, 257–8, 261. I am grateful to Donald Whitcomb for discussion on these issues.

36 See for recent discussion Morony, 'Economic boundaries?', pp. 181–3.

The late Roman urban landscape

The city was one of the most important features of the late ancient landscape, both in respect of the social organisation of production and the ownership and control of resources in land and manpower. Cities exist in a physical as well as a human social context, since the territory around urban centres was populated by a vast range of types of rural habitation whose occupants were responsible for the labour and effort that transformed the landscape. Evidence for village life varies according to the quality of the written sources and the extent to which archaeological investigation has focused on non-urban contexts, but the relationship between rural hinterland and village, on the one hand, and urban centre, whether large or small, on the other, is symbiotic, but in ways that cannot necessarily be used to interpret the processes of economic change and transformation evident from the archaeological and documentary record.[37]

There are three basic paths towards urban development. First, in the sense of urban centre or 'town' – that is, a location at which producers from the surrounding locality can meet on a regular basis to exchange goods and services, where local political power can be concentrated, which serve also as a cultic focus, that is to say, a religious centre, all of which presupposes physical accessibility (roads and transport from the locality to the town) and a water supply. Second, cities may grow out of settlements reflecting an original concentration of tribal or lineage population groups concentrated together for defence, which serve as centres of social and economic activity and which then evolve distinctive political and social institutions, acquiring thereby a specific status which distinguishes them from other rural settlements. Third, cities in suitable locations (the latter varying historically according to the demands of supra-local political authorities) attract administrative and institutional functions, as centres of military and fiscal activities. While these are somewhat broad, they can serve as a rough typological guide for urban centres in the late ancient world, and they are not exclusive, since the vast majority of larger and middling cities represent a mixture of all three elements.

As many studies have now shown, there had been a slow process of transformation in the pattern of late Roman urban society over the centuries preceding both the Persian wars and the Arab Islamic conquests. Although archaeological surveys and excavations demonstrate a revival in the fortunes

37 For a good comparative overview and analysis, see Wickham, *Framing the early Middle Ages*, pp. 591–692.

of many eastern cities in the later fifth and early sixth centuries, accompanied by substantial investment in public and private buildings, often on a monumental scale, they also show an almost universal tendency for cities to lose many of the features familiar from their classical structure – the lesser provincial towns first, followed at a somewhat later date, and influenced also by the extent to which the government intervened to assist them, by the larger, economically and politically more important centres. Major public buildings fell into disrepair, systems of water supply were often abandoned (suggesting a drop in population), rubbish was dumped in abandoned buildings, major thoroughfares were built on. These changes may not necessarily have involved any substantial reduction in economic or exchange activity in cities, and they happened at differentiated rates across the different provinces of the empire according to local economic and political conditions. The construction of defensive walls around many cities during the fifth and sixth centuries has generally been interpreted as a shrinkage of occupied areas of many cities, but this may not always have been the case.[38] On the other hand, the undoubted decline in the maintenance of public structures or amenities in the major, traditional Hellenistic–Roman cities – baths, aqueducts, drains, street surfaces, walls – does suggest a major shift in aspects of urban living, and of finance and administration in particular. The period after the arrival of the great Justinianic plague in the 540s is especially marked in this respect. But this shift is partly balanced by evidence for a considerable and widespread investment in church building (and related structures) of all kinds. An additional factor was the evolution of a more complex hierarchy of urbanism as many functions of the older cities began to be shared from the fourth century by smaller centres, often fortified, and often the focus of military or civil administration as well as of local exchange and production for their localities.[39]

Many older provincial cities, where they played a role in imperial civil or military structures, changed to conform to this pattern – from the later fourth

38 H. Vanhaverbeke, F. Martens, M. Waelkens and J. Poblome, 'Late Antiquity in the territory of Sagalassos', in Bowden, Lavan and Machado (eds.), *Recent research*, at p. 253 (Sagalassos); T. Gregory, 'Fortification and urban design in early Byzantine Greece', in R. L. Hohlfelder (ed.), *City, town and countryside in the early Byzantine era* (New York, 1982) (Corinth and other Greek cities).

39 A. W. Dunn, 'Heraclius' "reconstruction of cities" and their sixth-century Balkan antecedents', in *Acta XIII Congressus Internationalis Archaeologiae Christianae*, Studi di Antichità Cristiana 54 (Vatican City and Split, 1998); A. W. Dunn, 'Continuity and change in the Macedonian countryside from Gallienus to Justinian', in Bowden, Lavan and Machado (eds.), *Recent research*; Morrisson and Sodini, 'The sixth-century economy', pp. 179–81. See in particular the essays in J. Henning (ed.), *Post-Roman towns, trade and settlement in Europe and Byzantium*, vol. II. *Byzantium, Pliska, and the Balkans*, Millenium-Studien 5/2 (Berlin and New York, 2007).

and fifth centuries in the Balkans, somewhat later in less exposed parts of the eastern empire. Their evolution on imperial territory into the typical middle Byzantine *kastron* is not difficult to follow. But the path that urban development would take thereafter is determined also by the political histories of the areas in question. While they share a common late Roman heritage, the fate of towns in territories remaining to the empire after the middle of the seventh century was very different from that of the towns and cities that were in Islamic territory, for example – a reflection of the beleaguered and impoverished situation of the eastern Roman or Byzantine empire in the seventh and eighth centuries.

There was a series of interconnected factors in this long-term process. The partial confiscation of city lands which was made almost complete under Valens (r. 364–78) and Valentinian (r. 364–75) and then finalised under Justinian (r. 527–65), and a consequent decline in the independent economic resources of cities, was clearly important. An increasing level of intervention by imperial officials in local financial matters, culminating in the establishment of the *vindices* under Anastasius and the stipulations on civic building by Justinian, likewise played a key role. Significant changes in the relationship between the wealthier *curiales* and local magnates, on the one hand, and the less well-off, on the other, the so-called 'decline' of the curial order in general, also had an impact on the administrative and social function of cities. Cities *as corporate bodies* were less well-off than they had been before about the middle of the sixth century. But this did not mean that urban life declined, or that towns no longer fulfilled their role as centres of exchange and production. Indeed, the literary sources and the archaeological record show that commercial activity continues into the seventh century. The Church was also from the fourth century a competitor with the city for the consumption of resources, especially with the increasing importance of the bishop in local and provincial affairs and government. Citizens, particularly the wealthy, continued to donate funds or buildings to their cities, but this can hardly have compensated for the corporate loss of resources.

Archaeological investigation has revealed an increasing localisation of exchange activity from the later sixth century, although this does not have to mean a change in the role of cities as centres of such exchange. The Roman state had quite deliberately during the third, fourth and fifth centuries followed a policy of 'rationalising' patterns of distribution of cities. Many cities in over-densely occupied regions were deprived of the status and privileges of city, while others which were of importance to the state in its fiscal–administrative structure were 'incorporated' and received city status for the first time. This had nothing to do with economic interests, but reflected rather the desire of the emperors to establish a network of centres adequate to the demands of the fiscal system. Considerable numbers of the 'cities' that were suppressed in this process had been little more than villages representing the autonomous or semi-autonomous communities of the pre-Roman states incorporated into the empire. By endowing certain settlements with city status and, more especially, with local fiscal–administrative functions and responsibility, the state assured such cities of their continued existence and at the same time enhanced their local importance. It is a logical concomitant that, when the elites in such communities were no longer able adequately to fulfil this role for the state, and when the state began to supervise city fiscal affairs directly, the continued existence of such cities would become a matter of indifference to the central government, at least in functional terms. Within the bounds of the Roman world, it was the ideological and symbolic importance of cities and urban culture, expressed through imperial involvement in urban building and renewal in several cases, that prevented this happening at this stage. In addition, cities particularly associated with Christianity – through a local saint's cult, for example – enhanced their chances of flourishing where they did not already possess a primary economic character (Euchaita and Resafa (al-Ruṣāfa) are cases in point).[40]

Yet in spite of any general tendencies which can be said to mark the development of cities and urban economies in the fifth to early seventh centuries, strong regional variations have been detected in the archaeological record – and, in particular, a divergent trend between Anatolia and the European provinces of the empire, on the one hand, and Syria–Palestine and Egypt, on the other. In addition, while Syria and Palestine, with Egypt and possibly the North African provinces, continued to flourish well into the seventh century and beyond, much of Anatolia and the Balkans was suffering from economic contraction, urban recession and demographic decline by the mid-sixth century. As we have seen, there is also some evidence that northern Syria also experienced a different rate of change, beginning somewhat earlier, from the areas to the south.[41] If this interpretation of the available evidence is accepted, it has important implications

40 For Euchaita, see A. P. Kazhdan *et al.*, *The Oxford dictionary of Byzantium* (Oxford and New York, 1991), p. 737; for Resafa (Sergiopolis), see pp. 1877f.

41 See Morony, 'Economic boundaries?', pp. 178–80, with literature, following Ward-Perkins, 'Specialised production and exchange', pp. 354–61, and Morrisson and Sodini, 'The sixth-century economy', pp. 190–3, where the evidence and further literature are summarised; and now Wickham, *Framing the early Middle Ages*, pp. 613–34. For continuing prosperity and expansion in many areas of southern Syria and in Palestine beyond the middle of the seventh century, see now Magness, *Early Islamic settlements in Palestine*.

for the early stages of Islamic political development and the economies of the conquered territories.

Finally, the pattern of village communities in the eastern Roman world likewise varied from region to region, but in general it is the case that the vast majority of urban centres served as central places and thus also as markets for their surrounding districts and, until substantial changes occurred during the middle and later seventh century in what remained under imperial control in Anatolia and the Balkans, rural communities. Villages and more isolated farmsteads proliferated and there appears to have been a considerable expansion of such rural habitats across the late Roman world in the east from the fourth and in particular from the fifth century, associated with both a recession in villa-type estates and farms and a shift in the hierarchy of settlement towards an increase in the number and density of what have been referred to as 'secondary', often fortified, towns with their adjacent and 'dependent' villages.[42] This pattern seems to be found from the fifth into the seventh centuries in the Konya plain in central Anatolia, and in the territory of Sagalassos in Pisidia; in the southern Ḥawrān, the Decapolis and central Jordan plain and southern Jordan;[43] and elsewhere.[44]

Sasanian cities and urbanism

Cities and urban centres in the Sasanian world occupied a somewhat different role in the structure of the state, although they were similar in respect of some

42 Morrison and Sodini, 'The sixth-century economy', pp. 175–9 provides a brief summary with literature.

43 See D. Baird, 'Settlement expansion on the Konya plain, Anatolia: 5th–7th centuries AD', in Bowden, Lavan and Machado (eds.), *Recent research*; Vanhaverbeke *et al.*, 'Late Antiquity in the territory of Sagalassos' (Sagalassos territory); P.-L. Gatier, 'Villages du Proche-Orient protobyzantin (4ème–7èmes.): Étude régionale', in G. R. D. King and A. Cameron (eds.), *The Byzantine and early Islamic Near East*, vol. II: *Land use and settlement patterns* (Princeton, 1994) (north Syria); H. I. MacAdam, 'Settlements and settlement patterns in northern and central Transjordania, ca. 550–750', in King and Cameron (eds.), *Land use and settlement patterns*; and R. Schick, 'The settlement pattern of southern Jordan: The nature of the evidence', in King and Cameron (eds.), *Land use and settlement patterns*.

44 For central Syria and the limestone massif, see H. Kennedy and J. H. W. G. Liebeschuetz, 'Antioch and the villages of northern Syria in the 5th and 7th centuries: Trends and problems', *Nottingham Medieval Studies*, 32 (1988); C. Foss, 'The Near-Eastern countryside in Late Antiquity: A review article', in Humphrey (ed.), *Some recent archaeological research*; for Lycia, Isauria and Cilicia see C. Foss, 'The Lycian coast in the Byzantine age', *Dumbarton Oaks Papers*, 48 (1994); S. Mitchell, *Anatolia: Land, men and gods in Asia Minor*, vol. II: *The rise of the Church* (Oxford, 1993); for Macedonia, see Dunn, 'Continuity and change in the Macedonian countryside'; for Greece, see S. Alcock, *Graecia capta: The landscapes of Roman Greece* (Cambridge, 1993); A. Avramea, *Le Péloponnèse du IVe au VIIIe siècle: Changements et persistances* (Paris, 1997). See now the essays in J. Lefort, C. Morrisson and J.-P. Sodini (eds.), *Les villages dans l'empire byzantin (IVe–XVe siècle)* (Paris, 2005).

of their social and economic functions. They can be divided, very crudely, into two major types: those of the rich agricultural lands of Mesopotamia and Iraq; and those on the plateau and further east or north. One important difference between Roman and Sasanian cities, however, lies in the absence from the latter of the leading elements of the social elite, who seem to have preferred to live on their estates outside the towns, a social and cultural tradition that pre-dates the formation of the Sasanian royal state, and which may itself also be reflected in the pattern of royal residences.[45] Another is the absence from Sasanian urban centres, with a few exceptions, of major centres of Zoroastrianism – some of the most important fire-temples, for example, seem generally located away from towns, and often in remote areas.[46] Yet Sasanian cities did possess their own fire-temples, and they certainly housed an elite – indeed, the city elites, as reflected in a text such as the late sixth-century Syriac *History of Karka* (near mod. Kirkuk in northern Mesopotamia), were clearly vital to the ways Sasanian urban centres functioned and appeared.[47] Archaeological investigation of urban centres remains in many ways in its early stages, since generally accepted ceramic typologies and chronologies which make comparison across several such settlements in different regions of the empire possible have yet to be established for more than a few sites,[48] while many sites which have been excavated were examined without reference to the Sasanian levels.[49] Nevertheless, a number of regional surveys and comparisons have been carried out which permit admittedly broad generalisations about the areas in question to be made, and can be used to balance the textual evidence. At the same time, the textual evidence for

45 On the evidence for Sasanian cities and towns, see in particular Hugh Kennedy, 'From Shahristan to Medina', SI, 102, 3 (2006). For an example of what may be a noble residence in a rural location, see M. Arzanoush, *The Sasanian manor house at Hajjiabad* (Florence, 1994).

46 See K. Schippmann, *Die iranischen Feuerheiligtümer* (Berlin, 1971); M. Arzanoush, 'Fire temple and Anahita temple: A discussion on some Iranian places of worship', *Mesopotamia*, 22 (1987); M. G. Morony, *Iraq after the Muslim conquest* (Princeton, 1984; repr. Piscataway, NJ, 2006), pp. 283–4.

47 See J.-M. Fiey, 'Vers la réhabilitation de l'*Histoire de Karka d'Beit Sloh*', *Analecta Bollandiana*, 82 (1964). The text is edited by P. Bedjan in *Acta martyrum et sanctorum*, 7 vols. (Paris and Leipzig, 1890–7), vol. II.

48 R. M. Adams, 'Tell Abu Sarifa: A Sassanian Islamic ceramic sequence from south central Iraq', *Ars Orientalis*, 8 (1970), pp. 117–18; St J. Simpson, 'Partho-Sasanian ceramic industries in Mesopotamia', in I. Freeston and D. Gaimster (eds.), *Pottery in the making: World ceramic traditions* (London, 1997). See also the essays in D. Kennet and P. Luft (eds.), *Recent advances in Sasanian archaeology and history*, BAR Int. Ser. (forthcoming).

49 See St J. Simpson, 'From Tekrit to the Jaghjagh: Sasanian sites, settlement patterns and material culture', in K. Bartl and S. R. Hauser (eds.), *Continuity and change in northern Mesopotamia from the Hellenistic to the early Islamic period* (Berlin, 1996). The problem lies partly in the nature of the evidence for construction which, as Kennedy notes ('From Shahristan to Medina'), was largely of brick, mud brick and wood, so that few stone structures survive, in great contrast to the Roman cities of the eastern provinces.

the history of Iranian cities and urbanism during the late Sasanian era has to be derived almost entirely from later – Islamic – sources, which inevitably brings with it a series of methodological issues.[50]

It has for some time been established that there was a considerable expansion of irrigation systems in the fifth and especially sixth centuries, particularly associated with the reign of Khusrau I (531–79 CE), and concentrated in Iraq and Oman. These have been taken to imply increasing population, an absolute as well as a relative increase in production, and expanding urbanism.[51] In Mesopotamia and the western lands many of the most important urban centres were Hellenistic foundations, often constructed on or around pre-Hellenistic centres, but bearing many of the hallmarks of the *polis* familiar from the Roman and Hellenistic worlds. Such centres were foci of commerce and exchange as well as administration, and also housed substantial populations involved in the local agrarian economy, as did the majority of provincial cities in the Roman world. Yet the Sasanian world in general appears to have experienced a slow demographic downturn from the later third century onwards, as settlement surveys and sherd distribution analysis would seem to suggest; while the ceramic surveys of many of these sites and their hinterlands intimate that, while they continued to flourish into the fourth century, a recession set in towards the end of the fourth century which lasted through most of the fifth and into the sixth century, followed in many – but not all – cases by a recovery in the second half of the sixth century or a little later. This appears to be the case both in Mesopotamia, at some of the sites associated with Tesfōn (Ctesiphon), where evidence of severe and repeated flooding and gradual abandonment of some quarters has been identified, and an overall shrinkage of the city from the fourth into the later sixth century,[52] as well as on

50 See, for example, T. Daryaee (ed., trans. and comm.), *Šahrestānīhā ī Ērānšāhr: A middle Persian text on late antique geography, epic and history* (Costa Mesa, 2002), the core of which derives from sixth- and early seventh-century material, but which was recopied and interpolated at a much later date. See also J. Markwart, *A catalogue of the provincial capitals of Ēranshahr*, ed. G. Messina (Rome, 1931); and R. Gyselen, 'Les données de géographie administrative dans le "Šahrestānīhā-ī Ērān"', *Studia Iranica*, 17 (1988). See Kennedy, 'From shahristan to medina'.

51 For example, Adams, *Heartland of cities*, pp. 179–83, 209–11; Morony, 'Economic boundaries?', pp. 183f.; Morony, *Iraq after the Muslim conquest*, pp. 156–7. But see also M. Morony, 'Land use and settlement patterns in late Sasanian and early Islamic Iraq', in King and Cameron (eds.), *Land use and settlement patterns*, pp. 225f. for the methodological issues associated with the results of surface pottery surveys. See also, and in general on the expansion of irrigation schemes, Christensen, *The decline of Iranshahr*.

52 R. V. Ricciardi, 'The excavations at Choche', *Mesopotamia*, 5–6 (1970–1); M. Cavallero, 'The excavations at Choche (the presumed Ctesiphon), Area 2', *Mesopotamia*, 1 (1966). Choche is in fact Veh-Ardashīr.

the Iranian plateau, at sites such as Bard-i Neshāndeh and Masjid-i Soleimān;[53] in Khūzistān, at Qaṣr-i Abū Naṣr and Sūsa;[54] and in Fārs, at Iṣṭakhr or Naqsh-i Rustam, in these cases based on the numismatic material.[55] Although evidence for the continued expansion of the irrigation networks in Mesopotamia, the Diyālā basin and Khūzistān, and for royal sponsorship of major urban projects and new foundations in the period from the later third to the later sixth centuries, might suggest that these cities should have been flourishing economically, this seems problematic in the light of the ceramic and numismatic material which, as it is currently understood, appears to show a decline in urban fortunes during the fifth century, followed in the middle and later sixth by a limited recovery. The targeted deportation of Roman urban and rural populations from Syria and Mesopotamia from the fourth century onwards especially may perhaps also reflect these conditions.[56]

Cities had an important administrative and governmental role, as well as, in many cases, a military character, although they inevitably also attracted market activity and trade and, where their local hinterlands offered the necessary resources, substantial populations. Royal investment in cities in all the fertile and heavily irrigated western zones certainly involved the deliberate transplantation of substantial populations carried off from Roman cities in northern and central Syria, who brought with them artisanal, industrial and construction skills and knowledge, as well as some horticultural and agricultural expertise (in oleoculture, for example). The frequently circular or orthogonal plans of many Sasanian cities in Mesopotamia and Fārs implies a degree of central planning, or at least of an established or approved model for the establishment of towns. But this investment seems also to have involved the movement of substantial elements of the rural population into the urban

53 R. Ghirshman, *Terrasses sacrées de Bard-e Nechandah et Masjid-e Solaiman*, Mémoires de la Délégation Archéologique en Perse 45 (Paris, 1976), pp. 135, 143.

54 D. Whitcomb, *Before the roses and nightingales: Excavations at Qasr-i Abu Nasr, Old Shiraz* (New York, 1985), p. 104 (with fig. 3); R. N. Frye, *Sassanian remains from Qasr-i Abu Nasr: Seals, sealings and coins* (Cambridge, MA, 1973), p. 26 (Qaṣr-i Abū Naṣr); R. Boucharlat, 'Suse à l'époque sasanide', *Mesopotamia*, 22 (1987), at pp. 358–9 (Sūsa). But see also D. Kennet, 'The decline of eastern Arabia in the Sasanian period', *Arabian Archaeology and Epigraphy*, 18 (2007), pp. 115 n. 123, 118 n. 258 for some ambiguities with dating.

55 Whitcomb, *Before the roses and nightingales*, fig. 4 (heavy bias towards coins of Khusrau II with a very small proportion of earlier issues).

56 Brunner, 'Geographical and administrative divisions', pp. 758–62; Morony, *Iraq after the Muslim conquest*, esp. pp. 277ff.; A. Oppenheimer, *Babylonia Judaica in the Talmudic period*, Beihefte zum Tübinger Atlas des Vorderen Orients, B 47 (Wiesbaden, 1983), pp. 179–236; Boucharlat, 'Suse à l'époque sasanide', pp. 362–4. For population deportations, see Morony, 'Population transfers'; E. Kettenhofen, 'Deportations II: In the Parthian and Sasanian periods', in E. Yarshater (ed.), *EIr*, VII (Costa Mesa, 1994) and see also chapter 3 below.

centres, which were often very extensive: ceramic surveys in several regions suggest a reduction in the total number of rural settlements, accompanied by the construction or development of fewer but much larger urban centres.[57] Apart from the well-known cases from Mesopotamia,[58] the Diyālā basin and Khūzistān, other examples have now been identified, for example in the central Zagros region near the modern village of Firūzābād.[59] In the Dāmghān plain survey work has identified no obvious signs of population expansion in the later Sasanian period, but there does appear to have been a concentration of population in fewer and larger centres.[60] It is also clear that some of the very large new foundations were never fully occupied within their walls – this seems to have been the case with Jundīshāpūr and Ivan-i-Karkhah on the Susiana plain in Khūzistān, for example,[61] although it is less pronounced in other, similar urban centres in other regions such as Luristān, east of central Mesopotamia.[62] Nevertheless, this tendency, at least in those regions where major state-sponsored urban development took place, is the reverse of what was happening in the Roman countryside.[63] Together with the evidence for regionalised urban recession, it suggests that the economy was not without its problem areas,[64] even if the state was still able to extract a substantial amount of resources through the tax system, especially after the reforms of Khusrau I.

Mesopotamia profited from its geographical position, lying as it did between the wealthy provinces of Roman Mesopotamia and Syria, the trading routes east through the Indian Ocean and westwards to the east coast of Africa, the Central Asian steppes and, ultimately, China. The caravan cities or

57 D. Metzler, *Ziele und Formen königlicher Innenpolitik im vorislamischen Iran* (Münster, 1977), esp. pp. 177ff.

58 See Adams and Nissen, *The Uruk countryside*, pp. 59–63 for the Uruk district; Adams, *Heartland of cities*, pp. 179–85; St J. Simpson, 'Mesopotamia in the Sasanian period: Settlement patterns, arts and crafts', in J. Curtis (ed.), *Mesopotamia and Iran in the Parthian and Sasanian periods: Rejection and revival c.238 BC–AD 642* (London, 2000); but see also Howard-Johnston, 'The two great powers', p. 200 n. 91.

59 Abdi, 'Archaeological research in the Islamabad plain'; K. Abdi, 'Islamabad 1999', *Iran*, 38 (2000).

60 Trinkaus, 'Pre-Islamic settlement and land-use', pp. 133–40, 144; K. M. Trinkaus, 'Settlement of highlands and lowlands in early Islamic Dāmghān', *Journal of Persian Studies*, 23 (1985), pp. 130, 136–7.

61 A. Moghaddam and N. Miri, 'Archaeological research in the Mianab Plain of lowland Susiana, south-western Iran', *Iran*, 41 (2003), pp. 104–5; Wenke, 'Western Iran in the Partho-Sasanian period', pp. 255–6; Adams, *The land behind Baghdad*, pp. 115–16.

62 J. A. Neely, 'Sassanian and early Islamic water-control and irrigation systems on the Deh-Luran plain, Iran', in T. E. Downing and M. Gibson (eds.), *Irrigation's impact on society* (Tucson, 1974).

63 See Wenke, 'Imperial investments', esp. pp. 131–9.

64 See Howard-Johnston, 'The two great powers', p. 203.

ports along these routes also gained from the demand created by the markets of these cities and the royal court and its retinues: Marw,[65] Balkh, Samarqand and other cities of Khurāsān and Transoxania in the north-east (although also exposed to hostile activity from various nomadic peoples to the north), the cities of Khūzistān and Fārs along the southern route, and Hormuz and Sīrāf on the Persian Gulf.[66] In contrast, the cities of the Iranian plateau and of the eastern and south-eastern provinces were on the whole less fortunately placed, maintained chiefly through locations offering adequate water supplies, supplemented in the great majority of cases by *qanāt*s and related irrigation systems, and owing their vitality to a combination of both administrative and military (defensive) functions with which they were endowed by the state,[67] although the ports of the south-east were important links in the commercial chain that stretched along the coast towards India.[68] This does not mean that the cities of the plateau and mountain fringes were either culturally or economically unimportant – on the contrary, major towns such as Iṣṭakhr, Iṣfahān, Hamadhān or Rayy, along with many others in the west and north, or Bela, Panjgūr and Quzdar in the south-east, were centres of communications and commerce, in many cases had a vibrant local economy (the hinterland of Iṣfahān, for example, was famed for its grain production, and indeed the major centres around the desert fringes with which this city was connected by road were in general at the centre of relatively rich agricultural districts), and were located in relatively rich agricultural districts whose productivity was increased by extensive irrigation schemes.[69]

The political and administrative role of cities in the Sasanian empire is still poorly understood, although it is clear from the *Šahrestānīhā ī Ērānšāhr* that

65 See T. Williams, K. Kurbansakhatov *et al.*, 'The ancient Merv project, Turkmenistan: Preliminary report on the second season (2002)', *Iran*, 41 (2003).

66 D. Whitehouse and A. Williamson, 'Sasanian maritime trade', *Iran*, 11 (1973); Howard-Johnston, 'The two great powers', pp. 204–5; Brunner, 'Geographical and administrative divisions', pp. 755–7, 771–2; M. Tampoe, *Maritime trade between China and the west: An archaeological study of the ceramics from Sīrāf (Persian Gulf), 8th to 15th centuries AD* (Oxford, 1989), p. 2; T. Daryaee, 'Sources for the economic history of late Sasanian Fārs', in R. Gyselen and M. Szuppe (eds.), *Matériaux pour l'histoire économique du monde iranien* (Paris, 1999), pp. 135–8, 144–5; T. Daryaee, 'The Persian Gulf trade in Late Antiquity', *Journal of World History*, 14, 1 (2003); R. N. Frye, 'Byzantine and Sasanian trade relations with northeastern Russia', *Dumbarton Oaks Papers*, 26 (1972).

67 See R. N. Frye, 'The Sasanian system of walls for defense', in M. Rosen-Ayalon (ed.), *Studies in memory of Gaston Wiet* (Jerusalem, 1977); A. Christensen, *L'Iran sous les Sassanides* (Copenhagen, 1944), p. 287.

68 Howard-Johnston, 'The two great powers', pp. 206–10 for a useful survey of six such cities: Iṣṭakhr, Bishāpūr, Qaṣr-i Abū Naṣr, Iṣfahān, Sīstān and Ganzak. See also Brunner, 'Geographical and administrative divisions', pp. 750–3, 767.

69 Brunner, 'Geographical and administrative divisions', pp. 771–7.

they had both symbolic and ideological importance as well as administrative and fiscal significance.[70] It is also apparent from the surveys that have been carried out and from extant remains that many cities in the provinces, particularly along the northern and north-eastern fringes, served as significant military centres, with well-maintained fortresses either within the walls or closely associated with them.[71] Marw was an especially important centre on the north-eastern front, serving both as a control point for trade beyond the borders of the empire and as a major strategic centre. It seems clear that Sasanian kings pursued from the beginning a long-term policy of political centralisation, even if they were checked in much of their endeavour by the power of the Iranian landed elite or aristocracy, at least until the time of Khusrau I.[72] This policy was effected in part through the establishment of new royal cities, with their territories under centrally appointed officials, largely on territory that became part of the royal domain (*dastkart*).[73] Where refoundation or royal intervention affected the older Hellenistic foundations, particularly in the western parts of the empire, then their older civic institutions, including the role of the council and urban elite landowners, appears to have been superseded by the royal appointments and the installation of an administrative establishment responsible either to the provincial governor or directly to the king.[74] The evidence suggests that by the sixth century the state's fiscal administration was based at three levels, not dissimilar from the praefectural, provincial and civic levels in the Roman state, with state officials responsible in each city (perhaps to be identified with the reference to the *ummal al-harāj* of later Arabic accounts, a group of notables, perhaps local urban aristocrats, associated with the *dihqāns* of the cities) for the supervision of the assessment and collection of taxes in kind and in money, responsible in

70 The text seems to date in its final form from the ʿAbbāsid period, but seemingly represents the geographical extent of Sasanian authority during the later reign of Khusrau II, since it includes the cities of Roman Syria, as well as the Arabian Peninsula. But it is based in part on older material from the earlier sixth century: see Daryaee, *Šahrestānīhā ī Ērānšāhr*, pp. 1–11.

71 See Kennedy, 'From shahristan to medina'; and A. Petruccioli, *Bukhara: The myth and the architecture* (Cambridge, MA, 1999), p. 49.

72 R. N. Frye, 'The political history of Iran under the Sasanians', in E. Yarshater (ed.), *The Cambridge history of Iran*, vol. III: *The Seleucid, Parthian and Sasanian periods* (Cambridge, 1983); Howard-Johnston, 'The two great powers', pp. 158–64.

73 Morony, *Iraq after the Muslim conquest*, pp. 68–9; and P. Gignoux, 'Aspects de la vie administrative et sociale en Iran du 7ème siècle', in R. Gyselen (ed.), *Contributions à l'histoire et la géographie historique de l'empire sassanide*, Res Orientales 16 (Bures-sur-Yvette, 2004). But see Howard-Johnston, 'The two great powers', p. 215, n. 127.

74 V. G. Lukonin, 'Political, social and administrative institutions: Taxes and trade', in Yarshater (ed.), *The Seleucid, Parthian and Sasanian periods*, pp. 724–6.

turn to the next senior official at district level, and then beyond to the provincial instance.[75] The sigillographic evidence further suggests an effectively centralised administrative apparatus by the fifth century, if not from the very beginning under Ardashīr I (r. 224–40 CE), upon which Kawād I (r. 488–96, 499–531 CE) began to build in the late fifth and early sixth centuries, and which was the basis for the much more widespread reforms introduced under Khusrau I. These not only increased the efficiency of the whole fiscal apparatus and the methods of assessing and collecting taxable revenues, but also successfully challenged the power of the elite by limiting their access to resources and their political and economic independence – although it is entirely unclear as to how long after Khusrau's reign the effects of the reforms and the new arrangements they introduced were maintained. The strength of the Iranian merchant elite must also have played a role in these matters.[76] While there remains considerable disagreement among historians as to the exact import of Khusrau I's reforms, and the administrative apparatus of the state, it is clear that cities, as centres for local administration and taxation, and regardless of their size, were absolutely fundamental elements in Sasanian rule, and that the focus of Sasanian elite society, with the possible exception of the very highest levels of the aristocracy, was firmly anchored within them – even if we should beware of assuming too much uniformity across the provinces beneath the umbrella of the royal administration.[77]

75 See Christensen, *L'Iran sous les Sassanides*, pp. 113–16, 122–6, 132–40; Lukonin, 'Political, social and administrative institutions', pp. 681–746; R. Gyselen, *La géographie administrative de l'empire sassanide: Les témoignages sigillographiques* (Paris, 1989); R. Gyselen, *Nouveaux matériaux pour la géographie historique de l'empire sassanide: Sceaux administratifs de la collection Ahmad Saeedi*, Studia Iranica 24 (Paris, 2002) (especially for the sigillographic evidence for administrative structures); J. Wiesehöfer, *Ancient Persia from 550 BC to 650 AD* (London and New York, 1996), pp. 186–91. See also A. D. H. Bivar, *Catalogue of the western Asiatic seals in the British Museum. Stamp seals*, vol. II: *the Sassanian dynasty* (London, 1969); and R. Göbl, *Die Tonbullen vom Tacht-e Suleiman: Ein Beitrag zu spätsasanidischen Sphragistik* (Berlin, 1976), for seals and discussion, with the additional remarks of Howard-Johnston, 'The two great powers', pp. 216–18; G. Gnoli, 'The quadripartition of the Sasanian empire', *East and West*, 35 (1985), pp. 1–15; R. Gyselen, *The four generals of the Sasanian empire: Some sigillographic evidence* (Rome, 2001); and Gignoux, 'Aspects de la vie administrative et sociale'. For the tax officials, see F. Altheim and R. Stiehl, 'Die Lage der bauern unter den späten Sassaniden', in J. Herrmann and I. Sellnow (eds.), *Die Rolle der Volksmassen in der Geschichte der vorkapitalistischen Gesellschaftsformationen* (Berlin, 1975), p. 82.

76 E. de la Vaissière, *Sogdian traders: A history* (Leiden and Boston, 2005), pp. 227–32; Banaji, 'Precious metal coinages and monetary expansion', pp. 285–6.

77 See Morony, *Iraq after the Muslim conquest*, pp. 27–32, 51–6, 99–111, 125–64; Howard-Johnston, 'The two great powers', pp. 211–23; and on Khusrau's reforms, Z. Rubin, 'The reforms of Khusro Anūshirwān', in Cameron (ed.), *States, resources and armies*, with previous literature; and Wiesehöfer, *Ancient Persia*, pp. 190–1. For administrative and

The great emphasis placed upon cities can be explained at least in part as an effort to maximise and maintain some central control over resources, always an issue in states with substantial elites and extensive territory. If the evidence of movement or concentration of population in such centres has been correctly interpreted, therefore, then the bulk of the populace of these large cities must have been peasants, so that the cities served in effect as vast collection points for the payment of taxes. The locations of administrative centres, residential quarters, religious foci and public spaces such as markets all remain poorly understood, although some substantial structures of monumental proportions have been located and associated with administrative functions;[78] while royal palaces and related monumental or other structures both within and outside urban contexts have received a great deal of attention.[79] The *History of Karka* makes it clear that local urban elites invested considerable effort in the maintenance and improvement of the major public and private buildings in their towns, and the limited archaeological evidence bears this out.[80] The relationship of streets to the frontages of what appear to be residential and artisanal quarters at Khōkē (Choche), a suburb of Ctesiphon, appears to be not unlike that of some of the late antique towns of Syria, and in this respect determined to some extent the ensuing Islamic patterns of urban space, although at Qaṣr-i Abū Naṣr and Marw far less regular, unpaved streets with lanes leading off to either side seem to have been the norm.[81] Study of the layout of domestic dwellings is still in its infancy, although substantial urban residences as well as humbler dwellings have been excavated at Tell Baruda at Ctesiphon, at Seleucia, at Sūsa (where what appear to be major aristocratic residences have been identified), and at Dura-Europos, styles which represent the traditional Mesopotamian patterns, while a different regional architectural tradition in domestic architecture has been identified from the Sasanian levels at

social centrality see the *Sirat Anushirvan*, trans. in Grignaschi, 'Quelques specimens de la littérature sassanide', p. 20; and for administrative diversity see Gyselen, *Nouveaux matériaux pour la géographie historique*, pp. 28ff.

78 At early Sasanian Sūsa, for example: Boucharlat, 'Suse à l'époque sasanide', p. 358.

79 See the summary with literature in Wiesehöfer, *Ancient Persia*, p. 162; D. Huff, 'Zur Rekonstruktion des Turmes von Firuzabad', *Istanbuler Mitteilungen*, 19–20 (1969–70), pp. 319ff.

80 A point made by N. Pigulevskaya, *Les villes de l'état iranien aux époques parthe et sassanide* (Paris, 1963), see esp. pp. 141ff.

81 See Ricciardi, 'The excavations at Choche'; Whitcomb, *Before the roses and nightingales*, pp. 87–110; G. Herrmann, K. Kurbansakhatov *et al.* (eds.), 'The International Merv Project: Preliminary report on the fifth season (1996)', *Iran*, 35 (1997), pp. 1–33; see also the report for 1997 in *Iran*, 36 (1998), pp. 53–75.

Marw.[82] Institutional structures have, for the most part, not yet been properly recognised except through aerial survey and guesswork,[83] although what may be an early Sasanian governor's residence – a substantial colonnaded courtyard building – has been tentatively identified at Sūsa.[84]

Apart from the known fact of the transplantation of captive Roman urban populations, the question arises why the state should also have transferred substantial numbers of people away from their rural habitats into larger urban settings – if this is indeed how the evidence should be interpreted. Several hypotheses have been advanced, for the most part associating the change with an assumed desire or need to exercise greater supervision or control over resources, to enhance productive output and to increase market exchange. But in the first case it remains unclear why this particular policy would have been any more effective than maintaining a regular supervision of taxpayers through local landlords or notables – the *dihqāns* – which was the traditional means and must have continued to be the case in all those areas where such concentrations of population did not take place.[85] It has already been pointed out that distancing the agrarian producers more than a few hours from their fields and irrigation systems which, at field and farm level needed constant maintenance and care, would be counter-productive – indeed, would seriously damage the infrastructure necessary to maintain production in the first place.[86] The very partial nature of the archaeological record suggests that, for the moment, any conclusions based upon it should be seen as somewhat premature.

In comparison with what can be said about the evolution of cities, towns and the countryside in the late Roman east (including the Balkans), therefore, we remain very much in the dark about comparable developments in the Sasanian world. As we have seen, some have argued that there took place a

82 G. Herrmann, K. Kurbansakhatov and St J. Simpson (eds.), 'The International Merv Project: Preliminary report on the eighth year (1999)', *Iran*, 38 (2000), pp. 2–5. For the domestic structures at Ctesiphon, see R. V. Ricciardi and M. Ponzi Mancini, 'Choche', in E. Quarantrelli (ed.), *The land between two rivers: Twenty years of Italian archaeology in the Middle East. The treasures of Mesopotamia* (Torino, 1985), pp. 100–4; and for Sūsa, see Boucharlat, 'Suse à l'époque sasanide'; and M. Kervran, 'Transformations de la ville de Susa et de son économie de l'époque sasanide à l'époque abbaside', *Paléorient*, 11 (1985), pp. 91–100.

83 See R. W. Bulliet, 'Medieval Nishapur: A topographic and demographic reconstruction', *Studia Iranica*, 5 (1976), p. 67f.; Whitcomb, *Before the roses and nightingales*.

84 Boucharlat, 'Suse à l'époque sasanide', p. 358. For some discussion see P. Wheatley, *The places where men pray together: Cities in Islamic lands, seventh through the tenth centuries* (Chicago, 2001).

85 Morony, *Iraq after the Muslim conquest*, pp. 106–7, 11–13; F. Altheim and R. Stiehl, *Finanzgeschichte der Spätantike* (Frankfurt, 1957), pp. 57–9, 75–6; Christensen, *L'Iran sous les Sassanides*, pp. 112–13.

86 Wenke, 'Imperial investments', pp. 144–53.

reduction in population – and thus the size – of many large cities in the region in the early seventh century, a result of a combination of natural disasters (pestilence, flooding) and, in conditions of warfare and internal political unrest in the later 620s and 630s, the breakdown – or at least lack of state-supported maintenance for – the large irrigation networks. But the interpretation of the evidence on which this is based has been challenged, and the issue remains unresolved because of the absence of closer internal investigation of urban sites as well as reliably dated ceramic sequences from the surveys in question, and a lack of survey material as such from a wide enough range of samples.[87]

It is perhaps possible, however, to bring these developments into association with a range of other factors, in particular the possibility that they were a response to a long-term and incremental climatic change. We have already noted that there was a shift towards cooler climatic conditions from approximately the later fourth or early fifth century, lasting until the later eighth century. Now it is worth noting that the extensive irrigation systems of Mesopotamia and Khūzistān in particular must have been intended to support winter-rainfall agriculture, ensuring thereby the regularity of two crops per year (which would have been essential to the cultivation of rice, which is both water- and labour-intensive).[88] There is no reason to doubt that such a regularly high level of production per capita would lead to a demographic increase, higher demand for produce, enhanced market exchange and commercial demand, and greater revenues, as well as rental income for landlords. But these agricultural traditions evolved in the context of a relatively warm period, and a cooler climate, or at least a period of temperature fluctuations, which seems to have been characteristic of the fifth to seventh centuries, would destabilise the system. In the conditions prevalent in the Mesopotamian climatic region, reduced rainfall would require constant attention to, and expansion of, the irrigation system, and it may well be as much to such long-term and incremental pressures that the Sasanian kings of the fifth and especially the sixth centuries were responding, as well as the need or desire to maximise revenues, when they invested so massively in the canals and irrigation network of Mesopotamia, Khūzistān and the Diyālā basin.[89]

The ceramic survey material appears to suggest two phenomena: a clustering and concentration of population in fewer centres; and the

87 Morony, 'Land use and settlement patterns'; Morony, 'Economic boundaries?', p. 181.
88 Note Wenke, 'Imperial investments', pp. 144–6.
89 J. S. Veenenbos, *Unified report of the soil and land classification of Dezful project, Khūzistān, Iran* (Tehran, 1959); Wenke, 'Imperial investments', pp. 81–3.

deliberate development of a number of very large centres into which some of this population was moved, by means about which we are entirely uninformed. While this has been seen as a sign of a flourishing and expanding agriculture, increased levels of production, urban economic vitality and demographic expansion, it is possible in fact to see it in a somewhat different light. For in a situation in which reduced natural water resources impact on agrarian production – and thus state resources – and in which population is not expanding but contracting (which is an equally possible interpretation of the ceramic material), the kings would have had only one option if they were to maintain their own power and a degree of internal political stability: to expand irrigation and to concentrate populations where the levels of production could be most readily assured. It is not a coincidence that the work of expanding the irrigation systems of Mesopotamia undertaken by Kawād I in the early sixth century can probably be dated to the years following a serious drought around 500, which affected both Roman and Sasanian northern Mesopotamia.[90]

This is not to suggest that levels of production could not be maintained, or that the Sasanian state was impoverished – the quantity of silver and base-metal coinage minted alone militates against such a proposal.[91] The ambiguous evidence for the relatively limited treasury of the Persian kings at times in the fifth and sixth centuries,[92] and firmer testimony to famines or droughts (which also affected some of the eastern provinces of the Roman empire), may not offer much support either for an expanding and flourishing Sasanian economy[93] – but the numismatic evidence for a vast, and expanding, quantity of silver in circulation in the later sixth and early seventh centuries would appear to run counter to such an interpretation.[94] It does, on the other hand,

90 Christensen, *L'Iran sous les Sassanides*, pp. 352–3.

91 F. Thierry, 'Sur les monnaies sassanides trouvées en Chine', in R. Gyselen (ed.), *Circulation des monnaies, des merchandises et des biens* (Louvain, 1993), pp. 89–139; M. I. Mochiri, *Études de numismatique iranienne sous les Sassanides et Arabes-Sassanides*, 2 vols. (Louvain, 1983); and esp. A. Kolesnikov, 'The quantity of silver coinage and levels of revenue in late Sasanian Iran', *Cahiers de Studia Iranica*, 2 (1999), pp. 123–30.

92 Greatrex, *Rome and Persia at war*, pp. 47, 50–1. Yet this may reflect royal parsimony – other evidence suggests a vast treasury in bullion, coin and other materials by the end of the sixth century: see Morony, *Iraq after the Muslim conquest*, pp. 38–41, 61–3 with literature and sources.

93 See, for example, Christensen, *L'Iran sous les Sassanides*, pp. 290–1; Frye, 'Political history', p. 147; I. G. Telelis, Μετεωρολογικά Φαινόμενα *Φαινόμενα και κλίμα στο Βυζάντιο*, 2 vols. (Athens, 2003), vol. I, nos. 101, 103 (in 464–71 CE); 110, 112 (501–2 CE).

94 See J. Sears, 'Monetary revision and monetization in the late Sasanian empire', *Cahiers de Studia Iranica*, 2 (1999), pp. 149–67; Kolesnikov, 'The quantity of silver coinage and levels of revenue'.

offer an alternative model for the royal policy of investment in both irrigation and urban construction (as well as military predation on the wealthier cities of the nearest Roman provinces – see below), and allows us to place these in a context of gradually declining population, rather than assuming a general increase. And this in turn matches what appears to be the case, at the general level, and bearing in mind the regional fluctuations already noted, in the provinces of the eastern Roman state.

The Arabian Peninsula: a land between two empires

The Arabian Peninsula fits into this pattern politically because of the strategic importance of its coastlands as a source of resources and as a focus for long-distance trade. The semi-nomadic populations of the northern Arabian Peninsula occasionally posed a threat as small-scale raiders, but were also a source of mercenary and allied soldiers, as well as traders on a substantial scale to both Roman and Sasanian markets. The commercial centres of the south, such as Ṣanʿāʾ, or of the west, such as Medina and Mecca, maintained regular trading contacts between the cities of Syria and Palestine, the Indian Ocean, the East African littoral and the Aksumite kingdom of Ethiopia. The clans and tribes of the Ḥijāz were key players in trading a variety of goods, including perfumes as well as some non-luxuries, to the Roman provinces of Palestine, Syria and Arabia, and possibly beyond. The Quraysh of Mecca in particular were involved in what had by the later sixth century become a lucrative trade in leather, possibly supplying the Roman military. But gold and silver were also traded, and apparently in substantial quantities, a fact which may also contribute to explaining why Mecca in particular occupied such an important position economically.[95] Perhaps just as importantly, the role of the Ḥijāzī elites in the economic development of the region needs to be underlined, especially in view of their role in the new territories after the initial conquests – there is evidence for extensive irrigation works, dams and

95 See Crone, *Meccan trade*, pp. 98–101, 115–48; Patricia Crone, 'How did the Quranic pagans make a living?', *BSOAS*, 68 (2005), pp. 387–99; Patricia Crone, 'Quraysh and the Roman army: Making sense of the Meccan leather trade', *BSOAS*, 70 (2007), pp. 63–88. That leather played a key role in supplying the military is evident from its importance at Odessos (Varna) on the Balkan Black Sea coast, in the fifth and sixth centuries, where it was presumably destined for the armies along the Danube. The presence there of a substantial number of funerary inscriptions for leather workers or merchants, for example, largely of the sixth century, testifies to the significance of the military demand for leather from units along the Danube frontier, which Odessos served as a base for supplies and equipment. See V. Beševliev, *Spätgriechische und spätlateinische Inschriften aus Bulgarien* (Berlin, 1964), nos. 99, 100, 102, 103, 104. For precious metals: Heck, 'Gold mining in Arabia'.

reservoirs in some regions, for example, suggestive of large-scale estate management requiring the investment of substantial capital and manpower as well as organisational competence. The petty states of Aden and the Yemen (Ḥimyar) were a focus for diplomatic activity, and the kingdom of Ḥimyar in particular was a bone of contention between Persia and Rome, primarily because of its location in respect of the commercial interests of both states in the region, although ideological motives were also present. Indeed, by the later sixth century the Sasanians controlled, directly through the placement of garrisons and the building of forts or indirectly through client kings, most of the eastern coast of the Arabian Peninsula including Baḥrayn and Oman, as well as the Yemen.[96] The kingdom of Aksum, Christian since its conversion in the fourth century, figured likewise in the politics and commerce of the Arabian Peninsula, although the Aksumite rulers themselves remained entirely independent, and were key players in Roman politics in the Arabian Peninsula–Red Sea region. As a focus for exchange and the long-distance trade to both Rome's eastern provinces and Iraq, the significance of the region was clearly recognised, as the evidence of Persian political–military involvement throughout the region suggests (see below).[97]

Markets, exchange and taxation

Commerce played a crucial role in the history of those towns located in the right places – with good harbours, or at important crossroads and river crossings, for example, since they attracted not only local commercial activity but interregional or long-distance markets. Political boundaries could act as constraints on trade (as in the Roman–Persian frontier, for example, where long-distance trade between Rome and Sasanian Iran was regulated by a series of customs posts as well as by treaty throughout the fourth, fifth and sixth centuries), but many borders were in practice relatively permeable except in periods of warfare.[98] At the same time, exchange systems are rarely confined

96 Crone, *Meccan trade*, pp. 46–50.

97 D. Whitcomb, 'The "commercial crescent": Red Sea trade in Late Antiquity and early Islam', in L. Conrad (ed.), *Trade and exchange in the Late Antique and early Islamic Near East*, Studies in Late Antiquity and Early Islam 5 (forthcoming); Morony, 'The late Sasanian economic impact on the Arabian Peninsula'; D. T. Potts, *The Arabian Gulf in Antiquity*, vol. II: *From Alexander the Great to the coming of Islam* (Oxford, 1990), pp. 150–3, 211–18, 328–40; and note D. T. Potts, 'Late Sasanian armament from southern Arabia', *Electrum*, 1 (1997), pp. 127–37.

98 M. Morony, 'Trade and exchange: The Sasanian world to Islam', in Conrad (ed.), *Trade and exchange*; M. Morony, 'Commerce in early Islamic Iraq', *Asien Afrika Lateinamerika*, 20 (1993), pp. 699–710; A. D. Lee, *Information and frontiers: Roman foreign relations in Late Antiquity* (Cambridge, 1993), pp. 62–5; M. Gawlikowski, 'Some directions and perspectives of research: Graeco-Roman Syria', *Mesopotamia*, 22 (1987), p. 14.

to political boundaries, and both commercial and non-commercial exchange and the production that lies behind them generate social and cultural patterns across frontier or marginal regions which may be quite independent of the systems dominating in their hinterlands and core territories. The presence of armies in particular, with their demands for raw materials and foodstuffs, creates patterns of production and exchange which can directly impact upon the economies of regions outside their political or military reach through a process often referred to as 'incorporation'.[99] Although all the economies of the late ancient world were predominantly rural and agrarian, total self-sufficiency was relatively unusual, and involvement in a local, regional or supra-regional market was common. This applied as much to nomads as it did to sedentary populations. But there are clearly different levels of trade, exchange and market activity, and different levels of incorporation, and we shall now turn our attention to these.[100]

At the most basic level, within village communities and between such communities, the exchange of goods and products represented the long-term evolution of a pattern of production which reflected needs and local conditions of production. In some contexts each community might produce most of its requirements; in others, local conditions led to a specialisation in particular crops and the establishment of a more commercially orientated production. Thus in the limestone hills of northern Syria specialised production of olive oil on a large scale appears to have been a response first to local and then regional demand in the fourth and fifth to sixth centuries in particular,[101] and facilitated by the existence of a sufficiently monetised economy as well as the availability from other regional producers of products not otherwise available locally. The importance of this commerce in Syrian olive oil remains at issue, however. Tchalenko argued that the export of oil was crucial to the wealth of the villages he surveyed, and that it continued into the seventh century;[102] in contrast, it has more recently been argued that local demand in

99 A useful way into these issues is to be found in discussions about the value and application of 'world systems theory'. See in particular A. Gunder Frank, 'Abuses and uses of world systems theory in archaeology', in P. N. Kardulias (ed.), *World-systems theory in practice: Leadership, production and exchange* (Lanham, 1999), pp. 275–95; G. L. Stein, 'Rethinking world systems: Power, distance, and diasporas in the dynamics of interregional interaction', in Kardulias (ed.), *World-systems theory in practice*, pp. 153–77.

100 For good comparative analysis, see Wickham, *Framing the early Middle Ages*, pp. 693–720, 759–94.

101 But see U. Baruch, 'The late Holocene vegetation history of Lake Kinneret (Sea of Galilee)', *Paleorient*, 12 (1986), pp. 37–48.

102 G. Tchalenko, *Villages antiques de la Syrie du nord: Le massif du Bélus a l'époque romaine* (Paris, 1953–8), vol. I, pp. 435–7; M. Decker, 'Food for an empire: Wine and oil production in North Syria', in S. Kingsley and M. Decker (eds.), *Economy and exchange in the east Mediterranean during Late Antiquity* (Oxford, 2001), pp. 69–86.

northern and central Syria was sufficient to account for the apparent increase in production; that local production was by no means as monocultural and market-orientated as Tchalenko suggested; and that once the level of demand fell, beginning from the second half of the sixth century and culminating during the later seventh as the markets of the great urban centres of the region declined, so the prosperity of the region and its olive-oil production went into decline.[103] Yet at the same time, the extent of the trade remains disputed, with some suggesting that the oil export went much further afield, and for far longer (into the later seventh and eighth centuries, on the basis of the numismatic evidence) and, along with a range of other long-distance exports of agricultural produce, was an essential element of the late Roman economy. That there were such long-distance exports, penetrating the western Mediterranean as well as adjacent eastern provinces, is clear. The question is, how significant were they in respect of the interdependence of different regional economies?

This is a difficult question, because we immediately have to confront the issue of the role of the state. While it is generally agreed that the late Roman state intervened directly in the economy in such a way as to impact on a number of key areas of production, distribution and consumption, the extent to which this then further affected aspects of production less relevant to the state's needs remains unresolved. That this impact was felt both within and without the empire is clear.[104] Indeed, the Quraysh leather trade with the Roman army and other customers in Syria and Palestine may be a case in point, for it will have promoted both organisational potential and knowledge of the Roman provinces and military, exerting a powerful influence on the Ḥijāz and its politics.[105] State factories produced weapons; clothing and military equipment of all sorts were similarly organised or levied as an element of taxation; substantial parts of the land-tax were raised in kind to feed the army and provincial officials; government agents and senior officials

103 J. H. W. G. Liebeschuetz, *The decline and fall of the Roman city* (Oxford, 2001), p. 71; Morrisson and Sodini, 'The sixth-century economy', p. 196; Foss, 'The Near-Eastern countryside in Late Antiquity', pp. 219–20; in general, G. Tate, *Les campagnes de la Syrie du nord du IIe au VIIe siècle: Un exemple d'expansion démographique et économique dans les campagnes à la fin de l'Antiquité*, vol. I (Paris, 1992); for the later dating of this decline, see Magness, *Early Islamic settlement in Palestine*.

104 And the effect of the Roman economy on its neighbours is a significant issue which I cannot pursue here: see P. S. Wells, *The barbarians speak: How the conquered peoples shaped Roman Europe* (Princeton and Oxford, 1999); P. S. Wells, 'Production within and beyond imperial boundaries: Goods, exchange and power in Roman Europe', in Kardulias (ed.), *World-systems theory in practice*, pp. 85–101.

105 Crone, 'Quraysh and the Roman army'.

were maintained at the expense of taxpayers as they journeyed across the empire, either directly by being billeted on individuals, or indirectly through the public postal system, the *cursus publicus*, which was itself maintained through similar means. Rome and Constantinople were supplied with grain from North Africa or Egypt, and a vast tonnage of grain was transferred from one to the other as part of a regular tax arrangement. The army was likewise maintained directly by the taxpayer, even if soldiers were also paid, as a body, substantial sums, which then filtered back into the market. The issue of coin was a part of this process. Large quantities of precious-metal coinage ended up in private hands via commercial transactions and, perhaps more significantly, from state salaries paid to middle-ranking and senior officials across the provinces of the empire. The Roman government's insistence on the collection of money taxes in gold, the existence of a stable gold coinage throughout the fourth century and beyond the period of the Islamic conquests and the pressure exerted by the state elite in the use of this coinage for investment and purchases at all levels meant an extremely high degree of monetisation across the empire's territories, although the extent of the availability of the non-precious-metal coinage, on the one hand, and its value against gold (and silver), on the other, determined the extent to which the less wealthy in society could access market relations without resorting to means such as credit or barter. Indeed, it has been argued that extensive credit arrangements were also in place, permitting the transfer of values without the direct transfer of coin. Even if the pattern was in places uneven, fluctuating according to local circumstances, the presence of the army, and local patterns of agrarian production and levels of output, economic life was highly monetised throughout the sixth century and into the seventh, with increasing volumes of demand across most provinces of the empire in the east.[106] Further, while the state undoubtedly extracted, through taxation, sufficient quantities of the overall wealth produced across the empire to support its own activities, at least in the east and until the middle of the seventh century (the case of the west is

106 For the fourth century, see P. Garnsey and C. R. Whittaker, 'Trade, industry and the urban economy', in A. Cameron and P. Garnsey (eds.), *The Cambridge ancient history*, vol. XIII: *The late empire, AD 337–425* (Cambridge, 1998), pp. 316–17, 328–37; for the sixth century, see Liebeschuetz, *The decline and fall of the Roman city*, p. 45; Hendy, *Studies*, pp. 289–96, 602–7; Morrisson and Sodini, 'The sixth-century economy', pp. 214–19. Most forcefully, Banaji, *Agrarian change in Late Antiquity*, 39–88; Banaji, 'Precious metal coinages and monetary expansion', pp. 267–81. For credit arrangements, see P. Sarris, 'The early Byzantine economy in context', in M. Whittow (ed.), *Byzantium's economic turn* (Oxford, 2009). This situation changed fairly radically in the Anatolian provinces of the empire in the second half of the seventh century, and had already changed in much of the Balkan territory of the empire during the course of the later sixth century.

certainly very different), this may only be a relatively small proportion of the total wealth produced that then went onto the monetised market.[107]

The movement of some goods over long and short distances can be tracked either through references in texts and written evidence – as in Egyptian papyri – for fiscal records, delivery bills, receipts and so forth, or through the pottery in which many products were themselves transported, or which was itself exported as a marketable commodity in its own right, as in the case of finer tablewares as opposed to transport containers or cooking utensils. In the latter case the two dominant exports were: African red slip ware, the archaeological evidence for which shows a pan-Mediterranean distribution pattern, with a gradual reduction in the range and quality of products from the middle of the fifth century, with a revival from around 550 at a lower level of activity, and a reduction in the total number of sites at which it has been identified, especially in the eastern Mediterranean; and Phocaean red slip ware, which dominated the Aegean and eastern Mediterranean regions from the early fifth to late sixth / early seventh centuries. Both continued to make up a substantial proportion of the fine wares of the eastern Roman world until the middle of the seventh century, but the number of imitative types produced at a wide range of regional centres, and the increasing number of original local forms, show that both production and the market were increasingly fragmented.[108]

In the case of transport containers of coarser fabric, amphorae of various sizes, shapes and capacities were transported over very considerable distances carrying wine, oil, garum and other commodities to markets where demand

107 Estimates vary considerably: K. Hopkins, 'Rome, taxes, rent and trade', *Kodai: Journal of Ancient History*, 6–7 (1995–6), pp. 41–75 (repr. in W. Scheidel and S. von Reden (eds.), *The ancient economy* (Edinburgh, 2002), pp. 190–230), argues for a mere 5–7 per cent take by the Roman state; Wickham, *Framing the early Middle Ages*, pp. 64–6, argues for very much higher rates of extraction, 25 per cent or more in many cases, in the fifth–early seventh centuries. A global rate of taxation of between 15 and 23 per cent has been proposed for the eastern empire in the period from the eighth century onwards, for example, varying by time and place, degree of monetisation, and other related factors: see C. Morrisson and J.-C. Cheynet, 'Prices and wages in the Byzantine world', in Laiou *et al.* (eds.), *The economic history of Byzantium*, pp. 821f. – which would tend to support Wickham's higher levels. The problem lies in the nature of the evidence and the varying – and conflicting – calculations it can support.

108 For key issues, see Ward-Perkins, 'Specialised production and exchange'; J. F. Haldon, 'Production, distribution and demand in the Byzantine world, c. 660–840', in I. L. C. Hansen and C. J. Wickham (eds.), *The long eighth century* (Leiden, 2000), pp. 247–51; McCormick, *Origins of the European economy*, pp. 53–60; Morrisson and Sodini, 'The sixth-century economy', p. 210; A. Walmsley, 'Production, exchange and regional trade in the Islamic east Mediterranean: Old structures, new systems?', in Hansen and Wickham (eds.), *The long eighth century*, pp. 322–4.

was sufficient, primarily the major coastal cities of the Mediterranean world, with an onward network of routes by land to inland markets. To some extent, as with the movement of grain, oil and wine in particular, this was carried out by or at least for the state, through a system of contracting out cargoes to individuals and groups of ship-owners or masters. Thus Aegean wares reached the Balkan and Danube frontier forces as the government organised the supply of the field and garrison troops based along the *limes*, while other commodities reached the eastern front garrisons from northern Syria and in locally produced transport vessels. The best-known bulk movement of goods was, of course, that of grain from Egypt, but what is equally significant is the way in which smaller-scale enterprises and products were shipped on the back of the North African grain transport in particular, resulting in the import of a variety of goods by ports along the route taken by the grain convoys; and similar movements almost certainly accompanied other state-sponsored shipping of food or other products for the army, for example, as well as for the populace of Constantinople or Rome. The extensive movement of African fine wares and other products across the central and eastern Mediterranean can at least in part be explained through these means. But at the same time there can be little doubt that, on the basis of the numismatic and written evidence, far more trade was carried on through the medium of private entrepreneurs, markets and producers outside the state's purview.[109]

There is continued discussion about the point in time at which levels of production and consumption in the different parts of this eastern Mediterranean exchange zone began to fall off. The mid-sixth century (following plague and, in Syria, Persian inroads and economic disruption), the later sixth century (responding to loss of markets upon which certain areas depended), the first twenty or thirty years of the seventh century (a result of the Persian wars) and the mid-seventh century (Arab invasions) have all been proposed for different regions, the primary difficulty being the absence of any absolute dates for specific developments. What is not in dispute is the complexity, extent or wealth of the commerce of the late Roman world in the eastern Mediterranean (which, although regionally nuanced, as noted already, contrasts very strongly with parts of formerly Roman western Europe), and the high level of monetisation that facilitated it, or the fact that there was a marked decline in production levels and a narrowing and localisation of

109 C. Haas, 'Alexandria and the Mareotis region', in T. S. Burns and J. W. Eadie (eds.), *Urban centres and rural contexts in Late Antiquity* (East Lansing, 2001), pp. 47–62; P. Reynolds, *Trade in the western Mediterranean AD 400–700: The ceramic evidence*, BAR International Series 604 (Oxford, 1995).

exchange across the period around 550–700, even if it is also clear that trade and commerce across all political boundaries continued after 700, that ceramics from territories under Islamic control continued to be exported to the Aegean and south-west Anatolia, and that North African wares continued to appear in Constantinople into the early years of the eighth century at least. This narrowing of range is clearest in the Balkans, Anatolia and Africa, and less so in the Syria–Palestine region; although even here the evidence shows a shrinkage of urban space, a decline in the volume of traded imports and a reduction in port facilities. But in this area the evidence for thriving local production, if on a somewhat smaller scale than hitherto, is clear; while across the territory of the empire as a whole in the east, the decline of many middle-sized cities and the rise in importance of 'secondary' urban developments in the hinterlands of the largest cities suggests a shift both in patterns of settlement and in local exchange networks for reasons that remain to be determined. Yet again, however, regional variation is clear – while cities such as Apamea and others in the north appear to have gone into gradual decline from the middle of the sixth century onwards, others further south, in Palestine and Transjordan, such as Gerasa, Pella and Bostra, appear to have been flourishing until at least the early or middle years of the seventh century, and sometimes well beyond, and in the case of Gerasa, for example, as well as many others, to have produced substantial quantities of their own – often high-quality – pottery, and to have maintained their prosperity through the period of conquest and into the Umayyad period.[110]

The Sasanian world was, like the Roman, the location for regionally differentiated developments. As we have already seen, there is some evidence during the fifth century for economic expansion in some areas, most particularly the irrigable lands of Mesopotamia, Khūzistān and the Diyālā basin, and the central and western regions of Fārs, an expansion that may have been compromised during the later sixth century, perhaps becoming more acute in the first half of the seventh century.[111] Mesopotamia contrasts strongly with Roman northern Mesopotamia and Syria, however, in so far as the Romans rarely penetrated into Sasanian territory to conduct the sort of plundering

110 A. Walmsley, 'Byzantine Palestine and Arabia: Urban prosperity in Late Antiquity', in N. Christie and S. T. Loseby (eds.), *Towns in transition: Urban evolution in Late Antiquity and the early Middle Ages* (Aldershot and Brookfield, 1996), esp. pp. 147–51. Summaries of the evidence with literature can be found in Ward-Perkins, 'Specialised production and exchange', p. 354; Morrisson and Sodini, 'The sixth-century economy', pp. 193, 212; Wickham, *Framing the early Middle Ages*, pp. 613–25.

111 Balādhurī, *al-Balâdhurî, Kitâb futûh al-Buldân: The origins of the Islamic state*, trans. P. K. Hitti (London, 1916/Beirut, 1966), pp. 453–4.

operations that Sasanian armies regularly effected during the sixth century – in the 540s, 570s and 580s in particular, during which tens of thousands of people, including large numbers of craftsmen and artisans and their families were deported and resettled in new royal foundations near Ctesiphon, such as Vēh-az-antiok-Khusrau ('Khusrau's better-than-Antioch').[112] The result was that the rich western provinces of the Sasanian realm were allowed to prosper without serious interruption from the time of Julian's abortive invasion in 363, apart from occasional threats such as the campaign planned by Anastasius I (r. 491–518 CE) in 503 (or natural disasters such as flooding). Roman attacks invariably came from the north-west, and Sasanian defensive arrangements were such that they hardly ever penetrated beyond Arzanene and Atropatene. Only with Heraclius' (r. 610–641 CE) invasion from the north – also involving the sack of Ganzak, for example – in 628 and then the Islamic invasions in the 630s were these heartlands penetrated, and even then physical damage appears to have been relatively limited. In this respect there is a parallel between these regions of the Sasanian state and the more prosperous southern Syrian, Transjordanian and Palestinian towns and cities and their districts in Roman territory, which may be contrasted with those of the north, more frequently affected by Persian attacks.[113]

Although best known for the luxury goods such as silks that were traded to the north, Sasanian commerce was by no means confined to southward- or eastward-looking routes. Sogdian merchants imported and passed on to the east substantial amounts of Sasanian silver and precious metal wares, for example, although relations between the Sogdians and the Sasanian state, which had a powerful vested interest in a strictly controlled trade, were strained at times.[114] Merchants played an important role in the Sasanian state's economy, to the extent that a highly protectionist policy was maintained on all frontiers, particularly that with the Sogdian and other traders and middlemen in the north and north-east, and with the Romans in the west.[115] But it is significant that very little Roman-produced pottery appears to have been

112 Brunner, 'Geographical and administrative divisions', p. 758. The effects of such transfers are still unclear for the Roman towns and regions affected, although they must have been dramatic. See F. R. Trombley, 'War and society in rural Syria c. 502–613 AD: Observations on the demography', *Byzantine and Modern Greek Studies*, 21 (1997), esp. pp. 158, 168, 182ff.; and chapter 3 below.

113 See Lee, *Information and frontiers*, pp. 15–25, 109–28; M. Whitby, *The emperor Maurice and his historian: Theophylact Simocatta on Persian and Balkan warfare* (Oxford, 1988), pp. 195–218, for a survey of Roman–Persian relations.

114 See de la Vaissière, *Sogdian traders*, esp. pp. 171–6, 207–10, 227–37.

115 Ibid., pp. 228ff. Note also Amir Harrak, 'Trade routes and the Christianization of the Near East', *Journal of the Canadian Society for Syriac Studies*, 2 (2002).

found in Sasanian urban contexts, and what Sasanian material has been excavated from eastern Roman provincial sites is mostly small personal items and can probably be associated (with some exceptions) with the occupation of the eastern provinces in the period after 614.[116] To some extent this exchange pattern can be read off retrospectively from that of the early Islamic period, when locally produced fine wares from Palestine and Transjordan rarely moved east.[117] Commercial exchange certainly existed across the Romano-Persian frontier, but as I have noted it was carefully supervised (although the effectiveness of this is not clear), and appears to have consisted largely of luxury items. But this peaceful commercial activity was also supplemented by predation. Indeed, the chief characteristic of Roman–Persian exchange in the sixth century at least appears to be that the Sasanians took what they wanted when political circumstances allowed them to do so. Raiding for booty, labour and skills rather than for conquest (until the great war launched under Khusrau II (r. 590–628 CE)) was the key feature of Sasanian warfare in the west, and in so far as vast numbers of people and considerable quantities of gold were taken either in war or through 'subsidies' paid by the Roman government to hold off further attacks, it was extremely successful.[118]

A substantial commerce existed via the major routes that traverse northern Mesopotamia, and Sasanian rulers had invested in the construction of caravanserais to facilitate this activity, and the profits accruing to Persia from trade were noted by Roman commentators.[119] Trade in silks and other luxury items was important and profitable.[120] Trade eastwards, across the northern route and through Khurāsān, or via the Gulf and the Arabian Peninsula, was well established and requires little comment here,[121] although it is clear that the Sasanian kings actively encouraged certain commercial links, in particular the Silk Route and the Indian Ocean trade. Sasanian political intervention in South

116 E.g. A. M. Maier, 'Sassanica varia Palaestinensia: A Sassanian seal from T. Istaba, Israel, and other Sassanian objects from the southern Levant', *Iranica Antiqua*, 35 (2000), pp. 159–83.
117 See Walmsley, 'Production, exchange and regional trade', pp. 321–9.
118 Morony, 'Trade and exchange', pp. 000–00.
119 Wiesehöfer, *Ancient Persia*, pp. 192–7.
120 M. G. Raschke, 'New studies in Roman commerce with the east', in *Aufstieg und Niedergang der römischen Welt*, 2, 9.2 (1978), pp. 606–50, 821 (for caravanserais); J. I. Miller, *The spice trade of the Roman Empire, 29 BC to AD 641* (Oxford, 1969).
121 Thierry, 'Sur les monnaies sassanides trouvées en Chine', pp. 121–5 with maps 6 and 7, pp. 125–32; V. F. Piacentini, 'Ardashīr I Pāpakān and the wars against the Arabs: Working hypothesis on the Sasanian hold of the Gulf', *Proc. Seminar in Arabian Studies*, 15 (1985), pp. 57–77.

Arabia and the establishment of permanent military and commercial bases in the south and east of the Peninsula attest to the importance ascribed to the region. A chain of small fortresses and strongholds has been tentatively identified stretching from the Gulf as far as the mouth of the Indus, for example, presumably intended to protect the coastal trade and the major entrepôts.[122] But recent work re-assessing the archaeological evidence has cast some doubt on the picture of a flourishing eastern Arabian economy under Sasanian control; indeed an economic decline has been plausibly argued. While the advantages held by the Sasanians were considerable, there were no serious political hindrances in the Gulf and Indian Ocean to long-distance trade,[123] the investment by the kings in port facilities (if correctly identified) suggests that it was seen as a significant element in the royal economy. Yet, the ceramic evidence is ambiguous, and hardly supports the notion that the intensity of this trade was hardly surpassed in the later Middle Ages, or that there was a near monopoly operated by Sasanian merchants supported by the state.[124] There is also good evidence of a revival in trade overland with China – a highly monetised trade – in the last forty or so years of Sasanian rule, as political conditions in China stabilised and as Sasanian power and influence in the regions beyond Khurāsān was strengthened. Sasanian commercial activity in a wide range of luxury goods, both from west to east and vice versa was influential, and played also an important role in the economies of those regions of Central Asia as well as of China with which it was associated. Trade and exchange in urban contexts was certainly a major feature of urban life, as both the textual and archaeological evidence suggests.[125]

122 M. Kervran, 'Forteresses, entrepôts et commerce: Une histoire à suivre depuis les rois sassanides jusqu'aux princes d'Ormuz', in R. Curie and R. Gyselen (eds.), *Itinéraires d'Orient: Hommages à Claude Cahen* (Louvain, 1994), esp. pp. 331–8; Whitehouse and Williamson, 'Sasanian maritime trade', pp. 43–5.

123 M. Loewe, 'Spices and silk: Aspects of world trade in the first seven centuries of the Christian era', *JRAS*, n.s., 2 (1971), pp. 166–79; Thierry, 'Sur les monnaies sassanides trouvées en Chine'. For a significant challenge to the established view, see Kennet, 'The decline of eastern Arabia'.

124 Kennet, 'The decline of eastern Arabia', *passim*. Frye, 'Byzantine and Sasanian trade relations'; B. E. Colless, 'Persian merchants and missionaries in medieval Malaya', *Journal of the Malaysian Branch of the Royal Asiatic Society*, 42 (1969), pp. 10–47; Whitehouse and Williamson, 'Sasanian maritime trade', pp. 45f.; Kervran, 'Forteresses, entrepôts et commerce', pp. 338–9; summary of evidence in Banaji, 'Precious metal coinages and monetary expansion', pp. 285–90.

125 Thierry, 'Sur les monnaies sassanides trouvées en Chine', pp. 134–9; and esp. J. K. Skaff, 'Sasanian and Arab-Sasanian silver coins from Turfan: Their relationship to international trade and the local economy', *Asia Major*, 11, 2 (1998), pp. 67–114. See also E. de la Vaissière, 'Les marchands d'Asie Centrale dans l'empire khazar', in M. Kazanski, A. Nercessian and C. Zuckerman (eds.), *Les centres proto-urbains ruisses entre Scandinavie, Byzance et Orient* (Paris, 2000), pp. 367–78. For attitudes to commerce and the monetisation of exchange relations, see A. Panaino, 'Commerce and conflicts of religions in Sasanian Iran: Between

But it is also clear that, like Rome, the Sasanian state extracted substantial resources from the producing population in the form of crops or finished goods for its armies, as well as in terms of skills. Sasanian exchange systems seem also to have been heavily regionalised – a Mesopotamian zone overlapped to some extent with a south Iranian/Gulf/East Africa zone, which in turn connected with the Indian subcontinent – fine wares as well as domestic coarse wares from Gujarat as well as Sind and Maharashtra have been excavated from Sasanian levels at Ṣuḥār in Oman and Sīrāf, for example.[126] Yet this commerce seems hardly to have impinged, at least in terms of the movement of ceramics, on other zones to the north and east.[127] The pottery from Marw, for example, is associated stylistically with that from northern Bactria rather than Iraq or the northern Iranian plateau, while that from the Elburz regions is different again.[128] None of these types seems to have travelled far, except for certain fine wares, but these are also very limited in number.[129]

This picture contrasts with the Roman evidence, and largely reflects the different patterns of commerce and transport between coastal zones and maritime trade on the one hand, inland zones and the constraints of land transport, and on the other the types of goods that were traded. Silks and bullion, for example, which constituted two of the most important materials traded, leave no ceramic traces. But like the Roman economy, by the later sixth century the Sasanian economy also involved the circulation of a vast number of coins, reaching a peak in the period between 603 and 635 and directly impacting on the economy of the post-conquest period.[130] Indeed,

social identity and political ideology', in R. Rollinger and C. Ulf (eds.), *Commerce and monetary systems in the ancient world: means of transmission and cultural interaction* (Stuttgart, 2004), pp. 385–401.

126 See in particular Kennet, 'The decline of eastern Arabia', pp. 97–100. D. Whitehouse, 'Abbasid maritime trade: Archaeology and the age of expansion', *Rivista degli Studi Orientale*, 59 (1985), p. 344; M. Kervran, 'Indian ceramics in southern Iran and eastern Arabia: Repertory, classification, chronology', in H. P. Ray and J.-F. Salles (eds.), *Tradition and archaeology, early maritime contacts in the Indian Ocean: Proceedings of the international seminar Techno-archaeological perspectives of seafaring in the Indian Ocean 4th cent. BC–15th cent. AD* (New Delhi, 1996), pp. 37–58; D. Kennet, *Sasanian and Islamic pottery from Ras al-Khaimah: Classification, chronology and analysis of trade in the western Indian Ocean*, BAR International Series 1248 (Oxford, 2004), pp. 68–79.

127 D. Kennet, 'Sasanian pottery in southeastern Iran and eastern Arabia', *Iran*, 40 (2002); Adams, 'Tell Abu Sarifa', for southern Iraqi types.

128 G. Puschnigg, 'The pre-Islamic pottery', in G. Herrmann, K. Kurbansakhatov and St J. Simpson (eds.), 'The International Merv Project: Preliminary report on the ninth year (2000)', *Iran*, 39 (2001), pp. 22–3.

129 E.g. Kennet, 'Sasanian pottery in southeastern Iran', p. 159; Kennet, *Sasanian and Islamic pottery from Ras al-Khaimah*, pp. 68–71.

130 Kolesnikov, 'The quantity of silver coinage and levels of revenue'; de la Vaissière, *Sogdian traders*, pp. 228–32; Skaff, 'Sasanian and Arab-Sasanian silver coins from Turfan',

the evidence has been interpreted to suggest not only that coin production was inflected by military needs, as in the Roman world, but also that the Sasanian court was quite aware both of the need to circulate coin to meet commercial demands and of the possibility of manipulating the domestic market for its own purposes.[131]

The extent to which the Sasanian state, like Rome, transported large quantities of goods in bulk for its armies is unclear, but it is apparent that it was able to accommodate the logistical demands of substantial bodies of troops, and it is therefore very likely that its arrangements were not dissimilar from those of the Roman state.[132] There is some evidence for the long-distance movement of storage vessels, but these are found mostly in domestic or artisanal contexts rather than obviously military locations, and appear to reflect the regionalised exchange systems noted already, since they are confined largely (thus far) to sites in Mesopotamia, southern Iran and the Gulf.[133] For the most part its frontier provinces could support the burden of the soldiers based there, since the greater number of mints in both frontier and inner provinces serviced the needs of the military as well as the markets on which they depended very efficiently; while in the rich provinces of Mesopotamia the relatively high levels of agricultural production, combined with the possibility of riverine transport, gave the Sasanians an advantage in defensive terms.[134] The tax system, both before and after the reforms of Khusrau I, was certainly structured to support a considerable army, and involved levies of foodstuffs as well as livestock and equipment,

pp. 85–6; R. Gyselen, 'Un trésor de monnaies sassanides tardives', *Revue Numismatique*, ser. 6, 32 (1990), pp. 212–31; R. N. Frye, 'Sasanian-Central Asian trade relations', *Bulletin of the Asia Institute*, n.s. 7 (1993), pp. 73–7.

131 See esp. Sears, 'Monetary revision and monetization', pp. 161–3; Skaff, 'Sasanian and Arab-Sasanian silver coins from Turfan'.

132 Howard-Johnston, 'The two great powers', pp. 166–9, 185–6, 191–7; Morony, *Iraq after the Muslim conquest*, pp. 51–6, 61–2. Finds of Sasanian coins in districts distant from their mints may certainly reflect military as much as commercial movements: see N. Nakshabandi and F. Rashid, 'The Sassanian dirhams in the Iraq Museum', *Sumer*, 11 (1955), pp. 155–76; and esp. Sears, 'Monetary revision and monetization', pp. 161–2. For distribution of troops and arrangements for their provisioning and equipping, see Grignaschi, 'Quelques specimens de la littérature sassanide', p. 24 and notes.

133 In particular the so-called 'large incised storage vessels' and 'torpedo' jars: Kennet, 'Sasanian pottery in southeastern Iran', pp. 154, 158–60.

134 Howard-Johnston, 'The two great powers', pp. 88–91. On the mints, see esp. R. Gyselen, *Arab-Sasanian copper coinage*, Österreichische Akademie der Wissenschaften, Philosophisch-Historische Klasse, Denkschriften 284, Veröffentlichungen der numismatischen Kommission 34 (Vienna 2000), esp. p. 77; and cf. S. Tyler-Smith, 'Sasanian mint abbreviations', *Numismatic Chronicle*, 143 (1983), pp. 240–7.

although the details – recorded only obliquely in al-Ṭabarī[135] – remain obscure.[136]

It is apparent from this introductory survey that the eastern Roman and Sasanian empires had vast resources at their disposal. Both states had evolved complex administrative and social arrangements aimed at the extraction, redistribution and consumption of such resources, yet both were constrained by the geography, climate and technologies at their disposal or to which they were subject. Paradoxically, however, it was those territories that were not to be absorbed into the newly formed world of Islam which suffered most in their material infrastructure as a result of the conquests. For the process of conquest in both the Roman and Sasanian areas was in fact remarkably rapid. Within a ten-year period – from 632 to 642 – all Rome's eastern provinces, including Egypt, had been lost. Most cities surrendered with either no or only token resistance, their populations remained where they were, economic and social life continued. The changes that did take place were, therefore, both minimal – at least in the opening decades of Islamic rule – and gradual. An exception in both social and economic as well as political and cultural respects may be the fate of the elites in the formerly Roman provinces, where sometimes dramatic changes were effected as a result of the Islamic occupation and political restructuring from the 640s.[137] The fate of the Sasanian regional elites – as opposed to the senior aristocrats – was certainly milder, however. Apart from this, similar conditions following the conquest, with a few exceptions, applied in Iraq and Iran, and to a large degree the trajectory of development under way in the pre-conquest period continued on its course in the decades following, with certain notable exceptions (for example, the establishment of the *amṣār* (garrison cities) in Iraq and Egypt). The vast quantity of coined silver and gold circulating within and across these two spheres both united and separated them, through regionalised and long-distance overlapping trade and exchange networks. At the same time it emphasised their involvement and integration into a much wider Eurasian network of commercial as well as political ties or

135 Howard-Johnston, 'The two great powers', pp. 169–72; M. Morony, 'Land-holding in seventh-century Iraq: Late Sasanian and early Islamic patterns', in Udovitch (ed.), *The Islamic Middle East, 700–1900*, pp. 136–53; Altheim and Stiehl, *Finanzgeschichte der Spätantike*, esp. pp. 7–51; T. Daryaee, 'The effect of the Arab-Muslim conquest on the administrative division of Sasanian Persis/Fārs', *Iran*, 41 (2003), pp. 193–204; Trinkaus, 'Settlement of highlands and lowlands', pp. 129–30, 136–9, on the relationship between the local economy of the Dāmghān area and taxation.

136 On Khusrau's reform, see Rubin, 'The reforms of Khusro Anūshirwān'.

137 See Wickham, *Framing the early Middle Ages*, pp. 240–55.

associations. This had a crucial impact on the ways in which the Islamic successor state evolved its own patterns of resource distribution, exchange and commerce.[138]

In the surviving Byzantine lands, by contrast, a century and a half of debilitating and disruptive warfare ensued, which disrupted the provincial and rural economy and reduced the former eastern Roman imperial state to a shadow – and a relatively impoverished shadow – of its former self, contributing also to a radical transformation of urban life as well as of the state and eastern Roman society. But outside this war-damaged zone, urban life, inter-provincial and long-distance trade, and local economies in the conquered lands continued to evolve in directions set before the Islamic conquests with little or no interruption, although of course the social structure of landowning, elite culture and access to resources did change – in some cases substantially. Whatever the nature of the changes that affected the late ancient world in the wake of the early Islamic conquests, it was thus geography and landscape, on the one hand, and the demography and pattern of exploitation and distribution of resources of all kinds, on the other, that determined and constrained the initial trajectory of Islamic history.

138 P. Pourshariati, *Decline and fall of the Sasanian empire: The Sasanian–Parthian confederacy and the Islamic conquest of Iran* (London, 2008).

2

The late Roman/early Byzantine Near East

MARK WHITTOW

Rome was not 'declining' in Late Antiquity. In many ways it was thriving. Half a century of research – above all, archaeology – has shown in the Roman Near East a wealthy, well-populated world, whose inhabitants enjoyed a thriving economy and spent their money on lavish building projects, on silver and on high-quality textiles. In many areas of the Near East the Late Roman period, in terms of population size, settlement density and levels of exploitation, marks a pre-modern high.[1] On the other hand, there is no doubt that between the third and sixth centuries the Roman empire was transformed in ways that do much to explain what happened in the seventh century. The key to this process was conflict with Sasanian Iran. In response to that threat the structure, organisation and culture of the empire was reshaped; Rome's relations with the wider world were transformed; and the empire became involved in an escalating cycle of warfare that would culminate in the crisis out of which the Islamic world would emerge.

An obvious parallel is with the way the modern world is a product of the First World War. Without it we would have had neither Soviet Russia, nor Nazi Germany, nor the European Community, nor the United Nations, nor the current multi-state Middle East. That is not to say that peace in 1914 would have kept the world safe for imperialism and reaction, but that the war and its aftermath set the world on paths that would have been hardly imaginable six years earlier. In turn, the First World War can only be fully comprehended in the light of the European state system as it had evolved since the seventeenth century, a process that had divided the continent between powers equipped

1 J. Banaji, *Agrarian change in Late Antiquity: Gold, labour, and aristocratic dominance* (Oxford, 2001), pp. 15–22; B. Ward-Perkins, 'Land, labour and settlement' and 'Specialized production and exchange', in A. Cameron, B. Ward-Perkins and M. Whitby (eds.), *The Cambridge ancient history*, vol. XIV: *Late Antiquity: Empire and successors, AD 425–600* (Cambridge, 2000), pp. 315–91. See pp. 352–4, 358–61 for the prosperity of the Roman Near East in Late Antiquity.

and prepared to fight war on the grandest scale, and able to do so with the support and commitment of millions of their citizens.

In a similar way the Islamic world was the product of a war between Rome and Iran that broke out in 603 and lasted for twenty-five years. The war overturned an established order three centuries old, and created a power vacuum that allowed Arab armies to conquer two empires and create a third; but, although it had immediate causes, to be fully understood it needs, like the war that broke out in 1914, to be seen in terms of a political system that had evolved over several centuries, in this case since the third century CE.

To recognise this is not to say that Islam would not have come about without the wars of the Roman empire, but rather that God's purposes would have had to have been achieved in very different ways. The rise of Islam as it actually happened is comprehensible only in the context of the history of the Roman empire, a history that culminated in what James Howard-Johnston has evocatively dubbed the 'the last great war of Antiquity'.[2]

Rome and the Near East to the fourth century CE: making and re-making an empire

The expansion of Rome

At the beginning of the third century CE the Roman empire stretched from Hadrian's Wall in the north of England to the upper Tigris in eastern Turkey, a nominal distance of about 3,700 kilometres, and for any Roman traveller actually making this journey considerably more. The empire included not only the entire Mediterranean basin, but extended far beyond into a world whose rivers drained into the Persian Gulf, the Black Sea, the North Sea and the Atlantic Ocean. Its size in part reflected the attractiveness of Roman rule. Many inhabitants of this empire wanted to be citizens or at least clients of the Romans. For the elites or would-be elites of provincial society the Roman empire brought opportunities for riches and power, and the security to enjoy them: behave like a Roman and act in the name of Rome, and you would in effect be a Roman. The imperial administrative system was minimal and the tax burden light. In practice Rome's subjects governed themselves, and competed to display their loyalty to the emperor. The hundreds of temples to the cult of the emperor that dotted the Roman world are impressive

2 J. Howard-Johnston, 'al-Tabari on the last great war of Antiquity', in J. Howard-Johnston, *East Rome, Sasanian Persia and the end of Antiquity: Historiographical and historical studies* (Aldershot, 2006), chapter 6, p. 1.

testimony to an uncontested imperialism. Revolt and resistance was rare, and when it occurred was usually more a matter of pushing for further benefits than of any rejection of Roman rule as such.[3] The Jewish revolts of the first and second centuries CE, which were intended to rid Judaea of the Romans, were exceptional; the lack of any true network of fortifications in the Near East, whether to cow internal dissent or outside aggression, is a much better guide to the normal workings of the empire before the third century.[4]

The size of the empire also reflects Roman military superiority. At an operational level this was the product of a system honed in the later years of the republic and founded on the infantry of the legions; in strategic terms it was due to the lack of any great-power rival. Following the defeat and destruction of Carthage in the third century BCE, Rome was only opposed by local and regional powers. Had it been otherwise, Rome could not have conquered the east and at the same time sent its armies to the Rhine and distant Britain.

The territorial expansion of Rome began in earnest in the second century BCE, and had its roots in the competitive aristocratic politics of the republic.[5] Caesar's conquest of Gaul is typical in all but the fact that he wrote his own account of what happened. While his wars were fought chiefly to gain the very practical benefits of booty and glory, Caesar shows that he and his peers were not without a sense of strategy; not necessarily grand strategy, but certainly a practical awareness of the need to manage clients, control resources and avoid over-commitment. The destruction of Octavian's aristocratic rivals, the fall of the republic and the making of the empire at the end of the first century BCE slowed but did not halt Roman expansion. Emperors continued to fight wars for much the same trio of motives that had inspired Caesar, and after Claudius' conquest of Britain in 43 CE these tended increasingly to lead them east. The spoils were richer, the prestige of following in Alexander's footsteps greater, and the Parthians, if not a real rival, were at least worth

3 C. Ando, *Imperial ideology and provincial loyalty in the Roman Empire* (Berkeley and Los Angeles, 2000), pp. 1–15; J. H. W. G. Liebeschuetz, *The decline and fall of the Roman city* (Oxford, 2001), pp. 342–6; S. Price, *Rituals and power: The Roman imperial cult in Asia Minor* (Cambridge, 1984), pp. 76–7, 234–48; G. Wolf, *Becoming Roman: The origins of provincial civilization in Gaul* (Cambridge, 1998), pp. 238–49.

4 M. Sartre, *The Middle East under Rome*, trans. C. Porter and E. Rawlings (Cambridge, MA, 2005), p. 132; N. Pollard, *Soldiers, cities, and civilians in Roman Syria* (Ann Arbor, 2000), pp. 85–110; S. T. Parker, 'The defense of Palestine and Transjordan from Diocletian to Heraclius', in L. E. Stager, J. A. Greene and M. D. Coogan (eds.), *The archaeology of Jordan and beyond: Essays in honor of James A. Sauer*, Studies in the Archaeology and History of the Levant 1 (Winona Lake, IN, 2000), pp. 369–70; cf. B. Isaac, *The limits of empire* (Oxford, 1990), pp. 156–60.

5 W. V. Harris, *War and imperialism in republican Rome, 327–70 BC* (Oxford, 1979), pp. 30–1.

taking more seriously than the tribes of Germanic Europe. Under Trajan in the early second century CE, Rome's eastern frontier for the first time reached the Tigris, and his sack of the Parthian capital at Ctesiphon near modern Baghdad set a standard which his successors were keen to follow.[6]

The rise of the Sasanians

However, the political vacuum that lay behind the expansion of Rome could hardly be expected to last forever, and in the third century a new era began. In the west Rome was faced by an evolving Germanic world where tribes were coming together in more powerful confederations. Individually groupings such as the Marcomanni, the Alamanni (the archetypal name for a confederation) and the Goths did not pose a threat to Roman hegemony, but their management did require more resources than had their first-century predecessors. Half-hearted measures could – and did – lead to disaster.[7] The really significant change, however, was happening in the east.

The Parthian dynasty had signally failed to stop their aggressive western neighbours regularly invading Iraq through the second and early third centuries CE, and inevitably its legitimacy was called into question. The dynasty's failure was further emphasised by the inability to crush a long-running rebellion in western Iran. In 224 the rebel army defeated the Parthians for the third time; King Artabanus V fell on the battlefield, and the rebel leader, Ardashīr, moved rapidly to seize Iraq, so inaugurating the Sasanian regime that was to rule Iran until the Muslim conquest.[8] Rome was now faced by an entirely new situation. Ardashīr and his successors may initially have been drawn into war with Rome by the need to end any threat that former Parthian client states, such as Armenia, might serve as a base for a Parthian restoration, but soon war with

6 C. S. Lightfoot, 'Trajan's Parthian war and the fourth-century perspective', *Journal of Roman Studies*, 80 (1990), pp. 115–26; F. Millar, *The Roman Near East, 31 BC–AD 337* (Cambridge, MA, 1993), p. 99; S. P. Mattern, *Rome and the enemy: Imperial strategy in the principate* (Berkeley and Los Angeles, 1999), pp. 1–23, 81–122.

7 M. Todd, 'The Germanic peoples and Germanic society', in A. K. Bowman, P. Garnsey and A. Cameron (eds.), *The Cambridge ancient history*, vol. XII: *The crisis of empire, AD 193–337*, 2nd edn. (Cambridge, 2005), pp. 440–7; P. Heather, 'The Late Roman art of client management', in W. Pohl, I. Wood and H. Reimitz (eds.), *The transformation of frontiers: From Late Antiquity to the Carolingians* (Leiden, 2001). On the name 'Alamanni', see J. F. Drinkwater, *The Alamanni and Rome 213–496* (Oxford, 2007), pp. 62–9.

8 J. Howard-Johnston, 'The two great powers in Late Antiquity: A comparison', in A. Cameron (ed.), *The Byzantine and early Islamic Near East*, vol. III: *States, resources and armies*, Studies in Late Antiquity and Early Islam 1 (Princeton, 1995), pp. 158–62; M. H. Dodgeon and S. N. C. Lieu (eds.), *The Roman eastern frontier and the Persian Wars*, part 1: *AD 226–363: A documentary history* (London, 1991), pp. 9–33; cf. R. N. Frye, 'The Sassanians', in Bowman *et al.* (eds.), *The crisis of empire*, pp. 461–74.

the empire had become an end in itself. Victory demonstrated Sasanian charisma and brought huge profits. The experience of war bonded the Sasanian elite and created the infrastructure for further hostilities. Through to the 260s Sasanian armies raided throughout the Roman east, and the Roman response was largely ineffective. In 244 a Roman expedition to Ctesiphon ended with the emperor Gordian III's death and his successor, Philip the Arab,[9] making major concessions to ensure the army's retreat. In 253 the great Syrian city of Antioch was sacked, and in 260 the emperor Valerian himself was captured and put on display, in person for the rest of his life, and in stone for eternity.[10] The monumental rock-cut reliefs at Naqsh-i Rustam in Iran sum up the new order. The site lies 5 kilometres north-west of the ancient Persian capital of Persepolis. Here were buried the great Achaemenid shahs, Darius and Xerxes, who had ruled as far as the Mediterranean; and here, next to the tomb of the great Darius and close to the huge image of Ardashīr being given rule over Iran by the supreme God Ahuramazda, Ardashīr's son Shāpūr I celebrated his victories over Rome. Shāpūr's relief shows one emperor (Gordian III or Philip the Arab) kneeling at the feet of the mounted shah, and another, Valerian, held prisoner by the hand.[11] The message is clear. The Sasanians are divinely appointed rulers of the east, whose status as the legitimate heirs of the Achaemenids is demonstrated by victory over Rome.[12]

Palmyra and the third-century crisis

The very real danger of the break-up of the empire during these years is made clear by the so-called revolt of Palmyra. This oasis city, about 200 kilometres east of the Mediterranean, had been part of the empire since the early first century CE, and had made itself rich as one of the chief conduits for eastern trade into the Roman world. Inscriptions in Aramaic and Greek describe the system of protected caravans that crossed the Syrian desert, and Palmyrene merchants are attested resident as far afield as the Persian Gulf. Otherwise Palmyra was

9 On Philip's description in fourth-century sources as 'the Arab', see Millar, *The Roman Near East*, pp. 530–1: 'we must leave entirely open the question of what ethnic description we ought to give to the two Greek-speaking (and surely also Latin-speaking) sons of a local Roman citizen, Iulius Marinus, who both entered imperial service' (p. 531).

10 Dodgeon and Lieu (eds.), *The Roman eastern frontier*, pp. 34–67.

11 G. Herrmann, D. N. Mackenzie and R. Howell, *The Sasanian reliefs at Naqsh-i Rustam, Naqsh-i Rustam 6, The triumph of Shapur I*, Iranische Denkmaler 13 (Berlin, 1989).

12 Howard-Johnston, 'The two great powers in Late Antiquity', p. 160; G. Fowden, *Empire to commonwealth: Consequences of monotheism in Late Antiquity* (Princeton, 1993), pp. 28–9; cf. D. S. Potter, *Prophecy and history in the crisis of the Roman Empire: A historical commentary on the Thirteenth Sibylline Oracle* (Oxford, 1990), pp. 370–6, for the view that the Sasanians were unaware of their Achaemenid predecessors.

organised as an ordinary Roman city, ruled by a council of its leading citizens.[13] In the 260s, however, in the crisis that followed the capture of the emperor Valerian, one of its notables, Septimius Odenathus, came to prominence organising resistance to the Iranians and suppressing rivals to the new emperor, Gallienus. Odenathus' status at this stage is unclear. He was a Roman senator, and so a plausible person to exercise authority; he may have been governor of Syria, or he may have held a special regional command entrusted to him by Gallienus. The evidence is equivocal.[14] But in 268 Odenathus was murdered, and his power inherited by his wife Zenobia and son Vaballathus. Over the next few years their troops overran Syria and then Egypt, the wealthiest of the eastern provinces and a crucial source of Rome's grain supply. Gallienus had been killed in 268. His successor, Claudius, died in 270. It was not until 271 that the new emperor, Aurelian, marched east, defeated the Palmyrene armies, and in 272 sacked Palmyra, and brought Zenobia captive to Rome.[15]

At one level this was an ordinary piece of Roman imperial politics, and the fact that Palmyra was a commercial centre, bilingual in Aramaic and Greek, does not make its leading families any the less 'Roman'. Inscriptions such as those known from milestones in the province of Arabia (mod. Jordan) describe Vaballathus as 'Imperator Caesar L. Julius Aurelius Septimius Vaballathus Athenodorus', in other words as Roman emperor, and his ascent to power would have been no more extraordinary or exotic than that of the other Roman provincials who became emperors during the second and third centuries. A document from Egypt dated by the joint regnal year of the emperors Aurelian and Vaballathus is a plain indication of how the Palmyrene 'revolt' appeared at the time.[16] The fact that Aurelian defeated Vaballathus and Zenobia should not make us think that the former's power was in any way more legitimate or more 'Roman'. In many ways the story of Palmyra exemplifies the strength of the ties that bound the empire together, and enabled local notables to identify with it and use its structures for their benefit. Zenobia and Vaballathus were not Arab nationalists, nor were Palmyra's conquests the forerunners of those of the seventh century. To call Palmyra 'Arab' is a modern device with no contemporary usage.[17]

13 Millar, *The Roman Near East*, pp. 159–73, 319–36; M. Sartre, 'The Arabs and the desert peoples', in Bowman *et al.* (eds.), *The crisis of empire*, pp. 511–15.

14 For alternatives see Millar, *The Roman Near East*, pp. 165, 168–71; D. S. Potter, *The Roman Empire at bay, AD 180–395* (London, 2004), pp. 259–60; and U. Hartmann, *Das palmyrenische Teilreiche* (Stuttgart, 2001), pp. 91–6.

15 Dodgeon and Lieu (eds.), *The Roman eastern frontier*, pp. 68–110.

16 Ibid., pp. 88–9, 91.

17 J. Retsö, *The Arabs in Antiquity: Their history from the Assyrians to the Umayyads* (London, 2003), pp. 462–6.

But the 'revolt' did have more serious and genuinely contemporary implications. For the most part Palmyra's Aramaic inscriptions appear simply to convey Roman titles in a different idiom, but when Odenathus can be described on an inscription as 'King of Kings', in other words the title of the Iranian shah, and when Odenathus can give that same title to his elder son Herodian, who in turn can be depicted on a lead seal with a crown like that of the Parthian kings, then it indicates an ability among the Palmyrene elite to think in terms other than those derived from Rome.[18] The empire had grown up, and now rested on, the centripetal desire of local elites to be Roman. In the fifth century Roman power in Gaul would dissolve when local elites there came to realise that the empire could no longer provide them with security, and began to imagine a future without Rome – a process we now describe as the fall of the Roman empire in the west.[19] These Palmyrene inscriptions show the early stages of the same process. The crisis of the third-century east was short-lived compared with the problems that overwhelmed the fifth-century west; but the response of the Palmyrene elite to failure in the face of Sasanian aggression shows the early stages of the same process. If Rome could not provide the security and rewards for these elites that had bound them to the empire in the first place, then there were alternatives available, and, if followed, the empire would fail.

Re-making the empire

The implications of the rise of the Sasanians and the Palmyrene crisis were clear enough. Emperors needed more troops, and more resources to support them. That would require asking more from the empire's landowning elites, and to do that with any long-term success would require binding those individuals more closely into the administration and ideology of empire. If the early empire had flourished because it empowered local elites and asked for comparatively little in return, the empire's survival now demanded rather more.

Over the course of the late third and fourth centuries this agenda was largely achieved. It is traditional, and probably right, to give a great deal of the credit to Diocletian (r. 284–305) for increasing the size of the army and reorganising the empire's administrative and fiscal system, and to Constantine (r. 306–37) for

18 Dodgeon and Lieu (eds.), *The Roman eastern frontier*, pp. 77, 88; for the lead seal, see the illustration in E. Equini Schneider, *Septimia Zenobia Sebaste* (Rome, 1993), p. 98 and the discussion in Hartmann, *Das palmyrenische Teilreiche*, pp. 179–83.

19 P. Heather, 'The Huns and the end of the Roman Empire in Western Europe', *English Historical Review*, 110 (1995), pp. 38–9.

giving the empire a new ideological focus in Christianity, a new capital and senate in Constantinople and, arguably most important, a new gold-based currency. In both cases the changes had their roots in the earlier third century, and took more than a hundred years to be worked through, but it remains true that these two regimes took the crucial steps that were to shape the empire of Late Antiquity.[20]

The key factor was the need for more troops, from which followed the need to obtain more resources. There is no agreement on how large the increase in the size of the army was, but an increase by a third from about 350,000 at the end of the second century to nearly 500,000 by the end of the fourth would be a conservative estimate.[21] To meet the cost Italy lost its previous tax exemption, and city revenues were in effect nationalised. On top of this the system of requisitioning by which army units were provided with goods in kind was gradually expanded, first into an empire-wide system based on a census of people and land, and then commuted into a land tax which thenceforth formed the basis of the imperial budget.[22]

On the face of it, such changes should have been utterly unacceptable to the provincial elites whose commitment to the empire was essential for its survival, but in the event they were wooed by imperial propaganda emphasising how much the emperor shared their interests and concerns, and more importantly they soon found that they gained more by the opportunities that a more active central government provided than they had lost by the confiscation of civic revenues. Diocletian may have broken up the large provinces of the earlier empire into smaller units principally to make it more difficult for any governor thinking of revolt, but the consequence was many more posts in imperial government. Similarly, whatever Constantine's reasons for founding a new capital at Constantinople and reorganising the currency in a system based on gold, the eventual result was to take hundreds of leading provincial families from their cities to the imperial centre, and bind them there by golden ties. In the new world of Late Antiquity being paid in gold was akin to being paid in dollars or euros in a modern Third World economy. Gold went as

20 E. Lo Cascio, 'The new state of Diocletian and Constantine: From the tetrarchy to the reunification of the empire', in Bowman *et al.* (eds.), *The crisis of empire*, pp. 170–83; Potter, *The Roman Empire at bay*, pp. 367–400.

21 B. Campbell, 'The army', in Bowman *et al.* (eds.), *The crisis of empire*, pp. 123–4; H. Elton, *Warfare in Roman Europe AD 350–425* (Oxford, 1996), pp. 118–27; A. H. M. Jones, *The Later Roman Empire, 284–602: A social, economic, and administrative study*, 3 vols. (Oxford, 1964), pp. 56–60, 679–83; cf. Potter, *The Roman Empire at bay*, pp. 455–8.

22 M. Corbier, 'Coinage and taxation: The state's point of view, A.D 193–337', in Bowman *et al.* (eds.), *The crisis of empire*, pp. 370–86.

salaries to those who served the state, and in turn those who served the state had the resources to dominate provincial society.[23]

The culmination of these changes was the new role of the emperor which emerged in the early fifth century. In the past emperors had been soldiers, and they had needed to keep on the move. Even when they were not, they needed to cultivate this image. But in the fifth century it became possible for an emperor such as Theodosius II to spend his life in Constantinople, and to proclaim his status by presiding over Christian ceremonies, like a glorious spider at the centre of a web. By the fifth century the empire was centred as never before on a capital city, on a palace, and on the emperor who resided there.[24]

The transformation of the Roman empire inaugurated by Diocletian and Constantine enabled the empire to survive in a newly competitive world, and, as far as the Near East was concerned, to prosper too. Late Antique cities were generally less spectacular than their earlier Roman predecessors. With civic revenues in imperial hands and the foci of political life shifting elsewhere, the great building boom that had filled the region's cities with monumental public buildings was largely over by the fourth century, but the leaders of provincial society were still rich – indeed, paid in gold, their spending power was arguably greater than ever before, their investments fuelled growth, and the archaeological evidence, most obviously that from the limestone massif in northern Syria, suggests that the benefits reached a wide section of society.[25]

What was once seen as an age of decline has therefore come to look very different. Compared with the empire of the first and second centuries, that of Late Antiquity appears more, not less, effective at binding provincial elites to the centre and transmitting central authority to the periphery.[26] The imposition of Christianity is a good example. It may not have been as total or as uniform as emperors would have wished, but it represents a degree of central involvement in the lives of all imperial subjects unprecedented before the fourth century. The very concept of heresy would have been strange to pagan

23 P. Heather, 'New men for new Constantines? Creating an imperial elite in the eastern Mediterranean', in P. Magdalino (ed.), *New Constantines: The rhythm of imperial renewal in Byzantium, 4th–13th centuries* (Aldershot, 1994), pp. 11–33; Banaji, *Agrarian change*, pp. 39–40, 60–70.

24 A. D. Lee, 'The eastern empire: Theodosius to Anastasius', in Cameron *et al.* (eds.), *Late Antiquity*, p.35; M. McCormick, 'Emperor and court', in Cameron *et al.* (eds.), *Late Antiquity*, pp. 156–60; G. Dagron, *Naissance d'une capitale: Constantinople et ses institutions de 330 à 451* (Paris, 1974), pp. 77–92.

25 Liebeschuetz, *The decline and fall of the Roman city*, pp. 54–74; Banaji, *Agrarian change*, pp. 6–22; Ward-Perkins, 'Land, labour and settlement', pp. 315–45; C. Wickham, *Framing the early Middle Ages: Europe and the Mediterranean, 400–800* (Oxford, 2005), pp. 443–59.

26 P. Heather, 'Senators and senates', in A. Cameron and P. Garnsey (eds.), *The Cambridge ancient history*, vol. XIII: *The late empire, AD 337–425* (Cambridge, 1998), pp. 204–9.

Romans; the idea that an emperor should declare 'all heresies forbidden by both divine and imperial laws', as did Gratian, Valentinian and Theodosius in 379, would have been bizarre.[27]

If there was a fundamental weakness in the new order it lay in the inherent limits of such pretensions to central control. In the republic and early empire a Roman identity had been a privilege which provincials had struggled to obtain and display; now each city was as Roman as the next. The early empire was compensated for its minimal governmental structure by the desire of provincial families to be Roman. In the empire of Late Antiquity those same provincials were without question Roman citizens, and had nothing to prove. The ties that bound centre to periphery may have been stronger than before, but more depended upon them.[28]

The other weakness was that the empire's fortunes were thenceforth irretrievably tied to its relationship with Iran.

Rome and Persia

Fortunes of war, 284–628

The crisis of the mid-third century was surmounted, but it left emperors in no doubt that relations with the Persians had to be their first priority, and that major deployments anywhere other than the Persian front would depend on peace there. That fact did much to govern the history of the Roman empire through to the seventh century.

Much of the success of Diocletian's regime (284–305) followed from the victory secured in 298 by his junior colleague, the Caesar Galerius. His crushing defeat of the Persian shah Narseh was to win nearly forty years of comparative security, during which time many of the crucial reforms that were to reshape the empire took place. On the other hand, the long reign of Constantius II (337–61) was equally shaped by an inability to achieve a decisive victory over the Persians. Late in his reign his father Constantine had provoked a war with Persia, and this was inherited by Constantius, who found himself pinned to the east and unable adequately to deal with the threats posed by usurpers or barbarian neighbours in the Balkans and west. His need for someone to act as an imperial representative in Gaul eventually forced Constantius to appoint his nephew Julian as Caesar – in effect junior emperor.

27 *Codex Theodosianus*, XVI.5.5, ed. T. Mommsen and P. M. Meyer (Berlin, 1905), p.856, trans. C. Pharr as *The Theodosian Code* (New York, 1952), pp. 450–1.
28 Liebeschuetz, *The decline and fall of the Roman city*, pp. 346–51.

The step was risky because the emperor had been responsible for the death of many of Julian's relatives, including that of his brother Gallus in 354, and in the event failed. When in 358 Shāpūr captured the great fortress city of Amida (modern Diyarbakr) and Constantius ordered Julian to send troops to the east, the Caesar refused. In 360 Julian was proclaimed emperor in Paris, and marched east to seize power for himself.[29]

The expected showdown did not happen. Constantius died on the road, and Julian inherited the empire without a battle. Less than two years later the new emperor led his army into Iraq. The invasion force reached the Persian capital of Ctesiphon on the Tigris, but found the improved defences of the Persian capital too strong to storm. The retreat in the middle of an Iraqi summer turned to disaster when the emperor was mortally wounded in a skirmish. A group of junior officers proclaimed one of their number, Jovian, emperor. The retreat continued, but the army was now starving, and once frantic attempts to cross the Tigris back into Roman territory had failed, Jovian had little choice but to negotiate, and eventually concede a humiliating treaty in exchange for their escape.[30]

Julian's end has inevitably coloured all perceptions of the man and his decision to invade Persia. In Ammianus' carefully constructed narrative it seems a fated error, to which Julian was lured by visions of glory; but seen from the perspective of 361 it was arguably the obvious lesson of the previous sixty-three years. Galerius' victory had made the empire manageable; Constantius' inability to bring Shāpūr to battle had caused him to stumble from one crisis to the next. Julian 'the apostate' is famous as the emperor who wanted to roll back Christianity. If he were to have any chance of achieving that end he needed to begin with victory over Persia. A stalemate would have paralysed Julian as effectively as it had his uncle – not just as regards Christianity, but in terms of ruling the empire at all.

These conclusions were as true after 363 as before, but in the event both empires came to be preoccupied by other problems. In 376 the emperor Valens was confronting the Persians in Armenia when envoys arrived from two important Gothic groups, the Tervingi and Greuthungi, whose position

29 R. C. Blockley, *East Roman foreign policy: Formation and conduct from Diocletian to Anastasius* (Leeds, 1992), pp. 5–24; D. Hunt, 'The successors of Constantine', in Cameron and Garnsey (eds.), *The late empire*, pp. 39–43; Dodgeon and Lieu (eds.), *The Roman eastern frontier*, pp. 125–230.

30 Blockley, *East Roman foreign policy*, pp. 24–30; D. Hunt, 'Julian', in Cameron and Garnsey (eds.), *The late empire*, pp. 73–7; J. Matthews, *The Roman Empire of Ammianus* (London, 1989), pp. 130–79; Dodgeon and Lieu (eds.), *The Roman eastern frontier*, pp. 231–74.

north of the Danube was being rendered untenable by the impact of migrating Huns. The Goths were already clients of the Romans; they now wanted to be given land inside the empire. Pinned to the east by operations against the Persians, Valens had little choice but to agree for the moment, but as soon as he could disengage, the emperor marched his field army to the west, and set out to crush these unwanted immigrants. All looked set for an imperial triumph, but on 9 August 378 his army blundered into battle near Adrianople (mod. Edirne), and by the end of the day the emperor and two-thirds of his army (perhaps some 15,000 men) had been killed.[31]

The consequences of this unexpected disaster were played out over the following decades. The Romans recovered, but could not defeat the Goths; the Goths could not fight their way to security, and they found it very hard to force the Romans to negotiate in good faith or to abide by anything agreed. In the early fifth century the Goths, now led by Alaric, moved to Italy in an attempt to extract terms from the western empire, but with no more success. Threatening Rome itself, and even carrying out that threat on 24 August 410, did Alaric little good. His successor, Athaulf, led the Goths to Gaul, where eventually Goths and Romans made peace in 418. But by now the context was changing radically. In 406 several barbarian groups, including Vandals, Suevi and Alans, had crossed the Rhine into Roman territory. In 410 Britain slipped from imperial control; in 439 the Vandals conquered Carthage, and with it one of the chief sources of revenue for the western empire. Although the last emperor of the west was not deposed until 476, in reality the western empire had already fallen a generation before.[32]

During these years successive eastern regimes in Constantinople were pre-occupied first by the remaining Goths in the Balkans, then by the appalling implications of the Vandal conquest of Africa and the appearance of a Vandal war fleet in the Mediterranean, and from the late 430s by the Huns. The latter were a steppe nomad people, whose westward migration had triggered the Gothic crisis of 376–8 and quite likely the 406 Rhine crossings too. Up to about 440 the Huns had operated as small bands, exploiting whatever opportunities arose. At this point Attila and his brother Bleda managed to establish a powerful nomad state, which in effect operated a Europe-wide extortion racket for the next thirteen years. Attila's death in 453 paradoxically made the situation worse,

31 Blockley, *East Roman foreign policy*, pp. 30–9; P. Heather, *Goths and Romans 332–489* (Oxford, 1991), pp. 122–47.

32 P. Heather, *The fall of the Roman Empire: A new history* (Basingstoke, 2005), pp. 182–299; I. N. Wood, 'The barbarian invasions and first settlements', in Cameron and Garnsey (eds.), *The late empire*, pp. 516–37.

as former clients of the Huns, such as the Gepids and those Goths still in the Balkans, struggled for security and independence. It was only in 489, when Theodoric the Amal, who had eventually managed to establish his authority over the Balkan Goths, was persuaded to invade Italy, where he would rule in the name of the eastern emperor, that Constantinopolitan rulers could begin to look beyond successive crises on their Balkan doorstep.[33]

The Persians might have been expected to take ruthless advantage of Roman difficulties, and there were short wars in 420–1 and again in 440, but in general throughout the late fourth and fifth centuries the Persian response was tempered by a combination of internal political problems, Roman concessions and their own growing difficulties in the east. By themselves disputed successions and unstable regimes, such as followed Shāpūr II's death in 379, Yazdegerd I's in 420, Wahrām V's in 438, and Yazdegerd II's in 457, would have tended to provoke hostilities as new shahs looked to prove their charisma by victory over Rome, but in each case other factors worked to deter conflict. In 387 Theodosius I, heavily committed in the west, conceded effectively everything that the Persians demanded in Armenia, so giving up a Roman hegemony in this strategic mountainous region that went back to the first century CE. The Romans were also prepared to pay for peace. Whether this was a regular payment fixed by treaty, or whether it was envisaged as a Roman payment for Persian costs in blocking the Caucasian passes against enemies that might threaten both empires, or the dates when any of this happened, is all equally uncertain, but payments were made, and the Persians found these increasingly attractive the more they began to face serious difficulties on their own eastern frontiers.[34]

Through the fifth century Roman–Persian diplomacy was increasingly conducted in a language of brotherhood, friendship and coexistence as two sources of light. But we should be careful not to take this too seriously. Any diplomacy intended as more than sabre-rattling has to be conducted in mutually respectful terms. Peace was a product of Roman weakness and Persian satisfaction with their gains; before the end of the century neither condition would still apply.[35]

In about 469 Shāh Fīrūz was defeated and captured by the Hepthalites, an increasingly powerful nomad confederation on Persia's eastern frontier. To obtain his release he was forced to pay a huge ransom and promise not to

33 Heather, 'The Huns'; Heather, *Goths and Romans*, pp. 227–308.

34 Blockley, *East Roman foreign policy*, pp. 39–86; G. Greatrex and S. N. C. Lieu (eds.), *The Roman eastern frontier and the Persian Wars*, pt 2: *AD 363–630* (London and New York, 2002), pp. 16–17, 28–30, 32–3, 36–46.

35 Blockley, *East Roman foreign policy*, pp. 106–27.

attack the Hepthalites again. His son Kawād was left as a hostage while the necessary gold treasure was gathered. For the moment these events tended to preserve peace with Rome, but if victory against the Romans was important for a Sasanian shah, success against the nomads of Central Asia was essential. One of the fundamental tasks of Persian kings was to defend the settled land of Iran against the nomads of Tūrān. It was a duty with sacred dimensions that lay at the heart of the Zoroastrian religion, and Fīrūz returned with his charisma severely tarnished. Revolt could be expected. If Fīrūz was to survive, he needed to return to the field and bring victory. But the war of revenge, eventually launched in 484, led to the Sasanian Adrianople. The Persian army was destroyed and the shah himself killed on the battlefield. The dynasty faced ruin. The new shah, Fīrūz's brother, Balas, was toppled in 488; Kawād, the hostage of 469, lasted less than ten years, to be ousted by his brother, Zamasphes, but managed to regain power in 498. The success of the radical Zoroastrian Mazdakite movement during these years is a measure of how far the established order had been rocked by 484 and its aftermath. To survive Kawād needed money and military success. War with Rome was the obvious solution, and in 502 Persian armies invaded the empire.[36]

The war of 502 opened a cycle of conflict that would continue until 628, and in many ways set the pattern for what followed. Kawād's troops captured Theodosiopolis, the key to the defence of Roman Armenia, and then switched south to attack Amida, the largest and most heavily fortified city of Roman Mesopotamia, which fell at the beginning of 503 after a hard-fought siege of ninety-seven days. The Romans counter-attacked in 503 and 504, but achieved no more than stalemate. Having achieved his main war aims of prestige and booty, Kawād was ready to negotiate, and a seven-year truce was agreed in 506. The Romans recovered Amida and Theodosiopolis, and in exchange made what must have been a substantial payment to the Persian treasury.[37]

The Persians were to enjoy similar success on what one may call the 'central front', the traditional area of Roman–Persian conflict since the third century, during most years of the wars that followed. When fighting broke out again in 527, the year that Justinian succeeded as emperor, the Romans failed to take Nisibis, or any other major Persian stronghold in the region, and equally failed to inflict a decisive defeat on the Persian army. A Roman victory

36 G. Greatrex, *Rome and Persia at war, 502–532*, ARCA Classical and Medieval Texts, Papers and Monographs 37, (Leeds, 1998), pp. 43–52; K. Schippmann, *Grundzüge der Geschichte des sasanidischen Reiches* (Darmstadt, 1990), pp. 43–50; A. Christensen, *L'Iran sous les Sassanides*, 2nd edn (Copenhagen, 1944), pp. 290–7, 335–53.

37 Greatrex, *Rome and Persia at war*, pp. 73–119.

at Dara in 530 was enthusiastically celebrated in Constantinople, but there is no evidence that it seriously hindered Persian operations, and in any case it was offset by the defeat at Callinicum in 531. The payment of 11,000 pounds of gold, made by the Romans in order to secure the 'Eternal Peace' of 532, is comment enough on where the military advantage lay. When Khusrau broke the peace in 540, he managed to sack Antioch and extort huge sums from a series of Syrian cities before agreeing to a truce in 545 and again in 551. The latter involved regular Roman payments to the Persians, something Procopius tells us had not been conceded before, and were highly unpopular in Constantinople where the warm official welcome for Persian ambassadors carried its own message. The final treaty agreed in 561 was on much the same terms. The war that broke out in 572 was launched by Justinian's nephew and heir, Justin II, as a war of revenge, but Roman armies initially at least did no better in Mesopotamia than they had in the past. Another attempt on Nisibis failed, and the Persians responded by taking Dara, a disaster that seems to have sent Justin mad. During the 570s and 580s Roman raids deep into Persian territory did do something to alter the balance, but the war's triumphant conclusion in 591 owed everything to a political crisis among their enemies and little to any change of fortune in Mesopotamia. The last Roman–Persian war, which broke out in 603, repeated the pattern. Dara fell to the Persians in 604, but this time it was followed by a general collapse of the Mesopotamian front during the years 607–10, which opened the way for the Persian conquest of Syria in 613, Palestine in 614 and Egypt in 616. All Roman attempts at a counter-attack in this region failed utterly.[38]

The reasons for this Persian supremacy are not entirely clear. It presumably has something to do with the qualities of the Sasanian field army. Its heavy cavalry was famous, and despite some misleading comments from Ammianus and Procopius, one may deduce the existence of an effective infantry and system of supply from the accounts of successful siege operations against a series of heavily fortified and staunchly defended Roman cities.[39]

38 Greatrex and Lieu (eds.), *The Roman eastern frontier*, pp. 82–197; Greatrex, *Rome and Persia at war*, pp. 139–221; M. Whitby, *The emperor Maurice and his historian: Theophylact Simocatta on Persian and Balkan warfare* (Oxford, 1988), pp. 250–304; Sebeos, *The Armenian history attributed to Sebeos*, trans. R. W. Thomson, with commentary by J. Howard-Johnston, Translated Texts for Historians 31, 2 vols. (Liverpool, 1999), vol. II, pp. 193–213; M. Whittow, *The making of orthodox Byzantium, 600–1025* (Basingstoke, 1996), pp. 69–76.

39 Howard-Johnston, 'The two great powers in Late Antiquity', pp. 166–7, 174–5, 185–6; Greatrex, *Rome and Persia at war*, pp. 52–9; for misleading comments see Ammianus Marcellinus, *Rerum gestarum libri*, XXIII.6.83, ed. and trans. J. C. Rolfe, 3 vols. (Cambridge, MA, 1935–9; rev. edn. 1986), vol. II, pp. 394–7; Procopius, *History of the wars*, I.xiv.25, ed. and trans. H. B. Dewing, 5 vols. (Cambridge, MA, 1914–28), vol. II, pp. 120–1.

Some Roman troops did not perform well in face of the Persians, but one must be careful to compare like with like. The Roman army included four categories of soldier: *comitatenses*, *foederati*, *bucellarii* and *limitanei*. The *comitatenses* were the descendants of the earlier legions; the *foederati* were units recruited at least in theory from specific ethnic groups, sometimes outside the borders of the empire; the *bucellarii* were units raised personally by individual Roman generals. They were all in effect full-time soldiers and together made up the field army. The *limitanei* were troops permanently based in the frontier regions and supported by a mixture of tax-free estates and cash salaries. They were on occasion deployed as part of a field force, but normally it appears they were to be found scattered in small units garrisoning the empire's many hundreds of forts and cities. While there is no reason to view the *limitanei* as an ineffective peasant militia, they were unlikely to have been trained or equipped to match the shah's front-line soldiers.[40] How the soldiers of the sixth-century Roman field army compared to their Persian equivalents is hard to judge. There is no doubt that the Persians benefited from the fact that Roman resources were stretched thin, with the same front-line troops required in both the west and the east. Persian successes tended to come early in a war, before reinforcements could arrive, after which stalemate ensued. On the other hand, even in 572, when the Roman offensive had been planned in advance to catch the Persians unawares, it was the latter who came out on top.[41] In the third and fourth centuries it had been possible for Romans to assume that Persian success was merely the consequence of temporary Roman disorder; by the sixth and seventh that had long ceased to be the case, and Persian forces were recognised as formidable adversaries.[42]

But that was not the only respect in which the sixth and seventh centuries were different from the third and fourth. In the age of Diocletian, Shāpūr II and Julian, the Mesopotamian front had been in effect the only front, and the conflict had been almost solely between the armies of Rome and Persia. In the age of Kawād, Justinian and Heraclius, that was no longer the case. The conflict was waged as far afield as the Yemen, the

40 M. Whitby, 'Recruitment in Roman armies from Justinian to Heraclius (ca. 565–615)', in Cameron (ed.), *States, resources and armies*, pp. 61–124; M. Whitby, 'The army, c.420–602', in Cameron *et al.* (eds.), *Late Antiquity*, pp. 288–93, 300–8.

41 Whitby, *The emperor Maurice and his historian*, pp. 250–8.

42 For the third and fourth centuries see Whitby, *The emperor Maurice and his historian*, pp. 203–4; see in particular the comments of Dio Cassius in Dodgeon and Lieu (eds.), *The Roman eastern frontier*, p. 16; For the sixth and seventh centuries see Greatrex and Lieu (eds.), *The Roman eastern frontier*, pp. 179–81.

Transcaucasus and the steppes of Central Asia. Those waging it had come to include Arabs, Laz, Albanians, Armenians and Turks, acting as much for their own purposes as for the war aims of the two powers. What had been a war largely confined to Mesopotamia had expanded eventually to become a Eurasian world war. Persian supremacy on the central front was not repeated everywhere else, and the wider the war became, the more fragile did the Persian position prove to be.[43]

By the 620s the Roman empire appeared on the verge of extinction. The loss of Syria, Palestine and, above all, Egypt had taken away the empire's richest provinces. Roman rule in these regions was being supplanted by Persian administration that was set to stay. In 626 a combined siege of Constantinople by the Persians and Avars narrowly failed. The next year the emperor Heraclius opened operations in the Transcaucasus, the mountainous zone between Roman Anatolia to the west, Persia to the south and east, and the steppe world to the north. The Romans had been doing business with the powers of the steppe at least since the period of Hun dominance in Europe in the middle of the fifth century. Roman armies recruited heavily among the steppe peoples, and Roman ambassadors had learnt to negotiate with steppe rulers who spoke neither Greek nor Latin, and shared with the Romans neither religion nor political ideology. By 560 the Hepthalite hegemony in Central Asia had been replaced by that of the even more formidable Turks. In 568/9 a Turkish embassy arrived in Constantinople. In the following year a Roman embassy made a return journey of some 10,000 kilometres to visit the Turkish *khāqān*. With memories of fifth-century humiliations at the hands of the steppe powers, it is no wonder that the Persians made every effort to break these links, including the attempted ambush and murder of the returning envoys.[44] In the short term Roman hopes of a combined assault on Iran came to nothing, but in 627 these links paid off. The Turks crossed the Caucasus, and with these powerful allies Heraclius launched the great counter-attack that would save the Roman empire, and, after nearly twenty-three years of almost uninterrupted victory, finally bring Shāh Khusrau II's regime to defeat and disaster.[45]

43 Greatrex and Lieu (eds.), *The Roman eastern frontier*, pp. 78–80, 82–4, 94–5, 115–20, 136–42, 149, 153, 163, 167, 171, 178.

44 Ibid., pp. 136–7.

45 Ibid., pp. 198–226; J. Howard-Johnston, 'Heraclius' Persian campaigns and the revival of the East Roman Empire, 622–630', *War in History*, 6 (1999); J. Howard-Johnston, 'Pride and fall: Khusro II and his regime, 626–628', in *La Persia e Bisanzio*, Atti dei convegni Lincei 201, Roma, 14–18 ottobre 2002 (Rome, 2004).

Rome and the Arabs: centre and periphery in the Roman Near East

The initial Roman conquest of the Near East in the first century BCE had left most of the region in the hands of greater or lesser client rulers. Over the course of the first, second and third centuries CE these kingdoms and principalities were gradually abolished or annexed. Judaea became a province for the first time in 6 CE, and then definitively in 70 when it became Syria Palestina. The Nabataean kingdom in what is now Jordan and northern Saudi Arabia was annexed in 106 to create the province of Arabia. Further north, the kingdoms of Emesa (Homs) and Commagne were annexed in 72 CE. Only east of the Euphrates did such entities survive; the kingdom of Edessa was annexed only in 212–13, while that of Hatra survived as an ally until its destruction by the Sasanians in 242.[46]

Diocletian's response to the region's problems at the end of the third century would appear to have drawn on his experience of the empire's northern frontiers. The formerly very lightly fortified frontiers of the Near Eastern provinces were now lined with legionary fortresses, auxiliary forts and watchtowers to match those on the Rhine and the Danube.[47] Very soon, however, it must have been realised that the costs of completing this frontier, let alone garrisoning and maintaining it for the future, were unsustainable, and in a large degree out of all proportion to any likely threat. On the northern Mesopotamian front, where Roman and Persian armies faced each other across good campaigning country, such fortresses were essential – indeed, cost-effective – but further south the only possible threat was from Arab nomads, and these needed a policing operation rather than this extraordinary fortified belt stretching for hundreds of miles through a barely inhabited landscape.[48] The obvious and traditional answer to this fairly low-grade security problem was the use of clients and allies, but, possibly with the experience of Palmyra in mind, or perhaps simply because there was no

46 Sartre, *The Middle East under Rome*, pp. 70–87, 344–7; Sartre, 'The Arabs and the desert peoples', pp. 507–15.

47 Millar, *The Roman Near East*, pp. 180–90; Isaac, *The limits of empire*, pp. 161–71; Parker, 'The defense of Palestine and Transjordan', pp. 372–4; S. T. Parker, *The Roman frontier in Central Jordan: Final report on the Limes Arabicus Project, 1980–1989*, 2 vols., Dumbarton Oaks Studies 40 (Washington, DC, 2006), vol. II, pp. 541–50.

48 Isaac, *The limits of empire*, pp. 214–18; E. B. Banning, 'Peasants, pastoralists and Pax Romana: Mutualism in the southern highlands of Jordan', *BASOR*, 261 (1986); E. B. Banning, 'De Bello Paceque: A reply to Parker', *BASOR*, 265 (1987); cf. Parker, 'The defense of Palestine and Transjordan', pp. 374–9; Parker, *The Roman frontier in Central Jordan*, vol. II, pp. 538–41.

other realistic option, the traditional answer took a new form in the fourth century: Rome turned not to the sedentary elites of the Fertile Crescent, but rather to the nomads or semi-nomads of the desert and its margins.

There are references to phylarchs of the Arabs, in other words shaykhs and their tribal followers, serving the Romans and Persians in the first century. There is epigraphic evidence to suggest that nomads were settling on the fringes of the Fertile Crescent. There is also explicit literary evidence that between the fourth century BCE and the first century CE the Nabataeans had followed the same path.[49] Otherwise there are the so-called Ṣafaitic inscriptions, of which more than 20,000 have been recorded in the Syrian desert. They appear to date from the first century BCE to the fourth century CE, and they may be best regarded as the doodlings of bored nomads. Most give a name and some genealogy; some are prayers; and some talk of current events, mostly to do with the nomadic cycle, but occasionally referring to happenings in the world beyond the desert. These nomads hunt and occasionally make raids, but their primary occupation is tending their animals. Crucially, there is nothing here to suggest a powerful tribal confederation or any significant threat to the settled world.[50]

Banditry was a perennial issue throughout the region. Inscriptions from Palmyra show that it was necessary to organise merchants crossing the desert into caravans, and that security could be a problem. An inscription of 199 CE honours Ogēlos son of Makkaios, 'for having given satisfaction through continual commands against the nomads and for having provided safety for the merchants and caravans in all his caravan commands'.[51] But this is no more than dealing with crime; before the late third century at the earliest the desert nomads were, in military and political terms, of trivial importance.

From the fourth century this began to change. Ammianus Marcellinus, a Roman historian who had first-hand experience from serving in Syria in the 350s and 360s, talks of a new Persian strategy based on 'theft and robbery

49 Sartre, *The Middle East under Rome*, pp. 233–9. For the Nabataeans see Diodorus Siculus, *Bibliotheca historica*, ed. and trans. C. H. Oldfather, C. L. Sherman, C. Bradford Welles, R. M. Geer and F. R. Walton, 12 vols. (Cambridge, MA, 1933–67), II.48.26, XIX.94.2–4, 96.3; Strabo, *Geography*, ed. and trans. H. L. Jones, 8 vols. (Cambridge, MA, 1917–32), XVI.4.18, 21; Pliny, *Naturalis historia*, ed. and trans. H. Rackham, W. H. S. Jones and D. E. Eichholz, 10 vols. (Cambridge, MA, 1917–32), VI.32.143–4; Millar, *The Roman Near East*, pp. 400–1.

50 M. C. A. Macdonald, 'Nomads and the Hawran in the late Hellenistic and Roman periods: A reassessment of the epigraphic evidence', *Syria*, 70 (1993); cf. Parker, *The Roman frontier in Central Jordan*, vol. II, pp. 535–7.

51 For banditry see Matthews, *The Roman Empire of Ammianus*, pp. 346–7; for Palmyra see J. Starcky, *Inventaire des inscriptions de Palmyre*, X: *L'agora* (Damascus, 1949), no. 44, p. 31, cited in Millar, *The Roman Near East*, p. 332.

rather than on the pitched battles that had been their previous practice', a new strategy in which 'Saracen' allies who specialised in such raiding were essential.[52] One such ally on the Persian side described by Ammianus was a certain 'Malechus called Podosaces, phylarch of the Assanitic Saracens, a notorious robber who had long raided [the Roman] frontier districts with every kind of cruelty'. A Roman equivalent was Mavia, whose raids into Palestine and Phoenicia, and her defeat of the forces sent against her, forced the Roman authorities into recognising her as an ally in the 370s.[53] By the beginning of the fifth century at the latest a number of nomad shaykhs had made treaties with Rome and Persia. From these 'Saracen phylarchs', as Roman authors term them, the great powers gained cheap security and useful auxiliaries who could be used to ravage enemy territory and counter those of their opponents. In turn the shaykhs earned subsidies that enabled them to exercise a substantially new degree of authority in what had previously been a stateless tribal society. The fact that Podosaces is called 'Malechus', which is clearly the Semitic word for king, or that an inscription near the Roman fort at Namāra in the Ḥawrān south-east of Damascus and seemingly datable to 328 CE can describe a certain Imru' al-Qays son of ʿAmr as 'king of all the Arabs' are signs of how the desert world was changing.[54] The sixth-century citizen of Edessa in northern Syria who wrote the chronicle attributed to Joshua the Stylite was evidently right when he said that war between Rome and Persia 'was the cause of much enrichment to the Saracens of both sides'.[55] Bedouin impact on great-power politics was as yet very small, but the impact of great-power politics on the Bedouin world, or rather the impact of great-power conflict and the subsidies and employment it engendered, was clearly profound.

By the sixth century, nomad confederations, the most important being that of the Ghassānids, played a key role in the defences of the Roman Near

52 Ammianus Marcellinus, *Rerum gestarum libri*, XVI.9.1; XXIII.3.8; XXXI.16.5.

53 For Malechus called Podosaces see ibid. XXIV.2.4; for Mavia see Socrates, *Ecclesiastical history*, ed. G. C. Hansen, trans. P. Périchon and P. Maraval as *Histoire ecclésiastique*, vol. I (Paris, 2004), IV.36; Sozomen, *Ecclesiastical history*, ed. J. Bidez, trans. A.-J. Festugière as *Histoire ecclésiastique*, vol. I (Paris, 1983), VI.38.

54 Among the extensive literature on the Namara inscription, see P. Bordreuil, A. Desreumaux, C. Robin and J. Teixidor, in Y. Calvet and C. Robin, *Arabie heureuse Arabie déserte: Les antiquités arabiques du Musée du Louvre*, Notes et documents des musées de France 31 (Paris, 1997), pp. 267–9 (no. 205, Linteau inscrit: AO 4083); M. Zwettler, 'Imra'alqays, Son of 'Amr: King of ...???', in M. Mir and J. E. Fossu (eds.), *Literary heritage of classical Islam: Arabic and Islamic studies in honor of James A. Bellamy* (Princeton, 1993), pp. 3–37, pl. 1–5. I am very grateful to Michael Macdonald for advice on this text.

55 *The chronicle of Pseudo-Joshua the Stylite*, trans. with notes and introd. by F. R. Trombley and J. W. Watt, Translated Texts for Historians 32 (Liverpool, 2000), p. 97.

East. In 528 or 529 the emperor Justinian elevated the Ghassānid shaykh, al-Ḥārith ibn Jabala (known in Greek sources as Arethas), who was at that stage one of a number of allied phylarchs, to become supreme phylarch, and gave him the title of *basileus*, or king. Justinian was responding to the threat posed by the Sasanian shah's chief Arab ally, the Lakhmid leader, al-Mundhir, whose position seems to have allowed him to mobilise resources on a scale that none of the Romans' phylarchs could match. Procopius, who provides much of our information, was not an admirer of Saracens in general, or of al-Ḥārith in particular, and he blamed the latter for the Roman defeat at Callinicum in 531 and more generally for pursuing his own interests rather than the common good, but at least as a counter to the Lakhmids the policy appears to have been a complete success. Lakhmid raids had caused considerable damage in the early sixth century, but by the 550s the balance had shifted in favour of the Ghassānids. In 554 al-Mundhir himself was defeated and killed, and in 575, or shortly afterwards, al-Ḥārith's son and successor, al-Mundhir ibn al-Ḥārith, sacked the Lakhmid capital of al-Ḥīra in southern Iraq. Even after al-Mundhir's arrest and exile to Sicily in the 580s brought to an end the position of the Ghassānids as Rome's chief Arab allies, Lakhmid power did not recover.[56]

It is important not to exaggerate the scale of these groups or their importance to their employers. Despite their titles, Imru' al-Qays and Podosaces were no more than Bedouin shaykhs with subsidies – figures very similar to the Rashīdīs of Ḥāyil who acted as clients of the Ottomans on the eve of the First World War – and those subsidies are likely to have tailed off in the fifth century as Roman–Persian warfare went through an extended period of relative calm. Even the Ghassānids were no more than particularly successful examples of the phenomenon. They were Christians; they were generous patrons of the non-Chalcedonian Church; they were builders of monasteries; but the Ghassānids under the Jafnid dynasty, to which al-Ḥārith and al-Mundhir belonged, remained essentially a nomad tribal confederation. This point is sometimes missed or resisted because of the assumption that 'nomad' and 'sedentary' are mutually exclusive categories. The fact that the Jafnids were builders, that their regular campsites became permanent and no doubt relatively prestigious settlements, that they visited Constantinople, or that

56 Greatrex and Lieu (eds.), *The Roman eastern frontier*, pp. 85–8, 93, 100, 123, 129, 153, 162–5, 168; M. Sartre, *Trois études sur l'Arabie romaine et byzantine* (Brussels, 1982), pp. 162–72, 189–94; A. H. M. Jones, J. R. Martindale and J. Morris, *The prosopography of the later Roman Empire*, 3 vols. (Cambridge, 1971–92), vol. III, s.v. 'Alamundarus' and 'Arethas', pp. 34–7, 111–13.

they were regarded as among the leading laymen of the non-Chalcedonian Church, is not incompatible with a Bedouin identity and culture.[57]

By the 580s both Romans and Persians appear to have come to the conclusion that subsidising groups such as the Ghassānids or the Lakhmids on the scale that had made them the dominant forces among the tribes of the Syrian desert was no longer worthwhile. The story of Roman relations with the Ghassānids is told by the Syriac historian John of Ephesus in terms of Chalcedonian ingratitude to their loyal and orthodox allies, but John's is a very particular perspective. His is confessional history, and there can be little doubt that had al-Mundhir not been an anti-Chalcedonian John would have had little interest in or sympathy for his cause.[58] The Romans had built up the Jafnids as leaders of the Ghassānids in order to counter the threat from the Persian-subsidised Lakhmids. Once that threat was over there was apparently no need for Bedouin allies so powerful, or so independent minded.

But the genie could not be put back in the bottle. The inhabitants of the empire's desert periphery were richer, more organised and much more militarily effective than they had been three hundred years earlier.

The Roman Near East and the rise of Islam

Four centuries of Roman–Persian conflict had culminated in a twenty-five-year war that had left both empires exhausted. The state of Persia may be gauged by the fact that Heraclius' victories in 628 so rapidly triggered a

57 L. I. Conrad, 'The Arabs', in Cameron *et al.* (eds.), *Late Antiquity*, pp. 692–4; R. G. Hoyland, *Arabia and the Arabs from the Bronze Age to the coming of Islam* (London and New York, 2001), pp. 238–42; M. Whitby, 'Greek historical writing after Procopius: Variety and vitality', in A. Cameron and L. I. Conrad (eds.), *The Byzantine and early Islamic Near East*, vol. I: *Problems in the literary source material* (Princeton, 1992), pp. 74–80; M. Whittow, 'Rome and the Jafnids: Writing the history of a 6th-c. tribal dynasty', in J. H. Humphrey (ed.), *The Roman and Byzantine Near East*, vol. II: *Some recent archaeological research*, JRA Supplementary series 31 (Portsmouth, RI, 1999); D. Genequand, 'Some thoughts on Qasr al-Hayr al-Gharbi, its dam, its monastery and the Ghassanids', *Levant*, 38 (2006); cf. I. Shahid, *Byzantium and the Arabs in the sixth century* (Washington, DC, 1995–), vol. I; and his response to Whittow, 'Rome and the Jafnids', I. Shahid, 'Byzantium and the Arabs in the sixth century: *A propos* of a recent review', *Byzantinische Forschungen*, 26 (2000).

58 John of Ephesus, *Ecclesiastical history*, III.40–42, 54, 56, IV.36, 39, 40, 42, VI.3, 4, 16, 18, ed. E. W. Brooks, *Iohannis Ephesini Historiae Ecclesiastica pars tertia*, CSCO, Scr. Syr. III.3 (Louvain, 1935–6), text: pp. 173–7, 181–2, 216–21, 224–5, 280–7, 312–14; Latin translation: pp. 129–32, 135–6, 162–6, 168–9, 212–17, 237–8; English translation: R. Payne Smith, *The third part of the ecclesiastical history of John, Bishop of Ephesus* (Oxford, 1860), pp. 236–42, 294–300, 304–6, 370–9, 413–15; J. van Ginkel, 'John of Ephesus: A monophysite historian in sixth-century Byzantium', Ph.D. thesis, Groningen (1995), pp. 99–101, 166–8, 185–94, 216–17.

political crisis, the evacuation of the occupied territories and the Persian agreement to peace on the *status quo ante*. The Roman position was only a little less serious. The war had been fought largely on Roman territory, and some of the empire's richest provinces in Egypt and the Levant had been occupied for nearly two decades. A generation had grown up for whom Roman rule was no longer an inevitable fact of life. Nonetheless, the war had ended in a Roman victory, celebrated by Heraclius when he restored the True Cross to Jerusalem on 21 March 630, and, given time, the ties that bound Constantinople to the Near Eastern provinces would presumably have been refurbished.[59] In the event, of course, that was not to happen. Within ten years imperial forces were close to being expelled from the entire region, and Christian power would not return until the Byzantine conquests of the late tenth century and the Crusades in the twelfth.

Muslim success may owe something to Roman war-weariness, but that is a rather nebulous concept, possibly more appealing to scholars at their desks than to the sort of young men who actually filled the ranks of the Roman army. More important may have been the lack of ready cash. Heraclius had had to fight Persia without the revenues of Egypt and the Levant. To pay troops he had been forced to melt down silver treasures and bronze monuments, and having resorted to such expedients already, these reserves were not there to be used again in the 630s.[60] In any case it is worth remembering that all direct Roman attempts to expel the Persians from the Near East had signally failed, and Heraclius' final victory was won instead by an indirect approach through the Transcaucasus, where it had been possible to bring in the emperor's steppe nomad allies. Even then Heraclius only achieved his ends because Persia collapsed from within. None of these factors were applicable in the 630s. The Muslims did not have an accessible core territory to provide the target for such a counter-blow; Heraclius' nomad allies, the Turks of the western khāqānate broke up in civil war after 630;[61] and the first sign of exploitable political difficulties within the Muslim world would not come until the first *fitna* (656–61).

Muslim success clearly owes something too to the willingness of local elites to come to terms with the invaders. That willingness may have been

59 Whittow, *The making of orthodox Byzantium*, pp. 80–2; Howard-Johnston, 'Pride and fall'.

60 M. Hendy, *Studies in the Byzantine monetary economy, c. 350–1450* (Cambridge, 1985), pp. 494–5, 498–9; A. Cameron and J. Herrin (eds.), *Constantinople in the early eighth century: The* Parastaseis Syntomoi Chronikai (Leiden, 1984), pp. 116–17, 229–30.

61 P. B. Golden, *An introduction to the history of the Turkic peoples: Ethnogenesis and state-formation in medieval and early modern Eurasia and the Middle East* (Wiesbaden, 1992), p. 135.

reinforced by the experience of a relatively benign Persian occupation, under which life went on much as before.[62] Why risk sack and ruin if nothing fundamental was at stake? Yet this was hardly new. The Roman empire was based on a state monopoly of military force, and imperial defence did not rest primarily on local initiative. Although it is easy to cite cases through the fourth to seventh centuries where walled cities, often led by their bishops, had been prepared to resist Persian attack, there are as many examples where cities were willing to negotiate and pay their enemies off.[63] A key factor was usually the proximity or otherwise of an imperial army likely to bring relief, and the situation in the Levant in the 630s, where after the battle of Yarmūk in 636 such an army was notably lacking, was one in which Roman provincials of any era would have looked to make terms.

Later Syriac and Coptic literature portrays Roman rule as alien and heretic, with the implication that much of the population was only too ready to betray the empire; but this is a view that was developed to give a meaningful historical past to Christian communities now living as second-class citizens in an Islamic world, and needs to be discounted. It was comforting to believe that God's purpose in allowing the conquest might have been to protect them from oppression. The picture says little about the outlook of provincial society in 630 or before. Judging from contemporary accounts, such as the remarkable early sixth-century chronicle traditionally misattributed to Joshua the Stylite, what is actually striking is the degree of identification between Near Eastern provincials and the Roman empire. Roman–Persian warfare appears to have done more to bind the Near East to Rome than the reverse. Civilian–military tensions, exacerbated on occasion by high taxation and inadequate protection from Persian raids, were obviously a divisive factor, but against that war tended to point up the gulf between Christian Romans and pagan Persians, and the scale of Roman deployment in the region created jobs that tied local hierarchies to the imperial centre, and brought 'Romans' from elsewhere to settle in the Near East. There clearly were groups in Near Eastern society, such as the Jews and some anti-Chalcedonians, who had benefited from Persian patronage, who had no reason to celebrate with the emperor in 630, but there is no evidence that the core territories of the Roman Near East were animated by any strong separatist spirit in the early seventh century. It had taken over fifty years of complete neglect for Gaul to turn its back on the central government in the fifth

62 C. Foss, 'The Persian Near East (602–630 AD)', *JRAS*, 3rd series, 13 (2003).

63 For the various reactions of Syrian cities to Persian attacks in the 540s, see Procopius, *History of the wars*, II.xi.14–38, xii.1–2, 33–4, xiii.3–15, xx.1–16, xxi.30–32, xxvi.1–46, xxvii.1–46; ed. and trans. Dewing, vol. I, pp. 354–63, 372–7, 430–5, 448–51, 488–515.

century. Clearly such a process had started in the Near East during the Persian occupation, but it had not necessarily got very far.[64]

Rome and the Arabs

A further factor was the political and military transformation of Bedouin society that had taken place since the third century. It is certainly not accurate, as was once common, to talk of the invading Muslims as simply a nomad irruption into the Fertile Crescent. Nomads were already a familiar feature of the Levant, and in any case early Islam was in many ways profoundly a culture of the sedentary world. But the fact remains that thanks to Roman–Persian rivalry Arab tribal society had become much more militarised than it had been in the past, and, just as important, much more conscious of the possibility of gaining access to the wealth of the settled Near East. To judge from pre-Islamic poetry, the wealth of the Ghassānid and Lakhmid courts had had a profound impact on the Arab imagination.[65]

It has been argued – or implied – that if only the Romans had maintained Ghassānid hegemony rather than breaking it up, then they would have been there to act as a shield against the armies of Arabia in the seventh century.[66] Given the marginal impact of the phylarchs on the course of sixth-century warfare that may be hard to believe, but the end of the era of Roman and Persian subsidies may have had a less direct but equally profound effect. Writing in the ninth century, but copying an eighth-century Greek translation of an older Syriac chronicle, composed somewhere in Syria–Palestine,[67] Theophanes describes the origins of the Muslim invasions as follows.

> Now some of the neighbouring Arabs were receiving small payments from the emperors for guarding the approaches to the desert. At that time a certain eunuch arrived to distribute the wages of the soldiers, and when the Arabs came to receive their wages according to custom, the eunuch drove them away, saying, 'The emperor can barely pay his soldiers their wages, much less these dogs!' Distressed by this, the Arabs went over to their fellow-tribesmen,

64 J. Moorhead, 'The Monophysite response to the Arab invasions', *Byzantion*, 51 (1981); Whitby, *The emperor Maurice and his historian*, pp. 213–15; G. Dagron and V. Déroche, 'Juifs et Chrétiens dans l'Orient du viie siècle', *Travaux et Mémoires*, 11 (1991), pp. 22–32; Liebeschuetz, *The decline and fall of the Roman city*, p. 259.

65 Hoyland, *Arabia and the Arabs*, pp. 238–41; R. A. Nicholson, *A literary history of the Arabs* (Cambridge, 1930), pp. 37–54; R. Blachère, *Histoire de la littérature arabe des origines à la fin du xve siècle de J.-C.*, 3 vols. (Paris, 1952–66), vol. II, p. 344, vol. III, p. 786.

66 E.g. Shahid, *Byzantium and the Arabs in the sixth century*, p. xxviii; Parker, *The Roman frontier in central Jordan*, vol. II, p. 569.

67 Theophanes, *Chronographia*, trans. C. Mango and R. Scott as *The chronicle of Theophanes Confessor* (Oxford, 1997), pp. lxxxii–iii.

> and it was they that led them to the rich country of Gaza, which is the gateway to the desert in the direction of Mount Sinai.[68]

The story may not be strictly true, but nonetheless embodies the truth that Roman–Persian rivalry had created a society among the Arabs dependent upon subsidies. At the least the end of that subsidy era left a body of militarised tribesmen who were available to find new opportunities and even greater wealth in the service of Islam.

Conclusion

The rise of Islam is not explained by what had happened in the Roman Near East in Late Antiquity. But its phenomenal success owed much to the peculiar circumstances of the Roman Near East in the 630s, emerging from a twenty-five-year war with Persia, and to the militarised Arab society that more than three centuries of great-power rivalry had created. In the wake of the First World War Wahhābī forces headed north from Arabia to exploit the power vacuum created by Ottoman defeat. In the event the vacuum had already been filled by the British, and the Wahhābīs retired to the south. It is hard not to suspect that early Muslim expansion would have had rather different results had the Muslim armies appeared before or after what looks like a uniquely favourable moment in Near Eastern history.

68 Theophanes, *Chronographia*, AM 6123, ed. C. de Boor as *Theophanis Chronographia*, 2 vols. (Leipzig, 1883–5), vol. I, pp. 335–6, Mango and Scott (trans.), *Chronicle*, p. 466.

3

The late Sasanian Near East[1]

JOSEF WIESEHÖFER

The sources[2]

As opposed to the Arsacids, the Sasanians, like their Achaemenid 'ancestors' (see below), tell us a great deal about their notions of government, their public appearances and their political aspirations in both the domestic and foreign spheres. Their trilingual, bilingual or monolingual inscriptions (of the third century CE),[3] the most prominent of which are probably Shāpūr (Shābuhr) I's *res gestae* (ŠKZ),[4] and the inscriptions of Diocletian's rival Narseh from Pāikūlī (NPi),[5] tell us not only about the conflicts with Rome (ŠKZ) and

1 I would like to thank Henning Börm (Kiel) and James Howard-Johnston (Oxford) for their helpful comments and suggestions.

2 See J. Wiesehöfer, *Ancient Persia*, 2nd edn (London and New York, 2001), pp. 153–64 and 283–7; C. G. Cereti, 'Primary sources for the history of inner and outer Iran in the Sasanian period', *Archivum Eurasiae Medii Aevi*, 9 (1997) provides an excellent summary of the primary sources (epigraphy, archaeology, numismatics and sphragistics), with an extensive bibliography. The following books appeared too late to be considered in this chapter: V. S. Curtis and S. Stewart (eds.), *The Sasanian era* (London, 2008); T. Daryaee, *Sasanian Persia* (London, 2009); B. Dignas and E. Winter (eds.), *Rome and Persia in Late Antiquity* (Cambridge, 2007); R. E. Emmerick and M. Macuch (eds.), *The literature of pre-Islamic Iran* (London, 2008); A. Gariboldi, *Il regno di Xusraw dall'anima immortale: Riforme economiche e rivolti sociali nell'Iran sasanide del VI secolo* (Milan, 2006); P. Pourshariati, *Decline and fall of the Sasanian Empire* (London, 2008) (which, however, does not make me change my mind on the empire's end). For the Armenian sources see T. Greenwood, Sasanian reflections in Armenian sources', e-Sasanika 5 (2008), at www.humanities.uci.edu/sasanika/pdf/e-sasanika5-Greenwood.pdf.

3 Cereti, 'Primary sources', pp. 19–27; edition: M. Back, *Die sassanidischen Staatsinschriften: Studien zur Orthographie und Phonologie des Mittelpersischen der Inschriften zusammen mit einem etymologischen Index des mittelpersischen Wortgutes und einem Textcorpus der behandelten Inschriften*, Acta Iranica 18 (Leiden, 1978); cf., however, the reviews of this book by D. N. MacKenzie, 'Review of M. Back, *Die sassanidischen Staatsinschriften*', *Indogermanische Forschungen*, 87 (1982); P. Gignoux, 'Review of M. Back, *Die sassanidischen Staatsinschriften*', *Studia Iranica*, 13 (1984); and P. Huyse, *Die dreisprachige Inschrift Šābuhrs I. an der Ka'ba-i Zardušt (ŠKZ)*, CII, III, vol. I, texts I, vols. I–II (London, 1999), vol. I, pp. 14b–17a.

4 See the excellent edition of the inscription in Huyse, *Die dreisprachige Inschrift*.

5 See H. Humbach and P. O. Skjærvø, *The Sassanian inscription of Paikuli*, 3 parts (Wiesbaden, 1978–83).

dynastic enemies (NPi) respectively, but also reveal much about the early Sasanian court, its officials and the male and female members of the ruling family. In particular, they show how their rule was legitimised and how the kings represented themselves in their position as rulers (see below). It is no coincidence that Shāpūr had the 'account of his deeds' (*Tatenbericht*) placed on the Kaʿba-i Zardusht at Naqsh-i Rustam. This building had already been of particular importance in pre-Sasanian times (although the exact nature of this importance is not known to us), and it was situated at a place where the Achaemenids (who were no longer known to the Sasanians by name) had commemorated themselves in rock tombs and bas-reliefs.[6]

The trilingual nature of the inscriptions (in Middle Persian, Parthian and Greek) was also in imitation of 'the ancestors'. It is at the same time a reminder of the language policy the Arsacids adopted – one, however, in which Middle Persian had supplanted Parthian as the primary official royal language.[7] Narseh's bilingual inscription (in Middle Persian and Parthian) on the monument of Pāikūlī in Iraqi Kurdistan provides an account of his armed conflict with his rival Wahrām III. In addition, it also provides an account of the acknowledgement rendered to him there by the great dignitaries of the empire, as well as of his coronation, which probably also took place there.[8]

Apart from those of the kings, other important third-century inscriptions were only left behind by the mighty *mōbad* ('priest') Kerdīr (KKZ, KNRb, KNRm, KSM),[9] the governor of Bīshāpūr (Weh-Šābuhr) (ŠVŠ)[10] and the

6 For the latest account regarding the importance of Kaʿba-i Zardusht and Naqsh-i Rustam in Sasanian times, the history of the discovery of the inscriptions, the research related to them and how they were dated, see Huyse, *Die dreisprachige Inschrift*, vol. I, pp. 6a–17b.

7 For Greek–Iranian bilingualism in Sasanian times see M. Mancini, 'Bilingui greco-iraniche in epoca sasanide: Il testo di Šāhpuhr alla Kaʿba-yi Zardušt', *Bilinguismo e biculturalismo nel mondo antico: Atti del colloquio interdisciplinare tenuto a Pisa il 28 e 29 settembre 1987* (Pisa, 1988); for parallels between Achaemenid and Sasanian inscriptions see P. O. Skjærvø, 'Thematic and linguistic parallels in the Achaemenian and Sasanian inscriptions', *Acta Iranica*, 25 (1985); and P. Huyse, 'Noch einmal zu Parallelen zwischen Achaimeniden- und Sāsānideninschriften', *Archäologische Mitteilungen aus Iran*, n.s. 23 (1990).

8 See W. Sundermann, 'Review of H. Humbach and P. O. Skjærvø, *The Sassanian inscription of Paikuli*', *Kratylos*, 28 (1983); E. Kettenhofen, *Tirdād und die Inschrift von Paikuli: Kritik der Quellen zur Geschichte Armeniens im späten 3. und frühen 4. Jh. n.Chr.* (Wiesbaden, 1995).

9 For these inscriptions see D. N. MacKenzie, 'Kerdir's inscription: Synoptic text in transliteration, transcription and commentary', in G. Herrmann and D. N. MacKenzie (eds.), *The triumph of Shapur I (together with an account of the representation of Kerdir)*, Iranische Denkmäler, Lief. 13, Reihe II. Iranische Felsreliefs I: *The Sasanian rock reliefs at Naqsh-i Rustam, Naqsh-i Rustam 6* (Berlin, 1989); and P. Gignoux, *Les quatre inscriptions du mage Kirdīr: Textes et concordances* (Paris, 1991).

10 See Back, *Die sassanidischen Staatsinschriften*, pp. 378–83.

official Abnūn (ABD).[11] Kerdīr is, above all, concerned with publicly displaying his career, his actions in the field of religious policy and his religious and spiritual excellence. The inscription of Bishāpūr, however, is the one to which we owe the mention of a Sasanian era, which started in 205/6 CE.[12] Abnun, then again, confirms the victory of his king Shāpūr I over the Romans at Misikhe (244 CE). Middle Persian papyri and parchments bear witness to the Persian occupation of Egypt under Khusrau (Khusrō) II, and late Sasanian *ostraca* were discovered in archaeological digs in Iran.[13]

Secondary sources[14] pertaining to the period consist of, on the one hand, the contemporary, yet foreign, Greek and Latin tradition, and, on the other, the later, yet local, Syriac Christian and Manichaean tradition.[15] Cassius Dio and Herodian, who, to a certain extent, depended on the former, are among the most prominent Western authors of the early Sasanian period. In the fourth century they were joined by the partial eyewitness Ammianus Marcellinus,[16] as well as the

11 For this inscription see M. Tavoosi and R. N. Frye, 'An inscribed capital dating from the time of Shapur I', *Bulletin of the Asia Institute*, n.s. 3 (1990); P. Gignoux, 'D'Abnūn à Māhān: Étude de deux inscriptions sassanides', *Studia Iranica*, 20 (1991); V. A. Livshits and A. B. Nikitin, 'Some notes on the inscription from Nasrabad', *Bulletin of the Asia Institute*, 5 (1991); P. O. Skjærvø, 'L'inscription d'Abnūn et l'imperfait moyen-perse, *Studia Iranica*, 21 (1992); D. N. MacKenzie, 'The fire altar of Happy *Frayosh', *Bulletin of the Asia Institute*, 7 (1993); W. Sundermann, 'The date of the Barm-e Delak inscription', *Bulletin of the Asia Institute*, n.s. 7 (1993).

12 R. Altheim-Stiehl, 'Das früheste Datum der sasanidischen Geschichte, vermittelt durch die Zeitangabe der mittelpersisch-parthischen Inschrift aus Bīšāpūr', *Archäologische Mitteilungen aus Iran*, n.s. 11 (1978); but see also W. Sundermann, 'Shapur's coronation: The evidence of the Cologne Mani Codex reconsidered and compared with other texts', *Bulletin of the Asia Institute*, n.s. 4 (1990); and L. Richter-Bernburg, 'Mani's Dodecads and Sasanian chronology', *Zeitschrift für Papyrologie und Epigraphik*, 95 (1993).

13 D. Weber, *Ostraca, Papyri und Pergamente. Textband*, CII III, 4–5 (London, 1992); D. Weber, *Berliner Papyri, Pergamente und Leinenfragmente in mittelpersischer Sprache*, CII III, 4–5 (London, 2003); see also P. Gignoux, 'Une nouvelle collection de documents en pehlevi cursif du début du septième siècle de notre ère', *Comptes Rendus de l'Académie des Inscriptions et Belles-Lettres* (1991).

14 It is to P. Gignoux, 'Pour une nouvelle histoire de l'Iran sasanide', in W. Skalmowski and A. van Tongerloo (eds.), *Middle Iranian studies* (Louvain, 1984) that we owe a fundamental consideration of the respective weight of the sources.

15 For a summary of the literary sources of Sasanian history see A. Christensen, *L'Iran sous les Sassanides*, 2nd rev. edn (Copenhagen, 1944), pp. 50–83; G. Widengren, 'Sources of Parthian and Sasanian history', in E. Yarshater (ed.), *The Cambridge history of Iran*, vol. III: *The Seleucid, Parthian and Sasanian periods* (Cambridge, 1983), pp. 1261–83, 1269–82; R. N. Frye, *The history of ancient Iran*, Handbuch der Altertumswissenschaft III, 7 (Munich, 1984), pp. 287–91; K. Schippmann, *Grundzüge der Geschichte des sasanidischen Reiches* (Darmstadt, 1990), pp. 3–9; Wiesehöfer, *Ancient Persia*, pp. 153–9 and 283–5.

16 Ammianus Marcellinus, *Rerum gestarum libri*, books 23–5. For Ammian's oeuvre seen from the perspective of Iranian studies see P. Huyse, 'Vorbemerkungen zur Auswertung iranischen Sprachgutes in den Res Gestae des Ammianus Marcellinus', introduction to W. Skalmowski and A. Van Tongerloo (eds.), *Medioiranica*, Orientalia Lovaniensia Analecta 48 (Leuven, 1993); for Ammian and the Sasanians see chapters in J. W. Drijvers

biographies of the emperors found in the *Historia Augusta*, which, however, are to be used only with great caution. Yet what all these authors have in common is, above all else, an interest in the military conflicts between the Romans and Sasanians. Notwithstanding this and their bias against the enemy, many details in their accounts are of importance in the reconstruction of the Sasanian empire's internal affairs. Among the Byzantine witnesses of Byzantine–Sasanian contacts we find Procopius, who reported on the wars against the Persians in the sixth century in his capacity as confidant of the Byzantine general Belisar.[17] Procopius' historic 'successor' Agathias, who claims to have had access to the Sasanian state archives,[18] as well as Zosimus (late fifth/early sixth century), John Malalas (d. *c.* 570), Menander Protector (sixth/seventh century)[19] and Theophylactus Simocatta (d. *c.* 630)[20] were all such witnesses of Byzantine–Sasanian relations.

Within the Christian Syriac tradition,[21] numerous martyrs' accounts[22] illuminate the early history of Christianity in the Sasanian empire, its view of itself and the religious policies of the empire's rulers, despite all hagiographic distortions. We also owe valuable information to chronicles (the Chronicle of Arbela,[23] the

and D. Hunt (eds.), *The late Roman world and its historian: Interpreting Ammianus Marcellinus* (London and New York, 1999) (esp. H. Teitler, '*Visa vel lecta?* Ammianus on Persia and the Persians') and J. W. Drijvers, 'Ammianus Marcellinus' image of Sasanian society', in J. Wiesehöfer and P. Huyse (eds.), *Ērān ud Anērān: Studien zu den Beziehungen zwischen dem Sasanidenreich und der Mittelmeerwelt*, OrOCC 13 (Stuttgart, 2006).

17 For Procopius see mainly A. Cameron, *Procopius and the sixth century* (London and New York, 1985); A. Kaldellis, *Procopius of Caesarea: Tyranny, history, and philosophy at the end of Antiquity* (Philadelphia, 2004); and esp. H. Börm, *Prokop und die Perser*, OrOCC 16 (Stuttgart, 2007).

18 Agathias, *Historiae*, 2.27.2,4, 30. 2,3,5. See A. Cameron, 'Agathias on the Sassanians', *Dumbarton Oaks Papers*, 23–4 (1969–70).

19 R. C. Blockley, 'Subsidies and diplomacy: Rome and Persia in Late Antiquity', *Phoenix*, 39 (1985).

20 M. Whitby, *The emperor Maurice and his historian: Theophylact Simocatta on Persian and Balkan warfare* (Oxford, 1988).

21 S. Döpp and W. Geerlings (eds.), *Lexikon der antiken christlichen Literatur* (Freiburg, 1998); J. Aßfalg and P. Krüger (eds.), *Kleines Wörterbuch des christlichen Orients* (Wiesbaden, 1975); A. Baumstark, *Geschichte der syrischen Literatur mit Ausschluß der christlich-palästinensischen Texte* (Bonn, 1922; repr. 1968); and G. Graf, *Geschichte der christlichen arabischen Literatur*, 4 vols. (Vatican, 1944–53; repr. 1964–6) are still crucial accounts of the history of Christian literature; see now also S. P. Brock, *Brief outline of Syriac literature* (Kottayam, 1997).

22 Editions: S. E. Assemani, *Acta Sanctorum Martyrum Orientalium et Occidentalium in duas partes distributa* (Rome, 1748; repr. 1970); P. Bedjan, *Acta Martyrum et Sanctorum*, 7 vols. (Paris and Leipzig, 1890–7; repr. 1968); for translated extracts see G. Hoffmann, *Auszüge aus syrischen Akten persischer Märtyrer* (Leipzig, 1880); O. Braun, *Ausgewählte Akten persischer Märtyrer* (Kempten and Munich, 1915); S. P. Brock and S. Harvey (eds.), *Holy women of the Syrian Orient* (Berkeley, 1987).

23 P. Kawerau, *Die Chronik von Arbela*, CSCO 467–8, 2 vols., (Louvain, 1985); for the question of the authenticity of this chronicle see the dispute between J. M. Fiey, 'Review of P. Kawerau, *Die Chronik von Arbela*', *Revue d'Histoire Ecclésiastique*, 81 (1986) and

Chronicle of Se'ert (Arabic), Joshua the Stylite (sixth century)[24]) and Church histories, which sometimes show a remarkably exact chronology and offer information of great value.

As far as Manichaean material is concerned, there are original Coptic sources of Manichaeans from Central Egypt, wide-ranging discoveries of texts in Middle Persian, Old Turkic and Chinese from the Silk Route, and, finally, also findings in papyrus and parchment collections (the 'Cologne Mani Codex' (CMC)). All these have made it possible for the life and teachings of Mani, the early history of Manichaean missionary activity and the relationship between the Manichaeans and the Sasanian authorities to be appreciated from a point of view other than that of the enemies of Manichaeism.[25]

As far as Armenian historians are concerned, they are to be used only with the utmost caution, due to their predominantly antagonistic tendency towards the Sasanians and the specific problems related to their transmission.[26] Nevertheless, there is Łazar of Pharb's contemporary account of the 482–4 uprising, with detailed information about Sasanian commanders and disputation at court; the encomiastic biography of Smbat Bagratuni quarried by Pseudo-Sebeos, which includes an account of a grand reception at court; above all, the *History to 682*, incorporated into Movses Daskhurants'i's *History of the Caucasian Albanians*, the principal source for the 637 Persian counter-attack, noted below.

In late Sasanian and even Islamic times there appeared texts in Middle Persian, which were either commentaries on the Avesta, or which constituted

P. Kawerau, 'Correspondance', *Revue d'Histoire Ecclésiastique*, 82 (1987); for the problem of the authenticity of the data see E. Kettenhofen, 'Die Chronik von Arbela in der Sicht der Althistorie', in L. Criscuolo, G. Geraci and C. Salvaterra (eds.), *Simblos: Scritti di storia antica* (Bologna, 1995); and J. Wiesehöfer, 'Zeugnisse zur Geschichte und Kultur der Persis unter den Parthern', in J. Wiesehöfer (ed.), *Das Partherreich und seine Zeugnisse – The Arsacid Empire: Sources and documentation. Beiträge des Internationalen Colloquiums, Eutin (27.–29. Juni 1996)*, Historia-Einzelschriften 122 (Stuttgart, 1998).

24 A. Luther, *Die syrische Chronik des Josua Stylites*, Untersuchungen zur antiken Literatur und Geschichte 49 (Berlin and New York, 1997); F. R. Trombley and J. W. Watt (eds.), *The chronicle of Pseudo-Joshua the Stylite*, Translated Texts for Historians 32 (Liverpool, 2000).

25 Editions of Manichaean works and secondary literature until 1996 are gathered in G. B. Mikkelsen, *Bibliographia Manichaica: A comprehensive bibliography of Manichaeism through 1996*, Corpus Fontium Manichaeorum, Subsidia 1 (Turnhout, 1997). See now also the bibliography in I. Gardner and S. N. C. Lieu (eds.), *Manichaean texts from the Roman Empire* (Cambridge, 2004).

26 See the summaries in Christensen, *L'Iran*, pp. 77–9; Widengren, 'Sources of Parthian and Sasanian history', pp. 1274–6; for caveats see P. Gignoux, 'Pour une évaluation de la contribution des sources arméniennes à l'histoire sassanide', *Acta Antiqua Academiae Scientiarum Hungaricae*, 31 (1985–8); E. Kettenhofen, 'Review of E. Winter, *Die sāsānidisch-römischen Friedensverträge des 3. Jahrhunderts n.Chr.*', *Bibliotheca Orientalis*, 47 (1990), pp. 172–3; Kettenhofen, *Tirdād*.

a sort of epic or poetic literature related to a court setting.[27] A sort of 'Iranian national history' was created under Khusrau I and his successors in the form of the *X^w adāy-nāmag* (the 'Book of Lords'), which was a semi-official history of Iran from the first king of the world, Gayōmard, until the reign of Khusrau II.[28] After recalling Iran's glorious history in the face of a somewhat less magnificent present, this work, which has only survived in extracts, translations and later adaptations, recounts the reigns of fifty kings and queens. The text probably also had the aim of appeasing the needs of the ruled, and is characterised by certain mythical themes. An interesting feature of the Book of lords is that 'heroic' times generally alternate with periods in which soothsayers, 'holy men' or 'prophets' raise questions of ethics and morality, and in which the theme of war recedes into the background. In terms of genre, this 'national history' thus represents a mixture of heroic themes, proverbs of kings and sages, priestly disputes, philosophical meditations, moral precepts, and royal testaments and speeches. Time and again, these examine questions of justice, religiosity and the virtuous life. However, the Book of Lords was not just a semi-official book of 'history', but also a tool of literary entertainment and social education. It was meant to preach moral and socio-political ideals as well as the virtues of the ruled – ideals upon which Sasanian kings believed their rule to be founded and which they regarded as the means for safeguarding their continuing position of power. The biographies of kings, heroes and sages served as the background on the basis of which such ideals could be illustrated. The distinction between myth, legend and historical fact was therefore of secondary importance.[29]

Although much more written material has survived from the Sasanian era than from Parthian times, there has nevertheless been a serious loss of sources. Many texts were lost during the conquest of Iran by the Muslims, or through later invasions. Others were censored by religious zealots, or, in later times, were not deemed worthy or sufficiently interesting to be preserved. Translations and adaptations, as well as bibliographical collections and notes in Arabic and New Persian, only feebly reflect the breadth of Sasanian literature. But, at any rate, it is known that, alongside the religious writings,

27 J. C. Tavadia, *Die mittelpersische Sprache und Literatur der Zarathustrier* (Leipzig, 1956); M. Boyce, 'Middle Persian literature', in *Iranistik II, Literatur I*, Handbuch der Orientalistik I.IV.2.1 (Leiden, 1968); J. de Menasce, 'Zoroastrian Pahlavi writings', in Yarshater (ed.), *The Cambridge history of Iran*, vol. III; C. G. Cereti, *La letteratura pahlavi* (Milan, 2001).

28 A. S. Shahbazi, 'On the X^w adāy-nāmag', *Acta Iranica*, 30 (1990).

29 E. Yarshater, 'Iranian national history', in Yarshater (ed.), *The Cambridge history of Iran*, vol. III, part 1; for the role of the West ('Rum') in this tradition see below.

Middle Persian literature covered historical, geographical, didactic and astronomical works, and books on the natural as well as the social and cultural characteristics of countries. These included travel accounts, volumes on good manners and etiquette, legal manuals, historical novels, love stories and literature of popular entertainment.[30] However, much of the extant material is not contemporary to late Sasanian affairs and can only be used historically with great care.

Persian–Arabic historiography[31] (i.e. al-Ṭabarī and others[32]) owes its knowledge of Sasanian Iran to such late Middle Persian traditions. However, the extent of this knowledge needs to be examined in each specific case. It must also be investigated whether, in the process of being edited, facts might have been transformed organically, or adjusted to the exigencies of an Islamic view of 'salvation history'.[33]

The Sasanian inscriptions discussed above are at times juxtaposed, both in space and content, with artistically remarkable bas-reliefs, also mainly dating from the third and fourth centuries.[34] These usually portray the investiture of kings by gods. There also exist, however, bas-reliefs portraying scenes of victory, and some that depict the king on his throne surrounded by his entourage. Among the most impressive of the bas-reliefs portraying scenes of victory is the depiction of the battle of Hurmuzjān between Ardashīr I and Artabanus V in

30 Boyce, 'Middle Persian literature'.

31 See C. Brockelmann, *Geschichte der arabischen Literatur*, 2nd edn, 2 vols. (Leiden, 1943–9; suppl. 1–3, Leiden, 1937–42); F. Sezgin, *Geschichte des arabischen Schrifttums*, vol. I (Leiden, 1967); H. Busse, 'Arabische Historiographie und Geographie', in H. Gätje (ed.), *Grundriß der arabischen Philologie*, vol. II (Wiesbaden, 1987); J. C. Meisami and P. Starkey (eds.), *Encyclopedia of Arabic literature*, 2 vols. (London, 1998).

32 For al-Ṭabarī's outstanding role (Abū Jaʿfar Muḥammad ibn Jarīr al-Ṭabarī, *Taʾrīkh al-rusul waʾl-mulūk*, ed. M. J. Goeje *et al.*, 15 vols. in 3 series (Leiden, 1879–1901); translation of the Sasanian part: T. Nöldeke, *Geschichte der Perser und Araber zur Zeit der Sasaniden* (Leiden, 1878); C. E. Bosworth (ed.) *The history of al-Ṭabarī*, vol. V: *The Sāsānids, the Byzantines, the Lakmids, and Yemen* (Albany, 1999)), see Bosworth (ed.), *The history of al-Ṭabarī*, in particular vols. XV–XX; also *passim* for other works in Arabic, as well as Widengren, 'Sources of Parthian and Sasanian history', pp. 1280–1; Z. Rubin, 'Ibn al-Muqaffaʿ and the account of Sasanian history in the Arabic Codex Sprenger 30', *JSAI*, 30 (2005).

33 For the historical and intellectual background of Arab-Persian historiography of the Sasanian empire see M. Springberg-Hinsen, *Die Zeit vor dem Islam in arabischen Universalgeschichten des 9. bis 12. Jahrhunderts* (Würzburg and Altenberge, 1989). For the reliability of the material concerning late Sasanian affairs see Z. Rubin, 'Nobility, monarchy and legitimation under the later Sasanians', in J. Haldon and L. I. Conrad (eds.), *The Byzantine and early Islamic Near East*, vol. VI: *Elites old and new in the Byzantine and early Islamic Near East* (Princeton, 2004); Rubin, 'Ibn al-Muqaffaʿ'.

34 See the summary given in Cereti, 'Primary sources', pp. 33–7; and M. Abkaʿi-Khavari, *Das Bild des Königs in der Sasanidenzeit: Schriftliche Überlieferungen im Vergleich mit Antiquaria*, Texte und Studien zur Orientalistik 13 (Hildesheim, 2000), pp. 31–7.

three scenes,[35] as well as the five 'victory' reliefs of Shāpūr I (which depict the Roman emperors Gordian III, Philip the Arab and Valerian as 'victims').[36] The most impressive investiture reliefs are those of Ardashīr I from Naqsh-i Rustam and Naqsh-i Rajab.[37] The 'priest' Kerdīr, too, could not resist from drawing attention to himself by having his bust sculpted.[38] After a long interval devoid of depictions in stone, and in which silver vessels took on the role of bas-reliefs with regard to the art of royal representation,[39] it was Khusrau II who again had himself immortalised in stone. The reliefs of the great *iwān* of Ṭāq-i Bustān in Media (close to Kīrmānshāh) show him as the divinely chosen ruler and as an accomplished horseman, as well as in the midst of a wild boar and deer hunt.[40]

Even more remarkable than the colossal statues of Shāpūr I and Khusrau II, which represent rare examples of the Sasanian art of sculpture,[41] are the layouts of cities, palaces, religious buildings, bridges and dams of the time.[42] Worth mentioning among the cities are the round construction of Ardashīr Khwarrah (Gūr) on the plain of Firūzābād, from the time of the founder of the dynasty,[43] and the main residence of his son Shāpūr, Weh-Shābuhr (Bīshāpūr).[44] Both of these are situated in Fārs, alongside Jundīshāpūr (Mid. Pers. Weh-Andiyōk-Shābuhr; Syr. Bēth Lāpāṭ) close to Sūsa, which was not only home to a 'university', but also a centre of Persian silk manufacturing, and the main base of Khūzistān's Christians.[45] As far as the kings' palaces are concerned,[46] it is the

35 H. von Gall, *Das Reiterkampfbild in der iranischen und iranisch beeinflußten Kunst parthischer und sasanidischer Zeit*, Teheraner Forschungen 6 (Berlin, 1990), pp. 20–30.
36 M. Meyer, 'Die Felsbilder Shapurs I.', *Jahrbuch des Deutschen Archäologischen Instituts*, 105 (1990).
37 H. Luschey, 'Ardašīr I., II: Rock reliefs', *EIr*, vol. II, pp. 329–34.
38 W. Hinz, *Altiranische Funde und Forschungen* (Berlin, 1969), pp. 189–228.
39 P. O. Harper, *Silver vessels of the Sasanian period*, vol. I: *Royal imagery* (New York, 1981); P. O. Harper, 'Sasanian silver', in J. Boardman, I. E. S. Edwards, E. Sollberger and N. G. L. Hammond (eds.), *The Cambridge ancient history*, vol. III, part 2: *The Assyrian and Babylonian empires and other states of the Near East, from the eighth to the sixth centuries BC* (Cambridge, 1983); P. O. Harper, 'La vaisselle en métal', in *Splendeur des Sassanides: L'empire perse entre Rome et la Chine (224–642): 12 février au 25 avril 1993* (Brussels, 1993).
40 Cereti, 'Primary sources', p. 35, fn. 104 (with older literature); for the dating of the bas-reliefs, see now also von Gall, *Das Reiterkampfbild*, pp. 38–47.
41 For Sasanian sculpture, see Abkaʿi-Khavari, *Das Bild des Königs*, pp. 37–8.
42 For a summary see D. Huff, 'Sasanian cities', in M. Y. Kiani (ed.), *A general study of urbanization and urban planning in Iran* (Tehran, 1986); D. Huff, 'Architecture, III', *EIr*, vol. II, pp. 329–34; D. Huff, 'Architecture sassanide', in *Splendeur des Sassanides*; and Cereti, 'Primary sources', pp. 28–33.
43 For Sasanian city designs see Huff, 'Sasanian cities'; for Gūr see L. Trümpelmann, *Zwischen Persepolis und Firuzabad* (Mainz, 1991), pp. 61–71.
44 R. Ghirshman, *Bichapour I–II* (Paris, 1956–71).
45 D. T. Potts, 'Gundeshapur and the Gondeisos', *Iranica Antiqua*, 24 (1989).
46 L. Bier, 'Sasanian palaces in perspective', *Archaeology*, 35, 1 (1982); W. Kleiss, *Die Entwicklung von Palästen und palastartigen Wohnbauten in Iran*, Sitzungsberichte der Österreichischen Akademie der Wissenschaften, Philosophisch-historische Klasse 524 (Vienna, 1989).

two early residences of Ardashīr I,[47] the palace of Shāpūr I in Bīshāpūr, with its mosaics modelled on Roman patterns,[48] and the late Sasanian residence of Ctesiphon on the river Tigris – or rather, the one remaining monumental arch of its *iwān*[49] – that have left the greatest impression. Roman prisoners of war built many of the roughly twenty Sasanian bridges and dams that are still to be seen today.[50] The most important sanctuary of late Sasanian times, the Takht-i Sulaimān in Azerbaijān, was unearthed by German archaeologists.[51]

The products of Sasanian silk and textile manufacturing[52] also deserve mention, as well as Sasanian goldsmiths' art,[53] cameos,[54] glass manufacturing[55] and examples of the famous Sasanian stucco-work.[56] Historically more important, however, are the seals and *bullae*, which introduce Sasanian officials by their names, titles and functions,[57] as well as coins, the head of which generally depicted the ruler with his respective crown and legends, while the

47 G. Gerster and D. Huff, 'Die Paläste des Königs Ardaschir', *Bild der Wissenschaft*, 11 (1977).

48 Ghirshman, *Bichapour*.

49 E. J. Keall, 'Ayvān (or Tāq)-e Kesrā', *EIr*, vol. III, pp. 155–9.

50 L. Bier, 'Notes on Mihr Narseh's bridge near Firuzabad', *Archäologische Mitteilungen aus Iran*, n.s. 19 (1986).

51 R. Naumann, *Die Ruinen von Tacht-e Suleiman und Zendan-e Suleiman* (Berlin, 1977); D. Huff, 'Recherches archéologiques à Takht-i Suleiman', *Comptes Rendus de l'Académie des Inscriptions et Belles-Lettres* (1978); D. Huff, 'Der Takht-e Suleiman. Sassanidisches Feuerheiligtum und mongolischer Palast', in T. Stöllner *et al.* (eds.), *Persiens antike Pracht*, vol. II (Bochum, 2004).

52 E. H. Peck 'Clothing, IV', *EIr*, vol. V, pp. 739–52; A. Jeroussalimskaja, 'Soieries sassanides, A. Histoire culturelle', in *Splendeur des Sassanides*; D. de Jonghe, 'Soieries sassanides', in *Splendeur des Sassanides*.

53 Harper, *Silver vessels*; Harper, 'Sasanian silver'; Harper, 'La vaisselle'; P. O. Harper, 'Sasanian silver vessels: Recent developments', in V. S. Curtis, R. Hillenbrand and J. M. Rogers (eds.), *The art and archaeology of ancient Persia: New light on the Parthian and Sasanian Empires* (London and New York, 1998). For Sasanian jewellery see B. Musche, *Vorderasiatischer Schmuck zur Zeit der Arsakiden und Sasaniden*, Handbuch der Orientalistik VII.I.2B.5 (Leiden, 1988).

54 Von Gall, *Das Reiterkampfbild*, pp. 56–9.

55 S. Fukai, *Persian glass* (New York, 1977); D. Whitehouse, 'La verrerie', in *Splendeur des Sassanides*.

56 J. Kröger, *Sasanidischer Stuckdekor* (Mainz, 1982).

57 For a summary of Sasanian glyptography see Cereti, 'Primary sources', pp. 44–50; to this should be added *Catalogue des sceaux, camées et bulles sasanides de la Bibliothèque Nationale et du Musée du Louvre*, 2 vols., vol. I: R. Gyselen, *Collection générale* (Paris, 1993); R. Gyselen, *Sceaux magiques en Iran sassanide*, Cahiers de Studia Iranica 17 (Paris, 1995); R. Gyselen, *L'art sigillaire dans les collections de Leyde* (Leiden, 1997); R. Gyselen (ed.), *Sceaux d'Orient et leur emploi*. Res Orientales 10 (Bures-sur-Yvette, 1997); R. Gyselen, 'Sasanian glyptic: An example of cultural interaction between the Hellenistic world and the Iranian world', in M. Alram and D. Klimburg-Salter (eds.), *Coins, art and chronology: Essays on the pre-Islamic history of the Indo-Iranian borderlands*, Österreichische Akademie der Wissenschaften, philosophisch-historische Klasse, Denkschriften 280 (Vienna, 1999).

tail showed a fire-altar with assistant figures.[58] Since gold and copper coins were not in wide circulation, most coins were made of thin silver. As in the case of the Parthians, the basic unit was the drachma, with a weight of 4 grams. It began to be minted *en masse* under Shāpūr I, probably in order to attract mercenaries from Central Asia. Although coin factories and mint offices are mentioned, their number and kind are difficult to reconstruct. From the time of Kawād I, annual figures are given canonically. The so-called 'Kushano-Sasanian coins' pose yet another challenge. That is to say, the dating of coins issued by Sasanian governors in the provinces of the former Kushan empire, has produced extremely contradictory results.[59]

Sasanian history from Ardashīr I to Yazdgerd III[60]

As in the case of the Parthians, we know very little about the Sasanians' aims and activities in the field of foreign policy, most of which concerns their western

58 For a summary, see H. D. Malek, 'A survey of research on Sasanian numismatics', *Numismatic Chronicle*, 153 (1993); and Cereti, 'Primary sources', pp. 38–44. A *Sylloge Nummorum Sasanidorum* is about to be created (R. Gyselen *et al.*, 'Sylloge Nummorum Sasanidorum: Die Münzen der Sasaniden aus der Bibliothèque Nationale de France, dem Münzkabinett der Staatlichen Museen zu Berlin und dem Münzkabinett am Kunsthistorischen Museum in Wien (in Zusammenarbeit mit M. Alram u.a.)', *Anzeiger der philosophisch-historischen Klasse der Österreichischen Akademie der Wissenschaften*, 134 (1999); M. Alram and R. Gyselen, *Sylloge Nummorum Sasanidarum Paris – Berlin – Wien*, vol. I: *Ardashir I.–Shapur I.* (Vienna, 2003); N. Schindel, *Sylloge Nummorum Sasanidarum Paris – Berlin – Wien*, vol.. III, pts 1–2: *Shapur II.–Kawad I./2. Regierung* (Vienna, 2004)).

59 J. Cribb, 'Numismatic evidence for Kushano-Sasanian chronology', *Studia Iranica*, 19 (1990); R. Göbl, 'The Rabatak inscription and the date of Kanishka', in Alram and Klimburg-Salter (eds.), *Coins, art and chronology*; see now also Cereti, 'Primary sources', pp. 64–8.

60 For a summary, see R. N. Frye, 'The political history of Iran under the Sasanians', in Yarshater (ed.), *The Cambridge history of Iran*, vol. III; and Frye, *History*, pp. 287–339; see also A. D. Lee, *Information and frontiers: Roman foreign relations in Late Antiquity* (Cambridge, 1993). Single epochs are treated by F. G. B. Millar, *The Roman Near East 31 BC–AD 337*, 2nd edn (Cambridge, MA, and London, 1994); R. C. Blockley, *East Roman foreign policy: Formation and conduct from Diocletian to Anastasius* (Leeds, 1992); and N. G. Garsoian, 'Byzantium and the Sasanians', in Yarshater (ed.), *The Cambridge history of Iran*, vol. III. Information concerning Sasanian foreign policy can also be found in I. Shahid, *Byzantium and the Arabs in the fourth century* (Washington, DC, 1984); I. Shahid, *Byzantium and the Arabs in the fifth century* (Washington, DC, 1989) and I. Shahid, *Byzantium and the Arabs in the sixth century*, vol. I, parts 1–2 (Washington, DC, 1995). J. Howard-Johnston, 'The two great powers in Late Antiquity: A comparison', in A. Cameron (ed.), *The Byzantine and early Islamic Near East*, vol. III: *States, resources and armies*, Studies in Late Antiquity and Early Islam 1 (Princeton, 1995), provides an overview of the manifold relations between Rome/Byzantium and Persia. W. Felix, *Antike literarische Quellen zur Außenpolitik des Sāsānidenstaates*, vol. I: *224–309*, Österreichische Akademie der Wissenschaften, philosophisch-historische Klasse, Sitzungsberichte 456 = Veröffentlichungen der Iranischen Kommission 18 (Vienna, 1985), presents the classical (Greek and Roman) literary sources concerning

border. All lands of the former Parthian empire, except for Armenia, came under Sasanian control during the reign of the founder of the dynasty, Ardashīr (224–239/40?). It is under him that an offensive policy towards Rome is already discernible.[61] His son Shāpūr I (240–71/2 was more successful in this than his father, however: his campaigns affected not only Armenia, but even shook the foundations of the Roman empire. His armies advanced briefly as far as Antioch and Cappadocia, and Valerian became the first Roman emperor to be captured by the Sasanian enemy. Despite all later setbacks (e.g. against Odenathus of Palmyra), and if we believe his own account of his reign, Shāpūr's empire stretched from Mesopotamia in the west to Peshawar in the east.[62] Succession disputes, and Diocletian's aggressive eastern policy at the end of the century, caused the Sasanians to incur the loss of regions to the east of the Tigris and Armenia for several decades.[63] Only Shāpūr II could erase the memory of the 'Peace of Disgrace' concluded at Nisibis (298 CE), when he managed, after long battles, not only to drive Julian the Apostate away from Ctesiphon, but also

the foreign policy of the Sasanians (until 309 CE). A commented list of sources in translation with reference to Roman–Sasanian relations is given by M. H. Dodgeon and S. N. C. Lieu (eds.), *The Roman eastern frontier and the Persian wars*, part 1: *AD 226–363: A documentary history* (London and New York, 1991); G. Greatrex and S. N. C. Lieu, *The Roman eastern frontier and the Persian wars*, part 2: *AD 363–630* (London and New York, 2002); E. Winter and B. Dignas, *Rom und das Perserreich: Zwei Weltmächte zwischen Konfrontation und Koexistenz* (Berlin, 2001).

61 J. Wiesehöfer, 'Ardašīr I, I: History', *EIr*, vol. II, pp. 371–6; E. Winter, *Die sāsānidisch–römischen Friedensverträge des 3. Jahrhunderts n.Chr.: Ein Beitrag zum Verständnis der außenpolitischen Beziehungen zwischen den beiden Großmächten*, Europäische Hochschulschriften III, 350 (Frankfurt etc., 1988), pp. 45ff.; sources in Dodgeon and Lieu (eds.), *The Roman eastern frontier*, pp. 9–33; Winter and Dignas, *Rom und das Perserreich, passim.*

62 For Shāpūr's wars, see esp. E. Kettenhofen, *Die römisch-persischen Kriege des 3. Jahrhunderts n.Chr. nach der Inschrift Šāhpuhrs I. an der Kaʿbe-ye Zartošt*, Beihefte zum Tübinger Atlas des Vorderen Orients, series B, no. 35 (Wiesbaden, 1982), and Huyse, *Die dreisprachige Inschrift*. See also Winter, *Die sāsānidisch-römischen Friedensverträge*, pp. 80ff. (for this see Kettenhofen, 'Review of E. Winter, *Die sāsānidisch-römischen Friedensverträge*'); D. S. Potter, *Prophecy and history in the crisis of the Roman Empire: A historical commentary on the Thirteenth Sibylline Oracle* (Oxford, 1990), pp. 189ff.; K. Strobel, *Das Imperium Romanum im '3. Jahrhundert'*, Historia-Einzelschriften 75 (Stuttgart, 1993), pp. 220ff.; Millar, *The Roman Near East*, pp. 151ff. Sources can be found in Dodgeon and Lieu (eds.), *The Roman eastern frontier*, pp. 34ff., and Winter and Dignas, *Rom und das Perserreich, passim.*

63 Winter, *Die sāsānidisch-römischen Friedensverträge*, pp. 152ff.; E. Winter, 'On the regulation of the eastern frontier of the Roman Empire in 298', in D. H. French and C. S. Lightfoot (eds.), *The eastern frontier of the Roman empire: Proceedings of a colloquium held at Ankara in September 1988*, BAR International Series 553, part 1 (Oxford, 1989); Blockley, *East Roman foreign policy*, pp. 5ff.; Kettenhofen, *Tirdād, passim*; J. Wiesehöfer, 'Narseh, Diokletian, Manichäer und Christen', in M. Arafa, J. Tubach and G. S. Vashalomidze (eds.), *Inkulturation des Christentums im Sasanidenreich* (Wiesbaden, 2007); for sources regarding Roman–Sasanian relations until 298, see Dodgeon and Lieu (eds.), *The Roman eastern frontier*, pp. 111ff.; Winter and Dignas, *Rom und das Perserreich, passim.*

succeeded in wresting a great part of the lost territory from Julian's successor Jovian, both by military and diplomatic means (363 CE).[64] In the course and aftermath of these wars severe persecutions of Christians took place in the Sasanian empire. From a Christological point of view these Christians were *not yet* divorced from their fellow believers in the west, and after the 'Constantine Revolution' they thus became Rome's protégés and were regarded as partisans for the Roman cause by the Sasanian authorities.[65] The eastern part of Armenia also became Sasanian again in the year 387.[66]

During the subsequent century, however, the Hepthalites, or 'White Huns', were to become an even greater problem than the Romans, with whom a mutually satisfactory agreement was reached around 400.[67] The Hepthalites were tribes that had pushed forth from Dsugaria into Central Asia and now ruled, among other territories, Sogdia, Bactria, the western part of the Tarim plain and north-western India.[68] They utterly defeated King Fīrūz (Pērōz) twice (465 and 484) and forced him to pay tribute to them, which, combined with famines, led the Sasanian empire to the brink of internal collapse. It was at this time that a man by the name of Mazdak proclaimed a religious and ethical programme which called for the just distribution of ownership. His teaching, thanks to its 'Zoroastrian' terminology, its attractive dogmatics and theology and the charity practised within the Mazdakite communities in a time of widespread poverty and hardship, won over many people in Iran and Mesopotamia, not only those without means,

64 R. C. Blockley, 'The Romano-Persian peace treaties of AD 299 and 363', *Florilegium*, 6 (1984); Blockley, *East Roman foreign policy*, pp. 24ff.; for sources concerning the period up until 363, see Dodgeon and Lieu (eds.), *The Roman eastern frontier*, pp. 143ff.; Winter and Dignas, *Rom und das Perserreich, passim*.

65 W. Schwaigert, *Das Christentum in Ḫūzistān im Rahmen der frühen Kirchengeschichte Persiens* (Marburg, 1989), pp. 103–75; J. Wiesehöfer, 'Geteilte Loyalitäten: Religiöse Minderheiten des 3. und 4. Jahrhunderts n.Chr. im Spannungsfeld zwischen Rom und dem sāsānidischen Iran', *Klio*, 75 (1993).

66 R. C. Blockley, 'The division of Armenia between the Romans and the Persians', *Historia*, 36 (1987).

67 Blockley, *East Roman foreign policy*, pp. 52ff.; for Byzantium and the Sasanians in the fifth century, see Z. Rubin, 'Diplomacy and war in the relations between Byzantium and the Sassanids in the fifth century AD', in P. W. Freeman and D. L. Kennedy (eds.), *The defence of the Roman and Byzantine east: Proceedings of a colloquium held at the University of Sheffield in April 1986*, BAR International Series 297, part 2 (Oxford, 1986); Blockley, *East Roman foreign policy*, pp. 52ff.; G. Greatrex, *Rome and Persia at war, 502–532*, ARCA Classical and Medieval Texts, Papers and Monographs 37 (Leeds, 1998); Greatrex and Lieu, *The Roman eastern frontier*, pp. 31ff.

68 E. V. Zeimal, 'The Kidarite kingdom in Central Asia', in B. A. Litvinsky (ed.), *History of civilizations of Central Asia*, vol. III: *The crossroads of civilization AD 250 to 750* (Paris, 1996); B. A. Litvinsky, 'The Hephthalite empire', in Litvinsky (ed.), *History of civilizations of Central Asia*, vol. III; A. D. H. Bivar, 'Hephthalites', *EIr*, vol. XII, pp. 198–201.

but also members of the aristocratic elite. For a long time, the reign of King Kawād (488–96, 498–531) was shaped by the conflict between the new king and his pro-Hepthalite and pro-Mazdakite followers and a pro-Roman and anti-Mazdakite party. It was probably only Kawād's wish to establish his son Khusrau as successor to the throne in the 520s that broke the bonds between the king and the Mazdakites and led to violent action by the Mazdakites against the landowning aristocracy, to which many of the empire's non-urban population were liable for compulsory service and duties. Soon, however, Kawād and Khusrau would brutally suppress the uprising.[69] Both took advantage of the weakening of the aristocracy to implement fundamental social, economic and military reforms. Land ownership was registered, and a fixed land tax, as opposed to a changing income tax, was introduced. After a census had been taken, a new poll-tax was also established, according to different levels of wealth. In addition, the empire was divided into four military districts,[70] and special units took on policing and border-control duties. The creation of a new court elite and administration, which would no longer owe its privileges to reputation and descent, but to royal favour alone, was also in the interest of the kings, as was the backing of the lower, landowning aristocracy.[71]

The establishment of internal peace and stability allowed Khusrau to become active again externally.[72] In 540 he broke the 'Eternal Peace' that had been concluded with the Byzantine emperor Justinian.[73] The payment of

69 For this period, see Bosworth's historical commentary of al-Ṭabarī (Bosworth (ed.), *The history of al-Ṭabarī*, pp. 126–39, 146–62, including a bibliography). For the Mazdakites see W. Sundermann, 'Mazdak und die mazdakitischen Volksaufstände', *Altertum*, 23 (1977); M. Guidi and M. Morony, 'Mazdak', *EI2*, vol. VI, pp. 949–52; Z. Rubin, 'The reforms of Khusrō Anūshirwān', in Cameron (ed.), *The Byzantine and early Islamic Near East*, vol. III; G. Gnoli, 'Nuovi Studi sul Mazdakismo', in G. Gnoli and A. Panaino (eds.), *La Persia e Bisanzio*, Atti dei Convegni Lincei 201 (Rome, 2004); and J. Wiesehöfer, 'Chusro I. und das Sasanidenreich: Der König der Könige "mit der unsterblichen Seele"', in M. Meier (ed.), *Sie schufen Europa: Historische Portraits von Konstantin bis Karl dem Großen* (Munich, 2007).

70 See R. Gyselen, *The four generals of the Sasanian empire: Some sigillographic evidence* (Rome, 2001).

71 For the reforms of Khusrau see the different opinions of F. Altheim and R. Stiehl, *Finanzgeschichte der Spätantike* (Frankfurt, 1957), esp. pp. 31ff., M. Grignaschi, 'La riforma tributaria di Ḫosrō I e il feudalismo sassanide', in *La Persia nel medioevo* (Rome, 1971); Howard-Johnston, 'The two great powers', pp. 211ff., Rubin, 'The reforms'; and Wiesehöfer, *Ancient Persia*, pp. 190f. and 292f.

72 For Byzantine–Sasanian relations under Kawād see Luther, *Die syrische Chronik*; Greatrex, *Rome and Persia at war*; Greatrex and Lieu, *The Roman eastern frontier*, pp. 62ff.

73 For the 'Eternal Peace' see Greatrex, *Rome and Persia at war*, pp. 213ff.; Greatrex and Lieu, *The Roman eastern frontier*, pp. 96–7. For Justinian's Persian wars see B. Rubin, *Das Zeitalter Iustinians*, vol. I (Berlin, 1960), pp. 279–373; Greatrex and Lieu, *The Roman eastern frontier*, pp. 82ff. Cf. also Blockley, 'Subsidies and diplomacy'; G. Greatrex, 'Byzantium and the east in the sixth century', in M. Maas (ed.), *The Cambridge companion to the age of Justinian* (Cambridge, 2005).

tribute – a single payment had already been agreed upon in 532 – was raised in 562 with a new treaty. Khusrau's conquest of South Arabia, and the subsequent expulsion from there of the Aksumites (Ethiopians), who were in alliance with Byzantium, indirectly weakened Byzantium's position.[74] In the east he even managed to destroy the empire of the Hepthalites, with the help of the Western Turks, around 560.[75]

Khusrau I's reign was also the cultural climax of the history of the Sasanian empire. As a ruler with manifold interests, it was under him that Iran developed into a centre for the exchange of learning between East and West.[76] However, under Khusrau's son Hormezd IV (after 579) new conflicts were already arising between king and aristocracy, and severe warfare with the Turks aggravated the situation further.[77] The tide seemed to be turning again, however, both internally and externally, when Hormezd's son Khusrau II managed to crush the rebellion of Wahrām Chōbīn, a pretender to the throne, with Byzantine help in 591.[78] Moreover, he was able to reach as far as Egypt[79] and the gates of Constantinople (626) in his war with Byzantium (602–28). The fragments of the True Cross were taken from Jerusalem to Ctesiphon in 614.[80] The counterattack of the Byzantine emperor Heraclius, however, forced the Sasanians to surrender the newly conquered territories.[81] Khusrau II himself was brought down and killed by a revolt of the aristocracy (628). Following a period of

74 See Bosworth (ed.), *The history of al-Ṭabarī*, s.v. Wahriz.

75 Litvinsky, 'The Hephthalite empire', pp. 143–4; Bosworth (ed.), *The history of al-Ṭabarī*, pp. 152–3, 160.

76 Wiesehöfer, *Ancient Persia*, pp. 216–21, 298–300.

77 Bosworth (ed.), *The history of al-Ṭabarī*, s.v. Hurmuz, Hormizd IV. Cf. Whitby, *The emperor Maurice*, *passim*; Rubin, 'Nobility'.

78 A. S. Shahbazi, 'Bahrām VI Čōbīn', *EIr*, vol. III, pp. 519–22; Greatrex and Lieu, *The Roman eastern frontier*, pp. 172ff.; F. Altheim, *Geschichte der Hunnen*, vols. IV–V (Berlin, 1962), pp. 234ff. and Rubin, 'Nobility' (for the Wahrām romance).

79 For the Sasanian occupation of Egypt see R. Altheim-Stiehl, 'The Sasanians in Egypt: Some evidence of historical interest', *Bulletin de la Société d'Archéologie Copte*, 31 (1992); R. Altheim-Stiehl, 'Zur zeitlichen Bestimmung der sāsānidischen Eroberung Ägyptens', in O. Brehm and S. Klie (eds.), *Mousikos Aner. Festschrift für M. Wegner zum 90. Geburtstag* (Bonn, 1992).

80 R. Schick, *The Christian communities of Palestine from Byzantine to Islamic rule: A historical and archaeological study*, Studies in Late Antiquity and Early Islam 2 (Princeton, 1995), pp. 33–9, 46.

81 For Heraclius' Persian war, see now also Greatrex and Lieu, *The Roman eastern frontier*, pp. 198ff.; J. Howard-Johnston, 'Heraclius' Persian campaigns and the revival of the east Roman empire, 622–630', *War in History*, 6 (1999); W. E. Kaegi, *Heraclius: Emperor of Byzantium* (Cambridge, 2003), pp. 122ff. (including G. Greatrex, 'Review of W. E. Kaegi, *Heraclius*', *The Medieval Review* (2004), available at http://quod.lib.umich.edu/cgi/t/text/text-idx?c=tmr;cc=tmr;q1=2004;rgn=main;view=text;idno=baj9928. 0401.028). See also individual articles in G. Reinink and B. Stolte (eds.), *The reign of Heraclius (610–641): Crisis and confrontation* (Louvain, 2002).

anarchy with frequently changing rulers,[82] Yazdgerd III was made king by Rustam's aristocratic party, thus becoming the Sasanians' last ruler. However, the empire had been considerably weakened by wars and the self-interest of various parties, and Yazdgerd III was not able to defend it against the Muslim armies that were penetrating from the Arabian Peninsula. The Persians were indeed defeated, but only after making a real fight of it: after the first Arab attack (in 636), when they overran the irrigated alluvium and laid siege to Ctesiphon-Weh Ardashīr, Yazdgerd's forces staged a counter-attack (in 637) which drove the Arabs back into the desert; it has left a trace in the early Islamic sources, namely the battle of the Bridge; it then probably took several months for the Arabs to regroup, rally additional troops from all over Arabia, and finally dare to confront the Persians in open battle at al-Qādisiyya in Iraq on 6 January 638.[83] Following the defeats at al-Qādisiyya and at Nihāwand in Media (642), Yazdgerd retired to eastern Iran, where he was assassinated at Marw (651).[84] The Sasanian empire became part of the caliphate.

When attempting to assess the reasons for the fall of Sasanian rule, the following should be noted.[85] First, Sasanian defences, both natural and man-made, were strong: the outer line, the Euphrates fronted by forts, was much shorter than that of the Romans, who also had no convenient river to hold, except along the Jordan valley; the Euphrates line was backed by the Tigris (not forgetting the many canals to be crossed in the alluvium) and, behind the Tigris, by the Zagros. The main fighting force, the army which had conquered the Roman Near East, had not been defeated when it was withdrawn east under the terms of the agreement made between Heraclius and its commander, Shahrbarāz. Heraclius had achieved complete strategic surprise when he suddenly struck south across the Caucasus in autumn 627; the army which he defeated at Nineveh was a relatively small, scratch force sent north to bar the route to Ctesiphon. Of course, defeat in the war against the Romans must have had a devastating effect, but it was primarily political. It must have been a terrible

82 For the queens Pūrān and Āzarmīgdukht see A. Panaino, 'Women and kingship. Some remarks about the enthronisation of Queen Bōrān and her sister *Āzarmīgduxt', in Wiesehöfer and Huyse (eds.), *Ērān ud Anērān*.

83 This revised chronology is indebted to intensive discussions with J. Howard-Johnston (Oxford).

84 For the Arab conquest of Iran and the end of the Sasanian empire see Bosworth (ed.), *The history of al-Ṭabarī*, pp. 381–411.

85 The following points of argument are again strongly influenced by discussions with J. Howard-Johnston.

shock to the whole Sasanian governing class. At one moment they could contemplate something close to world dominance, with the Roman empire liquidated and the *shāhānshāh*'s authority extended to the whole basin of the east Mediterranean, from Egypt to Asia Minor, beyond which lay a series of minor sub-Roman, Germanic power, potentially open to Sasanian influence; the next, all of this had been suddenly snatched from them, when the age-old enemy from the steppes, Tūrān in the modern guise of the Turks, intervened to decisive effect. The immediate crisis, involving competing bids for the throne, may have been short, but in the longer term serious damage must have been caused to collective confidence. How could Iran cope for generation after generation if it were to remain caught between the great powers of the steppes and the west?

Second, Khusrau II's abrogation of Lakhm kingship – a bold, apparently foolish act, which was probably intended to prepare the way for a new system of multiple client princes to be introduced after the conquest of the Roman Near East – obviously weakened the outermost defence of Iran against the desert, provoking serious disturbances among neighbouring Bedouin tribes and providing an opportunity for the *umma* to exploit.

Third, regional particularism was to become a serious weakness, once the prestige of the crown was seriously harmed – after the battles of al-Qādisiyya and Nihāwand.

Fourth, it was Arab strength rather than Sasanian weakness that was the principal factor. It was a combination of (a) the driving faith of the Muslim community; (b) the well-developed statecraft and organisational capability of Mecca; (c) distant horizons of vision on the part of the leaders of the *umma*; and (d) the priority given to the conquest of Iran that generated and sustained an external force great enough to overwhelm the resources of the Sasanians and to overrun the whole of Iran within twenty years of the Prophet's death. The reasons for the priority for the conquest of Iran rather than the rump of the Roman empire might be the following: (a) it was Iran that had posed a steadily growing threat to the Ḥijāz throughout the Prophet's lifetime; (b) Islam acknowledged its affinity with Christianity, but could not but set itself against Zoroastrian dualism; (c) Iraq was much more exposed to counter-attack across the Zagros than was Palestine, shielded as it was by Syria to the north. The issue of priority is crucial. For it is plain that Byzantium was ripe for the taking by the early 650s, and that it was ultimately saved by the outbreak of civil strife within the caliphate in 656. Then, and only then, were the Byzantines able to revive their spirits and reactivate the ideology of a Christian, Roman, world-shaping power.

The 'King of Kings of Iran and Non-Iran' and his subjects[86]

It was a decidedly Iranian (as opposed to Parthian) attitude that characterised the Sasanian image of the ruler and his qualities. Ardashīr had put himself above all other dynasties of Ērānshahr as the 'King of Kings of Iran', while his son Shāpūr even included newly conquered territories (Anērān, or 'Non-Iran') and their dynasts.[87] The Sasanians also presented themselves as kings with divine qualities (MpI *bayān*) and as descendants and tools of the gods (*yazdān*).[88] Out of appreciation for the gods' favours, the Sasanian kings adopted the Zoroastrian cult, bestowed benefits on priests, founded 'fires', and thus multiplied places of worship.[89] 'Fires' were also established as 'Fires of Kings' and for the spiritual welfare and salvation of living and dead members of the royal household (cf. below).[90] Individual rulers derived their legitimacy not only through their descent but also through the 'divine grace' (Mid. Pers. *xwarrah*),[91] already known to us from the Parthians, and through their personal effort in war and at the hunt.[92] The dynasty in general derived its legitimacy by the invocation of earlier heads of the clan, and even kings of Iran the Sasanids themselves no longer knew by name, but whom they described as their 'forebears' (Gk. *pappoi*)

86 See Wiesehöfer, *Ancient Persia*, pp. 165–82, 287–91.

87 Among others ŠKZ 1/1/1. For the titles of (early) Sasanian kings, Huyse, *Die dreisprachige Inschrift*, vol. II, pp. 9b–11b and P. Huyse, 'Die sasanidische Königstitulatur: Eine Gegenüberstellung der Quellen', in Wiesehöfer and Huyse (eds.), *Ērān ud Anērān*.

88 Among others ŠKZ 1/1/1. W. Sundermann, '*Kē čihr az yazdān*: Zur Titulatur der Sasanidenkönige', *Archiv Orientalni*, 56 (1988); H. Humbach, 'Herrscher, Gott und Gottessohn in Iran und in angrenzenden Ländern', in D. Zeller (ed.), *Menschwerdung Gottes: Vergöttlichung von Herrschern* (Fribourg and Göttingen, 1988); A. Panaino, 'The baγān of the Fratarakas: Gods or "divine" kings?', in C. G. Cereti, M. Maggi and E. Provasi (eds.), *Religious themes and texts of pre-Islamic Iran and Central Asia: Studies in honour of Prof. Gherardo Gnoli on the occasion of his 65th birthday on 6th December 2002*, Beiträge zur Iranistik 24 (Wiesbaden, 2003).

89 See ŠKZ 22/17/38. See also K. Mosig-Walburg, *Die frühen sasanidischen Könige als Vertreter und Förderer der zarathustrischen Religion: Eine Untersuchung der zeitgenössischen Quellen* (Frankfurt and Bern, 1982).

90 ŠKZ 22ff./17ff./39ff. M. Macuch, 'Charitable foundations, I', *EIr*, vol. V, pp. 380–2; for the 'fires of kings' and other fires, see Huyse, *Die dreisprachige Inschrift*, vol. II, pp. 102b–3a, 105b–7a.

91 G. Gnoli, *The idea of Iran: An essay on its origin*, Serie Orientale Roma 62 (Rome, 1989), pp. 148–51; A. Hintze, *Der Zamyād-Yašt: Edition, Übersetzung, Kommentar*, Beiträge zur Iranistik 15 (Wiesbaden, 1994), pp. 15–17.

92 P. Gignoux, 'La chasse dans l'Iran sasanide', in G. Gnoli (ed.), *Essays and lectures*, vol. III: *Orientalia Romana* (Rome, 1983); M. Whitby, 'The Persian king at war', in E. Dabrowa (ed.), *The Roman and Byzantine army in the east: Proceedings of a colloquium held at the Jagiellonian University, Kraków in September 1992* (Crakow, 1994), pp. 227–63.

or their 'ancestors' (Gk. *progonoi*).[93] Later they would even associate themselves with the mythical kings of Iran, and in the Iranian 'national history', which they themselves decisively helped shape, they thus became the Iranian rulers par excellence, alongside the East Iranian Kayānids, who, like the mythical kings, are also not verifiable historically. They live on in Firdawsī and Niẓāmī's epics, just as in Islamic chronicles and popular literature. The Sasanians also created their own legend at the expense of the Arsacids, whose legitimate share in the Iranian success story was deliberately downgraded (see below).[94]

Just like the Parthians, the Sasanians held an aristocratic 'council of the king', which was composed of the heads of old Parthian and new south-west Iranian (that is to say, Persian) clans, and the aim of which was to confirm the rules for succession to the throne.[95] A special kind of worship of the founder of the empire can also be made out in their case.[96] Royal inscriptions of the early period distinguish between four specific 'groups' of aristocrats: the (Middle Persian) *šahrdārān* (regional dynasts and princes entrusted with rule over important parts of the empire), the *wāspuhragān* (probably members of the Sasanian dynasty, but without direct descent from the ruler), the *wuzurgān* (heads of the most important aristocratic families, as well as other members of the high aristocracy), and the *āzādān* (other noble Iranians).[97] The status of a Parthian or Persian aristocrat was, for a long time, virtually independent of the king's favour. He owed it, including all external signs of his dignity (such as tiaras with crest-like symbols, belts, earrings), to his name and descent; his

93 ŠKZ 21/16/35. For the partly different opinions on the identification of these ancestors, see T. Daryaee, 'National history or Keyanid history? The nature of Sasanid Zoroastrian historiography', *Iranian Studies*, 28 (1995); T. Daryaee, 'Memory and history: The reconstruction of the past in Late Antique Persia', *Nâme-ye Irân-e Bâstân*, 1, 2 (2001–2); A. S. Shahbazi, 'Early Sasanians' claim to Achaemenid heritage', *Nâme-ye Irân-e Bâstân*, 1, 1 (2001); P. Huyse, 'La revendication de territories achéménides par les Sassanides: Une réalité historique?', in P. Huyse (ed.), *Iran: Questions et connaissances: Actes du IVe congrès européen des études iraniennes organisé par la Societas Iranologica Europaea, t. 1: La période ancienne*, Studia Iranica, Cahier 25 (Paris, 2002); J. Wiesehöfer, 'Gebete für die "Urahnen" oder: Wann und wie verschwanden Kyros und Dareios aus der Tradition Irans?', in E. Dabrowa (ed.), *Tradition and innovation in the ancient world*, Electrum 6 (Crakow, 2002); and E. Kettenhofen, 'Die Einforderung der achaimenidischen Territorien durch die Sāsāniden: Eine Bilanz', in S. Kurz (ed.), *Festschrift I. Khalifeh-Soltani zum 65. Geburtstag* (Aachen, 2002). See also T. Daryaee, 'The construction of the past in Late Antique Persia', *Historia*, 55 (2006).

94 Yarshater, 'Iranian national history'.

95 NPi 33/29f.; 36f./33f.; 37f./34. P. O. Skjaervø, 'Commentary', in Humbach and Skjaervø, *The Sassanian inscription*, p. 13; Sundermann, 'Review', pp. 84–5.

96 NPi 31f./28f.

97 Among others NPi 2f./2f. For the hierarchical classes, cf. Sundermann, 'Review', p. 84; Rubin, 'Nobility', pp. 243ff.

rank was thus a sign of his special political and economic position.[98] This only changed in the later period, in particular due to Khusrau I's reforms, which not only extended direct taxation of the land to the possessions of the landowning aristocracy, but also defined the position of the ruler vis-à-vis the aristocracy in a fundamentally new way, with a new order for the court, the aristocracy and the armed forces (at least for a short while).[99] This was also the time when kings attached particular importance to the education of young court aristocrats (cf. *Husraw ud rēdag*)[100] as well as to an ever more elaborate court etiquette.[101] Female members of the royal family were granted a particular degree of esteem and attention in the Iranian sources of the third century .[102] A title such as 'Queen of Queens' (MpI *bāmbišnān bāmbišn*) is thus confirmation of the unique rank of the woman who carried it, and not a sign of the king's close or incestuous consanguineous marriage, which is certainly known to us from Sasanian Iran.[103]

Next to the aristocracy, it was religious dignitaries who carried special importance in the empire. These – Zoroastrian – 'priests' (*mōbads, hērbeds*) were not only experts in matters of religion (e.g. through the upholding of the religious tradition), but also in matters of administration and the law (as *dādwars*, i.e. 'judges'). Christians, for example, would get to know them as harsh judges in their trials. A real hierarchy of offices and functions, however, only developed from the fourth century on, in imitation of monarchical power. This hierarchy reached from simple officials on the ground, to the 'chief of the *mōbads*' (Syr. *rēš mauḥpātē*) at the top.[104]

98 Cf. Ammianus Marcellinus, *Rerum gestarum libri*, 18.5.6; KKZ 4/KNRm 9f./KSM 5; Procopius, *De bello Persico*, 1.6.13,13.16. For the signs of dignity see von Gall, *Das Reiterkampfbild*, pp. 23–6; Peck, 'Clothing, IV'.

99 See Theophylact Simocatta, *Historia*, 1.9,3.8; Procopius, *De bello Persico*, 1.17.26–28; al-Ṭabarī, *Ta'rīkh*, series I, p. 990, lines 16f.; al-Dīnawarī, *al-Akhbār aṭ-ṭiwāl*, ed. Vladimir Guirgass, Leiden, 1888, p. 85, line 6f.

100 J. M. Unvala, *Der Pahlavi-Text 'Der König Husrav und sein Knabe'* (Heidelberg, 1917).

101 Wiesehöfer, *Ancient Persia*, pp. 221–300; A. de Jong, '*Sub Specie Maiestatis*: Reflections on Sasanian court rituals', in M. Stausberg (ed.), *Zoroastrian ritual in context* (Leiden, 2004).

102 E.g. ŠKZ 23/18/39;25/20/46f.; 29/23/56. For the women of the royal family (and late Sasanian queens) see Wiesehöfer, *Ancient Persia*, pp. 174–5, 289–90, as well as Panaino, 'Women and kingship'.

103 M. Macuch, 'Inzest im vorislamischen Iran', *Archäologische Mitteilungen aus Iran*, 24 (1991); Wiesehöfer, *Ancient Persia*, pp. 181–2, 291; for Byzantine reactions to such relationships, see A. D. Lee, 'Close-kin marriage in Late Antique Mesopotamia', *Greek, Roman and Byzantine Studies*, 29 (1988).

104 For religious dignitaries and officials see P. Gignoux, 'Éléments de prosopographie de quelques mobads sasanides', *JA*, 270 (1982); P. Gignoux, 'Die religiöse Administration in sasanidischer Zeit: Ein Überblick', in H. Koch and D. N. MacKenzie (eds.), *Kunst, Kultur und Geschichte der Achämenidenzeit und ihr Fortleben* (Berlin, 1983); and P. Gignoux, 'Pour une esquisse des fonctions religieuses sous les Sasanides', *JSAI*, 7 (1986). For the position

Lower state functionaries, craftsmen, city merchants, physicians, astronomers, 'scientists' and 'singers', as well as the professional servants and staff of the court and the estates of the aristocracy, must be counted among the 'middle classes' of the empire.[105] Peasants represented the great bulk of Iran's population. But it was those lessees who for centuries had been the aristocracy's bondsmen who profited in particular from Khusrau's reforms, as they advanced to become free tillers of their own plots of land.[106]

Although legally defined as 'objects', in the Sasanian empire slaves were also seen as human beings, which distinguished them from other property, and, at the same time, protected them from excessively cruel treatment. This did not save them from being sold, rented or given as gifts, of course, and the products of a slave's labour would also always belong to his or her owner.[107]

Late Sasanian legal manuals also tell us a great deal about 'the household and family' at the time.[108] The members of a household, who represented a legal unit, as well as a unit of production and consumption, and a religious entity, were connected to each other through a wealth of regulations and responsibilities, control over which was usually in the hands of the *kadag-xwadāy* (the 'master of the house'). Detailed regulations also characterised marital law and the law of inheritance, as well as property law and the law of obligations.[109]

The royal court

The prime importance of the royal family at the Sasanian court is always apparent. First, the *res gestae* of both Shāpūr I (ŠKZ) and Narseh (NPi), which contain lists of court personalities graded in order of rank, give first rank to the members of the royal family, including queens and other 'ladies' (MpI *bānūg*).[110] It has rightly been stressed that social, not family, status was

of Kerdir under the early Sasanians, see P. Huyse, 'Kerdīr and the first Sasanians', in N. Sims-Williams (ed.), *Proceedings of the Third European Conference of Iranian Studies, held in Cambridge, 11th to 15th September 1995*, part 1 (Wiesbaden, 1998).

105 Wiesehöfer, *Ancient Persia*, pp. 176, 290; for 'singers', see V. S. Curtis, 'Minstrels in ancient Iran', in Curtis, Hillenbrand and Rogers (eds.), *The art and archaeology of ancient Persia*.

106 Wiesehöfer, *Ancient Persia*, pp. 176–7, 290–1.

107 M. Macuch, 'Barda and Bardadārī II', *EIr*, vol. III, pp. 763–6.

108 For Sasanian legal manuals and their function see the excellent work of M. Macuch, *Rechtskasuistik und Gerichtspraxis zu Beginn des siebenten Jahrhunderts in Iran*, Iranica 1 (Wiesbaden, 1993).

109 Ibid., *passim*; see also A. Perikhanian, 'Iranian society and law', in Yarshater (ed.), *The Cambridge history of Iran*, vol. III, part 2.

110 Many of those personalities have already prosopographically been dealt with by U. Weber, *Prosopographie des frühen Sasanidenreiches* (Kiel, 2004), available at www.uni-kiel.de/klassalt/projekte/sasaniden/index.html.

responsible for a man or woman's rank both in the royal genealogy and in the royal household. Female members of the royal family appear on the royal reliefs as well as on coins; they are also immortalised on gems and seals of their own. Both the epigraphically proven rank of queens, consorts and princesses and those works of art testify to the important social role of the women of the royal household; thus it is no longer surprising that shortly before the fall of the empire, women could even ascend the throne, as was the case with Pūrān and her sister Āzarmīgdukht, even if this happened for lack of male candidates.[111]

Second, the rule of succession to the throne was strictly patrilineal and restricted to members of the Sasanian family. The crises over the succession that arose in the third (Narseh vs. Wahrām III), fourth (Ardashīr II vs. Shāpūr III), and sixth centuries (Wistahm vs. Khusrau II) all demonstrate that these rules could not easily be circumvented. As already mentioned, rightful birth and election by predecessor were only two of the necessary prerequisites for ruling; there was also the idea that the future king should have divine grace (*xwarrah*), i.e. the necessary charisma of kingship.[112] In the inscriptions of the early kings, legitimacy could also be established by reference to preceding rulers, thus, in Shāpūr's case, by reference to his father Ardashīr, his grandfather Pābag, to the eponymous Sāsān, or even to the former great kings of Iran (the legendary Kayānids?).[113]

Third, as is shown by the title *māzdēsn bay kē čihr az yazdān* ('Mazdean divine Lord, whose origin [is] from the gods') for the reigning *shāhānshāh* ('King of Kings') in ŠKZ, the Sasanian kings stress the Mazdean quality of their royal power and their own divine nature (which, however, is different from that of the *yazdān*, i.e. Ohrmezd and the other gods).[114] The other male members of the royal family did not share this title with the reigning (and with the deceased) king(s). Fourth, Shāpūr I founded fire-temples 'for his own soul and glory' (*pad amā ruwān ud pannām*) and for the souls and the glory of his relatives and deceased ancestors, and endowed them with the necessary means. Apart from their social functions – material help for relatives and friends and provision of a special 'pension' for the founder's descendants – such endowments were also meant to provide the donor with prestige, to

111 Panaino, 'Women and kingship'.
112 See G. Gnoli, 'Farr(ah)', *EIr*, vol. IX, pp. 312–19.
113 For different identifications of those 'ancestors' and 'forefathers' see Daryaee, 'National history'; Daryaee, 'Memory and history'; Shahbazi, 'Early Sasanians' claim'; Wiesehöfer, 'Gebete'; Huyse, 'La revendication'; Kettenhofen, 'Die Einforderung'.
114 Panaino, 'The bayān of the Fratarakas', pp. 276–83.

establish his subjects' trust and loyalty and to maintain social structures of order. The deceased members of the royal family even became objects of organised worship, analogous to the Greek cult of dead heroes.[115] The fire-temples were normally named after their founders and benefactors (for example, the fire-temple founded by Shāpūr I for his own soul and glory was given the name *Husraw-Shābuhr* ('Glorious is Shāpūr')). Finally, consanguineous marriage (*xwēdōdah*), which the Zoroastrian theologians deemed meritorious and the Sasanians actually practised, served not only to keep property within the family but also to secure kingship by maintaining endogamy within the clan.[116] However, not all royal marriages were incestuous, as external alliances for political reasons are also recorded.

Both the royal inscriptions and Manichaean texts make it clear that not all members of the royal household were permanent members of the royal court; in particular, the king's grown-up sons (and other important relatives) were only temporarily in the ruler's personal vicinity, i.e. if their administrative duties or special occasions, such as festivities or wars, made it necessary to be present at court, or if the 'travelling king' with his entourage happened to come to a prince's province. Thus we may distinguish between a 'nuclear' court of permanent members and an 'extended' court of temporarily present people. It would appear that in early Sasanian times the 'nuclear' court mainly consisted of members of the royal family and household, with the great aristocratic landholders and magnates being part of the 'extended' court, since their main sphere of activity at that time was the management of their estates and the control of the peasants and tenant farmers dependent on them (see below).

In connection with the common duty to offer sacrifices for the benefit of the souls of the living and the dead, Shāpūr's *res gestae* list the contemporary members of the four aristocratic status groups mentioned above, as far as they were members of the ('extended') court society, both by their names and, if they held office, by their functions at court or in the empire. In early Sasanian times social ranking certainly also manifested itself at court, but, as far as the nobility is concerned, it was not only the court's head – the king – who set the rules of that ranking: descent could be still as important as royal favour. The fact that the Sasanians had not created these 'structures of standing' themselves, but had taken them over from the Parthians – while at the

115 Macuch, 'Charitable foundations'; M. Macuch, 'Die sasanidische Stiftung "für die Seele": Vorbild für den islamischen waqf?', in P. Vavroušek (ed.), *Iranian and Indo-European studies: Memorial volume of Otakar Klíma* (Prague, 1994); M. Stausberg, *Die Religion Zarathushtras*, vol. I (Stuttgart, 2002), pp. 219–20.

116 Wiesehöfer, *Ancient Persia*, pp. 180, 291.

same time enhancing the rank of the Persian, i.e. south-west Iranian, aristocracy – is proven by the end of the 'formula' in which the groups of nobility are presented in the Pāikūlī inscription: 'The landholders and the princes, the grandees and the nobles and the Persians and the Parthians'.[117] The loyal Parthian clans warranted continuity, but were now complemented by Persian clans without having to give up their leading position. At a later period, other 'clans' rose to the rank of magnates.

Depending on their social, political and economic standing, the high aristocracy was also able to play an advisory and corroborative role in the process of proclaiming the king: for Narseh and his predecessors, we might assume a 'mock consultation' of the highest dignitaries of the empire, documenting an ancient right of co-determination – or, rather, confirmation – held by the nobility.[118] In times of a powerful central authority, apart from the members of the royal household and of the higher and lower aristocracy, 'outsiders' and 'new men' had a good chance of being promoted to a position close to the king at the 'nuclear' court by arbitrary royal patronage.[119] A special exemplar of such a *homo novus* was the already mentioned ambitious Zoroastrian 'priest' Kerdīr, who, from the time of Shāpūr I to the time of Wahrām II, rose to great importance at court, and was even able to tell us about his promotion by means of inscriptions, which were carved into the rock façades or walls of important 'royal' places and monuments: 'The King of Kings Hormezd [i.e. the son of Shāpūr I] bestowed on me the tiara (*kulāf*) and the belt (*kamar*), and he raised my position (*gāh* ['throne', i.e. the place near the king]) and my dignity' (*pthšly*).[120] Kerdīr is a living example of a dignitary who started his career as a rather humble 'courtier', passed on to an extremely high position, not least because of his special abilities and the way he made himself indispensable, and probably lost his influence in the course of a new king's accession to the throne. It was his closeness to the king (i.e. the position of his *gāh* at royal declarations, audiences and banquets) and the function he fulfilled that reflected a person's standing at the early Sasanian court, and outward dress made it manifest to a broader public. Among the most prominent marks of dignity were the tiaras (*kulāf*), on which certain colours and symbols of a heraldic kind could point to

117 NPi 3 (§ 5) etc.
118 See Skjærvø, 'Commentary', p. 13, and Sundermann, 'Review', pp. 84–5. A 'king's council' is mentioned in NPi § 68, the 'sham consultation' in NPi §§ 73 and 75.
119 Ammianus Marcellinus, *Rerum gestarum libri*, 18.5.6.
120 KKZ 4/KNRm 9f./KSM 5 (in Gignoux, *Les quatre inscriptions*).

particular ranks or distinctions. Belts (*kamar*) studded with gems and earrings played a similar part.[121]

For the Iranian aristocracy, however, the real criterion for grandeur was for a long time not so much a title or royal distinction but lineage, and in times of crisis or during the reigns of 'weak' kings the higher nobility could even force a ruler to acknowledge established career structures. A respective case study is presented by Procopius for the extremely crisis-prone reign of King Kawād (fifth/sixth century), the father of the famous Khusrau I: 'He [Kawād] was mindful of the rule that did not allow the Persians to transfer any offices (*archai*) to strangers, but only to such men who were entitled to the respective position of honour (*timē*) through their lineage.'[122]

As we have seen, the rank of a Parthian or Persian nobleman had been more or less independent of the king's favour before the end of the fifth century; until then, the unruly heads of the great noble houses (such as Sūrēn, Kārin, the Lords of Andēgān and others) acknowledged only a nominal allegiance to the central power but were virtually independent from the king in their hereditary territorial domains, and royal power and influence depended to a large degree on effective control of the provincial governors (who were mostly members of the royal clan), as well as on the active support of the majority of the higher nobles. This changed only in the late Sasanian period, when the wearing of belts, rings, clasps and other marks of prestige required royal approval. As the Byzantine author Theophylactus maintains, (bestowed) rank now came to be esteemed more highly than name and descent.[123] This strengthening of royal power had become possible after the great crisis of state and empire that began in the mid-fifth century.[124] Crucial factors of the crisis were the disastrous defeats of Fīrūz I (r. 459–84) against the Hepthalites in the east, leading to tributary dependence on the Hepthalite 'state', in addition to several years

121 Peck, 'Clothing'.

122 Procopius, *De bello Persico*, 1.6.13; cf. 1.13.16 (Mihran is in fact the name of a noble clan).

123 Theophylact Simocatta, *Historia*, 1.9. 'Since it is a familiar habit of Persians to bear names according to distinguished positions, as if they disdained to be called by their birth names.' See Procopius, *De bello Persico*, 1.17.26–18 (a Mihran is punished by being deprived of a golden hairband: 'For in that country no one is allowed to wear a ring or a belt, a clasp or any other object of gold without royal bestowal'). For other examples see al-Ṭabarī, *Ta'rīkh*, series I, p. 990, lines 16f.; Theophylact Simocatta, *Historia*, 3.8; and al-Dīnawarī, *al-akhbār aṭ-ṭiwāl*, p. 85, lines 6f.

124 That the fifth and sixth centuries was a crucial period in Sasanian history is proven by the fact that a lot of important political developments as regards home affairs occurred during that time: the development of a hierarchical Zoroastrian clergy on the model of political power; a change in dynastic legitimisation which stresses the mythological Kayānid link, etc.

of drought and famine. Meanwhile, the twofold burden imposed on the peasants by landlords and state taxes, on the one hand, and the Hepthalite occupation of parts of the country, on the other, had led to a rural exodus and protests on the part of the peasant population. The latter had found a religious and ethical motivation for such actions in the social doctrine of Mazdak, especially in his call for communal ownership. King Kawād's wish to establish his son Khusrau as successor to the throne in the 520s put an end to the long collaboration between the ruler and the followers of Mazdak, and led to violent actions by the Mazdakites against the land-owning aristocracy, which were brutally suppressed by Kawād and Khusrau.[125] The subsequent reforms by the two kings were of a fundamental nature.[126] They not only extended direct land taxation to the estates of the landed aristocracy but, by establishing a new order for the nobility and the army, tried to change the empire's social structure and the position of the ruler with respect to the aristocracy: both the restoring of their old property to the nobility and the giving away of estates that no longer had owners were measures carried out at the behest of the king. In addition, a kind of 'administrative nobility' was created, and, in the case of the 'cavaliers' (MP *aswārān*), a military nobility whose duty was to follow the king in his campaigns. The latter was apparently meant to replace the retainer units formed by self-equipped members of the aristocracy, troops that had never really been at the king's command. Arab authors also introduce a new (or newly emerged) lower nobility, the *dehkānān*, who took over the administration of a village as its richest landowners, and sometimes even owned entire villages. These had been promoted by the king, who had granted them land, money and other assistance. They were to be his partisans on a local level (as against members of the high aristocracy, who were critical of the king, and the potentially rebellious peasantry), and were also, if necessary, to stand by him in military matters.[127] Al-Ṭabarī's report of Khusrau's reforms, quoted above, is quite unambiguous about the fact that the late Sasanian court underwent a change, too: whereas the 'nuclear' court had so far been determined by

125 For the Mazdakites see Sundermann, 'Mazdak'; Guidi and Morony, 'Mazdak'; Rubin, 'The reforms'; Gnoli, 'Nuovi studi'; and Wiesehöfer, 'Chusro I'.

126 For the reforms of Khusrau see the different opinions of Altheim and Stiehl, *Finanzgeschichte*, esp. pp. 31ff., Grignaschi, 'La riforma'; Howard-Johnston, 'The two great powers', pp. 211ff.; Rubin, 'The reforms'; and Wiesehöfer, *Ancient Persia*, pp. 190–1, 292–3.

127 For the 'cavaliers' and *dehkānān* see F. Altheim and R. Stiehl, *Ein asiatischer Staat* (Wiesbaden, 1954), pp. 129ff.; Altheim and Stiehl, *Finanzgeschichte*, pp. 57ff.

members of the king's personal household (family members and domestic staff), the other higher nobles being only temporarily members of the ('extended') court, Khusrau's 'nuclear' court now consisted both of royal relatives and of members of a kind of service nobility (*Dienstadel*), hand-picked and promoted by the ruler himself and more loyal to the king than to the clans they originally came from. It is this kind of court that is mirrored in most of the Middle Persian literary works (see below).

But as early as under Khusrau's immediate successors, renewed tensions arose between king and high aristocracy. It has been suggested that the king soon lost control of the 'cavaliers', who became again retainers of greater and virtually independent landlords, and that right from the start the king's supreme military commanders must have been powerful territorial lords.[128] The renewed political influence of the great landlords not only led, in the course of time, to the development of retinues of fighting men, but also to independent taxation in their own domains. In contrast to such powerful and ambitious nobles, who, as in early Sasanian times, again only temporarily visited the court, the members of the king's 'nuclear' court took the risk of losing their political weight in the case of a weak ruler and of becoming 'courtiers' in the strict sense of the word. Temporarily hindered in their ambitions because Khusrau II had centralised the financial administration, the landed and military aristocracy nevertheless managed to conspire against the king, who was reproached for his tyrannical attitude towards the nobility, his ruinous exaction of land taxes and his bloody wars against Byzantium. After Khusrau's death, kingship remained the instrument of different factions of the aristocracy. The rapid advances of the Muslim army and the sudden collapse of Sasanian sovereignty in Iran present a most eloquent testimony to the paralysing particularism of interests among the leading classes of the empire in this last phase of Iran's pre-Islamic history.

In his *res gestae*, Shāpūr I enumerates the dignitaries, officials and aristocrats of his empire who are, at least temporarily, close to him and in his vicinity at court, and who are therefore entitled to have offerings made for the benefit of their souls. Lists of this kind have come down to us in other inscriptions too, among them one more in the *res gestae* of the second Sasanian king (in which he refers to the reigns of Pābag and

128 Z. Rubin, 'The Sasanid monarchy', in A. Cameron, B. Ward-Perkins and M. Whitby (eds.), *The Cambridge ancient history*, 2nd edn, vol. XIV: *Late Antiquity: Empire and successors, AD 425–600* (Cambridge, 2000), p. 657.

Ardashīr I), and several in Narseh's Pāikūlī inscription. They are all similarly arranged, starting with the members of the royal house, followed by members of the (seven) most important noble clans and ending with other dignitaries and officials. As far as ŠKZ is concerned, the arrangement of names seems to be the result of a special mixture of personal and political considerations of the king; in other words, the list is evidence both for the dignitaries' personal relationships with the king and for Shāpūr's decisions to assign certain people to certain offices because of their characters and/or their professional skills.

Ardashīr, the king of Adiabene, is at the head of the sixty-seven dignitaries of Shāpūr's court. As this man is only mentioned in ŠKZ, we can only guess if he owed his outstanding position to his personal relationship with the king or to the importance of his province at that time, or to both. Probably due to the consolidation of power under the first two Sasanids, the 'extended' royal court increased considerably: whereas the court of King Pābag (Shāpūr's grandfather) had only consisted of eight members, and Ardashīr I had appointed thirty-one dignitaries, Shāpūr I doubled their number. In other words, empire building led to complexity in the court, and generated rationales and structures of its own. It is a pity that we do not have a comparable view of the Arsacid court, which would allow us to recognise the special Sasanian traits of court offices and court society. It is all the more deplorable that we also do not have a similar description of the 'nuclear' or 'extended' late Sasanian court: Byzantine historians go into detail for reports of Persian diplomatic missions to the emperor,[129] but they are rather taciturn the other way round. Even Menander the Guardsman, who says a lot about the content of Byzantine–Sasanian peace talks, does not provide us with a description of Khusrau's court. And the Iranian reports are either of a literary rather than historiographical kind (the contemporary works of Middle Persian literature; see below), or they are New Persian or Arabic adaptations of late Sasanian books (Firdawsī, *Shahnameh* etc.) which should be utilised only with great care, since they are not mere translations but rather epic or historiographical texts furnished in the style of their time of origin or with a special Islamic touch.[130] It is perfectly clear that in order to get an audience with the king in early Sasanian times, people had to go through the proper channels. King Wahrām, then dining with two very close 'friends', as is shown by the king's later gesture of embracement, orders Mani to wait; after the

129 See Constantine Porphyrogenitus, *De caeremoniis aulae Byzantinae*, 1.89f.

130 Abkaʿi-Khavari, *Das Bild des Königs*, although useful for its collection of sources, is quite uncritical in this respect.

end of the meal, he goes over to the waiting 'prophet' and gives him to understand that he is not welcome.

The 'Ardashīr romance' (*Kārnāmag ī Ardaxšīr ī Pābagān*), which was written in the late Sasanian period and subsequently revised,[131] projects the social conditions of the time when it was composed into the period of the empire's founder, and is sometimes considered as a description of the lifestyle of the court of the last Sasanians.[132] It is certainly true that after Khusrau's reforms and the creation of a service nobility, courtly manners were now also practised in the company of the king, the noble youths being royal courtiers and hostages for their fathers' loyalty at the same time. Obedience, elegant manners, culture, games and hunting were required and practised. It is no wonder then that among the late Middle Persian *andarz* texts ('wisdom literature') or their Arabic translations there are a number of works that – in the form of royal declarations, throne speeches or testaments – not only discuss or prescribe the proper character, behaviour and appearance of the king, but also that of his *bandagān* (his subjects) at court (at meals, at special occasions such as festivities, audiences etc.). At the same time, those texts were probably meant to foster the idea of a god-given political and social hierarchy in the empire and at court. The special position of the king[133] manifests itself also in the ruler's dress, jewellery, headgear, crown and throne, his display of luxury[134] and, last but not least, in the splendour and architectural layout of his residential palaces. Thus, the Arab conquerors of Iran in the seventh century were highly impressed by the enormous crown of Khusrau II[135] and by his huge carpet known as 'Khusrau's spring' in his winter residence at al-Madāʾin.[136]

It is also the time of Khusrau I and his successors that Middle Persian texts (such as the famous *Husraw ī kawādān ud rēdag-ē* ('Khusrau and his page'))[137]

131 *Kārnāmag ī Ardaxšīr ī Pābagān*, 2.5,10–12. An excellent edition with a French translation and commentary was published by Grenet (F. Grenet, *La geste d'Ardashir fils de Pâbag: Kārnāmag ī Ardaxšēr ī Pābagān* (Paris, 2001)).

132 For late Sasanian court culture see Altheim, *Geschichte der Hunnen*, vol. V, pp. 195ff.

133 For the titulature of the kings see above.

134 For the respective sources see Abkaʿi-Khavari, *Das Bild des Königs*.

135 For the famous crown of Khusrau II see al-Ṭabarī, *Taʾrīkh*, series I, p. 2446, lines 11ff.

136 Ibid., series I, p. 2452, lines 7ff.: 'Sixty times sixty yards as a single carpet by the dimension of its surface, on which the paths formed figures, the separating parts rivers, the intervals between them hills. On its border earth sown with spring growth out of silk against branches of gold, and its blossoms of gold, silver and the like.' See M. Morony, 'Bahār-e Kesrā', *EIr*, vol. III, p. 479.

137 Edition: J. M. Unvala, *The Pahlavi text King Husrav and his boy: Published with its translation, transcription and copious notes* (Paris, 1921). For the character of the text (and other similar texts) see Cereti, *La letteratura*, pp. 178–84.

present the court as a special place of *savoir vivre*: Waspuhr, a young man, poor and without employment, presents himself to the king, whom he asks to question him in order to test the extent of his knowledge of the most diverse aspects of luxurious living: fine food and tasty fowl, the preparation of jellied meat, ragout, preserves and stewed fruit; music, the scent of flowers; the best women, the best animals to ride and other pleasures. This text not only lists all the arts of military exercise and warfare and every kind of board game, but also all the animals that were hunted by the king and his courtiers: the bull, the wild ass, the stag, the wild boar, the young camel, the calf, buffalo, ass and gazelle, as well as hare and rabbit, partridge, pheasant, lark, crane, bustard, duck and peacock. The references to birds show that hunting, the Iranian royal 'sport' *par excellence*, was practised not only as a test of strength, but also for entertainment and subsequent consumption.[138]

Khusrau's interest in foreign games such as chess – the Middle Persian text *Wizārišn ī čatrang ud nihišn ī nēw-ardaxšīr* tells the story of its introduction to Iran[139] – leads us to his promotion of scholarship and the arts, a common feature in royal ways of self-manifestation and representation. Despite the unmistakable self-praise we notice in Khusrau's *res gestae (kārnāmag)*,[140] the king's efforts for higher learning cannot be denied. Agathias reports that Khusrau had offered hospitality to the Neoplatonic philosophers, who had become homeless after their school in Athens was closed down, and when – disappointed by the country and its inhabitants – they wished to return home, he had granted them exemption from punishment in their own country during his peace negotiations with Byzantium in 532.[141] The king's discussions with Zoroastrian, Christian and other authorities about questions of cosmogony and the end of the world, about God, primary matter and the elements are

138 For the royal hunt see the famous hunting reliefs of the Ṭāq-i Bustān grotto near Kīrmānshāh (K. Tanabe, 'Iconography of the royal-hunt bas-reliefs at Taq-i Bustan', *Orient* (Tokyo), 19 (1983); J. D. Movassat, *The large vault at Taq-i Bustan: A study in late Sasanian royal art* (Lewiston, 2005)).

139 Edition and commentary: A. Panaino, *La novella degli scacchi e della tavola reale: Un'antica fonte orientale sui due giochi da tavoliere più diffusi nel mondo eurasiatico tra Tardoantico e Medioevo e sulla loro simbologia militare e astrale. Testo pahlavi, traduzione e commento al Wizārišn ī čatrang ud nihišn ī nēw-ardaxšīr* (Milan, 1999). Cf. T. Daryaee, 'Mind, body, and the cosmos: Chess and backgammon in ancient Persia', *Iranian Studies*, 35 (2002).

140 Ibn Miskawayh, *The Tajârib al-umam or History of Ibn-Miskaway (Abu 'Ali Ahmad b. Muhammad)*, with a preface and summary by Leone Caetani, E.J. W. Gibb Memorial series 7, Leiden, 1913, pp. 206.4ff.

141 Agathias, *Historiae*, 2.30f. See U. Hartmann, 'Geist im Exil: Römische Philosophen am Hof der Sasaniden', in M. Schuol, U. Hartmann and A. Luther (eds.), *Grenzüberschreitungen: Formen des Kontakts zwischen Orient und Okzident im Altertum*, OrOcc 3 (Stuttgart, 2002).

famous.[142] Khusrau's interest in the East is shown by his initiative in commissioning a translation of a version of the Indian book of fables, the *Panchatantra*, which the physician Burzoy had brought from India.[143] Besides philosophy, theology and statesmanship, Khusrau was also interested in foreign contributions to law and medicine. Aside from medical inspirations from the West, Iranian and Indian traditions were also assimilated. Burzōy, himself a physician from Nīshāpūr, reports about them in his introduction to the collection of fables. According to an Arabic source, Khusrau I even wrote a medical book himself, or rather compiled it from Greek and Indian works. It was through the Sasanian–Middle Persian intermediary that not only medical and pharmaceutical literature from East and West, but also Romano-Byzantine agricultural writings and the *Almagest* of Ptolemy, found their way into Arabic literature.[144]

The late Sasanian period was altogether a time of literary flowering, much of it commissioned or sponsored by the royal court. Khusrau I Anūshirwān and his successors are credited with having especially contributed to promoting literature: thus Weh-Shāpūr, the head of the Zoroastrian clergy under Khusrau I, is said to have published the twenty-one *nasks* of the Avesta, and the *X^{w}adāy-nāmag* (the 'Book of Lords'), the semi-official 'Iranian national history', apparently existed in an initial authoritative version in Khusrau's reign and was later repeatedly revised (and continued).

142 Wiesehöfer, *Ancient Persia*, pp. 217, 299.

143 F. de Blois, *Burzōy's voyage to India and the origin of the Book of Kalilah wa Dimna* (London, 1990).

144 For the intermediary role of Sasanian Iran in philosophy, medicine, religion, mythology, magic, technical knowledge, law and science see P. Gignoux, 'Prolégomènes pour une histoire des idées de l'Iran sassanide: Convergences et divergences', in Wiesehöfer and Huyse (eds.), *Ērān ud Anērān*; R. Gyselen (ed.), *La science des cieux: Sages, mages, astrologues*, Res Orientales 12 (Bures-sur-Yvette, 1999); R. Gyselen (ed.), *Charmes et sortilèges: Magie et magiciens*, Res Orientales 14 (Bures-sur-Yvette, 2002); A. Panaino, 'Greci e Iranici: Confronto e conflitti', in S. Settis (ed.), *I Greci*, vol. III: *I Greci oltre la Grecia* (Torino, 2001); Z. Rubin, 'Res Gestae Divi Saporis: Greek and Middle Iranian in a document of Sasanian anti-Roman propaganda', in J. N. Adams, M. Janse and S. Swain (eds.), *Bilingualism in ancient society: Language contact and the written text* (Oxford, 2002); R. M. Schneider, 'Orientalism in Late Antiquity: The Oriental other in imperial and Christian imagery', in Wiesehöfer and Huyse (eds.), *Ērān ud Anērān*; M. Ullmann, *Islamic medicine* (Edinburgh, 1978); L. Richter-Bernburg, 'On the diffusion of medical knowledge in Persian court culture during the fourth and fifth centuries AH', in Z. Vezel *et al.* (eds.), *La science dans le monde iranien à l'époque islamique* (Tehran, 1998); L. Richter-Bernburg, 'Iran's contribution to medicine and veterinary science in Islam AH 100–900/AD 700–1500', in J. A. C. Greppin *et al.* (eds.), *The diffusion of Greco-Roman medicine into the Middle East and the Caucasus* (Delmar, 1999); L. Richter-Bernburg , 'Medicine, pharmacology and veterinary science in Islamic eastern Iran and Central Asia', in C. E. Bosworth and M. S. Asimov (eds.), *History of civilizations of Central Asia*, vol. IV: *The age of achievement: AD 750 to the end of the fifteenth century*, part 2: *The achievements* (Paris, 2000).

And finally, numerous compilations of *andarz* texts, as we have seen, and even the publication of treatises of this nature of his own, are attributed to Anūshirwān and his entourage.

Although former studies on Sasanian 'feudalism' very often drew unjustified and inaccurate parallels between Sasanian Iran and the medieval European monarchies, the theoretical parameters of studies on late medieval and early modern courts proved to be quite useful for cutting a swathe through the source material on the Sasanian court and on power and 'state building' in Sasanian Iran. However, a lot of work is still to be done: we urgently need fresh analyses of the Arabic and New Persian texts in the light of the extant late Sasanian and the contemporary Byzantine and Syriac literature, and a closer look at possible Iranian influence on Byzantine court institutions (and vice versa). And we would greatly appreciate further philological studies on the Middle Persian and Parthian vocabulary and word fields of 'court', 'rank' and 'dignity', as well as archaeological work on palace architecture and royal representation.[145]

Petty kings, satraps, craftsmen, merchants and soldiers

Sasanian royal inscriptions of the third century, as well as seal legends of later times, mention a host of dignitaries and officials. These included, for instance, 'petty kings' (MP *šāh*) in certain regions of the empire, such as Armenia and Mesene, 'satraps' (*šahrab*) in other provinces (*šahr*), their personal assistants, as well as the officials in the 'districts', and those on the ground. As we have heard, the royal court also maintained numerous functionaries and dignitaries at all times. There were administrative, military and educational functionaries and advisers, as well as those active in the fields of etiquette and the cult.[146] As already mentioned, following the reforms of Khusrau, most of these officials no longer represented the interests of their own families, but were now accountable to the king alone. In early Sasanian times some parts of the land were under the direct

145 But see Marion Hoffmann, 'Sasanidische Palastarchitektur' (Munich University, 2006), available at http://edoc.ub.uni-muenchen.de/9439/.

146 Important works on this topic are R. Gyselen, *La géographie administrative de l'empire sassanide: Les témoignages sigillographiques* (Paris, 1989) and R. Gyselen, *Nouveaux matériaux pour la géographie historique de l'empire sassanide: Sceaux administratifs de la collection Ahmad Saeedi*, Studia Iranica, Cahier 24 (Paris, 2002); see also Wiesehöfer, *Ancient Persia*, pp. 183ff., 291ff.

control of the king, while royal control (i.e. collection of taxes, conscription into the army) affected other parts of the land, namely those in the possession of the aristocracy, only by proxy. While at that time rulers could only found cities on 'royal land', the weakening of the aristocracy through the revolts of the late fifth century allowed the kings to turn land belonging to the aristocracy into royal land.[147] The fiscal reforms of Khusrau I (see above), which established fixed poll-taxes and land-taxes (Ar. *jizya* and *kharāj*), led, albeit only temporarily, to a strengthening of royal power, as well as a relaxation on the 'fiscal front'. They provided the king with greater leeway politically, in both the domestic and foreign arenas. The patronage of the sciences, arts and literature, as well as the renewed animosity towards Byzantium, can thus be explained.

As with virtually all states of Antiquity, agriculture was the fundamental economic activity in the Sasanian empire.[148] Apart from this, many subjects of the 'King of kings' earned their livelihood in the various crafts, in royal 'workshops', as well as in small private businesses. Many of the professionals employed by the king were men who had been deported from Syria and other regions and resettled in Iran during the reigns of Shāpūr I or Khusrau I, or their descendants.[149] Workers recruited by the state, or prisoners of war, worked in the textile industry of Khūzistān and in the construction industry, as well as as ironsmiths, goldsmiths, locksmiths and dyers.[150] The bridges, dams and irrigation works built by Roman prisoners of war are still impressive today.

Like the Parthians, the Sasanians were also trading their own and foreign products from west to east and vice versa; and like the Parthians, they cultivated contact with India by sea and China by land. But both the Byzantines and the Sasanians tried to find ways to further their own advantage in trade to the exclusion of the other side.[151]

As far as the equipment and tactics of their troops was concerned, the Sasanians also stuck to the Parthian model for a long time, especially regarding the cooperation of heavily armoured cavalry and mounted archers.[152] They

147 Altheim and Stiehl, *Ein asiatischer Staat*, pp. 12ff.; D. Metzler, *Ziele und Formen königlicher Innenpolitik im vorislamischen Iran* (Münster, 1977), pp. 177ff.; Wiesehöfer, *Ancient Persia*, pp. 189–91, 292–3.

148 Wiesehöfer, *Ancient Persia*, pp. 191–2, 293.

149 E. Kettenhofen, 'Deportations, II', *EIr*, vol. VII, pp. 297–308.

150 For crafts and craftsmen see Wiesehöfer, *Ancient Persia*, pp. 192–4, 293.

151 Ibid., pp. 194–7, 293–4.

152 Ammianus Marcellinus, *Rerum gestarum libri*, 23.6.83, 24.6.8; Procopius, *De bello Persico*, 1.14.24, 44,52; al-Ṭabarī, *Ta'rīkh*, series I, p. 964, lines 9f.; al-Dīnawarī, *al-akhbār aṭ-ṭiwāl*, p. 74, lines 15f.

also became experts in siege warfare,[153] this time imitating the Roman model. Battles were usually decided by a forceful attack of the cavalry, coupled with a shower of arrows from the archers. The king or general would be situated in the centre, near the imperial standard, and protected by elite troops.[154] This line-up, alongside the Persians' alleged lack of stamina in close-contact fighting, was the reason for many a Sasanian defeat. If the commander fled or fell, the soldiers, too, would give up the fight. And in the end, their heavily armoured cavalry would be overcome by the lightly armoured and more flexible horsemen of the Muslim armies.[155]

Religion and culture

The Sasanian empire was also characterised by the magnitude and diversity of its religious groups and communities. Most prominent among them were the Zoroastrians, who had populated Iran for centuries, but there were also Christians, Jews, Manichaeans and Mazdakites. Although Christians had settled in Mesopotamia in small numbers since the end of the second century, it was only the deportation of Roman citizens from Syria that served as the basis for a flowering of Christian communities in the Sasanian empire. Following the end of the persecution of Christians, and due to the Christological disputes that took place in the Roman empire, the Sasanian empire became a refuge for many persecuted Christians from the Roman East (Nestorians, Monophysites and others).[156]

Jews, with their old centres in Mesopotamia, and as loyal subjects of the Sasanian kings, were, by and large, not exposed to persecution, except in a few instances. This also explains how the great rabbinic schools of Mesopotamia could engage in the process of commentary and interpretation of the Mishna, which by the end of the sixth and beginning of the seventh centuries would eventually be concluded by the completion of the Babylonian Talmud.[157]

153 Ammianus Marcellinus, *Rerum gestarum libri*, 19.5f., 20.6f., 11.

154 For the ruler in battles, see Whitby, 'The Persian king at war'.

155 For the Sasanian military, see A. S. Shahbazi, 'Army, I', *EIr*, vol. II, pp. 489–99; Wiesehöfer, *Ancient Persia*, pp. 197–9, 294.

156 For Christians in the Sasanian empire see Wiesehöfer, 'Geteilte Loyalitäten'; and (for the early Sasanian era) C. Jullien and F. Jullien, *Apôtres des confins: Processus missionaires chrétiens dans l'empire iranien*, Res Orientales 15 (Bures-sur-Yvette, 2002) (both containing references to older literature). See now also M. Arafa, J. Tubach and G. S. Vashalomidze (eds.), *Inkulturation des Christentums im Sasanidenreich* (Wiesbaden, 2007).

157 J. Neusner, *A history of the Jews in Babylonia*, vols. II–V (Leiden, 1960–70); J. Neusner, *Israel and Iran in Talmudic times* (Lanham, 1986); and J. Neusner, *Israel's politics in Sasanian Iran* (Lanham, 1986); A. Oppenheimer, *Babylonia Judaica in the Talmudic period*,

Lastly, the Manichaeans were founded as a religious community by Mani, who had been born as a Parthian subject in Mesopotamia in 216 CE, but later concentrated his missionary activities on the Sasanian empire and beyond. Following the death of their prophet in a Sasanian prison, the Manichaeans diverted their activities to the Roman east, Arabia, and in particular further east along the Silk Route, where they would become serious rivals to Zoroastrians, Christians, Buddhists and Muslims for the hearts of those in search of religion.[158]

For a long time scholars have tried to juxtapose the religiously 'tolerant' Arsacids with the supposedly 'intolerant' rule of the Sasanians. Under the latter, a Zoroastrian 'state church' is supposed to have joined forces with the king, rigid in religious matters, in a so-called covenant of 'throne and altar' to the detriment of the non-Zoroastrian communities. Today we know that Sasanian Iran was indeed 'Zoroastrianised' to a greater extent than ever before in its history, and that the kings acted as sponsors of that faith. However, we also know that the religious and social identity of the kings and their subjects, as well as their relationships with each other, were characterised by features similar to those existent in the Roman empire. That is to say, the personal faith of each individual ruler was a factor – but, more importantly, so was the general internal and external situation of the empire and the political reaction of the kings to it (including their reaction in terms of religious policy). Also decisive was the conflict between the Zoroastrian priesthood, for whom Iranianism and Zoroastrianism were one and the same, and the faiths of the Christians and Manichaeans, which were not only theoretically directed towards universalism, but in fact had become 'universal' faiths. It was a conflict that can be described in the field of tradition as one between the 'People of the Book', on the one hand, and the followers of Zoroaster's message of salvation, on the other. Up until the fifth century, this message was only transmitted orally, in its distinctly 'Sasanian' attire. From the point of view of those affected by it, this was a conflict between 'God's people' (for the Christians), or the *electi* and *auditores* (for the Manichaeans), and the Zoroastrian 'priests', who were, above all else,

Beihefte zum Tübinger Atlas des Vorderen Orients, series B, no. 47 (Wiesbaden, 1983); R. L. Kalmin, *Jewish Babylonia between Persia and Roman Palestine: Decoding the literary record* (Oxford, 2006).

158 See above all S. N. C. Lieu, *Manichaeism in the later Roman empire and medieval China*, 2nd rev. edn (Tübingen, 1992); S. N. C. Lieu, *Manichaeism in Central Asia and China* (Leiden, 1998); and S. N. C. Lieu, *Manichaeism in Mesopotamia and the Roman east*, 2nd edn (Leiden, 1999); W. Sundermann, 'Studien zur kirchengeschichtlichen Literatur der iranischen Manichäer I/II', *Altorientalische Forschungen*, 13 (1986), pp. 40–92, 239–317; and W. Sundermann, 'Studien zur kirchengeschichtlichen Literatur der iranischen Manichäer III', *Altorientalische Forschungen*, 14 (1987).

especially concerned to safeguard the interests of the empire. However, state and religious authorities did not always act in harmony with each other in their interaction with minorities. The image of a covenant of 'throne and altar' is a construction of much later (Islamic?) times. There was never a Zoroastrian 'state church', or a single *religio licita* (officially authorised religion). Christians were persecuted not only when they were regarded as religious rivals, but also when they were believed to be politically unreliable subjects. However, from 424, when they organised themselves in a church with its own head, and when they finally broke with the Roman Church Christologically, after 484, through the definite adoption of the 'Nestorian' creed, the Sasanian kings contemplated this development with satisfaction. They used Christian dignitaries as ambassadors and advisers, and supported – also in their own interests – Nestorian education and science, such as in the 'School of the Persians', which was relocated from Edessa to Nisibis, or in the 'university' of Jundīshāpūr in Khūzistān.

As far as the Manichaeans are concerned, the exact historical circumstances under which they were supported (e.g. under Shāpūr I) or persecuted (e.g. under Wahrām I and II) should be noted. The Zoroastrian authorities abhorred the Manichaeans the way they did (as, incidentally, did the Christians), because the Manichaeans dressed their message within Iran partly in Iranian–Zoroastrian garb and, in addition to that, aspired to supersede and supplant all other religions. Thus, when the king needed the support of the priesthood in particular, this could very easily also lead to a persecution of Manichaeans.

The followers of Mazdak, whose call for a 'collective of possessions and women' and rejection of trial by ordeal and of oaths shook the foundations of Zoroastrian social and moral beliefs, were also 'heretics' in the eyes of the Zoroastrians. Their way of life threatened the fundamental bases and interests of the social order, grounded, as it was, in patrilineal descent and the preservation of the household in the male line. Thus, the Mazdakite 'reforms' could not in the long run be in the interests of the ruler either.[159]

Let us cast a quick glance at the cultural achievements of Sasanian artists and scientists. The influence of Sasanian architects extended far into the Byzantine, Armenian and Islamic Orient, with their cupola designs and *iwān* constructions, as well as their specific decorative ornamentation. Iranian toreutics and textiles spread into China and western Europe. Works of literature were transmitted from West to East, and vice versa, through the mediation of late Sasanian Iran. Graeco-Roman knowledge in the fields of

159 For the religious policy of the Sasanians see Wiesehöfer, 'Geteilte Loyalitäten'.

philosophy, medicine, law, geography and agriculture was transmitted at the academies, where, among other places, it would later be eagerly picked up by the Muslims. Finally, Manichaeans and Christians conducted their wide-reaching missionary activities from Iran, as we have seen above. Iranian literature, law, religious beliefs and *termini technici*, in their turn, also spread to both Orient and Occident.[160]

A semi-official version of Iranian history was also laid down in writing during the Sasanian era, in the form of the already mentioned 'Book of Lords' (*X^w adāy-nāmag/Khwadāy-nāmag*). This book would become the most important legacy of ancient Iran within Iran itself, its legends stemming from various great epic cycles. Pertaining, in time, to both the very distant and extremely recent past, and, in space, to geographical regions both near and far, these legends were arranged in a chronological system, and adapted to the religious, moral and ethical as well as literary 'ideals' of the time. Owing to its later adaptation by the brilliant poet Firdawsī, the 'Book of Kings' (*Shāhnāmeh*), as it was now called, would eventually become a piece of world literature.

Military encounters between Iran and Byzantium[161]

Whereas the fourth century was characterised by numerous military conflicts between the superpowers Iran and Byzantium, and, as a consequence, by massive persecutions of Christians in the Sasanian empire, the reign of Yazdgerd I (399–420), in particular, witnessed a Christian-friendly policy,[162] as well as an attempt at reconciliation with Byzantium. In 408/9, for example, an agreement concerning trade rules between East and West was reached.[163] Emperor Arcadius is even alleged to have expressed a wish that, after his death, the Sasanian ruler should become the 'guardian' of his son Theodosius,

160 For a summary of the cultural achievements of the (late) Sasanians and their role as cultural mediators see Wiesehöfer, *Ancient Persia*, pp. 216–21, 298–300; also Panaino, *La novella*; and J. Wiesehöfer, '"Randkultur" oder "Nabel der Welt"? Das Sasanidenreich und der Westen: Anmerkungen eines Althistorikers', in Wiesehöfer and Huyse (eds.), *Ērān ud Anērān, passim.*

161 The section is indebted to information found in Winter and Dignas, *Rom und das Perserreich*; Greatrex and Lieu, *The Roman eastern frontier*; and Sebeos, *The Armenian history attributed to Sebeos*, trans. R. W. Thomson with commentary by J. Howard-Johnston, Translated Texts for Historians 31, 2 vols. (Liverpool, 1999). More detailed literature regarding specific stages of Iranian–Byzantine encounters and clashes can be found below, in the section dealing with political and military history.

162 Socrates Scholasticus, *Historia ecclesiastica*, 7.8.1–20.

163 *Codex Justinianus*, IV.63.4.

still a minor at the time.[164] However, towards the end of Yazdgerd's reign there were renewed persecutions of Christians.[165] Numerous Persian Christians thus fled to the west with the new king, Wahrām V Gōr (r. 420–39), demanding their extradition. Furthermore, a war broke out with Byzantium in 421, which, due to lack of success on both sides, was brought to an end by a truce just a year later.[166] It subsequently only came to a limited military encounter between the two sides in 441. The reason for this may have been twofold. On the one hand, the Byzantine emperor had lost his claim to being the sole protector of the Christians. The Sasanian empire had become the new home for many of the followers of Nestorius's teaching of the dual nature of Christ following the Councils of Ephesus (431) and Chalcedon (451). Moreover, the 'Nestorianisation' of the Christian communities of the Sasanian empire, which came about at the Synod of Bēth Lāpāṭ in 484, and which was supported by King Fīrūz (r. 459–84), was proof for the Christians' loyalty toward the Sasanian 'state'. On the other hand, Yazdgerd I and Fīrūz had to fight off the assault of new peoples from the east, namely the Hepthalites or 'White Huns'. Although the Sasanians suffered injurious defeats at the hands of these 'Tūrānians' (see below), which would eventually plunge the empire into chaos, Byzantium apparently did not use her rival's difficult situation to her own advantage,[167] except for a short episode, which saw the temporary suspension of payments for the defence of the passes over the Caucasus.[168]

It was only with the return of Kawād to the throne in 499 that the focus of Sasanian foreign policy was again directed toward the west.[169] When, in 502, he needed money to pay the Hepthalites, with whom he had formed an alliance, he turned to Anastasius I. The latter was not forthcoming, but instead demanded the return of Nisibis, and Kawād thus used the opportunity to reopen hostilities.[170] The ensuing clashes, which extended over a number of years, saw Sasanian troops retain the upper hand for the most part, and in 503 led to the capture of the strategically important city of Amida. The war was temporarily halted in 505/6. After renewed troubles with Hunnic tribes, the

164 Procopius, *De bello Persico*, 1.2.7–10. See P. Pieler, 'L'aspect politique et juridique de l'adoption de Chosroes proposée par les Perses à Justin', *Revue Internationale des Droits de l'Antiquité*, 3 (1972).

165 Theodoret, *Historia ecclesiastica*, 5.39.1–6.

166 John Malalas, *Chronographia*, 14.23; Procopius, *De bello Persico*, 1.2.11–15.

167 See Procopius, *De bello Persico*, 1.3.8.

168 Priscus, *Historia Byzantiaca*, 41.1 (FHG IV fr. 31).

169 Procopius, *De bello Persico*, 1.6.1–18.

170 Johannes Laurentius Lydus, *De magistratibus populi*, 51–3; Joshua the Stylite, *Chronicle*, 7.11f.; Procopius, *De bello Persico*, 1.7.1f.

Iranians finally agreed to return Amida, and other territories they had conquered, for a substantial sum of money. A peace that was negotiated to last for only seven years in fact continued for more than twenty.[171] Although Emperor Anastasius irritated the Sasanians by his excessive border protection policy,[172] there were no more military clashes during his lifetime. War only erupted again under his successor Justin, probably due to disputes regarding the crucial border regions of Lazica and Iberia, as well as the Caspian Gates. Kawād's attempt to reach a diplomatic agreement with Byzantium, to secure his son Khusrau's succession, failed.[173] It is likely that war broke out in 526, that is to say, before Justin's death, a war that was still raging the year Kawād died (531). As neither side could attain a decisive advantage over the other, a truce was signed a year later. Byzantium agreed, on the one hand, to pay large sums for the upkeep of the Caucasus fortifications and the protection of the border there, while also agreeing to relocate the base of the *dux Mesopotamiae* from Dara, which was situated close to the border, to Constantia instead.[174] In return, the Sasanians gave up their claims to important sites in Lazica. Even though Procopius talks of the conclusion of an 'Eternal Peace' with regard to the treaty of 532,[175] the two powers were soon at war with each other again.

Diplomatic activities preceding the war were aimed at improving one's own position in the international balance of power of the time.[176] Apparently unresolved border disputes between the Arab tribes of the Lakhmids (clients of the Sasanians) and the Ghassānids (clients of Byzantium) and appeals for intervention in Roman Armenia served as a pretext for a new outbreak of war.[177] From spring 540, the two superpowers were fighting again. First it was Khusrau who was able to achieve a prestigious success with the conquest of Antioch. Heavily engaged in the west, Justinian had to accept a truce, which stipulated that Khusrau would withdraw, while Byzantium would pay a yearly tribute of five hundred pounds of gold.[178] Renewed military clashes erupted the following year. Khusrau, who had been called to help by the Lazicans against the deployment of Byzantine troops, agreed to provide the inhabitants

171 Procopius, *De bello Persico*, 1.9.1–25.
172 Ibid., 1.10.1–19.
173 Ibid., 1.11.6–11, 29f.
174 Ibid., 1.22.3–5, 16–18.
175 Ibid., 1.22.3.
176 Ibid., 2.2.4–11.
177 Ibid., 1.17.40f., 45–8. See Shahid, *Byzantium and the Arabs in the sixth century*, pp. 209–18; H. Börm, 'Der Perserkönig im Imperium Romanum: Chosroes I. und der sasanidische Einfall in das Oströmische Reich 540 n.Chr.', *Chiron*, 36 (2006).
178 Procopius, *De bello Persico*, 2.10.24.

of Lazica with protection.[179] Following a massive summons to arms, the Sasanians took Petra, a fortress on the east coast of the Black Sea.[180] However, the Byzantines were able to keep a balance in the battles of the subsequent years in Armenia and Mesopotamia. The Sasanians even ended the siege of Edessa in return for a payment of ransom.[181] While a truce concluded in 545 confirmed Khusrau's dominant position in Lazica and forced Justinian to commit to considerable payments,[182] a number of heavy defeats in 557 compelled Khusrau to acknowledge the status quo in a new truce that was supposed to precede a formal peace treaty.[183] This peace treaty was only concluded in 562,[184] and marked the climax of diplomatic relations between the two superpowers (see below).

The alliance between Byzantium and the western Turks, as well as the Sasanian advance into southern Arabia,[185] again led to the outbreak of a much longer war between Byzantium and the Sasanian empire in the spring of 572. Whereas Byzantine troops besieged Nisibis in vain, the Sasanians were able to take the Byzantine fortress of Dara towards the end of the following year, attack Syria and devastate it. The subsequent military encounters led to heavy losses on both sides. The war did not bring about any victories for Justin II, in particular. In addition, Byzantium was threatened by the Avars in the north, and faced a Lombard menace to its Italian possessions. As a result, Tiberius, whom Justinian had made fellow regent in 574 because of his own mental illness, decided to enter into negotiations with Khusrau I. They initially agreed a one-year truce, which was eventually extended (575–8). But the state of war continued because Armenia was not included in the truce, and diplomatic efforts for a peace there remained unsuccessful. The Sasanian king thus decided to attack Mesopotamia even before the truce had expired. Despite early Sasanian successes in Armenia and in the Byzantine part of Mesopotamia, the Byzantines managed to check the Persians and drive them back (the battle of Melitene), so that Khusrau was now prepared to sign a peace treaty after all. But the great Sasanian king died before an exchange of ambassadors could take place. His son and successor Hormezd IV (r. 579–90) presented the Byzantine ambassador with demands that could not possibly have been met from a

179 Ibid., 2.15.1–31.
180 Ibid., 2.17.3–28.
181 Ibid., 2.26.5–46, 27.1–46.
182 Ibid., 2.28.6–11.
183 Agathius, *Historiae*, 4.30.8–10.
184 Menander Protector, *Historiae*, fr. 6.1 (FHG IV fr. 11).
185 Theophylact Simocatta, *Historia*, 3.9.3–11.

Byzantine point of view. Consequently, the war continued for the entire reign of Hormezd, even after Maurice had succeeded as Byzantine emperor.

While the war continued in Mesopotamia, the Sasanians also were threatened by the Turks in the east, the Khazars in the north and Arab tribes in the south. The Western Turk danger in particular began to escalate in much the same way as the Hepthalite threat had done in the fifth century, and it was only due to the exceptional military capabilities of the Sasanian general Wahrām Chōbīn that the enemies in the east could be defeated and made to pay tribute in 588/9. He was subsequently sent to the southern Caucasus, in order to push for a fight with Byzantium from there. Triumphant at first, he then suffered a defeat in Azerbaijān.[186] When Hormezd IV accused him of cowardice and discharged him,[187] Wahrām revolted against the king, and with him the Persian army fighting in Mesopotamia.[188] In the end Hormezd was captured and blinded, and soon after the start of the new year in June 590[189] his son Khusrau II Abarwēz (Parwēz) (r. 590–628) was declared the new king. The latter tried in vain to come to an understanding with the rebels, but ultimately had to flee from Wahrām,[190] who ascended to the Sasanian throne as Wahrām VI Chōbīn on 9 March 590.[191] Maurice answered the territorial and financial offers of both pretenders to the throne with a clear stance in favour of Khusrau.[192] As a result, Byzantine and Sasanian troops fought side by side for the first and only time ever. In the spring of 591 Khusrau II began to move against Wahrām VI, and with Byzantine help he succeeded in defeating the rebel.[193] The latter fled to the western Turks, but was assassinated only a year later. The third great Iranian–Byzantine conflict of the sixth century thus ended with the renewed enthronement of Khusrau II Abarwēz in 591 and a peace treaty concluded the same year. Khusrau, who saw himself as the son of the Byzantine emperor,[194] made use of the subsequent period to consolidate his rule and restock the state treasury.

186 Ibid., 3.7.
187 Ibid., 3.8.1.
188 Ibid., 4.1f. See Rubin, 'Nobility'.
189 See S. Tyler-Smith, 'Calendars and coronations: The literary and numismatic evidence for the accession of Khusrau II', *Byzantine and Modern Greek Studies*, 28 (2004).
190 Theophylact Simocatta, *Historia*, 4.10.1–11.
191 Ibid., 4.12.6.
192 Ibid., 4.13.24, 14.8; Theophanes Confessor, *Chronicle*, 265.24–6.
193 Theophylact Simocatta, *Historia*, 5.11f.
194 Ibid., 5.3.11; Theophanes Confessor, *Chronicle*, 266.13.

The Arab allies of the superpowers had already been explicitly included in the great peace treaty of 562. This illustrates their crucial role as 'buffer states' in the conflicts. However, when the Lakhmid ruler Nuʿmān III (r. 580–602) converted to Christianity – his subjects had already turned towards the Nestorian creed – this initiated a break between the Lakhmids and the Sasanians.[195] Furthermore, Khusrau II, in whose eyes Nuʿmān had apparently become too powerful, accused the latter of not having supported him adequately at the time of his flight from Wahrām Chōbīn. The Lakhmid ruler was lured to the Sasanian court, where he was assassinated.[196] The fall of Nuʿmān III ended the Lakhmid kingdom, and Khusrau II entrusted an Arab of non-Lakhmid descent with the duties the old dynasty had hitherto carried out. At the same time a Sasanian governor was appointed to work alongside the new ruler.[197]

In the dispute between the murderer of Maurice, Phocas, and the alleged son of Maurice, Theodosius, Khusrau sided with the latter. Although the war was formally directed against the usurper of the Byzantine throne,[198] Khusrau was determined to seize the opportunity to push the borders of his empire further west. Within fifteen years almost the entire east of the Byzantine empire fell into Sasanian hands (the first and second phases of the war).[199] With the fall of Alexandria and Byzantium's loss of Egypt in 619, the Sasanian empire stood at the pinnacle of its power. The Sasanians planned the third and decisive phase of the war with resources of their own and those of foreign territories they had conquered. They planned to attack Anatolia from their positions on the Upper Euphrates and in Cilicia, and push on to Constantinople. At first everything proceeded according to plan, not least because they had arranged coordinated action with the Avars. The Persians attacked from the east (622) and advanced to conquer the entire northern edge of the Anatolian highland, while a vanguard sought to encircle the emperor and his army in Bithynia, while they were engaged in field exercises there. Although the emperor managed to break out and achieve some minor successes, he was soon called back to Constantinople, for the Avars had started attacking in the west. The Persian advance continued

195 G. Rothstein, *Die Dynastie der Laḫmiden in al-Ḥīra: Ein Versuch zur arabisch-persischen Geschichte zur Zeit der Sasaniden* (Berlin, 1899), pp. 139ff.; H. Preißler, 'Arabien zwischen Byzanz und Persien', in L. Rathmann *et al.* (eds.), *Geschichte der Araber*, 2nd edn, vol. I (Berlin, 1975), pp. 47–8.

196 T. Nöldeke, *Die von Guidi herausgegebene syrische Chronik: Übersetzt und kommentiert*, Sitzungsberichte der Akademie der Wissenschaften zu Wien, Philosophisch-Historische Klasse 128 (Vienna, 1893), pp. 13ff.

197 Rothstein, *Die Dynastie*, pp. 119–20.

198 Theophylact Simocatta, *Historia*, 8.15.7.

199 Al-Ṭabarī, *Ta'rīkh*, series I, p. 1002.

the following year, when they reached the north-western part of the Anatolian plateau and sacked Ancyra. Heraclius' hands were tied in the west, where he tried to come to an agreement with the Avars.

What was about to follow was one of the most astonishing turning-points in the history of Antiquity. Heraclius managed to turn the demoralised Byzantine military once more into a powerful army with a strong fighting spirit – an army convinced that it was engaged in a holy war against the Persians. In the spring of 624 Heraclius attacked Transcaucasia, where he was to stay for almost two years and wreak as much havoc and destruction as possible. He outmanoeuvred three Persian armies (625), called the Christians of the north to his assistance, and tried to convince the western Turks to enter the war on the Byzantine side. He even survived the crisis of 626, when two Sasanian armies attacked Anatolia, and an Avar one besieged the capital. In 627 he returned to Transcaucasia. In the meantime the Turks had responded to his plea for assistance by occupying Albania and launching an attack on Iberia.

In 627 Heraclius met Yabghu Khan, the 'viceroy' of the Turkic empire, outside Tiblisi, probably with the intention of conferring about coordinated action between them. The emperor then moved southwards to the Zagros, protected by the presence of a large Turkic contingent. The Turks left for the north in October, and Heraclius undertook a surprising push forward into the south, through the mountains. He gained a decisive victory at Nineveh (12 December 627) and threatened Khusrau II in the latter's favourite palace at Dastgerd. The Sasanian king fled to Ctesiphon, while Heraclius took Dastgerd. However, he soon retired to his winter quarters, as an attack on the heavily fortified main residence of the Sasanian king did not promise to be successful.

There was no further military conflict between the two sides. Khusrau II was deposed in a palace coup in the night of 23–24 February 628. His son Kawād II succeeded to the throne, and immediately petitioned for peace. Although negotiations proved difficult, the Sasanian occupying troops finally withdrew from Byzantine territory in 629. The return of peace and the victory of a Christian empire over the Zoroastrian opponent was celebrated ceremonially on 21 March 630. Heraclius entered Jerusalem triumphantly, with the relics of the True Cross, which the Sasanians had plundered in 614, in his possession.

Ideology, war and diplomacy

From their very beginning, Sasanian rock reliefs showed jousting scenes (probably derived from Hellenistic–Parthian models), which symbolically referred to important historical decisions and turning-points.[200] Most probably, those big-sized scenes of combat were originally designed for the mosaics and paintings of Sasanian palaces and then found their way into other genres of art. The fact that the Iranian heroic tradition also presents important historical and military decisions in the form of duels (as jousting or wrestling matches) seems to speak for a common root of the literary as well as iconographic conversion of such ordeal-like situations.

It has long been known that Romans and Sasanians, in the context of their triumphal art, tended to use each other's visual imagery and ideological vocabulary.[201] Iran's superiority over Rome is stressed both in the Sasanian royal inscriptions and in the Iranian mythological tradition.[202] The Sasanians also used other media to give expression to their striving for superiority over Rome. Particularly famous are the scenes of triumph on Sasanian rock reliefs[203] and the 'Shāpūr Cameo' of the Bibliothèque nationale in Paris, which was rightfully interpreted as a Roman piece of art on Sasanian instructions.[204] However, the ways in which the Iranians tried to deal with Roman ideas of world domination and the Roman language of visual art have not yet been properly analysed.

The Romans and, later, the Byzantines were never dismissed from their subordinate position in Sasanian royal ideology, even if the Sasanians had to be content with the acknowledgement of the equal rank of both realms and dynasties in diplomatic contact. It also seems that the Iranian rulers of the fifth and sixth centuries, in similar vein to Shāpūr's pecuniary demands on Philip the Arab in 244, passed off the Roman payments, which were meant to support Sasanian endeavours to protect the borders against nomads or mountain tribes, as Byzantine tributes, although in reality they were parts of well-balanced diplomatic treaties.[205]

Even if both the Sasanian and the Roman triumphal art leaves no doubt about the outcome of the respective duel portrayed,[206] and even if the two great

200 See von Gall, *Das Reiterkampfbild*, p. 97 for the temporary takeover of Roman imagery.
201 Schneider, 'Orientalism'.
202 Z. Rubin, 'The Roman empire in the Res Gestae Divi Saporis: The Mediterranean world in Sāsānian propaganda', in E. Dabrowa (ed.), *Ancient Iran and the Mediterranean world*, Electrum 2 (Crakow, 1998), pp. 181–2; J. Wiesehöfer, 'Rūm as enemy of Iran', in E. Gruen (ed.), *Cultural borrowings and ethnic appropriations in Antiquity*, OrOcc 8 (Stuttgart, 2005).
203 Schneider, 'Orientalism'.
204 Von Gall, *Das Reiterkampfbild*, pp. 56–9.
205 Yarshater, 'Iranian national history', p. 410; Rubin, 'The Roman empire', pp. 178–9.
206 Very often the enemy is unseated or taken by the hand.

powers ideologically stressed their respective superiority,[207] it is perfectly clear that both sides, in practice, had to recognise their equal rank and to get along with each other for better or for worse. Thus it is no surprise that the peace treaties of the Romans / Byzantines and the Sasanians were not only regarded as historically most relevant events, but were also arranged in a special ceremonial way.[208] This becomes particularly clear in Menander Protector's report on the peace treaty of 562 between Justinian and Khusrau I.[209] The author, a man with a profound rhetorical and legal education, and, as a member of the emperor Maurice's court, very familiar with Byzantine diplomatic customs, gives us an insight into all substantial aspects of the international law of his time.

In the preamble to the Sasanian document of ratification (in Menander's version) 'the divine, good, father of peace, ancient Chosroes [Khusrau], king of kings, fortunate, pious and beneficent, to whom the gods have given great fortune and a great kingdom, giant of giants, formed in the image of the gods'[210] calls his Roman opponent 'Justinian Caesar, our brother'.[211] Even if the titulature given to Justinian is plainly shorter than his own, the form of address ('brother') nevertheless shows clearly that the 'king who reigns over kings' and the 'victor of wars' grants the 'lord of all things and of the world'[212]

207 The Sasanians did not programmatically invent and systematically cultivate a preoccupation with the Occident as the Romans did with the Orient, although Rūm appears as one of the two deadly foes of Iran in the 'Iranian national history' (see below).

208 For the Romano-Sasanian diplomatic encounters and peace treaties see K. Güterbock, *Byzanz und Persien in ihren diplomatisch-völkerrechtlichen Beziehungen im Zeitalter Justinians* (Berlin, 1906); E. Winter, 'Legitimität als Herrschaftsprinzip: Kaiser und "König der Könige" im wechselseitigen Verkehr', in H.-J. Drexhage and J. Sünskes (eds.), *Migratio et Commutatio: Studien zur Alten Geschichte und deren Nachleben. Th. Pekáry zum 60. Geburtstag am 13. September 1989 dargebracht von Freunden, Kollegen und Schülern* (St Katharinen, 1988); Winter, 'On the regulation'; Winter and Dignas, *Rom und das Perserreich*, pp. 141–81.

209 Menander Protector, *Historiae*, fr. 6.1.

210 For the titulature of the Sasanian kings see Huyse, 'Die sasanidische Königstitulatur'. Justinian normally used for himself a titulature which was still in use in the tenth century: 'the pious, the lucky, the renowned, the victorious, the triumphant, always the illustrious emperor' (*pius* (*eusebês*), *felix* (*eutychês*),*inclutus* (*endoxos*), *victor* (*nikêtês*), *triumphator* (*tropaiouchos*), *semper augustus* (*aeisebastos augoustos*)).

211 Totally different is the protocol of Khusrau II's letter, when he asks the emperor Maurice for help: 'Chosroes king of the Persians greets the most prudent king of the Romans, the beneficent, peaceful, masterful, lover of nobility and hater of tyranny, equitable, righteous, saviour of the injured, bountiful, forgiving' (Theophylact Simocatta, *Historia*, 4.11, trans. M. Whitby and M. Whitby as *The history of Theophylact Simocatta: An English translation with introduction* (Oxford, 1986), pp. 117f.).

212 These are the words in Ammianus Marcellinus, *Rerum gestarum libri*, 19.2.12 (*rex regibus imperans et bellorum victor – dominus rerum et mundi*). Cf. 17.5.3: 'I, Sapor, king of kings, partner of the stars, brother of the sun and the moon, send my best regards to the Caesar Constantius, my brother' (*Rex regum Sapor, particeps siderum, frater Solis et*

equal rank in a diplomatic context. This is stressed particularly eloquently and colourfully in the words Byzantine authors such as Petrus Patricius and John Malalas put into the mouths of Sasanian kings and diplomats. There is mention of the two empires as two lights, which, 'like eyes, are adorned by each other's light',[213] or as two divinely planned centres of civilisation, which are called 'the moon of the west' and 'the sun of the east'.[214] Rome/Byzantium equally grants the same rank, the same dignity and the same autonomy to the eastern opponent, although, ideologically, the eastern *natio molestissima* ('most annoying nation') would actually deserve to be destroyed,[215] and although – or just because – Rome's claim to universal rule was in reality substantially limited by the existence of the Sasanian empire.

It was also usual for the two great powers to announce accessions to the throne by a special report, and to answer this report by a special message of greeting.[216] And it was also custom and practice to enquire of the foreign envoys after the well-being of the royal 'brother' during a solemn audience,[217] and to exchange gifts.[218] The fulfilment of requests also served the keeping of good terms with the neighbours.[219]

The Sasanians' view of the west[220]

We can only understand the neighbour's and opponent's special role in Iran in connection with the idea of Iran/Ērān and/or Ērānšahr ('Land/Realm of the

Lunae, Constantio Caesari fratri meo salutem plurimam dico), a formula which Constantius answers in the following way: 'I, Constantius, the victor on land and on the sea, always the illustrious Emperor, send my best regards to king Sapor, my brother' (*Victor terra marique Constantius semper Augustus fratri meo Sapori regi salutem plurimam dico*).

213 Petrus Patricius, *Fragmenta Historicorum Graecorum* (FHG), ed. C. Müller, vol. IV, Paris 1868, pp. 181–91, fr. 13.

214 John Malalas, *Chronographia*, 18.44 (p. 449).

215 Ammianus Marcellinus, *Rerum gestarum libri*, 23.5.19.

216 John Malalas, *Chronographia*, 18.34, 36 (p. 445, 448); Menander Protector *Historiae*, fr. 9.1; Theophylact Simocatta, *Historia*, 3.12; Theophanes Confessor, *Chronicle*, 250; *Chronicon Paschale*, 735. Such an announcement is omitted by Hormezd IV (Theophylact Simocatta, *Historia*, 3.17), whereas Khusrau II does not accept the letter of the murderer of his patron Maurice, Phocas (ibid., 8.15).

217 Petrus Patricius *apud* Constantine Porphyrogenitus, *De caeremoniis aulae Byzantinae*, 1.89.

218 Ibid., 1.89, 90; Procopius, *De bello Persico*, 1.24; gifts of the Augusta to the Persian queen: John Malalas, *Chronographia*, 18.61 (p. 467).

219 Thus, Justinian granted Khusrau I his wish and allowed the Neoplatonic philosophers, who had come to the Sasanian court at Ctesiphon, to return (Hartmann, 'Geist im Exil'); he also sent the physician Tribunus, whom Khusrau had asked for, to Persia for one year to cure the Sasanian king (Procopius, *De bello Gothico*, 4.10).

220 See Wiesehöfer, 'Rūm'.

Aryans / Iranians').[221] Although the Achaemenids had attached ethnic qualities to the word *ariya* which forms the basis of Middle Persian *ēr* (DNa), 'Iran' as an ethnic, religious and political term was first coined in early Sasanian times. It disappeared with the fall of the dynasty, and became a historicising term for its realm, only to be revived as a political concept in the time of the Ilkhanids and under the Pahlavi dynasty. It is obvious that the Sasanians, apart from alleged ethnic common ground, used this term to emphasise to their subjects both the experiences shared in the time of the Parthian overlords and the common cultural traditions of Iran. Those rather integrative factors were probably meant not least to prevent dangerous regional particularism within Iran and to legitimise the newly established rule. It has rightly been stated that the creation of a special Iranian identity is to be seen in connection with similar tendencies towards regionalism in the Roman empire.[222] That this Sasanian concept of a connection between 'Iranism' and 'Mazdaism' and of an ethnically, culturally and religiously self-contained Iranian community depended exclusively on royal ideology has correctly been postulated with reference to the numerous ethno-linguistic and religious minorities in the Sasanian empire, not least in its most fertile regions.[223]

Within the Sasanian concept of Iran, a special role is assigned to the royal 'ancestors' (MpI *niyāgān*, GkI *pappoi*) and 'forebears' (MpI *ahēnagān*, GkI *progonoi*) and their territories, as well as to Zoroastrian religious tradition and practice.[224] Specific means and institutions were meant to strengthen the idea that the ruler and his Iranian subjects shared the same destiny: symbolic references (e.g., an era, starting from 205/6); an iconography, tightly connected with the royal inscriptions and also underlining the kings' close relationship to the gods; special rites and practices (such as the lighting of royal and other fires, as well as donations for the welfare of the souls of deceased and living persons); and finally, important memorial places and monuments (as, for instance, the sacred shrine of Anahita at Iṣṭakhr, the big fire-temples, the cliff of Naqsh-i Rustam, and the towers there and at Pāikūlī). The process of the creation of a specific identity both for members of the Sasanian dynasty and for their subjects in (south-west) Iran had inclusive as well as exclusive features. Excluded from this close relationship were the

221 Gnoli, *The idea of Iran*; G. Gnoli, *Iran als religiöser Begriff im Mazdaismus*, Rheinisch-Westfälische Akademie der Wissenschaften, Vorträge G 320 (Opladen, 1993).
222 Gnoli, *Iran als religiöser Begriff*, p. 6.
223 R. Gyselen (personal communication).
224 For the scholarly debate on the identification of those 'ancestors' and 'forebears' see note 93.

inhabitants of Anērān, i.e. the areas that Shāpūr I and his successors had been able to conquer (temporarily), and all non-subjects of the 'King of kings' (in the *Res Gestae Divi Saporis* (ŠKZ) primarily the subjects of Rome). The term 'Iran' of Iranian tradition was not applied to the home countries of those people, and, ideologically, the people of Anērān remained second-class inhabitants of the empire.[225] In contrast, the members of the Parthian clans, who had changed sides in time or had been allowed to remain in office by the new lords for political reasons, were still considered worthy members of the 'imagined community' of Iranians. Possibly, terms such as Ērān and Anērān already had religious connotations, inasmuch as the first was considered to be under divine protection (domain of the *yazdān*), and the latter to be a place of idols (*dēwān*).[226] However, such a distinct, quasi-'nationalistic' Sasanian Iranism was a big drawback. It stood in the way of developing an integrative imperial ideology, which – as is shown by the Achaemenid royal inscriptions and reliefs – presents the ruler and all his subjects as a community of interests, chosen, fostered and legitimised by the gods. On the one hand, it is no wonder that the official Sasanian 'Iranism', also to be observed in Zoroastrian literature, was able to establish a kind of 'Iranian' identity (with which a universal religion such as Manichaeism had to cope and because of which it failed in the long run). On the other hand, this 'Iranism', which – not least in times of crisis – succeeded in strengthening thoughts of a clear distinction between friend and foe, stood in the way of a dissemination of an 'Iranian' (e.g. Zoroastrian) body of thought. Shāpūr's temporary interest in Mani's universal message, hinted at in Manichaean literature,[227] might have been an expression of royal discontent with the lack of integrative power of Zoroastrianism on an imperial level.

The epigraphic and archaeological testimony obviously never determined the Iranians' views of their neighbours and enemies in the west. This is evident in the fact that soon after the fall of the Sasanian empire in the seventh century, the rock reliefs were no longer regarded as the works of Shāpūr I and his successors by the inhabitants of Fārs, but were rather connected with characters of the Iranian legendary cycles such as Rustam.

225 For the term Anērān see Huyse, *Die dreisprachige Inschrift*, vol. II, pp. 10–11.
226 Ibid., p. 11.
227 M. Hutter, *Manis kosmogonische Šābuhragān-Texte: Edition, Kommentar und literargeschichtliche Einordnung der manichäisch-mittelpersischen Handschriften M 98/99 I und M 7980–7985*, Studies in Oriental Religion 21 (Wiesbaden, 1992), pp. 155–60.

The 'Book of Lords',[228] mentioned above, bundled together into a kind of semi-official Sasanian version the traditions of world and, more particularly, Iranian history. These had probably circulated previously in an independent fashion with each region of Iran undoubtedly possessing regionally specific versions of Iranian history, partly differing from those of other regions. Some of them, perhaps of an eastern Iranian provenance, must have been so popular that, in the end, they were able to displace or absorb the historical and partly legendary tradition of south-west Iran – a fact that is suggested by Sasanian ignorance of their Achaemenid forerunners. As it is out of the question that the Arsacids would have consciously wanted to erase the Achaemenids from the tradition, we should explain the loss of memory of the names of Cyrus and his successors as the result of a gradual process resulting from the oral character of Iranian tradition with its fascinating and entertaining traits, attributable in part perhaps to eastern traditions of historical interpretation that place particular emphasis on the gods' saving grace. As is well known, oral tradition is characterised by (a) the special attention given to the beginning and the contemporary end of history, while only little information is made available for the so-called floating gap, which bridges long periods of time; (b) the filling out of existing story patterns with new historical or mythical figures and themes. This subordinating of historical characters, events and details to the framework material, apart from other factors of deformation or transformation in oral cultures, might explain why popular knowledge of Cyrus and his successors faded or took another shape.[229] The Parthians, who had epic and poetic material performed at their courts,[230] are said to have helped in this process by collecting and saving the religious tradition of Iran. King Walakhsh (Vologeses I?) might be mentioned as an example.[231] Even if,

228 The following statements rely heavily on the observations of Yarshater, 'Iranian national history'. See also P. Huyse, 'Histoire orale et écrite en Iran ancien entre mémoire et oubli' (unpublished thesis). Huyse postulates a first compilation of 'historical' material in the time of Khusrau I. Khusrau II would then have been responsible for important additions to and revisions of that material (see Shahbazi, 'On the X^{w}adāy-nāmag', p. 214). There are even later additions in the time of Yazdgerd III (T. Nöldeke, *Das iranische Nationalepos* (Straßburg, 1896), pp. 12–13, §13). The first Sasanian attempt to collect all the legendary material circulating in Iran is probably to be dated to the early fifth century, when the Sasanian kings radically changed their royal titulature, not least by introducing the term 'Kayānid' into it. The first real Kayānid name of a Sasanian king is that of Kawād I (488–96, 499–531); see Huyse, 'Histoire orale'.

229 For the rules of oral tradition and the characteristics of Iranian oral tradition see Huyse, 'Histoire orale'.

230 See M. Boyce, 'The Parthian *gōsān* and Iranian minstrel tradition', *JRAS* (1957); M. Boyce, 'Gōsān', *EIr*, vol. XI, pp. 167–70 with the remarks of Huyse, 'Histoire orale'.

231 DkM 412 5–11.

as has rightly been stressed, the eastern Iranian epic cycles made up the core of the national saga and national history of Iran in (early) Sasanian times, this does not mean that the inhabitants of Fārs ('Kings', Magi etc.) did not contribute to the Sasanian version(s) of the 'national history'.[232] For example, their version of the Avestan tradition kept its formative strength in south-west Iran during Parthian rule and was finally canonised under the Sasanians. We find proof of this (partly older) south-west Iranian orientation of the Avesta in the throne names Ardakhshīr, Dārāyān and Manchihr of Parthian Fārs, and probably even in the Achaemenid use of Avestan names and concepts for their own needs.[233] This special 'Persian' development is also exemplified by the Sasanians' recollection of Achaemenid 'Aryanism', the affinity of Sasanian royal ideology for its Achaemenid counterpart, and the thematic and linguistic parallels in the Achaemenid and Sasanian royal inscriptions. A feeling for a special 'Persian', i.e. south-west Iranian, history and tradition (which differed from the Parthian version) was probably kept alive from late Achaemenid times through the time of the Frataraka and the sub-Parthian kings into the early Sasanian period with the help of the 'holy places' at Naqsh-i Rustam, Persepolis and elsewhere, including their iconography. When Shāpūr I 'worships' his 'forebears' (who, like his 'father' and his 'ancestors', have a special connection to Fārs), when he derives his own claims from their achievements and possession rights, when he stresses the special position of Ērānšahr in his empire, when a Sasanian prince as king of the Sacas prays for the builder of Persepolis at the beginning of the fourth century (the names of the place and the builder are, however, unknown to him), all these acts stand in causal connection to the impressive inheritance of the 'ancestors' and 'forebears'.[234] This can only mean that the Sasanians saw themselves as proud heirs to a glorious Iranian past of either a Kayānid–legendary or an uncertain 'historical' mould.

As already mentioned, 'Iranian national history' is shaped by a succession of dynasties. Among the mythical world rulers of the Pishdadian line, King Frēdōn is most important for us. He not only defeated the monster Dahāk, but also divided the world among his three sons Salm, Tūr and Ēraj. This touched off the disastrous strife between the Iranian kings (heirs of Ēraj, who were called Kayānids) and the descendants of Salm and Tūr, both of whom are

232 Yarshater, 'Iranian national history', pp. 390–1.

233 J. Kellens, 'L'idéologie religieuse des inscriptions achéménides', *JA*, 290 (2002). Huyse, 'Histoire orale', tries to show that the Kayānid legendary cycle(s) already played an important role in Achaemenid Fārs (and even among the Medes).

234 Wiesehöfer, 'Gebete'.

at home in the east and possess Iranian names. The Kayānid epic tradition shows a strong eastern Iranian legendary and religious slant, although some scholars would like to see in it allusions to western Iranian historical characters such as Cyrus the Great. The end of the third and last phase of Kayānid rule is heralded by the deeds of the conqueror Alexander of Rūm. It has long been known that two different Alexander traditions exist in Iran, the first of which, greatly influenced by the ancient 'Alexander Romance', presents Alexander as a Persian prince and mighty king, a Muslim sage or even a prophet, whereas the second one characterises him as evil incarnate, the 'devil's' henchman and a person who, like no one else, brought mischief and destruction to Ērānšahr. Thus, the first tradition, found in the works of Muslim poets, writers and historiographers, stands in sharp contrast to the second, Middle Persian, one, found in religious and didactic literature (including the 'Book of Lords'). Here, Alexander kills the last Kayānid king, Dārā, or plans his death; apart from that, the 'Roman' is said to have killed many members of the Iranian aristocracy and many priests and scholars, to have destroyed fire-temples or to have extinguished Holy Fires, to have razed cities and fortresses to the ground, to have robbed, burned or scattered the Holy Scriptures, and to have divided the empire into realms of powerless and quarrelling petty kings. The traditions competed with each other in late Sasanian and early Islamic times, after a version of the 'Alexander Romance' had been translated into Middle Persian. It seems as if the positive view of Alexander enjoyed particular popularity in aristocratic circles.[235]

The Arsacids probably followed the Kayānids in the Parthian version(s) of the 'national history'. After consciously displacing their predecessors from it in late Sasanian times, the Sasanians took their place, systematically revising the entire tradition and presenting themselves as Iranian kings par excellence, as if the history of Iran had culminated in their rule by law of nature. It is no wonder that for many Muslim authors the Arsacid era was the result of Alexander's misdeeds and a time of instability and chaos, when the numerous rivalries of petty kings jeopardised their predecessors' successes and afforded an opportunity to Iran's enemies to take advantage of its treasures. From the point of view of the late Sasanian compilers of the 'national history', the outstanding qualities of King Ardashīr were needed to restore Iran's former greatness and power. The extent to which the conflicts between Khusrau I and

235 J. Wiesehöfer, 'Zum Nachleben von Achaimeniden und Alexander in Iran', in H. Sancisi-Weerdenburg, A. Kuhrt and M. C. Root (eds.), *Achaemenid history VIII: Continuity and change* (Leiden, 1994).

his successors, on the one side, and the high nobility, on the other, especially in the fight for the throne between Khusrau II and Wahrām Chōbīn, have been responsible for the positive image of the founder of the Sasanian empire and the belittling of his Arsacid predecessor, has already been made clear.[236] That the Sasanian view of the Parthians must originally have been more favourable is suggested not only by the historically loyal Parthian clans of early Sasanian times, but also by the remains of a favourable assessment of the Arsacids in Muslim tradition. For example, Arsacid kings are genealogically affiliated to the Kayānid dynasty, and some of them are said to have been concerned about the promotion of scholarship, culture and religion.[237]

As far as Iran's enemies are concerned, 'Iranian national history' was subject to particularly flagrant changes and tendencies to updating in Parthian and Sasanian times. Whereas under the Arsacids, the eastern Iranian portion of the legendary material increased and displaced western Iranian tradition, there was a systematic adjustment of the tradition to the needs of the new Sasanian dynasty. As for the emphasis on the special position of Iran in world history, both dynasties introduced blatant new trends that affected the role of their neighbours in the west as well. Thus, in the long run, the sons of Fredon became the 'progenitors' of the royal dynasties of Iran, and of Tūrān and Rūm, the foreign arch-enemies of Iran. The early Sasanians referred to the legendary and the historical Parthian opposition to Rūm, as can be seen from their inscriptions and reliefs mentioned above. This was probably because they regarded south-western Iran as their home and the Romans as their worst enemies. We cannot determine how much historical information entered the 'national history' in this period, since the late Sasanian version of this tradition has survived almost alone. However, in the light of the character of this tradition, there is much to suggest that (as in Parthian times) the history of events gave way very early to the didactic and entertaining parts of the tradition, not only during the fourth/fifth[238] or even the sixth/seventh centuries. This follows from the disregard of the historically highly relevant Armenian question, from the rather casual treatment of the problem of social or religious minorities, and from absence of reference to the fights for the throne at the end of the third century.[239] It is hard to believe that only the Sasanian compilers in the time of Khusrau I and his successors wiped out such

236 Yarshater, 'Iranian national history', p. 474.
237 Ibid., pp. 475–6.
238 Daryaee, 'National history'; Daryaee, 'Memory and history'; Shahbazi, 'Early Sasanians' claim'.
239 Yarshater, 'Iranian national history', p. 477.

historical information, since the 'national history' does not even provide any information about the western campaigns of Khusrau II.[240]

Although there is more information about royal affairs, from the reign of Yazdgerd I onwards, we cannot speak of a real history of events, which normally analyses the motives of the people involved or the general political situation. Details of foreign, administrative or military affairs are only mentioned if they are of an entertaining kind or possess a narrative quality. The anecdotes that take centre stage are those that depict court life: the coronations of kings, their inaugural speeches, royal banquets, processions and merriments, as well as hunts and gift exchange, diplomatic contacts and military parades. Great victories of Iranian kings over their enemies in the west accompany those over the Tūrānians, and are partly presented as campaigns to avenge Alexander's misdeeds; non-Iranian forebears of Iranian kings and heroes are increasingly assessed as an apparent genealogical defect. In other words, the account of Romano-Sasanian relations in the 'Book of Lords' and its oral forerunners did not aim at determining the exact reasons for the conflicts between Iran and Rome. Where allusions to historical events are discernible at all and events and characters are not confused and mixed up, everything is determined by the effort to make Rūm appear as the arch-enemy of Iran and to be able to tell entertaining and didactic stories about the encounters between east and west. A good example of this is the account of the life of the famous Sasanian king Shāpūr II in Firdawsī's *Shahnameh*. This biography is nothing more than a description of his (unhistorical) rescue from Roman captivity with the help of a pretty young maiden of Iranian descent, and of his punitive Arabian war and two campaigns against the Romans, which prove to be a mixture of the wars of his time and those of the time of Shāpūr I. It is also in the reign of Shāpūr II that Mani, coming from China, is said to have been killed.

Initially unwilling to make themselves stand out at the cost of their royal Parthian predecessors, the new kings, in the course of time and in collaboration with the Zoroastrian clergy, gave the 'national history' a special Sasanian touch. They did so especially in the second half of their reign, and then with obviously anti-Parthian intentions. Rūm as a metaphor for their neighbours and the historical as well as contemporary enemies in the west now included the Byzantines. As with the Romans, we do not get much reliable historical

240 The question remains, however, whether the early Sasanians' claim to legitimisation already harked back to the Kayānids, since any allusion to the dynasty's Kayānid origin is absent in Narseh's Pāikūlī inscription and Kayānid names only enter royal nomenclature in the late fifth century.

information about them. The special character of the Sasanian view of history becomes particularly obvious through episodes that are related to Byzantium, but are anachronistically moved back to the time of the Kayānids.

Thus, Kai Kāwūs is said to have dispatched an envoy to the Kaisar, the young Gushtāsp to have made a journey to Rūm and to have married a Byzantine princess.[241] However, the late Sasanian revision of the 'national history' led to two remarkable changes, as far as the enemies of Iran are concerned: on the one hand, probably as a result of the disastrous invasions of Hepthalites and Turks, the role of Tūrān became more important than that of Rūm (finally leading to an identification of Tūrānians and Turks). On the other hand, within secular tradition, the pseudo-callisthenic Alexander in Iranian shape supplemented the Alexander as destroyer of Iranian greatness; he thus became a son of Dārā and the daughter of the king of Rūm.

In view of the character and the attractiveness of the 'national history', it is no wonder that an early Islamic historian of Iranian descent such as al-Ṭabarī, who had been interested in writing a Muslim account of pre-Islamic Iranian history within the framework of universal history, thereby stressing God's saving grace, had great difficulty extracting historical facts from the mythical, legendary and anecdotal material of the 'Book of Lords' and from other similar Sasanian sources. His world history from the early Muslims' point of view gives us information both about Muḥammad's historical forerunners and about the predecessors of the political leaders of the Islamic world. To accomplish this, it neither had to break with anti-Iranian taboos, as was postulated until recently, nor did it have to construct a national identity with an anti-Arabian or even anti-Islamic slant. The same applies to Firdawsī's epoch-making *Shāhnāmeh*. Like al-Ṭabarī relying on the late Sasanian view of history, the poet used the Iranian and non-Iranian dynasts' and peoples' special liking for Sasanian (especially royal) subjects, as well as the linguistic potential of the already Islamised New Persian language supremely well. He thereby helped to turn the pre-Islamic legendary sagas into a piece of world literature. It is the role of Alexander and the emperors of Rūm as neighbours and opponents of the mighty kings of Iran in the *Shāhnāmeh* and in other Persian epics and poems that has determined the Iranian view of the Graeco-Roman west in antiquity up to the present day.

241 Yarshater, 'Iranian national history', p. 403.

Genealogical table of the Sasanians

	Date	Name	Indigenous names	Genealogy	Commentary
1	224–41/2 CE	Artaxerxes (Artaxares) [Ardashīr] I	MP Ardašīr	son of Pābag	founder of the Sasanian empire
2	239/40–70/2	Sapor(es) [Shāpūr] I	MP Šābuhr	son of 1	until 241/2 co-regent of 1
3	270/2–3	Hormisdas (Hormizdes) [Hormezd] I	MP Hormezd-Ardašīr	son of 2	
4	273–6	Wahram (Va(ra)ranes) [Wahrām] I	MP Wahrām	son of 2	
5	276–93	Wahram (Va(ra)ranes) [Wahrām] II	MP Wahrām	son of 4	
6	293	Wahram (Va(ra)ranes) [Wahrām] III	MP Wahrām	son of 5	dispute for the throne with 7
7	293–302	Narses [Narseh]	MP Narseh	son of 2	dispute for the throne with 6
8	302–9	Hormisdas [Hormezd] II	MP Hormezd	son of 7	
9	309–79	Sapor(es) [Shāpūr] II	MP Šābuhr	son of 8	
10	379–83	Artaxerxes (Artaxares) [Ardashīr] II	MP Ardašīr	son (brother?) of 9	
11	383–8	Sapor(es) [Shāpūr] III	MP Šābuhr	son of 9	
12	388–99	Wahram (Va(ra)ranes) [Wahrām] IV	MP Wahrām	son (brother?) of 11	
13	399–421	Yazdgird I (Isdigerdes) [Yazdgerd]	MP Yazdgerd	son of 12	
14	421–39	Wahram (Va(ra)ranes) [Wahrām] V	MP Wahrām (Gōr)	son of 13	
15	439–457	Yazdgird II (Isdigerdes) [Yazdgerd]	MP Yazdgerd	son of 14	

Genealogical table of the Sasanians (cont.)

	Date	Name	Indigenous names	Genealogy	Commentary
16	457–9	Hormisdas [Hormezd] III	MP Hormezd	son of 15	
17	459–84	Peroz(es) [Fīrūz]	MP Pērōz	son of 15; brother of 16	
18	484–8	Balas (Blases)	MP Walaxš	son of 15; brother of 17	
19	488–96; 499–531	Kabades [Kawād] I	MP Kawād	son of 17	
20	496–8	Zamasphes (Zames)	MP Zamāsp	son of 17; brother of 19	
21	531–79	Chosroes [Khusrau] I	MP Husraw (Xusrō)	son of 19	epithet Anōširwān
22	579–90	Hormisdas [Hormezd] IV	MP Hormezd	son of 21	
23	590–628	Chosroes [Khusrau] II	MP Husraw (Xusrō)	son of 22	epithet Abarwēz
24	590–1	Wahram (Va(ra)ranes) [Wahrām] VI [Chōbīn]	MP Wahrām Čōbīn	rival claimant of 23	
25	628	Kabades [Kawād] II	MP Kawād	son of 23	
26	628–30	Artaxerxes (Artaxares) [Ardashīr] III	MP Ardašīr	son of 25	
27	630	Schahrbaraz [Shahrbarāz]	MP Šahrwarāz		
28	630	Chosroes [Khusrau] III	MP Husraw (Xusrō)	nephew of 23	
29	630–1	Boran [Pūrān]	MP Pūrān	daughter of 23	queen
30	631	Āzarmīgdukht	MP Āzarmīgduxt	daughter of 23; sister of 29	queen
31	631–2	Hormisdas [Hormezd] V	MP Hormezd	grandson of 23	
32	631–3	Chosroes [Khusrau] IV	MP Husraw (Xusrō)		
33	633–51	Yazdgird III (Isdigerdes) [Yazdgerd]	MP Yazdgerd	grandson of 23	

4

Pre-Islamic Arabia

MICHAEL LECKER

Tribal historiography

The literary sources in Arabic dealing with pre-Islamic Arabia are copious, but rarely give direct answers to questions which are of interest to modern research. Still, the following had to be based on these sources since Arabian archaeology is only emerging; one hopes that significant Arabian pre-Islamic sites incur no damage before they are excavated.

Arabian society was tribal and included nomadic, semi-nomadic and settled populations. The settled populations had genealogies similar to those of the nomads and semi-nomads, identifying them as either 'northern' or 'southern' through the identity of their presumed eponyms. Not only did genealogy define the individual tribe, it also recorded its links with other tribes within families of tribes or tribal federations, each including several or many tribes. Muḥammad's tribe, Quraysh, for example, was part of the Kināna, and hence the other tribes of the Kināna were its closest relatives. The settled populations, which probably included more people than the nomadic and the semi-nomadic populations put together, do not receive a proportionate share in the literary sources because the limelights are typically on the nomads, more precisely on their military activities, no matter how insignificant. Tribal informants focused on the military activities since the performance of town dwellers in the realms of trade and agriculture were less spectacular, and hence less contributive to tribal solidarity.

After the Islamic conquests the tribes underwent significant changes, but they preserved their genealogy and their rich oral heritage that was inseparable from the genealogy. The amount of the materials that were transmitted and preserved was naturally affected by the size and political influence of the individual tribes. It stands to reason, however, that tribes that lived in or around the main centres of intellectual endeavour, such as Baṣra and Kūfa, stood a better chance of having their heritage recorded when oral accounts became written literary history. Regarding the time of Muḥammad, the coverage of individual tribes was uneven since it was also affected by their role at that time. Tribes such as Ghifār, Muzayna, Juhayna and others roaming around Mecca and Medina (pre-Islamic Yathrib)[1] are better known to us than much stronger tribes such as Asad and Ghaṭafān, simply because the former played a more central role in Muḥammad's history.

The attention given in the literature to the military activities of the nomads led to an unrealistic and unbalanced perception of pre-Islamic Arabian society. While Mecca and Medina are described in much detail, many other settlements that were perhaps larger, wealthier and more populous than these two towns, such as Ḥajr (present-day Riyadh), which was the central settlement in the al-Yamāma area, are hardly taken into account in scholarly descriptions of pre-Islamic Arabia.

Much of the source material regarding Arabia goes back to tribal genealogists, each of whom specialised in a specific tribe or group of tribes. The tribal genealogists also mastered the tribal history and poetry, because they were both extensions of the genealogical information. Let us take for example the Taghlib. Al-Akhzar ibn Suḥayma was an early Taghlibī genealogist who transmitted part of the information on his tribe later incorporated in the genealogy books. Between the early genealogists and the philologists of the second/eighth century there were intermediaries who usually remained unidentified. But expertise in Taghlibī genealogy and tribal history was not an exclusive Taghlibī domain. The most famous genealogist and philologist of early Islam, Ibn al-Kalbī (d. 204/819), learned about Taghlibī matters from Abū Raʿshan Khirāsh ibn Ismāʿīl of the ʿIjl tribe who compiled a monograph about the tribal federation of Rabīʿa that included both his own tribe, the ʿIjl and the Taghlib. Khirāsh also reported about a battle that took place in early Islam (the battle of Ṣiffīn, 37/657), which indicates that his scholarly interests covered both the pre- and early Islamic periods. Indeed, tribal genealogists, and in their wake Muslim philologists whose scope was much wider, considered the pre- and early Islamic history of the tribes as an uninterrupted whole.

The members of each tribe shared a notion of common descent from the same eponym. The eponyms in their turn were interconnected by an intricate network of family links that defined the tribal system across Arabia; tribal alliances were often concluded along genealogical lines. From time to time genealogy fluctuated according to changing military, political and ecological

1 Both the tribes and their territories are referred to by the Arabic term *bādiya*; one speaks of the *bādiya* of such-and-such settlement.

circumstances. There were prestigious and famous lineages beside less prestigious ones. For example, detailed information about the Banū Zurāra, a leading family of the Tamīm, is included in a dialogue between a member of this family and an old man who lived in the south-eastern corner of Arabia but nevertheless had an impressive command of the intricacies of Tamīmī genealogy.[2]

By definition, tribal informants were biased and acted in an atmosphere of intertribal competition or even hostility. The formal state of truce that followed the tribes' conversion to Islam generally stopped their resort to violence. But polemics and friction, especially in the garrison cities of Iraq, were often intensified.

The bias of tribal informants must be taken into account and lead to greater prudence in using their reports. It can be demonstrated by the intertribal polemics surrounding the Arab bow of Tamīm's illustrious pre-Islamic leader Ḥājib ibn Zurāra, which holds a place of honour in Tamīm's pre-Islamic history. During a severe drought Ḥājib asked for Khusrau's permission to graze his tribe's herds on the fringes of the sown land in south-western Iraq. As a guarantee of good conduct Ḥājib pledged his bow, an unsophisticated item which nonetheless acquired great value through the eminence and authority of its owner. The Tamīm were very proud of this pledge, which showed the Sasanian emperor adopting their tribal values. Tamīm's adversaries in their turn attempted to belittle the importance of the gesture. 'Had they not been in my opinion of less value than the bow, I would not have taken it,' the emperor is made to say,[3] as if explaining why he did not take Tamīmī hostages instead of a worthless bow. Other anti-Tamīmī informants downgraded the authority with whom Ḥājib had negotiated. One version mentions Iyās ibn Qabīṣa al-Ṭā'ī who was 'Khusrau's governor in charge of Ḥīra and the Arabs in its vicinity'; while other versions mention 'the head of the *asāwira*, or heavy cavalry, charged with guarding the border between the Arabs and the Persians'[4] and 'one of Khusrau's *marzbāns*', or one of his (military, but also civil) governors.[5] Obviously, tribal polemicists were at work here, and they were anything but innocent.

2 Abū l-Baqā' Hibat Allāh al-Ḥillī, *al-Manāqib al-mazyadiyya*, ed. Ṣāliḥ Mūsā Darādika and Muḥammad 'Abd al-Qādir Khrīsāt, 2 vols. (Amman, 1404 AH [1984]), vol. I, p. 353. The late Ḥamad al-Jāsir wrote a monograph entitled *Bāhila al-qabīla l-muftarā 'alayhā* (Riyadh, 1410 AH [1989]). Tribal genealogies remain a delicate matter in contemporary Saudi Arabia.

3 Abū Manṣūr al-Tha'ālibī, *Thimār al-qulūb fī l-muḍāf wa-l-mansūb*, ed. Muḥammad Abū l-Faḍl Ibrāhīm (Cairo, 1965), p. 626.

4 Balādhurī, *Ansāb al-ashrāf* (MS Süleymanie Kütüphanesi, Reisülküttap Mustafa Efendi, 597, 598), 960a.

5 Abū l-Baqā', *al-Manāqib al-mazyadiyya*, vol. I, p. 61.

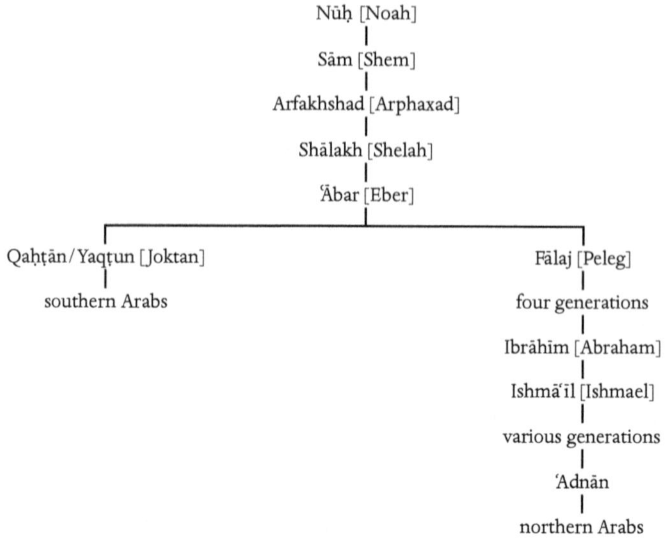

1. The 'northern' and 'southern' Arabs

Yet another example of tribal bias relates to Muḥammad's tribe, Quraysh, which was considered 'northern' from the genealogical point of view; unsurprisingly, many sources reveal a pro-Qurashī bias. Regarding the takeover of the Kaʿba in Mecca by Muḥammad's ancestor, Quṣayy, it is reported that a member of the Khuzāʿa tribe, which is usually considered a 'southern' tribe, sold the Kaʿba to Quṣayy. As usual, there are several versions regarding the mode of the takeover. However, the specific sale version that concerns us here did not come from an impartial party: it was reportedly promulgated by people fanatically hostile to the 'southern' tribes.[6] The Khuzāʿa did not remain indifferent to this hostile description of a crucial chapter in their tribal history: the historian al-Wāqidī (d. 207/823) concludes a variant of this version with the statement that it was denied by the elders of the Khuzāʿa.[7]

6 Al-Wazīr al-Maghribī, *al-Īnās fī ʿilm al-ansāb*, bound with Ibn Ḥabīb, *Mukhtalif al-qabāʾil wa-muʾtalifuhā*, ed. Ḥamad al-Jāsir (Riyadh, 1980), p. 114: *fa-yaqūlu l-mutaʿaṣṣibūna ʿalā l-Yamāniyya inna Quṣayyan shtarā l-miftāḥ*.
7 Taqī al-Dīn Muḥammad ibn Aḥmad al-Fāsī, *Shifāʾ al-gharām bi-akhbār al-balad al-ḥarām*, ed. ʿUmar ʿAbd al-Salām Tadmurī, 2 vols. (Beirut, 1985), vol. II, p. 87.

The nomadic and settled populations

Pre-Islamic Arabia was not lawless or wild since an unwritten legal code controlled the life of its people. The law of talion and various security arrangements protected the lives of tribesmen outside their tribal territories.

The boundaries of these territories were generally acknowledged; tribesmen were supposed to know when they left the territories belonging to their tribes. But just like tribal genealogies, tribal boundaries fluctuated to reflect changing circumstances on the ground. A tribe's territory often included enclaves belonging to other tribes, which necessitated cooperation between the tribes involved; indeed, such enclaves could only survive where a clear legal code prevailed.

Although the number of literate people was limited even in the settlements, resort to written documents during the conclusion of alliances and transactions was common.[8] The so-called Constitution of Medina concluded by Muḥammad shortly after the *hijra* shows that complex legal documents and legal terminology in Arabic had existed in Arabia before the advent of Islam.

The genealogical variegation of the settled populations was probably greater than that of the nomads; indeed, one expects the population of a settlement to include several or many tribes. This was the case with the Christian tribal groups living in al-Ḥīra, collectively referred to as al-ʿIbād, that preserved their original tribal affiliations. Pre-Islamic Medina provides further evidence of this: several towns in the Medina area were inhabited by *jummāʿ*, or groups from various tribes. 'The people of Zuhra' (*ahl Zuhra*) and 'the people of Zubāla', to give but two examples of such towns, were described as *jummāʿ*.[9]

The crucial relationship between the nomadic and settled populations across Arabia took many forms. Due to the size of their territory and their millstone-like roaming around their grazing grounds and water places, the Tamīm were one of the so-called 'millstones of the Arabs' (*arḥāʾ al-ʿarab*).[10]

8 See M. Lecker, 'A pre-Islamic endowment deed in Arabic regarding al-Waḥīda in the Ḥijāz', in M. Lecker, *People, tribes and society in Arabia around the time of Muḥammad* (Aldershot, 2005), no. IV.

9 ʿAlī ibn Aḥmad al-Samhūdī, *Wafāʾ al-wafā*, ed. Qāsim al-Sāmarrāʾī, 5 vols. (London and Jedda, 2001), vol. I, pp. 306–8.

10 Ibn Saʿīd al-Andalusī, *Nashwat al-ṭarab bi-taʾrīkh jāhiliyyat al-ʿarab*, ed. Naṣrat ʿAbd al-Raḥmān, 2 vols. (Amman, 1982), vol. I, p. 415.

But even the powerful Tamīmīs were vulnerable to outside pressure since they had to rely on the settlements for part of their subsistence. Their massacre in the battle of Yawm al-Mushaqqar could only take place because of their annual visit to Hajar on the coast of the Persian Gulf in order to receive their provisions.[11]

Sometimes the nomads roaming around a certain settlement and the people of the settlement belonged to the same tribe. The third/ninth-century geographer ʿArrām al-Sulamī's description of the stronghold of Suwāriqiyya south-east of Medina is generally true for pre-Islamic times as well. He says that Suwāriqiyya belonged to the Sulaym tribe alone and that each of the Sulamīs had a share in it. It had fields, dates and other kinds of fruit. The Sulamīs born in Suwāriqiyya lived there, while the others were *bādiya* and roamed around it, supplying food along the pilgrim roads as far as Ḍariyya seven days' journey from Suwāriqiyya.[12] In other words, the Sulamī farmers of Suwāriqiyya tilled the land and tended the irrigation systems, while the Sulamī nomads tended the beasts – above all the camels, which require extensive grazing grounds, and hence cannot be raised in significant numbers by farmers.

The biography of Muḥammad provides further evidence of the cooperation between the nomadic and settled populations. When the Jewish Naḍīr were expelled from Medina several years after the *hijra*, they hired hundreds of camels from a nomadic tribe roaming the vicinity of Medina; in normal circumstances these nomads would be transporting goods on behalf of the

11 Abū Jaʿfar Muḥammad ibn Jarīr al-Ṭabarī, *Taʾrīkh al-rusul wa-l-mulūk*, ed. M. de Goeje *et al.*, 15 vols. in 3 series (Leiden, 1879–1901), series I, p. 985: 'This was close to the days of the *luqāṭ* [the picking up of dates from the stumps of the branches of palm-trees after the cutting off of the dates]. The Tamīm used to go at that time to Hajar to get provisions and collect the dates left on the trees (*li-l-mīra wa-l-luqāṭ*).' Hajar was the largest date-producing oasis in northern Arabia. On the connection between *al-mīra wa-l-kayl*, or provisions, and obedience, see M. J. Kister, 'al-Ḥīra: Some notes on its relations with Arabia', *Arabica*, 15 (1968), p. 168. The Bedouin who came to Yamāma in the holy months (in which no warfare took place) in order to get provisions were called *al-sawāqiṭ*: Abū ʿUbayda Maʿmar ibn al-Muthannā, *al-Dībāj*, ed. al-Jarbūʿ and al-ʿUthaymīn (Cairo, 1991), p. 53: *wa-kāna l-sawāqiṭ min qabāʾil shattā wa-summū sawāqiṭ li-annahum kānū yaʾtūna l-Yamāma fī l-ashhuri l-ḥurum li-l-tamr wa-l-zarʿ*. At the time of the Prophet, when a certain Tamīmī came to Hajar in the holy month of Rajab in order to get provisions for his family (*yamīru ahlahu min Hajar*, i.e. as he used to do every year), his wife escaped from him; see e.g. Majd al-Dīn Ibn al-Athīr, *Manāl al-ṭālib fī sharḥ ṭiwāl al-gharāʾib*, ed. Maḥmūd Muḥammad al-Ṭanāḥī (Mecca, 1983), pp. 495–6.

12 ʿArrām al-Sulamī, *Asmāʾ jibāl tihāma*, in ʿAbd al-Salām Hārūn (ed.), *Nawādir al-makhṭūṭāt*, 2nd edn, vol. II (Cairo, 1973), pp. 431–2; Yāqūt al-Ḥamawī, *Muʿjam al-buldān* (Beirut, 1957), s.v. al-Suwāriqiyya.

Naḍīr. When the people of al-Khaybar cut off the fruit of their palm trees, the nomads would arrive with their camels and carry it for them to the villages, one camel load after the other (*ʿurwa bi-ʿurwa*, literally: one loop of the camel load after the other). The nomads would sell the fruit, keeping for themselves half of the return.[13]

In the battlefield, nomads fought against other nomads, while settled people fought against other settled people. A verse by the Prophet's Companion, the poet Ḥassān ibn Thābit (who was of the Khazraj, a 'southern' tribe) demonstrates this:

> Our settled men spare us the village dwellers,
> while our bedouins spare us the bedouins of the Maʿadd [i.e. the 'northern' tribes].[14]

During the *ridda* wars that followed Muḥammad's death there was a dispute within the Muslim army in al-Yamāma between the settled (*ahl al-qurā*, including the *muhājirūn* and the *anṣār*) and the nomads (*ahl al-bādiya/al-bawādī*), with each accusing the other of cowardice. The settled people claimed that they knew better how to fight against their like, while the nomads said that the settled people were not good fighters and did not know what war was.[15]

The military aspect was dominant in the relationship between the settled and the nomads, as shown by accounts dealing with Muḥammad and his Companions. Friendly nomads were considered Muḥammad's *bādiya*, with reference to their military role. Two tribes living near Medina once asked for Muḥammad's permission to build themselves a mosque in Medina similar to the mosques of other tribes. But he told them that his mosque was also their mosque, that they were his *bādiya* while he was their *ḥāḍira*, or their settled counterpart (lit., 'people dwelling by waters'), and that they should provide him with succour when called upon to do so.[16] The *hijra* of one of the *bādiya* meant that he had to provide succour when called upon to do so (*an yujība idhā duʿiya*) and to obey orders.[17] A 'good' Bedouin differed from a 'bad' one in that the former provided military aid. When ʿĀʾisha mentioned certain Bedouin, pejoratively calling them *aʿrāb*, Muḥammad corrected her: 'They

13 Samhūdī, *Wafāʾ al-wafā*, vol. II, p. 35.

14 Ḥassān ibn Thābit, *Dīwān*, ed. W. ʿArafat, 2 vols. (London, 1971), vol. I, p. 462, no. 287: *maḥāḍirunā yakfūnanā sākina l-qurā* [ ], *wa-aʿrābunā yakfūnanā man tamaʿdadā*.

15 Al-Ṭabarī, *Taʾrīkh*, series I, pp. 1946, 1947.

16 Ibn Shabba, *Taʾrīkh al-madīna al-munawwara*, ed. Fahīm Muḥammad Shaltūt, 4 vols. (n.p. [1979]; repr. Beirut, 1990), vol. I, p. 78.

17 Abū ʿUbayd al-Qāsim ibn Sallām, *Kitāb al-amwāl*, ed. Muḥammad Khalīl Harrās (Cairo, 1976), p. 280, no. 538.

are not *aʿrāb* but our *bādiya*, while we are their *ḥāḍira*; when summoned, they provide us with succour.'[18] A fuller version of this tradition makes it clear that the commitment to give succour was reciprocal.[19]

With regard to the relationship between the nomadic and settled populations the question of ascendancy arises. The conquest of settlements by nomads[20] must have been rare because the latter did not wish to become farmers. But Muḥammad's history shows that in the major military confrontations of his time the initiative was in the hands of his Qurashī enemies, and later in those of Muḥammad himself; this suggests that the ascendancy belonged to the settled people. Let us take for example the military activity of the Sulaym at that time: first they fought with Quraysh against Muḥammad, then they fought with Muḥammad against Quraysh.[21] In both cases the initiative was not theirs, and the same is true of the *ridda* wars and the Conquests.

Closely linked to the question of ascendancy is that of the food allocations granted by the settled people to the nomads. At first glance they appear to indicate the ascendancy of the latter, but this was not the case. The people of Medina granted an annual share of their date produce to the strong tribal leader of the ʿĀmir ibn Ṣaʿṣaʿa, Abū Barāʾ ʿĀmir ibn Mālik (nicknamed *Mulāʿib al-Asinna*, or 'the one playing with spears'). He received from them annually a certain amount (*kayla*) of dates in return for a guarantee of safe conduct for the Medinans travelling in Najd.[22] While protecting the lives and goods of these Medinans, the grant did not give the nomadic Banū ʿĀmir ascendancy over the settled Medinans. This state of affairs remains unchanged when other terms are employed in similar contexts. In connection with the conquest (or rather temporary takeover) of Fadak by the nomadic Kalb around 570 CE it is reported that the Kalbī leader involved was entitled to a payment (*jaʿāla*) from the people of Fadak. A *jaʿāla* is a payment for services such as the return of a missing camel or a fugitive slave. The Tamīm transported Khusrau's caravan from al-Yamāma to the Yemen in return for a *jaʿāla*, and the Kalb may well have earned their *jaʿāla* for providing similar services. Also, the leader of the Fazāra tribe, ʿUyayna ibn Ḥiṣn, received an annual

18 Ibid., no. 539.

19 Ibn Ḥajar al-ʿAsqalānī, *al-Maṭālib al-ʿāliya bi-zawāʾid al-masānīd al-thamāniya*, ed. Ḥabīb al-Raḥmān al-Aʿẓamī, 4 vols. (Kuwait, 1973), vol. IV, p. 144, no. 4185.

20 See M. J. Kister, 'On the wife of the goldsmith from Fadak and her progeny', *Le Muséon*, 92 (1979), pp. 321–30; repr. in M. J. Kister, *Society and religion from Jāhiliyya to Islam* (Aldershot, 1990), no. V.

21 M. Lecker, *The Banū Sulaym: A contribution to the study of early Islam* (Jerusalem, 1989), pp. 136–7.

22 Ḥassān ibn Thābit, *Dīwān*, vol. II, p. 176. The term *kayla* is derived from the root *k.y.l.*, which denotes a measure of capacity. Cf. above, n. 475.

grant from the date produce of Medina. The term used in his case, *itāwa*, sometimes means a tribute or tax. But here it designates an annual grant in kind to a nomadic leader, similar to those referred to by the terms *kayla* and *jaʿāla*.

Medina and the other settlements could afford to grant part of their huge surplus of dates to the leaders of large nomadic tribes in order to secure their goodwill. The size of the grants must have varied according to the harvest and the changing political circumstances on the ground; but even where they amounted to a sizeable part of the annual produce they did not indicate nomadic ascendancy.

Idol worship

The pre-Islamic Arabs were united by their love of poetry; many of them could probably appreciate the artistic value of the poems recited during major tribal gatherings, for example at the ʿUkāẓ fair, not far from Ṭāʾif. In their daily life, however, they spoke a large number of dialects. Many of them acknowledged the sanctity of the Kaʿba in Mecca and made pilgrimage to it, travelling under the protection of the holy months during which all hostilities ceased. The Arab idol worshippers were polytheists, but they also believed in a High God called Allāh whose house was in the Kaʿba and who had supremacy over their tribal deities.

Despite the diversity in the forms of idol worship, on the whole it was a common characteristic of pre-Islamic Arabian society. In the centuries preceding the advent of Islam Christianity and Judaism were competing with each other for the hearts of the Yemenite polytheists. Medina had a large Jewish population, while al-Yamāma and eastern Arabia had a large Christian one. Christianity, and to a lesser extent Judaism, penetrated several nomadic tribes. The celebrated *ḥanīfs*, or ascetic seekers of true religion who abandoned idol worship, were probably few; moreover, the identification of some of them as *ḥanīfs* is questionable. Several early Tamīmī converts to Islam were former Zoroastrians. However, on the eve of Islam idol worship prevailed, with the prominent exception of the Yemen, considered by medieval Muslim historians to have been predominantly Jewish.

Idols of every shape and material were ubiquitous, and their worship showed no signs of decline. Many conversion stories regarding both former custodians of idols and ordinary worshippers specifically refer to a shift from idol worship to Islam.

The most common deity was the household idol. Several conversion accounts that prove the proliferation of household idols in Mecca are associated with its conquest by Muḥammad (8/630). Al-Wāqidī adduces legendary accounts about the destruction of household idols. While the accounts aim at establishing the Islamic credentials of their protagonists, the background details are credible. One account has it that after the conquest of Mecca, Muḥammad's announcer ordered the destruction of every idol found in the houses. So whenever ʿIkrima ibn Abī Jahl (who belonged to the Qurashī branch Makhzūm) heard of an idol in one of the houses of Quraysh, he went there in order to smash it; it is specifically stated in this context that every Qurashī in Mecca had an idol in his house. In al-Wāqidī's account we find that the announcer proclaimed that every idol had to be destroyed or burnt, and that it was forbidden to sell them (i.e. to sell wooden idols to be used as firewood). The informant himself saw the idols being carried around Mecca (i.e. by peddlers); the Bedouin used to buy them and take them to their tents. Every Qurashī, we are told, had an idol in his house. He stroked it whenever he entered or left the house to draw a blessing from it.

Yet another account in the same source has it that when Hind bint ʿUtba (the mother of the future Umayyad caliph Muʿāwiya) embraced Islam, she started striking an idol in her house with an adze, cutting oblong pieces from it.[23] She probably destroyed her wooden idol using the very tool with which it had been carved. The authors of the legendary accounts about ʿIkrima and Hind sought to emphasise the zeal of these new converts, but the background information is accurate: idols were found in all Meccan households.

In Medina, which was in many ways different from Mecca, idols were associated with various levels of the tribal organisation. A house idol made of wood was an obstacle for Abū Ṭalḥa of the Khazraj when he proposed to his future wife. She refused to marry 'one who worshipped a stone which did neither harm nor good and a piece of wood hewed for him by a carpenter'.[24] Several young Medinans from both of the dominant Arab tribes of Medina, the Aws and Khazraj, smashed the idols found among their fellow tribesmen. Here too household idols were the most common form of idol worship. We have some evidence about the attributes of one of the Medinan household idols. Before one of them was destroyed with an adze, it had to be brought down, which indicates that it had been placed in an elevated place such as a shelf; the same idol had a veil hung over it.

One level up from the household idols we find those belonging to noblemen. Every nobleman in Medina owned an idol that had a name of its own.

23 Muḥammad ibn ʿUmar al-Wāqidī, *Kitāb al-maghāzī*, ed. Marsden Jones, 3 vols. (London, 1966), vol. II, pp. 870–1.

24 Ibn Saʿd, *al-Ṭabaqāt al-kubrā*, 8 vols. (Beirut, 1960–8), vol. VIII, pp. 425–6.

In addition, *baṭns*, or small tribal groups, had idols which, similarly, had names. The *baṭn*'s idol was placed in a sanctuary (*bayt*) and belonged to the whole *baṭn* (*li-jamāʿati l-baṭn*). Sacrifices were offered to it. One level above the *baṭns* in the tribal system of Medina stood the major subdivisions of the Aws and Khazraj. Evidence has so far emerged regarding the idol of one such subdivision: the Banū Ḥārith ibn al-Khazraj had an idol called Huzam that was placed in their *majlis*, or place of assembly, similarly called Huzam. One assumes that sacrifices were also offered to Huzam, since sacrifices were offered to the lower-level idols of the *baṭns*. The idol al-Khamīs was worshipped by the Khazraj,[25] while al-Saʿīda, which was located on Mount Uḥud north of Medina, was worshipped, among others, by the Azd – no doubt including the Aws and Khazraj, which belonged to the Azd.[26] At the top of the hierarchy of the idols worshipped by the Aws and Khazraj stood Manāt. A descendant of Muḥammad's Companion Saʿd ibn ʿUbāda reports that Saʿd's grandfather annually donated ten slaughter camels to Manāt. Saʿd's father followed suit, and so did Saʿd himself before his conversion to Islam. Saʿd's son, Qays, donated the same number of camels to the Kaʿba.[27] The report is not concerned with idol worship as such but with generosity, prestige and tribal leadership. Saʿd's donation of sacrifice camels to Manāt before his conversion to Islam shows that its cult continued to the very advent of Islam.

Household idols were ubiquitous in Medina, as in Mecca; noblemen, *baṭns* and major Aws and Khazraj subdivisions had idols. The Khazraj as a whole worshipped a special idol; the Aws and Khazraj were among the worshippers of another, and they were still worshipping their main idol, Manāt, when Muḥammad appeared. All this does not indicate a decline in idol worship.

Expressing his opinion about the influence of monotheism on the Arabs before Islam, Ibn Isḥāq says that 'it was merely superficial; the Arabs were illiterate and what they heard from Jews and Christians had no effect on their lives'. With regard to idol worship his statement is trustworthy.

Foreign powers

Pre-Islamic Arabia and its tribes were not isolated from the great empires of Byzantium and Persia, with the latter probably playing a more significant

25 Al-Ṭabarī, *Taʾrīkh*, series I, p. 1085.

26 Muḥammad ibn Ḥabīb, *Kitāb al-muḥabbar*, ed. Ilse Lichtenstaedter (Hyderabad, 1361 [1942]; repr. Beirut, n.d.), pp. 316–17.

27 Ibn ʿAbd al-Barr, *al-Istīʿāb fī maʿrifat al-aṣḥāb*, ed. ʿAlī Muḥammad al-Bijāwī, 4 vols. (Cairo, n.d.), vol. II, p. 595.

role. The Byzantine emperor, for example, is said to have been instrumental in the takeover of Mecca from the Khuzāʿa tribe by Muḥammad's ancestor Quṣayy.[28]

The Byzantines and Sasanians conducted their Arabian affairs through their respective Arab buffer kingdoms, Ghassān and al-Ḥīra. The king of al-Ḥīra appointed governors to the frontiers from Iraq to Baḥrayn, each of whom ruled together with a Bedouin leader who was in fact his subordinate.[29]

The same pattern was found in Oman: a treaty between the Sasanians and the Julandā family concluded in the second half of the sixth century stipulated that the Sasanians were entitled to station with the 'kings' of the Azd four thousand men including *marzbāns* (military, but also civil, governors) and *asāwira* (heavy cavalry), and an *ʿāmil* or official. The Sasanians were stationed in the coastal regions, while the Azd were 'kings' in the mountains, in the deserts and in the other areas surrounding Oman.[30] In other words, authority was divided between the Arabs and the Sasanians along geographical lines.

In Baḥrayn there was an Arab governor, with a Sasanian superior. Al-Mundhir ibn Sāwā al-Tamīmī is said to have been the governor of Baḥrayn. But the historian al-Balādhurī (d. 279/892) draws a clear line at this point between Sasanians and Arabs: 'The land of Baḥrayn is part of the Persian kingdom and there were in it many Arabs from the tribes of ʿAbd al-Qays, Bakr ibn Wāʾil and Tamīm living in its *bādiya*. At the time of the Prophet, al-Mundhir ibn Sāwā was in charge of the Arabs living there on behalf of the Persians.'[31] At the same time Baḥrayn had a Sasanian governor who was al-Mundhir's superior, namely Sībukht, the *marzbān* of Hajar.[32] On the eve of Islam the Yemen was under direct Sasanian control.

Roughly until the middle of the sixth century Medina was controlled by a *marzbān* whose seat was in al-Zāra on the coast of the Persian Gulf. The Jewish tribes Naḍīr and Qurayẓa were 'kings', and exacted tribute from the Aws and

28 Ibn Qutayba, *al-Maʿārif*, ed. Tharwat ʿUkāsha (Cairo, 1969), pp. 640–1; quoted in M. J. Kister, 'Mecca and the tribes of Arabia', in M. Sharon (ed.), *Studies in Islamic history and civilization in honour of David Ayalon* (Jerusalem and Leiden, 1986), p. 50; repr. in Kister, *Society and religion*, no. II. Cf. ʿUthmān ibn al-Ḥuwayrith's attempt to gain control of Mecca on behalf of the Byzantine emperor: Kister, 'al-Ḥīra', p. 154.

29 Abū l-Baqāʾ, *al-Manāqib al-mazyadiyya*, vol. II, p. 369.

30 J. C. Wilkinson, 'Arab–Persian land relationships in late Sasānid Oman', in *Proceedings of the Seminar for Arabian Studies*, 3 (1973), pp. 41, 44–7.

31 Al-Balādhurī, *Futūḥ*, ed. M. J. de Goeje (Leiden, 1863 –6), p. 78: *wa-kāna ʿalā l-ʿarab bihā min qibali l-furs*.

32 His name and title appear in connection with a letter allegedly sent by the Prophet to both al-Mundhir ibn Sāwā and Sībukht *marzbān* Hajar, calling upon them to embrace Islam or pay the poll-tax.

Khazraj on behalf of the Sasanians. In the last quarter of the sixth century the king of al-Ḥīra, al-Nuʿmān ibn al-Mundhir, declared a member of the Khazraj, ʿAmr ibn al-Iṭnāba, king of Medina or of the Ḥijāz.[33] At that time the Jews were no longer 'kings' and tribute collectors, but tribute payers. ʿAmr's appointment shows that Sasanian control in western Arabia continued in the latter half of the sixth century. Sasanian control there is also associated with al-Nuʿmān ibn al-Mundhir's father, al-Mundhir III (*c.* 504–54): the Sasanian emperor Khusrau I Anūshirwān (r. 531–79) made him king of the Arabs living between Oman, Baḥrayn and al-Yamāma to al-Ṭā'if and the rest of the Ḥijāz.[34]

Caravan trade was often behind the cooperation between certain nomadic tribes and the Sasanians. The Sulaym and the Hawāzin used to conclude pacts with the kings of al-Ḥīra, transport the kings' merchandise and sell it for them at the fair at ʿUkāẓ, among others.[35] With regard to the above-mentioned battle of Yawm al-Mushaqqar it is reported that Khusrau's caravan, having travelled from Ctesiphon via al-Ḥīra, was escorted by the Tamīm from al-Yamāma to the Yemen.

The evidence regarding military cooperation (or indeed any other form of cooperation) between the tribes and the courts of Ctesiphon and al-Ḥīra reveals a certain tension between the wish to praise the tribe's military exploits, even those carried out in the service of a foreign power, and the claim of independence from the same power; tribal historiography attempted to distance the tribes from the influence of the courts, while at the same time boasting of the close contacts between them.

Many Arabs probably saw the local representatives of the great power from behind bars: the kings of al-Ḥīra practised widespread incarceration as punishment and as a means of pressure. There were jails or incarceration camps at al-Quṭquṭāna in south-western Iraq and at al-Ḥīra itself.[36]

The Tamīm, the Taghlib and others took part in the institution of *ridāfa* (viceroyship) to the king of al-Ḥīra, which was essential in establishing al-Ḥīra's control over the tribes. The ceremonial and material privileges associated with it (perhaps exaggerated by the tribal informants) helped in buying

33 Kister, 'al-Ḥīra', pp. 147–9; Lecker, *People, tribes and society in Arabia*, index. It would seem that at that time Medina was no longer controlled from al-Zāra but directly from Ḥīra.
34 Al-Ṭabarī, *Ta'rīkh*, series I, pp. 958–9.
35 Abū l-Baqā', *al-Manāqib al-mazyadiyya*, vol. II, p. 375.
36 Abū Ḥātim al-Sijistānī, *al-Muʿammarūna*, bound with *Al-Waṣāyā* by the same author, ed. ʿAbd al-Munʿim ʿĀmir (Cairo, 1961), pp. 20–2. ʿAdī ibn Zayd was jailed at al-Ṣinnayn; al-Ṭabarī, *Ta'rīkh*, series I, p. 1023. A poet who lived in the transition period between *jāhiliyya* and Islam (*mukhaḍram*) was jailed by the Sasanians at al-Mushaqqar: Ibn Ḥajar al-ʿAsqalānī, *al-Iṣāba fī tamyīz al-ṣaḥāba*, ed. ʿAlī Muḥammad al-Bijāwī, 8 vols. (Cairo, [1970]), vol. II, p. 513.

off potentially dangerous tribes. Through trade, military cooperation and diplomacy Arab tribal leaders and merchants became acquainted with the courts of the buffer kingdoms and the great empires.

Mecca: trade and agriculture

Mecca and Medina, thanks to their association with the history of the Prophet Muḥammad and the rise of Islam, are better known to us than many other settlements in Arabia that may well have been larger, wealthier and more populous.

Mecca and its dominant tribe, Quraysh, reveal a high degree of internal cohesion; but Mecca's stability was in fact based on the preservation of a balance of power between two rival alliances of Quraysh rather than on any sense of tribal solidarity. As one can expect, in accounts of Mecca's pre-Islamic history – for example, concerning the establishment of its international caravan trade – the Prophet's ancestors receive more credit than is due to them. In any case, this trade was not a myth, but was Mecca's main source of revenue, regardless of the items and the income involved. In Arabian terms Mecca was a major trade centre, although it is impossible to establish whether or not it was the largest of its kind in Arabia.

Crossing evidence shows that the Prophet himself had been a merchant before receiving his first revelation. Trade partnerships were a significant aspect of the economic cooperation between Quraysh and the tribe controlling Ṭāʾif, the Thaqīf. Reportedly, the Qurashī Abū Sufyān and the Thaqafī Ghaylān ibn Salama traded with Persia, accompanied by a group of people from both tribes.[37] Both were Muḥammad's contemporaries.

In addition to trade, the entrepreneurial Qurashīs invested in agriculture. Since conditions in Mecca itself were uninviting for agriculture, they looked for opportunities elsewhere. It can be argued that the Qurashī expansion in Arabia preceded the advent of Islam.

There is a legendary story about the death of Ḥarb ibn Umayya, the father of the above-mentioned Abū Sufyān and the grandfather of the caliph Muʿāwiya. He was reportedly killed by the *jinn* at al-Qurayya north-west of Mecca, since together with a local partner he disturbed the *jinn* or killed one of them by mistake. This occurred while they were clearing a thicket in order to prepare the land for cultivation. The story probably owes its preservation to

37 Abū Hilāl al-ʿAskarī, *al-Awāʾil*, ed. Muḥammad al-Miṣrī and Walīd Qaṣṣāb, 2 vols. (Damascus, 1975), vol. II, p. 228.

the legendary elements; but the background details are no doubt factual.[38] There is rich evidence of pre-Islamic Qurashī involvement in agriculture in Ṭā'if, the town that supplied (and still supplies) most of Mecca's demand for fruit;[39] hence its appellation *bustān al-ḥaram*, or the orchard of the sacred territory of Mecca.[40] Side by side with the locals who cultivated small tracts of land, Qurashī entrepreneurs developed large estates in the valleys of Ṭā'if before the advent of Islam. Many Bedouin of the Qays ʿAylān and other tribes earned their living by transporting Ṭā'ifī products to Mecca. At Nakhla north-east of Mecca a caravan carrying wine, tanned skins and raisins[41] on its way from Ṭā'if to Mecca was attacked shortly after the *hijra* by the Prophet's Companions.

The best known and perhaps the largest Qurashī property in the vicinity of Ṭā'if is al-Waht̤, which is located in the valley of Wajj. The father of the Prophet's Companion ʿAmr ibn al-ʿĀṣ owned this estate before Islam. ʿAmr further developed it by raising the shoots of many thousands of grape-vines on pieces of wood made to support them.[42]

Numerous other Qurashīs owned estates near Ṭā'if. They included, among others, Abū Sufyān, ʿUtba and Shayba sons of Rabīʿa ibn ʿAbd Shams, the Prophet's uncle al-ʿAbbās and al-Walīd ibn al-Walīd ibn al-Mughīra (the brother of the famous general Khālid ibn al-Walīd).

The Muslim conquests in Palestine and elsewhere are unlikely to have been accompanied by large-scale devastation of agricultural land and facilities, since ʿAmr ibn al-ʿĀṣ and the other Qurashī generals had previous experience with agriculture and appreciated the economic value of cultivated land.

Medina: a precarious balance

The cluster of towns or villages known before Islam as Yathrib was called after the town of Yathrib on its north-western side. Under Islam the cluster

38 After the *hijra* it was one of Muḥammad's companions, Ṭalḥa, who introduced the sowing of wheat in Medina, while another companion, ʿAbdallāh ibn ʿĀmir, was famous for his talent for discovering water sources.

39 Muḥammad ibn ʿAbd al-Munʿim al-Ḥimyarī, *al-Rawḍ al-miʿṭār fī khabar al-aqṭār*, ed. Iḥsān ʿAbbās (Beirut, 1975), p. 379a.

40 Muḥammad ibn Isḥāq al-Fākihī, *Akhbār Makka*, ed. ʿAbd al-Malik ibn ʿAbdallāh ibn Duhaysh, 6 vols. (Mecca, 1987), vol. III, p. 206.

41 Wāqidī, *Maghāzī*, vol. I, p. 16.

42 Fākihī, *Akhbār Makka*, vol. III, p. 205 (read *ʿarrasha* instead of *gharasa*); Yāqūt, *Buldān*, s.v. al-Waht̤.

became known as al-Madīna. Major political and military upheavals preceding the *hijra* contributed to Muḥammad's success there in ways that are not yet fully clear.

Medina's large Jewish population was dispersed in both the Sāfila, or Lower Medina, in the north and the ʿĀliya, or Upper Medina, in the south. The Qurayẓa and Naḍīr are said to have inhabited the ʿĀliya, while a third large tribe, the Qaynuqāʿ, lived in the Sāfila. But the Naḍīr probably owned estates outside the ʿĀliya and on its fringe as well: the town of Zuhra is defined as the town of the Naḍīr (*qaryat banī l-naḍīr*); moreover, one of their notables, Kaʿb ibn al-Ashraf, owned land in al-Jurf north-west of Medina, at the upper part of the ʿAqīq valley.[43]

The oldest stratum in the Arab population of Medina was made up of members of the Balī and of other tribes, many of whom converted to Judaism. The Aws and Khazraj, who settled in Medina at a later stage, became known under Islam by the honorific appellation *al-anṣār* (the helpers). Unlike the earlier Arab settlers, most of the Aws and Khazraj remained idol worshippers. When they settled in Medina, their position vis-à-vis the Jewish tribes was weak. But gradually they gained strength, built fortresses and planted date orchards. The *anṣār* were ridiculed by other tribes for their initial subjection by the Jews, particularly with regard to the Arab Jewish king al-Fiṭyawn, 'the owner of Zuhra' (*ṣāḥib Zuhra*),[44] who reportedly practised the *ius prima noctis* on the Arab women. No wonder that al-Fiṭyawn figures prominently in *anṣārī* apologetic historiography. Admitting their initial weakness, they claimed that it came to an end with the killing of al-Fiṭyawn by a member of the Khazraj; from that moment onward the Jews were at the mercy of their former clients. However, *anṣārī* historiography should be taken with a grain of salt. The Jews suffered a setback, or the Khazrajī ʿAmr ibn al-Iṭnāba would not have become the king of Yathrib in the last quarter of the sixth century. But by the advent of Islam the main Jewish tribes Naḍīr and Qurayẓa had regained their power, as is shown by their victory at the battle of Buʿāth (615 or 617), together with their Awsī allies, over the powerful Khazraj.

ʿAmr ibn al-Iṭnāba and al-Fiṭyawn were not the only kings in Medina before Islam. Several generations before Islam there lived there a king called Ama ibn Ḥarām of the Khazraj subdivision called Salima whose powers included the confiscation and redistribution of agricultural land.

43 In due course Muḥammad himself owned agricultural land in al-Jurf.
44 Abū l-Faraj al-Iṣfahānī, *Kitāb al-aghānī*, 24 vols. (Cairo, 1927–74), vol. III, p. 40.

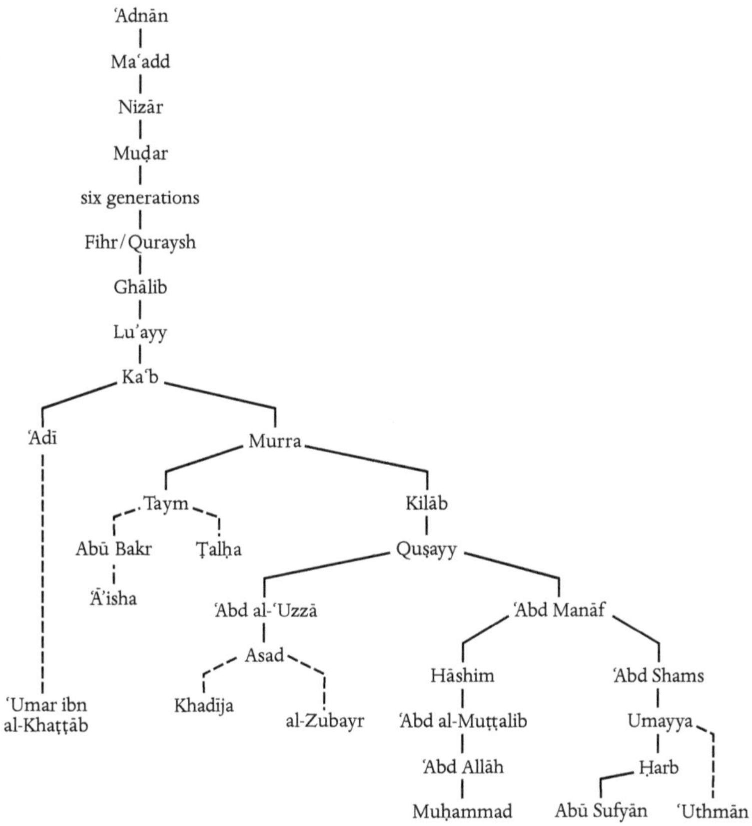

2. The Quraysh

On the eve of Islam a member of the Khazraj, ʿAbd Allāh ibn Ubayy, was nearly crowned. Masʿūdī reports: 'The Khazraj were superior to the Aws shortly before the advent of Islam and intended to crown ʿAbd Allāh ibn Ubayy ibn Salūl al-Khazrajī. This coincided with the arrival of the Prophet and his kingship ceased to exist.'[45]

Ibn Ubayy did not fight against the Jewish–Awsī coalition at Buʿāth, where his tribe, the Khazraj, was defeated. After Buʿāth he was the strongest leader among the Khazraj, and he showed great diplomatic skill in re-establishing the system of alliances that had existed before Buʿāth. In

45 Quoted in Ibn Saʿīd, *Nashwat al-ṭarab*, vol. I, p. 190.

this system the Naḍīr were allied with the Khazraj,[46] while the Qurayẓa were allied with the Aws. At the time of the *hijra* the Naḍīr and Qurayẓa were the main owners of fortresses and weapons in Medina, which made them the dominant power there.

46 Samhūdī, *Wafā' al-wafā*, vol. I, pp. 387–8, provides valuable evidence on the aftermath of Buʿāth.

PART II

*

UNIVERSALISM AND IMPERIALISM

5

The rise of Islam, 600–705

CHASE F. ROBINSON

The first Islamic century began in 622 of the Common Era with the *hijra* (Hegira), Muḥammad's 'emigration' from Mecca to the town of Yathrib, which lies about 275 miles to the north. As we shall see, the event was a turning-point in Muḥammad's life: delivered from the pagan opposition of the city of his birth, he was free to preach, teach and lead in Yathrib so successfully that he remained there until his death in 632. In time it would even come to be called 'the Prophet's city' or 'the city' (Medina) *tout court*. The *hijra* thus marked a new beginning for Muḥammad and his followers. It also illustrates a striking feature of Islamic history. For Muḥammad's decision to leave Mecca was in purpose both deeply religious and deeply political.

On the one hand, he and those who believed in his prophecy were escaping polytheist intolerance towards his uncompromising monotheism. They were making their way to a town where, as the Qur'ān seems to show, Muḥammad's ideas about God, man, this World and the Next, would evolve and sharpen, in part because he came into contact with the town's Jews, and in part because as Muslim numbers grew, so, too, did their demands upon him. Far more than in hostile Mecca, it was in Muḥammad's experience in Medina, as it is reflected in the Qur'ān (the great bulk of which was apparently revealed there) and Prophetic tradition, that so much of Islamic belief and law came to be anchored. At the same time, the emigration to Yathrib was not *merely* religious; for Muḥammad and his contemporaries lived in a pocket of western Arabia where institutionalised forms of governance were as underdeveloped as ties of real, imagined and adopted kinship were strong. (Even in the very different settled culture of South Arabia, kingship was relatively weak.[1]) In a society where social differentiation was relatively modest, it was as kinsmen (or confederates and the like) that the tribesmen married, shared and worshipped idols, herded, raided, defended and attacked, their skills often

1 A. F. L. Beeston, 'Kingship in ancient South Arabia', *JESHO*, 15 (1972).

overlapping. It was according to these ties, supplemented by traditional practices of cooperation, alliance and negotiation, that corporate action took place: they were the social ligature that organised society, constraining and conditioning the violence inherent in the fierce competition over scarce resources (especially water, pasture and animals) that characterised life in northern and central Arabian oasis settlements. There being no separate state agency, and religion being embedded as part of social life and identity, there was, then, no effective distinction between what we would regard as the 'religious' and 'political' spheres. Had he been inclined towards quietist introversion, Muḥammad might have satisfied his ambitions by making his *hijra* into desert solitude, as did many holy men of Late Antiquity. Instead, responding to an invitation to arbitrate between two tribes in Yathrib, he chose to take his message to a town where he could lead and organise men so as to organise a religious movement of radical reform. (Successful arbitration, like other forms of public diplomacy and martial valour, was an avenue towards higher social standing.)

So confessing belief in God and swearing loyalty to His Prophet meant working to effect a political order. As Muḥammad saw things, this order was willed by a God who, while promising Hellfire for polytheists, tolerated a variety of monotheist practices, on the condition that the monotheists – and indeed all creation – acknowledge His authority as delegated by Him to His Prophet Muḥammad, who was charged with the task of re-establishing this order on earth. It would thus be in Medina that Muslims embarked on the project, first by founding a simple but highly effective polity within the town, and second by launching a series of small but equally highly effective military campaigns outside it. In the short term, these brought the modest settlements of Arabia under the Prophet's control, each paying a tax or a tribute to symbolise their acknowledgement of God's authority, payable to His Prophet. In the long term, the campaigns grew into the conquest armies of the 640s and 650s (and beyond), which would overrun much of the Byzantine and all of the Sasanian Near East. Because the Prophet's and the caliphs' authority over these lands were understood to derive from God, it was as indivisible as His. It followed that prescribing and interpreting articles of Muslim belief, legislating, and ruling a multi-ethnic and religiously pluralistic empire – all these and other functions fell to the Prophet and the caliphs to carry out. The historical tradition preserves a letter purportedly written by the Prophet to a tribesman named ʿAmr ibn Ḥazm, whom Muḥammad had sent to govern south Arabian tribes; whatever its exact provenance – the authenticity of this document, like that of nearly all documents from the early period, is impossible to verify – it neatly expresses seventh- and eighth-century attitudes. We read that the Prophet instructs ʿAmr to fear God, to give instruction in the Qurʾān, in the attractions of Heaven and fears of Hell and in various rituals and rites (including prayer) – and also to tax and distribute booty according to a regime that distinguishes between rain- and spring-fed lands, on the one hand, and artificially irrigated land, on the other, between cows and bulls and calves and sheep, between Muslim and non-Muslim, male and female, free and slave.[2] Taxing was no less a religious activity than was praying.

The history made by seventh-century Muslims is thus at once religious, military and political history, and it is dominated by a prophet and then caliphs who, delegated by God, enjoyed His indivisible authority. In fact, we shall see that a great deal of the century's religious and political change was effected by three men: the Prophet Muḥammad and two long-ruling caliphs: Muʿāwiya ibn Abī Sufyān (r. 661–80) and ʿAbd al-Malik ibn Marwān (r. 685–705). Under their leadership the Near East would witness the last great religious movement of Antiquity. It almost goes without saying that in subsequent periods much in the Islamic religious tradition would evolve and transform; even so important a discipline as the study of Prophetic traditions only crystallised in the ninth century. Still, already by the end of the seventh century, what could be described as the core of Islamic belief had taken form: that the One God had made Himself known definitively and clearly in the Qurʾān and the experience of the Prophet Muḥammad and his community. Meanwhile, the century would also witness the founding of the last great empire of Antiquity, which, at its height in the decades following the death of ʿAbd al-Malik, would stretch from the Atlantic to the Oxus. In the space of three generations Arabs had moved from the periphery of the civilised world to the courts that ruled much of it, imprinting their language, culture and nascent religion upon millions. Recorded history has scarcely seen a more powerful fusion of belief and action than that effected by early Muslims.

How this happened can be answered theologically or historically. The theological answer – because God willed it so – generally lies behind all accounts provided by the pre-modern tradition, whether apologetic (Islamic) or polemic (usually Christian). According to these traditions, men may receive punishment or reward, but they always remain instruments of God's design. In the Islamic version, this design unfolds cyclically through history, as God, acting either

2 Abū Jaʿfar Muḥammad ibn Jarīr al-Ṭabarī, *Taʾrīkh al-rusul waʾl-mulūk*, ed. M. J. de Goeje *et al.*, 15 vols. in 3 series (Leiden, 1879–1901), series I, pp. 1727ff.; trans. I. K. Poonawala as *The history of al-Ṭabarī*, vol. IX: *The last years of the Prophet* (Albany, 1990), pp. 85ff.

mercifully or wrathfully, makes good on His promise to Man by sending prophets or other holy men, whom men then usually ignore; He also sends down chastisements of various kinds (evil men, plagues, earthquakes), which they cannot. (God's participation in human affairs is occasionally very direct, such as when He dispatches angels to fight alongside Muslims in an early battle against polytheists.) A rather more transcendent God stands behind some modern accounts, which typically replace God's miracles with His invisible hand, but the result is much the same – an Islamic 'exceptionalism', in which the laws of history are temporarily suspended.[3] Of course, God's agency is not something that we, as historians, should try to measure or describe; and even if we dismiss soldier-angels and similar miracles, such modern answers are by definition as persuasive to most historians as arguments for Intelligent Design are to most palaeontologists. We must therefore content ourselves with describing and explaining the conduct of men – that is, writing history without the benefit of divine intervention.

This said, when set out with any real precision, historical reconstructions – typically those that hold that Muḥammad was at once visionary, principled and pragmatic, and Ḥijāzī society was in a social or environmental crisis to which he offered answers,[4] that the Byzantine and Sasanian provinces of the metropolitan Near East were poorly defended, and thus relatively easily overrun by Muslims energised by a new faith – are vulnerable to near-lethal historiographic criticisms. As we shall see all too frequently throughout this chapter, the historiographic ground cannot bear interpretations that carry the freight of much real detail. For reasons made clear in chapter 15, the study of early Islam is plagued by a wide range of historiographic problems: the sources internal to the tradition purport to preserve a great deal of detailed history, but with very few exceptions they are late and polemically inclined; meanwhile, the sources external to the tradition are in many instances much earlier, but they know so little of what was happening in Arabia and Iraq that they are inadequate for detailed reconstruction.[5] What is abundant is in general unreliable; what is relatively reliable is invariably too little; meanwhile, the painstaking work

3 C. F. Robinson, 'Reconstructing early Islam: Truth and consequences', in H. Berg (ed.), *Method and theory in the study of Islamic origins* (Leiden, 2003).

4 For the most recent attempt at an environmental explanation, see A Korotayev, V. Klimenko and D. Proussakov, 'Origins of Islam: Political-anthropological and environmental context', *Acta Orientalia Academiae Scientiarum Hungaricae*, 52 (1999).

5 On the Prophet, see F. E. Peters, 'The quest for the historical Muhammad', *IJMES*, 23 (1991); Ibn Warraq (ed.), *The quest for the historical Muhammad* (Amherst, NY, 2000); but cf. R. Hoyland, 'Writing the biography of the Prophet Muhammad: Problems and solutions', *History Compass*, 5 (2007).

required to identify and isolate reliable accounts has only relatively recently begun.[6] Attempts to link Muḥammad's preaching to economic change or commercial dynamism in Arabia have been especially common; and not only are they typically based on unreliable sources, but they also very often reflect quaintly anachronistic models of economy, society and belief. There is nothing wrong in principle with proposing materialist interpretations of Islamic history, provided that the model is appropriate and the evidence sufficient.[7] So far neither condition is present.

Given the state of the evidence, the most one can do is to set out some historical answers very schematically. In what follows I endeavour to do precisely that, drawing upon the Islamic and non-Islamic literary evidence, in addition to the material evidence, as and when it is relevant. Alongside this historiographic prudence sits – perhaps uneasily – the conviction that, despite all the difficulties, early Islam *is* explicable, provided that it is explicated within the geographic, religious and political terms that are characteristic of the Late Antique Near East.

Ḥijāzī monotheism?

The Islamic tradition generally came to describe pre-Islamic Arabian history as the *jāhiliyya* – a period of 'ignorance' during which the pure monotheism that had been implanted in Arabia by Abraham was perverted by idol-worshipping polytheists, leaving only minority communities of Jews, the stray Christian and *ḥanīfs* (indigenous monotheists) to worship God.[8] Whatever its historicity, the construction of a naive *jāhiliyya* clearly formed part of a broader cultural re-orientation that took place during the Umayyad and ʿAbbāsid periods, when ethnic and religious identities took new shapes: as tribesmen settled in garrisons and towns of the Fertile Crescent during the seventh and

6 See, for some examples, M. Lecker, 'Did Muḥammad conclude treaties with the Jewish tribes Naḍīr, Qurayẓa and Qaynuqāʿ?', *Israel Oriental Studies*, 17 (1997); M. Lecker, 'The death of the Prophet Muḥammad: Did Wāqidī invent some of the evidence?', *ZDMG*, 145 (1995); G. Schoeler, *Charakter und Authentie der muslimischen Überlieferung über das Leben Mohammeds* (Berlin, 1996); and H. Motzki (ed.), *The biography of Muḥammad: The issue of the sources* (Leiden, 2000).

7 See P. Gran, 'Political economy as a paradigm for the study of Islamic history', *IJMES*, 11 (1980); M. Ibrahim, *Merchant capital and Islam* (Austin, 1990); and, for materialist-based sociology, M. Bamyeh, *The social origins of Islam: Mind, economy, discourse* (Minneapolis, 1999).

8 On the *ḥanīfs*, especially in terms of the epigraphic evidence (some of which is discussed below), see A. Rippin, 'RḤMNN and the Ḥanīfs', in W. B. Hallaq and D. P. Little (eds.), *Islamic studies presented to Charles J. Adams* (Leiden, 1991).

eighth centuries, what it meant to be an Arab and a Muslim came into sharper focus,[9] and this refocusing involved the elaboration of an Arabian past consistent with the Qurʾānic history. At least some of the traditional view of a pre-Islamic Ḥijāz dominated by paganism also seems to reflect generic monotheist polemic as much as it does authentic history; Arabian 'pagans', on this reading, were monotheists who came up short. It is certainly the case that in the middle of the eighth century Muslims would accuse Christians of being idolaters because they worshipped the Cross, and this can scarcely be taken to mean that eighth-century Syria was dominated by idolatry.[10] Unfortunately, there is relatively little evidence with which we might test the traditional views of things, but although there is little doubt that the worship of multiple gods through idols was the prestige form of religiosity,[11] what we happen to have does throw some doubt upon it. Strains of monotheism (rabbinic and non-rabbinic Judaism, varieties of Christianity and Jewish Christianity being its principal forms) may not have been as strong among the Arabs of the mid-Peninsula as they were among those in the south or in Iraq and especially Syria, where a Ghassānid Christianity has been voluminously documented,[12] but they seem to have been stronger than the Islamic tradition describes them.

Things are less clear in Arabia than we would wish them to be, but monotheism had certainly gained a solid foothold well before Muḥammad. The clearest example of this comes in the Yemeni town of Najrān, which was the centre of South Arabian Christianity from the fifth century.[13] Tradition

9 See S. Agha and T. Khalidi, 'Poetry and identity in the Umayyad age', *al-Abhath*, 50–1 (2002–3).

10 See, for example, G. R. Hawting, *The idea of idolatry and the emergence of Islam: From polemic to history* (Cambridge, 1999).

11 In general, see J. Retsö, *The Arabs in Antiquity: Their history from the Assyrians to the Umayyads* (London, 2003), pp. 600f.; R. Hoyland, *Arabia and the Arabs from the Bronze Age to the coming of Islam* (London and New York, 2001), pp. 139ff.; on Mecca in particular, C. Robin, 'Les "filles de Dieu" de Saba' à La Mecque: Réflexions sur l'agencement des panthéons dans l'Arabie ancienne', *Semitica*, 50 (2000).

12 I. Shahid, *Byzantium and the Arabs in the fifth century* (Washington, DC, 1989); I. Shahid, *Byzantium and the Arabs in the sixth century*, vol. I, parts 1 and 2 (Washington, DC, 1995 and 2002).

13 See J. S. Trimingham, *Christianity among the Arabs in pre-Islamic times* (London, 1979); Hoyland, *Arabia and the Arabs*, pp. 146–50; C. Robin, 'Judaisme et christianisme en Arabie du sud d'après les sources épigraphiques et archéologiques', *Proceedings of the Seminar for Arabian Studies*, 10 (1980); J. Beauchamp and C. Robin, 'Le Christianisme dans le péninsule arabique dans l'épigraphie et l'archéologie', *Hommage à Paul Lemerle, Travaux et mémoires*, 8 (Paris, 1981); on Najrān and Arab Christianity in general, there remain useful comments in T. Andrae, 'Der Ursprung des Islams und das Christentum', *Kyrkohistorisk Årsskrift*, 23 (1923), pp. 149–80.

explains one verse of the Qurʾān (Q 2:61) by adducing a visit to the Prophet by a delegation of Christians from the town, and some reports have the town's Jews join this delegation. As noted in chapter 4, Judaism was powerfully attractive to the Ḥimyarite kings that ruled in the south, who extended their authority during the fifth century towards the west and north, until the Christian Aksumite kingdom of Ethiopia reduced them to vassal status in the early sixth. This triggered the infamous massacre of the Christians of Najrān by Dhū Nuwās in 522–3,[14] an event that in turn led to an Ethiopian invasion of Arabia led by Abraha that avenged their martyrdom and brought Christian imperialism into the heart of the Peninsula. Abraha's ill-fated expedition to the Ḥijāz is known only to the Qurʾān, but it conforms to the pattern of his Arabian expansion, which is partially documented in a number of inscriptions.[15] In the east, the Nestorian Church, which is otherwise and less misleadingly known as the 'Church of the East',[16] was often tolerated and less often persecuted by the Sasanians; it had earlier penetrated the Gulf and eastern Arabia, and there it established an ecclesiastical organisation and claimed adherents well down the coast as well as among the Lakhmids, the Sasanians' client kingdom centred in al-Ḥīra. Several churches and monasteries survive in eastern Arabia, and although at least some were once thought to date from the Sasanian period, it seems that they actually belong to the eighth and ninth centuries,[17] a fact that says something about the tenacity of Christian belief even within the Peninsula.

Ringing the Peninsula's Byzantine, Sasanian and Aksumite periphery, monotheism was thus becoming an increasingly compelling language of political expression. How did these beliefs – monotheistic and quasi-monotheistic (in the eyes of many, Trinitarian Christianity might sit somewhere between monotheism and polytheism) – affect Arabian polytheism? Can we detect some faint signals for either parallel or related movements towards some variety of monotheism? The evidence of pre-Islamic inscriptions, though currently limited to southern Arabia, is particularly important in

14 See, in general, C. Robin 'Le judaïsme de Himyar', *Arabia*, 1 (2003); J. Beauchamp, F. Briquel-Chatonnet, and C. Robin, 'La persécution des chrétiens de Nagran et la chronologie Himyarite', *Aram*, 11–12 (1999–2000); and M. Lecker, 'Judaism among Kinda and the *ridda* of Kinda', *JAOS*, 115 (1995).

15 See below, note 19.

16 A recent summary can be found in J. F. Healey, 'The Christians of Qatar in the 7th century AD', in I. R. Netton (ed.), *Studies in honour of Clifford Edmund Bosworth*, vol. I: *Hunter of the East: Arabic and Semitic studies* (Leiden, 2000).

17 See now D. Kennet, 'The decline of eastern Arabia in the Sasanian period', *Arabian Archaeology and Epigraphy*, 18 (2007), pp. 86–122.

this regard: for there we can see how pagan formulae begin to be eclipsed by what appears to be the monotheistic marker of *al-raḥmān*, 'the merciful', which would come to be one of the principal epithets with which Muslims would describe Allāh, the one God. Dating these inscriptions is very difficult, but it has been argued that the eclipse begins in the fourth century.[18] One early sixth-century inscription, which glorifies Abraha, reads: 'By the might and aid and mercy of the Merciful and His Messiah and of the Holy Spirit. They have written this inscription: Behold Abraha … king of Saba' … and Dhu Raydan and Ḥaḍramawt and Yamanat and of "their" Arabs on the plateau and the Tihamat.'[19] With a dense fringe of Christians and Jews on the eastern and southern periphery, and some signs for the emergence of a supreme God in the inscriptions currently available from the south, one might expect to find similar developments at work in the Ḥijāz. In fact, the South Arabian inscriptions have sometimes been taken to demonstrate the presence of a religious movement (or community), which the sources describe as the Ḥanafiyya, and which began in the south and moved into the Ḥijāz.[20]

There is much to be said for this argument, not least of which is that it makes some sense of what the tradition itself says: pre-Islamic poetry and the language of early Islamic ritual hint at an earlier belief in a supreme God, one frequently known by the same name (*al-raḥmān*). From this perspective, Muḥammad's charge that his contemporaries were committing *shirk* ('association' and, by extension, polytheism) can be construed as a charge that they were associating other deities with the supreme God whom they already acknowledged, rather than as a blanket condemnation of polytheism.[21] Very telling is the testimony of the Qur'ān itself, which, whatever the precise course of its assembly and transmission, clearly has its origins in seventh-century Arabia. It is telling in two respects. The first is that it can be read to suggest a geography of belief in which the supreme God (Allāh) was acknowledged as the creator, and where lesser deities are called upon principally to intercede with Allāh. According to this view (or a version of it), the old gods were in

18 A. Beeston, 'Himyarite monotheism', in A. M. Abdulla *et al.* (eds.), *Studies in the history of Arabia*, vol. II: *Pre-Islamic Arabia* (Riyadh, 1984); C. Robin, 'Du paganisme au monothéisme', in C. Robin (ed.), *L'Arabie antique de Karib'īl à Mahomet: Nouvelles données sur l'histoire des arabes grâces aux inscriptions* (Aix-en-Provence, 1991).

19 For the inscription and the events, see S. Smith, 'Events in Arabia in the 6th century AD', *BSOAS*, 16 (1954), p. 437.

20 For criticisms, see above, note 8.

21 See, for example, K. Athamina, 'Abraham in Islamic perspective: Reflections on the development of monotheism in pre-Islamic Arabia', *Der Islam*, 81 (2004); M. J. Kister, 'Labbayka, allāhuma, labbayka: On a monotheistic aspect of a Jāhiliyya practice', *JSAI*, 2 (1980).

decline and the power of the supreme God was in the ascendant; Muḥammad's movement, it follows, accelerated a progress already in train.[22] Here it should be noted that tradition acknowledges the presence in other parts of Arabia, including the Najd and al-Yamāma, of prophetic figures whom it discredits as pseudo- and copy-cat prophets. The most notorious of these was named Musaylima ibn Ḥabīb, who preached in al-Yamāma with a book written in rhymed prose – the very prophetic portfolio that Muḥammad himself carried. Might it be that the sixth and seventh centuries, which produced messianic and prophetic figures among the Christians and Jews, produced among the incipient monotheists of Arabia a number of legislating prophets? If so, what we have in early Islam may be the culmination of a gradual process, in which the old gods grew gradually weaker and the supreme God gradually more powerful, one pushed along by several charismatic religious figures.

The Qurʾān is telling in another respect. It claims to express a 'clear Arabic', but it is an Arabic that may have been clearer to its contemporaries than it was to scholars of subsequent periods. In fact, a very conservative seventh- and eighth-century tradition of textual transmission has ironically conserved the text's polyglot origins: Qurʾānic language actually accommodates not only a wide range of non-Arabic loanwords, but also, perhaps, a Syriac Christian substrate of language and belief, which, though hardly detectable elsewhere, is what we might expect to find, given that Arabia was geographically and culturally contiguous to the heartland of Syriac Christianity. The argument for this substrate can be taken much too far, but to acknowledge it is in no sense to discredit Muḥammad or challenge the originality of his vision – at least any more than identifying the Jewish and Graeco-Roman context in which Jesus operated is to challenge his. It is merely to identify some of the ingredients with which Muḥammad forged his enormously powerful ideas. The fact is that terms as crucial as *Qurʾān* and *sūra* are Aramaic in origin, and postulating a Syriac substrate can unlock several obscure passages, while others are resolved by positing referents in the biblical, exegetical and liturgical traditions of eastern Christianity. An example can be found in Q 108, which, read as 'pure' Arabic, is scarcely meaningful either to medieval Muslim exegetes or modern critics:

> Surely we have given you abundance
> So pray to your Lord and make sacrifice
> Surely he who hates you will be disinherited / without posterity / cut off.

22 W. M. Watt, 'Belief in a "High God" in pre-Islamic Mecca', *JSS*, 16 (1971).

Read as an Arabic–Syriac hybrid, the text improves considerably:

> Surely we have given you [the virtue] of patience
> So pray to your Lord and persist [in your prayer]
> Your enemy [Satan] is thus vanquished.

Muḥammad was no crypto-Christian, and there is no good evidence for an Arabic bible in this period, but the dogma of his illiteracy obscures the presence of monotheistic ideas and practices with which he apparently had some real familiarity.[23]

Such, in very schematic form, is the evidence for movements of (or towards) monotheism in western Arabia. Though currently inadequate, it may improve in time. But it may also be that the Ḥijāz was not merely sluggish in following developments taking place in the south and east, but required nothing less than revolution. This should not necessarily surprise. For one thing, the area was not tightly stitched into the regional fabric by trade patterns. When the evidence is scrutinised carefully, the argument collapses for the movement of luxury goods (especially textiles and spices) through a Meccan entrepôt, leaving local trade in heavier (and thus lower profit) animal products, perhaps especially skins.[24] Again, the action was on the periphery: Sasanian pressure in the Gulf and north-eastern Arabia seems to have started by the middle of the third century, when cities were founded on both of its sides; by the latter half of the sixth century there seem to have been both military and trading colonies in the area.[25] For another – and again in contrast to the more promising south and east – a very forbidding environment and climate, combined with relatively modest natural resources,[26] meant that settlement in inner and western Arabia was sparse, levels of consumption and investment low, and the interest of Arabia's imperial neighbours

23 C. Luxenberg, *Die syro-aramäische Lesart des Koran*, 2nd edn (Berlin, 2004), trans. as *The Syro-Aramaic reading of the Koran* (Berlin, 2007), where this substrate becomes an 'original' version of a mixed-language text; the argument is occasionally forced and its readings often arbitrary; cf. C. Gilliot, 'Le Coran, fruit d'un travail collectif?', in D. De Smet *et al.* (eds.), *al-Kitāb: La sacralité du texte dans le monde de l'Islam* (Brussels, 2004). I draw the example from Gilliot, 'Le Coran', pp. 220–1.

24 P. Crone, *Meccan trade and the rise of Islam* (Princeton, 1987; repr. Piscataway, NJ, 2004); P. Crone, 'Quraysh and the Roman army: Making sense of the Meccan leather trade', *BSOAS*, 70 (2007).

25 See, for example, D. Whitehouse and A. Williamson, 'Sasanian maritime trade', *Iran*, 11 (1973); D. Potts, *The Arabian Gulf in Antiquity* (Oxford, 1990).

26 See G. W. Heck, '"Arabia without spices": An alternate hypothesis', *JAOS*, 123 (2003), where the argument for a 'vibrant and productive' macroeconomy, turning especially on silver mining, is put very robustly.

accordingly limited to its borders. Inscriptional evidence suggests that Rome had brought parts of the northern Ḥijāz under its direct control in the second century, but sustained and direct control ended well before Islam began to take root. There are accounts that have the Sasanians levy the occasional tax or tribute, but the Ḥijāz itself was unattractive to the Byzantine and Sasanian states in the long term: projecting power into inner and western Arabia was costly in many respects, and the benefits would not have repaid those costs.

Muḥammad in Mecca

According to the Islamic tradition of the late eighth and ninth centuries, it was within the relatively insulated and polytheist society of Mecca that Muḥammad was born in what it calls 'the year of the elephant'. The year is typically calculated to 570, when Mecca is said to have been threatened by an army sent by Abraha, the Ethiopian who had conquered South Arabia and was now moving into the west, his army outfitted with impressive African elephants that were presumably unfamiliar to the Ḥijāzīs. The events are vaguely known to the Qur'ān (105), but tradition attaches all manner of speculation, legend and polemic to the obscure verses. This – generating 'history' by assigning historical circumstances to verses that had become increasingly obscure – is a prominent feature of the early biographical tradition,[27] and it places near-insuperable obstacles in the path of writing detailed Prophetic history. Indeed, of Muḥammad's birth, childhood and early adulthood we know almost nothing that can properly be called knowledge.[28] In this period the general problem of writing Prophetic history (the great bulk of what is transmitted as Prophetic history was actually generated during the eighth and ninth centuries by exegetes attempting to make sense of those increasingly obscure Qur'ānic terms) is compounded by the indifference of early Muslims. For Muḥammad's experience before the Angel Gabriel first spoke to him appears to have been of little interest to the initial generations of Muslims, who focused on what he became rather than who he had been. Neither the non-Islamic sources nor material evidence can shed any real light.

When was Muḥammad born? According to fairly reliable literary and inscriptional evidence, the date of 570 is altogether too late for the tradition's invasion to have taken place, and if one is determined to retain the association

27 Crone, *Meccan trade*, pp. 203ff.
28 For a discussion of this and related problems, see chapter 15; on Muḥammad's date of birth, L. I. Conrad, 'Abraha and Muḥammad: Some observations apropos of chronology and literary topoi in the early Arabic historical tradition', *BSOAS*, 50 (1987).

between birth date and elephant army, it may be that he was born in the 550s instead. Muḥammad's name, which means 'the praised one', is an epithet that probably post-dates his prophetic claims. The legends proliferate. In some instances inspired by Qurʾānic obscurities, the tradition describes in striking detail an orphaned child who would be cared for by an uncle named Abū Ṭālib, the father of the fourth-caliph-to-be, ʿAlī ibn Abī Ṭālib, and who would travel to the north on trade. These journeys are often connected with his employment by a wealthy widow named Khadīja, whom he would marry, and who would bear him many children, although no sons who survived beyond childhood. As legends, these say more about how later Muslims understood prophecy than they do the circumstances of his life.[29] Thus when a monk (or holy man or Jew – the specifics are fluid) realises (such as by recognising a mark between the shoulder blades) that the youthful Muḥammad will be called to prophethood, the reader is to understand that other monotheists acknowledge one of the tradition's essential claims: this prophet belongs in a long chain of monotheist prophets sent by God. Other initiation accounts have a young Muḥammad's chest opened and miraculously closed; according to one version of this story, the surgery is performed by two eagle-like birds, who remove two black clots of blood, wash, and reseal the chest with 'the seal of prophethood'.[30] Other accounts have him participate in the purifying and rebuilding of the Kaʿba (the centre of the pagan sanctuary that would be converted into the centre of Islamic ritual). Still others describe an inchoate or incipient monotheist sensibility: we read that Muḥammad took to wandering in local hills, given over to quiet contemplation. If any of these accounts contain any kernel of truth, we cannot separate it from myth; because the non-Islamic sources that know of such accounts seem to rely upon the Islamic tradition, they cannot be called in as a control. That Muḥammad belonged to the clan of the Banū Hāshim of the tribe of the Quraysh, which was the leading tribe of Mecca, is probable, however.

Muḥammad only walks onto the set of history when God begins to speak to him through the Angel Gabriel. But the stage lights are very dim – virtually all we have that is early is the little that the Qurʾān tells us, and both the sequence and chronology of its chapters remain unclear. (In what follows, I accept that at least some Meccan and Medinan chapters can be disentangled from each

29 See J. Wansbrough, *The Sectarian milieu: Content and composition of Islamic salvation history* (Oxford, 1978).

30 For discussions, see U. Rubin, *The eye of the beholder: The life of Muḥammad as viewed by the early Muslims* (Princeton, 1995), pp. 59ff.; see also U. Rubin, *Between Bible and Qurʾān: The Children of Israel and the Islamic self-image* (Princeton, 1999).

other.) Tradition associates the turning-point with two Qur'ānic passages. The first (96:1–5) reads as follows:

> Recite in the name of your Lord who created
> Created man from a blood-clot.
> Recite – your Lord is the most generous
> Who taught by the pen
> Taught man what he did not know.

The second (Q 74:1–5) reads as follows:

> O you who are wrapped in your cloak
> Arise and warn
> And magnify your Lord
> Purify your clothes
> And shun pollution.

The tradition frequently holds that the first revelations were followed by a pause of three years, whereupon they came regularly for the next ten years or so. Traditional dating schemes, which generally turn on changes in style, associate short verses of striking imagery with the Meccan period. 'Arise and warn' (72:2), which is one of these, marks out Muḥammad as a 'warner', as does Q 26:214 ('And warn your nearest relatives'), a verse that is usually taken to signal the beginning of Muḥammad's public preaching. The Prophet thus follows in the footsteps of early monotheist warner-prophets – some 124,000 of them, according to one count, although only 135 are said to have combined prophecy with politics.[31] But whereas earlier prophets had typically warned their own communities of catastrophe (e.g. the 'painful chastisement' predicted by Noah), Muḥammad warned all mankind of nothing less than the Last Day (34:28 and 40:15). Thus the first verse of Q 81, which is usually said to be early: 'When the sun will be darkened, when the stars will be thrown down, when the mountains will be set moving … then will a soul know what it has produced.'

How did God make Himself understood through Muḥammad? According to tradition, God's messages were delivered orally by Gabriel to the Prophet, who subsequently dictated them from memory to a scribe for recording on the writing material that was available, such as bones, bark and stones; after the Prophet's death, contemporaries are said to have had what amounts to personal versions of the Qur'ān, but the task of establishing and distributing a single, authorised version was left to the third caliph, 'Uthmān ibn 'Affān (r. 644–656).

31 The numbers come from P. Crone, *Medieval Islamic political thought* (Edinburgh, 2004), p. 10.

How well Muḥammad could read and write – if he could do either at all – is left unanswered by the Qurʾān. Tradition would answer the question by asserting the dogma of his illiteracy, which functioned to insulate the Prophet from claims that his knowledge of monotheist history came from familiarity with the Torah or Gospels, as other monotheists had alleged. (For what they are worth, a late seventh-century Armenian chronicler has it that Muḥammad was 'learned and informed in the history of Moses' (that is, the Pentateuch), while John of Damascus (d. *c.* 750) held that Muḥammad knew the Old and New Testaments, and had met an Arian monk.[32]) The dogma also functioned to emphasise the 'miraculous inimitability' (*iʿjāz*) of the Qurʾān: Moses could transform walking-sticks into snakes, and Jesus could heal and resurrect, but Muḥammad spoke directly for God in God's perfect speech. Dogmas aside, what is clear from the text itself is that many Qurʾānic passages directly responded to problems that Muḥammad faced, both personal and communal. This is a pattern that becomes especially clear in Medina, such as when Muḥammad contravened social norms by marrying Zaynab, the divorced wife of his foster son, Zayd, a matter that was controversial enough not only to generate a Qurʾānic dispensation, but also to pass into the Christian tradition;[33] other examples include the raid at Nakhla (see below).

Exactly how the revelations were received cannot be known in any detail either. The lists and accounts of early converts more clearly reflect controversies about post-Prophetic politics than they do Prophetic history. Among the men, Abū Bakr (the first caliph) and ʿAlī (Muḥammad's son-in-law and later recognised as the fourth caliph) are the favoured candidates for pride of place; among the women, Khadīja is unrivalled. Nor can much be said about how the polytheist establishment responded to Muḥammad's prophetic claims. In the moments of revelation Muḥammad was given to shaking or even seizures of one sort or another, and according to one set of traditions, even Khadīja reacted to Q 96:1–5 by summoning a local monotheist, Waraqa ibn Nawfal, who reassured her that Muḥammad was indeed a genuine prophet. 'There has come to him the greatest law that came to Moses' (law (*nāmūs*)being glossed as 'Gabriel').[34] The Qurʾān itself makes plain that many Meccans quite naturally

32 Sebeos, *The Armenian history attributed to Sebeos*, trans. R. W. Thomson with commentary by J. Howard-Johnston, Translated Texts for Historians 31, 2 vols. (Liverpool, 1999), vol. I, p. 95; John of Damascus, *Écrits sur l'Islam,* ed. and trans. R. Le Coz (Paris, 1992), pp. 211–12; cf. A. Palmer, S. Brock and R. Hoyland, *The seventh century in the West-Syrian chronicles* (Liverpool, 1993), p. 130, note 293.

33 John of Damascus, *Écrits*, pp. 221–3.

34 Ibn Hishām, *al-Sīra al-nabawiyya*, ed. M. al-Ṣaqqā *et al.*, 4 vols. (Cairo, 1936), vol. I, p. 167.

took him to be a magician, soothsayer or otherwise possessed. There were other reasons to find Muḥammad objectionable. As a 'warner' in the tradition of early prophets, he emphasised man's accountability to God, His power, the rewards of Heaven and the punishment of Hell. He also levelled criticism against the prevailing social norms, railing against female infanticide and the abuses of wealth. None of this apparently sat well with the polytheist establishment, especially because he came to attack its gods and claim the Kaʿba for the One God. As his followers grew in number and Muḥammad grew in stature, the opposition to his movement stiffened. And when his uncle and guardian Abū Ṭālib died, Muḥammad became vulnerable; some measure of persecution then followed; a flight to Abyssinia was aborted; the *hijra* to Yathrib took place.[35] Muḥammad lived in a society where kinship ties provided such protection and safety as were possible, and, with the death of Abū Ṭālib, these ties, long stretched by Muḥammad's preaching, now snapped. He had to flee.

Muḥammad and his community after the *hijra*

That the *hijra* came to mark a watershed in the history of the Prophet and his community is made clear by several things, including the very frequent appearance and special significance in the Qur'ān of the derived Arabic word *muhājir* (pl. *muhājirūn*, '*hijra*-makers', 'Emigrants'), and the *anṣār* ('Helpers' – those in Medina who would follow Muḥammad). Borrowings of *muhājir* are used by Greek and Syriac writers as early as the 640s; there it is used to describe Muslims in general, a usage that is sometimes echoed in the Islamic tradition too. Early in the same decade, a bilingual papyrus receipt (in Arabic and Greek) refers to the 'month of Jumādā I of the year 22' (643), which signals the use (at least in Egypt) of the new Muslim calendar based on the *hijra*; and an epitaph written as far away from Arabia as Cyprus may provide an exceptionally early attestation (AH 29) for the term *hijra* itself.[36] Centuries later families would crow about their descent from the 'Emigrants'.

35 For details on this period, the standard work remains W. M. Watt, *Muhammad at Mecca* (Oxford, 1953), and, for the next, W. M. Watt, *Muhammad at Medina* (Oxford, 1956). Both are historiographically obsolete.

36 A. Grohmann, *Arabische Chronologie* (Leiden, 1966), pp. 13–14; E. Combe, J. Sauvaget and G. Wiet, *Répertoire chronologique d'épigraphie arabe I* (Cairo, 1931), pp. 5–6; and L. Halevi, 'The paradox of Islamization: Tombstone inscriptions, Qur'ānic recitations, and the problem of religious change', *History of Religions*, 44 (2004), p. 121.

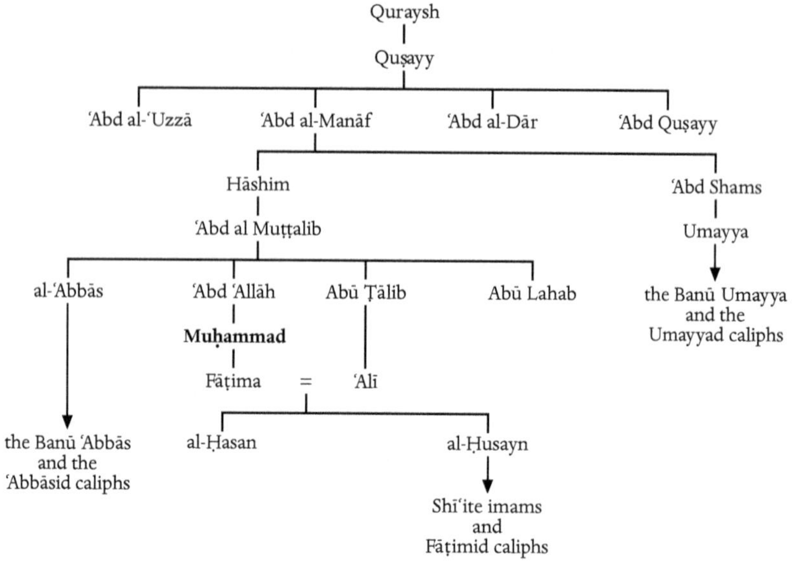

3. Muḥammad's family.
After Ira M. Lapidus, *A history of Islamic societies*, 2nd edn, 2002, p. 19, fig. 1. Copyright Cambridge University Press, reproduced with permission.

On this – the question of the *hijra* and associated terms – we can even do better than these relatively early attestations. The earliest use of the term 'Emigrants' comes in a contemporaneous set of documents, which are unfamiliar to the Qurʾān, but preserved in several versions in the eighth- and ninth-century Islamic tradition; they have come to be known as the Constitution of Medina. One version begins as follows:

> The Prophet, God's blessings and peace be upon him, wrote a document [governing relations] between the Emigrants and Helpers, in which he entered into a friendly compact with the Jews, confirmed their [claims] upon their religions and properties, and stipulated terms as follows:
>
> *In the name of God, the merciful and compassionate. This is a document from Muḥammad, God's prayers and peace be upon him, between the believers and Muslims of the Quraysh and Yathrib, and those who followed them, joined them and struggled with them. They are a single community* (umma) *to the exclusion of [other] people.*[37]

37 Ibn Hishām, *al-Sīra al-nabawiyya*, vol. I, p. 501; for different translations, see A. Guillaume, *The life of Muhammad* (Oxford, 1955), pp. 231–2, and now M. Lecker, *'The Constitution of Medina': Muḥammad's first legal document* (Princeton, 2004).

A series of stipulations about paying bloodwit, mutual aid and support, the conditions of just retaliation and practices of warfare are then enumerated. As the only documentary material to survive from Muḥammad's time, the Constitution of Medina is of immense historiographic significance. (Precisely how soon after the *hijra* these documents were drawn up is impossible to know, but none can date much beyond the battle of Badr in AH 2.) What the Constitution shows us is two interrelated processes.

The first was how Muḥammad assembled a community (*umma*) that he would lead. In other words, he was engaged in politics. Unlike the model of community upon which classical Islam would settle – a community of Muslims who, by professing a more-or-less settled creed and carrying out a more-or-less fixed set of rituals, were distinct both from polytheists and other monotheists – the *umma* of the Constitution appears to accommodate the Jews of Medina, although they occupy a subordinate status. This inclusive sense of community reflects the relatively catholic nature of early Islamic belief: we have already seen that Muḥammad had followed in the footsteps of earlier prophets (Moses and Abraham are especially prominent in the Qur'ān), and his call for monotheism was initially compatible with those made by his predecessors. In fact, the lines between Muslim and Jew were not yet firmly drawn,[38] evolving Muslim ritual (such as the fast of the tenth of Mūharram and 'the middle prayer ritual') being still closely patterned upon Jewish traditions (such as the fast of the tenth of Tishri and the second of the three ritual prayers).[39] Even a matter as important as the direction of prayer (*qibla*) was not yet settled: it seems that Muslims directed their prayers to Jerusalem until what the Qur'ān (see Q 2:142–150) and tradition describe as a decisive break with the Jews of Medina, which involved establishing Mecca once and for all as the normative *qibla*. The break would also involve expelling the Jewish tribes of the Banū Qaynuqāʿ and Banū al-Naḍīr and executing all of the men of a third, the Banū Qurayẓa.[40]

The fate of the Jewish tribes of Medina is closely related in our sources to the second process that the Constitution shows at work: Muḥammad putting his nascent community into shape for war-making against his polytheist opponents. In this, the Constitution conforms to the great stress laid in the

38 For a radical proposal along these lines, see F. M. Donner, 'From believers to Muslims: Confessional self-identity in the early Islamic community', *al-Abhath*, 50–1 (2002–3).
39 See, for example, S. Bashear, 'ʿĀ*shūrā*, an early Muslim fast', *ZDMG*, 141 (1991); repr. in S. Bashear, *Studies in early Islamic tradition* (Jerusalem, 2004).
40 M. J. Kister, 'The massacre of the Banū Qurayẓa: A re-examination of a tradition', *JSAI*, 8 (1986), pp. 61–96.

Qur'ān upon fighting on behalf of God in general, and upon the connection between emigration or 'going out' (*khurūj*, as opposed to 'sitting', *quʿūd*) and this fighting, as Q 2:218 ('those who emigrate and fight on the path of God'), and other verses put it. The Muslim is 'one who believes in God and the last Day and fights on the path of God' (Q 9:19). We have seen that Muḥammad's thinking and preaching in Medina evolved, particularly as relations with the town's Jews evolved. But in so far as the historical tradition offers anything like an accurate record of his concerns, his attention was focused upon fighting outside it. The Medinan phase is thus dominated by his campaigns against passing caravans, settlements and Bedouin tribes. These skirmishes and battles culminated in the capitulation of Mecca itself. *Jihād* (the struggle on behalf of God, which in this context meant nothing more or less than fighting on His behalf) was at the centre of Muḥammad's programme.

Why did Muḥammad take up arms? Leaving aside the vexed question of the vulnerability of Medina to its powerful neighbour, we can be fairly sure that Muḥammad wished his followers to be able to worship in Mecca or its environs, perhaps especially on the hills of Marwa and al-Ṣafā', which, as much as or even more than the Kaʿba itself, were integral to early Islamic ritual. Perhaps this wish, combined with the powerfully activist nature of his belief, led Muḥammad to begin hostilities soon after the *hijra*. His forces were typically small, but, with the exception of the battle of Uḥud, well managed and opportunistic.[41] The first skirmish, which is traditionally dated to AH 2, was a caravan raid at a settlement called Nakhla. Little blood was spilt, but what was spilt was spilt in Rajab, a 'forbidden' month, when fighting was proscribed by tribal convention; the event occasioned a revelation (Q 2:217) that allayed the resulting concerns.[42] The battle of Badr, a town that lay about 90 miles south-west of Medina, soon followed; the humiliating defeat for the Meccans – some seventy of whom are said to have been killed – is celebrated in Q 8:9, 12, 17 and 42 as proof of God's providential direction of Muḥammad's forces: angels fought alongside them.

Fortunes were dramatically turned at Uḥud, which is conventionally dated to AH 3 or 4. There, a relatively large Meccan force of 3,000 horsemen, led in part

41 On these armies, see E. Landau-Tasseron, 'Features of the pre-conquest Muslim army in the time of Muḥammad', in A. Cameron (ed.), *The Byzantine and early Islamic Near East*, vol. III: *States, resources and armies*, Studies in Late Antiquity and Early Islam 1 (Princeton, 1995), pp. 299–336. The material evidence for military technology only begins with the Marwānids; see D. Nicolle, 'Arms of the Umayyad era: Military technology in a time of change', in Y. Lev (ed.), *War and society in the eastern Mediterranean, 7th–15th centuries* (Leiden, 1997).

42 See M. J. Kister, '"Rajab is the month of God": A study in the persistence of an early tradition', *Israel Oriental Studies*, 1 (1971).

by Khālid ibn al-Walīd, who would later command spectacularly successful conquest armies, avenged the defeat of Badr by killing sixty-five or seventy Muslims. (The numbers are stereotypical and probably unreliable.) We read that the Prophet himself was wounded. Jewish *Schadenfreude* about the events of Uḥud is traditionally adduced to explain Muḥammad's growing hostility towards them in this period. The Meccans were dilatory in following up the advantage they had gained at Uḥud, giving Muḥammad something like two years to dig a defensive ditch around Medina, which would give its name to the battle of the Ditch in about AH 5. With their cavalry unable to negotiate this obstacle, the Meccans were forced to break off their siege of the town. The Prophet's fortunes had been reversed again. In the meantime, and continuing thereafter, Muḥammad led or sent several successful expeditions against Ḥijāzī tribes. We can attach names to those who fought here and elsewhere because Prophetic biography (*sīra*) includes what appear to be some relatively early lists of expedition participants. What we cannot say is how they conducted themselves on the battlefield: just as conversion narratives reflect subsequent history, so, too, do battle narratives such as these. We shall never know what ʿAlī, Abū Bakr, ʿUmar and ʿUthmān did (or failed to do) at Uḥud; what we can know is how claims about status were made in historical narrative.

At this point – the fifth and sixth year of the *hijra* – the traditional chronology leads in two directions. The first is towards Mecca. In AH 6 Muḥammad, confident in the aftermath of the battle of the Ditch, led a group of Muslims on pilgrimage to Mecca, and although he had to abort it, he nonetheless came away from the settlement of al-Ḥudaybiya with an agreement that a pilgrimage could be conducted the following year; a ten-year truce was also signed with the Meccans. The following year the oasis town of al-Khaybar fell, delivering such large amounts of booty and spoils into Muslim hands that it merits mention in Q 48:18–21. Meanwhile, Muḥammad carried out the pilgrimage that had been agreed the previous year. Medina's strength had thus grown at the expense of Mecca's, and the almost bloodless capitulation of Mecca in AH 8 may have come as something of an anti-climax: the Prophet had been carrying on what amounted to a charm offensive against influential Meccans. Most of those notable Qurashīs who had failed to acknowledge Muḥammad during the previous year did so now, although there were apparently some spectacular exceptions, such as Abū Sufyān, the *de facto* leader of the Meccan establishment and father of the second Umayyad caliph, Muʿāwiya. Although Muḥammad had apparently been clement towards his Meccan adversaries – tradition generally has him spare everyone save a few exceptionally offensive poets – one imagines that Mecca remained inhospitable (and in some respects hostile) to the Muslims. The Prophet would return to Medina for the final two years of his life.

From AH 5 and 6, the traditional chronology also leads in a second direction – towards the conquests in general and Syria in particular. The oasis town of Dūmat al-Jandal lay about fifteen days' march north from Medina; it also lay about half that distance from Damascus. Its strategic position perhaps explains why it was the object of no fewer than three raids, the first of which was led by the Prophet himself in AH 5. It fell for good in AH 9 to Khālid ibn al-Walīd, who had been dispatched by Muḥammad, who had himself taken another town in north-western Arabia, Tabūk, in the summer of that year, having heard that a coalition of Byzantine and Arab forces had amassed there. In fact, as early as AH 6 or 7, the tradition has Muḥammad dispatch letters to Heraclius, the Negus of Abyssinia and the Sasanian Shah, among others, inviting them to acknowledge his prophecy and convert to Islam. (They all declined.) The terms of capitulation for Dūmat al-Jandal and Tabūk, as they had been for al-Khaybar, called for a tribute payable to Muḥammad. At least in part because the Qurʾānic injunction that the People of the Book (that is, monotheists who acknowledge scripture) pay a tribute (*jizya*) is so vague, these capitulation accounts would function as partial models for conquest arrangements.[43] After the conquest of Mecca, Muḥammad is also said to have extended his influence in eastern and southern Arabia, chiefly by treaty rather than conquest. At least one non-Islamic source has Muḥammad lead a conquest army into Palestine, but this must be mistaken.[44]

Whatever the accuracy of the sequence and chronology of the Prophet's campaigns, not to mention the authenticity of the texts of letters and treaties ascribed to him, the tradition – and, following it, much modern scholarship – have seen in these events the origins of the great conquest movements that post-dated Muḥammad's death. In broad strokes, this must be true. The dynamic that Muḥammad had set into motion in the 620s did not go still in the 630s: manifesting and exemplifying belief by fighting on behalf of God, and reaping the rewards of this world and the next as a result, continued to exert a powerful and widespread influence long after 632. Put another way, after Muḥammad's death, God would continue to effect His will through the

43 On these and related problems, see W. Schmucker, *Untersuchungen zu einigen wichtigen bodenrechtlichen Konsequenzen der islamischen Eroberungsbewegung* (Bonn, 1972).

44 P. Crone and M. Cook, *Hagarism: The making of the Islamic world* (Cambridge, 1977), p. 4; R. Hoyland, *Seeing Islam as others saw it: A survey and evaluation of Christian, Jewish and Zoroastrian writings on early Islam* (Princeton, 1997), p. 555.

agency of tribesmen campaigning on the order of caliphs who had inherited the Prophet's authority. Only gradually – and incompletely, as subsequent Islamic history would show – was taking up arms disengaged from belief, as armies were professionalised and the state claimed the exclusive right to carry out legitimate violence. 'There shall be no *hijra* after the conquest [of Mecca]' is a widespread tradition that was circulated to discourage eighth- and ninth-century Muslims from doing exactly what Muḥammad had urged them to do – to emigrate and fight in order to prove and manifest their belief.[45]

That Muḥammad had set that dynamic into motion within Arabia is not to say it was an exclusively Arabian phenomenon. The seventh century was a time of Holy War. When Muḥammad was campaigning within the Ḥijāz on behalf of God, the Byzantine emperor Heraclius, having broken from the emperors' tradition by leading armies in person, was campaigning in Armenia and Iraq on behalf of Christ and God.[46] It may even be that in the very year that the Prophet entered into the treaty at al-Ḥudaybiya, thus ensuring a peaceful pilgrimage to Mecca, Heraclius' army was storming into Sasanian Iraq, thus ensuring the return of fragments of the Cross to Jerusalem. Events in and outside Arabia had been running in parallel, but they would now intersect.

The death of Muḥammad and its aftermath

Muḥammad died in early June 632 (AH 11) after a short illness. According to what emerged as the prevailing tradition, he left behind devoted followers, revelations that would subsequently be assembled into the Qur'ān, clear views on matters of belief and action, and several wives and daughters; but no sons, successors or clear plan of succession. If this, the Sunnī tradition, is correct, one way to square Muḥammad's careful coalition building and prudent politics with the absence of any succession arrangement is to imagine that ensuring the success of his radical monotheism required holding to traditional tribal practices, which gave short shrift to authority that was purely inherited or transferred (rather than also earned). It may also be that, the community being so fragile, Muḥammad thought it unwise to make his wishes clear. Another is to posit on his part an impending sense of the End. There are other possibilities, but there is no way of choosing between them.

45 P. Crone, 'The first-century concept of *Hiǧra*', *Arabica*, 41 (1994).

46 J. Howard-Johnston, 'The official history of Heraclius' Persian campaigns', in E. Dabrowa (ed.), *The Roman and Byzantine army in the east: Proceedings of a colloquium held at the Jagiellonian University, Kraków in September 1992* (Crakow, 1994).

This is not to say that there is little to choose from: the sources of the eighth and ninth centuries have a great deal to say about the events that followed the Prophet's death. They do so not because Muslims shared a Christian fascination with death, but because it was in the events of 632 that the Sunnī–Shīʿite divide would be anchored. Might it be that Muḥammad *had* appointed a successor? If not, who was present at the crucial moments after he died, when the fateful decisions were taken? Sunnīs answered the first question in the negative, holding that the community rallied around Abū Bakr, who, as both the first to convert and the most senior, was the natural choice. He would reign only briefly, from 632 to 634; unlike Muḥammad, however, he did appoint a successor, ʿUmar ibn al-Khaṭṭāb, during whose ten-year reign (634–44) the conquests exploded into the Fertile Crescent. Shīʿa came to answer this question of succession in the affirmative, adducing a number of arguments that Muḥammad *had* appointed ʿAlī as his successor: to the Shīʿite way of thinking, kinship (ʿAlī was Muḥammad's son-in-law and cousin) dictated it, and the facts were recorded not only by the historical record (Muḥammad presented ʿAlī as his successor to assemblies of Muslims), but also scripture (where indications of Muḥammad's wish to appoint ʿAlī are either read into the text or said to have been read out of it – that is, suppressed by the Sunnī tradition). For Sunnīs the succession arrangements were legitimate, if a bit chaotic, and the arrangements *ad hoc* – and this as late as 644, when an electoral conclave (*shūrā*) of six notables was chosen to elect ʿUmar's successor. For Shīʿa of the so-called Rāfiḍī variety, the succession amounted to a *coup d'état*: Abū Bakr, ʿUmar and ʿUmar's successor, ʿUthmān, were all usurpers.[47]

The tradition thus gave answers about who legitimately succeeded Muḥammad (or who did not). Written as it was by authors who lived under the direct or indirect patronage of eighth- and ninth-century caliphs, governors and rulers of various sorts, it takes for granted that the earliest Muslims should wish to fall behind a ruler. But since there was no tradition of stable rulership in either Mecca or Medina – had there been one, one imagines the succession to Muḥammad would have gone altogether more smoothly – we might wonder why so many of the tribesmen would have chosen to do so. (In describing the 'wars of apostasy', the *ridda* wars, when Arab tribes outside the Ḥijāz dissolved the treaties they had entered into with Muḥammad, the tradition concedes that many tribesmen did not.) The answer must be that

47 For a version of the Shīʿite case, see W. Madelung, *The succession to Muḥammad* (Cambridge, 1997).

belief was a strong compound, strengthened by the deep conviction that Muḥammad was a prophet acting for God, and that God rewarded those who held such a conviction – in this world and the next. Worldly success was distinct from (and, according to some, inferior to) the Heavenly rewards of faith, but faith brought its rewards in the here and now as well. When the Umayyad commander and governor-to-be ʿAmr ibn al-ʿĀṣ volunteered that he had converted, not out of any desire for wealth and possessions, but rather because of his devotion to Islam and Muḥammad, the Prophet responded: 'How good is wealth righteously gained for a righteous man!'[48] From this perspective, we can see that believers had organised themselves into a polity that had enjoyed such miraculous success and generated such extraordinary resources that belief in its corporate survival survived Muḥammad's death. What held the polity together was thus both belief in the next world and confidence in this one because of the rewards God offered through the spread of His dominion – that is, conquest. 'The earth belongs to God, Who bequeaths it to whom He wishes amongst His servants', as Q 7:128 puts it. The early Islamic polity survived in large part because it conquered.

If the conquest movement was an important ingredient in the success of early Islam, it is also very hard to describe. Neither their precise course nor their chronology can be established in any detail. In some instances, there is no prospect for recovering any authentic history; in others, a careful examination of the Arabic sources, combined with the judicious use of non-Islamic sources when they are available, can lead to a reliable sequence, an outline chronology and a small handful of solid facts.[49] What follows is appropriately schematic.

As we have seen, Muḥammad's *jihād* in the Ḥijāz was the ultimate inspiration for the conquests that would follow his death; but at least as far as Syria is concerned, their actual trigger seems to have been the small battles and skirmishes that are said to have broken out upon the Prophet's death, when tribesmen repudiated treaties negotiated by Muḥammad.

> The Islamic conquest of the Near East cannot be viewed, then, as something separate from the career of Muḥammad the Apostle or from the conquest of

48 M. J. Kister, 'On the papyrus of Wahb b. Munabbih', *BSOAS*, 37 (1974), p. 559.

49 See L. I. Conrad, 'The Conquest of Arwād: A source-critical study in the historiography of the early medieval Near East', in A. Cameron and L. I. Conrad (eds.), *The Byzantine and early Islamic Near East*, vol. I: *Problems in the literary source material* (Princeton, 1992); M. Hinds, 'The first Arab conquests of Fārs', *Iran*, 22 (1984); C. F. Robinson, 'The conquest of Khūzistān: A historiographic reassessment', *BSOAS*, 67 (2004); C. F. Robinson, *Empire and elites after the Muslim conquest: The transformation of northern Mesopotamia* (Cambridge, 2000), chapter 1; the standard account remains F. M. Donner, *The early Islamic conquests* (Princeton, 1981).

> Arabia during the *ridda* wars. It must be seen as an organic outgrowth of Muḥammad's teachings and their impact upon Arabian society, of Muḥammad's political consolidation, pursued by traditional and novel means, and especially of his efforts to bring nomadic groups firmly under state control, and of the extension of that process of consolidation by the Islamic state and its emerging élite under the leadership of Abū Bakr.[50]

Commanders such as Khālid ibn al-Walīd, Shuraḥbīl ibn Ḥasana and ʿArfaja ibn Harthama were accordingly sent out to Najd and beyond – to the west and north, where the desert stretches into the Syrian steppe and southern Iraq. Extending power over Arab tribal groups thus brought Muslim armies within hailing distance of the two great powers of the day. And once in contact with imperial armies, the Muslims were extraordinarily successful. In three decisive battles in Syria (Ajnādayn, Fiḥl and, most important, Yarmūk), the back of the Byzantine defence was broken. The provincial city of Damascus fell around 636; within twenty-five years, it would be the capital of the caliphate. The principal cities of northern Syria (Ḥimṣ, Aleppo, Qinnasrīn) followed suit soon after 636, as did Jerusalem, which ʿUmar himself apparently visited; there, according to some accounts, he led prayers and began the construction of a mosque.[51] From the occupation of Palestine that followed sprang a separate conquest movement to Egypt led by ʿAmr ibn al-ʿĀṣ, in the course of which Alexandria fell in 642; Muslims would establish their main garrison in Fusṭāṭ, towards the southern edge of current-day Cairo.

Alongside the conquest of Syria took place the conquest of Iraq, which was apparently opened from the south. After a disastrous defeat at the battle of the Bridge in late 634, the Muslims sent Saʿd ibn Abī Waqqāṣ in command of a relatively large army, which he led to al-Qādisiyya, a small settlement lying south-west of al-Ḥīra. There, in Muḥarram (February or March) of either 636 or 637, the Sasanian commander Rustam was routed. Soon thereafter came the defeat of the Sasanians at Jalūlāʾ, and then, also in 637, fell al-Madāʾin (Ctesiphon), the Sasanian capital. With the fall of Nihāwand (641), the Sasanian defence collapsed entirely, forcing the Sasanian shah, Yazdegerd, to flee to Khurāsān, where he was murdered in 651. By the late 630s or very soon after, the two garrisons of Baṣra and Kūfa had been founded; both would grow into major cities. Meanwhile, northern Mesopotamia had by around 640 fallen

50 Donner, *Early Islamic conquests*, p. 90. On the matter of the Islamic 'state', see below.
51 See H. Busse, 'Omar b. al-Haṭṭāb in Jerusalem', *JSAI*, 5 (1984).

to armies marching from the Syrian steppe in the west and armies marching up the Tigris from the south. The conquest movement did not end in the early 640s – it seems that it was not until well into the 650s that a measure of control over the Mediterranean islands of Cyprus, Rhodes and Crete was extended, and ʿUqba ibn Nāfīʿ projected Islamic rule further west in north Africa in the 660s and 670s – but the first great push had ended. The Sasanian empire had collapsed, and the frontiers with Byzantium would remain relatively stable for centuries.

What explains the success of the early conquests? The size of the armies is impossible to measure with any accuracy. Some Christian sources, which are generally keen to exaggerate the catastrophe of the defeat, speak of extraordinary casualties: a contemporaneous Syriac account has 50,000 killed in a single battle in Syria; another early source, which was probably written some time in the 670s, has the Arabs kill no fewer than 100,000 Byzantines in Egypt.[52] The figures given by the Islamic sources for the numbers of combatants are generally much more reasonable, often in the hundreds or low thousands; even a large army, such as the one that fought at al-Qādisiyya, probably numbered no more than 10,000 or 12,000 men.[53] These more modest armies, which would be much easier to provision and manage, make considerably more sense. Since there is no good evidence for any substantial reduction in Byzantine manpower (and virtually no evidence at all for Sasanian numbers, reduced or otherwise),[54] it is probably safe to assume that Muslims were often outnumbered. Unlike their adversaries, however, Muslim armies were fast, agile, well coordinated and highly motivated. The speed of the conquests on both fronts – as we have seen, the decisive battles took place in the space of four or five years – also suggest that, whatever their numbers, both the Byzantine and Sasanian defences were brittle. In contrast to the large-scale, resource-intensive and protracted campaigns that were so typical of Byzantine–Sasanian warfare of the sixth and early seventh centuries, and which in at least some places resulted in widespread violence and social dislocation,[55] the Islamic conquests of the mid-seventh century read like a series of relatively short engagements (the great battle of al-Qādisiyya is

---

52 Robinson, 'Khūzistān', p. 39.

53 Donner, *Early Islamic conquests*, p. 221.

54 C. Whitby, 'Recruitment in Roman armies from Justinian to Heraclius (*ca.* 565–615)' in A. Cameron (ed.), *The Byzantine and early Islamic Near East*, vol. III: *States, resources and armies* (Princeton, 1995), pp. 120–2.

55 For Asia Minor, see C. Foss, 'The Persians in Asia Minor and the end of Antiquity', *The English Historical Review*, 90 (1975); for Syria, see below, note 58.

said to have lasted three days), which were made by relatively small and hit-and-run armies that rarely laid sieges of any length or produced casualties in large numbers. In many and perhaps most cases in the Byzantine provinces, local elites cut deals that avoided large-scale violence. Modern descriptions of systematic conquest-era violence targeted at non-Muslims, in addition to those of post-conquest persecution before the Marwānids, are usually nothing more than poorly disguised polemics.[56]

If the historical tradition would have us infer that large-scale mortality and dislocation were very occasionally the exception to a general rule, the archaeological evidence clinches this inference. Unlike the barbarian invasions of the fourth- and fifth-century western Mediterranean,[57] the effects of the Islamic conquests were in many respects modest. There is a fair amount of regional variation, but there is no sure archaeological evidence for destruction or abrupt change in settlement patterns that we can directly associate with the events of the 640s and 650s. In Palestine and Syria, where rural settlement seems to have reached a peak in the middle or late sixth century, the conquests bore no impact upon a decline that had apparently begun before they took place.[58] In Syria, we also know that transformations in urban space that earlier generations of historians had attributed to Muslim rule may have actually been under way before the Muslims arrived.[59] Patterns of occupation and use in the towns of the northern Negev, to take an example that is particularly striking, seem to carry on through the seventh century with little appreciable change; the story changes in the course of the eighth and ninth centuries, when decline sets in, presumably accelerated by the shift of the caliphate to Iraq, although the earthquake of 747 had deleterious effects elsewhere.[60] The evidence is very poor for Iraq, but there, too, archaeology suggests that

56 See B. Ye'or, *The decline of Eastern Christianity under Islam: From jihad to dhimmitude* (Cranbury, NJ, 1996); cf. D. J. Constantelos, 'The Moslem conquests of the Near East as revealed in the Greek sources of the seventh and eighth centuries', *Byzantion*, 42 (1972).

57 For a provocative discussion of the west, see B. Ward-Perkins, *The fall of Rome and the end of civilization* (Oxford, 2005).

58 See C. Foss, 'Syria in transition, AD 550–750: An archaeological approach', *Dumbarton Oaks Papers*, 51 (1997); C. Foss, 'The Near Eastern countryside in Late Antiquity: A review article', *The Roman and Byzantine Near East: Journal of Roman Archaeology*, supplementary series 14 (1995); A. Walmsley, *Early Islamic Syria: An archaeological assessment* (Bath, 2007), esp. pp. 44ff.

59 H. Kennedy, 'From polis to madina: Urban change in Late Antique and early Islamic Syria', *Past and Present*, 106 (1985); but cf. J. Magness, *The archaeology of the early Islamic settlement in Palestine* (Winona Lake, IN, 2003), and Walmsley, *Early Islamic Syria*, pp. 37f.

60 Such as in parts of Palestine, on which see Magness, *Early Islamic settlement*; cf. Fiḥl (Pella) in A. Walmsley, 'The social and economic regime at Fihl (Pella)', in P. Canivet and J.-P. Rey Coquais (eds.), *La Syrie de Byzance à l'Islam* (Damascus, 1992), p. 255.

conquest effects were far from catastrophic.[61] Of course the shift of the caliphate from Syria to Iraq may have resulted at least in part from underlying economic changes, but precisely how the political history of the early caliphate relates to the economic history of the Near East remains unclear. It is certainly the case that locating the centre of the caliphate in Syria, which was enjoying an Indian summer of a flourishing eastern Mediterranean economy, initially made much more sense than doing so in or around the Gulf, which had apparently suffered several centuries of economic decline.[62] In this connection it is noteworthy that the political frontier in northern Syria that would long separate Byzantium from the caliphate, unlike the political frontier that had separated Byzantium from the Sasanian empire, appears to coincide with an economic (and geographic) frontier that had separated Anatolia from Syria on the eve of the Islamic period. If the waves of conquest only reached as far as the highest tide of economy had reached earlier, one might think that economy and conquest *were* fairly closely related.[63]

Whatever the precise course of victory, to the victors went the spoils. How much wealth came into the hands of the Muslim conquerors? We know that churches and monasteries possessed objects of great value, and major Byzantine cities such as Damascus, Antioch, Edessa, even more so the Sasanian capital, Ctesiphon, must have had very considerable wealth, perhaps especially in the form of silver.[64] Although we read that Byzantine elites moved north in advance of Muslim armies, and that the conquering Muslims found al-Madāʾin empty of Sasanian royalty and their retainers, not everyone with movable wealth had the time or the inclination to take it with them. Indeed, it must be that many more stayed behind; and many who did leave would have left their wealth behind, as some of the hoards of coins deposited during the seventh century suggest.[65] That all the wealth added up is made clear if we consider that the first step in the direction of a rudimentary administrative system was taken in ʿUmar ibn al-Khaṭṭāb's establishment of a

61 M. Morony, 'The effects of the Muslim conquest on the Persian population of Iraq', *Iran*, 14 (1976).

62 On the archaeological evidence from the western Gulf, see D. Kennet, 'On the eve of Islam: Archaeological evidence from eastern Arabia', *Antiquity*, 79 (2005).

63 M. Morony, 'Economic boundaries? Late Antiquity and early Islam', *JESHO*, 47 (2004), p. 180.

64 See, for example, S. Boyd and M. Mango (eds.), *Ecclesiastical silver plate in sixth-century Byzantium* (Washington, DC, 1992).

65 On some early seventh-century hoards, see S. Heidemann, 'The merger of two currency zones in early Islam: The Byzantine and Sasanian impact on the circulation in former Byzantine Syria and northern Mesopotamia', *Iran*, 36 (1998), p. 96; cf. R. Gyselen and L. Kalus, *Deux trésors monétaires des premiers temps de l'Islam* (Paris, 1983).

bureau (*dīwān*) to measure and redistribute conquest booty among the tribesmen.[66] The principle of distribution described to us by our sources is called 'precedence' (*sābiqa*), according to which the earlier in the conquest movements a given tribesman enrolled, the higher his annual stipend (*ʿaṭā*ʾ). We read that a stipend of 3,000 *dirhams* was awarded to soldiers who had participated in the earliest raids into Iraq, while those who took part in the campaigns leading up to the crucial battle of al-Qādisiyya in Iraq, which was the turning-point in the war against the Sasanians, received 2,000.[67] Whatever the accuracy of these figures, it is clear that the wealth of many early Islamic families was rooted in conquest-era spoils and booty.

Of course, most of the wealth available to the conquerors was immovable because it came in the form of land. Much of the most productive land was Crown Land, and this, in addition to the land owned by local elites (including bishops and monks), became available to conquering Muslims through abandonment and confiscation. In the Sawād – the 'black' area of alluvial soil in central and southern Iraq, where information is fullest – Crown Lands included not only all the properties of the Sasanian royal house, but also those attached to fire-temples, post-houses and the like; ʿUmar is said to have distributed four-fifths to the soldiers and kept one-fifth as his share as caliph, which was to be used for the benefit of the community. As far as labour was concerned, ʿUmar's policy was conservative: the peasants were left to work the land, this being part of a more general *laissez-faire* style of ruling, in which non-Muslims – who in the first decades of Islamic rule were generally lumped together with non-Arabs – enjoyed wide-ranging autonomy. Elsewhere abandoned lands were snatched up, and lands owned by those who had resisted (or could be said to have resisted) the conquests were confiscated. It may be that redistribution to conquering tribesmen was left to the discretion of local authorities; in some cases (such as well-irrigated – and thus valuable – land in the northern Mesopotamian city of Mosul), it is clear that 'precedence' was in operation, as we would imagine it to be: first come, first served; the best lands often went to the earliest settlers, although there was no land-grab, it appears.

Whatever the value of the booty and confiscated land, conquerors and conquered alike had to make sense of the momentous events. For Muslims, the conquests demonstrated God's continued participation in human affairs (the Islamic sources typically have it that God 'conquered by the hands of the

66 See G. Puin, *Der Dīwān von ʿUmar ibn al-Haṭṭāb: Ein Beitrag zur frühislamischen Verwaltungsgeschichte* (Bonn, 1970).

67 For an overview of this system, see Donner, *Early Islamic conquests*, pp. 231–2, 261–2.

Muslims'). The conquests were compelling proof that Muslims enjoyed God's favour and generosity. What could be more persuasive than the enormous bounty of booty taken from Ctesiphon, where the Shah's storehouses were thrown open and all manner of treasure – precious metals, vessels, garments, regalia, even foodstuffs – carried off? Arabian tribesmen were inheriting the riches of empire:

> We marched into al-Madāʾin and came upon Turkish tents filled with baskets sealed with leaden seals. At first, we did not think they would contain anything but food, but later they were found to contain vessels of gold and silver. These were later distributed among the men. At the time ... I saw a man running and shouting, 'Who has silver or gold in his possession?' We also came upon large quantities of camphor which we mistook for salt. So we began to knead it (in our dough) until we discovered that it made our bread taste bitter.[68]

The Qurʾān had made clear that God delivered bounties in this world and the next. Delivering dominion was one of these bounties. Accounts that enumerate the great treasure and booty that fell into Muslim hands thus functioned to illustrate the rewards that God delivered to His believers, and also to contrast the piety and *naïveté* of early Muslims with the wealth-induced arrogance and complaisance of the empires that they had conquered.

Of course things were very different for non-Muslims. Here the events of the conquests were typically assimilated into pre-existing patterns of monotheistic history, and the agents of those conquests, the 'Arabs', 'Saracens' or 'Hagarenes', were assimilated into ready categories of monotheistic belief. In other words, the conquests were proof of God's wrath, and Muslims were heretical monotheists. Put another way, although the deep syntax of historical explanation – history is made as God operates through men – was shared by all monotheist historians, whether Muslim or Christian, for non-Muslim monotheists the events signalled a wrathful rather than a merciful God. As early as about 634, the patriarch of Jerusalem wrote of the 'Saracens who, on account of our sins, have now risen up against us unexpectedly and ravage all with cruel and feral designs, with impious and godless audacity'.[69] Twenty or thirty years later, a chronicler in northern Mesopotamia asked: 'How, otherwise, could naked men, riding without armour or shield, have been able to win, apart from divine aid, God having called them from the ends of the earth so as to destroy, by them, "a sinful kingdom" [i.e. Byzantium] and to bring

68 Al-Ṭabarī, *Taʾrīkh*, series II, pp. 244f. trans. G. H. A. Juynboll as *The history of al-Ṭabarī*, vol. XIII: *The conquest of Iraq, southwestern Persia, and Egypt* (Albany, 1989), p. 24.
69 Hoyland, *Seeing Islam*, p. 69.

low, through them, the proud spirit of the Persians?'[70] Daniel's apocalyptic vision proved especially accommodating to Christians struggling with the significance of the conquests and early Islamic rule. Thus Daniel conditions the words of an Armenian chronicler writing some time in the early 660s: 'I shall describe the calamity which beset our time, the rupture of the vein of the old south and the blowing on us of the mortal hot wind which burned the great, leafy, beautiful, newly planted trees of the orchards. This [happened] rightly, because we sinned against the Lord and we angered the Holy One of Israel.'[71]

Muslims thus drew very different lessons from the spectacular success of the conquests; for them, it was in post-conquest events – the first, great civil war (*fitna*) of the 650s – that God came to express His disfavour. Disunity among Muḥammad's successors imperilled the successes that his unifying vision had produced.

The early caliphate: succession, civil war and opposition movements

In Islamic historiography of the eighth and ninth centuries, the civil war between ʿAlī and Muʿāwiya is a topic of enormous interest, Shīʿa and Sunnīs taking their respective sides and narrating contrasting accounts. For many Muslims of this and later periods, the *fitna* marked a decisive break: before it, the short but inspired moment of the time of the Prophet, the conquests, just rule and political unity; after it came the altogether more ambivalent and controversial periods of Umayyad and ʿAbbāsid rule. Because the events of the *fitna* were accordingly shaped and re-shaped in historical narrative,[72] knowing exactly what happened is out of the question, even if names can be identified and alignments sketched out.[73] Still, there can be little doubt that the

70 S. P. Brock, 'North Mesopotamia in the late seventh century: Book xv of John Bar Penkāyē's *Rīš Mellē*', *JSAI*, 9 (1987), pp. 57–8.

71 Sebeos, *Armenian history*, vol. I, p. 132; in general, H. Suermann, *Die geschichtstheologischen Reaktion auf die einfallenden muslime in der edessenischen Apokalyptik des 7. Jahrhunderts* (Frankfurt, 1985).

72 E. L. Petersen, *ʿAlī and Muʿāwiya in early Arabic tradition: Studies on the genesis and growth of Islamic historical writing until the end of the ninth century*, 2nd edn (Odense, 1974 [Copenhagen, 1964]); R. S. Humphreys, 'Qurʾanic myth and narrative structure in early Islamic historiography', in F. M. Clover and R. S. Humphreys (eds.), *Tradition and innovation in Late Antiquity* (Madison, 1989); B. Shoshan, *Poetics of Islamic historiography: Deconstructing Ṭabarī's* History (Leiden, 2004), pp. 173ff.

73 M. Hinds, 'Kūfan political alignments and their background in the mid-seventh century AD', *IJMES*, 2 (1971); for a very different view, see Madelung, *Succession*.

significance of the dreadful events – murder, Muslim set against Muslim, a divided caliphate – was recognised in its day. As an Armenian chronicler, writing within a generation of the events, put things: 'Now God sent a disturbance amongst the armies of the sons of Ishmael, and their unity was split. They fell into mutual conflict and divided into four sections ... They began to fight with each other and to kill each other with enormous slaughter.'[74] Seventh- and early eighth-century Syriac historians were equally impressed, borrowing the Arabic term, *fitna*, a term which presumably was in broad circulation among Muslims of the period. In sum, the significance of the *fitna* is hard to overstate.[75]

What does *not* seem to have been at issue – at least for those who took their principles seriously enough to try to apply them – was how God's authority was to be effected after the Prophet had died.

Our relatively late sources generally reflect ninth- and tenth-century realities, when caliphs functioned for the most part as guardians of a society with a more-or-less independent religious elite. The earlier evidence shows, however, that virtually all shared the view that the office of the caliphate combined religious and political authority, and that the caliph provided salvation to those who paid him allegiance. For most, the age of prophets had come to an end, succeeded by the age of caliphs, whose status was equal (and, according to some, superior) to that of the prophets. The caliph led the community in this world towards the next one: he was 'the *imām al-hudā*, an imam of guidance who could be trusted to show his followers the right paths. He was compared to way-marks, lodestars, the sun, and the moon for his ability to show the direction in which one should travel.'[76] Early disagreement, then, lay not in the powers that the caliph was to exercise, but in the person (or family) who was to exercise those powers.

Civil war was thus about succession to the office of caliphate, which all Muslims acknowledged should be the ruling institution of the nascent state. We have seen that amidst the chaotic atmosphere of Muḥammad's death, Abū Bakr had been acclaimed as caliph, and he, in turn, had designated ʿUmar as his successor. This engendered very little debate, since, according to tradition, ʿUmar had been so close to the Prophet: his name had even been mooted directly after Muḥammad's death. For his part, ʿUmar nominated a group of six men who were to choose his successor: this group included ʿAlī, ʿUthmān and

74 Sebeos, *Armenian history*, vol. I, p. 154.
75 See H. Djait, *La grande discorde: Religion et politique dans l'Islam des origines* (Paris, 1989).
76 Crone, *Political thought*, p. 22; P. Crone and M. Hinds, *God's caliph: Religious authority in the first centuries of Islam* (Cambridge, 1986).

(usually) four other figures, two of whom were al-Zubayr ibn al-ʿAwwām and Ṭalḥa ibn ʿUbayd Allāh, both revered as close Companions of the Prophet himself. This electoral conclave (*shūrā*) produced ʿUthmān, a Qurashī who belonged to the Umayyad clan that had earlier been so resistant to Muḥammad's preaching in Mecca. ʿUthmān did not prove to be a popular choice: initial resentment was fuelled by his family's chequered past and the disappointment felt by those who supported the claims of ʿAlī. This resentment was compounded by his uninspiring character and conduct: according to our sources, he accepted gifts, which were called bribes, and appointed kinsmen to important (and lucrative) posts, a practice that was branded nepotism. All this emboldened his opponents, and in June 656, while reading the Qurʾān, ʿUthmān was murdered. ʿAlī's supporters immediately acclaimed him as the caliph in the Prophet's Mosque in Medina.

The problem for ʿAlī was that he never enjoyed much support outside Medina and Kūfa. Almost immediately upon his accession he was challenged by Ṭalḥa and al-Zubayr, who were joined by ʿĀʾisha, the most influential of the Prophet's surviving wives. The three gathered an army and engaged ʿAlī in what history would come to call 'the battle of the Camel', after the memory of ʿĀʾisha, posed as she purportedly was upon a camel; this battle took place in December 656 in Iraq. ʿAlī was victorious, but it was a Pyrrhic victory, the principal cost being to his reputation. More pious and gentle than he was shrewd, ʿAlī was quickly outmanoeuvred by Muʿāwiya, ʿUthmān's governor of Syria, who argued that the murderers of ʿUthmān had gone unpunished. He is said to have displayed to a Damascus crowd ʿUthmān's bloody shirt and the fingers of a wife, which were severed as she tried to defend her husband. Muʿāwiya's challenge to ʿAlī soon led to the battle of Ṣiffīn, which lay on the Euphrates south of al-Raqqa, in 657. The two armies hesitated to fight, and when they finally did, tradition tells us that ʿAlī, though on the verge of victory, agreed to a truce. Arbitrators were chosen, and although the events are unclear, it seems that they agreed that neither ʿAlī nor Muʿāwiya was fit to rule. As caliph, ʿAlī had everything to lose from this decision, which was taken in 659, while Muʿāwiya had everything to gain from it. In its wake ʿAlī was hopelessly weak; within two years he had been murdered, and Muʿāwiya was proclaimed caliph in Jerusalem (or Damascus) in 660–1. The civil war had ended. Muʿāwiya would rule for nearly twenty years.

If the trigger for civil war was a dispute about succession and the killing of a just (or unjust) caliph, the underlying causes were rooted in patterns of post-conquest settlement and competing models of status and privilege. It seems that the conquest polity had growth pains. In crude terms, ʿUmar's policy of 'first come, first served' had meant a system that favoured the *muhājirūn* – those who had joined Muḥammad early on – at the expense of those who had enjoyed high prestige in the clan-based social order of the pre-Islamic period. As the initial surge of the conquests ebbed, tensions rose, particularly over the terms on which tribesmen-believers would negotiate their status. We can see this most clearly in Kūfa, where the status of older settlers, who possessed 'precedence', began to be challenged by more recent settlers, who in some cases were being paid higher and higher stipends. As a result, the older settlers came to oppose not only these parvenus, but also the Umayyad governors who had permitted them to settle. In the long term, the effective bonds of kinship – symbolised most clearly by the *ashrāf* (tribal chiefs), who emerged victorious – would dissolve, as tribesmen settled in far-flung towns and cities, and took up a variety of professions and vocations. But this took some time, and a modified kinship politics of the old style was carried out by these *ashrāf*, who, either chosen or acclaimed because they could wield influence among fellow kinsmen, received the salaries, favours and gifts of the caliph, in return for which they offered their loyalty and ability to muster tribal units on his behalf.[77] It took the death of Muʿāwiya and a second civil war that broke out in 683 to demonstrate that the *ashrāf* had outlived their usefulness.

Kinship politics of this variety was thus cultivated by Muʿāwiya, and it had a relatively short shelf-life. Of much more enduring significance were two religio-political movements that issued from these early disputes about succession and the events of the first *fitna*, and that would mature during the second *fitna*. Shīʿism and Khārijism flourished as powerful movements of opposition to the Umayyad clan, which staked its claim to the caliphate, first with ʿUthmān in 644, and second – and considerably more successfully – with Muʿāwiya, who began to rule in 661, and who would name his son Yazīd ibn Muʿāwiya as heir-apparent shortly before he died in 680. Several things distinguished the Shīʿa and Khārijites, but we can start with what they had in common.

Although Shīʿa and Khārijites alike shared with the Umayyads the emerging conception of the caliphate, as opposition movements concentrated in the garrison towns of southern Iraq they both fed off resentment towards the Umayyads, whose late conversion had made them appear opportunistic and cynical in the past, and whose heavy-handed and iniquitous policies, on the one hand, and alleged impiety, on the other, made the present intolerable too. They accordingly held that the Umayyads were entirely unqualified to occupy the

77 Hinds, 'Kūfan political alignments'; P. Crone, *Slaves on horses: The evolution of the Islamic polity* (Cambridge, 1980), pp. 30–2.

office. To most Shīʿa and all Khārijites, then, Abū Bakr and ʿUmar had ruled legitimately, but things went very wrong with the first Umayyad, ʿUthmān (some Shīʿa came to hold that the Prophet had designated ʿAlī, which meant that even Abū Bakr and ʿUmar were usurpers). Although the Umayyads would eventually fall to an ʿAbbāsid movement that was in some measure Shīʿite in inspiration, neither movement had any success in replacing Umayyad imams with imams of their own, and they survived into classical Islam only in so far as they were able to reconcile themselves to what became, during the course of the eighth and ninth centuries, Sunnī rule. In practice this eventually meant exchanging revolution for secession and political activism for sectarian quietism, a process that was nearly complete by the end of the ninth century.

If the Shīʿa and Khārijites shared some common concerns, they differed in others. The chief difference lay in the qualifications they attached to the office of the caliphate. The Shīʿa, who were numerous in Kūfa, insisted on kinship, holding that their imams had to be drawn from the Prophet's family. Since Muḥammad had left no male heirs, in practice this meant candidates from the clan of Hāshim, which included descendants of al-ʿAbbās (the Prophet's uncle) and the relatives and descendants of ʿAlī (Muḥammad's cousin and son-in-law). Throughout the Umayyad period, candidates for the imamate came from several different branches of the Hāshim clan, and the ʿAbbāsid revolution of 750 was successful in no small part because it capitalised upon the view that the ʿAbbāsid family might offer such candidates. But for some Shīʿa the field would by the end of the seventh century begin to narrow towards the line that issued from ʿAlī himself, and what would turn out to be the most important lines ran through al-Ḥusayn (a son of his marriage with the Prophet's daughter Fāṭima), who led a spectacularly unsuccessful rebellion near Kūfa in 680, and through Muḥammad ibn al-Ḥanafiyya (a son from a concubine), in whose name a nebulous figure named al-Mukhtār led an altogether more successful rebellion seven years later. (There were some exceptions, most notably a mid-eighth-century rebellion led by a descendant of ʿAlī's brother, but most Shīʿite rebellions were no more successful than these.) The line that ran from al-Ḥusayn through Mūsā al-Kāẓim (d. 799) would in the long term emerge as the single most important of three main Shīʿite branches (the Twelvers or Imāmīs, Zaydīs and Ismāʿīlīs); it would come to an end only in the late ninth century, when, allegedly, the twelfth and last of these imams disappeared into occultation. But it was from Muḥammad ibn al-Ḥanafiyya that the most successful of all Shīʿite movements – the ʿAbbāsids – would claim to have inherited the imamate. By the time of the ʿAbbāsid revolution (750), genealogical claims had come to be buttressed by historical claims: not only was ʿAlī said to have been designated by the Prophet, but successive imams were said to be designating their successors. Thus the ʿAbbāsids claimed that they inherited the imamate from a descendant of Muḥammad ibn al-Ḥanafiyya, according to his last will and testament.[78]

The Shīʿa were thus devoted to a family in general (the Hāshimīs) and a person in particular (ʿAlī), and this devotion is neatly expressed by their appellation: *shīʿī* ('partisan of ʿAlī'; 'Shīʿite') derives from *shīʿat ʿAlī*, 'the party of ʿAlī'. The Shīʿa's ʿAlid imams came to be endowed not only with religious authority, but also characteristics that others associated with prophets and holy men, such as inerrancy and foresight. In so far as early Shīʿa had a political programme, it lay in rebellion for the sake of restoring effective political rule to the family of the Prophet – the rest would take care of itself. By contrast, the Khārijites were committed not to a family, but to an idea, and this is neatly expressed by their most common appellation: a *khārijī* is 'one who goes out [to fight on behalf of God]', just as a *muḥakkim* (a rarer Khārijite label) is one who proclaims that 'there is no judgement but God's', a slogan associated with the battle of Ṣiffīn, where the Khārijites, pinning Qurʾāns to their lances, abandoned ʿAlī. According to the Khārijite way of looking at things, ʿAlī had fatefully agreed to respect the 'judgement' of men by agreeing to enter into arbitration. If the slogan was clearly potent, we cannot say why, although it may constitute very early evidence for scripturalist attitudes that characterised Khārijite thought of a later period, especially as it is reflected in the Ibāḍī literature, which is the only Khārijite tradition to survive.[79] In any event, within a year (658) ʿAlī had defeated his Khārijite opponents at the battle of Nahrawān, but far from ending the Khārijite threat, the defeat inspired more tribesmen to rebel. As we shall see, in the second *fitna* and the early Marwānid period that would follow it, Khārijites would challenge Umayyad authority and effective power.

Under whose leadership did the Khārijites 'go out' to fight on behalf of God's 'judgement'? For those who made the case for the Umayyads, Qurashī blood was sufficient, while those who made the Shīʿite case insisted upon Hāshimī blood; the Khārijites imposed no genealogical restrictions whatsoever on their imams, insisting for the most part that merit and merit alone was determinant. This

78 For an overview, Crone, *Political thought*, pp. 87–94; more generally, H. Halm, *Shiism* (Edinburgh, 1991).

79 G. R. Hawting, 'The significance of the slogan *lā ḥukma illā lillāh* and the references to the *ḥudūd* in the traditions about the *fitna* and the murder of ʿUthmān', *BSOAS*, 41 (1978); M. Cook, ''Anan and Islam: The origins of Karaite scripturalism', *JSAI*, 9 (1987), pp. 169–72. On the Khārijites more generally, see P. Crone and F. Zimmermann, *The epistle of Sālim ibn Dhakwān* (Oxford, 2001); K.-H. Pampus, *Über die Rolle der Ḫāriǧīya im frühen Islam* (Wiesbaden, 1980).

repudiation of kinship is striking, and must reflect the egalitarian thinking of those living in Baṣra and Kūfa more than that of the Khārijite tribesmen who had broken off from ʿAlī and who, often operating in kinship groups (the Shaybān and Tamīm tribes produced many Khārijites), rebelled against Umayyad and early ʿAbbāsid rule. Just how committed these tribesmen were to Khārijite ideals of merit is hard to know; what is clearer is that Khārijite bands were committed to violent rebellion according to a fairly consistent pattern: secession through emigration (*hijra*) and *jihād* against those whom they considered unbelievers. (In some exceptional cases, the Khārijite commitment to violence extended to non-combatant women and children.) In practising emigration and *jihād*, the Khārijites were falling foul of the Umayyads, but they were holding fast to ideas that had powered Muḥammad and his contemporaries out of Arabia.[80] That they had so little success says something about how quickly things had changed in the space of a couple of generations.

The early Islamic polity: instruments and traditions of rule in the Sufyānid period

We saw earlier that ʿUmar (r. 634–44) is credited with establishing the first *dīwān*, which distributed stipends to conquering soldiers. Several other administrative innovations are similarly ascribed to the second caliph, such as the introduction of the Muslim calendar and the office of the *qāḍī* (judge). So, too, is an indulgent and conservative fiscal policy towards indigenous cultivators: taxes were kept reasonable, the peasants left undisturbed, and the remnants of the Byzantine and Sasanian bureaucracies left intact. Fewer such innovations are attributed to the altogether more controversial ʿUthmān and ʿAlī. With the longer and more stable reigns of Muʿāwiya (r. 661–80) and ʿAbd al-Malik (r. 685–705), the innovations appear with greater frequency: the former is commonly credited with establishing a number of other *dīwān*s, and the latter with a wide range of administrative and bureaucratic measures. These include translating the tax documents from Greek and Persian into Arabic, and reforming weights, measures and coins, as we shall presently see.

The tradition, in sum, lays the foundation of the Islamic state in the inspired rule of the second of the four 'rightly guided caliphs', and describes its growth as evolutionary.[81] Does it have things right? The material and documentary

80 Robinson, *Empire and elites*, pp. 109–26.
81 For a modern version, see A. Ibrahim, *Der Herausbildungsprozeß des arabisch-islamischen Staates* (Berlin, 1994), esp. pp. 163ff.

evidence tells a story that is different from that of the tradition – a story of deferred revolution, rather than gradual evolution.

The conquerors put in place a rudimentary system for the redistribution of conquest resources among the tribesmen, and tribal chieftains (*ashrāf*) played a crucial role in the overlapping networks of indirect rule that characterised Muʿāwiya's caliphate. Similarly rudimentary was the division of authority in the newly conquered territories: the caliph seems to have ruled northern Mesopotamia, Syria, Palestine and Arabia directly, and the rest of the empire was divided into three huge governorships: North Africa and Egypt; Baṣra and those eastern provinces associated with it; and Kūfa and associated provinces. By later Umayyad and ʿAbbāsid standards, administrative geography was thus undifferentiated and monolithic. So, too, were administration and bureaucracy. Governorships were awarded for a number of reasons, but kinship was always a criterion; and when genuine kinship was lacking, it was invented, as in the case of a famous governor of Baṣra, Ziyād ibn Abīhi ('Ziyād, the son of his father'), whose services were so valuable to Muʿāwiya that the caliph made him a foster brother.[82] (Muʿāwiya himself married into the Kalb tribe, thus consolidating his tribal support in Syria.) Sitting in small courts atop rump bureaucracies, his governors seem to have enjoyed broad and undifferentiated civil and military authority; the law remaining underdeveloped and authority undifferentiated, they played roles that would subsequently be played by judges, tax collectors and commanders of the later Marwānid and ʿAbbāsid periods. Moreover, such power as Muʿāwiya and his governors possessed was mediated by tribal chiefs, upon whom they relied to raise armies, and non-Muslim local elites, upon whom they relied to raise taxes.[83] Gifting and bestowing favours and privileges were the currency of these transactions. Similarly, non-Muslim subject populations generally did not experience Islamic rule, or experienced it only indirectly: local authority was usually in the hands of non-Muslim authorities, and Muʿāwiya seems to have been considered a benevolent, hands-off ruler.[84]

That Muʿāwiya apparently handled the *ashrāf* as in some measure as *primi inter pares* does not mean that he failed to develop a language of caliphal authority. As the seat of the caliphate moved from Medina to Kūfa to

82 On Ziyād and his rule in the east, see M. Morony, *Iraq after the Muslim conquest* (Princeton, 1984), *passim*.

83 Crone, *Slaves on horses*, pp. 30–3.

84 For northern Mesopotamia and Iraq, see Robinson, *Empire and elites*, pp. 33–62; Morony, *Iraq*; for Egypt, K. Morimoto, *The fiscal administration of Egypt in the early Islamic period* (Kyoto, 1981).

Damascus – that is, from a corner of Arabia to one of Late Antique Syria's major cities – ideas of authority and rule naturally transformed to some degree. Such as it is, the evidence does suggest that Muʿāwiya innovated in ways that anticipate the later caliphate. According to the historical tradition, which is generally less than sympathetic to the caliph, Muʿāwiya introduced, *inter alia*, the *maqṣūra* (a private enclosure inside the mosque), a number of ceremonial practices, and a caliphal guard. Although the epigraphic record leads back to the 640s, it was Muʿāwiya who appears to have been the first caliph to publicise his name and claim to rule: already in 662 or 663, his name and title appear in Greek in a monumental inscription in Palestine ('Muʿāwiya, commander of the believers'), and other examples (from Egypt and Arabia) follow in graffiti, coins and papyrus protocols.[85] It is also with Muʿāwiya that a record of correspondence begins – much spurious, but some at least partially authentic – between the caliph and his neighbouring sovereigns, Constans II (r. 641–68) and Constantine IV (r. 668–85).[86] Although nothing remains of it, Muʿāwiya's palace in Damascus was apparently an impressive building complex, which announced itself clearly enough in the formerly Byzantine capital;[87] like other Syrian properties of his, it would be reoccupied by subsequent caliphs, including ʿAbd al-Malik. The evidence is very thin, but it may even be that the ingredients for what became the standard form of the mosque – a large courtyard enclosure with a hypostyle hall at one end – were first mixed in Iraq during Muʿāwiya's reign.[88] In sum, he may have come to power through civil war, but his vision – of caliphal rule projected from Syria principally by Syrian tribesmen – was a powerful one, which survived nearly a century after his death.

Still, if ideas of authority and rulership were transforming during the reign of Muʿāwiya, the instruments of power and persuasion remained relatively undeveloped. Muʿāwiya's was a conquest polity in which regionalism was the rule;

85 J. Johns, 'Archaeology and the history of early Islam: The first seventy years', *JESHO*, 46 (2003), pp. 419–20; cf. R. Hoyland, 'New documentary texts and the early Islamic state', *BSOAS*, 69 (2006).

86 For a survey and discussion, see A. Kaplony, *Konstantinopel und Damaskus: Gesandtschaften und Verträge zwischen Kaisern und Kalifen 639–750* (Berlin, 1996).

87 For a description, see F. B. Flood, *The Great Mosque of Damascus: Studies on the makings of an Umayyad visual culture* (Leiden, 2001), pp. 147ff.

88 For reconstructions of the Kūfan mosque, which was built, according to tradition, by Ziyād ibn Abīhi, see B. Finster, *Frühe iranische Moscheen* (Berlin, 1994), pp. 23f.; and J. Johns, 'The "House of the Prophet" and the concept of the mosque', in J. Johns (ed.), *Bayt al-Maqdis: Jerusalem and early Islam*, Oxford Studies in Islamic Art 9, part 2 (Oxford, 1999), pp. 64f. The appearance of the *miḥrāb* is less clearly datable to the Sufyānid period; see Finster, *Moscheen*, pp. 113ff.; and Flood, *Great Mosque of Damascus*, p. 194.

an ambitiously centralising state, one that patronised not only building projects on an unprecedented level, but also relatively stable institutions, emerged only during the reign of ʿAbd al-Malik. This – the very modesty of very early Islamic rule – is clearly reflected in the coinage.

Although circulation and minting patterns are clearer in the former Byzantine provinces than they are in the east, undated issues make sequences and chronologies difficult to establish and highly controversial, even in Syria and Palestine. Even so, some basic patterns are well established, and the most important of these is an early conservatism. The pre-conquest divide in precious metal (Byzantine gold and Sasanian silver) was preserved throughout most of the seventh century. Within greater Syria, where the evidence is fullest, we know that the coinage of vanquished adversaries continued to circulate, small handfuls of Sasanian issues left over from the Sasanian occupation of 612–30, and large fistfuls of Byzantine coinage, some having survived from Byzantine rule, others filtering in across a porous frontier: thus one finds large numbers of Byzantine issues struck during the reign of Constans II (641–68), and others struck as late as the reign of Constantine IV (r. 668–85). In design, too, Byzantine and Sasanian models were closely followed, the issues of Constans II and Khusrau II (r. 590–628) proving the most popular.[89] Muʿāwiya appears on a silver coin in the fifty-fourth or fifty-fifth year of the *hijra* as the 'commander of the believers'; but the coin, which was minted in the southern Iranian town of Dārābjird, retains strikingly pre-Islamic elements: its dating is to the era of the Sasanian shah Yazdegerd, and its language is Pahlavi, or Middle Persian.[90] Within this broad conservatism there was thus a measure of innovation in the coinage, but this innovation is clearest in Iraq and Iran – that is, outside the metropolitan capital of Syria, where the caliph's influence was presumably strongest. An argument that Muʿāwiya *did* have a hand in minting reform has been tentatively made, but it turns more on a single (and controversial) line in an early Syriac chronicle than on the surviving numismatic record. Whether any minting took place under caliphal supervision before the 690s therefore remains unproven, although the regional coinages of Syria from the 660s and 670s apparently show some increased organisation.[91]

89 C. Foss, 'The coinage of Syria in the seventh century: The evidence of excavations', *Israel Numismatic Journal*, 13 (1994–9); C. Morrison, 'La monnaie en Syrie byzantine', in J. M. Dentzer and W. Orthmann (eds.), *Archéologie et histoire de la Syrie II* (Saarbrücken, 1989); on this and the coinage more generally, see below, chapter 16.

90 For a description, see S. Album and T. Goodwin, *Sylloge of Islamic coins in the Ashmolean*, vol. I: *The pre-reform coinage of the early Islamic period* (London, 2002), p. 15 and plates 17 and 18.

91 H. Bone, 'The administration of Umayyad Syria: The evidence of the copper coins', Ph.D. thesis, Princeton University (2000), esp. pp. 26ff.; C. Foss, 'A Syrian coinage of

What is indisputable is that clearly centralised and coordinated minting appears only in the last decade of the seventh century as and when state institutions were crystallising. For much of the seventh century a bewildering array of coins was in circulation in Syria, some genuine Byzantine issues, others imitations (particularly of Constans II), others imitations of imitations.

There is, then, no reliably early evidence for anything beyond very rudimentary instruments of rule that we can attribute to the caliphs or their courts. There is compelling evidence for a fairly sophisticated state apparatus at work throughout the seventh century, however. We find it in Egypt, where a wealth of Greek papyri (receipts of various sorts, requisitions, entagia, protocols) reflect the continuity – and, as recent scholarship has shown, an apparent expansion – of an early Islamic fiscal system rooted in Byzantine traditions. (Layers of the Sasanian administrative apparatus survived into the early Islamic period, too, but there is virtually no documentary or contemporaneous evidence for it.) In what ways was the Byzantine system affected by Islamic rule? Arab-Muslim officials of various sorts figure in the papyri from soon after the conquest, where they appear to have been both knowledgeable about, and assertive in, the management of the fisc. As a bilingual (Greek and Arabic) papyrus dated to AH 22 puts it (in the Greek): 'In the name of God, I, Abdellas [ʿAbd Allāh], *amīr* [commander] to you, Christophoros and Theodorakios, pagarchs of Herakleopolis. I have taken over from you for the maintenance of the Saracens being with me in Herakleopolis, 65 sheep.'[92] In fact, the early Islamic papyri document some reorganising of Egypt's administrative geography, and perhaps also the introduction of the poll-tax to Egypt, which would reflect the practical imposition of the *jizya* as it is promised in Q 9:69.[93] It now appears that the Muslim rulers of early and mid-seventh-century Egypt were not the passive receptors of Byzantine bureaucratic traditions, as some earlier scholars had argued, but assertive participants in their transformation.[94]

Muʿawiya?', *Revue Numismatique*, 157 (2002); C. Morrison, 'Monnayage omeyyade et l'histoire administrative et économique de la Syrie', in P. Canivet and J.-P. Rey-Coquais (eds.), *La Syrie de Byzance à l'Islam* (Damascus, 1992), esp. p. 312.

92 A. Grohmann, *The world of Arabic papyri* (Cairo, 1952), pp. 113–14.

93 See F. Morelli, *Documenti Greci per la fiscalità e la amministrazione dell'Egitto Arabo* (Vienna, 2001), pp. 19–20.

94 See J. Gascou, 'De Byzance à l'Islam: Les impôts en Egypte après la conquête arabe', *JESHO*, 26 (1983); P. Sijpesteijn, 'New rule over old structures: Egypt after the Muslim conquest', in H. Crawford (ed.), *Regime change in the Ancient Near East and Egypt, from Sargon of Agade to Saddam Hussein*, Proceedings of the British Academy 136 (London, 2007), pp. 183–200.

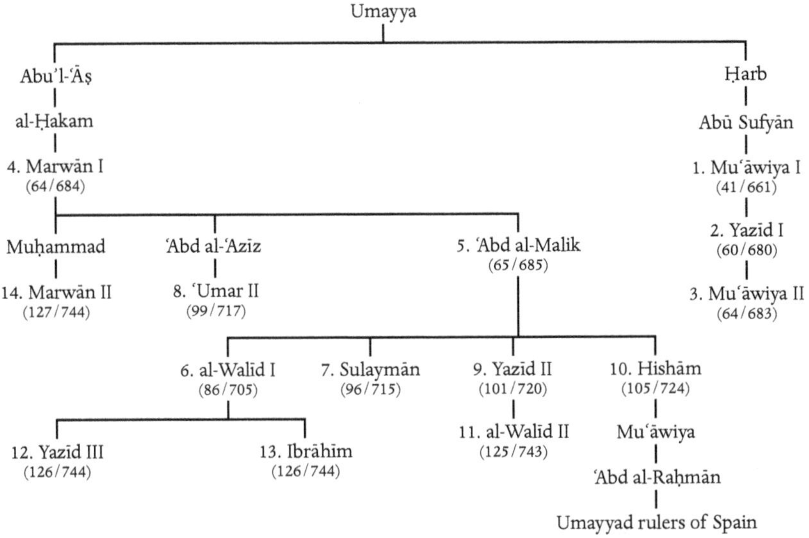

4. The Umayyads (dates of accession).
After Hugh Kennedy, *The Prophet and the age of the caliphates*, 2004, p. 403. Copyright Longman, reproduced with permission.

The papyri from Egypt, like the many fewer that survive from Palestine, thus demonstrate the continuity of Byzantine traditions and, in the Egyptian case, an expansion and elaboration of Byzantine traditions during the first half-century of Islamic rule. But if Egypt possessed a sophisticated tax regime, nowhere do we find anything reliable that connects it to the imperial capital, either in Arabia, southern Iraq or Syria. Nor do we find any indication that the Arab-Muslim oversight of the Byzantine machinery that they had inherited was conditioned by an imperial programme projected by Medina, Kūfa or Damascus. In fact, that the impetus for maximising tax revenue was a local initiative is suggested by the contrasting histories of other provinces, such as Northern Mesopotamia, where taxation appears to have been relatively low and irregular for most of the seventh century – that is, until the Marwānids imposed an altogether new and more robust tax administration.[95] To judge from a small clutch of papyri that survive from Nessana, an irregular regime seems to have been in place there too.[96]

95 Robinson, *Empire and elites*, pp. 33ff.
96 Johns, 'Archaeology and the history of early Islam', p. 421; cf. Hoyland, 'New documentary texts', pp. 399ff.

In sum, there is good reason to think that first- and second-generation conquerors may have been hesitant imperialists, who, settling more frequently at some distance from local inhabitants than next to them, looked after themselves rather than their subjects. 'What, then, did the Arabs do with the regions they conquered?', an archaeologist asks: 'For the most part, they seem to have left them alone.'[97] This is what the evidence says,[98] and it is what sense dictates: why emulate the traditions of the Byzantine and Sasanian states when God had delivered victory over them to austere monotheists, and when there already were people in place to do the job well? Precisely the same conservatism that led the early caliphs to leave indigenous Greek- and Persian-speaking and writing bureaucrats in place in the provinces acted as a brake upon administrative innovation at the empire's centre.

And being conservative came naturally: all of the caliphs who ruled until 680 had been born and bred in Arabia, and had witnessed the glorious moments of early Islam.[99] Muʿāwiya, whose father had been a very prominent opponent of Muḥammad's and had converted only late and opportunistically, himself converted only when Mecca was conquered by Muḥammad, whereupon he entered his circle of advisers and confidants (he is conventionally identified as one of the Prophet's secretaries). He was thus very much the product of the same world that had produced Muḥammad himself: a Qurashī schooled in the ways of tribal politics of Mecca and Medina, he was already in his fifties when he became caliph in 40/661. By contrast, ʿAbd al-Malik was born in 26/646f., that is, at the beginning of ʿUthmān's reign. His formative experience was not of Qurashī Mecca or Muḥammad's community in Medina, nor even of Medina filled with the spoils of ʿUmar's spectacular conquests. It was of a town riven by the controversies of ʿUthmān and ʿAlī's reigns. In other words, what ʿAbd al-Malik knew of Islam's glorious origins was mediated by others, and the lessons he learned during his childhood were about the

97 Foss, 'Syria in transition', p. 266.

98 Even much later, in the middle decades of the eighth century – that is, when state institutions had developed considerably, and the instruments of state power had become more coercive – conquering Muslims seem to have balked before imposing state structures in their newly acquired territories: Islamic coinage began to circulate in northern Afghanistan only after a full century of hands-off rule; and although the tradition describes a late seventh- and eighth-century programme of Arabicising official documents, the surviving material remains in Bactrian. See N. Sims-Williams, *Bactrian documents from northern Afghanistan*, vol. I: *Legal and economic documents* (Oxford, 2000), pp. 116, 134 ('Arab dirhams in silver' appear in 507/739 and again in 525/757); the poll-tax only appears in the latter.

99 See Crone, *Slaves on horses*, p. 5: 'Rarely have a preacher and his followers lived in such discontinuous environments: what made sense to Muḥammad made none to Muʿāwiya, let alone to ʿAbd al-Malik.'

fragility of the early Islamic elite. These lessons would be repeated during the second civil war, when the elite fragmented further. Historical discontinuities may have taken an enormous toll on the preservation of their history, but it freed Muslims of the early period to innovate and experiment.

Little wonder, then, that it is only with ʿAbd al-Malik and his generation of Muslims that we have clear evidence for a programme of state building that was driven by the Muslim ruling elite, and which systematically diffused new ideas of power and authority.[100] Since the evidence for all of this explodes onto the scene within a short time – the late 680s and early 690s – we must accordingly describe the process of early Islamic state building as revolutionary, rather than evolutionary.

The second *fitna* and the Marwānid revolution

The second *fitna*,[101] like the first, was triggered by problems of succession. Muʿāwiya's appointment of his son as heir-apparent seems to have been unpopular in principle, since it departed from traditions of acclamation and election. Yazīd's difficulties were compounded by his conduct: the son possessed little of the father's nous and forbearance, and it was at the beginning of Yazīd's reign that an Umayyad army suppressed a rebellion led by the Prophet's grandson, al-Ḥusayn. In the long term, his gruesome slaying at Karbalāʾ (680) came to exemplify Umayyad brutality and provide inspiration to subsequent Shīʿite movements, especially as it followed earlier instances of Sufyānid abuse of the Shīʿa, such as Muʿāwiya's execution of the Kūfan Shīʿite al-Ḥujr ibn ʿAdī; in the short term, it deepened the crisis for Muʿāwiya's successor. Umayyad rule was further weakened with the succession in 683 of the sickly and incompetent Muʿāwiya II, who ruled for a matter of months. Umayyad authority outside Syria had started to dissolve earlier, but now it collapsed almost entirely, with the result that several Umayyads and non-Umayyads emerged as candidates for the caliphate. Of these, four are especially prominent in the sources: ʿAbd Allāh ibn al-Zubayr, the pious son of a revered Companion who would rule effectively from Mecca; al-Ḍaḥḥāk ibn Qays al-Fihrī, a governor of Muʿāwiya's; Ḥassān ibn Malik ibn Bahdal, a cousin of his son, Yazīd; and ʿAmr ibn Saʿīd, an Umayyad who had served Muʿāwiya.

100 For a different view, see F. M. Donner, 'The formation of the Islamic state', *JAOS*, 106 (1986), pp. 283–96.

101 The fullest discussion remains G. Rotter, *Die Umayyaden und der Zweite Bürgerkrieg (680–692)* (Wiesbaden, 1982).

In the event, Umayyad rule would be reconstituted, but the process would be slow and difficult. It started in the early summer of 684 with the acclamation in al-Jābiya (near Damascus) of Marwān ibn al-Ḥakam, a well-respected and senior member of the Umayyad house; Marwān promptly set about establishing himself in Syria, defeating al-Ḍaḥḥāk at Marj Rāhiṭ, and then moving to Damascus. He died in the spring of the following year, and was succeeded by his son, ʿAbd al-Malik. It was ʿAbd al-Malik who, after several false starts and heavy campaigning, completed the process eight years later by defeating his Syrian rivals (notably ʿAmr ibn Saʿīd), campaigning in Iraq and Northern Mesopotamia, and eventually sending an army against Ibn al-Zubayr's Mecca. There, in March 691, ʿAbd al-Malik's most trusted commander and future governor of the east, al-Ḥajjāj ibn Yūsuf, laid siege to the city and put an end to the caliphate of Ibn al-Zubayr.[102] Although ʿAbd al-Malik's bid for the caliphate dates from 685, when he received the oath of allegiance in Syria, it was probably only with the death of Ibn al-Zubayr late in 692 that he was widely acknowledged as caliph. Regnal dates that conventionally put the beginning of his caliphate in 685 say more about subsequent Umayyad claims than they do about contemporaneous attitudes.

Indeed, there can be little doubt that Ibn al-Zubayr, although portrayed by much of the primary and secondary literature as a pretender or rebel (one most frequently described as 'he who takes refuge in the house', i.e. the Kaʿba),[103] had been widely acknowledged as caliph – certainly much more so than Yazīd, Muʿāwiya II, Marwān and, at least until 692, ʿAbd al-Malik himself. A political and dynastic dead-end who had the great misfortune to have been overthrown by the extraordinarily successful ʿAbd al-Malik, Ibn al-Zubayr then had his caliphate written out of most (if not all) of the history books. History itself was different. Almost universally respected because of his descent from al-Zubayr, the Prophet's Companion who had rebelled alongside ʿĀʾisha in the battle of the Camel, Ibn al-Zubayr had firm control of the Prophet's homeland and the emerging cultic centre of Mecca, and minted coins as early as 684 (using what was becoming the standard caliphal title, 'the commander of the faithful'). He ruled lands stretching from Egypt in the west to eastern Iran and parts of Afghanistan in the east by appointing governors,

102 The following is spelled out in much more detail in C. F. Robinson, *ʿAbd al-Malik* (Oxford, 2005). The politics of the period is very usefully summarised in A. A. Dixon, *The Umayyad caliphate 65–86/684–705 (a political study)* (London, 1971).

103 In addition to Robinson, *ʿAbd al-Malik*, pp. 31ff., see Abū al-Fatḥ al-Sāmirī, *The continuatio of the Samaritan chronicle of Abū al-Fatḥ al-Sāmirī al-Danafī*, ed. and trans. M. Levy-Rubin (Princeton, 2002), pp. 54f.

levying taxes and dispatching armies, and successfully suppressed the most potent opposition movement of the civil war, a Shīʿite rebellion in southern Iraq (685–7) led by a shadowy figured named 'al-Mukhtār', who championed the right to the caliphate of Muḥammad ibn al-Ḥanafiyya, a son of ʿAlī's by a concubine. It is true that his vision of a Ḥijāzī-based empire turns out to have been naive and nostalgic, but in several respects he was an innovator: for example, it is during his reign that part of the Muslim profession of faith ('Muḥammad is the messenger of God') first appears on coinage, one of several practices that would survive his death in 692. He also undertook what appears to have been a substantial rebuilding programme in Mecca, which anticipates ʿAbd al-Malik's. In overthrowing Ibn al-Zubayr, ʿAbd al-Malik thus defeated the man who was at once the most effective spokesman for the interests of the Ḥijāzīs left behind by Umayyad rule, the most respected opponent of Umayyad dynastic claims, and the one most widely acknowledged as caliph.

ʿAbd al-Malik's revolutionary impulse carried him beyond his defeat of Ibn al-Zubayr. For it was during his reign that we witness nothing less than the transformation of the loosely federal, ideologically inchoate conquest polity of the early caliphs into the land-based, bureaucratic state that lay at the heart of the Marwānid empire – and one that, within a generation of ʿAbd al-Malik's death, would reach its greatest size. Just how fragile the conquest polity had been can be seen in its catastrophic collapse upon the death of Muʿāwiya. Just how robust ʿAbd al-Malik's state was can be seen in the events following his death, when he was succeeded by no fewer than four sons, three grandsons and two nephews. And because his and his sons' rule was so successful in the short term, the traditions, institutions and ideas they put in place survived in the longer term, underpinning the ʿAbbāsid empire of the eighth and ninth centuries.

The changes were military, administrative and ideological; all contributed to the complex process – itself already under way – in which Islamic society became in many respects increasingly differentiated and complex, and the instruments of rule more powerful and persuasive. We may begin with the army.

Having settled in the provinces in the 640s and 650s, by the 670s and 680s many conquering tribesmen would have begun to take up a variety of occupations, depending on their resources, abilities and opportunities; and in some instances we know that sedentarisation was encouraged among pastoralists, and that garrisons were being transformed into towns.[104] Even

104 For an overview, see K. ʿAthamina, 'Arab settlement during the Umayyad caliphate', *JSAI*, 8 (1986).

so, the contrast between civilian and soldier remained indistinct until ʿAbd al-Malik's military reforms, when the tribesmen-soldiers of the conquest armies, generally mustered and led by chieftains drawn from high-status kinship groups, began to be replaced by a professional soldiery of Syrians. The lesson taught by the civil war, when fickle chieftains had abandoned the Sufyānids for rival candidates, was duly learned. What resulted was thus an altogether clearer contrast between civilian and soldier, which, in the view of a state claiming a monopoly on legitimate violence, transformed the armed civilian into a brigand or rebel. At the same time, because the army was overwhelmingly Syrian in composition, it also resulted in an altogether clearer distinction between (ruling) Syrian and (ruled) non-Syrian.

In the short term, the new-style Syrian army was a success: within three years of defeating Ibn al-Zubayr, ʿAbd al-Malik had launched what would turn out to be a four-year campaign on the Byzantine frontier, and parts of Armenia would fall under Islamic rule for the first time. (The *jihād* would be expanded with considerable success by ʿAbd al-Malik's son and successor, al-Walīd, especially in North Africa and Sind.) But problems naturally appeared. We occasionally read of desertion and the soldiers' reluctance to fight; we also read of spectacular rebellions led by commanders on extended campaigns (thus a dangerous revolt in the east led by the celebrated Kindī commander, Ibn al-Ashʿath, in 699) and of soldiers who had fallen off the *dīwān* and thus out of favour with the Umayyads (thus the Khārijite rebellion led by Shabīb ibn Yazīd al-Shaybānī in Northern Mesopotamia and Iraq in late 695 and 696).[105] Perhaps most important, the distinction between Syrian and non-Syrian became politically explosive. The occupation of Iraq and Iran by Syrian soldiers – Syrian garrisons were established in Iraq and Iran, the garrison of Wāsiṭ being built in 702 or 703, equidistant between Baṣra and Kūfa as a base against their restive tribesmen – provided the coercion necessary to extract taxes and tribute from non-Syrians. This would lead in the short term to endemic rebellion in the provinces, most notably by Khārijites, and, in the long term, to the catastrophic revolution of 749–50. Meanwhile, the professionalisation of the army led to the emergence of two rival factions (the Qays/Yaman, or 'northerner'/'southerner'); and this rivalry would also subvert Umayyad rule until its end.[106]

105 On Ibn al-Ashʿath, see R. Sayed, *Die Revolte des Ibn al-Ashʿat und die Koranleser* (Freiburg, 1977); on Shabīb, see Robinson, *Empire and elites*, pp. 109ff.

106 P. Crone, 'Were the Qays and Yemen of the Umayyad period political parties?', *Der Islam*, 71 (1994).

Military reforms thus strengthened Umayyad power in the short term, as they reflected the shift away from a relatively undifferentiated conquest society. The same processes characterised the administrative and fiscal reforms of the period. Here, too, we find indirect influence being replaced by direct control. The scale of these reforms is hard to exaggerate. As the Islamic historical tradition makes clear, the changes were in part linguistic: the language of tax administration, which until this period had remained unchanged in Greek and Persian, was now replaced by Arabic. The surviving documentary evidence offers some corroboration for this shift, although the pace of change in the Islamic east seems to have been considerably slower than the historical tradition would have it.[107] The introduction of Arabic into the tax administration had the effect of opening up bureaucratic careers to Arabs and to non-Arab converts (*mawālī*), who were incorporated into Islam through admission as clients by Arab patrons, although Christians and Jews would continue to serve; the Marwānid period is consequently filled with examples of extraordinary social climbing, as Arabs and *mawālī* alike joined the ranks of administrators and tax officials. A relatively closed elite of tribesmen-soldiers was cracking open. Effects aside, the intention of this linguistic change must have been to extend Umayyad control over tax revenues so as to maximise the elite's share. Indeed, there is no doubt that the last two decades of the seventh century and first two of the eighth were a watershed in the fiscal history of the Near East, as irregular and inconsistent tribute taking was replaced by regular and more systematic taxing. The documentary and Syriac historical traditions show this at work in Syria and Northern Mesopotamia; in the latter we have a handful of apocalypses and apocalyptic histories that describe in hyperbolic detail the devastating effects of the new taxing regime.[108] Even in Egypt, where the engines of the Byzantine tax machine had never stopped firing, we read of the unprecedented extension of tax liabilities to mobile peasants and monks, and the unrest that resulted from the new regime. Arabs, too, now became increasingly liable to taxation, as the poll- and land-taxes were firmly established for the first time, the former on non-Muslims, the latter on non-Muslim and Muslim alike.[109]

The scale and nature of these changes are reflected in the material evidence. Leaving aside all the papyri generated by the Byzantine machinery of Egypt,

107 See above, note 98.

108 For a survey, see Hoyland, *Seeing Islam*, pp. 257ff.; Robinson, *Empire and elites*, pp. 48ff.

109 See J. B. Simonsen, *Studies in the genesis and early development of the caliphal taxation system* (Copenhagen, 1988), esp. pp. 113ff.; Morimoto, *Fiscal administration of Egypt*, pp. 139ff.

we have precious little elite-sponsored documentary and inscriptional material (which is to be distinguished from occasional graffiti) dating from the conquest and Sufyānid periods, but with the Marwānids the corpus not only grows larger, but also more consistent. For example, while no pre-Marwānid milestones have been discovered, no fewer than six date from the reign of ʿAbd al-Malik.[110] Patterns of non-elite settlement and land use may have been slow to change in this period, but new tools and techniques of rule were being adopted: it is at the tail end of the seventh and early eighth centuries, to take another example, that mobile non-Muslim taxpayers were made to wear seal pendants to mark their tax status.[111] The best evidence for the scale and nature of change comes in the coinage. We saw earlier that coinage had been diverse, preserving (and elaborating upon) the varieties of Byzantine and Sasanian minting traditions that had carried on through the conquests. Starting almost immediately upon the defeat of Ibn al-Zubayr, ʿAbd al-Malik's minters abandoned the conservatism of their forebears, first (starting in *c.* 692) by introducing distinctively Islamic designs and motifs (such as a portrait of ʿAbd al-Malik; what may be a spear in a prayer niche), and second, starting with gold coins in around 696–7, by abandoning altogether the figural imagery and languages of pre-Islamic coinage in favour of purely non-figural, epigraphic coins with exclusively Arabic legends that expressed in formulaic ways distinctively Islamic ideas.[112] Alongside these coinage reforms, which centralised minting and imposed standard weights,[113] sits a reform of weights and measures. In addition to circulating tokens that broadcast legitimising and universalising claims, the elite was thus taking an unprecedented interest in fostering economic exchange. The Marwānids certainly patronised commercial building projects in Palestine and Syria.[114]

What we have, in sum, is the relatively sudden appearance of a cluster of institutions and practices: an imperial state designed for the systematic extraction of agricultural revenues was being engineered. It was to be effected by a professional soldiery resourced by an increasingly thorough tax regime, which

110 A. Elad, 'The southern Golan in the early Muslim period: The significance of two newly discovered milestones of ʿAbd al-Malik', *Der Islam*, 76 (1999).

111 C. F. Robinson, 'Neck-sealing in early Islam', *JESHO*, 48 (2005).

112 Bone, 'Copper coins'.

113 P. Grierson, 'The monetary reforms of ʿAbd al-Malik: Their metrological basis and their financial repercussions', *JESHO*, 3 (1960).

114 See R. M. Foote, 'Commerce, industrial expansion, and orthogonal planning: Mutually compatible terms in settlements of Bilad al-Sham during the Umayyad period', *Mediterranean Archaeology*, 13 (2000); and S. Berthier (ed.), *Peuplement rural et aménagements hydroagricôles dans la moyenne vallée de l'Euphrat, fin VIIe–XIXe siècle* (Damascus, 2001).

was managed by new cadres of bureaucrats and administrators. Its authority was to be anchored in that unitary conception of authority with which this chapter began, and which was now crystallising. As the poetry and prose of this and subsequent periods shows, ʿAbd al-Malik was 'God's caliph', heir to the Prophet's authority and God's 'shadow on earth', a legislator, judge, guide, warrior, rain-maker, prayer-leader, perhaps an editor (the Qurʾānic text may have been fixed only in the early Marwānid period)[115] – and certainly a builder of what remains the oldest intact Islamic building: the domed, octagonal building in Jerusalem that is called the Dome of the Rock. Completed in around 72/691f., the Dome of the Rock sits atop the Temple Mount, which looks down upon Christian Jerusalem. The building is a monument to victory: not merely victory over Ibn al-Zubayr (its construction seems to have taken place during or soon after the end of the *fitna*) but, more importantly, victory over rival monotheisms. In fact, it was an imposing reminder of their obsolescence: just as the building was made to sit at the heart of the Holy Land, literally upon the foundations of the Jews' Temple, so did the faith that it symbolised claim to reform and perfect earlier revelations. Thus its inscriptions announce that God is merciful and compassionate, that He is alone and has no sons ('The messiah Jesus, son of Mary, was only a messenger of God … [Who] is too exalted to have a son'), that Muḥammad is His Prophet, and that:

> Religion with God is Islam. Those who received the scripture differed only after knowledge came to them, out of envy for one another. Whoever denies the signs of God [beware], for God is swift to call to account.[116]

Conclusion

Given the extraordinarily modest cultural and political traditions generally associated with western Arabia in Late Antiquity, how is it that Muḥammad and the Arab caliphs and commanders who immediately succeeded him had both the vision and perspicacity to forge a new religio-political tradition that would survive in post-conquest Syria and Iraq? Sophisticated religious traditions generally emerge in societies with relatively high levels of social differentiation; the rule of history calls for the assimilation of conquering pastoral

115 Thus M. Sfar, *Le coran est-il authentique?* (Paris, 2000), pp. 83ff.; Robinson, *ʿAbd al-Malik*, pp. 100ff.
116 Hoyland, *Seeing Islam*, pp. 696ff.

and semi-pastoral tribesmen, along with their political and cultural traditions, into the more developed, sedentary culture so conquered, be it fifth-century Roman Italy or twelfth-century Saljūq Iraq. Why were seventh-century Arabs so different? These questions can be answered in a variety of ways, but it may be useful to contrast two of them.

The first, here put in its most extreme form, is to argue that the Ḥijāz had nothing to do with earliest Islam. Because religious traditions have a habit of misrepresenting their origins, and because we lack corroborating evidence that is contemporaneous to the crucial events of the seventh century, there is no reason to suppose that everything happened as the Islamic tradition tells us it happened. One may accordingly assert that Muḥammad did not exist, that the conquests – that is, the Ḥijāzī Arabs' violent seizure of power from the Byzantines (and Sasanians) – did not take place, and that the Qurʾān, with all of its debts to Judaism and Christianity, was compiled at least a century (and perhaps two centuries) later.[117] (Islamic history would thus be comparable to Israelite history, its scripture, conquest and early polity as enigmatic as those ascribed to Moses and David.) There being no historical basis for early Islamic narratives, the problematic Ḥijāzī context of earliest Islam is thus solved at a stroke: Islam's origins lie not in Arabia, but in the Late Antique world of the eighth- and ninth-century Fertile Crescent, in the religious, ethnic and linguistic matrix that produced comparable forms of monotheism, such as, especially, rabbinic Judaism. According to this line of argument, Arabian origins reflect not historical reality, but an invented tradition.

Now, it can hardly be doubted that the early Islamic historiographic tradition was at once deeply conditioned by polemical assertions regarding identity, origin and social status, and preserves only very incompletely any authentic material from the seventh century. But if it is one thing to envision the growth of the Islamic tradition as part of a much broader process, in which monotheist identity of several varieties took shape, it is altogether something else to reject in its entirety the tradition's claim for Arabian origins. In fact, revisionism of this sort can readily be blunted by adducing a variety of seventh-century evidence. The fact is that Christian and Jewish sources confirm that Muḥammad *did* exist and did make prophetic claims, that some kind

117 For revisionism of the most radical kind, see Y. Nevo and J. Koren, *Crossroads to Islam: The origins of the Arab religion and the Arab state* (Amherst, NY, 2003), inspired, in part, by the work of Wansbrough, which is usefully discussed in H. Berg, 'Islamic origins reconsidered: John Wansbrough and the study of early Islam', *Method and Theory in the Study of Religion*, 9 (1997); cf. I. Olagüe, *Les arabes n'ont jamais envahi l'espagne* (Paris, 1969).

of violent political change effected by monotheist tribesmen-soldiers from Arabia *did* occur, and that, at least in some fragmentary form, some kind of an Islamic scripture *can* be dated to the seventh century. Non-Islamic and material evidence is far too sketchy to produce a coherent account of Islam's beginnings, but it securely locates those beginnings in events that are familiar to us from the Islamic tradition itself. In any case, if one deprives the conquests of the great motive force of Muḥammad's revelations and politics, one makes them altogether harder to understand.

One solution to the problem of the Ḥijāz's cultural insularity is thus to pull Islamic origins entirely out of Arabia and into the Late Antique Fertile Crescent of the eighth and ninth centuries. The second, which is more promising, is to pull Late Antiquity into the seventh-century Ḥijāz. For the more evidence we have that it was open to the political, cultural and religious currents of Late Antiquity, the easier it is for us to understand not merely the Qur'ān – that 'text without a context' – but also early Islam more generally. There is disappointingly little of it that we can securely date to the sixth and early seventh centuries, however. (Arguments for Christian, Jewish or Manichaean influence upon Muḥammad and his contemporaries typically adduce the biographical and historical tradition, especially Prophetic *sīra*, which generally dates from eighth- and ninth-century Iraq;[118] until the genesis and transmission of this tradition are understood more fully, evidence such as this is far from clinching.) The political and cultural circumstances for Arabian archaeology are admittedly very unfavourable, but, such as the archaeology is, it yields virtually no sure evidence for the extension of political and cultural influences from the Late Antique heartland into the sixth- and seventh-century Ḥijāz; this contrasts with earlier periods and other regions of Arabia, particularly the south and the east, which, according to the material and historical record, were frequently brought into the orbit of the Byzantine and Sasanian empires.[119] To assemble the thin evidence for local monotheisms, we must fall back upon the incidental references in the slim non-Islamic tradition, and, as we have already seen, the testimony of the one text that was generated in the seventh-century Ḥijāz – the Qur'ān.

In the present state of our knowledge, the most we can do is propose hypotheses that accommodate the available evidence according to models appropriate to the Late Antique world in which early Muslims evolved. Arabia

118 For a Manichaean example, see M. Gil, 'The creed of Abū ʿĀmir,' *Israel Oriental Studies*, 12 (1992).
119 For an overview, Hoyland, *Arabia and the Arabs*.

was moving – perhaps sluggishly – towards monotheism, and Muḥammad seems to have greatly accelerated this process. Beyond adducing the force of his personality, political acuity and the victories of the early Medinan period, explaining why his vision of reform and political action should have been so successful is very difficult, but it may be because western Arabia lay outside the dense network of Christian and Jewish belief and institutions that Muḥammad was free to innovate in the long-abandoned style of a Hebrew prophet, legislating, leading and warring, and that this style had such appeal; had he been born and raised in Syria, one might expect a very different career, perhaps as a more typical (but equally charismatic) holy man. What is clearer is that he articulated a religious vision that was at once reassuringly familiar and passionately revolutionary – and this, in a distinctively Arabian idiom. Thus paganism is repudiated, but the pagan sanctuary of Mecca is reinterpreted as Abrahamic and integrated into the new dispensation; similarly, the Arabic Qurʾān rejects the *jāhiliyya* ethos, but draws upon registers of orality that had been closely associated with the very kinship patterns that were at the heart of *jāhilī* paganism.[120] While the universality of Islam took some time to develop, the special role of the Arabs and their traditions of kinship had to have a place from the start. Indeed, from as early as we can trace things, we know that the central institution of rule (the caliphate) was dominated by Arabs, while, at least in theory, the only institution of incorporation (conversion) was effected through the adoption of Arab tribal lineage.

Whatever their Ḥijāzī origins, Arab identity and the nascent religious tradition were subsequently conditioned by patterns of post-conquest settlement and assimilation. There is no reason to doubt that the garrisons founded apart from or adjacent to pre-Islamic settlements were intended at least in part to insulate Arab Muslims from non-Arab non-Muslims; but they inevitably attracted and generated trade and exchange, and, with it, the influx of non-Arabs. What appears to have been an initial experiment, in which an ethnic and religious elite would rule at arm's length, was overtaken by the realities of settlement. From this perspective, the late seventh-century programme of Arabisation marks a transitional phase between the relative insularity of the first generations, born and bred in Arabia and among the Arabs of Syria, and the clear universalism and cosmopolitanism of the Iraqi-based caliphate of the ʿAbbāsid period. In the meantime Muslims developed their religious tradition in response to, and in interaction with, their fellow monotheists, even if the

120 A. Jones, 'The language of the Qur'an', in K. Dévéni, T. Iványi and A. Shivtel (eds.), *Proceedings of the Colloquium on Arabic Lexicology and Lexicography* (Budapest, 1993).

early Islamic tradition is disappointingly taciturn about the world in which these interactions took place. Muslims having been small minorities throughout the seventh, eighth and ninth centuries, classical Islam – that is, the religious and political system that crystallised during the ninth century – owes innumerable debts to the prevailing, majority cultures of the day,[121] which were evolving and transforming as well, at least sometimes in response to Islam.[122] Disputation and controversy began very early on,[123] but much of classical tradition was forged in multi-ethnic Iraq and the Islamic east. As Muslim rulers left Arabia and Arabian Syria, Islamic society and belief were changing.

121 For Muslim debts to the rabbis, see M. Cook, 'The opponents of the writing of tradition in early Islam', *Arabica*, 44 (1997), pp. 437–530; M. Cook, 'Magian cheese: An archaic problem in Islamic law', *BSOAS*, 47 (1984); for background, M. J. Kister, 'Ḥaddithū ʿan banī isrāʾīla wa-lā ḥaraja', *Israel Oriental Studies*, 2 (1972).

122 For Karaite debts to Muslims, see Cook, 'ʿAnan and Islam'.

123 See S. H. Griffith, 'Disputes with Muslims in Syriac Christian texts: From Patriarch John (d. 648) to Bar Hebraeus (d. 1286)', in B. Lewis and R. Niewöhner (eds.), *Religionsgespräche in Mittelalter* (Wiesbaden, 1992).

6
The empire in Syria, 705–763

PAUL M. COBB

Introduction

Syria is usually where empires end, not where they begin. Throughout its long history the region between the Euphrates and the Mediterranean has been a theatre for imperial designs concocted elsewhere: in Babylon, Rome, Constantinople, Cairo. After the collapse of the Seleucid state (323–64 BCE), only once, and only briefly, did Syria itself serve as the metropole to an empire. Like its Seleucid ancestor, the Marwānid experiment in Syria showed that a far-flung Middle Eastern empire was still possible without Iraq or Egypt to serve as its centre. Yet without the intensively harvested revenues of the Nile Valley and Mesopotamia and the military and cultural production they allowed, the Marwānid caliphate would not have lasted as long as it did. And if the Seleucid empire was a successor state to Alexander's Hellenistic venture, then the Marwānid reprise must be reckoned a precursor state. Providing as it did the framework in which Islam and Arabic culture spread beyond the Nile-to-Oxus core of the caliphate, the Marwānid caliphate set Islamic civilisation on course to be fully realised by other polities. Greater in size if not duration than the Seleucid empire, the Marwānid caliphate gave Islamic Syria its place, however fleeting, in the sun.

The fruitful combination of empire and monotheism that cemented the ascendancy of ʿAbd al-Malik and his successors was a transregional – indeed, universal – system of ideas. But the fact that the Marwānid house depended so heavily for its might upon Syrian troops meant that the world-view that the caliphs encouraged was expressed in Syrian terms and backed up by Syrian muscle. For all that the Marwānid caliphs saw themselves as God's caliphs, from France to Farghāna it was the Syrian tribal armies who were the real world conquerors. In the end, the contradictions inherent in a theoretically universalist ruling ideology based upon the privileges of a small regional elite caused the Marwānid structure of empire to come crashing down. It is no accident that opposition to the caliphs was expressed in resentment against Syrian privilege, in tribal factionalism, and in claims for Islamic alternatives to the empire of Marwānid Syria.

The Marwānid dynasty and its structure: an overview

Even before the death of ʿAbd al-Malik, succession disputes created tensions within the Marwānid house. Two mutually exclusive modes of succession kept family tensions simmering until the overthrow of the dynasty in 750. On the one hand, the sons of Marwān were expected to share the office of caliph 'horizontally' from brother to brother, following common Arab tribal political traditions. This meant that after ʿAbd al-Malik, his brother ʿAbd al-ʿAzīz was expected to rule, though in the end the latter predeceased him. On the other, this fraternal arrangement conflicted with a desire for primogeniture, which hoped to see the caliphate passed 'vertically' from father to son. Thus, ʿAbd al-Malik tried to get his brother to renounce his claim and to confirm the succession instead to his son al-Walīd, but he refused, noting, according to one account, that he cherished hopes for his own sons just as much as ʿAbd al-Malik did for his. Nonetheless, of ʿAbd al-Malik's ten successors, four were his sons, and three his grandsons. The Marwānids were thus in many ways more the dynasty of ʿAbd al-Malik than of his father Marwān. But the dynasty was not without its fault-lines and, given the growing problem of tribal factionalism under the later Marwānids, it is remarkable that dynastic tensions did not explode into open conflict sooner than they did.

When ʿAbd al-Malik died in 705, the caliphate, and the new vision of Islamic empire that he had fostered, passed smoothly to his own son, al-Walīd. The reign of al-Walīd I (r. 705–15) is often seen as the high-water mark of the Umayyad period, but it is not clear whether this is a result of any of the caliph's own talents or of the accomplishments of his father. Certainly, given the contentious decades of civil war that preceded it, the reign of al-Walīd seems a miracle of calm and prosperity. Al-Walīd also continued his father's interest in public statements of Marwānid religious authority, and the 'Umayyad Mosques' that he founded or restored in Medina, Jerusalem, and Damascus are every bit the fitting sequels to ʿAbd al-Malik's projects in Jerusalem. And as Marwānid troops continued the conquest of North Africa, Sind and Central Asia (to name only the most active fronts), the caliphate achieved its greatest territorial extent.

The impression of continuity is no doubt partly a result of the continued presence of the mighty and irascible al-Ḥajjāj, who served both ʿAbd al-Malik and al-Walīd as governor of Iraq and the east. It was he who directed the conquests and maintained pressures on the caliphate's foes on the eastern frontier, who continued to develop the infrastructure of Iraq and who, in return, was given a relatively free hand in appointing his own men to whatever positions in the caliphate he wished, even when it discomfited members of the dynasty, among whom, it is worth noting, was the next caliph, Sulaymān, al-Walīd's brother. Sulaymān had long before been named heir apparent, and, although there is some indication that al-Walīd hoped he could pass the caliphate on to his own son, Sulaymān succeeded without controversy.[1]

Sulaymān ibn ʿAbd al-Malik (r. 715–17) had been governor of the sub-district of Filasṭīn during his brother's caliphate, so he had had ample time to foster ties with the all-important Syrian tribal armies. Indeed, his reign witnessed the first stirrings of what would in later years become full-fledged factional politics among the Syrian troops. That Sulaymān was sensitive to these developments in the army can be seen both in his efforts to 'clean house' by appointing new men to provincial positions almost across the empire, and in his desire to keep the armies on campaign. By previous accord, Sulaymān was to pass the caliphate on to his brothers Yazīd and Marwān but, Marwān having died, Sulaymān too tried to get his own son recognised as his heir. In the end, this son himself died unexpectedly, and so Sulaymān's ambitions were thwarted. On his death-bed, Sulaymān was persuaded to pass over his remaining sons as too young and to name his cousin, ʿUmar ibn ʿAbd al-ʿAzīz, to succeed him, with Yazīd ibn ʿAbd al-Malik, now bumped from the previous succession arrangement, to follow ʿUmar.[2]

ʿUmar II (r. 717–20) came to power without any significant opposition. Of all his kinsmen, he alone has a distinctively positive reputation among later writers as a pious figure who tried to rein in the fiscal and military excesses

1 For the reign of al-Walīd, see Abū Jaʿfar Muḥammad ibn Jarīr al-Ṭabarī, *Taʾrīkh al-rusul wa al-mulūk*, ed. M. J. de Goeje *et al.*, 15 vols. in 3 series (Leiden, 1879–1901), series II, pp. 1172–281; Julius Wellhausen, *Das arabische Reich und sein Sturz*, Berlin, (1902, trans. M. G. Weir as *The Arab kingdom and its fall* (Calcutta, 1927), pp. 224–57; G. R. Hawting, *The first dynasty of Islam: The Umayyad caliphate, AD 661–750*, 2nd edn (London, 2000), pp. 58–71. On what has been called 'the Age of Ḥajjāj', see M. A. Shaban, *Islamic history: A new interpretation*, 2 vols. (Cambridge, 1971–6), vol. I, pp. 100–26.

2 On Sulaymān, see Reinhard Eisener, *Zwischen Faktum und Fiktion: Eine Studie zum Umayyadenkalifen Sulaiman b. ʿAbdalmalik und seinem Bild in den Quellen* (Wiesbaden, 1987).

of his predecessors, consciously evoking the right-guidance of his earlier namesake, ʿUmar ibn al-Khaṭṭāb. Such reform as he may have intended, however, did not outlive his short reign. Moreover, some of the remaining sons of ʿAbd al-Malik are said to have expressed their dissatisfaction at the fact that the caliphate had, with ʿUmar, left the line of ʿAbd al-Malik. This dissent seems not to have been warranted, as ʿUmar himself appears to have had no dynastic ambitions of his own, and at his death (which some said was engineered by his resentful cousins), the caliphate passed, as agreed, back to the line of ʿAbd al-Malik via Yazīd ibn ʿAbd al-Malik, known as Yazīd II (r. 720–4). Somewhat to his later regret, Yazīd was persuaded to forgo his own inclinations to pass the caliphate on to his sons and instead to acknowledge his brother Hishām as heir. As a consolation, Yazīd's son, al-Walīd ibn Yazīd, was named to succeed Hishām.[3]

The accession of Hishām ibn ʿAbd al-Malik (r. 724–43), which some sources describe as the work of his brother Maslama, brought to power someone who consistently extended the power of the caliphate: on its rapidly expanding frontiers, over its tax-paying subjects, and its diplomatic contacts. Indeed, Hishām's success as a state builder can be seen both in the ʿAbbāsids' grudging praise of his ability and the many outbursts of provincial unrest during his reign: a sure sign that the state was making new inroads. Hishām's reign also marks the end of the line for the sons of ʿAbd al-Malik. At his death in 743 there were no sons of ʿAbd al-Malik left to take the throne. The likeliest candidate was probably Maslama himself, but he had died in 738. And so, as planned, al-Walīd II (r. 743–4), the son of Yazīd II and grandson of ʿAbd al-Malik, came to the throne; Hishām's own sons seem not, initially, to have contested the arrangement.[4]

The fact that the horizontal succession arrangements between the sons of ʿAbd al-Malik had now run their course may have contributed to the onset of

3 On ʿUmar II, C. H. Becker, 'Studien zur Omajjadengeschichte. A) ʿOmar II', *Zeitschrift für Assyriologie*, 15 (1900) is the starting-point; see also Wellhausen, *Arab kingdom*, pp. 267–311. On the succession, see C. E. Bosworth, 'Rajāʾ b. Ḥaywa al-Kindī and the Umayyad caliphs', *Islamic Quarterly*, 15 (1971). See most recently Antoine Borrut, 'Entre tradition et histoire: Genèse et diffusion de l'image de ʿUmar b. ʿAbd al-ʿAzīz', *Mélanges de l'Université Saint-Joseph*, 58 (2005). On Yazīd II, see Wellhausen, *Arab kingdom*, pp. 312–25; and H. Lammens and K. Blankinship, 'Yazīd (II) b. ʿAbd al-Malik', *EI2*, vol. XI, pp. 310–11.

4 On Hishām, see Francesco Gabrieli, *Il Califatto di Hishām: Studi di storia omayyade*, Mémoires de la Société Royale d'Archéologie d'Alexandrie 7 (Alexandria, 1935); Khalid Yahya Blankinship, *The end of the jihād state: The reign of Hishām Ibn ʿAbd al-Malik and the collapse of the Umayyads* (Albany, 1994). On the reign of al-Walīd II, see Francesco Gabrieli, 'al-Walīd b. Yazīd, il califfo e il poeta', *RSO*, 15 (1935); Dieter Derenk, *Leben und Dichtung des Omaiyadenkalifen al-Walīd ibn Yazīd* (Freiburg im Breisgau, 1974).

civil war following the succession of al-Walīd II. The field, in effect, was now wide open, and al-Walīd's personal conduct and reputation for impiety seem to have provided enough of a pretext for other claimants to contest his right to rule, sparking what became known as the third *fitna* or civil war. From 744 until as late as 754 the office of caliph was contested by members of a younger generation of Umayyad claimants, most of them by this time solidly entrenched in the factional politics of the Syrian army (on this aspect of the third *fitna*, see below). With the Marwānids themselves barely able to agree upon the legitimacy of a given caliph during these years, it was perhaps inevitable that other bloodlines, with their own dynastic ambitions, would enter the fray. But few would have imagined that the ʿAbbāsids, from an entirely separate clan within Quraysh, would be the claimants who won the caliphal prize, and put an end to Marwānid – and Syrian – power.[5]

Imperial expansion, from France to Farghāna

Despite the tensions surrounding succession within the Marwānid family, the territorial expansion of the caliphate proceeded apace without any noticeable slowing until the eve of the third *fitna* (744). In keeping with the imperial vision established by the time of ʿAbd al-Malik, Marwānid imperial designs were in theory limitless. In practice, however, an Islamic empire centred upon Syria and based upon the military capabilities of Syrian tribal armies could only expand so far before breaking apart. Nevertheless, the immense territorial expansion of the caliphate is one of the Marwānid dynasty's great lasting achievements, establishing as it did the boundaries of the *dār al-islām* (the 'abode of Islam'), which, excepting the case of Spain, would remain essentially the same well after the Marwānids had left the scene and Syria had ceased to be the centre of empire.

The west: North Africa, al-Andalus and the Berber revolt

At the death of ʿAbd al-Malik, the Maghrib – the region of North Africa excluding Egypt – was still an active military zone and an expanding imperial frontier. Indeed, by the reign of al-Walīd, Cyrenaica was largely under control and securely attached to Egypt, and so a second base was required, close to the western lands that remained unconquered and nominally under Byzantine and Visigothic control. It was thus probably around 705 that Ifrīqiya was created as an administrative district (*wilāya*) in its own right. This region

5 On the third *fitna* and the rise of the ʿAbbāsids, see below.

(roughly modern Tunisia) had long been a theatre for raiding by Muslim troops from Egypt, though it had only recently been pacified in any definitive fashion. Its small garrison-settlement at Qayrawān became the district's capital.[6]

Starting in 705, the Marwānids' western conquests, led by the talented commander and governor Mūsā ibn Nuṣayr, were directed at securing the central and western Maghrib. To extend their conquests the Marwānids, whose armies were already overextended on other fronts, badly needed cooperation from the Berber peoples of North Africa. This was not easily obtained. On the one hand, if most of the Berbers appear at least to have superficially converted to Islam and recognised Marwānid authority, many still provided fierce resistance. On the other, and perhaps because of this resistance, the Marwānids insisted upon exacting a levy of slaves from Muslim Berber tribes – a practice unknown in any other part of the caliphate.[7] But Mūsā was ultimately able to make allies in the region and, with every mile westward, the importance of Berber manpower increased. By 710 the conquest of northern Africa was effectively complete. Mūsā withdrew to Qayrawān, leaving his *mawlā*, the Berber Ṭāriq ibn Ziyād, with a small body of Berber, Arab and black African troops in Tangier to take charge of affairs at the western limit of the Islamic world.[8]

With the Sahara providing an effective obstacle to expansion in the south, Spain – or al-Andalus, as it became known – was Ṭāriq's next logical destination. The Iberian Peninsula was a wealthy and fertile land, and the kingdom of the Visigoths under Roderic was politically divided. After a desultory test raid onto its southern shores, Ṭāriq led a full-scale invasion in April 711, occupying the Straits and the area immediately around Algeciras. In July he decisively defeated the forces of Roderic in Sidonia; by October, Muslim troops had captured the old Visigothic capital of Toledo and what would later become

6 On the Muslim conquest of al-Andalus, the classic point of departure is Evariste Lévi-Provençal, *Histoire de l'Espagne musulmane*, 3 vols. (Leiden, 1950–3), vol. I, pp. 1–89. More recently, and with more coverage of North Africa, Pedro Chalmeta, *Invasión e islamización: La sumisión de Hispania y la formación de al-Andalus* (Madrid, 1994), is superb; see also Michael Brett, 'The Arab conquest and the rise of Islam in North Africa', in J. D. Fage and Roland Oliver (eds.), *The Cambridge history of Africa*, 8 vols. (Cambridge, 1978), vol. II: *From c. 500 BC to AD 1050*; Hugh Kennedy, *Muslim Spain and Portugal: A political history of al-Andalus* (London, 1996), pp. 1–29.

7 On the Berber slave levy, see Brett, 'Arab conquest', pp. 506–7; and Elizabeth Savage, *A gateway to hell, a gateway to paradise: The North African response to the Arab conquest* (Princeton, 1997), pp. 67–79.

8 Against claims that the 'Arab conquests' in the west were really mass conversions in disguise, see the response of Pierre Guichard, 'Les Arabes ont bien envahi l'Espagne: Les structures sociales de l'Espagne musulmane', *Annales*, 29 (1974).

one of the capitals of al-Andalus, Cordoba. In the mountainous north and north-east, Visigothic elements held on by making separate treaties with the Muslims. In the summer of 712 Mūsā returned to Spain and captured Seville, which became his seat in the province. The next year he took Mérida, while another body of troops, under his son ʿAbd al-ʿAzīz, turned its attention to Málaga and the south-east and, later, central Portugal, establishing treaties with cities such as Lisbon and Coimbra. By 714 Muslim troops had followed the remnants of the Visigothic army into the Cantabrian mountains, finally subduing Galicia and Asturias.

Further campaigns continued intermittently after 714, but by this time news of the startling successes of Ṭāriq and Mūsā had reached al-Walīd in Syria. Significantly, he is said to have been most alarmed at Mūsā's ambitions and, one presumes, that he was acting a little too independently in such a remote and wealthy province.[9] Mūsā and Ṭāriq were ordered back to Syria at once, and they brought with them a vast amount of plunder and slaves intended to propitiate the caliph. But even without Mūsā and Ṭāriq, Muslim troops continued to make raids. To the south, armies penetrated deep beyond the Atlas into the Sūs around 736, reaching 'the land of the Blacks' and taking great plunder. In the north, from al-Andalus, armies raided across the Pyrenees into southern Gaul and the Languedoc, occupying some towns and establishing a short-lived base at Narbonne. But, like the contemporary naval raids from Ifrīqiya into Byzantine Sicily and Sardinia, these forays into southern France were ephemeral. Toulouse was attacked in 721, Autun pillaged in 725 and, near Poitiers, a Muslim army was defeated by Charles Martel in 732. Although raids would continue across the Pyrenees, historical hindsight would view this otherwise unimportant failure near Poitiers as the high-water mark of Muslim expansion in the west.[10]

It is tempting to view the remarkable expansion of the caliphate's western borders as testimony of the strength of the caliph in Syria. But such a view ignores the high degree of autonomy that commanders in the field possessed and the rather uneven spread of caliphal authority in lands that had been conquered. Indeed, on almost every front, Muslim armies that were engaged in external conquests of expansion were also called upon to pacify populations

9 See, for example, Abū al-Qāsim ʿAbd al-Raḥmān ibn ʿAbd al-Ḥakam, *Futūḥ Miṣr wa-akhbāruhā*, ed. C. C. Torrey (New Haven, 1922), pp. 210–11, where al-Walīd is angered that Mūsā has thrown Ṭāriq in prison without consulting the caliph.

10 On transpyrenean conquest and settlement, see Philippe Sénac, *Musulmans et Sarrazins dans le Sud de la Gaule du VIIIe au XIe siècle* (Paris, 1980); Roger Collins, *The Arab conquest of Spain, 710–797* (Oxford, 1989), pp. 86–96.

well within the frontiers of the caliphate who had not yet been subdued or who had thrown off their allegiance to the caliphs.

The Berber revolt of 740–1 is instructive for what it reveals not only about the ethnic exclusivity of Marwānid Islam, but also about the ebb and flow of central power in the Maghrib.[11] The revolt spanned territories from Spain to Tunisia, pitted Berbers against their conquerors and effectively removed the Maghrib from control of Syria under Hishām. It is often described in medieval and modern sources as a 'Khārijite' rebellion, but the causes for the revolt have more to do with the unequal treatment of the Berbers at the hands of their Arab conquerors than with issues of doctrine or leadership of the Muslim community. And while the revolt at times adopted the language of Islam to validate its actions, rebel leaders identified as Khārijites (especially of the Ṣufriyya variety) were only part of the larger movement. Indeed, it may best be seen as the response of one conquered region's formerly non-Muslim populace to the pressures of a centralising administrative apparatus and the cultural contradictions that were imported with it, as the provincial populace found themselves squeezed by the demands of the central government and blocked by prevailing notions of Arab privilege.

Hishām, like his predecessors, endeavoured to keep the distant Maghrib tight in the administrative grip of Syria, transferring, in 734, the governor of Egypt, 'Ubayd Allāh ibn al-Ḥabḥāb, to Ifrīqiya in the hope of bringing the taxation and fiscal administration of the Maghrib into step with the rest of the caliphate. The reaction to his policies took time, but was explosive. In 740 'Ubayd Allāh's representatives in Tangier and Tlemcen were murdered by the followers of a Berber who is described as a Ṣufrī Khārijite and who took the caliphal title of *amīr al-mu'minīn*.[12] 'Ubayd Allāh sent a large body of troops from Qayrawān against the rebels, but, in a bloody confrontation known as the 'battle of the Nobles', they were defeated. At this point Hishām reacted decisively, sending in a massive new army recruited from various sub-districts of Syria and from Egypt. The Syrians reached the rebels late in 741 on the Sebou river in northern Morocco and were, once again, roundly defeated.

In the meantime, the Berber revolt had had its impact in al-Andalus, where Berber troops revolted in the north of the peninsula and marched on Cordoba. Desperate for support, the governor there joined forces with the Syrians who

11 On the Berber revolt, see Brett, 'Arab conquest', pp. 517–21; Savage, *Gateway to hell*, pp. 43–5 and *passim*, and Blankinship, *Jihād state*, pp. 203–22.

12 Aḥmad ibn Muḥammad ibn 'Idhārī, *al-Bayān al-mughrib fī akhbār al-Andalus wa al-Maghrib*, ed. G. S. Colin and E. Levi-Provençal, 4 vols. (Leiden, 1948–51), vol. I, p. 53; cf. Ibn 'Abd al-Ḥakam, *Futūḥ Miṣr*, p. 218.

survived the debacle at the Sebou river and urged them to join him across the Straits. These combined forces finally defeated the Berbers outside Toledo in 742. All seemed well, but the arrival in al-Andalus of large numbers of Syrian troops brought with it traditions of tribal factionalism and tensions with the early settlers already in place, and these would frustrate further attempts at central control from Syria.[13]

Finally, things fell apart in Qayrawān and Tunis, where Khārijite rebels had taken over. A new army was sent from Egypt (significantly not from Syria) that finally took Qayrawān back in 742, pushing the rebels into the oases of southern Ifrīqiya. But in 743 Berber rebels seized Tripoli, and ʿAbd al-Raḥmān ibn Ḥabīb al-Fihrī, a commander who had survived the battle of the Nobles and fled into al-Andalus, now returned to North Africa and seized power as autonomous governor of the Maghrib. With the murder of the caliph al-Walīd II in 744, as Syria descended into the third *fitna*, the Maghrib and al-Andalus were autonomous regions themselves divided by unabated Berber revolts and military factionalism. The Maghrib would have to wait until the arrival of ʿAbbāsid authorities from Baghdad before feeling the firm hand of central authority again. But by then it was Iraq and Khurāsānīs that established order, and al-Andalus would in any case be removed altogether, taken by a Marwānid prince fleeing the horrors of an ʿAbbāsid revolution in the east.

The north: Byzantium and the Caucasus

In most medieval and modern accounts of the expansion of the Marwānid caliphate, the Byzantine empire is taken to be the caliphate's primordial enemy. And while there is ample evidence of non-military contact between Byzantium and the caliphate – in the realms of commerce and intellectual culture, for example – it is war that is the defining feature of Byzantine–Muslim relations under the Umayyads.[14] However, the historical record of actual conquest on this frontier pales in comparison to the activities of Marwānid armies on other fronts in the west, and most notably on the

13 On the situation in al-Andalus during the Berber revolt and the coming of the Syrians and its fallout, see Chalmeta, *Invasión*, pp. 307–48; Kennedy, *Muslim Spain and Portugal*, pp. 23–9.

14 On non-military contacts, see H. A. R. Gibb, 'Arab–Byzantine relations under the Umayyad caliphate', *Dumbarton Oaks Papers*, 12 (1958); Hugh Kennedy, 'Byzantine–Arab diplomacy in the Near East from the Islamic conquests to the mid eleventh century', in J. Shepard and S. Franklin (eds.), *Papers from the twenty-fourth Spring Symposium of Byzantine Studies* (Aldershot, 1992). On the alleged influence of Islamic attitudes towards images upon Byzantine iconoclasm, see Sidney H. Griffith, 'Images, Islam and Christian icons', in Pierre Canivet and Jean-Paul Rey-Coquais (eds.), *La Syrie de Byzance à l'Islam, VIIe–VIIIe siècles* (Damascus, 1992).

Caucasus frontier to the immediate east, where the Khazars threatened to strike into eastern Anatolia and even northern Iraq. The stasis on the Byzantine frontier is especially marked in the period after the failed siege of Constantinople in 718. By then, both the caliphate and Byzantium had their own concerns that kept them from further conquests of any significance.[15]

While the Byzantine emperor Justinian II reigned, Marwānid armies in Anatolia were not able to conquer any significant new lands (the capture of the fortress of Tyana in 708 being an important exception), even if they did repeatedly defeat their Byzantine adversaries in the field. After Justinian II's murder in 711, however, the Byzantine empire destabilised, and so Sulaymān seized the moment to embark on a massive campaign aimed at nothing less than the conquest of Constantinople. By 717 a massive army under Maslama was encamped before the Byzantine capital, while a fleet blockaded the port. The siege stretched on for months, with supplies for the Muslims becoming scarce. When ʿUmar II succeeded as caliph, therefore, he inherited an expensive campaign that was more and more obviously fruitless; and so, in 718, he ordered Maslama and the armies to lift their siege. ʿUmar further withdrew all troops from the frontiers to the region of Malaṭya, and sent no further troops against the Byzantines.

Thenceforth, until the collapse of the Umayyad dynasty itself, most military activity directed against the Byzantines consisted of desultory raiding rather than permanent conquest. After the failed siege of 718, it was the reign of Hishām that saw the most significant action. The year 725 was particularly busy, with Hishām's son Muʿāwiya raiding deep into Anatolia around Dorylaeum, and a fleet attacking Cyprus. In the next year Maslama made an equally stunning raid into Cappadocia, followed by a lightning raid by Muʿāwiya ibn Hishām on Nicaea itself, the closest the Muslims would come to Constantinople until the reign of the ʿAbbāsid caliph al-Rashīd. But in 739, at Ancyra, the Umayyad dynasty made its last capture of a Byzantine town, a success as minor as the defeat that followed was grand, when a Byzantine campaign in 740 led in person by the emperor Leo III and his son Constantine destroyed the Muslim army. Hishām himself took to the field to defend

15 On Umayyad–Byzantine warfare, a starting-point is E. W. Brooks, 'The Arabs in Asia Minor 641–750, from Arabic sources', *Journal of Hellenic Studies*, 18 (1898), a collection of reports from some of the better-known Arabic sources. On sieges of Constantinople, see Marius Canard, 'Les expéditions des Arabes contre Constantinople dans l'histoire et dans la légende', *JA*, 208 (1926). On the siege of 718, see Rodolphe Guilland, 'L'expédition de Maslama contre Constantinople (717–718)', *Revue des études byzantines*, 17 (1959). For the reign of Hishām, see Blankinship, *Jihād state*, pp. 117–21, 162–3, 168–70, 200–2.

Malaṭya from the reinvigorated Byzantines, but territorial conquest was still out of the question. The Umayyads' last raid was under al-Walīd II in 743, an uneventful foray whose destination is not even recorded. Shortly thereafter al-Walīd ordered the Muslim populace of Cyprus to be evacuated. On the eve of the third *fitna* Muslims on the Byzantine front were running scared.

Further to the east, on the Caucasus front, Marwānid troops acquitted themselves much more admirably, establishing by the beginning of the third *fitna* a secure frontier south of the Caucasus bolstered by fortresses and garrisons at the major passes.[16] But this was not an easy achievement, requiring as it did a quiescent Armenia and the subjugation of the Khazar khāqānate, which was, now that the Byzantines were on the defensive, the greatest threat to the survival of the caliphate. Indeed, by the time al-Walīd took power in 705, the Marwānids and the Khazars were Transcaucasia's principal 'superpowers', Byzantium having been eclipsed as a political (but not cultural) force. Only the neighbouring Christian region of Georgia would resist outright annexation by the Marwānids or the Khazars, but it would be devastated in the process.[17]

The provinces of Armenia, with its capital at Dabīl (Dvin), and Azerbaijan, with its capital at Ardabīl, provided the main jumping-off points for Marwānid expansion into Transcaucasia. Of these two provinces, Christian Armenia was the latecomer to caliphal rule. In 705 the Muslim governor had to brutally crush a widespread rebellion of Armenian princes who had, with Byzantine help, resisted Muslim annexation. But after 711, when a Muslim garrison was established at Dabīl, local elites more or less acquiesced to the situation and Armenia was integrated into the caliphate, even supplying local troops as needed. Conflicts between the Khazars and the Muslim armies in the region intensified only after 715, when a Muslim garrison was established at al-Bāb (or Bāb al-Abwāb). In the winter of 722, for example, the Khazars made a spectacular raid into Muslim-held Armenia and inflicted heavy losses. This was followed by a Muslim retaliatory raid in the same year, which drove the

16 On the Caucasus in Umayyad times, see J. Laurent, *L'Arménie entre Byzance et l'Islam depuis la conquête arabe jusqu'en 886*, rev. Marius Canard (Paris, 1980); René Grousset, *Histoire de l'Arménie des origins à 1071* (Paris, 1947). On the Khazars, see Peter B. Golden, *Khazar studies: An historico-philosophical inquiry into the origins of the Khazars*, 2 vols. (Budapest, 1980); D. M. Dunlop, *A history of the Jewish Khazars* (New York, 1954); Blankinship, *Jihād state*, pp. 106–9, 121–5, 149–54, 170–5.

17 On Marwānid raids into Georgia, see B. Martin-Hisard, 'Les Arabes en Géorgie occidentale au VIIIe siècle: Étude sur l'idéologie politique Géorgienne', *Bedi Kartlisa*, 40 (1982).

Khazars back across the Caucasus. Subsequent Khazar raids on Armenia were repelled until the reign of Hishām.

In 725 Maslama ibn ʿAbd al-Malik was named governor of Armenia and Azerbaijan, and we find him campaigning in Khazar territory in 727 and successfully repelling the Khazars' raids into Azerbaijan, which seems to have attracted Khazar attention now that Armenia was denied them. Indeed, in 730, with Maslama removed from office, the Khazars inflicted a huge disaster on the Muslims there. While most of the Muslim army was scattered in the field, the Khazars outmanoeuvred them and attacked the capital, Ardabīl. A desperate attempt by the Muslim armies to save the city failed at the battle of Marj al-Sabalān outside the city, during which the governor was killed. A large number of Muslim troops and civilians were likewise killed or taken prisoner. All of Azerbaijan was given over to plunder, and outliers of the Khazar forces even turned up in the vicinity of Mosul, a clear demonstration of the vulnerability of the central lands of Iraq and Syria should the northern front collapse. Hishām ordered a massive and immediate riposte. By 731 Azerbaijan had been recaptured and the war had been brought to the Khazars, who were regrouping in the northern steppe.

In 732 Marwān ibn Muḥammad, the future caliph Marwān II, was named governor of Armenia and Azerbaijan. So desperate were the Marwānids for assistance against the Khazars (who had themselves allied with Byzantium in the meantime) that Marwān granted Armenia virtual autonomy under Ashot Bagratouni in return for military support. Marwān also embarked on a fiscal reorganisation of the province, and re-garrisoned the northern front almost exclusively with his Qaysī troops. With regard to Marwān's immediate military concerns, these steps seem to have resulted in a stable frontier. Most subsequent campaigns north of the Caucasus were unspectacular: no lasting conquests, but no startling defeats either. The only exception was in 737, when Marwān campaigned deep into Khazar lands, reaching the *khāqān*'s capital on the Volga, al-Bayḍāʾ (Itil). While this did not eliminate the *khāqān* or the Khazar threat, many prisoners were taken, and there were no further Khazar raids south of the Caucasus in Umayyad times.

The east: Transoxania and Sind

In the eastern reaches of the caliphate, the Marwānids expanded primarily on two fronts: in Transoxania in the north-east and Sind in the south-east. These two fronts were separated by a third region of conflict, comprising Sīstān and neighbouring Ẓābulistān, which never yielded to Umayyad attempts to control it. Indeed, in 727, its ruler, the *zunbīl*, annihilated a Muslim army in the region, including its commander. The region, with its imposing deserts and mountains, remained a glaring exception to Marwānid imperial success.[18]

In the north-east, Khurāsān served as the base for the conquest of Transoxania, including the rich trading cities of Sogdia, and for attempts to subjugate the Turkish Türgesh confederation that dominated the region.[19] Al-Walīd's governor of Khurāsān, Qutayba ibn Muslim, was responsible for some of the most significant early conquests into Transoxania, thanks largely to his close (if not always warm) cooperation with al-Ḥajjāj. Starting in 705, Qutayba subjugated much of Ṭukhāristān, capturing Balkh, Āmul and Bukhārā by 709. Nearby Samarqand remained unconquered, but paid Qutayba tribute. The next few years were years of consolidation, with mopping-up campaigns in Ṭukhāristān (whose ruler, the *jabghu*, was sent to Damascus as a trophy). As in North Africa and the Caucasus, local levies played an important role in furthering the conquests for a caliphate that was finding itself overstretched. By 712 the rear-position of Khwārazm had been conquered and colonised, allowing Qutayba to return in force to Transoxania, capturing Samarqand outright and establishing a garrison there.

A more prudent commander would have stopped to strengthen his hold over these newly conquered territories. But Qutayba pressed on, leaving much of Sogdia unsubdued, and headed for the lands across the Jaxartes. While his Iranian troops subdued Shāsh, Qutayba pushed into Farghāna. To the rear, however, the local princes of Sogdia took advantage of Qutayba's preoccupations far to the east, and called out for aid to rid them of Muslim rule. They first appealed to the Türgesh *khāqān* without success, and then to the Chinese emperor. As a result, in 713 Qutayba (or al-Ḥajjāj) was likewise obliged to open negotiations with the Chinese emperor to make his claims. According to Chinese sources, the Muslim embassy was favourably received despite the fact that the ambassadors refused to kow-tow before the emperor.[20]

The raids into the Jaxartes provinces recommenced, with the outright conquest of Farghāna the clear goal. But the death of al-Ḥajjāj in 714 and

18 On Sīstān in early Islamic times, see C. E. Bosworth, *Sīstān under the Arabs, from the Islamic conquest to the rise of the Ṣaffārids (30–250/651–864)* (Rome, 1968).

19 On Umayyad expansion in the north-east, see H. A. R. Gibb, *The Arab conquests in Central Asia* (London, 1923); and M. A. Shaban, *The ʿAbbasid revolution* (Cambridge, 1971).

20 On Muslim embassies to China, see E. Chavannes, *Documents sur les Tou-Kiue (Turcs) occidentaux* (St. Petersburg, 1903); and H. A. R. Gibb, 'Chinese records of the Arabs in Central Asia', *BSOAS*, 2 (1922); Zhang Jun-yan, 'Relations between China and the Arabs in early times', *Journal of Oman Studies*, 6 (1983).

then of al-Walīd in 715 prevented any such activity. Later in 715, unwilling to relinquish command to any new governor that the new caliph, Sulaymān, might send, Qutayba revolted. But he had misjudged his own men, who turned on him, and killed him in Farghāna. Sulaymān ordered these troops to be immediately withdrawn to Marw, where they were disbanded. As it would happen, Qutayba's death marked the end of Umayyad expansion in the north-east. When ʿUmar II took power he ordered the garrisons in Transoxania disbanded, but he died before they were obliged to obey. Trouble for the Muslim garrisons continued as the local princes of the region were increasingly restless and sent many embassies appealing to the Chinese emperor or his Türgesh vassals for aid. The Chinese never became directly involved in Transoxanian affairs, but the Türgesh were not shy. In 720 they came to the aid of some Sogdian rulers and marched on Samarqand, but this only elicited a Muslim counter-attack, which routed the Türgesh and recaptured all of Sogdia.

Under Yazīd II, raiding into Transoxania culminated in the 'Day of Thirst' (724), a debacle from which the Muslims of the north-east never fully recovered. Thenceforth the Muslims were on the defensive, their hold on lands east of the Oxus shaky. The Türgesh raided across into Khurāsān and local populations rose in revolt, even in long-subdued locales such as Khwārazm. In 731 a further blow came at the battle of the Pass, in which the Muslims barely managed to fend off a joint Türgesh–Sogdian assault on Samarqand. To make matters worse, in 734 a pious and battle-scarred veteran named al-Ḥārith ibn Surayj revolted against what he perceived to be Marwānid iniquities in the province. After capturing Balkh he and his Khurāsānī followers were forced to retreat into Ṭukhāristān, and from there he joined the side of the Türgesh *khāqān*. In 737 the Türgesh and their new allies renewed their attacks, launching raids into Transoxania, Ṭukhāristān, and even Khurāsān itself. But this time, at the battle of Kharīstān, the Muslims were prepared and, with help from Iranian allies, they captured the *khāqān*'s encampment, and the Türgesh were thrown into confusion and fled. Al-Ḥārith escaped to Shāsh, but later a second attempt at rebellion on his part ended in his death. In 738 the *khāqān* was assassinated and the Türgesh confederation dissolved amidst internal rivalries. While this put an end to any further threat from the Türgesh to the Muslims, it also removed the only buffer in Central Asia between the Muslim caliphs and the Chinese emperors.

In the same year Naṣr ibn Sayyār was named governor of Khurāsān; he would be the last Umayyad governor of the province. An old Khurāsān hand, Naṣr seems to have been well liked by locals, and he did his best to remain above tribal factionalism in the army. In 741 he launched a campaign on Shāsh, and passed through but did not formally conquer the region of Ushrūsana, and raided into Farghāna, where the local king agreed to pay tribute. In 744, in recognition of the new political situation between them, Naṣr sent a huge delegation to China, including representatives of many of the local princes of Transoxania and Ṭukhāristān. As the caliphate slipped into civil war, then, it seemed as if the Umayyads would finally have the success they had sought in the north-east, with a subjugated Transoxania, an expanding frontier of influence, a respected governor and a relatively calm population.

In the south-east, the Marwānids experienced equally spectacular successes and failures as their armies consolidated their hold on Sind and, briefly, extended their conquests into India.[21] At the death of ʿAbd al-Malik Sind was still unconquered, a largely Hindu kingdom with a Buddhist minority ruled by a monarch named Dāhir from his capital, Daybul. In 711, however, al-Ḥajjāj appointed Muḥammad ibn Qāsim al-Thaqafī at the head of a large body of Syrian troops over the district of Makrān, entrusting him with the task of extending Marwānid rule into Sind. By the time of his death three years later, Marwānid rule extended over the lower Indus Valley and even beyond. Resistance was fiercest at Daybul, which fell after a few months of siege, in 711. The king, Dāhir, was later killed in battle near Rāwar, and the country was opened to Marwānid conquest.

Still, control of these distant lands stretched the abilities of the caliphate, and for most of the Marwānid period the Indus river formed the border between the western lands of Sind under Marwānid control and eastern lands in, at best, a tributary relationship. In 723 the Qaysī commander Junayd ibn ʿAbd al-Raḥmān al-Murrī was named governor, and he extended Marwānid control east of the Indus for the first time, securing Daybul and subduing rebellious princes by 724. He then embarked on extensive campaigns in the wealthy lands of north-west India, Rajasthan and Gujarat, but information on the precise locales involved, not to mention the chronology, is very unclear.[22] But whatever the case, these conquests, even Daybul, were soon lost, perhaps a result of local rebellions against attempts at Muslim rule.

Some time in the 730s two new forward positions were established at al-Maḥfūẓa and al-Manṣūra, near Brahmānābād. These were to serve as

21 On Sind, see Francesco Gabrieli, 'Muḥammad ibn Qāsim ath-Thaqafī and the Arab conquest of Sind', *East and West*, n.s., 15 (1964–5); and Derryl N. Maclean, *Religion and society in Arab Sind* (Leiden, 1989).

22 Blankinship provides a convincing reconstruction: *Jihād state*, pp. 131–4, 147–9, 186–90, 202–3.

bases from which to consolidate Muslim rule over Sind and to relaunch conquests into India: many lands in Gujarat that had been lost earlier were now recaptured, and even Kashmir appears to have been threatened. By 739 Marwānid armies ranged as far south as Navasarika in southern Gujarat, the furthest into India the Umayyads would ever go. It was not to last. After the Muslim defeat at Navasarika a new governor arrived in 740, the son of the great conqueror Muḥammad ibn Qāsim. But an alliance of local princes revolted against the Muslims, rolling back definitively the conquests east of the Indus and besieging the governor at al-Manṣūra. New troops arrived to crush the rebellious Sindīs, but, as the constant see-sawing of conquests in the area suggests, the Marwānids had reached the limits of their expansion.

Administrative centralising

The Marwānids are said to have taken the decentralised system of regional leaders and tribal groupings that made up the Sufyānid conquest state and transformed it into a centralised empire. This is true in broad terms, and the later heavily centralised state of the ʿAbbāsids certainly owes its existence to the experiments of the Marwānids.[23] In general, the expanding empire under Marwānid control was divided into a number of provinces (*wilāyāt*), themselves divided and subdivided down to the local district (the *kūra*, *rustāq* or *tassūj*), and each level of the administration had, in theory, its responsible official in charge of, at the very least, revenue collection. At the highest level, that of the provincial governor (known variously as the *wālī*, *amīr* or *ʿāmil*), responsibilities were often divided between a military official and an administrative/fiscal official, who might be appointed by the caliph himself. Any provincial governor might be expected to have subordinates and a staff assigned with him, a body of guardsmen (*shurṭa*), and perhaps a judge (*qāḍī*). As provincial administration was the most lucrative and powerful position one could obtain, these positions attracted the most competition among tribal factions and the most anxiety from caliphs wary of overpowerful governors in distant corners of the caliphate.

But centralisation is a slow and messy process. Indeed, one should properly speak of Marwānid *centralising* rather than Marwānid centralisation, as the direct power of the caliph over provincial matters was at no time a *fait accompli*. This was largely due to practical concerns: it was easier for central

23 Irit Bligh-Abramski, 'Evolution vs. revolution: Umayyad elements in the ʿAbbāsid regime 133/75–32–932', *Der Islam*, 65 (1988).

control to take root in those provinces that were closer to Syria and in which Muslim populations had long been resident. In newly conquered or distant provinces other arrangements prevailed. Thus Greek continued to be used as the administrative language in Egyptian papyri until early in the reign of al-Walīd, in 706; in Khurāsān Arabic did not take over as the administrative language until 742. Moreover, provincial and sub-provincial boundaries were not etched in stone and could change as circumstances, and individual governors, warranted.

There is sufficient numismatic and literary evidence to suggest that most of the provinces of the caliphate were grouped into three or four 'superprovinces': Ifrīqiya and the West; al-Jazīra and the North; and Iraq and the East (with an occasionally independent Khurāsān).[24] However, it is likewise clear that, from the point of view of Syria's governing elite, the caliphate was divided into a core zone of firmly held provinces frequently governed by close kinsmen or protégés of the caliphs and a periphery of more remote provinces administered by other parties, who might enjoy a certain autonomy from Syrian demands.

The heart of the caliphate was thus the core area of provinces that experienced frequent direct rule by Umayyad kinsmen, a family preserve that included Egypt, al-Jazīra, Iraq and the Ḥijāz. But the heart of this heart was of course Syria, the metropolitan province, where, until the Marwānid system collapsed during the third *fitna*, all the caliphs made their home. Unique among all other provinces, Syria was originally divided into four sub-districts or *ajnād* (sing. *jund*), a term designating both these districts and the armies (most of them Yamanī tribes) levied in them. They were, from south to north: Filasṭīn (with its capital at al-Ramla); al-Urdunn (with its capital at Tiberias); Damascus; and Ḥimṣ (these last two named after their capital cities). At a later date, perhaps under the Sufyānids, the *jund* of Qinnasrīn, with its heavy concentrations of Qaysī tribes, was created, and detached from Ḥimṣ. This unique administrative arrangement can be explained by the importance of the Syrian tribal armies as props of the Marwānid dynasty and as the elite military forces of their expanding caliphate. Although the Qaysī troops of the nearby province of al-Jazīra would come to dominate political and military matters more and more, it was upon the troops of Syria that the Marwānids relied in

24 I borrow the term 'superprovince' from Blankinship, *Jihād state*, p. 39. For numismatic evidence, see Denise A. Spellberg, 'The Umayyad North: Numismatic evidence for frontier administration', *American Numismatic Society Museum Notes*, 33 (1988); Michael Bates, 'History, geography and numismatics in the first century of Islamic coinage', *Revue Suisse de Numismatique*, 65 (1986).

their rise to power after the second *fitna*, and it was these troops, the *ahl al-Shām*, that they used to subdue and occupy Iraq, and were sent as needed even to the most distant provinces of the caliphate – not without tensions with the Muslim armies and settlers who had preceded them.

Of the remaining provinces of this core area, Egypt, al-Jazīra and Iraq served as the centres of larger superprovinces – but only in the case of Egypt, thanks to the papyri, do we have any detailed sense of the actual mechanics of Marwānid administration and the stakes involved. Here, the earliest Muslim administrators adopted much of the extant Byzantine administrative system. But by Marwānid times the system had become much more efficient and centralised within the province, with greater powers for the local-level tax officials (called pagarchs) who were placed directly under the control of the governor in Fusṭāṭ.[25] And a succession of skilled, if not ruthless, administrators such as Qurra ibn Sharīk (709–15) and ʿUbayd Allāh ibn al-Ḥabḥāb (724–34) initiated land surveys and censuses, reorganised the *dīwān*, built and expanded mosques, improved irrigation, imposed new taxes on Muslims, limited movement of the subject population, settled new areas, built up the Umayyad fleet and encouraged conversion to Islam. The result was an increase in state revenues and central authority, and, inevitably, revolts of segments of the indigenous Coptic populace.[26]

But even in these more centralised core areas, flexibility and change were the rule. Thus, even in Egypt caliphal appointees had to bow to local sentiment when choosing subordinate officials and, at least in some places, the central power of Fusṭāṭ was diffused at the local level.[27] In parts of the province of Mosul (which was often separate from al-Jazīra) the governors had little influence in the countryside, and instead relied upon the Christian

25 On the generalities of Umayyad administration in Egypt, see H. I. Bell, 'The administration of Egypt under the Umayyad khalifs', *Byzantinische Zeitschrift*, 28 (1928); G. Frantz-Murphy, *The agrarian administration of Egypt from the Arabs to the Ottomans* (Cairo, 1986). Petra M. Sijpesteijn, 'Shaping a Muslim state: Papyri related to a mid-eighth-century Egyptian official', Ph.D. thesis, Princeton University (2004), pp. 18–33, 92–118, offers the clearest exposition to date.

26 On Qurra, see Nabia Abbott, *The Ḳurrah papyri from Aphrodito in the Oriental Institute* (Chicago, 1930); Y. Ragib, 'Lettres nouvelles de Qurra ibn Šarīk', *JNES*, 49 (1981). On ʿUbayd Allāh, see N. Abbott, 'A new papyrus and a review of the administration of ʿUbaid Allāh b. al-Ḥabḥāb', in G. Makdisi (ed.), *Arabic and Islamic studies in honor of Hamilton A. R. Gibb* (Cambridge, MA, 1965). On the 'alms-tax' levied on Muslim lands to cope with fiscal shortfalls, see Sijpesteijn, 'Shaping a Muslim state', pp. 119–88.

27 As stressed in H. Kennedy, 'Egypt as a province in the Islamic caliphate, 641–868', in C. F. Petry (ed.), *The Cambridge history of Egypt*, vol. I: *Islamic Egypt, 640–1517* (Cambridge, 1998). For a revision of the strict centralisation model based on papyri from the Fayyūm, see Sijpesteijn, 'Shaping a Muslim state', pp. 92–118.

shahārija (the local gentry) to do their administrative dirty work.[28] And Iraq, with its Syrian occupying forces and recently demobilised tribes in the *amṣār*, had its own unique challenges for its governors. Here, men such as al-Ḥajjāj and Yūsuf ibn ʿUmar al-Thaqafī kept an eye on the east, and on Kūfa in particular. The Ḥijāz and Yemen were excluded from the superprovinces (eastern Arabia fell under al-Baṣra's control), no doubt because they lacked any active military fronts or waves of settlement. Only the prestige of the Holy Cities of Mecca and Medina obliged the Marwānids to keep the region within the control of the family circle. In other aspects the region had become a backwater: major roads were not even built until the reign of the ʿAbbāsid caliph al-Mahdī.

Beyond these core regions dominated by the ruling family lay a periphery of distant frontier provinces where the authority of the Marwānid dynasty was felt less directly.[29] To the west, the authority of the caliph weakened as it spread further from Syria, filtered first through Egypt, and then through Ifrīqiya, so as to be in al-Andalus more of an ideal than a reality. On the caliphate's eastern flank, Iraq might be governed by loyal Thaqafī strongmen, but in Iraq's eastern dependencies such as Khurāsān the men chosen to govern often did so with little input from the caliph. If al-Andalus and the west barely felt the authority of the caliphs, Khurāsān and the east toed the line only slightly better, oscillating between local autonomy and direct Syrian rule. Finally, compared with the western and eastern flanks, the northern provinces governed from al-Jazīra – Armenia, Arrān and Azerbaijan – were long the preferred arenas of Marwānid kinsmen, perhaps reflecting the gravity of the Khazar and Byzantine threats. With this one possible exception in the north, as much as the Marwānids could rely upon relatively easy administration of their core territories, the imposition of authority in the periphery was never a given.

Settlement and economy

The economic forces that undergirded Syria's role as the centre of empire remain poorly understood. That said, the two most significant forces shaping

28 On Mosul and al-Jazīra in Marwānid times, see C. F. Robinson, *Empire and elites after the Muslim conquest: The transformation of northern Mesopotamia* (Cambridge, 2000).

29 What follows can be easily seen by comparing appointments to provincial governorates. See Eduard von Zambaur, *Manuel de généalogie et de chronologie pour l'histoire de l'Islam*, 2nd edn (Bad Pyrmont, 1955). For the Maghrib, see Hicham Djaït, 'Le Wilaya d'Ifriqiya au IIe/VIIIe siècle', *SI*, 27 (1967); Salvador Vilá Hernández, 'El nombramiento e los wālīes de al-Andalus', *al-Andalus*, 4 (1936–9).

the economy in this period are undeniable, and have already been discussed: imperial expansion and administrative centralising. Along with these two forces were a number of associated trends, most of which have their roots in Late Antiquity, and the Sasanian economy in particular, but which underwent greater intensification during the early and middle eighth century.[30]

The monetarised economies of Late Antiquity continued unabated under Islam, and here we are best informed about the core areas of the caliphate.[31] In Egypt, Iraq, Iran and Syria, for example, copper coins continued to be minted locally throughout the Umayyad period. Although gold and silver coins were not minted in Egypt until the ʿAbbāsid period, there is abundant evidence in the papyri and in glass weights of foreign gold and silver being used in commercial and fiscal transactions.[32] In Syria, Iraq and the east, reformed gold and silver issues are well documented for the Marwānid period.[33] Nevertheless, we should imagine that a customary economy revolving around barter and payments in kind existed to some degree alongside the monetarised economy. This can be documented in Egypt, and was undoubtedly true of other regions as well.[34]

The Late Antique tendency for large estates, worked by tenant farmers, to proliferate in the hands of the powerful – and to grow ever larger – also continued in Marwānid times. 'And if you are able to, obtain for me the land of Bilatūs ibn Bīhawīh's which you mentioned, if you think it a good idea. Or tell Yuḥannis ibn Sawīrus to give it to me, for he has already promised me ten

30 For the broader context, see Chris Wickham, *Framing the early Middle Ages: Europe and the Mediterranean, 400–800* (Oxford, 2005). For a synthetic sketch, see Alan Walmsley, 'Production, exchange and regional trade in the Islamic East Mediterranean: Old structures, new systems?', in Inge Lyse Hansen and Chris Wickham (eds.), *The long eighth century* (Leiden, 2000). Specific trends have been identified in greatest detail by Michael G. Morony, 'Economic boundaries? Late Antiquity and early Islam', *JESHO*, 47 (2004).

31 Morony, 'Economic boundaries', pp. 170–2.

32 Michael L. Bates, 'Coins and money in the Arabic papyri', in Y. Ragib (ed.), *Documents de l'Islam medieval: Nouvelles perspectives de recherche* (Cairo, 1991). On the continued monetisation of Egypt throughout the eighth century, see Jairus Banaji, *Agrarian change in Late Antiquity: Gold, labour, and aristocratic dominance* (Oxford, 2001), p. 188. On the copper coinage of Syria, see Shraga Qedar, 'Copper coinage of Syria in the seventh and eighth century AD', *Israel Numismatic Journal*, 10 (1988–9).

33 John Walker, *A catalogue of the Muhammadan coins in the British Museum*, vol. I: *A catalogue of the Arab-Sassanian coins* (London, 1941); vol. II: *A catalogue of the Arab-Byzantine and post-reform Umaiyad coins* (London, 1956). Michael L. Bates, 'The coinage of Syria under the Umayyads, 692–750 AD', in M. A. Bakhit and R. Schick (eds.), *The history of Bilad al-Sham during the Umayyad period: Proceedings of the third symposium* (Amman, 1989), vol. II.

34 On the mixed economy of Egypt, see Sijpesteijn, 'Shaping a Muslim state', pp. 71–2, n. 141.

feddans.' These were the orders issued in 735 from one such landlord to his estate manager in the Fayyūm, preserved in a papyrus letter that testifies to the brisk business of land-grabbing in Egypt and, incidentally, one of the first attested Muslim large estate-holders known to the documentary record.[35] Large estates are likewise attested in Iraq and North Africa, but the situation was mixed in Syria and Mesopotamia, where, on the whole, small farms and villages seem to dominate the literary and archaeological record. The proliferation and growth of large estates are related to another trend: the spread of irrigated agriculture. Under the Marwānids some areas of the caliphate came under cultivation that had either never been cultivated, or that had at least been neglected for generations.[36]

What all this implies, of course, is a market in agricultural produce and, one should add, specialised processed goods such as oil and wine, and industrial goods such as pottery and glass. 'Make sure, O Abu 'l-Ḥārith, that you help out for my sake Yuḥannis ... the old man, with the mill-wheat and sift it and take it. And when each one is done, send Zayd and have him measure each one, and order Sanbā not to forget to improve the field.' Thus ran more advice from our over-anxious Fayyūmī landlord, himself miles away from the estate, selling part of his wheat harvest in Alexandria (he also made wine). These were the classic consumer goods of the ancient world, of course, but now available by Marwānid times in greater volume and variety.[37]

And what all this commercial activity implies is building, and lots of it. From their new cities and their markets to their new estates and their irrigation works, the Marwānids were the great builders of the early Islamic period, and there is fortunately abundant record of this in Syria alone. For what Egypt is to Umayyad documents, Syria is to Umayyad monuments. The

35 The letter (slightly amended here) is edited and translated in Petra M. Sijpesteijn, 'Travel and trade on the river', in P. Sijpesteijn and L. Sundelin (eds.), *Papyrology and the history of early Islamic Egypt* (Leiden, 2004), esp. pp. 135–6.

36 On the broader phenomenon of large estates and agricultural expansion, see Banaji, *Agrarian change*; and Morony, 'Economic boundaries?', pp. 168–70. On continuities in elite incomes from land from Umayyad to ʿAbbāsid times, see Hugh Kennedy, 'Elite incomes in the early Islamic state', in John Haldon and L. I. Conrad (eds.), *The Byzantine and early Islamic Near East*, vol. VI: *Elites old and new in the Byzantine and early Islamic Near East* (Princeton, 2004).

37 On commercialised agriculture and specialisation of certain industries, see Morony, 'Economic boundaries?', pp. 172–8 and the introductions to two volumes edited by him: *Production and the exploitation of resources*, The Formation of the Classical Islamic World 11 (Princeton and Aldershot, 2002) and *Manufacturing and labour* (Aldershot, 2003); Rebecca M. Foote, 'Commerce, industrial expansion, and orthogonal planning: Mutually compatible terms in settlements of Bilad al-Sham during the Umayyad period', *Mediterranean Archaeology*, 13 (2000). On the Fayyūmī letter, see note 35.

most famous of these are the 'desert castles', which is rather a misnomer since many of these structures are neither castles nor located in the desert. The Arabic term for them – *quṣūr* – is a vague one that denotes form more than anything else,[38] but is suitably flexible to describe the many uses to which these buildings were put, as hunting lodges, defensive strongholds, urban cores, spas, palaces and, especially for present purposes, country estates: these are sites of the farmer's life as much as they are of *la dolce vita*.[39] The diversity of the *quṣūr* is readily apparent even to the untrained eye, ranging as they do from the massive structure(s) at the complex known as Qaṣr al-Ḥayr al-Sharqī in the Syrian desert to the many others that, by comparison, seem like mere hovels, as at Khān al-Zabīb, near Qatrana in Jordan.

But for all the diversity of form and function, the location of the Umayyad *quṣūr* in the economic trends discussed above cannot be denied.[40] Surely at Qaṣr al-Ḥayr al-Sharqī we are looking at the sort of thing that the historians mean when they refer to 'the growth of large estates'. Here, in a cultivable seam in the desert midway between Palmyra and the Euphrates, two fine stone chateaux and other outbuildings (including an olive-press) were built in 727 in the reign of Hishām, surrounded by a village of mud-brick dwellings, as well as a circuitous enclosure wall that marked off an immense area of cultivated land served by dams, canals and cisterns. Other humbler brick *quṣūr* were later added to the ensemble. Many similar arrangements can be found throughout Syria, as at al-Bakhrā', where al-Walīd II was assassinated in 744, and where the surrounding village extends for some 40 hectares (at least).[41]

38 Lawrence I. Conrad, 'The *quṣūr* of medieval Islam: Some implications for the social history of the Near East', *al-Abḥāth*, 29 (1981).

39 And possibly the traveller's life, too: see G. R. D. King, 'The distribution of sites and routes in the Jordanian and Syrian deserts in the early Islamic period', *Proceedings of the Seminar for Arabian Studies*, 17 (1987), which posits a connection between the *quṣūr* (at least some of them) and the Umayyad road-network.

40 The literature on the *quṣūr* is dauntingly large and diffuse. A definitive inventory and analysis of the dozens of structures that can claim to be Umayyad *quṣūr* has yet to be written. Older starting-points include Jean Sauvaget, 'Châteaux umayyades de Syrie: Contribution à l'étude de la colonisation arabe aux Ier et IIe siècles de l'Hégire', *REI*, 35 (1967); and Fawwāz Ṭūqān, *al-Ḥā'ir: Baḥth fī al-quṣūr al-umawiyya fī al-bādiya* (Amman, 1979). More recently, see Jere L. Bacharach, 'Marwānid building activities: Speculations on patronage', *Muqarnas*, 13 (1996) (not limited to the *quṣūr* alone); and the summary reports of Denis Genequand's project 'Implantations umayyades de Syrie et de Jordanie', for the Schweizerisch-Liechtensteinische Stiftung für archäologische Forschungen im Ausland (SLSA) in the *SLSA-Jahrsbericht 2001* (Zürich, 2001) and *SLSA-Jahresbericht 2002* (Zürich, 2003).

41 Oleg Grabar, R. Holod, J. Knustad and W. Trousdale, *City in the desert: Qasr al-Hayr East*, 2 vols. (Cambridge, MA, 1978). But cf. Denis Genequand, 'Rapport préliminaire de la campagne de fouille 2002 à Qasr al-Hayr al-Sharqi (Syrie)', in *SLSA-Jahresbericht 2002*

But for all the attention that they lavished on cultivating the rural landscapes of their core lands, the Marwānids and their servants were really thinking in the end about their cities, where their surplus could be brought to market, and their income and rents spent.[42] Here too the monuments can help us, revealing a vigorous commercial and industrial economy. This is evident in both Antique urban landscapes that were maintained or retooled and in *de novo* foundations. Examples of the former include Baysān in Palestine, where Hishām ordered the construction of a complex of some twenty shops and a notable covered walkway on the site of a ruined Byzantine basilica; or Palmyra (Tadmur), where an impressive new market, some 200 metres long and containing some fifty stalls, was inserted into the colonnade of the old Roman *decumanus*. Examples of the latter include ʿAnjar in the Biqāʿ valley of Lebanon, probably built by al-Walīd I's son, ʿAbbās, to house his troops. It was built from scratch in the style of a Roman legionary camp, but is unambiguously Umayyad, with its palaces, mosque, Syrian-style houses, baths and shops; or al-Ramla, capital of the *jund* of Filasṭīn, built by the future caliph Sulaymān, though its original plan is unknown. So identified with city building were the Marwānids that at Mosul the family cut new canals, developed the land and added some new buildings, but were nevertheless held by tradition to have founded the city itself.[43] When we add to these examples in the core areas the propensity of Marwānid governors in the provinces for agricultural development and urban expansion,[44] we can begin to appreciate that we are dealing with a society and an elite committed to urban living.

Whether there were enough people to keep the economy going is a debatable question. The demographic trends of the early Islamic period are really only the subject of clever guesswork. Conventional wisdom suggests that a recovery from the demographic downturn caused by the plagues, famines, deportations and wars of Late Antiquity was in the offing, but

(Zurich, 2003); Denis Genequand, 'Rapport préliminaire de la campagne de fouille 2003 à Qasr al-Hayr al-Sharqi et al-Bakhrāʾ (Syrie)', in *SLSA-Jahresbericht 2003* (Zurich, 2004).

42 On Marwānid urbanism in Syria, see Alastair Northedge, 'Archaeology and new urban settlement patterns in early Islamic Syria and Iraq', in G. R. D. King and A. Cameron (eds.), *The Byzantine and early Islamic Near East*, vol. II: *Land use and settlement patterns* (Princeton, 1994); Bacharach, 'Speculations'; and, esp. Foote, 'Commerce'.

43 Robinson, *Empire and elites*, pp. 86–9.

44 On settlement and development in the provinces, see Ira M. Lapidus, 'Arab settlement and economic development of Iraq and Iran in the age of the Umayyad and early Abbasid caliphs', in A. L. Udovitch (ed.), *The Islamic Middle East, 700–1900: Studies in economic and social history* (Princeton, 1981); Khalil ʿAthamina, 'Arab settlement during the Umayyad caliphate', *JSAI*, 8 (1986).

would have to wait until after the Marwānids had left the scene.[45] Certainly, Marwānid investment in this labour-intensive economy of farming, building, mining and so on created a demand for labour, either in the form of slaves or corvée, which may suggest that economy was outstripping demography. It also suggests a certain mobility, at least for labourers, such as the Ḥimṣīs sent by Hishām to build Qaṣr al-Ḥayr al-Sharqī, the Iraqi Christians and Copts enlisted to build ʿAnjar, or the Zuṭṭ peoples, captured in Sind and resettled on the Syrian coast in the reign of al-Walīd I, presumably as labourers and not as sailors.

The mobility of certain populations (to which we should add the well-travelled troops, scholars and administrators of the period), the integration of regional markets and merchant communities, and the administrative centralising of this period also led to a greater regional interdependence. But one should not exaggerate such a process. We are dealing principally with small-scale local economies that were only beginning to connect to one another and to a broader world. Nevertheless, the increasingly integrated economies of the Marwānid caliphate would set the stage for the increasingly integrated Islamic civilisation of later periods. In sum, even if the economic history of the period is patchy and resistant to synthesis, the confluence of trends is clearly recognisable: urbanism and economic expansion were as much a part of the Marwānid programme as were monotheism, centralisation and empire.

Elite culture and the Marwānid transformation

As has already been noted, the Marwānid caliphs who ruled over this spreading and centralising empire were holders of imperial might – latter-day avatars of Khusrau and Caesar – and also religious guidance – signposts and lodestars. But the caliphs were also sources of wealth and patronage. Their cash-parched poets eulogised them in panegyric as storm-clouds, rivers and falling rain. They were, in their munificence, elemental. The *ashrāf* – the Arab elite who served the caliphs as commanders, soldiers and, increasingly, administrators – will have felt the same, even if they expressed it in less mellifluous terms. The entire system of Marwānid loyalty hinged upon patronage emanating from the caliph filtered through networks of patronage headed by the *ashrāf* on down to their tribal constituents. The caliphs were always the head of this system, the fount of any benefits that might accrue to the populace. But on the

45 Morony, 'Economic boundaries?', pp. 181–3. On Late Antique economic trends more generally, see chapter 1 in this volume.

basis of their wealth and noble ancestry the *ashrāf*, the descendants of Islam's early conquest elite, could aspire too to be rivers to their people.

Nowhere can the aspirations of the Marwānid elites be better glimpsed than in the *quṣūr* built by caliphs and *ashrāf* throughout the caliphate. Some of these were quite humble, but others were clearly sites dedicated to elite distraction and self-representation. A particularly well-preserved case, Quṣayr ʿAmra, can serve as a convenient example, though other equally lavish *quṣūr*, such as those at Khirbat al-Mafjar near Jericho or Qaṣr al-Ḥayr al-Gharbī south-west of Palmyra, would do as well. Located in the Jordanian steppe south-east of ʿAmmān, Quṣayr ʿAmra is perhaps to be attributed to al-Walīd II. And, while the decoration of the structure can certainly tell us much about the ideals of caliphs, it is also revealing of the broader world of the *ashrāf* who served them.[46] The site itself consists of a small hall attached to a bath-house, with a nearby well and cistern. The ruins of other structures, including a mosque and a residence of some kind, are located in the vicinity. What the site lacks in external appeal, it makes up for in interior decoration.

In Quṣayr ʿAmra's frescoes we see the cultural world of the Marwānid elite as its putative caliphal patron wanted it to be represented to his household, clients, allies and rivals. In an alcove directly opposite the entrance one confronts an image of a prince enthroned, in a style evocative of Late Antique representations of Adam. The rest of the hall is given over to images that call forth the pastimes of the men who frequented it: hunting scenes, musicians, workers, acrobats, dancers, scores of voluptuous women and, lest one get jaded, personifications of Philosophy, History and Poetry, identified by Greek inscriptions. Similar frescoes can be found in the adjoining bath-house, where the *caldarium* is crowned by a zodiacal dome. Amidst the general riot, one is drawn to three panels in the western aisle, which may be taken to represent three concurrent scenes. In the centre, a nearly naked woman emerges Venus-like from her bath while attendants (and a peeping Tom) look on. In the panel to the right, and thus outside the building in which the bathing woman is busied, acrobats perform in celebration. Finally, to the left, a dour delegation awaits entry: six kings humbled by the might of the caliph and the *ashrāf*, identified in matching Greek and Arabic inscriptions: the Byzantine Caesar; the Visigoth Roderic; the Persian Khusrau; the Abyssinian negus; and

46 For a study of the messages conveyed by the decoration of Quṣayr ʿAmra, to which most of the following discussion is indebted, see Garth Fowden, *Quṣayr ʿAmra: Art and the Umayyad elite in Late Antique Syria* (Berkeley, 2004). On the elite cultural world associated with the *quṣūr*, see also Robert Hillenbrand, '*La dolce vita* in early Islamic Syria: The evidence of later Umayyad palaces', *Art History*, 5 (1982).

two unidentified monarchs, probably a Turkish or Khazar *khāqān* and an Indian *rāja*. These are expressions of an elite that embraced the finer things of Antiquity, that valued manliness, genealogy, ostentatious display, power over nature and dominion over foes on every horizon. Such artistic expressions are not, as in the coins and monuments of ʿAbd al-Malik, the loud clamourings of a newcomer to the dance of empire, but rather the subtler gestures of the heirs of conquerors, supremely confident of their place in history.

In this sense, Quṣayr ʿAmra is a testament to the blinkers worn by Syria's elite. For by the time the workers who are depicted in its frescoes were mixing its mortar, the political horizons of the *ashrāf*, like the conquest society that they created, had undergone a radical transformation.[47] The close-knit conquest society of earlier days, in which a small tribal elite of Arab Muslims sequestered themselves in the *amṣār*, was now disintegrating. There were two principal mechanisms of this momentous social change. The first was conversion to Islam. What little we know about this process suggests that, other than simple opportunism, such conversion as happened at this early date occurred primarily by two means: conversion due to voluntary religious conviction; and conversion through enslavement, the result of being taken captive in war and brought into Muslim households. There slaves learned some Arabic, encountered and accepted Islam and, in the ideal, were freed, entering the ever-growing (and, to the *ashrāf*, ignoble) stratum of non-Arab converts (*mawālī*). Muslims became more and more common, in every sense of the word.

The second mechanism was the professionalisation of the army. Under ʿAbd al-Malik and his successors the role of imperial army now went to a loyal, professional body of troops from Syria and al-Jazīra, who were sent to various hot-spots when needed and to replenish garrisons on active frontiers.[48] This meant that the old tribal armies of the *amṣār* and the old-style *ashrāf* who led them were effectively demobilised, and many (though not all) of the once-proud families of the conquests settled down and took to civilian pursuits such as trading, landownership and scholarship. Garrison towns became cities and soldiers became civilians. Having assimilated into this emergent civilian

47 On the Marwānid transformation and the development of factionalism, see Patricia Crone, *Slaves on horses: The evolution of the Islamic polity* (Cambridge, 1980); Patricia Crone, 'Were the Qays and Yemen of the Umayyad period political parties?', *Der Islam*, 71 (1994).

48 On the military reforms of ʿAbd al-Malik, see Chase F. Robinson's discussion in chapter 5 of this volume.

society, there was now little beside their genealogies that distinguished the *ashrāf* from the *mawālī* so many of them had scorned.

None of these changes boded well for the Marwānids. Given that non-Muslim subjects and non-Arab Muslims carried the bulk of the tax burden of the caliphate, conversion theoretically meant a reduction in revenues, precisely in an era when building projects, urbanism and military expansion demanded more, not less, returns from the peasantry. Indeed, it is said that al-Ḥajjāj, a man ever attentive to fiscal matters, was obliged to send back to their villages the peasant cultivators who – if only for the tax-break – flocked to the towns clamouring for conversion to Islam. Such practices will only have angered the populace: the *mawālī* of course, but also a growing number who worried that their caliphs had become better at collecting taxes than at offering God's guidance. Among these concerned civilians were scholars, and it is surely no accident that it is, so far as one can tell, in these late Umayyad times that scholars with clear claims to religious authority emerge. Significantly, it was especially in Iraq, not metropolitan Syria, that such scholars began to delve into the lore of other monotheisms and start policing the perimeters of right-guidance themselves, in *ḥadīth* and in theological disputation (*kalām*); it is also the time when the first chronicles – among them a *History of the caliphs* – were composed, a sign perhaps of contested caliphal legitimacy.[49]

Meanwhile, in Syria, the caliphs, their kinsmen and the old Syrian *ashrāf* dominated political affairs until just before the collapse of the dynasty, no doubt working out their alliances and shared political goals through meetings arranged at places just like Quṣayr ʿAmra.[50] But outside the metropole, the old noble families of Sufyānid times, replaced by the Syro-Jazīran imperial troops, were now merely the children of conquerors, not conquerors themselves. Those members of the old-style *ashrāf* who remained involved in the military did so primarily as local troops in garrisons on active frontiers such as Khurāsān. As a result, the Syro-Jazīran troops were bitterly resented by old Arab families and their *mawālī* in the provinces, who came to see them as an

49 For two examples from the world of Marwānid scholars, see Alfred-Louis de Prémare, 'Wahb b. Munabbih, une figure singulière du premier islam', *Annales HSS*, (2005); and Gerhard Conrad, *Die Quḍāt Dimasq und der Madhab al-Auzāʿī: Materialen zur syrischen Rechtsgeschichte* (Beirut, 1994). See also Christian Décobert, 'L'autorité religieuse aux premiers siècles de l'islam', *Archives de Sciences Sociales des Religions*, 125 (2004). On early history writing, see Fred M. Donner, *Narratives of Islamic origins: The beginnings of Islamic historical writing* (Princeton, 1998).

50 On the role of the *quṣūr* in Umayyad tribal politics, see the suggestive study by Heinz Gaube, 'Die syrischen Wüstenschlösser: Einige wirtshaftliche und politische Gesichtspunkte zu ehrer Entstehung', *Zeitschrift der Deutschen Palästina-Vereins*, 95 (1979).

occupation force, and an insult to their honourable past service. It also meant that, for those few groups of *ashrāf* who still held on to positions of power and privilege in the provinces, old-style tribal politics had given way to the new-style factional politics that had become endemic in the army, what the sources call tribal partisanship or *ʿaṣabiyya*.

ʿAṣabiyya was the defining feature of political life in the provinces. In the course of governing a province, governors were inclined to rely upon their own kinsmen and allies for their sub-governors or other positions. As a result, various groups – Syro-Jazīran troops, local Arabs, *mawālī* – competed for access to the power and patronage that a given governor might offer to his kinsmen in return for loyal service. Although it was usually the case for South Arabian tribes to line up with the Yaman faction and North Arabian tribes to align with Qays/Muḍar, this was not always the case, and it is not uncommon to find genealogically 'southern' tribesmen supporting Qays and 'northerners' supporting Yaman in their rivalries against one another and feuding over provincial appointments. For example, the revolt in 720 of the former governor of Khurāsān, Yazīd ibn al-Muhallab, was backed by Qaysīs and Yamanīs alike. But because the Muhallabids were of Azd/Yaman and his revolt was crushed by largely Qaysī troops under Maslama ibn ʿAbd al-Malik, it became part of a Yamanī narrative of Umayyad oppression that they would later exploit. Indeed, as only one faction can be on top, such partisanship quickly became polarised and, as resentment at the Syro-Jazīran troops and the caliphs who sent them grew, factional complaints, especially by the out-of-favour, became increasingly shrill. In the end, as the musicians played on at Quṣayr ʿAmra, factional politics in the provinces would finally boil over into Syria and bring civil war with it.

Rebellion and the alternatives to Marwānid imperium

For the growing crowd who resented Umayyad rule, it helped that other groups – Khārijites and Shīʿa – had been organised against the dynasty since the battle of Ṣiffīn and remained steadfast in their opposition. However, since the second *fitna*, Khārijites and Shīʿa were in a tighter spot than they had ever been before. Under ʿAbd al-Malik Khārijite rebellions had threatened Marwānid control over southern Iraq at a moment when the dust of the civil war had barely begun settling. However, the rebellions were soon subdued when ʿAbd al-Malik stationed Syrian troops under al-Ḥajjāj in Iraq. With this new aggressive stance Khārijites were obliged to move further afield, to Iran and, in particular, to Mosul and al-Jazīra. This latter region was the scene of some Khārijite activity in the last decades of Marwānid rule, but even in these cases rebellion for the moment involved small numbers and little hope for success. When a son of the old Khārijite leader Shabīb ibn Yazīd rose in revolt, he could only raise a few score men for an unsuccessful raid on one of the governor's country estates. Only during the third *fitna* would Khārijism regain its power to contest the caliphate.[51]

Before the third *fitna*, Shīʿite movements faced the same situation, and the same odds. None of the Shīʿite revolts in southern Iraq in Marwānid times came close to the threat posed by al-Mukhtār's rebellion during the second *fitna*. However, they did adopt some of its ideas, a testament to the popularity in the Iraqi *amṣār* of radical expressions of Shīʿism spiked with gnostic concepts, and these movements were duly dismissed by later observers as extremists (*ghulāt*).[52] And if the specific creeds of the *ghulāt* are hard to piece together from the hostile and patchy sources that relate them, their gnostic flavour and focus on the Banū Hāshim as imams are clear.[53] Thus, Bayān al-Nahdī, who rebelled in Kūfa and was executed some time in the 730s, is said to have claimed to have worked for Abū Hāshim, the son of Muḥammad ibn al-Ḥanafiyya, himself a son of ʿAlī by a concubine, though he is also said to have claimed to be the emissary of Muḥammad al-Bāqir, from the Ḥusaynid branch of ʿAlī's descendants. To these figures all manner of beliefs were attributed, including the doctrine of continuous prophecy, transmigration of souls, the divinity of ʿAlī and his sons and the belief in a pair of Gods – an earthly and a heavenly one.[54]

In comparison with the small-scale political agitation of the *ghulāt*, the revolt in 740 led by a grandson of al-Ḥusayn, Zayd ibn ʿAlī, seemed to hold

51 On Jazīran Khārijite activities after the second *fitna*, see Julius Wellhausen, *Die religiös-politischen Oppositionsparteien im alten Islam* (Berlin, 1901), trans. R. C. Ostle as *The religio-political factions in early Islam* (Amsterdam, 1975), pp. 79–80; Robinson, *Empire and elites*, pp. 125–6, 147–8.

52 On the term, see Wadād al-Qāḍī, 'The development of the term *ghulāt* in Muslim literature with special reference to the Kaysāniyya', in A. Dietrich (ed.), *Akten des VII. Kongresses für Arabistik und Islamwissenschaft* (Göttingen, 1976). On the gnostic influence see Patricia Crone, *God's rule: Government and Islam: Six centuries of medieval Islamic political thought* (New York, 2004), pp. 80–2.

53 Though, as Crone notes, the imams of the *ghulāt* were not expected by their followers to be politicians: Crone, *God's rule*, pp. 82–4.

54 On these rebellions and other Umayyad *ghulāt* movements, see M. G. S. Hodgson, 'Ghulāt', *EI2*, vol. II, pp. 1093–5; M. G. S. Hodgson, 'Bayān b. Samʿān al-Tamīmī', *EI2*, vol. I, pp. 1116–17; and the series of articles by William F. Tucker, 'Bayān ibn Samʿān and the Bayāniyya: Shīʿite extremists of Umayyad Iraq', *MW*, 65 (1975); 'Rebels and gnostics: al-Mugīra Ibn Saʿīd and the Mugīriyya', *Arabica*, 22 (1975); 'Abū Manṣūr al-ʿIjlī and the Manṣūriyya: A study in medieval terrorism', *Der Islam*, 54 (1977).

more promise for those seeking an ʿAlid imam.[55] He is said to have called his followers in Kūfa to 'the Book of God and the *sunna* of His Prophet, holy war against the tyrants, defending the oppressed, giving pensions to those deprived of them, distributing plunder (*fayʾ*) equitably amongst those entitled to it, restitution to those who have been wronged, recall of those detained on the frontiers, and help the household of the Prophet against those who oppose us and disregard our cause', a fairly generic appeal to settle old Kūfan grievances.[56] Syrian troops quashed Zayd's revolt, and he was killed. His son Yaḥyā survived, and fled to Khurāsān, where he too was tracked down and killed. Given the ease with which the Marwānids suppressed their revolt, the cause of Zayd and his son posed no real danger, and it is the claims made later upon them for which they are remembered. Zayd was claimed as the founder of a small but flourishing Shīʿite sect, the Zaydiyya. And some sources relate that Yaḥyā – or rather, vengeance for his murder – moved into action one Shīʿite partisan in Khurāsān: Abū Muslim, chief missionary for the Hāshimiyya, a Shīʿite movement that would, very soon, topple the Marwānid house.

Fitna and *dawla*: the end of Syrian centrality

The maelstrom that toppled the Umayyad dynasty from power and replaced them with an ʿAbbāsid dynasty, and ultimately ended Syria's short-lived role as the centre of empire, is best conceived of in three closely connected phases: the conflict that broke out over disputes about the succession of al-Walīd II; the *dawla* or revolution of the Hāshimiyya movement, which joined the fray of the third *fitna* under its own candidate for imam; and the Manṣūrid victory, by which, on the heels of a Hāshimī victory, the ʿAbbāsid notable Abū Jaʿfar al-Manṣūr consolidated ʿAbbāsid power, neutralised his rivals within the revolution and secured the succession to rule in his own line. It is the first two phases that principally concern us here.

The third fitna

Upon the succession of al-Walīd II (r. 743–4), the prognosis for Marwānid rule was not good. True, the territory controlled by the caliph was vastly larger than it had been at the death of ʿAbd al-Malik. But all indications suggested

55 On this revolt, see al-Ṭabarī, *Taʾrīkh*, series II, pp. 1676–8, 1698–1711; Aḥmad ibn Abī Yaʿqūb al-Yaʿqūbī, *Taʾrīkh al-Yaʿqūbī*, ed. M. T. Houtsma, 2 vols. (Leiden, 1883), vol. II, pp. 391–2; Wellhausen, *Religio-political factions*, pp. 161–4.

56 Al-Ṭabarī, *Taʾrīkh*, series II, p. 1687.

that the caliphate had overreached itself, and that the ideals of Marwānid rule were unable to extend to its furthest borders. The fissures were everywhere: in the stark disconnect between provincial administrative practice and central administrative demands; in the exhaustion of the Syrian troops; and in the growth of tribal factionalism. To Khārijites, Shīʿa and others who sought an imam who better represented their understanding of God's plan for the faithful, it was equally clear that Marwānid-style Islam had reached its limits, too. Taxation, the military, factionalism and Islamic alternatives were all at work behind the overthrow of al-Walīd II and, ultimately, of the Umayyad dynasty itself.

Al-Walīd II's father, Yazīd II, had named Hishām as heir, but he had specified that al-Walīd II was to succeed Hishām in turn. Hishām had tried to overturn this arrangement and keep the caliphate within the line of his own sons, but was unable to do so. It was little comfort to the sons of Hishām that when al-Walīd finally did succeed, he showed little talent or love for his job. An accomplished poet, the sources also describe him as a bit of a *debauché* who liked to pass his time as he pleased, generally ignoring his duties amidst the *otium* of one of his *quṣūr*.[57] Yet for all his alleged disdain for caliphal responsibilities, al-Walīd seemed determined to remain in power, and he swiftly acted against any who opposed him. Some of the tribal notables who resented his succession he had killed. His main Marwānid rival, Sulaymān ibn Hishām, he had beaten and imprisoned. And when he named his two minor sons as his heirs, and Hishām's beloved governor of Iraq and the east, the pro-Yamanī Khālid al-Qasrī, refused to recognise them, al-Walīd handed Khālid over to his enemy and successor as governor, who had him tortured and killed. The rift between al-Walīd II, on the one hand, and the Yamanī faction and the rest of the Marwānid house, on the other, was complete.

Al-Walīd's cousin, the future Yazīd III, backed by disgruntled Umayyads such as Sulaymān ibn Hishām and members of the infuriated Yamanī faction, led the charge against him. Most of Yazīd's Yamanī followers were seasoned veterans, many of them with connections to the deeply factionalised armies. Still others came from the villages surrounding Damascus, especially al-Mizza, a town noted as a centre of Yamanī settlement and a hotbed of a heretical doctrine called Qadarism. As a result of this association, elements of Yazīd's

57 For a whimsical sampling, see Robert Hamilton, *Walid and his friends: An Umayyad tragedy*, Oxford Studies in Islamic Art 6 (Oxford, 1988). On al-Walīd's literary shaping, see Steven Judd, 'Narratives and character development: al-Ṭabarī and al-Balādhurī on late Umayyad history', in Sebastian Guenther (ed.), *Ideas, images, and methods of portrayal: Insights into classical Arabic literature and Islam* (Leiden, 2005).

supporters are referred to as belonging to the Qadariyya or, less frequently, the Ghaylāniyya. While later sources use the term Qadarī to refer to Muslims who uphold human free will in contrast to the prevailing Muslim doctrine of predestination, it is not entirely clear what being a Qadarī meant in the middle of the eighth century. Free will does not necessarily breed rebels, and the political content of Yazīd's programme and the claims of his followers seem fairly limited (see below). As for the Ghaylāniyya, these were the disciples of the rebel Ghaylān al-Dimashqī, a *mawlā* and Marwānid bureaucrat who was executed by Hishām. Although little is known about his teachings, Ghaylān, too, is later named as a Qadarī. Whatever their exact political and theological claims, it was their military support and their loathing of al-Walīd II that most mattered to Yazīd.[58] With the Yamaniyya behind him, Yazīd entered Damascus, neutralised any sources of resistance in the city, was proclaimed caliph in the Umayyad Mosque and received the oath of allegiance from the troops. He then sent a detachment of men to intercept al-Walīd who had, in the meantime, relocated to the *qaṣr* of a loyal supporter of his at al-Bakhrāʾ, not far from Palmyra. Al-Walīd was apprehended and executed.

The resistance on the part of the old *ashrāf* of Syria was immediate. Despite the fact that many of them hailed from genealogically Yamanī tribes, they and their troops from the *ajnād* had every reason to fear for their future under a rebel caliph and the upstart Yamaniyya faction. In both Ḥimṣ and Filasṭīn, loyalist *ashrāf* and local troops rebelled against Yazīd III in the name of the sons and heirs of al-Walīd II, whom Yazīd III had thrown into prison. Yazīd, aided by Sulaymān ibn Hishām, crushed the revolt in Filasṭīn (led by a son of the caliph Sulaymān), and apprehended the leader of the Ḥimṣīs (a descendant of Muʿāwiya). Further north, the grizzled general Marwān ibn Muḥammad (a grandson of Marwān I) had prepared to march from Armenia to support the cause of al-Walīd II's heirs against the rebel Yazīd III, but the Yamanī troops with him on the frontier deserted, and he was forced to interrupt his plans. He further mollified the troops by retaining some of their *ashrāf* in power and paying their stipends.

With most of the immediate threats to his power neutralised, Yazīd could focus on his duties as caliph. His first duty, of course, was to his factional

58 On the events of this phase of the *fitna* and the reign of Yazīd III see al-Ṭabarī, *Taʾrīkh*, series II, pp. 1775–875, esp. pp. 1784–836; 1870–4; Josef van Ess, 'Les Qadarites et la Gailaniyya de Yazīd III', *SI*, 31 (1970); Crone, *Slaves on horses*, pp. 46–8; Paul M. Cobb, *White banners: Contention in ʿAbbasid Syria, 750–880* (Albany, 2001), pp. 71–5. On the later literary shaping of Ghaylān al-Dimashqī, see Steven Judd, 'Ghaylān al-Dimashqī: The isolation of a heretic in Islamic heresiography', *IJMES*, 31 (1999).

following and, sure enough, Yamanīs came to dominate provincial affairs under Yazīd III, notably in Iraq. But was Yazīd's revolt just a Yamanī coup? Certainly the references to the Qadariyya or Ghaylāniyya suggest some kind of ideological basis to his actions. But if a Qadarī programme was behind Yazīd's rebellion, it seems to have more to do with concerns about the imamate than with free will. In a speech he gave upon seizing power in 744,[59] Yazīd claimed to be rebelling in righteous anger in the name of God, His Book, and the *sunna* of His Prophet. The wicked al-Walīd II had forfeited his rights through his tyrannical conduct, and by extinguishing 'the light of pious folk'. On a more practical level, Yazīd pledged that he would 'not place stone upon stone nor brick upon brick' or cut any canals, an evident gripe against the profligate building projects of the Marwānids. The rest of his speech addresses grievances common to much of the Umayyad period involving taxation, military service and justice. As it happens, Yazīd was unable to keep any of these promises, as he died after ruling only a few months.

The coup of Marwān II

Yazīd had named his brother Ibrāhīm (r. *c.* September–November 744) to succeed him but, given the context, the people's allegiance to him wavered. As a result, he barely gets a notice in the sources.[60] As under Yazīd III, the troops of Ḥimṣ refused to recognise this new caliph at first, and Ibrāhīm was beset with rivals almost from the moment he took power. Chief of these was his kinsman Marwān ibn Muḥammad, who now saw his moment to renew his plan to march on Damascus in the name of the two young heirs of al-Walīd II, who were still locked away in prison. Marwān and his Qaysī troops were intercepted on their way to Damascus by a Yamanī army under Sulaymān ibn Hishām. Marwān's battle-hardened frontier troops easily held the day, and Sulaymān's forces were routed. Sulaymān himself fled to Damascus and, it is said, arranged with a cabal of Yamanī leaders to murder al-Walīd II's young heirs. Not long afterwards Marwān arrived in Damascus and received the oath of allegiance as caliph from the troops and *ashrāf*, who were happy to be rid of a caliphal line associated with the odious Yazīd and his Yamaniyya. The reigning caliph, Ibrāhīm ibn al-Walīd, followed suit and joined Marwān's retinue.

59 Al-Ṭabarī, *Ta'rīkh*, series II, pp. 1834–5; *Fragmenta historicorum arabicorum*, ed. M. J. de Goeje, 2 vols. (Leiden, 1869), vol. I, pp. 150–1; Khalīfa ibn Khayyāṭ, *al-Ta'rīkh*, ed. Akram al-ʿUmarī, 2 vols. (Najaf, 1967), vol. II, pp. 382–3.

60 On Ibrāhīm ibn al-Walīd and the coup of Marwān, see al-Ṭabarī, *Ta'rīkh*, series II, pp. 1876–9; *Fragmenta*, vol. I, pp. 154–6; Ibn Khayyāṭ, *Ta'rīkh*, vol. II, pp. 391–3.

As in Yazīd III's revolt, which resulted in the Yamaniyya faction acquiring a new position of authority, Marwān II (r. 744–50) owed his rise to power to the factional loyalties of the Qaysī troops of the frontier. Marwān was thus as obliged, as Yazīd had been, to reward his factional supporters. In some provinces Qaysīs did come to dominate positions of power. But in Syria itself the Qaysīs made only slight headway. This might have been enough to mollify the army and *ashrāf* of Syria, had Marwān not made the decision to move, with the treasury, from Syria to Ḥarrān in al-Jazīra. For Marwān this was a sensible move back to familiar territory long associated with his kinsmen and the homeland of his Qaysī supporters. But for other Umayyads and the *ashrāf* and armies of Syria it was a further sign of their growing irrelevance in the new political landscape. The result was predictable, and the *ashrāf* and the Syrian *ajnād* (most of them Yamanīs) revolted in concert against this new caliph. Marwān thus spent much of 745 pacifying Syria, subduing revolts in Filasṭīn, Tiberias, Ḥimṣ, Palmyra, and even Damascus. Syria's old guard rallied behind Sulaymān ibn Hishām, who had recently been pardoned by Marwān for his association with the regime of Yazīd III. Together with two other sons of Hishām, Sulaymān received the allegiance of a host of Yamanī troops, and attempted to seize cities throughout Syria. In the end Marwān was just able to counter the uprising of the sons of Hishām, razing the walls of the cities that had dared to revolt; but Sulaymān managed to escape and flee to Iraq.

At this point the Syrian troops garrisoned in Iraq were divided between Yamanīs loyal to Yazīd III and his governor (a son of the caliph ʿUmar II) and Qaysīs loyal to Marwān and his governor. This situation should have made Marwān's subjugation of the province an easy one, but it was complicated by a Khārijite uprising among the Rabīʿa tribes, traditional rivals of Qays despite their 'northern' origins. They were led by Shaybānīs of northern Mesopotamia under al-Ḍaḥḥāk ibn Qays.[61] But this was a Khārijite uprising quite unlike the recent raids by small bands of Shaybānī bandits. Al-Ḍaḥḥāk's men (and women, who joined them in battle) numbered in the thousands, were well paid and included seasoned veterans of the frontier. Al-Ḍaḥḥāk marched into Iraq and overwhelmed the Syrian troops. The Qaysīs fled but the Yamanīs, under their noble governor, submitted to the Khārijites, recognising al-Ḍaḥḥāk as their caliph with authority in Iraq, western Persia and Mosul. It was a unique sight, even for a civil war: 'A Qurayshite of the ruling family now prayed behind a Khārijite of Bakr ibn Wāʾil!' as Wellhausen

61 On this revolt, see al-Ṭabarī, *Taʾrīkh*, series II, pp. 1897–916, 1938–49; Wellhausen, *Religio-political factions*, pp. 80–2. Robinson, *Empire and elites*, pp. 110–13, 125–6.

exclaimed, echoing the amazement of a contemporary poet at how badly fragmented Islam's ruling dynasty had become.[62] At Mosul, the mendicant Umayyad Sulaymān ibn Hishām also joined al-Ḍaḥḥāk's cause. Marwān first sent his son ʿAbd Allāh to pen in al-Ḍaḥḥāk in al-Jazīra, but the caliph was soon obliged to join the fray himself, and he ultimately triumphed, killing al-Ḍaḥḥāk and scattering his forces. By 746 the remnants had crossed over the Tigris, and were forced to flee into the mountains to the east. Iraq submitted to Marwān's authority.

Perhaps inspired by these events, Khārijites in the Ḥijāz seized control of Mecca and Medina.[63] This group recognised as caliph a Khārijite judge in the Hadramawt who took the sobriquet 'the Seeker of Justice' (*ṭālib al-ḥaqq*), but were led locally by a Baṣran troublemaker named Abū Ḥamza ibn ʿAwf. With a small group of followers, Abū Ḥamza took over Mecca during the pilgrimage, railed against the iniquities of the Marwānids – Marwān II in particular – and convinced the city's governor to flee. A lieutenant then took charge of Medina. Without delay Marwān sent an army under a trusted commander to take charge of the situation in Arabia. Abū Ḥamza's forces were overcome, and Medina and Mecca were secured. The army then proceeded into Yemen, where they captured the Khārijite leader, sending his head back to Marwān.

With Egypt only recently subjugated and the Maghrib still reeling from the effects of the Berber revolt, Iran and the east next drew Marwān's attentions. The focus of opposition here was the Shīʿite rebel ʿAbd Allāh ibn Muʿāwiya, a descendant of ʿAlī's brother Jaʿfar.[64] In 744, after the death of Yazīd III, he had rebelled in Kūfa against the governor and his garrison, but was forced to flee to western Iran. He was joined by Zaydī Shīʿa, a disgruntled *mawālī*, even the remnants of the Khārijite followers of al-Ḍaḥḥāk ibn Qays (among them the Umayyad Sulaymān ibn Hishām), who had fled Marwān II's armies into Ibn Muʿāwiya's domains. His following even included a few members of the ʿAbbāsid family, a notable lineage of the Banū Hāshim who were only now beginning to manifest their opposition to generations of Umayyad rule. At its height the dominion of Ibn Muʿāwiya included most of south-western Iran, but it was short-lived. In 746–7 the bulk of his forces were on the run and

62 Wellhausen, *Arab kingdom*, p. 390.

63 On this revolt, see al-Ṭabarī, *Taʾrīkh*, series II, pp. 1942–3, 1981–3, 2005–15; Wellhausen, *Religio-political factions*, pp. 85–8; C. Pellat, 'al-Mukhtār ibn ʿAwf al-Azdī', *EI2*, vol. VII, p. 524.

64 On the revolt of ʿAbd Allāh ibn Muʿāwiya, see al-Ṭabarī, *Taʾrīkh*, series II, pp. 1879–88; Wellhausen, *Religio-political factions*, pp. 164–5; William Tucker, 'ʿAbd Allāh b. Muʿāwīya and the Janāḥiyya: Rebels and ideologues of the late Umayyad period', *SI*, 51 (1980).

defeated by Marwān's troops near Marw. The rebel Umayyad Sulaymān ibn Hishām managed to escape with a few men to Sind, the very margins of the Islamic world, where death caught up with him. Ibn Muʿāwiya himself escaped and fled into Khurāsān, where Abū Muslim, the leader of another Shīʿite revolt, had him captured and executed as a rival.

Hāshimiyya and ʿAbbāsids

It is traditional at this point in medieval and modern narratives of the fall of the Umayyads to pick up our story in Khurāsān, whence Abū Muslim's Shīʿite movement, called the Hāshimiyya, exploded, defeating Marwān and his badly overstretched armies, overturning the Umayyad dynasty and replacing it, after some sleight of hand, with a line of caliphs from the ʿAbbāsid family. It is this sequence of events that modern historians usually call 'the ʿAbbāsid revolution'. But there are good reasons for questioning the precise role of the ʿAbbāsids in all this – and, furthermore, just how revolutionary it all was.[65]

We may consider first whether the revolution was really ʿAbbāsid. Given that the movement began with a clandestine phase (called the *daʿwa*), puzzling out what really happened before the public uprising (called the *dawla*) of the Hāshimiyya is a fraught pursuit. A few points can be taken as relatively certain, however.[66] The Hāshimiyya movement, as its name suggests, was a Shīʿite opposition group originating in Kūfa whose members believed that the leadership of the Muslim community should be drawn solely from the Banū Hāshim, the Prophet's clan, which they also called variously the *ahl al-bayt* (People of the Household) or simply the *āl Muḥammad* (the Family of Muḥammad). The goals of the Hāshimiyya thus automatically excluded an imam/caliph drawn from the broader pool of Quraysh such as the earliest caliphs, Abū Bakr and ʿUmar. More to the point, it considered the current line of Umayyad caliphs a terrible deviation, an iniquitous dynasty that should

65 There is a large and diverse body of scholarship devoted to the ʿAbbāsid revolution. For a convenient summary discussion, see R. Stephen Humphreys, *Islamic history: A framework for inquiry*, rev. edn (Princeton, 1991), pp. 104–27, with the addition of Saleh Said Agha, *The revolution which toppled the Umayyads: Neither Arab nor ʿAbbāsid* (Leiden, 2003).

66 On the *daʿwa*, see Moshe Sharon, *Black banners from the east* (Jerusalem, 1983); Moshe Sharon, *Revolt: The social and military aspects of the ʿAbbāsid revolution* (Jerusalem, 1990); Hugh Kennedy, *The early Abbasid caliphate: A political history* (London, 1981); Tilman Nagel, *Untersuchungen zur Entstehung des abbasidischen Kalifates* (Bonn, 1972); Patricia Crone, 'On the meaning of the ʿAbbasid call to al-Riḍā', in C. E. Bosworth *et al.* (eds.), *The Islamic world from classical to modern times: Essays in honor of Bernard Lewis* (Princeton, 1989), pp. 95–111; and most recently, Agha, *Revolution*.

never have come to rule. For the Hāshimiyya, restoring the imamate to the family of the Prophet was a clear solution to the error of Marwānid rule.

The Hāshimiyya thus revolted to vindicate the claims of a clan, not an individual. They referred to their future unspecified leader as *al-riḍā min āl-Muḥammad* ('the one selected from the family of Muḥammad'), which suggests that, like so many rebel movements before them, they considered selection by *shūrā* (electoral council) to be the mechanism that would determine their imams. As the pool was limited to the Banū Hāshim, the new imams could be either ʿAbbāsid or ʿAlid. During the clandestine phase of the revolution, and even afterwards, many may well have assumed this really meant an ʿAlid imamate, but others seem to have supported the claims of the ʿAbbāsid Ibrāhīm ibn Muḥammad (dutifully called Ibrāhīm al-Imām in the sources) as being the most worthy of the Banū Hāshim.

Strictly speaking, this is not how the ʿAbbāsids themselves came to remember their role in the *daʿwa*.[67] In the ʿAbbāsid version of these events it is the Imām Ibrāhīm's father, Muḥammad ibn ʿAlī, who was the first ʿAbbāsid to become involved in the Hāshimiyya. And he was no mere disgruntled notable, but rather the chosen heir of Abū Hāshim, the son of the ʿAlid imam Muḥammad ibn al-Ḥanafiyya (this last is the same ʿAlid to whom al-Mukhtār had tied his fortunes back in the second *fitna*). From the ʿAbbāsid family *qaṣr* at Ḥumayma in southern Transjordan, Muḥammad ibn ʿAlī directed the growing network of propagandists who spread his claims in Kūfa and elsewhere, above all Khurāsān. When he died in 743, his son Imām Ibrāhīm took over as head of the movement, and it was he who, in response to demands from the Khurāsānīs, appointed a mysterious *mawlā* of his, Abū Muslim, as chief propagandist there. As it happens, Marwān II seems to have caught on to what the ʿAbbāsids were up to, and he had Ibrāhīm dragged in chains from Ḥumayma and thrown into prison in Ḥarrān, where, in 749, he died. By then the revolution was in full swing, and claims about old caliphs took a back seat to struggles with current ones.

The ʿAbbāsid story of their origins thus posits an early connection with the *daʿwa* of the Hāshimiyya and irrefutable Shīʿite credentials through the 'testament' of Abū Hāshim. And if it provides as many problems for us as it did solutions for ʿAbbāsids worried about legitimacy, it is nevertheless the official version of events and worthy of note in that respect. But an unproblematic

67 I base my paraphrase of the 'official version' here on the anonymous *Akhbār al-dawla al-ʿAbbāsiyya wa-fīhi akhbār al-ʿAbbās wa-wuldihi*, ed. ʿAbd al-ʿAzīz al-Dūrī and A. J. al-Muṭṭalibī (Beirut, 1971), on which see Elton Daniel, 'The anonymous history of the Abbasid family and its place in Islamic historiography', *IJMES*, 14 (1982), pp. 419–34.

direct line between the 'Abbāsid caliphs and Muḥammad ibn al-Ḥanafiyya certainly sounds more like post-revolutionary wishful thinking than a straightforward guide to what transpired in the last days of the Marwānids. Unfortunately, the evidence does not offer us much with which to construct an alternative. For both historiographical and political reasons 'the relationship between the 'Abbasids and the revolution customarily named after them is nothing if not problematic'.[68]

Although Kūfan in origin, the Hāshimiyya found its most ardent supporters in Khurāsān. It was an ideal place to start a revolution.[69] While Marwān II was stamping out the fires of rebellion in Egypt, Arabia, Syria and Iraq, Khurāsān was governed almost autonomously by Naṣr ibn Sayyār, Hishām's octogenarian governor, who had steadfastly refused all attempts to replace him. Naṣr faced two principal local challenges. On one hand, there was the civilian population, comprising both non-Arabs and Arabs, who had created an 'archipelago' of settlement in the towns and villages of the province.[70] In the aftermath of the early waves of conquest the traditional barriers between Arab settlers and Iranian *mawālī* were breaking down and, as both sides intermarried and commingled, their interests began to converge. One of these interests was taxation. For decades the Arab settlers had complained that local non-Muslim elites in charge of tax collection were favouring their fellow natives and co-religionists, which meant that Muslims paid more than their share of the taxes. Naṣr attempted to resolve these issues by making some significant tax reforms, but these seem to have arrived too late to quell all opposition to him.

On the other hand, there was the army, based most prominently in Marw. As in other provinces, the army was divided by factional disputes between Yaman and Qays. Naṣr here also tried to resolve differences, but to no avail. A dispute over pay led one Yamanī commander to revolt and gather his kinsmen and factional followers in opposition to Naṣr, whom he was able to oust from Marw. Naṣr's appeals to Marwān II for help went unanswered but, gathering Qaysī supporters from other settlements, he camped before Marw in the summer of 747. It was at this juncture that, in the nearby village of Sikadanj, the Hāshimiyya under Abū Muslim proclaimed a new turn of fortune's favour

68 Crone, 'al-Riḍā', p. 103, which also treats the political reasons. The evidence for historiographical re-shaping is discussed in Jacob Lassner, *Islamic revolution and historical memory: Abbasid apologetics and the art of historical writing* (New Haven, 1986).
69 On the public manifestation of the revolution, Wellhausen, *Arab kingdom*, is fundamental. See also Shaban, *'Abbasid revolution*; Sharon, *Revolt*.
70 The allusion is to Agha, *Revolution*, pp. 185–6.

(*dawla*) to replace the loathsome Umayyads, and prayers were said on behalf of Imām Ibrāhīm. By adopting such techniques as using black banners as their insignia, and later giving their caliphs apocalyptic-sounding epithets, the Hāshimiyya tapped into a strain of apocalyptic expectation that had never really died down among Muslims – or, for that matter, non-Muslims – in the region.[71] Naṣr briefly came to terms with the Yamanī opposition, and was able to retake Marw, but Abū Muslim was too deft an intriguer for Naṣr and, in early 748, with overwhelming Yamanī and even Qaysī support, he and his Hāshimī followers, Arabs and *mawālī*, took the city. Naṣr once again took flight.

Abū Muslim's commander-in-chief in Khurāsān was a Yamanī soldier named Qaḥṭaba ibn Shābīb. It was Qaḥṭaba who pursued Naṣr and his men westward across Iran, dislodging him from Nīshāpūr and Qūmis, and penning him in at Hamadhān, where Naṣr finally fell. Iraq was in reach. Qaḥṭaba made for Kūfa, but was forced to contend with the Umayyad garrison at Wāsiṭ, where he himself fell in August 749. His son al-Ḥasan now took command and proceeded to Kūfa, which was already in the midst of a Yamanī-led pro-ʿAbbāsid revolt, perhaps by prior arrangement. It was in this period, the early autumn of 749, that several members of the ʿAbbāsid family made their way to Kūfa. Among them was the man whom, it is said, Imām Ibrāhīm named as his successor: his brother Abū al-ʿAbbās. Although some members of the Hāshimiyya were reluctant to accept these claims, when Abū al-ʿAbbās was proclaimed caliph on 28 November 749 in the main mosque of Kūfa his opponents in the movement could do little but acquiesce, and thereby transformed the Hāshimī revolution into an ʿAbbāsid *coup d'état*.

Acquiescence was not an option for Marwān II, however. In al-Jazīra he was convinced to take to the field against a Khurāsānī army that had been sent to take Mosul, under the command of Abū al-ʿAbbās's uncle, ʿAbd Allāh ibn ʿAlī. Marwān's exhausted force of Syro-Jazīran troops had little hope against the Khurāsānī army under ʿAbd Allāh ibn ʿAlī and, in January 750, on the banks of a flooded tributary of the Tigris called the Greater Zāb, the last Umayyad caliph's army was broken, and Marwān fled. He fled first into Syria, where, after years of revolt, nearly every city closed what was left of their ruined gates to him. Passing through Palestine, he reached Egypt where, in August 750, ʿAbbāsid troops caught up with him at Būṣīr, where he had taken refuge in a

71 ʿAbd al-ʿAzīz al-Dūrī, 'al-Fikra al-mahdiyya bayna al-daʿwa al-ʿabbāsiyya wa-al-ʿaṣr al-ʿabbāsī al-awwal', in W. al-Qāḍī (ed.), *Studia arabica et islamica: Festschrift for Iḥsān ʿAbbās* (Beirut, 1981); H. Suermann, 'Notes concernant l'apocalypse copte de Daniel et la chute des Omayyades', *Parole de l'Orient*, 11 (1983).

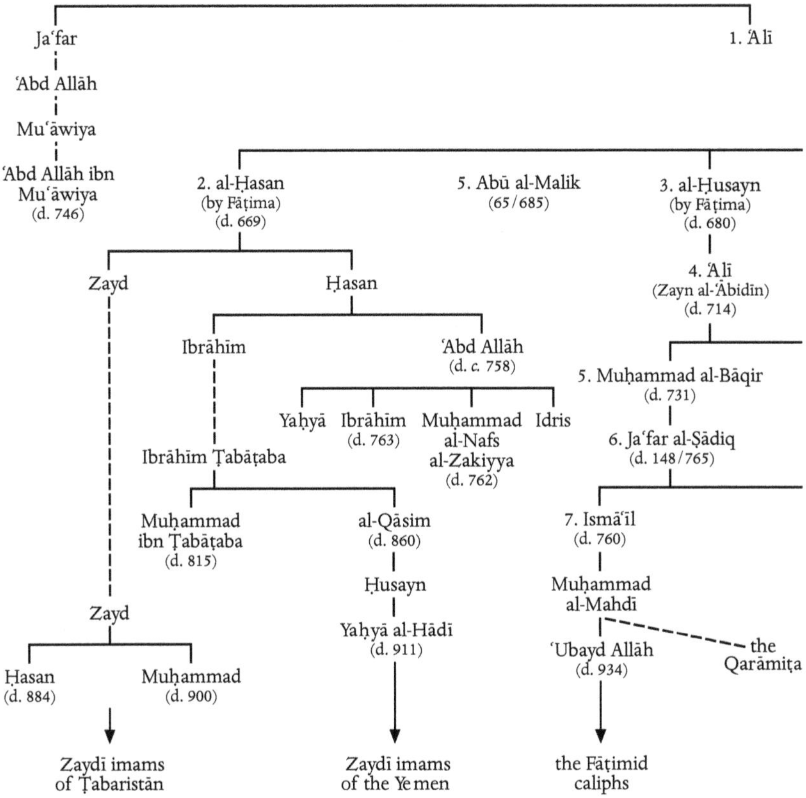

5. The Shi'ite imams.
After Ira M. Lapidus, *A history of Islamic societies*, 2nd edn, 2002, pp. 96f., fig. 4. Copyright Cambridge University Press, reproduced with permission.

church.[72] Although Marwān's men reportedly outnumbered his pursuers, in a short skirmish under cover of night, the Khurāsānīs prevailed. At first unrecognised in the midst of the mêlée, Marwān, a soldier to the end, was killed fighting alongside his men. Back in Syria, city after city surrendered almost without incident to 'Abd Allāh ibn 'Alī and his Khurāsānī troops. At Damascus, where Mu'āwiya had built his green-domed palace and al-Walīd I his sublime mosque, Yamanī townsmen enthusiastically opened the gates to an 'Abbāsid general bearing black banners from the east.

72 On the contested location of Būṣīr, see G. Wiet, 'Buṣīr', *EI2*, vol. I, p. 1343.

Conclusion: 750 and all that

If the ʿAbbāsids played a minor part in the planning and execution of the Hāshimiyya's activities and only later claimed a central, starring role, then the ʿAbbāsid revolution can only be said to be ʿAbbāsid in hindsight. But was it really a revolution? Even if the passing of authority from one branch of Qurashī caliphs to another hardly seems revolutionary, the question is about more than semantics. In considering the ʿAbbāsid dynasty's role in the passing of Syria's moment as the heart of empire we would do well to recall that the ʿAbbāsid revolution was, after all, merely the final fillip to an Umayyad civil war rooted in Syria, and to remember that, from a Syrian point of view, the battle for the caliphate was far from over even in 750.

Abū al-ʿAbbās (r. 749–54) staked his claim to be caliph with the suitably apocalyptic-tinged title al-Saffāḥ ('the blood-letter'), thanks to his role (rather exaggerated in the sources) in the massacre and collective desanguinisation of the Umayyad family. Yet even under a caliph whose name was so literally made in Umayyad misfortune, Syrians had varied options.[73] Many members of the Marwānid army, of course, simply surrendered, hoping for a continued future under the ʿAbbāsids. Others, however, were more pessimistic about their future under the new regime, and so continued to fight so long as there were suitable Umayyad claimants with good odds. Umayyad kinsmen with factional followings continued to fight throughout the reign of al-Saffāḥ, proof that the question of ʿAbbāsid sovereignty was still an open one. In Palestine, Damascus, Ḥimṣ, Qinnasrīn, Aleppo and on the Syrian frontier, garrisons fought behind members of the Umayyad family (Sufyānid and Marwānid) to stake their claims. In the end all of them were subdued by Khurāsānī armies.

That Syria could not yet be written off as a centre of power was amply demonstrated early in the reign of al-Saffāḥ's successor, his brother Abū Jaʿfar al-Manṣūr (r. 754–75). Al-Manṣūr's succession was disputed by his powerful uncle ʿAbd Allāh ibn ʿAlī, who was al-Saffāḥ's governor of Syria, and who claimed he had been named to succeed al-Saffāḥ in return for his duties in overthrowing Marwān II. To back up his claim he convinced prominent commanders of the Syro-Jazīran army to join with his Khurāsānī troops

73 On the reactions of Syrians and surviving Umayyads to the coming of the ʿAbbāsids and their diverse fates thereafter, see Cobb, *White banners*.

(i.e. the very men responsible for their downfall) and march with him to confront his upstart nephew in Iraq. In the end, thanks to dissension within his ranks, ʿAbd Allāh was defeated and al-Manṣūr was secure as caliph. The Syrians involved in the action sent a delegation to the new caliph, who pardoned them. From al-Manṣūr's time onward the Syro-Jazīran troops were assured a continued role in the new ʿAbbāsid empire, but it would be an increasingly limited one. Outside Spain (where a grandson of Hishām managed to flee and set up his own caliphate) the descendants of the Umayyad dynasts who survived the unpleasantness of 750 settled in as courtiers and comfortable, if not privileged, members of ʿAbbāsid society.[74]

From the early eighth century and, arguably, even before, the region of Syria and its populace broke from its prevailing historical role as a province of empire and became instead the heartland of a burgeoning Umayyad caliphate, making manifest what had been only a potential future created by the reforms of ʿAbd al-Malik. Syria's rise to prominence was made possible principally for one reason: it was Syria's tribal armies that manned the machinery of Marwānid imperium. As a result, Syria became a clearing-house for commerce and tribute from France to Farghāna and, as such, Syria suited the ruling dynasty. As much as Umayyad elites lived and served throughout the caliphate, only Syria offered the dynasty room for its penchant for settlement, frontier warfare, urban consumption and the pastimes of the steppe. But it was the Syrians, not the Umayyads, who elevated the region. For, as we have seen, Syria's peculiar imperial moment ended not when Marwān II was cut down in 750, but only when al-Manṣūr, who would root his empire in Baghdad, accorded the Syrians an honourable but circumscribed place in the new regime. In so doing, he ensured that when the Syrians revolted it would be not to overturn the ʿAbbāsid state, but to grumble over better treatment within it, and that when surviving Umayyads revolted in Syria they did so not as caliphal rivals, but as bandits, messiahs and madmen.

The revolutionary deed of the ʿAbbāsids in these events was therefore not so much in replacing the Umayyads, for there is little in ʿAbbāsid statecraft that is not recognisably Marwānid in precedent, but in providing answers to some of the problems that the Marwānid experiment posed and by meeting the needs of a growing populace that was increasingly Muslim and increasingly non-Arab. The Umayyads never stopped depicting themselves as God's

74 Specific cases of Umayyad elites in ʿAbbāsid times have been studied in Amikam Elad, 'Aspects of the transition from the Umayyad to the ʿAbbāsid caliphate', *JSAI*, 19 (1995). On the second Umayyad caliphate of Spain, see chapter 14.

caliphs and as figures of immense Islamic sacrality.[75] But they could never avoid the fact that they were Islamic rulers who came to power when being Muslim was almost identical with being Arab, and they simply could not – or would not – provide legitimacy to the newfangled political unity required in the 740s. With its origins as an Arab kingdom in a practical sense, the Umayyad state fell short of a caliphate in a symbolic sense. It was symbolism of what was viewed as Islamic rule as opposed to Arab rule that the ʿAbbāsids, as members of the sacred lineage of the Prophet, backed by their devoted Khurāsāni troops and 'Sons of the Revolution', could provide, and it is this that stands as their earliest and most durable achievement.

75 Wadād al-Qāḍī, 'The religious foundation of late Umayyad ideology and practice', in *Saber religioso y poder político en el Islam: Actas del simposio internacional (Granada, 15–18 octubre 1991)* (Madrid, 1994).

7

The empire in Iraq, 763–861

TAYEB EL-HIBRI

The consolidation of power

Although the Umayyad dynasty fell rapidly in the face of the Hāshimite–Khurāsānī revolution in 132/750, the ʿAbbāsid dynasty's hold on power took until 145/762 to become firmly established. The second ʿAbbāsid caliph, Abū Jaʿfar al-Manṣūr (r. 136–58/754–75), rightly recognised by historians as the real founder of the ʿAbbāsid state, was well aware, immediately after his accession to power, that he had to subdue a range of the revolution's heroes if the caliphate was to remain in his family line. His first political move in 754 was to force the allegiance of his uncle, ʿAbd Allāh ibn ʿAlī, thereby redefining the hierarchy within the ʿAbbāsid house. This step was quickly followed by the overthrow of Abū Muslim al-Khurāsānī. In spite of his outward loyalty to the Hāshimite family, Abū Muslim commanded popular support in Khurāsān as an Iranian political leader, and to some he resembled a messianic figure. The latter aspect became apparent only after his downfall, when a series of rural rebellions, collectively known as the 'Abū Muslimiyya' revolts, sprang up in Khurāsān, challenging ʿAbbāsid rule. Although these heterodox (*ghulāt*) rebels did not seriously threaten the ʿAbbāsid state, they did point to both the lingering hope for an Iranian revival and a syncretistic belief in continuous prophecy, which at that juncture included such beliefs as Abū Muslim's occultation, reincarnation and future return.[1]

By far the greatest potential threat that al-Manṣūr expected, however, came from the ʿAlid branch of the Hāshimite family, which had the closest kin ties to the Prophet, and was thus viewed by Hāshimite sympathisers as the most legitimate inheritor of the caliphate. The ʿAbbāsids had long sensed the prestige of the ʿAlid imams, and contented themselves during the propaganda

1 E. Daniel, *The political and social history of Khurasan under Abbasid rule, 747–820* (Minneapolis and Chicago, 1979), pp. 125–47.

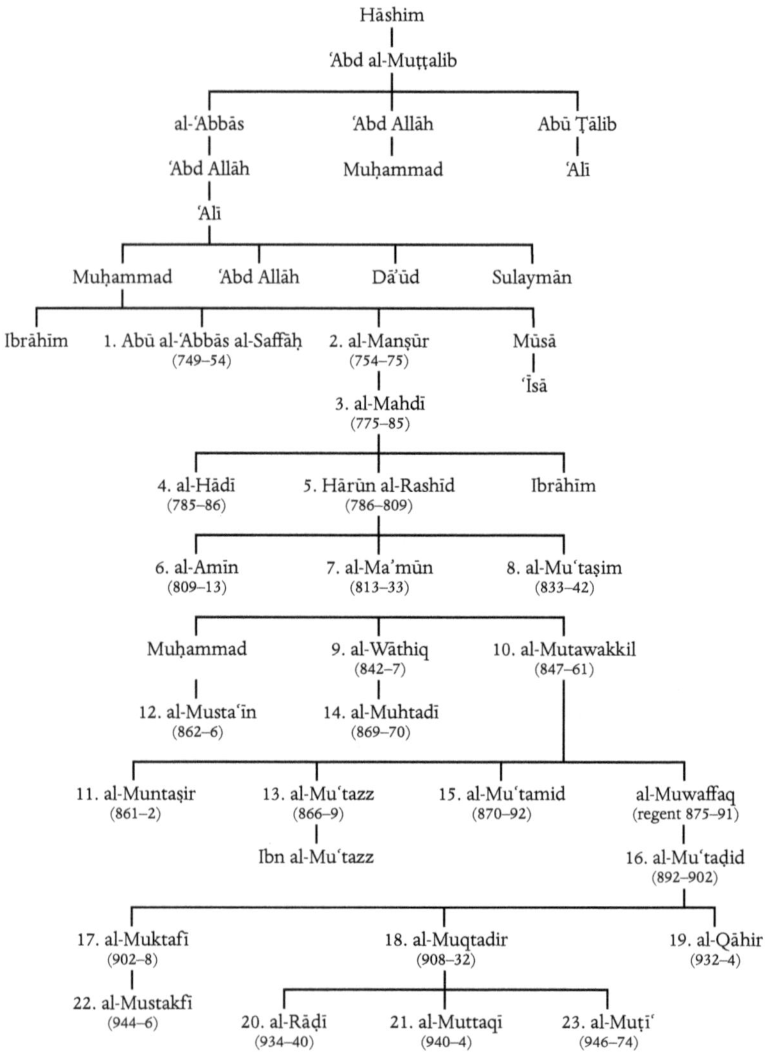

6. The ʿAbbāsids.
After Ira M. Lapidus, *A history of Islamic societies*, 2nd edn, 2002, p. 55, fig. 3. Copyright Cambridge University Press, reproduced with permission.

phase of the revolution with generalising the aim of the anti-Umayyad opposition for a Hāshimite leader rather than specifying a candidate branch for the caliphate (whether ʿAbbāsid or ʿAlid). The name of the 'Hāshimiyya' movement reflected this by pointing to the wider Banu Hāshim clan, thereby allowing the ʿAbbāsids to share with the ʿAlids the image of religious mystique and pretension to esoteric religious knowledge. Meanwhile, the leadership objective of the revolution was also kept general in the slogan that called for eventual rule by 'the one agreed upon or satisfactory from the family of Muḥammad' (*al-riḍā min āl-Muḥammad*).[2]

The main ʿAlid challenger to al-Manṣūr was Muḥammad al-Nafs al-Zakiyya, an illustrious scion to the Ḥasanid branch of the ʿAlid family, who was born the year the *daʿwa* began and was surrounded with a measure of reverence in the wider clan, such that some reports assert that he was given a *bayʿa* in Medina by the leading Hāshimites during the early phase of the *daʿwa*. Whatever the truth behind his claims, Muḥammad al-Nafs al-Zakiyya seems to have garnered enough support to declare his rebellion in 145/762 not only in Medina, but also in Baṣra, where an uprising was led by his brother Ibrāhīm ibn ʿAbd Allāh, and was to find support in traditionalist religious circles that included the renowned scholars Mālik ibn Anas and Abū Ḥanīfa as sympathisers. An exchange of letters between caliph and pretender before the outbreak of conflict may have been significantly embellished in the chronicle of al-Ṭabarī, but it sufficiently summarises the crux of the competing arguments between the two Hāshimite branches. Muḥammad al-Nafs al-Zakiyya stressed the primacy of his direct descent from Fāṭima, the Prophet's daughter, while al-Manṣūr pointed to pre-Islamic patriarchal tradition that stressed the priority of the uncle – in this case al-ʿAbbās – inheriting from a man who left no male offspring. The ʿAlid rebel also stressed that his campaign was a return to the simple society and government of early Islam, in contrast to the imperialistic – even heretical – pretensions of the new caliph.

While the ʿAlids were in full command of the rhetoric of opposition and sentimental memory, the ʿAbbāsids ultimately controlled the battlefield and strategic policies. In spite of its important religious symbolism, Medina was a non-strategic centre for rebellion, a fact that quickly became evident when al-Manṣūr disrupted the grain supplies from Egypt on which the Ḥijāz depended. The second rebellion in Baṣra, led by Ibrāhīm ibn ʿAbd Allāh, met with greater success, but even there the ʿAlids stood no chance against al-Manṣūr's ability to muster troops from Khurāsān. Matters were further complicated for the ʿAlids by division within their family, reflected by the lack of support from

2 P. Crone, 'On the meaning of the ʿAbbāsid call to al-Riḍā', in C. E. Bosworth *et al.* (eds.), *The classical and medieval Islamic world: Essays in honor of Bernard Lewis* (Princeton, 1990), pp. 98–9.

Jaʿfar al-Ṣādiq and much of the Ḥusaynid branch of the ʿAlids for what was largely viewed as the Ḥasanid rebellion of Muḥammad al-Nafs al-Zakiyya.

Although the rebellion did not last long, it did signal the beginning of a new phase of rivalry between the ʿAlid imams and the ʿAbbāsids, which would erupt intermittently over the next century, even while the caliphs tried to bring it under control through a mix of coaxing and coercive policies. The ʿAlid revolt of 145/762 did also have the important effect of influencing some changes in religious attitudes and policies. Sunnī religious scholars, for example, who had previously supported al-Nafs al-Zakiyya's political bid, thereafter renounced millennial activism altogether in favour of political quietism, and began distancing themselves from the ʿAlid cause as a sectarian Shīʿite movement. Also at around the same time, the ʿAbbāsid caliphs, probably reacting to the resonance of the ʿAlid claim for the imamate, began cultivating their own rival conception of an ʿAbbāsid imamate, which centred on the caliphs and had its own claims for ideas of *ʿilm* (gnosis), *wasiyya* (official succession designation) and reference to early Hāshimite (ʿAbbāsid) patriarchs.

The foundation of Baghdad

Having consolidated his political leadership against his two main rivals, the ʿAlids and the Persian sympathisers of Abū Muslim, al-Manṣūr set about laying the foundations of the new ʿAbbāsid state, the most prominent signal of which was the establishment of a new capital: Baghdad, or Madīnat al-Salām (the city of peace), as it was known in its time. After initial experiments to establish a capital named 'al-Hāshimiyya' in the environs of Kūfa, al-Manṣūr finally decided on a location for the new capital in the heart of Mesopotamia, at the point where the Tigris and Euphrates rivers came closest, some fifteen miles north of the former Sasanid capital of Ctesiphon. Baghdad was meant to be the fortress of the new dynasty in times of crisis, as well as a strategically situated city in times of peace in economic and political terms. Its river surroundings permitted rapid communication with distant provinces of the empire through the Persian Gulf, and its central location made it a vital link for merchant traffic between Syria and Iran. Later medieval geographers, such as al-Yaʿqūbī (d. 284/897) and Ibn Khurdādhbeh (d. 272/885), marvelled not only at the wealth of the city's markets, but also at its ideal climate, which they related to the brilliance and good nature of its people.

The foundation of Baghdad did more than provide control over the wealthiest agricultural province of the empire and facilitate tax collection; it provided the ʿAbbāsids with a new space for inventing their own political mythology and religious pretensions. The original kernel of the city, founded in 145/762, was the Round City of Baghdad, which housed the adjoining complex of the caliph's palace and mosque at its centre and was lined around its perimeter with the military barracks of the ʿAbbāsid troops and administrative buildings. With its circular design, and the caliph's palace and mosque standing at its centre, the Round City was meant to mirror the cosmological disc of the heavens, while its four main gates (Kūfa, Baṣra, Khurāsān and Damascus) pointed towards the cardinal directions, symbolising the varied directions of ʿAbbāsid control. The overall message was clear: the caliph's authority was divinely sanctioned, and the new caliphate seemed to lay a universal claim of succession to previous Near Eastern empires. Astrologers predicted that no caliph would meet death while living in the Round City, and a free-turning statue towering over the palace pointed to where the caliph's enemies could come from next.

The new Islamic capital resonated with new ideological pretensions about the position of the ʿAbbāsid caliphs as imams and representatives of divine rule. Iranian notions about the divine right of kings were fused with Islamic messianic expectations centred on the family of the Prophet, or a utopian community ruler, to shape the ʿAbbāsid political institution. This mixture was best reflected in the messianic titles that various caliphs were given as successors even before they assumed caliphal authority. The caliphs ruled as blessed members of the Prophet's family, as guardians of the Islamic faith, and as just rulers who were faithful to the Persian monarchal ideal. The strength of the caliphal institution thus lay in its universality and ability to communicate different things to different subjects of the empire, an achievement that surpassed all the particular shades of previous Near Eastern empires.[3]

Within this milieu of competing religious expectations, al-Manṣūr crafted the path of his successor when he designated his son, Muḥammad, as heir to the throne and gave him the more formally suggestive title 'al-Mahdī' (the rightly guided one) in 141/758. At the time, al-Mahdī was just being readied to depart to Rayy to rule as viceroy of the eastern provinces and confront the challenges of the Khurāsānī rebellion (led by ʿAbd al-Jabbār al-Azdī). In that climate the title 'al-Mahdī' was clearly meant to bring a closure to all hopes of millennial change, both Arab and Iranian. Over the next decade al-Mahdī's governorship gave a certain stability to the ʿAbbāsid image in this context. His provincial capital, Rayy, was renamed 'al-Muḥammadiyya' in his honour, and

3 J. Lassner, *The shaping of ʿAbbāsid rule* (Princeton, 1980), pp. 169–75; C. Wendell, 'Baghdad: *Imago Mundi* and other foundation-lore', *IJMES*, 2 (1971).

the city's fortunes quickly grew in the second half of the eighth century, as it became both a trading hub for the Caspian region and a monetary centre that issued a volume of ʿAbbāsid coinage that rivalled Baghdad's.[4]

Aside from crafting the charismatic image of the new state, al-Manṣūr was a methodical planner of centralising policies, a quality that was reflected in his military and provincial organisation. While the institution of the vizierate had not yet assumed a significant role, a range of advisers (Abū Ayyūb al-Muryānī, Khālid ibn Barmak and al-Rabīʿ ibn Yūnus) helped facilitate policies planned by the caliph. Al-Manṣūr's primary reliance on the Khurāsānī troops who brought the ʿAbbāsids to power during the revolution remained his main policy. Various commanders who had formed the nucleus of lieutenants (*nuqabāʾ*) of the early revolutionary summons (*daʿwa*) now assumed leading roles as commanders (*quwwād*) in the new state, holding positions of governorship and heading important campaigns. The most prominent in this group included Khāzim ibn Khuzayma al-Tamīmī, Mālik ibn al-Haytham al-Khuzāʿī, Muḥammad ibn al-Ashʿath al-Khuzāʿī, Muʿādh ibn Muslim al-Dhuhlī, ʿUthmān ibn Nahīk al-ʿAkkī, al-Musayyab ibn Zuhayr al-Ḍabbī and kin relations of the famous Qaḥṭaba ibn Shabīb al-Ṭāʾī. This was a formidable circle of commanders, who commanded support both in their land of Arabian origin and in the Khurāsānī settlements they had inhabited in the late Umayyad period. The caliph often called on them in situations of crisis, and they invariably proved successful in defending the ʿAbbāsid cause. In honour of their role in founding the ʿAbbāsid regime, the caliphs bestowed on them the honorary title 'al-Abnāʾ,' an abbreviation of *abnāʾ al-daʿwa* or *abnāʾ al-dawla* ('the sons of the state') which gradually was applied to their descendants who served in a similar capacity as well. The Abnāʾ formed both a social and a military solidarity group drawn from the larger army of the Khurāsāniyya, and they became the crack troops of the caliphs for a period of half a century. Their unique identification with the historical moment of the revolution was only strengthened with their settlement in Baghdad and their acquisition of landed estates in Iraq (*qaṭāʾiʿ*).[5]

Another group that al-Manṣūr relied on extensively was the ʿAbbāsid family itself. Al-Manṣūr's succession coup, in which he claimed the succession for himself and his son at the expense of ʿAbd Allāh ibn ʿAlī, did not prevent him from relying on his other uncles to govern important provinces. These individuals often included Sulaymān ibn ʿAlī (in Baṣra), Ṣāliḥ ibn ʿAlī (Syria),

4 Thomas Noonan, 'The ʿAbbāsid mint output', *JESHO*, 29 (1986), pp. 150–3.
5 H. Kennedy, *The early Abbasid caliphate: A political history* (London, 1981), pp. 78–85.

Ismāʿīl ibn ʿAlī (Mosul) and ʿĪsā ibn Mūsā (in Kūfa). Their children often occupied government positions as well, albeit not necessarily in the same town or for a significant length of time. A key pattern of the early ʿAbbāsid state was that, whereas the Abnāʾ and the Khurāsānī commanders often served in distant provinces (al-Jibāl, Fārs, Khurāsān or North Africa), members of the ʿAbbāsid family took appointments in regions closer to Baghdad (Kūfa, Baṣra, Syria, Egypt and the Ḥijāz).[6] Ceremonial functions such as leading the pilgrimage caravan to Mecca were also entrusted to members of the ʿAbbāsid family.

Beyond these two groups of officials, al-Manṣūr tried to reach out to veteran commanders of the Umayyad period, including those who had once fought against him during the revolution. In this group one finds commanders such as Salm ibn Quṭayba ibn Muslim, Maʿn ibn Zāʾida al-Shaybānī and a slew of Muhallabī commanders (Sufyān ibn Muʿāwiya ibn Yazīd ibn al-Muhallab, governor of Baṣra; Rawḥ ibn Ḥātim ibn Qabīsa ibn al-Muhallab; Yazīd ibn Ḥātim al-Muhallabī; and Muḥammad ibn ʿAbbād). These commanders did not always thoroughly defend the ʿAbbāsid interest, such as in the wavering role Sufyān ibn Muʿāwiya assumed in Baṣra during the ʿAlid revolt of Ibrāhīm ibn ʿAbd Allāh, but al-Manṣūr seems to have been willing to forgive some lapses. It appears that, while religiously his propaganda addressed an eastern constituency, politically and militarily his focus was on the Arab tribal elite, even if this sometimes meant rehabilitating former Umayyad commanders.[7] This trend towards an accommodation with Syria was best reflected in 154/771, when al-Manṣūr ordered the building of the garrison city of al-Rāfiqa, modelled after Baghdad, adjacent to the town of al-Raqqa as the ʿAbbāsid base in Syria. Al-Raqqa and Rāfiqa would quickly surpass Damascus as the largest urban centre in Syria, and Hārūn al-Rashīd would later choose al-Raqqa as his political centre and residence during the period 180–92/796–808.

There is less information about the economic organisation of the ʿAbbāsid empire in those decades than its political and military order. Iraq was the wealthiest province of the empire, and had been undergoing a process of agricultural development since the Umayyad period. Al-Manṣūr continued the practice of allocating various revenue-generating projects to his supporters;

6 D. Nicol, 'Early ʿAbbāsid administration in the central and eastern provinces, AH132–218/AD750–833', Ph.D. thesis, University of Washington (1979), pp. 208, 211, 271.

7 On the continuity in some governmental patterns from the Umayyad to the ʿAbbāsid period, see I. Bligh-Abramski, 'Evolution vs. revolution: Umayyad elements in the ʿAbbāsid regime 133/75–32–932', *Der Islam*, 65 (1988); A. Elad, 'Aspects of the transition from the Umayyad to the ʿAbbāsid caliphate', *JSAI*, 19 (1995).

however, this time the main share went to members of the ruling family. These were encouraged to reclaim lands in the marsh area (the territory known as al-Baṭāʾiḥ) for agricultural use, to develop irrigation in the area, and were granted commissions for canals initiated by the caliph in the region.[8] The tax regime in Iraq seems to have been flexible, and even light, favouring the continued satisfaction of the ruling elite over fiscal control from the central government. In a region that was historically the breeding-ground for ʿAlid rebellion, this policy was partly intended to sway political sympathies towards the ruling dynasty. Information about taxation in other provinces is not abundant, but anecdotal evidence from an important source such as al-Balādhurī's *Futūḥ al-buldān* also shows a trend of government flexibility whereby caliphs sometimes modified the taxation rate of particular towns upon petition from the populace.[9] This flexibility was to change in the reign of al-Maʾmūn, who demanded greater revenues from the provinces, and this resulted in famous rebellions, in Egypt in 217/832 and in some Iranian towns (at Qumm in 210/825).

Al-Manṣūr's image in the sources is that of a thoroughly authoritarian ruler, consistently centralising but never arbitrary. He is said to have compared himself with the Umayyad caliph ʿAbd al-Malik ibn Marwān as a consolidator of caliphal power, and he probably went further in keeping track of his governors' policies through a network of provincial agents (*ṣāḥib al-khabar*), although this may well be exaggerated as a political exemplum in the sources.[10] Various accounts also give a vivid picture of al-Manṣūr's pragmatism and his parsimony, which built the ʿAbbāsid treasury. When he decided to build a wall enclosure and a moat around Kūfa, he reportedly offered residents of the town, who participated in the project, five *dirhams* each before the work began. But then, using this to establish a population census, he later ordered that each resident of the town be taxed forty *dirhams*.[11] Poets and courtly visitors found little patronage at al-Manṣūr's court, but he left behind a rich

8 Aḥmad ibn Yaḥyā Balādhurī, *Futūḥ al-buldān*, ed. S. al-Munajjid, 3 vols. (Cairo, 1957), vol. I, pp. 445, 451, 453–4; Michael Morony, 'Landholding and social change: Lower al-ʿIrāq in the early Islamic period', in Tarif Khalidi (ed.), *Land tenure and social transformation in the Middle East* (Beirut, 1984).

9 This happened mainly during the reign of al-Rashīd: Balādhurī, *Futūḥ al-buldān*, vol. I, p. 182, vol. II, p. 456: Qudāma ibn Jaʿfar, *Kitāb al-kharāj wa ṣināʿat al-kitāba*, ed. M. H. al-Zubaydi (Baghdad, 1981), p. 377; Yāqūt al-Ḥamawī, *Muʿjam al-buldān*, 5 vols. (Beirut, 1957), vol. IV, p. 343.

10 A similar policy of monitoring governors is attributed to ʿUmar ibn al-Khaṭṭāb earlier: al-Jāḥiẓ (attrib.), *Kitāb al-tāj fī akhlāq al-mulūk*, ed. A. Zaki (Cairo, 1914) p. 168.

11 Abū Jaʿfar Muḥammad ibn Jarīr al-Ṭabarī, *Taʾrīkh al-rusul waʾl-mulūk*, ed. M. J. de Goeje, 15 vols. in 3 series (Leiden, 1879–1901), series III, p. 374.

treasury and a stable empire for his successor. It was left to al-Mahdī to decide on a new direction in official policy.

Al-Mahdī, al-Hādī and al-Rashīd

Al-Mahdī's decade-long reign was by all accounts a prosperous time for the caliphate. Al-Manṣūr's efforts to build the name of the dynasty and its treasury allowed his successor to explore new paths for developing ʿAbbāsid authority, especially in the religious sphere and in foreign policy towards the Byzantines. Al-Mahdī's policies aimed at making the caliphate more popular with its subjects. He began his reign with an amnesty for political prisoners and established a high court that examined public grievances (*maẓālim*), and sought to lessen the tax burden in Iraq by establishing the system of *muqāsama*, a tax ratio that was established in proportion to the agricultural yield, in place of the existing fixed tax rate (*misāḥa*).[12] Messianic rebellions against the caliphate greatly diminished (especially from the ʿAlids, with whom the caliph established some measure of reconciliation), with the important exception of the Iranian revolt initiated in 159/776 by the famous 'veiled prophet' (al-Muqannaʿ). This revolt, which began in the town of Kish in Khurāsān, eventually spread to Samarqand, and lasted for three years before it was defeated, thus showing the continued resilience of the millennial message in the east.

Al-Mahdī's more immediate response after al-Muqannaʿ's revolt was to draw a clearer boundary between Islam and *zandaqa* (heresy),[13] as well as to foster a greater affinity between the caliphate and traditional Islam. Toward this effort, he invested heavily in the upkeep of Mecca, the pilgrimage road and charities associated with the *ḥajj*. In 161/778 he refurbished the Kaʿba (removing previous layers of veiling piled up since the time of Hishām ibn ʿAbd al-Malik), and undertook an expansion of its mosque that included the adding of significant decorative mosaics. He improved the pilgrimage road from Iraq to Mecca by building better travel stations along the way, lavished charities on the Meccan inhabitants, and in 166/782 added a postal network

12 The switch in tax regimes was in part due to reduced expectations of revenues from Iraq's agricultural lands after the area was affected by war in the last decades of Umayyad rule. The system of *muqāsama* also varied according to amount of cultivated land, irrigation methods being used, types of crops and proximity to the market: ʿAbd al-ʿAziz al-Duri, *al-ʿAṣr al-ʿAbbāsī al-awwal* (Baghdad, 1945), pp. 85, 204–6; R. Le Tourneau, 'Bayt al-Māl', *EI2*, vol. I, pp. 1141–9.

13 The charge of *zandaqa* had previously been applied by the Zoroastrians to the Manichaeans.

between Mecca, Medina and Yemen.[14] All this attention came in addition to the already established practice of the ʿAbbāsid caliphs of making frequent pilgrimage trips to Mecca (or assigning a member of the family to lead the ceremony in their place), as well as making occasional visits to Jerusalem and devoting resources to its preservation.[15] Al-Mahdī is noted for having completely rebuilt al-Aqṣā Mosque after it was damaged by an earthquake in 130/747.[16]

There was also from this period a greater turning at the ʿAbbāsid court towards the traditionist culture of *jamāʿī-sunnī* practices, dicta and customs of Medina. Sunnī Islam, as later generations came to know it from the canonical *ḥadīth* texts of the ninth century and the Ḥanbalī responses to the Muʿtazila, had not yet flowered, but the key trends of *jamāʿī* beliefs and practices, as well as the method for reasoning legal opinion, were already in place. Mālik ibn Anas (d. 179/795) and Abū Ḥanīfa (d. 150/767) were the two leading exponents of normative religious practice. The first contributed his classic compilation *al-Muwaṭṭaʾ*, which preserved the sayings and practices of the Prophet and the early Medinan community as a code of religious practice, and the second introduced the use of reasoned argument (*al-raʾy*) to adduce jurisprudential opinion. Unlike the Umayyads, the ʿAbbāsids displayed an interest in the activities of religious scholars and tried to have them serve in official capacities. Al-Manṣūr did not make much progress in this, but his successors, especially al-Rashīd, later did, and attracted a diverse circle of traditionalist scholars to their court.[17] Among these individuals were sages, such as ʿAbd Allāh ibn al-Mubārak (d. 181/797), Qurʾān scholars, such as al-Kisāʾī (d. 189/805), and jurists, such as Abū Yūsuf (d. 182/798), a student of Abū Ḥanīfa who became the chief *qāḍī* of Baghdad.

But perhaps the most public sign of the ʿAbbāsid rediscovery of Islamic symbols was the revival of the Arab–Byzantine *jihād*. Arab campaigns in Asia Minor, which had been a major pillar of Umayyad imperial expansion, had come to a halt during the period of the dynastic transition. In place of official

14 Al-Ṭabarī, *Taʾrīkh*, series III, p. 483. ʿIzz al-Dīn ʿAlī ibn Aḥmad ibn al-Athīr, *al-Kāmil fīʾl-taʾrīkh*, 13 vols. (Beirut, 1965–7), vol. VI, pp. 55, 76.

15 Al-Manṣūr had already introduced the custom of caliphal visits to Jerusalem, after his pilgrimage in 140/757, and al-Mahdī made a similar journey in 163/779. Al-Manṣūr also journeyed from Baghdad as far as Jerusalem in 154/771, accompanying the army of Yazīd ibn Ḥātim al-Muhallabī, which was heading to North Africa: Balādhurī, *Futūḥ al-buldān*, vol. I, p. 275.

16 Shams al-Dīn Muḥammad ibn Aḥmad al-Muqaddasī, *Aḥsan al-taqāsīm fī maʿrifat al-aqālim*, ed. M. J. de Goeje (Leiden, 1906), p. 168; R. W. Hamilton, *The structural history of the Aqsa Mosque* (Jerusalem, 1949), pp. 71–3.

17 Muhammad Q. Zaman, *Religion and politics under the early ʿAbbāsids: The emergence of the pro-Sunnī elite* (Leiden, 1997), pp. 147–62.

campaigns, during the early ʿAbbāsid period the frontier became open to local warlords, who were occasionally joined by religious volunteers who took up residence in improvised *ribāṭs* (frontier forts).[18] Starting with al-Mahdī, the caliphate began to reassert its presence in organising campaigns, which on occasion the caliph led in person, such as in 163/780, when he was accompanied by his twenty-year-old son Hārūn. Two years later Hārūn was put in command of his own army, which mounted a daring expedition that reached as far as the coastline opposite Constantinople and forced the Byzantine empress Irene to pay a heavy tribute of 160,000 *dīnārs* for the next three years.[19] It was probably in light of Hārūn's savvy strategy in this campaign that he was given the title 'al-Rashīd' the following year and designated as second successor, after al-Hādī.

Al-Mahdī's attention to the Arab–Byzantine conflict formed a major pillar in his religious propaganda on behalf of the caliphate. These expeditions set in place the image of the '*ghāzī*-caliph' who was resuming the unfinished mission of the early Islamic conquests, and reviving the potential for conquering Constantinople. Aside from its religious significance, the increased ʿAbbāsid attention to the Byzantine frontier underscored the policy of restoring a military role for former tribal sources of support in Syria. As such, the Byzantine front helped bridge differences between the Iraqi and Syrian military elite, and the situation was reinforced in a new administrative context when in 189/805 al-Rashīd established the new frontier province of al-ʿAwāṣim, which ran along the southern side of the Taurus mountains in northern Syria. The new unit was placed under the leadership of a prominent member of the ʿAbbāsid house, Hārūn's nominee for the third succession, al-Muʾtaman, who from then on became responsible for commanding annual raids, supervising conscription and ransoming prisoners of war.

Al-Mahdī died suddenly in 169/785 – from eating a poisoned pear, according to one account, or in a hunting accident, according to another. The sources give little biographical information about him in comparison with al-Manṣūr or al-Rashīd, which may indicate a redaction in the extant early medieval chronicles from a once-larger collection of narratives. Al-Mahdī was succeeded by al-Hādī, who ruled for one year and died in mysterious circumstances. The main event of his reign was another attempt at revolt by an ʿAlid leader from the Ḥasanid line, al-Ḥusayn ibn ʿAlī, who chose Mecca as his base

18 Michael Bonner, 'Some observations concerning the early development of jihād on the Arab–Byzantine frontier', *SI*, 75 (1992), p. 30.

19 Warren Treadgold, *The Byzantine revival 780–842* (Stanford, 1988), pp. 67–70.

this time. The revolt was a dismal failure and ended with the tragic death of its leader, which the caliph reportedly deeply regretted and claimed had happened against his will. A more important result of this rebellion was the escape of two of al-Ḥusayn's ʿAlid supporters, Idrīs ibn ʿAbd Allāh and Yaḥyā ibn ʿAbd Allāh, brothers of Muḥammad al-Nafs al-Zakiyya, to distant provinces where they set up ʿAlid bases away from ʿAbbāsid control. Idrīs fled to the Maghrib, where he succeeded in rallying Berber support in establishing the first ʿAlid dynasty in Islamic history, while Yaḥyā fled to Daylam, where he found refuge with Persian princes of the area before he was captured during al-Rashīd's reign.

When the ʿAbbāsid succession passed on to Hārūn al-Rashīd, it was finally the anticipated moment which different factions wanted. The ʿAbbāsid family, the Barmakid viziers and the army had all favoured al-Rashīd for his achievements in al-Mahdī's time, and he appeared ready to take the ʿAbbāsid state to a new height. While al-Manṣūr had established the concept of the ʿAbbāsid caliphate, it was Hārūn al-Rashīd who came to establish the character of its monarchy. His relatively long (twenty-three-year) rule helped institutionalise the image of the ʿAbbāsid court at home and abroad. Through numerous anecdotal accounts set during his reign, the medieval sources describe patterns of courtly order and ceremony that were surely new to the caliphate and that probably reflected a revival of Persian Sasanid principles of a ruler's behaviour and conduct.

The ʿAbbāsids went even further than the Umayyads in announcing their political absolutism and its religious foundation, claiming titles such as 'imam' and 'God's caliph' (especially from al-Maʾmūn's time onwards). But whereas Umayyad absolutism was characterised negatively by Islamic texts as *mulk* (kingship), the ʿAbbāsids were accommodated by *jamāʿī-sunnī* writers, mainly because the new caliphs postured as guardians of Islamic law and ritual. More than any previous caliph, al-Rashīd cultivated a public image of piety, often leading the pilgrimage to Mecca and just as frequently leading an expedition across the Byzantine frontier. Following al-Mahdī's policy, he established generous endowments at Mecca and Medina, and he went further by welcoming a range of *ḥadīth* and *fiqh* scholars and ascetics at his court.[20] Al-Rashīd's

20 Hārūn's times in general were a period when important religious sciences were undergoing critical systematisation and contributing to the shaping of orthodox principles. After an earlier generation of mentors, such as Abū Ḥanīfa, Mālik ibn Anas and Ibn Isḥāq, a diverse cadre of successors contributed to the shaping of detail in the grammar and message of the Islamic text. This included the jurist Shāfiʿī (d. 204/819); Abū Ḥanīfa's student Muḥammad ibn al-Ḥasan al-Shaybānī (d. 189/804), the grammarians al-Khalīl ibn Aḥmad al-Farāhīdī (d. 175/791) and Sībawayhi (d. 183/799), and Qurʾān reciters such as Warsh (d. 197/812) and Ḥafṣ (d. 189/805).

wife, Zubayda, also earns a wide reputation in the sources for funding the construction of the water stations (the famous Darb Zubayda) between Kūfa and Mecca, to facilitate the *ḥajj* journey and bring water to pilgrims in Mecca.

On the international stage, Hārūn also devoted considerable effort to projecting an image of ʿAbbāsid power. The story of Charlemagne's embassies to Baghdad in 797 and 802, and the arrival of envoys from the caliph in Aachen, is well known from Western medieval sources and, although never mentioned in the Arabic chronicles, does seem historically genuine.[21] The aim of these ties was primarily to build on the mutual hostility of the two leaders to the Spanish–Umayyad emirate in Cordoba and the Byzantine empress Irene and her successor, Nicephorus. In studying ʿAbbāsid–Carolingian relations, F. W. Buckler has argued that at a crucial moment, around 803, with simultaneous pressures on the Byzantine empire in Venice and the Dalmatian region as well as in Asia Minor, Nicephorus was forced to recognise Charlemagne as emperor in the west.[22] Even more important to ʿAbbāsid foreign policy were relations with the Khazar kingdom, situated north of the Caucasus. The Khazars, a people of mixed Altaic and Turkic background, had generally harboured a pro-Byzantine policy. They had helped them turn back the tide of Sasanid conquest in the reign of Heraclius (610–41), and were later to intervene in similar contexts (their invasion of the Caucasus in 183/799 helped distract al-Rashīd from his campaign against the Byzantines). Al-Manṣūr had tried to improve relations with the Khazars in 760 when he ordered his governor of Armenia, Yazīd ibn Usayd al-Sulamī, to betroth himself to the daughter of the Khazar *khāqān*, but an alliance failed to materialise after the accidental death of the Khazar princess, which led to the initiation of raids against the caliphate. Al-Rashīd seems to have also tried, albeit unsuccessfully, to improve ties with the Khazars.[23]

In internal government, an important innovation by al-Rashīd was to develop the powers of the vizierate, which promoted a new class of bureaucrats (the *kuttāb*), who mediated political control in the provinces. Among the *kuttāb*, the Barmakid family rose to unprecedented prominence for a period of nearly two decades. Khālid ibn Barmak, the family's chief representative during the revolution, was a trusted adviser to the caliph al-Manṣūr, but it was in Hārūn's time that the fortunes of Khalid's son, Yaḥyā, and grandsons,

21 Among the well-known Western accounts of these embassies are those by Einhard and Notker Stammerer, *Two lives of Charlemagne*, trans. L. Thorpe (Penguin, 1969), pp. 70, 145–9.

22 F. W. Buckler, *Harunu'l-Rashid and Charles the Great* (Cambridge, MA, 1931), p. 27.

23 W. Barthold and P. Golden, 'Khazars', *EI2*, vol. IV, pp. 1172–8.

al-Faḍl and Jaʿfar, became increasingly dominant. The ʿAbbāsids had probably long appreciated the elite Persian roots of the Barmakid family, as former priests of the Buddhist temple of Balkh, and their ties with princely families in Khurāsān, and tried to establish a closer link with them through a milk brotherhood, which was repeated in two generations such that it made Hārūn al-Rashīd and al-Faḍl ibn Yaḥyā milk brothers, and Yaḥyā a kind of foster parent for the caliph.

During their tenure as viziers the Barmakids succeeded not only in reducing Iranian revolts, but also in garnering a more realistic share of Khurāsān's tax revenues for the central government, and were able to defuse ʿAlid revolts as well. It was clear that Hārūn relied on the Barmakids to give an Iranian character to the caliphate in the east, and that through the vizierate he sought to project an image of partnership between the Arab and Iranian elements in ruling the empire.[24] The energetic Barmakids played a key role in making this equilibrium between east and west work, and it seems they may have pushed to translate it to the sphere of dynastic succession as well. After designating his son al-Amīn to the caliphal succession in 175/791, Hārūn assigned al-Maʾmūn as second successor in 183/799. The maternal ties of the two successors were influential in these decisions, since al-Amīn was born to Zubayda and her illustrious Arab line of descent from al-Manṣūr, while al-Maʾmūn was the son of a Persian concubine from the region of Bādhghīs. Selecting a second successor with Khurāsānī ties was clearly symbolically important for future government, and was undoubtedly an evolution of the policy of relying on the Barmakids. The culmination of this symbolic refinement of administration came in 186/802 with Hārūn's famous plan to 'divide' the empire between his two successors upon his death. Thus, while al-Amīn was to reign as caliph in Baghdad, he would rule effectively only in the western provinces (west of Iraq), while al-Maʾmūn would be the autonomous ruler of the eastern provinces until he succeeded al-Amīn, when he would reign as caliph over a reunited empire.

The details of this plan are described in a covenant of succession included in al-Ṭabarī's chronicle. There is, however, reason to doubt the full authenticity of this document, since it often sounds like an apologetic text written in the aftermath of the civil war to defend al-Maʾmūn's counterclaims against al-Amīn during the succession conflict in 195–8/811–13. The assertions in the

24 The story of the influential Barmakids remains mired in a mix of historical fact and literary legend. For a traditional survey of their prosperous career and sudden downfall from power in 187/803, see D. Sourdel, *Le vizirat abbaside de 749 à 936*, 2 vols. (Damascus, 1959–60), vol. I, pp. 127–81.

succession covenant of 186/802 about full independence for al-Ma'mūn in the east may well be an exaggeration of an earlier attempt by Hārūn to give al-Ma'mūn a position of governorship that would remain under the central rule of Baghdad. While keeping Khurāsān under the central rule of Baghdad, however, Hārūn did envisage a unique, new image for 'Abbāsid governorship in the east that would replace the crucial role previously played there by al-Faḍl ibn Yaḥyā.

Within a year of establishing the covenant of succession Hārūn ordered the sacking of the Barmakids. Whether the caliph believed that the 'Abbāsid dynasty had become self-sufficient with the new succession arrangement, and that the Barmakids had served their purpose of coopting the loyalty of the east, or whether he feared that this family of ministers had become too powerful, cannot easily be determined. However, the years that followed were marked by the return of 'Abbāsid government to the centralising policies of al-Manṣūr. The caliph now relied increasingly on the Abnā' to enforce provincial control. 'Alī ibn 'Īsā ibn Māhān, one of the more assertive members of the Abnā', though not their most experienced, was dispatched to Khurāsān to control the province. His policies alienated the population, however, and it did not take long before rebellion broke out. Provincial disaffection surfaced this time in the garb of a rebellion by the governor of Samarqand, Rāfi' ibn al-Layth, grandson of the last Umayyad governor in Khurāsān, Naṣr ibn Sayyār. Al-Rashīd's previous options, using the *quwwād* and the Barmakids, had now been exhausted, and he resorted to a new strategy altogether, which was to head to Khurāsān in person, accompanied by al-Ma'mūn. This was the first time a caliph had journeyed to Khurāsān, and the gesture was intended as much to introduce 'Abbāsid charismatic presence on the Khurāsānī arena as to subdue the challenge of Rāfi' ibn al-Layth. A chain of army command was established between the caliph in Ṭūs, al-Ma'mūn in Marw and the commander, Harthama ibn A'yan, in Samarqand.

Not long afterwards Hārūn died in Ṭūs from a lingering illness he had contracted before leaving Baghdad, and the stage was set for rivalry between his sons, al-Amīn in Baghdad and al-Ma'mūn in Marw. This ended the famous 'golden prime' of the 'Abbāsid caliphate. Hārūn's relatively stable reign became a reference point for nostalgia by later Muslim chroniclers who wrote after the civil war. For Sunnī writers his reign symbolised a time of harmony within the *jamā'a* before the onset of *fitna* (conflict), while for literary writers it represented the last days of a prosperous time. Religious writers saw in him a loyal champion of *ḥadīth*, unlike the innovative al-Ma'mūn, while literary writers depicted his court as the purveyor of massive wealth and patronage for poets and all those with talent. And yet, notwithstanding an element of myth, the prosperity of the caliph's time does appear to have been real. The archaeological evidence of pottery and numismatic finds outside the caliphate in the Baltic Sea region, the coast of East Africa and China point to a wide network of long-distance trade in which Baghdad stood as the most important metropolis.[25] The cooperative relation between the ʿAbbāsids and the Tang dynasty (r. 618–907) in China facilitated not only overland trade through Transoxania, but also helped establish a commercial presence for Muslim traders in the Indian Ocean, which contributed in time to the emergence of a Muslim community in South Asia.[26] In the absence of reliable literary accounts about al-Rashīd, the main image of the caliph remains the popular, romantic one of the *Thousand and one nights*. There, Hārūn remains the caliph who would journey the streets of Baghdad at night in disguise, accompanied by his minister Jaʿfar, mingling with the ordinary population in search of mystery and adventure while being attentive to his subjects' well-being.

The succession crisis

The formal agreement that Hārūn drafted between his two sons mainly established a line of first and second succession. This had become necessary, as previous political experience showed that a ruling caliph often tried to change the path of succession from a relative (often a brother) to his own son. Al-Manṣūr did this when he pushed away ʿĪsā ibn Mūsā from the succession in favour of al-Mahdī, and al-Hādī tried to do the same when he sought to place his son Jaʿfar ahead of al-Rashīd. The document of 186/802 helped to formalise the succession through covenants. However, the gubernatorial role given to al-Maʾmūn in the east, combined with the unrest in Khurāsān at the time of Hārūn's death in 193/809, made the situation open for ambitious contention. Almost immediately al-Maʾmūn became a political magnet for Iranian sympathisers (in place of Rāfiʿ ibn al-Layth), who saw in him a national representative against the central government. Meanwhile, al-Amīn's hasty attempt to

25 Richard Hodges and David Whitehouse, *Mohammed, Charlemagne and the origins of Europe: Archaeology and the Pirenne thesis* (Ithaca, 1983), p. 158.

26 Philip Curtin, *Cross-cultural trade in world history* (Cambridge, 1984), p. 107. G. Hourani, *Arab seafaring in the Indian Ocean in ancient and early medieval times* (Princeton, 1951), pp. 68–73. Remarkably, the most convenient path for trade between the caliphate and Europe through the Mediterranean was blocked by the Byzantine navy, which tried to thwart contacts between Charlemagne and the ʿAbbāsids.

exert a traditional centralising policy by recalling his brother from the east in favour of leaving the Abnāʾ commanders to handle the situation further strengthened the polarisation between al-Amīn and al-Maʾmūn.

Each side was advised by a capable minister who sought to protect a privilege or an ambition at the cost of war. Al-Faḍl ibn al-Rabīʿ, who had replaced the Barmakid family in the vizierate, strengthened the bias against Khurāsān by pushing to have al-Amīn drop al-Maʾmūn from the succession altogether, while in Khurāsān al-Faḍl ibn Sahl, a Khurāsānī aristocrat and a protégé of the Barmakids, urged al-Maʾmūn to remain in the east, and set about organising a local army under the command of Ṭāhir ibn al-Ḥusayn. Ṭāhir's family, although Iranian (from the town of Būshanj near Herat), had joined ʿAbbāsid service since the revolution, but they had been eclipsed by bigger stars among the Abnāʾ. Al-Maʾmūn thus represented to diverse groups (the Sahlids, the Farrkhusraws and the Ṭāhirids) an opportunity for changing the status quo. When al-Amīn finally summoned his brother to the capital and the latter refused, al-Amīn dropped al-Maʾmūn's name from coinage as successor in favour of his own son, Mūsā, 'al-Nāṭiq bi'l-Ḥaqq', and the situation became one of open war from 196/812 onwards.

During the next two years the succession conflict between al-Amīn and al-Maʾmūn translated into a myriad of regional conflicts across the Islamic empire as local leaders championed the cause of one ʿAbbāsid leader against the other. The central military confrontation between al-Amīn's armies, which were led by ʿAlī ibn ʿĪsā ibn Māhān, and al-Maʾmūn's troops, who were led by Ṭāhir ibn al-Ḥusayn, happened at the town of Rayy, where, after a clear victory, al-Maʾmūn's army advanced on to Baghdad in 198/813. After a siege that lasted over a year, al-Maʾmūn's forces finally broke through the defences of the city, and in the chaos that followed the caliph was captured and quickly put to death. This resolution must have gone against the strategy of al-Faḍl ibn Sahl, who then feared a backlash against al-Maʾmūn and sought to alleviate the crisis by transferring Ṭāhir to a relatively inferior military command in al-Jazīra soon afterwards. The regicide of al-Amīn was the first time that an ʿAbbāsid caliph had been violently overthrown, and this was something that no doubt shook the credibility of the ʿAbbāsid monarchal institution and altered how it was perceived by an Islamic and Persian public.

Far from providing stability, Ṭāhir's conquest of Baghdad triggered a new phase of turmoil, as local vigilante groups took control of the city and ousted the new governor of Iraq, al-Ḥasan ibn Sahl. A rebellion in southern Iraq on behalf of an ʿAlid imam, led by a former army commander Abu 'l-Sarāyā, further added to the chaos. Iraqi resentment was further enhanced by al-Ma'mūn's curious policies during the next four years. Instead of returning to Baghdad after his victory he remained in Marw after 198/813, and allowed al-Faḍl ibn Sahl a free hand in ruling the empire, after having bestowed on him the title of Dhu 'l-Riyāsatayn. To the Iraqi populace, attached to the primacy of their province in the empire, this was a subversive Iranian action, designed by the Sahlids to undermine the Arab caliphate. When al-Ma'mūn decided in 201/816 to enhance his religious authority by assuming the title 'God's caliph' and simultaneously nominating the ʿAlid imam ʿAlī ibn Mūsā al-Riḍā to the caliphal succession and changing the official colour of the ʿAbbāsid state from black to green, the Baghdadīs decided to respond by putting forward their own nominee for the caliphate, Ibrāhīm ibn al-Mahdī, and dismissed al-Ma'mūn as a prince manipulated by the Persians.

However, when the situation in Baghdad spiralled completely into chaos al-Ma'mūn's priorities now shifted to the west, and he resolved to return to Baghdad and reduce his partisan association with Khurāsān. His journey west, which took a whole year to complete, began conveniently with the death of ʿAlī ibn Mūsā al-Riḍā (who died poisoned in mysterious circumstances). Al-Ma'mūn's political rapprochement with the Baghdad opposition was helped even more when al-Faḍl ibn Sahl was assassinated soon after in the town of Sarakhs, again possibly at the caliph's instigation. He had been the architect of al-Ma'mūn's bid for power from the beginning, but had also come to be viewed as the reason for the ʿAbbāsid civil war, and had alienated both the Abnā' and his own Ṭāhirid military base. When the new caliph finally arrived in Baghdad in 204/819, all disturbances in the city subsided. The populace was now eager for a return to more peaceful days and for the restoration of Hārūn's legacy.

The age of reunification and transition (204–18/819–33)

When al-Ma'mūn began the new phase of his rule from Baghdad, only the eastern provinces of the empire were politically stable. Nearly all the others had lapsed, in varying degrees of autonomy, from ʿAbbāsid rule. Egypt had broken up into two districts ruled by competing commanders, ʿUbayd Allāh ibn al-Sariyy in the south and ʿAlī al-Jarawiyy in the north. Syria had fallen to local tribal rivalries in which a Qaysī strongman, ʿAbd Allāh ibn Bayhas, emerged as a leader. Al-Jazīra had fallen under the sway of another amibitious Qaysī chief, Naṣr ibn Shabath al-ʿUqaylī, while Yemen drifted under various ʿAlid rebellions, first led by Ibrāhīm ibn Mūsā ibn Jaʿfar al-Ṣādiq in 199–202/814–17, and later resumed by another ʿAlid rebel, ʿAbd al-Raḥmān ibn Aḥmad, in 206/821. Most dangerous of all was the heterodox movement of Bābak al-Khurramī, who, starting in 201/816, took control of the mountainous region of Azerbaijan and Armenia and declared an open war against Islam and Arab rule. Reunifying these diverse provinces demanded a kind of military force that was not available to al-Maʾmūn at that time, so for the next decade he used a mix of diplomacy and incremental conquest to restore his control of the empire.

The cornerstone of al-Maʾmūn's new government was a continued reliance on the Ṭāhirid family that had brought him to power. Now, under the command of ʿAbd Allāh ibn Ṭāhir, a new and more Iranian nucleus of the ʿAbbāsid army set about achieving provincial centralisation. After achieving reconciliation with the ʿAbbāsid family and granting amnesty to former opponents in Baghdad, al-Maʾmūn dispatched ʿAbd Allāh ibn Ṭāhir on the mission of reunification. This began first in 209/824 with a move north against Naṣr ibn Shabath, who was brought to submission after difficult negotiations, and the same ʿAbbāsid army then moved south-west into Syria, gaining the allegiance of Ibn Bayhas along the way, and then marched towards Egypt. Although the two Egyptian commanders were not directly hostile to al-Maʾmūn's leadership as caliph they were clearly interested in autonomy, and had succeeded in rebuffing an earlier army sent by al-Maʾmūn in 209/824, led by Khālid ibn Yazīd ibn Mazyad. ʿAbd Allāh ibn Ṭāhir must have shown a distinct military talent on his campaign, since through tactical manoeuvring and negotiation he was able to outmatch the two experienced governors. When he returned to Baghdad in 212/827 with news of the submission of Egypt, Ibn Ṭāhir was received with a parade and a hero's welcome, and was soon afterwards designated the new governor of Khurāsān, thus beginning the most prosperous phase of Ṭāhirid rule in the east (213–30/828–45).

The caliph's success in the west was not matched in the north, where a series of armies sent out against the Khurramiyya met with catastrophic failure. Several key ʿAbbāsid commanders of these campaigns were killed during these wars including, al-Sayyid ibn Anas, governor of Mosul, and Muḥammad ibn Ḥumayd al-Ṭūsī, governor of Azerbaijan. The persistence of the Khurramiyya revolt was partly due to their knowledge of the region's difficult terrain and their alliance with the Byzantines, but over time, and from the perspective of the central government in Baghdad, the situation provided a sharp reminder of the empire's shortage of military resources, which had reached a crisis point with the defeat of Muḥammad ibn Ḥumayd in 214/829.

It is therefore not a coincidence that the first significant appearance of the new Turkish slave military units – when Abū Isḥāq (al-Muʿtaṣim) is reported to have commanded an army of 4,000 Turkish troops – happened around this time.[27] This military development signalled a new strategy by al-Maʾmūn for dealing with the crisis on the northern front. The Ṭāhirids and the Sāmānids, while aware of the increased military demands of the caliphate, appear to have been reluctant to join in such intractable wars.[28]

At the same time that he sought to achieve political centralisation in the empire, the caliph also undertook other steps that reflected administrative changes. The most salient of these was perhaps the coinage reform for the empire, which changed both the fineness and the style of *dirhams* and *dīnārs*. In place of the varied inscriptions on Islamic coinage, which previously included names of local governors and officials as well as the caliph, al-Maʾmūn ordered the removal of all names, including his own, from the coinage. This trend towards anonymity was perhaps meant to simplify the test of political control in the provinces and the continuity of the minting process. A remarkable artistic feature of the new coinage was a marked refinement in the style of Arabic Kūfic script. This change in script mirrored accounts in the sources about the caliph's command to scribes and chanceries at around the same time, when he reportedly ordered an improvement in the styles of calligraphy. These monetary reforms came at a time when al-Maʾmūn was also reorganising tax assessments in Iraq and making some changes to systems of measuring the agricultural harvest.[29]

By 215/830 al-Maʾmūn had restored control over most of the empire, and essentially turned a new leaf in ʿAbbāsid government, moving away from the traditional system of al-Manṣūr and al-Rashīd. Provinces were now organised into larger administrative units than those that had prevailed before. The province of al-Jibāl, for instance, was now subsumed under Khurāsān, and smaller town governorships, such as Kūfa and Baṣra, were merged into Iraq. The principle of hereditary and family-centred gubernatorial appointment was introduced in provincial administration. The Ṭāhirids were the first and most prominent example of this new pattern of administration: Ṭāhir ibn al-Ḥusayn was appointed governor of Khurāsān in 205/820, and his family continued as governors in the province until 259/873. Their domain was vast (from the outskirts of Baghdad to the border of Transoxania), and they had control over

27 Muḥammad ibn Yūsuf al-Kindī, *Wulāt Miṣr*, ed. H. Nassar (Beirut, 1959), p. 212.

28 ʿAbd Allāh ibn Ṭāhir declined the offer to assume command of the war against the Khurramiyya in 212/827.

29 Al-Ṭabarī, *Taʾrīkh*, series III, p. 1039.

the tax revenues. They were also in charge of providing security in Baghdad, a task that would become even more important when the capital shifted to Sāmarrā'. The Persian identity of the Ṭāhirids greatly helped them to gain local political support. In cultural terms, however, they made every effort to identify with Arab culture, inviting eminent poets from Baghdad to come to their court and publicising their ancestral clientage to the tribe of Khuzāʿa (purportedly this began with the clientage of the family's ancestor, Ruzayq, to Ṭalḥa ibn ʿAbd Allāh al-Khuzāʿī, who was governor of Sīstān (62–4/681–3)). Khuzāʿa was especially important because in pre-Islamic times it had been considered a host and protector for the tribe of Quraysh; as such this helped enhance the symbolism of Ṭāhirid support for al-Ma'mūn.[30] Various strands in their image as just rulers, loyal governors to the caliph and their affinity to Arab culture were strengthened further by their religious policy, which favoured the *jamāʿī-sunnī*. As such, they succeeded in distancing themselves from the previous stigma of religious syncretism, especially in its messianic aspects, which had previously characterised – and often undermined – Iranian political movements in Khurāsān.

Across the Oxus river, the Sāmānids provided what proved to be an even more important example of family government, as al-Ma'mūn put various children of Asad ibn Sāmān-khudā (Nūḥ, Yaḥya and Aḥmad) in charge of the important provinces in Transoxania (Samarqand, Shāsh and Farghāna). The early history of the Sāmānids, when they first supported al-Ma'mūn's cause against Rāfiʿ ibn al-Layth, and later, during the civil war, is less known than that of the Ṭāhirids, but the key fact about them is that they had an aristocratic background – priestly, and probably princely as well – that resembled the background of the Barmakids. Unlike the Ṭāhirids, the Sāmānids identified strongly with Persian culture, even though they were also ardent Sunnīs who attracted *ḥadīth* scholars to their capital, Bukhārā, and essentially set the standard for the non-Arab Sunnī emirate. While the Ṭāhirids were in power the Sāmānids were dependent on their support, receiving investitures of governorate from Nīshāpūr rather than from Baghdad. The Sāmānids were not alone in their dependence on Ṭāhirid political approval. The same applied to Māzyār, the Iranian ruler of Ṭabaristān, and possibly to Afshīn in Ushrūsana. Accustomed to longstanding independence, particularly in Ushrūsana, which only cooperated with the caliphate during the governorate of al-Faḍl al-Barmakī, the two leaders would later rebel against al-Muʿtaṣim

30 C. E. Bosworth, 'The Ṭāhirids and Arabic culture', *JSS*, 14 (1969).

because of his insistence that they continue to report to the Ṭāhirid governor of Khurāsān.

With this reshaping of the provincial administration in favour of a new Iranian elite, al-Ma'mūn had essentially pushed aside the two key groups that had previously served as governors, the ʿAbbāsid family and the Abnāʾ. The power of the Abnāʾ was also deliberately reduced as a response to their previous support for al-Amīn. Their political influence, however, may have already been on the decline for some time, with their increasing attachment to their economic interests and landed estates in Iraq. Still, for all the loyalty of the eastern governors to al-Ma'mūn, the caliph gradually became wary of Baghdad's singular dependency on the Iranian political element, and to counterbalance this he presided over the organisation of two other wings of the military. The first of these was the newly created Turkish military slave corps, which was put under the direction of the future al-Muʿtaṣim, who became the caliph's viceroy in the western provinces of Syria and Egypt and a likely candidate for succession. And the second was the grouping of a tribal army under the direction of the caliph's son, al-ʿAbbās, who became the governor of al-Jazīra and was put in charge of organising campaigns against the Byzantines.

This new tripartite structure of the ʿAbbāsid army allowed the caliph to balance his diverse troops (Arab, Iranian and Turkish) and preserve the autonomy of caliphal decisions. With these and other administrative changes in place, al-Ma'mūn began to pursue a systematic strategy of confrontation with the Byzantine empire. The beginning of these hostilities can be dated to 215/830, when relations between the ʿAbbāsids and the Byzantines rapidly deteriorated. Byzantine attempts to restore their military pride in Asia Minor, along with ʿAbbāsid suspicion of Byzantine support for the revolt of the Khurramiyya, were key factors in igniting cross-border raids. Unlike previous caliphs, whose conflicts with Byzantines tended to stabilise after a momentous confrontation, such as al-Rashīd's conquest of Heraclea in 190/806, al-Ma'mūn showed a surprising determination to escalate the war to the extent of showing an ambition to subdue the entire empire. This can partly be gauged from the impossible conditions he put on Theophilus in 218/830 (that all his subjects convert to Islam or all, including the emperor, pay the poll-tax), and from the extra military recruitments the governors ordered in the regions of Syria, Jordan, Palestine, al-Jazīra, Baghdad and Egypt.[31]

31 Al-Ṭabarī, *Ta'rīkh*, series III, p. 1112; Abū Zakariyā Yazīd ibn Muḥammad al-Azdī, *Ta'rīkh al-Mawṣil*, ed. ʿAlī Ḥabība (Cairo 1967), pp. 410, 412.

For all its religious appearances, al-Ma'mūn's ambitious thrust against the Byzantines may have also had secular components that rested on a cultural and civilisational rivalry between Baghdad and Constantinople. Al-Ma'mūn was most famous among the caliphs for his interest in retrieving the classical heritage of the ancient Greeks from the Byzantines and for his patronage of the translation of classical texts. In his reign Iraq became renowned not only for gathering specialists in different fields, but also for synthesising knowledge from diverse cultures: Persia, India and the Byzantine domains. In the light of this, it is not unlikely that the caliph viewed his political ambitions in synchrony with his scientific ones, and considered regional dominance a catalyst for the acquisition of knowledge in various fields. Whatever his exact motives were, however, al-Ma'mūn's campaign ended with his sudden death after his armies had assembled in Tarsus. He was accompanied by his brother Abū Isḥāq (al-Muʿtaṣim) and his son al-ʿAbbās, and there are conflicting reports about whether the caliph had intended to transfer the succession to the throne from al-ʿAbbās to al-Muʿtaṣim, who in fact assumed the caliphal title soon after.

Intellectual life: the religious policy of al-Ma'mūn

Just as al-Ma'mūn's political achievements radically transformed the ʿAbbāsid government, his religious policies were equally new and daring. Unlike previous caliphs who had tried to ally themselves with existing systems of religious authority, al-Ma'mūn challenged *ḥadīth* and *fiqh* scholars directly. His adoption of the title *imām al-hudā* ('the guide to righteousness') in 195/811 and of 'God's caliph' in 201/816 gave an early sign of his ambition for a dominant religious authority. However, the more wide-ranging plan for religious influence surfaced later, when he showed favour for the Muʿtazilī religious movement over other traditional sects. The Muʿtazila school of speculative theology had branched off some time in the early ʿAbbāsid period from the rationally oriented approach to forming legal opinion, the *ahl al-ra'y*. Whereas the latter were concerned with practical juristic problems and solutions, however, the Muʿtazila debated sophisticated questions that dealt with the meaning of the divine word, the concept of divine justice, individual free will and predestination.[32] Al-Ma'mūn's first clear patronage of the Muʿtazila occurred in 212/827, when he proclaimed as official doctrine the Muʿtazilī creed concerning the 'createdness' of the Qur'ān.

32 M. Watt, *Islamic philosophy and theology* (Edinburgh, 1962), p. 42.

The idea of the createdness of the Qur'ān was a Muʿtazilī refinement of the traditional religious belief in the Qur'ān as the speech of God. This issue was controversial because it had a bearing on how orthodox belief ought to interpret the attributes of God, their eternity and the definition of an absolute monotheism. The Muʿtazilī logic behind the refinement considered that mere assertions about the Qur'ān as the speech of God risked making the word of God something that existed outside the frame of time and therefore co-eternal with the Creator. Philosophical belief in a Prime Mover demanded that all contingent events be viewed as created in time (*muḥdath*). *Ḥadīth* scholars, however, who were dubious about any discussion of revelation and prophecy in relation to philosophy and linguistic detail, rejected this interpretation and abided by the letter of the text without attempts at redefinition. The Qur'ān, to the traditionalists, was simply the 'Word' of God that cannot be characterised further.

When al-Ma'mūn first declared the official adoption of the createdness creed in 212/827, he remained tolerant of other *jamāʿī* opinions on this issue for a period of six years. During that time he experimented with other official declarations that had diverse religious implications, including declaring the superiority of ʿAlī's merits over those of other Companions of the Prophet, rejecting the merits of Muʿāwiya, adding the *takbīr* ritual after the prayer and prohibiting puritanical zealousness – as per the slogan *al-amr bi'l-maʿrūf wa'l-nahy ʿan al-munkar* (commanding right and forbidding wrong). Then, in 218/833, the caliph returned to the issue of the createdness creed when he decided to impose this interpretation, along with other Muʿtazilī opinions, on traditional *ḥadīth* scholars in a programme known as the *miḥna* (lit., 'ordeal' or 'inquisition').

Why the creed issue interested al-Ma'mūn to the point of making it official doctrine, and why the *ḥadīth* scholars stood so solidly against it, is still not clear. Although it may seem that, by contextualising the Qur'ān as 'created' in time, al-Ma'mūn was trying to override the text's authority, there is no evidence that the caliph was trying to override the authority of the Qur'ān as a source of religious law. Rather, the confrontation with the *ʿulamā'* probably related indirectly, but more importantly, to the authority of *ḥadīth*.[33] *Ḥadīth* had long been the primary field of specialty among traditionalists, who professed knowledge not only about the authority of *ḥadīth* content but also about those who narrated it. This exclusive exercise, which had grown to govern a variety of topics, including interpreting the law, Qur'ānic exegesis, and narrating an authoritative

33 M. Hinds, 'Miḥna', *EI2*, vol. VII, pp. 2–6.

version of early Islamic history (the *sīra* and biographies of the Companions), gave the *ʿulamāʾ* a religious authority that surpassed that of the caliph. The *miḥna* sought to change this by applying scrutiny to the content of selected examples of religious commentary: the createdness creed; the controversy over the attributes of God (the issue of *tashbīh*, anthropomorphism); the beatific vision; and stories about Final Judgement. The ensuing debates quickly showed that these issues needed *ḥadīth* to be interpreted in the way the *ʿulamāʾ* demanded, and it was in this sphere that al-Maʾmūn probably perceived the conflict to be truly happening. By forcing the *ʿulamāʾ* to abide by a new official policy, the caliph was making state approval (and the logical system that the Muʿtazila demanded) – and not the books of *ḥadīth* – the source of final authority. Had he succeeded in enforcing the case of the 'createdness creed', al-Maʾmūn would have been on his way to creating a formal religious hierarchy tied to the court that would have been instrumental in centralising the process of legal and theological interpretation in the empire.[34]

In some sense this was not the first attempt by the ʿAbbāsid state to centralise religious authority. As early as the reign of al-Manṣūr, the palace counsellor Ibn al-Muqaffaʿ had advised of the need for the caliph to codify a law for the empire that would eliminate provincial variations in religious custom and interpretative practices.[35] At the time (during the 750s) the concept of Medinan and Prophetic *sunna* was just beginning to gain popularity as an authoritative source of law alongside the Qurʾān. Al-Manṣūr's times, however, were still secure enough for the caliphate to maintain its religious authority on the basis of its connection to the Prophet's family. It was not until al-Maʾmūn's time that a caliph would attempt to define the system of religious authority in a new way. That he sought to achieve it on a philosophical ground only partly explains his failure to dominate prevailing currents of popular piety. More importantly perhaps, al-Maʾmūn's religious programme came too late. For, during the time he was in Khurāsān, a process of systematisation of legal and doctrinal principles had already been pioneered by Muḥammad ibn Idrīs al-Shāfiʿī (d. 204/819) in his famous *Risāla*, which established a synthesis between the two main currents of religious interpretation: the '*ḥadīth* folk' (*ahl al-ḥadīth*), who followed Prophetic sayings and established Medinan customs as precedents; and the group that favoured rationalist interpretation (*ahl al-raʾy*). This synthesis was to bridge different

34 John Nawas, 'A reexamination of three current explanations for al-Maʾmūn's introduction of the *miḥna*', *IJMES*, 26 (1994).

35 A. Lambton, *State and government in medieval Islam: An introduction to Islamic political theory* (Oxford, 1981), pp. 53–4.

regional religious cultures as well, since the *ḥadīth* method was predominant in the Ḥijāz, while the rationalist approach was predominant in Iraq. Shāfiʿī's contributions were of a wide-ranging scope, and he had essentially invented the science of Islamic jurisprudence (*fiqh*). His achievement strengthened the concept of *sunna* by associating it with *ḥadīth* sayings, universalised the legal authority of Medinan *sunna* to the exclusion of other customs attributed to the Companions in the provinces, and toned down the range of rationalist interpretation to something that needed to be grounded in the texts of the Qurʾān and the *ḥadīth* rather than drawing on other interpretations and customs. *Raʾy* therefore became more a matter of *qiyās* and *ijtihād* (interpretation through analogy and a limited degree of interpretation) that is grounded on a set basis of religious texts, rather than being a free exercise of rationalism and the incorporation of provincial customs that pre-dated the advent of Islam. And in the event of a remaining controversy among religious scholars on addressing a certain case, al-Shāfiʿī established the principle of *ijmāʿ*, a kind of collective agreement in the community on interpreting outstanding issues, and this ultimately meant a scholarly circle of *ḥadīth* and *fiqh* scholars.[36] With a system in place that favoured the *ḥadīth* text to the degree of giving it a near-infallible authority, it was no wonder that al-Maʾmūn would face overwhelming opposition.

Thus al-Maʾmūn's programme of imposing the Muʿtazilī interpretation was doomed to be unsuccessful. For about eight years various kinds of pressure were applied by al-Maʾmūn and his successors, al-Muʿtaṣim and al-Wāthiq, particularly in the western provinces of Iraq, Syria and Egypt, to make the *ʿulamāʾ* abide by the 'createdness creed'. Scholars who refused to follow the official doctrine were not allowed to serve in an official capacity as judges, prayer leaders or teachers; nor was their word in court testimony considered bona fide. In Egypt there are stories about some scholars being prevented from praying in the main mosque because they were in the opposition group.[37] The creed of the 'created Qurʾān' itself was given great publicity when al-Maʾmūn commanded that it be included in inscriptions at the entrances of some mosques.

In the end, however, the campaign not only failed, but also had a negative effect on the image of the caliphate as a source of religious authority and increased the popularity of *ḥadīth* scholars. It was not so much the arguments

36 N. J. Coulson, *A history of Islamic law* (Edinburgh, 1964), pp. 53–60.

37 Abū ʿUmar Muḥammad ibn Yūsuf al-Kindī, *Kitāb al-wulāt waʾl-quḍāt*, ed. R. Guest (Leiden and London, 1912), p. 446.

of the ʿ*ulamāʾ* that won them support as their principled stance against political authority and their seeming devotion to simple belief.[38] Aḥmad ibn Ḥanbal (d. 241/855), whose name later became a lightning-rod for traditionalist Islamic movements, became famous primarily as one of the few scholars who held out against the *miḥna* till the very end. When the caliph al-Mutawakkil finally decided to lift the *miḥna* in 233/848, the *ḥadīth* group emerged as a stronger and more cohesive network that commanded not just scholastic allegiance across the provinces, but the loyalty of a Baghdad commune as well. The Ḥanbalīs (named after Ibn Ḥanbal) became the spearhead of *jamāʿī-sunnī* Islam, resistant to mixing philosophy with religion, wary of the esoteric path of Sufism and hostile to Shīʿite Islam and to People of the Book. By the third quarter of the ninth century *ḥadīth* became more rigid than it had ever been, codified in canonical texts, and its authority was matched only in importance by the reputations of its narrators.

Al-Maʾmūn's reign can easily be misperceived as a time of decline in the fortunes of Islam, in light of the *miḥna* and the rise in provincial decentralisation in Khurāsān. In reality, however, his reign marks a watershed moment of growth in the social history of Islam, as it was a time of acceleration in the pace of conversion to Islam.[39] An entire period of religious rebellions in Khurāsān and Transoxania, which had been unknown in the Umayyad period but had littered the landscape of the early ʿAbbāsid period, came to an end with al-Maʾmūn's rise to power. The caliph's Persian identity, his long residence in Marw, his reliance on Khurāsān's local elites and his eventual tolerance for the autonomy of these groups were all factors that increasingly made Islam appear less the political emblem of outside conquerors and more the new domestic cultural identity. The Sahlids, Ṭāhirids, Sāmānids, Māzyār of Ṭabaristān and Afshīn of Ushrūsana were all groups and leaders who either converted to Islam in al-Maʾmūn's reign or brokered the dissemination of the traditional tenets of the faith while serving as governors. The effect of this was to make Islam the defining culture for political change and social mobility to a much greater extent than had been the case in the Umayyad or early ʿAbbāsid periods. In time this development represented a prelude to the emergence of autonomous provincial dynasties in the east, which would relate to the caliphal centre in nominal terms of loyalty only.

38 Michael Cooperson, *Classical Arabic biography: The heirs of the Prophet in the age of al-Maʾmūn* (Cambridge, 2000), p. 40.

39 Richard Bulliet, *Conversion to Islam in the medieval period: An essay in quantitative history* (Cambridge, MA, 1979), p. 47.

The caliphate at Sāmarrāʾ

Soon after al-Maʾmūn's death al-Muʿtaṣim seized control of the caliphate, called a halt to the invasion of Asia Minor, and returned to Baghdad. With the accession of al-Muʿtaṣim there began a clear and decisive shift in the political and military foundations of the empire towards a new regime that was militaristic and centred on the Turkish corps. Whereas al-Maʾmūn had created a coalition of Arab, Iranian and Turkic-Transoxanian troops that balanced one another, al-Muʿtaṣim relied almost exclusively on the newly recruited Turkish troops. The exact nature of his military power base is difficult to know precisely, and has been the subject of debate. Some of the new commanders who became his chief lieutenants were probably of aristocratic Transoxanian or Central Asian background, such as Afshīn, prince of Ushrūsana, Khāqān ʿUrṭūj and al-ʿAbbās ibn Bukhāra Khuda, who brought with them their personal military retinues (*chakars*). In these situations the loyalty of these troops to the caliph was mediated through a princely figure for some time before it became direct to the caliph.[40] The majority in the rank and file of the new army, however, were slave troops who were dispatched from beyond the Oxus river by the Sāmānid governor to al-Muʿtaṣim.[41] Little is known about these latter recruits, who are collectively labelled 'Turks', a term that referred to diverse people in a wide region stretching from the Khazar domain in the Caucasus to the Central Asian steppes. Be that as it may, al-Muʿtaṣim's Sāmarrān troops were both ethnically and linguistically – and probably for some time religiously – different from the mainstream of the Perso-Arab society of the empire, which created the first paradigm of a political rift between a ruling elite and Islamic society.

It was not long before al-Muʿtaṣim realised both the need for new quarters for his fledgling army and the problems the latter had in mixing with the Baghdad population. After considering places in the suburbs of Baghdad as locations for a new military encampment, he finally decided to reach further out. At a distance of some 60 miles north of Baghdad, and with enough good portents from astrologers and soothsayers, he decided to build his new capital of Sāmarrāʾ in a lightly settled area, mostly steppe land, on the eastern bank of the Tigris. The name of the capital probably derived from a more ancient toponym (*Souma* in Greek, *Sumere* in Latin), but soon a clever play on words in

40 C. I. Beckwith, 'Aspects of the early history of the Central Asian guard corps in Islam', *Archivum Eurasiae Medii Aevi*, 4 (1984), p. 39.
41 Matthew Gordon, *The breaking of a thousand swords: A history of the Turkish military community of Samarra (AH 200–275/815–889 CE)* (Albany, 2001), p. 8.

Arabic established its more widely famous name: Surra man Raʾā ('he who sees it is pleased').[42] For the next fifty years the new city not only became the centre of the empire, but also witnessed a rapid and astonishingly ambitious wave of construction. Sāmarrāʾ served not only the practical purpose of providing lodging for al-Muʿtaṣim's army, but, just as importantly, it enhanced the prestige of the ʿAbbāsid dynasty. The ruling authority was now set at a distance from the populace of Baghdad and protected by a new guard of foreign troops, and amid a new royal culture revolving around sprawling palatial grounds, public spectacle and a seemingly ceaseless quest for leisurely indulgence. The relationship between Sāmarrāʾ and the metropolis of Baghdad, as Oleg Grabar has noted, became like that between Versailles and Paris during the seventeenth and eighteenth centuries.[43] Different caliphs competed in building their own palaces. Al-Muʿtaṣim's al-Jawsaq, al-Wāthiq's Hārūnī and al-Mutawakkil's al-ʿArūs provide a few such examples – as does the occasional palace for an heir apparent, such as the palace of Bulkawara built for al-Muʿtazz. Eventually al-Mutawakkil, still unsatisfied, went on to build his own city, al-Jaʿfariyya (also known as Madīnat al-Mutawakkiliyya) to the north of Sāmarrāʾ.

Unlike in Baghdad, where the city began with the Round City and then developed around this nucleus, Sāmarrāʾ was laid out on a vertical plan along the east bank of the Tigris, which allowed more spacious development in a mostly grid street design. The key features of the new town included the separation of residential areas from the markets and the organisation of its military residents in a series of large cantonments. Under the ordinances of al-Muʿtaṣim these military personnel were not encouraged to mix with the local population. In addition, each community had its exclusive neighbourhood (the Turks, the Farāghina, the Shākiriyya and the Maghāriba), while more established commanders such as Afshīn, Ashnās and Khāqān ʿUrṭūj had their own *qaṭāʾiʿ* (large estates) and mansions. The city's grand mosque, built by al-Mutawakkil between 848 and 852, probably as a statement of his orthodox piety after the lifting of the *miḥna*, remains to this day something of a legend as the largest mosque in the Islamic world, with its massive dimensions (240 × 156 m), bastioned walls, and famous spiral minaret (the *malwiya*), reminiscent of ancient ziggurats at Babylon. The minaret rises to a height of 60 metres, and has thus far defied explanations of function. Sāmarrāʾ quickly came to influence provincial

42 Alastair Northedge, 'Samarra', *EI2* , vol. VIII, pp. 1039–41.
43 Oleg Grabar, *The formation of Islamic art* (New Haven, 1973), p. 166.

styles in architecture (the Mosque of Ibn Ṭūlūn in Egypt, for example, shows a similar design), and set a new artistic style and sensibility. A famous decorative pattern emerged in Sāmarrāʾ that favoured naturalistic representation, albeit in abstract terms (the so-called 'bevelled' style), which appeared in stucco building panels as well as in wooden doors, and glass design. This predominant pattern, however, did not entirely overshadow pictorial representation, which remained evident in interior palace murals.

In Sāmarrāʾ the greatest emphasis was placed on its palaces, which represented a distinct break in style from the famous Umayyad summer palaces. Here, al-Muʿtaṣim's palace of al-Jawsaq (also known as Dār al-Khilāfa) set the standard for the new designs and later Sāmarrān architecture. Whereas the Umayyad palaces tended to have a clear linear axis of courtly progression, along with adjoining apartments (at Mshatta and even Ukhayḍir), al-Jawsaq shows more complexity with its sprawling clusters of courts, gardens, public and private assembly rooms, and tunnels. The overall design showed a strong concern with security as much as an aesthetic that valued mystery. Outside, al-Jawsaq's palace grounds, covering an area of 71 hectares, boasted a range of space types, including review stands, hunting reserves, a polo maydan and various pools.[44] The caliphs were increasingly kept at a distance from the public, and the caliph's public appearances became carefully staged events. Whether it was al-Mutawakkil's trip to the mosque on a holiday festival or the event of announcing the designation of his three sons (al-Muntaṣir, al-Muʿtazz and al-Muʾayyad) for succession in 236/850, the court went to great effort and expense to mount a parade spectacle that went on for miles.[45]

In spite of their focus on Sāmarrāʾ, the concerns of the first three caliphs who built the city were very different. Al-Muʿtaṣim was a military personality, whereas his son al-Wāthiq was more concerned with literary matters, and seems to have been little interested in government.[46] Al-Muʿtaṣim tried to invest greater authority in the office of the chief judge, most notably Aḥmad ibn Abī Duʾād, in place of the vizierate, while al-Mutawakkil tried to consolidate more power with himself and dealt directly with the military. Perhaps

44 A. Northedge, 'The palaces of the ʿAbbāsids at Samarra', in C. F. Robinson (ed.), *A medieval Islamic city reconsidered: A multidisciplinary approach to Samarra*, Oxford Studies in Islamic Art 14 (Oxford, 2001).

45 Muḥammad ibn ʿAlī ibn al-ʿImrānī, *al-Inbāʾ fī taʾrīkh al-khulafāʾ*, ed. Q. al-Samarrāʾī (Leiden, 1973), pp. 117–18.

46 *Kitāb al-aghānī* preserves many anecdotes related to al-Wāthiq and his interests in poetry and song: Abūʾl-Faraj al-Iṣfahānī, *Kitāb al-aghānī*, ed. A. Muhanna, 27 vols. (Beirut, 1992), vol. IX, pp. 315–35.

the most important difference, however, was the reversal in caliphal religious policy that al-Mutawakkil introduced when he abandoned the pro-Muʿtazila programme and the *miḥna*, and instead began backing the Ḥanbalī and *ḥadīth* scholars as the propagators of orthodoxy. This was a crucial turning-point in Islamic history, since it signalled the triumph of Sunnī ideology and its ability from that time onwards to shape not only orthodox religious doctrine but the whole narrative of the Islamic past in a way that legitimised the primacy of the *jamāʿa*. And part of the fallout of the new policy had polemical dimensions as well, as boundaries were now drawn more rigidly between Sunnīs and Shīʿa, Muslims and non-Muslims (Christians and Jews), and some restrictions were placed on the latter to stress the supremacy of Islam. These restrictions were probably projected on the past as the 'ordinances of the caliph ʿUmar' during that time.

Al-Mutawakkil inherited a caliphate that was greatly strengthened by the military triumphs of al-Muʿtaṣim and the sustained loyalty of the new military system. This allowed his reign to be characterised by stability and prosperity. With the exception of a revolt in Armenia in 236/850, there is little evidence of regional disaffection. All political and financial power was consolidated at the centre in Sāmarrāʾ, in the army, its officers and a class of palace ministers. Al-Mutawakkil tried to scale back the influence of these groups by sacking their main leaders, Itākh in the army and Ibn al-Zayyāt, the chief minister; but the limits on the caliph's ability to form new and independent policies did not radically change. This became evident in 244/858, when the caliph's attempt to shift the capital to Damascus was strongly resisted by the Turkish corps and had to be abandoned. Al-Mutawakkil's possible expectation that his orthodox religious policy would garner popular social and military support for the caliphate and counter the influence of the Turks did not materialise either, leaving him still reliant on the Turkish military.

The critical factor that ultimately undermined al-Mutawakkil's caliphate, however, was probably financial, and related to his extravagant lifestyle. It is not difficult to establish an image of al-Mutawakkil's personality from anecdotal literature and the vast archaeological remains of Sāmarrāʾ. He appears to have been anxious to leave a significant legacy in ʿAbbāsid history, which led him to try to outdo the achievements of his predecessors (especially al-Rashīd, al-Maʾmūn and al-Muʿtaṣim). This he set out to do in a palace-building spree, through extravagant festivals for commemorative events, and with the construction of the new city of al-Jaʿfariyya, where he built his most magnificent palace, Qaṣr al-Jaʿfarī. Several medieval sources give a lengthy list of the palaces that al-Mutawakkil built, sometimes providing the cost of each in an effort to highlight their exorbitant cost and perhaps to signal a reason for the eventual decline of the ʿAbbāsid government after him.[47]

Less than a year after he moved into the new city of al-Jaʿfariyya, al-Mutawakkil was assassinated by a clique of palace commanders working in league with al-Mutawakkil's eldest son, al-Muntaṣir, who apparently feared that his father was about to shift the succession to his other son, al-Muʿtazz. After a reign of nearly two decades, this was a momentous event. Up until then the idea of military intervention in politics had been successfully suppressed (with the downfall of al-ʿAbbās ibn al-Maʾmūn, Afshīn and Itākh, all suspected of seeking to foment such conspiracies). With al-Muntaṣir the plan had finally succeeded, and it set in place the paradigm of palace coups for later Turkish commanders. Al-Muntaṣir himself died suddenly only six months after his accession. He was succeeded by several short-lived caliphs (al-Mustaʿīn, al-Muʿtazz and al-Muhtadī), who were installed and deposed through the domination of one faction of Turkish commanders or another. Caliphal authority underwent a dramatic collapse during this period, and with it came a general decline in the fortunes of Sāmarrāʾ (and the total abandonment of al-Jaʿfariyya) until the capital eventually was moved back to Baghdad in 279/892. Modern historians, following the the opinion of medieval chroniclers, are prone to blame al-Mutawakkil for the decline of the caliphate at Sāmarrāʾ. The famous remark that 'what al-Maʾmūn, al-Muʿtaṣim and al-Wāthiq had accumulated [in wealth], al-Mutawakkil spent completely'[48] finds support in the amounts he spent building palaces.

But the reasons for the decline of the ʿAbbāsid caliphate at Sāmarrāʾ are not exclusively al-Mutawakkil's policies. They also have to do with the choice of Sāmarrāʾ as a new capital, as well as the policy of reliance on the Turkish troops. From its very beginning Sāmarrāʾ was an artificial city, where life revolved more around palatial construction and imperial display than its urban population or commerce. Unlike Baghdad, Sāmarrāʾ lacked the necessary resources for cohesive growth or steady communication. The built-up area was entirely on the east bank, where the land was arid, fresh water scarce and its canals were few and flawed in their original levelling and construction. Whatever resources existed were channelled primarily to the palace and, with its regimented military and social divisions, the city could not have been an inviting place for commerce. Sāmarrāʾ could only survive as long as the caliphs

47 Yāqūt, *Muʿjam al-buldān*, vol. III, p. 175.
48 Abū Manṣūr ʿAbd al-Malik ibn Muḥammad Thaʿālibī, *Laṭāʾif al-maʿārif*, ed. P. de Jong (Leiden, 1867), p. 71.

poured wealth into its upkeep, which reached a point of culmination with al-Mutawakkil's excessive palace building.[49]

The relationship between the Turkish military and the court had also undergone some important changes. In al-Muʿtaṣim's reign the loyalty of the leading commanders, such as Ashnās, Bughā and Itākh, to the caliph was strong because they had been dependent on the success of his faction, and probably because of their own rivalries with the Transoxanian leaders, such as Afshīn. In al-Mutawakkil's reign, however, a generational turn must have occurred that brought in younger, more ambitious generals who felt little obligation to the caliphal office. The radical switch in caliphal religious policy probably played a role in shaping this change as well. Al-Mutawakkil's lifting of the *miḥna* and abidance by the *ḥadīth* and *jamāʿī-sunnī* principles of the traditional *ʿulamāʾ* constituted an admission that the caliph derived his legitimacy from defending *ḥadīth* principles and was no longer himself the anchor of religious and political authority, as had been the case in al-Maʾmūn's time. In this new environment the roads of Islamic legitimacy had diversified, reaching to any credible authority figure (the Ṭāhirids, the Sāmānids or the Turks), so long as such a group kept *sunnī* and *ḥadīth* interests paramount. After al-Mutawakkil the locus of political power in the Islamic empire shifted decisively to the provinces, even though the economic and cultural fortunes of Baghdad continued to ascend.

The twilight of the high caliphate after the end of al-Mutawakkil's reign invites a comparison with the earlier conditions of the Umayyad empire. As early as the ninth century Muslims began comparing the two dynasties, such as when the famous essayist al-Jāḥiẓ (d. 255/869) remarked that the main difference was that whereas the Umayyad state was Arab, the ʿAbbāsid state was Iranian and Khurāsānī (*ʿajamiyya khurāsāniyya*).[50] While this juxtaposition is valid for the period after al-Maʾmūn's caliphate, the situation during the period before (132–98/750–813) is more complex. It may be true that the early ʿAbbāsids surrounded themselves with Persian courtly culture and bureaucratic arrangements, but they also, as noted earlier, invested heavily in coopting Arab tribal support and used Syria (al-Raqqa) as much as Baghdad as their base for government and military preparation. Indeed, it was their continuous attempt to reconcile the Arab tribal armies (of the central lands) with the Khurāsānī troops (the emigre Arabs of Khurāsān and non-Arabs) that

49 J. M. Rogers, 'Samarra: A study in medieval town-planning', in A. Hourani and S. M. Stern (eds.), *The Islamic city: A colloquium* (Oxford, 1970), pp. 140–2, 152–4.

50 ʿAmr ibn Baḥr al-Jāḥiz, *al-Bayān wa'l-tabyīn*, ed. A. H. Harun, 4 vols. (Cairo, 1960), vol. III, p. 366.

eventually resulted in tensions. The system could work only through a combination of religious/ideological propaganda and under a leadership of proven skill, such as al-Manṣūr, or charisma, such as al-Rashīd. In the absence of a uniting force the ʿAbbāsid armies were prone to division and conflict, as occurred in al-Amīn's reign.

A more glaring difference between the two empires, however, was territorial, and was reflected in the rapid loss of ʿAbbāsid control over Spain and North Africa and the cessation of the tide of conquest on virtually every front (and with this, one should add, ended any further mention of tribal tensions between Qaysiyya and Yamaniyya). With the exception of al-Maʾmūn's attempt to revive full-scale campaigns against the Byzantines, official ʿAbbāsid wars were generally fought out of necessity, either to deter and impress or to protect a vital interest. Al-Muʿtaṣim's spectacular campaign against ʿAmmuriya in 223/838 is an example of the former, while al-Mutawakkil's expedition against a tribal grouping called al-Beja in Nubia in 241/855 illustrates a retaliatory measure after this group attacked the gold and mineral mines in southern Egypt. The ʿAbbāsids never built up a significant navy, nor did they attempt to take Constantinople. They seem to have had a sense of territorial or civilisational self-sufficiency in their control over the central lands, and a belief in Islamic fulfilment with the establishment of their rule as the Hāshimite caliphs. All of their efforts were devoted to consolidating control over the existing empire, which eventually they accomplished through a variety of arrangements.

Still, for all their chiliastic pretensions and political confidence, the early ʿAbbāsids faced a continuous trend of populist, religious rebellions from 750 onwards, and in this lies a major difference with the Umayyad experience. In Umayyad times political challenges were often counter-claims to the caliphate or – more commonly – mutinies over taxation, which targeted the Umayyads in the provinces as much as it did their regional allies, such as the *dihqāns* in Khurāsān. Rebellions against the ʿAbbāsids, however, were often modelled after the *daʿwa* of the revolution. They were little concerned with economic issues, but were rather centred around a compelling religious belief, either in a revivalist prophecy or imamate or in an imminent redemptive moment. The syncretistic rebellions in Khurāsān during 136–60/754–75 were examples of this philosophy, and these were eventually brought under control when the caliphate stood as the defender of Islamic orthodoxy and in alliance with the Iranian aristocracy (the Barmakids). However, in North Africa the ʿAbbāsid cause proved more vulnerable, and soon lost ground there for good. There it was the Khārijites who made inroads among the local Berber tribes and succeeded in creating a rival imamate. From their remote bases in Tāhert and Sijilmāsa the Khārijites launched attacks that battered the isolated ʿAbbāsid garrison city of Qayrawān starting in 141/758. The caliphate was, with difficulty, able for a time to regain the initiative, such as during the successful governorship of Yazīd ibn Ḥātim al-Muhallabī, who arrived in 154/771 with a massive army of 60,000 troops. But the province suffered from additional problems which had to do with the restive situation within the provincial army of Qayrawān over issues of pay and promotion. Eventually, the problems of security and managing the province were solved when the ʿAbbāsids finally conceded provincial authority to an experienced, permanently resident local governor, Ibrāhīm ibn al-Aghlab, who established the hereditary governorship of the Aghlabids in Tunisia starting in 184/800.

The Khārijites were not the only competitors for the ʿAbbāsids in the west. Spain had already drifted from the authority of the caliphate in 138/756 when an adventurous member of the Umayyad family, ʿAbd al-Raḥmān ibn Muʿāwiya ibn Hishām (r. 138–72/756–88), escaped the dynasty's downfall in Syria and succeeded in establishing an Umayyad emirate in Spain with Cordoba as its capital. ʿAbd al-Raḥmān's rule had to contend for some time with various challenges, including a pro-ʿAbbāsid attempted coup encouraged by al-Manṣūr, a resistance movement from the local governor, Yūsuf al-Fihrī, who led a Qaysī tribal coalition against ʿAbd al-Raḥmān in 141/748, and a challenge from Charlemagne to control the northern cities of Saragossa and Barcelona in 162/778. Eventually the Umayyad emirate of Spain stabilised as a hereditary dynasty, and although its *amīrs* did not assume the title 'caliph' (which would happen in the early tenth century), they were able to cultivate a strong image of their rule as orthodox Sunnī leaders who were defending the western Islamic frontier. The legitimacy of their authority was strengthened further when they adopted the Mālikī school of law during the reign of Hishām ibn ʿAbd al-Raḥmān (r. 172–80/788–96), which allowed them to connect with the most popular current of Sunnī Islam at the time. Although they remained politically hostile to the ʿAbbāsids for some time, the Umayyads kept up an avid interest in cultural and intellectual developments in Baghdad, and succeeded in attracting talented luminaries from the east. This happened particularly during the reign of ʿAbd al-Raḥmān II (206–38/822–52), who presided over what can be termed the first golden age of Islamic Spain.

Another, more politically challenging, rival to ʿAbbāsid authority was Idrīs ibn ʿAbd Allāh, a prominent Hāshimite descendant, who arrived in the western extremity of the Maghrib in 173/788. After an odyssey of escape from the Ḥijāz following the failed ʿAlid rebellion in Mecca in 171/786, Idrīs represented the quintessential ʿAlid victim of ʿAbbāsid persecution, and quickly succeeded in rallying the sympathy and support of the largest Berber confederation of the Walila in Morocco, who saw in him both a patron saint and a political leader for their autonomous aspirations. The rise of the Idrīsid dynasty, which became the first ʿAlid state in Islamic history, represented the counter-image to al-Maʾmūn's organisation of a Khurāsānī movement during the civil war with Baghdad. Both leaders, Idrīs and al-Maʾmūn, provided examples of a Hāshimite leadership with important religious pretensions that attached itself to a movement of regional particularism. The long-standing restiveness of the Berbers against central caliphal rule came to an end, as in Khurāsān, after the establishment of a local religious and political leadership.

As the ʿAbbāsid state turned increasingly to a decentralised system of government in the ninth century, the North African principalities, which included the Idrīsids (r. 188–305/804–917), the Rustamids (r. 161–296/778–909) and the Aghlabids (r. 184–296/800–909), blended well with the picture of the semi-autonomous eastern governorates of the Ṭāhirids (r. 206–59/821–73) and Sāmānids (r. 204–389/819–999) in the east, the Ziyādids in the Yemen (r. 202–371/817–981) and the Ṭūlūnids (r. 253–93/868–906) in Egypt. Although these states emerged in different contexts and varied in their degrees of autonomy, they all inherited key patterns of the caliphal government in the mid-ninth century and (with the exception of the Khārijite Rustamids) adopted its orthodox ideology. Provincial cities, such as Bukhārā, Nīshāpūr, Fusṭāṭ, Qayrawān and Fez grew into important centres of religious learning and commerce, and the provincial states sometimes projected an Islamic assertiveness, such as in the conquests of the Aghlabids, that had previously been a key prerogative of the caliphate. In this environment, the caliphate in Baghdad increasingly became mainly a cultural symbol for Islamic society, rather than being a politically dominant institution as it had been in the seventh and eighth centuries. In spite of all the political upheavals that it endured, however, Baghdad remained the pre-eminent city in the Islamic world, favoured as it was by its ideal location, commercial importance and historical memory as the last capital of the great caliphs.

8

The waning of empire, 861–945

MICHAEL BONNER

The assassination of al-Mutawakkil

On a winter night in Sāmarrāʾ in 247/861, the caliph Jaʿfar al-Mutawakkil held a carousing session with some companions and courtiers. The caliph had a fondness for wine, as well as for the foolery of clowns and other entertainments,[1] and we are told that on this occasion, after openly insulting his son and heir apparent, al-Muntaṣir, he proceeded to drink himself into a stupor. By this time al-Muntaṣir had already made his way out of the door, but the courtiers and servants who remained in the caliph's presence were reluctant to leave. However, the Turkish commander Bughā the Younger ordered most of them to go since, he said, the caliph's womenfolk were within hearing distance. Soon afterwards al-Mutawakkil was awakened, as a band of armed men took up positions before him. He asked who these were, and Bughā replied that they were merely the night guard. But now the band, led by Bughā himself, rushed with drawn swords against the caliph and his confidant, al-Fatḥ ibn Khāqān. Al-Fatḥ threw himself over the caliph in a desperate attempt to defend him and then, after receiving a fatal wound, cried out 'Death!' (*al-mawt*). The others dispersed as the assassins hacked the caliph into pieces. The *bayʿa*, or oath of accession, was offered that same night to al-Muntaṣir, who accepted immediately. Al-Muntaṣir's involvement in the plot seemed even more certain when he put out the patent lie that it had been al-Fatḥ who had killed his father and that he, al-Muntaṣir, had then ordered the killing of al-Fatḥ.

1 Julia Bray, 'Samarra in ninth-century Arabic letters', in Chase F. Robinson (ed.), *A medieval Islamic city reconsidered: An interdisciplinary approach to Samarra*, Oxford Studies in Islamic Art 14 (Oxford, 2001), p. 24.

This dark scene[2] marked a low point for the ʿAbbāsid caliphate. Since the days of the Rāshidūn (632–61) several caliphs had been deposed[3] and a few had met violent deaths, but only after civil wars or other open conflicts.[4] Al-Mutawakkil's assassination was all the more shocking for having been carried out by men of servile origin: as one court poet put it, 'The Commander of the Faithful has been killed by his slaves, / Slaves, who are always the bane of kings.'[5] Finally, and most terribly, we have the implication of al-Muntaṣir in the plot, indicated in most versions of the story that we have.[6]

The Islamic world in 861 still had a palpable sense of its own unity, which it projected squarely onto the figure of its caliph. But now, literally overnight, the humiliation or murder of a caliph became thinkable, and before long it would be unremarkable. And as the ruler proved vulnerable and fragile, so too did the empire. In 861 the ʿAbbāsids still controlled most of Iraq, Syria, the Byzantine frontier district in Anatolia (the Thughūr), Egypt, Arabia and Iran, even if they had to share some of their authority with local dynastic rulers such as the Ṭāhirids and Dulafids. But over the next several years, as internal struggles raged at the empire's heart, the provinces were largely left to fend for themselves, in a variety of ways that this chapter will seek to chart. Meanwhile, the loss of control over the provinces aggravated the crisis at the centre. As a result, a number of transformations now became visible. These included changes in the ownership and taxation of agricultural lands, in the role of the military in the administration and government, and in several other areas. Thus when a new generation of caliphs, commanders and administrators began, only a decade later, to assemble a reformed ʿAbbāsid caliphate, this enterprise stood on a different basis from the old 'classical' caliphate of Hārūn al-Rashīd and the

2 The version described here is found in Abū Jaʿfar Muḥammad ibn Jarīr al-Ṭabarī, *Taʾrīkh al-rusul waʾl-mulūk*, ed. M. J. de Goeje *et al.*, 15 vols. in 3 series (Leiden, 1879–1901), series III, pp. 1471–84; see also vol. XXXIV, trans. Joel L. Kraemer as *Incipient decline* (Albany, 1989), pp. 170–84.

3 Franz-Christoph Muth, '"Entsetzte" Kalifen, Depositionsverfahren im mittelalterlichen Islam', *Der Islam*, 75 (1998).

4 Including the ʿAbbāsid revolution and the fourth *fitna* or civil war between al-Amīn and al-Maʾmūn. Suspicions about al-Hādī's death in 170/786 may have had some basis but were never proved: see Michael Bonner, 'al-Khalīfa al-Marḍī: The accession of Hārūn al-Rashīd', *JAOS*, 109, 1 (1988); and Richard Kimber, 'The succession to the caliph Mūsā al-Hādī', *JAOS*, 121, 3 (2001).

5 ʿAlī ibn al-Jahm, quoted by ʿIzz al-Dīn ibn al-Athīr, *al-Kāmil fī l-taʾrīkh*, 11 vols. (Beirut, 1418/1998), vol. VI, p. 140. Contempt for the 'slaves' is underlined by the verb in the feminine plural.

6 Samer Ali, 'Praise for murder? Two odes by al-Buḥturī surrounding an ʿAbbasid patricide', in Beatrice Gruendler and Louise Marlow (eds.), *Writers and rulers* (Wiesbaden, 2004).

Barmakids. Now many people would look back with nostalgia to that lost era, regarding it as a golden age of unity and prosperity.

For these and other reasons, political disenchantment prevailed in many places. We may detect some of this in our historical sources, which change markedly during the eight decades covered in this chapter. The unitary caliphate of the Rāshidūn, Umayyads and earlier ʿAbbāsids received its greatest memorial in the *History* of al-Ṭabarī (d. 310/923), who settled in Baghdad around nine years after the death of al-Mutawakkil. As he looked back over nearly three centuries of the history of the caliphate, this office, even in its most difficult moments, still inspired respect and awe, evoked in the phrase *hādhā l-amr*, 'this [caliphal] authority'. As al-Ṭabarī left off and other historians took up the story after him, the caliphate remained an important fact; now, however, the phrase *hādhā l-amr* could connote political ambition and instrumentality, at times verging on cynicism.[7]

By the end of this chapter we shall find that some people remained loyal to the ʿAbbāsid caliphate, even though they understood that its authority was symbolic – or even fictitious. Others sought new sources of charismatic authority, in ways that the following pages will attempt to chart. At the same time, values were now projected and interests advanced through networks of associations and groups, and through the leadership that these networks generated. The practices of negotiation were never far away and, one way or another, the old unity was gone. A new, more complex, world was emerging, a world whose contours were still not quite clear.

If these were the lessons of al-Mutawakkil's murder, they were not yet apparent. What was clear was that during his lifetime al-Mutawakkil had pursued dangerous policies. By reversing the *miḥna* he had renounced the prerogative of caliphs to pronounce on matters of right belief. By instituting measures against Shīʿa, Christians and Jews he had risked alienating large groups. One reason for these moves may have been a desire to cultivate new constituencies, such as the budding Ḥanbalī movement in Baghdad. However, the caliph's isolation in Sāmarrāʾ made such constituencies unreachable. For despite Sāmarrāʾ's building boom, its population still did not approach Baghdad's. And while Sāmarrāʾ attracted soldiers, courtiers, poets, craftsmen and builders, for men of religious learning it remained merely a passing destination.[8]

7 E.g. ʿArīb ibn Saʿd al-Kātib al-Qurṭubī, *Ṣilat taʾrīkh al-Ṭabarī* (Leiden, 1897), pp. 20–1.
8 Sāmarrāʾ has no biographical literature of its own: Bray, 'Samarra in ninth-century Arabic literature', p. 22.

Al-Mutawakkil brought down several powerful figures, including the administrator Ibn al-Zayyāt, the *qāḍī* Ibn Abī Duʾād and the commander Itākh. The men who took their places did not lack ability, but some of them lacked clear places in the hierarchy. The crucial post of *ḥājib* (chamberlain) was typically held by several men simultaneously.[9] Of all the caliph's courtiers, the one closest to him was al-Fatḥ ibn Khāqān, who apparently held no formal position at all. Al-Mutawakkil went further than most of his predecessors in this matter of having his highest officials answer to him personally and almost informally. In the matter of lavish spending he may have outdone all his predecessors, with his mind-numbing expenditures on palaces, gardens, ceremonies, and gifts to poets and other courtiers.[10]

We may also detect a gambler's instinct in al-Mutawakkil's handling of the succession to himself. Early in his reign he set up three of his sons, al-Muntaṣir, al-Muʿtazz and al-Muʾayyad, as successors to one another, in a manner reminiscent of Hārūn al-Rashīd's arrangement in 803. As in that earlier instance, the politics of succession intermeshed with other matters, chief among which was al-Mutawakkil's desire to get free of the Turkish officers who surrounded him. In this he proceeded imprudently, without establishing an alternative base of support, which, as we have seen, was just about unachievable in any case. Only three years before his death al-Mutawakkil had to renounce his plan for establishing his capital at Damascus.[11] He then returned to Sāmarrāʾ and built himself yet another costly palace. Meanwhile, we are told that he sought to remove al-Muntaṣir from the position of heir apparent and to elevate al-Muʿtazz, who thus became associated with an 'anti-Turkish' policy. Despite all this manoeuvring, al-Mutawakkil remained isolated and vulnerable, as everyone learned on that dismal winter night.

Sāmarrāʾ and civil war

At the outset of this chapter on the waning of empire we may affirm that we are, in fact, dealing with an empire. Imperial structures in the western Mediterranean had collapsed long before, and while they survived in the eastern Mediterranean and Near East, it was a colossal task to maintain

9 Matthew Gordon, *The breaking of a thousand swords: A history of the Turkish military of Samarra (AH 200–275/815–889 CE)* (Albany, 2001), pp. 79–80.

10 Ibid., p. 88; Chase F. Robinson, introduction to Chase F. Robinson (ed.), *A medieval city reconsidered: An interdisciplinary approach to Samarra*, Oxford Studies in Islamic Art 14 (Oxford, 2001,) pp. 10–12; chapter 7 above.

11 Paul Cobb, 'al-Mutawakkil's Damascus: A new ʿAbbāsid capital?', *JNES*, 58 (1999).

them. The caliphate inherited this task from its Byzantine and Sasanian predecessors. At the same time, however, the Islamic caliphate went in new directions in the matter of religion, and also in the recruitment and organisation of its armies. Eventually it took quite a new path when it established its capital in Sāmarrāʾ. This militarisation of the empire's centre resulted in the dominance of a military elite and the isolation of the ruler. Al-Mutawakkil tried to reverse all this; the result was the plot against him. After his death came a decade-long crisis, which we often call 'the anarchy of Sāmarrāʾ'. Here the structures of empire were shaken so severely that afterwards they only recovered in part, and then not for very long.

The Turkish rank-and-file soldiers were, in their origins, slaves from the eastern steppes, whereas their commanders were generally free men of aristocratic or royal lineage. There were also units of free soldiers from the Islamic west (Maghāriba) and Central Asia (Farāghina). This was the situation when Sāmarrāʾ was first built, and it remained broadly so during the next decades.[12] Relations between commanders and rank-and-file were thus far from easy. The commanders, moreover, did not constitute a unified group among themselves. However, the most powerful figures among them provided at least passive support for the conspiracy against al-Mutawakkil. The *wazīr* ʿUbayd Allāh ibn Yaḥyā ibn Khāqān (not related to al-Fatḥ) immediately organised resistance against the conspirators. This meant supporting al-Muʿtazz, next in line to the succession after al-Muntaṣir. ʿUbayd Allāh gathered many soldiers (by some reports, as many as 20,000), but the attempt fizzled. Backing al-Muntaṣir was the chamberlain Waṣīf, who had provided tacit support for the plot against al-Mutawakkil, and who now emerged as the leader of the ruling elite within the palace.

Al-Muntaṣir's caliphate lasted only six months, during which he completed his parricidal work by razing his father's palace.[13] Al-Muntaṣir tried to establish his footing in an increasingly slippery Sāmarrāʾ, now dominated by the Turkish commanders, especially Waṣīf, and by the new *wazīr*, Ibn al-Khaṣīb. Al-Muntaṣir's brothers al-Muʿtazz and al-Muʾayyad were compelled to abdicate their places as heirs. Meanwhile Waṣīf fell foul of Ibn al-Khaṣīb and was sent off to the Byzantine frontier. Then, when al-Muntaṣir died under suspicious circumstances, the most powerful commanders selected a new

12 See chapter 7 above.

13 Al-Ṭabarī, *Taʾrīkh*, series III, p. 1439, and vol. XXXIV, trans. Kraemer as *Incipient decline*, p. 156; Julie Scott Meisami, 'The palace-complex as emblem: Some Samarran *qasidas*', in Chase F. Robinson (ed.), *A medieval Islamic city reconsidered: An interdisciplinary approach to Samarra* (Oxford, 2001), p. 69.

caliph, Abu 'l-ʿAbbās, a grandson of al-Muʿtaṣim, who took the regnal title al-Mustaʿīn. This time, however, conflict broke out and led gradually to a war, sometimes known as the fifth *fitna*, which took up all of 251 (865–6) and culminated in a siege of the city of Baghdad.

This conflict had several parties. The ruling elite of Turkish officers included Waṣīf, Utāmish, Bughā the Younger and Bughā the Elder, who, when he died in 248/862, was replaced by his son, Mūsā ibn Bughā. These men consolidated their position by ridding themselves of the *wazīr* Ibn al-Khaṣīb. However, there was rivalry among them, while their relations with their own soldiers and lower-ranking officers were far from harmonious. For in the caliphate's declining fiscal circumstances,[14] it was becoming impossible to keep these men paid and equipped. Any new caliph – and anyone who wished to manipulate the caliph and the government – would have to deliver arrears of pay, as well as the special grants or donatives that the soldiers expected on the occasion of a new reign. As resources grew scarcer the soldiers felt increasing resentment against their own commanders. Their fears were exacerbated by the hostility of the civilian population. This hostility now emerged in the Turks' home base of Sāmarrā', but it remained, as before, most intense in Baghdad. It was accordingly in Baghdad that Muḥammad ibn ʿAbd Allāh ibn Ṭāhir, commander of the *shurṭa*, or security forces in the city, led the fight against the Sāmarrān Turkish ruling elite.

As civil war loomed, and then broke out in earnest in 251/865, al-Mustaʿīn transferred to the old capital of Baghdad, where he allied himself with Waṣīf, Bughā the Younger and the Ṭāhirid Ibn ʿAbd Allāh. The opposing commanders, who remained in Sāmarrā', reclaimed their supremacy by proclaiming al-Muʿtazz as caliph. Al-Mutawakkil, at the end of his life, had favoured al-Muʿtazz over al-Muntaṣir as part of his anti-Turkish policy. However, the fight that now erupted was not a contest of Turks against non-Turks: al-Muʿtazz's partisans included both Turks and Maghāriba (men from the western Islamic world), and the situation was much the same for al-Mustaʿīn's side in Baghdad. But al-Mustaʿīn made a fatal error when he spoke in public about his lower-ranking Turkish officers as 'uncouth foreigners' (*qawm ʿajam*) and sent these off to Sāmarrā' where, not surprisingly, they went over to the

14 Abū l-Qasim ʿUbaydallāh ibn Khurradādhbih, *al-Masālik wal-mamālik* (Leiden, 1889), pp. 8–14, reports budget figures for the Sawād of Iraq during the time of al-Mutawakkil and just following. The yearly revenue here is 94 million *dirhams*, a loss of 18.5 million since the budget for 204/819 (reign of al-Ma'mūn), reported by Qudāma ibn Jaʿfar, *Kitāb al-kharāj wa-ṣināʿat al-kitāba*, ed. M. H. al-Zubaydi (Baghdad, 1981), pp. 162–7; cf. D. Waines, 'The third century internal crisis of the ʿAbbasids', *JESHO*, 20 (1977), p. 286.

other side. The struggle acquired yet more of an ethnic character as ragtag irregulars (*ṣaʿālīk*) took part in the fighting in Baghdad, seeking Turkish heads, for which Ibn ʿAbd Allāh had promised to pay bounty. All this recalled the siege of Baghdad of a half century earlier, as did the devastation wrought on the city and the land around it. Waṣīf and Bughā, cut off from their sources of wealth and authority in Sāmarrāʾ, yielded leadership in the fight to Ibn ʿAbd Allāh who had, in turn, to confront angry crowds shouting 'Hunger!' before his palace. In the end, the Sāmarrān leadership held and al-Mustaʿīn abdicated in favour of al-Muʿtazz. Shortly afterwards a young officer named Aḥmad ibn Ṭūlūn conveyed al-Mustaʿīn to Wāsiṭ, conspicuously showing him honour and politeness. Some days later the deposed caliph was found dead.

The four-and-a-half years of al-Muʿtazz's caliphate were consumed by violence and intrigue. Waṣīf and Bughā the Younger were reinstated in Sāmarrāʾ, but Waṣīf was killed in 253/867 by soldiers angry over delays in their pay, while Bughā, after a long, deadly dance with the caliph, finally knelt on the executioner's mat in 254/868. The new generation of officers who emerged, led by Ṣāliḥ, the son of Waṣīf, and Mūsā, the son of Bughā the Elder, faced fiscal collapse. To meet the army's demands for its pay, Ṣāliḥ tried to extort large sums from administrators in Iraq, but to no avail. As soldiers marched on the palace, Ṣāliḥ and his fellow officers directed their wrath against al-Muʿtazz, who was tortured and killed.

During the brief reign of al-Muhtadī (255–6/869–70), in al-Ṭabarī's words, 'the entire Islamic realm was engulfed in civil strife'.[15] Ṣāliḥ ibn Waṣīf held as much effective control as there was, until Mūsā ibn Bughā arrived in Sāmarrāʾ, sent out search parties for Ṣāliḥ, found him and put him to death. Mūsā also came into conflict with al-Muhtadī, who insisted on recovering some of the dignity of his office. The quarrel turned into an armed confrontation, which the caliph naturally lost; and so al-Muhtadī became the latest in the series of caliphs killed by mobs of angry soldiers. Meanwhile, however, negotiations had begun between the caliph and the rank-and-file of the army, apparently circumventing the high commanders. An opportunity now presented itself for the assertion of caliphal authority, and this time the ʿAbbāsid house proved equal to the challenge. The accession of al-Muʿtamid in 257/870 marked an end to the nightmare of the 'the anarchy of Sāmarrāʾ'.

In their negotiations with al-Muhtadī in 256/869f. the soldiers are reported to have demanded that their Turkish commanders be replaced by the caliph's brothers, and that guilty commanders and officials be punished

15 Al-Ṭabarī, *Taʾrīkh*, series III, p. 1739; Gordon, *The breaking of a thousand swords*, p. 101.

for looting the treasury.[16] The call for restoration of the tried-and-true order extended also to tax revenues, as the soldiers demanded the abolition of abuses that had damaged the *kharāj* lands and estates (*ḍiyāʿ*), 'as a result of the awarding of concessions (*iqṭāʿāt*) to their officers'.[17] This may be the first evidence that we have for the new type of *iqṭāʿ* that would later become widespread in Iraq under Būyid rule, and eventually throughout the Islamic world. The evidence is sketchy, but here we can perceive crisis and change in both the land regime and the army.

The *kharāj* or land-tax was the staple element of the fiscal system of early Islam, both in theory and practice. In the later Umayyad and early ʿAbbāsid periods it was assessed and levied according to a centralised model, with taxpayers dealing directly with the fiscal agents of the state. This system must have proved unwieldy, for the fiscal authorities resorted to contracts of tax-farming (*ḍamān*) at least from the early ninth century onward.[18] In the course of the century other, related, arrangements became widespread, including *muqāṭaʿa*, the contracting out of a rural district (that owed *kharāj*) to an individual in return for payment to the treasury of a specified sum; and *īghār*, fiscal immunity, amounting to much the same thing.[19] At the same time, ever since the arrival of Islam there had been lands classified as estates (*ḍiyāʿ*), which did not owe the heavy *kharāj*, but only the lighter tithe or *ʿushr*. Caliphs often made grants of such estates to their entourages and family members. This, according to the late ninth-century writer al-Yaʿqūbī, is how Sāmarrāʾ was first built: al-Muʿtaṣim distributed grants (*qaṭāʾiʿ*, sing. *qaṭīʿa*) to his commanders and ordered them to build up the city and its environs, applying their names and patronage to the new urban quarters and rural districts.[20]

From al-Ṭabarī's report of the negotiations between al-Muhtadī and the soldiers in 256/870, we see that high-ranking officers were benefiting from the revenues of estates (*ḍiyāʿ*) and *kharāj* lands. Again, modern scholars have looked here for the beginnings of the new *iqṭāʿ*, but this is looking ahead to the end of

16 Al-Ṭabarī, *Taʾrīkh*, series III, p. 1824; Gordon, *The breaking of a thousand swords*, p. 104. The demand for ʿAbbāsid commanders may be related to the subsequent rise of Abū Aḥmad al-Muwaffaq: see Gordon, *The breaking of a thousand swords*, p. 142.

17 Al-Ṭabarī, *Taʾrīkh*, series III, pp. 1798–9; Gordon, *The breaking of a thousand swords*, pp. 125–7.

18 M. Brett, 'The way of the peasant', *BSOAS*, 47, 1 (1984), pp. 49–50, referring to Egypt but broadly applicable to Iraq as well.

19 C. Cahen, 'L'évolution de l'*iqṭāʿ* du IXe au XIIIe siècle: Contribution à une histoire comparée des sociétés médiévales', in C. Cahen, *Les peuples musulmans dans l'histoire médiévale* (Damascus, 1977).

20 Aḥmad ibn Abī Yaʿqūb ibn Wāḍiḥ al-Yaʿqūbī, *Kitāb al-buldān* (Leiden, 1892), pp. 256–64.

this chapter and beyond.[21] The point to keep in mind here is that revenues coming not only from estate lands, but now also from *kharāj* lands, were being directed towards the high-ranking officers, and away from the control of the fiscal agents of the ʿAbbāsid caliphate. One result was a deterioration of the caliphate's cash flow, especially since the rank-and-file soldiers still depended upon the central treasury for their pay. Another result was change in the countryside itself. Here the fate of individual landowners is difficult to follow: no doubt there were cases of outright expropriation, but more often we detect small landholders seeking to lighten their burden of taxes (or rents) by taking refuge (*iljāʾ*) with powerful individuals who then consolidated these properties with what they already held. The result, of course, was the disappearance of the weak and the enhancement of the strong.

Together with this turmoil on the land came what we may call the privatisation and factionalisation of the army, trends that had been perceptible at least since the foundation of Sāmarrāʾ. Even if the commanders grew rich from their holdings, in the end they had to rely on the support of soldiers who were, as we have seen, prone to anger and alienation. The 'decade of anarchy' in Sāmarrāʾ was not a case of domination by a group of men united in solidarity by their Turkish ethnicity, military function and non-free status over free civilians and soldiers. It was rather a series of manoeuvres by desperate individuals looking for leaders whom they could safely follow, or followers whom they could safely lead.

Periphery and centre

With Sāmarrāʾ and Baghdad absorbed by inner conflict in the 860s and trying to recover from it during the following decades, most of the empire fell apart. We are best able to perceive this process when it takes the form of the emergence of new dynastic states on the periphery. These were remembered afterwards as the wilful expression of military men who carved out territories for themselves and their descendants within the physical and moral space of the ʿAbbāsid caliphate. At the same time, several of these successor states were also built out of the principles and practices of warfare against the enemies of Islam, which is to say, the *jihād*. In other words, these were frontier societies, negotiating new Islamic identities for individuals and groups.

21 Gordon, *The breaking of a thousand swords*, pp. 118–24. Cahen, 'L'évolution de l'*iqṭāʿ*', pp. 236–8, argued that the new *iqṭāʿ* did not derive from the estates, but rather from the *muqāṭaʿa* and *īghār* arrangements imposed on lands that owed *kharāj*: see below, p. 353.

We may well ask whether the inhabitants of these provinces really wished to renegotiate their relations with the caliphate. In general, however, relief from ʿAbbāsid fiscal pressure was welcome, and in some places a measure of local identity began to emerge. These were, after all, the years in which Islam became the majority religion in most places,[22] which meant that a local or provincial identity, expressed in Islamic (or even religiously neutral) terms, no longer had to pose a threat to the governing authorities. So while the Sāmarran crisis of 861–70 precipitated the expression of these local identities, they would doubtless have emerged sooner or later.

When al-Muʿtamid, a son of al-Mutawakkil, succeeded to the caliphate in 256/870, he was compelled to make a special place for his brother Abū Aḥmad, who received a regnal title of his own, al-Muwaffaq. Abū Aḥmad, like his grandfather al-Muʿtaṣim, was a military man through and through. Having acted as chief commander for al-Muʿtazz's side during the civil war of 865, he enjoyed the respect of the soldiers. And so, after a chaotic decade during which Turkish commanders had intrigued against one another and deposed or killed at least four caliphs, the solution arose of putting the army under the command of an ʿAbbāsid prince with a general's résumé. In the event, al-Muwaffaq's decisive leadership was to save the ʿAbbāsid caliphate from destruction on more than one occasion. Not surprisingly, however, al-Muʿtamid chafed at this arrangement.

Under these circumstances it became clear that the ties between periphery and centre were severely frayed. Nothing illustrates this so well as the vicissitudes of the Ṭāhirid dynasty. Now well into their third generation of high office, the Ṭāhirids remained firmly rooted in their native Khurāsān, where the leading member of their family held the office of governor or *amīr*. At the same time, ever since the days of Ṭāhir ibn al-Ḥusayn (d. 822) the Ṭāhirids had governed in conjunction with the ʿAbbāsids. In Baghdad the crucial job of *ṣāḥib al-shurṭa* (chief of the security force) was theirs by hereditary right. They also held other positions, in addition to estate properties in Iraq and elsewhere. Their relations with the caliphs were not easy: the transfer of the capital to Sāmarrāʾ had never suited them, and may have been made, in part, to diminish their importance. Nonetheless, the Ṭāhirids maintained their position securely in Khurāsān and Baghdad, astride the great route known now as the Silk Route, enjoying the support of the Khurāsānian landholding classes. In the eyes of modern historians, even

22 R. Bulliet, *Conversion to Islam in the medieval period: An essay in quantitative history* (Cambridge, MA, 1979).

though the Ṭāhirids come first in the well-known sequence of ninth- and tenth-century 'eastern dynasties', they appear different from the dynastic rulers who come after them in Iran: 'not a separate dynasty, but merely the hereditary governors of Khurasan, always as servants of the commander of the faithful in Baghdad', their true fame resting 'in their cultural patronage', especially of Arabic letters.[23]

It may be useful to think of the Ṭāhirid phenomenon as a remnant of the centripetal politics of the Umayyad and early ʿAbbāsid periods, from a time when provincial ambition, especially in the all-important frontier province of Khurāsān, looked obsessively to the centre of the Islamic world. The Ṭāhirids loyally held the eastern frontiers against external enemies. However, it was not this activity that defined them as much as their stable place within the political system of the caliphate and their embodiment of the aristocratic cultural values expressed, in Arabic, at the ʿAbbāsid court in Sāmarrāʾ and the Ṭāhirid court in Nīshāpūr.[24]

With Sāmarrāʾ in deep crisis, a centrifugal pattern set in that, as much as anything else, comes near to defining this entire period of Islamic history. Now we find ambitious military commanders (most often social upstarts) establishing themselves in the provinces through forcible conquest, and through peaceful alliance with local elites. In their relations with the caliphal government, these new men were mostly content with formal recognition of their status as provincial *amīrs*. Only one of them, in the third/ninth century, made a serious attempt against the heart of the ʿAbbāsid empire (see following paragraphs). This change from a centripetal to a centrifugal pattern[25] became visible rather suddenly, in the east, with the rapid decline of the Ṭāhirids. (The west is a different story, to be discussed below.) Thus Muḥammad ibn ʿAbd Allāh ibn Ṭāhir's defeat in Baghdad in 865 (see above) was followed in 873 by the ousting of his brother Ṭāhir ibn ʿAbd Allāh from the governorship of Khurāsān, at the hands of Yaʿqūb ibn al-Layth al-Ṣaffār ('the Coppersmith' in Arabic, from which comes the name of the dynasty he founded, the Ṣaffārids). Now visibly out of date, the Ṭāhirid enterprise was reduced, though not yet swept aside.

This Yaʿqūb ibn al-Layth, a charismatic soldier of humble origins, had emerged as the major power in the eastern Islamic world during the decade

23 Richard N. Frye, *The golden age of Persia: The Arabs in the east* (London, 1975), pp. 191–2.

24 C. E. Bosworth, 'The Ṭāhirids and Arabic culture', *JSS*, 14 (1969); see chapter 7 above.

25 This distinction was stated in a conference paper by Michael Cook in 1984. See now Patricia Crone, *God's rule: Government and Islam* (New York, 2004), esp. pp. 36–9.

of strife in Sāmarrāʾ. His home was the eastern Iranian province of Sīstān (Sijistān), a marginal region which had never come under the firm control of the caliphate. But now Sīstān was destined to enjoy the limelight for a while, for three main reasons. The first of these was its position as a frontier province, connecting to the mountains of present-day Afghanistan and the fringes of India. The second reason was Sīstān's internal condition. For generations it had harboured Khārijite rebels who had, under Ḥamza ibn Ādharak (d. 213/828), controlled much of it. The Ṭāhirid governors did not seriously try to control the countryside, but limited themselves to the large towns of Bust and Zaranj. But there too central authority suffered, as bands of local urban roughnecks (*ʿayyārūn*) set out to fight the Khārijites.

The third reason for Sīstān's sudden fame was Yaʿqūb's rare combination of ability and ambition. Yaʿqūb and his brothers joined the *ʿayyārūn* in Bust, fighting hard and rising quickly. In 247/861, the year of al-Mutawakkil's murder, Yaʿqūb gained control over Zaranj and, in the next four years, over all of Sīstān. He then turned eastward to lead armies against the frontier regions of Zābulistān, Kabul and Bādhghīs, acquiring plunder and prestige. During these operations many Khārijites joined his side, an early sign of the waning of Khārijism. After opening hostilities against the Ṭāhirids in Herat, Yaʿqūb began to look westward. In the early 870s he invaded Kirmān and Fārs, receiving reluctant acknowledgement as governor from the caliph al-Muʿtamid. In 259/873 he turned north, invaded Khurāsān and seized Nīshāpūr, thus toppling the Ṭāhirids, as we have seen. Now al-Muʿtamid declared that Yaʿqūb had gone too far. In 262/876 Yaʿqūb replied by marching into Iraq, but there, near Dayr al-ʿĀqūl, some 50 miles from Baghdad, an ʿAbbāsid army defeated him, to everyone's surprise. Yaʿqūb withdrew, retaining control over most of Iran, but three years later he died and was succeeded by his brother ʿAmr.

The brilliant, though uneven, career of the Coppersmith has provoked much interest. Two questions emerge in particular. First, what did Yaʿqūb have in mind when he assaulted the ʿAbbāsid caliphate at its seat? (Though still based in Sāmarrāʾ, the caliphate was already repositioning itself to Baghdad.) Perhaps this question has no answer, other than Yaʿqūb's fury against the ʿAbbāsids and their rejection of his claim. It was generally understood during this era that a provincial governor would indicate his loyalty to the caliphate through two symbolically loaded acts: by including the caliph's name on coins struck in the provincial mint (*al-sikka*); and by making an invocation in the caliph's name during the sermon (*al-khuṭba*) pronounced on the occasion of the Friday prayer. Now Yaʿqūb did try to secede from caliphal rule in some way. However, he remained within these limits of *sikka* and *khuṭba*: even during his campaign against the ʿAbbāsids he proposed no alternative to the caliphate, and may have intended merely to replace al-Muʿtamid with another ʿAbbāsid prince.[26] He rejected overtures from the most important rebels in southern Iraq at the time, the Zanj (see below). Above all, his rebellion carried no religious message – Khārijite, Shīʿite, Zoroastrian or anything else.

The second question regards the reasons for Yaʿqūb's success. These included a superb military organisation,[27] and also an appeal to Iranian group feeling or, more precisely, to memories of the traditions of Persian kingship.[28] Yaʿqūb was notorious for his ignorance of Arabic, as well as his rough manners and lowly birth. But what is the meaning of his rise to prominence as a leader of *ʿayyārūn* in Bust and Zaranj? These groups were utterly local in character: something more was necessary if they were to become the vehicle for the formation of a new state and regional power. Deborah Tor has argued that Yaʿqūb, and the Ṣaffārid dynasty as a whole, lived and breathed for one purpose only, which was performance of holy war against infidels and heretics. If so, then the bands of *ʿayyārūn* were actually *mutaṭawwiʿa* (volunteers) and *ghāzīs* (warriors for the faith). By remaining true to the ascetic ideals of these *ghāzī* bands, Yaʿqūb and his successor ʿAmr would have won justification for their wars of conquest.[29] In particular, they won the support of religious learned groups in the cities in this way,[30] although here the evidence remains slim. This view of Yaʿqūb and ʿAmr as frontier fighters for the faith provides welcome relief from the views that have often prevailed of them, as well as of other *amīrs* of the 'eastern dynasties', as either overambitious soldiers of fortune, or else as Iranian patriots and nationalists *avant la lettre*. On the other hand, it may be too much to ascribe the entire Ṣaffārid enterprise to a single motivating principle of holy war.[31] Be that as it may, we can see in the rise and expansion of the

26 Deborah G. Tor, 'A numismatic history of the first Ṣaffārid dynasty (AH 247–300/AD 861–911)', *Numismatic Chronicle*, 162 (2002) p. 298; C. E. Bosworth, *The history of the Ṣaffārids of Sīstān and the Maliks of Nimrūz (247/861 to 949/1542)* (Costa Mesa and New York, 1994), pp. 153, 156–7.

27 C. E. Bosworth, 'The armies of the Ṣaffārids', *BSOAS*, 31 (1968); Bosworth, *History of the Ṣaffārids*, pp. 341–57.

28 Samuel Miklos Stern, 'Yaʿqūb the Coppersmith and Persian national sentiment', in C. E. Bosworth (ed.), *Iran and Islam, in memory of Vladimir Minorsky* (Edinburgh, 1971); Bosworth, *History of the Ṣaffārids*, pp. 160–80.

29 At least until 287/900, when ʿAmr went soft and 'betrayed his original *ʿayyar* ideals of *ghazw* and ascetic zeal', as a result of which his army handed him over to the Sāmānids, who sent him on to Baghdad for execution: Tor, 'A numismatic history', p. 309.

30 Ibid., pp. 304–5.

31 As was done by Paul Wittek, *The rise of the Ottoman empire* (London, 1938). By advancing *jihād* – or, in Wittek's case, *ghazā* – as an explanatory principle or cause, we risk falling into a circular argument, just as when we advance Islam itself.

Ṣaffārids a drama of state formation, with stage and backdrop provided by the eastern frontier. Unlike the Khārijites, they did not accuse other Muslims of unbelief, but rather sought to expand the territory of Islam, as they gathered legitimacy and strength along the eastern frontier.

Centrifugal forces had become noticeable earlier on in the other, western, end of the Islamic world, where the caliphal authorities had yielded to them much sooner. This was especially true of al-Andalus, or Islamic Spain, which had precociously dropped out of the ʿAbbāsid caliphate in the 750s. As the country grew more prosperous, the Umayyad *amīrs* of al-Andalus consolidated their position and then, after 852, lost ground to internal opposition and anarchy. Meanwhile, al-Andalus lived in a condition of low-density warfare against the Christian kingdoms on its northern borders. This meant that it developed as a frontier society, where the performance of *jihād* against external enemies was critical not only for territorial defence and expansion, but also for upholding the legitimacy of rulers, and for articulating the claims to leadership made by various legal and religious authorities.[32]

More important in the eyes of the caliphal government was the province of Ifrīqiya, corresponding to modern-day Tunisia and parts of Algeria and Libya. Here, since 184/800, the *amīrs* of the Aghlabid dynasty enjoyed substantial autonomy, including the right to transfer the emirate within their bloodline. The Aghlabids showed formal loyalty to the ʿAbbāsids as they conducted religious quarrels with Khārijites, especially the Berber Ibāḍīs of the Rustamid state which formed the western border of Aghlabid Ifrīqiya.[33] At the same time, the Aghlabids faced internal opposition from the Arab fighters of the *jund* (army), and also from urban men of religious learning, above all those of the Mālikī *madhhab* (school of law), which was establishing its dominant position in Muslim North Africa in the course of the century.

In 827 the Aghlabids began the conquest of Byzantine Sicily. This operation, which required three-quarters of a century to complete, met with enthusiastic support. Mass participation in the Sicilian campaigns, together with frequent turmoil among the Muslim fighters there, provided the Aghlabids with an escape valve for tensions building up among the soldiers

32 Hugh Kennedy, *Muslim Spain and Portugal: A political history of al-Andalus* (London and New York, 1996), pp. 30–62; Cristina de la Puente, 'El Ŷihād en el califato omeya de al-Andalus y su colminación bajo Hišām II', in Fernando Valdés Fernández (ed.), *Almanzor y los terrores del Milenio* (Aguilar de Campoo, 1999).

33 Elizabeth Savage, *A gateway to hell, a gateway to paradise: The North African response to the Arab conquest* (Princeton, 1997).

of the *jund* and the scholars of the Mālikī *madhhab*.[34] Meanwhile the coasts of Ifrīqiya itself remained exposed to attack. The Aghlabids and their subjects devoted considerable resources to defensive structures, known as *ribāṭs*, where volunteer garrisons could reside. It was, however, in its project of conquest in Sicily that Aghlabid Ifrīqiya revealed its character as yet another provincial frontier society. This was in some ways the last of the early Islamic conquests, performed largely by volunteers fighting for religious reward and the promise of plunder.[35] Operations began successfully with the fall of Palermo in 216/831, but were soon bogged down in quarrels that reflected the conflicts of Ifrīqiya itself, between Arabs and Berbers and between the Aghlabid ruling house and its unruly subjects. With the accession of Ibrāhīm II in 261/875, the Muslims had a series of successes, culminating in the fall of Syracuse in 264/878. Otherwise an unpopular ruler, Ibrāhīm found in the *jihād* an activity to his liking, and later he relinquished the emirate and devoted himself to the Sicilian war, achieving the conquest of Taormina in 289/902. This was precisely when the Fāṭimid *dāʿī* (missionary) Abū ʿAbd Allāh al-Shīʿī began to lead his Kutāma Berber force against the Aghlabid state from its western edge. It now turned out that the Aghlabids had made a fatal error by concentrating upon Sicily and neglecting their land frontiers.

Egypt, despite its economic and political problems earlier in the ninth century, now enjoyed prosperity, with its borders secure and its commerce increasing in the Red Sea and the Mediterranean.[36] However, it still played a subordinate role as provider of foodstuffs and cash. Indeed, as Iraq became beset by economic difficulties, Baghdad and Sāmarrāʾ depended all the more on the Egyptian revenues that in centuries past had gone to their imperial predecessors (Byzantine Constantinople, Medina under the Rāshidūn, Umayyad Damascus). Now, however, an Islamic Egyptian voice was emerging, audible in Arabic among scholars such as the Ibn ʿAbd al-Ḥakam family, authors of major works on history and law. And the country was about to acquire, for the first time, a front-rank place in the politics of the Islamic world, with the arrival of Aḥmad ibn Ṭūlūn and the founding of the Ṭūlūnid dynasty.

34 Michael Brett, *The rise of the Fatimids: The world of the Mediterranean and the Middle East in the fourth century of the hijra, tenth century CE* (Leiden, 2000), p. 80.

35 R. Traini, 'Siḳilliyya', *EI2*, vol. IX, pp. 582–9.

36 Thierry Bianquis, 'Autonomous Egypt from Ibn Ṭūlūn to Kāfūr, 868–969', in Carl F. Petry (ed.), *The Cambridge history of Egypt*, vol. I: *Islamic Egypt, 640–1517* (Cambridge, 1998), pp. 87–8.

We have already met Aḥmad ibn Ṭūlūn as he conveyed the deposed caliph al-Mustaʿīn to his doom in Wāsiṭ at the end of the civil war in 865.[37] The freeborn son of a Turkish father, Ibn Ṭūlūn had grown up in Baghdad and Sāmarrāʾ, and received a literary and religious, as well as a military, education. His youthful experience also included military service on the Arab–Byzantine frontier, where he received instruction from the *ḥadīth* scholars and pious men (*zuhhād*) of Tarsus.[38] In 254/868 he was appointed deputy governor of Egypt by his patron Bayākbak (or Bākbāk), a member of the ruling elite in Sāmarrāʾ who had been granted control over the province. At this point Ibn Ṭūlūn was just one of several junior officers under the patronage of high-ranking men such as Bayākbak, Ṣāliḥ ibn Waṣīf and Mūsā ibn Bughā. Indeed, Bayākbak was in competition against Ṣāliḥ, who around this time named Abu ʾl-Sāj – another capable officer who would soon make a name for himself – as his proxy in northern Syria.[39] Ibn Ṭūlūn arrived in Egypt to find the fiscal administration under the control of Ibn al-Mudabbir, a wily bureaucrat with long experience. Four years went by before Ibn Ṭūlūn succeeded in getting rid of him, during which time he also faced local opposition in several parts of Egypt. But now, with the administration (both military and fiscal) of the entire country finally under his control and with his Sāmarrān patron, Bayākbak, removed from the scene, Ibn Ṭūlūn found himself in a position of strength and autonomy. He maintained this position in part by timely interventions and gift-giving at the caliphal court in Sāmarrāʾ, and in part by building a powerful army of slave-soldiers at home in Egypt. In the manner of all rulers of Egypt before and since, Ibn Ṭūlūn paid special attention to the situation along the country's north-eastern border.

We have seen that the caliph al-Muʿtamid was compelled to share power with his brother al-Muwaffaq, and Ibn Ṭūlūn now found himself in the midst of the quarrel. He began by favouring al-Muʿtamid, sending him the lion's share of the Egyptian tribute in 263/876[40] and assuming, after 265/878, the title *mawlā amīr al-muʾminīn* ('client of the commander of the faithful'). Meanwhile al-Muʿtamid, like several of his predecessors, divided his realm into two regions, each assigned to a viceregent who was also a prince of the ʿAbbāsid house. In 875 he assigned

37 Al-Balawī, the author of an encomiastic biography of Ibn Ṭūlūn, absolves his hero from involvement in the crime: *Sīrat Aḥmad ibn Ṭūlūn* (Damascus, 1939), pp. 40–1.

38 Ibid., pp. 34–5; Bianquis, 'Autonomous Egypt', p. 91; Gordon, *The breaking of a thousand swords*, pp. 99f., 117, 226.

39 Gordon, *The breaking of a thousand swords*, p. 100; al-Ṭabarī, *Taʾrīkh*, series III, p. 1697.

40 1.2 million *dinars* to Muwaffaq and 2.2 million to Muʿtamid: Bianquis, 'Autonomous Egypt', p. 95.

the western provinces to his son and heir Ja'far, while the eastern provinces went to al-Muwaffaq. However, al-Muwaffaq held the real power and did not feel constrained to operate in the eastern provinces only. With al-Muwaffaq threatening both Syria and Egypt, Ibn Ṭūlūn asked al-Mu'tamid for the command over the Arab–Byzantine frontier district of the Thughūr. He moved against Āmājūr, the 'Abbāsid governor in Damascus, who then died in 264/877f. As Ibn Ṭūlūn occupied the great cities of Syria, al-Muwaffaq named Mūsā ibn Bughā governor of Egypt and sent him to Syria; lacking funds, however, Mūsā's expedition collapsed and he returned to Iraq.

Ibn Ṭūlūn then marched on Tarsus, chief stronghold of the frontier district of the Thughūr. This move had much in common with Ya'qūb ibn al-Layth's activity, in the 860s, on the eastern frontiers. Ibn Ṭūlūn already had credentials as a participant in the Byzantine wars, as well as in the learned and pious activities characteristic of Tarsus. However, Ya'qūb had built up the Ṣaffārid state by commanding *ghāzīs* on the eastern frontiers, whereas the Ṭūlūnid project of state formation was now already substantially complete. The residents of Tarsus, for their part, felt no desire for an Egyptian occupation. Ibn Ṭūlūn withdrew, but left his lieutenant Lu'lu' in command in Aleppo. In this way he combined control over Syria, Palestine and some of al-Jazīra (northern Mesopotamia), in addition to Egypt, briefly anticipating the later pattern of the Ayyūbid and Mamlūk sultanates.[41]

It was in Egypt that Ibn Ṭūlūn's achievement was most lasting, as is apparent today to anyone who stands in the courtyard of the great Ibn Ṭūlūn Mosque in Cairo. This mosque was completed in 266/880 and was soon accompanied by a palace for the *amīr* and residential quarters for the army, called al-Qaṭā'i' ('the land-grants'). While these buildings announced Egypt's arrival as a military and political power, many things about them, including the Mesopotamian architectural idiom of the mosque, also recalled Sāmarrā'. Just as al-Mu'taṣim had done in Sāmarrā' a half-century earlier, Ibn Ṭūlūn now settled his army in al-Qaṭā'i', assigning a land-grant to each unit. Thenceforth these slave-soldiers formed the backbone of Ṭūlūnid power, and much of Egypt's wealth would be spent on a standing army which, in the year of Ibn Ṭūlūn's death, included 24,000 Turks and 42,000 black Africans, both slave and free.[42]

In 269/881 Ibn Ṭūlūn's deputy in Syria, Lu'lu', was summoned by al-Muwaffaq to serve against the Zanj in Iraq (see below). Ibn Ṭūlūn departed

41 Ibid., p. 96.
42 Ibid., p. 98.

for Syria, where again he found trouble in Tarsus. There the governor, the eunuch Yāzmān, refused to acknowledge his authority. As Ibn Ṭūlūn passed through Syria in 882 he received a message from the caliph al-Muʿtamid, saying that he had secretly left Sāmarrāʾ and was on his way to Syria. Ibn Ṭūlūn waited for al-Muʿtamid in Damascus, hoping to escort him to Fusṭāṭ; in this way Egypt might become the centre of a restored ʿAbbāsid caliphate, under Ṭūlūnid protectorate. However, al-Muwaffaq's agents got wind of the scheme and a commander loyal to him, Isḥāq ibn Kundaj, encountered al-Muʿtamid near Ḥadītha, in western Iraq, and forced him to return to Sāmarrāʾ.

In Damascus Ibn Ṭūlūn now convened an assembly of religious scholars and judges from all the territories under his control. *Khuṭba* (Friday sermon) after *khuṭba* denounced al-Muʿtamid's imprisonment and al-Muwaffaq's arrogance. However, there was some disagreement among the judges and scholars, and when Ibn Ṭūlūn demanded a declaration of *jihād* against al-Muwaffaq, the assembly refused to go that far. All the same, the event was the first of its kind, an indication of the ties that Ibn Ṭūlūn cultivated among the learned classes. Al-Muwaffaq replied by having curses against Ibn Ṭūlūn pronounced from the pulpits of the territories under direct ʿAbbāsid control.[43] Meanwhile, Ibn Ṭūlūn tried unsuccessfully to dislodge Yāzmān from Tarsus in 270/883. He fell ill during the campaign and returned to Fusṭāṭ, where he died in 270/884.

Opposition

For the ʿAbbāsid leadership these new dynastic enterprises were ultimately manageable. An adroit player of the game such as al-Muwaffaq could even use them to his own advantage. During these years, however, new threats arose that can only be described as existential. A series of movements and groups made religious and ideological claims that left no room for the ʿAbbāsid caliphate and empire. Some of these sought autonomy, resistance and revenge. Others aimed to restore the caliphate, in a reformed and purified version. Questions relating to universal dominion and just rule were debated constantly and passionately. These questions were at once historical, relating to the Islamic past and its interpretations, and theological, relating to God's plan for the world and the community of believers. Our historical sources for these movements and groups are largely absorbed by

43 Al-Balawī, *Sīrat Aḥmad ibn Ṭūlūn*, pp. 298–300; Bianquis, 'Autonomous Egypt', pp. 101–2.

these arguments. Accordingly, the study of what has been called 'the revolt of Islam'[44] requires attention to some historiographical problems.

At the beleaguered centre of the Islamic empire, al-Muʿtamid and his brother al-Muwaffaq began to share power in 870, as we have seen. Despite the conflict between them, this arrangement worked reasonably well, since it allowed al-Muwaffaq to maintain the loyalty of the armies and to meet military challenges. Thus it was al-Muwaffaq, together with Mūsā ibn Bughā, who commanded the force that stopped Yaʿqūb the Coppersmith in 876 at Dayr al-ʿĀqūl. Meanwhile, as the Sāmarrān crisis of the 860s abated and the officers loosened their grip on the caliphal administration, the scribes (*kuttāb*) gained in visibility and influence. Al-Muʿtamid began by appointing as his *wazīr* ʿUbayd Allāh ibn Yaḥyā ibn Khāqān, who had held the office at the time of al-Mutawakkil's death. This allowed al-Muʿtamid to maintain some independence; but, after ʿUbayd Allāh's death in 262/877, al-Muwaffaq intervened by appointing men of his own choice as al-Muʿtamid's *wazīrs*. Al-Muʿtamid's position grew weaker, and after his failed attempt to escape to Egypt in 882 he found himself under house arrest. Meanwhile, as the administrators became more powerful, the factional divisions among them grew. This bureaucratic factionalism would prove characteristic of the coming decades, as would the chronic lack of money in the treasury.

The great crisis of the era of al-Muʿtamid and al-Muwaffaq was the revolt of the Zanj. This Arabic word denotes blacks originating from the East African coast. Large numbers of East African slaves had, in the later first/seventh century, been brought to work in southern Iraq under harsh conditions.[45] In the third/ninth century we find gangs of Zanj kept in conditions of acute hardship and misery and working in the marshlands (*al-baṭāʾiḥ*) of lower Iraq, removing the nitrous topsoil (*sibākh*) to reclaim the land for cultivation. This swampy region was ideally suited to guerrilla warfare, as everyone would soon know. Our information here comes almost exclusively from al-Ṭabarī, who does not tell us all we would like to know about the ownership and management of these lands. It appears, in any case, that the owners were concentrated in the nearby city of Baṣra, and that they availed themselves of the provision in Islamic law for 'reviving dead lands' (*iḥyāʾ al-mawāt*) under fiscally advantageous terms. We know of no other instances of plantation-style slavery of this kind in the early Islamic world – as opposed to domestic and military slavery, which were widespread.

44 Bernard Lewis, *The Arabs in history* (London, 1958).
45 Alexandre Popovic, *The revolt of African slaves in Iraq in the 3rd/9th century* (Princeton, 1998), pp. 22–3.

The revolt got under way in 255/869 with the arrival of one ʿAlī ibn Muḥammad, whom al-Ṭabarī describes as an adventurer and jack-of-all-trades, but who had considerable charisma and leadership skills.[46] ʿAlī's appeal to the Zanj had a markedly Shīʿite character, although it was not until around two years later, after the destruction of Baṣra, that he actually claimed membership, through Zayd ibn ʿAlī, in the Prophet's family.[47] ʿAlī ibn Muḥammad promised the Zanj revenge against their oppressors, riches and slaves of their own, and in the next few years he made good on these promises to a remarkable extent. The local and caliphal authorities were unable to defend against the Zanj, who moved swiftly on interior lines, hidden by the swamps. They seized the main cities of lower Iraq and neighbouring Khūzistān, including Baṣra, Wāsiṭ, ʿAbbādān and Ahwāz. They slaughtered many inhabitants, but did not occupy these cities permanently: all the ʿAbbāsid forces could do was to enter these ruined centres of early Islamic civilisation and survey the devastation. Meanwhile, ʿAlī ibn Muḥammad established himself in al-Mukhtāra, a fortress town astride several canals to the east of Baṣra, where he minted coins and tried to create alliances with the Ṣaffārids and the Qarāmiṭa (see below). The ʿAbbāsid authorities, led by al-Muwaffaq, did not mobilise effectively against the Zanj until 266/879, the year of Yaʿqūb the Coppersmith's death. But now they moved resolutely, driving the Zanj back into the swamps and canals. Command of the armies was shared between al-Muwaffaq and his son Abu 'l-ʿAbbās, the future caliph al-Muʿtaḍid. The ʿAbbāsid forces pressed slowly through the canals, forcing the Zanj to concentrate their forces and to undergo a siege at al-Mukhtāra. Finally, in 893, when al-Muʿtaḍid had already succeeded to the caliphate, the Zanj were defeated, their leader killed and his chief companions taken for execution to Baghdad.

If the revolt of the Zanj had begun only a few years earlier, it probably would have brought an end to the ʿAbbāsid caliphate. As is, it stands out as the greatest slave rebellion in the history of Islam. At the same time, its appeal went beyond the slaves of the swamp region. Its commanders, including ʿAlī ibn Muḥammad himself, seem to have been of Arab origin – in any case, not Zanj. The movement's Shīʿite character may seem rather vague, although this may be a result of the hostility of al-Ṭabarī and his sources. Of special interest is the fact that Arab nomads or semi-nomads (*aʿrāb*) are described as fighting

46 Al-Ṭabarī, *Ta'rīkh*, series III, pp. 1742–6, vol. XXXVI trans. D. Waines as *The revolt of the Zanj*, (Albany, 1992), pp. 30–3; Popovic, *Revolt*, pp. 33–43.

47 Al-Ṭabarī, *Ta'rīkh*, series III, p. 1857; vol. XXXVI, trans. Waines as *The revolt of the Zanj*, p. 133.

side by side with the Zanj, especially in the early phase of the rebellion when cities such as Baṣra were targeted and destroyed.[48]

Until this time Khārijism was the form of Islam preferred by many dissidents who inhabited the borderlands between the desert and the sown. In earlier times there had been Khārijites (notably al-Ḍaḥḥāk ibn Qays al-Shaybānī, d. 128/746) who attempted to take over the entire Islamic polity. But in the ʿAbbāsid period Khārijism was more often the creed of people who wanted nothing to do with the centre of empire except, where convenient, to do it harm. Khārijites sought to establish virtuous polities in fringe provinces, as Ḥamza ibn Ādharak had done in Sīstān (see above).

We have seen that in the later ninth century provinces were falling into the hands of local *amīrs* who desired autonomy from the imperial centre. In doctrinal terms these new rulers tended to remain Sunnī (if it is not too early to use this word), although some of them, notably Yaʿqūb the Coppersmith, mounted political and cultural resistance against the hegemony of Sāmarrāʾ and Baghdad. Meanwhile, Shīʿism provided the structure and idiom for a wide – and, in many ways, new – range of opposition movements. At least in some areas (such as North Africa and northern Syria), where formerly we found Khārijites, we now find more adherents of Ismāʿīlism and other forms of radical Shīʿism. But though radical Shīʿism now spread widely, it had its beginnings at the heart of the ʿAbbāsid empire, in the fertile farmland of southern and central Iraq and in the marginal lands – whether desert or marsh – that surrounded it. In this way the revolt of the Zanj was a harbinger of what was to come.

Our literary sources for these Shīʿite movements of the later third/ninth century present difficulties. Many of these sources are heresiographical in character: their purpose is to identify false belief (whether from a Shīʿite, Sunnī or other perspective) and to refute it. The historical chronicles also show sectarian disagreement. Sunnī chronicles, such as the *History* of al-Ṭabarī, often have an anti-Ismāʿīlī viewpoint. On the other hand, there is also an Ismāʿīlī historiography which connects these events to the rise of the Fāṭimid dynasty, the major manifestation of Ismāʿīlism in this period. In recent decades a large body of scholarship has emerged regarding these questions of Ismāʿīlī and Fāṭimid origins. Before we discuss this, however, we may quickly review the situation of Shīʿism in the later ninth century.

48 Al-Ṭabarī, *Taʾrīkh*, series III, pp. 1850–1; vol. XXXVI, trans. Waines as *The revolt of the Zanj*, pp. 127–8.

Most Shīʿa agreed that rightful authority – the true imamate and caliphate – belonged, after the Prophet, to a series of imams, beginning with the Prophet's son-in-law and cousin ʿAlī ibn Abī Ṭālib. With the exception of ʿAlī himself, who ruled as caliph from 35/656 to 40/661, these imams did not actually command armies and governments on earth. Nonetheless, they held rightful authority, and all the Umayyads and ʿAbbāsids were mere usurpers. In this view each imam inherited his rank both through ties of blood and through designation by the current imam of his heir.

In the later ninth century the Shīʿa of Iraq underwent a crisis of leadership, coinciding with the crisis of the ʿAbbāsid caliphate – of which, whether they liked it or not, they were subjects. They disagreed over several matters, one of which regarded events over a century old. The sixth in the line of imams had been the highly respected Jaʿfar al-Ṣādiq (d. 148/765). According to some Shīʿa, Jaʿfar had designated as his heir his son Ismāʿīl who, however, predeceased him; the imamate then went to Jaʿfar's grandson, Muḥammad the son of Ismāʿīl. Shīʿa of this persuasion became known as Ismāʿīlīs or Seveners.[49] Many of them believed that Muḥammad ibn Ismāʿīl, the last of their imams, had not died but had disappeared into occultation (*ghayba*), from which he would return one day to rule the earth.

Other Shīʿa disagreed, claiming that Jaʿfar al-Ṣādiq had been followed in the imamate not by Ismāʿīl, but by another son, Mūsā al-Kāẓim. For people of this persuasion the series ended with the death of the eleventh imam, al-Ḥasan al-ʿAskarī, in Sāmarrāʾ in 260/874, early in the reign of al-Muʿtamid. Some of al-Ḥasan's followers held further that a son of his, Muḥammad ibn al-Ḥasan, was the rightful twelfth imam, even though he had disappeared at around the same time. Agreement on all this was not achieved until some time afterwards, with the consolidation of what we know as Imāmī or Twelver Shīʿism. Shīʿa of this persuasion believed (and believe) that the twelfth imam, Muḥammad ibn al-Ḥasan the Mahdī, the 'rightly guided', had entered a state of occultation (*ghayba*) from which he will emerge eventually to rule the world. It is important to remember, in any case, that it was during the later ninth century that these doctrines were taking form; and that many Shīʿa, and Ismāʿīlīs in particular, expected that their imam would return from occultation very soon.

Ismāʿīlīs were not the only political activists during these years. Zaydī Shīʿa, concentrated in Kūfa and elsewhere, had already been involved in a long series of revolts against the ʿAbbāsid caliphate, especially in its early decades. Their

49 For the arithmetic leading to seven, see Heinz Halm, *The empire of the Madhi: The rise of the Fatimids*, trans. Michael Bonner (Leiden, 1996), p. 19.

doctrine achieved maturity in the work of the imam al-Qāsim ibn Ibrāhīm al-Rassī (d. 246/860). Now, in the later ninth century, Zaydīs emerged in force in two peripheral areas. In Ṭabaristān, south of the Caspian, a Zaydī state was established in 250/864 by the Ḥasanid al-Ḥasan ibn Zayd, followed by his brother Muḥammad. External resistance and internal turmoil overcame this enterprise, but a renewed Zaydī state was established by a Ḥusaynid, al-Nāṣir ilā 'l-Ḥaqq (d. 304/917). This Zaydī presence in the southern Caspian provided a constant challenge to the ʿAbbāsid governors and other rulers of this turbulent region. Meanwhile in Yemen a Zaydī state emerged in 284/897, led by a grandson of al-Qāsim ibn Ibrāhīm, al-Hādī ilā 'l-Ḥaqq, followed by a long line of imams. From their capital in Ṣaʿda the Zaydīs achieved a remarkable level of stability, maintaining distance from the politics of the larger Islamic world.[50]

Regarding the rise of Ismāʿīlism and the Fāṭimid caliphate, recent research on the literary sources[51] points to a sequence of events that may be sketched as follows. The doctrine and sect first became visible in the early 870s, in the activity of ʿAbd Allāh the Elder (ʿAbd Allāh al-Akbar) who lived in ʿAskar Mukram in Khūzistān. ʿAbd Allāh preached that Muḥammad ibn Ismāʿīl was *al-mahdī*, 'the truly guided one' and *al-qāʾim*, 'the one who appears', destined to return and to rule the world; he was also the seventh and last within an Islamic cycle of imams, itself the last within a larger series of cycles. Upon his arrival Muḥammad ibn Ismāʿīl would reveal the 'true religion', known until then only to small circles of the initiated. This revelation would result in the abolition of Islamic law (*rafʿ al-sharīʿa*), together with a renewal of the Edenic religion of Adam, without any rites, commandments or prohibitions.[52] In this way ʿAbd Allāh the Elder combined Shīʿite principles regarding the imamate with gnostic teachings and secret rites of initiation. (The Neoplatonism that we associate with Ismāʿīlism did not enter the picture until afterwards.) ʿAbd Allāh and his family established themselves quietly in Salamiyya (or Salamya) in eastern Syria on the desert's edge. There, acting as chief *dāʿīs* (callers) for Muḥammad ibn Ismāʿīl, they sent out other *dāʿīs* who created a network of communities in northern Iran, the Gulf, Yemen and elsewhere. They scored an early success in the Sawād of Iraq.

50 W. Madelung, 'al-Rassī, al-Qāsim b. Ibrāhīm', *EI2*, vol. VIII, pp. 453–4; W. Madelung, 'Zaydiyya', *EI2*, vol. XI, pp. 477–81 with bibliography; W. Madelung, 'The minor dynasties of northern Iran', in R. N. Frye (ed.), *Cambridge history of Iran*, vol. IV: *The period from the Arab invasion to the Saljuqs*, (Cambridge, 1975).

51 Recent summaries of this approach can be found in Halm, *Empire of the Mahdi*; Paul Walker, 'The Ismāʿīlī daʿwa and the Fatimid caliphate', in Carl F. Petry (ed.), *The Cambridge history of Egypt*, vol. I: *Islamic Egypt, 640–1517* (1998); and Paul Walker, *Exploring an Islamic empire: Fatimid history and its sources* (London and New York, 2002).

52 Halm, *Empire of the Mahdi*, p. 21.

> It has already been mentioned that al-Ḥusayn al-Ahwāzī was sent to the Sawād of Kufa as a *dāʿī* … Along the way he met a man called Ḥamdān ibn al-Ashʿath, who was known as Qarmaṭ, since he was short and had short legs … [Qarmaṭ] had with him an ox, on which he was carrying goods. Al-Ḥusayn asked him, 'Which is the way to Quss Bahram?' 'That's my village,' replied Qarmaṭ … After they had gone for a while, Ḥamdān said to him, 'I suppose you've had a long journey, since you're exhausted. Come sit on this ox of mine!' Al-Ḥusayn replied, 'I have not been instructed to do that.' [Ḥamdān Qarmaṭ's interest is aroused, and al-Ḥusayn continues:] 'A sack has been entrusted to me which contains the knowledge of one of God's secrets. I have been instructed to cure the people of this village, to make them rich, to save them, and to take the kingdoms of the world out of the hands of those who now control them, and to place them under their rule.'[53]

Ḥamdān Qarmaṭ takes the vow 'which God took from his prophets and messengers'. He and his brother-in-law ʿAbdān become zealous partisans of the *mahdī*. The *dāʿī* lives in their village until his death, when Ḥamdān Qarmaṭ takes his place. This Iraqi mission recognises the authority of Salamiyya, where the entire network is directed by a series of descendants of ʿAbd Allāh the Elder, each bearing the title of *ḥujja*, or 'proof'.

It is rare for medieval Arabic historical writing to carry us so deep into the countryside, riding on the back of an ox. For a while the narrative tarries in the village, as the community shares its possessions and contributes to the *mahdī*'s cause. Soon, however, we find ʿAbdān preaching to the Bedouin around Kūfa.[54] Within a few years these nomads and semi-nomads were threatening the cities of Iraq and Syria, where the ʿAbbāsid authorities referred to them by the (abusive) term Qarmaṭīs, or Qarāmiṭa. However, if the Qarāmiṭa were now predominantly Bedouin, their leadership came from the settled lands of the Sawād,[55] just as the leadership of the Zanj had not come from the Zanj themselves.

Another brilliant success was reserved for the resourceful Abū ʿAbd Allāh al-Shīʿī, originally from Kūfa, who was recruited and sent to Egypt and Yemen in 891. While on the pilgrimage Abū ʿAbd Allāh met a group of Kutāma Berbers from what today is north-eastern Algeria. Sensing an opportunity, he plied his new acquaintances with questions.

53 Ibid., pp. 28–9, combining several sources that rely ultimately on the anti-Ismāʿīlī polemicist Ibn Rizām. A readily accessible version of the story is in Aḥmad ibn ʿAlī al-Maqrīzī, *Ittiʿāẓ al-ḥunafāʾ bi-akhbār al-aʾimma al-fāṭimiyyīn al-khulafāʾ* (Cairo, 1967), pp. 151–8.

54 Halm, *Empire of the Mahdi*, pp. 48, 64.

55 Hugh Kennedy, *The Prophet and the age of the caliphates*, 2nd edn (Harlow, 2004), p. 286.

> He asked them whether the [Aghlabid] rulers of Ifrīqiya had any governors [in the region where they lived], and they said they did not. There were individual men who ruled alone over the various cities, but these had nothing to do with the rulers, beyond having the prayer said for them in the pulpits … 'Then do you owe them obedience?' 'Not at all; they rather fawn on those of us who go to them, for we are superior to them in strength.' Then who rules over you?' 'Each of us has power over himself' … 'How large is your country?' 'Five days' journey in length and three in width.' And are you a single tribe?' 'The name Kutāma unites us, but we are divided into tribes, subtribes and clans.' 'Then are you unified among yourselves?' 'No, we fight one another, and after someone has gained the victory, we join together again' … 'But if a stranger tries to force his way in among you, do you hold together?' 'No one has yet tried that.' 'And why not?' 'Because we are many and our country is impassable.' 'How many are you then?' 'No one, neither from among us, nor so far as we know from outside, has ever counted us.' 'Do you have horses and weapons?' 'They are our most important possessions and all our pride; we collect these things because we need them in our fights against one another.' … [Abū ʿAbd Allāh] retained everything and got them to report everything he wanted to know. For he had high expectations and hopes in them, whereas they had no inkling of what he wanted … He was content with everything he heard and thought that with them he would arrive at his goal.[56]

Abū ʿAbd Allāh travelled to the Kutāma homeland and established himself there. The Kutāma admired him for his knowledge of the law and his ascetic way of life, and soon most of them were enthusiastic converts to the cause of Muḥammad ibn Ismāʿīl.

In Salamiyya in 899 the leadership of the *daʿwa* or 'summoning' devolved upon a descendant of ʿAbd Allāh the Elder named Saʿīd ibn al-Ḥusayn. This Saʿīd now declared that he was not merely the 'Proof' and the leader of the *daʿwa*, but the actual imam himself. He claimed to be a direct descendant of Muḥammad ibn Ismāʿīl and, through him, of ʿAlī and the Prophet Muḥammad. In this view the imamate would have been passed on continuously within this family, instead of ending with the disappearance of the seventh imam. Saʿīd's claim, which was sorely contested on genealogical grounds, roiled the Ismāʿīlī movement. Some, including Abū ʿAbd Allāh al-Shīʿī in the west, accepted the imamate of Saʿīd, who now took the name ʿAbd Allāh (and thereby became known to his enemies as ʿUbayd Allāh, 'little

56 Halm, *Empire of the Mahdi*, pp. 40–1, quoting Qāḍī Nuʿmān, *Iftitāḥ al-dawla wa-btidāʾ al-daʿwa*, ed. F. Dachraoui [Dashrāwī] (Tunis, 1975), paragraphs 31 ff.; ed. W. al-Qāḍī (Beirut, 1970), pp. 54–8.

'Abd Allāh'), and the title al-Mahdī. Others, including the followers of 'Abdān and Ḥamdān Qarmaṭ in Iraq, rejected it, insisting on the imamate of Muḥammad ibn Ismāʿīl. Meanwhile, Saʿīd/'Abd Allāh escaped to Egypt and from there to North Africa. He did not join Abū 'Abd Allāh and the Kutāma, but pushed ahead to the western fringe of the Islamic world in Sijilmāsa, where he tried to remain anonymous.

Abū 'Abd Allāh emerged with a Kutāma fighting force in 902 and attacked the Aghlabid emirate. We have already seen that the Aghlabids had made a fatal error in committing most of their resources to the war in Sicily, while leaving their western borderlands in the hands of Berber tribesmen and a few Arab warlords in the cities (as the Kutāma informed Abū 'Abd Allāh). The enthusiastic Kutāma overcame the demoralised Aghlabid force. In 297/909 Abū 'Abd Allāh took the Aghlabid capital, al-Raqqāda, near Qayrawān, as well as Qayrawān itself. In the same year the Rustamid state also fell victim to Abū 'Abd Allāh and the Kutāma, who destroyed their capital, Tāhert. As Ziyādat Allāh III, the last of the Aghlabid *amīrs*, escaped from Ifrīqiya to Egypt, Abū 'Abd Allāh led a rescue expedition westward to Sijilmāsa. When 'Abd Allāh the Mahdī arrived in Ifrīqiya in 297/909f., he formally assumed the imamate and caliphate. Here we have the beginning of what we know as the Fāṭimid caliphate of North Africa and (from 358/969 onwards) of Egypt.

Counter-caliphs and Shīʿite rebellions had risen before, but since the 'Abbāsid revolution none of them had come so far. For whatever one thought of his credentials, the Fāṭimid *mahdī* ruled over a large part of the Islamic world, at a time when the 'Abbāsid caliphate was ill-equipped for the challenge. However, the *daʿwa* network that the *mahdī*'s ancestors had knit together now came unravelled. In Iraq we hear nothing more of Ḥamdān Qarmaṭ,[57] but, as we have seen, the 'Abbāsid authorities applied the term 'Qarmaṭī' to Bedouin movements that threatened them much as the Zanj had done earlier, but now over a wider area. These 'Qarmaṭīs' of Syria, Iraq and al-Baḥrayn were sworn enemies not only of the 'Abbāsids, but also of the Fāṭimid *mahdī*.

In Ifrīqiya, however, the *mahdī* set about establishing a state that broadly resembled its Umayyad and 'Abbāsid predecessors. Again we have an imperial centre deriving the bulk of its revenues from a land-tax levied directly upon

57 There is, however, the interesting (and solitary) passage in Ibn Ḥawqal, *Ṣūrat al-arḍ* (Leiden, 1938), p. 96, which identifies a Fāṭimid supporter and courtier named Abū 'Alī as none other than Ḥamdān Qarmaṭ. According to Walker, 'The Ismāʿīlī daʿwa and the Fatimid caliphate', pp. 126–7, Abū 'Alī/Ḥamdān would have been responsible for the conversion of Abū 'Abd Allāh al-Shīʿī and his brother Abu 'l-'Abbās in Kūfa.

the taxpayers. The bureaucracy resembled its ʿAbbāsid counterpart, with the lack of a formal office of *wazīr* amounting to an archaic trait. And, like the earliest Islamic state, the Fāṭimid enterprise owed its success to a tribal army, the Kutāma, who remained eager for further conquest. Before long, however, the Fāṭimids brought their state into line with prevailing trends, by resorting to tax-farming[58] and – already in the reign of al-Mahdī – by bringing slave-soldiers into their armies. On the other hand, the Fāṭimids had a different theory of succession to the imamate.[59] Their imam was a charismatic figure, surrounded by an ever more complex processional and ceremonial, rising above the religious and social divisions of the Islamic world over which he reigned.[60]

This sketch of Ismāʿīlī and Fāṭimid origins is based on the analysis of modern scholars who have used a rich and growing collection of medieval sources. However, it is important to mention other approaches, especially that of Michael Brett.[61] Brett sees ninth-century Ismāʿīlism as part of a larger brew of oppositional trends, the 'sectarian milieu' which John Wansbrough described as the religious and doctrinal environment of early Islam.[62] Thus, when the Fāṭimid dynasty came to power in North Africa in 909, and again when it conquered Egypt in 969, its historians and other advocates – including the Qāḍī al-Nuʿmān (d. 975), a brilliant jurist and gifted writer – retrospectively cast a view of unity over the entire Ismāʿīlī past. More precisely, these pro-Fāṭimid writers presented a story of a united origin followed by sectarian division: those who believed in the imamate of the Fāṭimids were the trunk of the Ismāʿīlī tree, the followers of the authentic teaching, whereas the various dissenting groups were branches that had diverged into wrong belief. In Brett's view it is likely that the so-called Qarmaṭīs of Iraq and Baḥrayn were not even part of the original Ismāʿīlī movement, but became associated with it later on.[63] At the same time, the idea of an unbroken connection between the beginning of Ismāʿīlī doctrine and the foundation of the Fāṭimid caliphate also suited the purposes of anti-Ismāʿīlī writers who sought, all at once, to

58 Halm, *Empire of the Mahdi*, pp. 358–60.

59 Though not entirely different from the Umayyad doctrine, if we follow Patricia Crone and Martin Hinds, *God's caliph: Religious authority in the first centuries of Islam* (Cambridge, 1986).

60 Brett, *Rise of the Fatimids*, pp. 176–99.

61 Brett, 'The Mīm, the ʿAyn, and the making of Ismāʿīlism', *BSOAS*, 57 (1994), repr. in Michael Brett, *Ibn Khaldūn and the medieval Maghrib* (Aldershot, 1999); Brett, *Rise of the Fatimids*, esp. pp. 29–47, 176–218.

62 John Wansbrough, *The sectarian milieu: Content and composition of Islamic salvation history* (Oxford, 1978).

63 Brett, *Rise of the Fatimids*, pp. 46–7.

denounce Ismāʿīlī doctrines as heresy, and to discredit Fāṭimid claims to legitimacy as genealogical lies. Accordingly, in Brett's view, the fact that pro- and anti-Ismāʿīlī sources often agree in their description of events does not constitute proof for the historicity of these events: the two camps, each for its own reasons, embraced a similar (unitary) view of Fāṭimid and Ismāʿīlī origins.

Restoration

Before and during this challenge from a vigorous rival, the ʿAbbāsids, together with their soldiers and administrators, worked hard to rebuild their own caliphate, and for a time they achieved considerable success. Here, in a world of reduced resources and proliferating red tape, technocrats and bureaucrats held the key. Soldiers, though needed at every turn, were mainly content to follow the caliph, a military man like themselves. At the same time, this restored ʿAbbāsid caliphate imitated some of the practices of its neighbours, especially in the search for legitimisation through performance of *jihād* and through control of the frontiers against the enemies of Islam.

When al-Muwaffaq died in 278/891 his son Abu ʾl-ʿAbbās inherited his position as high commander and strongman. In the following year al-Muʿtamid died, and Abu ʾl-ʿAbbās pushed aside his cousin, Jaʿfar ibn al-Muʿtamid, to become caliph in his own right, assuming the regnal title al-Muʿtaḍid. Al-Muʿtaḍid cut a figure similar to his father's: an energetic military man, respected by the troops. Unlike his father, however, he now enjoyed sole control over the caliphate and, with the defeat of the Zanj in 280/893, a generally improved situation. He achieved a reputation and popularity that went beyond the army, and his reign (279–89/892–902) constituted the high point of what is known as the 'ʿAbbāsid restoration'.

This restored caliphate was militarised in a way that the old caliphate of al-Manṣūr and al-Rashīd had not been. This did not mean that the soldiers could simply have their way: the Sāmarrān crisis of the 860s had made everyone averse to such a situation. The bureaucracy, meanwhile, saw a net gain in its power and influence. Al-Muʿtaḍid's *wazīr*, ʿUbayd Allāh ibn Sulaymān ibn Wahb, held wide power over both civil administration and military affairs. But in a situation where both caliph and *wazīr* were often preoccupied with military affairs, the leading bureaucrats learned to impose themselves. After all, the army could not live (let alone fight) unless it received its pay from the *dīwān al-jaysh*, the Bureau of the Army. The caliphate was reduced in territory and could rely on regular income from only a few areas, apart from the Iraqi heartland of the Sawād. Al-Muʿtaḍid set about remedying this situation by bringing the *amīrs* of remote provinces into line and, where possible, by reconquering territory for the caliphate to administer directly. However, these expeditions cost large amounts of money, which the bureaucrats had to exert all their skills to provide.

By this time the ʿAbbāsid bureaucracy had achieved a high level of technical proficiency and complexity. It provided the very model for Islamic administration, a model that would be imitated by, among others, the Sāmānids (see below), who would then transmit these procedures, together with the cultural styles associated with them, to later dynastic states in the east. Employment in the *dīwāns* (bureaux) required an array of accomplishments which included, on the humanistic side, mastery of the Arabic language together with poetry, history, calligraphy and many other subjects. On the technical side, scribes needed expertise in arithmetic, accounting and surveying, together with familiarity with the fiscal districts and the procedures governing them; this technical work seems especially daunting because what we now call the 'Arabic numerals' were not yet in everyday use. The skills required for the *dīwāns* were thus quite demanding, but educational networks, including the practices of apprenticeship within the *dīwāns* themselves, produced them in abundance, and there were more than enough qualified scribes available for the jobs.

The *dīwāns* became ever more complex, hierarchical and costly. And as they grew larger the fiscal districts grew smaller, to allow the officials to exercise closer oversight. Under al-Muʿtaḍid the *dīwāns* of all the provinces were united in one central location in Baghdad, the *dīwān al-dār*, or Bureau of the Palace. Afterwards these were divided again into the *dīwāns* of the west, the east and the Sawād, while the *dīwān al-dār* became an accounting or records office for the others.[64]

The reign of al-Muʿtaḍid saw a growth of factionalism within this bureaucracy, observable also in the army and in urban civilian life.[65] A leading role in financial administration was played by two brothers of the Banū al-Furāt family, Aḥmad and ʿAlī, until 286/899, when their place was taken by the Banū al-Jarrāḥ, led by Muḥammad ibn Dāwūd and his nephew ʿAlī ibn ʿĪsā. In the following decades ʿAbbāsid administration would be largely dominated by

64 R. Mottahedeh, 'The ʿAbbāsid caliphate in Iran', in R. N. Frye (ed.), *The Cambridge history of Iran*, vol. IV: *The period from the Arab invasion to the Saljuqs* (Cambridge, 1975), pp. 79–84.

65 R. Mottahedeh, *Loyalty and leadership in an early Islamic society* (Princeton, 1980; repr. 2001), esp. pp. 158–68 (factions).

these two clans, the Furātids and Jarrāḥids; employees of the bureaucracy had little choice but to establish ties of patronage with one or the other. Thus whenever the man at the top was dismissed, his network would collapse and be replaced by the rival network. The scribes were usually civil and restrained in their dealings with members of the opposing faction, since they knew well that the situation could turn against them at any moment. At times we find them taking indirect action against each other, as in a caliphal decree (issued under al-Muqtadir, in 296/909) that Jews and Christians must not be hired for administrative work;[66] this seems to have been a Furātid measure directed against the Jarrāḥids, recent converts to Islam whose rank and file still included numbers of unconverted Christians.

However, things could become uncivil – and worse – during the investigative and confiscatory procedure known as *muṣādara*, in existence since the days of the Umayyads. It was common, whenever a *wazīr* or other high official fell from power, for his successor in the office, with approval of the caliph, to 'encourage' the fallen official to hand over the properties and funds that he had supposedly embezzled during his term of office. The mulcting procedure involved imprisonment and torture, sometimes extended to the victim's family. One result was that a holder of high office had no choice but to stow away large amounts of property and cash, so as to avoid being tortured to death when the moment arrived. At the same time, it was necessary not to give everything away at once, which would lead the investigators to suspect the existence of even more. We may view all this as a routinised combination of embezzlement and extortion: at least since the days of al-Maʾmūn there had been a *dīwān al-muṣādarāt*, a 'Bureau of Mulcted Properties'.[67] Confiscations could also be directed against a wider range of targets, and not only former office-holders. It seems, moreover, that the confiscated wealth was turned over to the caliph's 'private' treasury or privy purse, the *bayt māl al-khāṣṣa*.[68] During this period of the restored ʿAbbāsid caliphate and the precipitate decline that followed it, this caliphal treasury frequently held more money than the 'public treasury', the *bayt māl al-ʿāmma*. Thus, on the accession of al-Muqtadir in 295/908, the 'private' treasury held 15 million *dīnārs*, the 'public' treasury only 600,000.[69] The privy purse had its own *dīwāns* and a cohort of bureaucrats to administer them, a source of frustration for those who tried to make the entire machine work more efficiently.

66 Sibṭ Ibn al-Jawzī, *Mirʾāt al-zamān*, British Museum, OR 4169, vol. 2, 42b.
67 C. E. Bosworth, 'Muṣādara', *EI2*, vol. VII, pp. 652–3.
68 A. K. Lambton, 'Ṣāfī', *EI2*, vol. VIII, pp. 798–800.
69 Al-Ṭabarī, *Taʾrīkh*, series III, p. 2281; ʿArīb, *Ṣila*, pp. 22–3.

The balance among competing factions of bureaucrats and soldiers was precarious. One thing that held it all together under al-Muwaffaq and al-Muʿtaḍid was the example set by the ruler, especially in his personal involvement in the wars. The role of '*ghāzī*-caliph', invented by Hārūn al-Rashīd[70] and enhanced by al-Muʿtaṣim, now had its greatest performance, in al-Muʿtaḍid's tireless campaigning. This allowed him to foster ties of patronage among the army, so that many soldiers proudly called themselves 'al-Muʿtaḍidī' ('so-and-so the client or follower of al-Muʿtaḍid') for their entire lives. Al-Muʿtaḍid also enjoyed popularity among civilians, which made it easier for him to transfer the capital from Sāmarrāʾ to Baghdad. This move had begun decades earlier, when al-Muwaffaq made Baghdad a base of operations against the Zanj. But now al-Muʿtaḍid established himself in what became Baghdad's centre of gravity, on the east bank of the Tigris downstream from the Round City of al-Manṣūr.[71]

At the outset of his reign al-Muʿtaḍid did not control much territory beyond Iraq. His project of restoration would succeed only if he could gain control over the revenues of other provinces. He proceeded accordingly and, where he could not achieve this goal directly, he sought the formal allegiance of the rulers in question. He chose his targets shrewdly, alternating diplomacy with the use of force. His accomplishments now seem all the more remarkable when we consider how unwieldy and expensive the ʿAbbāsid army and bureaucracy had become.

In Egypt, upon the death of Ibn Ṭūlūn in 270/884 the emirate had been taken over by his son Khumārawayh. Al-Muwaffaq opposed this move and mounted a challenge, which Khumārawayh fended off in 271/885. Khumārawayh managed to extend Ṭūlūnid power over most of al-Jazīra, and he even compelled Yāzmān, the strongman of Tarsus, to acknowledge him as overlord. In 273/886 al-Muwaffaq made peace with Khumārawayh, granting to the Ṭūlūnid line the right to govern Egypt for the next thirty years. Thus, even though Khumārawayh lacked his father's charisma and energy, he achieved a measure of success. He also seems to have made a good choice by entrusting the country's finances to the Mādharāʾīs, a family of administrators who would maintain fiscal continuity in Egypt for decades to come, over several changes of regime.

When al-Muʿtaḍid became caliph he tolerated the Ṭūlūnid position in Syria, al-Jazīra and the Thughūr. In 280/893 he made a new accord with Khumārawayh, this one more favourable to the ʿAbbāsid side. The Ṭūlūnids

70 Michael Bonner, *Aristocratic violence and holy war: Studies in the jihad and the Arab–Byzantine frontier* (New Haven, 1996), pp. 99–106.
71 Kennedy, *The Prophet and the age of the caliphates*, p. 181.

were to pay an annual tribute of 300,000 *dīnārs*, with 200,000 *dīnārs* of arrears to be provided forthwith. Khumārawayh also agreed to hand over the Jazīran provinces of Diyār Rabīʿa and Diyār Muḍar. Al-Muʿtaḍid was prepared to coexist with the Ṭūlūnids: this is evident in his marriage to Khumārawayh's daughter Qaṭr al-Nadā, who brought a record-breaking dowry of a million *dīnārs*.[72] However, the young bride did not live long afterwards, nor did her father: Khumārawayh was assassinated in Damascus in 282/896, by his court eunuchs. He was followed by his fourteen-year-old son Jaysh, who was soon deposed, and then by another son, Hārūn. With the Ṭūlūnids disabled, Tarsus and the Arab–Byzantine frontier district opted for al-Muʿtaḍid, who then assumed, after a long hiatus, the old caliphal prerogative of commanding the annual summer expedition and arranging the defence against the Byzantine empire. The crumbling Ṭūlūnid state then had to face the onslaught of the Qarāmiṭa, who defeated the Ṭūlūnid commander, Ṭughj ibn Juff, near al-Raqqa in 289/902, and then besieged Damascus. Now many Ṭūlūnid officers left to join the more promising enterprise of the ʿAbbāsids.

Al-Muʿtaḍid also devoted attention to al-Jibāl, in west central Iran. Since the days of Hārūn al-Rashīd this had been the home of the Dulafids, descendants of the poet and commander Abū Dulaf (d. *c.* 225/840), centred on Karaj, between Hamadhān and Iṣfahān.[73] The Dulafids enjoyed a hereditary position within the ʿAbbāsid caliphate, rather like that of the Ṭāhirids. Now, with the death of Aḥmad ibn ʿAbd al-ʿAzīz ibn Abī Dulaf in 280/893, al-Muʿtaḍid saw an opening. He went to the province and imposed his son ʿAlī al-Muktafī as governor of Rayy, Qazvīn, Qumm and Hamadhān, and in 283/896 he stripped the last Dulafid *amīr* of his remaining lands.[74] However, the affairs of the province remained turbulent, in part because of the Zaydī ʿAlid mini-state lodged in the lowlands of nearby Ṭabaristān.

The Ṣaffārids remained the dominant power in the Persian-speaking world. After the death in 265/879 of Yaʿqūb ibn al-Layth, his brother, ʿAmr ibn al-Layth, proved a shrewd leader. Though mainly active in the east, ʿAmr still held Fārs in south-western Iran, a province that the ʿAbbāsids coveted for themselves. However, al-Muʿtaḍid chose the path of cooperation here (since ʿAmr was clearly too big to take on), recognising ʿAmr's position in Fārs as well as in Khurāsān. In 285/898 al-Muʿtaḍid allowed ʿAmr to go one step further, when he appointed him governor of Transoxania. This province was

72 Bianquis, 'Autonomous Egypt', p. 106.

73 C. E. Bosworth, *The new Islamic dynasties: A chronological and genealogical manual* (New York, 1996), p. 153.

74 Kennedy, *The Prophet and the age of the caliphates*, pp. 183–4.

already in the possession of the Sāmānid *amīr* Ismāʿīl ibn Aḥmad, whose brother Naṣr had previously been recognised as governor by al-Muʿtamid. With these conflicting investitures, al-Muʿtaḍid may have thought it in his own best interest to let ʿAmr and Ismāʿīl fight it out. When the decisive battle occurred, ʿAmr met utter defeat.[75] Ismāʿīl sent him as a prisoner to Baghdad, where he was executed soon after the death of al-Muʿtaḍid in 289/902. However, this did not mark the end of the Ṣaffārids. In Fārs, still an object of desire for the ʿAbbāsids, a grandson of ʿAmr ibn al-Layth named Ṭāhir ibn Muḥammad held out against armies sent by al-Muʿtaḍid. The province would not fall to the ʿAbbāsids until 910; later the Ṣaffārids would reappear as local rulers in Sīstān and adjoining regions, beginning in 923.

Al-Muʿtaḍid died in 289/902, after a reign of ten years. If he had ruled as long as his ancestors al-Manṣūr and al-Rashīd, things might have turned out differently for the ʿAbbāsid caliphate, which now found itself in an improved but still precarious position. The new caliph was ʿAlī al-Muktafī, a son of al-Muʿtaḍid who already had experience of governing in Rayy and Qazvīn. In his policies al-Muktafī provided continuity, but in his character and comportment he did not, being a sedentary figure who did not instill much loyalty, let alone inspiration, in the soldiers. However, loyalty and inspiration were now sorely needed, as the ʿAbbāsid caliphate faced the gravest threat it had seen since the days of the Zanj.

The Ismāʿīlī network of the late ninth century included a community in north-eastern Arabia, in the region known as al-Baḥrayn (corresponding broadly to the modern Saudi province of al-Ḥasā, not the island known nowadays as Bahrain). Here, in the last years of the caliphate of al-Muʿtaḍid, Abū Saʿīd al-Jannābī established himself at the head of this community and challenged the caliph's forces in Iraq, with considerable success. The ʿAbbāsid authorities called these Arabian sectarians Qarāmiṭa or Qarmaṭīs, as we have seen. Having previously encountered this threat from the south-east, the authorities were unprepared for the Qarmaṭī threat that now erupted in the west.

In the turmoil that followed the announcement by Saʿīd/ʿAbd Allāh of his own status as *mahdī* and imam, the Ismāʿīlīs in Iraq found themselves divided. Some, led by Ḥamdān Qarmaṭ's brother-in-law ʿAbdān, denied the claim, as we have seen. Others, who supported it, arranged for ʿAbdān to be treacherously murdered. Implicated in the deed was one Zikrawayh or Zikrōye, a former protégé of ʿAbdān who now went into hiding. In Syria, Zikrawayh's

75 See above, n. 29.

son Yaḥyā emerged at the head of a force of Bedouin from the tribal confederation of the Kalb. Yaḥyā read from a book containing divine instructions, he wore a veil which left only his eyes uncovered, and he rode a camel mare (*nāqa*) which provided a rallying-point (and totemic emblem) for the warriors. Accordingly, Yaḥyā became known as *ṣāḥib al-nāqa* (the 'man with the she-camel').[76] In 289/902 he defeated a Ṭūlūnid force, sacked al-Ruṣāfa and besieged Damascus, as we have seen. Meanwhile 'Abd Allāh the *mahdī* began his westward flight. Yaḥyā pressed on with the siege of Damascus, but in the summer of 290/903 he died before the city walls, and the siege was lifted. However, his brother al-Ḥusayn, known as *ṣāḥib al-shāma* (the 'man with the birthmark' (or mole)), took over, briefly establishing the *mahdī*'s rule in several Syrian towns. Awkwardly, the *mahdī* himself did not arrive, though he sent messages promising he would do so.

Meanwhile, al-Muktafī sent an army to Syria, commanded by Muḥammad ibn Sulaymān, who bore the title 'scribe of the Bureau of the Army' (*kātib dīwān al-jaysh*). (Significantly, Ibn Sulaymān had risen in the bureaucracy, and not the army.) Ibn Sulaymān encountered the Bedouin fighters, now referred to as 'Fāṭimids' (*Fāṭimiyyūn, Fawāṭim*), and routed them. 'Abd Allāh the *mahdī* still maintained a prudent distance, and the 'man with the birthmark', in his rage, slaughtered those members of the *mahdī*'s household who still remained in Salamiyya. This atrocity did not endear him to the surviving Bedouin 'Fāṭimids', who returned to their pasturages. Ibn Sulaymān tracked him down and delivered him to Baghdad where, in an elaborate public spectacle in the winter of 291/904, the 'man with the birthmark' was maimed and tortured to death, together with over 300 of his followers and some common criminals. The gruesome show gave vent to the fear that the 'Qarmaṭīs' inspired among the population. But although al-Muktafī could claim victory this time, this fear would return many times in the coming decades.

The other notable success of al-Muktafī's five-year reign involved the end of the Ṭūlūnid state. Ṭughj ibn Juff, who had been the Ṭūlūnid commander against the sons of Zikrawayh before the arrival of the Iraqi army commanded by Ibn Sulaymān, now came to an understanding with the 'Abbāsid forces. Fusṭāṭ surrendered in 292/905, the Ṭūlūnid complex of al-Qaṭā'i' was razed to the ground, except for the great mosque, and a train of prisoners was dispatched to Baghdad. Nonetheless, the restoration of 'Abbāsid rule did not bring an improvement in Egypt's fortunes. Having to send large sums to Iraq every year, and saddled with an expensive military

76 Al-Ṭabarī, *Ta'rīkh* II, series III, p. 2224; Halm, *Empire of the Mahdi*, pp. 71–2.

establishment at home, the Egyptian administrators apportioned *iqṭāʿāt* (concessions of revenues from fiscal districts), as had happened in Iraq perhaps as early as the 860s. Lands were assigned to soldiers and administrators, and periodically confiscated. This practice immobilised a large proportion of Egyptian lands and properties, and reduced the ability of rulers and administrators to take effective action.[77]

Not surprisingly, direct ʿAbbāsid rule in Egypt did not last long. After several governors had come and gone, a Turkish commander named Takīn gained control and received confirmation from Baghdad in 301/913f. Takīn then had to confront the first attack against Egypt launched by the Fāṭimids in North Africa. He was removed in the following year, and in the end it was Muʾnis, a general from the court of the caliph al-Muqtadir, who came from Iraq and repelled the invasion. A second Fāṭimid invasion followed five years later; Takīn took control, only to see Muʾnis enter Egypt again with a force of 3,000, defeating the Fāṭimids in 922. Takīn was reappointed a third time in 924, in a time of turmoil and insecurity. After he died in 933 a struggle took place over the leadership; and now the ʿAbbāsid authorities were unable to intervene. The winner was Muḥammad ibn Ṭughj, son of that Ṭughj ibn Juff who had fought the sons of Zikrawayh and brought about the collapse of the Ṭūlūnid state. Ibn Tughj staved off a third Fāṭimid invasion in 323/935, this time without outside help. He received confirmation of his governorship, and in 327/939 the caliph al-Rāḍī granted him the right to be called *ikhshīd*, a princely title harking back to the land of his ancestors, Farghāna in Central Asia. The *ikhshīd*'s position resembled that of the Ṭūlūnids before him, even if he lacked their brilliance. Egypt in the Ikhshīdid period (until 968) was a major power within the new configuration of politics in the Mediterranean, which included a revived Byzantine empire, a Holy Roman empire occupying much of southern Italy, and two new Islamic caliphates in the west, those of the Fāṭimids (from 909) and the Spanish Umayyads (from 929).

New centres of power

As the ʿAbbāsid caliphate in Baghdad collapsed during the first half of the tenth century, in other places – especially along the edges of the Islamic world – new rulers achieved successes and new states emerged.

77 Bianquis, 'Autonomous Egypt', p. 109.

Fāṭimid North Africa

The Fāṭimid *dawla*, or dynastic state, that emerged in Ifrīqiya in 909 harked back, in many ways, to the Umayyad and early ʿAbbāsid caliphates, as we have seen. Of course it was built on the foundations of the Aghlabid emirate.[78] At the same time, this new *dawla* was the achievement of one man, the austere Abū ʿAbd Allāh al-Shīʿī. But now, for Abū ʿAbd Allāh and some of his fellow *dāʿīs*, the new reality proved disappointing. The *mahdī* whom they had placed on the throne did not lead an exemplary life, let alone usher in a new age. A measure of messianic expectation can be seen in the name and title of his son and heir, Abu ʾl-Qāsim Muḥammad ibn ʿAbd Allāh al-Qāʾim (where the genealogically ordered name is precisely that of the Prophet Muḥammad, and the title, 'the present one', is millennarian), but for the most part the new ruler was concerned with establishing a state and army in conventional ways. Within two years matters came to a head. The *mahdī* found out about a plot against him, and he executed Abū ʿAbd Allāh together with several other *dāʿīs* and Kutāma commanders. The similarity to the execution of Abū Muslim, a century and a half previously, has often been noted: like Abū Muslim, Abū ʿAbd Allāh had become a burden to the ruler he had placed on the throne. And like the ʿAbbāsid caliph al-Manṣūr, the Fāṭimid *mahdī* had to struggle afterwards to maintain the loyalty of his base; but in the end he prevailed.

The history of the Fāṭimid caliphs in North Africa conveys a sense of movement towards a great consummation: not the End of Days, but rather the worldly conquest of Egypt. This great province, whose revenues dwarfed those of Ifrīqiya, was the first step on the way to dominion over the entire Muslim world, which the Fāṭimid claim to imamate and caliphate entailed. Moreover, Egypt was vulnerable following the Ṭūlūnid collapse and ʿAbbāsid takeover. To exploit the situation, the *mahdī* sent an expedition in 301/914. His son and heir Abu ʾl-Qāsim took part, holding Alexandria, Giza and the Fayyūm before yielding to the ʿAbbāsid commander Muʾnis, as we have seen. Five years later another expedition was sent, nominally under Abu ʾl-Qāsim's command. This expedition included a fleet of around eighty ships, which the ʿAbbāsids destroyed. Meanwhile, Abu ʾl-Qāsim occupied much of the country before he became trapped, in 922, in the Fayyūm and was forced to escape with heavy losses. Afterwards, early in his own reign, Abu ʾl-Qāsim al-Qāʾim made a last attempt to take Egypt. Despite the failure of these

78 The basic work on the Aghlabid emirate is still Mohamed Talbi, *L'émirat aghlabide (184–296/800–909): Histoire politique* (Paris, 1966). Much of the recent work relating to the Aghlabids has dealt with their operations in Sicily.

expeditions, they are a testimony to Fāṭimid power. Egypt is nearly impregnable from its western side: the Fāṭimid expedition that ultimately succeeded, that of Jawhar in 969, met little opposition, and the only serious invasion from the west since then has been that of Rommel, which came to grief in 1942 at El Alamein.

Ismāʿīlīs were probably not as scarce in the Fāṭimid domains as we often think: proselytising 'sessions of wisdom' (*majālis al-ḥikma*) were held, at first under Abū ʿAbd Allāh al-Shīʿī himself, and from a later time we hear, from the Qāḍī al-Nuʿmān, that the audiences for these sessions were eager and large.[79] However, there is no denying that the ruling elite was a religious minority. Al-Mahdī built himself a new capital, al-Mahdiyya, a fortified stronghold on a spit of land jutting into the Mediterranean, thus isolating himself from the hostile Sunnī and Mālikī populace of Qayrawān. In fact, his Aghlabid predecessors had done much the same, in establishing themselves at al-Raqqāda (near Qayrawān) and Tunis (like al-Mahdiyya, looking out to sea); afterwards the Fāṭimids would return inland, to a new foundation in al-Manṣūriyya. However, even if the Fāṭimid caliphs maintained a degree of physical separation from the population, their relations with non-Ismāʿīlīs were not uniformly hostile. Mālikī biographical works with a hagiographical character lament the oppression inflicted by the heretical rulers, but they do not name a single victim who suffered martyrdom at their hands.[80] There were confrontations over matters of ritual, along Sunnī–Shīʿite lines, but the Fāṭimids learned to leave other religious groups considerable latitude in their religious practice and communal organisation. Like the Aghlabids before them, the Fāṭimids found that the campaigns in Sicily and southern Italy, together with the activity of volunteers in the *ribāṭs*, or fortresses guarding the North African coastlines, provided a minimal measure of solidarity between rulers and ruled. Above all, this was a time of prosperity for North Africa. Trade with western Europe was on the rise. The naval technology of the time required frequent stops, which worked to the advantage of the North African and Sicilian ports. In this way the Fāṭimids benefited from the conquest of Sicily, and Palermo became one of the largest cities of Islam. This did not, by itself, quell opposition to the Fāṭimids, but many North Africans must have noticed the relative increase in prosperity that came with their rule.[81]

79 Halm, *Empire of the Mahdi*, pp. 374–6, citing Qāḍī al-Nuʿmān, *al-Majālis wal-musāyarāt* (Tunis, 1978), paragraphs 201, 224, 467, 487.

80 Halm, *Empire of the Mahdi*, pp. 221–47, citing the *Riyāḍ al-nufūs* of Abū Bakr al-Mālikī (Beirut, 1981).

81 Brett, *Rise of the Fatimids*, pp. 247–66.

Effective and deadly opposition to the Fāṭimids came from another direction. Many North African Muslims remained loyal to Khārijism, especially along the fringes of the Sahara and among Berber tribal confederations that were rivals of the Kutāma. It was among one of these, the Zanāta, that the great enemy of the Fāṭimids arose: Abū Yazīd Makhlad ibn Kaydad, known as the *ṣāḥib al-ḥimār* (the 'man with the donkey'). Abū Yazīd set out in 943 and quickly swept over most of Ifrīqiya, including Qayrawān. He besieged the caliph al-Qāʾim (r. 322–34/934–46) in al-Mahdiyya where, some said afterwards, it had been prophesied that the entire Fāṭimid realm would become reduced to a single narrow space. Things looked all the worse for the Fāṭimid cause because of al-Qāʾim's reclusiveness and passivity, which contrasted strangely with the energy he had shown in his youth. However, Abū Yazīd and his back-country followers severely alienated the urban Mālikī population when they occupied Qayrawān. The Fāṭimids and the Kutāma managed to regroup and to drive the Khārijites back. The hero of the encounter was al-Qāʾim's son, the future caliph Ismāʿīl al-Manṣūr (r. 334–41/946–53). After years of hard campaigning he defeated the Khārijites and finally got hold of the 'man with the donkey' himself, whose corpse, flayed and stuffed with straw, was then paraded throughout the Fāṭimid domains. Al-Manṣūr is alone among the Fāṭimid caliphs, Egyptian as well as North African, in being a military figure, a '*ghāzī*-caliph', through and through. This, together with his early death, contributed to the favourable image he had among his subjects, including and beyond his fellow Ismāʿīlīs.[82]

Al-Andalus

The arrival of a new caliphate in North Africa in 909 was followed, two decades later, by yet another one, this one in al-Andalus or Islamic Spain. We have seen that in the second half of the ninth century al-Andalus suffered from internal strife. Meanwhile, it remained a frontier society, in constant low-density warfare against the small Christian kingdoms to its north.[83] All this changed with the Umayyad *amīr* ʿAbd al-Raḥmān III, who, from the beginning of his rule in 300/912, campaigned energetically against local lords installed in cities, mountain redoubts and frontier posts. ʿAbd al-Raḥmān also looked to the north, where Christians from León had advanced to the Duero and were raiding Muslim territory. ʿAbd al-Raḥmān personally led campaigns of *jihād* five times. In 924 he arrived in the Ebro valley, sacking Pamplona and

82 Halm, *Empire of the Mahdi*, p. 337.
83 Above, p. 318.

burning its cathedral. In this way he extended Umayyad power to the north, including the Mediterranean coast.

ʿAbd al-Raḥmān also faced a challenge in the south, from the Fāṭimid al-Mahdī and his successors. Ismāʿīlism on its own never gained ground in al-Andalus, but, with the rise of the new caliphal power, rebels against ʿAbd al-Raḥmān could compel the mosques in the territory under their control to say the *khuṭba* in favour of the Fāṭimid.[84] Fighting between Umayyads and Fāṭimids did not take the form of direct conflict and invasion. Instead, the two sides acted against each other through proxies in the western reaches of North Africa. There the earlier division of territory, with the Midrārids based in Sijilmāsa, the Idrīsids in Fez and the Rustamids in Tāhert, had already been upset by the arrival of the Fāṭimids. In 921 a Fāṭimid campaign took Fez (though the Fāṭimids did not hold it for long), bringing an end to what remained of the Idrīsid dynasty. Meanwhile ʿAbd al-Raḥmān fortified his ports and sought bases on the North African coast near Spain.[85]

Encouraged by his successes and seeking to counter the Fāṭimid threat to his south, ʿAbd al-Raḥmān made a bold move in 929, by assuming the title commander of the faithful, with the regnal title al-Nāṣir ('the victorious'). The Umayyads of Spain had never claimed the caliphate before, but now they had good reasons for trying. The decline of ʿAbbāsid power was felt throughout the Islamic world. The Umayyads had a plausible claim to the caliphate, based on their simply being Umayyads: for them the usurping, butchering ʿAbbāsids had deprived all generations of Umayyads of their rightful place. The decisive reason, however, must have been rivalry with the Fāṭimids. ʿAbd al-Raḥmān made contact with Byzantium and the German emperor Otto I (r. 938–73), with the goal of restraining a common enemy. A new configuration of power in the Mediterranean was emerging, as we have already seen.

This new – or renewed – Umayyad caliphate constituted a high point of prosperity and cultural production for al-Andalus. However, there was turbulence, some of it caused by the caliph's slave-soldiers, many of whom were Slavs or Europeans (*ṣaqāliba*). Holding this prosperous but fractious enterprise together required energy and determination. In this ʿAbd al-Raḥmān resembled the ʿAbbāsid al-Muʿtaḍid, and here too the restored caliphate of al-Andalus did not long survive the disappearance of its '*ghāzī*-caliph' from the scene.

84 As was done in 909 by the rebel Ibn Ḥafsūn, who also sent an embassy to Qayrawān and received a return visit of Ismāʿīlī *dāʿīs* bearing robes of honour from al-Mahdī.

85 Kennedy, *Muslim Spain and Portugal*, pp. 95–7; Halm, *Empire of the Mahdi*, pp. 264–74.

The Sāmānid emirate in Khurāsān and Transoxania

In the east, the family that we know as the Sāmānids first rose to prominence as sub-governors in the service of the Ṭāhirids in Khurāsān and Transoxania, in the early third/ninth century.[86] In 875, after the fall of Nīshāpūr and the collapse of the Ṭāhirids, the Sāmānid Naṣr ibn Aḥmad, already de facto governor of Transoxania, received confirmation from the caliph al-Muʿtamid. Rather like al-Muʿtamid in those same years, Naṣr found himself under the domination of an ambitious brother, Ismāʿīl, who assumed sole control when Naṣr died in 279/892. As we have seen, Ismāʿīl defeated the Ṣaffārid ʿAmr ibn al-Layth in 287/900, after which al-Muʿtaḍid awarded him the governorship of Khurāsān and Transoxania. These two provinces together then constituted the core of the Sāmānid emirate. Though Nīshāpūr, in Khurāsān, remained a great city, the Sāmānids maintained their court and capital on the other side of the Oxus river, in Bukhārā.

This choice of capital guaranteed that the Sāmānid emirate would be a frontier state. Ismāʿīl inaugurated his reign with an expedition into the steppe in 280/893, defeating the Qarluq Turks and capturing Talas, far to the north-east. In addition to ruling directly over their core provinces, Ismāʿīl and his successors asserted over-lordship over the rulers of Ushrūsana and Farghāna to the east, Khwārazm to the north, and other regions. This position on the frontier brought prosperity to the Sāmānids and at least some of their subjects: in an age when Turkish slaves were in high demand, the Sāmānids had a monopolistic control over the supply. Their raiding expeditions took captives who either went on to the slave markets further west or remained in the Sāmānids' service. Meanwhile, like the Ṭāhirid *amīrs* before them, the Sāmānids constructed systems of defensive fortresses, as well as walls and ramparts for the cities. Under Ismāʿīl these were so effective that the fortifications of Bukhārā and Samarqand became neglected, unfortunately for later generations.[87] Large numbers of 'volunteers' served in these frontier posts, known here, as in Aghlabid North Africa, as *ribāṭs*, while many religious scholars took part in the affairs of the emirate. Their role consisted largely of preaching and exhorting, but there is also evidence for men of learning at the head of units of *ghāzīs* (fighters for the faith), apparently not organised directly by the Sāmānid state.[88] This participation of 'volunteers' in defence of the frontiers may be

86 See chapter 7.

87 R. N. Frye, 'The Samanids', in R. N. Frye (ed.), *The Cambridge history of Iran*, vol. IV: *The period from the Arab invasion to the Saljuqs* (Cambridge, 1975), p. 140.

88 Jürgen Paul, 'The histories of Samarqand', *Studia Iranica*, 22 (1993), esp. pp. 82–7; Jürgen Paul, *The state and the military: The Samanid case*, Papers on Inner Asia 26 (Bloomington, 1994); Jürgen Paul, *Herrscher, Gemeinwesen, Vermittler: Ostiran und Transoxanien in vormongolischer Zeit* (Beirut and Stuttgart, 1996), esp. pp. 93–139.

connected to the social peace that prevailed under Sāmānid rule: the Sāmānids, who may have been descendants of petty landowners from near Balkh, enjoyed good relations with the *dihqāns*, or landed gentry.

The high regard for scholarship at the Sāmānid court appears in an anecdote in which the *amīr* Ismāʿīl ibn Aḥmad rises publicly before a man of learning, and is then chided by his brother: 'You are the ruler of Khurāsān, and you rise before one of your subjects when he enters your presence? This is the end of statecraft and good policy!' Ismāʿīl's comportment then receives approval in a dream in which the Prophet announces the confirmation of Ismāʿīl's rule and that of his descendants, and the end of his brother's rule. In this way the theme of respect for scholars is related to the rivalry between the brothers Ismāʿīl and Naṣr at the beginning of the independent Sāmānid emirate.[89]

During the long reign of Naṣr II ibn Aḥmad ibn Ismāʿīl (301–31/914–43), the Sāmānid court took the lead in a remarkable flourishing of the arts and sciences. Two of Naṣr's *wazīrs*, al-Jayhānī (302–10/914–22 and 327–31/938–41), and Abu 'l-Faḍl al-Balʿamī (310–27/922–38), had leading roles in this activity, which may be further described, in general terms, as bilingual.[90] The Ṭāhirids had made scant use of Persian, though the Ṣaffārids used it considerably more. But under the Sāmānids Persian emerged as a full-fledged language of literature and (to a lesser extent) administration. Court patronage was extended to Persian poets, including the great Rūdakī (d. *c.* 940). Meanwhile Arabic continued to be used abundantly, for administration and for scientific, theological and philosophical discourse.

Relations with the ʿAbbāsid caliphate tended to be correct but cool. Although the names of the caliphs duly appeared on their coins, the Sāmānids did not forward these coins to Baghdad in the form of tribute or tax. Of course the ʿAbbāsids were far away and increasingly powerless. In some ways, however, the Sāmānids paid them the compliment of imitation: their well-ordered administration was modelled largely on ʿAbbāsid precedent. Afterwards it provided the model for administrative structures and

'Fighting scholars' are discussed also by Michael Bonner, *Jihad in Islamic history: Doctrines and practices* (Princeton, 2006), pp. 97–117; and in Deborah Tor's *The ʿAyyārs: A study in holy warfare, chivalry and violence* (forthcoming).

89 Abū Bakr Aḥmad al-Khaṭīb al-Baghdādī, *Ta'rīkh Baghdād*, 14 vols. (Cairo, 1931), vol. III, p. 318, entry for Abū ʿAbdallāh Muḥammad ibn Naṣr al-Marwazī, d. 295. This date of death indicates that the losing brother must be Naṣr ibn Aḥmad (d. 279/892), and not Isḥāq, who is named in the story. This Isḥāq ibn Aḥmad was another brother of Ismāʿīl and Naṣr who revolted later on, after the accession of the underage *amīr* Naṣr II ibn Aḥmad ibn Ismāʿīl (r. 301–31/914–43). The narrator of the story, Abu 'l-Faḍl al-Balʿamī, was *wazīr* for Naṣr II from 310/922 to 327/938.

90 Frye, 'The Samanids', pp. 142–3, 145–6.

techniques for, among others, the Ghaznavid and Saljūq states; the Saljūq *wazīr* Niẓām al-Mulk (d. 485/1092) admired the Sāmānid example beyond all others.

The Sāmānids were Sunnī in their religious doctrine and Ḥanafī in their legal affiliation. However, the Ismāʿīlī *daʿwa* achieved some success in their domains, and in the reign of Naṣr II it attracted converts at the court and in adjacent circles. The *amīr* himself tolerated and even, to some extent, adopted this Ismāʿīlism, which here, in the Sāmānid north-east, took on a markedly philosophical (Neoplatonic) character. The response came in 331/943, when a *coup d'état* brought Naṣr II down and elevated his son Nūḥ to the throne. One result was an affirmation of the Sunnism and anti-Shīʿism of the Sāmānid state, especially since its chief rival was now the pro-Shīʿite Būyid emirate of Iraq and western Iran.

Like the Fāṭimids and the Spanish Umayyads, and indeed like most of the political formations that emerged during these decades, the Sāmānids relied on units of slave-soldiers, to the point where Turkish commanders came to outweigh the Sāmānid *amīrs* and bureaucrats. This resulted in a crisis that had some points in common with that of the ʿAbbāsid caliphate in Sāmarrāʾ in the 860s; however, since it came a good century later than that crisis, it lies beyond the scope of this chapter.

Daylam and the rise of the Būyids

This tour of the edges of the Islamic world ends with mountainous Daylam, at the south-western end of the Caspian Sea.[91] Because of its difficult terrain, Daylam had never been integrated into the unitary caliphate. Islam also arrived late, and then often in the form of Zaydī Shīʿism. Daylam might have remained obscure and marginal, but for the fact that in the early tenth century it began to export soldiers throughout northern Iran, and then to much of the Islamic world. The phenomenon seems difficult to explain. In a military scene dominated by cavalry, the Daylamīs were infantry, known for their use of the javelin and tall shield. The most sought-after units consisted of Turkish slaves who had been born outside the Islamic world and then converted to Islam; the Daylamīs were free-born Iranians. One reason for their popularity was their reputation for endurance and strength. Another reason must have been that unlike slave-soldiers they did not have to be bought and cared for, and unlike tribal levies – such as the Kutāma in North

91 'Daylam' in the sources for this period often refers to the entire southern Caspian region, including Jurjān, Ṭabaristān and Gīlān, in addition to Daylam proper.

Africa or the Arab tribal confederacies of the Syrian desert – they were largely immune to what Ibn Khaldūn would later call ʿ*aṣabiyya*, the passion of group feeling. Despite their Zaydism they did not usually fight out of religious or ideological passion. In a world where loyalties were under negotiation, where military needs were often short term, but where religious and ethnic identity had sharp edges, the Daylamīs had the potential for being truly effective mercenaries, and thus in great demand.

The Daylamī commanders, often compared to the *condottieri* of the Italian Renaissance, sought power and fame, and some of them became rulers of fledgling dynastic enterprises. Daylam and the neighbouring areas lay between the spheres of control of the Sāmānids to the east and the ʿAbbāsids to the west. In the early tenth century there was another power on the scene, Ibn Abi ʾl-Sāj, the ruler of Azerbaijan, whose departure for Iraq in 314/926, to fight the Qarāmiṭa, left an opening. Several commanders fought one another, and one of these, Mākān ibn Kākī, became master of Ṭabaristān, Jurjān and even of Nīshāpūr in Khurāsān in 318/930. Meanwhile, the fierce and extravagant Mardāvīj ibn Ziyār, who had risen in the service of yet another commander, Asfār ibn Shīrawayh, rebelled against his master in 319/931 and killed him. Mardāvīj then captured some of the cities of western Iran from the ʿAbbāsids, before seizing Ṭabaristān and attacking Mākān ibn Kākī. However, the Sāmānid Naṣr II intervened, and Mardāvīj agreed to a peace settlement.[92] It was at around this time that three Daylamī brothers in Mākān's service, ʿAlī, Ḥasan and Aḥmad, sons of a Caspian fisherman named Būya (or Buwayh), transferred their allegiance from Mākān to Mardāvīj. ʿAlī, the eldest, received an appointment as governor over the old Dulafid capital, Karaj. Later on, Mardāvīj made threats against Baghdad and the caliphate, declaring his intention to restore the Iranian monarchy and the Zoroastrian religion. Before he could do this, however, he was murdered by his own Turkish slaves in Iṣfahān in 323/935. His brother Wushmgīr held on to the Caspian regions of Ṭabaristān and Jurjān, where the Ziyārid line continued afterwards.[93] These Daylamī commanders, Mardāvīj above all, are interesting as players of the rough game of military politics in the post-caliphal Islamic world, and also as seekers of new kinds of local and Iranian identity. However, it was the three sons of Būya, whom we know as the Būyids (or Buwayhids), who were going to leave a profound mark on the history of Islam.

92 C. E. Bosworth, 'Mākān b. Kākī', *EI2*, vol. VI, pp. 115–16; W. Madelung, 'Mardāwīdj b. Ziyār b. Wardanshāh', *EI2*, vol. VI, p. 539.
93 Madelung, 'The minor dynasties of northern Iran'.

Well before Mardāvīj's death ʿAlī ibn Būya found an independent base in the south-western Iranian province of Fārs. The ʿAbbāsid caliphate had previously won Fārs back from the Ṣaffārids, but now, with general anarchy threatening, some local magnates there invited ʿAlī to provide them with protection. Backed by this alliance, ʿAlī settled in with his soldiers and sought recognition of his position from Baghdad. Mardāvīj's death then allowed ʿAlī to avoid a confrontation with his former master and to recruit some of his troops. The power void in west central Iran eventually enabled ʿAlī to place his brother Ḥasan over a large region, including the cities of Rayy and Iṣfahān, in 335/947. Meanwhile the third brother, Aḥmad, had an unsuccessful adventure in the province of Kirmān, just to the east. Now, however, he looked westward to Iraq and joined the military commanders who were competing there for the new position of *amīr al-umarāʾ* (chief commander), circling like vultures over an ʿAbbāsid caliphate that had nearly come to its end.

End of the independent ʿAbbāsid caliphate

During the four decades between the accession of al-Muqtadir in 295/908 and the arrival of Aḥmad ibn Būya in Baghdad in 334/945, all of the ʿAbbāsid caliphate's hard-won gains of the previous decades vanished. We know a good deal about these events because of the coverage provided by several historians who wrote in Arabic during the tenth and eleventh centuries.[94] These historians valued eyewitness testimony, and while they were acutely aware of the legacy of al-Ṭabarī, who died in the middle of this period in 310/923, they also went in directions that the master had not taken, as some of them displayed intimate knowledge of the protocol and inner life of the court, while one of them, the philosopher-historian Miskawayh, proved to be a world-class observer and analyst of politics. For readers accustomed to the work of al-Ṭabarī and his predecessors, this historical writing can have a bracing effect.[95] Nowadays, however, historians often neglect the history of the first half of the tenth century, perhaps because they see it as a painful transition between effective ʿAbbāsid rule and the ensuing period of Būyid domination in Iraq and western Iran, famous for its 'renaissance of Islam'.[96]

94 There are summaries of the historiographical 'succession to al-Ṭabarī' in Kennedy, *The Prophet and the age of the caliphates*, pp. 362–5; and Franz Rosenthal, *A history of Muslim historiography* (Leiden, 1968), pp. 81–3.

95 See the beginning of this chapter.

96 Joel L. Kraemer, *Humanism in the Renaissance of Islam: The cultural revival during the Buyid age* (Leiden, 1993).

When al-Muktafī, still in his early thirties, died of an intestinal disorder in 295/908, the situation of the caliphate seemed favourable, with Egypt recently conquered from the Ṭūlūnids, the Qarāmiṭa repelled, and the treasuries reporting a modest surplus.[97] At this point the bureaucrats had matters in hand as never before, and the group that gathered to choose a new caliph included only administrators, but no soldiers or princes of the blood. The reports of this meeting are filled with refined calculation of political interest. The *wazīr* at the time, al-ʿAbbās ibn Ḥasan, backed by ʿAlī ibn al-Furāt and his faction, desired to keep power for himself, as he had grown accustomed to exercising it during al-Muktafī's illness. This led him to declare for al-Muktafī's brother Jaʿfar, a child of thirteen. The meeting concluded in agreement and Jaʿfar was acclaimed as caliph, with the regnal title al-Muqtadir. Much of the money in the treasury went into donatives for the army and other gifts, as was customary on these occasions. The boy-caliph immediately lived up to ʿAbbās's expectation, being naive, gullible and open to manipulation.

There is nothing so dangerous as the fulfilment of one's dearest wish, and in the following year the ambitious *wazīr* fell victim to a *coup d'état*. This was organised by administrators of the Jarrāḥid faction and by officers led by the dashing Arab commander al-Ḥusayn ibn Ḥamdān, who deposed al-Muqtadir and replaced him with ʿAbd Allāh ibn al-Muʿtazz.[98] At the time Ibn al-Muʿtazz seemed a plausible candidate, notwithstanding (or because of?) his reputation as a poet and man of letters. However, a group of officers and administrators closed ranks around al-Muqtadir, while Ibn al-Muʿtazz's partisans disintegrated because of their inept planning. Ibn al-Muʿtazz and several of his followers were put to death and others suffered prison or exile, while the ruling faction saw its power confirmed. Now it was necessary to distribute yet another round of donatives and gifts, eliminating whatever surplus still remained in the treasury.

Bureaucratic factions dominated the long reign of al-Muqtadir. One soldier kept the remnants of the army together and saved the caliphate on several occasions: this was Muʾnis al-Khādim ('the eunuch'), who had been in the ʿAbbāsid service since the days of al-Muʿtaḍid and who, after his first triumph over the Fāṭimids in Egypt in 301/914 (see above) received the honorific title al-Muẓaffar ('the Victorious'). Meanwhile, a long string of *wazīrs* came and went, facing the impossible task of maintaining the caliphate's finances and

97 See above, p. 334.

98 Son of that al-Muʿtazz who was declared caliph in a failed *coup d'état* after the murder of his father al-Mutawakkil, and later became counter-caliph against al-Mustaʿīn in 865, and then caliph until his miserable death in 869 (see above).

periodically undergoing the ordeal of *muṣādara* (see above). Most prominent of these were the two rivals, ʿAlī ibn ʿĪsā and ʿAlī ibn al-Furāt, who each served as *wazīr* three times. ʿAlī ibn ʿĪsā, allied with Mu'nis, was known for piety, efficiency and attempts at limiting expenditure.[99] ʿAlī ibn al-Furāt, also admired for his knowledge and skill, was given to displays of generosity, which led him to accumulate large sums for himself. Like other members of his clan Ibn al-Furāt favoured Imāmī Shīʿism, though not quite openly. It was still possible for a high-ranking official to have such a sympathy, though it could provide Ibn al-Furāt's enemies with a weapon when they wanted one.

The precarious balance among factions in the administration and court suffered damage during the tumult of the trial and execution of the mystic al-Ḥusayn ibn Manṣūr al-Ḥallāj. Born in 244/857f., al-Ḥallāj ('the carder') travelled widely, including stints on the eastern frontiers and in India. When he came to Baghdad during the reign of al-Muktafī he resumed the impassioned preaching that had made him famous as 'the carder of hearts' (*ḥallāj al-qulūb*). A first trial of al-Ḥallāj ended in his release since, as one jurist said, the authorities had no jurisdiction in the matter. Already, however, al-Ḥallāj had friends and enemies at court. The failed *coup d'état* in favour of Ibn al-Muʿtazz was a debacle for al-Ḥallāj's supporters the Jarrāḥids, and he fled into exile. He was brought back, however, and made to stand trial a second time. Now ʿAlī ibn ʿĪsā was the *wazīr*, and he managed to end this trial in 301/912. For a long time afterwards al-Ḥallāj was kept at the palace, with the factions swirling around him. The third and final trial took place in 308–9/921–2. The *wazīr* at the time, Ḥāmid ibn al-ʿAbbās, went to great lengths to destroy al-Ḥallāj. The mystic, who had been accused of claiming to have achieved substantial union with God (*ḥulūl*, as in the saying that his enemies attributed to him, 'anā 'l-ḥaqq', 'I am the Truth'), was now accused, somewhat improbably, of being a Qarmaṭī. Finally a conclave of jurists, under prodding, signed a death warrant. Al-Muqtadir concurred, and al-Ḥallāj was gibbeted, tortured and dispatched. It is noteworthy that this death warrant included signatures from representatives of different *madhhab*s, or schools of law. The Ḥanbalīs, however, took al-Ḥallāj's side, aggravating the urban unrest that was already brewing. Angry mobs threatened the jurist and historian al-Ṭabarī, now near death, who had declared against al-Ḥallāj.

The episode of al-Ḥallāj illustrated many things, beginning with the precariousness of life at court and of ʿAbbāsid rule itself. It revealed the very

99 Harold Bowen, *The life and times of ʿAlī ibn ʿĪsā, the 'Good Vizier'* (Cambridge, 1928), still the most gripping account (in a European language) of this period.

palpable importance of the *madhhabs*, which had been growing as juridical and intellectual affiliations for a long time, but were thenceforth a major element of identity for large urban groups, and often for angry mobs. Not least of all, the episode shows that Sufism was becoming more and more noticeable within urban life, as the central authority of the caliphate declined. Sufism of the 'Baghdad school' had flourished in the previous century as a set of moral and intellectual doctrines with, for example, the introspective teachings of al-Muḥāsibī enjoying popularity among many of the townspeople. But now, with the growing division between the followers of the so-called 'drunken' al-Ḥallāj and their more 'sober' rivals, Sufism offered an enormous range of doctrines and experiences, as well as new styles of leadership. Together with other forms of mystical and ascetic expression it spread far beyond Baghdad, especially in the Sāmānid east, and became a major element of social aggregation.[100]

Al-Ḥallāj's death brought little advantage to ʿAlī ibn al-Furāt who, in his third wazirate, struggled to sustain the failing machine of government. In his rage at the situation he faced, and having recently endured a long imprisonment himself, Ibn al-Furāt, together with his son al-Muḥassin, extorted and tortured beyond the customary limits of *muṣādara*. Father and son fell from power and were executed in 312/924. ʿAlī ibn ʿĪsā returned to the wazirate, but when he was brought down in 317/929, the loyal Mu'nis finally turned against al-Muqtadir and attempted a *coup d'état*. A brother of al-Muqtadir, Muḥammad al-Qāhir, was briefly installed on the throne, before al-Muqtadir was restored and Mu'nis driven away. In 320/932, however, Mu'nis returned, and in the ensuing fight al-Muqtadir was killed. Now al-Qāhir became caliph and Mu'nis, as kingmaker and head of the army, held the reins of power.

During the decade before al-Muqtadir's death the situation was severely aggravated by the renewed attacks of the Qarāmiṭa of Baḥrayn. Under their leader, Abū Ṭāhir Sulaymān, the Qarāmiṭa sacked Baṣra in 311/923, and in 315/927 they nearly took Baghdad itself. Qarmaṭī bands repeatedly attacked the Meccan caravans. In 317/930 they stormed Mecca and, amid great slaughter, they removed the Black Stone and brought it to their capital, where it would remain for some years.[101] Unable to meet this challenge with its own resources, the government offered Ibn Abi 'l-Sāj, the *amīr* of Azerbaijan and Armenia, a splendid reward for fighting the Qarāmiṭa in 314/926. He accepted

100 Jacqueline Chabbi, 'Remarques sur le développement historique des mouvements ascétiques et mystiques au Khurasan', *SI*, 46 (1977).

101 C. E. Bosworth, 'Ṣanawbarī's elegy on the pilgrims slain in the Carmathian attack on Mecca (317/930): A literary-historical study', *Arabica*, 19, 3 (1972).

the offer and proceeded to attack the enemy, but was defeated and killed. Factional divisions within the government aggravated differences over policy, as ʿAlī ibn ʿĪsā advocated the unpopular view that it was better to appease the Qarāmiṭa than to endure their attacks.

Although the Qarmaṭī threat subsided after 930, it was clear that if the ʿAbbāsid state was to survive it would have to resolve its military crisis. In fact, al-Muqtadir's violent death marked a new domination of the government by the military, as was widely noted at the time. As in Sāmarrāʾ in the 860s, the factional fighting became intense. Its early victims included Muʾnis, killed in 321/933 by al-Qāhir, whom he himself had placed in power. Once again the provinces fell away, this time including al-Jazīra, now in the hands of the Ḥamdānids (see below). Only the Sawād of Iraq remained, and even this was compromised, as the Barīdī family held sway around Ahwāz, in Khūzistān to the south. Though the Barīdīs were administrators rather than soldiers, they interacted skilfully with the soldiers by allocating revenues and lands. For these were now at stake, as the fiscal system of the caliphate fell to pieces.

In these years, together with the following period of Būyid domination, the land regime emerges that we sometimes call the 'new' *iqṭāʿ*. The term *iqṭāʿ* means the act of apportioning a land-grant or *qaṭīʿa*, but it can also refer to the land-grant itself. As we have seen, perhaps as early as the 860s such grants were made to army commanders not only out of 'estate' lands (*ḍiyāʿ*), but also out of *kharāj* lands, supposedly under direct control of the administration (see above, p. 312). The evidence for this is slender. By 945, however, *iqṭāʿ* clearly referred to the allocation of the revenues of a district, made directly to an individual – most often a high-ranking officer – who received these revenues in lieu of regular pay from the central treasury.

There are two ways of conceptualising this 'new' *iqṭāʿ*. The first is at the level of the provincial governor, a military man who could be granted the right to all the revenues of his province, with the stipulation that he would forward a specified sum to the central treasury. An example is the deal made with Ibn Abi ʾl-Sāj in 314/926. In this instance, Ibn Abi ʾl-Sāj died in combat against the Qarāmiṭa and the deal was never completed. However, there was only one step from this 'provincial' *iqṭāʿ* to employing the same procedure in the Sawād of Iraq itself. This meant, in effect, militarising the central administration and, indeed, the lands.

The second way of conceptualising the 'new' *iqṭāʿ* involves considering the administration of all the lands within a particular province – here, the Sawād of Iraq. We have already seen that the land regime of the 'classical' caliphate included two main categories, lands paying the heavy *kharāj* (land-tax) directly to the central treasury; and *ḍiyāʿ* ('estates'), lands in the possession of privileged individuals who paid only the lighter *ʿushr* (tithe). The holders of *ḍiyāʿ*, or estate lands, would collect their revenues (or rents) from the taxpayers (or tenants) who resided on their lands; these revenues (or rents) were assessed at the same (high) rate as the *kharāj*. The estate-holders would then forward to the central treasury a smaller amount, assessed according to the *ʿushr*. They would keep the difference between the two – a very tidy sum – for themselves.

As for the *kharāj* lands, we have seen that throughout the third/ninth century the work of levying taxes from them was often not performed directly by the fiscal authorities of the ʿAbbāsid state, but instead by intermediaries. The legal instruments of these transactions were contracts of tax-farming (*ḍamān*), and then also of *muqāṭaʿa* and *īghār* (see above, p. 312). Here the contracting party collected the taxes from the taxpayers at the *kharāj* rate, paid a stipulated amount to the central treasury, and kept the rest for himself as a fee.

Now, beginning in the later third/ninth century, came a further step, which we identify with the 'new' *iqṭāʿ*. A military officer would no longer draw his pay directly from the central treasury, but instead would be assigned the revenues from a particular district in the Sawād. He was expected to forward a stipulated amount to the treasury (though in reality he often sent less than that amount, or nothing at all). On the one hand, the position of this *muqṭaʿ*, or recipient of *iqṭāʿ*, resembled that of someone who had signed a contract of tax farming (*muqāṭaʿa* or *īghār*). On the other hand, the *muqṭaʿ* was still a soldier, and not a professional administrator. And the officers who found themselves in this position apparently felt a strong – even proprietary – interest in their assigned districts, beyond that of a functionary or tax-collector. As in the case of the 'provincial' *iqṭāʿ* (see above), the result was the militarisation of what had previously been a civilian contract or arrangement. And now the entire countryside became open, at least potentially, to this new regime: not only *ḍiyāʿ*, but even *kharāj* lands, which were theoretically the property of the civilian owners who held title to them, became open to the domination of military landholders.

Unlike the *iqṭāʿ* of the later Saljūq, Ayyūbid and other periods, which was partly the result of planning, the *iqṭāʿ* of this period emerged out of crisis-mode improvisation. With the treasury empty and the soldiers constantly demanding their pay, it offered liquidity and security: once assured of a comfortable income, the officers would presumably remain loyal. On the negative side, however, the soldiers of the rank and file still had to be paid out of the central treasury.[102] And together with the new *iqṭāʿ* came a decline in the professional standards of the bureaucrats, whose main task became (or so they complained) the demarcation of districts for *iqṭāʿ*. Since an *iqṭāʿ* assignment was, in principle and largely in fact, for a fixed time only, the officers sought upgrades, and competed avidly for the desirable holdings. However, they had little motivation and no expertise for maintaining the lands in good condition and performing vitally needed infrastructural work. The decline of the agricultural lands is painfully visible in budget data: in the century between 204/819 (in the reign of al-Maʾmūn) and 303/915 (in the reign of al-Muqtadir) the revenues of the Sawād shrank from 112,416,000 *dirhams* to 22,500,000, with most of the loss occurring from the reign of al-Mutawakkil.[103] The historian Miskawayh describes these converging processes in a Thucydidean passage that is remarkable for its analytic power and economy of expression.[104]

While civilian administrators such as the Barīdīs could participate in this competition for revenues and lands, the big players were the military commanders. After Muʾnis's death, the next powerful figure to emerge was Muḥammad ibn Rāʾiq, military governor in Baghdad, Baṣra and then Wāsiṭ. The caliph was now al-Rāḍī (r. 322–9/934–40), a son of al-Muqtadir, who in 324/936 reluctantly agreed to appoint Ibn Rāʾiq as *amīr al-umarāʾ* ('chief commander'), with control over the civilian administration (or what remained of it) as well as the military. However, the violent competition among the officers did not let up. Ibn Rāʾiq killed al-Rāḍī's household troops, and then, in the following year, seeking a momentary advantage over his opponents, he destroyed the Nahrawān canal, undoing the work of generations and causing untold ecological damage. Meanwhile, new soldiers arrived from the east, following the assassination of Mardāvīj ibn Ziyār (see above). These included the Turks Bajkam and Tūzūn, who afterward held the new office of *amīr al-umarāʾ*. Ibn Rāʾiq himself was assassinated in 942 by Ḥasan ibn Abī al-Hayjāʾ, who then briefly held the office of *amīr al-umarāʾ* himself.

This Ḥasan was a member of the family known as the Ḥamdānids. Unusually for high-level players in the military politics of this age the Ḥamdānids were Arabs, of the tribe of Taghlib. In the late third/ninth century they had changed their affiliation from Khārijism to mild Shīʿism, not

102 Cahen, 'L'évolution de l'*iqṭāʿ*', pp. 244–5.
103 Budget data are collected by Waines, 'Internal crisis', pp. 286–7.
104 Miskawayh, *Tajārib al-umam*, ed. A. Emami (Tehran, 2001), vol. VI, pp. 129–32, trans. D. S. Margoliouth in *The eclipse of the ʿAbbasid caliphate: Original chronicles of the fourth Islamic century*, vol. V (Oxford, 1921), pp. 100–5.

uncommon for inhabitants of the borderlands between desert and sown at the time (see above, p. 325). We have already met al-Ḥusayn ibn Ḥamdān, a leader in the failed coup in favour of Ibn al-Muʿtazz in 296/909. Afterwards al-Ḥusayn came in and out of ʿAbbāsid service, before ending on the executioner's mat in 306/918. Meanwhile his brother Abū al-Hayjāʾ performed brilliantly in the expeditions against the Dulafids, the Qarāmiṭa (including 'the man with the birthmark') and the Ṭūlūnids. Loyal to Muʾnis al-Khādim, he died defending al-Qāhir during the abortive attempt at overthrowing al-Muqtadir in 317/929. By then, however, Abū al-Hayjāʾ had established a foothold in the province of Mosul. His son al-Ḥasan took his place there, holding several provinces as *iqṭāʿ*s, and playing a role in the murderous intrigue of the following years. Al-Ḥasan was thus all at once a provincial ruler ensconced in Mosul, and a product of the power politics of Baghdad. He acquired the honorific title Nāṣir al-Dawla ('helper of the dynasty') while his younger brother ʿAlī received the title Sayf al-Dawla ('sword of the dynasty').

In the end it was the younger brother who brought lasting fame to the Ḥamdānid line. From 944 onwards Sayf al-Dawla became established in northern Syria and the district of the Byzantine frontier, a position which made him a '*ghāzī-amīr*', which is to say, a provincial ruler who gloried in his role of fighter for the faith. The Ḥamdānid emirate of Aleppo was accordingly a frontier state, like so many we have seen in this chapter. Although Sayf al-Dawla did not succeed in the end, his dynastic enterprise achieved renown because of its Arabism, because of the unparalleled collection of literary talent that Sayf al-Dawla assembled to sing his praises, and because of the stand that the Ḥamdānids took against the onslaught of a restored and strengthened Byzantine empire. All this, however, belongs to a later chapter.

When al-Rāḍī died in 329/940, several candidates for the caliphate declined to be considered since, they are reported to have said, 'the executive power belonged to someone else [other than the caliph]'.[105] Finally the choice fell upon al-Rāḍī's brother Abū Isḥāq, who chose the regnal title al-Muttaqī. The *amīr al-umarāʾ* was now Bajkam, who died soon afterwards. Turks and Daylamīs in the army began to quarrel, as the Barīdīs threatened Baghdad and Ibn Rāʾiq tried to get back his old job of *amīr al-umarāʾ*. Al-Muttaqī tried to save himself through an alliance with Nāṣir al-Dawla, who did away with Ibn Rāʾiq, as we have seen. However, Nāṣir al-Dawla's stint as *amīr al-umarāʾ* ended when the Turkish commander Tūzūn occupied Baghdad in 331/943.

105 Abū Bakr Muḥammad al-Shaṭranjī al-Ṣūlī, *Akhbār al-Rāḍī wal-Muttaqī* (London, 1935), p. 186, 'wal-tadbīr li-ghayrihi'.

Al-Muttaqī then tried to form an alliance with the *ikhshīd*, the ruler of Egypt who also controlled Syria at the time. When this attempt failed, al-Muttaqī received assurances and oaths from Tūzūn that he could come back and resume his place in Baghdad. However, when al-Muttaqī did return in 333/944, Tūzūn had him blinded and then deposed, an act that deeply shocked the Islamic world.[106] Tūzūn himself died within the year, an act of divine justice in the eyes of many observers.

Now it was the turn of Aḥmad ibn Būya. As we have already seen, Aḥmad had been previously in Fārs and Kirmān. He came to Khūzistān to ally himself with the Barīdīs, but then turned against them and ruled Khūzistān on behalf of his brother ʿAlī, from 330/941 onward. In 334/December 945 Aḥmad seized his opportunity and entered Baghdad with his troops. He assumed the position of *amīr al-umarā*ʾ and the honorific title Muʿizz al-Dawla ('strengthener of the [ʿAbbāsid] dynasty'). Despite this title, when Aḥmad found the current caliph (al-Mustakfī, since 333/944) not to his liking, he cast him aside and appointed a new one (al-Muṭīʿlillāh, r. 334–63/946–74).

The arrival of Muʿizz al-Dawla in Baghdad marks a turning-point. Now the Būyids ruled over Baghdad and the Sawād, centre of the caliphate and the old Islamic empire, together with their holdings in western and central Iran. It is reported that Muʿizz al-Dawla considered doing away with the ʿAbbāsids – like other Daylamīs, the Būyids were sympathetic to Zaydī Shīʿism – but thought better of it. A powerless ʿAbbāsid caliphate was still indispensable to the Būyids for several reasons, including their need for formal legitimacy. Thus began a century of unhappy cohabitation between Būyid *amīrs* and enfeebled ʿAbbāsid caliphs.

Conclusion

With Tūzūn's treacherous blinding of al-Muttaqī we seem to have come full circle since the assassination of al-Mutawakkil, as once again an outrage against a caliph's body reveals the fragility of dynasty, empire and state. Now, however, the ʿAbbāsid empire and state no longer exist, except as a legal or sentimental fiction. People feel horror over Tūzūn's perjury, but not because of damage done to the sacred office of the caliphate and the community of believers so much as because oaths and vows are now the essential way of making binding arrangements for the long and the short term. The

106 Mottahedeh, *Loyalty and leadership*, pp. 46–8.

caliph's body is no longer the focal point of unity, but merely a visible patch within the great fabric of loyalties and associations.

During the eight decades between the assassination of al-Mutawakkil and the blinding of al-Muttaqī, people came to identify themselves more completely with the associations they were born into or entered into voluntarily, in their religious activities, professions, legal affiliations, urban neighbourhoods and other things. More than before, life was a matter of negotiation and renegotiation among groups and individuals, at all levels of society including that of high politics. The rulers now acted as mediators among these formations and groups, understanding full well that they could not govern without the approval of the civilian elites.[107]

We often think of corruption as a component of the fall of empire, and this period of Islamic history has its share of conspicuous overconsumption, bribery, fraud, embezzlement and extortion. However, many of these practices were routinised, as in the *muṣādara* (see above). The rules and expectations were complex, as we see in a report from the courtier and historian al-Ṣūlī describing how, in 329/940, he drew up a list of possible regnal titles for the new caliph, one of which, al-Muttaqī, was eventually selected.

> On Tuesday evening al-Tarjumān said to me, 'Choose a name [regnal title] for the caliph.' I wrote out thirty names on a piece of paper and then did the same on another piece. I sent one to him and the other to Aḥmad ibn Muḥammad ibn Maymūn. They assured me that I would receive a consideration for having chosen the names (*wa-ḍaminā lī ikhrāj ḥaqq al-tasmiya*). However, they did not keep their word in the least, they did not intercede with anyone on my behalf, and they did not lead anyone else to think favourably of me.[108]

Al-Ṣūlī expects a monetary reward or tip for his exertions.[109] He is furious over his patrons' failure to extend protection during the perilous time of an interregnum. It might be argued that during the earlier, 'classical', caliphate of Hārūn al-Rashīd and the Barmakids, the machinery of government had been constantly and systematically greased with gifts and bribes. Now, however, with the caliphate at its end and the bureaucracy in disrepair, these costs increase disproportionately. It is likely that 'considerations', such as the one that al-Ṣūlī expected here for a small, discrete piece of work, were exacted

107 Ibid., esp. pp. 175–90; Michael Chamberlain, *Knowledge and social practice in medieval Damascus, 1190–1350* (Cambridge, 1994).

108 Ṣūlī, *Akhbār al-Rāḍī wal-Muttaqī*, p. 187; trans. Marius Canard as *Histoire de la dynastie abbaside de 322 à 333/933 à 944*, 2 vols. (Algiers, 1950), vol. II, p. 6. I follow Canard in reading Ṣūlī's interlocutor as 'al-Tarjumān', and not 'al-Barjmālī(?)'.

109 In fairness to Ṣūlī, it has to be remembered that he was a *nadīm*, a courtier, and not a salaried bureaucrat.

constantly and routinely, thereby increasing the hidden expense of government and aggravating the decline that we see in the budget figures and elsewhere. The great fabric of loyalties and associations came, quite literally, at a cost.

The decline and fall of the ʿAbbāsid empire coincided with the rise and flourishing of many new successor states. Among these we have seen three basic types which we may quickly review here, bearing in mind that any real-life example can combine characteristics of more than one type.

The first is the dynastic state pure and simple, resulting from the activity of a military adventurer who seizes control over a territory and then tries to make his rule palatable to the local population (which does not actually have much say in the matter), to rival centres of power and to the central authorities of the empire. Though rough and unpredictable, the state that forms in this way still belongs to the older value system of the caliphate: the new dynast does not aspire to overthrow the imperial centre, but needs that centre to provide confirmation of his own authority. The Būyids are a good example of this, ironically enough since they came to occupy the physical space of the ʿAbbāsid caliphs themselves.

The second type, which forms along the frontier, applies to such dynastic states as the Ṣaffārids, Sāmānids and Ḥamdānids. These are frontier societies not only because they emerge and grow on the physical periphery, but also because they are constantly discovering and testing the inner limits and meanings of Islamic society. Their characteristics include lots of movement, as volunteer fighters, ascetics and men of religious learning come to these borderlands to take part in the fight against the infidel.[110]

The third and final type is the state that forms out of a volatile combination of tribal group feeling and the propagation of a new religious message. This is the process familiar to us from Ibn Khaldūn, and which is often discussed as the most common – or even normal – mode of state formation in Islam. In this period the notable examples of state formation of this type involve radical Shīʿite states, especially those of the Fāṭimids in North Africa and the Qarāmiṭa in Baḥrayn. The Fāṭimids are, at the same time, the outstanding instance of a restoration of the caliphate and a revival of the old, battered structures of empire.

How can we set this shifting grid of new dynastic states together with the all-pervasive fabric of loyalties and associations mentioned just before,

110 Bonner, *Jihad in Islamic history*, chapters 7 ('Embattled scholars') and 8 ('Empires, armies and frontiers').

in such a way as to obtain an accurate, three-dimensional picture of the Islamic world in 334/945? We may well think of this world as an Islamic commonwealth, as some have done. We should also remember that some of the best writers of this age were interested in the problem of how to name and portray the Islamic world they lived in. We have seen that al-Ṭabarī recorded the history of the old unitary caliphate in loving detail, but showed reticence and discomfort when he arrived at his own troubled times. Younger writers, however, were willing to take on the problem, and we may single out two of these. Qudāma ibn Jaʿfar was a scribe in the ʿAbbāsid service in Baghdad during the first half of the tenth century, and the author of a comprehensive work on 'the land tax and the secretary's art'. Abū Isḥāq Ibrāhīm al-Iṣṭakhrī was a lifelong traveller and geographical writer; we do not know how he actually made his living. Both Qudāma and al-Iṣṭakhrī describe the late or post-caliphate world as *mamlakat al-islām*, 'the realm of Islam'. In their books this is an enormous space traversed by itineraries, trade routes, religious and cultural affinities, frontiers, shared administrative practices and other affiliations.[111] The realm of Islam is thus an idealised, intensely networked geographical and political entity which, strictly speaking, happens to lack a head. Later geographical writers would take up the idea, but already we see what a varied and interesting place this post-imperial Islamic world has become.

111 André Miquel, *La géographie humaine du monde musulman*, 4 vols. (Paris and the Hague, 1967), vol. I, pp. 271–5.

9

The late ʿAbbāsid pattern, 945–1050

HUGH KENNEDY

The decline and fall of the ʿAbbāsid caliphate in the first half of the fourth/tenth century led to the emergence of a new political order. The most fundamental change was the collapse of the resource base and fiscal system that had sustained the caliphate. The ʿAbbāsid caliphate had owed its wealth and hence its political survival to the revenues derived from the rich agricultural lands of the Sawād of Iraq. A rough calculation suggests that during the reign of Hārūn al-Rashīd this area produced a large proportion of the gross revenue of the caliphate, four times as much as the next most productive area, Egypt.[1] During the course of the third/ninth and fourth/tenth centuries this happy state of affairs changed forever. The once-rich landscapes of the alluvial plain of southern Iraq were ruined and impoverished by a mixture of maladministration, military campaigning and lack of investment. Such meagre revenues as they continued to yield had been appropriated by the military nominally serving the government in Baghdad or by independent adventurers, and no longer filled the coffers of the state.

This economic decline profoundly affected the political geography of the Islamic world. Even under the Umayyads, whose courts were predominantly to the west in Syria, Iraq had been the resource base of the caliphate, and this status had been reinforced under the early ʿAbbāsids by investment in agricultural infrastructure. By the mid-fourth/tenth century, however, Iraq was probably no more productive than many other areas.[2] This fiscal realignment was the prelude to a political shift that resulted in the centrifugal dispersal of power; polities based in Fārs, Khurāsān or Egypt could be just as wealthy and powerful as those based in the old heartland. With the collapse of the centre, power passed to new regimes in the provinces.

1 See David Waines, 'The third century internal crisis of the ʿAbbāsids', *JESHO*, 20 (1977).
2 Hugh Kennedy, 'The decline and fall of the first Muslim empire', *Der Islam*, 81 (2004), repr. in H. Kennedy, *The Byzantine and Islamic Near East* (Aldershot, 2006).

Social and religious changes were also in progress. In the first century-and-a-half of Islam the caliphate was inhabited largely by non-Muslims ruled over by an elite class of Muslims, most of whom were – or claimed to be – of Arab descent. By the third and fourth centuries, however, this had changed. The central administration of the Middle ʿAbbāsid caliphate was increasingly dominated by men of non-Arab – usually Turkish or eastern Iranian – origin. One effect of this was to alienate the Bedouin tribes of the Arabian and Syrian deserts from the formal government, as can be seen from the increasing level of nomad attacks on the *ḥajj* in the late third/ninth and early fourth/tenth centuries. At the same time, increasing conversion to Islam in provinces and outlying regions meant that these areas produced native Muslim elites, whether landowners in Fārs or the chiefs of transhumant Kurdish tribes. They were all Muslims, but saw no need to show any deference or obedience to the authorities in Baghdad and Iraq. It is a striking fact that, with one exception, none of the dynasts and warlords who took power in the lands that the ʿAbbāsids had ruled made any attempt to reject Islam or establish Christian or Zoroastrian states.

The lands that had once formed the domains of the ʿAbbāsid caliphate became a commonwealth in the sense that they were linked by many ties: by the shared elite religion, Islam; the use of Arabic as the language of administration and high culture; and by patterns of trade and pilgrimage which brought together people from all over the area. Baghdad itself remained a centre of scholarship that attracted seekers of knowledge from all parts of the Muslim world. But these links no longer provided the basis for political unity. In place of the caliphate, numerous different ruling polities emerged, each striving to maintain itself in its chosen area.

That the only man who tried to reverse the tide of Islamic rule, the Daylamite warlord Mardāvīj ibn Ziyār, had little success speaks to the degree of Islam's entrenchment in the culture of Iran.[3] Mardāvīj (d. 323/935) was one of the most remarkable personalities of his age. Brutal and aggressive as he was, he had a vision of a restored Iranian monarchy, ordering that the old Sasanian palaces at Ctesiphon (al-Madāʾin, near Baghdad) should be restored to await his arrival. He rejected the authority of the ʿAbbāsid caliphate entirely, and sought to displace Islam as the dominant religion and restore the old Zoroastrian faith, ostentatiously reviving the old ceremonies of fire

3 The Daylamites inhabited the mountainous province of Daylam at the south-west corner of the Caspian Sea. They were to be the military foundation of Būyid power: see below.

worship. It is therefore with some satisfaction that Muslim writers record his death at the hands of some disillusioned Turkish troops in 323/935. Despite his personal power, his efforts to revive the old faith seem to have met with little popular support.

Apart from Mardāvīj, all the dynasties that emerged to fill the power vacuum caused by the collapse of ʿAbbāsid power were, despite their differing geographical and ethnic affinities, Muslim. The post-ʿAbbāsid history of the central Islamic lands is usually presented in dynastic terms (e.g. the Būyids, Ghaznavids etc.), the names of the dynasties often being distinct from those of the tribes that supported them: thus the Banū Mazyad or Mazyadids were chiefs of the Asad tribe, the Mirdāsids of the Kilāb etc., the name of the ruling dynasty usually being derived from that of the father or grandfather of the first important ruler. This may seem somewhat arbitrary and show cavalier disregard for regional identities and economic realities; it can certainly result in a bewildering multitude of unmemorable names. It does, however, reflect the terminology of the sources on which we depend and the reality of political power, and these conventional dynastic divisions are probably the most satisfactory way of presenting these developments. And if the modern reader is confused, we can imagine that many people at the time were equally perplexed about what was going on around them.

Typology of successor regimes

The ʿAbbāsid caliphate did not disappear. The three caliphs who succeeded the unfortunate al-Muttaqī,[4] al-Mustakfī (r. 333–4/944–6), al-Muṭīʿ (r. 334–68/946–74) and al-Ṭāʾī (r. 363–81/974–91), were effectively powerless puppets confined to their palace in Baghdad, without any possibility of independent action. All three were deposed, al-Mustakfī and al-Ṭāʾī because they were felt to be resisting the demands of the Būyids. Al-Muṭīʿ was paid a pension of 2,000 *dirhams* per day by the Būyid Muʿizz al-Dawla, who insisted on choosing the members of the caliph's household himself. However powerless and impoverished they were in reality, their continued existence did, however, provide a constitutional façade for the different dynasts who did control the Muslim world and their survival meant that the ʿAbbāsids could take on a new and important role as leaders of the Sunnī community from the time of al-Qādir (r. 381–422/991–1031).

4 See chapter 8 above, for the ʿAbbāsid caliphs of the early fourth/tenth century.

The regimes that took over effective political power from the ʿAbbāsids can be divided, very simply, according to the type of fiscal and military structure on which they based their power. In one group were the polities were based on the employment of the *ghulām*, and in the second those based on the support of fellow tribesmen. The term *ghulām* (pl. *ghilmān*), originally meaning 'young man', is used in Arabic sources of this period to describe professional soldiers, usually but not always of Turkish origin. From the fifth/eleventh century such soldiers would come to be known in Arabic-speaking countries as *mamlūks*. Legally, the *ghilmān* were unfree, but in practice this made little difference to their ability to further their own financial and political interests and, unlike true slaves, they were paid for their work. During the third/ninth century the *ghilmān* had emerged as the undisputed elite soldiers of their time, fighting as cavalry and often as mounted archers.[5] They were efficient, usually loyal and always very expensive. Many of the post-ʿAbbāsid regimes attempted to continue the old system and employ *ghilmān*, with their salaries being paid out of the receipts of taxation. With the exception of the Ghaznavids, who acquired additional resources out of the proceeds of *jihād* in India, regional regimes such as the Būyids mostly encountered major financial problems, and their precious *ghilmān* went looking elsewhere for paid employment or mutinied to try to extort their pay.

On the other hand, regional dynasts who based their power on the services of their fellow tribesmen were not under this constant financial pressure, since their followers were interested in access to good pastures and occasional booty rather than regular cash salaries. But tribal supporters brought other sorts of problems. They were often difficult to discipline, and unwilling to accept commands from a chief whom they regarded as no more than *primus inter pares*. Among these states were the ʿUqaylids of Mosul, whose support was based on Arab Bedouin; another was the Marwānids of Mayyāfāriqīn, and their transhumant Kurds.[6]

In *ghulām*-based states the traditions of ʿAbbāsid bureaucracy were continued, with greater or lesser success: revenues still had to be collected and salaries paid. The Ghaznavids on the far eastern frontiers of the Muslim world developed an administrative system which was ultimately based on those that had been developed by the ʿAbbāsids in Baghdad and Sāmarrāʾ. Tribal polities needed no such infrastructure: their rulers were often on the move and their viziers served not as heads of a complex bureaucratic structure, but rather as

5 See chapter 7 above for the emergence of this new army.
6 On these dynasties see below.

intermediaries with local peoples and to compose such diplomatic correspondence as was required.

Almost without exception the rulers of these polities looked to ʿAbbāsid structures to provide a form of legitimisation. They took titles that claimed them to be supporters of the *dawla* – that is, the ʿAbbāsid dynasty – so we find ʿImād al-Dawla (ʿsupport of the *dawla*'), Rukn al-Dawla (ʿpillar of the *dawla*') and so on. In fact, this allegiance rarely impinged on their independence, nor did it provide any support against their enemies; but it did allow some dynasts, most notably the Ghaznavids, to claim a legitimacy within the Muslim commonwealth which these newly converted Turkish ex-slaves would otherwise have lacked.

The Būyid confederation

The Būyids[7] were the dynasts who took over the lands in Iraq and western Iran that had formed the core of the ʿAbbāsid caliphate in the ninth and early tenth centuries. They also took over some, at least, of the administrative traditions of the ʿAbbāsids and dominated the caliphate itself as 'protectors' of the ʿAbbāsid caliphs, who remained in their palace in Baghdad, powerless in all practical ways but still important as legitimising figureheads. The Būyids themselves came originally from Daylam, at the south-western corner of the Caspian Sea. They were complete outsiders – descendants, it was said, of a simple fisherman called Būya from an area that had never produced important figures in the politics of the Islamic world. The local inhabitants, the Daylamites, fought as foot-soldiers, taking service with military leaders in Iran and Iraq as mercenaries. This meant that they had to find allies – usually Turks, sometimes Kurds – who could provide the cavalry to make up a balanced fighting unit. Family ties were very important to the Būyids, and much of Būyid politics was family politics.

The Būyids' initial success was due to their military abilities. In 320/932 ʿAlī ibn Būya, with a force of just 400 men, made himself master of the rich and comparatively peaceful province of Fārs. In 315/927 the province had been

7 On the Būyids, see H. Busse, *Chalif und Grosskönig: Die Buyiden im Iraq (945–1055)* (Beirut, 1969); John J. Donohue, *The Buwayhid dynasty in Iraq 334H/945 to 403H/1012: Shaping institutions for the future* (Leiden, 2003); R. Mottahedeh, *Loyalty and leadership in an early Islamic society*, 2nd edn (Princeton, 2001). On the cultural achievements of the period, Adam Mez, *The Renaissance of Islam*, trans. Khuda Bakhsh (London, 1937; repr. New York, 1975) is still valuable. See also chapter 8 above.

taken over by a Turkish soldier called Yāqūt, who made himself unpopular with the local people by his misgovernment and oppressive taxation.ʿAlī achieved power by allying with important landowners in the area, some of whom claimed ʿAlid descent. They provided the revenues, while ʿAlī and his Būyid followers supplied the military power to maintain law and order and protect the province from outside invasions. It was an arrangement that generally worked well until the coming of the Saljūqs in the 1050s, and during this period Fārs was one of the most stable and agriculturally prosperous areas of the Muslim world.

ʿAlī ibn Būya's brother al-Ḥasan was able to establish himself as ruler of central Iran, from Rayy to Iṣfahān, in 335/947, and Aḥmad, the third brother, turned to Iraq. In 332/944 he attempted to take Baghdad for the first time, but was beaten off by the Turkish *amīr al-umarāʾ* ('commander of commanders', the title adopted by the military rulers of the ʿAbbāsid caliphate), Tūzūn. A year-and-a-half later, however, Tūzūn was dead, and so Aḥmad easily occupied the city with his forces and was accepted by the caliph al-Mustakfī as *amīr al-umarāʾ* in 334/945. By 335/946 the brothers were rulers of Fārs, Iraq and Rayy, and their descendants were able to maintain themselves in most of those areas until the coming of the Saljūqs a hundred years later.

In theory, the Būyid brothers exercised authority as governors for the ʿAbbāsid caliphs. Aḥmad was appointed *amīr al-umarāʾ* by the ʿAbbāsid caliph in Baghdad. His brothers were 'appointed' to provincial governorates, and both the structures of ʿAbbāsid government and the old provincial boundaries remained largely unchanged. The brothers took titles that expressed their support of the ʿAbbāsid *dawla* (dynasty): ʿAlī was to become ʿImād al-Dawla ('support of the state'), al-Ḥasan, Rukn al-Dawla ('pillar of the state'), while Aḥmad was to be Muʿizz al-Dawla ('glorifier of the state'). Some Būyids also revived the old Sasanian title of *shāhānshāh* (king of kings).[8] By this they intended to establish their legitimacy with their Iranian subjects and, above all, with their fellow Daylamites.

The Būyid lands formed a family federation, not a centralised empire, and family concerns and rivalries remained central to their political outlook. The possessions of the family were always considered as the property of the whole kin, rather than of individual branches, and relatives felt that they had the right – even the duty – to interfere in times of trouble. The Būyids never

8 See W. Madelung, 'The assumption of the title shāhānshāh by the Būyids and "the reign of the Daylam *(dawlat al-Daylam)*"', *JNES*, 28 (1969).

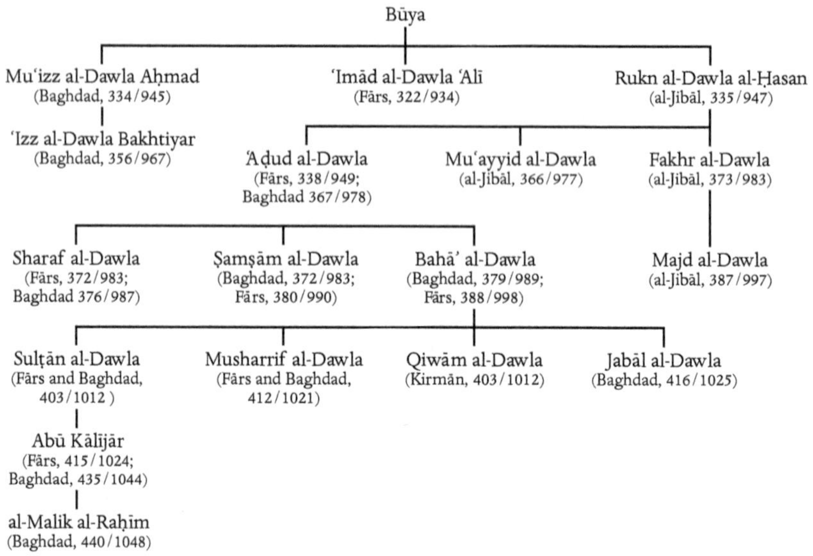

7. The Būyids.
After Hugh Kennedy, *The Prophet and the age of the caliphates*, 2004, p. 405. Copyright Longman, reproduced with permission.

developed a clearly defined system of inheritance; each powerful ruler sought to provide a suitable inheritance for all his sons, even if it had to be done at the expense of his cousins. The tensions between the traditional Daylamite clannishness and the needs of settled government were a continuing source of conflict.

The major political units were the principalities centred on Fārs, with its capital at Shīrāz, al-Jibāl, based on Rayy, and Iraq, including Baghdad, Baṣra and, very briefly, Mosul. After the death of the last of the original Būyid brothers, Rukn al-Dawla al-Ḥasan, in 366/977, the western half of the principality of al-Jibāl was detached to form a new unit based on Hamadhān and Iṣfahān, while from time to time Kirmān in the east enjoyed independence from Fārs, an independence which became permanent after the death of Bahā' al-Dawla in 403/1012. Of these principalities, Fārs was the most important, maintaining its power and prosperity well into the fifth/eleventh century. Baghdad enjoyed prestige as the seat of the caliphate, and remained a cultural and intellectual centre of great importance. Politically and economically, however, it was very weak, and after the death of its first Būyid ruler, Mu'izz al-Dawla, in 356/967 it became apparent that the only Būyid rulers who could exercise power effectively in Baghdad were those like ʿAḍud al-Dawla and Bahāʾ al-Dawla, who also ruled Fārs. The fortunes of the rulers of Shīrāz and Baghdad were therefore closely linked. The principality of Rayy, on the other hand, remained somewhat separate, never being ruled by the same prince as Fārs and facing different problems, notably the danger of attack from the east by the Sāmānids[9] and later the Ghaznavids.

On some occasions, especially in the second half of the Būyid century after the death of ʿAḍud al-Dawla in 372/983, princes were persuaded or obliged to take the offensive against other members of the family by different groups of their followers. After ʿAḍud al-Dawla's death a group of wealthy Iraqis, whom he had sent into exile in Fārs, persuaded his son Sharaf al-Dawla, against the advice of his Fārsī counsellors and his own better judgement, to attack Iraq so that they could be restored to their possessions. It was Fakhr al-Dawla's vizier, the Ṣāḥib ('the master') Ibn ʿAbbād, who induced him to attack Iraq in 379/989. The most serious and lasting source of such quarrels was the rich lands of southern Iraq and Khūzistān whose lush *iqṭāʿ*s (the rights to revenues from lands and districts given to troops as payment) were the envy of troops from less favoured areas. With the ravaged lands around Baghdad almost useless as a source of revenue, the lands of Khūzistān and Wāsiṭ were now vital for the support of the largely Turkish garrison of Baghdad; at the same time, they were also coveted by the Daylamite troops from Fārs. No Būyid prince could afford to ignore demands from his soldiers that he should seize these areas, and they were a continuing source of conflict between the princes of Baghdad and Shīrāz until Bahāʾ al-Dawla's administrators worked out a careful division of the territories around the turn of the fifth/eleventh century.

Būyid rule in Baghdad was always precarious. The first problem that faced Muʿizz al-Dawla after he took over the city in 334/945 was that of relations with the Ḥamdānids, who were now firmly in control of Mosul and northern Iraq. Nāṣir al-Dawla had been *amīr al-umarāʾ* before, and sought to regain his position by launching an attack on Baghdad which was only beaten off with difficulty. From then on, Muʿizz al-Dawla's relations with the Ḥamdānids were based on an uneasy balance of forces, tested from time to time when the Būyids tried to take the Ḥamdānid base at Mosul. Nāṣir al-Dawla was able to maintain his independence by withdrawing to his mountain fortresses when attacked, but was obliged to promise tribute, only intermittently paid. The failure to subdue al-Jazīra (the lands between the middle

9 For the Sāmānids see chapter 8 above.

Tigris and Euphrates rivers) had important consequences in Baghdad since the area had been a major source of grain for the city, and its loss was one of the reasons for the repeated famines which caused much misery in Būyid times.

Muʿizz al-Dawla had taken Baghdad by peaceful agreement, and had had to reach an accommodation with existing forces in the city. He brought with him his own Daylamite followers, but was also obliged to employ the troops, most of them Turks, who were already there. These arrangements seem to have meant that he had a military establishment that was much larger and more expensive than the country could support, and as soon as he arrived he was faced with a major economic crisis, resulting in famine and appalling hardship for the civilian population. It also became clear that the revenues were totally inadequate to pay regular salaries to the inflated numbers of soldiers, and he was forced to grant out much of Iraq as *iqṭā*ʿs to his Daylamite and Turkish soldiers. This meant that much of the tax revenue from Iraq never reached the Būyid government, which became increasingly impoverished. In any case these measures merely postponed the problem, however, since the troops soon complained that their revenues were inadequate, while it became very difficult for the government to recover its financial and political power because the tax base was now so small.

The granting of *iqṭā*ʿs did not solve the problems of military discontent. This was in part because the *iqṭā*ʿ-holders were often cheated by the agents they employed to collect their revenues, or because the lands they relied on had been ruined by war. The problem was made worse by the fact that the Turkish cavalry were paid more than the Daylamite infantry, and there was constant tension between the two groups as each struggled to obtain a share of the diminishing resources of the state.

Until the end of the fourth/tenth century Būyid administration was vigorous and moderately successful. The high point of their power in Iraq was under the rule of the great ʿAḍud al-Dawla (366–72/977–83). He was already ruler of Fārs, and brought the resources of that province to the government of Baghdad. He also succeeded in taking control of Mosul, expelling Abū Taghlib, the last of the Ḥamdānids, in 369/979 and so bringing al-Jazīra back under the control of Baghdad. ʿAḍud al-Dawla took effective measures to discourage violence between Sunnīs and Shīʿa, to revive the economy of Iraq, and to keep the restless Bedouin away; but when he died in 372/983 his possessions were divided up. Constant rivalries among his heirs and the continuous financial crises meant that Būyid rule in Baghdad became increasingly enfeebled. Under Jalāl al-Dawla (416–35/1025–44) the city became a lawless environment made up of fortified and mutually hostile villages presided over by a powerless *amīr* who could not afford to pay his servants or feed his horses. The Saljūq conquest of 1055 must have come as a relief to many of the city's inhabitants.

The Būyid emirate of Rayy was less bureaucratic and more financially secure than Iraq. This was not because the country was richer, but rather because the *amīrs* never recruited Turkish *ghilmān*, relying instead on Daylamite troops. They kept on good terms with the leading families of Daylam, with whom they made marriage alliances, and with the Ḥasanwayhid Kurds of the Zagros mountains, who provided some cavalry in exchange for being allowed effective independence in their own lands. The Būyids of Rayy were served by a series of viziers who made an enormous contribution to Arabic literature. Rukn al-Dawla relied from the beginning of his reign on the services of his great vizier, Ibn al-ʿAmīd, who served him loyally until his death in 360/970 when he was succeeded by his son, also known as Ibn al-ʿAmīd. The most famous of all Būyid viziers was Ismāʿīl ibn ʿAbbād, known as the Ṣāḥib, who served the Būyids of Rayy for a quarter of a century from 360/970f. to 385/995.

The viziers of the Būyids were prominent patrons of the Arabic literature of the period, and it is as patrons of culture, rather than for their administrative achievements, that they are chiefly remembered.[10] The elder Ibn al-ʿAmīd was renowned for his knowledge of classical Arabic poetry, while Ibn ʿAbbād was the patron of Abu ʾl-Faraj al-Iṣfahānī, whose *Kitāb al-aghānī* (Book of songs) is the most important record we have of early Arabic poetry and poets; he was also an accomplished Arabic stylist himself. The most important Muslim intellectual of his generation, Abū ʿAlī ibn Sīnā (d. 428/1037), known in the West as Avicenna, served for the last nine years of his life as vizier to a member of the Būyid clan, the Kākwayyid ruler of Iṣfahān and Hamadhān. Despite the Iranian origins of the dynasty, the high culture of the Būyid courts was almost entirely Arabic, in contrast to both the Sāmānids and the Ghaznavids further east, who patronised the emerging new Persian literature.

The Būyid period can be seen as a confusing and unimpressive period in Islamic history. The Shīʿite religious affiliations of the dynasty[11] also meant that they were the victims of hostile reports among contemporaries and later historians. This is not really fair. It is true that the dynasty did not supply the strong centralised government historians tend to admire, but the way local

10 For the literary and philosophical milieu of the Būyid period see J. L. Kraemer, *Humanism in the renaissance of Islam: The cultural revival of the Buyid age* (Leiden, 1992).
11 On which see below pp. 387–90.

urban elites and tribes worked out a measure of autonomy within the general framework of Būyid rule may actually have benefited most people much more than strong government and the fierce taxation that inevitably went with it. A study of the small Iranian city of Qazvīn has shown how authority was divided between members of two prominent local families: on the one hand, the ʿIjlīs of Arab tribal origin and the Jaʿfarīs, descended from Jaʿfar, brother of ʿAlī ibn Abī Ṭālib, who held the unofficial but important title of *raʾīs*; and, on the other, the *amīr*, effectively the military governor appointed by the Būyid rulers in Rayy. The *qāḍīs* were appointed by the rulers in Rayy but were almost always chosen from prominent local Qazvīnī families. Far from exercising absolute power, the Būyids of Rayy, like many contemporary rulers, had to negotiate authority with local elites and respect the interests of the urban community in such matters as curbing the factionalism that was such a destructive feature of the life of many towns in this period.[12] It is also true that there were many wars, but it must be remembered that armies were small, much smaller than those of the early ʿAbbāsid period or of the Saljūq Turks, and the campaigns were seldom very destructive. The great failure of the dynasty was the failure to secure the prosperity and stability of Iraq, but this was a problem whose origins went back before Būyid times and whose solution was probably beyond the powers of any contemporary government. In central Iran, and above all in Fārs, their rule seems to have been an era of prosperity and development, an era brought to a premature close by the influx of the Ghuzz Turkmen in the middle of the fifth/eleventh century.

The Ghaznavids

From the beginning of the fifth/eleventh century the position of the Būyids on the Iranian plateau was threatened by the rise of the Ghaznavids.[13] Like the Būyids, the Ghaznavids were rulers who followed the middle ʿAbbāsid practice of recruiting an army of Turkish *ghilmān* and collecting taxes to pay them. In other ways, however, they were very different. The Ghaznavids sought to challenge the legitimacy of the Būyids by proclaiming themselves militant Sunnīs, supporters and avengers of the ʿAbbāsid caliphs. They also claimed legitimacy because of their role as *ghāzīs*, leaders of the Muslims in their struggle to conquer India from the infidels.

12 See R. Mottahedeh, 'Administration in Būyid Qazwīn', in D. S. Richards (ed.), *Islamic civilisation 950–1150* (Oxford, 1975).

13 For the Ghaznavids see C. E. Bosworth, *The Ghaznavids: Their empire in Afghanistan and eastern Iran* (Edinburgh, 1963).

The establishment of the Ghaznavid dynasty as rulers in Khurāsān in 389/999 marks the moment when the *ghulām* system came of age in the eastern Islamic world. For the first time in the history of the Islamic world, a group of Turkish *ghilmān* took power in their own right. Rather than being the elite soldiers and servants of dynasties of Arab or Iranian origin, they were independent sovereigns, exercising authority in their own names. The authority of the Ghaznavids was not based on tribal connections, claims to tribal leadership or the complicated family alliances of the Būyids. They were very much part of the post-ʿAbbāsid pattern in that they used the proceeds of taxation to pay a professional army. The dynasty owed its power to the ability of the rulers to attract and above all pay enough *ghilmān* and other soldiers to ensure that their army was the strongest in the region. Financial strength and military success were essential to Ghaznavid power, and when these began to falter there were no wider or more ancient loyalties on which they could call.

The Ghaznavid state was thus based firmly on the power of the army. For any *amīr*, the most important concern was to raise enough money to make sure that the military were regularly paid. The collection of revenues was the responsibility of the civil bureaucracy with the vizier at its head. This bureaucracy differed from the military in recruitment and ethnic background. While the leading *ghulām* soldiers were all Turks, the bureaucrats all came from Persian backgrounds and used New Persian (the Persian language written in Arabic script with many Arabic loanwords which became the lingua franca of the Iranian world from the third/ninth century on) as the language of administration. In the first years many of them had previously worked for the Sāmānids in Khurāsān and had been trained in the traditions of Iranian bureaucracy. The revenues came from royal lands, regular land-tax (*kharāj*) and war plunder. When these proved insufficient, Ghaznavid rulers and their agents resorted to illegal taxes (that is, taxes not sanctioned by Islamic law) and the confiscation of the possessions of disgraced subjects.

The founder of the dynasty, Sebüktegin, was born on the southern shores of the Issyk Kul, the vast freshwater lake surrounded by snow-capped mountains in what is now Kyrgyzstan. It seems he was captured when young by members of a rival tribe and sold in the slave markets of Transoxania. Here he was purchased by Alptegin, the chief *ghulām* of the Sāmānid rulers of Bukhārā. The young *ghulām* soon showed his talents, and rose rapidly in his master's favour. In 350/961 Alptegin attempted to intervene in a succession dispute at the Sāmānid court and, finding himself on the losing side, he set out with his *ghilmān*, perhaps heading for India. In the event, he took the frontier town of Ghazna, hitherto a comparatively unimportant agricultural and trading centre on the road from Kabul to Kandahar. Sebüktegin accompanied his master, and even at this early age he commanded a small body of *ghilmān*. In Ghazna, Alptegin became ruler with an ambiguous relationship with his erstwhile masters, the Sāmānids, for whom Ghazna was a small and remote frontier town of no great value. He established his Turkish followers in *ʿiqṭāʿ*s in the countryside around Ghazna and set up what was essentially a small, independent state.

Alptegin designated one of his sons as his heir, but he died shortly afterwards and the attempt to start a dynasty failed. For a while Ghazna was ruled by Alptegin's *ghilmān*, who continued to acknowledge Sāmānid overlordship until in 366/977 when they chose Sebüktegin as their new ruler. He then set about consolidating his position. In 367/977f. he took Bust from its Turkish *ghulām* rulers and so came to control most of what is now southern and eastern Afghanistan. He also reformed the simple administration of his realm, setting up three *dīwāns* to ensure that all his Turkish followers were properly rewarded. He also minted his own, rough and ready, coins.

The continuing decline of the power of the Sāmānids gave Sebüktegin further opportunities. In 383/993 he went to Khurāsān at the invitation of the Sāmānid *amīr*, Nūḥ ibn Naṣr, who was faced by a rebellion of his military commander Fāʾiq, supported by a powerful noble, Abū ʿAlī Sīmjūrī. When Sebüktegin defeated the rebels the next year he was rewarded with the governorships of Balkh, Ṭukhāristān, Bāmyān, Ghūr and Gharchistān – that is, almost all of modern Afghanistan – and was given the title of Nāṣir al-Dīn wa-al-Dawla. His able son Maḥmūd was made commander of the Sāmānid army in Khurāsān and given his own title, Sayf al-Dawla.

Sebüktegin died in 387/997 as a loyal, though very powerful, subject of the Sāmānids. He divided his possessions between his brother and three of his sons. His brother, Bughrachuq, was to be governor of Herat; his son Naṣr of Bust; and his youngest adult son, Ismāʿīl, was given the homelands around Ghazna – perhaps because he alone was a grandson of Alptegin through his mother, and hence was felt to have a firmer claim. Meanwhile, his most able and experienced son, Maḥmūd, inherited his position as head of the Sāmānid army in Khurāsān. Sebüktegin's succession arrangements mark the first time in Islamic history that *ghilmān* were able to establish a dynastic succession, and he treated his possessions like a Bedouin or Kurdish tribal chief, making sure that all his family had shares.

Meanwhile the power of the Sāmānid dynasty was failing rapidly. The last *amīr*, Abu'l-Ḥārith Manṣūr, was faced by the opposition of many of the leading magnates, including the Sīmjūrids of Khurāsān and the Turkish

Qarakhānids, who were already in control of the Jaxartes river valley. Maḥmūd, who had by this time deposed his brother Ismāʿīl and taken control of Ghazna, was determined to secure for himself effective control of Khurāsān and make himself protector of the enfeebled Sāmānids. In 389/999 Manṣūr was deposed and blinded by the leading figures in his army, who were afraid that he would make an agreement with Maḥmūd that would exclude them. They appointed the deposed *amīr*'s brother, but the fate of Manṣūr gave Maḥmūd the chance to pose as his avenger. After the failure of negotiations Maḥmūd quickly defeated the opposition and became the effective ruler of Khurāsān.

He moved now from being the most successful military commander of his generation to being an independent sovereign. He repudiated the Sāmānid dynasty entirely and proclaimed himself the loyal subject of the ʿAbbāsid caliph al-Qādir (r. 381–422/991–1031). The letter he wrote to the caliph offering his allegiance claimed that he had only acted because of the Sāmānids' disobedience to the ʿAbbāsid dynasty. The argument may well have been specious, but the acceptance of ʿAbbāsid sovereignty was to prove of great importance. In return for his profession of obedience Maḥmūd received formal investiture with the governorate of Khurāsān, a crown and the two titles of Yamīn al-Dawla and Amīn al-Milla ('right hand of the dynasty' and 'trustworthy supporter of the faith') This endorsement gave legitimacy to Maḥmūd's position, which no previous Turkish *ghulām* had ever achieved. At the same time it bound Maḥmūd firmly to the Sunnī cause. At this time al-Qādir was consistently asserting his role as leader of the Sunnīs, in opposition to the Fāṭimids of Egypt and Ismāʿīlī groups throughout Iran. In this way Maḥmūd began the association of Turkish rule with Sunnī Islam that was to be inherited by the Saljūqs and later by the Ottomans. In everyday usage Maḥmūd was often referred to as *sulṭān*. In early Islamic usage this term was an abstract noun meaning 'the authorities', but in the fifth/eleventh century it was increasingly used to refer to an individual, much in the same way as the abstract noun 'majesty' in English comes to refer to the person of the monarch ('Her Majesty'). The term also distinguished its bearer from the largely powerless caliph.

Maḥmūd made the persecution of Shīʿa in general and Ismāʿīlīs in particular a central part of his policy. By claiming to rid his lands of these 'heretics' he justified his often brutal repressions in his own lands and interventions in neighbouring areas. This opposition to the Shīʿa was especially useful when he began to intervene in the Būyid kingdom of Rayy after 419/1028.

It remained for Maḥmūd to come to a *modus vivendi* with his neighbours to the north and east. Shortly after he became ruler he made peace with the

Qarakhānids who had occupied the eastern parts of the former Sāmānid lands. It was agreed that the Oxus should form the frontier between the two domains, and the peace was sealed by a marriage alliance when Maḥmūd married the daughter of the Qarakhānid ruler. Peace did not last long. In 1006, when Maḥmūd was in India, Qarakhānid troops crossed the river and took Balkh and Nīshāpūr. Maḥmūd hurried back and drove them out. According to the defeated Qarakhānid commanders, Maḥmūd's elephants had played an important part in his victory. In 1008 the Qarakhānids made a last attempt on Khurāsān, recruiting allies from Khotan, far to the east. Again Maḥmūd's military ability and the 500 elephants in his army ensured victory, and Qarakhānid power was soon paralysed by internal feuds.

Maḥmūd was never able to reunite the lands once ruled by the Sāmānids in Iran and Central Asia. Transoxania and the great cities of Bukhārā and Samarqand remained in the hands of the Qarakhānids. He did, however, establish control over the rich and fertile lands of Khwārazm. The pretext was the marriage of his sister to the brother of the ruling *amīr* in 406/1015f. When he attempted to exploit this connection by demanding that he be recognised in the *khuṭba* (the Friday sermon in the main mosque at which the ruler's name was invoked) his brother-in-law was assassinated by the angry Khwārazmians. This gave Maḥmūd the excuse for direct military intervention; the country was conquered by the Ghaznavid army and the Maʾmūnid dynasty replaced by a Turkish *ghulām*.

On his western frontiers, Maḥmūd was for most of his reign content to accept Būyid control over Rayy. It was not until 1028, when the Būyid ruler Majd al-Dawla asked Maḥmūd to support him against his own Daylamī followers, that he intervened. Using the excuse that he was cleansing the area of 'Bāṭinis' (literally those who believe in the hidden meaning of the Qurʾān; the term is used as a disparaging description of Shīʿa) and other heretics, he invaded, sacked Rayy and established Ghaznavid rule over the city.

In the south, Maḥmūd invaded Sīstān in 1002 and deposed the last of the Ṣaffārids.[14] The Hindus in his army behaved with great savagery, destroying both the great mosque and the church in the capital Zaranj, and Ghaznavid rule was harsh and rapacious. The province, with its vast deserts and scattered settlements, was never an easy place to govern, and there was continuous guerrilla activity against the Ghaznavid governors. When the Turkmen appeared in the area in 427/1036 local people welcomed them and offered them their support.

14 For Sīstān in this period see chapter 8 above.

Maḥmūd's authority was enforced by what was probably the largest and most formidable army in the Islamic world at the time. Essentially this was a *ghulām*-based state, but on a much larger scale than the Būyids or other contemporaries in western Iran and the Fertile Crescent. Sebüktegin had been a *ghulām* himself, and the Ghaznavids had no tribe on which they could call for support. At the heart of the army there was a comparatively small force of some 4,000 *ghilmān*, mostly Turks of slave origin. In addition to this full-time professional nucleus there were numerous other troops: in 414/1023 Maḥmūd is said to have reviewed 54,000 men and 1,500 elephants at Ghazna, though this was probably exceptional.[15]

As with later ʿAbbāsid administration, which it imitated in many ways, the Ghaznavid civil administration was sharply differentiated from the military. It was staffed by Persians steeped in the traditions of Persian bureaucracy and Arabic literary culture. At the same time, Ghaznavid administration seems to have been more systematic and developed than that of most contemporary regimes in the Middle East. There were five main *dīwāns*, the most important of which were the *dīwān-i risālat* dealing with correspondence and the *dīwān-i ʿarīḍ* concerned with the military. In many ways, as Niẓām al-Mulk recognised, the administration of the Ghaznavids laid the foundations for later Saljūq systems but, like Saljūq administration, it was fairly fluid, with different officials exercising the same offices in many different ways. Like the Sāmānids who preceded them, but unlike their Būyid contemporaries in western Iran, the Ghaznavid court used Persian as the language of administration and culture. The leading court poet al-ʿUnṣurī (d. 431/1039f.) wrote in Persian and the court of the Ghaznavids was chronicled in Persian by Abu 'l-Faḍl Bayhaqī (d. 470/1077), while his older contemporary Abū ʿAlī Miskawayh (d. 421/1030) wrote the history of the Būyids in Arabic.

Much of this splendour was financed by Maḥmūd's most famous military exploits, his raids into India, which became almost annual winter expeditions. The object of the military forays was not permanent conquest, or even the spread of Islam among the conquered populations. The element of prestige was certainly important: being a *ghāzī* (warrior for the faith) prince and leading the Muslim armies against the Hindu idolators was an important way for Maḥmūd to assert his legitimacy as a Muslim ruler and answer the claims of critics and rebels within the Muslim world. News of his victories was always sent to Baghdad, where it was publicised and new honorific titles were

15 For the numbers of troops in the Ghaznavid armies, see Bosworth, *The Ghaznavids*, pp. 126–8.

awarded in return. Like his older contemporary in al-Andalus, al-Manṣūr ibn Abī ʿĀmir, he used the *jihād* as a way to legitimise political authority acquired by brute force. But it was above all the constant need for money to pay the army and maintain the court that drove Maḥmūd. The Ghaznavids paid their armies in cash, and the need for funds usually seems to have dominated Maḥmūd's actions. In areas such as Khurāsān, already under Ghaznavid control, this took the form of sweating their assets ruthlessly by imposing heavy and oppressive taxation, to the great distress of their inhabitants. The plains of Hindustān (today Pakistan and northern India) and its rich temples offered the possibility of plunder and of serving the cause of Islam.

Muslim penetration of the Indus Valley had begun in Umayyad times with the expedition of Muḥammad ibn Qāsim al-Thaqafī in 90–2/709–11. These early Muslim attacks had come by sea or by the long desert route through Makrān. The Ghaznavids were the first Muslims to exploit the northern route through the Khyber Pass, and the fact that their bases in Afghanistan were so much closer meant that their attacks were much more devastating. One of Maḥmūd's first objectives was the main Muslim city of Multān, first settled in the second/eighth century. The presence of a substantial Ismāʿīlī community in the city meant that Maḥmūd could justify his aggression as a campaign against 'heretics', and in 401/1010 he deposed the local ruler, Abu 'l-Fatḥ Dāʾūd. The Ghaznavid takeover of the city was followed by a massacre of the Ismāʿīlīs.

Winter was the campaigning season, and Ghaznavid armies, along with volunteer *ghāzīs* attracted from all over the Muslim world, would descend. The next targets were the Hindūshāhid rulers of the kingdom of Wayhind in the Punjab. Since their domains lay at the foot of the Khyber Pass, they bore the brunt of Maḥmūd's aggression. In 392/1001 Maḥmūd won his first great victory when he defeated and captured the *rāja* Jaipāl in a battle near Peshawar. The struggle was continued by his son Ānandpāl, but he too was defeated in 399/1009. Resistance continued until the death of the last Hindūshāhid, Bhīmpāl, in 417/1026, after which virtually all the Punjab was in Ghaznavid hands.

The great Hindu temples were especially attractive because not only did they contain enormous stores of wealth, but Hindus were not People of the Book and could not claim the status of *dhimmīs*, so pillaging their shrines was a religious duty as well as an economic opportunity. In 405/1014 the temple at Thānesar just north of Delhi was sacked, but his most celebrated triumph was the expedition to Somnāth on the coast of Gujarat in 416–17/1025–6. When the temple was taken and burned to the ground, the loot is said to have amounted

to the vast sum of 20 million *dīnārs*. News of the sack of Somnāth spread throughout the eastern Islamic world, and the ʿAbbāsid caliph sent his congratulations and more honorific titles to Maḥmūd. Along with the money and the prestige, the campaigns in India brought back large numbers of captives – 53,000 from the expedition of 409/1018 alone, we are told – and they were sold to merchants from all over the Middle East. Others were incorporated into the Ghaznavid armies. Unlike Turkish *ghilmān* they were not required to convert to Islam, and in some difficult areas such as Sīstān the Ghaznavids used them against their own Muslim subjects.

Maḥmūd's expeditions to India are an interesting example of the use of *jihād* as an instrument of state policy. The campaigns provided legitimacy for Ghaznavid rule, and the sultan became a hero of Islam. It is probable that the booty provided the resources to maintain the army and build mosques in Ghazna and the vast palace at Lashkar-i Bāzār on the Helmand river in southern Afghanistan. The campaigns, however, did little to spread Islam or Muslim power in the Indian subcontinent. The Ghaznavids made no effort to hold onto the areas they raided, and there is no evidence for widespread conversion of the local population to Islam.[16]

Maḥmūd died in 421/1030. The obvious successor was his son Masʿūd, who had had considerable military experience, having recently distinguished himself in the struggle against the Būyids, and was governor of Herat. However, Maḥmūd passed him over in favour of another son, Muḥammad, who was in Ghazna at the time of his father's death. Masʿūd had the advantages of experience and reputation and, with the support of senior members of the family and commanders of the army, he was able to seize power from his hapless brother. Like his father, the new sultan was an energetic warrior, but he was also a suspicious and difficult man, surrounding himself with cronies and unwilling to accept unpalatable advice.

The account of his reign by the historian Abu ʾl-Faḍl Bayhaqī casts a clear and often cruel light on the sultan and his court, but he also describes the splendour with which Masʿūd used to dazzle his subjects. The historian describes him at one great *majlis* (formal reception) on his golden throne, with his crown suspended on a golden chain above his head and wearing a cloak of crimson so heavily embroidered with gold that almost nothing of the original material could be glimpsed. 'All around the hall, standing against the panels, were the household *ghilmān* with robes of Saqlāṭūnī [apparently

16 For the early history of Islam in India see A. Wink, *Al-Hind: The making of the Indo-Islamic world*, 3 vols. (Leiden, 1990–2004).

of unknown origin] Baghdādī and Iṣfahānī cloth, two-pointed caps, gold-mounted waist sashes, pendants and golden maces in their hands. On the dais itself, to both left and right of the throne, were ten *ghilmān*, with four sectioned caps on their heads, heavy, bejewelled waist sashes and bejewelled sword belts.' After describing more groups of *ghilmān* and their golden bejewelled accoutrements, he describes the celebrations.

> The great men of state and the holders of high ranks came forward. Enormous quantities of largesse were distributed. The prominent people, governors and great men were invited to sit on that dais and the Amīr [Mas'ūd] held court, seated on his throne, until morning when the *nadīms* [boon-companions] came in, and distributed largesses. Then the Amīr rose, mounted and made off to the garden. He changed his robes, rode back and sat down to feast in the splendidly adorned hall. The nobles and great men of the state came forward to the table too. Other tablecloths were spread outside the hall, to one side of the palace and groups of the army sat down there and began to eat. Musicians struck up and wine flowed like water so that, gradually, those who had become drunk left the tables. The Amīr rose up from the table in a mood of great joy, mounted and rode off to the garden.[17]

Such were the pleasures of wealthy monarchy, and it is worth remembering that his Būyid contemporary in Baghdad, Jalāl al-Dawla, was so poor that he could not pay his servants or feed his horses. No wonder the courts of the Ghaznavids achieved such fame in the Muslim world.

In the early years of his reign Mas'ūd was able to pursue the same aggressive policies as his father had done. Further conquests were made in India, and in 429/1037f. he personally led an expedition which took the fortress of Hānsī near Delhi. But all was not well with the Ghaznavid army in India. Aḥmad Ināl-Tagīn, whom he had appointed to command the Ghaznavid garrisons, led a rebellion among the Turkish *ghilmān* stationed in the Punjab. Mas'ūd was obliged to rely on an Indian commander called Tilak to crush the rebellion in 425/1034.

While Mas'ūd was able to continue an aggressive policy in India, the position was very different in Khurāsān. Already by Maḥmūd's time, Ghaznavid rule had been resented for its brutality and harsh taxation. Furthermore, even Maḥmūd had been unable to take the Transoxanian cities of Bukhārā and Samarqand and the Farghāna valley from the Qarakhānids, who always provided a focus for rivalry and opposition. Maḥmūd's conquest of Khwārazm had helped to neutralise this threat, but under the strong rule of 'Alī Tegīn the Qarakhānids

17 Bayhaqī, *Ta'rīkh-i Mas'ūdī*, in Bosworth, *The Ghaznavids*, pp. 136–7 (slightly abridged).

once again became a real threat to Ghaznavid power. Masʿūd's problems were compounded by his own suspicious nature. The *khwārazmshāh*, Altūntāsh, appointed by his father, had always proved a loyal ally against the Qarakhānids, but Masʿūd resented his semi-independent power and large army, and made an attempt to assassinate him. When Altūntāsh was killed in 423/1032, still fighting for the Ghaznavids against ʿAlī Tegīn, his son Hārūn swiftly changed sides, allying himself with the Qarakhhānids against the Ghaznavids. In 425/1034 Hārūn and ʿAlī Tegīn launched a joint campaign to drive the Ghaznavid forces out of Transoxania. Masʿūd had Hārūn assassinated and ʿAlī Tegīn died in the same year of natural causes, but Hārūn's brother and ʿAlī Tegīn's sons continued the fight, and the lands of the lower Oxus were lost to the Ghaznavids for ever.

If they had only had to contend with the Qarakhānids, the well-equipped Ghaznavid armies might have prevailed, but there was a new, much less conventional, threat that they had to face. This is not the place to give a full account of the origins and growth of Saljūq power, but we need to recount the stages by which these bands of impoverished and apparently disorganised nomads effectively defeated the most powerful army in the eastern Islamic world.

The Ghuzz tribesmen, who formed the foundation of Saljūq power, first entered Ghaznavid territory in 416/1025 when the men of 4,000 tents asked to be able to use the pastures in the areas of Sarakhs and Abīvard, in return for which they would guard the frontiers against other nomads. Inevitably friction arose between the nomads and the people of the towns and villages in the area, and just three years later Masʿūd had to lead in person an expedition to disperse them. Some fled west where they entered into service with the Būyids and other western Iranian dynasts, while others went back across the Oxus to join the Saljūq leaders, Ṭughril Beg and Chaghri Beg, now allies of the Qarakhānids. After the death of ʿAlī Tegīn the Saljūqs were threatened by the power of another Ghuzz leader, Shāh Malik, from the steppes around the lower reaches of the Jaxartes river. Defeated and destitute, some 10,000 of them petitioned Masʿūd to be allowed to enter his lands and, once more, to take service as frontier guards. This time Masʿūd was resolute in his refusal, determined to crush the unruly Turkmen once and for all; but the armies he sent against them were defeated, and by 428/1037 the Saljūqs were demanding that Sarakhs and the great city of Marw itself should be granted to them. The Turkmen became increasingly bold, pasturing their flocks throughout the settled lands of Khurāsān as far west as Nīshāpūr, which they occupied in 429/1038.

The Saljūqs did not take these great cities by siege or by force; they did not have the forces to do that. Local elites chose to make agreements with the

Saljūq leaders rather than rely on the sporadic and ineffective protection offered by Masʿūd in distant Ghazna. At this time both Marw and Nīshāpūr were prosperous cities, and the new suburbs that had sprung up since the Muslim conquests were unwalled. There were no local military forces and, in the absence of the sultan's army, making peace was the only sensible option.

Masʿūd remained determined to crush the nomads. In 430/1039 his armies defeated the Turkmen at Sarakhs and retook Nīshāpūr. The next year he mounted another campaign with the intention of driving the Turkmen from the steppes around Marw. A large army, including elephants, set out across the semi-desert from Sarakhs, but at the isolated desert city of Dandānqān they met a group of some 16,000 Turkmen. The Ghaznavid army, weakened by thirst and exhaustion, was cut to pieces, the survivors fleeing back towards Ghazna in complete disarray. Masʿūd himself retired to his capital, where he carried out a purge of all those whom he blamed for his defeat. He then seems to have decided to abandon Iran altogether and retreat to India, but his troops mutinied and he was killed in 432/1040.

Masʿūd was succeeded by his son Mawdūd who took over in Ghazna, and the dynasty survived for the next 130 years in eastern Afghanistan and the Punjab. Nonetheless, the battle of Dandānqān marked a major turning-point in the history of Iran. The Ghaznavids could not hope to retrieve their position in Khurāsān, and the Saljūqs were accepted, even welcomed, by the towns-people of the cities they had once ruled.

The Kurdish dynasties

Kurds had inhabited much of the area of the Zagros mountains and the uplands to the north of Mosul for many centuries before the coming of Islam.[18] Like the Daylamites, however, they had only played a marginal part in the politics of the Islamic state until the fourth/tenth century, being mentioned as rebels or mercenaries in the chronicles. The failure of centralised ʿAbbāsid government, coinciding with the spread of Islam among the Kurdish tribes, however, allowed the emergence of a number of independent Kurdish principalities alongside, and sometimes in competition with, the Daylamite ones. This Kurdish efflorescence survived until the coming in the

18 On the geography of Kurdish settlement in this period, see I. C. Vanly, 'Le déplacement du pays kurde vers l'ouest', *RSO*, 50 (1976); for a general political history, see Hugh Kennedy, *The Prophet and the age of the caliphates*, 2nd edn (London, 2004), pp. 248–64.

430s / 1040s of the Ghuzz Turkmen, who sought to take over their pastures and effectively squeezed them out of many of their traditional areas.

The main Kurdish dynasties which emerged in the second half of the fourth / tenth century were the Ḥasanwayhids and ʿAnnāzids of the central Zagros, the Rawwādids and Shaddādids of Azerbaijan and the Marwānids of south-eastern Anatolia. They were based in different areas and never developed any common political ties, but they had much in common. All emerged in mountainous regions, the natural pasture grounds of the Kurdish tribes, and many were based on the great transhumance routes between summer and winter pastures. On the whole their administrations were primitive; some, such as the ʿAnnāzids in southern Kurdistan and Luristān (381 / 991 to *c*. 500 / 1107), seem to have lacked any bureaucratic structures at all. But the picture is not one of chaos and anarchy, as might at first appear. Some of the Kurdish rulers, notably Badr ibn Ḥasanwayh (r. 370–404 / 980–1013 in the Central Zagros around Qarmāsīn / Kīrmānshāh) and Naṣr al-Dawla the Marwānid (r. 401–53 / 1011–61 in Amida and Mayyāfāriqīn), left reputations for good government which few of their contemporaries could match. Equally telling are the good relations Kurdish leaders frequently developed with leading citizens of the towns in their domains, frequently working in partnership with them. The collapse of ʿAbbāsid rule allowed local elites to emerge, and it is fascinating to see how the people of each area developed their own political solutions, a pattern of variety and local autonomy soon to be extinguished by the coming of the Turks. At Amida (Diyarbakr) for example, real power in the city was exercised by the *qāḍī* Ibn Damna, a member of a prominent local family who agreed to pay a tribute to the Marwānid ruler in exchange for effective autonomy for the city and its inhabitants. Even after his death in a domestic intrigue in 415 / 1024f., the Marwānids were obliged to accept the authority of his successor as *qāḍī*, Ibn Baghl.

In the mid-fourth / tenth century the Kurds were distributed all along the Zagros chain from Fārs in the south to Azerbaijan and the Araxes river in the north. They were also influential in south-east Anatolia as far west as Amida and northern Syria. They were largely sheep-rearers who exploited the pastures of the high Zagros and eastern Anatolia in the summer and the warm plains of Iraq and al-Jazīra in the winter. The Hadhbānī Kurds, one of the most powerful tribes in the period, are described as spending the summer in Azerbaijan around the area of Salmās, north-east of Lake Urmiyya, and the winter on the plains along the Greater and Lesser Zāb rivers east of Mosul. Not all Kurds, however, were transhumant shepherds, and their leaders often seem to have maintained fortresses along the migration routes where their valuables were kept and where they could take refuge in time of danger. There were Kurdish populations in many of the small towns of the mountain area such as Shahrazūr and Salmās, and there were also Kurds who lived in villages; the Marwānid rulers of Mayyāfāriqīn came from a family who were headmen of a village near Sīʿird (modern Siirt). With the decline of ʿAbbāsid power, leaders of the Kurdish tribes came to assume military control in the areas they moved through and became effectively independent rulers while still acknowledging the theoretical overlordship of the caliph.

The Kurdish dynasts all based their power on the military prowess of the Kurdish tribesmen. They never needed to employ Turkish *ghilmān*, as the Būyids did, because they provided mounted soldiers from their own ranks. The rise to power of the Kurdish dynasties also changed the political geography of the area: the ʿAbbāsid, Būyid and Ḥamdānid states were all based on cities and their surrounding agricultural land. By contrast, the power of the Kurdish rulers (with the possible exception of the Shaddādids (340–468/951–1075 in Ganja and Dvin in Armenia) was based on their control of the transhumance routes, and it was the valleys of the Zagros and anti-Taurus that formed the nucleus of these states. This was not because they were especially rich and fertile and thus produced high tax-yields, but because it was there that the tribesmen passed on their biannual migrations. The relationship of the Ḥasanwayhids with the town of Hamadhān, like the relationship of the Marwānids with Amida or the Shaddādids with Dvin and Ganja, was based on indirect influence rather than direct control; the Shaddādids and the Marwānids especially established close links with local, non-Kurdish urban elites. The administration of the Kurdish states tended to be very basic; the Marwānids employed viziers, but there is no indication that the other groups employed any bureaucrats at all: the cities paid an agreed tribute, and for the rest, the traditional mechanisms of tribal authority were sufficient. The *ḥimāya* (protection agreement) was the underlying basis of government.

This Kurdish ascendancy was soon threatened, as elsewhere in the Zagros and southern Anatolia. As early as 420/1029 these pasture-hungry nomads had reached Marāgha and killed a number of Kurds. Thereafter the pressure from Turkish tribes was almost continuous. The Turks, by the arrival of the Ghuzz Turkmen tribes, precursors of the Saljūqs, were much more of a threat to the Kurds than their traditional rivals, the Daylamites or the Armenians, had been. Daylamites and Armenians, being settled farmers, could coexist with transhumant pastoralists such as the Kurds; clearly there were sometimes clashes of interests – when flocks strayed into cultivated fields, for example – but these could be adjudicated. The Turks, on the other hand, were sheep-rearing nomads, in direct competition for the rich summer grazing on the mountain uplands, and the days of Kurdish dominance were accordingly numbered. The Saljūqs took control of the ʿAnnāzid lands in the Central Zagros in 447/1055, and the Rawwādid capital at Tabrīz in 463/1071. In 468/1075 they took control of Shaddādid lands in Azerbaijan, and the Marwānids of Diyarbakr were extinguished by the armies of Malik Shāh in 478/1085.

The Bedouin dynasties[19]

The Muslim world had come into being because lands from Central Asia to North Africa had been conquered by armies largely made up of Arab Bedouin tribesmen. In the first century-and-a-half of Muslim rule, Bedouin – or at least the descendants of men who had been Bedouin – formed an important part of the ruling class. There had always been Bedouin who had refused to pay taxes or accept the authority of the caliphs, both Umayyad and ʿAbbāsid, and formed themselves into Khārijite bands. From the third/ninth century, however, the Bedouin were increasingly excluded from the rewards of being part of the ruling elite. No longer receiving military salaries or government subsidies, some began to resort to more ancient methods of extracting revenues from settled populations. We begin to hear of Bedouin disturbances in the Ḥijāz during the reign of al-Muqtadir, suppressed by Turkish soldiers sent from Baghdad. At the same time, the Bedouin also began to attack pilgrim caravans crossing Arabia from Iraq to Mecca and Medina, a clear sign that they felt they were not benefiting from this traffic. In the early fourth/tenth century many of them joined the religio-political movement known as the Qarāmiṭa (Carmathians)[20] and launched devastating attacks on the pilgrim caravans and even on important Iraqi cities such as Baṣra (sacked in 311/923). By the end of al-Muqtadir's reign (320/932) they were a real threat to the existence of the ʿAbbāsid caliphate. The alienation of many Bedouin from the Islamic state their ancestors had helped to create was virtually complete.

With the collapse of the Qarāmiṭa in the 350s/960s and the weakening of Būyid and Ḥamdānid power in the 370s and 380s/980s and 990s, the chiefs of the larger Bedouin tribes began to establish themselves as independent rulers. A number of dynastic polities were founded in which the ruling families were chiefly by lineages of Bedouin tribes, and the tribesmen provided the military muscle. The important cities of Mosul and Aleppo were

19 For a general account see Kennedy, *Prophet and the age of the caliphates*, pp. 283–306.
20 See chapter 8 above.

ruled by men such as Ṣāliḥ ibn Mirdās al-Kilābī (d. 415/1024) and Qirwāsh ibn al-Muqallad al-ʿUqaylī (d. 442/1050), whose power ultimately derived from their status as tribal chiefs, a position usually inherited from their fathers or other members of their kin. In other areas of the Fertile Crescent, from southern Iraq to Palestine, we find Bedouin tribes and their leaders establishing or attempting to establish small independent states. The Banū ʿUqayl of Mosul (*c.* 380–478/*c.* 990–1093), the Banū Mirdās of Aleppo (415–72/1024–80), the Banū Asad (Mazyadids) in the Kūfa area from around 350/961 to 558/1163 and the Numayrīs in Ḥarrān (380–*c.* 474/1081) are all examples of tribes that came to dominate important towns and establish independent dynastic polities. Other large and influential tribes such as the Banū Kalb in the Damascus area and the Banū Ṭayy in southern Palestine failed to achieve control over major urban centres, largely as a result of Fāṭimid military intervention, and never established settled states.

The Qarāmiṭa had profoundly affected the balance of power among the tribes in the north Arabian and Syrian deserts, and in the main it was tribes that had been involved in the movement that came to dominate the area. Now, however, they did not do so in the name of a religious ideal but for their own tribal interests, and they were led not by missionaries from the settled peoples but by their own tribal shaykhs. Kilāb and ʿUqayl had been the leading supporters of the Qarāmiṭa of Baḥrayn, and it seems that in the second half of the fourth/tenth century many of them, disillusioned with the decline of the power of the movement, drifted north to join fellow tribesmen already established in the hinterlands of Mosul and Aleppo. The influence of the Kalb in central Syria had probably been consolidated by their leading role in the rebellion of the Syrian Qarāmiṭa, while the Ṭayy seem to have moved from northern Arabia to Palestine during the last waves of Qarmaṭī attacks on the area. Of the tribes that founded Bedouin states at this period, only the Asadīs in the Kūfa area had played no part in the movement.

The founders of these Bedouin states all owed something to the patronage of rulers of settled states. The Mirdāsid chiefs of Kilāb owed much of their predominance in northern Syria to the support given them by Sayf al-Dawla the Ḥamdānid (d. 381/991). The primacy of the ruling clan of the ʿUqayl was greatly aided by the Būyid ʿAḍud al-Dawla, who made them responsible for the disciplining of their fellow tribesmen. It was the attempts of the last Ḥamdānids to counter the influence of the Kurds in the Mosul area by granting lands to the ʿUqaylids that ensured their control of northern Iraq. Equally, the Mazyadid leaders of the Asad tribe owed much to the patronage of Bakhtiyār (d. 367/978) and later contenders for power in Būyid Baghdad who sought their support, while Ibn Ustādh-hurmuz (Būyid governor of Baghdad, 392–401/1002–10) was to rely on them to discipline the Bedouin of the area. None of the dynasties would have achieved power without the patronage of settled rulers.

The dynasties that prospered were only able to do so because they had access to the revenues of towns and settled areas with which to reward their followers. The power of ʿUqaylid rulers lay in their tribal following, but it was control of Mosul that brought them the wealth these followers needed. Ṣāliḥ ibn Mirdās was simply one of a number of Kilābī chiefs until he took possession of Aleppo, a position which assured his primacy in the tribe. In the desert a nomad state was impossible since no chief could command absolute authority. Contact with settled powers and peoples enabled some ruling clans to establish themselves as effective dynasts, even while retaining a nomad lifestyle. The possession of the revenues of settled lands also helped the chiefs to increase their tribal following. The dominant position of the ʿUqayl in northern Iraq looks at first glance to have been the product of a vast influx of tribesmen from Arabia, and there certainly were new immigrants from northern Arabia at this time; but it may also be, although it is hard to find specific examples, that many of the members of these newly dominant tribes in fact came from other groups and had attached themselves to the successful tribe, adopting their names and thenceforward being counted among the ʿUqayl or Kilāb.

In economic terms, the changing relationships between the nomads and the settled population can be seen in the laments of numerous sources about the decline of settled agriculture and the occupation of farmland by the Bedouin. The areas worst affected were probably Transjordan, where almost all urban and much village life seems to have come to an end at this time, the Ḥawrān, south of Damascus, and the northern Jazīra, where Ibn Ḥawqal describes the process most clearly. It is probable that other areas on the desert margins of Syria and Iraq were also affected. There can be no doubt that the century 950–1050 saw a vast increase in the area used for nomad pasture and the collapse of the agricultural economy in districts that had once been the granaries of the ʿAbbāsid caliphate.[21] It would be wrong to present a purely negative view of these changes. There were cities that benefited from the Bedouin ascendancy; Aleppo seems to have been more prosperous under the Kilābī Mirdāsids than

21 See for example the collapse of the irrigation systems of the middle Euphrates valley described in Sophie Berthier, *Peuplement rural et aménagements hydroagricoles dans la moyenne vallée de l'Euphrate, fin VIIe–XIX siècle* (Damascus, 2001), esp. pp. 161–70.

it had been under the Ḥamdānids. It may have been that tax levels were lower under Bedouin rule than under regimes such as the Būyids or Ḥamdānids with their expensive *ghilmān* to pay. Certainly the city that suffered the best-documented urban crisis in this period, Baghdad, was never under Bedouin control, while nearby Ḥilla, 'the camp' of the Mazyadid clan of the Banū Asad, developed into a flourishing city which has remained one of the main towns of central Iraq to the present day.[22]

The rise and fall of a Bedouin dynasty can be observed in the history of the ʿUqaylids of Mosul.[23] The Banū ʿUqayl are found in al-Jazīra from Umayyad times, but until the death of the Būyid ʿAḍud al-Dawla in 372/983 they were subject to the authority of the Ḥamdānids or the Būyids. In the confusion that followed the great man's death, the ʿUqaylī chief Muḥammad ibn al-Musayyab was able to make himself master of the city of Mosul in 386/996. The chiefs did not, however, live in the city but exercised power from the nomad camps. An attempt by one member of the ruling family, al-Muqallad ibn Muḥammad, to establish himself in the city and recruit Turkish *ghilmān* – in fact, to make the ʿUqaylids into a settled dynasty like the Ḥamdānids or Būyids – met with failure in the face of opposition from his fellow tribesmen. In 391/1001 leadership of the tribe was assumed by Qirwāsh ibn al-Muqallad, who was to reign until 441/1049. During this half-century his main priorities were to preserve his political independence and ensure access to sufficient summer and winter pastures for his tribesmen. He lived in his camp and seldom visited Mosul or any of the other towns that paid him tribute. The most dangerous and persistent of his enemies were the rival Bedouin chiefs of the Khafāja and Asad tribes to the south, who challenged ʿUqaylid access to winter grazing. In contrast, the ʿUqaylids had generally good relations with the Kurds in the mountains to the north, with whom they were not in competition for resources.

The ʿUqaylids are sometimes described as a Shīʿite dynasty, but this gives a rather misleading impression. In fact, Qirwāsh and his followers seem to have paid little attention to the demands of formal religion. It is true that in 401/1010 Qirwāsh had his allegiance to the Fāṭimid caliph al-Ḥākim proclaimed in the mosques of the cities under his control, which at that time included Mosul, Anbār, Kūfa and al-Madāʾin. However, in the absence of any military support from Cairo he soon abandoned this attempt at independence and reverted to his allegiance to the ʿAbbāsids.

22 G. Makdisi, 'Notes on Ḥilla and the Mazyadids in medieval Islam', *JAOS*, 74 (1954).

23 On whom see H. Kennedy, 'The Uqaylids of Mosul: The origins and structure of a nomad dynasty', *Actas del XII Congreso de la UEAI* (Madrid, 1986), repr. in H. Kennedy, *The Byzantine and Islamic Near East* (Aldershot, 2006), XIII.

Like all the other states in the area, the ʿUqaylids were challenged by the arrival of the Ghuzz Turks. At first things went badly for the ʿUqaylids, and in 433/1041f. the Turks took Mosul. However, the newcomers were in direct competition for pasture with both Kurds and Arabs, and Qirwāsh was able to put together a coalition which inflicted a major defeat on the Turks in Ramaḍān 435/April 1044, a victory which effectively ensured that the plains of northern Iraq should remain in Arab, rather than Turkish, hands. Qirwāsh's most important successor, Muslim ibn Quraysh (453–78/1061–85), was able to maintain his independence for a while by playing off Fāṭimids and Saljūqs, but after his death in battle the Saljūqs gradually asserted their authority, and in 486/1093 the city was taken by Tutush ibn Alp Arslān.

Sunnism and Shīʿism

The period from 945 to 1050, which we can call that of the Muslim commonwealth, was in some ways a period of dissolution and disintegration, and the elaborate and powerful state structures so admired by many historians collapsed. But at the same time it was like fifteenth-century Italy, in that great political diversity went along with immense cultural achievement. It was also a time when many provincial centres acquired their own Muslim identity for the first time.

It was also a period when religious divisions within the Islamic community hardened. Perhaps the most important and long-lasting development within the Islamic *umma* during this period was the formalisation of the divisions between Sunnī and Shīʿite branches in the Muslim world. It would be fair to say that in 900 many Muslims did not consider themselves either Shīʿite or Sunnī. It is true that many Muslims venerated the house of ʿAlī, and that some fervently believed that only with the accession to power of a member of that house could a truly just Muslim society be established. There was no body of Shīʿite ritual, however, which distinguished its adherents from other Muslims, and no distinctively Shīʿite festivals.

It was in Baghdad during the period of Būyid rule (945–1055) that 'Twelver' Shīʿism developed more distinctive religious practices and a clearer sense of communal identity.[24] The last of the widely acknowledged imams of the house of ʿAlī, al-Ḥasan al-ʿAskarī, died in Sāmarrāʾ in 260/874, leaving no

24 For the history of Shīʿism in general, see H. Halm, *The Shiʿites*, 2nd edn (Princeton, 2007). On the history of early Shīʿism, S. H. M. Jafri, *The origins and early development of Shiʿa Islam* (London, 1979).

generally accepted heir. During the course of the fourth/tenth century, however, it came to be believed among the Shīʿa that he had left a son who had remained hidden and never died, but would come again to establish the rule of true Islam. Meanwhile, he had left representatives in the world to guide the faithful in his absence. Acceptance of the imam remained, however, fundamental to true belief, since he was the *ḥujja*, the proof of God, without whom there could be no Islam. This theory of the imamate was developed in Baghdad by such scholars as al-Kulaynī (d. 329/940f.) and above all al-Shaykh al-Mufīd (d. 413/1022), who produced the view of the imamate generally held by Twelvers down to the present day. Despite the violence and the economic problems of the former capital city, this intellectual activity was centred on Baghdad, especially on the old commercial quarter of al-Karkh, which became the main stronghold of the Shīʿa, and scholars from all over the Muslim world, such as the famous Muḥammad ibn al-Ḥasan al-Ṭūsī (d. 460/1067) from Khurāsān, were attracted to the city.

This newly emerging Shīʿism was not formally the state religion of the Būyids (in the sense that Ismāʿīlī Shīʿism was in the Fāṭimid caliphate). Remote Daylam, the original homeland of the dynasty, was an area in which members of the ʿAlid family had sought refuge and made converts, and the Būyids were, in some sense, Shīʿa. They made no attempt, however, to replace the ʿAbbāsid caliphs with rulers from the house of ʿAlī. There were good practical reasons for this. Such a move would have alienated many in Iraq and western Iran who were otherwise prepared to accept Būyid rule in exchange for a measure of peace and security. It would also have meant finding an imam from the house of ʿAlī, and such an imam might well have wanted to take real power in his own name. However, Shīʿite scholars were given some support by figures at the Būyid court, such as the vizier, Sābūr ibn Ardashīr, who established a major Shīʿite library in al-Karkh in 381/991f. The scholars were also patronised by rich local families of ʿAlid descent who were in many cases close to the Būyid court, such as the *sharīfs* al-Raḍiyy (d. 406/1015) and al-Murtaḍā (d. 436/1044). While some Būyid rulers, notably ʿAḍud al-Dawla (d. 372/982), seem to have discouraged speculation that might divide the Muslim community, others at least tolerated it and allowed their courtiers to provide patronage for the needy intellectuals involved.

New elements distinguished the Shīʿa from other sects, specifically its distinctive and exclusive religious observances. These included the public denigration of the first two caliphs (Abū Bakr and ʿUmar), who were held to have usurped the rights of ʿAlī, and the development of certain particularly Shīʿite public festivals. The most important of these festivals was the mourning for al-Ḥusayn on 10 Muḥarram and the celebration of Ghadīr Khumm on 18 Dhū al-Ḥijja, in commemoration of the event when the Prophet was said to have acknowledged ʿAlī as his successor during the Farewell Pilgrimage in 10/632. There also took place the development of the tombs of members of the ʿAlid family as centres of pilgrimage. These three elements characterise the development of the mature Shīʿism of the fourth/tenth century as distinct from the reverence for ʿAlī or support of ʿAlid pretenders to the caliphate which had been common in previous centuries. This Shīʿism was basically quietist in that its adherents did not demand the immediate installation of an ʿAlid as caliph, nor did they feel that they had to take up arms to achieve this. The three distinguishing features of the new Shīʿism described above were all essentially public acts, and at least two were exclusive; while any Muslim could accept the veneration of the tomb of ʿAlī, if not those of all his descendants, no one could accept the celebration of Ghadīr Khumm or the cursing of the first two caliphs without cutting himself off from a large number of other Muslims. Sectarian tension between supporters and opponents of the house of ʿAlī had been increasing in Baghdad before the coming of the Būyids, but the policies of Muʿizz al-Dawla (d. 356/967) and Bakhtiyār (d. 367/978) escalated the situation by taking deliberately provocative positions on the three elements outlined above. From the time of their arrival in Baghdad, the Daylamites became associated with the Shīʿite point of view, and allowed and encouraged the development of a Shīʿite party in the capital, partly to secure the support of at least one constituency among the Baghdad populace. In 351/962 Muʿizz al-Dawla provoked public anger by having curses of the first two caliphs painted on walls in Baghdad. In the end his astute vizier, al-Muhallabī, persuaded him that only the first Umayyad caliph, Muʿāwiya, who had few admirers in Iraq, should be condemned, and so Abū Bakr and ʿUmar were spared. In 353/964 Muʿizz al-Dawla encouraged the public celebration of the important Shīʿite festivals of 10 Muḥarram and Ghadīr Khumm, to the intense annoyance of many in Baghdad. In the same period the Shīʿite shrines of Iraq and Iran were increasingly revered, and they came to replace Mecca and Medina, increasingly difficult to reach because of the lawless conditions in the Arabian Peninsula, as the goal of pilgrimage for many Shīʿa. In 342/953 an officer from Baṣra requested to be buried beside al-Ḥusayn at Karbalāʾ, and the practice of Shīʿite burial *ad sanctos* soon grew in popularity. On his death in 399/1009, Aḥmad ibn Ibrāhīm al-Ḍabbī, the vizier of the Būyid rulers of Rayy, instructed that his body be taken to Karbalāʾ for burial, as did al-Ḥusayn ibn al-Maghribī (d. 418/1027), vizier of the Marwānid ruler of Mayyāfāriqīn. Under Būyid patronage most of the famous Shīʿite shrines were embellished – not only the tombs of ʿAlī and al-Ḥusayn, but also that of Fāṭima in Qumm and of ʿAlī al-Riḍā near Ṭūs (now known as Mashhad).

A further step in the differentiation of sects within Islam came with the establishment of the Fāṭimid caliphate in Egypt in 358/969.[25] As long as the Fāṭimids, with their claims to be imams directly descended from ʿAlī and Ismāʿīl, were confined to the Maghrib, they did not constitute a serious threat and could be dismissed as provincial dissidents. When they took over Egypt, began to move into southern Palestine and to send missionaries throughout the Middle East, it became essential for the Shīʿa of Baghdad to distinguish themselves from these newcomers. The Fāṭimids claimed to be caliphs of the entire Islamic world, so it was important for the Būyids too that the Shīʿite ideology they espoused did not accept Fāṭimid claims to the imamate.

The tensions between the Sunnī and Shīʿite parties in Baghdad came to a head during the reign of the feeble Būyid ruler Bakhtiyār from 361/972 onwards. A powerful Turkish leader in Būyid service, Sebüktegin,[26] diverted the enthusiasm of the Baghdadīs for the *jihād* against the Byzantines into attacking the Būyids and their Daylamite and Baghdadī supporters on the grounds that they were heretics and so legitimate targets for holy war. The Shīʿa were fewer in number, and their centre, the al-Karkh area, was burned down twice during this period. Miskawayh, a contemporary observer, is quite specific about the nature of the change that resulted: 'the dispute between the two factions [Sunnī and Shīʿite], which had formerly been on religious questions, now became political as well, as the Shīʿa adopted the watchword of Bakhtiyār and the Daylamites while the Sunnīs adopted that of Sebüktegin and the Turks'.[27] The fighting resulted in the arming of both factions and the increasing division of the city into fortified quarters, each with its own sectarian character. These divisions persisted after the immediate political quarrel was over, and in the end became permanent.

It was also at this time that the Turks became identified with the anti-Shīʿite party. There is no evidence that the Turks of Sāmarrāʾ in the third/ninth

25 See Yaacov Lev, 'The Fatimid caliphate (358–567/969–1171) and the Ayyubids in Egypt (567–648/1171–1250)', in Maribel Fierro (ed.), *The new Cambridge history of Islam*, vol. II (2010).

26 Not to be confused with the Sebüktegin who founded the Ghaznavid dynasty.

27 Ibn Miskawayh, *Tajārib al-umam*, ed. and trans. H. Amedroz and D. S. Margoliouth in *The eclipse of the ʿAbbasid caliphate*, 7 vols. (London, 1920–1), vol. II, p. 328.

century had shown any hostility at all to the house of ʿAlī, and many of them had supported the Muʿtazilite movement. From Bakhtiyār's reign, however, they became associated with the Sunnī cause, a development which became firmly established in the next century when Turkish rulers such as Maḥmūd of Ghazna and the Saljūqs emphasised their role as champions of Sunnism. The identification of Turkish rulers with Sunnism was to persist throughout the Saljūq and Ottoman periods, outside Ṣafavid Iran.

Throughout the second half of the Būyid period, processions on sectarian feast days and the writing of inflammatory slogans, particularly the cursing of the Companions of the Prophet and the first three caliphs, were to provide flash-points for continuing violence. Despite the efforts of determined rulers of Baghdad such as ʿAḍud al-Dawla to put an end to the growth of sectarian tension, the divide between the Shīʿa and their opponents continued to harden. In the years after the death of ʿAḍud al-Dawla in 372/983 those who can now confidently be described as Sunnīs who opposed the claims of the Shīʿa were developing their own festivals, notably the feast of the Cave, just eight days after Ghadīr Khumm; in this way the Sunnīs memorialised how the Prophet and Abū Bakr had taken refuge together in a cave during the *hijra* from Mecca to Medina, emphasising the unique closeness of the first caliph to Muḥammad. Again the processions and public festivities were an occasion for violence.

In the early fifth/eleventh century a new element was added to the deepening divisions between the sects when the ʿAbbāsid caliphs assumed the role of champion of the Sunnī community. As Būyid power in Baghdad decayed, so the ʿAbbāsids began to explore ways of increasing their power and status. The ʿAbbāsid caliphs became firmly attached to the Sunnī cause, and they were encouraged in this by the rising power of Maḥmūd of Ghazna, who linked himself firmly to the Sunnī, anti-Būyid position.

The last decades of Būyid rule in Baghdad, despite the political chaos, witnessed a religious development which was to affect the whole subsequent history of Islam: the so-called Sunnī revival.[28] This was not, in fact, so much of a revival as the formulation and definition of Sunnism in response to the contemporary emergence of Imāmī (Twelver) Shīʿism. The new Sunnism was based on the ideas of the *muḥaddithūn* (Traditionists), first developed in the third/ninth centuries. They had held that the traditions of the Prophet (his *sunna*) were the only true foundation of Islamic law and religious practice, and

28 See G. Makdisi, *Ibn ʿAqīl et la résurgence de l'Islam traditionaliste au XI siècle* (Damascus, 1962).

that no imam, whether descended from ʿAlī or not, should presume to interfere. In Baghdad this division was intensified by political strife: while Shīʿism was intermittently patronised by the Būyids and their representatives in Baghdad, the lead in the elaboration of Sunnism was taken by the ʿAbbāsid caliph.

The caliph al-Qādir (r. 381–422/991–1031) worked to codify a Sunnī doctrinal and ritual position to counter that of the Shīʿa and to strengthen his position against the absent Būyid ruler of Baghdad, Bahāʾ al-Dawla. His first opportunity came in 394/1003 when Bahāʾ al-Dawla was rash enough to propose a leading member of the family of ʿAlī, Abū Aḥmad al-Mūsawī, as chief *qāḍī* in Baghdad. For the first time the ʿAbbāsid caliph put himself at the head of the popular protest and, successfully, refused to accept the nomination. Thereafter he began to defend the cause of the Traditionists against the claims of Twelver Shīʿism. He did, however, find common ground with the Būyids in his opposition to the claims of the Fāṭimids, and so established himself as spokesman for both Sunnīs and Twelver Shīʿa.

The death of Bahāʾ al-Dawla allowed him more scope. In 409/1018 he took a major step, issuing a decree which condemned Muʿtazilism and Shīʿism and asserted that the Companions of the Prophet and all the first four caliphs should be venerated by 'true' Muslims. These doctrines were repeated and elaborated in 420/1029 when the doctrine of the createdness of the Qurʾān was explicitly condemned. This creed, the so-called *al-Risālat al-Qādiriyya*, marks a fundamental development for two reasons. The first was because Sunnism was defined explicitly and positively. Hitherto, the supporters of the *sunna* had largely been defined by their opposition to the claims of the Twelver Shīʿa; now there was a body of positive belief which had to be accepted by anyone claiming to be a Sunnī. Like the Twelver doctrines developed during the previous century, it was exclusive; the acceptance of the veneration of the first four caliphs meant rejecting the claims of the Twelvers that ʿAlī had been unjustly deprived of the caliphate. It was no longer possible to be simply a Muslim: one was either Sunnī or Shīʿite.

The second important development was that the ʿAbbāsid caliph had emerged as spokesman for the Sunnīs. The early ʿAbbāsid caliphs were not, in the classical sense, Sunnī; an important part of the ʿAbbāsid claim to the caliphate was dependent on a recognition that the family of the Prophet, of which they could claim to be a branch, had a unique claim to leadership. They usually opposed the claims of the ʿAlids to political power, but that did not make them Sunnīs. As part of their attempted rapprochement with the ʿAlids, al-Maʾmūn and his immediate successors had espoused or sympathised with the Muʿtazilite doctrines which al-Qādir explicitly condemned. By his action al-Qādir had become the champion of the Sunnīs and Traditionists against the claims of Twelver Shīʿa and Fāṭimids alike. He had also created a new and lasting role for the ʿAbbāsid caliphate. As Jaʿfar al-Ṣādiq had shown in the second/eighth century, it was possible to be an imam from the house of ʿAlī without taking an active role in politics or making claims to the caliphate, so al-Qādir showed that there was a religious role for the ʿAbbāsid caliphs, a role which they could fulfil despite the fact that their temporal power was non-existent.

Al-Qādir was able to take this position because he had more political independence. To begin with, the Būyid emirate of Baghdad had become so weak that it could not afford to take action against the caliph. He could also count on a large body of support in Baghdad itself; the people might not fight to restore the political power of the ʿAbbāsid caliph, but many of them would support the Sunnī cause against the pretensions of the Shīʿa. In addition he received powerful moral support from Maḥmūd of Ghazna. He was a fierce opponent of the Būyids on a political level, but he also gave a religious dimension to the conflict by accusing them of being heretics and claiming that he was the champion of Sunnī Islam. He established himself as protector of the *ḥajj*, a role traditionally played by the caliphs as leaders of the Muslim community. This moral support from the east enabled al-Qādir to distance himself from the Būyids. But this did not lead to direct political power. By the time of his death al-Qādir had established his moral and religious authority, but the ʿAbbāsid caliph had no troops to command and no land to call his own beyond the gates of his palace.

By this time Baghdad was firmly divided between the adherents of the two rival religious groups, each armed and defending its own areas. The divisions soon spread to other Iraqi towns such as Wāsiṭ and to other parts of the Islamic world. It is probable that the divisions between Sunnī and Shīʿiite would have hardened in this period in any case, partly because of the establishment of the Fāṭimid caliphate, but there can be no doubt that the political rivalries in Baghdad accelerated and defined the process, not just because sectarian differences were encouraged for local political reasons but because Baghdad remained such an important intellectual centre for Sunnī and Shīʿite alike.

PART III

*

REGIONALISM

10

Arabia

ELLA LANDAU-TASSERON

The history of the Arabian Peninsula after the shift of the capital of the empire to Damascus is largely neglected by the universal histories. For example, al-Ṭabarī mentions in one line the conquest of Oman in 280/893, completely ignoring the major civil war that had led to it. Local sources for certain regions, such as Oman, Ḥaḍramawt and Najd, are very deficient as well.[1] This fact is perhaps the reason for the assumptions sometimes voiced by modern scholars: that the central government was not interested in the Peninsula (except in the holy places), and that its history was largely tribal, cyclical and trivial. As will be shown below, these assumptions may be correct when applied to certain regions, such as Najd and Ḥaḍramawt, but not to others, such as Oman, Baḥrayn and the main parts of the Yemen.

Only a few generalisations may be made. The Peninsula never constituted one province, or one political unit, and its internal administrative and political divisions often changed. From the second/eighth century independent and semi-independent polities appeared, and regions underwent cycles of unification and fragmentation. Broadly speaking, society in Arabia, both settled and nomad, remained tribal, and ruling dynasties usually never became full-fledged states. The Peninsula in general lacked the features characteristic of other parts of the Islamic world, namely, court society, sophisticated central bureaucracy, highly developed civilisation and a fixed system of raising standing armies. Apart from that, there were great differences between the various regions.

This chapter is divided into four sections, following a certain division into regions: the Ḥijāz, the Yemen, Oman, and Central and Eastern Arabia. Each section opens

1 Abū Jaʿfar Muḥammad ibn Jarīr al-Ṭabarī, *Taʾrīkh al-rusul wa-l-mulūk*, ed. M. A. Ibrāhīm, 10 vols. (Cairo, 1960), vol. X, p. 33; Saʿīd ʿAwaḍ Bāwazīr, *Ṣafaḥāt min al-taʾrīkh al-ḥaḍramī* (Aden, n.d.), pp. 76, 79; R. B. Serjeant, 'Historians and historiography of Ḥaḍramawt', in R. B. Serjeant, *Studies in Arabian history and civilization*, Variorum Collected Studies X (Aldershot and Vermont, 1981), pp. 241–7; R. B. Serjeant,, 'Materials for South Arabian history', *BSOAS*, 13 (1950), pp. 283–4, 289–302; M. A. Cook, 'The historians of pre-Wahabī Najd', *SI*, 76 (1992), pp. 163–76. For Oman see below.

with an overview, followed by more detailed information arranged chronologically. When the chronological arrangement was not adequate, it has been complemented by thematic arrangement. The outline of the chapter is therefore the following:

(1) The Ḥijāz
 Outline of Ḥijāzī history in the first/seventh and second/eighth centuries
 Administration from the first/seventh to the third/ninth century
 The special status of Mecca and Medina
 Sanctity violated: rebellions and disorders in the holy cities
(2) The Yemen
 The Yemen from the first/seventh to the end of the second/eighth century
 Non-sectarian dynasties
 Religious activity and sectarian states
(3) Oman
 Oman from the first/seventh to the third/ninth century
 Oman from the third/ninth to the fifth/eleventh century
(4) Central and Eastern Arabia: Najd, Yamāma and medieval Baḥrayn
 Central and Eastern Arabia from the first/seventh to the third/ninth century
 The Qarmaṭīs

Finally, two points should be made. First, there is much more material about the Ḥijāz and the Yemen than about Oman and Eastern Arabia. The sections of the chapter are therefore of varying length. Second, contradictory information is not explicitly discussed in the chapter, but contradictory reports are included in the references.

The Ḥijāz

The Ḥijāz, which lies between the plateau of Najd and the Red Sea coast, is the heart of Arabia, for it is the cradle of Islam and contains the holy cities of Mecca and Medina. Information about these cities in the period discussed here is better than information about other places in the Ḥijāz.[2]

The Ḥijāz is varied in landscape, containing desert as well as oases of various sizes.[3] Accordingly, its population on the eve of Islam was made up of sedentary, nomadic and semi-nomadic tribes, most of them pagan but some Jewish and

2 Ḥamad al-Jāsir, 'Mu'allafāt fī ta'rīkh Makka', *al-ʿArab*, 4 (1970); Ḥamad al-Jāsir, 'Mu'allafāt fī ta'rīkh al-Madīna', *al-ʿArab*, 4 (1969); ʿA. ʿA. Drees, 'A critical edition of *Ta'rīkh al-Madīna* by al-Shaykh Quṭb al-Dīn', Ph.D. thesis, University of Edinburgh (1985), part I, pp. 12–23; Ṣāliḥ Aḥmad al-ʿAlī, *al-Ḥijāz fī ṣadr al-Islām: dirāsāt fī aḥwālihi al-ʿumrāniyya wa-l-idāriyya* (Beirut, 1990/1410), pp. 568–91.

3 Detailed geographical description: ʿAlī, *al-Ḥijāz*, pp. 61–156.

Christian. The main settlements were the three towns, Mecca, Ṭā'if and Yathrib, and the oases of Khaybar and Fadak to the north of Yathrib. Mecca, which was ruled by the Quraysh tribe, thrived on international – or at least trans-peninsular – trade, whereas the other towns lived off agriculture and local trade. Each of these towns had an array of nomadic and semi-nomadic tribal groups attached to it in one way or another. Political, economic and religious leadership lay in the towns, in particular Mecca, and not in the nomadic tribes, even though, generally speaking, the latter were militarily superior.

Outline of Ḥijāzī history in the first/seventh and second/eighth centuries

Yathrib was the base of the Prophet's activity after he had migrated there in 622, and it came to be known as Medina. Mecca surrendered to the Prophet in 8/630, and soon Ṭā'if followed suit. The Prophet recognised the high status traditionally accorded to the dominant sedentary tribes, the Quraysh of Mecca and the Thaqīf of Ṭā'if. This attitude helped many of the Ḥijāzī satellite tribal groups to decide to convert.[4] The extent of the Prophet's rule in the Ḥijāz cannot be established, but winning the Ḥijāz over to his side was certainly his greatest political achievement. It was mainly Ḥijāzī tribes that coalesced around Abū Bakr after Muḥammad's death in 11/632 and that helped him subdue the whole of the Arabian Peninsula; and it was mainly the elite of the Ḥijāzī towns, in particular Mecca, that led Islam to become a world religion and that continued for a long time to assume the roles of political and economic leadership in the empire.

In spite of tribal emigration to the conquered territories, the cities of the Ḥijāz were not depleted or relegated to a marginal position during the Rāshidūn period (11–40/632–61). Medina in particular attracted many new inhabitants, being the political capital of the new empire. Great wealth flowed into the Ḥijāz, and the standard of living rose considerably. As early as 'Umar's reign (r. 13–23/634–44) food supplies from Egypt arrived in Medina and Mecca through the ports of al-Jār and al-Shu'ayba. 'Uthmān (r. 23–35/644–56) reportedly abandoned the port of al-Shu'ayba and chose Judda instead.[5]

4 See chapter 6 in this volume. For details about the tribes see 'Alī, *al-Ḥijāz*, pp. 177–90; M. F. von Oppenheim, *Die Beduinen*, vol. II, ed. E. Bräunlich and W. Caskel (Leipzig, 1943), pp. 314–16 and *passim*.

5 Aḥmad ibn Abī Ya'qūb al-Ya'qūbī, *Ta'rīkh*, 2 vols. (Beirut, 1379/1960), vol. II, p. 154; 'Abd al-Qādir ibn Muḥammad ibn Muḥammad ibn Faraj al-Juddī al-Ḥijāzī, *al-Silāḥ wa-l-'udda fī ta'rīkh Judda*, ed. M. al-Ḥudrī (Damascus, Beirut and Medina, 1988), pp. 25–6; Ḥamad al-Jāsir, *Fī shimāl gharb al-Jazīra* (Riyādh, 1981), pp. 167–214; 'Alī, *al-Ḥijāz*, pp. 429–32. A. Dietrich, 'al-Djār', *EI2*, vol. II, p. 454; R. Hartmann and Phebe Ann Marr, 'Djudda', *EI2*, vol. II, p. 571; G. F. Hourani, *Arab seafaring in the Indian Ocean in ancient and medieval times*, (Princeton, 1951), pp. 60–82.

As a result of the assassination of the third caliph, ʿUthmān, the capital shifted, first to Kūfa (under ʿAlī, r. 35–41/656–61), and then to Damascus (under the Umayyads, 40–132/660–750). The Ḥijāz nevertheless remained prosperous. Provisions continued to arrive from Egypt, and the local agriculture was greatly developed as well, being based on the labour of war prisoners sent from the conquered territories. Existing settlements grew and new villages and towns came into being, such as al-Rabadha. New crops were introduced, dams were constructed and wells were dug by the government and by private entrepreneurs. Roads were improved, milestones and way marks were set up, and road stations were built. As a result administration, tax collecting, pilgrimage and commerce were facilitated. Economic prosperity, which was occasionally interrupted by crises (for instance during the time of Hishām, r. 105–25/724–43), was accompanied by both intellectual and leisure activities in Mecca and Medina. Such activities are usually associated with courts, but here they developed after the court had moved away. Descendants of Companions of the Prophet, among others, took it upon themselves to hand down his heritage. Thus, Islamic law, theology, tradition (*ḥadīth*), Islamic history and the Prophet's biography (*sīra*) began to develop in the holy cities. Among the most famous Ḥijāzī scholars of the first two centuries of Islam were ʿUrwa ibn al-Zubayr, Ibn Shihāb al-Zuhrī, Ibn Jurayj, Ibn Isḥāq, al-Wāqidī, Nāfiʿ and Mālik ibn Anas. At the same time the high standard of living contributed to the growth of social gatherings, poetry and music.

The shift of the court to Iraq in the middle of the second/eighth century did not at first affect the Ḥijāz. The main political, economic and intellectual activities now took place in Iraq, but the first ʿAbbāsids continued to give their attention to the Ḥijāz, because of its holy places, its political significance and the status of its city-dwellers (see below). Heavy damage was sometimes inflicted on Ḥijāzī settlements as a result of rebellions, but recovery usually followed. The prosperity of the towns was due not only to the attention of the government but also to the fact that they were largely free of Bedouin pressures. By this time many Ḥijāzī tribal groups had migrated, either on their own initiative or because ordered or encouraged to do so by the government. It was only after the middle of the third/ninth century that conditions in the Ḥijāz really deteriorated, as detailed below.[6]

6 Drees, 'A critical edition', part II, pp. 64–93; Juddī, *al-Silāḥ wa-l-ʿudda*, p. 26; Ḥamad al-Jāsir, 'al-Rabadha fī kutub al-mutaqaddimīn', *al-ʿArab*, 1 (1966); ʿAlī, *al-Ḥijāz*, pp. 199–206, 379–434, 441–5, 479–81, for the crops see pp. 157–76; Oppenheim, *Beduinen*, vol. II, pp. 317–20; Saʿd al-Rāshid, *al-Rabadha: A portrait of early Islamic civilization in Saudi Arabia* (Riyadh, 1986).

Administration from the first/seventh to the third/ninth century

Information about the administrative status and divisions of the Ḥijāz is contradictory. Various men are mentioned as governors for the Prophet, for the Rāshidūn and for Muʿāwiya (r. 41–60/661–80) in each of the three towns. Sometimes Mecca and Ṭāʾif had one governor, Medina another, and at other times all three cities constituted one jurisdiction, but the Ḥijāz as such does not generally figure as a single administrative unit. The great number of governors indicates frequent replacements, although it may also reflect various versions of historians.[7] The logic of the various divisions is not always clear. For example, it is reported that the whole of the Peninsula, excepting Mecca and Yemen, was attached to Medina, until Muʿāwiya removed Baḥrayn and Oman from the jurisdiction of the Ḥijāz and attached them to Iraq. Yet the area of al-Ṭaff, to the west of Kūfa (and closer to Kūfa than to the Ḥijāz), is said to have paid its taxes to Medina until the time of al-Mutawakkil (r. 232–47/847–61). According to other reports Mecca and Medina, and sometimes also Ṭāʾif, were joined together with Yamāma, or the Yemen.[8] The different administrative divisions of the Ḥijāz reflect in part changes over time, in part a hierarchy of governors and sub-governors, and perhaps also confusion in the sources. All this is difficult to follow, but some facts seem to emerge out of the plethora of contradictory details. First, Mecca and Medina constituted separate governorships in the early period. Second, the early caliphs attached great importance to the holy cities. Until the middle of the third/ninth century most of the governors were members of the royal family or other people of high standing, mainly Qurashīs. Third, Medina remained an important economic and administrative centre throughout the Umayyad period. The governors often served the private interests of the Umayyad caliphs in agriculture and in business.

Economic crises: Muḥammad ibn Aḥmad al-Fāsī, *Shifāʾ al-gharām bi-akhbār al-balad al-ḥarām*, vol. II, ed. ʿU. ʿA. Tadmurī (Beirut, 1405/1985), pp. 429–31; Ibn Ẓahīra, *al-Jāmiʿ al-laṭīf*, in F. Wüstenfeld, *Akhbār Makka al-musharrafa*, 3 vols. (Göttingen, 1274/1857), vol. II, pp. 309–11. Scholars of the first two centuries: Muḥammad ibn Aḥmad al-Fāsī, *al-ʿIqd al-thamīn fī taʾrīkh al-balad al-amīn*, ed. M. Ḥ. al-Faqī, F. Sayyid and M. M. al-Ṭanāḥī, 8 vols. (Cairo, 1378–88/1958–69), *passim*; S. Muṣṭafā, *al-Taʾrīkh al-ʿarabī wa-l-muʾarrikhūn*, vol. I (Beirut, 1979), pp. 149–68; J. Horovitz, *The earliest biographies of the Prophet and their authors*, ed. L. Conrad (Princeton, 2002); H. Motzki, *The origins of Islamic jurisprudence: Meccan fiqh before the classical schools* (Leiden, 2002). Poetry and social life: A. Arazi, 'Sukayna', *EI2*, vol. IX, p. 802.

7 ʿIzz al-Dīn ʿAbd al-ʿAzīz ibn ʿUmar Ibn Fahd, *Ghāyat al-murām bi-akhbār salṭanat al-balad al-ḥarām*, vol. I, ed. Fahīm Muḥammad Shaltūt (Mecca, 1406/1986), pp. 35–114, 127; ʿAlī, *al-Ḥijāz*, pp. 61–2; ʿA. ʿAbd al-Ghanī, *Umarāʾ al-Madīna al-munawwara* (Damascus, n.d.), pp. 25–58, 492–4.

8 Al-Ṭabarī, *Taʾrīkh*, vol. VIII, p. 40; ʿAli ibn Tāj al-Dīn al-Sinjārī, *Manāʾiḥ al-karam fī akhbār Makka wa-l-bayt wa-wulāt al-ḥaram*, ed. J. ʿA. Muḥammad al-Miṣrī, 6 vols. (Mecca, 1998/1419), vol. II, p. 150, read Ḥamdawayh for 'Ḥamdūn' (see on him below).

It was Muʿāwiya or his son Yazīd (r. 60–4/680–3) who first combined Mecca and Medina; or Medina and the Ḥijāz; or Mecca, Medina and Ṭāʾif under one governor. Such arrangements were more common subsequently, but were never followed on a regular basis.[9] In the early ʿAbbāsid period the office was occasionally only a nominal one. So, for example, al-Maʾmūn (r. 198–218/813–33) appointed his minister al-Ḥasan b. Sahl to 'the Ḥijāz, the Yemen, Fārs, al-Ahwāz and Iraq'. Obviously this was a delegation of general authority, and not a nomination to specific governorship. Such an appointee would assign governors to govern the provinces directly. A remarkable fact is that, although seemingly people worthy of the caliphs' trust, most governors served only short terms.[10] The pilgrimage was usually led by the governor of the holy cities, unless the caliph himself performed it, or appointed a person for the task (*amīr al-ḥajj*), or unless a rebel took over.[11] The office of *amīr al-ḥajj* had great political significance, as illustrated by the choice of the caliph al-Qādir (r. 381–422/991–1031) who appointed the Alid Shīʿī leader, the *sharīf* al-Raḍiyy, to this office, and, when necessary, reminded him and his relatives of this favour.[12] This appointment was meant to conciliate the Shīʿites and to counter the influence of the Fāṭimids in the Ḥijāz (see below).

Outside of the towns, the tribes were apparently left to their own devices, except that they had to pay the alms-tax (*ṣadaqa*) to the governor of Medina. There is hardly any information about tax-collectors sent to the tribes, or indeed about their tribal daily life and about their contacts with the government.[13]

ʿAbbāsid governors in the Ḥijāz are still mentioned in the sixties of the third/ninth century. Some of the governors of this period served long

9 Fāsī, *Shifāʾ*, pp. 259, 261, 266, 273–5; Fāsī, *ʿIqd*, vol. III, p. 419; Ibn Fahd, *Ghāya*, pp. 82, 108, 116, cf. pp. 91, 315–16, 318.

10 Muḥammad ibn Aḥmad al-Fāsī, *al-Zuhūr al-muqtaṭafa min taʾrīkh Makka al-musharrafa*, ed. A. M. al-Ghazāwī (Beirut, 2000), pp. 208–24; Fāsī, *Shifāʾ*, pp. 251–303; Sinjārī, *Manāʾiḥ*, vol. I, pp. 513–29, vol. II, pp. 8, 11–14, 37, 39, 47–8, 50, 55–61, 69–70, 72, 77, 79, 86, 90–5, 98, 100–3, 109–10, 119–20, 127–8, 142, 150–1, 155, 157–60, 164–5, 168–9, 171, 175; Ibn Fahd, *Ghāya*, pp. 191–389, 408–64; ʿAlī, *al-Ḥijāz*, pp. 282–315, 322–37; ʿAbd al-Ghanī, *Madīna*, pp. 107–90 (al-Ḥasan ibn Sahl, pp. 160, 164; other examples, pp. 174, 182, 185, 193); Edward von Zambauer, *Muʿjam al-ansāb wa-l-usarāt al-ḥākima fī al-taʾrīkh al-Islāmī* (Beirut, 1980), pp. 27–9, 35–7.

11 E.g. al-Ṭabarī, *Taʾrīkh*, vol. VIII, pp. 238–9, 254, 272; Sinjārī, *Manāʾiḥ*, vol. II, p. 148; Ibn Fahd, *Ghāya*, pp. 318, 325; ʿAbd al-Ghanī, *Madīna*, p. 174.

12 Taqī al-Dīn Aḥmad ibn ʿAlī al-Maqrīzī, *Ittiʿāẓ al-ḥunafāʾ bi-akhbār al-aʾimma al-Fāṭimiyyīn al-khulafāʾ*, ed. Jamāl al-Dīn al-Shayyāl (Cairo, 1368/1948), p. 39.

13 See e.g. ʿAbd al-Ghanī, *Madīna*, p. 129; ʿAlī, *al-Ḥijāz*, pp. 292–3, 316–17, 339–57; Oppenheim, *Beduinen*, vol. II, pp. 320–1.

terms, a fact that gives the wrong impression of stability in the Ḥijāz.[14] As a matter of fact, the central government had lost its grip on the region by this time.

The special status of Mecca and Medina

The holy cities had great political significance, not only as symbols of a faith that was also a polity, but also as cultic centres regularly visited by Muslims from all over the empire. This explains why the caliphs reserved for themselves, as long as they were able, the power to appoint governors to the Ḥijāz. It also explains the huge investments made by the caliphs and other rulers, not only in public but also in private property. In addition to renovations of mosques and infrastructure, caliphs and high officials built and purchased houses for themselves in Mecca, preferably near the Kaʿba.[15]

It appears that, in the early period, the caliphs' willingness to invest was the result of genuine concern for the believers' welfare. ʿUmar established a food storehouse in Medina, and watering-places on the road between Mecca and Medina, for the benefit of pilgrims. He also enlarged the mosques since they could no longer accommodate the growing numbers of believers. ʿUthmān bought and demolished houses adjacent to the Kaʿba in order to enlarge the mosque there.[16] Attention to decoration began with Muʿāwiya, who sent from Damascus incense, candles, a cover (*kiswa*), and slaves to serve in the Kaʿba. ʿAbd Allāh ibn al-Zubayr, who ruled from Mecca in the years 64–73/683–92, enlarged the mosque of the Kaʿba and repaired the damages inflicted on it during the Syrian siege of 64/683. Having defeated Ibn al-Zubayr in 73/692, the general and governor al-Ḥajjāj b. Yūsuf returned the building to its previous state.[17] The caliph al-Walīd (r. 86–96/705–15) invested not only in the Kaʿba but also carried out extensive works in the central mosque in Medina, turning it into a magnificently decorated edifice; a special militia was assigned to guard it (*ḥaras al-masjid*). In addition, al-Walīd ordered that a mosque be built at every place

14 E.g. Sinjārī, *Manāʾiḥ*, vol. II, p. 157. See further ʿA. ʿAbd al-Ghanī, *Taʾrīkh umarāʾ Makka al-mukarrama* (Damascus, 1413/1992), pp. 85–440.

15 See e.g. Muḥammad ibn Isḥāq al-Fākihī, *Taʾrīkh Makka*, in Wüstenfeld, *Akhbār Makka*, vol. II, pp. 13–17.

16 Quṭb al-Dīn al-Nahrawālī, *al-Iʿlām bi-aʿlām bayt allāh al-ḥarām*, in Wüstenfeld, *Akhbār Makka*, vol. III, pp. 74–9; Sinjārī, *Manāʾiḥ*, vol. I, p. 529; Drees, 'A critical edition', part II, pp. 169–70, 173–4; ʿAlī, *al-Ḥijāz*, pp. 204–5.

17 Sinjārī, *Manāʾiḥ*, vol. II, pp. 17–26, 30–1, 45–51; Fāsī, *Zuhūr*, pp. 60–2, 68–9, 91, 104–5; Ibn Fahd, *Ghāya*, p. 188; Nahrawālī, *Iʿlām*, in Wüstenfeld, *Akhbār Makka*, vol. III, pp. 73–86; ʿAlī, *al-Ḥijāz*, pp. 596–610.

where the Prophet had prayed. From the Marwānid period (beginning in 65/684) onwards, the caliphs donated gold, silver, ivory and mosaics to decorate the two cities' mosques. Renovations sometimes aroused opposition. Some refused to give up their homes, which had to be pulled down in order to enlarge the mosques. Others objected to adornments, which they associated with luxury and which they considered as deviation from the Prophet's custom. The protests had no effect, and they soon disappeared. Moreover, the inhabitants came to realise that they could benefit from the government's attention, and started to appeal directly to the authorities outside the Ḥijāz for help in repairing, for instance, the damage caused by floods, and their requests were usually granted. Such appeals, however, were not generally necessary, for the caliphs and governors often took the initiative in making repairs.[18] It appears, however, that after the Rāshidūn, investments were meant to enhance the rulers' authority and to earn them legitimacy and prestige rather than merely to contribute towards the welfare of the Muslims. From the third/ninth century such investments served as a major tool in the competition between rival Muslim states. Destruction of renovations carried out by a political rival was rare,[19] but its occurrence points yet again to the political significance of maintenance works in the holy cities.

Governors occasionally engaged not merely in renovations but also in innovations. In the Marwānid period Khālid al-Qasrī, for example, enforced the separation of men from women during the circumambulation (*ṭawāf*) of the Kaʿba. This particular innovation was accepted, but others were resented or rejected.[20] Innovations, like renovations, had political significance, as illustrations of sovereignty.

The fact that the Ḥijāz had been the seat of the Prophet's rule and the centre of the new empire not only led to its development but also meant that its people, in particular the dwellers of the holy cities, claimed a special status. Some of the closest Companions of the Prophet and other important personalities remained in the Ḥijāz, profiting from their high status and from lands that had been granted them by the Prophet. Some of them further purchased

18 Fāsī, *Shifā'*, pp. 267–8; Sinjārī, *Manā'iḥ*, vol. I, pp. 7–8, vol. II, pp. 92–3, 109–15, 122–3, 151–8, 161–3, 170, 178, 182–4, 186; Nahrawālī, *Iʿlām*, in Wüstenfeld, *Akhbār Makka*, vol. III, pp. 86–162; Ibn Fahd, *Ghāya*, pp. 204, 212–13, 231, 300, 309, 335, 370, 410–13, 424–5, 443; Drees, 'A critical edition', part II, pp. 128–42, 155–7, 181–2, 201, 203–6, 217, 234, 323–6; 'Alī, *al-Ḥijāz*, pp. 205, 306–7.

19 E.g. Ibn Fahd, *Ghāya*, p. 300.

20 Fāsī, *ʿIqd*, vol. IV, p. 272; Ibn Fahd, *Ghāya*, pp. 194–200, see also pp, 409, 414, 426, 431, 444, 448.

lands and invested great sums of money in agricultural enterprises. Chief among them were the Prophet's cousin and son-in-law ʿAlī b. Abī Ṭālib, al-Zubayr b. al-ʿAwwām, Ṭalḥa b. ʿUbayd Allāh and ʿAbd al-Raḥmān b. ʿAwf, all Qurashīs. It is perhaps no accident that the ʿAlids and the Zubayrids were the greatest opponents of the Umayyads, who competed with them over the economic opportunities of the Ḥijāz, in addition to usurping their position as leaders of the Muslims.[21] In the early period actual rebellions were few, but the Meccans and Medinans did defy the caliphs in various ways, and kept their dignity and status in the local arena even after their defeat in the second civil war (*fitna*, 61–73/680–92). Umayyad and early ʿAbbāsid caliphs tried to reconcile the members of the elite (e.g. by giving them generous gifts and pensions, *ʿaṭāʾ*, by granting their requests, sometimes by the choice of governors), while at the same time keeping an eye on them. The caliphs did not hesitate to suppress rebellions, nor, when they saw fit, to confiscate lands, to deprive the Ḥijāzī notables of their pensions and to humiliate them.[22]

Of the two local families just mentioned, the Zubayrids came to prominence first, but it was the ʿAlids, descendants of the Prophet, who had the more enduring influence. They were mainly based in the area of Yanbuʿ, to the west of Medina, and in Fadak, to the north, where they owned large tracts of land. Yanbuʿ occasionally suffered from destruction as a result of ʿAlid revolts, yet in the fourth/tenth century it was even more prosperous than Medina. The property, among other things, became a cause of quarrel between the various groups of the family of the Prophet.[23] It may also partly explain why the ʿAlids never constituted a united front against any government.

21 Details of land ownership: Ḥamad al-Jāsir, *Bilād Yanbuʿ* (Riyadh, n.d.), pp. 23–4, 139; ʿAlī, *al-Ḥijāz*, pp. 304, 445–80; S. A. al-ʿAlī, 'Mulkiyyāt al-arḍ fī al-Ḥijāz fī al-qarn al-awwal al-hijrī', *al-ʿArab*, 3 (1969). See also M. J. Kister, 'The battle of the Ḥarra: Some socio-economic aspects', in M. Rosen-Ayalon (ed.), *Studies in memory of Gaston Wiet* (Jerusalem, 1977).

22 Ibn Fahd, *Ghāya*, p. 187; ʿAlī ibn Aḥmad ibn Ḥazm, *Jamharat ansāb al-ʿArab*, ed. ʿA. M. Hārūn (Cairo, 1382/1962), p. 39 (al-Manṣūr appoints an ʿAlid as governor of Medina); Jāsir, *Yanbuʿ*, p. 24; ʿAlī, *al-Ḥijāz*, pp. 301–4, 379–434, note that after Hārūn no state pensions are mentioned (p. 411); Kister, 'Ḥarra'. Defiance of caliphal authority (short of rebellion): Aḥmad ibn Yaḥyā al-Balādhurī, *Ansāb al-ashrāf*, vol. V, ed. S. D. Goitein (Jerusalem, 1936), pp. 28–9, 41; Yaʿqūbī, *Taʾrīkh*, vol. II, p. 250; Muṣʿab ibn ʿAbd Allāh al-Zubayrī, *Nasab Quraysh*, ed. E. Levi-Provencal (Cairo, n.d.), p. 154; Ibn Fahd, *Ghāya*, pp. 201, 282, 284; Sinjārī, *Manāʾiḥ*, vol. II, pp. 62, 68–9. Generosity of caliphs: ibid., pp. 90, 111, 119, 123; Fāsī, *Shifāʾ*, pp. 342–3, cf. p. 353; Drees, 'A critical edition', part II, p. 156.

23 Yanbuʿ: Jāsir, *Yanbuʿ*, pp. 13–16, 19–28. Disputes among ʿAlids over property: al-Ṭabarī, *Taʾrīkh*, vol. VII, pp. 161–3, cf. Ibn Fahd, *Ghāya*, p. 120.

Sanctity violated: rebellions and disorder in the holy cities

The Ḥijāz was rarely a target for attacks by non-Muslims, though this did occur – for example, in 173/790 and 183/799, when Ethiopians landed on the coast.[24] As a rule it was Muslims who stirred up violence, despite the prohibition on spilling blood in the holy places. Rebels, both local and others, did not hesitate to clash in Mecca, usually during the holiest of times, the pilgrimage. Robbery of pilgrim caravans, and even of the Kaʿba itself, became ever more common from the third/ninth century onwards. It was not only Bedouin who committed such acts, but also local leaders descending from the Prophet's family (*ashrāf*). The caliphs themselves sometimes ignored the sanctity of Mecca and Medina, even when it was not absolutely necessary, for example, the first ʿAbbāsid governor of the region executed the Umayyads in Mecca, paying no heed to protests.[25]

The first civil war (*fitna*) started with the assassination of the caliph ʿUthmān in Medina (in 35/656), but subsequent events took place outside of the Peninsula, and those who remained in the Ḥijāz were not involved. Hostilities almost broke out in Mecca in 39/660 between supporters of ʿAlī and a representative sent by Muʿāwiya, but the parties avoided it and reached an agreement.[26] During Muʿāwiya's reign (41–60/661–80), which followed that war, resentment in the Ḥijāz grew, and after his death many refused to recognise his son Yazīd as caliph. Al-Ḥusayn b. ʿAlī left for Kūfa as a claimant to the throne, to be killed at Karbalāʾ (61/680); ʿAbd Allāh ibn al-Zubayr demanded that a caliph be elected by consultation, but claimed the throne himself after Yazīd's death (64/683); the Medinans acted under their own leadership and drove the Umayyads out of their town, but were defeated by a Syrian army at the battle of al-Ḥarra (64/683).[27] The Ḥijāzī opposition was not united until after al-Ḥarra. Thereafter it was the Zubayrid family that gained prominence. Between the years 64 and 73/683 and 692 hegemony in the Ḥijāz (and in fact in most of the Islamic lands) was in the hands of ʿAbd Allāh ibn al-Zubayr, but he was eventually defeated by the Umayyads. The Zubayrids remained in the Ḥijāz and continued to own lands there, and even to serve as

24 Sinjārī, *Manāʾiḥ*, vol. II, pp. 121, 126.

25 Ibn Fahd, *Ghāya*, pp. 300–1. For Bedouin violence across the centuries, see al-Ṭabarī, *Taʾrīkh*, vol. IX, p. 553; Fāsī, *Shifāʾ*, pp. 344–5, 352, 364; Sinjārī, *Manāʾiḥ*, vol. II, pp. 147, 174, 204; Ibn Fahd, *Ghāya*, pp. 174, 399, 433; ʿAbd al-Ghanī, *Madīna*, pp. 175–7, on the *ashrāf* see below.

26 Fāsī, *Shifāʾ*, pp. 338–9.

27 Al-Ṭabarī, *Taʾrīkh*, vol. V, pp. 381–467, 479–81; Ibn Fahd, *Ghāya*, pp. 122–6; Kister, 'Ḥarra'.

governors of Medina for the early ʿAbbāsids, but their political role was minor.[28] The stage in the Ḥijāz was thenceforth occupied by ʿAlids and by non-local forces.

The first non-local rebel to take Mecca and Medina, in 129/746, was the Yemenī Khārijite al-Mukhtār Abū Ḥamza. He was acting on behalf of ʿAbd Allāh b. Yaḥyā Ṭālib al-Ḥaqq, who had seized the Yemen shortly before. The caliph Marwān II (r. 127–32/744–50) dispatched troops from Syria, which suppressed the movement in both Mecca and the Yemen.[29]

The local ʿAlids first rebelled in 144/762 led by Muḥammad al-Nafs al-Zakiyya, who was a Ḥasanid (namely, a descendant of al-Ḥasan b.ʿAlī) . Battles took place in Mecca and Medina, and the revolt was suppressed.[30] Another ʿAlid–Ḥasanid revolt, led by al-Ḥusayn b. ʿAlī, 'the man of Fakhkh', occurred in 169/786 and was suppressed during the Pilgrimage, its leader killed while being in the state of *iḥrām*.[31] The caliph al-Amīn (r. 193–8/809–13) violated the sanctity of the Kaʿba, albeit not by spilling blood. In 196/811 he removed from it the document regulating the succession to the caliphate that had been drawn up by his father Hārūn. He then burnt it, an action that marked the beginning of yet another civil war. The Ḥijāzīs rejected al-Amīn and gave their allegiance to his brother Maʾmūn. But they did not take to arms, and the actual civil war took place outside the Ḥijāz.[32] Rarely did a governor refrain from fighting a rebel in order to avoid bloodshed in Mecca, the holy city. Thus al-Maʾmūn's governor preferred to leave Mecca (in 199/815) rather than to fight the ʿAlid rebel al-Ḥusayn al-Afṭas.

The latter took control of Mecca and its port Judda on behalf of Abū al-Sarāyā, who had rebelled in Iraq in 199/815. Abū al-Sarāyā gained control not only of Mecca but Medina too, through another agent, the Ḥasanid

28 Balādhurī, *Ansāb*, pp. 150–9, 188–204, 355–78; Ibn Fahd, *Ghāya*, pp. 139–87; G. Rotter, *Die Umayyaden und der zweite Bürgerkrieg* (680–692) (Wiesbaden, 1982). Zubayrids as governors: ʿAbd al-Ghanī, *Madīna*, pp. 154–5.

29 Fāsī, *ʿIqd*, vol. V, pp. 511–12; Sinjārī, *Manāʾiḥ*, vol. II, pp. 73–7; Ibn Fahd, *Ghāya*, pp. 282–97; Sālim b. Ḥamūd al-Sayyābī, *al-Ḥaqīqa wa-l-majāz fī taʾrīkh al-Ibāḍiyya bi-l-Yaman wa-l-Ḥijāz* (Muscat, 1400/1980), pp. 81, 99–125 (note the author's strong penchant for Ibāḍism); ʿAbd al-Ghanī, *Madīna*, pp. 104–7. Ṭālib al-Ḥaqq and the Syrian army: see below.

30 A. Elad, 'The rebellion of Muḥammad b. ʿAbdallāh b. al-Ḥasan (known as al-Nasf al-Zakiyya) in 145/762', in J. E. Montgomery (ed.), *ʿAbbasid Studies: Occasional papers of the School of ʿAbbasid Studies, 6–10 July 2002* (Leuven, Paris and Dudley, MA, 2004).

31 Sinjārī, *Manāʾiḥ*, vol. II, pp. 115–19; Ibn Fahd, *Ghāya*, pp. 349–55; Abū al-Faraj al-Iṣfahānī, *Maqātil al-Ṭālibiyyīn*, ed. Aḥmad Ṣaqr (Beirut, n.d.), pp. 435–60.

32 Al-Ṭabarī, *Taʾrīkh*, vol. VIII, pp. 438–40; Fāsī, *Shifāʾ*, pp. 284–5.

Muḥammad b. Sulaymān b. Dāʾūd. After Abū al-Sarāyā had been killed in 200/816, al-Ḥusayn al-Afṭas looked for another leader. He turned to the local Ḥusaynid (namely, a descendant of al-Ḥusayn b. ʿAlī), Muḥammad b. Jaʿfar al-Ṣādiq, and persuaded him to declare himself caliph. Muḥammad mustered support among Ḥijāzī Bedouins and defeated an ʿAbbāsid army, but he was eventually defeated (in 200/816) by a coalition of Meccans, Medinans and the ʿAbbāsids. His nephew, Ibrāhīm b. Mūsā al-Kāẓim (brother of the well-known ʿAlī al-Riḍā), was involved as well, but the reports about his career are contradictory.[33]

Despite the turbulent events, the ʿAbbāsids did not change their policy towards the Ḥijāz during the first half of the third/ninth century. They continued to appoint governors (again from their own family), but their control of the region grew ever weaker. This was due partly to their general decline and the rise of other forces, partly to the arrival of new Bedouin groups from the south and the east to the vicinity of Mecca and Medina, and partly to the disturbances caused by ʿAlids inside the cities. The general picture is that of a growing number of forces trying to gain control of the Ḥijāz.

In about 230/845 the caliph al-Wāthiq (r. 227–32/842–7) had to dispatch an army to fight the Sulaym and other tribes which were troubling Ḥijāzī cities. The Turkish general who led this expedition, Bughā al-Kabīr, acted against tribes in Najd as well, and emerged victorious, though only after several defeats.[34]

The other threat to the caliphs, the ʿAlids, was growing more menacing. Some early ʿAbbāsid caliphs tried to conciliate them, but Mutawakkil (r. 232–47/847–61) reversed this policy.[35] Perhaps in response to this pressure, the Ḥasanid Ismāʿīl b. Yūsuf rebelled in 251/865 or 252/866 and wreaked havoc in Mecca, Medina and Judda. He robbed the Kaʿba, starved the Meccans under siege, and killed more than a thousand pilgrims. The governor used gold taken from the Kaʿba to finance the struggle against the rebel, but he also needed reinforcements from Baghdad. Eventually Ismāʿīl died of the

33 Al-Ṭabarī, *Taʾrīkh*, vol. VIII, pp. 531–3, 536–40; Iṣfahānī, *Maqātil*, pp. 533, 537–41; Fāsī, *Shifāʾ*, pp. 285–8, 289–90, a confused version on p. 344; Fāsī, *ʿIqd*, vol. III, pp. 264–5, vol. VII, p. 466; Sinjārī, *Manāʾiḥ*, vol. II, pp. 142–50; Ibn Fahd, *Ghāya*, pp. 376–8, 389–400, 405–7; Juddī, *al-Silāḥ wa-l-ʿudda*, p. 30 ; ʿAbd al-Ghanī, *Madīna*, pp. 161–4. On Ibrāhīm see also below.

34 Al-Ṭabarī, *Taʾrīkh*, vol. IX, pp. 129–35, 146–50; Oppenheim, *Beduinen*, vol. II, p. 318; see also note 25 above (refs. to Bedouin violence), and below.

35 See e.g. Iṣfahānī, *Maqātil*, p. 599.

plague. His brother succeeded him, but was forced out of Mecca into Yamāma, where he established the long-lasting Ukhayḍir dynasty. One of the results of Ismāʿīl's revolt was economic decline, which forced many Meccans to leave their city.[36] In Medina, other ʿAlid claimants rose in the second half of the third/ninth century – some Ḥasanids, some Ḥusaynids and some Jaʿfarids (namely descendants of Jaʿfar b. Abī Ṭālib). Muslim sources vilify some of these claimants for their sinful conduct. They sometimes turned against one another, as well as against the cityfolk and the pilgrims. The Shīʿa ideology does not seem to have meant much to the Ḥijāzī ʿAlids of this period.[37]

In addition to the various ʿAlid groups, there is mention of other local notables, members of the ancient aristocratic Makhzūm clan, who fought against one another (or against the governor) over Mecca and Judda (in 262/876 and 266/880). One of these notables may have been acting on behalf of the leader of the Zanj, whose rebellion in Iraq (254–69/868–83) deeply shook the caliphate.[38] To add to the confusion, non-local Muslim rulers intervened in the Ḥijāz, namely Ibn Ṭūlūn, ruler of Egypt and Syria (254–70/868–884) and Yaʿqūb b. Layth al-Ṣaffār, ruler of Sīstān (253–65/867–79).[39] The latter appointed (in 266/880) a governor to the holy cities, Muḥammad b. Abī al-Sāj al-Afshīn, who in turn appointed his own representatives. Forces of Ibn Ṭūlūn and al-Ṣaffār clashed in Mecca in 269/882, and the battle ended with Ibn Ṭūlūn's defeat.[40] During the same period, there is mention also of representatives sent directly by the government in Iraq, both to Mecca and to Medina; naturally, clashes occurred between the various appointees. Amazingly, one functionary, Hārūn b. Muḥammad of the ʿAbbāsid family, led the pilgrimage through the many vicissitudes of the period, for sixteen successive years (264–79/878–93). Certain sources call

36 Al-Ṭabarī, *Taʾrīkh*, vol. IX, pp. 436–7; Fāsī, *Shifāʾ*, pp. 294–6, 298; Sinjārī, *Manāʾiḥ*, vol. II, pp. 165–7; Shams al-Dīn al-Sakhāwī, *al-Tuḥfa al-laṭīfa fī taʾrīkh al-Madīna al-sharīfa*, 3 vols. (Cairo, 1376/1957), vol. I, pp. 308–9; Ibn Fahd, *Ghāya*, pp. 434–7, 443; ʿAbd al-Ghanī, *Madīna*, pp. 186–7.

37 Al-Ṭabarī, *Taʾrīkh*, vol. IX, pp. 552–3, 621, vol. X, p. 7; Iṣfahānī, *Maqātil*, pp. 716–20; Ibn Ḥazm, *Jamhara*, p. 39; ʿAbd al-Ghanī, *Madīna*, pp. 189 (feuds in 255/868), 192 (in 271/884), 194 (in 265–6/878–9), 197–203 (several rivals, all in 271/884), 206–8.

38 Fāsī, *Shifāʾ*, pp. 300–1; Sinjārī, *Manāʾiḥ*, vol. II, pp. 172–4; Ibn Fahd, *Ghāya*, pp. 456–62, 464; Juddī, *al-Silāḥ wa-l-ʿudda*, p. 32.

39 Sinjārī, *Manāʾiḥ*, vol. II, p. 172; Ibn Fahd, *Ghāya*, pp. 450, 456–7; ʿAbd al-Ghanī, *Madīna*, pp. 194–6.

40 Al-Ṭabarī, *Taʾrīkh*, vol. IX, pp. 652–3; Sinjārī, *Manāʾiḥ*, vol. II, pp. 172, 175–7; Ibn Fahd, *Ghāya*, pp 450, 454–7; ʿAbd al-Ghanī, *Madīna*, pp. 194–6.

him 'governor of Mecca, Medina and Ṭā'if', but he did not occupy this post during all these years.[41]

Events in the Ḥijāz at the beginning of the fourth/tenth century are obscure, and certain sources admit their bewilderment. References are made to governors; to army commanders sent to fight Bedouins; to Jaʿfarids who took Medina; and to a claimant to the throne, the Ḥasanid Muḥammad b. Sulaymān, who proclaimed himself imam in Mecca in 301/913. It appears that the caliphs had only nominal control. This is indicated by the facts that they distributed huge sums of money in the holy cities, and that they entrusted the Ḥijāz to Turkish generals.[42] In 300/912 Mu'nis al-Muẓaffar was in charge of the 'two holy cities and the frontiers', which means that conditions in the Ḥijāz were unstable, to the point that not a governor, but a general was needed to handle them.

In 317/930 the Qarmaṭīs of Baḥrayn entered Mecca during the pilgrimage, massacred thousands of people, wreaked destruction on the holy places and stole the black stone; it was only returned in 339/951. The pilgrimage ceased for a number of years, and anarchy prevailed.[43] Under these circumstances, it is not surprising that in 331/943 the caliph agreed that Mecca and Medina should be brought under the nominal jurisdiction of the Ikhshīdids, the semi-independent dynasty that ruled Egypt and Syria (325–58/935–69). Nevertheless, the caliphs continued to contribute towards renovations in the holy places, and the actual governors, as far as anything is known of them, were still drawn from the 'Abbāsid family. These caliphs' policies did not prevent clashes in Mecca between representatives of the Ikhshīdids on the one hand, and on the other, the Buwayhids. 'Alid leaders also played a part in local political and military events.[44]

41 'Abbāsid governors after al-Ma'mūn and until the end of the third/ninth century: Ibn Fahd, *Ghāya*, pp. 419–67; Fāsī, *Shifā'*, pp. 277–305; Sinjārī, *Manā'iḥ*, vol. II, pp. 177, 179; 'Abd al-Ghanī, *Madīna*, pp. 190, 201, 203, 204–5, 211; Zambauer, *Muʿjam al-ansāb*, pp. 28–9, 37; Hārūn ibn Muḥammad: al-Ṭabarī, *Ta'rīkh*, vol. X, p. 31; Ibn Fahd, *Ghāya*, pp. 453–4; 'Abd al-Ghanī, *Madīna*, pp. 204–5. Clashes between various appointees: Fāsī, *Shifā'*, pp. 299–301, 303–4.

42 Fāsī, *Shifā'*, p. 303; Sinjārī, *Manā'iḥ*, vol. II, pp. 179–81, 185, cf. Ismāʿīl ibn 'Umar ibn Kathīr, *al-Bidāya wa-l-nihāya*, 14 vols. (Beirut, n.d.), vol. XI, p. 200; 'Abd al-Ghanī, *Madīna*, pp. 208–17. The systematised lists of rulers in *Mir'āt* do not match the information given in the other sources: see A. Ṣabrī Bāshā, *Mir'āt jazīrat al-ʿArab*, trans. A. F. Mutawallī and A. al-Mursī (Cairo, 1419/1999), pp. 93–7, 101.

43 Sinjārī, *Manā'iḥ*, vol. II, pp. 187–95, 198, and see below. The pilgrimage was suspended many times: see Fāsī, *Shifā'*, pp. 346–9, 351–2, 354–7, 359–60, 364.

44 Fāsī, *'Iqd*, vol. II, pp. 31, 33–4; Fāsī, *Shifā'*, pp. 305–6, 349–50; Sinjārī, *Manā'iḥ*, vol. II, pp. 181–2, 192, and on renovations 198–202; Ibn Fahd, *Ghāya*, pp. 470, 474–9. On the Buwayhids, who were the actual rulers behind the caliphs in the years 946–1055, see chapter 9 in this volume.

Some time before 329/940 the Ḥusaynid ʿUbayd Allāh b. Ṭāhir founded in Medina the Banū Muhannā dynasty, which lasted until the end of the tenth/sixteenth century. It is not known precisely how he came to power, and whether he wrested the city from Jaʿfarids or from an appointed governor. Mecca followed suit, and after (or shortly before) the death of Kāfūr the Ikhshīd in 356/967, the Ḥasanid Jaʿfar b. Muḥammad established a dynasty that lasted until 453/1061. Henceforth Ḥasanid and Ḥusaynid families ruled Mecca and Medina respectively, fighting one another, the Jaʿfarids, Bedouins and non-Ḥijāzī Muslim powers.[45] These descendants of the Prophet (*ashrāf*) were closer in spirit to the Bedouin of the Peninsula than to the sophisticated urban Islamic elites elsewhere. Not only were they often engaged in internal wars, but they also treated the Ḥijāz, its people and the pilgrims mainly as a source of income. Whereas rulers of other provinces often expressed their status in grand architecture and by acting as patrons of art and science, the *ashrāf* of the Ḥijāz paid no heed to such matters, and they sometimes even robbed the Kaʿba themselves.[46] It is no accident that the renovations of the holy places were as a rule carried out by one of the competing Islamic states that flourished outside the Peninsula. The *ashrāf* for their part were under constant pressure to choose between the competitors, whether the Western ones like the Ikhshīdīs and the Fāṭimids after them, or the Eastern ones, namely, the ʿAbbāsid caliphs, the Buwayhids and later the Saljūqs, and even the distant Ghaznavids. Competing rulers would offer to support one of the rival *ashrāf* against another, and would also intervene directly, attempting to gain their allegiance by a variety of means: military force, lavish gifts and food supplies (the last being sent from Egypt). The *ashrāf* not only transferred their loyalty from one power to another (as tribal leaders would), but also occasionally played an active role in the political struggles of the Islamic world. Muḥammad b. ʿUbayd Allāh, son of the founder of the Banū Muhannā (Ḥusaynid) dynasty of Medina, may have played a part in the Fāṭimid takeover of Egypt in 359/969.[47] That same year the founder of the dynasty

45 Fāsī, *Shifāʾ*, pp. 306–7; Sinjārī, *Manāʾiḥ*, vol. II, pp. 211–16; Ibn Fahd, *Ghāya*, pp. 480–500; Ibn Ḥazm, *Jamhara*, p. 47; Maqrīzī, *Ittiʿāẓ*, pp. 145–6; ʿAbd al-Ghanī, *Madīna*, pp. 217ff.

46 E.g. Fāsī, *Shifāʾ*, pp. 310, 312.

47 Sinjārī, *Manāʾiḥ*, vol. II, pp. 203, 206–7, 221 (siege, and gifts), 230–1, 236 (gifts); Fāsī, *Shifāʾ*, p. 353. There is a confusion regarding the relations of ʿUbayd Allāh ibn Ṭāhir and his sons with the Ikhshīdīs and the Fāṭimids: see Ibn Kathīr, *Bidāya*, vol. XI, pp. 310–11; ʿAbd al-Ghanī, *Madīna*, pp. 222–3, 226–7. Contacts with the Ghaznavids: ibid., pp. 228–9, with the Saljūqs, p. 236. See also Oppenheim, *Beduinen*, vol. II, pp. 321–2.

in Mecca, Jaʿfar b. Muḥammad, was already paying allegiance to the Fāṭimids, perhaps as gratitude to the Fāṭimid caliph al-Muʿizz, who reportedly mediated in the 348/959 feud between the Ḥasanids and Jaʿfarids.[48] Jaʿfar's son and successor, Ḥasan b. Jaʿfar Abū al-Futūḥ, paid allegiance to the Fāṭimids as well, and took Medina from the Ḥusaynids (in 390/1000) on their command. For part of his long rule (384–430/994–1038) he became disaffected with the Fāṭimids and proclaimed himself caliph under the name al-Rāshid bi-Allāh. He was even acknowledged as caliph by the Bedouins of Syria, who were anxious to free themselves of the Fāṭimids. Eventually, however, Abū al-Futūḥ renounced the caliphal title and returned to pay homage, first to the Fāṭimid al-Ḥākim (r. 386–411/996–1021) and later to the ʿAbbāsid caliph, al-Qādir (r. 381–422/991–1031).[49] Abū al-Futūḥ's son and successor (from 430/1039), Shukr, re-conquered Medina, but he was embroiled in wars with his own relatives, and he had no offspring. Various ʿAlid branches fought one another upon Shukr's death in 453/1061, and anarchy prevailed. Peace returned when ʿAlī b. Muḥammad al-Ṣulayḥī, the Fāṭimids' agent in the Yemen, entered Mecca in 455/1053. The sources describe al-Ṣulayḥī as just and considerate. At the request of some of the Ḥasanid leaders ʿAlī al-Ṣulayḥī left the city after he had chosen a representative, the Ḥasanid Muḥammad b. Jaʿfar Abū Hāshim (son-in-law of the former ruler, Shukr). Muḥammad was thus the founder of a new Ḥasanid dynasty, the Hawāshim, which lasted until 597/1201. He was temporarily expelled from Mecca by his rivals, but eventually regained his position and held it for thirty-three years. He also succeeded in temporarily wresting Medina from the Ḥusaynid Banū al-Muhannā.[50] The Saljūqs, acting on behalf of the ʿAbbāsids, and the Fāṭimids continued to exert pressure on the *ashrāf*, the Ḥasanid Hawāshim in Mecca and the Ḥusaynid Banū al-Muhannā in Medina. Even Muḥammad b. Jaʿfar, who had been appointed by the Fāṭimid agent al-Ṣulayḥī, vacillated between the two powers. Other *ashrāf* followed the same pattern and also transferred their allegiance from

48 Fāsī, *Shifāʾ*, p. 351; al-Muʿizz: Maqrīzī, *Ittiʿāẓ*, pp. 145–6 (Maqrīzī's dates differ from those given in other sources).

49 Very different versions of the events are given: see Fāsī, *Shifāʾ*, pp. 307–9; Sinjārī, *Manāʾiḥ*, vol. II, pp. 208–9, 216–20, 221–2; Ibn Fahd, *Ghāya*, pp. 485–94; Ibn Kathīr, *Bidāya*, vol. XI, pp. 309–10; ʿAbd al-Ghanī, *Madīna*, pp. 230–1; Oppenheim, *Beduinen*, vol. II, p. 322.

50 Fāsī, *Shifāʾ*, pp. 310–12, note the confusion about the identity of Banū Abī al-Ṭayyib; ʿImād al-Dīn, *ʿUyūn al-akhbār wa-funūn al-āthār*, vol. VII, ed. A. F. Sayyid (London, 2002), pp. 22–36; Sinjārī, *Manāʾiḥ*, vol. II, pp. 222–34, 242–66, note the confusion regarding the names of the petty dynasties; Ibn Fahd, *Ghāya*, pp. 500–2, 509–10; ʿAbd al-Ghanī, *Madīna*, pp. 236, 238, 240ff, 505, note the confusion about the years 390–469/999–1076 on pp. 230–7.

one power to the other, sometimes in return for huge gifts, at other times under pressure. For example, in 484/1091, and again in 486/1093 or 487/1094, Saljūq forces conquered Mecca, and plundered it. In addition, attacks by the *ashrāf* themselves on pilgrims and merchants were not uncommon, and the same applies to clashes between pilgrims representing competing dynasties or rival ideologies.[51] It is remarkable that in the early days of Islam, no one had dared to rob the pilgrims, and enemies performed the pilgrimage side by side, deliberately avoiding clashes in Mecca during the pilgrimage.[52]

The political instability that started in the third/ninth century had a devastating effect. Some of the land still prospered in the fourth/tenth century, but in general, agriculture declined, settlements were deserted and the Bedouin way of life spread and affected the towns and their rulers. According to the traveller Nāṣir-i Khusraw (middle of the fifth/eleventh century), many edifices in Mecca had fallen in ruin and the population was only 2,500 people (one fifth of whom were temporary residents, *mujāwirūn*). The population of Judda was 5,000, and Ṭā'if was 'a wretched little town'. No central authority was recognised, and, he says, 'the people were robbers and murderers'.[53] The unstable conditions also influenced intellectual activity and the creativity of the first two centuries disappeared. It is mainly from the fifth/eleventh century onwards that pilgrims in increasing numbers resided in Mecca or in Medina, for shorter or longer periods. Many received and transmitted religious knowledge, namely *ḥadīth*, *fiqh* and various readings of the Qur'ān (*qirā'āt*). Among the famous scholars who settled temporarily in Mecca were Juwaynī (d. 478/1085) and Zamakhsharī (d. 538/1144). It may be noted that of the historians who lived there, only ten were active from the third/ninth to the fifth/eleventh century. The remaining 177 were active from the sixth/twelfth to the thirteenth/nineteenth century.[54]

After the fall of the Fāṭimids in 566/1171, the Ḥijāz was generally under the patronage of whoever held power in Egypt.

51 Fāsī, *Shifā'*, pp. 311–13, 357–8, 362–4; Sinjārī, *Manā'iḥ*, vol. II, pp. 231, 234–43; Ibn Fahd, *Ghāya*, pp. 510–23; 'Abd al-Ghanī, *Madīna*, pp. 238–43.

52 Fāsī, *Shifā'*, pp. 338–9, 340–1 (first and second civil wars, the 'Abbāsid revolution); Sinjārī, *Manā'iḥ*, vol. II, pp. 73–7 (Abū Ḥamza's revolt).

53 Nāṣer-e Khosraw, *Book of travels (Safarnāma)*, trans. W. M. Thackston Jr., Bibliotheca Persica (Albany, 1986), pp. 67, 69, 82–3.

54 Fāsī, *'Iqd*, *passim*; Muḥammad al-Ḥabīb al-Hayla, *al-Ta'rīkh wa-l-mu'arrikhūn bi-Makka min al-qarn al-thālith al-hijrī ilā al-qarn al-thālith 'ashar* (Mecca, 1994). Prosperity in Yanbu' in the fourth/tenth century: Jāsir, *Yanbu'*, pp. 27–8.

The Yemen

The Yemen is characterised by the great variety of landscapes and tribes. Its topography effected a division into a great number of administrative provinces, tribal territories, domains of warlords and dynasties, and strongholds of ideological groups.[55] The boundaries of all of these were constantly shifting, as were the loyalties of the tribal groups. Furthermore, because of its remoteness, on the one hand, and its proximity to the holy cities in the Ḥijāz, on the other, the Yemen served as a haven for many rebels. Among those were Khārijites, Shīʿites and many other claimants who vied for power and for the local resources, including international maritime trade. The history of the Yemen is largely made of the struggles between all these groups and dynasties, on the one hand, and, on the other, the interaction between them and the pre-Islamic Yemenite social structures and institutions that survived the advent of Islam. Certain modern scholars have noted that, broadly speaking, the north tended to remain anarchic throughout the centuries, whereas the southern parts tended to be more manageable to governments. This distinction is somewhat schematic. Ḥaḍramawt, in the south, was certainly anarchic, perhaps even more so than the north.[56]

The early tenth century historian and geographer al-Yaʿqūbī (d. 284/897) lists eighty-four provinces, and 'a multitude of tribes'. Often, however, only a few main geographical divisions are mentioned, for example, from west to east: (1) the coastal plain (Tihāma), a region of great importance, due to its seaports; (2) the highlands, called Najd of Yemen; (3) al-Jawf and Ma'rib; (4) Ḥaḍramawt, which lies along the southern coast. There are other ways of division, for example: Ṣanʿā' and its provinces; Ḥaḍramawt and its provinces; al-Janad and its provinces (which include the coastal plain).[57] The whole of the

55 ʿUmāra al-Yamanī, *al-mufīd fī akhbār Ṣanʿā' wa-Zabīd wa-shuʿarā' mulūkihā wa-aʿyānihā wa-udabā'ihā*, ed. Muḥammad b. ʿAli al-Akwaʿ (Ṣanʿā', 1985), pp. 77–83; Ayman Fu'ād Sayyid, *Ta'rīkh al-madhāhib al-dīniyya fī bilād al-Yaman* (Cairo, 1988/1408), pp. 57, 78–81; R. W. Stookey, *Yemen: The politics of the Yemen Arab Republic* (Boulder, 1978), pp. 96–7.

56 Stookey, *Yemen*, p. 50; D. T. Gochenour, 'The penetration of Zaydī Islam into early medieval Yemen', Ph.D. thesis, Harvard University (1984), pp. 10–26, see also pp. 35–8, 90–147, for the persistence of ancient structures. Local resources: see e.g. Ṣāliḥ al-Ḥāmid, *Ta'rīkh Ḥaḍramawt* (Jiddah, 1968), pp. 93–5. International trade: Hourani, *Arab seafaring*, pp. 69–84. Conditions in Ḥaḍramawt: Bāwazīr, *Ṣafaḥāt*, pp. 78–80. See also G. R. Smith, 'Yemenite history: Problems and misconceptions', in G. R. Smith, *Studies in the medieval history of the Yemen and Arabia Felix* (Aldershot and Brookfield, VT, 1997), II, pp. 131–9.

57 Yaʿqūbī, *Ta'rīkh*, vol. I, p. 201; ʿAbd al-Muḥsin Madʿaj M. al-Madʿaj, *The Yemen in early Islam 9–233/630–847: A political history* (London, 1988), p. 5; Gochenour, 'Penetration', pp. 1–10. Detailed geographical description: Ḥasan ibn Aḥmad al-Hamdānī, *Ṣifat jazīrat al-ʿArab*, ed. M. ibn ʿAlī al-Akwaʿ (Beirut and Ṣanʿā', 1403/1983), pp. 90ff.

Yemen was rarely, if ever, unified, and the political frameworks often did not overlap any of the geographical divisions.

The Yemen from the first/seventh to the end of the second/ eighth century

The main large tribal confederations in the Yemen on the eve of Islam were Ḥimyar, Hamdān, Madhḥij, Kinda, Ḥāshid, Bakīl and Azd. In addition, an aristocratic group of Persian origin, the Abnāʾ, was scattered throughout the country, and prominent in Ṣanʿāʾ.[58] The Abnāʾ presumably adhered to Zoroastrianism, but throughout the Yemen, Christianity and Judaism were widespread. At the time of the Prophet Ṣanʿāʾ was ruled by the Abnāʾ whereas the rest of the country was divided among local kings and chiefs, power struggles being a constant feature. Islam was thus introduced into the Yemen, and became yet another factor in the struggles between local leaders and groups. Yemenite delegations to the Prophet are reported, as well as the names of tax-collectors, judges and instructors who were sent by the Prophet to Yemenite regions and tribes.[59] The extent of conversion during the Prophet's time cannot be determined. The sources are tendentious, reflecting the efforts made by each group to prove its early conversion and its contribution to Islam. It should also be noted that the sources are in the habit of applying the names of whole confederations to mere parts thereof. Thus, a report that the Prophet sent someone over Madhḥij, for instance, should not be taken literally: the person may have been appointed over merely a small group pertaining to Madhḥij. Finally, the sources tend to ignore the fact that although formally part of the Islamic domain, much of the Yemen remained as it had been in pre-Islamic times.

Islam initially contributed to the local struggles rather than to the unity of the Yemen and its tribes. As elsewhere in the Peninsula, certain tribal chiefs adhered to Islam to enhance their status against other chiefs. Rivals were branded as apostates even if the rivalry did not revolve around religion. The

58 Yaʿqūbī, *Taʾrīkh*, vol. I, p. 201; S. ʿA. al-Kāf, *Ḥaḍramawt ʿabra arbaʿat ʿashar qarnan* (Beirut, 1990/1410), pp. 26–30; Ḥāmid, *Taʾrīkh Ḥaḍramawt*, pp. 13–53; Madʿaj, *Yemen*, pp. 6–7; Gochenour, 'Penetration', pp. 10–26.

59 Al-Ṭabarī, *Taʾrīkh*, vol. III, pp. 120–2, 126–38, 147, 227; Aḥmad ibn ʿAbd Allāh al-Rāzī, *Taʾrīkh madīnat Ṣanʿāʾ*, ed. Ḥ. ibn ʿAbd Allāh al-ʿAmrī (Ṣanʿāʾ, 1401/1981), pp. 140, 249, 255, 293; ʿAbd al-Raḥmān ibn ʿAlī ibn al-Daybaʿ, *Qurrat al-ʿuyūn bi-akhbār al-Yaman al-maymūn*, ed. M. ibn ʿAlī al-Akwaʿ al-Ḥiwālī (Cairo, n.d.), pp. 36–75; Ḥusayn ibn ʿAbd al-Raḥmān al-Ahdal, *Tuḥfat al-zaman fī taʾrīkh al-Yaman*, ed. ʿA. M. al-Ḥibshī (Beirut, 1407/1986), pp. 124–7; Ḥāmid, *Taʾrīkh Ḥaḍramawt*, pp. 113–34; al-Kāf, *Ḥaḍramawt*, pp. 30–1; Madʿaj, *Yemen*, pp. 10–15; Stookey, *Yemen*, p. 29.

most prominent among the 'apostates' was al-Aswad al-ʿAnsī, who reportedly claimed to be a prophet and mustered large support in 10/632. The fact that he conquered Ṣanʿāʾ has led some scholars to believe that his efforts were mainly directed against the foreign Abnāʾ, some of whom may have been Muslim by this time. Be that as it may, a coalition of members of the Abnāʾ and deserters from al-Aswad's own camp succeeded in killing him that same year.[60] The role of Islam and the Prophet in this so-called apostasy was apparently minor. The Prophet's successor, Abū Bakr, played a more active role in establishing Muslim authority in the Yemen. He recruited local forces, reinforced them with troops sent from Medina, and eventually succeeded in adding the Yemen to the domains of Islam, at least formally. The most important foci of his military activity were in Ṣanʿāʾ, Ḥaḍramawt and the Tihāma. Leaders of the 'apostates', such as Qays b. al-Makshūḥ, ʿAmr b. Maʿdikarib and the Kindī al-Ashʿath b. Qays, repented, were pardoned and played important roles in the subsequent Islamic conquests.[61] Thereafter, Yemenites left their homeland by the thousands to participate in the conquests and to settle in the new provinces. They played increasingly important roles in the army and in politics.[62] Despite the fact that it was depleted of much of its manpower, the Yemen in general did not become a deserted backwater, as is sometimes assumed.[63]

The Rāshidūn sent governors to the Yemen. Occasionally the sources specify the assignments as Ṣanʿāʾ, or Ḥaḍramawt, or al-Janad, but even if the assignment is given as 'the Yemen', these governors never controlled the whole country. Nevertheless, Ṣanʿāʾ was sometimes the base of a governor who controlled some junior officials in other regions. The appointees were mostly Companions of high status, such as Abān b. Saʿīd b. al-ʿĀṣ, al-Mughīra b. Shuʿba and Yaʿlā b. Umayya. The last governed Ṣanʿāʾ for twenty-four years, serving the first three caliphs, and was dismissed by the fourth. ʿUmar is said to have intervened in affairs in Ṣanʿāʾ, and to have called the governor to

60 Al-Ṭabarī, *Taʾrīkh*, vol. III, pp. 228–40; Sulaymān ibn Mūsā al-Kalāʿī, *al-Iktifāʾ bi-mā taḍammanahu min maghāzī rasūl allāh wa-l-thalātha al-khulafāʾ*, ed. M. K. ʿAlī, 4 vols. (Beirut, 1417/1997), vol. III, pp. 95–8; Madʿaj, *Yemen*, pp. 25–32; Stookey, *Yemen*, pp. 30–1.

61 Kalāʿī, *Iktifāʾ*, vol. III, pp. 99–108; Ḥāmid, *Taʾrīkh Ḥaḍramawt*, pp. 149–61; al-Kāf, *Ḥaḍramawt*, pp. 32–7; Madʿaj, *Yemen*, pp. 41–55; Stookey, *Yemen*, p. 32.

62 Details in Madʿaj, *Yemen*, pp. 64–101.

63 E.g. by ibid., pp. 156, 159, and Stookey, *Yemen*, p. 42. Ḥaḍramawt was an exception: see Ḥāmid, *Taʾrīkh Ḥaḍramawt*, pp. 166–80, 197–200, 227, 245–6; A. Shalabī, *Mawsūʿat al-taʾrīkh al-Islāmī wa-l-ḥaḍāra al-Islāmiyya*, vol. VII (Cairo, 1982), pp. 299–301.

account when necessary. The Rāshidūn also reportedly appointed judges and Qur'ān instructors.[64] All this indicates that they attached importance to the Yemen, although in the tribal territories, pre-Islamic chiefs often retained their positions, with or without the recognition of the caliphs. Special measures were taken by 'Umar against the powerful Christian tribes of Najrān. In spite of previous treaties that they had with the Prophet and Abū Bakr, 'Umar evicted them from the area. Jews, however, were allowed to remain in return for the payment of poll-tax.[65]

The main events of the first civil war (36–41/656–61) took place outside the Arabian Peninsula, but those Yemenites who remained in their homeland were divided, like the rest of the Muslims. Both 'Alī and Mu'āwiya sent troops to the Yemen. For some time 'Alī's party had the upper hand, but opponents of his revolted against his governors in Ṣan'ā' and al-Janad. Eventually, Mu'āwiya's general conquered Najrān and Ṣan'ā' in 40/660.[66]

Like their predecessors, the Umayyads attached great importance to the Yemen, even though their capital shifted away from the Arabian Peninsula. Governors were appointed directly by the caliph, but the jurisdiction of the Yemen was sometimes attached to that of other regions. Thus 'Abd al-Malik (r. 65–86/685–705) appointed al-Ḥajjāj b. Yūsuf over Yamāma, the Ḥijāz and the Yemen. Al-Ḥajjāj remained in the Ḥijāz and sent his brother to represent him in the Yemen. As a rule the governors were high-ranking individuals, whether they were outsiders or locals. One of the latter was Fayrūz, a leader of the Abnā', who served under Mu'āwiya. How much each governor's control extended outside of the city that was his base is not clear, but the pre-Islamic aristocracy certainly retained its status.[67]

During the second civil war, the Meccan caliph, 'Abd Allāh ibn al-Zubayr (64–73/683–692), had control of Ṣan'ā', but he constantly replaced his governors,

64 Rāzī, *Ta'rīkh*, pp. 153, 158, 163–5, 294; Ḥāmid, *Ta'rīkh Ḥaḍramawt*, pp. 162–4; Mad'aj, *Yemen*, pp. 102–21; G. R. Smith, 'The political history of the Islamic Yemen down to the first Turkish invasion (1–945/622–1538)', in G. R. Smith, *Studies in the medieval history of the Yemen and Arabia Felix*, Variorum Collected Studies (Aldershot and Brookfield, VT, 1997), I, pp. 129–30.

65 Al-Ṭabarī, *Ta'rīkh*, vol. III, p. 446; Mad'aj, *Yemen*, pp. 111–13; W. Schmucker, 'Die Christliche Minderheit von Najrān', *Studien zum Minderheitenproblem im Islam*, 1 (1973).

66 Al-Ṭabarī, *Ta'rīkh*, vol. V, pp. 139–40; Yaḥyā ibn al-Ḥusayn, *Ghāyat al-amānī fī akhbār al-quṭr al-yamānī*, ed. S. 'A. 'Āshūr and M. M. Ziyāda (Cairo, 1388/1968), pp. 95–8; Mad'aj, *Yemen*, pp. 123–49.

67 Ḥāmid, *Ta'rīkh Ḥaḍramawt*, pp. 201–2; Mad'aj, *Yemen*, pp. 156–60, 169–70; Stookey, *Yemen*, p. 41. Lists of governors: Ahdal, *Tuḥfa*, pp. 134–40; Ibn al-Dayba', *Qurrat*, pp. 89–114.

sometimes appointing locals to the post. This indicates, first, that he was not indifferent to the situation there, and, second, that his control was not firm. Lack of central control is also apparent in the events of 67/686 and 68/687. Challenged by Khārijites from Oman and Baḥrayn, the people of Ṣanʿāʾ paid the invaders a large sum of money in the first case, and gave their allegiance to the invader, Najda b. ʿĀmir, in the second. In these reports there is no mention of a governor. It was the scholar Wahb b. Munabbih who tried, in vain, to incite the cityfolk to repel the invaders.[68] That Ibn al-Zubayr did not enjoy strong Yemenite support was finally proven in 73/692, when Ṣanʿāʾ offered no opposition to the Marwānid forces. After the re-conquest of the Yemen the Umayyad caliphs continued to be directly involved in its affairs, and some invested great sums in its infrastructure, so that the country's economy prospered.[69] Typically, ʿUmar b. ʿAbd al-ʿAzīz (r. 99–101/717–20) took care to redress the wrongs done to the Yemenites by previous Umayyad caliphs and their governors. As elsewhere, ʿUmar became a model of justice, even for local Ismāʿīlī and Zaydī historians.[70]

The Yemen was not unified under the authority of the government, yet the sources do not report many revolts. Some Khārijites settled there directly after their defeat by ʿAlī in the battle of Nahrawān (38/658), but no open revolts are recorded. Khārijites from al-Yamāma invaded Ḥaḍramawt and Ṣanʿāʾ in 67–8/687–8, but they did not stay to rule. A rebel named ʿAbbād al-Ruʿaynī rose in 107/725–6, and the sources are divided as regards his precise identity and sectarian affiliation. Some say that he claimed to be the Ḥimyarite messiah, but others identify him as a Khārijite. The number of his supporters was 300.[71] A much more serious revolt occurred in 128–30/745–7 during the caliphate of the last Umayyad, Marwān II. The Kindī ʿAbd Allāh b. Yaḥyā, the appointed judge of the Umayyad governor in Ḥaḍramawt, assumed the title Ṭālib al-Ḥaqq ('The One who Pursues the Truth'), and proclaimed himself caliph. Supported by the Ibāḍiyya Khārijites in Oman (see below), he succeeded in seizing Ḥaḍramawt, Ṣanʿāʾ and even Mecca and Medina (through his agent Abū Ḥamza); the number of his followers is estimated by some sources at about thirty thousand (this number may of course be a topos, for it is recurrent, but it conveys large numbers). Allegiance was sworn to him in

68 ʿIzz al-Dīn ibn al-Athīr, *al-Kāmil fī al-taʾrīkh*, 10 vols. (Beirut, 1415/1995), vol. IV, p. 21; M. ʿI. al-Ḥarīrī, *Dirāsāt wa-buḥūth fī taʾrīkh al-Yaman al-Islāmī* (Beirut, 1418/1998), pp. 19, 21; Muḥammad ibn Muḥammad Zabāra al-Ḥasanī, *al-Inbāʾ ʿan dawlat Bilqīs wa-Sabaʾ* (Ṣanʿāʾ, 1404/1984), pp. 40–1.

69 Madʿaj, *Yemen*, pp. 161–3, 170; Ḥarīrī, *Dirāsāt*, p. 31; see also Hamdānī, *Ṣifat*, p. 105.

70 ʿUmāra, *Mufīd*, p. 66; Zabāra, *Inbāʾ*, pp. 41–3.

71 Yaḥyā ibn al-Ḥusayn, *Ghāyat*, p. 119; al-Ṭabarī, *Taʾrīkh*, vol. VII, p. 40; Zabāra, *Inbāʾ*, p. 43; Madʿaj, *Yemen*, pp. 161, 163–4.

Baṣra too, which is an indication not only of his power, but also of the fact that the Yemen was not politically isolated. Ṭālib al-Ḥaqq was defeated in 130/747 by Marwān's general, ʿAbd al-Malik ibn ʿAṭiyya, who on that occasion suppressed yet other rebels in the region, Yaḥyā b. ʿAbd Allāh al-Sabbāq and Yaḥyā b. Karib; both were Ḥimyarites who were active in their tribal territories, in al-Janad and the coastal areas respectively. By order of the caliph, Ibn ʿAṭiyya left before completing his operation, to lead the pilgrimage in his name. Before leaving he reached a peace agreement with the Ibāḍiyya of Ḥaḍramawt, granting them the right to choose their own governors. Thus Ḥaḍramawt remained under local Ibāḍī rule until the reign of al-Manṣūr (136–58/754–75).[72]

The early ʿAbbāsids continued their predecessors' policies. Again, sometimes the Yemen was attached to the jurisdiction of the governor of Ḥijāz, who would appoint a representative there. And again, people of high standing received governorships, and the caliphs sometimes replaced governors at the Yemenites' request. Members of the ʿAbbāsid family served as governors, as well as *mawālī* of the caliphs, members of the Arab Muslim aristocracy (occasionally Yemenite themselves), and even a member of the Barmakid family. At the time of the latter, who served under Hārūn (r. 170–93/786–809), Ṣanʿāʾ prospered, yet it is reported that the number of poor people was great.[73]

The Yemen remained fragmented, and pre-Islamic local conflicts continued, sometimes intertwined with sectarian opposition to the government. For example, a governor of local origin, ʿAbd Allāh b. ʿAbd al-Madān, declared his independence in 142/759, which induced al-Manṣūr to send his general, Maʿn b. Zāʾida, to restore order. During his nine years in office (142–51/759–68) Maʿn suppressed insurrections in various parts of the Yemen, including Ṣaʿda, al-Janad and Ḥaḍramawt, where Ibāḍī Khārijism was active. He applied harsh measures that resulted in thousands of casualties, and led to his assassination.[74] In this period the ʿAbbāsids also stationed a garrison in Ṣanʿāʾ, but it was not

72 Yaḥyā ibn al-Ḥusayn, *Ghāyat*, pp. 124–6; Ḥāmid, *Taʾrīkh Ḥaḍramawt*, pp. 203–13; Sayyābī, *al-Ḥaqīqa*, pp. 89–96, 125–30 (according to this source the Ḥimyarite chiefs were Ibāḍīs, and the Ibāḍiyya was suppressed as early as 132/750); Madʿaj, *Yemen*, pp. 164–7; E. Francesca, 'Ṭālib al-Ḥakk', *EI2*, vol XII, p. 785.

73 Hamdānī, *Ṣifat*, pp. 108, 112–13; Ahdal, *Tuḥfa*, pp. 140–50; Rāzī, *Taʾrīkh*, pp. 105–8, 111–12; Yaḥyā ibn al-Ḥusayn, *Ghāyat*, pp. 31–2, 141–2, 146–7; Ibn al-Daybaʿ, *Qurrat*, pp. 115–131; Ḥāmid, *Taʾrīkh Ḥaḍramawt*, pp. 214–24; Madʿaj, *Yemen*, pp. 180–2, 190–6, 220–3.

74 Ahdal, *Tuḥfa*, p. 143; Sayyābī, *al-Ḥaqīqa*, pp. 45–6; Ḥāmid, *Taʾrīkh Ḥaḍramawt*, pp. 214–19; Madʿaj, *Yemen*, pp. 183–5; Stookey, *Yemen*, p. 44.

always adequate. For example, around 184/800 a Ḥimyarite chief, al-Hayṣam b. ʿAbd al-Ṣamad, stirred up a rebellion against Hārūn (reigned 170–93/786–809), which coincided with an insurrection in the Tihāma. The caliph sent reinforcements headed by his trusted *mawlā*, Ḥammād al-Barbarī, to restore order. As a result of the activity of this governor (184–94/800–10) the trade routes between Ṣanʿāʾ, al-Yamāma and Mecca became relatively secure, and economic prosperity followed. Ḥammād's success, however, was achieved by treating the Yemenites harshly. Their complaints to the caliph al-Amīn did not go unheeded, and Ḥammād was replaced in 194/810.[75] Nevertheless, the Yemenites did not remain loyal to al-Amīn. During the struggle between him and his brother al-Maʾmūn (r. 193–8/809–13) the latter's general, Ṭāhir b. al-Ḥusayn, sent a representative to the Yemen, Yazīd b. Jarīr. Yazīd caused the Yemenites to transfer their allegiance to al-Maʾmūn by employing unorthodox means. For example, he forced the Yemenites of Persian origins to divorce their Arab wives. Another one of al-Maʾmūn's appointees acted against all things Ḥimyarite. Among other things, he is reported to have cut down all Ḥimyarite apricot trees.[76]

Al-Maʾmūn appointed and replaced some 15 governors.[77] In 200/815 an ʿAlid pretender from Mecca, Ibrāhīm b. Mūsā al-Kāẓim (brother of the well-known ʿAlī al-Riḍā), occupied Ṣanʿāʾ and controlled much of the highlands to the north; it is not certain whether he did so on behalf of the ʿAlid rebel in Kūfa, Ibn Ṭabāṭabā, or on his own accord. However, *dīnār*s were struck in Ṣanʿāʾ in his name, he stirred up tribal conflicts, indulged in murder and robbery of Yemenites, and perhaps took Mecca as well. He clashed with ʿAbbāsid troops on the outskirts of Mecca during the pilgrimage of 200/815, and shortly afterwards he was defeated by al-Maʾmūn's army in Ṣanʿāʾ. His fortunes changed, however, with al-Maʾmūn's change of policy. When in 201/817 the caliph decided to appoint the eighth Imāmī imam, ʿAlī al-Riḍā, as his successor, he also appointed ʿAlī's brother, Ibrāhīm b. Mūsā, first to Mecca, then to the Yemen. Al-Maʾmūn's governor since 200/815, Ḥamdawayh (or Ibn Māhān), refused to step down and rebelled against the caliph. Armies sent

75 Ahdal, *Tuḥfa*, pp. 146–7; Rāzī, *Taʾrīkh*, pp. 108–9; Yaḥyā ibn al-Ḥusayn, *Ghāyat*, pp. 143, 146; Ibn al-Daybaʿ, *Qurrat*, pp. 131–6 (here al-Hayṣam's revolt is a response to Ḥammād's harsh treatment); Madʿaj, *Yemen*, pp. 186–8, 203.

76 Yaḥyā ibn al-Ḥusayn, *Ghāyat*, pp. 146–7; al-Ṭabarī, *Taʾrīkh*, vol. VIII, p. 440 (cf. p. 593: harsh treatment by governors incurred an ʿAlid revolt in 207/822); Ibn al-Daybaʿ, *Qurrat*, pp. 139–41; Stookey, *Yemen*, p. 44.

77 Ahdal, *Tuḥfa*, pp. 147–9; Madʿaj, *Yemen*, pp. 220–2; Stookey, *Yemen*, p. 44. See the full list in Zambauer, *Muʿjam al-ansāb*, pp. 175–6.

from Baghdad defeated Ḥamdawayh in 205/820, and Ibrāhīm remained to represent al-Maʾmūn in the Yemen until 213/828.[78]

Ṣanʿāʾ was to remain under the caliphs' control for some time. By the end of the third/ninth century it was greatly reduced due to the struggles between Zaydīs, Ismāʿīlīs (see below) and local contenders.[79] In other parts of the Yemen independent dynasties were established as early as al-Maʾmūn's time. Some of them came into being out of mere personal ambition, whereas others were the expression of sectarian ideologies. As opposed to other parts of the empire, dynasties here often did not cause fragmentation, but rather unified parts of the country that had long been fragmented.

Non-sectarian dynasties

The first of these dynasties was of al-Maʾmūn's own making (just as was the case in Khurāsān). In 202/817, faced with a continuous tribal rebellion in the coastal area, he appointed Muḥammad b. ʿAbd Allāh b. Ziyād, a descendant of the famous general Ziyād b. Abīhi, to restore order. Ibn Ziyād remained in the Yemen but he did not always live up to the task, and the caliph had to send him reinforcements. Nevertheless, Ibn Ziyād established the town of Zabīd in Tihāma and the Ziyādī dynasty, that lasted until 409/1019. The dynasty retained its base there, at times extending its influence over most of the Yemen, including Ṣaʿda, Najrān, Ṣanʿāʾ, Aden, Shiḥr and Ḥaḍramawt. Ziyādī Zabīd is described as a prosperous city, deserving of the name 'Baghdad of the Yemen'. Even when effectively independent, the Sunni Ziyādīs remained loyal to the ʿAbbāsids in appearance, and to orthodox (Sunni) Islam. Consequently, they constantly fought the Zaydīs and the Ismāʿīlīs (see below). By the second half of the fourth/tenth century the Ziyādīs had lost most of their holdings and had become nominal rulers in their own court, with their black slaves holding the real power. In 407/1016 or 409/1018 the last of the Ziyādīs was assassinated and one of his slaves founded a new dynasty, the Najāḥīs. Like its predecessor this dynasty was loyal to the *sunna* and the ʿAbbāsids, and therefore it engaged in constant struggle with the Ṣulayḥī Ismāʿīlī state. During the fifth/eleventh century the Najāḥīs were vassals to the ruler of Aden, and they lost many of their territories – some of them to local and tribal rulers; others, including their capital, Zabīd, to the Ṣulayḥīs

78 Al-Ṭabarī, *Taʾrīkh*, vol. VIII, pp. 535–6; Ahdal, *Tuḥfa*, pp. 147–9; Yaḥyā ibn al-Ḥusayn, *Ghāyat*, pp. 148–51; Ibn al-Daybaʿ, *Qurrat*, pp. 144–7; Ibn Fahd, *Ghāya*, pp. 399, 405–7; Madʿaj, *Yemen*, pp. 205–8; cf. Sayyid, *Taʾrīkh*, p. 52. The reports of Ibrāhīm's career are contradictory, see also above.

79 Rāzī, *Taʾrīkh*, pp. 112–15; Yaḥyā ibn al-Ḥusayn, *Ghāyat*, pp. 151–4, 165–7, 219.

and the Zaydīs. The Najāḥīs reasserted their rule several times, and survived until the middle of the sixth/twelfth century, when they were brought down by ʿAlī b. Mahdī, founder of the Mahdī dynasty in Zabīd.[80]

The Ziyādī dynasty in Tihāma had the blessing of the caliphate from its inception. Other dynasties, however, were opposed to the caliphate. Thus the Ḥimyarī chiefs, the Manākhīs, seized the southern part of the highlands, where they held sway from 214/829 until they fell to the Ismāʿīlī ʿAlī b. al-Faḍl in 293/906. In the central and northern highlands another Ḥimyarī chief, Yuʿfir b. ʿAbd al-Raḥmān al-Ḥiwālī, based in Shibām, challenged ʿAbbāsid authority. The latter was represented by the governors of Ṣanʿāʾ, and was also supported by some local chiefs and tribes. The conflict between the two lasted some twenty years (214–33/829–47). In 247/861 the Yuʿfirīs established control over Ṣanʿāʾ and a large part of the highland, from Ṣaʿda in the north to al-Janad in the south, and in 258/871–2 they conquered Ḥaḍramawt as well. Being Sunnī, however, the Yuʿfirīs were recognised by the ʿAbbāsids in 257/870, to make a Sunnī front against the Zaydīs and the Ismāʿīlīs in the Yemen. They sometimes paid homage, and even taxes, to the stronger Sunnī state, the Ziyādīs of Tihāma. Their state lasted until the end of the fourth/tenth century.[81]

Religious activity and sectarian states

The Yemen was the theatre of intense religious activity, both political and literary. From the religio-political point of view it was the Shīʿa, both Zaydī and Ismāʿīlī, who were the most active. Ibāḍism, suppressed in the early second/eighth century (see above), recovered in Ḥaḍramawt, and the community was largely autonomous under the aegis of the Ziyādīs. During the first half of the fourth/tenth century Ibāḍism in Ḥaḍramawt faltered, reportedly due to the activity of the Shīʿa. This activity was introduced by Aḥmad b. ʿĪsā, a descendant of the ʿAlid imam Jaʿfar al-Ṣādiq. Aḥmad left Baṣra in 318/930 as a result of the Qarmaṭī attacks, and migrated to Ḥaḍramawt (subsequently

80 Ahdal, *Tuḥfa*, pp. 150–1; ʿUmāra, *Mufīd*, pp. 49–77, 154–84; Nāṣer-e Khosraw, *Travels*, p. 71; Shams al-Dīn al-Muqaddasī, *Aḥsan al-taqāsīm fī maʿrifat al-aqālīm*, ed. M. J. de Goeje (Leiden, 1906), pp. 85, 104; Ibn al-Daybaʿ, *Qurrat*, pp. 322–60; Ḥarīrī, *Dirāsāt*, pp. 179–213; Sayyid, *Taʾrīkh*, pp. 82–3; Madʿaj, *Yemen*, pp. 208–12; Smith, 'Political history', pp. 130–2; Stookey, *Yemen*, pp. 45, 65–6, 75–6, 98; Zambauer, *Muʿjam al-ansāb*, pp. 179, 181–2.

81 Ahdal, *Tuḥfa*, pp. 148–52; ʿUmāra, *Mufīd*, pp. 55–9; Yaḥyā ibn al-Ḥusayn, *Ghāyat*, pp. 155, 160, 164–7; Ibn al-Daybaʿ, *Qurrat*, pp. 154–77, 182, 200–12, 218–21; Ḥarīrī, *Dirāsāt*, pp. 96–7, 181–2; Sayyid, *Taʾrīkh*, pp. 54–5; A. ibn A. al-Muṭāʿ, *Taʾrīkh al-Yaman al-Islāmī min sanat arbaʿ wa-miʾatayn ilā sanat alf wa-sitt*, ed. ʿA. M. al-Ḥibshī (Beirut, 1986/1407), pp. 70–4; Madʿaj, *Yemen*, pp. 213–18, 233; Gochenour, 'Penetration', pp. 38–46; Stookey, *Yemen*, p. 54; Smith, 'Political history', pp. 130–1; Zambauer, *Muʿjam al-ansāb*, pp. 179–80.

the descendants of the Prophet in Ḥaḍramawt came to be known as '*sayyids*'). The Shīʿa started to gain supporters in Ḥaḍramawt, but Ibāḍism reasserted itself in the fifth/eleventh century. The proximity of Ḥaḍramawt to Ibāḍī Oman certainly encouraged the Ḥaḍramī Ibāḍīs, and in the fifth/eleventh century Ḥaḍramawt was incorporated into the Omanī Imamate. The collapse of the latter, and the conquest of Ḥaḍramawt by the Ismāʿīlī al-Ṣulayḥī (see below), brought an end to Ibāḍism there, so that it left no lasting imprint.[82]

Religio-political as well as spiritual activity sometimes blended into the pre-Islamic Yemenite institutions. Traditionally, the arms-bearing tribes were the dominant class and so they remained after the advent of Islam. It was such tribes that protected the *ḥawṭas* (sacred enclaves) in Ḥaḍramawt, and the *hajar/hijras* (protected areas and protected status), in Northern Yemen. Under the aegis of these institutions many leaders, scholars and saintly people were active. Some of them were descended from the Prophet (or pretenders), whereas others were descended from ancient saintly local families.[83]

From the literary point of view, the cultural achievements of the Yemen are quite impressive. There were many historians and poets, some astronomers and mathematicians; but, above all, there were scholars of the religious sciences. Qurʾān exegesis, jurisprudence, *ḥadīth* and theology thrived throughout the Yemen from the first/seventh century onwards, and some Yemenite scholars acquired fame all over the Islamic world.[84] Theological debates were common from an early date, given the presence of scholars, on the one hand,

82 Al-Kāf, *Ḥaḍramawt*, pp. 40–1, 44; Bāwazīr, *Ṣafaḥāt*, pp. 56–79; Ḥāmid, *Taʾrīkh Ḥaḍramawt*, pp. 245–7, 250, 261–72, 296–336, 360 (the author is a Shīʿite, and he plays down the Khārijite revival, while emphasising the role of Aḥmad ibn ʿĪsā); Sayyābī, *al-Ḥaqīqa*, pp. 130–51 (the author is an Ibāḍī and he emphasises the exploits of this sect); Stookey, *Yemen*, p. 42; Serjeant, 'Historians', p. 241; R. B. Serjeant, 'The sayyids of Ḥaḍramawt', in R. B. Serjeant, *Studies in Arabian history and civilization*, Variorum Collected Studies VIII (Aldershot and Brookfield, VT, 1981), p. 9.

83 Serjeant, 'Sayyids'; R. B. Serjeant, 'South Arabia', in R. B. Serjeant, *Studies in Arabian history and civilization*, Variorum Collected Studies IX (Aldershot and Brookfield, VT, 1981); R. B. Serjeant, 'The interplay between tribal affinities and religious (Zaydi) authority in the Yemen', *al-abḥāth*, 30 (1982); Gochenour, 'Penetration', pp. 165–73, 295; W. Madelung, 'The origin of the Yemenite *hijra*', in A. Jones (ed.), *Arabicus Felix: Luminosus Britanicus, essays in honour of A F. L. Beeston on his eightieth birthday* (Oxford, 1991), pp. 25–44 (according to Madelung, the institution of *hijra* in the Yemen is not pre-Islamic).

84 Hamdānī, *Ṣifat*, pp. 103–7; Ḥarīrī, *Dirāsāt*, pp. 81–9. Full details: Rāzī, *Taʾrīkh*, pp. 294–454; Aḥmad ibn Muḥammad al-Shāmī, *Taʾrīkh al-Yaman al-fikrī fī al-ʿaṣr al-ʿAbbāsī*, 4 vols. (Beirut, 1407/1987); ʿA. M. al-Ḥibshī, *Maṣādir al-fikr al-Islamī fī al-Yaman* (Beirut, 1408/1988); ʿA. M. al-Ḥibshī, *Muʾallafāt ḥukkām al-Yaman*, ed. Elke Niewoehner-Eberhard (Wiesbaden, 1979); Sayyid, *Taʾrīkh*; Serjeant, 'Historians'.

and the involvement of the Yemen in the empire's events, on the other.[85] It may be noted that both the Yemen and the Ḥijāz suffered from long periods of instability. But whereas in the Ḥijāz this (among other things) led to a depletion of cultural activity, in the Yemen the rivalry between the schools, sects and enclaves produced a vast literature.

Some sources report that during the Umayyad period the idea of *jabr* (predestination) was widespread in the Yemen, and that the most popular schools of law until the third/ninth century were the Ḥanafī and the Mālikī. Whether or not these statements are accurate, it is clear that the third/ninth century represents a turning-point in Yemen's history. The Shāfiʿī school of law was introduced, and it subsequently became increasingly prevalent. Zabīd became the main centre of Shāfiʿism, but the school was popular also in al-Janad, Ḥaḍramawt, Aden and Ṣanʿāʾ.[86] Towards the end of the century Zaydism and Ismāʿīlism entered the Yemen simultaneously, against the background of political division: the Ziyādī state in the Tihāma; the Ḥimyarite Yuʿfirīs in Ṣanʿāʾ and part of the highland southwards to Janad; the Ḥimyarite Manākhīs in the southern highland; and the tribes of the north, who were busy fighting one another and paying allegiance to no central power. It was in the latter, fragmented area that the Zaydīs established themselves, whereas the Ismāʿīlīs (called 'Qarāmiṭa' by the Zaydīs, to be distinguished from the real Qarmaṭīs of Baḥrayn) entered the south, as well as the western part of the central mountain ranges.[87]

The Zaydīs

In 284/897 Yaḥyā b. al-Ḥusayn al-Ḥasanī, entitled al-Hādī ilā al-Ḥaqq (the 'Leader to the Truth'), arrived in the northern highlands from the Ḥijāz. As a descendant of ʿAlī and Fāṭima and a respected religious authority, he was invited by chiefs of quarrelling Yemenite tribes to restore peace and order. His mission in the area a few years earlier had ended in failure and his departure, but this time he remained and succeeded in establishing a Zaydī regime (*imāma*) based in Ṣaʿda. Striving to extend his influence he fought the Yuʿfirīs and other tribal chiefs over Ṣanʿāʾ, as well as the Ismāʿīlī claimant to

85 See e.g. Rāzī, *Taʾrīkh*, pp. 356, 387, 393, 401.

86 Yaḥyā ibn al-Ḥusayn, *Ghāyat*, p. 203; Ḥarīrī, *Dirāsāt*, pp. 79–80; Sayyid, *Taʾrīkh*, pp. 44–69; Serjeant, 'Historians', p. 239.

87 Yaḥyā ibn al-Ḥusayn, *Ghāyat*, p. 167; Sayyid, *Taʾrīkh*, p. 55; P. Dresch, *Tribes, government and history in Yemen* (Oxford, 1989), p. 167; Gochenour, 'Penetration', pp. 38–46; Stookey, *Yemen*, p. 45.

power, ʿAlī b. al-Faḍl. Having failed to gain firm control of Ṣanʿāʾ, al-Hādī returned to Ṣaʿda, where he died in 298/911.[88]

The period between 284–444/897–1052 is sometimes called the first Zaydī Imamate, but Zaydī imams continued to rise after this date as well, although not consecutively. The initial purpose for which the founder, al-Hādī, was invited to the Yemen was in general not achieved. Although some of the imams were strong enough to unify the northern region of the Yemen, the Imamate did not succeed in establishing permanent peace or unity. In fact, the Zaydī regime can hardly be considered a state. There was no formal administrative apparatus and no fixed pattern of succession. The main criterion for eligibility, in addition to ʿAlid descent, was military activity aimed at establishing Zaydism. This had several consequences. First, there were many interregna. Second, Zaydī imams were constantly struggling against non-Zaydīs – occasionally also against their own tribal supporters, because the latter might oppose the imam's enforcement of the Qurʾānic punishments (*ḥudūd*) and the levying of *zakāt* (alms-tax). Indeed, Islamic law often clashed with the entrenched customary law. This explains why Zaydī imams are sometimes portrayed as fighting tribalism as such. Third, Zaydīs were also often at war among themselves. Members of the Prophet's family, backed by different tribal groups, fought one another over leadership. Imams often became entangled in tribal disputes that had nothing to do with Zaydism.

The Zaydī imams were associated with tribal protected status and sacred enclaves (*hajar* or *hijra*), but their influence usually extended beyond one tribe. This ancient Yemenite institution served to spread Zaydism in the northern Yemen (although it should be noted that not all enclaves were Zaydī). There were many enclaves throughout the tribal territories that may have been independent from one another, but were regarded by the Zaydī historiography as parts of a single Zaydī state. Although entangled in tribal life and politics, the imams, also called *sayyids*, differed from the tribal leaders (shaykhs), in that they called to *jihād*, practised the Commanding of Right and Forbidding Wrong (*al-amr bi-'l-maʿrūf wa-'l-nahy ʿan al-munkar*), rendered educational and spiritual services, dispensed Islamic justice, and enforced Islamic law as far as they could. It is remarkable that, although considered holy by virtue of descent from the Prophet, Zaydī imams were

88 Yaḥyā ibn al-Ḥusayn, *Ghāyat*, pp. 166–90; ʿAlī ibn Muḥammad ibn ʿUbaydallah, *Sīrat al-Hādī Yaḥyā b. al-Ḥusayn*, ed. Suhayl Zakkār (Beirut, 1972); al-Muṭāʿ, *Taʾrīkh al-Yaman*, pp. 74–146; Gochenour, 'Penetration', pp. 46–56; Smith, 'Yemenite history', pp. 137–8; Stookey, *Yemen*, p. 79. On the turbulent events in Ṣanʿāʾ during the late third/ninth and fourth/tenth centuries see also ibn al-Daybaʿ, *Qurrat*, pp. 218–42.

characterised by learning and knowledge of the law, rather than supernatural powers. They were nevertheless distinguished not only from tribal leaders but also from the religious elite that was not descended from the Prophet. Although highly regarded, and although they functioned as leaders of *jihād*, the Zaydī imams remained dependent on the tribes for protection. And therefore, although they served as mentors, judges, arbiters, political leaders and military commanders, they cannot be considered as the ruling elite.[89]

The first Zaydī Imamate was active in Ṣaʿda and Najrān, occasionally in Ṣanʿāʾ and the Jawf, but Tihāma was generally out of its reach. The first half of the fifth/eleventh century was a period of deterioration and sectarian division. One major new sect, led by a Yemenite, Muṭarrif b. Shihāb, became known as Muṭarrifiyya. Although originating as a schism, this sect was beneficial to Zaydism as a whole, and it upheld and spread the mission when the descendants of the Prophet were unable to do so. By the middle of the century the first Zaydī Imamate had come to an end at the hands of the Ismāʿīlī dynasty, the Ṣulayḥīs. The Zaydīs established their second Imamate in 532/1138, simultaneously with the demise of the Ṣulayḥīs; it lasted until 980/1585.[90]

The Ismāʿīlīs

Ismāʿīlī activity (*daʿwa*) in the Yemen started perhaps in the second half of the third/ninth century. There is a report about a missionary, al-Ḥasan b. Faraj al-Ṣanādīqī, who based himself in Mudhaykhira, acquired many followers and conquered the Yemen. He pretended to be a prophet, committed many atrocities, and was the cause of a massive emigration.[91] Reports about all this are, however, sparse even in Yemenite sources. We have better information about the organised mission and military activity of the Ismāʿīlīs towards

89 Ḥarīrī, *Dirāsāt*, pp. 62–8; C. van Arendonck, *Les débuts de l'imamat zaidite du Yemen*, trans. J. Ryckmans (Leiden, 1960), pp. 127–255; Gochenour, 'Penetration', pp. 64–294 (list of enclaves on p. 172); Dresch, *Tribes*, pp. 136–97; Serjeant, 'Interplay'; E. Landau-Tasseron, 'Zaydī imams as restorers of religion: *Iḥyāʾ* and *tajdīd* in Zaydī literature', *JNES*, 49 (1990).

90 Stookey, *Yemen*, pp. 57, 61, 95, 98; Dresch, *Tribes*, pp. 171–2. On the Muṭarrifiyya see Gochenour, 'Penetration', pp. 186–201. Further details on Zaydī imams and their exploits: Yaḥyā ibn al-Ḥusayn, *Ghāyat*, pp. 204–52; al-Muṭāʿ, *Taʾrīkh al-Yaman*, pp. 146–61, 179–233, 291–312; Muḥammad ibn Muḥammad Zabāra al-Ḥasanī, *Itḥāf al-muhtadīn bi-dhikr al-aʾimma al-mujaddidīn* (Ṣanʿāʾ, 1343/1925); Muḥammad ibn Muḥammad Zabāra al-Ḥasanī, *Taʾrīkh al-Zaydiyya*, ed. M. Zaynahm (Cairo, n.d.).

91 Maqrīzī, *Ittiʿāẓ*, pp. 222–3, see also Muḥammad ibn Aḥmad al-Dhahabī, *Siyar aʿlām al-nubalāʾ*, ed. S. al-Arnāʾūṭ and M. N. al-ʿArqasūsī, 23 vols. (Beirut, 1413/1993), vol. X, p. 285.

the end of the third/ninth century. Two Ismāʿīlī missionaries were sent to the region. One of them, Abū al-Qāsim ibn Ḥawshab, succeeded in conquering the entire Jabal Miswar massif (north-west of Ṣanʿāʾ) and became known as 'Manṣūr al-Yaman' ('the God-aided one from the Yemen'). The other, ʿAlī b. al-Faḍl, was active in the south, took the former Manākhī capital, Mudhaykhira, in 293/906, then went to Ṣanʿāʾ. The city was contested for several years between the Yuʿfirīs, the Zaydī al-Hādī ilā al-Ḥaqq and ʿAli b. al-Faḍl, and finally fell to the latter in 298/911. Encouraged by his success, ʿAlī defected from the Ismāʿīlī cause, became independent and turned to fight his former partner, Manṣūr al-Yaman. ʿAlī was assassinated by an agent of the Yuʿfirīs in 303/915, whereupon his regime collapsed. Manṣūr al-Yaman remained loyal to the Ismāʿīliyya and to the Fāṭimids – who meanwhile had taken power in the Maghrib (in 297/909). He continued to send Ismāʿīlī missionaries to other regions, such as Oman, Yamāma and Sind. His regime was brought to an end by the internal quarrels after his death in 302/914. One of his successors transferred his allegiance to the ʿAbbāsids, and the Ismāʿīliyya in the Yemen became mostly an underground movement until the rise of the Ṣulayḥīs, an aristocratic family of the tribe of Hamdān.[92]

ʿAlī b. Muḥammad al-Ṣulayḥī, son of a Sunnī judge from the Ḥarāz district (to the west of Ṣanʿāʾ), was chosen as agent for the Fāṭimids in the Yemen. During the first half of the fifth/eleventh century he engaged in clandestine activity, and acquired fame and support. Towards the middle of the century he received permission to act in public, and he based himself at the mountain of Masār in his native district. Having defeated the Zaydī imam of Ṣaʿda and the local rulers of Ṣanʿāʾ and the Ḥaḍūr district to the north, ʿAlī proceeded to consolidate his authority by military exploits, diplomacy and intrigue. After few clashes with the ruler of Zabīd, Najāḥ, the latter died (in 452/1060), apparently of poisoning arranged by ʿAlī himself. ʿAlī thus gained control of the Tihāma, whereupon he conquered the southern part of the Yemen, including Aden and Ḥaḍramawt. By 455/1063 he had unified the Yemen as it had been under the pre-Islamic Ḥimyarites, although some anarchic tribal areas remained, as well as petty chiefdoms, such as Āl Qaḥṭān, Banū al-Daʿʿār and Āl Fāris in Ḥaḍramawt.[93] Based in Ṣanʿāʾ, ʿAlī personally appointed governors to the provinces and supervised their work, as well as the work

92 Ahdal, *Tuḥfa*, pp. 153–64, 168–71; ʿUmāra, *Mufīd*, pp. 59–63; Yaḥyā ibn al-Ḥusayn, *Ghāyat*, pp. 191–209, 219; Ibn al-Daybaʿ, *Qurrat*, pp. 182–217; Ḥarīrī, *Dirāsāt*, pp. 188–90; Stookey, *Yemen*, pp. 52–7; W. Madelung, 'Manṣur al-Yaman', *EI2*, vol. VI, p. 438.

93 Al-Kāf, *Ḥaḍramawt*, pp. 45–8; Ḥāmid, *Taʾrīkh Ḥaḍramawt*, pp. 403–28.

of the missionaries sent to spread the Ismāʿīlī ideology. He remained attached to the court in Cairo, received his orders from the caliph al-Mustanṣir, and often appealed to him for advice and authorisation of his actions. ʿAlī al-Ṣulayḥī acted in the Ḥijāz as well on behalf of his patrons, secured the allegiance of Mecca to Cairo, and carried out renovations in the holy places. However, his relations with the *sharīf* of Mecca sometimes necessitated the mediation of the Fāṭimid caliph.[94]

ʿAlī al-Ṣulayḥī was constantly at war, whether against Ethiopian invasions or against numerous internal enemies, including tribal chiefs, rival dynasties and sects and Ismāʿīlīs who had gone astray. His staunchest enemies, however, were the Najāḥīs. The struggle between these two states continued, with Zabīd frequently changing hands, until both dynasties came to a simultaneous end in the middle of the sixth/twelfth century. It appears that the issue in this struggle was not only Sunnism versus Ismāʿīlism, but also control of the Tihāma, which ensured control of the trade via the Red Sea.

It was the Najāḥīs who killed ʿAlī al-Ṣulayḥī in 460/1067, while he was on his way to perform the pilgrimage. His son al-Mukarram took over, and successfully withstood both rebellions and attacks by traditional enemies, namely, the Zaydīs and the Najāhīs. He avenged his father's death, rescued his mother from captivity in the hands of the Najāḥīs, and brought the Ṣulayḥī state to its peak. The extent of his power may be gauged from the fact that in 460/1068 he reportedly succeeded in defeating a tribal coalition numbering 30,000 men (this number may be a topos, but it conveys large numbers). Another indication of his eminence is that in 468/1075 the caliph entrusted him with conducting the Ismāʿīlī mission in India.[95] However, al-Mukarram became too ill to conduct the affairs of the state, and the throne went to his wife Arwā even before his death (that occurred in 477/1094). The Free Lady (al-Sayyida al-Ḥurra) was recognised by the caliph in Cairo, moved her court to Dhū Jibla in the southern mountains and continued the struggles against the Najāḥīs and other opponents. She was also involved in the Ismāʿīlī movement at large. In the schism that broke out in 487/1094 she sided with the Egyptians who supported al-Mustaʿlī bi-Allāh (as against his brother Nizār). Al-Mustaʿlī in turn reconfirmed her position as both ruler and chief missionary.

94 See e.g. A. F. Sayyid, P. Walker M. A. and Pomerantz, *The Fāṭimids and their successors in Yaman: The history of an Islamic community*, Arabic edn and English summary of Idrīs ʿImād al-Dīn's *ʿUyūn al-akhbār*, vol. VII (London and New York, 2002) (henceforth ʿImād al-Dīn, *ʿUyūn*), p. 36.

95 Ibid., pp. 117–27, 131–44, 152.

The Ismāʿīlī missionary ʿImād al-Dīn (d. 872/1468) describes Arwā as a pious and learned woman who successfully implemented both her political and religious tasks.[96] But it appears that, being a woman, Arwā could not herself act as a missionary, just as she did not herself lead troops to battle. A chief judge sent from Cairo, Lamak b. Mālik, and his son, acted by her side as auxiliary missionaries. Other major officials were Sabaʾ b. Aḥmad, al-Mufaḍḍal b. Abī al-Barakāt and Ibn Najīb al-Dawla (the latter sent from Cairo in 513/1119, and sent back as a prisoner in 519/1125). Perhaps her gender was also one of the causes that led to the undermining of Arwā's authority by her own appointees (although ʿImād al-Dīn expressly denies this). In addition, she was unable to retain Ṣulayḥī military superiority, and her armies were soundly defeated by a coalition of the Zaydīs and Najāḥīs in 479/1087. Ṣanʿāʾ, which had been changing hands between Ṣulayḥī governors and local Hamdānī rulers already in al-Mukarram's time, fell to the Āl Ḥātim family in 493/1098.[97] In the Cairo crisis of 526/1130 Arwā remained loyal to the marginalised Fāṭimid heir, al-Ṭayyib, and refused to follow the regent (ʿAbd al-Majīd al-Ḥāfiẓ). This crisis estranged her from the Fāṭimid court and further weakened the Ṣulayḥī state, which shrank and deteriorated.[98] After Queen Arwā's death in 532/1137, the Banū Zurayʿ of Aden took over. This petty dynasty had ruled Aden (after having replaced the local Banū Maʿn) since 476/1083, under the patronage of the Ṣulayḥīs. Its relations with Arwā, however, were not always peaceful. Fifteen years after her death they bought the main castles and towns from al-Manṣūr b. al-Mufaḍḍal, the son of her former official, became independent, and sided with the Egyptian Ismāʿīlī mission, which had been rejected by Arwā. The Zurayʿīs fell to the Ayyūbids with the rest of the Yemen in 569/1173.[99] Ismāʿīlī missionaries, however, with tribal backing from the Hamdān, continued their activities underground for centuries. They were

96 Ibid., pp. 278–9.
97 Ibid., pp. 304–9.
98 On the Ṣulayḥī dynasty from its foundation see ibid., pp. 5–36, 98–177, 199–200, 213–15, 271–310; ʿUmāra, *Mufīd*, pp. 83–138; Yaḥyā ibn al-Ḥusayn, *Ghāyat*, pp. 253–301; Ibn al-Daybaʿ, *Qurrat*, pp. 218–304; Ḥāmid, *Taʾrīkh Ḥaḍramawt*, pp. 340–64; Ḥarīrī, *Dirāsāt*, pp. 190–211; Sayyid, *Taʾrīkh*, pp. 91–169; Stookey, *Yemen*, pp. 58–77; Smith, 'Political history', p. 132. The career of the founder, ʿAlī, is especially difficult to follow: see Gochenour, 'Penetration', pp. 307–16.
99 ʿImād al-Dīn, *ʿUyūn*, pp. 274–8, 310; ʿUmāra, *Mufīd*, pp. 139–52; Ibn al-Daybaʿ, *Qurrat*, pp. 304–20; Ḥāmid, *Taʾrīkh Ḥaḍramawt*, pp. 345–53; Ḥarīrī, *Dirāsāt*, p. 105; Smith, 'Political history', p. 133; Zambauer, *Muʿjam al-ansāb*, p. 181. Al-Mukarram, grandfather of Zurayʿ, is not to be confused with al-Mukarram, son of ʿAlī al-Ṣulayḥī. See further on the Ismāʿīlīs in the Yemen and all their rivals: al-Muṭāʿ, *Taʾrīkh al-Yaman*, pp. 121–295.

mostly based in strongholds around Ṣan'ā', monitoring the *da'wa* not only in the Yemen but also in the Ḥijāz, Sind and Oman.

Oman

Oman had many peculiar features to its economy, its social organisation, its internal divisions and the patterns of authority and government. These were strongly affected by its location and by its geography and topography.[100]

Oman lies on the south-eastern corner of the Arabian Peninsula, and contains a coastal plain, mountain ranges and desert. The coastal area, known as the Bāṭina, is easily accessible from Iraq on the one hand, and from the Far East and Africa on the other. Its inhabitants on the eve of Islam were fishermen, sailors, pearl divers, traders, textile manufacturers and farmers. Many were Persian, and in the coastal town of Ṣuḥār the spoken language was Persian even in the fourth/tenth century. The interior, known as the Ẓāhira or Jawf, lies beyond the range of the Ḥajar and the al-Akhḍar mountains, and is much less accessible than the coast. Its inhabitants were settled and nomadic tribesmen. The Azd tribes, who were considered Southern Arabs, were dominant from ancient times, but many tribal groups from other parts of the Peninsula moved into the region before as well as after the advent of Islam. Among them were those from amongst the so-called 'Northern' tribes, namely the Quraysh, Tamīm, 'Āmir, 'Abs and Dhubyān, to name but a few. These facts played a decisive role in Oman's turbulent history. The coastal area with its capital, Ṣuḥār, took part in the international trade that brought much wealth and power. It was therefore a bone of contention between the coastal population, the inland tribes and foreign powers that attacked Oman recurrently. The inland tribes, thanks to their geographical position, were often able to retain their independence, even when the Bāṭina was occupied by foreign powers.

The details of Oman's history are immensely confused due to incessant invasions, the division between the coast and the interior, the internal wars and the biases of the local historians. The latter were mainly religious scholars of the Khārijite Ibāḍī sect, and the scope of their interest in history was relatively limited. According to the Omanī historian Sālimī (d. 1332/1914), 'the Omanis are not interested in history, so most of the reports about the [Ibāḍī] imams are lost, to say nothing of reports about others'. Indeed, Sālimī, among other historians, often points to lacunae in the historical

100 See J. C. Wilkinson, *The imamate tradition of Oman* (Cambridge, 1987). Detailed geographical description in C. Holes , ''Umān', *EI2*, vol. X, p. 814.

information. To add to the difficulties, many of the Omanī sources are still in manuscript form.[101]

Oman from the first/seventh to the third/ninth century

At the beginning of the first/seventh century Oman was under Persian influence, and its internal affairs were run by a local family of the Azd tribe, the Julandā. Towards the end of the Prophet's lifetime the rulers, Jayfar and ʿAbd (or ʿAbbād), sons of al-Julandā, were converted to Islam. After Muḥammad's death in 11/632 a movement of opposition to Islam and to the Julandā occurred, referred to in Islamic historiography as 'the apostasy of the Omanīs' (*riddat ahl ʿUmān*). The Julandā overcame the revolt with the assistance of troops sent by Abū Bakr. It may be noted that the conversion of Oman to Islam was coupled with the expulsion of the Persians.[102]

Universal histories record the names of several governors appointed by Abū Bakr (r. 11–13/632–4) and ʿUmar (r. 13–23/634–44) to Oman. The region was usually attached to Baṣra, but occasionally it belonged to the same jurisdiction as Baḥrayn or Yamāma. Governors sent from Medina were based in the coastal town of Ṣuḥār and had the tasks of collecting taxes and leading military expeditions eastwards.[103] The general sources, however, tend to ignore the role of Jayfar and ʿAbd after the *ridda*. It appears from the local sources that the brothers remained in office, just as they had in the Prophet's time. During ʿUmar's time the two Julandā brothers Jayfar and ʿAbd died and were succeeded by the

101 Shalabī, *Mawsūʿa*, pp. 11–24; ʿA. ʿA. al-ʿĀnī, *Taʾrīkh ʿUmān fī al-ʿuṣūr al-Islāmiyya al-ūlā* (London, 1420/1999), pp. 44–53; J. C. Wilkinson, 'Bibliographical background to the crisis period in the Ibāḍī imamate (end of the ninth to end of the fourteenth century)', *Arabian Studies*, 3 (1976); Wilkinson, *The imamate*, pp. 364–72; Ḥasan M. Naboodah, 'Banū Nabhān in the Omani Sources', in G. R. Smith , J. R. Smart and B. R. Pridham (eds.), *New Arabian Studies*, 4 (Exeter, 1997), pp. 181–4. See also Sālimī's remark: Nūr al-Dīn ʿAbd Allāh ibn Ḥumayd al-Sālimī, *Tuḥfat al-aʿyān bi-sīrat ahl ʿUmān*, vol. I (Cairo, 1380/1961), p. 353, see also pp. 338, 342. International trade: ʿĀnī, *Taʾrīkh*, pp. 79–81, 85; Hourani, *Arab seafaring*, pp. 61–83. Tribes: Sālim ibn Ḥamūd al-Sayyābī, *Isʿāf al-aʿyān fī ansāb ahl ʿUmān* (Beirut, 1384/1965); ʿĀnī, *Taʾrīkh*, pp. 57–69.

102 Al-Ṭabarī, *Taʾrīkh*, vol. III, pp. 95, 314–16; Yāqūt ibn ʿAbd Allāh, *Muʿjam al-buldān*, 5 vols. (Beirut, n.d.), vol. III, p. 27; Yaʿqūbī, *Taʾrīkh*, vol. II, p. 122; Sālimī, *Tuḥfa*, pp. 53–69; Anonymous, *Taʾrīkh ahl ʿUmān*, ed. S. ʿA. ʿĀshūr (Oman, 1986), pp. 40–4; Kalāʿi, *Iktifāʾ*, vol. II, pp. 398–401, vol. III, pp. 92–4; ʿĀnī, *Taʾrīkh*, pp. 95–109; Shalabī, *Mawsūʿa*, pp. 228–30; Wilkinson, *The imamate*, p. 205; J. C. Wilkinson, 'The Julandā of Oman', *Journal of Oman Studies*, 1 (1975); M. Kervran, 'Ṣuḥār', *EI2*, vol. IX, p. 774.

103 Al-Ṭabarī, *Taʾrīkh*, vol. III, pp. 479, 623; Yūsuf ibn ʿAbd Allāh ibn ʿAbd al-Barr al-Qurṭubī, *al-Istīʿāb fī maʿrifat al-aṣḥāb*, ed. ʿA. M. al-Bījāwī, 4 vols. (Beirut, 1412/1992), vol. III, pp. 1035, 1082, 1187; Aḥmad ibn ʿAlī ibn Ḥajar al-ʿAsqalānī, *al-Iṣāba fī tamyīz al-ṣaḥāba*, ed. A. M. al-Bījāwī, 8 vols. (Beirut, 1412/1992), vol. II, p. 44; Dhahabī, *Siyar*, vol. II, p. 374; Khalīfa b. Khayyāṭ al-ʿUṣfurī, *Taʾrīkh*, ed. A. Ḍ. al-ʿUmarī, 2 vols. (Beirut and Damascus, 1397/1976), vol. I, pp. 124, 278; ʿĀnī, *Taʾrīkh*, p. 116.

latter's son, ʿAbbād b. ʿAbd, who in turn was succeeded by his two sons, Sulaymān and Saʿīd.[104]

In addition to highlighting the role of the Julandā family, local sources tend to play down the *ridda* in Oman, and to emphasize the loyalty and support that the Omanīs gave to Medina at that difficult time, and later as well.[105] Indeed, in the Rāshidūn period many Omanīs departed for the conquered territories and played an important role in the conquests and settlement of Iran and territories further east. Omanī maritime expertise was of great service in launching military expeditions against the west coast of India. The Omanī Muhallabī family, among others, left a deep mark on both the military exploits and the politics of the Umayyad period. In addition, Oman gradually replaced coastal Baḥrayn as the main centre of maritime trade in the Persian Gulf.[106]

Oman did not participate in the first civil war of 36–41/656–661. When this war ended with the Umayyads' victory, the Julandā brothers, Sulaymān and Saʿīd, became independent. During the second civil war (61–73/680–92) Najda b. ʿĀmir, leader of an extremist Khārijite faction, conquered Oman for a short period of time, but the Julandā brothers succeeded in re-establishing their position.[107] Khārijite migration from Baṣra, however, which began after the first civil war, continued through the second half of the first/seventh century, turning Oman into a centre of Khārijite activity. The most prominent among the Khārijites in Oman were the Ibāḍīs, that is, the followers of Ibn Ibāḍ, who represented a moderate form of Khārijism.

It was only under the caliph ʿAbd al-Malik (r. 65–86/685–705) that the governor of Iraq, al-Ḥajjāj b. Yūsuf, dispatched troops that re-conquered Oman, albeit with great difficulty. The Julandā brothers fled to East Africa, and governors representing the Umayyads were henceforth sent to Oman. The governor of Iraq shouldered the responsibility of appointing these, but when there were complaints about them, the caliph sometimes intervened.[108] There is no information about Omanī insurrections during the Marwānid period (64–132/684–749), but a certain report suggests that such

104 Sirḥān ibn Saʿīd ibn Sirḥān al-Izkiwī (attrib.), *Annals of Oman to 1728*, trans. and annotated E. C. Ross (Cambridge and New York, 1984), p. 10; Anonymous, *Ta'rīkh*, pp. 45–7; ʿĀnī, *Ta'rīkh*, pp. 113–17, 214.

105 E.g. Anonymous, *Ta'rīkh*, pp. 40–5; Izkiwī (attrib.), *Annals*, pp. 9–10; Sālimī, *Tuḥfa*, pp. 69–73.

106 Aḥmad ibn Yaḥyā al-Balādhurī, *Futūḥ al-buldān*, ed. R. M. Riḍwān (Beirut, 1983/1403), p. 420; P. Casey Vine (ed.), *Oman in history* (London, 1995), pp. 136–60; ʿĀnī, *Ta'rīkh*, pp. 140, 177–84. The Muhallabīs: M. Hinds, 'An early Islamic family from Oman: al-ʿAwtabī's account of the Muhallabids', *JSS*, Monograph 17 (Manchester, 1991).

107 Ibn al-Athīr, *Kāmil*, vol. IV, p. 21; ʿĀnī, *Ta'rīkh*, pp. 117–19.

108 Khalīfa, *Ta'rīkh*, vol. I, pp. 297, 310, 319, 367; Abū Nuʿaym al-Iṣbahānī, *Ḥilyat al-awliyā'*, 10 vols. (Beirut, 1405/1985), vol. V, p. 290, see also vol. IX, p. 31 (the caliph intervenes in

events did occur. It is related that ʿUmar II (r. 99–101/717–20) issued a decree concerning Muslim Omanī captives.[109] These captives may have been rebels, supporters of Yazīd b. al-Muhallab, one of the chiefs of the Omanī Azd and governor of Khurāsān and Iraq for ʿAbd al-Malik and Sulaymān (r. 96–9/715–17) respectively. Yazīd b. al-Muhallab made many enemies during his long career, including the caliph ʿUmar II, who had him deposed and imprisoned in 99/717. In 101/720 Yazīd staged a revolt and succeeded in extending his control over Iraq, southern Iran and Oman. His revolt lasted only a few months, and after having defeated him, the Umayyads returned to control Oman.[110]

Despite Umayyad rule, the ancient local Julandā family remained powerful. Shortly after the advent of the ʿAbbāsids in 132/750, the Ibāḍiyya elected al-Julandā b. Masʿūd as their ruler (imam), although his family did not support the sect. The ʿAbbāsids, on their part, appointed governors to Oman. The Ibāḍiyya seems to have taken over with the help of the second ʿAbbāsid governor, who sympathised with them. Al-Julandā was powerful enough to repel an invasion by Ṣufrī Khārijites in 134/752, and to inflict heavy casualties on ʿAbbāsid troops sent to Oman. He was, however, eventually killed by these troops, reportedly together with 10,000 Omanīs. His rule was brief, but it is remembered in Omanī history as just and righteous, the precursor of the first Imamate, and al-Julandā himself is lauded as the best of all the subsequent imams.[111] After his death a period of unrest ensued, characterised by fragmentation and constant feuds. Despite the ʿAbbāsid victory it seems that no governors were sent to Oman.[112] Two leaders of the Julandā family, Muḥammad ibn Zāʾida and Rāshid b. Shādhān (or al-Naẓr), stand out in Ibāḍī historiography as oppressors, presumably because they acted as agents of the ʿAbbāsids.

the matter of the *ṣadaqa* tax); Muḥammad ibn Ismāʿīl al-Bukhārī, *al-Taʾrīkh al-kabīr*, ed. H. al-Nadwī, 8 vols. (Beirut, n.d.), vol. III, p. 79, vol. VI, p. 348; Sālimī, *Tuḥfa*, pp. 74–7; Sirḥān ibn Saʿīd ibn Sirḥān al-Izkiwī (attrib.), *Kapitel XXXIII der anonymen arabischen Chronik Kašf al-ǧumma al-ǧāmi li-ahbār al-umma*, ed. and trans. Hedwig Klein (Hamburg, 1938), pp. 11–15; Izkiwī (attrib.), *Annals* pp. 10–12; Anonymous, *Taʾrīkh*, pp. 47–51; ʿĀnī, *Taʾrīkh*, pp. 120–2; Sayyābī, *Isʿāf*, pp. 74–6; Shalabī, *Mawsūʿa*, pp. 231–2. On the Ibāḍiyya, see Lewicki, 'Ibāḍiyya', *EI2*, vol. III, p. 648.

109 ʿAbd al-Razzāq al-Ṣanʿānī, *Muṣannaf ʿAbd al-Razzāq*, ed. Ḥ. al-Aʿẓamī, 11 vols. (Beirut, 1403/1983), vol. X, p. 105.

110 ʿĀnī, *Taʾrīkh*, p. 121. On Yazīd see P. Crone, 'Muhallabids', *EI2*, vol. VII, p. 358.

111 Al-Ṭabarī, *Taʾrīkh*, vol. VII, pp. 462–3, cf. p. 353; Ibn Kathīr, *Bidāya*, vol. X, p. 57 (Julandā is identified here as leader of the Ṣufriyya, instead of the Ibāḍiyya); Izkiwī (attrib.), *Annals*, pp. 12–13; Anonymous, *Taʾrīkh*, pp. 54–5; Sālimī, *Tuḥfa*, pp. 88–102, 276; Casey Vine (ed.), *Oman*, pp. 164–5; Laura Veccia Vaglieri, 'L'Imāmato Ibāḍita dell' Oman', *Annali* (Istituto Universitario Orientale, Napoli), n.s. 3 (1949).

112 Only one governor is mentioned: see al-Ṭabarī, *Taʾrīkh*, vol. VIII, p. 204.

In 177/793 the Ibāḍīs succeeded in overcoming other powers and established a state. Their religious leaders elected a man of the Azdī Yaḥmad confederation as imam, and when he displeased them, they deposed him and chose another.[113] This pattern of government was relatively stable for about a century. Imams, mostly Yaḥmadīs (from either the Kharūṣ or the Fajḥ clan), ran a unified Imamate that extended from Baḥrayn to the Yemen, and that was also recognised by the Ibāḍī community of Ḥaḍramawt. Many imams reigned for long periods.[114] In its structure and ideas the Imamate differed considerably from the Caliphate. There was no ruling family and no hereditary succession. It was a tribal community in which the leader was elected by a group of elders (namely, religious scholars), took his decisions by consultation, had no privileged position, and had only limited authority to compel military service. The Imamate was intertwined with the tribal concepts and cultures, yet the imams were not merely tribal leaders, and the latter did not disappear from the scene.[115] Such a pattern of government would suggest instability and weakness, but the imams of the second/eighth and third/ninth century successfully repelled attacks by several enemies, among them invaders from India, and troops sent by Hārūn al-Rashīd (r. 170–93/786–809). Oman prospered in this period, mainly due to the role it played in international maritime trade. Not only did it serve as a depot but its trade also expanded overseas, in the Indian Ocean as well as on the East African coast. But stability was not to last. Contenders for power and for wealth, among them descendants of the ancient ruling family, the Julandā, repeatedly challenged the imams.[116] These internal struggles turned into a major civil war in the last third of the third/ninth century.

Oman from the third/ninth to the fifth/eleventh centuries

The civil war is usually portrayed simply as a struggle between the two factions that are known to have been rivals in many parts of the empire, namely the 'Southerners' ('Yaman') and the 'Northerners' (known variously as 'Qays', 'Muḍar' or 'Nizār'). In Oman the 'Southerners' meant in particular the Azd and the

113 Izkiwī (attrib.), *Annals*, pp. 13–14; Anonymous, *Ta'rīkh*, pp. 56–8; Sālimī, *Tuḥfa*, pp. 107–17; Wilkinson, *The imamate*, p. 9. Casey Vine (ed.), *Oman*, pp. 165–6.

114 Ten, twelve, eighteen and even thirty-five years: see Anonymous, *Ta'rīkh*, pp. 60, 62, 63, 67; Wilkinson, *The imamate*, pp. 9–10; Wilkinson., 'Bibliographical background', p. 137.

115 Wilkinson, *The imamate*, pp. 91–212.

116 Izkiwī (attrib.), *Annals*, pp. 14–19; Izkiwī (attrib.), *Kapitel*, pp. 18–27; Anonymous, *Ta'rīkh*, pp. 58–68; Wilkinson, 'Bibliographical background', p. 138; Casey Vine (ed.), *Oman*, pp. 168–9. For the attacks by Hārūn in 170/786 and 189/804, see Khalīfa, *Ta'rīkh*, vol. I, p. 447; al-Ṭabarī, *Ta'rīkh*, vol. VIII, p. 317; Sālimī, *Tuḥfa*, pp. 118–19.

'Northerners' meant in particular the Banū Sāma group. In actuality, however, the conflict was a complex matter that involved not only tribes, but also regions (the Bāṭina and the eastern valleys of Jabal al-Akhḍar as against the interior), as well as factions within the Ibāḍiyya. The caliph al-Muʿtaḍid and the governor of Baḥrayn were drawn into the struggle as well. The latter, Muḥammad b. Thawr (or Nūr, or Būr), conquered Oman in 280/893, wreaked devastation and caused many Azdīs to emigrate.[117] Thus ʿAbbāsid intervention in the civil war helped bring down the first Imamate of Oman.

The period that followed was extremely turbulent, and the sources are very confused. While tribal, ideological and regional motives stirred up internal conflicts, there was also a growing interest on the part of foreign powers in controlling the Gulf. The country was divided, the coastal area alternately occupied by the ʿAbbāsids, the Qarmaṭīs from Baḥrayn (who first invaded Oman in 318/930), the Ṣaffārids, the Buwayhids, and later the Saljūqs, while the inland tribes continued to elect imams or tribal chiefs, to fight one another, and to struggle against the foreign powers all at the same time. Imams and tribal chiefs were elected over various tribes and areas simultaneously, so that the authority of each was very limited and struggles continued incessantly. The Ibāḍiyya became increasingly divided between two schools, known as the Nizwā school and the Rustāq school, after their respective centres (Nizwā was the capital of the interior, Rustāq the capital of the Ghadaf, i.e. the eastern valleys of Jabal al-Akhḍar). Ostensibly the major divide was the question of blame for the major civil war of the third/ninth century, a matter that was never resolved.[118] An attempt to bridge the internal differences was made after 323/934 when the Ibāḍī scholars agreed to suspend further judgement and refrain from quarrelling among themselves. They then elected an imam, Rāshid b. al-Walīd of the Kinda tribal confederation (the majority of the imams were of the Azdī Kharūṣī group). Based in Nizwā, this imam is said to have gained wide recognition. However, he was subsequently deserted by his followers and

117 Izkiwī (attrib.), *Annals*, pp. 20–3; Izkiwī (attrib.), *Kapitel*, pp. 27–37; Anonymous, *Taʾrīkh*, pp. 68–74; Sālimī, *Tuḥfa*, pp. 196–263; ʿĀnī, *Taʾrīkh*, pp. 137–8; Shalabī, *Mawsūʿa*, pp. 741–2; Wilkinson, *The imamate*, pp. 9–10, 202–10; Wilkinson, 'Bibliographical background', p. 138; Casey Vine (ed.), *Oman*, pp. 170–1.

118 Izkiwī (attrib.), *Kapitel*, pp. 38, 40; Anonymous, *Taʾrīkh*, pp. 75–91; Sālimī, *Tuḥfa*, pp. 263–78, 288–94, see also 349, 352; Wilkinson, *The imamate*, pp. 11, 166–8, 201, 209, 349 note 20; Casey Vine (ed.), *Oman*, pp. 171–2. See also ibn Kathīr, *Bidāya*, vol. XI, p. 120: 'Oman's ruler' (*ṣāḥib*) sends presents to the ʿAbbāsid caliph, in 301/914, probably a token of submission. For a list of imams see Zambauer, *Muʿjam al-ansāb*, pp. 191–3 (they seem to be represented as a dynasty, which is misleading).

forced to capitulate to the sultan. The source mentions neither the date of these events nor the identity of the 'sultan'.[119]

In the fourth/tenth century there is mention of 'the ruler of Oman' (*ṣāḥib ʿUmān*), one Yūsuf b. Wajīh, a non-Ibāḍī who apparently controlled the coastal plain. Very little is known of him, although he almost conquered Baṣra in 331/943 and again in 340/951 (and perhaps also in 341/952).[120] In 354/965 Yūsuf's assassin and successor, his black *mawlā* Nāfiʿ, submitted to the Buwayhids, but the Omanīs rejected this move and turned to pay allegiance to the Qarmaṭīs of Hajar (Baḥrayn). Under nominal Qarmaṭī rule conflicts continued, among them clashes within the army between units of white soldiers against the black ones (Zanj, East African blacks who reportedly numbered 6,000 men).[121]

In 355/966 the Buwayhids conquered Oman, but they had to re-conquer it subsequently. It appears that their main objective was to destroy the maritime strength of the port of Ṣuḥār and to secure for themselves the route from the Gulf into the Indian Ocean. A major battle occurred in 362/972, when Zanj (blacks, presumably from the Omanī army) killed the Buwayhids' appointee, ʿUmar b. Nabhān, and appointed one Ibn Ḥallāj as a ruler. Buwayhid armies dispatched from Kirmān defeated the Zanj on land and at sea. Another Buwayhid army, sent against the inland Ibāḍiyya, was victorious as well, and caused the Ibāḍī imam to flee Nizwā for Yemen. In 394/1003 Bahāʾ al-Dawla, then ruler of the Buwayhid confederacy, appointed his friend and father-in-law, Abū Muḥammad b. Mukram, as governor. Thereafter members of this family ruled Oman for about half a century. They kept close relations with the Buwayhids, and were sometimes embroiled in their quarrels.[122] It appears,

119 Izkiwī (attrib.), *Annals*, pp. 26–30; Sālimī, *Tuḥfa*, pp. 279–85; Sayyābī, *Isʿāf*, p. 136; cf. Wilkinson, *The imamate*, pp. 210–12; Anonymous, *Taʾrīkh*, pp. 84–91.

120 Ibn al-Athīr, *Kāmil*, vol. VII, pp. 173, 241 (but on p. 185 he has Yūsuf assassinated already in 332/943); Ibn Kathīr, *Bidāya*, vol. XI, pp. 224, 225; Muḥammad ibn ʿAbd al-Malik al-Hamdānī, *Takmilat taʾrīkh al-Ṭabarī*, ed. A. Y. Kanʿān (Beirut, 1957), pp. 135, 165; Izkiwī (attrib.), *Kapitel*, p. 65 of the German text, Klein's note to p. 40.

121 Ibn al-Athīr, *Kāmil*, vol. VII, pp. 290–2; Sālimī, *Tuḥfa*, pp. 289–91; Casey Vine (ed.), *Oman*, pp. 174–5. See also Zambauer, *Muʿjam al-ansāb*, p. 193. The latter (p. 194) also mentions two rulers of Banū Sāma between 300 and 316, based only on ibn Khaldūn's *ʿIbar*.

122 Ibn al-Athīr, *Kāmil*, vol. VII, pp. 292–3, 348–9, 354–5, vol. VIII, pp. 14, 224, 233–4, 253; Sālimī, *Tuḥfa*, pp. 285–93, 318–20; Wilkinson, *The imamate*, pp. 10, 213, and p. 349 note 20. The latter seems to identify the Nabhānīs with the Mukramids. The Nabhānīs rose to power in the sixth/twelfth century, but Sālimī, *Tuḥfa*, p. 352 records an earlier phase of this dynasty (mentioning no dates), while omitting mention of the Mukramids. Zambauer omits mention of the Mukramids as well. Abū Muhammad ibn Mukram also served the Buwayhids outside Oman, and was deeply involved in Būyid politics: see e.g. ibn al-Athīr, *Kāmil*, vol. VII, p. 496, vol. VIII, pp. 137, 144–5, 166. See also Casey Vine (ed.), *Oman*, pp. 175–6.

however, that the dynasty mainly controlled the coastal plain, while Ibāḍī imams continued to be elected in the interior.[123] It is remarkable that Oman continued to be a centre for maritime trade connecting the Far East and Africa with the caliphate despite the unstable political conditions of the third/ninth and the fourth/tenth centuries. Ṣuḥār, and to a lesser extent Masqaṭ, served as centres for this trade and enjoyed prosperity.[124]

A special feature of the period from the end of the third/ninth to the middle of the sixth/twelfth century is the distinction made between different types of Ibāḍī imams. Some of them were recognised as leaders of offensives, in keeping with the Khārijī tradition (*imām ʿalā al-shirāʾ*) which meant that they were expected to wage *jihād* on non-Khārijites in order to spread the true faith. Others were not expected to engage in such activity, and pledged to lead only wars of defence (*imām ʿalā al-difāʿ*). It should also be noted that, although an imam's son would occasionally inherit his father's office, the Imamate was not hereditary in principle, and no dynasties were formed. The imams' authority was often contested by rivals from within, and challenged by outsiders too. Some regularly made themselves scarce whenever a representative of the real – that is, foreign – power happened to come to the country.[125]

According to *al-Kāmil* (a general history of the Muslim world, written by Ibn al-Athīr, d. 630/1233), by 442/1050 Oman was no longer ruled by the Mukramids, but by a Buwayhid governor, the son of Abū Kalījār, king of Fāris. This governor was defeated by the Khārijites, led by 'Ibn Rāshid'.[126] Ibn al-Athīr here apparently refers to the imam Rāshid b. Saʿīd, who was elected in Rustāq in 425/1033 (or later), remained in power until he died in 445/1053, and succeeded in driving the Buwayhids out of the coastal plain. The Imamate under him was a unified and powerful state that incorporated Ḥaḍramawt and expanded overseas as well, not only conducting trade but also propagating Ibāḍism.[127]

123 Sālimī, *Tuḥfa*, pp. 295, 304: al-Khalīl ibn Shādhān and Rāshid ibn Saʿīd were elected before 442/1050, while the Mukramids were still in power.

124 Muqaddasī, *Aḥsan al-taqāsīm*, p. 92; R. D. Bathurst, 'Maritime trade and imamate government: Two principal themes in the history of Oman to 1728', in D. Hopwood (ed.), *The Arabian Peninsula, society and politics* (London, 1972), pp. 92–3; on the traded commodities see ʿĀnī, *Taʾrīkh*, pp. 147–68, on the extent of the trade pp. 178–208.

125 Izkiwī (attrib.), *Annals*, pp. 20–30; Izkiwī (attrib.), *Kapitel*, pp. 27–40; Anonymous, *Taʾrīkh*, pp. 75–91. Cf. the distinction made (for other reasons) between Zaydī imams who were both warriors and scholars, and those who were only warriors: Landau-Tasseron, 'Zaydī imams'.

126 Ibn al-Athīr, *Kāmil*, vol. VIII, p. 295; Sālimī, *Tuḥfa*, pp. 293–4, 319 (quoting ibn al-Athīr).

127 Sālimī, *Tuḥfa*, pp. 304–14; Wilkinson, *The imamate*, p. 210; Wilkinson, 'Bibliographical background', p. 139. Ibn Kathīr, *Bidāya*, vol. XII, p. 61, refers in one sentence to the imam's success, among the events of the year 442/1050.

The Imamate collapsed under the pressures of both foreign powers and internal quarrels. In 455/1063 the coast came under the nominal rule of the Saljūqs. The Omanīs, however, remained largely independent in their activities overseas. More destructive than this occupation was the edict issued in 443/1052 by the Rustāq school which declared their opponents to be renegades, thus perpetuating the rift between the schools. As a result, many tribes abandoned the Ibāḍī creed, tribal and regional wars increased, and rival imams and local non-Ibāḍī rulers constantly sought to establish their power.[128] The death of the imam Muḥammad b. Khanbash in 557/1161 marks the beginning of a period that is often considered an interregnum, but Ibāḍī imams continued to be elected, albeit intermittently, until the ninth/fifteenth century.[129] A non-Ibāḍī local dynasty of the Azd tribe, the Nabhānīs, seized power at the end of the sixth/twelfth century.[130]

Central and eastern Arabia: Najd, Yamāma and medieval Baḥrayn

These three regions extended from the eastern border of the Ḥijāz, through the central plateau and as far as the Persian Gulf. Not only are they adjacent, but they also were often under the same regime or influence, and certain tribes, such as Banū ʿĀmir and Tamīm, were dispersed over all three. Yamāma is in fact often considered to be geographically a part of Najd.[131] It may be added that events in Islamic Baḥrayn are much better documented than those in Najd and Yamāma.

Central and eastern Arabia from the first/seventh to the third/ninth century

Najd is the remotest and least known of these regions. At the beginning of the seventh century CE it was mainly populated by numerous nomadic and semi-nomadic tribal groups. Most of these opposed the Prophet, but some joined him at various stages of his career, in particular after he had conquered Mecca in 8/630. Certain Najdī groups, including some that had been converted before Muḥammad's death, participated in the so-called 'Wars of Apostasy' of 11–12/632–3. After these events all the tribes

128 Sālimī, *Tuḥfa*, pp. 320–42; Wilkinson, *The imamate*, pp. 210–12; Wilkinson, 'Bibliographical background', pp. 139–40; Casey Vine (ed.), *Oman*, pp. 176–8.

129 Izkiwī (attrib.), *Kapitel*, pp. 15–18; Anonymous, *Ta'rīkh*, pp. 60–93; Shalabī, *Mawsūʿa*, pp. 234–6.

130 Casey Vine (ed.), *Oman*, pp. 178–81; Naboodah, 'Banū Nabhān'; Zambauer, *Muʿjam ansāb*, p. 194.

131 A. Grohman, 'Nadjd', *EI2*, vol. VII, p. 864; U. M. al-Juhany, *Najd before the Salafī reform movement* (Reading and Riyadh, 2002), pp. 23ff.; Shalabī, *Mawsūʿa*, pp. 44–6, 80.

and their domains became part of the Muslim state. The sovereignty of the state in the area is perhaps best illustrated by the *ḥimās*, the large pasture areas that the state confiscated from Najdī tribes for its own use. The best known of these are Ḍariyya and al-Rabadha. The system, established by ʿUmar b. al-Khaṭṭāb, only fell out of use in the middle of the second / eighth century, after the advent of the ʿAbbāsids.[132]

To the east of Najd lay Yamāma, a densely populated, cultivated area. Its main towns were Ḥajr and al-Jaww, also called al-Khiḍrima. The importance of pre-Islamic Yamāma lay in the fact that it supplied wheat to the Ḥijāz, and that trade routes from Iraq, the Yemen and Mecca ran through it. In the Prophet's day the dominant tribe, Ḥanīfa, was ruled by Hawdha b. ʿAlī, a Christian loyal to Persia. After Hawdha's death in 8 / 630, his successor, Musaylima, offered staunch opposition to Islam, both during the Prophet's lifetime and after it. Yamāma was conquered by the caliph's armies in 11 / 632, though only with great difficulty.

The eastern part, extending as far as the western shores of the Persian Gulf, was known in medieval Islam as al-Ḥasā, al-Aḥsāʾ, Hajar and Baḥrayn (to be distinguished from the island of Baḥrayn). The precise meaning of these terms and the boundaries of the regions to which they refer cannot be determined. The names al-Ḥasā and Hajar refer both to the entire region and to specific towns. Al-Ḥasā sometimes designates the oases part of the region, but the southern part of these, which lies on the shores of the Persian Gulf, is known as al-Qaṭīf.[133] For the sake of convenience I shall refer to the region by a single term, Baḥrayn.

At the time of the Prophet the inhabitants of Baḥrayn comprised mainly groups of the Arab confederations of ʿAbd al-Qays, Bakr and Tamīm, most of whom lived off agriculture, fishing, textile production, pearl diving and trade. Many were Christians or Zoroastrians, and some were Jews. The region was under Persian rule, the Persians being represented by a local Tamīmī, al-Mundhir b. Sāwā. His clan was apparently under heavy Persian influence, and its members were known by the mysterious appellation *asbadhiyyūn*, usually rendered as 'horse-worshippers'. Persian troops were stationed in al-Qaṭīf, but they did not offer any resistance to Muḥammad. Reportedly the local ruler was converted to Islam after negotiations with the Prophet, and the

132 Al-Rāshid, *al-Rabadha*, pp. 2–4, see also the references in note 139 below.
133 Ḥamad al-Jāsir, *al-Muʿjam al-jughrāfī li-l-bilād al-ʿArabiyya al-Suʿūdiyya*, 3 vols. (Riyadh, 1399–1401 / 1979–81), vol. I, p. 31; F. S. Vidal, *The oasis of al-Ḥasā* (Dhahran, 1955), pp. 4–9; F. S. Vidal, 'al-Ḥasā', *EI2*, vol. III, p. 237; G. Rentz, 'Ḳaṭīf', *EI2*, vol. IV, p. 763.

inhabitants either followed suit or became subject to the poll-tax. Al-Mundhir retained his post until he died, shortly after the Prophet. Names of the Prophet's appointees to Baḥrayn are mentioned as well.[134]

After the Prophet's death the 'Wars of Apostasy' encompassed almost every settlement in Baḥrayn. Troops sent by Abū Bakr, reinforced by loyal groups from Yamāma, succeeded in suppressing them. Some Persian resistance persisted until about 19/640, but most Arab tribesmen converted and left for the conquests and the conquered areas.

The Rāshidūn appointed Companions of high standing as governors of Baḥrayn. The first of them, already appointed by the Prophet, was the Meccan al-ʿAlāʾ b. al-Ḥaḍramī, who served until 16/637. Administrative divisions, however, were not rigid. Baḥrayn and Yamāma sometimes constituted one division, and at other times Oman and Baḥrayn, or the Yemen and Baḥrayn, were joined under a single governor, who would reside in one place and appoint representatives to the others. Thus, although adjacent, the three regions were attached to different centres in this period. When Muʿāwiya came to power in 40/661, Yamāma was attached to Medina whereas Baḥrayn and Oman were administratively part of the Ḥijāz. Muʿāwiya at first appointed to Baḥrayn one of his own relatives, but later he added it, as well as Oman, to the jurisdiction of his powerful governor in Iraq, Ziyād b. Abīhi. His reason for doing this was, perhaps, that it was easier to control eastern Arabia from Iraq than from western Arabia. Administration in Iraq was more developed, and military power stationed there was much superior to that present in Arabia. Henceforth the governors of Iraq often shouldered the responsibility of appointing representatives to Baḥrayn, or to Baḥrayn and Yamāma, or to Baḥrayn and Oman.[135]

The importance of Baḥrayn lay especially in its location: in the Rāshidūn period it was a convenient base for raids into Persia. Later it received attention as lying on the road from Iraq to the holy places in the Ḥijāz. It also played a part in the maritime trade with the Far East, although Oman's role in this trade

134 References for all three regions: Yaʿqūbī, *Taʾrīkh*, vol. II, pp. 76, 82; al-Ṭabarī, *Taʾrīkh*, vol. III, pp. 137, 147, 301; Yāqūt, *Muʿjam al-buldān*, vol. I, p. 172; Dhahabī, *Siyar*, vol. I, pp. 261, 263; Muḥammad ibn Mukram ibn Manẓūr, *Lisān al-ʿArab*, 15 vols. (Beirut, n.d.), vol. III, p. 493; Jāsir, *Muʿjam*, vol. I, pp. 48–52, 56–7; Shalabī, *Mawsūʿa*, pp. 412–15; M. F. von Oppenheim, *Die Beduinen*, vol. III, ed. W. Caskel (Wiesbaden, 1952), pp. 7–10 and *passim*; Juhany, *Najd*, pp. 39–42.

135 Ibn Ḥajar, *Iṣāba*, vol. I, p. 34 (s.v. al-Aḥwaṣ ibn ʿAbd), see also vol. II, p. 457; Balādhurī, *Ansāb*, p. 126; al-Ṭabarī, *Taʾrīkh*, vol. V, p. 217; Ibn al-Athīr, *Kāmil*, vol. IV, p. 367; ʿAlī, *Ḥijāz*, p. 293; Ḥamad al-Jāsir, 'Wulāt al-Aḥsāʾ fī al-ʿahd al-Umawiyy', *al-ʿArab*, 1 (1966–7). See also p. 401 above for contradictory information on administration.

increasingly superseded that of Baḥrayn. Yamāma and Baḥrayn also supplied the Ḥijāz with grain, and were a source of revenue for the caliphate.[136] During Muʿāwiya's reign Baḥrayn yielded 15 million *dirhams*, and benefited from investments in agriculture and infrastructure, as did Yamāma and other parts of the Arabian Peninsula. Some such investments in Najd were made already by the Rāshidūn, mostly connected with the *ḥimās*.[137]

Not much is known about central and eastern Arabia during the Umayyad period, except that it became the theatre of tribal hostilities, often under the Khārijite banner. According to one report, a local Tamīmī chief, ʿUmayr b. Sulmiyy, took control of Yamāma during the first civil war.[138] The Khārijite Najda b. ʿĀmir rose in Yamāma during the second civil war and, supported by the local tribes of Bakr, took control of Baḥrayn (as well as Ḥaḍramawt and Ṭāʾif) from 67/686. Muṣʿab b. al-Zubayr, governor of Iraq for his brother ʿAbd Allāh (r. from Mecca 64–73/683–92), continually attacked Baḥrayn, but to no avail. Najda was killed in 72/691 by another Khārijite leader, Abū Fudayk. The latter's revolt was suppressed the next year by Umayyad troops from Iraq, with great difficulty and at the cost of 6,000 lives on the rebels' side. Further Khārijite revolts occurred in 79/698, 86/705 and 105/723. The leader of the revolt of 105/723, Masʿūd al-ʿAbdī, is said to have ruled Baḥrayn and Yamāma for nineteen years, until the Umayyad representative to Yamāma killed him and vanquished his followers. Throughout the Marwānid period Baḥrayn and Yamāma remained under the jurisdiction of the governor of Iraq, who would appoint sub-governors and send troops to combat rebels.[139]

136 The Rāshidūn period in all three regions (including the *ridda*): Yaʿqūbī, *Taʾrīkh*, vol. II, pp. 131, 134, 138, 153, 161, 201; Balādhurī, *Futūḥ*, pp. 90–5, 378, 420; al-Ṭabarī, *Taʾrīkh*, vol. III, pp. 301–13, 427, 479, vol. IV, pp. 39, 79, vol. V, p. 155; Yāqūt, *Muʿjam al-buldān*, vol. I, p. 430, vol. III, p. 113, vol. IV, pp. 227, 455; Jāsir, *Muʿjam*, vol. I, pp. 69–75; Ḥamad al-Jāsir, *Madīnat al-Riyāḍ ʿabra aṭwār al-taʾrīkh* (Riyadh, 1386/1966), pp. 52–60; Shalabī, *Mawsūʿa*, pp. 416–19; Oppenheim, *Beduinen*, vol. III, pp. 10–13; E. Shoufani, *al-Riddah and the Muslim conquest of Arabia* (Toronto and Beirut, 1975), pp. 112–34; M. J. Kister, 'The struggle against Musaylima', *JSAI*, 27 (2002). The raids from Baḥrayn into Persia may have been initiated by the governor rather than the caliph: see Ibn Kathīr, *Bidāya*, vol. VII, p. 84. On maritime trade: Hourani, *Arab seafaring*, pp. 64–76; ʿĀnī, *Taʾrīkh*, pp. 175–9.

137 Yaʿqūbī, *Taʾrīkh*, vol. II, p. 233; Jāsir, *Muʿjam*, vol. I, pp. 75–6; Oppenheim, *Beduinen*, vol. III, p. 12; Juhany, *Najd*, p. 42.

138 Hamdānī, *Ṣifat*, p. 254, but see below note 140.

139 Yaʿqūbī, *Taʾrīkh*, vol. II, pp. 272–3; Khalīfa, *Taʾrīkh*, vol. I, pp. 267, 278, 279, 313, 359, 336; al-Ṭabarī, *Taʾrīkh*, vol. V, p. 619, vol. VI, pp. 174, 913; Ibn al-Athīr, *Kāmil*, vol. IV, pp. 366, 491; Yūsuf ibn al-Taghribirdī, *al-Nujūm al-ẓāhira fī mulūk Miṣr wa-l-Qāhira*, 12 vols. (Cairo, n.d.), vol. I, p. 199; Jāsir, *Muʿjam*, vol. I, pp. 76–7; Jāsir,, 'Wulat al-Aḥsāʾ'; Shalabī, *Mawsūʿa*, pp. 420–4; Oppenheim, *Beduinen*, vol. III, p. 13.

Rebellions were not motivated only by religion. In 126/744 a rebel of the Banū Ḥanīfa in Yamāma simply wanted his country back and expelled the Umayyad governor. Yamāma was left to tribal feuds for a time, until another governor was sent from Iraq. As a result of these and other tribal feuds in the Umayyad period, the Banū Ḥanīfa completely lost their pre-Islamic eminence, a process already begun upon their defeat in the Wars of Apostasy. Najd was largely left to its own feuds, and was hardly involved in the major political struggles of the Islamic world.[140]

With the shift of the capital to Iraq in 132/750, the pilgrim road to the Ḥijāz through eastern Arabia grew in importance and attracted large investments by the caliphs and members of their family. The pilgrim road from Kūfa is named Darb Zubayda after al-Rashīd's wife, who expended great effort and wealth on it. The eastern region of the Peninsula, which had been depleted by the migration of the tribes for the conquests, was now filled again with tribes coming from the south and the west. Villages along the route prospered, and some tribal groups became sedentarised through a long process that appears to have lasted into the third/ninth century.[141] In contrast to Umayyad practice, the first ʿAbbāsid caliphs appointed the governors of the region themselves, often choosing their own family members. Baḥrayn still yielded considerable revenues, and occasionally it was administratively attached to provinces in southern Iraq and/or southern Persia, rather than to Yamāma. However, a governor's jurisdiction would occasionally comprise Yamāma, Mecca, Medina and Ṭāʾif (in the years 163–4/779–80), Yamāma, Baḥrayn and the route to Mecca (in 236/850), or Yamāma, Baḥrayn and Baṣra (in 252/866). The appointment of governors remained in the hands of the caliphs; but the fact that al-Mutawakkil (r. 232–47/847–61) appointed to Baḥrayn (and Yamāma) a poet who had praised him, perhaps indicates that he despaired of holding on to a region that had grown too difficult to control.[142]

As early as 151/768 or 152/769 the people of Yamāma and Baḥrayn killed al-Manṣūr's governor, and insurrections during al-Mahdī's reign (r. 158–69/775–85) are mentioned as well. These revolts were harshly suppressed, and the government apparently continued to have fairly firm

140 Ibn al-Athīr, *Kāmil*, vol. IV, pp. 491–3; Jāsir, *Madīnat*, pp. 65–7; Juhany, *Najd*, pp. 40, 42–3; Shalabī, *Mawsūʿa*, p. 95. The name of the rebel in 126/743 is al-Muhayr ibn Sulmiyy, so perhaps the unique report of Hamdānī (above note 138) is a distortion of this one.

141 Oppenheim, *Beduinen*, vol. III, pp. 13–14; Juhany, *Najd*, p. 42; Saʿd al-Rāshid, *Darb Zubayda: The pilgrim road from Kūfa to Mecca* (Riyadh, 1980).

142 Al-Ṭabarī, *Taʾrīkh*, vol. VII, pp. 459, 465, vol. VIII, pp. 134, 149, 151, vol. IX, pp. 140, 183; Ibn al-Athīr, *Kāmil*, vol. IV, p. 493, vol. V, p. 199, vol. VI, pp. 140, 183; Sinjārī, *Manāʾiḥ*, vol. II, pp. 86–7, 90–1; Juhany, *Najd*, p. 44; Shalabī, *Mawsūʿa*, pp. 62–3; Jāsir, *Muʿjam*, vol. I, pp. 79–81.

control until the third/ninth century. By this period Bedouin groups of the Banū ʿĀmir had replaced the once-powerful Tamīm and Bakr in central and eastern Arabia. These newly arrived groups were continually disturbing the peace in these regions, and the caliph al-Wāthiq (r. 227–32/842–7) sent against them armies from Baghdad, headed by his Turkish general Bughā al-Kabīr. He was soundly defeated in Najd in 230/845 and 232/847, but eventually had success against these tribes and others, in Najd as well as in the Ḥijāz.[143]

Following these events the ʿAbbāsids allowed Yamāma and Baḥrayn to fragment and be ruled by several local tribal chiefs. An ʿAbbāsid governor is still mentioned in Baḥrayn in 280/893 as involved in bringing down the imamate of Oman.[144] But, it was chiefs of the ancient local tribes who succeeded, albeit with great difficulty, in expelling the ʿAlid pretender who mustered support in the region in 249/863. This pretender, ʿAlī b. Muḥammad, started his mission in Baḥrayn, reportedly because 'its people were stupid and easily deceived'. After his defeat at the hand of the local chiefs he left for Baṣra to become the leader of the Zanj revolt that wreaked havoc in Iraq between 255–70/868–83.[145] In Yamāma the local chiefs were marginalised by the Ukhayḍirs, an ʿAlid family that came from the Ḥijāz and ruled Yamāma from the middle of the third/ninth century. The large emigration from Yamāma that is reported in the third/ninth century is imputed by cetain sources to the evil regime of this family.[146]

The revolt of ʿAlī b. Muḥammad, 'Lord of the Zanj', was but a precursor to the other serious threat to the caliphate in Baghdad, namely, the extreme Shīʿī movement called the Qarmaṭī.

The Qarmaṭīs

The foundation of the Qarmaṭī state is shrouded in mystery. Some sources describe the founder, Abū Saʿīd al-Jannābī, as a poor Baṣran corn measurer who staged a revolt at the head of the remnants of the Zanj. Others connect him with clandestine activity of extremist Shīʿīs begun in Baḥrayn a few years

143 Yaʿqūbī, *Taʾrīkh*, vol. II, pp. 385, 396; al-Ṭabarī, *Taʾrīkh*, vol. VIII, p. 39, vol. IX, pp. 129–35, 146–50; Juhany, *Najd*, pp. 44–5; Oppenheim, *Beduinen*, vol. III, p. 14.

144 See above.

145 Dhahabī, *Siyar*, vol. XIII, pp. 132–6; Ibn al-Athīr, *Kāmil*, vol. VI, pp. 206–7; Shalabī, *Mawsūʿa*, pp. 431–2; Oppenheim, *Beduinen*, vol. III, p. 15. For the 'kings' of al-Yamāma see also Hamdānī, *Ṣifat*, p. 276.

146 Jāsir, *Madīnat*, pp. 71–2. On the Ukhayḍirs see ibid., pp. 69–78; Ibn Ḥazm, *Jamhara*, pp. 47–8; Sakhāwī, *Tuḥfa*, vol. I, p. 309; Juhany, *Najd*, pp. 45–7; Zambauer, *Muʿjam al-ansāb*, p. 177, records their end at the hand of the Qarmaṭīs, but see below and above (p. 409).

before his appearance.[147] He was probably a missionary sent by the extremist Shīʿite agent Ḥamdān Qarmaṭ. When the latter seceded from the Ismāʿīlī Fāṭimids who came to power in North Africa in 296/909, Abū Saʿīd may have remained loyal to them, but the information about his conduct is contradictory. Be that as it may, Abū Saʿīd gained support among certain Bedouin tribes in Baḥrayn, mainly the ʿUqyal and other sections of the Banū ʿĀmir, who had migrated there during the third/ninth century. Abū Saʿīd first conquered al-Qaṭīf, then the other oases and towns of Baḥrayn, as well as Ṭāʾif and a few oases in Najd. Troops sent by the caliph al-Muʿtaḍid could not rout him, and he continued his military activity after he had consolidated his reign. He raided Oman to extract tribute and booty, and extended Qarmaṭī influence (but not direct rule) to Yamāma, which was ruled by the Ukhayḍirs. His rule, begun in 286/899, ended with his assassination in 301/913.[148]

The great exploits of the Baḥrayn Qarmaṭīs were initiated by Abū Saʿīd's son, Abū Ṭāhir, who took the reins of power in 305/918 or 310/923 and ruled until he died in 332/943. He subordinated the Ukhayḍirs of Yamāma, then carried onto the heart of the caliphate, after years of peaceful relations with the ʿAbbāsids. He captured Baṣra in 311/923, raided Iraq and the pilgrim caravans repeatedly, conquered Kūfa in 313/925 and almost reached Baghdad by 317/929, after having defeated a large ʿAbbāsid army. In these campaigns he was leading the nomads of the Arabian Peninsula into the Fertile Crescent to plunder in the traditional Bedouin way, but he also received support from Qarmaṭīs in southern Iraq, apparently on an ideological basis. The strength of his army is estimated at between 1,500 and 2,700 troops, but the ʿAbbāsid government failed in vanquishing it, and attempted to secure peace by other means. In 327/939 it was proposed that Abū Ṭāhir act as the pilgrimage protector in exchange for tribute and a fee to be paid by the pilgrims. He accepted the offer, but did not refrain from raiding Iraq in subsequent years. After the mid-fourth/tenth century, the Buwayhids avoided Qarmaṭī hostility by granting them extensive privileges in addition to those arising from their

147 ʿAbd al-Ḥayy ibn Aḥmad ibn al-ʿImād, *Shadharāt al-dhahab fī akhbār man dhahab*, 4 vols. (Beirut, n.d.), vol. I, p. 192; Ibn al-Athīr, *Kāmil*, vol. VI, pp. 396–7; Muḥammad al-Khalīfa Mayy, *Min Sawād al-Kūfa ilā al-Baḥrayn* (Beirut, 1999), pp. 239–43; Suhayl Zakkār, *al-Jāmiʿ fī akhbār al-Qarāmiṭa fī al-Aḥsāʾ, al-Shām, al-Irāq, al-Yaman* (Damascus, 1407/1987), p. 147.

148 Al-Ṭabarī, *Taʾrīkh*, vol. X, pp. 71, 75, 104; Ibn al-Athīr, *Kāmil*, vol. VI, pp. 419, 482; Ibn Kathīr, *Bidāya*, vol. XI, p. 83; Yāqūt, *Muʿjam al-buldān*, vol. IV, p. 359; Maqrīzī, *Ittiʿāẓ*, pp. 214–21; Mayy, *Min Sawād al-Kūfa*, pp. 244–8, 265–8; Zakkār, *al-Jāmiʿ*, pp. 460–8, 541–7; Oppenheim, *Beduinen*, vol. III, pp. 14, 15–17; W. Madelung, 'The Fāṭimids and the Qarmaṭīs of Baḥrayn', in F. Daftary (ed.), *Medieval Ismāʿīlī history and thought* (Cambridge, 1996), pp. 22–9 (the last two references include discussions of the origins of the Qarmaṭī movement as a whole).

protection of the caravans. Among other things, the Qarmaṭīs received land holdings in southern Iraq and kept a permanent representative in Baghdad.[149]

Abū Ṭāhir's murderous and sacrilegious activities reached their peak in 317/929, when he conquered Mecca, massacred its population and removed the black stone from the Kaʿba. It was kept in the Qarmaṭī capital for twenty-two years, and was only returned when the ʿAbbāsid caliph paid a large ransom. The raids on the pilgrims and the robbery of the black stone reflected Abū Ṭāhir's belief that the end of the Islamic era was nearing with the imminent advent of the *mahdī*. In 319/931 this belief led him to transfer all powers to a Persian pseudo-prophet, and even to deify him. This impostor reportedly committed murders and other atrocities, and tried to rid himself of the ruling family. Encouraged by his minister, Ibn Sanbar, Abū Ṭāhir removed him and his influence from Baḥrayn, and re-established state control. In view of Abū Ṭāhir's career it is not surprising that Muslim historians were not satisfied with reporting the shocking events, but imputed additional atrocities to him, such as making permissible homosexuality and intercourse between brothers and sisters. It is also reported that the Fāṭimid caliph tried to induce him to burn mosques and Qurʾān copies. Less hostile reports have it that the Qarmaṭī government failed to build mosques or hold Friday prayers.[150] In actuality, the order and justice that prevailed within the Qarmaṭī state have evoked the admiration, if not the envy, of non-Qarmaṭīs. The state was run by descendants of the founder, Abū Saʿīd, either collectively or as a council acting at the ruler's side. The council included other dignitaries, chief among whom were the Sanbars, a local family, perhaps of humble origin, who had supported the Qarmaṭī state from its inception. The revenues were distributed with a view to the welfare of the inhabitants at large. The state took care of production, education, security and trade in a way that has led certain modern scholars to describe it as 'communist', and even to impute to it a liberal attitude towards women. It may also be noted that crises of succession, rebellions and civil wars were much less frequent than in other dynasties.[151] This is proved not only by the sparsity of

149 Maqrīzī, *Ittiʿāẓ*, pp. 239–46; Mayy, *Min Sawād al-Kūfa*, pp. 269–92; Zakkār, *al-Jāmiʿ*, pp. 154, 403, 489–501, 517; W. Madelung, 'Ḳarmaṭī', *EI2*, vol. IV, p. 660; Juhany, *Najd*, pp. 47–9.

150 Fāsī, *Shifāʾ*, pp. 346–7; Ibn al-ʿImād, *Shadharāt al-dhahab*, vol. I, p. 305; Yāqūt, *Muʿjam al-buldān*, vol. II, p. 224; Dhahabī, *Siyar*, vol. XV, pp. 320–5; Ibn al-Taghribirdī, *Nujūm*, vol. III, p. 287; Ahdal, *Tuḥfa*, p. 165; Mayy, *Min Sawād al-Kūfa*, pp. 293–307; Zakkār, *al-Jāmiʿ*, pp. 149, 152–3, 503–7, 595; Oppenheim, *Beduinen*, vol. III, p. 17; Madelung, 'The Fāṭimids', pp. 21–2, 30–3, 37, 46–9.

151 Cases of internal division: Madelung, 'The Fāṭimids', pp. 38–40; Zakkār, *al-Jāmiʿ*, pp. 155–6, 225–6, cf. Shalabī, *Mawsūʿa*, pp. 462, 465. Descriptions of the state: Nāṣer-e Khosraw, *Travels*, pp. 86–90; Mayy, *Min Sawād al-Kūfa*, pp. 226–8, 245–58; Zakkār, *al-Jāmiʿ*, pp. 148–51; Oppenheim, *Beduinen*, vol. III, p. 18; Madelung, 'Ḳarmaṭī'. List of rulers: Zambauer, *Muʿjam al-ansāb*, p. 180.

accounts about such crises, but also by the fact that the ruler and his army stayed away for long periods of time, presumably without fear of rebellion.

The Qarmaṭīs of Baḥrayn attacked not only Iraq but also Syria – aided, and perhaps propmpted to action, by local Bedouin. Al-Ḥasan al-Aʿṣam, a nephew of Abū Ṭāhir who was leading the Qarmaṭī armies between 357–66/968–77, took Damascus from the Ikhshīdīs in 357/968 and extracted annual tribute of 300,000 *dīnārs*. This payment was later stopped by the Fāṭimids when they conquered parts of Syria in 359/970. Al-Ḥasan al-Aʿṣam then fought the Fāṭimids in Syria, sometimes cooperating with the Ikhshīdīs, his former enemies. He also invaded Egypt, supported by the ʿAbbāsid caliph, to whom he paid allegiance despite his own sectarian persuasion. The Fāṭimids, however, wrested Syria from the Qarmaṭīs, and bought their peace in Egypt in 363/974. Hostilities between the Fāṭimids and the Qarmaṭīs on Syrian soil were resumed on the death of the Fāṭmid caliph al-Muʿizz in 365/976. Al-Ḥasan al-Aʿṣam formed an alliance with the Turkish warlord Alftakīn, who had taken Damascus a few years earlier. After a few initial victories this coalition was defeated. Al-Ḥasan died in 366/977, and his successor continued the struggle against the Fāṭimids until a new peace treaty was signed in 368/978. This treaty secured Qarmaṭī allegiance to the Fāṭimids in exchange for annual tribute.[152]

Little is known of the Qarmaṭīs of Baḥrayn from the end of the fourth/tenth century. They may have vacillated between the ʿAbbāsids and the Fāṭimids, and attempted military adventures at the same time.[153] These adventures eventually cost them their influence in Iraq and their privilege of escorting the pilgrim caravans. In 373/983 they attacked Baṣra, and in 375/985 they occupied Kūfa. The Buwayhid government in Iraq felt prompted to act, and defeated them. The Qarmaṭīs now began to lose the support of the Bedouins who had followed them to campaigns and to the gain of booty. Moreover, Baḥrayn itself fell prey to Bedouin attacks, and the Qarmaṭīs suffered defeats at their hands as well (as in 378/988, the raid of the ʿUqaylīs led by al-Aṣfar). Much weakened, they remained to rule Baḥrayn until they began losing their domains to local rebels, from the first half of the fifth/eleventh century. In the 430s/1040s Abū al-Bahlūl, a chief of the local ʿAbd al-Qays tribe, took the island of Uwāl and destroyed the port of al-ʿUqayr (on the mainland). The Qarmaṭīs suffered another major defeat at his hand in a naval battle off al-Qaṭīf, in 450/1058. By this time they had lost their influence in

152 Maqrīzī, *Ittiʿāẓ*, pp. 177–9, 181–2, 247–65; Mayy, *Min Sawād al-Kūfa*, pp. 307–20; Zakkār, *al-Jāmiʿ*, pp. 226–44, 401–2, 508–17, 528–32, 565–83, 595–8, 606; Shalabī, *Mawsūʿa*, pp. 455–60; Madelung, 'Ḳarmaṭī'. Note the contradictory reports about al-Aʿṣam's correspondence and relations with the Fāṭimids.

153 Ibn Kathīr, *Bidāya*, vol. XI, p. 311; Madelung, 'Ḳarmaṭī'.

Yamāma, and the Ukhayḍirs were completely independent of them. The traveller Nāṣir-i Khusraw presumably refers to the Ukhayḍirs when he states (in the 440s/1050s) that Yamāma was ruled by a strong dynasty that relied on three or four hundred mounted soldiers. Notwithstanding these events and processes, the same traveller describes Baḥrayn as a prosperous state run with equity and efficiency, based on the labour of 30,000 slaves and on military power of 20,000 soldiers.

The Qarmaṭī state came to an end in 470/1077, brought down by a tribal chief from the ʿAbd al-Qays of Baḥrayn, ʿAbd Allāh b. ʿAlī al-ʿUyūnī. The new regime was formally subject to the Ismāʿīlī Ṣulayḥīs of the Yemen, and stayed in power until the seventh/thirteenth century.[154]

The policy and exploits of the Qarmaṭīs during the fourth–fifth/tenth–eleventh centuries boosted the wave of nomad migrations from the Peninsula into the Fertile Crescent and Egypt, apparently set in motion by droughts. No less importantly, they caused huge damage to settlements along the pilgrim routes and to agriculture in large areas of the Peninsula. Among other places, the town of al-Rabadha was destroyed and deserted. Yamāma under the Ukhayḍirs was still relatively prosperous in the fourth–fifth/tenth–eleventh centuries, but in general central and eastern Arabia did not recover with the waning of the Qarmaṭīs of Baḥrayn.[155] Events in Yamāma and Najd between the fifth/eleventh and the eighth/fourteenth centuries are very poorly known. The regions appear to have been fragmented and constantly engaged in tribal feuds, mostly unattractive to external powers, save sometimes to the rulers of Baḥrayn.[156] It is also worthy of note that in general, eastern Arabia contributed very little, if anything, to Islamic scholarship.[157]

The Arabian Peninsula of the first–fifth/seventh–eleventh centuries was a place of many variations. Its society – both nomad and settled – and its culture, were mostly tribal, yet the different regions followed various ideologies and various forms of political order. Sunnīs, Khārijites and Shīʿites of many kinds, centralised regimes, petty dynasties and tribal polities, local and foreign powers, all contributed to the complex history of Arabia in this period.

154 Ibn al-ʿImād, *Shadharāt al-dhahab*, vol. II, p. 55; Maqrīzī, *Ittiʿāẓ*, p. 68; Ibn al-Taghribirdī, *Nujūm*, vol. IV, p. 74; Nāṣer-e Khosraw, *Travels*, pp. 86–90; Mayy, *Min Sawād al-Kūfa*, pp. 321–3; Shalabī, *Mawsūʿa*, pp. 462–3, 468–9; Zakkār, *al-Jāmiʿ*, pp. 517, 583; Madelung, 'Ḳarmaṭī'; Madelung, 'The Fāṭimids', pp. 34–5, the question of the Qarmaṭīs' allegiance or otherwise to the Fāṭimids is discussed in detail throughout this article; Oppenheim, *Beduinen*, vol. III, pp. 17–19; M. Canard, 'al-Ḥasan al-Aʿṣam', *EI2*, vol. III, p. 246.

155 Juhany, *Najd*, pp. 42, 47–9. On the damages to the pilgrim road see al-Rāshid, *Darb Zubayda*, pp. 47–52; al-Rāshid, *al-Rabadha*, p. 11.

156 Shalabī, *Mawsūʿa*, pp. 48–59, 63, 81–3, 91; Jāsir, *Madīnat*, p. 79.

157 See Ḥamad al-Jāsir, 'al-Ḥafṣī wa-kitābuhu ʿan al-Yamāma', *al-ʿArab*, 1 (1967); A. b. ʿA. Āl Mubarak, ''Ulamā' al-Aḥsā' wa-makānatuhum al-ʿilmiyya wa-l-adabiyya', *al-ʿArab*, 17, 1 (1982–3), pp. 361–83; Cook, 'The historians'.

11

The Islamic east

ELTON L. DANIEL

The concepts of both the 'Islamic east' and 'regionalism' are nebulous enough to require some definition for the purposes of this discussion. In the case of the 'Islamic east' there are two terms sometimes found in Muslim geographical and historical works that could be understood as referring to such an area: *al-sharq* and *al-mashriq*.[1] *Al-sharq*, the east in general, should probably be understood, at least in the conceptual framework of most medieval Muslim geographers, as referring to everything to the east of Egypt. *Al-mashriq*, the eastern lands, refers to a smaller and more distinct component of this territory; as a term, it was certainly in usage by 203/818f., as it appears on a coin of that date.[2] It was precisely defined by the geographer al-Muqaddasī (d. *c.* 380/990) as encompassing Khurāsān, Sīstān (Sijistān) and Transoxania (Mā Warā' al-Nahr), an area which he saw as a unity but which his predecessor, Abū Zayd al-Balkhī (d. 322/934) had regarded as a group of regions (*aqālīm*).[3] Neither of these concepts is well suited for the present purpose: *al-sharq* is much too broad, as it would include areas such as Syria, while *al-mashriq* is perhaps too narrow, as it would exclude Ṭabaristān and other areas.

In a more practical sense for modern usage, 'Iran and the Islamic east' can be understood as referring to those parts of the Islamic oecumene that had formerly been part of the Sasanian empire and where Islam came to be the dominant religion, but where Arabic did not establish itself as the vernacular language of the majority of the population. Such a definition has the advantage of eliminating the need to discuss areas west of the Euphrates or even most of Iraq, which became Arabic speaking, as well as those such as Armenia, which remained Christian. Given the shadowy eastern boundaries of the Sasanian

1 See A. Miquel, 'Mashriḳ', *EI2*, vol. VI, p. 720.
2 G. C. Miles, 'Numismatics', in R. N. Frye (ed.), *The Cambridge history of Iran*, vol. IV: *The period from the Arab invasion to the Saljuqs* (Cambridge, 1975), p. 370.
3 Shams al-Dīn Muḥammad ibn Aḥmad al-Muqaddasī, *Aḥsan al-taqāsīm fī maʿrifat al-aqālīm*, ed. M. J. de Goeje (Leiden, 1906), p. 260.

empire, it also reduces the need to consider all the remote principalities of Central Asia as well as the Indus and India, the subject of separate chapters elsewhere in this series.[4] It is still not entirely satisfactory, however, as it leaves for consideration a large number of territories such as Arrān, al-Jibāl or Qūhistān, about which we are poorly and unevenly informed in the available sources and which would be difficult to treat in any comprehensive fashion. Moreover, defined in this way, the 'Islamic east' was a region only in the generic dictionary sense of 'a large and indefinite part of the surface of the earth'.[5] If one assumes 'regionalism' to be based upon some criteria of geographical, political, administrative, economic, social and/or cultural unity, then the Islamic east was not 'a region' so much as a group of regions – or, better still, a network of cities and their hinterlands – with great variations in terms of relations both with each other and with the greater commonwealth of the caliphate.

Finally, 'regionalism' in the strict sense should be understood as a concept implying a high degree of political, economic and cultural autonomy. One can detect a great many examples of provincialism or localism or nativism in the Islamic east as defined above, but there are far fewer areas that can be said to have a truly regional culture and history in this way. Of these, the region par excellence of the Islamic east was *al-mashriq* as understood by al-Muqaddasī, i.e. Khurāsān and adjacent territories. Tremendously important both as a critical frontier province and an avenue for trade, it developed into a centre of political and cultural development that rivalled the centre of the caliphate itself. Of necessity, it will be the primary focus of this chapter.

The conquest of the Islamic east

The history of the conquest of the Islamic east, like that of other phases of the Muslim wars of expansion, is difficult to reconstruct and to interpret.[6] The extant sources provide often lengthy accounts, but they are also full of contradictions and inconsistencies when it comes to matters of chronology, the personalities involved and the course of events. They show a marked

4 See Edmund Bosworth, 'The steppe peoples in the Islamic world' and André Wink, 'The early expansion of Islam in India', in David Morgan and Anthony Reid (eds.), *The new Cambridge history of Islam*, vol. III: *The eastern Islamic world, eleventh to eighteenth centuries* (Cambridge, forthcoming).

5 *Webster's new world dictionary of the American language* (Cleveland and New York, 1974), p. 1196.

6 For a good overview of this problem, see Chase Robinson, 'The rise of Islam, 600–705', chapter 5 in this volume.

preference for repetitious *topoi* and moralising tales rather than any meticulous concern for historical detail or actual military tactics and strategy. Any modern description of the phenomenon must therefore be tentative and to some extent conjectural.

The opening phase of the conquest of the east apparently had its origins in the need to provide the newly established garrison city of Baṣra with a supporting agrarian hinterland, comparable to that available to its counterpart at Kūfa, by expanding into the plains of Khūzistān.[7] Skirmishing between Baṣran forces and those of the local Persian ruler of those areas, Hurmuzān (Hormizdān), began in AH 16 or 17 (637–38). Hurmuzān proved to be a wily and tenacious opponent, but was eventually forced to surrender. The districts around Ahwāz, Sūs, Tustar and Rāmhurmuz all came under Arab rule, either by force or capitulation.[8]

Having completed the detachment of the western provinces from the Sasanians and established a line of control all along the foothills of the Zagros, the caliph ʿUmar seems to have been reluctant to push further. He is said to have urged the Baṣrans to be content with the cultivated lands around Ahwāz and to have wished that 'a mountain of fire' would separate the Baṣrans and Kūfans from the people of Fārs and al-Jibāl, 'through which they cannot get at us, nor we at them'.[9] Whether this caution was due to the need to consolidate what had already been conquered, a shift in focus to the western campaigns, a fear of overextending his forces, or the realisation that further expansion would dilute the Arab character of the newly created empire is open to debate. In any case, ʿUmar's hesitation was trumped by other factors. One was the eagerness of individual warriors to carry out raids on their own initiative, sometimes dragging the caliph into fights he might have wished to avoid. Thus al-ʿAlāʾ ibn al-Ḥaḍramī reportedly disregarded the caliph's instructions discouraging both further expansion and undertaking raids that required the use of ships in order to initiate a piratical attack of his own from Baḥrayn on Fārs. He raided as far inland as the provincial capital at Iṣṭakhr, but his expedition turned into a near disaster when his troops were cut off from their ships. ʿUmar, though furious at this act of disobedience, felt

7 Abū Jaʿfar Muḥammad ibn Jarīr al-Ṭabarī, *Taʾrīkh al-rusul waʾl-mulūk*, ed. M. J. de Goeje *et al.*, 15 vols. in 3 series (Leiden, 1879–1901), series I, p. 2539.

8 See Chase Robinson, 'The conquest of Khūzistān: A historiographical reassessment', *BSOAS*, 67 (2004) for a detailed review of the problems regarding the conquest of these areas.

9 Al-Ṭabarī, *Taʾrīkh*, series I, p. 2545. This may well be a kind of *topos* – ʿUmar, for example, makes a similar remark later about Khurāsān – but probably reflects a genuine ambivalence about further expansion.

obliged to send a relief force to extricate al-ʿAlāʾ, thereby becoming involved in the fighting in Fārs.[10]

Another important consideration for ʿUmar was the possibility that the Sasanians might attempt to drive the Arabs back from the conquered territories. It is debatable whether the defeated Sasanian king, Yazdegerd III, was really engaged in trying to organise such a counter-offensive, but it does seem that a number of Persian magnates in the Zagros principalities feared that the Arabs would not be content with what they had already conquered and would seek to expand further – in which case their territories, like those of Hurmuzān, might be lost. A number of these Persian commanders – their names are given differently in various sources – began to gather in the area of Nihāwand, near a key pass through the central Zagros, but what they actually intended to do is not known. Reports about this supposed massing of forces persuaded ʿUmar to authorise a pre-emptive strike, drawing on troops from both Kūfa and Baṣra. The date of the consequent battle of Nihāwand is disputed in the sources (it was most likely in 21/642, though perhaps as early as 18/639), and the actual course of events is blurred by the intrusion of the colourful anecdotes to which those sources are prone. It does appear to have been a fierce fight extending over several days; both the Arab and Persian commanders are said to have been killed, but in the end the Persian forces were decisively defeated.

After the 'Victory of Victories' at Nihāwand ʿUmar endorsed a comprehensive invasion of the remaining Sasanian territories[11] (at that point it is unlikely he could have restrained the armies in any case). This might better be described as an occupation rather than an invasion, since further Persian resistance was isolated and sporadic. Many places, or at least some local authorities anxious to preserve as much of their lands and privileges as possible, chose to capitulate and sign treaties rather than resist. As a result, the Arabs – who by now had been joined by many defectors such as some Iranian cavalrymen (the *asāwira*) and other non-Iranian irregular forces that had been in Sasanian employ (such as the Zuṭṭ)[12] – were able to advance fairly rapidly to the east. Not long after Nihāwand, the Fādhūsafān (*pādhgōspān*) of Iṣfahān agreed to surrender the area on terms to the Arabs. From there a mostly Kūfan army moved along the northern rim of the central desert basin of the

10 See Martin Hinds, 'The first Arab conquests in Fārs', *Iran*, 22 (1984) for a critique of the problems in accounts of these campaigns.
11 Al-Ṭabarī, *Taʾrīkh*, series I, p. 2643.
12 See, for example, Aḥmad ibn Yaḥyā al-Balādhurī, *Kitāb futūḥ al-buldān*, ed. M. J. de Goeje (Leiden, 1866), pp. 365–74.

Iranian plateau towards Rayy, while a mostly Baṣran army set out along the southern perimeter of the basin towards Fārs, and perhaps Kirmān.

In the northern campaign, the difficulty the Persians had in maintaining a united opposition against the Arabs was quite apparent. Hamadhān was besieged immediately after the battle of Nihāwand, and the commanding general, Khusrawshunum, agreed to surrender on the usual terms of immunity in exchange for tribute. After the surrender of the city one of the local aristocrats, Dīnār, managed to pass himself off as the 'king' of Media in order to sign a treaty with the Arabs and thereby enhance his own authority in the area. Other leaders – and perhaps the general population – were not so submissive: Hamadhān had to be retaken and a force of 12,000 troops stationed there. They were challenged by a combined force of Persians from Daylam, Azerbaijan and Rayy that reportedly put up a significant fight at a place called Wāj al-Rūdh but were defeated (*c.* 22/643). Thereafter, the Arabs established a number of small garrisons in fortresses throughout Media to pacify the area and serve as a frontier zone adjacent to unconquered Daylam. The overlord of Rayy, Siyāwakhsh ibn Mihrān, also tried to resist the Arab advance; he was, however, betrayed by one of his vassals, a *dihqān* (village landlord and minor military officer) named Zīnabī, who showed the Arabs a way into the city and then arranged a treaty with them.[13] The Mihrānids were removed from power and their estates demolished; Zīnabī and his family were recognised as the new *marzbāns* (military governors) of the city. Treaties of capitulations with other cities and rulers soon followed: with Qūmis, Ruzbān Ṣūl of Jurjān, Farrukhān of Ṭabaristān and the Jīl-Jīlān, and Shahrbarāz at al-Bāb.

In the south, Baṣran forces were joined by Arabs from Baḥrayn and the Gulf who had renewed their assault on the coastal areas of Fārs. In 23/643f. they took Tawwaj (an important town probably located near the confluence of the Shahpur and Dalaki rivers, just inland from what is today the port of Bushire) and made it into a permanent base of operations.[14] Shahrak, the *marzbān* of Fārs, tried once again to cut the Arabs off from their lines of communication but was defeated and killed in what is described as a major battle near Rīshahr. Presumably leaderless, demoralised and facing the combined Arab armies, the people of most of the other major towns of Fārs – Sābūr, Arrajān, Fasā, Dārābjird, Iṣṭakhr – made treaties of submission and agreed to pay tribute. Places that did resist, such as Jahram or the forts at Shabir and Jannābā, were

13 Al-Ṭabarī, *Ta'rīkh*, series I, pp. 2653–5.

14 Rather typically, al-Ṭabarī's source (*Ta'rīkh*, series I, p. 2694) attributes the conquest to the Baṣrans under Mujāshiʿ ibn Masʿūd, and al-Balādhurī (citing Abū Mikhnaf) (*Futūḥ*, p. 386) to the Gulf Arabs under ʿUthmān ibn Abi 'l-ʿĀṣ.

soon subdued. An apparent uprising of Persians and Kurds at Birūdh, to the rear of the Arab armies, was also suppressed.

Virtually all of the recently conquered areas from Azerbaijan to Fārs revolted after hearing news of the caliph ʿUmar's assassination in 644, and had to be pacified again. It was not until 29/649f., after meeting fierce resistance, that the new governor of Baṣra, ʿAbd Allāh ibn ʿĀmir, was able to regain firm control of Iṣṭakhr. One of his lieutenants, Mujāshiʿ ibn Maʿsud al-Sulamī, reportedly went on to take Kirmān and Sīrjān. Mujāshiʿ also attempted to invade Sīstān, but most of his army perished near Bīmand in a sudden blizzard.[15] After raising another army he was able to take control of the area south of Kirmān, including Bamm, Jiruft and Hormuz. A second attempt to conquer Sīstān was made under Rabīʿ ibn Ziyād al-Ḥārithī. After sporadic fighting and the capture of several small towns, Rabīʿ besieged the capital, Zaranj. The *marzbān*, Abarwīz (or according to the *Tārīkh-i Sīstān*, the shah of Sīstān, Īrān ibn Rustam ibn Āzādkhū, and the high priest), decided to capitulate, out of a mixture of respect for the religion of the invaders and shock at the barbarity of their actions.[16] While this was going on, the bulk of Ibn ʿĀmir's army moved into Qūhistān as a prelude to the systematic conquest of Khurāsān.

Accounts of the conquest of Khurāsān and eastern Iran are usually connected to the pursuit of Yazdegerd, the last Sasanian shah. After the initial Arab victories he had supposedly tried to rally resistance from Rayy, Jūr, Kirmān, Sīstān, and finally Marw and Marw al-Rūdh, but in case after case he had been obliged to leave after disputes with the local governors – usually over access to funds from the treasury, but sometimes also due to fears his presence would be an invitation for the Arabs to attack. According to some of al-Ṭabarī's sources, an effort to capture him began as early as 23/543f.: as the Baṣran forces advanced from Fārs to Sīrjān, Kirmān, Sīstān and Makrān, a detachment under Aḥnaf ibn Qays crossed the desert directly from Iṣfahān to enter Khurāsān at Ṭabasayn and proceeded to take Herat, Nīshāpūr, Sarakhs and Marw.[17] If this expedition took place at all, however, it could hardly have been more than a passing raid. Other reports have Yazdegerd still in Fārs, either having returned from Khurāsān or perhaps not yet having left the area, at the time of the revolts and Ibn ʿĀmir's campaign.

15 Al-Ṭabarī, *Taʾrīkh*, series I, p. 2863. The *Tārīkh-i Sīstān* (ed. Malik al-Shuʿarāʾ Bahār, (Tehran, 1935), p. 63), however, says he was defeated in battle. Balādhurī, *Futūḥ*, p. 391 simply says that his army was wiped out.

16 *Tārīkh-i Sīstān*, p. 81 (trans. Milton Gold as *The Tārikh-e Sistān* (Rome, 1976), p. 64); cf. Balādhurī, *Futūḥ*, pp. 393–4.

17 Balādhurī, *Futūḥ*, p. 403 attributes the conquest of Ṭabasayn about this same time to ʿAbd Allāh ibn Budayl, who perhaps led an autonomous raid of his own.

Following the crushing defeat of the Persians at Iṣṭakhr he set out (again?) from Jūr for Khurāsān in 30/650f. Stories about his movements and activities are thus numerous, but differ greatly in their details; it is clear enough, however, that he had no success in organising any general resistance to the Arab advance, either among the local population or from the Hepthalites, Sogdians, Turks and Chinese, to whom he supposedly appealed for help. Even the armed forces remaining with him were destroyed, most likely because of a treacherous betrayal by the *marzbān* of Marw, Mahūya; Yazdegerd himself was murdered in 31/651f., though by whom, how and why is much disputed.[18]

There are reports that an army under Qārin, apparently a scion of the famous noble family of Sasanian times, attempted to resist Aḥnaf's advance in 32/652f. but was defeated. There may also have been an effort at resistance in 655 by Yazdegerd's son, Fīrūz, with some Chinese backing and the support of troops from Ṭukhāristān; if so, it too failed.[19] For the most part, the various towns and cities of Khurāsān, without any semblance of coordinated resistance, fended for themselves with the various detachments of Ibn ʿĀmir's army. Most of the smaller towns, such as Zām, Bayhāq or Baghgh, are said to have been conquered (one suspects they were attacked mostly because they lacked adequate fortifications and made easy targets). Larger cities, particularly those with military governors anxious to preserve their positions and privileges, generally agreed to capitulate on terms. Thus Nīshāpūr, Nasā, Abīvard, Herat, Marw and Marw al-Rūdh capitulated; the *kanārang* (the local ruler) of Ṭūs apparently sought out a treaty arrangement even before his city came under attack. The most determined resistance came from the mostly Hepthalite areas of Ṭukhāristān. That region was invaded by a detachment under Aḥnaf ibn Qays, who defeated a large opposing army, took the cities of Juzjān, Ṭālaqān, Fāryāb and Balkh, and even attempted to raid down the Oxus to Khwārazm.

Although virtually the whole of the former Sasanian empire was thus overrun, it was hardly subdued. Just as the agreements that had hastily been made in western Iran soon broke down and resulted in open rebellion, so too did those in eastern Iran. In most cases these 'revolts' were efforts to avoid the regular payment of taxes and tribute, taking advantage of the civil strife that had broken out among the Arabs after the murder of ʿUthmān. This was represented, for example, in the revolt of Nīshāpūr in 37/657f. as well as in a major revolt in Fārs and Kirmān in 39/659f., when the inhabitants are said to

18 Al-Ṭabarī, *Ta'rīkh*, series I, pp. 2872–84.
19 H. A. R. Gibb, *The Arab conquests in Central Asia* (London and New York, 1923), p. 16.

have driven the tax-collectors out of every district.[20] It would seem that agreeing to pay tribute to encourage a marauding army to move on was one thing, but actually having to pay them taxes year after year quite another. A major turning-point in terms of alleviating this problem and consolidating the conquests apparently came with ʿAlī's appointment of Ziyād ibn Abīhi as governor of Fārs and Kirmān to deal with the revolt there. Ziyād established a new fortress and treasury near Iṣṭakhr, restored order, and gradually won the support of the populace through what seems essentially to have been a policy of the carrot and the stick.[21] Later, as governor of Baṣra under Muʿāwiya, Ziyād also brought to an end a series of revolts in Khurāsān, reorganised the administrative structure of the province, and established a large permanent garrison of Arab forces at Marw.

At the same time that so many areas were restive, other areas on the periphery of the conquests were only under nominal control, or were openly hostile. The 'conquests' in Ṭabaristān, for example, amounted to nothing more than the acceptance of mutual non-aggression pacts by which the local hereditary rulers remained in place but paid some token tribute. The treaty was broken by a Kūfan army under Saʿīd ibn al-ʿĀṣ in 30/650f. that attempted, with minimal success, to invade Ṭabaristān from Jurjān after it had failed in its effort to advance towards Khurāsān. Arab armies sent against Ṭabaristān in 41/661 and 61/680 were both routed. In Jurjān itself the Arabs had to deal with the local Turkic ruler, the *ṣūl*, until he was finally defeated in 98/716f. Even more troublesome were areas such as the principalities of Bādhghīs and Ṭukhāristān in the highlands of what today would be north-west Afghanistan. The Arabs frequently raided these areas from their bases at Marw al-Rūdh or Balkh, but were fiercely resisted by the Hepthalite inhabitants, perhaps in coalition with Turkish, Sogdian and Tibetan allies. Nīzak Ṭārkhān, the Hepthalite ruler of Bādhghīs, was the wiliest of these adversaries. An opportunist, he (or a predecessor with the same name/title) had supposedly been involved in the murder of Yazdegerd, campaigned against Rabīʿ ibn Ziyād in Qūhistān in 51/671f., and alternately collaborated with or fought Arab commanders until he was finally killed in 91/710. A similar situation prevailed to the south in Sīstān. The Arabs were in relatively firm control of Zaranj, where, as noted earlier, the ruler and inhabitants had decided to capitulate. Their efforts to raid or control adjacent territories,

20 Al-Ṭabarī, *Taʾrīkh*, series I, p. 3449. Al-Ṭabarī (ibid., pp. 3350, 3390) curiously attributes the revolt in Nīshāpūr to the people's espousal of unbelief (*kufr*), but it hardly seems possible that they would have converted and apostatised at such an early date.

21 Ibid., pp. 3349–50.

however, were contested fiercely and mostly successfully by the existing rulers, notably the *zunbīl*[22] of Rukhkhāj and Zamīndāwar and the *kābulshāh*, neither of whom could be subdued. For the better part of two centuries the *zunbīl* was 'a bone in the throat' of the Muslims.[23]

Another, and essentially final, phase of the conquests in the Islamic east can be said to have begun after Ziyād's reforms in Khurāsān and to have concluded in 751 with the great victory of Ziyād ibn Ṣāliḥ over a coalition of Central Asian forces at the battle of Talas. This expansion, which brought Transoxania as well as Sind under Muslim rule, appears rather different in character from the earlier phases of the conquests. It was made possible by Ziyād's administrative reforms and the settling of large, permanent Arab military garrisons in Khurāsān, but it was also marked by a much greater degree of collaboration between the Arabs and local military forces in joint operations of mutual benefit. As a result, it soon acquired the features of a systematic war of expansion rather than the rather haphazard filling of a political vacuum by the disorganised raids that typified earlier periods.

The initial forays across the Oxus were aimed at Bukhārā in 54/673f. and Samarqand in 56/675f. Details about both campaigns, the first led by ʿUbayd Allāh ibn Ziyād and the latter by Saʿīd ibn ʿUthmān, are sketchy, but they are said to have succeeded in extracting promises to pay tribute. An effort to follow up on these campaigns was apparently undertaken by Salm ibn Ziyād in 61/68 of., but it achieved little before being disrupted by the civil war that broke out during the reign of Yazīd I. As noted by H. A. R. Gibb, circumstances in Central Asia were at that time actually rather propitious for an Arab advance,[24] but the political upheavals of the late Sufyānid and early Marwānid periods resulted in a long hiatus of a quarter-century in the campaigns and a reversal of many of the earlier successes. This changed dramatically with the appointment of Qutayba ibn Muslim as governor of Khurāsān on behalf of al-Ḥajjāj in 86/705.

Several important developments are noticeable in the period of Qutayba's administration. First of all, he was from a 'neutral' tribe, Bāhila, and thus not beholden to the existing Arab factions in Khurāsān while being in a good position to keep them united. Second, in his inaugural address in Khurāsān he emphasised the importance of *jihād* and the struggle on the frontier[25] (typical

22 This term, which also appears in the sources in orthographical variants such as *rutbīl*, could have been a personal name but was most likely the hereditary title of a priest-king who ruled over the upper Helmand valley: see e.g. G. Scarcia, 'Zunbīl or Zanbīl?', in *Yádnáme-ye Jan Rypka: Collection of articles on Persian and Tajik literature* (Prague, 1967), pp. 41–5.

23 Al-Ṭabarī, *Taʾrīkh*, series I, p. 2706.

24 Gibb, *Arab conquests*, pp. 22–3.

25 Al-Ṭabarī, *Taʾrīkh*, series II, p. 1179.

of his religious policy but also a convenient means of keeping the tribal factions united and too busy for the internecine political rivalries that had proven so disruptive). Third, he left little room for doubt that the conquests carried out were meant to be permanent and treaty arrangements to be honoured accordingly; cities or people that revolted or reneged on the payment of tribute were severely punished,[26] in stark contrast to the milder renewal of terms that had earlier been the norm. Finally, he encouraged the fraternisation of Arabs and the local peoples (having Arab troops quartered in native houses in Bukhārā, for example[27]), and made extensive use of indigenous soldiers willing to help in his campaigns, both as auxiliaries and as members of the standing army. Taken together, these policies led to a decade of spectacular military successes in the Islamic east, which have been described in detail by Gibb:[28] the re-establishment of control over the rebellious areas of Ṭukhāristān in 86/705; the conquest of Bukhārā and its suburbs, Samarqand and Khwārazm (over the period 87–93/706–12); and excursions across the Jaxartes and deep into the Farghāna valley (where Qutayba was murdered during an army mutiny in 96/715 or 716). Qutayba also took a hand in the affairs of Sīstān and helped direct a new campaign against the *zunbīl* in 92/711. Not exactly to his credit, he also had Nīzak Ṭārkhān murdered.

The expansion again lost momentum after Qutayba's murder, and it was not long before the Arabs were placed on the defensive by the emergence of a powerful alliance of Sogdian and Turkish (Türgesh) forces, backed by Chinese support. The Turkish counter-offensive began with a surprise attack on the fortress of Qaṣr al-Bāhilī in 102/720. In 106/724 the Turks routed an army in Farghāna led by Muslim ibn Saʿīd al-Kilābī, and by 110/728 they were threatening Samarqand. An infusion of reinforcements by Syrian troops eventually helped turn the tide: in 119/737 the Turks were able to cross the Oxus and invade Khurāsān, but were defeated in a skirmish at Kharīstān. The Turkish camp, including its flocks of sheep, was captured; not long afterwards the Turkish *khāqān* was murdered and his confederation collapsed. Under the governorship of Naṣr ibn Sayyār virtually all that the Arabs had lost was retaken by 123/741. The definitive victory marking the consolidation of the

26 For example, the severe punishment of the rebels in Bukhārā or the execution of Nīzak.

27 Abū Bakr Muḥammad Narshakhī, *Tārīkh-i Bukhārā*, ed. Mudarris Raḍavī (Tehran, 1972), p. 66, ed. and trans. R. N. Frye as *The history of Bukhara* (Cambridge, MA, 1954). p. 48.

28 Gibb, *Arab conquests*, pp. 29–57.

Islamic east would come ten years later, after the ʿAbbāsid revolution, with Ziyād ibn Ṣāliḥ's defeat of a Chinese-led army at Talas – an event of world historical significance, though one curiously neglected in works by the early Arab historians.

The conquests and the development of regionalism

The Arab conquests in what would become the Islamic east entailed a number of demographic, social, economic, political and cultural changes that would help determine the parameters for the development of this area. These changes are not easy to follow or to explain: even in the most obvious and important case – the transition from a very diverse religious population to a predominantly Muslim one – the best available interpretations of the process of conversion still involve a considerable degree of conjecture. The early Arabic sources tend to deal with such matters only in incidental or anecdotal fashion, and provide little in the way of solid historical data. At the same time they are overwhelmingly interested in the affairs of the Arab conquering elite, while largely ignoring the vastly greater subject population, giving only minimal attention to non-Arab Muslims and virtually none at all to non-Muslims. Occasionally, though, there are bits of information that surface to suggest the broad outlines of regional developments. In addition, there have survived some provincial histories – works on areas such as Sīstān or Ṭabaristān and clearly written from the perspective of the periphery rather than the imperial centre – that can provide important correctives to the usual narratives; they are, however, generally in Persian and of a relatively late date, and consequently have often been discounted or ignored by modern historians.

In terms of demographic change, it is obvious that the conquests did lead to the intrusion of a substantial number of Arab settlers, either as occupying forces or outright colonists. Exactly how large this new Arab population was and where it was concentrated is more difficult to say. As noted earlier, accounts of the conquest often mention or imply the establishment of more or less permanent military garrisons in strategic locations such as Tawwaj, Iṣṭakhr, Kirmān, Zaranj, Iṣfahān, Hamadhān, Qazvīn, Rayy, Ardabīl and Bāb al-Abwāb; when numbers are mentioned, they are usually in the range of 4,000–8,000 per garrison (the number stationed at Bāb al-Abwāb, a critical frontier post, was much larger). At least some of these forces remained in place, and several petty dynasties (such as the Rawwādids or Dulafids) that eventually emerged in western Iran could trace their origins back to early commanders of these garrisons. The same pattern was followed at first in

Jurjān and Khurāsān, but military necessity there dictated settlement on a much larger scale. In 51/671 Rabīʿ ibn Ziyād is supposed to have settled 50,000 warriors and their families in Khurāsān, and several thousand more were sent a few years later by Salm ibn Ziyād, perhaps to replace those who elected not to stay permanently. Al-Balādhurī and Balʿamī give a similar number of 47,000 Arab troops in Khurāsān at the time of Qutayba's governorship.[29] Most of these settlers seem to have resided in the Marw oasis, but groups of Arab settlers can also be identified in other cities of Khurāsān such as Balkh and Marw al-Rūdh. These numbers can certainly be questioned but are not inherently unreasonable, and if the soldiers' families in fact came to settle with them, one could assume an immigrant population of approximately 150,000 Arabs in the area.[30]

As is implied by the history of the conquests, three basic zones of Arab settlement in the Islamic east can be distinguished. The area to the north and west of a line from around Nihāwand to Jurjān was conquered, for a while administered, and mostly colonised by Arab tribesmen from Kūfa. The area to the south and west was similarly conquered, administered and settled by Arabs from Baṣra. Initially, Khurāsān was also regarded as a predominantly Baṣran territory, but its emergence as a crucial frontier province soon dictated an expanded presence of Arab forces that included both Kūfans and Baṣrans and, later, Syrians as well. These patterns of settlement had significant implications for regional political and religious development. Kūfa was well known for its anti-Umayyad and pro-ʿAlid sentiments, and its dissident tribesmen often found it convenient to remove themselves, apparently in rather substantial numbers, to more isolated areas of al-Jibāl. The area around Qumm was a particularly popular location for such immigrants, attracting former supporters of al-Mukhtār, rebels against al-Ḥajjāj and Shīʿite Ashʿarī tribesmen. Likewise, dissidents from Baṣra tended to seek refuge in Khūzistān, Fārs, Kirmān and Sīstān. These were mostly Khārijites: after failing to hold Baṣra, Khārijites led by Nāfiʿ ibn al-Azraq (perhaps a non-Arab in origin) controlled Ahwāz down to 65/685,

29 Balādhurī, *Futūḥ*, p. 423; Abu 'l-Faḍl Muḥammad Balʿamī, *Tarjamah-yi Tārīkh-i Ṭabarī*, ed. M. Rawshan as *Tārīkh-nāmah-ye Ṭabarī*, 3 vols. (Tehran, 1988), p. 873. Zotenberg's French translation of Balʿamī (*Chronique de Abou-Djafar Mohammed ben Djarir ben-Yezid Tabari*, 4 vols. (Paris, 1867–74)) claims 40,000 Baṣran and 47,000 Kūfan troops; although this figure has sometimes been accepted (e.g. P. Oberling, ''Arab IV: Arab tribes of Iran', *EIr*, vol. II, p. 215), it is clearly erroneous and is given correctly as 40,000 Baṣran and 7,000 Kūfan troops in the Rawshan edition.

30 Saleh Said Agha, *The revolution which toppled the Umayyads: Neither Arab nor ʿAbbāsid* (Leiden, 2003), pp. 177–85 reviews the evidence and concludes that the Arab population was at least 115,000 but no more than 175,000.

and Azraqī Khārijites virtually ruled Fārs and Kirmān until their 'caliph', Qaṭarī ibn al-Fujā'a, was defeated and killed around 79/698f. In Khurāsān and Transoxania, political problems developed not so much from 'unofficial' settlement by rebels and dissident sects as from factional disputes among the 'official' settlers – rivalries between Baṣran troops and settlers and the more recent Kūfan arrivals and, later, friction between both of them and the new influx of Syrian troops. Perhaps as a result, religious trends there tended to develop almost as a reaction to the Shī'ism and Khārijism of other areas. Although they often seemed to express affection for the family of the Prophet and made pious calls for rule in accordance with the Qur'ān and the *sunna*, they also attempted to defuse sectarian tensions and to foster better relations between Arab and non-Arab Muslims. Thus two of the strongest religious trends in that part of the Islamic east were the theological school of the Murji'a, which emphasised avoiding contention over the relative merits of 'Uthmān and 'Alī (but could also be quite critical of the Umayyad central government and was heavily involved in revolts against it),[31] and the Ḥanafī school of law, which appealed greatly to non-Arab Muslims – in its willingness, for example, to legitimise the uses of languages other than Arabic for religious purposes.

As for the overall impact of these demographic developments, it is probably safe to say that the conquests and subsequent influx of Arabs settlers did little to displace the existing population, or even to disrupt the existing social structure – at least initially. There are, of course, in non-Muslim sources some allegations of destruction and persecution that contrast rather sharply with the much more benign picture of the conquests suggested by the Muslim historians. The 'Khūzistān Chronicle' claims that the Arabs 'shed blood there as if it were water' and killed a number of Christian religious notables.[32] Various Zoroastrian texts such as the *Zand-i Vohuman Yasht*, which claims the Arabs killed righteous men as easily as they would a fly, or the *Qiṣṣa-i Sanjan*, which alludes to the persecutions that eventually caused the Parsees to flee to Gujarat, also raise this possibility. Even in Muslim accounts there are occasionally references, if of debatable reliability, to mass killings: Sa'īd ibn al-'Āṣ is supposed to have treacherously slaughtered all the defenders of a fortress in Ṭabaristān save one,[33] and Yazīd ibn al-Muhallab to have murdered

31 See Wilferd Madelung, 'The early Murji'a in Khurāsān and Transoxania and the spread of Ḥanafism', *Der Islam*, 59 (1982); Khalil Athamina, 'The early Murji'a: Some notes', *JSS*, 35 (1990).

32 Translation in Robinson, 'Conquest of Khūzistān', p. 18.

33 Al-Ṭabarī, *Ta'rīkh*, series I, p. 2837; however, the story, like those in most of this section of the narrative, sound suspiciously like fables or folklore.

thousands of Turks in Jurjān, as their leader, Ruzbān, had neglected to secure an amnesty for them.[34] The *Tārīkh-i Qumm* claims that the defenders of Shustar (Ar. Tustar) killed their families and destroyed their belongings rather than surrender them to the Arabs, and it portrays the Arab and Iranian populations in Qumm as living in rather frosty isolation from each other for quite some time,[35] a pattern apparently followed in several other areas as well. Many Sogdians are also said to have fled, against the advice of their king, to more remote parts of Inner Asia out of fear of reprisals.[36] These probably represent extreme cases, however, and it is likely that the experience of the conquests by the population of south-western Iran was rather different from that in areas such as Ṭabaristān or Sīstān, which were barely affected, or Khurāsān, where circumstances really demanded cooperation between the Arab forces and their subjects.

The formation of a new Arab social elite in the Islamic east also had less of an impact on the existing social structure than one might think. Sasanian society was organised in a fairly rigid system of four classes (bureaucracy, military, clergy and subjects) and a hierarchy of officials: the monarch and great imperial officers (such as the commander-general of the army, the *Iranspahbad*); the de facto local rulers (*shahrdārān*); the military grandees (*wāspuhragān*); the lesser nobility (*wuzurgān*); freemen (*āzādān*); and ordinary subjects, mostly peasants.[37] A good deal of this structure is still apparent well into the conquest period, if in slightly modified form, under different names, with changes in personnel, and with the integration of the new Arab military elite into it. In the longer term, the most important changes probably derived from the stimulation of the urban environment in the form of more and larger cities, along with the commercial activities and social classes that accompanied them.

Obviously, the top of the old structure, the Sasanian monarchy and its attendant imperial institutions, was obliterated in the course of the conquests, culminating in the murder of Yazdegerd and the destruction of the retinue and praetorian guard he had with him. The supposed efforts of his son and

34 Balādhurī, *Futūḥ*, p. 336, trans. P. K. Hitti and F. C. Murgotten as *The origins of the Islamic state*, 2 vols. (New York, 1916–24), vol. II, p. 41.

35 Ḥasan ibn Muḥammad Qummī, *Kitāb-i tārīkh-i Qumm* (Tehran, 1353/1934), p. 300. It has been noted that this tendency to keep Arab and Zoroastrian populations physically separated may have been due to the important Zoroastrian beliefs regarding ritual purity and pollution; see Jamsheed K. Choksy, *Conflict and cooperation: Zorastrian subalterns and Muslim elites in medieval Iranian society* (New York, 1997), p. 44.

36 Al-Ṭabarī, *Ta'rīkh*, series II, p. 1439.

37 For a survey of the Sasanian social hierarchy, see A. E. Christensen, *L'Iran sous les Sassanides*, 2nd edn (Copenhagen, 1944), pp. 97–113; see also Josef Wiesehöfer, 'The late Sasanian Near East', chapter 3 in this volume.

pretender to the throne to restore the regime came to nothing, as most of his help came from outside forces and received little support from within the conquered areas. The Zoroastrian clergy probably suffered almost as much as the monarchy; their popular support had been dwindling for some time, and they were heavily dependent on state support, which was now cut off. Some members of the aristocracy who had remained loyal were also eliminated: Hurmuzān was sent to Medina, where he narrowly escaped being executed, only to be murdered after the assassination of ʿUmar. As noted earlier, the valiant *marzbān* of Fārs, Shahrak, fell in battle. The *marzbān* of Kirmān was killed, as was Zadhūya, the *marzbān* of Sarakhs.[38] The wholesale slaughter that occurred at places such as Iṣṭakhr after the revolt of 29/649f. must also have done away with many members of the officer corps and other officials.

However, it is also clear that a very substantial number of aristocrats, military governors, prefects and administrators survived, and even thrived, by choosing to collaborate with the invaders. The notorious Mahūya of Marw is but the best-known example; he was still in a position of authority as late as 36/656f., when he hastened after the assassination of ʿUthmān to secure recognition of his position from ʿAlī. Other provincial lords who managed to stay in place for some time included Mardānshāh, the *maṣmūghān*[39] of Dunbāwand; Ruzbān Ṣūl, the Turkish ruler of Jurjān; Farrukhān of Ṭabaristān; and the tenacious Nīzak Ṭārkhān of lower Ṭukhāristān.[40] Although less frequently mentioned in the sources, it is likely that a large percentage of lower-ranking military nobles also remained: Shahrbarāz secured his position and the status of tax-exempt auxiliaries for his troops at Darband, and he probably expressed a common sentiment when he told his Arab counterpart that they should cooperate since noblemen associate with noblemen and both were facing a common 'rabid enemy' and people of ignoble descent (i.e. the Khazars). Likewise, the letter ʿAlī sent confirming Mahūya in office was addressed to the 'landlords of Marw, cavalry, and army officers (*dahāqīn*, *asāwira*, and *jundsalārīn*)', which indicates that a significant section of the old military-aristocratic hierarchy was still in existence in Khurāsān.[41] It is not uncommon to find mention of other lesser

38 Balādhurī, *Futūḥ*, p. 405.
39 Translated in Wilferd Madelung, 'The minor dynasties of northern Iran', in Frye (ed.), *The Cambridge history of Iran*, vol. IV, p. 199 as 'Great One of the Magians', perhaps suggesting here as in other places the existence of a kind of local priest-king.
40 Al-Ṭabarī, *Taʾrīkh*, series I, pp. 2656, 2658, 2659; on Nīzak, see E. Esin, 'Ṭarkhān Nīzak or Ṭarkhān Tīrek? An enquiry concerning the prince of Bādhghīs ...', *JAOS*, 97 (1977).
41 Al-Ṭabarī, *Taʾrīkh*, series I, p. 3249.

officials who were still exercising authority after the conquests, such as Bahmana, administrator of Abīvard,[42] or the *yazdānfādhār* of Abarishtjān, who provided land for the Ashʿarī colonists who came to Qumm.[43] As late as 61/680f. there was still in existence some kind of council of the 'kings of Khurāsān' to coordinate their activities.[44] Finally, and most importantly, at the base of the old Sasanian social structure were the *dihqāns*, the village landlords, who clearly survived as a class and were indispensable to the Arabs as tax-collectors, auxiliaries and administrators. They also served as significant cultural interlocutors, both keeping alive old Iranian social traditions and using them to influence the customs and behaviour of the Arab conquerors. For example, ʿAbd Allāh ibn al-Zubayr, during his stay in Sīstān, was reportedly given advice on how to govern by Rustam ibn Mihr-Hurmuzd al-Majūsī in the form of proverbs known to the *dihqāns*.[45] Likewise, the governor of Khurāsān, Asad ibn ʿAbd Allāh, attended a Mihrijān feast at Balkh in 120/737f. organised by the *dihqāns* of Khurāsān, who lavished gifts on him and praised him for his conduct (which they saw as in keeping with the Sasanian principle of justice in the sense that neither weak nor strong, rich nor poor, could be oppressed).[46]

Finally, there is the key – but most difficult – issue of how the conquests and resulting demographic and social changes can be connected to the conversion of most of the population (previously a mix of Zoroastrians, Christians, Buddhists, Manichaeans, Jews and other faiths) to Islam. This turns on two basic questions: what were the motives for conversion; and at what rate did they proceed?

The problem of motivation (and along with it the matter of sincerity and exactly what it meant to 'convert') is particularly difficult to address. If one looks, for example, at the hagiographical literature (such as the collection of biographies of Sufi saints by Ḥujwīrī, d. *c.* 469/1072), it might be concluded that conversion was a largely random process that involved some kind of personal spiritual crisis and resolution leading to a profound faith. The historical literature, on the other hand, often implies much more mundane factors such as a desire to maintain social status or to avoid taxes. It also suggests that 'conversion' was, at least initially, a rather superficial change – Narshakhī (*fl.* 332/943), for example, says that the people of Bukhārā thrice

42 Balādhurī, *Futūḥ*, p. 404.
43 Qummī, *Tārīkh-i Qumm*, p. 32.
44 Al-Ṭabarī, *Taʾrīkh*, series II, p. 394.
45 *Tārīkh-i Sīstān*, p. 106 (trans. Gold as *The Tārikh-e Sistān*, p. 85).
46 Al-Ṭabarī, *Taʾrīkh*, series II, pp. 1635–8.

converted to Islam and then apostatised before Qutayba ibn Muslim 'planted Islam in their hearts', and even then they still worshipped idols in secret.[47] We can, however, be fairly sure that outright coercion – as opposed to various social pressures – was a factor of minimal importance in bringing about conversions: the best-known evidence is probably the letter of Bishop Ishoyahb III of Rev Ardashir that complains about how quickly and readily the Christian population of Marw had decided to embrace Islam even without the threat of persecution.[48] We are also told that plans by Ziyād ibn Abīhi to execute Zoroastrian religious leaders and destroy fire-temples in Sīstān were blocked by protests from the local Muslim population, who insisted on honouring the principle of tolerance embedded in the peace treaties they had concluded.[49] Proselytising and inducement as official policy, however, did play a role in converting the general population. There are several indications of this in, for example, the *Tārīkh-i Sīstān*. ʿAbd al-Raḥmān ibn Samura is supposed to have brought Ḥasan al-Baṣrī to Sīstān in 43/663 to help reform the government and to teach Islam to the people, and many Zoroastrians converted because of their impression of the virtue and justice of the administration of Rabīʿ al-Ḥārithī. A great adversary of al-Ḥajjāj, ʿAbd al-Raḥmān ibn Muḥammad ibn al-Ashʿath, also courted the people of Sīstān (i.e. Zaranj), Bust, Zābul and other eastern lands, and used scholars and popular preachers 'to capture the minds of the people' there and 'to make Islam and the Shariʿa attractive to them' while simultaneously complaining about al-Ḥajjāj's oppression.[50] Proselytising also seems to have been a conscious and deliberate aspect of Qutayba ibn Muslim's strategy in Transoxania, as he not only founded new mosques there but subsidised attendance at the prayer services.[51] It is well known that ʿUmar II strongly endorsed efforts to promote conversion, inviting the 'kings of Transoxania' to accept Islam and ordering the governor of Khurāsān, al-Jarrāḥ ibn ʿAbd Allāh al-Ḥakamī, to make it easier for people to convert and to remit their taxes.[52] Similarly, al-Ḥārith ibn Surayj and the Murjiʾa in Khurāsān encouraged conversion by championing the rights of non-Arab Muslims while insisting that the non-Muslims be held strictly to the payment of *dhimmī* taxes, and conversion was probably an important aspect of the ʿAbbāsid propaganda mission (*daʿwa*) too.

47 Narshakhī, *Tārīkh-i Bukhārā*, p. 66, trans. Frye as *History*, pp. 47–8.
48 See Thomas Walker Arnold, *The preaching of Islam* (London, 1913), pp. 82–3.
49 *Tārīkh-i Sīstān*, p. 92, trans. Gold as *The Tārikh-e Sistān*, p. 74.
50 *Tārīkh-i Sīstān*, pp. 83, 114–15, trans. Gold as *The Tārikh-e Sistān*, pp. 66, 92.
51 Narshakhī, *Tārīkh-i Bukhārā*, pp. 67–8, trans. Frye as *History*, pp. 47–9.
52 Balādhurī, *Futūḥ*, p. 426; al-Ṭabarī, *Taʾrīkh*, series II, p. 1354.

The most systematic effort thus far to trace the pace of conversion in the Islamic east has come from a quantitative analysis by Richard Bulliet of data in medieval Islamic biographical dictionaries.[53] It suggests that the conversion process proceeded slowly until about the time of the ʿAbbāsid revolution, and then accelerated rapidly until the mid-third/tenth century, by which time 90 per cent of the population had become Muslim. Of course, the biographical data on which this study was based tend to be confined to a fairly narrow social class (religious scholars) and discrete urban environments; it is not entirely clear how far the results can be extrapolated to reflect the conversion process in general. There are at least a few indications in narrative sources that in some places early conversion, or at least nominal conversion, might have been more common than this scenario suggests: al-Balādhurī, for example, reports that the people of Qazvīn, facing defeat, decided to become Muslims because they disliked the prospect of paying the poll-tax; the *Tārīkh-i Sīstān* says that many Zoroastrians became Muslims because they were impressed by the justice and equity of the administration of Rabīʿ al-Ḥārithī; and the *Tārīkh-i Bukhārā* also claims that the people of that city converted very readily to Islam in the days of Qutayba ibn Muslim, who was flexible enough to allow prayer services to be conducted in Persian – as well as to pay a dole for attendance at Friday prayers.[54] Conversion stories in the historical literature may be somewhat more common for the period before the ʿAbbāsid revolution, but this is probably due to their novelty (and the status of the converts) rather than their number. It may also be that some places resisted conversion much longer than others: there are reports that Fārs still had a substantial Zoroastrian population even towards the end of the tenth century.[55] For the most part, however, Bulliet's results seem to track well both with anecdotal material about conversion and with what is known about overall historical developments. Reports about the size of the Muslim army in Khurāsān just before the ʿAbbāsid revolution, for instance, suggest that non-Arab Muslims (*mawālī*) made up about 15 per cent of the military forces, roughly the same percentage as the quantitative study indicates for the general population. If the pattern

53 Richard W. Bulliet, *Conversion to Islam in the medieval period: An essay in quantitative history* (Cambridge, MA, 1979), summarised in Richard W. Bulliet, *Islam: The view from the edge* (New York, 1994), pp. 38–9. An outdated but still useful study of anecdotal evidence about conversion in the Islamic East can be found in Arnold, *Preaching of Islam*, pp. 82–6, 209–20; more recent, but rather unsatisfactory in its handling of the source material, is Choksy, *Conflict and cooperation*.

54 Balādhurī, *Futūḥ*, p. 321; *Tārīkh-i Sīstān*, p. 91, trans. Gold as *The Tārikh-e Sistān*, p. 74; *Tārīkh-i Bukhārā*, pp. 67–8, trans. Frye as *History*, p. 48.

55 For example, Muqaddasī, *Aḥsan al-taqāsīm*, p. 429.

holds, the tipping-point when the majority of the population became Muslim came during the mid-second/ninth century; by the early third/tenth century the conversion process was largely complete. These, as will be seen, are also critical times in the political evolution of the Islamic east, corresponding to the periods when autonomous and then fully independent dynasties of regional rulers appeared. The implication would thus seem to be that a unified Islamic empire was viable as long as it involved a small Muslim elite ruling over a vast non-Muslim population, but much harder to justify as that population converted: religious homogeneity magnified the importance of other differences. In that sense, ironically enough, conversion would seem to be an essential ingredient, not in consolidating and assimilating the population of an Islamic empire, but in the formation of regional identities in a Muslim oecumene. It is also particularly important to note that in the Islamic east, and virtually nowhere else during this period, conversion to Islam did not also produce a transition to Arabophone culture; vernacular languages and culture remained dominant.[56] This was of considerable significance since it helped ensure that Islam evolved into a multicultural world religion instead of remaining an essentially Arab religion.

The political development of the Islamic east

The classical Arabic historical sources, and a good many modern historians who follow them, generally tend to convey the impression of an Islamic east that was for some time a well-integrated part of an imperial system, with the caliphs appointing and dismissing governors, directing wars and policy, and systematically collecting taxes and tribute. Nonetheless, it is unlikely that such a highly centralised empire actually existed for any substantial length of time, or even at all. As has already been indicated here, the conquered areas were riddled with largely autonomous enclaves. Numerous local rulers and nobles from the old order remained in place. The administration of the fiscal apparatus depended heavily on the same class that had played that role in Sasanian times. Even many of the governors designated by the caliph came from powerful families of the Arab elite in the provinces, and frequently used that local power base to rebel, so that it might be more accurate to say that they were 'recognised' rather than 'appointed'. In the century or so following

56 On this phenomenon, see in particular Ehsan Yarshater, 'The Persian presence in the Islamic world', in R. G. Hovannisian and Georges Sabagh (eds.), *The Persian presence in the Islamic world* (Cambridge, 1998), pp. 4–125.

the conquest period, a tension between the forces of central authority and regional autonomy was quite noticeable before it was definitively resolved in favour of the latter; this transformation from empire to regional commonwealth is perhaps the overarching theme of the history of the Islamic east during the period of the high caliphate.

At least in theory, the conquest of the Islamic east replaced the Sasanian administrative structure of the four 'quarters' and their subordinate *kūras* with a set of provinces connected to the central government via Kūfa and Baṣra (or later as part of what has been called the 'superprovince' of Iraq[57]). This network of provinces and sub-provinces is familiar from the works of the medieval Arabic geographers, and has been comprehensively described in Guy LeStrange's classic *Lands of the eastern caliphate*. Leaving aside the Mesopotamian areas (parts of eastern Anatolia, al-Jazīra, Iraq and Khūzistān) as well as those along or beyond the Indus, there were approximately twenty such provinces, most with many subdivisions, distributed among what we might regard as six or seven quite distinct geographical regions: the Caucasian provinces (Armenia, Arrān, Shirwān), the Caspian provinces (Mūqān, Jīlān, Ṭabaristān, Jurjān), the provinces of the western Zagros (Azerbaijan, al-Jibāl), the provinces of southern Persia (Fārs, Kirmān), the provinces of north-eastern Iran (Qūmis, Qūhistān, Khurāsān), Chorasmia (Khwārazm), the Transoxanian provinces (Sogdia, Ushrūsana, Shāsh), and the provinces of south-eastern Iran (Sijistān / Sīstān and Makrān).

The political history of these provinces – either individually or collectively – is not, however, a very satisfactory framework for discussing regionalism in the Islamic east, partly because we are told a great deal more about events in some provinces than others, and partly because the divisions themselves are somewhat arbitrary. Political economy, rather than fiscal administration, provides a better guide to distinguishing the various regions of the Islamic east and following their development. The key fact in this regard was the growing importance of Khurāsān and Transoxania, *al-mashriq* par excellence, as a frontier for expansion, as a centre of trade and commerce and as a hotbed for political upheaval – so important, indeed, that its history is virtually impossible to separate from that of the caliphate in general. Other areas, notably Azerbaijan and Sīstān, might have played comparable roles, but both became essentially static and defensive frontiers, rather than the dynamic type of frontier represented by Khurāsān, and neither had a comparable place in the

57 Khalid Yahya Blankinship, *The end of the jihād state: The reign of Hishām Ibn ʿAbd al-Malik and the collapse of the Umayyads* (Albany, 1994), p. 57.

commercial networks of the time (the areas north of the Caucasus being of minor economic importance and maritime routes to South Asia providing alternates to transit via Sīstān). The relative importance of the various components of the Islamic east was also greatly affected by the opening of the 'Great Highway' to Khurāsān via Rayy and Nīshāpūr. Up until the time of Qutayba ibn Muslim, as al-Ṭabarī notes in a particularly revealing incidental remark,[58] the most common route to Khurāsān was from the south, from Baṣra and Ṣuḥār to Shīrāz, Zaranj, Herat and Balkh – the route followed by the Baṣran invasion. The Kūfans, moving along the northern rim of the desert basin, could advance no further than Jurjān, and failed to establish firm control even there. Qutayba managed to subdue the area around Qūmis, probably by freeing it from Hepthalite marauders, and thereafter the northern route eclipsed the southern route. Naturally, the tendency was for the areas along the older southern route to become more isolated and to decline in importance, while those along the northern route increased in importance. Moreover, since there was generally no interior threat to the new line of communication between the metropolitan centre and its most important eastern province, there was little reason for either the government or historians to concern themselves much with the affairs of such areas. Were it not for the chance survival of sources such as the *Tārīkh-i Sīstān*, the history of the southern areas in the early Islamic period would be very obscure indeed. Finally, the pacification of Jurjān opened up a venue for a new effort of expansion into the coastal plains south of the Caspian.

Taking all this into account, it is possible to suggest a framework for discussing the regional history of the Islamic east based not on individual provinces but three rather distinct areas: Khurāsān and Transoxania, which are of the greatest importance and about which we are best informed; the secondary frontier areas, primarily Sīstān and Ṭabaristān, about which we are relatively well informed due to the survival of local histories dedicated to them; and the interior areas, including virtually all of western Iran, Fārs, and Kirmān, about which we know the least.[59] The last of these will not be treated in any detail here, partly because of the relative lack of information but also because its history is so closely tied to that of the successor states in Iraq.[60]

58 Al-Ṭabarī, *Ta'rīkh*, series I, p. 2839.

59 There is a very comprehensive and authoritative survey of the available information about the numerous petty dynasties that flourished in this area in Madelung, 'Minor dynasties'.

60 See Michael Bonner, 'The waning of the empire, 861–945' and Hugh Kennedy, 'The late 'Abbāsid pattern, 945–1050', chapters 8 and 9 in this volume.

Khurāsān and Transoxania

As Khurāsān became the most important component of the Islamic east, it also became the most politically volatile. Each change of governorship, each new infusion of troops, each change in fiscal and administrative policy carried the potential to touch off conflict among factions within the local elite or between the local elite and the central authorities. The severity of these disturbances tended to escalate whenever the momentum of the wars of expansion declined. The sources and many modern accounts generally depict them as conflicts between Arab tribal blocs (perhaps with links to geographic centres in Baṣra, Kūfa and Syria), but tribal identity is neither an infallible guide to individual allegiances in the disputes nor a particularly informative indication of their motivation. In early cases, the disturbances may have been little more than quarrels over the division of political and economic spoils, but they soon came to represent much more than that. In the revolt of al-Ḥārith ibn Surayj (beginning in 116/734), for example, questions of religion and ideology are apparent in his ties to the Murji'a, as are the issues of relations between the Arabs and the native and non-Muslim population, and between both of them and the central government. These issues culminated in the great upheaval known as the ʿAbbāsid revolution.

The ʿAbbāsid revolution was clearly a pivotal event for both the Islamic east and the Islamic empire as a whole, but what is of key interest here is the regional dimension of this revolt and its consequences.[61] The impression given in most of the traditional sources is of an externally organised and centrally directed movement, covert and conspiratorial in nature, which had as its secret goal the installation of a member of the ʿAbbāsid family as caliph. For over twenty-five years this organisation conducted a campaign of propaganda and manipulation to undermine the Umayyad regime in Khurāsān, and in 129/746f., under the leadership of a formerly obscure agent called Abū Muslim al-Khurāsānī, it launched an open revolt there that swept away Umayyad power, not only in Khurāsān but the metropolitan centres of power as well. Unfortunately, few of the details of this story can be taken at face value, and many defy credibility. There is not much reason to doubt that the movement was conspiratorial in nature, but the notion that it was consistently run by an outside organisation working for the ʿAbbāsid family can be regarded as mostly a myth concocted by propagandists after the dynasty came to

61 For more details on these events and their background, see Tayeb El-Hibri, 'The empire in Iraq', 763–861, chapter 7 in this volume.

power.[62] Even the date at which the movement committed itself to the ʿAbbāsids is uncertain; the slogans on the earliest revolutionary coins could easily be interpreted as pro-ʿAlid, and some were actually minted in the name of ʿAbd Allāh ibn Muʿāwiya.[63] The received tradition is quite obviously the result of much reworking and rewriting to accord with various political agendas, and it is anything but clear what the real nature and mechanics of the movement were. At least at the regional level, however, the vague slogans said to have been used by the revolutionary propagandists seem to suggest that the movement had two general goals: (1) to provide a thoroughly Islamised framework of government; and (2) to redefine the nature of the relationship between the local Arabo-Persian Muslim elite and the caliphal authorities.

The implication of the first objective was that the mixed Muslim and non-Muslim administrative structure of the conquest and early Umayyad period would be replaced by an exclusively Muslim one, but on the basis of an Islam that welcomed conversion and was open to all ethnicities equally. Controversies over these issues had been simmering for some time, and it seems highly probable that a crisis was precipitated by the policies of the governor Naṣr ibn Sayyār, such as switching the language of administration from Persian to Arabic, removing *dihqāns* as tax agents, and bringing in more Syrian troops. These policies may well have been unwisely imposed on him by the central authorities against his own better judgement, but in any case they could hardly have been seen as anything other than an effort to Arabise the governing regime in the Islamic east. It was in reaction to this that the ʿAbbāsid movement was able to construct a popular coalition of anti-Umayyad forces that cut across tribal loyalties and in which distinctions between Arab and non-Arab became largely irrelevant. As long as non-Arabs had converted, there would be no barrier to their participation in the governing elite, but the system by which a non-Muslim such as Nīzak could serve as a vassal-lord or an unconverted *dihqān* could act as a tax agent would be dismantled. This principle was exemplified above all in the person of Abū Muslim al-Khurāsānī, who emerged as the leader of the overt revolution in Khurāsān. As often noted, his very name (actually a deliberately chosen *nom de guerre*) proclaimed the fusion of religious and local identity. He is said to have made sure that those Iranians joining the revolutionary army were Muslims, but by the same token he insisted that those Iranian Muslims who did join should be welcomed

62 See especially Agha, *The revolution which toppled the Umayyads.*
63 See the very useful Miles, 'Numismatics', p. 369.

and treated well;[64] one of his first acts after seizing power was to establish a new army register which abolished the distinction between Arab and non-Arab forces.

The second objective, the forging of a new centre–periphery balance of power, is perhaps less obvious and more controversial to assert; indeed, it is likely that at least some of the factions involved in the revolution would not have agreed with it. It can be argued, however, that this message was implied in the call for rule by a chosen one from the family of the Prophet (*al-riḍā min āl Muḥammad*),[65] which was widely cited as a slogan of the revolutionaries. It was an invitation to replace the impious, despotic and increasingly intrusive rule of the worldly Umayyads with that of a charismatic holy man, chosen from the family of the Prophet in accordance with the will of the believers (or rather the elite leadership of the believers), who would give legitimacy to a system of government but would himself be uninvolved in secular affairs beyond perhaps mediating disputes between the regional components of the Islamic commonwealth. That there was to be some sort of deliberative and consensual process in the recognition of *al-riḍā* is suggested by the substantial delay between the victory of the revolutionary army and the decision to install Abū al-ʿAbbās al-Saffāḥ as caliph. The desire for the separation and recalibration of the powers of the caliph and the local authorities is best attested by the actual results of the revolution, namely the attempt to create a system in which there was an unrestrained exercise of independent authority conducted by Abū Salama al-Khallāl as *wazīr āl Muḥammad* in the west and Abū Muslim al-Khurāsānī as *amīn* (or *amīr*) *āl Muḥammad* in the Islamic east. That this was a strategic objective, and not just a temporary tactical necessity, is confirmed by the tenacious efforts Abū Muslim made to preserve his prerogatives as the leader of the Islamic east against caliphal demands. Indeed, so successful was he that the later ʿAbbāsid propaganda designed to demean his stature and minimise his importance could not succeed in effacing the memory of his all-important role in the revolution and the foundation of the new regime.

From the regional perspective, however, and with this aspect in mind, the ʿAbbāsid revolution in fact turned out to be a *revolution manqué* that achieved at best only part of its agenda. The will of the believers may have played some role in the appointment of al-Saffāḥ as caliph (though no doubt a good many of

64 *Akhbār al-dawla al-ʿAbbāsiyya wa-fīhi akhbār al-ʿAbbās wa-wuldihi*, ed. ʿAbd al-ʿAzīz al-Dūrī and ʿAbd al-Jabbār al-Muṭṭalibī (Beirut, 1971) (hereafter *Akhbār al-ʿAbbās*), p. 280.

65 On a possible interpretation of this slogan, see Patricia Crone, 'On the meaning of the ʿAbbāsid call to al-Riḍā, in C. E. Bosworth *et al.* (eds.), *The Islamic world: Essays in honor of Bernard Lewis* (Princeton, 1989).

the revolutionaries were surprised to find that an ʿAbbāsid had been selected rather than a descendant of Muḥammad), but none at all in that of his successor, Abū Jaʿfar al-Manṣūr. Al-Manṣūr was not only the most forceful and overbearing personality in the ʿAbbāsid family, he was if anything even more absolutist in his conception of the caliphate than the Umayyads had been. He was clearly the leader of a reactionary faction perfectly willing to co-opt elements of the former regime and to suppress the interests of those who had put him in power, and he was busily engaged in intrigues against the revolutionary agenda even before assuming office himself. Although it is true that a good many of the Khurāsānīs, such as the Abnāʾ expatriates who came to reside in Iraq or various social classes such as merchants who had a vested interest in a strong centralised administration to provide security and freedom of movement for trade, became firm supporters of al-Manṣūr and ʿAbbāsid rule, the sympathies of the Khurāsānī population in general towards the ʿAbbāsids proved highly ambivalent. Indeed, there are many hints in the sources that a significant segment of the Khurāsānī elite preferred another member of the ʿAbbāsid family, ʿĪsā ibn Mūsā, to al-Manṣūr and to his successors al-Mahdī and al-Hādī, and that pro-ʿAlid sympathies were very strong among the general population.

In the case of the Islamic east, the most important and immediate aspect of al-Manṣūr's plans was the elimination of Abū Muslim. The sources are full of reports about the cat-and-mouse game that developed between the powerful king-maker and his erstwhile ʿAbbāsid masters: an apparent attempt to implicate Abū Muslim in the murder of Abū Salama; Abū Muslim's interference with Abū Jaʿfar's efforts to secure a pardon for the Umayyad governor Ibn Hubayra; Abū Jaʿfar's resentment at Abū Muslim's perceived slights of him; efforts to stir up revolts against Abū Muslim in various parts of the Islamic east; and Abū Muslim's rejection of ʿAbbāsid attempts to assert suzerainty over him in matters pertaining to provincial administration and control of the army. In one particularly telling example, Abū Muslim's governor in Fārs would not accept even the caliph's uncle as governor without a patent from Abū Muslim.[66] Finally though, Abū Muslim, perhaps overconfident of his position, was lured away from his power base in Khurāsān and treacherously murdered in 137/755. With good reason, al-Manṣūr reckoned that day as the true beginning of his rule as caliph.

After Abū Muslim's death al-Manṣūr was able to move to affirm ʿAbbāsid control over the Islamic east, but with decidedly mixed results. In 140/757f. the

66 Al-Ṭabarī, *Taʾrīkh*, series III, pp. 71–2.

deputy Abū Muslim had left in Khurāsān, Abū Dāwūd Khālid ibn Ibrāhīm, died – or, more likely, was murdered. This enabled the ʿAbbāsids, for the first time, to make a direct appointment of a governor for the province. Al-Manṣūr's choice for the job was ʿAbd al-Jabbār ibn ʿAbd al-Raḥmān al-Azdī, formerly the chief of his security forces. It is fairly clear from the sources that ʿAbd al-Jabbār was given a mandate to root out any elements in Khurāsān suspected of loyalty to the cause of Abū Muslim or the ʿAlids, but accounts of how he carried out his instructions differ wildly. According to some he was so overzealous in imposing new taxes and killing and arresting members of the local elite that he threatened to provoke an all-out revolt and had to be recalled, at which point he himself decided to revolt. In others he is depicted as being secretly in league with anti-ʿAbbāsid elements in Khurāsān before openly proclaiming his own revolt. In either case, it is obvious that caliphal authority in the Islamic east was not yet fully established. To suppress the revolt al-Manṣūr had to send out a substantial army under the nominal command of his son and heir, Muḥammad al-Mahdī. ʿAbd al-Jabbār was captured and executed no later than 143/761.[67]

Among the string of ʿAbbāsid governors who followed ʿAbd al-Jabbār, the sources tend to distinguish between those who worked with the local elite and in the local interest, the exemplar among them being al-Faḍl ibn Yaḥyā al-Barmakī (governor 178–9/794–5), and those who excessively taxed, oppressed, exploited and manipulated the population. Of the latter, the worst and most unpopular by far was the notorious ʿAlī ibn ʿĪsā ibn Māhān, who was appointed in 180/796. By 189/804f. so many protests and revolts had broken out that the caliph Hārūn al-Rashīd investigated his conduct; but instead of removing him, Hārūn confirmed him in office (largely because of the lavish bribes offered up by ʿAlī ibn ʿĪsā). That touched off such a serious and massive revolt throughout the Islamic east – nominally under the banner of Rāfiʿ ibn al-Layth, an army officer in Samarqand (and reputed grandson of Naṣr ibn Sayyār), but one in which many different dissident groups joined – that Hārūn was finally obliged to dismiss and arrest ʿAlī ibn ʿĪsā in 191/806 and come to Khurāsān in person to try to restore order. To do so he not only had to correct the abusive policies of ʿAlī ibn ʿĪsā, he had to rely on the support of key elements of the local elite, notably Ṭāhir ibn al-Ḥusayn, the chief landlord and de facto local ruler of Būshanj, to buttress the army he had brought with him under the command of Harthama ibn Aʿyan. While engaged in this

67 See E. Daniel, *The political and social history of Khurasan under Abbasid rule 747–820* (Minneapolis and Chicago, 1979), pp. 159–62.

campaign, Hārūn died at Ṭūs in 193/808. Under the terms of the succession arrangement he had made in 186/802, one son, al-Amīn, was to become caliph in Baghdad while another, al-Ma'mūn, would essentially become an autonomous vicegerent in the Islamic east.

Al-Ma'mūn, guided by the advice of his minister al-Faḍl ibn Sahl (a recent convert and protégé of the Barmakids), managed to associate himself very closely with the local political, military and religious elites and their interests; in particular, he reversed the oppressive fiscal policies that ʿAlī ibn ʿĪsā had followed and pledged to act in accordance with the principles of religious law. He behaved much as Abū Muslim had done in asserting his power on a regional basis and resisting any effort by the caliph and central government to interfere with it, and he was reportedly lionised by the local population, especially the *dihqāns*, for his judicious conduct. When al-Amīn challenged al-Ma'mūn's autonomy and attempted to reinstall the hated ʿAlī ibn ʿĪsā as governor of the province, civil war was the inevitable result. The troops brought to the Islamic east by Hārūn al-Rashīd and commanded by Harthama were conspicuous by their absence, apparently desiring to remain neutral in the initial phase of this conflict. Instead, al-Ma'mūn relied on a military force led by Ṭāhir ibn al-Ḥusayn and composed mainly of *dihqāns* and their followers from Khurāsān and especially Transoxania. Ṭāhir routed the army of al-Amīn at a great battle near Rayy in 195/811, in the course of which ʿAlī ibn ʿĪsā was killed. Al-Ma'mūn was then proclaimed caliph in Khurāsān, and al-Faḍ l ibn Sahl became governor of the whole of the Islamic east, with a huge salary and military and administrative authority from Hamadhān to the borders of China and from the Caspian Sea to the Persian Gulf.[68] Ṭāhir, now joined by the regular forces (commanded by Harthama ibn Aʿyan and Zuhayr ibn al-Musayyab), commenced a siege of Baghdad in 196/812. When it became clear that the city would fall, al-Amīn attempted to surrender to Harthama, but was captured and murdered by troops loyal to Ṭāhir in 198/813. Al-Ma'mūn then ruled from Marw as sole caliph and sent al-Ḥasan ibn Sahl, brother of al-Faḍl, to be governor of Baghdad and the central provinces.

The civil war thus did not end simply with a restoration of provincial autonomy: in effect, the Islamic east had suddenly become the locus of power and the former metropolitan centre its dependency – it is thus not surprising that it is just at this time that coins bearing the term *al-mashriq* appeared. This generated its own set of problems, including continued resistance by supporters of the old regime in Baghdad, ʿAlid revolts in Iraq and the

68 Al-Ṭabarī, *Ta'rīkh*, series III, p. 841.

fear of moderates in al-Maʾmūn's camp (notably Harthama) that events were getting out of hand. At first al-Maʾmūn appeared to be supporting the more radical aspects of Sahlid policy. Harthama was executed in 200/816, and in 201/816 al-Maʾmūn appointed an ʿAlid, ʿAlī ibn Mūsā al-Riḍā, as his heir. This essentially revived the civil war and led to the declaration of a counter-caliphate under Ibrāhīm ibn al-Mahdī in the west. In the face of these difficulties, al-Maʾmūn, supposedly with reluctance, left Marw in 202/818 to return to Baghdad. With so many issues occupying him there, from war with the Byzantines to theological disputes to local revolts, he entrusted the governorship of all the Islamic east to Ṭāhir in 205/820. Ṭāhir and his descendants would continue to rule the region on a hereditary – and, for all practical purposes, autonomous – basis down to 259/872.

Although it is fairly clear that the issue of central authority and regional autonomy was at the heart of these events, there are many difficulties in understanding exactly how this played itself out. Among them is the question of whether al-Maʾmūn was really the reluctant caliph and champion of the forces of regionalism he might appear to be from traditional accounts. If his actual goal was to preserve and enhance his position after al-Amīn became caliph, he had no realistic alternative to cultivating the regional elites, and his actions can be interpreted as merely tactical moves towards that end. His appointment of ʿAlī al-Riḍā as heir, for example, served to shock his dynastic opponents in Baghdad and to blunt the appeal of pro-ʿAlid sentiments not only in Iraq but in the Islamic east as well. His return to Baghdad may have been much less forced by circumstances and reluctantly undertaken than is claimed; he certainly used the opportunity to shed past commitments by dispensing with both al-Faḍl ibn Sahl and the need for an ʿAlid heir. Exactly how and why he appointed Ṭāhir as governor is even more obscure, and there is reason to think al-Maʾmūn was not happy with the arrangement; as will be discussed below, there are indications that the two were on a collision course averted only by Ṭāhir's untimely, and rather suspicious, death in 207/822. All in all, however, an effective compromise had been struck through which regional elites could act without interference in return for nominal allegiance to the caliphs and cooperation with them when it was in their mutual interest, thus effectively achieving what appears to have been the abortive goal of the earlier ʿAbbāsid revolution. This was the political pattern that would hold thereafter.

The intra-elite dispute over the balance of central and regional authority was by no means the only manifestation of turbulence in the post-revolutionary Islamic east. Khurāsān and much of the larger region were affected for several decades by a sequence of movements variously depicted as heterodox, chiliastic and insurrectionary or revolutionary.[69] They are usually described as led by heresiarchs, charismatic figures teaching syncretistic religious doctrines who sometimes claimed to be prophets and employed various tricks to dupe the simple-minded into following them. The sources often attribute low social origin to these heresiarchs, but on closer inspection they rather appear to have been wealthy and powerful local magnates. Most of the movements and revolts are said to have shared a common ideology of radical social egalitarianism (even wearing garments of the same colour) and thus to be directly related to each other in some way; several also supposedly connected themselves with the legacy of Abū Muslim and claimed to be avenging his murder (they are thus often referred to as the sects of the Khurramiyya, Abū Muslimiyya, Muḥammira, Mubayyiḍa, etc.). One, Bihāfarīd, however, appeared in the rural districts of Nīshāpūr while Abū Muslim was establishing his administration at that city and was ruthlessly suppressed by him. In 138/755f. a certain Sunbādh the Magian declared a revolt to avenge the murder of Abū Muslim, and seized the treasury at Rayy to finance it before finally being defeated somewhere in the mountains of Ṭabaristān. Somewhat paradoxically, he is also said to have believed that Abū Muslim was not dead but in concealment with Mazdak and the *mahdī*, awaiting their messianic return. He supposedly called, among other things, for the slaughter of the nobles and aristocrats, for the overthrow of the empire of the Arabs, and for the restoration of a religion based on a form of sun-worship. Whether he actually propounded any or all of these ideas is open to question; they may simply have been attributed to him in order to legitimise the suppression of the insurgency. Another large uprising, around 148/765, was led by Ustādhsīs and concentrated in the area around Bādhghīs. Ustādhsīs reportedly cooperated with a contemporary Khārijite uprising (and is sometimes described as a Khārijite himself) but is also said to have taught his own doctrines based on the ideas of Bihāfarīd (i.e. combining aspects of Islam and Zoroastrianism). His army, however, appears to have been composed primarily of peasants armed with hoes, shovels and axes. The revolt was brutally suppressed by the ʿAbbāsid general Khāzim ibn Khuzayma, who is said to have slaughtered tens of thousands of the rebels. The sources disagree on the fate of Ustādhsīs himself; some suggest that he was taken captive at his mountain fortress and presumably executed, while others indicate that he

69 On these revolts, see G. H. Sadighi, *Les mouvements religieux iraniens* (Paris, 1938); B. S. Amoretti, 'Sects and heresies', in Frye (ed.), *The Cambridge history of Iran*, vol. IV; Daniel, *Khurasan*, pp. 125–47; R N. Frye, *The golden age of Persia* (New York, 1963), pp. 126–49.

received a pardon, probably because he had earlier played a role in supporting the ʿAbbāsid revolution. (There are even claims that Marājil, the concubine of Hārūn al-Rashīd and mother of the caliph al-Maʾmūn, was his daughter.[70]) Yet another spectacular revolt around 159–63/776–80 was led by the so-called 'veiled prophet of Khurāsān', al-Muqannaʿ. He and his followers, the 'wearers of white' (*mubayyiḍa* or *safīd-jāmagān*), apparently controlled the whole of the Kashka Darya valley from their strongholds at Nasaf and Kish, and at times threatened Bukhārā itself; they were also strong in areas around Samarqand and the upper Zarafshan valley. Muqannaʿ himself had a fortress near a place called Sanām (described as a lavish, almost paradisal, enclosure reminiscent of those later attributed to the Assassins); he supposedly claimed to be not just a prophet but a god, taught a form of Mazdakism, and used tricks such as causing a false moon to rise from a well or using mirrors to focus sunlight on his person in order to overawe his sectarians. When it was clear that his fortress would fall, he, along with his wives and followers, committed suicide to avoid capture. A similar sectarian ideology is also attributed to the great insurrection led by Bābak in Azerbaijan (201–22/816–37). These are by no means the only such movements and revolts, but simply the best known.

How should this phenomenon be interpreted? The source material is badly deficient since we have no documents from the movements themselves, only from writers who are generally hostile to them, and modern opinions about the nature of the movements – religious, political or social – vary greatly. Two basic features of these revolts, though, appear certain and must be taken into account: they occurred in a very discrete time period, the half-century or so after the ʿAbbāsid revolution, and only in parts of the Islamic east (mostly in peripheral, rural areas). This makes it very difficult to accept the notion, as dear as it was to later polemicists such as Niẓām al-Mulk, that the revolts were the continuation – in thinly disguised form – of the Mazdakite and Manichaean traditions of earlier times as well as the precursors of subsequent Ismāʿīlī heterodox movements. The idea, popular with nineteenth-century European racial historians and twentieth-century Iranian chauvinists, that they were part of some more generalised 'national' or 'anti-Arab' insurgency can also safely be discarded. They would rather seem to be connected in some way with specific changes brought about by the ʿAbbāsid revolution and by the regional characteristics of the Islamic east.

If one emphasises the religious syncretism apparent in the revolts they might be explained as the product of the accelerating process of conversion to

70 Abū Saʿīd Gardīzī, *Zayn al-akhbār*, ed. ʿA.-Ḥ. Ḥabībī (Tehran, 1347/1969), p. 125.

Islam brought about by the ʿAbbāsid revolution in the especially mixed religious enviroment of Khurāsān and Transoxania. It is also possible that they grew out of popular disenchantment with the political and social results of the ʿAbbāsid revolution, crystallised and epitomised above all by the murder of Abū Muslim. Most revolutions attract coalitions of actors, some more radical than others, united only by their antipathy to the status quo; once the revolution succeeds these components clash, and the weakest are eliminated. In this regard, there are many indications that the ʿAbbāsid revolution stirred up the messianic and utopian dreams of the masses, especially the desire of the peasantry for social justice and an end to economic exploitation as well as the hopes of indigenous people to live free from outside interference. These sentiments and groups were not ones with which all the revolutionary leadership was comfortable, and efforts were made to suppress them even in the time of Abū Muslim; naturally, the early ʿAbbāsid caliphs tolerated them even less. A variation of this interpretation would place greater emphasis on the social aspects of the heterodox revolts: they may not have been literally and directly connected to earlier religious movements or to each other, but they did share an aversion to the imposition of a religious system favoured by the state and urban elites and the social injustices that went along with it. In this view, many of the religious doctrines attributed to these movements and the stories about their leaders may have been little more than myths, distortions and *topoi* used to discredit and justify suppressing the remaining autonomous peasant communities of the region. (For example, the allegations about al-Muqannaʿ's claim to divinity take on a different cast when one remembers that documents from Mount Mugh only a few decades earlier regularly referred to local rulers in that same region as 'god-kings'.[71])

Yet another interpretation, which has become popular in recent years, essentially sees all of these revolts as a last, desperate, and rather cynical effort by the vestiges of the pre-Islamic aristocracy in certain sub-regions to hold on to an autonomous position of privilege by deliberately manipulating and exploiting the religious sensibilities, superstitions and class hatreds of the masses.[72] It should be noted, however, that some of these movements do seem to have been genuinely popular in character and to have achieved a

71 See R. N. Frye, 'Ṭarxūn-Türxūn and Central Asian history', *Harvard Journal of Asiatic Studies*, 14 (1951), p. 127.

72 See, for example, Fuzuko Amabe, 'The lords of Khurāsān and Mā warāʾan-Nahr', in Fuzuko Amabe, *The emergence of the ʿAbbāsid autocracy: The ʿAbbāsid army, Khurāsān and Adharbayjān* (Kyoto, 1995), pp. 87–104; the same general approach has been applied to other revolts such as those of Bābak and Māzyār (see below).

remarkable degree of communal solidarity. Women, peasants, tribesmen, and perhaps merchants and artisans as well, all appear to have joined in what could be regarded as a coherent guerrilla insurgency led by al-Muqanna‘.[73]

Whatever particular interpretation one follows, it is difficult to escape the conclusion that these movements represented some kind of response to the imposition of a greater degree of political, economic and/or doctrinal control over the whole of the Islamic east in the aftermath of the ‘Abbāsid revolution. As the frontier stabilised and the expansion that characterised earlier periods came to an end, the focus of both the caliphal authorities and the local elites turned to internal expansion, i.e. tightening up their hold on previously isolated or neglected areas within the borders of the Islamic east, and the potential for conflict increased. All of the revolts just mentioned reflected a reaction to this intrusion; their suppression coincided with the destruction and subjection of the autonomous communities that had supported them.

The Caspian

As noted earlier, the Caspian region, shielded to the west and south by a formidable mountain barrier, was hardly touched by the early Arab conquests. Indeed, the Arab destruction of the Sasanian monarchy gave the local magnates an expanded opportunity to assert their authority. There is much confusion in the sources about the names, titles and relative positions in the hierarchy of these nobles. At the beginning of the Islamic era a dynasty of military governors (*iṣbahbadhs*) known as the Dābūyids claimed rule over everything from Jīlān in the west to Nīshāpūr in the east, the contemporary ruler being a son of Dābūya named Farrukhān.[74] Rulers of this line are known to have minted their own coinage at least as early as 93/711 (year 60 in the Yazdegerdī era used by the coins), and they seem to have made a rather conscious effort to keep alive Zoroastrian and Iranian traditions and to isolate their subjects from contact with Arabs and Muslims. The control of the Dābūyids over Jīlān and Daylam was more nominal than real, and they also recognised as subordinate vassals various relatives and de facto local rulers of the mountainous areas of Ṭabaristān, of whom the most important were Bāwandids and the Qārinids. The ruler of Damāwand, the *maṣmūghān*, maintained his own independence and was in some ways a rival to the *iṣbahbadhs*. The main focus of the Arab efforts at conquest was a struggle with the Dābūyids for control of the coastal plain. None of the early

73 See the perceptive comments of Amoretti, 'Sects and heresies', p. 502.

74 Al-Ṭabarī, *Ta'rīkh*, series I, pp. 2659–60. There was apparently a later Dābūyid by the same name, who ruled 93–110/711–28; see W. Madelung, 'Dabuyids', *EIr*, vol. VI, pp. 541–4.

Arab raids made much progress, and even the major attempt at conquest launched in 98/716 by Yazīd ibn al-Muhallab ultimately failed, although it did exact a new agreement to pay tribute.[75] Following the ʿAbbāsid revolution, Abū Muslim sought and received a pledge of allegiance from the *iṣbahbadh* Khurshīd.[76] After al-Manṣūr had Abū Muslim murdered, Khurshīd seems to have thrown his support to Sunbādh, leader of the revolt in 137/754f. to avenge Abū Muslim and perhaps to bring about a restoration of Zoroastrianism (neither Sunbādh nor the Dābūyids had converted). One of his relatives, however, betrayed and murdered Sunbādh, supposedly because of a personal offence but perhaps also as part of an internal dynastic rivalry exploited by the ʿAbbāsids.[77]

Khurshīd managed to remain in power by paying lavish tribute to al-Manṣūr. Nonetheless, the accusation of support for Sunbādh, coupled with al-Manṣūr's avarice and absolutist tendencies, sealed his fate. According to Ibn Isfandiyār, Āmul was taken over as the ʿAbbāsid capital in 140/757f. and numerous small garrisons were established throughout the lowlands.[78] In 141/759 the caliph launched a major new invasion of Ṭabaristān. The *iṣbabadh* and *maṣmūghān*, warring with each other at the time, set aside their differences to resist the mutual threat, but they were worn down in what al-Ṭabarī describes as a relentless war.[79] Judging from Ibn Isfandiyār's account, the ʿAbbāsid offensive enjoyed two advantages over earlier efforts to subdue the region. First, the campaign was advised by ʿUmar ibn al-ʿAlāʾ, a man who had gained intimate knowledge of the area during a period when he lived as a political refugee under the protection of the *iṣbahbadh* (and who was appointed at the recommendation of Abarwīz, brother or son of the *maṣmūghān*). Second, the *iṣbahbadh* had lost the support of much of the civilian population in the plains; thus, the people of Āmul are said to have tired of the *iṣbahbadh* and to have welcomed the opportunity to surrender and to convert to Islam after ʿUmar ibn al-ʿAlāʾ had established a just administration there. The *iṣbahbadh* finally fled to Daylam, but after his family was captured he despaired and committed suicide in 144/761. The *maṣmūghān* was also captured, and his principality collapsed into a state of anarchy.[80]

75 Balādhurī, *Futūḥ*, p. 338.

76 *Akhbār al-ʿAbbās*, p. 333, ʿIzz al-Dīn ʿAlī ibn Aḥmad ibn al-Athīr, *al-Kāmil fī ʾl-taʾrīkh*, 13 vols. (Beirut, 1965–7), vol. V, p. 397.

77 Al-Manṣūr clearly exploited such rivalries to gain control over the area: not only did he try to supplant Khurshīd by recognising his brother(?) Wandād as *iṣbahbadh*, he managed to win over one of the sons of the *maṣmūghān* (al-Ṭabarī, *Taʾrīkh*, series III, p. 131) who had quarrelled with his brother.

78 Ibn Isfandiyār, *Tārīkh-i Ṭabaristān*, ed. ʿAbbās Iqbāl (Tehran, 1944), pp. 175ff.

79 Al-Ṭabarī, *Taʾrīkh*, series III, pp. 136–7.

80 Ibid., p. 137.

Although the coastal plains of Ṭabaristān thus became integrated into the caliphal system of provinces, ʿAbbāsid authority over the rugged interior remained minimal; both Bāwandids and Qārinids, along with lesser families, continued to hold power there. They were willing to make token obeisance to the ʿAbbāsids, but they firmly resisted any real encroachment (destroying, for example, the towns Khālid ibn Barmak had attempted to found in their territory). When people in the area under caliphal control tired of the onerous new tax regime they turned to the Qārinid ruler, Wandād-Hurmuzd, for support. After rallying the other local princes Wandād-Hurmuzd led an uprising around 165/781, beginning, according to Ibn Isfandiyār, with a general massacre of the Arabs in Ṭabaristān. He repeatedly defeated the forces sent against him until, in 169/785, he was persuaded by Mūsā ibn al-Mahdī (the future caliph al-Hādī and nominal leader of the ʿAbbāsid campaign) to surrender in return for a pardon. He was detained briefly in Baghdad but soon returned to resume his position in Ṭabaristān. In 189/805, after the murder of an ʿAbbāsid tax official, Hārūn al-Rashīd obtained a more formal treaty arrangement with Wandād-Hurmuzd and the vassal-princes, spelling out the requirement for them to pay tribute and provide auxiliary troops to the caliph but recognisng their autonomy in the highlands.

Both Wandād-Hurmuzd and his Bāwandid counterpart, Sharwīn, died during the reign of the caliph al-Maʾmūn (apparently at its outset, *c.* 198/813), and were succeeded by their sons, Qārin and Shahriyār. Qārin was a much less capable ruler than Wandād-Hurmuzd had been, and the Bāwandid Shahriyār became more and more powerful. After Qārin's death Shahriyār defeated his son and successor, Māzyār, and seized his lands. Māzyār was somehow able to make his way to al-Maʾmūn and win his assistance: the colourful account in Ibn Isfandiyār claims he was imprisoned by his uncle, Wandā-Umīd, but managed to escape, while al-Ṭabarī suggests that the ʿAbbāsids had taken advantage of the internecine conflict to expand their presence in Ṭabaristān and took Māzyār as a captive or hostage in 201/816f.[81] In any case, al-Maʾmūn decided to support Māzyār, but on condition he convert to Islam and become the caliph's *mawlā* – something that had long been an objective of the caliphs but never accepted by the earlier local rulers. The caliph's motivation in this is not clear: Ibn Isfandiyār attributes it in part to his appreciation of Māzyār's valour during a campaign against the Byzantines. However, he also saw an opportunity to use him to displace the new and unpopular Bāwandid ruler, Shāpūr ibn Shahriyār, and he almost certainly saw

81 Ibn Isfandiyār, *Tārīkh-i Ṭabaristān*, pp. 206–7; al-Ṭabarī, *Taʾrīkh*, series III, p. 1015.

Māzyār as a valuable counterweight to the growing power of the Ṭāhirids in Khurāsān. Back in Ṭabaristān by 207/822f., technically as a co-governor on behalf of the ʿAbbāsids, he supposedly soon began acting in the same imperious manner as the earlier *iṣbahbadhs*. At least on the face of it, judging from sources that are universally hostile to him, Māzyār managed to alienate all the major groups of society. He carried out a purge of his former enemies and rivals, killing Wandā-Umīd and Shāpūr, and the lesser nobility resented his increasing power and favour with the caliph. He outraged the urban Muslim elite, apparently by trying to impose taxes on them and restricting their efforts to gain control of agricultural lands, and they, led by the *qāḍī* of Āmul, reciprocated by accusing him of apostasy and collaboration with Bābak and the Khurramdīn heretics of Azerbaijan. He also offended the Ṭāhirids, who were trying to extend their influence over Ṭabaristān, by refusing to submit taxes to the caliph via their officials (which would have implied subordination to them) and by becoming embroiled in a plot with al-Afshīn (a general, himself of Central Asian origin, who had commanded the forces of al-Muʿtaṣim against Bābak) to overthrow ʿAbd Allāh ibn Ṭāhir.

Māzyār's relations with the peasantry are more ambiguous: on the one hand, he seems to have required them to provide corvée labour to construct forts and guard-houses; yet he is also said to have encouraged them to carry out a jacquerie in which a number of landlords (presumably the new Muslim landlords, not the native nobility) were slaughtered. He supposedly deceived the caliph and resisted orders to appear at court by claiming he was engaged in warfare against Daylamites and ʿAlid pretenders. Some of these allegations are less than convincing. Māzyār certainly had enemies and rivals among the native elite, but others, including some very capable generals, remained loyal to him. Moreover, despite the numerous complaints and the reports of his own spies, al-Maʾmūn continued to support Māzyār, and even recognised him as sole governor. Indeed, al-Maʾmūn addressed Māzyār with the same grand titulature used by the ancient Dābūyid rulers: Jīl-Jīlān, Iṣbahbadh-i Iṣbahbadhān, Bishwār Jirshāh (or Khurshāh), and perhaps even Iṣbahbadh-i Khurāsān.[82] Rather revealingly, Māzyār is said to have referred to himself not as the client (*mawlā*) but as the ally (*muwālī*) of the caliph. It may well be that in tightening up the government, taxing the urban classes and challenging the Ṭāhirids, Māzyār and the caliph were willing partners. It was not

82 Aḥmad ibn Abī Yaʿqūb al-Yaʿqūbī, *Kitāb al-buldān*, ed. M.J. de Goeje (Leiden, 1892), p. 276; Aḥmad ibn Abī Yaʿqūb al-Yaʿqūbī, *Taʾrīkh*, ed. M. Houtsma as *Ibn Wādhih qui dicitur al-Jaʿqubī historiae*, 2 vols. (Leiden, 1883), vol. II, p. 582; al-Ṭabarī, *Taʾrīkh*, series III, p. 1298.

until 224/838f. that ʿAbd Allāh ibn Ṭāhir succeeded in turning al-Muʿtaṣim against Māzyār, provoking the latter to declare an open revolt and to cut off all payment of taxes. The forces arrayed against Māzyār were formidable, but he was ultimately defeated by exploitation of petty dynastic rivalries: his own brother Qūhyār seized him and turned him over to the Ṭāhirid general al-Ḥasan ibn al-Ḥusayn in the hope of assuming his position. Māzyār was sent to Sāmarrāʾ, put on trial, and executed in 225/840. About the same time Qūhyār was murdered by members of Māzyār's former bodyguard, and the Qārinid dynasty effectively came to an end, although people said to be Qārinids continued to appear in minor positions of power for quite some time.

Despite its brevity, Māzyār's revolt is by far the most extensively discussed of these events in the sources, and was certainly a key moment in the regional history of the Caspian component of the Islamic east. Its political, social and cultural implications have been much debated by modern historians, and those debates reflect some important questions in terms of the phenomenon of regionalism in the Islamic east that have already been noted in connection with the heterodox revolts in Khurāsān and Transoxania. Thus, some older scholarship tended to see the revolt of Māzyār, like others, as a manifestation of 'national' anti-Arab or anti-Islamic sentiments; more recent studies see him as little more than a political opportunist who used whatever means were at hand to preserve his personal position.[83] Both views are probably exaggerated. Māzyār certainly did not hesitate to use conversion and caliphal support to hold on to his claim to authority, but in terms of regional dynamics he was also making a last-ditch stand against the spread of a Muslim and commercial urbanism in the lowlands that was bringing agricultural land and the peasantry under the domination of urban elites and thereby disrupting the traditional social and economic structure of the region. He may not have been a neo-Mazdakite in the way he is presented in some sources, but there is little reason to doubt that he used the Mazdakite technique of pitting peasants against rival aristocrats in his struggle. The irony is that the final collapse of the nativist resistance to the spread of Islamic urbanism and its political economy worked not to the benefit of a centralising caliphate but to another regional power, the Ṭāhirids of Khurāsān, who now acquired hegemony over the area.

The Bāwandid Qārin ibn Shahriyār survived this last upheaval by throwing in his lot with the Ṭāhirids and at last converting to Islam. This can be explained not only by political expediency but by the appearance of a new

83 See M. Rekaya, 'Māzyār: Résistance ou intégration d'une province iranienne au monde musulman au milieu du IXe siècle ap. JC', *Studia Iranica*, 2 (1973).

and rather unexpected element in the development of the Caspian region: the emergence of Zaydī Shīʿa as competitors to nativist, caliphal and Ṭāhirid authorities alike.

The stronghold of Zaydism was in western Ṭabaristān, carried there, it seems, by survivors of the revolt of Yaḥyā ibn ʿAbd Allāh, who had himself been given refuge in 176/792 by a local Daylamite ruler from a line known as the Justanids. Zaydism was then propagated to adjacent areas, especially by missionaries loyal to al-Qāsim ibn Ibrāhīm al-Rassī (d. 246/860).[84] In an uprising against the Ṭāhirids in 250/864 the people of Daylam and western Ṭabaristān invited a Ḥasanid, al-Ḥasan ibn Zayd, then living in Rayy, to become their leader. Although he was not recognised as an imam, he was able to found a Zaydī state that expanded to control most of Ṭabaristān, with its capital at Āmul. Not only did the Zaydīs and their supporters oust the forces of the waning Ṭāhirids, they repeatedly defeated and expelled local Bāwandids who opposed them. The most effective of the Zaydī rulers was no doubt al-Ḥasan ibn ʿAlī al-Uṭrūsh (d. 304/917), who successfully resisted challenges from both the Sāmānids of Khurāsān and the local Bāwandids and Justanids. Zaydism and Zaydīs continued to be the dominant forces in Ṭabaristān right down to the time of the rise of the Ziyārids, at which point the regional history of the Caspian begins to merge with that of western Iran and Iraq and is thus outside the range of this account. The question of exactly why Zaydism should have become such a fundamental element in Caspian regionalism is not easy to answer. To some extent it filled the void created by the erosion of sympathy among the population for either the local aristocracy or the outside powers trying to supplant them. It was perhaps a way of acceding to what seemed the inevitable spread of Islam while retaining some sense of local identity. It tapped into sentiments of affection for the ʿAlids that appeared in the Kūfan zone of conquest and the Islamic east in general. The appeal in the Caspian context of Zaydī theology and spirituality is difficult to explain, but there is testimony that there was an appreciation among the populace of the justice and ethical conduct of the Zaydī leaders,[85] and that may be the most basic factor in their success.

Sijistān/Sīstān

Sīstān and the Caspian are dramatically different places in many respects, but their local histories share a surprising number of similar features. Not the least

84 See W. Madelung, *Der Imam al-Qāsim b. Ibrāhīm und die Glaubenslehre der Zayditen* (Berlin, 1965).
85 Al-Ṭabarī, *Taʾrīkh*, series III, p. 2292.

of them is that we are fortunate to have available in both cases unique narrative texts that flesh out the sparse details about the history of these provinces found in the major chronicles. Ibn Isfandiyār's *Tārīkh-i Ṭabaristān*, however, seems to have been motivated by a simple antiquarian interest in the area, while the anonymous *Tārīkh-i Sīstān* (a composite work, the bulk of which was probably written in the late eleventh century CE) reflects the author's sense of a distinct local identity and a pride in it as it moved from being little more than an appendage of Khurāsān to the seat of the Ṣaffārid emirate and a regional power in its own right.

At least in the early conquest period the Arabs probably viewed Sīstān as a frontier province of prime importance, as it offered a prosperous urban and agrarian base in Zaranj and its hinterlands; prospects for raids and plunder in the still unsubdued marches of Zamīndāwar, Rukhkhāj and Ghūr; and the potential to serve as a springboard for further imperial expansion towards India. As time went on all these attractions must have lost their initial appeal, especially when contrasted to the opportunities developing in Khurāsān.[86] The old trade routes, as noted earlier, were shifting dramatically, and settled agrarian life in Sīstān was hardly easy, as Qutayba ibn Muslim found out when he had crops planted at Zaranj but then could not harvest them because of the infestation of serpents.[87] The people of Zaranj and other cities that had accepted Arab rule displayed a remarkable streak of independence; they were known on occasion to shut their gates to newly appointed governors of whom they disapproved, or even to chase unpopular officials out of town. In these disputes the Arab tribes often wound up fighting each other rather than any local enemies.

Meanwhile, the *zunbīls* and *kābulshāhs* proved to be formidable adversaries whose power could not be broken and whose lands were difficult to penetrate. Even when they agreed to pay tribute in exchange for the withdrawal of Arab armies, the amounts represented a rather poor return for the costs of the campaigns. One Arab general, having spurned an offer from the *zunbīl* to pay tribute of a million *dirhams*, had to accept an offer of 300,000 after a typically disastrous campaign, much to the disgust of the caliph, ʿAbd

86 Ibid., series I, p. 2705 notes that the strategic importance of Sīstān was greater than that of Khurāsān down to the time of Muʿāwiya.

87 Balādhurī, *Futūḥ*, p. 400. It is interesting that the peace treaties concluded in Sīstān sometimes included the provision that weasels should not be killed, in the interest of helping to keep down the snake population! In general, there is good reason to think that agricultural productivity in Sīstān had already begun a downward spiral that eventually impoverished the area.

al-Malik.[88] His successor fared even worse, and actually had to give tribute and hostages to the *zunbīl*; when a faction of the army protested and tried to continue to fight, it was annihilated.[89] The vigorous efforts of al-Ḥajjāj to subjugate the area fared little better (he was eventually obliged to strike a bargain with the *zunbīl* in order to obtain his help against the rebel Ibn al-Ashʿath), and we are told that after the death of al-Ḥajjāj the *zunbīl* declined to pay any tribute at all.[90] A declining interest in Sīstān in the later Umayyad period can be detected in the rapid turnover of obscure governors there, as well as Khālid ibn Yazīd's frank advice to ʿAbd al-Malik to ignore any political troubles in Sīstān and worry about those in Khurāsān.[91]

None of this was much changed by the ʿAbbāsid revolution. Judging from the *Tārīkh-i Sīstān* (the text unfortunately has some lacunae at this point) the people of Zaranj were unenthusiastic about the regime change, and refused to hand over the Umayyad governor to the ʿAbbāsid forces sent by Abū Muslim until he was guaranteed safe conduct back to Syria. Abū Muslim's next governor, ʿUmar ibn ʿAbbās, stirred up so much controversy among both the townspeople and the tribesmen of Tamīm in Zaranj that his chief of police was murdered, and ʿUmar had to flee to Bust. He was killed in subsequent fighting, and his successor, the prominent ʿAbbāsid propaganda chief (*dāʿī*) Abu ʾl-Najm ʿImrān ibn Ismāʿīl, was blocked by local forces led by a renegade from Bust named Abū ʿĀṣim, who became the effective ruler of Sīstān for four years and even attempted, unsuccessfully, to invade Khurāsān before being killed by a new ʿAbbāsid governor, Sulaymān ibn ʿAbd Allāh al-Kindī, in around 138/755. ʿAbbāsid authority was still quite tenuous: Sulaymān himself rebelled when al-Manṣūr appointed a new governor in 140/757; that replacement, Hannād al-Sarī, likewise rebelled when his term of office came to an end. Only under the governorship of Maʿn ibn Zāʾida al-Shaybānī was there some semblance of stability as well as some success against the *zunbīl*, but even Maʿn wound up being murdered by dissidents in 152/769. In sum, the appeal of caliphal authority in Sīstān to certain circles of the urban elite was more than offset by a general dislike of outside interference in local affairs – and especially the taxation that accompanied it – by most of the rest of the population.

One of the most powerful counteracting forces of localism in Sīstān was manifested in Khārijism, which played at least as important a role in the

88 Ibid., p. 399; cf. the apparently confused account in *Tārīkh-i Sīstān*, pp. 105–6 (trans. Gold as *The Tārikh-e Sistān*, pp. 86–97).
89 Balādhurī, *Futūḥ*, p. 399.
90 Ibid., p. 400.
91 Al-Ṭabarī, *Taʾrīkh*, series II, p. 1059.

history of that province as Zaydism did in the Caspian. Whatever may be said about the supposed Khārijite propensity for violence and divisiveness, the sect's indifference to ethnicity and its uncompromising insistence on virtue and justice could have great appeal, and certainly did in the case of Sīstān. The earliest Khārijite presence there was largely due to the collapse of the Azraqī principality in Fārs. Its last 'caliph', Qaṭarī ibn al-Fujā'a, had once served with Muhallab ibn Abī Ṣufra in Sīstān, where, according to the *Tārīkh-i Sīstān*, he was 'an illustrious man' (*buzurgwarī*) who won over many people as friends. He appealed to the Sīstānīs for help in his struggle against al-Ḥajjāj, and was supported by them, both nobles and commoners.[92] After his defeat and death (*c.* 79/698) surviving remnants of the movement sought refuge in Sīstān.[93] It is clear that these Khārijites were not long regarded as interlopers; they quickly established deep roots in Sīstānī society and found considerable support among the native population. In Sīstān, as C. E. Bosworth has noted, Khārijism managed to achieve a fusion of piety and politics that transformed it into a movement 'with some local foundations and with a concern about such grievances as excessive taxation and unjust tax-collectors'.[94] As such, its main base was outside the urban areas and especially among the peasantry, but even people in the big cities might collude with them against an unpopular governor (as is probably exemplified, for example, in the ease with which Khārijites were able to penetrate into Zaranj to murder Ma'n ibn Zā'ida in 152/769[95]). At times the Khārijite disturbances in Sīstān could spill over into the countryside of adjacent provinces as well.

All of these trends are illustrated in the most important and climactic of the Khārijite revolts, led by Ḥamza ibn 'Abd Allāh. He was himself of Iranian, and probably Zoroastrian, origin (other sources give his father's name as Ādharak and the *Tārīkh-i Sīstān* says he was from the family of Zawtahmāsb) but had many Arab followers. He is described in the *Tārīkh-i Sīstān* as a pious man who first gained notoriety by killing an oppressive tax-collector and then became

92 *Tārīkh-i Sīstān*, pp. 109–10 (trans. Gold as *The Tārikh-e Sistān*, p. 88).

93 It is interesting that the early peace treaty with the Sīstānīs, perhaps in conformity with traditional practices, specified that the wasteland areas served as a sanctuary for dissidents of various kinds and was regarded as off-limits to the regular Muslim forces (al-Ṭabarī, *Ta'rīkh*, series I, p. 2705); this practice may well have provided an ideal refuge for the defeated Khārijites, who gradually banded together with the local inhabitants.

94 C. E. Bosworth, *Sīstān under the Arabs, from the Islamic conquest to the rise of the Ṣaffārids (30–250/651–864)* (Rome, 1968), p. 87.

95 *Tārīkh-i Sīstān*, pp. 143–8 (trans. Gold as *The Tārikh-e Sistān*, pp. 113–17); Ya'qūbi, *Historiae*, vol. II, pp. 462–3; cf. Chase Robinson, *Empire and elites after the Muslim conquest: The transformation of northern Mesopotamia* (Cambridge, 2000), pp. 147–52.

the leader of a Khārijite sub-sect in the vicinity of Ūq, an obscure town that had become notorious as a bastion of brigands and Khārijites.[96] At first he was mostly engaged in fighting rival sects, but he soon became the champion of a much broader and more popular struggle against the policies of the governor ʿĪsā ibn ʿAlī ibn ʿĪsā ibn Māhān, who was as hated in Sīstān as his father was in Khurāsān. He defeated ʿĪsā in 182/798; spared the provincial capital, Zaranj; and abolished the land-tax. According to the *Tārīkh-i Sīstān*, the people of Zaranj negotiated a settlement with Ḥamza whereby they continued to recognise the caliph as ruler, but the payment of taxes and tribute to Baghdad ceased and was not resumed.[97] When ʿAlī ibn ʿĪsā sent an ʿAbbāsid army to try to reclaim Sīstān in 186/802, Ḥamza simply moved his insurgency to Khurāsān, killing tax-collectors wherever he could.

At that point the struggle between the Khārijites and the ʿAbbāsids took a particularly brutal turn, with reports of devastation, mass slaughter and bloody reprisals carried out by both sides. Eventually the disturbances became so widespread and severe that the caliph Hārūn al-Rashīd had to come in person to lead the campaign against Ḥamza. Hārūn sent an ultimatum to Ḥamza calling on him to submit, to which Ḥamza replied by using exactly the same titulature for himself as the caliph had employed and emphasising that he was fighting against the misconduct and oppression of government officials.[98] Hārūn's death in 193/809 averted the need for a decisive battle; Ḥamza apparently then dispersed his forces and returned to Sīstān, where he may have devoted himself to *jihād* against various non-Muslim territories.[99] Al-Maʾmūn was, as we have seen, too preoccupied with larger problems to expend much effort in dealing with Sīstān. As the *Tārīkh-i Sīstān* explains it, the governors sent by al-Maʾmūn governed lightly and did not demand much in the way of taxes, the Khārijites concentrated on raiding frontier areas, and the two sides generally left each other alone. That began to change after the Ṭāhirids took over the administration of Sīstān in 206/821, in part because of feuding between some of the Ṭāhirid officials and those sent to replace them.

96 C. E. Bosworth, *The history of the Saffarids of Sistan and the Maliks of Nimruz* (Costa Mesa, 1994), pp. 77–8 locates it north of Zaranj, probably near the earlier Zoroastrian cult centre of Karkūya.

97 *Tārīkh-i Sīstān*, p. 158 (trans. Gold as *The Tārikh-e Sistān*, pp. 124–5).

98 The exchange of letters is preserved in the *Tārīkh-i Sīstān*, pp. 162–4 (trans. Gold as *The Tārikh-e Sistān*, pp. 128–34); on them, see G. Scarcia, 'Lo scambio di lettere fra Hārūn al-Rašīd e Hamza al-Ḫāriǧi secondo il "Ta'riḫ-i Sistān"', *Annali dell'Instituto Universitario Orientale di Napoli*, n.s. 14 (1964).

99 His supposed campaigns as far as India are part of the popular legends that make up the fabulous work known as the *Ḥamza-namah*, followed also in part by the *Tārīkh-i Sīstān*.

One of the governors named by Ṭalḥa ibn Ṭāhir actually had to ally himself with Ḥamza to secure his office against his rivals. Ḥamza died in 213/218, not long after defeating a Ṭāhirid army and driving the governor back to Khurāsān. Inconclusive fighting between the Khārijites and Ṭāhirid governors continued for quite some time.

The Ṭāhirid intrusion into Sīstān coincided with both the collapse of the last vestiges of caliphal authority in the area and the rise of the popular militia forces known as the *ʿayyārs*.[100] The origins and exact nature of these groups are uncertain and controversial. At least in the case of Sīstān they have been well and succinctly described by C. E. Bosworth as 'anti-Kharijite vigilantes'.[101] There the *ʿayyār* groups were fairly clearly, if paradoxically, composed of non-sectarian brigands from the countryside and the lumpenproletariat (young, poor or unemployed, unmarried men) of the towns, especially Bust, under the sponsorship of an urban elite that, having despaired of the ability of the central government to maintain order, turned to these gangs to maintain some semblance of security. Although they were at first directed against the Khārijites, they soon became fierce opponents of Ṭāhirid policies and methods in Sīstān – primarily fiscal oppression and the depredations of the Turks who were beginning to figure in the Ṭāhirid military forces. One of the *ʿayyār* leaders, Ṣāliḥ ibn Naḍr (or Naṣr), succeeding in driving out the last Ṭāhirid governor in 239/854.

The great regional dynasties

Following al-Maʾmūn's accession to the caliphate and return to Baghdad, the history of the Islamic east becomes primarily that of largely autonomous, hereditary, regional dynasties: the Ṭāhirids, Ṣaffārids, Sāmānids and Ghaznavids (leaving aside the plethora of petty local rulers and dynasties). To these one could add the Būyids as well, but the history of that dynasty is so closely interwoven with that of Iraq that it is best considered in the context of the caliphate's history. The purpose here is not to give anything like a systematic account of the eastern dynasties, for which many excellent studies

100 See Claude Cahen, 'Mouvements populaires et autonomisme urbain dans l'Asie musulmane du moyen âge', *Arabica*, 5 (1958, pp. 225–50, and 6 (1959), pp. 25–56, 233–65; F. Taeschner, 'Futuwwa: Eine gemeinschaftbildende Idee im mitelalterlichen Orient und ihre verschiedene Erscheinungsformen', *Schweizerishes Archiv für Volkskunde*, 52 (1956), pp. 122–58; Mohsen Zakeri, *Sāsānid soldiers in early Muslim society: The origins of ʿAyyārān and Futuwwa* (Wiesbaden, 1995); Bosworth, *Saffarids of Sistan*, pp. 68 ff.

101 Bosworth, *Saffarids of Sistan*, p. 69.

are now available,[102] but simply an overview of their significance for the development of regionalism.

The Ṭāhirids

The appointment of Ṭāhir ibn al-Ḥusayn ibn Muṣʿab al-Bushanjī as governor of Khurāsān and the whole of the Islamic east in 205/821, the beginning of a governorship that would be held on a hereditary basis for some fifty years, can be regarded as a key turning-point in the history of the region. Some modern historians downplay the importance of this event, emphasising that the Ṭāhirids retained the status of governors and 'faithfully acknowledged and fulfilled the constitutional rights of their overlords the caliphs' or that they were 'partners in the Abbasid state' rather than 'independent dynasts'.[103] There was indeed nothing novel about a powerful family dominating the province for a generation or more (much the same could be said about governors going as far back as Ziyād ibn Abīhi), and the relationship between the caliphs and the governors was no doubt correct in its adherence to the formalities of appointment. There was, however, a crucial difference. Up until the time of al-Maʾmūn, a caliph might be obliged by circumstances to recognise an individual as governor, but he retained the ability to remove him, albeit with difficulty, or even – as we have seen – by military force. Beginning with the Ṭāhirids, there is not the slightest reason to suppose that the caliphs had any such option or ability in the Islamic east – but plenty of hints that they wished they did.[104] There is also at least one case in which the caliph's choice as governor was rejected by other members of the Ṭāhirid family, and he was compelled to accede to their wishes.[105] The fact is that the Ṭāhirids achieved a military power, political autonomy and fiscal independence beyond anything the caliphs could control; the caliphs were merely fortunate that on a good many matters their interests and those of the Ṭāhirids happened to coincide.

102 Among them Munjī Kaʿbī, *Les Tāhirides: Étude historico-littéraire de la dynastie des* Banū *Ṭāhir b. al-Ḥusayn au Ḫurāsān et en Iraq*, 2 vols. (Paris, 1983); Bosworth, *Saffarids of Sistan*; R. N. Frye, *Bukhārā: The medieval achievement* (Norman, OK, 1965); W. Luke Treadwell, 'The political history of the Samanid state', D. Phil. thesis, Oxford (1991); C. E. Bosworth, *The Ghaznavids*, 2nd edn (Beirut, 1973).

103 C. E. Bosworth, 'Tahirids', *EI2*, vol. IX, pp. 104–5; Hugh Kennedy, *The early Abbasid caliphate: A political history* (London, 1981), p. 167.

104 Al-Maʾmūn was suspected of wanting to kill Ṭāhir; al-Muʿtaṣim is said to have detested ʿAbd Allāh ibn Ṭāhir; and al-Mustaʿīn was relieved to hear of Ṭāhir ibn ʿAbd Allāh's death since there was 'no one he feared more' (Yaʿqūbī, *Historiae*, vol. II, p. 604).

105 The caliph al-Wāthiq reportedly attempted to install Isḥāq ibn Ibrāhīm ibn Muṣʿab as governor but eventually had to recognise the succession arrangement that ʿAbd Allāh ibn Ṭāhir had specified, giving the office to Ṭāhir ibn ʿAbd Allāh.

It is certainly difficult to describe the relationship between Ṭāhir and al-Ma'mūn as harmonious. Al-Ma'mūn had turned to Ṭāhir mostly out of necessity, and it can be argued that he came to be as distrustful of Ṭāhir as al-Manṣūr had been of Abū Muslim. In this case, the grievances went beyond resentment over being in debt to the kingmaker; much of what Ṭāhir had done was decided entirely on his own, and al-Ma'mūn seems to have been genuinely disturbed by Ṭāhir's role in the murder of al-Amīn and perhaps also over having been manipulated by him into acceding to the execution of Harthama. Just as al-Manṣūr had endeavoured to keep Abū Muslim from returning to Khurāsān by entangling him in the suppression of revolts and the managing of affairs in western provinces where he had no base of support, so al-Ma'mūn tried to keep Ṭāhir in Iraq and gave him the task of fighting the rebel Naṣr ibn Shabath in al-Jazīra. There are likewise claims that he was plotting to kill Ṭāhir (and that Ṭāhir was aware of this).[106] However, the governors al-Ma'mūn had attempted to place in Khurāsān had proven corrupt or ineffective or both, and disturbances there enabled Ṭāhir to engineer his return as governor despite al-Ma'mūn's misgivings and the hostility of al-Ḥasan ibn Sahl. Al-Ma'mūn could not risk an open breach with the regional elite that had put him in power, and he may well have been beginning to feel uneasy, after his return to Baghdad, with the prospect of living under the shadow of Ṭāhir in the west. Conceding him the governorship of the Islamic east was an effective and necessary response to both realities.

It is equally difficult to think of Ṭāhir as simply the faithful and loyal servant of the caliph. Indicative of his true attitude is the rebuke he gave al-Ḥasan ibn Sahl when pressed to fight Naṣr ibn Shabath: 'I made war on a caliph, and I handed over the caliphate to a caliph, and he gives me an order like this? He should send one of my subordinates for that!'[107] Obedience to the caliph figures hardly at all in the admonishments Ṭāhir gave his son ʿAbd Allāh when the latter took over the job of fighting rebels in al-Jazīra. While in Iraq he did not hesitate to rely on spies, and bribed officials to keep himself informed about the caliph's plans. Upon returning to Khurāsān, he minted coins in his own name, and reportedly omitted the customary mention of the caliph's name in the Friday sermons. All indications are that an open break was prevented only by Ṭāhir's sudden death in 207/822.

After Ṭāhir's death his son Ṭalḥa took charge of the army and succeeded him as governor of Khurāsān. It is not entirely clear whether his formal

106 Al-Ṭabarī, *Ta'rīkh*, series III, p. 1042.
107 Ibid., p. 1043.

appointment was made by al-Maʾmūn, or whether he assumed the post as deputy of his brother ʿAbd Allāh, who inherited the post of governor of all the Islamic east but continued to conduct operations in the west. Not a great deal is known about Ṭalḥa's governorship (207–13/822–8), but he does not seem to have been a particularly capable ruler; he had to face at least two serious problems, the rebellion of another member of his family (al-Ḥasan ibn al-Ḥusayn ibn Muṣʿab) and the Khārijite insurgency led by Ḥamza ibn ʿAbd Allāh. This gave al-Maʾmūn one last chance to assert some caliphal authority over the Islamic east by sending Aḥmad ibn Abī Khālid, ostensibly to direct campaigns against the Turks in Ushrūsana and Farghāna but more likely to spy on Ṭalḥa or even to try to replace him as governor. A huge bribe sufficed to defuse any trouble for Ṭalḥa that Aḥmad ibn Abī Khālid might have made.

Meanwhile, the far more talented and ambitious ʿAbd Allāh ibn Ṭāhir had carved out a base of support in the central lands that rivalled that of the Ṭāhirids in the east. He had proven himself indispensable by restoring order to al-Jazīra and Egypt, and was preparing to attack the rebel Bābak when Ṭalḥa died and he was supposedly given the choice of prosecuting the war or going to take over Khurāsān. He had also acquired vast wealth, including lands and a palace in Baghdad that had the same status as a royal residence. Even after he returned to Khurāsān he left a cousin in charge of the security forces in Baghdad, thereby keeping an important instrument of leverage vis-à-vis the caliph. Most sources (notably al-Yaʿqūbī, who seems to have held a position in the late Ṭāhirid administration) paint a glowing picture of ʿAbd Allāh's governorship of the Islamic east, and that is probably accurate from the point of view of the classes and interests it protected. What is known about it generally reflects the idealised form of government envisaged in the famous 'Epistle' addressed to ʿAbd Allāh by his father Ṭāhir: the cultivation of an image of piety; close association with the religious scholars; adherence to religious law coupled with a sense of justice; maintenance of security and public order; a fair and scrupulous collection of taxes; and a paternalistic fiscal policy that promoted the welfare of the subjects.[108] Perhaps the most basic change was a shift in the primary role of the governor of the Islamic east from

108 The text is preserved in Abu ʾl-Faḍl Aḥmad ibn Ṭāhir ibn Abī Ṭāhir Ṭayfūr, *Baghdād fi taʾrīkh al-khilāfa al-ʿabbāsiyya* (Baghdad, 1968), pp. 19–28 and al-Ṭabarī, *Taʾrīkh*, series III, pp. 1046–61; see C. E. Bosworth, 'An early Arabic mirror for princes: Ṭāhir Dhuʾl-Yaminain's epistle to his son ʿAbdallāh (206/821)', *JNES*, 29 (1970). Although Bosworth sees the ideas of the 'Epistle' as a reaction to 'new, Persian, hierarchic practices' that looks for 'a return to the simplicities of the Arab past', much of it actually seems in full accord with the values known to have been encouraged by the Iranian *dihqān* class to which the Ṭāhirids had assimilated themselves.

being a marchlord and leader of wars of external expansion to a director of internal development. ʿAbd Allāh certainly retained an interest in the affairs of Inner Asia (not least because of the increasingly lucrative market for Turkish slaves) and carried out some campaigns there, but his general policy was to entrust the defence of the frontier to local lords, the best known being the Sāmānids. In keeping with this, he moved the capital from Marw to Nīshāpūr and took a great interest in the promotion of agricultural development; among other things, he was responsible for a codification of law pertaining to canals and water rights.[109]

The darker side of ʿAbd Allāh's policies and those of the Ṭāhirids in general was the extent to which they wanted to dominate the whole of the Islamic east, not just Khurāsān and Transoxania. As we have seen, their efforts to take control of Ṭabaristān certainly generated some friction with the caliphs. In both Ṭabaristān and Sīstān they also produced a considerable amount of local resistance: obviously not everyone in those areas was as impressed with the benefits of Ṭāhirid rule as people in their homelands supposedly were. The Ṭāhirid hold on Sīstān was broken rather quickly by the *ʿayyārs*, as we have seen, and this helped create the circumstances conducive to the rise of the next great dynasty of the Islamic east, the Ṣaffārids.

The Ṣaffārids

The Ṣaffārids represented in almost every conceivable way the antithesis of the Ṭāhirid version of regionalism. The Ṭāhirids were aristocrats with a distinguished lineage going back to the time of the ʿAbbāsid revolution; the first of the Ṣaffārids was a plebeian upstart and unabashed, even proud, of it (the fanciful genealogy ascribed to him in some texts notwithstanding[110]). The Ṭāhirids maintained at least outwardly correct and respectful relations with the caliphs; the Ṣaffārid ruler made no secret of his disdain for the ʿAbbāsid caliphate (which he described as founded on treachery and deceit and not to be trusted), and may even have dreamed of overthrowing it. The caliphs may have resented the Ṭāhirids, but they collaborated with them; they detested and distrusted the Ṣaffārids, and used every opportunity to undermine them.

109 Gardīzī, *Zayn al-akhbār*, p. 137.

110 The *Tārīkh-i Sīstān*, pp. 200–2 (trans. Gold as *The Tārikh-e Sistān*, pp. 159–60) gives an elaborate, and completely unbelievable, lineage for Yaʿqūb ibn al-Layth going back to Ardashīr ibn Bābak and Kayūmarth; while the famous poem, most likely by Ibn Mamshādh, has him claiming to be a descendant of Jam: see S. M. Stern, 'Yaʿqūb the Coppersmith and Persian national sentiment', in C. E. Bosworth (ed.), *Iran and Islam* (Edinburgh, 1970). As noted by Bosworth, *Saffarids of Sistan*, p. 179, it is most improbable that Yaʿqūb would ever have taken such flattery seriously.

The regional character of the Ṭāhirids was diluted by their territorial expansion and their vast holdings of property in the central lands; although the conquests of the Ṣaffārids were even more extensive, the dynasty remained distinctly Sīstānī in character and orientation. The Ṭāhirids cultivated religious scholars and acted as defenders of orthodoxy; though pious in their own way, the Ṣaffārids had no perceptible sectarian biases, and welcomed support from groups such as the Khārijites. The Ṭāhirids supported and participated in the high culture in Arabic of their time; the unpretentious Ṣaffārids viewed elite culture with contempt, and valued vernacular and popular culture instead.

Yaʿqūb ibn al-Layth, the founder of the dynasty, was a coppersmith (*ṣaffār*) by profession. He emerged as one of the most popular and successful *ʿayyār* leaders after Ṣāliḥ ibn Naḍr had expelled the last of the Ṭāhirid governors, distinguishing himself in several battles against the Khārijites. Thanks to what the *Tārīkh-i Sīstān* calls his 'manliness, bravery, and splendor' (for which we might read his skilful exploitation of rivalries between *ʿayyār* factions and the cities of Zaranj and Bust), he was able in 247/861 to take control of Zaranj.[111] The following year he also displaced Ṣāliḥ ibn Naḍr, the *ʿayyār* commander of Bust. When Ṣāliḥ sought refuge with the *zunbīl*, Yaʿqūb responded by invading Zābulistān and accomplishing what no previous Muslim army had been able to do: decisively defeat and kill the *zunbīl* himself. Not only that, Yaʿqūb began to expand his army by co-opting and assimilating the very brigands and Khārijites the *ʿayyār* had been formed to resist. His great ideological tool in uniting such previously hostile groups appears to have been an appeal to Sīstānī nativist sensibilities; in a letter to one of the Khārijite leaders, for example, he emphasised the common task of fighting injustice by government officials (*aṣḥāb-i sulṭān*), resisting rule by 'foreigners' (*ghurabāʾ*) and a pledge not to surrender Sīstān to anyone (from outside).[112]

With a solid base in Sīstān, Yaʿqūb began to move into adjacent areas, consolidating his hold on Zābulistān and taking the area of Herat and Bādhghīs – which, as mentioned earlier, had long been a centre of local resistance and Khārijite activity – from the Ṭāhirids. Around 254/868 (according to the *Tārīkh-i Sīstān*) he occupied Kirmān, and the following year captured Shīrāz, the capital of Fārs. Also in 255/869 (or 259/873 according to other sources) he was able to take Nīshāpūr without a battle, and imprisoned the last of the Ṭāhirid governors of Khurāsān, Muḥammad ibn Ṭāhir. He also made a rather half-hearted effort to invade Jurjān and Ṭabaristān. The motivation

111 *Tārīkh-i Sīstān*, p. 199 (trans. Gold as *The Tārikh-e Sistān*, p. 158).
112 *Tārīkh-i Sīstān*, p. 203 (trans. Gold as *The Tārikh-e Sistān*, p. 160).

behind these spectacularly successful campaigns is open to debate. They were surely mercenary – robber's raids, as Nöldeke puts it[113] – to some extent, especially given the hardships that had befallen Sīstān because of recent droughts and famine. The attack on the Ṭāhirids could be interpreted as striking back at those who had formerly dominated Sīstān, as Yaʿqūb thought that it was his divine destiny 'to exterminate the Tahirids and end their tyranny over Muslims'.[114] The conquests in Kirmān and Fārs and the great importance attached to them, however, also suggest a larger strategic interest of reviving the trade routes and consequent importance of Sīstān that had prevailed in the early Islamic period.

The conquests in Fārs, along with the overthrow of Muḥammad ibn Ṭāhir, brought into the open the question of Yaʿqūb's relationship with the caliphate. To begin with, Yaʿqūb probably did not have a clear idea of the actual power possessed by the caliph, or his sentiments, and sought to appease him by sending rich tribute, including fifty 'gold and silver idols' seized at Kabul and the head of a Khārijite opponent who had posed as a counter-caliph. For his part, the caliph al-Muʿtamid was alarmed by Yaʿqūb's actions but responded politely to him since, as the *Tārīkh-i Sīstān* bluntly states, he had no other choice.[115] He indicated that he was willing to recognise Yaʿqūb's authority in Sīstān on the basis of his claims to be restoring order there, but that his actions in Khurāsān and Fārs were unacceptable.[116] When Yaʿqūb found that the people of Nīshāpūr would not include his name in the Friday sermon (*khuṭba*) because he did not have a patent (letter) of investiture from the caliph, he derisively dismissed this as the charade that it was, making a display of his military might before the notables of the city and telling them that his authority, no less than the caliph's, was based on the sword: 'My patent and the caliph's are one and the same'.[117] If the *Tārīkh-i Sīstān* is to be believed, he began acting much like a caliph himself, being addressed as 'king of the world' (*malik al-dunyā*), receiving embassies from foreign countries, and planning to lead a holy war against the Byzantines.[118] In any case, a break between al-Muʿtamid and Yaʿqūb was not long in coming. Neither efforts at appeasement nor inciting rebels in proxy wars against Yaʿqūb having produced satisfactory results, al-Muʿtamid publicly repudiated Yaʿqūb's authority over Khurāsān in 261/874,[119] and Yaʿqūb responded by invading Iraq

113 Theodore Nöldeke, 'Yakub the Coppersmith and his dynasty', in Theodore Nöldeke *Sketches from eastern history*, trans. J. S. Black (London, 1892; repr. Beirut, 1963), p. 181.
114 *Tārīkh-i Sīstān*, p. 220 (trans. Gold as *The Tārikh-e Sistān*, p. 175).
115 *Tārīkh-i Sīstān*, p. 225 (trans. Gold as *The Tārikh-e Sistān*, p. 178).
116 Al-Ṭabarī, *Taʾrīkh*, series III, p. 1882.
117 *Tārīkh-i Sīstān*, p. 223 (trans. Gold as *The Tārikh-e Sistān*, p. 176).
118 *Tārīkh-i Sīstān*, p. 234 (trans. Gold as *The Tārikh-e Sistān*, pp. 182–3).
119 Al-Ṭabarī, *Taʾrīkh*, series III, p. 1887.

and marching on Baghdad, quite possibly with the intention of deposing al-Muʿtamid.[120] Probably to everyone's surprise, the caliph's forces actually managed to stop 'the accursed renegade called Yaʿqūb b. al-Layth'[121] at a battle near Dayr al-ʿĀqūl in Rajab 262/April 876. The *Tārīkh-i Sīstān* seems to imply that Yaʿqūb had been lured into an ambush by a letter in which the caliph lavished praise on Yaʿqūb and invited him to visit the court;[122] others attribute the defeat to Yaʿqūb's naive overconfidence that the caliph would capitulate. There is no doubt, however, that Yaʿqūb found himself fighting, quite uncharacteristically, with an inferior number of troops on unfamiliar terrain under disadvantageous circumstances. Despite this setback, Yaʿqūb retired in good order to Jundīshāpūr and continued to control Fārs and Khūzistān until his death in 265/879.

Yaʿqūb was succeeded by his brother ʿAmr ibn al-Layth. ʿAmr had earlier had a falling out with Yaʿqūb and they had only recently been reconciled, and he was acclaimed ruler by the army somewhat reluctantly; he may well have represented a minority faction in the Ṣaffārid regime that favoured a more conciliatory policy towards the caliphate.[123] Sīstān remained firmly under his control, but he had to engage in a protracted and complicated struggle to suppress major revolts in Khurāsān while simultaneously trying to hold on to the lucrative province of Fārs in the face of ʿAbbāsid intrigues to recover it for the caliphate. Much like the Ṭāhirids, ʿAmr seemed perfectly willing to pay regular tribute to the caliph in return for patents of investiture, but the ʿAbbāsids granted them only reluctantly and grudgingly, and revoked them whenever an opportunity presented itself. Thus in 271/885 al-Muʿtamid proclaimed that ʿAmr was to be deposed from all his posts and publicly cursed in the prayer services. The caliph's brother (and effectively the co-caliph) al-Muwaffaq invaded Fārs and drove ʿAmr back to Zaranj in 274/887 before being obliged to renew the arrangement of recognising ʿAmr in return for payment of tribute. In 276/890 al-Muwaffaq again proclaimed ʿAmr's deposition, but to no avail; he had to reconfirm ʿAmr as governor of Khurāsān in 279/892. After defeating his rivals in Khurāsān ʿAmr had managed to make himself master of most of the Islamic east by 283/896.

120 Gardīzī, *Zayn al-akhbār*, p. 141.

121 The description in the caliph's victory letter, quoted in al-Ṭabarī, *Ta'rīkh*, series III, p. 1895.

122 *Tārīkh-i Sīstān*, pp. 231–2 (trans. Gold as *The Tārikh-e Sistān*, p. 183).

123 See B. Skladanek, 'External policy and interdynastic relations under the Saffarids', *Rocznik Orientalistycny*, 36 (1974).

As has been noted, the Ṭāhirids had followed a policy of entrusting the defence of the frontier in Transoxania to a network of local lords as their subordinate governors. Of these the family known as the Sāmānids had emerged as the most important, becoming the rulers of Sogdia, with a capital at Samarqand. After the overthrow of the Ṭāhirids the caliph al-Muʿtamid had recognised one of them, Naṣr ibn Aḥmad, as governor of Transoxania in 261/875 (presumably as a counterweight to the Ṣaffārids; Yaʿqūb had defeated Naṣr's uncle Ilyās and removed him from the governorship of Herat, so relations between the Ṣaffārids and Sāmānids were likely to be hostile). As it happened, Yaʿqūb ibn al-Layth showed little or no interest in challenging this system or adding Transoxania to his domains, so the Sāmānid family continued to rule there. But ʿAmr, after his victory over the rebels in Khurāsān, made the mistake of asserting a claim to Sāmānid territory. In 285/898 he induced al-Muʿtamid to depose the Sāmānid Ismāʿīl ibn Aḥmad as governor of Transoxania and recognise him instead. Ismāʿīl reportedly pleaded with ʿAmr to be content with the vast territories he already possessed and leave him in control of his frontier zone, but ʿAmr refused. He apparently also ignored the warnings of his own military advisers about the difficulty of mounting a campaign across the Oxus.[124] Ironically, Transoxania had developed almost as strong a sense of local identity and resistance to outside interference as Sīstān had, and ʿAmr quickly found that he had overextended himself. Ismāʿīl rallied the *dihqāns* and landlords of the area to resist him, defeated a Ṣaffārid army, and scornfully dismissed an offer from ʿAmr to negotiate a settlement. In 287/900 he managed to surround and beseige ʿAmr near Balkh, and finally to take him prisoner. Although some sources emphasise that Ismāʿīl treated ʿAmr magnanimously, he was soon sent to Baghdad, where he was publicly humiliated, imprisoned, and most likely murdered in 289/902.

The unexpected and abrupt fall of ʿAmr did not mean the end of the Ṣaffārid dynasty, but it did mark the beginning of its transformation from a great regional power to one of purely local significance. The Ṣaffārid army and administration were still largely intact and acclaimed ʿAmr's grandson Ṭāhir ibn Muḥammad as ruler. Ṭāhir faced serious problems both in holding on to Fārs against claims on it by the caliph and in managing factional strife within the Ṣaffārid regime, and he did not deal with either of them very satisfactorily. He was also threatened by Ismāʿīl ibn Aḥmad, who was now laying claim to

124 Al-Ṭabarī, *Ta'rīkh*, series III, p. 2194; cf. Abu 'l-Faḍl Muḥammad Bayhaqī, *Tārīkh-i Bayhaqī*, ed. ʿAlī Fayyāḍ (Mashhad, 1350/1971), p. 615. The *Tārīkh-i Sīstān*, pp. 254–5 (trans. Gold as *The Tārikh-e Sistān*, p. 202) suggests that the caliph had approved ʿAmr's request in order to lure him into just such a trap.

Sīstān itself. In many ways the most important power in the Ṣaffārid realm was now the Turkish general Subkarā, who was in control of Fārs and its revenues, rather than Ṭāhir. Not even the *Tārīkh-i Sīstān* has much of a positive nature to say about Ṭāhir, depicting him as a kind-hearted but pleasure-seeking and fiscally irresponsible ruler, who may also have been mentally unstable (sometimes spending days alone with pigeons and mules, which he regarded as his friends).[125] His various successors were not much better. In 298/910 the caliph al-Muqtadir formally recognised a Sāmānid, Aḥmad ibn Ismāʿīl ibn Aḥmad, as governor of Sīstān, and within a year Sāmānid forces had captured Zaranj and brought the first line of Ṣaffārid rulers to an end. The Sāmānid occupation of Sīstān was not popular, however, and met with protracted resistance led by a collateral branch of the Ṣaffārid family, which was in power in the period 297–393/911–1002.

The Sāmānids

The Sāmānids, who now became the most important dynasty in the Islamic east, traced their origins back to one Sāmān-khudā, a *dihqān*, probably from near Balkh, although this is uncertain (the claim that they were descended from the Sasanian general Wahrām Chobin is intriguing but of course ultimately unverifiable). Sāmān-khudā was among the many *dihqāns* of that area who admired Asad ibn ʿAbd Allāh for his administration of Khurāsān. He presumably converted to Islam (his son was named after Asad and all his grandsons have Muslim names), but it is not clear whether he became Asad's *mawlā*. It is also not clear how his association with Asad, a notorious persecutor of the ʿAbbāsid propagandists, might have affected the family after the overthrow of the Umayyads. Asad ibn Sāmān-khudā's sons reappeared in the time of Hārūn al-Rashīd, when they provided valuable assistance against the rebel Rāfiʿ ibn al-Layth (perhaps inducing him to sign a peace accord). For this they were rewarded in 202/817f., when al-Maʾmūn had his governor of Khurāsān, Ghassān ibn ʿAbbād, assign each of them districts to govern: Nūḥ at Samarqand, Aḥmad in Farghāna, Yaḥyā in Shāsh and Ilyās at Herat.[126] Eventually the line of Aḥmad became the most important branch of the family. His senior son, Naṣr, ruled at Samarqand and a younger son, Ismāʿīl, took over the administration of Bukhārā. As noted earlier, it was Naṣr ibn

125 Bosworth, *Saffarids of Sistan*, pp. 243–59 attempts to rehabilitate Ṭāhir's reputation somewhat, and it may be that he suffers in the sources from the wreckage that had been really been inflicted on the state by the more glamorous ʿAmr.

126 Following the detailed account of the family's origins in Narshakhī, *Tārīkh-i Bukhārā*, pp. 104–6 (trans. Frye as *History*, pp. 76–7).

Aḥmad whom al-Muʿtamid recognised as governor of Transoxania in 261/875. Around 272/885 there was some kind of conflict between Naṣr and Ismāʿīl over the revenues from Bukhārā. Ismāʿīl prevailed in the fighting and captured his brother in 275/888, but magnanimously arranged for him to continue in office at Samarqand. From then on, however, Ismāʿīl was the de facto Sāmānid ruler and Bukhārā his capital. He was recognised as sole ruler after Naṣr's death in 279/892 and, as discussed earlier, successfully fended off the challenge posed by ʿAmr ibn al-Layth.

Clearly the caliphs felt more comfortable with the Sāmānids than the Ṣaffārids as the regional power in the Islamic east. The Sāmānid attitude towards the caliphs was somewhat less deferential than that of the Ṭāhirids, but far less insolent than that of the Ṣaffārids. They followed the time-honoured Iranian tradition of sending 'gifts' to a nominal sovereign, but there is no indication they ever paid regular taxes or tribute. They minted coins (in great abundance) in their own names. They usually honoured the tradition of obtaining patents of investiture from the caliphs, still something necessary for legitimacy at least in the eyes of the urban elites and *ʿulamāʾ*, but it may be remembered that they also granted recognition of authority to the caliphs – and on some occasions declined to do so. The complicating factor in the relationship was the rise of the Būyid rulers in western Iran and Iraq, particularly after their capture of Baghdad in 334/945, when the ʿAbbāsid caliphs became essentially Būyid puppets. Muʿizz al-Dawla deposed al-Mustakfī in 334/946, installed al-Muṭīʿ as caliph, and pressured him to appoint Abū ʿAlī al-Ṣaghānī governor of Khurāsān, a clear affront to the Sāmānids (the issue was not so much his authority there as whether he received it from the Sāmānids or directly from the caliph). In consequence, the Sāmānids did not recognise al-Muṭīʿ as caliph until 344/955. Similarly, when Bahāʾ al-Dawla deposed al-Ṭāʾī in 381/991, the Sāmānids withheld recognition until they were satisfied with the new caliph's policies (*c.* 390/1000). It is this tension that probably explains the reports that the Sāmānid *amīr* Naṣr ibn Aḥmad (r. 301–31/914–43) at least flirted with the possibility of switching his allegiance to Ismāʿīlī Islam and perhaps the Fāṭimids. If the Ṭāhirids can be described as only an autonomous hereditary dynasty, the Sāmānids were a fully independent one.

In his justification for resistance to ʿAmr, Ismāʿīl ibn Aḥmad had pointed in particular to his role as a leader of *ghāzīs*, protectors of a remote frontier and warriors for the faith in unconquered lands. This role provided a key prop for the maintenance of their legitmacy as rulers. Just as the Ṭāhirid change of capital from Marw to Nīshāpūr had reflected a reorientation of policy towards internal expansion, the move of the capital from Nīshāpūr to

Bukhārā symbolised a return of interest in external expansion. Sometimes this was done by encouraging peaceful missionary activities to convert the Turks of Inner Asia, sometimes through diplomacy, and sometimes through active warfare. Ismāʿīl's first major expedition as governor of the Islamic east came in 280/893, when he successfully conquered Ushrūsana, ending the rule of a local dynasty there, and then invaded the lands of the Qarluq Turks in the steppes near Ṭarāz. When the Turkish tribes responded by attempting to invade Sogdia, Ismāʿīl proclaimed a *jihād* and soundly trounced them in a major battle around 292/904. These victories justified his boast that he would spare the people of Bukhārā the trouble and expense of maintaining their defensive walls because 'while I live, I am the wall of the district of Bukhārā'.[127] Not long afterwards the Turks began to convert in significant numbers to Islam. One perhaps unintended consequence of this was that the Sāmānid homeland began to be flooded with Turkish slaves and converts, fuelling the rise of Turks as slave-soldiers in the armies of the Sāmānids and others and rather dramatically changing the demographics and then the politics of the Islamic east.

Of course, it was not only activities in the northern steppes that interested the Sāmānids. Like the Ṭāhirids, they took their role as a regional power rather seriously, but their direct control over adjacent principalities was tenuous, and generally exercised by accepting the nominal vassalage of local rulers (not unlike the relation of the regional ruler himself to the caliph). This was the case, for example, in Khwārazm, where the Afrīghid *khwārazmshāhs* remained in office; in Jurjānj, with the Ma'mūnids; and in Juzjān, governed by the Farīgūnids. In the case of Sīstān, Aḥmad ibn Ismāʿīl (295–301/907–14) sent two armies into Sīstān and captured Zaranj in 298/911. As indicated earlier, Sāmānid rule was never very popular in Sīstān, thanks largely to its rapacious taxation policies and the rowdiness of the troops (now mostly Turkish) sent to occupy the province. There was a revolt and a short-lived attempt to bring about a Ṣaffārid restoration in 299/912, and a more successful one that brought a collateral branch of the Ṣaffārid line to power in 311/923. Aḥmad ibn Ismāʿīl also attempted to assert authority over Ṭabaristān after a rebellion broke out there under Nāṣir al-Kabīr. He was murdered before accomplishing this, and the Zaydī imam al-Uṭrūsh repelled Sāmānid invasions in 301–2/914–15. To the south-west, however, Rayy was brought under Sāmānid rule in 314/926. Down to around 333/945 the Sāmānid military governor of Khurāsān, Abū ʿAlī al-Ṣaghānī, endeavoured to maintain some control over these areas; he

127 Narshakhī, *Tārīkh-i Bukhārā*, p. 48 (trans. Frye as *History*, p. 34).

contested parts of western Iran with the rising power of the Būyids and restored Sāmānid rule in Rayy. With the rise of the Būyids, however, the Sāmānids and some of the local rulers of northern Iran found it prudent to cooperate against a common rival. Thus the Ziyārids of Jurjān became nominal vassals of the Sāmānids in return for Sāmānid assistance against the Būyids; they secured an uneasy peace with Rukn al-Dawla in 344/955. Thereafter the main thrust of Sāmānid policy seems to have been to avoid doing anything that might provoke the Būyids into attempting an invasion of Khurāsān.

In the discussion thus far the focus has been on the political development of the Islamic east as a region, but with the Sāmānids the question of whether there was also a development of a cultural regionalism takes on special importance. There is no doubt that the cultural accomplishments of the Sāmānid period were prodigious, but many of them, like those of preceding periods, can be seen as part and parcel of general Islamic culture. In the case of figures such as the physician-philosopher Ibn Sīnā (d. 428/1037) or the polymath al-Khwārazmī(d. *c.* 232/847), for example, it would seem pointless to try to distinguish their work as representative of regional rather than metropolitan culture. Likewise, the influence of the legal school of Abū Ḥanīfa and the theology of al-Māturīdī were pervasive in the Sāmānid Islamic east, but were neither monolithic there nor absent elsewhere. The collection and compilation of traditions of the Prophet (*ḥadīths*) was carried out as enthusiastically in the Islamic east as anywhere else,[128] but this can hardly be regarded as regional culture. Nonetheless, the culture of the Samānid period did have a certain regional flavour, and some of its particular style and mannerisms in things such as speech, dress and social customs were identified by the geographer al-Muqaddasī, who visited the area at that time.[129]

In terms of high culture, it is also possible to identify some important tendencies that mark out a kind of regionalism. One, in keeping with the frontier location and spirit of the region, is a marked interest in geography, especially as it pertains to those areas outside the Islamic world that were of special importance to the Sāmānids: the northern steppes, China, Tibet and India. That interest is also notable in works from earlier periods, as in the history and geography of al-Yaʿqūbī, probably as the result of his work for the

128 The remarkably extensive activity in this regard has been noted by R. Mottahedeh, 'The transmission of learning: The role of the Islamic northeast', in N. Grandin and M. Gaborieau (eds.), *Madrasa: La transmission du savoir dans le monde musulman* (Paris, 1997).

129 Muqaddasī, *Aḥsan al-taqāsīm*, esp. pp. 327–40.

Ṭāhirids, both of which give more attention to these areas than one normally finds in the conventional Arabic texts. It is quite apparent during the Sāmānid period in the patronage the Sāmānid rulers provided to Ibn Faḍlān during his journey (albeit on behalf of the caliph al-Muqtadir) to the Bulghār lands (309–10 / 921–2)[130] and to Abū Dulaf in his travels among the Turks and Chinese (*c.* 331 / 943?).[131] It was probably also characteristic of the unfortunately lost works of Abū ʿAbd Allāh al-Jayhānī (*fl.* 310 / 922?) and Abū Zayd al-Balkhī (d. 322 / 934), judging from what is said about them in later books by Gardīzī and Bīrūnī. It may also be that in historiography there was now a more pronounced interest in a specifically regional history, exemplified in the (again, unfortunately no longer extant) *Taʾrīkh wulāt Khurāsān* by al-Sallāmī (*fl.* fourth / tenth century).

Much more important for regional culture than any of these trends, however, was the emergence of Persian as a literary language, ending in the Islamic east the monopoly of Arabic in this regard. As a spoken vernacular language, recognisable dialects of Persian had been in use for some time, and had even been adopted by Arab settlers in the Islamic east: al-Ṭabarī, for example, often quotes military commanders as giving orders or making comments in Persian, and records that the dying words of Ṭāhir ibn al-Ḥusayn were in Persian (ʻdar marg nīz mardī wāyadhʼ: ʻone must be a man even in dyingʼ).[132] Al-Muqaddasī gives a fascinating overview of the various dialectical forms of this language spoken throughout the Islamic east and at the Sāmānid court (in the form called *darī*).[133] It was also adopted at various times as the language of the bureaucracy – although this seems to have been a very contentious matter, as some factions pressed for the use of Arabic.[134] The issue was probably not so much the language itself, as most officials were certainly bilingual in Arabic and Persian, as the implications of using one or the other: was the Islamic east an autonomous region or part of a larger commonwealth? Would the interests of local groups, speaking languages such as Sogdian or Khwārazmian, be better served through the use of Arabic or Persian as an official language? Should the Turks now entering the Islamic east in great numbers be acculturated in Arabic or Persian? Exactly how all this played out is not clear, but the turning-point

130 See A. Zeki Velidi Togan, *Ibn Faḍlan's Reisebericht* (Leipzig, 1939); A. P. Kovalevskii, *Kniga Akhmeda Ibn Fadlan o ego puteshestvii na Volgu* (Kharkov, 1956); M. Canard, *La relation du voyage d'Ibn Faḍlān chez les Bulgares de la Volga* (Algiers, 1958).

131 A. von Rohr-Sauer, *Des Abu Dulaf Bericht über seine Reise nach Turkestan, China und Indien* (Bonn, 1939).

132 Al-Ṭabarī, *Taʾrīkh*, series II, p. 1063.

133 Muqaddasī, *Aḥsan al-taqāsīm*, pp. 334–6.

134 See Treadwell, 'Samanid state', pp. 173–180.

would seem to be Aḥmad ibn Ismāʿīl's futile effort to reimpose Arabic as the language of administration; thereafter, Persian was dominant. The victory of Persian in the chancery was accompanied by the rise of literary Persian, sometimes under the patronage of the *dihqāns* and local lords and eventually by the Sāmānid rulers themselves. In poetry, there may have been some tentative efforts under the Ṭāhirids and Ṣaffārids to produce Persian verse; under the Sāmānids there was a galaxy of great Persian poets, including Rūdakī (d. *c*. 329/940) and Daqīqī (d. *c*. 370/980?). For prose, a critical development was the decision of the Sāmānid *amīr* Manṣūr ibn Nūḥ (350–65/961–76) to order Persian 'translations' (actually redactions) of al-Ṭabarī's *Taʾrīkh* and *Tafsīr*, thereby extending Persian into realms of scholarship and religion that had always been the exclusive preserve of Arabic. The magnitude of the change in mindset that this required is indicated by the fact that he felt the need to secure a *fatwā* affirming that the use of Persian for such a purpose was legitimate. It served both to affirm the regional identity of the Islamic east under the Sāmānids and to assimilate sub-regional identities into a common fabric: 'In this land, the language is Persian (*pārsī*), and the kings of this realm are Persian kings (*mulūk-i ʿajam*).'[135]

The downfall of the Sāmānids, ironically, was the product of their greatest success – their triumphs over the Turks – aggravated by disputes within the family itself. The acquisition of large numbers of Turkish slaves and their use as *ghulām*-troops led to the eclipse of the Iranian *dihqān* forces which had been the backbone of earlier armies in the Islamic east. The Islamisation of the Turks and the appearance of Muslim Turkish states negated, at least in theory, the possibilities for *jihād* and enslavement. It was not long before the Sāmānids were under both internal pressure from their less than obedient *ghulāms* and external pressure from the new Turkish state of the Qarakhānids. The problem is obvious at least as early as 301/914, when Aḥmad ibn Ismāʿīl was murdered by his own Turkish troops (supposedly because of his overly deferential attitude towards the religious scholars, although one suspects there was a good deal more than that behind the assassination). He was succeeded by his eight-year-old son Naṣr (301–31/914–43), and from then on it is difficult to avoid the impression that the Sāmānid rulers were mostly figureheads, with the real power behind the throne being Iranian ministers such as Jayhānī and Abu ʾl-Faḍl al-Balʿamī and later Turkish generals such as Tāsh and Fāʾiq. If Naṣr's encouragement of the Ismāʿīlīs was part of an attempt to reassert his independence and authority, it failed. He was compelled to

135 *Tarjumah-i Tafsīr-i Ṭabarī*, ed. Ḥabīb Yaghmāʾī, 7 vols. in 4 (Tehran, 1961), vol. I, p. 5.

abdicate in 331/943 after the discovery of a plot in the army to overthrow him. Perhaps as part of this same conspiracy, his successor, Nūḥ ibn Naṣr (331–43/943–54), sought to install the Turkish general Ibrāhīm ibn Sīmjūr as military governor of Khurāsān, which provoked a rebellion by the previous Iranian commander, Abū ʿAlī al-Ṣaghānī. This continuing quarrel over Khurāsān both weakened the dynasty and increased the dependency of the ruler on Turkish troops to stay in power (Nūḥ had to fend off an effort by Abū ʿAlī to set up another member of the Sāmānid family as *amīr*). In the best-known and most consequential case of Turkish insubordination, the governor of Khurāsān, Alptegin, having failed in an effort to install a candidate of his choosing as the successor to ʿAbd al-Malik ibn Nūḥ in 350/961, went off with his supporters and seized control of Ghazna. There he acted ostensibly as a Sāmānid governor devoted to leading *jihād* in India while actually being in a state of semi-rebellion, probably driving back at least one Sāmānid army sent against him.

The death pangs of the Sāmānid dynasty were protracted but inexorable. By the reign of Nūḥ ibn Manṣūr (r. 365–87/976–97) the struggle between Iranian and Turkish elements in the army for control of Khurāsān had become a competition between rival factions of Turks: on the one hand, the *amīr*'s nominal choice as governor, Abu ʾl-ʿAbbās Tāsh; and on the other, a coalition of the chamberlain, Fāʾiq, and the governor of Qūhistān, Abu ʾl-Ḥasan Sīmjūrī (who also took the opportunity to orchestrate the murder of the minister Abu ʾl-Ḥusayn al-ʿUtbī in 371/982). Tāsh, despite an appeal to the Būyids for help, was defeated in 377/987. Sīmjūrī's son, Abū ʿAlī, then defeated Fāʾiq in 380/990. As a result, Sāmānid rule over Khurāsān was completely lost. Meanwhile, the Qarakhānids were bearing down on the Sāmānids from the north, taking Isfījāb in 370/980. In 381–2/991–2 Bughrā Khān, the chief Qarakhānid ruler, attacked the Sāmānids and occupied Bukhārā, probably at the instigation of Fāʾiq or Abū ʿAlī Sīmjūrī or both of them. Nūḥ soon recovered his capital after Bughrā Khān fell fatally ill and returned home. Fāʾiq and Abū ʿAlī then attempted to overthrow Nūḥ, but Sāmānid rule was saved by the intervention of Sebüktegin, who had become the chief of the Turkish troops at Ghazna; as a reward Sebüktegin's son, Maḥmūd, was recognised by the Sāmānids as governor of Khurāsān. Nūḥ also sought Sebüktegin's help against an invasion by the new Qarakhānid ruler, Ilik-Naṣr, in 386/996. Sebüktegin, however, did not entirely trust the Sāmānid ruler and had little interest in becoming embroiled in a fight with the Qarakhānids. Consequently he negotiated a settlement with Ilik-Naṣr that recognised Qarakhānid supremacy north of the Jaxartes and Sebüktegin's in Khurāsān, leaving a Sāmānid principality now reduced to what had been its homeland areas around Samarqand and Bukhārā as a buffer between them. After Fā'iq, in league with the Turkish general Baktuzun, engineered yet another plot to put a puppet on the throne, even that was lost. Maḥmūd ibn Sebüktegin reached an agreement with the Qarakhānids on the division of territory, confirming his supremacy south of the Oxus, and in 398 / 999 Ilik-Naṣr occupied Bukhārā. Clearly the Sāmānid ruler was no longer a 'wall' for the city against the Turks or anyone else, and the religious leadership, which had invited a Sāmānid to rule in the first place, now declared that the dynasty was not worth fighting for since the Turks had become Muslims. There was eventually one last effort to bring about a Sāmānid restoration, but it ended with the death of Ismāʿīl ibn Nūḥ in 395 / 1005.

The fall of the Sāmānid dynasty marks an appropriate end for a history of the Islamic east in the classical period, although this is masked somewhat by the afterglow provided by the Ghaznavid rulers, especially during the reign of Maḥmūd of Ghazna (388–421 / 998–1030). The Ghaznavid period was a transitional one, and it is certainly possible to regard it as the end rather than the beginning of an era. It is true that the Ghaznavids vigorously defended their hold on the former Sāmānid territories south of the Oxus before finally being driven out by the Saljūq Turks at the battle of Dandānqān in 431 / 1040. It is also true that many of the cultural trends of the Sāmānid period, such as the Persian literary revival, the reconstruction of the Iranian national epic, and the perfection of the Persian bureaucratic system, continued into early Ghaznavid times. Nonetheless, the Ghaznavids and the Qarakhānids represented the advent of a new Turkish political power unlike anything that had existed before. And, well before Dandānqān, the Ghaznavid vision was fixed on new conquests and new lands in Afghanistan and India, which is where the real significance of that dynasty resides.[136] The unity and shape of the Islamic east had fundamentally changed, but not before creating a synthesis of Islamic, Arab, Persian and Turkish culture that would prevail over a much larger area for many centuries to come.

136 See Wink, 'The early expansion of Islam in India'.

12

Syria

R. STEPHEN HUMPHREYS

Syria is a name, not a country. It comprises a vast region whose boundaries, political or 'natural', cannot be defined with any precision. The Arabs called it (and still do) al-Shām or Bilād al-Shām – literally, 'the lands to the left', i.e. to the north for a person in the Arabian Peninsula facing east towards the rising sun. In its broadest sense it is simply the western half of the Fertile Crescent, reaching north to south from the foothills of the Taurus and Anti-Taurus mountains to the Gulf of ʿAqaba and the Wādī Sirḥān, and east to west from the middle Euphrates to the Mediterranean. On the south, it fades imperceptibly into the great deserts of Sinai and the Arabian Peninsula. On the north, it adjoins the Cilician plain. The lands stretching from the Euphrates east and to the upper Tigris are both an extension of Syria and a separate entity. Usually called Mesopotamia – or, in Arabic, al-Jazīra – this region had, and still retains, a distinctive profile of its own, for it formed the frontier zone between Islam and Byzantium, and between the Kurdish and Armenian highlands on the north and the Arab-dominated lowlands on the south. Even so, western Mesopotamia/al-Jazīra is so deeply intertwined with Syria proper that it must be included in this chapter. Localism and political fragmentation were the inevitable consequence of Syria's geography. Even so, the interaction between the region's disparate elements was constant and intense. One could never regard Syria as a single unit, but on every level – political, economic, social, cultural – it certainly constituted a coherent system.

Syria falls into several geographical zones: a narrow plain that runs the length of the Mediterranean coast from Antioch to Jaffa; behind this plain, linked chains of hills and moderately high (but easily traversed) mountains; and finally, a vast interior steppe. The coastal plain north of Tyre receives extensive albeit seasonal rainfall, and northern Syria and the northern Jazīra typically see enough to support rainfed agriculture. With a few exceptions the centre and south are far more arid, and here agriculture is only possible with skilfully managed irrigation. Because of its complex geography Syria has always possessed a diverse population and wide range of cultures. The coastal plain is dotted with major and minor seaports, and has been a hive of commercial and cultural exchange since the earliest times. The hills and mountains have generated an interwoven series of village-based peasant societies, each jealously guarding its lands and way of life against its neighbours as well as any outside powers that might try to intrude. The western edge of the interior steppe is favoured by a series of oases and small rivers, and has been quite densely sprinkled with cities and villages for several millennia. In some ways this region, marked by famous names such as Damascus, Homs and Aleppo, seems the heart of Syria. The interior steppe, finally, has been dominated at least since the early first millennium BCE by tribally organised nomadic pastoralists, whose economy has been based largely (though never exclusively) on camel herding.[1]

The demography of Syria, both now and in the past, does not permit a simple description. On the eve of the Arab conquest both the coastal and interior cities were dominated by a Greek-speaking elite of landowners, imperial officials and senior ecclesiastics. However, the bulk of the urban population (at least in the interior cities and towns) spoke one or another dialect of Aramaic as their first language. Almost the entire village population, whether in the mountains or the western edge of the steppe, also spoke Aramaic, which was (in its Syriac form) already the predominant written language in al-Jazīra. The steppe and desert were dominated by Arabic speakers, as they had been for many centuries past. The boundaries between language groups were hardly crisp: most townsmen must have had some Greek, however rough and ungrammatical, and the Arab tribesmen on the western fringes of the steppe could move in and out of sedentarised modes of life.

When Heraclius entered Jerusalem in triumph in March 630, he retook possession of a region that was the most deeply Christianised part of his empire, and also one that Hellenistic and Roman culture had profoundly shaped in its own image over the course of more than nine centuries. Three centuries later, however, the changes in the region would have been striking even to a casual observer. Roman rule was now only a dim memory, recalled in the ruins of its monuments and in the resurgence of Byzantine military power along Syria's northern borderlands. Some districts, especially those on the western fringes of the interior steppe, were distinctly poorer and less populous than they had been in Roman times, though whether this was true

1 The most systematic recent survey, with a strong historical dimension, is E. Wirth, *Syrien: Eine geographische Landeskunde* (Darmstadt, 1971).

of Syria as a whole is open to question. Greek had been supplanted by Arabic as the language of educated discourse throughout the region, and in most places Arabic was probably the main vehicle of everyday speech as well. In many areas (especially in Mount Lebanon, northern Syria and northern Mesopotamia) Christians surely still constituted a demographic majority, with their institutions and cultural life largely intact. However, Islam had sunk deep roots and was arguably a more dynamic force in the country's social and cultural life. In short, by the mid-fourth / tenth century Syria was no longer a Roman–Christian land, but rather one that was largely Arabic-speaking and increasingly Muslim.

The late Roman milieu

In 630 no one could have imagined that such a thing might be possible. The imprint of *romanitas* and Christianity was obvious in every dimension of life. On the level of sheer visual grandeur, there were the impressive colonnaded streets, public basilicas, churches and agoras of major and lesser cities stretching from Antioch and Apamea in the north, to Beirut and Damascus in the centre, and finally to Caesarea Maritima and Gerasa in the south. By the end of the Persian war in 628 – and perhaps well before that time – the urban fabric of Greece, the Balkans and central Anatolia may have been seriously damaged, but even the smaller towns of Syria were still largely intact, though their surface areas (and presumably their populations) had shrunk somewhat since the third century.[2] Certainly their agricultural hinterlands seem to have been flourishing and highly developed. If the traditional organs of urban life – temples, gymnasia and monumental public baths – had been abandoned or converted to new uses, their loss was compensated by a host of churches thickly strewn across the landscape. Even remote mountain towns or settlements on the edge of the Jordanian steppe might have several churches, built and endowed by both private and official donors. Most were fairly small structures, but even these were beautifully constructed and richly decorated. A few imperial foundations, such as St Simeon Stylites in the limestone massif south-west of Aleppo, St Sergius in Rusafa (al-Ruṣāfa) and of course the Church of the Holy Sepulchre in Jerusalem, were imposing indeed. Like churches, monasteries were everywhere – always outside the city walls, but

2 J. H. G. Liebeschuetz, *Decline and fall of the Roman city* (Oxford, 2001), pp. 54–63, 295–317; C. Wickham, *Framing the early Middle Ages: Europe and the Mediterranean, 400–800* (Oxford, 2005), pp. 613–30.

often in rather close proximity to them. Beyond such formal institutions there was the dense network of holy men, living and dead, whose mighty deeds demonstrated God's ever-present power and protection.[3] In the realm of Greek thought and letters (both pagan and Christian), Syria had played an extraordinary role since Eusebius of Caesarea and Libanius of Antioch in the fourth century. In the early first/seventh century alone the monastery of Mar Sabas east of Jerusalem had produced such luminaries as John Moschos, Maximus the Confessor and Sophronius – and its great days were far from over. Greek was the language of law and administration everywhere. Even such marginal places as Petra (east of the Dead Sea) and Nessana (in the Negev) could produce complex legal and administrative documents written in serviceable Greek.

Looked at more closely, of course, the picture was more complicated. To begin with, not everyone shared in the region's cosmopolitan Graeco-Roman culture. Indeed, except in imperial administrative centres such as Antioch or Caesarea the majority of townspeople, and the vast majority of country dwellers, spoke Greek as a second language, if at all. For the most part they relied on their ancestral Aramaic or (in the interior steppe) on Arabic. The peoples of Syria and Palestine were overwhelmingly Christian by this time, but in some areas – among the desert Arabs, for example – Christianity had only begun to take hold in the course of the sixth century, and Syria's many traditional cults must still have survived in patches that escaped the vigilance of imperial and ecclesiastical authorities. (The most striking case would be the astral religion of Ḥarrān, a substantial town in this period.) More important than such 'pagan' survivals was the presence of substantial Jewish communities (including the Samaritans), present in many places but especially concentrated in Jerusalem and northern Palestine. Certainly there were enough Jews to attract the unwelcome attention of Christian activists – not least the emperor Heraclius himself – who were embittered by the Jews' alleged treason during the Persian war (602–28), and fearful that their knowledge of the Old Testament might confuse ordinary Christians and tempt them away from the true faith.[4]

3 P. Brown, 'The holy man in Late Antiquity', *Journal of Roman Studies*, 61 (1971), pp. 80–101, repr. in P. Brown, *Society and the holy in Late Antiquity* (Berkeley and Los Angeles, 1979), pp. 103–52. On the spread of the cult of St Sergius of Rusafa, see E. Fowden, *The barbarian plain: Saint Sergius between Rome and Iran*, Transformation of the Classical Heritage 28 (Berkeley, 1999), maps 2–3, pp. 101–5 and *passim*.

4 G. Dagron, 'Judaiser', in G. Dagron (ed.), *Travaux et mémoires*, 11 (1991), pp. 359–80; survey of anti-Jewish tracts in V. Déroche, 'Polémique anti-judaique au VIe et au VIIe siècle', in G. Dagron (ed.), *Travaux et mémoires*, 11 (1991), pp. 275–84.

Christians themselves were not of one mind. Palestine, most of the coastal cities and the districts around Damascus followed the imperial Church with its Chalcedonian creed. The imperial Church was run by Greek-speaking bishops and used a Greek liturgy, however, and this created a real barrier between clergy and laity. In Palestinian churches the Greek liturgy was typically interspersed with Aramaic paraphrases so that the congregation could follow along, and something like this must have been true elsewhere.[5] However, among Christian Arabs (most notably the Ghassānid confederation which dominated the interior steppe from al-Ruṣāfa to the Ḥawrān) and in the towns and countryside of northern Syria and Mesopotamia most people adhered to rival confessions, conveniently if somewhat misleadingly called Monophysite and Nestorian. In so far as they had the power to do so, imperial authorities strove to control the major bishoprics and enforce doctrinal and liturgical conformity, but for the most part they won for themselves only a reputation for brutal persecution. Even in the first/seventh century, to be sure, adherents of the Monophysite and Nestorian creeds did not regard themselves as a separate church; rather, like their Chalcedonian opponents, they were struggling for the soul of the one true Church. Even so, they dominated the monasteries in the north and tried to install bishops (or counter-bishops) of their own wherever possible. Most important, they conducted their liturgy and wrote most of their theological, didactic and hagiographical works not in Greek but in Syriac – i.e. Christian Aramaic. Their religious discourse was thus carried on in the most widely used spoken language – more precisely, in a learned form of that language – and this fact connected them more closely with their flocks than most Greek-speaking clergy in Syria–Palestine could ever hope to be.

None of this should lead us to suppose that Rome was widely viewed as an alien power, that Hellenism was only a veneer, or that the peoples and cultures of Syria were too divided against themselves to resist the Arab armies and their new religion. There is no good evidence that Syrians hailed the Arab armies as liberators from Roman oppression. On the contrary, our first/seventh-century witnesses portray the coming of the Arabs as a divine chastisement, like the Assyrians and Chaldaeans of old, and they took it for granted that this chastisement would end as soon as the Christian people repented of their sins, or the emperor at last saw the light of the true faith. The new rulers

5 S. H. Griffith, 'The monks of Palestine and the growth of Christian literature in Arabic', *Muslim World*, 78 (1988), p. 5, repr. in S. H. Griffith, *Arabic Christianity in the monasteries of ninth-century Palestine* (Aldershot, 1992).

themselves feared a Byzantine *revanche* down to the end of the first/seventh century, and not without reason. As for Islam, sophisticated Christian observers initially regarded it as little more than the inchoate cult of a few thousand barbarians; it could hardly threaten so deep-rooted and richly elaborated a faith as Christianity.[6]

Whatever residual loyalties to Rome there might have been among Syrian Christians, however, the Arab–Muslim conquest incontestably altered the balance of social forces in the country; it created an environment in which Arab political domination and the religion of Islam could take root. By the time Arab armies pushed into Syria in the early 630s there was much discontent with Byzantine rule, even if there was no active desire to overthrow it. Byzantine military and fiscal resources, drained by the long Persian war, were further depleted in the vain struggle against the Arabs in the 630s. After the grave defeat suffered by his forces at the Yarmūk river in 636 Heraclius was unable to raise a new army, and was compelled to leave the surviving Byzantine garrisons in Syria and Mesopotamia to their fate. Even Byzantium's powerful navy was sidelined for decades after the catastrophic battle of the Masts, which took place off the south-western coast of Anatolia near Phoenix (modern Finike) in 655. Under these circumstances a serious Byzantine counter-attack was more a phantom hope than a realistic possibility. Syrians might soon come to feel that a relatively stable and tolerant Arab–Muslim government was no worse than the disruption and turmoil of the last decades of Byzantine rule. Islam in turn was a more formidable competitor than the earliest Christian commentators supposed. To begin with, it had the prestige of being the victors' religion – a manifest sign of divine favour. With time, as Islam asserted a distinctive identity of its own and developed a more nuanced set of practices and teachings, it might well compete effectively with Christianity for the spiritual allegiance of Syrians. In short, the brilliant victories of the 630s opened the door to a new Arab–Islamic order of things in Syria, but it was anyone's guess whether this new order would take root and endure.

The shape of early Islamic rule

The immediate changes brought to Syria and Mesopotamia by the Arab conquests were minimal on many levels. First of all, the degree of physical

6 B. Flusin, 'Démons et Sarrasins', in G. Dagron (ed.), *Travaux et mémoires*, 11 (1991), pp. 382–409, esp. pp. 407ff.; V. Déroches, 'Polémique anti-judaique et émergence de l'Islam (7e–8e siècles)', *Revue des études byzantines*, 57 (1999).

destruction was slight. Except for Caesarea Maritima (stormed and sacked in 638 or 640) almost all cities and towns surrendered on terms and were left undamaged. We have ample testimony from both Muslim and Christian sources that the countryside was scoured by Arab raiding parties; apart from the destruction of villages and crops, vast numbers of captives were seized in these raids. But crops could be replanted, and many captives were soon returned to their lands through ransom, exchange and manumission. These processes may have cost bishops and monasteries many of their treasures, but in aggregate terms that only represents a transfer of wealth from one owner to another. As for the goods carried off to Mecca and Medina, they were typically luxury fabrics or ceremonial objects – very costly, but not the kind of liquid wealth that fuelled everyday economic life. The battles of the 630s were sometimes very bloody; at Gaza, Fiḥl, Ajnādayn (all 634) and the Yarmūk (636) Arab forces gave no quarter. However, Byzantine armies were a mix of Anatolian, Armenian and Christian Arab troops. They were not recruited from Syrian peasants and townsmen, so the bloodshed had no significant impact on the indigenous sedentary population. It does seem that many high officials, great landowners and senior ecclesiastics (especially from the imperial Church) fled the country as Byzantine forces withdrew into Anatolia. However, enough experienced people remained to run things under the Arabs; there is no evidence of an administrative breakdown in either fiscal or ecclesiastical affairs. Finally, and perhaps most important, the conquest of Syria brought about no major Arab immigration and settlement. Long-established Bedouin tribes – Judhām in the south, Quḍāʿa in the centre, Tanūkh and Ṭayyiʾ in the north – continued to dominate the Syro-Jordanian steppe. The Arab armies that had come from the Peninsula were not large, and most of the troops who remained in Syria – in particular their commanders, drawn largely from Quraysh – could be quartered in existing cities such as Damascus and Homs. The experiment of creating a separate garrison town in al-Jābiya, the old Ghassānid encampment in the Ḥawrān, was quickly abandoned due to a murderous outbreak of the plague there in 639. In sum, the Arab conquest of Syria and Mesopotamia was rather like a summer thunderstorm (to borrow an image proposed by Clive Foss) – terrifying while it lasted, but soon past and the damage promptly repaired.[7]

At the conclusion of the fighting in 639–40, Syria was exceptionally fortunate in its newly appointed governor, Muʿāwiya ibn Abī Sufyān. In many ways

7 F. M. Donner, *The early Islamic conquests* (Princeton, 1981), pp. 91–155, 245–50; W. Kaegi, *Byzantium and the early Islamic conquests* (Cambridge, 1992).

Muʿāwiya was not the obvious choice for this critical position. He belonged to the notorious Umayyad clan – fellow tribesmen of Muḥammad but (with a few important exceptions) bitterly hostile to his prophetic claims. His father, Abū Sufyān, had been one of Muḥammad's most obdurate opponents, and accepted Islam only on the eve of the latter's occupation of Mecca in 630. Muʿāwiya himself was a late convert, though perhaps a bit in advance of his father, and many doubted the depth of his attachment to Islam. He began as an obscure mid-level commander in the Syrian campaigns of 634, but by the end of the decade he had won his way to senior positions. The Plague of ʿAmwās, which decimated the Arab forces gathered at al-Jābiya, also killed the three leading Arab generals, including Muʿāwiya's older brother Yazīd. The post of governor fell to him almost by default, and he retained it unchallenged for the next sixteen years, through the caliphates of ʿUmar (r. 634–44) and ʿUthmān (r. 644–56).[8]

His long governorship gave him the opportunity to build an unrivalled power base among the Arab tribes and Muslim notables of Syria – an opportunity he did not miss – but it also gave him a chance to develop his skills as a ruler. In contrast to his counterparts in Iraq and Egypt, Muʿāwiya did not have to deal with a large influx of Arabian tribesmen from disparate lineages. Such newcomers needed to be settled and supervised, and they were easily filled with jealousy and resentment focused on the division of the spoils of the conquests. In contrast, the numerous tribes under his authority continued to live more or less in their traditional areas, and hence seldom fell into conflict with one another. He assiduously cultivated his connections with the old Syrian tribes, especially Kalb, the largest lineage in the Quḍāʿa group and the one that dominated the countryside around his capital, Damascus.[9] These tribes in fact supplied the manpower for Muʿāwiya's armies. Since they resided in the steppe and desert they required little bureaucratic oversight, but could rather be recruited and paid as needed. We know very little about military administration in Muʿāwiya's Syria, but most likely it was done through subsidies to the tribal leaders rather than by centrally controlled stipends assigned to individual soldiers. No doubt all these factors, combined with his extraordinary political acumen, helped Muʿāwiya make Syria and Mesopotamia into the most stable provinces in the emerging Islamic empire.

8 On Muʿāwiya there is a surprisingly thin literature: for his early career, see Aḥmad ibn Yaḥyā al-Balādhurī, *Futūḥ al-buldān*, ed. M. J. de Goeje, (Leiden, 1866), pp. 117–18, 126–9, 133–4, 139–42; R. S. Humphreys, *Muʿawiya ibn Abi Sufyan: From Arabia to empire* (Oxford, 2006), pp. 43–53.

9 J. Wellhausen, *The Arab kingdom and its fall*, trans. M. G. Weir (Calcutta, 1927), pp. 131–3; H. Lammens, *Le califat de Yazid Ier* (Beirut, 1921), pp. 5–6, 103.

Muʿāwiya used his Syrian base to pursue the war with Byzantium, dispatching expeditions into central Anatolia and Armenia almost every summer (and often during the winter). These expeditions were not aimed at permanent conquest and occupation, but they should not be regarded merely as glorified raiding parties.[10] Rather, they represented a strategy of attrition, grinding down Byzantine military resources until a strike could be mounted against Constantinople itself. In addition to overland expeditions Muʿāwiya opened a new front on the sea, and indeed he must be regarded as the founder of the Muslim navy. Partly this was a defensive move, since the Syrian coast suffered repeatedly from Byzantine naval raids throughout the 640s. Muʿāwiya may also have been impressed by the Byzantine naval expedition against Alexandria in 645. That effort enjoyed only a brief success, but it both demonstrated the danger of leaving Byzantine naval power unchecked and suggested the possibilities that command of the sea might offer. Muʿāwiya's initiative bore fruit almost from the outset, with lucrative raids against Cyprus in 649–50 and Rhodes in 653, and a spectacular victory by a combined Syrian and Egyptian fleet against the Byzantine navy (under the personal command of the emperor Constans II) in the battle of the Masts (655). The Syrian littoral was henceforth secured, and this would ultimately open the way to a resettlement of the coastal towns in Muʿāwiya's later years.[11]

Muʿāwiya's aggressive stance against Byzantium was not mirrored in his dealings with the Christian populations of Syria and Mesopotamia, who of course constituted the overwhelming majority of his subjects. Although we have no way of making any systematic comparison between Byzantine and early Islamic tax assessments, and the situation may well have differed between one province and another, the oldest Syriac sources imply that they were moderate and relatively stable. Churches and monasteries were left unmolested, and the archaeological evidence (admittedly very difficult to

10 Anatolian expeditions: Abū Jaʿfar Muḥammad ibn Jarīr al-Ṭabarī, *Taʾrīkh al-rusul wa-l-mulūk*, ed. M. J. de Goeje *et al.*, 15 vols. in 3 series (Leiden, 1879–1901), series I, pp. 2806–9, 2907, series II, pp. 16, 27, 67, 82, 84, 85, 86, 87, 111, 157, 158, 163, 171, 173, 180, 181, 188; Balādhurī, *Futūḥ*, pp. 163–5, 178, 183–5, 197–8, 204; Theophanes, *The Chronicle of Theophanes Confessor*, trans. C. Mango and R. Scott (Oxford, 1997), pp. 479–82, 484, 486–90, 492–6; J. Wellhausen, 'Arab wars with the Byzantines in the Umayyad period', in M. Bonner (ed.), *Arab–Byzantine relations in early Islamic times* (Burlington, VT, 2005); Humphreys, *Muʿawiya*, pp. 50–3, 58–60, 104–10.

11 Naval expeditions, Cyprus: al-Ṭabarī, *Taʾrīkh*, series I, pp. 2820–7, 2865, 2867–71, 2888–9, series II, pp. 67, 85, 86, 87, 158, 163, 173, 181; Balādhurī, *Futūḥ*, pp. 128, 152–4; Theophanes, *Chronicle*, pp. 478–9, 481–2, 493–5; Dionysius of Tell Mahré, trans. in A. Palmer, S. Brock and R. Hoyland, *The seventh century in the West-Syrian chronicles* (Liverpool, 1993), pp. 73–5, 179–80; Humphreys, *Muʿawiya*, pp. 53–8.

date and interpret) suggests that they continued to be built and maintained. Indeed, an early Christian source tells us that Muʿāwiya restored the great church of Edessa, one of the finest in the region, when it was damaged in an earthquake in 679. Public worship was mostly unhindered, and the bishoprics and major churches were left in the hands of the confessions that controlled them when the Byzantines withdrew.[12]

The Monophysite and Nestorian churches were indeed better off under the new order, since Muʿāwiya was determined to keep peace between the rival sects and refused to favour one against the others. For the first time Monophysites and Nestorians were free to appoint their own bishops and teach their doctrines without hindrance. A policy of evenhandedness was not easy to bring off, since tolerance was a strange and unwelcome concept to most Christians, but to a remarkable degree Muʿāwiya and his sub-governors made it work. (Sometimes Muslim troops had to be posted during church services to keep the peace.) On balance, it is little wonder that Syrian churchmen did not worry much about the 'Saracen heresy' during the early decades of Muslim rule.

As benign as Muʿāwiya's rule might have seemed, however, the churches were now operating in a radically changed environment, and over time this would have significant effects. On the material level, bishops and monasteries were no longer supported by public revenues and imperial benefactions. Thenceforth they had to live from private gifts and endowments, and in the long term, as taxes bit harder and conversion to Islam took hold, such gifts would be a declining resource. The former imperial (Chalcedonian) Church suffered a greater immediate loss than the Monophysites and Nestorians, to be sure, but on some level all the churches were affected. If not subject to slow starvation, they were at least living in reduced circumstances. The administrative and judicial authority of the bishops, which was very extensive in Byzantine times, was certainly altered, but it is impossible to be precise. We can at least be sure that conflicts between Muslims and Christians, which must have been numerous, were now handled by Muslim officials. The symbolic impact of Muslim rule may have been even greater, for the new regime was no longer a Christian commonwealth, a providential vehicle of salvation. In a sense, as in the Roman empire before Constantine, Christians were again

12 S. Brock, 'North Mesopotamia in the late seventh century: Book xv of John Bar Penkāyē's *Rīš Mellē*', *JSAI*, 9 (1987), p. 61; Dionysius of Tell Mahré, trans. in Palmer, Brock and Hoyland, *Seventh century*, pp. 186–7, 195. Archaeological evidence reviewed in R. Schick, *The Christian communities of Palestine from Byzantine to Islamic rule: A historical and archaeological study*, Studies in Late Antiquity and Early Islam 2 (Princeton, 1995).

strangers in a strange land. Under such circumstances the goal of the Church was not to infuse the state with a divine purpose, but simply to survive.

In 656 Syria ceased to be just another province within the vast Islamic empire. For the next five years it would be, along with Iraq, one of the two axes of the great civil war that brought the nascent Islamic empire to the verge of ruin. When the caliph ʿUthmān was killed by mutinous Egyptian troops in his own residence in Medina, his second cousin Muʿāwiya was inevitably implicated in the crisis. Though at first he made no claims on his own behalf, he demanded justice for his murdered kinsman, and used this demand to manoeuvre ʿAlī ibn Abī Ṭālib out of the caliphate in spite of initial support from the Kūfan and Egyptian garrisons and many Medinan Companions. By July 660 Muʿāwiya was in a position to advance his own claim to the caliphate. His adherents swore the oath of obedience to him in Jerusalem, where he visited the Holy Sepulchre and the grave of St Mary the Virgin – a striking act whose real purpose is a matter of conjecture, but which must have been meant to reassure his Christian subjects that he was not only head of the Muslim community, but their emperor and protector as well.[13] His grip on the office was assured the following year when ʿAlī was assassinated by a Khārijite, and even the Iraqis were at last compelled to recognise him as caliph.

Muʿāwiya is commonly regarded as the founder of the first hereditary dynasty in Islam, the Umayyads. More important, however, was his decision – bitterly but ineffectually resented by many Medinans – to remain in Syria, with Damascus as his administrative centre. Syria thus became the metropolis of a great empire for the first time since the Seleucids a millennium before. Muʿāwiya acted partly for pragmatic reasons, since his power rested on the Arab tribes of Syria – in particular the Kalb, whom he had cultivated and nurtured for two decades. He could not possibly recreate such a support network in the Ḥijāz or anywhere else in the Islamic empire. But his decision not to return to Medina, the traditional and religiously sanctified capital, rested on broader calculations as well. He recognised that an empire spanning the entire Nile-to-Oxus region could not be governed from a remote oasis in the Arabian Peninsula, but only from within the urban–agrarian heartland, where the main lines of commerce and communication intersected and where experienced administrators could be found. In many respects Damascus filled the bill admirably. It was close to the critical Byzantine frontier and centrally located between Iraq, Egypt, the Ḥijāz and the Mediterranean ports. Its

13 Muʿāwiya's accession to the caliphate: Wellhausen, *Arab kingdom*, pp. 101–2, 134; Humphreys, *Muʿawiya*, pp. 83–4.

drawback was that it was only a medium-sized city with limited resources in its immediate hinterland. Syria was a prosperous region, but it did not produce anything remotely approaching the tax revenues of Iraq and Egypt. Syria's structural limitations would only gradually come into play, however; whatever the causes of the fall of the Umayyads, a lack of adequate Syrian financial resources was not among them.

As caliph Muʿāwiya largely continued the same policies in Syria that he had followed as governor, albeit on a larger scale. His central administration was of the most rudimentary kind – essentially a mechanism for maintaining communications with (and control over) the powerful provincial governors of Iraq, Egypt and the Ḥijāz. He almost certainly received some surplus revenues from Iraq and Egypt, but to a large degree he ran Syria (including payments to the nomadic tribesmen who constituted the core of his army) on the basis of its own resources. Syria was in a sense his personal domain, but it was divided into sub-provinces (the famous *ajnād*, lit., 'army commands': originally Filasṭīn, al-Urdunn, Dimashq and Ḥimṣ, with Qinnasrīn added in the north under his son Yazīd I), and these in turn into sub-districts. No doubt there was some sort of centralised fiscal apparatus, but the only direct evidence from his reign (a few papyri from the Negev town of Nessana) suggests a highly localised system of tax assessment and collection: bi-monthly requisitions issued by the district sub-governor to indigenous local officials, ordering them to send specified provisions to troops under his command. In Syria the fiscal system as well as everyday economic life continued to rely on Byzantine (or imitation Byzantine) gold and bronze coinage. According to a contemporary Christian source Muʿāwiya endeavoured to introduce a gold and silver coinage of his own early in his reign, but his coins were rejected because they lacked a cross – striking evidence both of the continuing prestige of Byzantium in Syria and of the strong Christian identity of its people.[14]

Perhaps Muʿāwiya's main innovation was a systematic effort to repopulate the almost abandoned coastal cities through a mix of incentives (e.g. hereditary land grants) and compulsory population transfers. As governor he had established a community of Jews or Persians in Tripoli shortly after its conquest during ʿUthmān's caliphate. Now he brought Persians, Malays and Djats from Iraq (especially the port city of Baṣra) to Antioch, Tyre and Acre. His decision to look so far afield for appropriate settlers is intriguing but hard to interpret.

14 C. J. Kraemer, *Excavations at Nessana*, vol. III: *The non-literary papyri* (Princeton, 1958); Maronite Chronicle, in Palmer, Brock and Hoyland, *Seventh century*, p. 32; C. Foss, 'A Syrian coinage of Mu'awiya?', *Revue numismatique*, 158 (2002).

Possibly the indigenous population of Syria was too decimated by a century of violent turmoil to provide the needed colonists, or perhaps they simply refused to return to places that still seemed insecure. More likely, Muʿāwiya simply did not trust them; as Christians they were all too likely to collaborate with Byzantine naval raids. Outsiders would be more reliable and easier to control. Whatever Muʿāwiya's thinking, his resettlement policy represents the beginnings of an Umayyad effort to restore and develop the Syrian economy.

Ambitious in many ways, Muʿāwiya was not a builder of monuments: his palace in Damascus elicited derisory remarks from a Byzantine embassy, he erected no major mosques, and only one or two rural residences. He may have cleared the debris from the Temple esplanade in Jerusalem and enhanced a primitive mosque (the first al-Masjid al-Aqṣā) erected there by ʿUmar, but the evidence for this is terse and hard to interpret.[15] His most important contribution to Syria and Mesopotamia was security and public order, a welcome respite after the turbulent century between Justinian's later years and the end of Islam's first civil war. According to John Bar Penkāyē, a Nestorian monk of Sinjār: 'Justice flourished in his time and there was great peace in the regions under his control; he allowed everyone to live as they wanted … Once Mʿaway [*sic*] had come to the throne, the peace throughout the land was such that we have never heard, either from our fathers or grandfathers or seen that there had ever been any like it.'[16] John's words, written about a decade after Muʿāwiya's passing in 680 at the height of a bitter civil war, may be nostalgic rather than descriptive, but they surely reflect an authentic memory of better times.

The Pax Muʿāwiya ended soon enough after his death. The reign of his son and successor Yazīd I (r. 680–3) left Syria and al-Jazīra undisturbed, despite serious revolts in Iraq and the Ḥijāz. But when he died things rapidly came unglued. Most disturbing perhaps was the emergence of a bitter rivalry between the two main tribal groups in the country, Kalb in the centre and the newly settled Qays in the north along the Byzantine frontier. The rivalry did not stem from some atavistic quarrel. Rather, it was rooted in a profound political crisis. With the death of Yazīd, and that of his young son Muʿāwiya II a few months later, there was no viable candidate for the succession in the Sufyānid branch of the Umayyad house. At the same time ʿAbd Allāh ibn al-Zubayr in the Ḥijāz now revived his bid for the caliphate, which Yazīd's

15 B. Flusin, 'L'esplanade du temple à l'arrivée des arabes, d'après deux récits byzantins', in J. Raby and J. Johns (eds.), *Bayt al-Maqdis: ʿAbd al-Malik's Jerusalem*, Oxford Studies in Islamic Art 9, part 1 (Oxford, 1992), pp. 17–32.

16 Brock, 'North Mesopotamia', p. 61.

forces had all but crushed. As the son of a prestigious Companion who had been closely affiliated with Abū Bakr and ʿUmar, Ibn al-Zubayr could attract a wide spectrum of followers. Lacking an acceptable Umayyad candidate, the Qaysī tribes of northern Syria joined his cause. Umayyad rule was on the verge of extinction when Marwān ibn al-Ḥakam, second cousin to Muʿāwiya I and almost eighty years old, emerged to rally the Kalb. Marwān and the Kalb confronted the Qays at Marj Rāhiṭ near Damascus (684) and won a decisive but bloody victory. Umayyad hopes (now represented by the Marwānid branch of the family) were saved, though eight years of desperate struggle would pass before they at last vindicated their claim to the caliphate. The Kalb retained their pre-eminent place in the Umayyad structure of power, but the Qays were humiliated and embittered. Successive Umayyad caliphs strove to reconcile the Qays and their allies in other regions of the empire, but it was a difficult task, all the more as excessive deference to Qays would inevitably alienate Kalb. In the 740s the delicate balancing act finally collapsed, as rival contenders for power within the Umayyad house lined up with different tribal factions. The manipulation of tribal politics, which had been the original foundation of Umayyad power, ended by destroying it.[17]

Marwān ruled for less than a year, but his victory at Marj Rāhiṭ at least bequeathed a relatively secure position within Syria to his son and successor, ʿAbd al-Malik (r. 685–705). Only in 692 did ʿAbd al-Malik at last crush Ibn al-Zubayr and impose his authority throughout the caliphate – although the struggle against the Khārijites in Iraq took many years more – but he did not wait for the final outcome of the struggle to begin instituting important changes in the regions he did control. The Nessana papyri suggest a much stricter tax regime by the late 680s, with rates severe enough to provoke protest delegations. In part such changes may reflect ʿAbd al-Malik's urgent need for cash to pay his troops in a period of crisis and constant warfare, but they also reflect the temperament of a state builder. Like Muʿāwiya, ʿAbd al-Malik had to reconstruct an empire on the verge of dissolution, but too much had changed for him to rely simply on his predecessor's tools of conciliation, patronage and personal loyalty.[18]

ʿAbd al-Malik's fiscal reforms were certainly instituted wherever he established his government, and they were continued if not intensified under his son

17 Tribal conflicts: Wellhausen, *Arab kingdom*, pp. 180–2, 202–12, 397–491 and *passim*; G. L. Hawting, *The first dynasty of Islam: The Umayyad caliphate, AD 661–750* (London and Sydney, 1986), pp. 53–5, 73–6 and *passim*; P. Crone, 'Were the Qays and Yemen of the Umayyad period political parties?', *Der Islam*, 71 (1994).

18 On ʿAbd al-Malik, see most recently C. Robinson, *ʿAbd al-Malik* (Oxford, 2005); for ʿAbd al-Malik as a state-builder, pp. 59–80, 105–21.

al-Walīd (r. 705–15). Dionysius of Tell Mahré (d. 846) comments that 'this Walīd was a learned man. But he raised the taxes and increased the general suffering more than any of his predecessors.' He describes the policy of the caliph's brother Maslama more concretely: 'Maslama's first action on coming to Mesopotamia and taking over the governorship of all the Jazira was to commission a survey of the arable land and a census of vineyards, orchards, livestock and human beings. They hung a leaden seal on each person's neck.'[19]

In the early Islamic state taxpayers were by definition non-Muslims, so the polities of ʿAbd al-Malik and al-Walīd were clearly aimed at the Christians of Syria and Mesopotamia. In addition, the caliphs began eroding the position of their Christian subjects in symbolic ways. Michael the Syrian (d. 1199, probably paraphrasing Dionysius) states that in about 696–7 'the Arab king ʿAbd al-Malik decreed that crosses should be taken down and pigs slaughtered'.[20] That is, the visible signs of a Christian society were to be removed from public view, and Muslim dietary taboos were to be enforced on everyone. We do not know just what circumstances occasioned these decrees – possibly ʿAbd al-Malik was seeking to curry favour among the more rigorously minded Muslims, for example – nor do we know to what degree they were actually enforced. Nevertheless, there is a change of tone. The coinage reform, which replaced the sign of the cross with the Muslim *shahāda*, and the gradual institution of Arabic as the sole language of official administration, tended in the same direction. That is, the key words and symbols of Christian identity were gradually being removed from public life.

ʿAbd al-Malik's most spectacular gesture was no doubt the building of the Dome of the Rock in 692. On one level he was following in Muʿāwiya's footsteps some thirty years earlier by recognising the special sanctity of Jerusalem. But on another level this act demonstrates the striking difference between the policies of the two men. Muʿāwiya, for whatever reason, went out of his way to honour two Christian shrines dedicated to key doctrines of the faith – the virgin birth, and the crucifixion and resurrection. ʿAbd al-Malik, in contrast, revivified the Temple Mount, the holiest of Jewish sites. Moreover, the inscriptions inside the Dome of the Rock quite explicitly denounce the doctrine of the Trinity and proclaim that Islam had supplanted all other religions. A more forthright statement of the religious identity and

19 *Chronicle of 819* and Dionysius, both in Palmer, Brock and Hoyland, *Seventh century*, pp. 79, 209; C. Robinson, 'Neck-sealing in early Islam', *JESHO*, 48 (2005).
20 Michael the Syrian, *Chronique de Michel le Syrien, patriarche jacobite d'Antioche (1166–1199)*, ed. and trans. J.-B. Chabot, 4 vols. (Paris, 1899–1924), vol. II, p. 475; G. R. D. King, 'Islam, iconoclasm, and the declaration of doctrine', *BSOAS*, 48 (1985).

purpose of his empire, or of the reduced status that non-Muslims (and Christians in particular) would have in it, is hard to imagine.[21]

Apart from its general ideological import, the Dome of the Rock also marks the beginning of the Islamisation of the Syrian landscape. Until ʿAbd al-Malik, the public monuments of Syria marked it as a Christian country – a point noted by the geographer al-Muqaddasī in the mid-fourth/tenth century, when he asked his uncle why al-Walīd had squandered such immense sums on the Umayyad Mosque in Damascus. His uncle spoke directly to the point:

> Al-Walīd was right, and he was prompted to a worthy work. For he saw that Syria was a country long occupied by the Christians, and he noted the beautiful churches still belonging to them, so enchanting and so renowned for their splendor, like the Church of the Holy Sepulchre and the churches of Lydda and Edessa. So he sought to build for the Muslims a mosque that would be unique and a wonder to the world. Likewise, is it not obvious that ʿAbd al-Malik, seeing the grandeur and magnificence of the Dome of the Holy Sepulchre, was concerned lest it dazzle the thoughts of the Muslims, and thus he erected above the Rock the Dome now seen there?[22]

In following up his father's initiative, al-Walīd was not content with the mosque in Damascus. He continued ʿAbd al-Malik's emphasis on the Temple esplanade with al-Aqṣā Mosque, and he also launched a programme of great imperial mosques throughout the caliphate. (The mosque in Damascus had involved razing the Church of St John the Baptist, but such 'conversions' were very rare in Umayyad times.) Sulaymān (r. 715–17) was mostly preoccupied with the siege of Constantinople, but he found time to undertake the Great Mosque in Aleppo. Thereafter there was a pause for a few years, but the construction of new mosques was energetically pursued by Hishām (r. 724–43). Though the ones he erected were on a more modest and practical scale than the grand monuments of al-Walīd, there were certainly a great many of them. By the end of the Umayyad dynasty Islam had already left a deep imprint on Syria, even if Christian monuments still predominated.

At least in its earlier phases the policy of Islamisation set in motion by ʿAbd al-Malik probably did not aim at encouraging conversion to Islam. The Umayyad state still rested (as it had under Muʿāwiya) on a sharp distinction between an Arab Muslim ruling class and non-Muslim tax-paying subjects, even though that distinction was becoming difficult to maintain even by the

21 O. Grabar, *The formation of Islamic art* (New Haven, 1973), pp. 61–7 (though he hedges his conclusions in the revised edn, 1987), O. Grabar, *The shape of the holy: Early Islamic Jerusalem* (Princeton, 1996).

22 Grabar, *Formation* (1973), pp. 64–5 (translation slightly revised).

mid-680s. However, the Islamising and Arabicising reforms of ʿAbd al-Malik and al-Walīd certainly encouraged an increasing flow of converts in Iraq, and it is fair to assume a similar situation in Syria, though in the present state of research we know very little about it.

These tendencies were reinforced and consolidated by the policy initiatives of ʿUmar ibn ʿAbd al-ʿAzīz (r. 717–20), the brevity of whose reign belies its tremendous importance. The oldest Christian sources characterise him as 'a good man and a king more merciful than all those who had preceded him',[23] and state that 'as much honor and praise is bestowed on him by all, even foreigners, as ever has been offered to anyone in his lifetime holding the reins of power'.[24] That fits with his reputation among Muslim writers, who praised his piety, justice and commitment to equality for the heretofore despised and maltreated *mawālī*, the non-Arab converts to Islam. But the story is more complex. Michael the Syrian (d. 1199, but citing much earlier sources) concedes his personal piety and uprightness, but asserts that he was hostile to Christians and pressured them in every way to adopt Islam. To encourage this, converts were exempted from the poll-tax. At the same time, Christians were not permitted to bear witness against Muslims, serve as government officials or pray with loud voices, along with many other restrictions. Theophanes even claims that Christians who would not convert were put to death, but this is certainly erroneous.[25] ʿUmar's decrees represented a major shift in Umayyad policy, an effort to marginalise the practice of Christianity. In principle (though as yet seldom in reality) Christianity was to be enclosed within the walls of home, church and monastery; public space would belong to Islam.

This tendency was further confirmed by the Iconoclast decree of Yazīd II (r. 720–4), who commanded the destruction of all images of animate beings – first and foremost Christian icons, of course – throughout the caliphate. Yazīd apparently died before the decree could be enforced, but it set the stage for the parallel decree issued by the Byzantine emperor Leo III in 726. Obviously the two decrees struck a chord among many Christians, for the Iconoclast Controversy in Syria was a bitter one, to which the widespread defacing of mosaics in Jordanian churches, sometimes repaired with clumsily executed vegetal or geometric motifs, bears eloquent witness. St John of Damascus's

23 *Chronicle of 819*, in Palmer, Brock and Hoyland, *Seventh century*, p. 80.

24 *Hispano-Arab Chronicle* (=*Anon. Chronicle 741*), trans. in R. Hoyland, *Seeing Islam as others saw it: A survey and evaluation of Christian, Jewish, and Zoroastrian writings on early Islam* (Princeton, 1997), p. 625.

25 Michael the Syrian, *Chronique*, vol. II, p. 489; Theophanes, *Chronicle*, p. 550.

famous defence of religious images reflects local conditions as much as it does the theological quarrels in distant Constantinople. In any case Iconoclasm in Syria was a matter between Christians, in which the Muslim authorities were involved only in minor ways.

We might speculate that the Iconoclast Controversy demoralised some Syrian Christians and hence did something to encourage conversion to Islam. We do know at least that by the late second/eighth century Christian discourse in Syria and Iraq had moved to an apologetic register, a defence of Christian truths against the attacks of Muslim critics, and these apologetics were composed in Arabic – i.e. in a language strongly inflected by Islamic scripture and religious discourse. We know also that no Syrian bishops attended the Council of Nicaea (787), which restored the veneration of icons. The Syrian churches would no longer have any role in the debates and controversies that embroiled Byzantine and Roman Christianity. These facts do not necessarily imply isolation or intellectual stagnation, to be sure. Apart from their sheer numbers, Syro-Jazīran Christians could draw on the great theological tradition of their region. Down through the fifth/eleventh century, at least, Christian apologetics were conducted with growing ingenuity and sophistication. By the late second/eighth century, however, Syrian and Mesopotamian Christians were on their own; they had to explain and defend their faith and practice within a world whose cultural and intellectual parameters were increasingly fixed by Islam.

The trends sketched above continued to evolve during the long reign of Hishām (724–43), though he seems to have had a more sympathetic attitude towards Christianity than his two immediate predecessors. Even if his policies represented in themselves no real innovation, however, he pushed them vigorously, and they ended up by bringing about some important changes. The most important of these concerned the caliphate as a whole, but their effects were strongly felt in Syria and Mesopotamia. Hishām strove (with reasonable success for most of his reign) to maintain the balance between the great tribal factions of Muḍar, Yaman and Rabīʿa – or, in Syro-Mesopotamian terms, Qays and Yemen (i.e. Kalb and the other Quḍāʿa tribes). He was notorious for his unrelenting efforts to squeeze more money from his subjects. More important, however, was his resolution of the fiscal dilemma created by ʿUmar II's reforms in favour of the *mawālī*. Finally, he strove to reignite the project of imperial expansion pursued with such brilliant success by his father ʿAbd al-Malik and his brother al-Walīd.

The last of these was critical on an ideological as well as a purely political level, since conducting the *jihād* was a foundation-stone of Umayyad legitimacy. Unfortunately Hishām's *jihād* was at best a stalemate. There were occasional victories, but just as many defeats, some of them extremely serious. Nineteen years of warfare ended with almost no changes in the caliphate's frontiers, and this at an enormous cost in money and manpower. Although these wars were usually waged in places remote from Syria and Mesopotamia (except on the Byzantine and Armenian frontiers), they had a serious impact on these two regions, because Syrian and Mesopotamian troops were by far the most reliable and effective forces available to Hishām. As one military crisis or revolt succeeded another, he was compelled to send expeditionary forces recruited in Syria to deal with the situation, and often to remain there, hundreds of miles from home, in order to keep things patched together when the immediate emergency was past. These measures both depleted military manpower in Syria to an alarming degree and eroded the Syrian tribes' morale and loyalty to the regime. In brief, Hishām's *jihād* policy ended by subverting the chief bulwark of Umayyad rule since the days of Muʿāwiya.[26]

It is very hard to know the numbers involved in all this. Blankinship has estimated that Syria and Mesopotamia supplied about 175,000 and 75,000 men respectively out of the roughly 400,000 that made up the caliphal armies as a whole. The total number of troops is a reasonable one given the vast size of the caliphate, and it is roughly similar to the nominal strength of the Roman army in the fourth century.[27] However, the estimates for Syria seem very high in view of that region's limited fiscal resources, all the more as Syrian and Jazīran troops were drawn from widely scattered tribes in the interior steppe, not from densely settled garrison cities such as Kūfa and Baṣra. However, these numbers do include the Syrian garrisons that came to be posted all over the empire – in Iraq, Khurāsān, North Africa, even distant al-Andalus – and presumably these garrisons were paid from local revenues. Moreover, Egypt was easily controlled from Damascus. Since it had only a small standing garrison, a substantial proportion of its revenues (which totalled at least twice those of Syria) could have been used to support Syria's tribesmen. Likewise, as the Arab tribesmen quartered in Iraq were progressively reduced to second-line status after the rebellion of Ibn al-Ashʿath in 701, an increasing

26 K. Y. Blankinship, *The end of the jihad state: The reign of Hishām ibn ʿAbd al-Malik and the collapse of the Umayyads* (Albany, 1994), pp. 230–6.

27 Ibid., pp. 82, 303, n. 38. Cf. W. Treadgold, *Byzantium and its army, 284–1081* (Palo Alto, CA, 1995), pp. 44–59. The Saljuqid vizier Niẓām al-Mulk gives 400,000 as the total number of troops available to Malikshāh, around 1080, in an empire that stretched from Syria to Transoxania.

proportion of Iraq's lucrative tax receipts might have been redirected to Syria. At the current stage of research, however, all this can only be speculation.

In Syria itself, Hishām directed his attention to two very disparate areas: (1) the sponsorship (and of course control) of Islamic learning and thought; and (2) an extensive construction programme, with an emphasis on the interior steppe of Syria. As to the former, a concerted effort to define the theological doctrines and moral obligations of Islam had been rapidly developing among pious circles in several centres, especially Mecca, Medina, Baṣra and Kūfa, since the end of the great civil war in the early 690s. Since the Umayyad caliphs claimed to be God's vicegerents on earth and the authoritative spokesmen for Islam, they could not stand aside from this effort, all the more as the Ḥijāz and Iraq had often been staging-grounds for rebellions against the regime and were never well reconciled to it.

Umayyad Syria has usually been regarded as only a secondary centre of Islamic thought, but that judgement may rest more on the surviving sources – which are overwhelmingly Iraqi and Medinan – than on second/eighth-century realities. Both ʿAbd al-Malik and ʿUmar ibn ʿAbd al-ʿAzīz, both of whom had spent many years in the Ḥijāz, were regarded as highly learned, and serious theological discourse in Islam may have begun (though the matter is disputed) with ʿAbd al-Malik's assertion of the dogma of predestination. Hishām was both severe in temperament and personally observant, and he actively cultivated such eminent scholars as Ibn Shihāb al-Zuhrī (d. 742), Maʿmar ibn Rāshid (d. 750?) and several others. Apart from such prominent individuals, the great biographical compilations of Ibn ʿAsākir (d. 1176) and Ibn al-ʿAdīm (d. 1262) contain entries for many hundreds of learned figures who resided in Syria during the Umayyad period. A substantial majority – some three-quarters – of those whose occupation is recorded held political, military or administrative offices, but since scholars were only beginning to emerge as an identifiable group, that fact should not be surprising.

Hishām's construction programme reveals a different facet of his rulership. He certainly was no innovator in this area, although things seemed to reach their apogee during his reign. In some cases we are dealing with alternate capitals. Thus Qinnasrīn, near the Byzantine frontier, was the regular residence of the otherwise polar opposites Yazīd I and ʿUmar ibn ʿAbd al-ʿAzīz. Hishām himself spent hardly any time in Damascus. His principal residence was al-Ruṣāfa south of the Euphrates, adjacent to the great Byzantine shrine city dedicated to St Sergius. Both Qinnasrīn and al-Ruṣāfa were close to Mesopotamia and to the northern frontier, and were probably chosen in part for strategic reasons.

It is, however, the still-puzzling 'desert castles' (*quṣūr*) that have attracted most attention.[28] Again, Hishām was not doing anything essentially new; he simply acted on a larger scale than his predecessors. Even Muʿāwiya preferred to spend as much time as he could in a rural residence outside the formal capital, Damascus – he particularly favoured Sinnabra near the southern shore of Lake Tiberias – and later caliphs and princes enthusiastically followed his lead. They expended great sums to build an extremely varied group of structures in the countryside, some very simple and some extremely large and elaborate ensembles. A few of these were placed in pleasant, well-watered areas, such as the new town of ʿAnjar in the southern Biqāʿ valley, or Hishām's own winter palace of Khirbat al-Mafjar in the Jordan valley near Jericho. The majority, however, were located on the edge of the steppe, or even far within it. What drove the Umayyads to such a fever of construction? Few now believe that it stemmed from a romantic nostalgia for the life of the desert. On the other hand, an idea first put forth by Sauvaget – that these ensembles represented large-scale economic development projects – has recently come in for serious criticism. Unfortunately the extant monuments have almost no inscriptions, and there are very few direct references in our textual sources.

As things stand, it is probably best to recognise that they were meant to serve many different purposes – though often we can only guess at just what the builders had in mind. Some, like Qaṣr al-Kharāna, were probably no more than way-stations in the desert for soldiers and officials as they moved across the steppe from one locale to another. Others might have served as gathering-places for the provincial governors or even the caliph to renew bonds of loyalty and negotiate terms of service with the tribal leaders, and to distribute pay and bonuses to the tribesmen who made up Syria's armies. Qaṣr al-Ḥallabāt may be a case in point. Some were certainly retreats, where the princes and their entourages could get away from the health hazards, congestion and prying eyes of the cities and enjoy the princely pleasures of hunting, music, wine and the company of singing-girls. Quṣayr ʿAmra, with its small but wonderfully painted reception hall and bath, almost surely belongs in this group.

Finally, there were indeed some very ambitious ensembles that clearly did involve a major investment in irrigation, agriculture and horticulture, and even permanent settlement. The clearest and most impressive example is

28 G. Fowden, *Quṣayr ʿAmra: Art and the Umayyad elite in Late Antique Syria* (Berkeley, 2004), pp. 1–30, reviews the large but uneven literature.

Qaṣr al-Ḥayr al-Sharqī, far out in the desert north-east of Palmyra, and clearly built at Hishām's direction.[29] This complex encloses some 10 square kilometres. Two large and handsomely constructed walled enclosures – probably a palace and a vast residential compound – were embedded in the midst of numerous villages, elaborate irrigation works, agricultural and pasture lands, etc. The palace, one assumes, would have been occupied only when the caliph or governor was in residence. The residential compound, with its impressive mosque and carefully laid-out apartment complexes, might have had a permanent garrison or police force, but space must have been reserved for the entourages accompanying the caliph or governor during their occasional visits. Whether Qaṣr al-Ḥayr al-Sharqī represented a serious economic investment, or whether it was chiefly meant to assert government control over the nomadic tribesmen in this remote part of the steppe, is still open to debate. Whatever questions there are in regard to specific structures, however, the 'desert castles' show that the Umayyads viewed the Syrian interior as a vital part of their domain. Their active engagement in the region on many levels ensured their cultural, political and economic ties with the tribesmen who were the foundation of their power.

The apparently abrupt collapse of the Umayyad regime after the death of Hishām in 743 was in part connected with antagonisms and fissures within the ruling house, in part with the last caliphs' failure to manage tensions between the Qays and Yaman tribal factions in Syria itself. In the end these tensions led to the total triumph of Qays under the leadership of the governor of Mesopotamia, Marwān ibn Muḥammad, and thus to the alienation of Kalb, the dynasty's traditional bulwark.[30] (As noted above, Kalb's loyalties may already have been severely eroded by Hishām's unending wars on the remote frontiers of the caliphate.) Marwān made Ḥarrān his principal residence, and his caliphate was certainly not welcomed by the Syrian Arabs. He was compelled to reduce Homs and Damascus to obedience by force. When the ʿAbbāsid armies crossed the Euphrates into Syria in 750 after Marwān's forces were shattered at the Zāb, they faced surprisingly feeble resistance from the Syrians, demoralised as they were by Marwān's harshness and the internal disintegration of the Umayyad family.

29 O. Grabar, R. Holod, J. Knustad and W. Trousdale, *City in the desert: Qasr al-Hayr East*, 2 vols. (Cambridge, MA, 1978); D. Gènequand, 'The early Islamic settlement in the Syrian steppe: A new look at Umayyad and medieval Qasr al-Hayr al-Sharqi (Syria), *al-ʾUsur al-Wusta*, 17 (2005).

30 Wellhausen, *Arab kingdom*, pp. 377–80.

ʿAbbāsid Syria

What changes did the new regime bring to Syria? It was long argued that the ʿAbbāsid victory meant that Syria was reduced to the status of a minor, though sometimes troublesome, province. Various facts do seem to favour this interpretation. First of all, the capital was moved to Iraq, a far richer region than Syria, and the burgeoning new metropolis of Baghdad rapidly eclipsed Damascus in size and wealth. The great opportunities for land speculation and commercial agriculture were now in Iraq. Second, the ʿAbbāsids took bloody vengeance on as many princes of the Umayyad house as they could reach. Though they did not succeed in liquidating them all, they did eradicate much of the propertied elite that had sustained Syrian prosperity during the first half of the second/eighth century. Third, the Syrian Arabs were progressively demobilised, beginning under al-Manṣūr (r. 754–75) and ending with the reign of al-Maʾmūn (813–33). As their names were struck off the army registers they lost an irreplaceable source of income, and were driven back into the traditional poverty of pastoral nomadism.

These arguments have merit, but they overlook some factors and exaggerate others. First of all, calls for a return to Umayyad rule evoked a very shallow response; the ʿAbbāsids had no difficulty in suppressing a series of revolts by various Umayyad (or pseudo-Umayyad) pretenders in the early 750s. Most of these revolts, however, should be seen as struggles by Yaman and Kalb tribesmen to reclaim lost military status and financial privileges, or even (as with the uprising led by Abū Ḥarb al-Mubarqaʿ in 841) as simple peasant revolts. In general, challenges to central power in ʿAbbāsid Syria were no different from those in any other province of the caliphate; they stemmed from ambitious provincial governors, dissatisfied urban notables and tribal leaders, local factionalism, and rural banditry. A more serious cluster of revolts during the 810s displayed a brief outbreak of millenarianism and Umayyad legitimism, but these events reflected the crisis of ʿAbbāsid authority during the civil war between al-Amīn and al-Maʾmūn. None of these outbreaks posed a serious threat to ʿAbbāsid rule.[31]

The ʿAbbāsids in fact did not regard Syria as a minor province; for more than half a century at least major parts of it were held as an apanage by one branch of the new ruling house.[32] The first governor was ʿAbd Allāh ibn ʿAlī,

31 P. M. Cobb, *White banners: Contention in Abbasid Syria, 750–880* (Albany, 2001), argument summarised pp. 125–36.

32 H. Kennedy, *The early Abbasid caliphate: A political history* (London and Sydney, 1981), pp. 48–50, 74–5, 168–9.

the powerful uncle of al-Saffāḥ and al-Manṣūr who had led the victorious ʿAbbāsid armies into Syria. When ʿAbd Allāh was removed from the picture after his failed *coup d'état* against al-Manṣūr, Syria was assigned to another uncle, Ṣāliḥ ibn ʿAlī, and remained in his descendants' hands until 803. Ṣāliḥ took over many of the Umayyad estates (including, no doubt, the desert castles), and apparently made new investments of his own in northern Syria. To legitimise his position he even married the widow of Marwān II, the last Umayyad caliph. Whatever her feelings about the matter may have been, the marriage was probably advantageous for her as well. His sons Faḍl and ʿAbd al-Malik (the latter's mother was Marwān's former wife) continued in the same way, and ʿAbd al-Malik ibn Ṣāliḥ was highly influential at Hārūn al-Rashīd's court. Finally, Ṣāliḥ inherited the Umayyad mission of pursuing the *jihād* against Byzantium. In addition to leading numerous campaigns into Anatolia, he rebuilt a number of fortresses in Cilicia and the Taurus that had been lost or destroyed in the Byzantine counter-offensives under Constantine V (r. 741–75): Marʿash, al-Maṣṣīṣa (Mopsuestia), Malaṭya (Melitene) and Adana.

The commitment of Ṣāliḥ ibn ʿAlī and his family to the region was echoed in the career of Hārūn al-Rashīd (r. 786–809), both before and after he became caliph. From 796 to 808 Hārūn resided mainly at Raqqa on the Euphrates, not far from Hishām's old capital of al-Ruṣāfa, partly because he disliked Baghdad and partly because of his personal commitment to the Byzantine *jihād*. He strove to distinguish himself as the *ghāzī*-caliph – the first caliph to lead troops against the infidel. In this framing of his public persona we may well detect the influence of his Syrian cousins Faḍl and ʿAbd al-Malik.[33] Hārūn's interest in the Byzantine frontier was maintained at least sporadically by two of his sons. Al-Ma'mūn (r. 813–33) spent the last three years of his caliphate there, and died at Tarsus. Al-Muʿtaṣim (r. 833–42) devoted most of his reign to building his new capital at Sāmarrāʾ and to quashing rebellions in Iraq and north-western Iran, but in 838 he led a triumphant expedition against Amorion. However, this would be the last major offensive against the Byzantines by any Muslim ruler for more than a century.

Archaeological evidence supports the textual sources. Recent excavations and redatings of previously studied sites indicate that many Umayyad buildings and ensembles remained inhabited and economically active down into the early or mid-third/ninth century, well over half a century after the fall of

33 M. Bonner, *Aristocratic violence and holy war: Studies in the jihad and the Arab–Byzantine frontier* (New Haven, 1996), pp. 88–9, 99–106.

the Umayyads. Only then do we see clear signs of abandonment and impoverishment. Even some of the Christian churches in Jordan (most strikingly St Stephen's at Umm al-Raṣāṣ near Ma'daba) show signs of embellishment and new construction in the first decades of ʿAbbāsid rule, though by this time a distinctly more hostile and restrictive attitude towards the old religion was growing up among Muslim officials and scholars.[34]

In the struggle against Byzantium the ʿAbbāsids significantly reshaped the army in northern Syria and the Thughūr (i.e. the military districts along the Byzantine frontier, established by Hārūn, and stretching from Tarsus in the west to Samosata in the east), by stationing there a substantial number of Khurāsānī troops, the so-called *abnāʾ al-dawla* who constituted the core of the caliphal army.[35] The Khurāsānī forces supplemented rather than replaced the Arab tribesmen (mostly from Qays) who had been the mainstay of the Umayyad armies in the region. There is no basis on which to estimate the proportion of Khurāsānī to Syrian troops, but it seems likely that the Syrian tribesmen (i.e. the former Umayyad army) remained in the majority. Nor did the new Khurāsānī forces represent any fundamental ethnic change, since many were ethnic Arabs drawn by the Umayyads from the Iraqi and Syrian armies and stationed as garrison forces in north-eastern Iran over a period of several decades. Still, they were newcomers to northern Syria and represented a new set of interests and ambitions. At the very least they kept the existing Syrian tribesmen under close surveillance, to ensure their loyalty to the new regime. The old Umayyad forces were still crucial to the job of maintaining the frontiers, but they were relegated to second-line status and some were struck off the official registers. Likewise, the senior commanders in the region were now all drawn from the *abnāʾ al-dawla* as well.

These changes did not greatly affect ʿAbbāsid policy on the Byzantine frontier. After the catastrophic failure of the siege of Constantinople in 717–18 the Umayyads had been content to maintain a stalemate. They could launch very destructive raids deep into Anatolia during the summer expeditions, but they never tried to expand their holdings in a permanent way, or even resettle their side of the half-abandoned frontier zone. The first three ʿAbbāsid caliphs followed the same pattern: the summer expeditions were regarded as important, but they were not expected to lead to permanent conquests. Moreover, under the emperor Constantine V the Byzantine army was tenacious and

34 J. Magness, *The archaeology of the early Islamic settlement in Palestine* (Winona Lake, IN, 2003).

35 The following paragraphs are based largely on Bonner, *Aristocratic violence*, pp. 56–68, 85–92, 107–9, 135–56.

effective. With Hārūn al-Rashīd (r. 786–809) there was, as noted above, a new emphasis on the Byzantine frontier. Hārūn's motives are not certain. He too did not aim at permanent conquest (although his reign fell in a period of Byzantine political and military disarray) and so from a strategic point of view he was simply repeating a policy of limited war and stalemate. It has been argued that he was striving for legitimacy. He had after all come to the throne via the assassination of his elder brother, and even though he was not personally implicated in this event, he was inevitably tainted by it. He could thus demonstrate his right to rule the Muslims only by taking personal command of armies of Islam and leading them against the greatest infidel power, or at least symbolically the most important one.

The major social, religious and cultural changes on the Byzantine frontier during the period 750–861 resulted from a spontaneous flow of immigrants towards that frontier – immigrants motivated by the desire for *jihād*, in the conviction that full obedience to God's commandments required every believer to undertake the struggle against the infidel. The caliphs certainly attached themselves to this process and encouraged it; especially important was the restoration and refortification of Tarsus after 786. Still, it is hard to see it as a consciously planned policy. Even those immigrants who did not personally take up arms felt the need to live in a region where the confrontation between Belief and Infidelity was stark and immediate. In the century after 750 these immigrants created the first real Muslim community along the frontier, a community of merchants, artisans, scholars – people whose life was anchored in the mosque and marketplace, so to speak. Nothing of the sort existed there before that time. The indigenous populace of the towns and villages must still have been solidly Christian, albeit much diminished and impoverished by the endemic frontier warfare of the previous century. Muslims were present only as administrators and landowners (much the same thing), scattered fortress garrisons and nomadic tribes in the adjoining steppe. So for the Syrian and Cilician towns north of Antioch, the ʿAbbāsid revolution did bring about something truly new.

Where did these Muslim immigrants come from? Among those few whose origins we can identify with certainty, the great majority came from two regions: Iraq and Khurāsān. Very few came from Egypt, the Ḥijāz, or even Damascus and central Syria. The Khurāsānīs included the famous ascetic Ibrāhīm ibn Adham (d. 777), who developed a large following in northern Syria, and the scholar Ibn al-Mubārak (d. 802), whose *Kitāb al-jihād* (more a collection of *ḥadīth* on martyrdom than a treatise on warfare) is the oldest extant work in this genre. Among the Iraqis, Aḥmad ibn Ḥanbal is a crucial figure, since he was imprisoned in Tarsus by al-Maʾmūn for refusing to agree that the Qurʾān was created. The number of scholars in the Byzantine frontier who are presented as his followers or disciples is remarkable – but of course his austerity, traditionalism, absolute commitment to principle and militant piety were a perfect match for the ethos of that region.

The Iraqi migration to the frontier seems more a puzzle than the Khurāsānī migration. Iraq, after all, was not a frontier zone and presumably did not breed the same frontier ethos. However, we might surmise that many Iraqi scholars of a particularly ascetic, militant character wanted to get away from the stifling, corrupting presence of the ʿAbbāsid court, and perhaps from the 'hothouse' academic atmosphere of Baṣra and Kūfa. Possibly the Islamic scholarship of the Byzantine frontier (with its emphasis on *ḥadīth* and *furūʿ al-fiqh*) was rooted in Iraq – both the migration of Iraqi scholars to the frontier and the travels of frontier scholars to Iraq for study. On the other hand, the peculiar militancy and austerity of Islam in the Thughūr were largely owed to Khurāsānī immigrants.

Developments in northern Syria and Mesopotamia can thus be seen as a natural outgrowth of processes already under way in Umayyad times. That is much less true of central Syria (Homs and Damascus) and Palestine, however. Especially by the mid-third/ninth century, textual and archaeological evidence points to economic decline, some degree of cultural stagnation (especially after the death of the eminent jurist al-Awzāʿī in 777) and a climate of social tension, expressed in repeated revolts and social disturbances.[36]

Although Christians probably remained a majority in the villages and small towns throughout Syria and Mesopotamia throughout the third/ninth century, and some major centres such as Edessa (Ar. Ruhā) and Antioch were still predominantly Christian, Islam was now gaining converts rapidly and making its presence felt everywhere. By this time most of the once-Christian Arab tribes – Kalb, Tanūkh, even much of stubborn Taghlib – had gone over to Islam. As we have seen, the cities and fortresses of the Thughūr were attracting a strong flow of ardently Muslim immigrants. In central Syria, as well as Palestine and Jordan, Muslims were an important part of the social and demographic landscape from the 630s on. They constituted the ruling elite in the major towns, especially the political-administrative centres of Damascus and Homs, and they were densely interwoven with the native Christian

36 M. Abiad, *Culture et éducation arabo-islamiques au Šam pendant les trois premiers siècles de l'Islam, d'après Taʾrīkh madīnat Dimasq d'Ibn ʿAsākir (499/1105–571/1176)* (Damascus, 1981), pp. 155–207; Cobb, *White banners*, pp. 34–42, 92–102, 116–124.

populations in the villages and small towns along the edge of the interior steppe. Just from the fact of constant interaction they would exert a certain pressure and influence on Christian communities in those regions. By the second/eighth century, if not earlier, Muslims were permeating smaller cities such as Jerash. This close intermingling of Christian and Muslim populations, combined with the conversion of most nomadic tribesmen to Islam and the strongly pro-Islamic policies of the later Marwānids and ʿAbbāsids, do much to explain the trend of conversion to Islam in the districts between Homs and the Negev. A further element would be the fact that this part of Syria-Palestine was largely Chalcedonian. The Chalcedonian leadership had in effect been decapitated during the conquests, and the Church's official Greek language was unintelligible to most of the faithful. The capacity of the former imperial Church to shelter and nurture its flock was thus gravely weakened.

In the north – the Thughūr and the Jazīran–Armenian borderlands east of the Euphrates – things were quite different. The new Muslim settlers there were not much concerned with the established Christian populations and seem to have interacted with them only in limited, though rather destructive, ways – e.g. foraging military expeditions, harsh tax collections etc. For that reason the old Christian communities, especially those that were somewhat out of the way of armies marching back and forth, could continue their life much as before. These districts were heavily Monophysite. Here the clergy and monks shared a language (Syriac or Armenian) and common ethnic origins with their flock, so the close-knit ties of pre-Islamic times were not broken or strained by the conquests. Likewise, Monophysite ecclesiastics might well feel liberated by the disappearance of Roman rule, as witnessed by the oft-cited comment of Dionysius of Tell Mahré: 'When [God] saw that the measure of the Romans' sins was overflowing and that they were committing every sort of crime against our people and our churches ... He stirred up the Sons of Ishmael and enticed them hither from their southern land ... It was by bargaining with them that we secured our deliverance. This was no small gain, to be rescued from Roman imperial oppression.'[37] So long as the Muslim authorities were tolerant or indifferent, the position of Christianity seemed strong. As we have seen, however, Muslim tolerance grew narrower in late Umayyad and especially ʿAbbāsid times, and fiscal exactions grew more severe.

ʿAbbāsid fiscal policy was initially moderate, and northern Mesopotamia seems to have been very prosperous during these years. However, in 773, near

37 Dionysius, in Palmer, Brock and Hoyland, *Seventh century*, p. 141.

the end of al-Manṣūr's reign, he named a new governor for the province, one Mūsā ibn Muṣʿab, whose brutality, extreme demands and arbitrary assessments became a byword.[38] He was at least not discriminatory, since his agents pursued Arab Muslim landowners with almost the same ferocity as they did Christians. He held office only for a few years, so it is hard to know whether his actions did any long-term damage. In any case, it must have been clear to the Christians of Mesopotamia how vulnerable they were to sudden shifts in government policy. From these things, and from a growing Muslim population, the churches could not insulate their people or even always protect their own interests. The trend of conversion to Islam would be much slower than in the south, the pockets of Christian believers would remain much larger. But here too a process was under way that would in the long run sap the churches of their vitality and erode the loyalty and confidence of their members, even though the full impact of that process would only be felt with the coming of the Turkomans in the fifth/eleventh century and the Crusades in the period following.

Some aspects of the problem are visible in the fate of the Greek and Syriac languages. Language change is a problem in its own right and does not explain the rise of Islam, since it was always perfectly possible to be a Muslim without speaking Arabic (as in Iran or the Berber highlands), or to become an Arabic speaker without becoming also a Muslim (as with the Christians and Jews of Egypt and the Fertile Crescent). Nevertheless, the processes of Arabicisation and Islamisation run in parallel, and language change may reveal important aspects of religious identity. It was the Chalcedonians (or Melkites) of central Syria and Palestine who first adopted Arabic as their primary vehicle of literary expression.[39] By the end of the second/eighth century Greek had almost disappeared as a literary, scientific and theological language in Syria and Palestine – an astonishing collapse in view of Syria's role in Patristic and Late Antique writing. Even in early Islamic times one finds such names as Anastasius of Sinai, St John of Damascus, George Syncellus and Theodore Abu Qurra. But the writings of this last figure tell a story: Theodore Abu Qurra was thoroughly at home in Greek, and yet by the 780s he found it more useful to

38 *Chronicle of Zuqnin*, parts 3 and 4, trans. Amir Harrak (Toronto, 1999), pp. 215, 223ff.; C. Cahen, 'Fiscalité, propriété, antagonismes sociaux en Haute-Mésopotamie au temps des premiers ʿAbbāsides, d'après Denys de Tell Mahré', *Arabica*, 1 (1954); C. Robinson, *Empire and elites after the Muslim conquest: The transformation of northern Mesopotamia* (Cambridge, 2000), pp. 156–8.

39 S. Griffith, 'The Gospel in Arabic: An inquiry into its appearance in the first Abbasid century', *Oriens Christianus*, 69 (1985), pp. 160–7.

compose his theological treatises in Arabic. By that time the first language even of educated Christians in Palestine, including monks and lower clergy, was clearly Arabic. A similar process was under way in Iraq, as witnessed in the famous dialogue between the Nestorian Catholicos Timothy I and the caliph al-Mahdī (r. 775–85).[40]

Syriac enjoyed a much longer career, at least in Mesopotamia. But elsewhere it too began to fade quite early on. Central and northern Syria retained Aramaic speech somewhat longer than Palestine, but the appearance of Agapius of Manbij's chronicle in Arabic around 940 demonstrates that by then Arabic had become the language of literate Chalcedonians in that region as well. In Mesopotamia Syriac remained a living tongue on every level well into the third/ninth century, as witnessed by the great chronicle of Dionysius of Tell Mahré (d. 846), though some time thereafter it slowly began to fade. By the sixth/twelfth century Syriac had clearly fallen out of use outside the monasteries and the liturgy, save in isolated regions such as Ṭūr ʿAbdīn. The late sixth/twelfth and seventh/thirteenth centuries saw a brief literary renaissance, but the last flourish of literary production came from Gregory Abū al-Faraj (Bar Hebraeus, d. 1283), a converted Jew for whom Syriac was clearly a grammar-book language, and who also wrote in Arabic.

Later ʿAbbāsid Syria

In the late third/ninth century Syria suddenly entered on an era of sustained turbulence, in common with many parts of the Islamic world. The assassination of the caliph al-Mutawakkil (r. 847–61) and the temporary seizure of power by the Turkish troops of Sāmarrāʾ opened a period of political devolution, during which provincial governors or self-made warlords were able to assert control of broad territories within the caliphate. For the most part the new rulers maintained formal obeisance to the caliphs, but they had a free hand to run the territories they had seized. Thus in 868 Egypt fell into the hands of its governor, Aḥmad ibn Ṭūlūn (r. 868–84), himself one of the Sāmarrāʾ Turks, and by 882 he had brought most of Syria under his control. In 890 his son and successor Khumārawayh (r. 884–96) occupied much of al-Jazīra as well as the strategic frontier city of Tarsus. For the first time in Islam, but hardly the last, Syria was ruled (in a manner of speaking) from Egypt. The Ṭūlūnid interlude was a brief one, since ʿAbbāsid forces

40 Dialogue of Timothy and al-Mahdī: A. Mingana (ed. and trans.), 'The apology of Timothy the Patriarch before the caliph Mahdi', *Woodbrooke Studies*, 2 (Cambridge, 1928).

reoccupied Syria in 903 and Egypt two years later, and there is no reason to think that the Ṭūlūnids had attempted to alter established fiscal and administrative patterns there.

Far graver issues were posed by the Ismāʿīlī revolt at the beginning of the fourth/tenth century. During the 870s a clandestine revolutionary movement emerged in Iraq which aimed at overthrowing the ʿAbbāsids and replacing them with an imam descended from ʿAlī ibn Abī Ṭālib through Muḥammad ibn Ismāʿīl ibn Jaʿfar al-Ṣādiq, a shadowy figure of whom we know nothing save his name, and who probably died some time around 800. The Ismāʿīlīs quickly gained followers in many parts of the Islamic world – Iraq, northern and eastern Iran, Yemen and Syria – but suffered a grave crisis in 899 when one of their leaders, ʿUbayd Allāh (residing in the small Syrian town of Salamiyya) proclaimed that he himself was the awaited *imām*. His claims were accepted by some – enough to allow him to found the Fāṭimid dynasty, which governed North Africa and then Egypt from 909 until 1171. But they were violently rejected by another Ismāʿīlī faction, the Qarāmiṭa (also called Carmathians), so named after their chief, Ḥamdān Qarmaṭ. Although the Qarāmiṭa had their greatest long-term impact in southern Iraq and eastern Arabia, where they would be a major political and military force into the eleventh century, they first exploded onto the scene in Syria.[41] Especially in its earlier years, the movement was extremely fluid, with cross-cutting alliances and rivalries that are almost impossible to trace. The Qarāmiṭa were in fact not a single sect, but rather a congeries of Ismāʿīlī factions who rejected the claims of ʿUbayd Allāh and his Fāṭimid successors.

One branch of the movement, directed by a man named Zikrawayh and variously connected both with ʿUbayd Allāh and the Qarāmiṭa, succeeded in converting several sections of the Kalb tribe to its cause. Zikrawayh himself remained in Iraq, but he sent his newly recruited forces to lay siege to Damascus in 903. They failed to capture it, but, nothing daunted, turned on the other cities of Syria. Aleppo also fended them off; however, they did seize Homs, Hama and several other towns, though they did not try to occupy them permanently. In 906 Adhriʿāt and Buṣrā were sacked by Zikrawayh's men, who then attacked Damascus for a second time, again without success. At this point Zikrawayh turned his attention away from Syria and towards the more crucial arena of Iraq. Brief successes there, including the massacre of an Iranian pilgrimage caravan returning from Mecca, soon ended with

41 W. Madelung, 'Ḳarmaṭī', *EI2*, vol. IV, pp. 660–5; W. Madelung, 'Fatimiden und Bahrainqarmaten', *Der Islam*, 34 (1959).

Zikrawayh's own death in battle in 907. With this event the Ismāʿīlī revolt in Syria faded away. The leadership of the revolt had lain with townsmen, largely Iraqi in origin, but (as in many areas) its followers were largely recruited among Bedouin tribesmen. It is impossible to gauge the depth and character of the latter's commitment to Ismāʿīlism. Only the Kalb seem to have been brought into the Ismāʿīlī orbit and, with two minor exceptions, none of the major tribal revolts of the mid-fourth/tenth century can be linked to this movement.

The definitive collapse of ʿAbbāsid power in the 920s and 930s led to a new local dynasty centred in Egypt but with Syrian ambitions. The Ikhshīdid era (935–69) was likewise brief and troubled, and they were never able to extend their control much beyond Damascus. Northern Syria (Homs and Aleppo), the Thughūr and western Mesopotamia instead fell in 947 to Sayf al-Dawla ʿAlī ibn Abī al-Hayjāʾ ibn Ḥamdān, a brilliant young officer who had previously made his career in the maelstrom of caliphal politics in Iraq. By the mid-940s this vast region was in effect a power vacuum, and Sayf al-Dawla had no difficulty in seizing it from the Ikhshīdids. His elder brother Nāṣir al-Dawla had been trying (with uneven success) to establish his own principality in Mosul since the mid-930s, and to some degree Sayf al-Dawla was able to draw on his brother's resources and position. But while Sayf al-Dawla was in principle the junior partner in the Ḥamdānid enterprise, he quickly established himself as a far more effective and prestigious ruler.[42] The extent of his territories led Sayf al-Dawla to establish two capitals, Aleppo in the west and Mayyāfāriqīn (modern Silvan) in the north-east. Until this time both had been minor cities; thenceforth both would become important political centres, and Aleppo the most prominent city in northern Syria. Sayf al-Dawla devoted great efforts to fortifying and embellishing both towns, and a number of major monuments date from his reign. Given the nature of the times, he of course focused on the defences of the two cities, but a fine palace outside Aleppo, along with gardens and a new aqueduct, indicate his intentions to make a showpiece of his Syrian capital.

Sayf al-Dawla's personal fame rests on two things: his indefatigable though ultimately disastrous warfare against the Byzantines; and the brilliant circle of poets, scholars and thinkers whom he brought to Aleppo. These were a remarkable group: the poets Abū Firās (Sayf al-Dawla's cousin) and al-Mutanabbī, the preacher and rhetorician Ibn Nubāta, the philosopher

42 M. Canard, *Histoire de la dynastie des H'amdanides de Djazira et de Syrie* (Algiers, 1951); but now see T. Bianquis, 'Sayf al-Dawla', *EI2*, vol. IX, pp. 103–10.

al-Fārābī (admittedly very late in his life) and many others of only moderately less attainment. Though a soldier by training and temperament, Sayf al-Dawla enjoyed intellectual debates on all subjects as well as the verbal display of court poetry. In his time Aleppo could certainly have held its own with any court in Renaissance Italy.

Sayf al-Dawla was himself a Shīʿite (of the Twelver school), and he encouraged Shīʿite observance in his domains, which had until this time been quite solidly Sunnī and traditionalist in outlook. Beginning in the mid-fourth/tenth century, however, Shīʿism would strike root in northern Syria, and ultimately gain the wide popular following it had there by the sixth/twelfth century. Whether this is due largely to Sayf al-Dawla's efforts, or can also be connected in some way with currents of revolutionary Ismāʿīlism in Syria during this period, is open to debate. Sayf al-Dawla's religious initiatives seem broadly similar to those of the Būyids in Iraq during the same period, and Būyid patronage of Twelver Shīʿism unquestionably had an important long-term impact on the development of this sect.

Sayf al-Dawla had an unusual ethnic background in a period when most of the warlords of the Nile-to-Oxus region were of Turkish or Iranian descent, for he traced his ancestry to the Arab tribe of Taghlib in northern Iraq (though he may have had Kurdish connections as well). His background surely aided him in asserting control over the various Arab tribes of central and northern Syria and in establishing effective relations with them. On the other hand, it required a decade of negotiation and fighting, and the repression of a major revolt in 955, before this task was really completed. After 955 he was able to rely on the support of the Banū Kilāb, the most powerful tribe still remaining in northern Syria. However, Sayf al-Dawla did not use Bedouin tribesmen as the core of his army. Rather, he relied on the same mix as everyone else in this period: Daylamī infantry and Turkish mounted archers, along with Arab auxiliary cavalry and Sudanese spearmen.

Sayf al-Dawla was a soldier of undoubted courage and skill, as well as a resourceful commander. Perhaps inspired by the *ghāzī* mentality of northern Syria and the Thughūr, he was deeply committed to the *jihād* against Byzantium. It was his misfortune to live in a time when the resurgent Byzantines were threatening the Muslims' hard-won positions, not only in Cilicia and the Taurus mountains, but throughout all northern Syria. Sayf al-Dawla's forces more than held their own in the early years of his reign. After 960, however, he had to face generals such as Nicephorus Phocas and John Tzimisces. In 962 Nicephorus overwhelmed Sayf al-Dawla's capital, Aleppo, and pillaged the city, though fortunately he did not try to retain it. In 963 the ferocious John Tzimisces obliterated Sayf al-Dawla's army near Adana. Worst of all, in 964–5 al-Maṣṣīṣa and Tarsus fell to the Byzantines, and the Muslim inhabitants of Cilicia were forced to evacuate the region. The geographer Ibn Ḥawqal, writing about 980, laments the perilous situation of the Muslims in northern Syria and the Thughūr. Many, he points out, are now under Byzantine rule; compelled to live in humiliation and pay a heavy capitation, it cannot be long before they give up their religion and go over to Christianity.[43]

Two years after the Byzantine conquest of Cilicia (967) Sayf al-Dawla died, after suffering a long, debilitating illness. In spite of the dire circumstances, however, he was able to pass Aleppo on to his son Saʿd al-Dawla Sharīf. The dynasty endured another forty years, perhaps because its very weakness made it useful to its enemies, the Byzantines and the rising power of the Fāṭimids.

The extraordinary political instability and periodic violence of fourth/tenth-century Syria and Mesopotamia would naturally lead us to suppose that the negative economic trends of the third/ninth century must have continued, if not intensified. That is not necessarily the case, however, at least not everywhere. Travellers and geographers such as Ibn Ḥawqal and al-Muqaddasī, who had detailed, first-hand knowledge of this region, do not give us a bleak picture of the towns and countryside, apart from the war-ravaged Byzantine frontier. In their portrayal the cities seem active and prosperous, while the land is actively cultivated with a wide range of crops. The nomadic Arab tribes do seem more in evidence than in the first/seventh and second/eighth centuries; they now dominated stretches of territory that had been devoted to agriculture in early Byzantine and Umayyad times – the Balqāʾ east of the Jordan river, parts of the upper Orontes basin, etc. On the other hand, much of this land was quite marginal and could only be brought under cultivation through extraordinary levels of investment. Pastoralism was not necessarily a less productive use of it. Moreover, some of the tribes were by now at least partly settled, either at their own initiative or that of the regional rulers. We should perhaps hypothesise a levelling-off of third/ninth-century trends, perhaps a consolidation of economic life within reduced but now stable parameters. However, any serious conclusions, either as to long-term trends or underlying causes, must await further research.[44]

43 Ibn Ḥawqal, *Kitāb ṣūrat al-arḍ*, ed. M. J. de Goeje, rev. J. H. Kramers, BGA 2 (Leiden, 1938), pp. 187–9.

44 M. D. Yusuf, *Economic survey of Syria during the tenth and eleventh centuries*. (Berlin, 1985), pp. 177–82: well documented, but a more optimistic interpretation than most other scholars have given.

By 970 Syria and Mesopotamia had unquestionably changed greatly since Byzantine, and even Umayyad, times – on every level – but there was much continuity as well. Greek had disappeared and Arabic was now the dominant language both of high culture and everyday speech; on the other hand, Syriac continued to flourish in the monasteries and many of the villages and towns of Mesopotamia. Islam was clearly the paramount religion – not only politically privileged, but also the one that set the parameters for religious and philosophical discourse. However, Christianity still commanded a demographic majority in many areas, its institutions were still largely intact, and intellectually it was far from moribund. Indeed, the fourth/tenth century witnessed an unusually high level of serious debate between Muslim and Christian thinkers. On the level of material life, Syria and Mesopotamia were still highly urbanised; if some cities, such as Antioch, Apamea or Caesarea, had shrunk to a fraction of their former size, others such as Aleppo had risen to replace them. The balance between agriculture and pastoral nomadism had shifted somewhat in favour of the latter, but there is no evidence of agrarian crisis. A Byzantine official from the early seventh century might have had some trouble getting his bearings in tenth-century Damascus or Aleppo, but he would surely sense that these places still had strong links to their Roman and Christian past.

13

Egypt

MICHAEL BRETT

Muslims and Christians

In Egypt the Arab conquest initiated a cultural transformation that left unchanged the constants of the country's history over the past three thousand years. The country itself was an anomaly, a vast oasis formed in the desert by the Valley and Delta of the Nile, a great tropical river bringing an immense amount of water to a rainless land. From the first cataract at Aswan to the sea, it made possible irrigated agriculture on a grand scale, a large agricultural population and a centralised state. To the north, the Delta or Lower Egypt looked to the Mediterranean and Near East; to the south, the Valley or Upper Egypt looked to Nubia, the Red Sea and the Indian Ocean. The arc became a full circle with Islam, which added the western and central Sudan, and a systematic relationship with North Africa. Politically, the state had the resources to expand north-eastwards into Syria, westwards to (modern) Cyrenaica in Libya and southwards into Nubia, but the country was equally open to invasion and conquest, so that for the past fifteen hundred years it had alternated between the status of a province and a seat of empire ruled by immigrants. The history of the first four hundred years of Muslim rule is the history of its further progress from province to empire under the impulsion of fresh waves of conquest. The novel feature was the accompanying passage from Christianity, Coptic and Greek to Islam and Arabic.

The sources generated by this passage are twofold. The Muslim tradition begins with Ibn ʿAbd al-Ḥakam (d. 257/870) in the ninth century and al-Kindī (d. 350/961) in the tenth, who celebrate the creation of an expanding Islamic community in the country.[1] On the other hand are those of the Christians: that of the Orthodox Melkites, compiled by Eutychius under his Arabic name of

1 Ibn ʿAbd al-Ḥakam, *Kitāb futūḥ Miṣr wa ʾl-Maghrib*, ed. C. C. Torrey (New Haven, 1922); al-Kindī, *Governors and judges of Egypt*, ed. R. Guest (Leiden and London, 1912).

Saʿīd ibn Baṭrīq (d. 328/940) in the tenth, and that of the Monophysite Copts in the eleventh-century edition of *The history of the Coptic patriarchs of Alexandria*, which document the acceptance by the original majority of the population of an inferior status and numerical decline.[2] Apart from these literary sources, the archaeological evidence of settlement is matched by that of the papyri, a unique if fragmentary contemporary record, which for the first three centuries after the conquest supplements and controls the sectarian versions of events.[3] Ibn ʿAbd al-Ḥakam's *Futūḥ Miṣr* (The conquests of Egypt) is a legal text that served to establish the legality of the conquerors in accordance with the criteria of the Islamic law some two hundred years after the event.[4] Al-Kindī's *Wūlāt wa qūḍāt Miṣr* (Governors and judges of Egypt) brought the story down to his own time in notices of the two principal officers of the Muslim community: on the one hand, the governor responsible for obedience to the caliph; on the other, the judge responsible for obedience to the law.[5] On the same principle the *History of the Coptic patriarchs of Alexandria* recounts the events of each ecclesiastical reign, confirming the dependence of the two religious communities upon the government of their respective pastors. In the case of the Muslims this was in effect the *qāḍī* or judge who, since his original appointment by the Umayyads to act on behalf of the caliph, had come to represent the supreme authority of the *sharīʿa* or law of God. In consequence, although he depended for his appointment upon the governor or the caliph himself, he stood apart as the magistrate who met the supreme requirement of the community for government in accordance with the law. So too, on the principle of the apostolic succession, did the Coptic patriarch, who long before the Arab conquest had taken his stance in opposition to the Christian emperor on a point of doctrine, upholding the Monophysite view of the single divine nature of Christ against the Orthodox view of His duality, both human and

2 Saʿīd ibn Baṭrīq [Eutychius], *Eutychii Patriarchae Alexandrini Annales*, ed. L. Cheikho, CSCO, Scriptores Arabici, 3rd series, vols. VI, VII (Beirut, Paris and Leipzig, 1906, 1909); (Severus ibn al-Muqaffaʿ), *History of the patriarchs of the Coptic Church of Alexandria/the Egyptian Church*, ed. and trans. B. T. A. Evetts, Y. ʿAbd al-Masih, O. H. E. Burmester and A. Khater, 3 vols. (Paris, 1901; Cairo, 1943–59, 1968–70).

3 Most accessible in A. Grohmann (ed. and trans.), *Arabic papyri in the Egyptian Library*, 6 vols. (Cairo, 1934–62); see also J. Karabacek, *Papyrus Erzherzog Rainer: Führer durch die Ausstellung*, Vienna, 1892. Cf. L. Sundelin, 'Papyrology and the study of early Islamic Egypt', in P. M. Sijpesteijn and L. Sundelin (eds.), *Papyrology and the history of early Islamic Egypt* (Leiden, 2004), pp. 1–19.

4 See R. Brunschvig, 'Ibn ʿAbdalh'akam et la conquête de l'Afrique du Nord par les Arabes', in R. Brunschvig, *Études sur l'Islam classique et l'Afrique du Nord*, ed. A.-M. Turki, Variorum Reprints XI (London, 1986).

5 For the list of governors, *qāḍīs* and other officers down to the arrival of Ibn Ṭūlūn, see S. Lane-Poole, *A history of Egypt in the Middle Ages*, 4th edn (London, 1925), pp. 45–58.

divine. The conflict this had generated between Byzantine state and Coptic Church was a major factor in the success of the Arab invasion.

Arabs and Egyptians

Written more than a hundred and fifty years later than the events themselves, the account of that invasion in the extant Muslim sources begs many questions. The contemporary account in the *History of the Coptic patriarchs* is brief to the point of ignoring almost everything except the reappearance of the Coptic patriarch Benjamin I after years of hiding from Byzantine persecution directed by 'al-Muqawqas'. In the Melkite account of Eutychius, on the other hand, 'al-Muqawqas' figures not only as the financial controller of Egypt, but as a Jacobite, a heretical Copt who betrayed the country to the Arabs out of hatred of Byzantium. It was the late seventh-century chronicle of John, Coptic bishop of Nikiu, which survives only in Ethiopic translation,[6] that was largely used by Butler to settle the question of his identity, and establish a convincing account of the conquest.[7] The mysterious Muqawqas was Cyrus, bishop of Phasis in Colchis, appointed by the emperor Heraclius not only as the Orthodox Melkite patriarch of Alexandria in the last of many attempts by Constantinople to recover the Church in Egypt from the Monophysite heresy, but also as the governor of the country. When the Arabs under ʿAmr ibn al-ʿĀṣ invaded Egypt from Palestine in Dhū al-Ḥijja 18 / December 639, advancing up the eastern side of the Delta to besiege the fortress of Babylon at its head, he negotiated its surrender at Easter 641 (Rabīʿ II AH 20). When the Arabs advanced down the west side of the Delta to the siege of the capital Alexandria, he returned after a brief dismissal to negotiate in Dhū al-Ḥijja 20 / November 641 its evacuation by the Byzantines in Shawwāl 21 / September 642. The city was reoccupied by the Byzantines in 24 / 645, but finally relinquished the following year.

Between the Arabs, the Orthodox Greeks and the Monophysite Copts, however, there is no clear-cut opposition. The conquest took two or three years of confused warfare in the Delta, in which it appears from John of Nikiu that the invaders found allies as well as enemies among both Greeks and

6 John of Nikiou, *Chronique de Jean, Evêque de Nikiou*, ed. and trans. A. Zotenberg (Paris, 1883), trans. R. M. Charles as *The Chronicle of John, Bishop of Nikiu* (Oxford, 1916).

7 A. J. Butler, *The Arab conquest of Egypt and the last thirty years of the Roman dominion*, 2nd edn, with critical bibliography by P. M. Fraser (Oxford, 1978). For Byzantine Egypt, see W. E. Kaegi, 'Egypt on the eve of the Muslim conquest', in C. F. Petry (ed.), *The Cambridge history of Egypt*, vol. I: *Islamic Egypt, 640–1517* (Cambridge, 1998).

Copts, and were not invariably successful.[8] The situation was clarified by the Byzantine withdrawal, when Duke Sanutius (Shenute), prefect of the Rīf (coast), brought the Egyptian fleet over to ʿAmr, and was instrumental in bringing the Coptic patriarch Benjamin out of hiding in 23/644, to be reinstated as the rightful successor to the see of St Mark. The Egyptian fleet, manned by Egyptians, is an important but neglected aspect of the country's history throughout the period of this chapter; in 24/645 it aided the Arab conquest of Cyrenaica and its annexation to Egypt as the province of Barqa.[9] The Coptic Church regained possession of all the extensive ecclesiastical property in the country, which it held in trust under the Roman law of *piae causae*, with appropriate tax exemptions. In return for this patronage it helped to ensure a smooth transition to Arab rule. The initial levies of food and clothing were regularised as the Arabs took control of the state and its fiscal system, documented for this as for previous periods by the surviving papyri.[10] Existing taxes were paid in tribute to the conquerors by the Christian population, categorised as *dhimmiyyūn* or protected subjects. The land-tax in particular remained as before, levied by village quota in accordance with an assessment of what the land would bear. Responsibility was for the most part left to the district administration or pagarchy, at the beginning of yet another phase in the age-long conflict between peasant and state that characterised the history of the country down to the nineteenth century.[11]

The conditions were laid down on the one hand by the Nile flood, and on the other by the fiscal demands of the state. Out of the flood had emerged the system of 'basin' irrigation, under which the floodwater was formed into artificial lakes by long earthen banks to allow it to soak into the soil.[12] A collective effort was required to build the banks, and to open and close the entrances each year. This effort called for collective organisation, not only to irrigate the land, but to allocate it each year to the villagers for cultivation,

8 See M. Brett, 'The Arab conquest and the rise of Islam in North Africa', in J. D. Fage and Roland Oliver (eds.), *The Cambridge history of Africa*, vol. II: *From c. 500 BC to AD 1050* (Cambridge, 1978), pp. 495–9.

9 See R. G. Goodchild, 'Byzantines, Berbers and Arabs in seventh-century Libya', *Antiquity*, 51 (1967), repr. in R. G. Goodchild, *Libyan studies: Selected papers of the late R. G .Goodchild*, ed. J. Reynolds and Paul Elek, London, 1976; F. R. Trombley, 'Sawīrus ibn al-Muqaffaʿ and the Christians of Umayyad Egypt: War and society in documentary context', in Sijpesteijn and Sundelin (eds.), *Papyrology*, pp. 199–226.

10 See Grohmann (ed. and trans.), *Arabic papyri*, vol. III. See also Sijpesteijn and Sundelin (eds.), *Papyrology*; and P. M. Sijpesteijn, 'The Muslim conquest and the first fifty years of Muslim rule in Egypt', in R. S. Bagnall (ed.), *Egypt in the Byzantine World, 300–700* (Cambridge, 2007).

11 See M. Brett, 'The way of the peasant', *BSOAS*, 47 (1984).

12 See H. E. Hurst, *The Nile* (London, 1952), pp. 38–46.

depending on the extent of the flood. Village custom was important for this purpose,[13] but never independently of central government, which drew the bulk of its revenue from agriculture. While recording the area of land, the number of people and the amount due, the state went beyond the mere collection of taxes in its provision for the cultivation of the floodplain. Central control of the flood itself was not possible before the introduction of permanent irrigation through barrages and dams in the nineteenth and twentieth centuries, while central supervision of the task in each village was beyond the capacity of the pre-modern state to sustain. The historical solution was a local manager responsible for ensuring the productivity of the land and its yield in taxation, somewhere between a landowner and an official. In Roman Egypt he had been a tax-farmer. In Byzantine Egypt the nobility had moved in the direction of autonomy with their self-governing estates or *autopracts*. With the Arab conquest, estates reappeared in the hands of the Arab nobility, but for most of the country the pendulum swung towards the opposite extreme in a uniform system of small administrative districts called *kuwar* (sing. *kūra*), under pagarchs or governors appointed by the state.

The pagarchs were native Egyptians, drawn from a class of property owners described in the Aphrodito papyri as *proteuontes*, who were entrusted by the Arabs with responsibility for the collection of taxes and thereby for agricultural production, beginning with the management of the irrigation system through their subordinates, the village heads. The instrument of control was the list of cultivators in each village who were liable for tax. Upon the number of such cultivators depended the extent of the land under cultivation, and the size of the village tax quota.[14] Peasants and pagarchs alike, however, belonged to the Coptic Christian community, while the administrative language was Greek. In the absence of expert supervision by the Arabs, this centralised system, which required the pagarchs to pay regular visits to the capital, served the purpose of their subjects, as peasants and pagarchs connived to keep the tax lists short and the quotas correspondingly low. Such profitable collusion between taxpayers and tax-collectors, combined with the recognition of the Coptic Church as representative of the Christian population, went far to keep Egypt quiet under its new rulers down to the end of the seventh century.

13 See T. Sato, 'Irrigation in rural Egypt from the 12th to the 14th centuries', *Orient*, 8 (1972).

14 See D. C. Dennett, *Conversion and the poll-tax in early Islam* (Cambridge, MA, 1950), pp. 81, 91–105; K. Morimoto, *The fiscal administration of Egypt in the early Islamic period* (Kyoto, 1981), pp. 96–104; Brett, 'Way of the peasant'.

The new rulers were the Arabs. Those who first conquered Egypt were Yemenites – southern, as distinct from northern, Arabians – whose commanders became a hereditary Arab aristocracy. They abandoned the Byzantine capital of Alexandria for Babylon, the fortress commanding the junction of the Nile Valley and Delta, which they incorporated into an army camp that rapidly became a city under the name of Fusṭāṭ (from Greek *phossaton*, '(defensive) ditch', which acquired the meaning of 'tent' in Arabic). Generically it was a *miṣr* (pl. *amṣār*), 'a garrison city', a common noun of Syriac origin homonymous with Miṣr, the Arabic name of Egypt. Miṣr in consequence became an alternative name of the city, so that it is often difficult to know whether the city or the whole country is intended. Situated on the right bank of the river, and centred on the Mosque of ʿAmr, the new foundation was divided into *khiṭaṭ* (sing. *khiṭṭa*) quarters for the tribal regiments.[15] The building up of these quarters in high-rise blocks marked a change of character from military to civilian which corresponded to the evolution of the army of conquest into a cross-section of the population. As it did so the exclusive Arab host of *muʾminūn*, or faithful original followers of God and His Prophet, was gradually outnumbered in an eclectic community of *muslimūn*, those who had submitted to the Arabs and been accepted into the ranks of believers. The factors were recruitment and reproduction, which by the end of the seventh century had turned the Arabs of the *jund* (army), warriors who received their pay out of the revenues of the state under the name of *ʿaṭāʾ* (gifts), into a dwindling minority of the religious community. Recruitment appears in the papyri as a distinction between *moagiritai* and *mauloi*, *muhājirūn* and *mawālī*, Arab 'emigrants' and non-Arab clients.[16] Many of these were of slave origin, and many composed the armed retinues of the Arab aristocracy.[17] Reproduction followed from the acquisition of women, again very often as slaves, and led to an increase in numbers far beyond what the state was prepared to support. This new, dynamic element in the population, Muslim and Arabic speaking, was in marked contrast to the native Christian, Coptic-speaking majority. After the confusion of the conquest this mainly rural population was not liable to enslavement or eligible for recruitment, but was excluded from the ranks of conquerors and their burgeoning community as tax-paying subjects locked into their own society and economy.

15 See W. Kubiak, *al-Fustat: Its foundation and early urban development* (Cairo, 1987); S. Lane-Poole, *The story of Cairo* (London, 1902); A. Raymond, *Le Caire* (Paris, 1993).

16 For *moagiritai/muhājirūn*, see P. Crone and M. Cook, *Hagarism: The making of the Islamic world* (Cambridge, 1977), pp. 8–9.

17 For examples see Brett, 'Arab conquest', pp. 502–4.

Only as conscripts did Copts figure alongside the Muslim *mawālī* as *maqāmiṣa* (Greek *machismoi*), 'fighters' called up for military service as one of the liturgies or labours they were obliged to perform.[18]

Between Syria and the west

While the Arab colonisation of Egypt was taking hold of its government and society, the country played a dual role in the development of the new Islamic empire. While serving as a base for the conquest of North Africa and Spain, it was active in the establishment and growth of the Umayyad caliphate at Damascus. The two roles emerged under ʿAbd Allāh ibn Saʿd ibn Abī Sarḥ, governor of Egypt from 25/645 to 35/656, who made the country tributary to Medina while leading a successful raid into Byzantine Africa in 27/647f., and one to Nubia in 31/651f. The expedition to Christian Nubia resulted in the *baqṭ* (pact), a treaty which at least in its later recensions provided for a Nubian tribute of 360 slaves a year, and established a peaceable relationship across the frontier at Aswan.[19] The raid into Byzantine Africa may have based itself on Tripoli; it was followed in the 650s by raids conducted by Muʿāwiya ibn Ḥudayj, the principal Arab commander settled in Egypt. But permanent conquest was deferred until after the first civil war (*fitna*) that broke out after the murder of the caliph ʿUthmān in 35/656. Arabs from Egypt had a prominent hand in the assassination, which is evidence of the way in which local resentment at the amount sent each year to Medina flowed into the more general resentment of the growing inequalities within the community, splitting it into factions. As the affair developed into the contest between ʿAlī and Muʿāwiya ibn Abī Sufyān for the caliphate, the protesters lost their battle when ʿAmr ibn al-ʿĀṣ returned to Egypt in 38/658 to gain the country for Muʿāwiya and the partisans of ʿUthmān. Their cause, however, was temporarily won when ʿAmr was left to govern on his own account, keeping the country's revenues for his own and the army's benefit.[20]

At ʿAmr's death in 43/664 the alliance between governors sent from Damascus and the Arab aristocracy of the province (*wujūh*) kept the peace with only a brief interruption in 64–5/683–4, in the course of the second civil war, when the proclamation of Ibn al-Zubayr as caliph at Mecca briefly stirred

18 Ibid. Cf. M. A. Shaban, *Islamic history: A new interpretation*, 2 vols. (Cambridge, 1971–6), vol. I: *AD 600–75 (AH 132)*, pp. 157–8.

19 See Y. F. Ḥasan, *The Arabs and the Sudan* (Edinburgh, 1967), pp. 20–4.

20 For the political history of this period, see H. Kennedy, 'Egypt as a province of the Islamic caliphate, 641–868', in Petry (ed.), *The Cambridge history of Egypt*, vol. I.

up opposition to the Umayyad establishment. His partisans, however, were defeated by the incoming Umayyad caliph Marwān, who left his son ʿAbd al-ʿAzīz to rule the country while his other son, ʿAbd al-Malik, succeeded at his father's death to the caliphate at Damascus. In this family empire, Egypt was largely independent under a monarchical regime whose shift of government away from the *miṣr* (garrison city) to the princely court was a notable feature of the growth of the community out of a conquering army into a population of civilian subjects. While the Mosque of ʿAmr was rebuilt, ʿAbd al-ʿAzīz not only constructed a new palace, the Dār al-Mudhahhab (Gilded hall), but a summer residence at Helwan to the south of Fusṭāṭ. Outside the city altogether, this became a seasonal capital in which the district governors were each required to build a house, while the Coptic patriarch erected a church for his regular visit from Alexandria. Meanwhile the conquest of Byzantine Africa, interrupted yet again by the warfare of the 680s, was resumed and eventually completed by 705. After the expeditions of Muʿāwiya ibn Ḥudayj in the 650s and 660s this was no longer a specifically Egyptian initiative but, as the point of departure for subsequent expeditions, the province and its government supplied men, money and ships. ʿAbd al-ʿAzīz was thus well placed to take over the conquest effected by his brother's nominee Ḥasan ibn al-Nuʿmān. In 85/704 Ḥasan was dismissed and replaced with ʿAbd al-ʿAzīz's own man, Mūsā ibn Nuṣayr, as governor of the new province of Ifrīqiya, which was thus annexed to his Egyptian dominion. As far as Egypt itself was concerned, the attraction of ʿAbd al-ʿAzīz's court coupled with the ongoing conquest of Ifrīqiya made for a vigorous immigration which thrived on the opening up of the way to the west. While Fusṭāṭ flourished, however, the condition of the Coptic majority worsened as the state set out to increase its revenues to meet the demands of an ambitious regime. The imposition in 74/693f. of a poll-tax on Coptic monks by al-Aṣbagh, the son of ʿAbd al-ʿAzīz, marked the beginning of a major change.

Helwan was an echo of the palaces that the Umayyad caliphs had begun to construct in the Syrian desert in anticipation of the palace cities built by their ʿAbbāsid successors. But the evolution of monarchy in Egypt, and any pretension to an Egyptian empire, was halted by the death of ʿAbd al-ʿAzīz in 86/705, preceded by that of his son and heir, al-Aṣbagh. ʿAbd al-ʿAzīz was succeeded by ʿAbd Allāh, son of the caliph ʿAbd al-Malik; but after ʿAbd al-Malik's own death later in the year, ʿAbd Allāh himself was dismissed in 90/709 by his successor al-Walīd, and an officer, Qurra ibn Sharīk, appointed to complete the return of the country to the status of a province under the direct authority of the caliph. Under the new regime the efforts of ʿAbd al-ʿAzīz and his son to take a tighter grip on the revenues developed into a systematic reform of the administration. A *dīwān* (register) of the Arabs eligible for pay as warriors of the *jund* was drawn up, clearly distinguishing between this residue of the original community of the faithful and the much larger Muslim population that had grown out of it over the past fifty years. At the same time Arabic was introduced as the official language of the administration in place of Greek, requiring its predominantly Coptic staff to work in the new language, and making possible a much closer supervision of their practice. For the first time monks were registered for tax, but the chief victims were the Coptic peasants, as the government attempted to match their numbers with the tax-lists. Such an attempt was difficult at the best of times as new generations took the place of old,[21] but in this case was aggravated by the perpetual migration of peasants, leaving the villages where they were registered for others where they were not. A practice previously condoned by the pagarchy, it became the principal form of resistance to taxation, and a major problem for the regime. The administration resorted to passports and the forcible return of peasants to their original villages; those who pretended to be monks without the iron ring with which monks were now branded had their hands cut off. With penalties for officials who failed to enforce these measures, the old complicity between the peasantry and the district administration was broken. Reform of the system itself culminated in the appointment in 105/724 of ʿUbayd Allāh ibn al-Ḥabḥāb as *ʿāmil* (head of the financial administration), directly responsible to the caliph Hishām. His appointment accelerated the substitution of Muslims for Christians in the administration, and the transfer of responsibility for local taxation from the pagarchs and village headmen to treasury officials. A land survey and a population census provided the basis for a revision of taxes and tax liabilities, which finally separated the poll-tax under the name of *jizyat raʾs* ('on the head') from the land-tax under the name of *jizyat arḍ* ('on the land'): the first was to be paid by Christian subjects, the second by Muslims as well. The revision entailed a review of village and monastery quotas, and fresh lists of taxpayers and their dues; receipts were given for payment.[22]

The entry of Muslims on the land-tax lists is a sign that the growth of the Muslim community into a cross-section of the population had extended into

21 The problem is well illustrated in Norman Sicily: see J. Johns, *Arabic administration in Norman Sicily: The royal* dīwān (Cambridge, 2002), pp. 144–69.

22 See Morimoto, *Fiscal administration*, pp. 120–6. This is the standard history of the financial administration in the period of this chapter. Cf. C. Robinson, 'Neck-sealing in early Islam', *JESHO*, 48, 3 (2005), pp. 409–41.

the countryside, helped by the policies of Ibn al-Ḥabḥāb, who established a colony of Syrian Bedouin around Bilbays to the north-east of Fusṭāṭ in the eastern Ḥawf or margin of the Delta. Their appearance in the lists, however, was not a sign of growing conversion of the Coptic population, since to become Muslim Copts had to be accepted into the Muslim community as *mawālī* (clients), giving up their previous livelihood, including their land. With no escape from increasing fiscal control they turned to sporadic revolt, beginning in the Delta in 107/725f.; a second outbreak occurred in Upper Egypt in 121/739, after the departure of Ibn al-Ḥabḥāb for the Maghrib in 117/734, and the succession of his son al-Qāsim. Al-Qāsim's legendary severity during years of famine in Egypt was matched by the unpopularity of Ibn al-Ḥabḥāb and his other sons in North Africa, where their fiscal demands provoked the revolt of the Berbers that in 740 overthrew the Umayyad dominion in the west. Such discontent in Egypt, however, was overshadowed by the succession crisis of the dynasty that broke out on the death of Hishām in 125/743. The conflict that this brought into the open between northern and southern Arabians, and between Syria and the rest, was manifested in Egypt when the governor, Ḥafṣ ibn al-Walīd al-Ḥaḍramī, from a local Yemenī or southern Arabian family, created an Egyptian force out of the largely Yemenī Arab *jund*, the *mawālī* and the Coptic *maqāmiṣa* (military conscripts) in opposition to the immigrant northern Arabian Syrians. In 128/745 the country was reconquered by a Syrian army sent by the new caliph, Marwān II, but its sentiments resurfaced in 131/749, when Marwān's governor Ḥawthara left to help combat the advance of Abū Muslim's revolutionary ʿAbbāsid armies from Khurāsān. Both Arabs and Copts were in rebellion when Marwān himself arrived in flight from Syria in 132/750, only to be pursued and killed by the victors. Their messianic message of deliverance from tyranny was echoed in Egypt by John the Deacon, the contemporary author of the biography of the patriarch Michael I in the *History of the patriarchs*, where the kingmaker Abū Muslim comes under the sign of the Cross as a man sent from God to deliver His people, Christian and Muslim alike.

The end of Arab supremacy

John may have spoken for Egypt; he was certainly speaking for his Church and his people in his wary welcome of the new regime, whose distance from its new subjects was established with the building of a second *miṣr*, al-ʿAskar (the army), to house its Khurāsānī troops and its government. The adherence of the Copts to the revolution was briefly rewarded with fiscal concessions but, in accordance with the new egalitarianism, the Muslim community was opened up to Christian converts. The patriarchate was in a difficult position, responsible both to the infidel state and to its flock, a dilemma rendered all the more acute by the evolution of Arab practice into Islamic law. Evident in the establishment of the *jizya* as a poll-tax, this converted the original subject status of the Christian into a legal condition by which he was categorically defined. In such circumstances, a Church that identified itself with the warrior St George, but which owed its liberties to its submission to rulers of a different faith, resisted extortionate demands but distanced itself from rebellion, counselling reluctant resignation. Over the next half century, as the hoped-for deliverance failed to materialise, and the administrative reforms begun by the Umayyads were pursued by the ʿAbbāsids, the patriarchate was left to lament the renewed rebellion and repression of the Coptic peasantry, and the desertion of the Church by those tempted to escape the poll-tax by conversion to Islam, while still retaining their land.

Administratively, the poll-tax under the name of *jizya* was definitively separated from the land-tax under the name of *kharāj*. Collection remained in the hands of an *ʿāmil* (financial controller) responsible either to the governor or, between 152/769 and 161/778, to Baghdad; his collectors appear to have dealt directly with the village heads to the exclusion of the pagarchs.[23] But collection continued to be problematic when the tax concessions of 133/750 were abolished in 134/752. The Coptic peasant revolt that this precipitated was the beginning of a tale of growing resistance and rebellion down to the death of the caliph Hārūn al-Rashīd in 193/809, in which the Coptic revolts of 150–2/767–9 and 156/773 blended by the end of the century into those of the Arabs settled in the eastern Ḥawf, and these in turn into the renewed opposition of the Arabs of Egypt to imperial government from abroad. For Baghdad as for Damascus, the problem lay in the rapid turnover of governors required to prevent the independence of the province under a viceroy such as ʿAbd al-ʿAzīz, at the price of lack of support for a regime whose prime purpose was to raise revenue for Iraq. For the first twenty-five years the balance was achieved between governors from the elite of the new regime and the members of the old elite of the province. Through the office of *ṣāḥib al-shurṭa* (prefect of police) the latter commanded the local *jund*, while the former were as much concerned with the protracted reconquest of Ifrīqiya from Arab and Khārijite Berber rebels as with Egypt: in 142/760 the governor Ibn al-Ashʿath, and in 152/769 the governor Yazīd ibn Ḥātim al-Muhallabī, were sent westwards

23 Morimoto, *Fiscal administration*, p. 150.

with their armies for the purpose. In the meantime a revolt in 145/762f. in favour of the ʿAlid pretender to the caliphate, Muḥammad al-Nafs al-Zakiyya, was suppressed without difficulty. Not so that of the Umayyad pretender Diḥyā ibn Muṣab, a descendant of ʿAbd al-ʿAzīz, who rebelled at Ahnās (Ihnāsiyat al-Madīna, ancient Herakleopolis) in the Valley to the south of the Fayyūm in 167–9/783–5.

Yazīd was succeeded by governors from the local elite, but following the death of the caliph al-Manṣūr in 158/775, the accession of al-Mahdī and the renewed appointment of governors from Baghdad, the alliance with the Egyptians broke down over taxation. While Diḥyā took control of Upper Egypt, the Arabs of the eastern Ḥawf rose in revolt against a system that taxed their land at the same rate as the Copts, and included them in an attempt to increase the revenue of the province. With the compliance of the *jund* the governor, al-Khathʿamī, was killed in 784, and a major invasion was required to put down the two rebellions, with no clear victory for government. Over the next twenty years the strained relationship between a string of fleeting governors and recalcitrant Egyptian Arabs was punctuated by further revolt in the Ḥawf, in 178/794, 186/802 and 190–1/806–7. Copts as well as Arabs appear to have been involved, calling for further invasions in 178/794 and 191/807. On the death of the caliph Hārūn al-Rashīd in 193/809, the conflict came to a head.

As the contest for the caliphate developed between al-Amīn and al-Maʾmūn from 195/811 onwards, the army in Egypt divided into the *ahl Miṣr* (men of Egypt) and the Khurāsānī regiments brought in from Iraq over the previous ten to fifteen years to stiffen the *jund*. While the Egyptians, including the Arabs of the Ḥawf, declared for al-Amīn, the Khurāsānians were enlisted on the side of al-Maʾmūn by Harthama ibn Aʿyan, one of his principal supporters, who had restored order in Egypt in 178/794, whose son Ḥātim had been appointed governor in 194/810, and who had at his disposal the wealth of his Egyptian estates for the purpose. Ḥātim, however, was dismissed in 196/812 and, following the death of al-Amīn in 198/813, the claims of al-Maʾmūn and his nominees were effectively ignored by the leader of the Khurāsānī faction, Sarī ibn al-Ḥakam. Ruling the Valley and the southern Delta from Fusṭāṭ, he confronted the Arabs under ibn al-Wazīr al-Jarawī, who controlled the central and northern Delta from Tinnis on the coast to the north-east. Sarī was finally recognised as governor in 202/817, but after both he and ibn al-Wazīr died in 205/820 the division of the country was maintained by their sons, Muḥammad followed by his brother ʿUbayd Allāh at Fusṭāṭ, and ʿAlī at Tinnis. The picture was further complicated in 199/815 when Alexandria was captured by a fleet of Andalusians who allied themselves with a party of zealots called the Ṣūfiyya to seize the city and massacre the Banū Ḥudayj, the principal members of the old Arab nobility. As Kennedy remarks, what is surprising, and significant, is that this nobility, so essential to government under the Umayyads and early ʿAbbāsids, failed to seize the opportunity of the civil war to take over the country.[24] While its wealth and patronage were doubtless offset by that of a new and for the most part absent nobility represented by Harthama and his son, in neither case were these sufficient to take control of the military whose commanders seized power.

The success of the two regimes, and especially that of ibn al-Wazīr, which represented the interests of the rebels against taxation in the Delta, was evidently a consequence of their light hand. They survived, however, only until al-Maʾmūn was in a position to recover the country in 211/826 through the agency of ʿAbd Allāh ibn Ṭāhir, his viceroy of the western provinces of the empire. Ibn al-Sarī and ibn al-Jarawī both submitted, while the Andalusians were driven away from Alexandria to Crete in 212/827. But when ibn Ṭāhir was replaced by the future caliph al-Muʿtaṣim in 213/828f. the Delta revolted, just as in 134/752, against the attempt of his nominees to reimpose the old level of taxation. In 214/829 al-Muʿtaṣim's governor was killed; in 215/830 al-Muʿtaṣim himself put down the rising by both Arabs and Copts, but only briefly. In 216/831 it was systematically suppressed by al-Muʿtaṣim's Turks under their commander al-Afshīn; but only after the arrival of al-Maʾmūn himself in 217/832 were the Copts of the Basharūd (the coastal marshes) finally put down after ignoring the appeal of the patriarch to submit. It was the culmination of a century of revolt. Provoked by the fiscality of the regime, the long series of rebellions was both the cause and the consequence of long-term social and political change. While the original Arab supremacy, like that of the Greeks before them, was at an end, the appearance of Arabs in the peasant population, in contrast to the Greeks, signalled an alteration in the composition of the population as a whole.

Arabisation and Islamisation

The end of the Arab supremacy was complete when in 219/834 the Arabs were struck from the *dīwān*, the list of those entitled to pay as members of the *jund*, despite their protest that it was theirs by right. According to al-Maqrīzī (d. 845/1442) it was matched by an end to the Coptic majority, when in the fifteenth century he said of the Copts that after the suppression of the revolt in the

24 Kennedy, 'Egypt as a province', p. 81.

Basharūd in 217/832: 'ghalabahum al-Muslimūn ʿalā ʿāmmat al-qurā'.[25] Meaning either that the Muslims were in the majority or simply dominant in all the villages, the statement is ambiguous, made all the more questionable by the following statement that the Copts then turned from rebellion to plotting against the Muslims, notably by controlling the collection of taxes – an attack upon the Coptic staff of the Mamlūk treasury. While it may be doubtful as a statement of fact, it nevertheless points to the emergence of that tax-paying Arab peasant population which by al-Maqrīzī's time was indeed in the vast majority. As to when it attained that majority, his comment remains the basic ground for the contention that the corresponding passage of the Copts from the people of Egypt into the community of a minority came about in the course of the ninth century.[26] In support of this contention is the evidence from the province of Ashmunayn to the south of Fusṭāṭ for the destruction of small local churches dedicated to local saints with local, Coptic names, and their replacement by fewer, larger churches with dedications to major saints, most notably St George, in the course of the revolts of the late eighth and early ninth centuries.[27] In the course of that century, moreover, insecurity was such as to oblige the monasteries to turn themselves into fortresses.[28] The Coptic community was evidently hard hit, and felt threatened by desertion to Islam and the ways of the Arabs.[29] On the other hand, it survived, resisting conversion down to the present day. The tax lists of the ninth century contain numerous Christian names, as well, perhaps, as Arab names for Christians. In the tenth century ibn Ḥawqal considered the Qibṭ (Copts) to be the people of Egypt, noting their presence in the places he described.[30] So did al-Muqaddasī, noting that they still spoke Coptic, still numerous enough to form a language community.[31] Despite their undoubted retreat, the Copts may still have been in the majority.

25 Al-Maqrīzī, *Kitāb al-mawāʿiẓ wa 'l-iʿtibār fī dhikr al-khiṭaṭ wa 'l-āthār (al-Khiṭaṭ)*, ed. G. Wiet, 4 vols. only (Cairo, 1911), vol. II, pp. 1–3.

26 See e.g. I. M. Lapidus, 'The conversion of Egypt to Islam', *Israel Oriental Studies*, 2 (1972); S. I. Gellens, 'Egypt, Islamization of', in A. S. Atiya (gen. ed.), *The Coptic encyclopedia* (New York, 1991), vol. III, pp. 936–42.

27 See M. Martin, 'La province d'Ashmunayn', *Annales Islamologiques*, 23 (1987).

28 See C. C. Walters, *Monastic archaeology in Egypt* (Warminster, 1974), chs. 1 and 3.

29 See C. Décobert, 'Sur l'arabisation et l'islamisation de l'Egypte médiévale', in C. Décobert (ed.), *Itinéraires de l'Egypte: Mélanges offerts au père Maurice Martin, SJ*, (Cairo, 1992), pp. 288–300.

30 Ibn Ḥawqal, *Ṣūrat al-arḍ*, ed. J. H. Kramers, 2 vols. (Leiden, 1938–9), p. 153 and *passim*, trans. G. Wiet as *Configuration de la terre*, 2 vols. (Beirut and Paris, 1964), p. 151.

31 Al-Muqaddasī, *Aḥsan al-taqāsīm fī maʿrifat al-aqālīm* (Damascus, 1980), p. 185; cf. A. Miquel, 'L'Egypte vue par un géographe arabe du IVe/Xe siècle: al-Muqaddasī', *Annales Islamologiques*, 11 (1972), p. 124.

The explanation of the Copts' survival after the ʿAbbāsids had removed the barrier to conversion will have lain in the internal solidarity of their community as its members weighed the disadvantages of conversion against the obvious advantage of freedom from the poll-tax. Long after the regime had broken the solidarity of pagarchy and peasantry, al-Maqrīzī's denunciation of a Coptic conspiracy at the level of government takes a sour view of their continued operation in the fisc, an occupation in which their expertise gave employment up to the higher levels of the administration. The same was true of the Church, a still more reserved occupation which drew upon the same membership, socially as well as economically united through patronage and family connections. For such as these, the benefits of remaining Christian evidently outweighed any to be gained by conversion, all the more because the adoption of spoken and written Arabic to the point at which it became a native language included them in the dominant society and culture. In the same way, the traditional skills of the Coptic artisan, such as the textile workers of Tinnis, may have helped to preserve the religious community.[32] At Fusṭāṭ, in the capital city founded by the Arabs, such factors certainly contributed to the actual growth of a Coptic community, whose festivals became a major feature of the calendar for centuries to come. Such occupational benefits will not have accrued to the illiterate Coptic peasant, progressively losing his monopoly of his traditional occupation, the cultivation of the soil. It is clear, however, that the advantages of conversion were similarly offset by reluctance to abandon a community which still maintained a hold upon the land, and the possibility of unemployment for any who left to make their way in the circle of the mosque. It would certainly seem that the desertions bemoaned in the time of troubles from the early eighth to the mid-ninth century were countered by a closing of the ranks, which was rewarded with the return of a less oppressive regime from the end of the ninth century onwards. Given such solidarity, the explanation for the gradual attrition of the Coptic population must lie elsewhere.

It is most probably to be found in demography, to which al-Maqrīzī referred when he spoke of the taking of Christian wives by Muslim men as a factor in the prevalence of Muslims over Christians after 832.[33] Despite the

32 See Y. Lev, 'Tinnīs: An industrial medieval town', in M. Barrucand (ed.), *L'Egypte fatimide: Son art et son histoire* (Paris, 1999).

33 See M. Brett, 'Population and conversion to Islam in the mediaeval period', in U. Vermeulen and J. Van Steenbergen (eds.), *Egypt and Syria in the Fatimid, Ayyubid*

famous fertility of the Nile Valley and Delta, the pre-modern population of Egypt was small even if comparatively large for the period; in the absence of statistics the best estimate is that it fluctuated between two and six million around a norm of four to five.[34] It was kept low by high mortality attributable to poverty and disease associated with the precariousness of agriculture, at the mercy of the river, the climate and the state.[35] The land was in consequence undercultivated, certainly by the middle of the ninth century, when the lament of the financial controller ibn Mudabbir that only some 2 million *feddans*, a third to a half of the cultivable area, were down to crops reflects a shortage of labour, doubtless worsened by the insecurity of the previous hundred years.[36] By the eleventh century, when Issawi plausibly estimates the population at around four to five million, the situation had improved; but the ceiling on population growth remained, with important implications for its composition. In such a situation the growth of one sector can only have occurred to the detriment of another, in this case that of the Muslims vis-à-vis the Copts. The evident growth of the Muslim sector derived from immigration, which created the city of Fusṭāṭ, settled the Arab Bedouin on the land, and continued with a constant trickle of such settlement by Bedouin forced out of the desert. It was certainly assisted by conversion, but maintained by natural reproduction, which, if al-Maqrīzī is correct, was at the expense of the Coptic population, which lost its women to its rival. The extent to which Muslim men did indeed take Christian wives may be unknown, but in an essentially static population differential fertility would have been all that was required to achieve a growing imbalance between the two communities from generation to generation. An added factor in the case of the Copts would have been the celibacy of the clergy with its monks and nuns. Whatever the weight of any one factor, the Islamisation of Egypt, accompanied by its Arabisation, is likely to have come about less by choice than by gradual substitution of the one community for the other.

and Mamluk eras, vol. IV (Leuven, 2005). The general question is discussed by T. Wilfong, 'The non-Muslim communities: Christian communities', in Petry (ed.), *The Cambridge history of Egypt*, vol. I.

34 C. Issawi, 'The area and population of the Arab empire', in A. Udovitch (ed.), *The Islamic Middle East, 700–1900* (Princeton, 1981).

35 C. Issawi, *Egypt: An economic and social analysis* (London, New York and Toronto, 1948), pp. 45–6; H. H. Rabie, 'Technical aspects of agriculture in medieval Egypt', in Udovitch (ed.), *The Islamic Middle East*.

36 Ibn Ḥawqal, *Ṣūrat al-arḍ*, p. 135, trans. Wiet as *Configuration*, pp. 133–4.

From province to empire: the Ṭūlūnids

Population was certainly the underlying factor in the policies and politics of the regime after the restoration of caliphal control in 217/832. Under the system of provincial government introduced by al-Maʾmūn, Egypt was incorporated with Syria in the domain of a member or intimate of the dynasty – al-Maʾmūn's son and successor al-Muʿtaṣim, followed by the Turks Ashnās and Itākh, and finally by the son and successor of al-Mutawakkil, al-Muntaṣir. Their government was an exercise in patronage rather than administration, which was delegated to the governors they appointed. Revenues once again went to the capital, now Sāmarrāʾ. But discontent was not in evidence for some thirty years, and the chief opposition to the regime came from the Arab bourgeoisie of Fusṭāṭ, who gave vent, perhaps, to their dissatisfaction with government from abroad in their resistance to the doctrine of the created Qurʾān from 227/842 until its abandonment by al-Mutawakkil in 235/850. Much more important was the attempt by the fisc to remedy the shortage of cultivators through the introduction of tax-farming. This was in effect an admission of defeat, since it encouraged rather than forbade the migration of peasants when the farmer contracted for uncultivated land on favourable terms, and offered it for cultivation at a reduced rate of *kharāj* – rent or tax, depending on the point of view. The flight from the villages which had undermined the system instituted by the Arabs in the seventh century was not condoned in principle, but employed in practice as an essential feature of the new order. Tax-farming itself remained central to the financial and eventually the political system of Egypt down to modern times.

The matter of population meanwhile took a different turn with the opening up of gold and emerald mines in the desert to the south-east of Aswan. The gold rush that this provoked brought the Arab Bedouin tribes of Egypt southwards to the point at which they came to dominate Aswan, to push back the indigenous Beja nomads of the south-eastern desert, and threaten Nubian control of the Māris, the valley to the south of Aswan. It was the beginning of a long migration which took the Arabs deep into the Sudan, and brought about the elimination of Christian Nubia by the fourteenth and fifteenth centuries.[37] As far as Egypt was concerned, the state rapidly lost control of the gold-mining operation, together with much of its authority over the frontier at Aswan, a situation which remained a permanent feature of its history.

37 See Ḥasan, *The Arabs and the Sudan*, pp. 50–62.

As the country settled down in this fashion there was little to suggest its spectacular rise to independence and empire following the murder of al-Mutawakkil in 247/861, when the death or killing of the next four caliphs by the Turkish soldiery was followed by the rising of the Zanj in southern Iraq under the messianic leadership of the ʿAlid pretender ʿAlī ibn Muḥammad. Beginning in 255/869, the rising inaugurated a century of such revolutionary movements that looked for the coming of the *mahdī*, a second Muḥammad who would bring in the final, golden age of the world. These culminated exactly a hundred years later in the Fāṭimid conquest of Egypt, after governing the course of its history from the outset. In the climate of revolutionary expectation building up to the rising of the Zanj, the revolt was preceded by persecution of the Shīʿa, the party of ʿAlī, around whose descendants such expectations centred. In Egypt, wealthy and influential members of the family were either deported to Iraq or forbidden to leave Fusṭāṭ, to own an estate or more than one slave, and to ride a horse. But in 252/866 the fragile peace of the country was broken by renewed rebellion, when one such ʿAlid, ibn al-Arquṭ, was proclaimed by an alliance of militiamen and peasants, Muslims and Copts, under the leadership of one Jābir ibn al-Walīd. These took over ibn al-Wazīr al-Jarawī's old lands in the Delta with the similar aim of collecting the taxes for themselves. Put down in 253/867, they reappeared in 254/868 to the west of Alexandria under a second ʿAlid pretender, only to be followed in 255/869 by a third such pretender in Upper Egypt, ibn al-Ṣūfī, who massacred the inhabitants of Esna, and crucified the commander sent against him. Such rebellions reflected the persistence of popular discontent, but also the appeal of Islam, as the legalistic claims of the Arab *jund* to its pay faded into Islamic messianism on the part of a disenfranchised Muslim population. Whatever the relative size of that population, its creed had finally taken the place of Christianity as the ideology of political action.[38]

This wave of rebellion was bracketed by two major appointments to the government, both in accordance with previous practice, but which combined in the circumstances to break decisively with the past. Al-Muntaṣir's appointment of the experienced ibn al-Mudabbir to the post of *ʿāmil* (financial controller) of Syria and subsequently Egypt was an attempt to bring the revenues of the two provinces under his direct control, first as their overlord and then as caliph. Recorded by al-Maqrīzī in a diatribe against the 'cunning

38 See Brett, 'Arab conquest', pp. 589–91; M. Brett, *The rise of the Fatimids: The world of the Mediterranean and the Middle East in the the fourth century of the hijra, tenth century CE* (Leiden, 2001), pp. 56–7.

devils of scribes' who oppressed the people with unjust taxes despite the efforts of enlightened rulers to bring the fiscal system into line with the Islamic law,[39] Ibn al-Mudabbir's reputation for raising old and introducing new taxes presumably reflects his efficiency and determination, but also his partial responsibility for the revolts of the decade. Those revolts in turn contributed to the appointment in 254/868 of the Turk Bayākbak as overlord of the western provinces of the empire, followed by the appointment of Bayākbak's stepson Aḥmad ibn Ṭūlūn as governor at Fusṭāṭ. Al-Muntaṣir's long-serving governor Yazīd ibn ʿAbd Allāh al-Turkī (242–53/856–67) had been unable to deal with ibn al-Walīd and ibn al-Arquṭ, and his successor Muzāḥim, who had put down the revolt, had died. Aḥmad's own captains were initially routed by ibn al-Ṣūfī and al-ʿUmarī, the adventurer who had established himself in the land of the mines and the valley to the south-east and south of Aswan, and it was six or seven years before Upper Egypt was pacified. Meanwhile at Fusṭāṭ Aḥmad was confronted by Ibn al-Mudabbir, in control of the revenue and answerable only to Sāmarrāʾ. The situation, however, was favourable. The outbreak of the Zanj rebellion in 869 meant the preoccupation of the caliphate with the war in Iraq for the next fourteen years. In 256/870 Bayākbak was succeeded by Aḥmad's father-in-law Yārjūkh, who in 257/871 extended his appointment to include Alexandria and Barqa in (modern) Cyrenaica. Ibn al-Mudabbir was finally transferred back to Syria, and replaced as *ʿāmil* in Egypt by Aḥmad himself. The accumulation of power was complete in 258/872, when Yārjūkh died at Sāmarrāʾ and was only nominally replaced by al-Mufawwaḍ, the young son of the caliph al-Muʿtamid.

By that time Aḥmad's ambition was apparent in the construction of a new palace city, beyond al-ʿAskar to the north-east of Fusṭāṭ. Its name, al-Qaṭāʾiʿ (the wards), for the quartering of the various regiments of his army, reveals its military purpose in connection with the eclectic force of Turks, blacks (Sūdān, ʿAbīd) and probably Greeks which he was now able to afford. Blacks and Greeks are first mentioned in 256/870, the year of the foundation of al-Qaṭāʾiʿ, when Aḥmad led a brief expedition into Palestine. The blacks probably came as slaves from both Nubia via Aswan and the central Sudan via Zawīla in the Fezzan; the origin and indeed identity of the Greeks (the Rūm) is less clear. But the new city was palatial, with a royal residence and adjoining garden; recreational, with its *maydān* (hippodrome); governmental, housing the offices and officers of state; commercial, with its markets; and charitable, with its hospital. With the building of its great mosque, the Mosque of Ibn Ṭūlūn, it

39 Al-Maqrīzī, *Khiṭaṭ*, vol. II, p. 81.

acquired a great fortress, and a crowning symbol of its status as a royal capital in the style of Sāmarrā'. From the time the building was begun in 262/876, indeed, al-Qaṭā'iʿ developed into a rival to Sāmarrā', as Aḥmad's ambitions came into conflict with the effort of al-Muwaffaq, brother of the caliph al-Muʿtamid, to prosecute the Zanj war from his base at Baghdad. His ambitions centred on Syria under its governor at Damascus, Āmājūr, and its *ʿāmil*, his old opponent Ibn al-Mudabbir. The conflict stemmed from the unequal division between al-Muʿtamid and his brother of the tribute that Aḥmad continued to send to Iraq, and more generally from al-Muwaffaq's evident alarm at the liaison between Aḥmad and the caliph. In 263/877, while al-Muʿtamid conferred upon Aḥmad the defence of the Thughūr – the northern border of Syria with Byzantium, and thus in effect the government of Syria – al-Muwaffaq attempted to depose him, entrusting to his senior general Mūsā ibn Bughā the task of installing Āmājūr as governor at Fusṭāṭ. Mūsā, however, never got beyond al-Raqqa on the Euphrates, Āmājūr died, and in 264–5/878 Aḥmad marched through Syria to Cilicia, evicting Ibn al-Mudabbir and taking over its government. He returned to Egypt to deal with the revolt of al-ʿAbbās, his son, heir and regent in his absence, who fled westwards in an unsuccessful attempt to displace the Aghlabids of Ifrīqiya, and was eventually captured and imprisoned by his father in 268/881. But in 266/879f. Aḥmad's name first appeared on the coinage in association with that of the caliph; and when in 269/882 the defection to al-Muwaffaq of Lu'lu', his commander at al-Raqqa, brought him back to Damascus, he prepared to welcome al-Muʿtamid as a refugee from his brother. When the flight from Sāmarrā' was halted by al-Muwaffaq, Aḥmad summoned the *fuqahā'* (jurists) to declare al-Muwaffaq a traitor who had forfeited his claim to obedience, imprisoning the *qāḍī* (chief judge) of Egypt, Bakkār ibn Qutayba, for his refusal. For this, it is said, he died penitent, returning from Cilicia in 270/884 to die at al-Qaṭā'iʿ, the city that might have become the new capital of the caliphate.

Founded by a *ghulām* (pl. *ghilmān*), a so-called slave-soldier, Aḥmad's empire was what Kennedy has called a *ghulām* state, in which the pay of such troops was the principal charge upon the exchequer, as well as the means to secure their crucial loyalty.[40] The resulting onus upon the fisc led in this case to the appointment in 265/879 of a replacement for Ibn al-Mudabbir in the shape of the Iraqi Aḥmad al-Mādharā'ī, the founder of a dynasty of such *ʿāmils* who ensured the continuity of the financial administration through the

40 H. Kennedy, *The Prophet and the age of the caliphates* (London and New York, 1986), pp. 208–10.

vicissitudes of the next seventy years. The foundation of a *dīwān al-inshā'* (chancery) with the appointment of the equally Iraqi Muḥammad ibn ʿAbd al-Kān as secretary of state was likewise required to conduct the correspondence of the regime, not least with the caliphate. On this firm basis Khumārawayh, the second son of Aḥmad, not a professional soldier like his father, but like him brought up as a member of the Arab–Persian aristocracy of the caliphate, took possession of his inheritance in the aftermath of the Zanj war, when al-Muwaffaq was at last free to challenge him. But invasions of Syria in 271/885 and 272/886 failed to install ibn Kundājik, the governor of Mosul, at Damascus, and by caliphal diploma Khumārawayh was confirmed in his father's dominions for thirty years in exchange for a modest tribute. In 274/887 he went on to campaign in northern Mesopotamia, while the governor of Tarsus in Cilicia returned to his former obedience. His success was crowned after the death of al-Muwaffaq in 278/891 and that of al-Muʿtamid in 279/892, when his daughter was married to the new caliph, al-Muʿtaḍid, at fabulous expense, and the accord of 273/886 was renewed for a further thirty years. The marriage was a token of the wealth at his disposal now that the revenues of Egypt were retained in the country, and an indication of the prosperity this engendered. But it was at the same time a sign of the legendary luxury in which he lived, and which by all accounts precipitated the downfall of his dynasty.

In contrast to Aḥmad, Khumārawayh enjoys a bad reputation in the sources, in which the sins of the father against the caliphate have been visited on the son as a figure of immorality and extravagance. Murdered, appropriately, in his harem at Damascus in 282/896, he allegedly left an empty treasury. He certainly left a succession that was murderously disputed among his sons and brothers. While his young son Jaysh was almost immediately deposed and killed, the still younger Hārūn survived until murdered in 292/904 by his uncle Shaybān, who had himself survived the execution of several of his brothers. Ṭūlūnid troops from Syria defected to Iraq, and in 285/898 the caliph seized the opportunity to revise the original agreement with Khumārawayh, raising the tribute while recovering Cilicia and Aleppo for the empire. Just as Aḥmad had risen to power on the back of the Zanj rebellion, however, so his dynasty was finally brought down by a second wave of Mahdism in Iraq, which spread into Syria. Unlike the Zanj, the Qarāmiṭa (or Carmathians) had no single leader; the term is applied in the sources to a range of movements at least partially focused on the expected appearance of the *mahdī* in 290/902f.[41] Certainly in Syria the

41 See Brett, *Rise of the Fatimids*, pp. 61–72.

Ṭūlūnids, 254–92/868–905

1.	254/868	Aḥmad ibn Ṭūlūn
2.	270/884	Khumārawayh, Abū al Jaysh (son of 1)
3.	282/896	Jaysh, Abū al-ʿAsākir (son of 2)
4.	283/896	Hārūn, Abū Mūsā (son of 2)
5.	292/904	Shaybān, Abū al-Manāqib (son of 1)

292/905 reconquest by the ʿAbbāsid general Muḥammad ibn Sulaymān

Ikhshīdids, 323–35/935–69

1.	323/935	Muḥammad ibn Ṭughj, Abū Bakr al-ikhshīd
2.	334/946	Ūnūjūr, Abū al-Qāsim (son of 1)
3.	349/961	ʿAlī, Abū al-Ḥasan (son of 1)
4.	355/966	Kāfūr al-Lābī, Abū al-Misk
5.	357/968	Aḥmad, Abū al-Fawāris, d. 371/981 (son of 3)

358/969 conquest of Egypt by Fāṭimids

Fāṭimids, 297–567/909–1171

1.	297/909	ʿAbd Allāh (ʿUbayd Allāh) ibn Ḥusayn, Abū Muḥammad al-Mahdī
2.	322/934	Muḥammad, Abū al-Qāsim al-Qāʾim (son of 1?)
3.	334/946	Ismāʿīl, Abū Ṭāhir al-Manṣūr (son of 2)
4.	341/953	Maʿadd, Abū Tamīm al-Muʿizz (son of 3)
	358/969 caliph in Egypt	
5.	365/975	Nizār, Abū Manṣūr al-ʿAzīz (son of 4)
6.	386/996	al-Manṣūr, Abū ʿAlī al-Ḥākim (son of 5)
7.	411/1021	ʿAlī, Abū al Ḥasan al-Ẓāhir (son of 6)
8.	427/1036	Maʿadd, Abū Tamīm al-Mustansir (son of 7)

8. The rulers of Egypt, 868–1036.
After Carl F. Petry (ed.), *The Cambridge history of Egypt* vol. I, 1998, p. 517. Copyright Cambridge University Press, reproduced with permission.

year saw the siege of Damascus by the messianic *ṣāḥib al-nāqa* ('man with the she-camel'), whose place was taken after his death in battle by the *ṣāḥib al-shāma* ('man with the birthmark'). Although Damascus was held against them, the Ṭūlūnid forces under Ṭughj ibn Juff were unable to crush them. A Mahdist state was proclaimed at Salamiyya, Homs and Hama, which was only overthrown in 291/903 by the forces of Baghdad under their commander-in-chief, the minister Muḥammad ibn Sulaymān al-Kātib. In 292/904, joined by Ṭughj ibn Juff at Damascus and fortified by the Cilician fleet, these moved by land and sea against Egypt. In December Hārūn, awaiting the invasion at the head of his army out beyond Bilbays on the eastern edge of the Delta, was murdered by Shaybān, who withdrew to Fusṭāṭ before the advance of Muḥammad, to whom he surrendered in Ṣafar 292/January 905. The radical hostility of Baghdad to Ṭūlūnid pretentions was demonstrated not by the execution of Shaybān and his relatives, who were deported to Iraq, but by the total destruction of al-Qaṭāʾiʿ apart from the mosque.

From province to empire: The Ikhshīdids

The extirpation of the Ṭūlūnids brought the return of Egypt to provincial status with a recrudescence of provincial unrest, immediately manifested in the welcome at Fusṭāṭ to one ibn al-Khalīj, or al-Khalījī. An Egyptian officer deported to Baghdad, he had escaped at Aleppo and returned to Egypt to proclaim the restoration of the Ṭūlūnids under Ibrāhīm ibn Khumārawayh. Not only did he drive out the ʿAbbāsid governor al-Nūsharī, but he repelled an initial expedition from Baghdad before his defeat and capture by a second in 293/906. His success and failure are equally significant. With the defection of Turks such as Ṭughj ibn Juff to the ʿAbbāsids, and the massacre by Muḥammad ibn Sulaymān of the black troops of the Ṭūlūnids, the fallen dynasty was identified with the cause of the men of Egypt, half military, half popular, going back to the beginning of the previous century. His failure was the failure, yet again, of that cause to provide the country with a government, either for or against Baghdad.

In the thirty years that followed, the question of for and against Baghdad was exacerbated, on the one hand by the descent of the caliphate under al-Muqtadir and his successors into an ultimately fatal struggle for power between its Men of the Pen and Men of the Sword, and on the other by the third and ultimately triumphant wave of Mahdism, that of the Fāṭimids. Where the death in 260/874 of al-Ḥasan al-ʿAskarī, the eleventh imam in line from ʿAlī, had left his followers to await the return of his vanished son as the second Muḥammad, the Fāṭimid *mahdī* ʿAbd Allāh and his son Muḥammad al-Qāʾim claimed a different line of descent from Jaʿfar al-Ṣādiq, the sixth imam. 'Arising with the sword' as 'the Sun of God in the West', ʿAbd Allāh came to power in Ifrīqiya in 297/910, two years after the accession of al-Muqtadir, and promptly turned his attention to Egypt.[42] For Baghdad the country was held, along with Syria, not so much by its governors as by the *ʿāmils* of the Mādharāʾī family, members of the administrative elite of Iraq, and consequently involved in the factional politics of the period. Having been introduced by Aḥmad ibn Ṭūlūn, they survived the downfall of his dynasty as tax-farmers on a gigantic scale, undertaking responsibility for the fiscal regime of the two provinces in return for annual payments to Baghdad. In the process they built the Egyptian treasury into the central organ of government, but found difficulty in paying the troops stationed in the country. These, however, were relatively few and the governors who commanded them

42 See ibid., pp. 29–132.

correspondingly weak, in no position as yet to repeat the exploit of Aḥmad ibn Ṭūlūn in disposing of ibn al-Mudabbir and creating their own state. By the same token they were in no condition to repel an invasion, all the more because the country was not united behind them. Against Baghdad were not only those who regretted the demise of the Ṭūlūnids but those who favoured the Fāṭimids, whose *mahdī* had passed through Egypt on his way to the west in 292/905 with the connivance of sympathisers.

Like the rebellion of ibn al-Khalīj, the Fāṭimid invasions of 301–2/914–15 and 306–9/919–21 were nevertheless defeated. Determined attempts by the Fāṭimid al-Qāʾim, the *mahdī*'s son and heir Abu 'l-Qāsim Muḥammad, to carry the revolution in the west eastwards to Baghdad were thwarted by logistics. Barqa in Cyrenaica was a long way from Fusṭāṭ, and easily taken and retained by the Ifrīqiyans. From there Alexandria, isolated on the coast to the west of the Delta, was on both occasions taken with the aid of the Fāṭimid fleet. But Fusṭāṭ was still some 200 kilometres further for an expedition whose lines of communication were already long, and on both occasions was not reached before the arrival of reinforcements. In 302/915 the invaders were defeated at Giza by the governor Takīn with the aid of troops from Syria, and retreated to Alexandria and finally Ifrīqiya as Muʾnis al-Muẓaffar, the principal ʿAbbāsid commander, arrived from Baghdad. The Iraqis were unpopular, and quickly withdrew, while the new governor, Dhukā al-Rūmī (Ducas the Greek), imprisoned those who had been in correspondence with the invaders; many had hands and feet cut off. Agitated by Fāṭimid propaganda, however, the country was divided. When slogans appeared on the doors of the Mosque of ʿAmr extolling the first three caliphs, Abū Bakr, ʿUmar and ʿUthmān, in defiance of their denunciation as usurpers by the Fāṭimids, crowds demonstrating their support with the approval of the chief of police were dispersed by troops, and the slogans themselves effaced. In 306–7/919 the regime almost collapsed as the Fāṭimid al-Qāʾim returned to claim not only Egypt but Iraq for the rightful heirs of the Prophet. Alexandria was occupied, the Berber tribes to the west of the Delta revolted, and the governor, Dhukā, died and was not immediately replaced. But al-Qāʾim waited until the next year for the arrival of the Fāṭimid fleet to escort the army upriver to Fusṭāṭ, and when it came it was caught on a lee shore by the fleet from Cilicia and destroyed – most probably in Aboukir Bay, where Nelson in similar fashion destroyed the French fleet in 1798. God's wind, said al-Kindī for the Egyptian opposition, had saved Islam, not least by allowing time for Muʾnis to arrive yet again from Baghdad. For a year al-Qāʾim occupied the Fayyūm until the

Cilician fleet recaptured Alexandria and he was obliged once again to retire.[43]

Barqa in Fāṭimid hands remained a forward base for raiding in the western desert, but no third expedition was forthcoming for the next fifteen years, until Egypt was again on the verge of independence. After the retreat of al-Qāʾim, discontent in the country reverted to that of the army with its irregular pay, but subsided with the replacement of the governor Aḥmad ibn Kayghalagh by the former governor Takīn in 312/924, and the return, after four years' absence, of Ḥusayn followed by Muḥammad al-Mādharāʾī to the post of ʿāmil in 313/926. The crisis came in 933: with the death of Takīn in the same year as the execution of Muʾnis at Baghdad the rapid dissolution of the central government of the empire began. Not only did the troops mutiny over pay, but fighting broke out between Takīn's son Muḥammad at the head of the Mashāriqa (Easterners), the Turkish soldiery, and the former governor Aḥmad ibn Kayghalagh at the head of the Maghāriba (Westerners), most probably Berbers and blacks. Used for the first time, these two terms reflected the long-standing divisions within the army and the equally long-standing hostility of the Egyptians to the Iraqis. The contest between the two rival governors was juggled by the *ʿāmil*, Muḥammad al-Mādharāʾī, until cut short by the arrival of Muḥammad ibn Ṭughj in 323/935. The son of the Ṭūlūnid commander Ṭughj ibn Juff, he had served Takīn in Egypt, then risen as a client of Muʾnis to become governor of Damascus in 319/931. Appointment to Egypt on the death of Takīn was halted by Muʾnis's execution, but renewed in 323/935 with the support of Muʾnis's ally al-Faḍl ibn Jaʿfar, member of the great vizieral family of the Banū al-Furāt at Baghdad and political opponent of the Mādharāʾīs. Like Muḥammad ibn Sulaymān thirty years previously, ibn Ṭughj came as an invader by land and sea to put down a rebel. Like Shaybān, ibn Kayghalagh abandoned Fusṭāṭ but, fleeing westward to Fāṭimid Barqa, procured from al-Qāʾim, now imam–caliph in succession to the *mahdī*, a third expedition which in 324/936 retook possession of Alexandria. It was, however, rapidly expelled. Muḥammad al-Mādharāʾī was imprisoned until restored to his essential role in 327/939, by which time ibn Tughj had welcomed at Fusṭāṭ in 325/937 his ally at Baghdad, Faḍl ibn Jaʿfar ibn al-Furāt, in flight from ibn Rāʾiq, the new master of the empire. In 327/939 his own effective independence was recognised with the grant of the title *al-ikhshīd*, the designation of the princes of his original homeland in Farghāna to the east of Transoxania.

43 Details in H. Halm, *The empire of the Mahdi*, trans. M. Bonner (Leiden, 1996), pp. 196–213.

Coming to Egypt from Damascus, Ibn Ṭughj had no difficulty in returning to Syria to secure its possession, and reconstitute the empire created by Ibn Ṭūlūn when he invaded Syria from Egypt. That invasion had been justified by the holy war with Byzantium, which turned the northern borders of Syria, including Cilicia, into a militarised zone of conflict for which Ibn Ṭūlūn had claimed responsibility. But Cilicia in particular had proved recalcitrant, and had been returned to Baghdad in 285/898, while for Ibn Ṭughj the championship of the holy war was an obligation that he was happy to lose at a time of renewed Byzantine aggression: in 322/934 the frontier city of Malaṭya was taken, and in 331/943 the Byzantines raided deep into northern Iraq and Syria. Syria itself proved difficult to retain when ibn Rāʾiq, driven from Baghdad, entered Damascus and held it from 328/940 to his death in 330/942. Ibn Ṭughj was then able to obtain from Baghdad in 331/943 the prestigious custodianship of the holy places of Mecca and Medina, and was tempted in 332/944 to repeat Ibn Ṭūlūn's offer of hospitality to the caliph al-Muʿtamid, making a similar offer to the caliph al-Muttaqī in a meeting at al-Raqqa on the Euphrates. But that was after he had been obliged to recover Aleppo from the Ḥamdānids of Mosul. The offer to al-Muttaqī was declined, and the Ḥamdānids in the person of the adventurous Sayf al-Dawla ʿAlī ibn Ḥamdān not only returned to Aleppo but occupied Damascus. In 334/945 Ibn Ṭughj agreed to a partition which left him in possession of Damascus as ruler of the centre and south, and gave Aleppo to Sayf al-Dawla as commander of the holy war on the frontier. At his death in 335/946 the second Egyptian empire to emerge from the troubles of Iraq had taken permanent shape.

Its internal character was likewise in formation. Like that of the Ṭūlūnids, that of the Ikhshīdids was a *ghulām* state, in which the payment of the army was central to the administration. Founded and ruled by a *ghulām*, it was moreover ruled after his death by a *ghulām* of very different origin, the black eunuch Abu 'l-Misk Kāfūr. Coming from Nubia, and acquired by ibn Ṭughj at Fusṭāṭ in the 310s/920s, Kāfūr represented the strong African element underlying the dominant Turkish and Iraqi presence in the government of the country. As the lieutenant of his master in command of the army, he had the power as well as the authority, not only to secure the succession for his patron's sons, first Ūnūjūr (r. 335–49/946–61), then ʿAlī (r. 349–55/961–6), but to rule in their name as their *ustādh* (tutor). Despite a brief attempt by Ūnūjūr to take power in 343/954, they remained condemned to a life of idleness. Kāfūr's position was quickly consolidated in Syria vis-à-vis the Ḥamdānids, and in Egypt with the defeat of Ghalbūn, rebel governor of Ashmunayn, in 336/947, leaving him free to govern as a statesman rather than a politician or administrator. His recruitment of a household regiment of guardsmen, the Kāfūriyya, alongside the Ikhshīdiyya of ibn Ṭughj, reinforced his control of the army, while his prompt dismissal of Muḥammad al-Mādharāʾī in 335/946 removed his most obvious rival from control of the administration. This was then handed to a different figure in a different capacity, Jaʿfar, son of the refugee al-Faḍl ibn al-Furāt whom ibn Ṭughj had welcomed in 325/937, whom he appointed to the position of *wazīr*. The Banū al-Furāt were only the greatest of such immigrants into Egypt, executives of the caliphate displaced by the collapse of central government in Iraq,[44] who provided the nascent Ikhshīdid regime with staff, and helped to create it on the model of Baghdad. With the appointment of Jaʿfar, the principal feature of that model was introduced into the country. The ʿAbbāsid *wazīr* had been head of government on behalf of the sovereign, although in the latter years of increasingly murderous competition for control of the caliphate, his position had been undermined by rivalry within his own secretarial class and with the military. Under Jaʿfar the wazīrate became central to the administration which the Mādharāʾīs had directed as heads of finance, and which now expanded to embrace the whole range of offices developed by the ʿAbbāsids for the government of the empire. Of these the most notable, as in Ṭūlūnid times, was the *dīwān al-inshāʾ* (chancery).

The Fāṭimid conquest

After the retreat from Alexandria in 324/936 the threat of Fāṭimid invasion receded. The revolutionary *élan* that had sought to extend 'the rising of the sun of God in the West' in the person of the *mahdī* ʿAbd Allāh to the east in the person of his son Muḥammad al-Qāʾim had subsided before the son succeeded his father in 322/934. The claim to universal sovereignty remained, and with it the design upon Egypt. But the years that saw the foundation of the Ikhshīdid empire by Muḥammad ibn Ṭughj culminated in Ifrīqiya in a crisis that brought his dynasty to the verge of extinction. The final suppression in 336/947 of the rising of Abū Yazīd, 'the man with the donkey', was the occasion for a revival of Fāṭimid imperialism that culminated twenty years later in the final invasion and conquest of Egypt. For most of that time, however, the dynasty was preoccupied with the restoration of its position in the western Mediterranean, and with the redevelopment by al-Muʿizz, the fourth imam–caliph, of its

44 See E. Ashtor, 'Migrations de l'Irak vers les pays méditerranéens', in E. Ashtor, *The Medieval Near East: Social and economic history*, Variorum Series IV (London, 1978).

appeal to the Shīʿa in the east. At a time when the followers of Muḥammad al-Muntaẓar, the expected twelfth imam, had reconciled themselves to his occultation, al-Muʿizz declared himself the lineal descendant of Muḥammad ibn Ismāʿīl ibn Jaʿfar al-Ṣādiq, and the second founder of his dynasty, with whom the original promise of the *mahdī* would at last be fulfilled. The conquest of Egypt was the necessary proof of that claim, but al-Muʿizz waited for the death of Kāfūr in 357/968, two years after the regent had himself ascended the throne with the title of Ustādh, and opened up the question of the succession in the absence of a son and heir.

For many years, therefore, Kāfūr was left in peace. The prestigious role of protector of the holy places was carried out by supplies of grain to feed the annual multitude, and payments to the Qarāmiṭa of Baḥrayn to secure the passage of the pilgrimage from Egypt and Syria. To the south, incursions from Nubia in 339/951 and 344/956 provoked a retaliatory expedition to the frontier fortress of Qaṣr Ibrīm in 345/957. A more serious invasion in the early 350s/960s, however, seems to have brought the Nubians 200 miles north of Aswan to Ikhmim, and kept them there for three years.[45] By then the general situation had deteriorated. The Byzantines took Crete in 350/961 and Cyprus in 354/965, provoking anti-Christian riots in Egypt and a disastrous naval expedition, whose destruction exposed the coast of Egypt and Syria to Byzantine attack. In 353/964 the Qarāmiṭa of Baḥrayn invaded Syria in concert with their Bedouin allies, who plundered the pilgrim caravan from Damascus in 355/966. In Egypt itself a prolonged period of famine from 352/963 to 357/968 led to Bedouin raids. At Fusṭāṭ, in anticipation of Kāfūr's death, rivalry was intensified by the rise of the Iraqi Jewish ibn Killis to control of the fisc, and his aspiration to the wazīrate. When Kāfūr died in 357/968, the crisis came to a head. The child Aḥmad ibn ʿAlī ibn Muḥammad ibn Ṭughj was enthroned with the *wazīr* Jaʿfar ibn al-Faḍl as regent supported by the *ghulām* Shamūl in command of the army. But Yaʿqūb ibn Killis fled to Ifrīqiya, where al-Muʿizz had long since prepared his invasion, and now set it in train.

As befitted the logistical nature of the enterprise, wells had been dug and depots established along the route as far as Barqa, while its commander, Jawhar al-Ṣiqlabī, was chosen as an administrator rather than a soldier to take over the country on behalf of his master. With an end to the ʿAbbāsid empire, Egypt was isolated, and the imam–caliph the strongest candidate for a throne effectively left vacant by Kāfūr's death. Mustered over the summer and

45 See Ḥasan, *Arabs and the Sudan*, p. 91; P. L. Shinnie, 'Christian Nubia', in Fage and Oliver (eds.), *The Cambridge history of Africa*, vol. II, p. 579.

winter of 357–8/968–9, the Fāṭimid host set out in February, to arrive outside Alexandria in May. At Fusṭāṭ Jaʿfar had been deserted by Shamūl, who had left for Syria with the Ikhshīdid prince Ḥasan, and sued for peace through the agency of the *ashrāf* (nobles), like the Fāṭimids of ʿAlid descent. This was granted by Jawhar, who took from them an oath of fidelity in the *ʿahd* (pact) by which he granted the protection of the imam–caliph in return for their obedience.[46] At Fusṭāṭ in July the regiments of the Ikhshīdiyya and Kāfūriyya made a stand, but were rapidly overwhelmed; and Jawhar proceeded to lay the foundations of al-Muʿizziyya (the city of al-Muʿizz), out beyond the ruins of al-Qaṭāʾiʿ to the north-east of Fusṭāṭ. Laid out on the model of al-Mahdiyya, the Ifrīqiyan capital of the dynasty on the coast of (modern) Tunisia, it was divided by a central street with a palace on either side and, as al-Qāhira (the victorious), eventually gave its name to the Egyptian metropolis. It was certainly intended as the new capital of Islam.

The acquiescence of Jaʿfar in the assumption of power by Jawhar on behalf of his master ensured the continuity of government, with the two men sitting together to hear the petitions that occupied a central place in the routine of government, and a similar duplication of personnel in control of the police and finance. Arriving after yet another low Nile in 357/968, Jawhar was obliged to take emergency measures to force grain onto the market, while funds to meet his expenses were probably obtained from the estates whose income had been assigned to the Ikhshīdiyya and Kāfūriyya. Normality returned with a good harvest in spring 360/970, by which time Jawhar had set in train the invasion of Syria. Between May and October the resistance of the Ikhshīdid prince Ḥasan at al-Ramla was overcome, Jawhar's general Jaʿfar ibn Falāḥ took Damascus, and the *ghulām* Futūḥ began to summon volunteers to the holy war. The enemy was Byzantium, whose own holy war had overwhelmed the defences of the Syrian borders and culminated in the siege and capture of Antioch in 358/969. At the time of Jawhar's arrival in Egypt this assault upon Islam had added urgency to the claim of the imam–caliph to the throne. The muster elicited an enthusiastic response in Palestine and Tiberias, but the campaign was called off in 360 (June 971), when Damascus came under attack from a different quarter. Brutally treated by Jaʿfar ibn Falāḥ, the citizens of Damascus appealed to the Qarāmiṭa of Baḥrayn, whose subsidy from the Ikhshīdids had been stopped by Jawhar. A coalition of Qarāmiṭa, Arab Bedouin and refugee Ikhshīdid *ghilmān*, formed with the blessing of the ʿAbbāsid caliph and the aid of the Ḥamdānids of Mosul, then defeated and killed Jaʿfar in August. In

46 See Brett, *Rise of the Fatimids*, p. 301.

September the horde entered Egypt and overran the eastern Delta. It was only driven out in 361 (December 971), after defeat at Fusṭāṭ, where a wall and ditch thrown up from the river to the Muqattam cliffs was held by the citizens whom Jawhar had conscripted and armed.

Syria was lost together with the momentum of the Fāṭimid invasion, but Egypt was ready to welcome the imam–caliph himself. Al-Muʿizz left Ifrīqiya in 362 (November 972), to arrive at Fusṭāṭ in June 973, and take up residence in the palace city of al-Muʿizziyya. Jawhar was retired and Jaʿfar ibn al-Faḍl dismissed by a monarch who took personal control of the state. Yaʿqūb ibn Killis was appointed with an Ifrīqiyan colleague to the position he had enjoyed under Kāfūr in charge of the revenue. Such resolution carried the regime through the crises of the next two years. On behalf of Egypt the *ashrāf*, certified descendants of the Prophet and putative kinsmen of the imam–caliph, were prepared to welcome the new sovereign; but one of their number, Akhū Muslim, defected to the Qarāmiṭa, who remained deaf to al-Muʿizz's appeal for recognition. It required the defeat of a second assault upon Fusṭāṭ in 363/974 to put an end to their threat, and permit the reoccupation of Damascus by Fāṭimid forces. In 364/975, however, the rebellious citizenry found a new ally in the Turkish *ghulām* Aftakīn, in flight from Būyid Baghdad; and the death of the heir apparent ʿAbd Allāh was followed by that of al-Muʿizz himself at the end of the year.

The Fāṭimid empire

His death meant that the reign of the Fāṭimids in Egypt began with a new monarch, his son and successor al-ʿAzīz, under whom the dynasty assumed its Egyptian character and Egyptian outlook.[47] Through the work of Ibn Zūlāq, the pro-Fāṭimid continuator of the anti-Fāṭimid al-Kindī's *Wulāt*, the dynasty took over the historiographical tradition of Egypt, and made it their own in a court chronicle on which al-Maqrīzī based his history of the dynasty, his *Ittiʿāẓ al-ḥunafāʾ*.[48] The dynasty's remarkably determined pursuit of the Mahdist aim of restoring to the community its true faith and true government at the

47 See ibid., chs. 10 and 11; Y. Lev, *State and society in Fatimid Egypt* (Leiden, 1991), chs. 1, 4 and 5; P. Sanders, 'The Fāṭimid state, 969–1171', in Petry (ed.), *The Cambridge history of Egypt*, vol. I. The most recent history of the Fāṭimids in Egypt down to 1074 is H. Halm, *Die Kalifen von Kairo. Die Fatimiden in Ägypten 973–1074* (Munich, 2003). For the history of their doctrine, see F. Daftary, *The Ismāʿīlīs: Their history and doctrines* (Cambridge, 1990).

48 Al-Maqrīzī, *Ittiʿāẓ al-ḥunafāʾ*, ed. J. D. al-Shayyāl and M. H. M. Aḥmad, 3 vols. (Cairo, 1967–73).

hands of the true heirs of the Prophet was similarly modified. The pursuit was based on two requirements: belief in their imamate; and acceptance of their caliphate. The first was the principle of their *daʿwa*, their call to join the ranks of the *muʾminūn* (faithful), those for whom belief in the imam was the way to God. The second was that of their *dawla* (state), in which the generality of *muslimūn* was summoned to obedience on the strength of their *islām*, or submission to God. While all *muʾminūn* were *muslimūn*, most *muslimūn* were not such believers, a division of the community which was reflected in the reach of the *daʿwa* to a minority across the Muslim world, while the *dawla* was restricted to the territory controlled by the caliph. But since it was of the essence of his mission that he should rule the entire world, and certainly the whole of the *dār al-islām*, the extension of the *dawla* continued to be a fundamental aim of the dynasty after the appropriation of Ikhshīdid Egypt. The way it was pursued and accomplished by al-ʿAzīz determined the character of the empire for the next hundred years.

The principle of the *dawla* in Egypt remained that of the *ʿahd* concluded by Jawhar with the representatives of the Ikhshīdid regime on behalf of the population. Its accent upon the *dhimma* (protection accorded to that population) effectively placed Muslims on the same level as the *dhimmiyyūn*, the Christians and Jews under the protection of the Muslim community, under the sway of a monarch situated on an altogether higher plane. But under al-ʿAzīz, the son and successor of al-Muʿizz, the father's close direction of both *dawla* and *daʿwa* gave way to an extensive delegation of responsibility to a new generation of servants. Of these, the sons of the great Qāḍī al-Nuʿmān, whose *Daʿāʾim al-Islām* (Pillars of Islam) had spelled out the doctrine of the law on the authority of the imam, established a dynasty which held the post of chief *qāḍī* almost continuously down to the 430s / 1040s. In that capacity they represented the monarch in his dual capacity as imam and caliph, laying down the law and supervising its administration by subordinates often belonging to other schools. But both as administrators of the law and as custodians of the doctrine of the imamate enunciated by their father, they were challenged by Yaʿqūb ibn Killis, for whom the post of *wazīr* was reintroduced in 368 / 979. For the Fāṭimids this was a major innovation which relieved the monarch of the care of government, including the all-important task of hearing petitions in his capacity as the fount of justice. In this judicial role ibn Killis clashed with the sons of al-Nuʿmān, all the more because he had joined the ranks of the *muʾminūn* as an initiate who composed a treatise on the law in place of the *Daʿāʾim*, endowed a number of scholars to teach in al-Azhar, the dynastic mosque of al-Qāhira, and as an arbiter of the faith conducted doctrinal disputations which included Severus Ibn al-Muqaffaʿ, Coptic bishop of Ashmunayn.[49] The conflict only ended with his death in 380/991.

More importantly for Egypt, ibn Killis had presided over a renewal of prosperity which began when he supervised a reallocation of tax-farms, in effect inviting the Egyptians to buy into the new regime. Such investment in the fiscal yield of the economy was matched by investment in its agricultural and industrial production and commercial activity. Waste land was reclaimed for the cultivation of the old winter crops of grain and flax, while artificial irrigation supported the more recent summer crops of sugar cane and cotton. While grain came onto the market largely through taxation of the harvest, flax, sugar cane and cotton were cash crops that fed major industries. Peasant initiative was important, but only at the base of a commercial and industrial enterprise dominated by the wealthy landholding aristocracy of the regime: at his death ibn Killis left a huge stock of linen and perhaps other cloth to be sold by merchants on his behalf. The export of such manufactures was matched by the import of commodities from across the Mediterranean, ranging from timber and metals, olive oil and leather, to silks and other textiles, carried increasingly in Italian ships. The Mediterranean was paired with the Sahara, across which came slaves and gold; but these were only the western extension of an intercontinental commercial network centred upon Egypt. With the decline of Iraq and the Persian Gulf, Egypt had returned to its position in Antiquity as the focus of exchange between the Indian Ocean and the Mediterranean via the Red Sea.[50] Pepper and spices were only the most exotic of the commodities that travelled from east to west.

With such economic growth a rise in population is indicated, which may have slowed if not halted the long-term decline of the Coptic community.[51] It certainly favoured the Jews, as we see from the Geniza documents of the immigrant North African Jewish community at Fusṭāṭ, employed by Goitein to paint a broad picture of urban society in the Fāṭimid period.[52] But as we see

49 See, in addition to Brett, *Rise of the Fatimids*, pp. 386–8, M. Brett, 'al-Karāza al-Marqusiya: The Coptic Church in the Fatimid empire', in Vermeulen and Van Steenbergen (eds.), *Egypt and Syria in the Fatimid, Ayyubid and Mamluk Eras*, vol. IV (Leuven, 2005).

50 See M. Lombard, *The golden age of Islam* (Amsterdam, Oxford and New York, 1975); K. N. Chaudhuri, *Trade and civilisation in the Indian Ocean* (Cambridge, 1985).

51 See Brett, 'Way of the peasant'; Brett, 'Population and conversion', pp. 10–11.

52 Studied by S. D. Goitein, *A Mediterranean society: The Jewish communities of the Arab world as portrayed in the documents of the Cairo Geniza*, 5 vols. (Berkeley and Los Angeles, 1967–88), vol. I: *The economic foundations*. See also Lev, *State and society*, chs. 9 and 10, 'The urban society of Fusṭāṭ–Cairo' and 'The non-Muslim communities'.

in the case of ibn Killis, the greatest beneficiaries were the great men, and women, of the dynasty, whose wealth was increased by investment in long-distance trade, and redistributed in lavish expenditure.[53] Through such expenditure the dynasty reaped a further reward in the association of the populace with its political and religious programme. Construction work in the capital afforded employment while creating the setting for the celebration of its grandeur. The mosque built by the queen mother Durzān became the centrepiece of the royal cemetery and residential suburb of al-Qarāfa, a place of Shīʿite devotion and popular rendezvous.[54] Al-Qāhira itself developed as the ritual city, in Paula Sanders' phrase,[55] of what Geertz has described in Java as the theatre state, whose spectacular ceremony was at the heart of government.[56] (For army and bureaucracy, see below.)

Egypt nevertheless remained a *ghulām* state, with an army whose character was determined by the protracted effort of al-ʿAzīz to regain possession of Syria, first by the reoccupation of Damascus, second by the annexation of Ḥamdānid Aleppo. The opposition of Damascus was not finally overcome until 373/983, and a governor from al-Qāhira not installed until 378/988; Aleppo, defended by its citizens in alliance with Byzantium, remained independent at al-ʿAzīz's death in 386/996. In the process, however, the Turkish *ghulām* (see above for preference for the Arabic) Aftakīn, whom Damascus had welcomed as its champion, was defeated in 368/978, captured and received into the Fāṭimid army, which thus acquired the nucleus of a force of Turkish cavalry alongside the more lightly armed Kutāma Berbers from Ifrīqiya. Meanwhile a force of Daylamī infantry from Iran was recruited alongside blacks from the Sudan. In this way the army became permanently, and dangerously, divided between westerners and easterners. Their rivalry came into the open at the death of al-ʿAzīz, when the veteran Ifrīqiyan Ḥasan ibn ʿAmmār at the head of the Kutāma regiments of the army took power as regent for the infant al-Ḥākim, only to be defeated by the Turks and ousted by the boy's tutor Barjawān.[57]

The death of al-ʿAzīz in 386/996, and the accession for the first time of a minor to the imamate and caliphate, put an end to the formidable build-up of

53 For the nature of this economy, see Brett, *Rise of the Fatimids*, pp. 286–7, 332–9.

54 See D. Cortese and S. Calderini, *Women and the Fatimids in the world of Islam* (Edinburgh, 2006), pp. 167–9, 187.

55 P. Sanders, *Ritual, politics and the city in Fatimid Cairo* (Albany, 1994).

56 C. Geertz, *Islam observed: Religious development in Morocco and Indonesia* (Chicago and London, 1968), pp. 36–8.

57 See Lev, *State and society*, ch. 5, 'The evolution of the tribal army'.

forces in Syria for an attack upon Aleppo, whose possession was essential for any advance into Iraq. Instead, the pause that it induced in the expansion of the empire set the seal upon the direction this had taken under al-ʿAzīz. The long drive to recover the Ikhshīdid and Ṭūlūnid territories in Syria had been accompanied by withdrawal from the government of Ifrīqiya, where the death in 373/984 of Buluggīn, the viceroy installed by al-Muʿizz, had been followed by an unsuccessful attempt by al-ʿAzīz to demote his son al-Manṣūr. The killing by al-Manṣūr of Muḥammad al-Kātib, the minister at Qayrawān whom the caliph had endeavoured to promote, marked the independence of the Zīrid dynasty in return for recognition of Fāṭimid suzerainty. Forced upon al-Qāhira, this solution to the question of its relationship to the state that the dynasty had left behind became the means to the extension of Fāṭimid sovereignty over the Islamic world. Outside the *dawla* proper, where the imam–caliph ruled as well as reigned, there formed a circle of territories over which he reigned but did not rule, from Ifrīqiya, Sicily and Barqa through al-Raqqa, Baḥrayn and Sind to the holy places of Mecca and Medina; their various princes offered the Friday prayer in his name, while the Christian king of Nubia offered the equivalent in the form of the *baqṭ*. Beyond this circle was what might be called the *Dawla Irredenta*, the lands where the caliph neither ruled nor reigned, but where he strove for recognition to achieve the goal of universal empire. While conquest remained focused on Aleppo, a propaganda campaign conducted by the *duʿāt* (missionaries) of the imam aimed to bring about the necessary revolution by peaceful or violent means.

The patrimonial state

In Egypt the accession of al-Ḥākim proved to be the beginning of a revolution of a different kind. The Fāṭimids provided Max Weber with a prime example of the institutionalisation of charisma in the patrimonial state, of the way in which government passed out of the hands of a dynasty founded by a religious revolutionary into those of its servants, who governed its patrimony in the ruler's name.[58] This is indeed the story of their reign in the eleventh century, which began with a rapid and frequently sanguinary turnover of personnel that resolved itself into a more stable ministerial regime before a second crisis ended in government by the commander of the army. Initial responsibility lay with the new caliph. Controversial in his lifetime, al-Ḥākim has remained an

58 See B. S. Turner, *Weber and Islam* (London, 1974), ch. 5, 'Patrimonialism and charismatic succession'.

enigmatic figure, with insanity an unsatisfactory explanation for his behaviour.[59] Controversy was both religious and political, leading to conflict within the dynasty and its following; with the Sunnī population; and with the ʿAbbāsids, who formally challenged the claim of the dynasty to descent from the Prophet. Analysis is not helped by the paucity of information on the last seven years of the reign, perhaps because of subsequent censorship of the court chronicle of al-Musabbiḥī (d. 420/1029). What is clear is that, after a century of firm direction, the dynasty wavered under al-Ḥākim, uncertain of its religious policy and unsure of its servants.

The institutionalisation of the *daʿwa* with the creation of the post of chief *dāʿī* (caller to the faith) was symptomatic of the underlying problem. While the appointment reflected the consolidation of the Fāṭimid following into a worldwide congregation, it emphasised its constitution as the Ismāʿīliyya, the sectarian name by which the faithful were distinguished from the similarly sectarian followers of the twelfth imam, and *a fortiori* from the body of Sunnī Islam. A movement predicated upon its universal appeal to the entire Muslim community was becoming increasingly separate and increasingly minoritarian. The contrast became apparent in the course of al-Ḥākim's reign, as he struggled to come to terms with his role as representative of God on earth. Apart from a string of moral and curious dietary prohibitions, repeated from year to year, policy was inconsistent over the three main periods of the reign, after he took power with the murder of his tutor Barjawān in 390/1000. In the first, he broke with the previously generous interpretation of Jawhar's *ʿahd* to curse the Companions and the first three caliphs, and impose their distinctive dress upon Christians and Jews. In 395–8/1005–7, however, he was confronted by the Mahdist rising of Abū Rakwa ('the man with the goatskin waterbottle') in the western desert, prompting a *rapprochement* with the Sunnī population in which the cursing was forbidden, Sunnī observances tolerated and the caliph himself came to lead the prayer in the Mosque of ʿAmr in 402–3/1012. In contrast, prohibitions on Christians and Jews hardened into outright persecution. Perhaps in response to Christian millenarianism, around 398–400/1007–10 the Church of the Holy Sepulchre in Jerusalem was destroyed, along with many others. But in 401–4/1011–13 revolt in Syria briefly installed a rival caliph at al-Ramla, and in 404/1013 the toleration of Sunnism came to an end along with the persecution of Christians, who were allowed to return, to rebuild

59 See M. Canard, 'al-Ḥākim bi-Amri'llāh', *EI2*, vol. III, pp. 76–82; Lev, *State and society*, pp. 25–37; T. Bianquis, 'al-H'âkim bi amr Allâh ou la folie de l'unité chez un souverain fât'imide', in C. A. Julien *et al.* (eds.), *Les Africains*, vol. XI (Paris, 1978); J. Forsyth, *The Byzantine-Arab chronicle (938–1034) of Yaḥyā b. Saʿīd al-Anṭākī* (Ann Arbor, 1977).

their churches and resume their faith. Much more radical was the designation in 404/1013 of a cousin, ibn Ilyās, as heir apparent (*walī ʿahd al-muslimīn*), while he himself withdrew from public life. The most plausible explanation of this departure from the dynasty's fundamental rule of patrilineal succession is that al-Ḥākim considered himself to be the ninth and last imam from the ancestral Muḥammad ibn Ismāʿīl, after whom only the caliphate would continue in his line. No record of the consternation in the palace has survived, but in 409/1018f. there were riots in Fusṭāṭ against the preaching of his divinity by two Iranians, al-Darazī and Ḥamza. The *dāʿī* in Iraq, al-Kirmānī, was summoned to clear al-Ḥākim himself of responsibility, but the conjunction of extreme sectarianism with so radical a departure from dynastic orthodoxy dramatically demonstrated the difficulty faced by the Fāṭimids in sustaining their appeal after their triumph in the previous century. The crisis only ended with al-Ḥākim's disappearance, presumed murdered, in the desert in 411/1021.

Al-Ḥākim's seclusion in the last seven years of his reign was in contrast to his earlier accessibility, walking in Fusṭāṭ and hearing petitions in person. Equally in contrast to what had gone before was the length of the wazīrate of ʿAlī, son of the Jaʿfar ibn Falāḥ slain at Damascus in 360/971, a member of the Berber military aristocracy who governed with the title of Dhu 'l-Riyāsatayn (the man of two headships, the Pen and the Sword) from 405/1015 until he was murdered by unknown attackers in 409/1019. From the assassination of Barjawān onwards his fellows from the coterie of Ifrīqiyan, Ṣiqlabī, Berber, Coptic and Iraqi families in the upper echelons of the regime, officiating as judges, generals and ministers, usually with the lesser title of *wāsiṭa* (middle-man), had been regularly dismissed, and in the previous period frequently executed or mutilated. The pattern resumed in 409/1019, but ended with al-Ḥākim's presumed murder, when ibn Ilyās was put to death, and the succession reverted to al-Ḥākim's youthful son under the name of al-Ẓāhir li-iʿzāz Dīn Allāh ('he who appears openly to strengthen the religion of God').

The title is significant of the return of the dynasty to its previous orthodoxy, but not of a return to firm direction by the sovereign. Until her death in 413/1023 the government was controlled by al-Ḥākim's sister Sitt al-Mulk, and thereafter manipulated by the queen mother Ruqiyya, with whose support al-Jarjarāʾī became *wazīr* in 418/1028. An immigrant from Iraq whose hands had been cut off in one of al-Ḥākim's many purges, al-Jarjarāʾī had returned to office as a skilled administrator and consummate politician, who came to the wazīrate at the head of a patronage party whose members formed his government. After the turbulence of the previous reign the palace and the personnel of the dynasty colluded in a regime that excluded the monarch but satisfied the expectations of his servants in the administration and the army. As head of the administration the *wazīr* presided over a miscellany of boards, departments and offices collectively known as the *dawāwīn* or *dīwāns*, broadly divided between the permanent bureaux dealing with the main areas of revenue, expenditure and documentation, and others created for specific and perhaps temporary purposes, such as the affairs of Syria or the property of the queen mother.[60] In an age when specific revenues were typically assigned to specific purposes, many of these boards would have arisen within the main departments to take care of special interests, most notably a *dīwān khāṣṣ* or 'privy purse' to meet the expenses of the palace. All of them came under the supervision of the *dīwān al-majlis*, the meeting of the heads of department in the presence of the *wazīr*, which had its own secretary. Among the main departments the *dīwān al-rasāʾil* or *inshāʾ*, the chancellery dealing with state correspondence, was prestigious but peripheral to the *bayt al-māl* or treasury, divided between the supervision of taxation and the direction of expenditure. Taxation of all kinds was now generally farmed out on the basis of treasury assessments and valuations. The most essential item of expenditure in this *ghulām* state was the army, which in this period seems to have been paid out of central funds, with specific revenues assigned to specific regiments under the name of *iqṭāʿāt*, (sing. *iqṭāʿ*, 'portions'). It was a large and composite force, ethnically divided between Turks, Berbers, Slavs, Greeks, blacks, Iranian Daylamīs and Arab Bedouin, and technically between heavy and light cavalry, heavy and light infantry, archers and spearmen, which required all the political skills of the *wazīr* to control.[61] The navy was a major expense, but from its low profile in the sources lacked a corporate identity and political significance.[62]

Outside Egypt the main aim of al-Jarjarāʾī was to restore the Fāṭimid position in Syria, where after the death of al-ʿAzīz the dynasty had been forced back onto the defensive by the Arab Bedouin: the Kilāb in the north, who in 1015 established the Mirdāsid dynasty at Aleppo in succession to the Ḥamdānids, and the Jarrāḥid chiefs of the Ṭayyiʾ in the centre and south. At Uqhuwāna in northern Palestine the Mirdāsids and Jarrāḥids were

60 See A. F. Sayyid, *al-Dawla al-fāṭimiyya fī Miṣr/Les Fatimides en Egypte* (in Arabic) (Cairo, 1992), pp. 255–90; Brett, *Rise of the Fatimids*, pp. 341–4.

61 See Brett, *Rise of the Fatimids*, pp. 342–5; M. Brett, 'The origins of the Mamluk military system in the Fatimid period', in U. Vermeulen and D. De Smet (eds.), *Egypt and Syria in the Fatimid, Ayyubid and Mamluk Periods*, vol. I (Leuven, 1995).

62 See Y. Lev, 'The Fatimid navy, Byzantium and the Mediterranean sea, 909–1036 CE', *Byzantion*, 54 (1984).

overwhelmingly defeated in 420/1029. The victor, the Turkish *ghulām* al-Dizbirī, became governor of Damascus, while negotiations with Constantinople led to an agreement which not only permitted the Byzantines to rebuild the Church of the Holy Sepulchre, but opened the way for his conquest of Aleppo in 429/1038. This, however, was far from being a resumption of the dynasty's offensive against Baghdad. Politics took precedence over imperial ambitions when al-Dizbirī was ousted from Damascus in 433/1041 by an army revolt provoked by the *wazīr*, and Aleppo was lost. Following the death of al-Ẓāhir in 427/1036, the accession of the infant al-Mustanṣir and the replacement of his patroness Ruqiyya by a new queen mother, Raṣad, al-Jarjarāʾī no longer had the palace on his side. Raṣad's own protégé, the Iranian Jewish al-Tustarī, was not in a position to replace him as *wazīr*, and his party survived in office after his death in 436/1045. An alternative party had nevertheless begun to form, prompting the murder of al-Tustarī in 439/1047, for which the *wazīr*, al-Fallāḥī, was arrested and executed in 440/1048. Al-Fallāḥī was succeeded by the nephew of al-Jarjarāʾī; Abu 'l-Barakāt; but Raṣad's patronage continued to grow at the hands of al-Yāzūrī, the steward of her estates. When the failure of the attack upon Aleppo ordered by the new *wazīr* in 440/1049 prompted his dismissal in 442/1050, al-Yāzūrī had the necessary support to form a government. While never able to command the same broad following as al-Jarjarāʾī, he was strong enough vigorously to react to the rapidly developing crisis east and west.

The growth of the *daʿwa* under al-Ḥākim had been marked by the shift of its intellectual centre from al-Qāhira to Iran and Iraq, where the *dāʿī* al-Kirmānī emerged as a major philosopher, and from where al-Darazī and Ḥamza came to proclaim al-Ḥākim's divinity before Ḥamza and his followers fled into Syria as the Druzes. The fading of Fāṭimid imperialism since the beginning of the century, however, had been matched by the growth of ʿAbbāsid propaganda, which by the 430s/1040s threatened not only the mission of the dynasty but the whole fabric of its empire. By the time al-Yāzūrī came to power the Zīrids of Ifrīqiya had turned to Baghdad; more seriously, the incoming Saljūqs had taken up the ʿAbbāsid cause.[63] In 443–4/1052 al-Yāzūrī scored a military victory over the Zīrids' allies the Banū Qurra at Barqa, and in 445/1053f. a propaganda victory over the Zīrids themselves after their defeat by the Banū Hilāl at the battle of Ḥaydarān in 443/1052; by 449/1057 they had returned to Fāṭimid

63 See Brett, *Rise of the Fatimids*, pp. 404–7, 429–30; and M. Brett, 'ʿAbbasids, Fatimids and Seljuqs', in David Luscombe and Jonathan Riley-Smith (eds.), *The new Cambridge medieval history*, vol. IV (Cambridge, 2004).

allegiance.[64] An unsought bonus was the conquest of the Yemen by the *dāʿī* al-Ṣulayḥī between 429/1038 and 455/1063. To counter the Saljūqs after the arrival of Ṭughril Beg at Baghdad in 447/1055 al-Yāzūrī then turned to the *dāʿī* al-Shīrāzī, who had worked to win the last Būyids for al-Qāhira, and was now entrusted with the raising of an army in Syria for an invasion of Iraq to restore al-Basāsirī, the former governor of Baghdad, to the ʿAbbāsid capital. In 450/1058 the invasion was unexpectedly successful, to the delight of al-Mustanṣir; but not before al-Yāzūrī had been accused of treasonable correspondence with Ṭughril Beg, and executed. Domestic politics had once again proved decisive in determining the direction of both *dawla* and *daʿwa*, on this occasion with disastrous consequences. The offensive in Iraq may have been doomed; sixty years after the death of al-ʿAzīz the *élan* of the dynasty had been lost, and under the *wazīrs* of the Pen the regime was in no shape to repel the Saljūqs, let alone resume the drive for universal empire. It was in Egypt, however, that its fundamental weakness was exposed. The execution of al-Yāzūrī grievously backfired, since now there was no one with sufficient support to form a government. When Ṭughril Beg finally re-entered Baghdad in 452/1060 al-Qāhira was in disarray.[65]

As *wazīrs* came and went with increasing rapidity, the inability of the caliph to take back control of the government was demonstrated by the fiasco of al-Mustanṣir's attempt to hear petitions himself. A scholarly man, unlike his father, who had the mission of the dynasty at heart, his failure to do so was a measure of the distance travelled by the regime since its installation in Egypt, and a sign of worse to come. The failure of al-Yāzūrī's general, the Ḥamdānid prince Nāṣir al-Dawla, to recapture Aleppo brought him back to Egypt in 454/1062. In 455/1063 the Turks and the blacks, the Mashāriqa and the Maghāriba, came to blows on the parade ground; from 458/1066 onwards the Turks held the caliph to ransom in al-Qāhira, while Nāṣir al-Dawla based himself at Alexandria in a bid for power; the countryside was plundered by soldiers and Bedouin. Only after Nāṣir al-Dawla was murdered in 465/1073 was order restored by Badr al-Jamālī, the governor of what remained of Fāṭimid Syria at Acre, with whom the wazīrate passed out of the control of the Men of the Pen into the hands of a Man of the Sword. The pretentions of the imam–caliph to universal sovereignty remained, and were indeed revived by the new regime.

64 See Michael Brett, 'The central lands of North Africa and Sicily until the beginning of the Almohad period', in *The new Cambridge history of Islam* (Cambridge, 2010), vol. II: Maribel Fierro (ed.), *The western Islamic world, eleventh to eighteenth centuries*, ch. 2.

65 See M. Brett, 'The execution of al-Yāzūrī', in U.Vermeulen and D. De Smet (eds.), *Egypt and Syria in the Fatimid, Ayyubid and Mamluk Eras*, vol. II (Leuven, 1998).

For Egypt as well as the Fāṭimids, however, it was the end of an era. In the great Shidda, the prolonged famine that accompanied the conflict, the population fell;[66] and with an end to the demographic buoyancy of the previous hundred years it is likely that the balance tipped finally for the Muslims against the Copts.

66 See Brett, 'Way of the peasant', pp. 51–5; Brett, 'Population and conversion', pp. 28–30.

14

The Iberian Peninsula and North Africa

EDUARDO MANZANO MORENO

The expansion in the west

The Arab conquests in North Africa began soon after the fall of Alexandria to the army commanded by ʿAmr ibn al-ʿĀṣ in 21/642. Unlike previous expansion in the Near East, the march westwards of the Arab soldiers was not marked by sweeping victories and the resigned acquiescence of the conquered populations. Widespread revolts, crushing defeats and hasty evacuations of recently conquered territories fill the terse accounts of the few Arab sources that provide some information on this huge area. In contrast, the narrative of the conquest of Hispania in 92/711 recalls a similar pattern to the invasions in Byzantine and Sasanian territories: after one pitched battle and the defeat of the king's army the Visigothic administration crumbled, clearing the way for an Arab rule which consolidated with remarkable ease and no serious challenges.

The resistance met by the conquerors in the southern Mediterranean was due to the political and social diversity of the region. In the land extending from Alexandria to Tangier the Arabs did not meet one single enemy, but rather a number of enemies whose actions and motivations were diverse, and not always comprehensible to modern historians. Arguably, the main opponent of the invading armies was the Byzantine empire, whose foothold in North Africa went back to the times when, in 534, the generals of the emperor Justinian conquered the Vandal kingdom. As shown by the rescripts he issued in the aftermath of the conquest, Justinian's grandiose idea had been to restore the ancient limits of Roman Africa, from Tripolitania, adjoining Egypt, to Mauritania on the Atlantic shores, from coastal cities to pre-desert enclaves.[1] This ambitious scheme was doomed to failure, however. In classical times North Africa had become a vast frontier, which stood against the sporadic

1 *Codex Iustinianus*, ed. P. Krueger (Berlin, 1954), 1, 27, 1, 7–12 and 1, 27, 2, 1ª.

attacks of peripheral Berber tribes. Its government rested on the loyalty of assimilated native populations, on a complex network of diplomatic dealings with tribal chieftains, and on tight control, through military operations by police and garrisoned checkpoints, of the tribes' nomadic movements. This system gradually collapsed from the second half of the fourth century onwards. The inability of the Roman frontier (*limes*) to protect the rich coastal cities against tribal incursions and the growing disaffection of the class of indigenous landowners, who became tribal warlords at the final stages of imperial rule, made up the awkward legacy left by the late empire to its successors in North Africa. Tribal pressure on Tripolitania increased throughout the Vandal period as witnessed by the devastation of Leptis Magna (Lebda in modern-day Libya) or the heavy defeat inflicted on the Vandal army before 523 by the Laguantan, a tribe which came from the oases of western Egypt. The last Vandal kings were familiar with the names of Ortaias, Iaudas or Antalas, Berber warlords whose rule over pastoralist tribes and sedentary communities of pre-desert regions in the Hodna, the Aurès or the Tunisian Dorsal posed a serious threat to their domains in *Africa Proconsularis* and northern *Byzacium*, broadly speaking the same land that the Arabs later called Ifrīqiya.

The Vandal kingdom disintegrated before the Byzantine army, but the complex socio-political conditions of North Africa remained almost unchanged. Some tribal leaders switched their loyalty to the new rulers and were invested with insignia and emblems of power following a Roman practice, which had been maintained by the Vandal kings. The most skilled Byzantine generals (*duces*) and governors (*exarchs*) managed to draw other warlords into this sort of alliance, either extolling force or resorting to diplomacy. Berber troops swelled the field armies in the capacity of auxiliary troops, not always trustworthy but nevertheless always at hand, even in the final moments of imperial rule. However, relations were often strained. The plundering of cities and rural areas by uncommitted tribes such as the Laguantan continued throughout the whole period, particularly in Tripolitania and Byzacium; ill-timed killings or humiliations of hitherto allied tribal chieftains by Byzantine officials sparked fierce rebellions, which were also inflamed by the depredations of imperial troops in tribal territories.

If we bear these precedents in mind, it is hardly surprising that Arab sources do not mention any serious opposition from the Berber tribes found by the conquerors in the lands bordering on Egypt. The troublesome Laguantan (Ar. Lawāta), who inhabited the vicinity of Barqa, agreed to come to terms with the newcomers. Perhaps the key to this understanding was the fact that Arab governors of Egypt led the early campaigns in the form of raids against cities in Tripolitania and Byzacium, very much in the same way that this tribe had been doing until then. The most successful of these expeditions was commanded by ʿAbd Allāh ibn Abī Sarḥ, which defeated the army of the Byzantine exarch Gregorius near Sufetula in 27/647. However, ʿAbd Allāh did not attempt to gain a territorial foothold in the region, and retreated to Egypt after having exacted tribute from the province.[2]

The actual occupation of North Africa was only carried out under the Umayyad caliphs of Damascus. Raiding expeditions were abandoned when the caliph Muʿāwiya (41–60/661–80) entrusted Ifrīqiya to ʿUqba ibn Nāfiʿ. The campaigns of the previous decades had somehow ensured the occupation of Tripolitania, and at this juncture (50/670) ʿUqba managed to found a new city, Qayrawān, in a strategic location at the heartland of former Byzacium, which rapidly became the main outpost of Arab settlement in North Africa. Although still in possession of Carthage, the Byzantines were unable to prevent this move, and in the following decades the main opposition to the Arabs came from Berber tribes throughout the extensive lands, which lay outside the former *limes*.

Umayyad governors of Qayrawān soon had to face the same dilemma as their Byzantine predecessors: how to accommodate these Berber populations into the imperial scheme the governors represented. Military conquest and cooperation were the mutually exclusive options considered from the very beginning, as shown by the fierce rivalry that pitted the governor ʿUqba ibn Nāfiʿ, an advocate of aggressive warfare, against his successor, Abu ʾl-Muhājir Dīnār (55–61/674–680), who seems to have been more inclined to reach compromises with Berber chieftains. Although the former option prevailed during ʿUqba's second tenure of governorship (61–3/680–3), it was handicapped by the vastness of the region and the military strength that tribal warlords were able to assemble. The celebrated campaign led by ʿUqba against the Maghrib allegedly reached the Atlantic shores of today's Morocco, but ended with his death and the defeat of his army in Tahūda (south-east of Biskra) at the hands of a confederation of Berber and Byzantine troops led by a shadowy figure called Kusayla (or Kasīla). The disaster forced the Arabs to evacuate Qayrawān, allowing a brief Byzantine recovery from Carthage. It took a vast number of troops mobilised with characteristic

2 This tribute was presumably paid in gold, which seems to have circulated in significant amounts in the province in this period: see R. Guéry, C. Morrison and H. Slim, *Recherches archéologiques franco-tunisiennes à Rougga. 3: Le trésor de monnaies d'or byzantines* (Rome, 1982), pp. 76–94.

boldness by the caliph ʿAbd al-Malik (65–86/685–705) to dispose of Kusayla. Arab sources claim that the new governor, Ḥasan ibn al-Nuʿmān, entered Qayrawān again and conquered Carthage for the first time in 78/697, but these events suggest that at this juncture Arab rule still depended exclusively on military might, without affecting the social fabric of North African populations.

The weaving of this social fabric involved a long and complex process. Arab sources encapsulate it in a narrative whose main character is a riveting female figure called al-Kāhina ('the sorceress'), who fought Ḥasan ibn al-Nuʿmān with her Jarāwa tribe from the Aurès mountains. The broad 'historical' details of her deeds are quite similar to those mentioned in the war against Kusayla: under al-Kāhina's leadership Berber tribes massacred Ḥasan's army, forcing him to evacuate Qayrawān, while a short-lived reconquest of Carthage by the Byzantine navy once again shook the foundations of Ifrīqiya. But, more than the historical circumstances, it is the legend that matters in these accounts. Al-Kāhina is depicted as a soothsayer and mother of two sons: one Berber, the other of a Greek father. The family grows when al-Kāhina adopts an Arab prisoner through a rite of simulated suckling. But she is well aware that it is not her destiny to reign over this mixed progeny, as she foresees her own defeat and death at the hands of the reshuffled troops of Ḥasan ibn al-Nuʿmān. The recognition that the rule of the Arabs will prevail moves her to entrust her sons to Ḥasan, who fulfils the prophecy by defeating and killing al-Kāhina, but also by giving to one of her sons the command of the Berber troops of his army. The death of al-Kāhina and the assimilation of her offspring were the preconditions for the establishment of the new administration: the account ends with the Arab governor peacefully ruling in Qayrawān and organising the fiscal system which taxed Christians of both Byzantine (*ʿajam*) and Berber origin.

As the final narrative of the conquest of Ifrīqiya, the legend of al-Kāhina enshrines an interpretation of the consolidation of Arab rule over Berber tribal chieftains. Under these new circumstances, joining the ranks of the conquerors as troops in the service of Arab military leaders was the way to fit into the new order, as al-Kāhina had prophesied to the son who was later promoted in the army of Ḥasan ibn al-Nuʿmān. In what may be seen as a fulfilment of al-Kāhina's vision, a few years after the pacification of Ifrīqiya, in 92/711, Berber troops took part in the Arab expedition that crossed the Straits from Ceuta, landed in the Iberian Peninsula and defeated the Visigothic army. Most of the 18,000 soldiers who allegedly took part in this early campaign were Berbers who had joined the Arab army of the governor Mūsā ibn Nuṣayr. The conquered had become the conquerors, and for a moment it seemed that further expansion offered the possibility of a smooth integration of the Berbers into the empire of the Umayyads.[3]

The consolidation of Arab rule in the Iberian Peninsula took a different path. The Arab and Berber troops who landed in Hispania in 92/711 had responded to an appeal made by one of the factions fighting in a dynastic dispute, which opposed the sons of the late Visigothic king, Witiza (d. 710), against the partisans of Roderic, who was considered a usurper by his foes. Lacking enough military resources, the sons of Witiza appealed to the new authority, which had emerged beyond the Straits. The expedition was commanded by Ṭāriq ibn Ziyād, probably a Berber chieftain acting as a lieutenant of Mūsā ibn Nuṣayr, the new Arab governor of Ifrīqiya. The defeat of Roderic at the battle of Guadalete and the success of the ensuing campaign convinced Mūsā that a full-fledged conquest was feasible. He decided to lead the expeditions personally, rapidly conquering the main cities – Cordoba, Seville, Toledo and Saragossa – while Visigothic administration broke down.[4] When Mūsā was summoned to the east by the caliph al-Walīd (86–96/705–15), who was increasingly worried by the independence his warlike governor was showing, he could boast that he had left behind a territory that, although perhaps not wholly subdued, certainly lacked any unified opposition against the new rulers.

The sudden fall of the Visigothic kingdom was caused by its own political and social fragmentation. The bitter dispute, which had involved King Roderic and the sons of his predecessor, was the outcome of decades of internal turmoil marked by an increasing estrangement of the landowning class from the monarchy. A number of military laws issued by the last kings show this class ignoring summonses to join the royal army or turning up with a minimal part of their private retinues. Harsh penalties and fines were decreed for those who failed to comply with royal appeals, but the fact that the problem had to be addressed again and again indicates a growing alienation of the monarchy from its social base.[5] When the kingdom had to face a threat as serious as the Arab invasion, the aristocracy reacted as the kings had been fearing: after the defeat of Guadalete cities and territories were left to their own devices, and resistance was only possible where local defences could be gathered. In the absence of any centralised authority the Visigothic aristocracy opted to

3 M. Brett and E. Fentress, *The Berbers* (Oxford, 1996), pp. 83–7.

4 P. Chalmeta, *Invasión e islamización: La sumisión de Hispania y la formación de al-Andalus* (Madrid, 1994).

5 A. Barbero and M. Vigil, *La formación del feudalismo en la Península Ibérica* (Barcelona, 1978), pp. 201–7; A. Isla, 'Conflictos internos y externos en el fin del reino visigodo', *Hispania*, 62 (2002), pp. 619–36.

safeguard their own interests. Local and personal pacts were established, which explain the variety of situations that the conquest engendered. Characteristically, these different outcomes expressed themselves in terms of ethnicity, of the assimilation into the Arab stock of some members of the aristocracy, while others preserved their indigenous identity even though they also converted to Islam at a very early stage.

Assimilation was the path followed by those who chose to collaborate with the conquerors from the very beginning. Among them the sons of Witiza – Arṭubās, Waqīla and Alamund – were the most outspoken partisans of the new order. As its beneficiaries they prospered in the aftermath of the conquest. Their wealth was based on the extensive lands inherited from their father, whose undisputed property was recognised by the Arabs. The senior brother, Arṭubās, is described as a great landowner, revered and respected by the conquerors, who entrusted to him the collection of taxes among the Christians. He was still alive several decades later, when the first Umayyad *amīr*, ʿAbd al-Raḥmān I (138–72/756–88), confiscated some of his extensive landholdings. Nothing is known of Arṭubās's offspring. If we are to believe the Arab sources the only descendants of this family were those of Sara, daughter of Alamund, who managed to preserve her father's extensive properties in the Seville region against the rapacity of her uncle Arṭubās. Sara was married twice, to prominent members of the Arab army, and her descendants became leading Arab families of Seville in later centuries, such as the Banū Ḥajjāj or the Banū Maslama. The unyielding system of Arab kinship, which was based on patrilineal descent, obscured the distant Visigothic ascendancy of these lineages, and in fact we would be unaware of their distinguished ancestry were it not for the fact that one of her descendants, Ibn al-Qūṭiyya (d. 361/971), wrote an account of the conquest in which the deeds of his great-grandmother were described in some detail.[6]

A similar case was that of Theodomir, a Visigothic *dux* who ruled in the south-east of the Peninsula, in a region which the Arabs named Tudmīr after him. At the time of the conquest Theodomir entered into a pact with the conquerors, a pact whose wording has been preserved in late compilations and which bears strong resemblances to similar post-conquest agreements in the Near East: in exchange for recognition of his rule and the guarantee of safety for his subjects and religion, Theodomir undertook to pay a certain amount of taxes in cash and kind to the Arabs. Whether the wording of this

6 Ibn al-Qūṭiya, *Ta'rīkh iftitāḥ al-Andalus*, ed. P. de Gayangos, E. Saavedra y F. Codera (Madrid, 1868), pp. 2–4.

pact is genuine or not, it is clear that Theodomir established a close relationship with the new rulers, which led to the marriage of his daughter to a member of the Arab army, one ʿAbd al-Jabbār ibn Khaṭṭāb. The descendants of this union were called the Banū Khaṭṭāb, and became a rich and influential family of local *ʿulamāʾ* until the end of Islamic rule in the region of Murcia in the eighth/thirteenth century.

In the decades after the conquest this kind of marriage alliance may have been quite common. Echoes of this practice reached even Rome, as witnessed by a letter written by Pope Hadrian around 785, in which he complained that in Hispania some who called themselves Catholics had no objection to marrying their daughters to the heathen breed. Bishops who met at a council held at Cordoba in 836 also condemned mixed unions. The concerns of the Church were fully justified, as marriage of indigenous women with members of the conquering army resulted in their integration into the rigid structures of Arab patrilineal kinship and their detachment from the social networks where the Church had hitherto maintained its influence.[7]

However, not all members of the Visigothic aristocracy who reached agreements with the conquerors were assimilated into Arab kinship. Some accounts in early Latin chronicles refer to diehards who continued to resist for several years after 92/711, sheltered in their domains in the rural areas.[8] Eventually they also came to terms with the conquerors, but they managed to preserve not only their realms but also their own distinctive identity. This was the case with Casius, a military man who was stationed in the Upper Ebro valley, on the northern frontier that the Visigothic kings had established against the restless northern populations. When the conquerors arrived in his domains Casius came to an agreement with them, and it is even claimed that he converted to Islam in Damascus at the hand of the caliph al-Walīd, becoming his *mawlā*. Be this as it may, the offspring of Casius, the so-called Banū Qasī, were Muslims, and in the two centuries following the conquest they ruled, with a high degree of independence, a territory which stood as a frontier (*thaghr*) against the northern Christian kingdoms.

7 *Monumenta Germaniae Historica, Epistolae Merowingici et Karolini. Aevi*, III/I, ed. E. Dummler and W. Gundlach (1892), p. 643. 'Concilium Cordubense', in *Corpus Scriptorum Muzarabicorum*, 2 vols., ed. I. Gil (Madrid, 1973), vol. I, p. 140. On the role of women in networks of kinship and power, see M. Marín, *Mujeres en al-Andalus* (Madrid, 2000), pp. 395–597.

8 *Crónica Mozárabe de 745*, ed. J. E. López Pereira (Saragossa, 1980), p. 54; *Crónica de Albelda*, in *Crónicas Asturianas*, ed. J. Gil, J. L. Moralejo and J. I. Ruiz de la Peña (Oviedo, 1985), p. 183.

Like the Banū Qasī, other powerful Muslim families of indigenous stock were in command of rural districts in different parts of the Peninsula. Their agreements with the conquerors guaranteed their rule over territories, which included fortifications and villages (*castris et vicis*) where they collected taxes which were forwarded to the Arab governors, provided the latter had enough political and military resources to enforce their authority. Arab chroniclers of the fourth/tenth century called them *muwalladūn* in the accounts of the endless struggles that Umayyad *amīrs* faced in order to subdue them, as will be seen below.

Although most written Arab sources from the third and fourth (ninth–tenth) centuries in Umayyad Cordoba insist that the conquest had been accomplished following the legal rules regarding territories conquered 'by the force of arms' (*ʿanwatan*), such claims were designed to support legal claims based on Mālikī law, which decreed that a territory conquered on these conditions belonged to the Muslim community. The descendants of the conquerors upheld a different interpretation, however: the conquest had been carried out by means of ad hoc agreements, and the lands they possessed had been acquired through dealings with the indigenous population and not as concessions that the Umayyad *amīrs* had bestowed upon them in their capacity as administrators of the lands of the Muslim community. As we have seen, this view of the conquest was the closest to reality, but late Umayyad historiography and legal opinions staunchly rejected it, as it also denied central government the control of that fifth (*khums*) of the lands that legally would have corresponded to the *amīrs* had al-Andalus been conquered 'by the force of arms'.[9]

It is doubtful, therefore, whether the way the conquest had in fact been conducted justified the collection of large tax revenues for the caliphal administration – and even more doubtful that tax receipts ever reached Damascus. If coinage is an indicator of tax-collection, the limited number of coins issued by the first governors shows a poor fiscal harvest. Soon after his arrival Mūsā ibn Nuṣayr coined gold pieces in Hispania which were imitations of the Byzantine *solidi* from North Africa. These early coins date from as early as 93/711f., and give testimony to a conquest led by a strong and self-aware military command. They bear Latin inscriptions which translate the Muslim profession of faith, 'There is no god but God': *Non Deus Nisi Deus Non Deus Alius*. Soon the model changed, incorporating bilingual legends in Latin and Arabic, which proves that al-Andalus, the name given by the conquerors to

9 E. Manzano Moreno, 'Las fuentes árabes sobre la conquista de al-Andalus: Una nueva interpretación', *Hispania*, 202 (1999), pp. 389–432.

Hispania, was already in use by 98/716f. Finally, the coins issued in al-Andalus adopted the reformed model of the caliph ʿAbd al-Malik in 102/720f. However, gold coinage stopped in 127/744f. The governors minted silver *dirhams* more or less regularly, but they do not seem to have circulated in large amounts, judging from the number of preserved specimens.[10]

The extent to which the conquest of al-Andalus may have been unprofitable for the caliphal treasury is further confirmed by the fact that most of its governors were appointed by rulers of Ifrīqiya. The caliph ʿUmar II (r. 99–101/717–20) even considered the idea of abandoning the new territory altogether, possibly because the resources it yielded to the caliphate did not justify the deployment of the army in such a distant land.[11] However, ʿUmar was convinced to give up his plans, and instead he appointed al-Samḥ ibn Mālik al-Khawlānī as governor of al-Andalus. His short tenure (100–2/718–21) was important for two reasons: first, he ordered the first tax census of the whole province; and second, he led the first Arab expeditions into southern France. Both decisions had the same aim (to improve the meagre resources yielded by the province) but in the long run their success was uneven. Military campaigns in southern France achieved the occupation of Septimania, the last stronghold of Visigothic rule, which served as a base for further raids into the land where Carolingian rule was emerging. However, the crushing defeat of one of these expeditions at Poitiers by the Carolingian Charles Martel in 732 and the conquest of Narbonne by the Carolingians in 759 marked the end of these adventures beyond the Pyrenees. In contrast, the organisation of the tax administration had far-reaching consequences. Al-Samḥ's was the first of the three surveys conducted under the rule of the governors. They were probably carried out every fifteen years, as in other parts of the empire.[12] Once the expansion was over, the conquerors began to turn to a more systematic exploitation of the new province. The achievement of this goal was possible through the invaluable help of fresh troops, who arrived in al-Andalus in the dramatic circumstances of a revolt, which shook the foundations of Arab rule in the west.

10 A. Balaguer, *Las emisiones transicionales árabe-musulmanas de Hispania* (Barcelona, 1976), pp. 105–11. On the name 'al-Andalus', see J. Vallvé, *La división territorial de la España Musulmana* (Madrid, 1986), pp. 17–62; F. Corriente, *Léxico estándar y andalusí del* Dīwān *de Ibn Quzmān* (Saragossa, 1993), pp. 22–3.

11 Ibn al-Qūṭiya, *Ta'rīkh*, p. 12; *Akhbār majmūʿa*, ed. and trans. E. Lafuente Alcántara (Madrid, 1867), pp. 23/34.

12 *Crónica de 754*, pp. 84, 104, 122. After the first census by al-Samḥ, the other two were conducted by governors ʿUqba ibn al-Ḥajjāj (117–23/735 or 736–40) and Yūsuf al-Fihrī (130–8/747–56). Note that an interval of fifteen years fits the periods of tenure of these three governors.

The Berber revolt

The earliest surviving account of the conquest of North Africa was written not by a chronicler but by a jurist, Ibn ʿAbd al-Ḥakam (d. 257/870), who belonged to the Mālikī circles of Egypt. One of the pieces of information he included in his work was supported by other Mālikī jurists and described the submission of the Lawāta Berbers from Cyrenaica during the first campaign led by ʿAmr ibn al-ʿĀṣ. Under the terms of a pact they agreed to pay a tax (*jizya*) of 13,000 *dīnārs*, but in order to gather this cash they were given permission to sell their own children. This historical account bears witness to the interest of Egyptian religious scholars in the narratives of the early conquests as a means to justify certain legal interpretations, in this case how to deal with heathen peoples. In this connection, there is no doubt that some Egyptian *fuqahāʾ* (jurists) deemed the buying and selling of certain Berbers as lawful.[13] There was no lack of arguments for this position: the difficulties of the conquest, the paganism – or, at least, the uncertain religious persuasion of some tribes – and the number of revolts that the Berbers had led against Arab rule all justified their harsh treatment. Slaves taken in triumphant campaigns were counted by the thousand, and once the conquests were over their flow to the east did not stop. Even the ʿAbbāsid caliph al-Manṣūr (r. 136–58/754–75) is reported to have been enraged when at the time of his accession he did not receive the usual shipment of slaves as a gift from Ifrīqiya; its governor, ʿAbd al-Raḥmān ibn Ḥabīb, claimed that all the population of his province had become Muslims and that their enslavement was therefore unlawful.[14]

These harsh conditions contrasted with the fact that many Berber chieftains had agreed to join the Arab armies as auxiliary troops. They had taken part in the conquest of al-Andalus, where they had settled in extensive regions in the eastern and central Peninsula, or had joined the ranks of the Arab army stationed in North Africa. These Berbers realised now that their submission (*islām*) had been 'employed as an instrument of government', and they decided to resist.[15] When the Arab governor of Ifrīqiya, Yazīd ibn Abī Muslim, ordered his Berber body-troops to be tattooed, as was the custom

13 Ibn ʿAbd al-Ḥakam (d. 257/870), *Futūḥ Miṣr wa-l-Magrib wa-l-Andalus*, ed. C. C. Torrey (New Haven, 1922), pp. 170–1; R. Brunschvig, 'Ibn ʿAbdalhakam et la conquête de l'Afrique du Nord par les Arabes', *Annales de l'Institut d'Etudes Orientales Université d'Alger*, 6 (1942–7).

14 M. Talbi, *L'émirat aghlabide (184–296/800–909): Histoire politique* (Paris, 1966), pp. 25–35.

15 M. Brett, 'The Arab conquests and the rise of Islam in North Africa', in J. D. Fage and R. Oliver (eds.), *The Cambridge history of Africa*, 8 vols. (Cambridge, 1978), vol. II: *From c. 500 BC to AD 1050*, p. 512.

with slaves, they killed him (102/720). Twelve years later, in al-Andalus, a Berber called Munuza, who was stationed in the garrison posts near the Pyrenees, rebelled against the governor of Cordoba due to the oppression suffered by his people.[16] Munuza was easily disposed of, but his revolt shows that al-Kāhina's vision was waning as former subjects were becoming restless foes. An account highly sympathetic to Berber claims describes an attempt made by ten military chieftains to transmit their grievances to the caliph Hishām (r. 105–25/724–43): they felt utterly discriminated against by governors who, favouring the Arabs, humiliated them in the distribution of booty, deployed Berber soldiers in sieges while the Arabs were retained at the rear and, finally, imposed harsh levies in cattle and slave-girls on Berber tribes. The petitioners waited in vain for an audience with the caliph and, once they became convinced that their complaints would never receive attention, they decided to raise the standard of rebellion in 122/740.[17]

It was a long and complex revolt. Its first leader was Maysara al-Madgharī, allegedly one of the frustrated ambassadors to the caliph Hishām. Under his command the rebels occupied Tangier and most of today's Morocco. Soon afterwards the rebels decided to depose him and appointed Khālid ibn Ḥumayd al-Zanātī as their leader. An Arab army sent by the Ifrīqiyan governor 'Ubayd Allāh ibn al-Ḥabḥāb was annihilated at what came to be known as the battle of the Nobles (123/740) due to the large number of principals killed on the field. By then the rebellion had extended to al-Andalus: three columns of Berber troops marched against Toledo, Cordoba and the Straits.[18] Alarmed by the news coming from the west, the caliph Hishām dispatched the imperial troops of the Syrian army (*jund*) led by Kulthūm ibn 'Iyāḍ, who also recruited troops in Egypt. The army, plagued by dissent between its Syrian commanders and North African Arabs, was routed in the battle of the river Sebou, another disaster in the long list of military calamities that filled the caliphate of Hishām.[19]

The outcome of this defeat was very different in al-Andalus and North Africa. Most of the remnants of the Syrian army gathered in the garrison harbour of Ceuta. Surrounded by enemies who denied any possibility of return, the survivors had no choice but to cross the Straits towards al-Andalus. An initial

16 *Crónica de 754*, p. 96.
17 *The history of al-Ṭabarī*, vol. XV: *The crisis of the early caliphate*, trans. R. S. Humphreys (Albany, 1990), pp. 20–2 [2815–16].
18 *Crónica de 754*, pp. 108–10.
19 K. Y. Blankinship, *The end of the jihād state: The reign of Hishām ibn 'Abd al-Malik and the collapse of the Umayyads* (New York, 1994), pp. 206–12.

refusal to admit them by the governor, ʿAbd al-Malik ibn Qaṭan, changed to a conditional approval once he realised that he lacked the resources necessary to quell the Berber rebels threatening his own rule. The arrival of the Syrians in the Peninsula helped to crush this revolt, but they soon made it clear that, contrary to the governor's desires, they had no intention of returning to their own country or of crossing the Straits again to face the rebellion that was still active on the African shores. They decided to settle in al-Andalus, a move that found staunch opposition from the early conquerors. The Syrians finally got the upper hand, but only after a decade of fighting which coincided with the fall of the Umayyad caliphate in the east and the de facto independence of the province.

The conditions that regulated the final settlement of the Syrian army had far-reaching consequences. In al-Andalus the *jund* kept its original organisation of troops divided into a number of army districts. The original names of these districts were maintained, and each of them was allotted a territorial circumscription. Thus, the *jund* of Ḥimṣ settled in the province (*kūra*) of Seville; Damascus received the *kūra* of Elvira; Palestine the *kūra* of Algeciras; Qinnasrīn the *kūra* of Jaén; Jordan the *kūra* of Rayyo whereas the troops of the *jund* of Egypt were divided among the *kūra*s of Niebla and Tudmīr. In these conscriptions the troops did not remain garrisoned in cities; they settled in villages (*qaryā*; pl. *qurā*) where they were in charge of the collection of taxes from the indigenous populations: a fixed amount of the tax receipts were forwarded to the governor's coffers in Cordoba, while the rest was kept by the troops as their means of living. Whenever the army was mustered for an expedition, both the commanders and the rank and file received stipends. By the terms of this arrangement the Syrians were accommodated and the rights of the early conquerors, who had become landowners and were obliged to pay the tithe (*ʿushr*), were respected. When the Umayyad ʿAbd al-Raḥmān ibn Muʿāwiya arrived in al-Andalus a few years later, the foundations of the fiscal administration of this territory had already been laid.[20]

Meanwhile, what remained of Umayyad North Africa was plunged into chaos. After their victory at Sebou the rebels advanced eastwards to Qayrawān, gaining the support of Berber groups from Ifrīqiya led by ʿUkkāsha ibn Ayyūb al-Fazārī, perhaps a Persian who had deserted the ranks of the Syrian army. The capital would have fallen to the rebels had it not been for the victories gained at its gates by the former governor of Egypt, Ḥanẓala

20 E. Manzano Moreno, 'The settlement and organization of the Syrian junds in al-Andalus', in M. Marín (ed.), *The formation of al-Andalus*, vol. I: *History and society* (Aldershot, 1998), pp. 85–115.

ibn Ṣafwān, in 125/743. But the times of hasty expansions and recoveries were definitively over. Caliphal rule never extended again beyond the Zab. Western North Africa became a distant territory populated by countless tribes whose chieftains were convinced that al-Kāhina was wrong when she had predicted that Berbers were doomed to assimilation into the imperial scheme of the Arabs. Consequently, local dynasties replaced caliphal governors. The origins of these dynasties were very varied – some indigenous, some founded by oriental exiles – and their ideological justification is not always clear, as it is possible that their dogmas were not so well established at this period as later accounts would lead us to believe. But it is difficult to overlook the fact that eastern preachers and fugitives, sharing, in one way or another, the deep impact of the new order, succeeded where caliphal armies had previously failed.

The arrival of eastern ideologies and dynasties

The last governor appointed by the Umayyads in Ifrīqiya was Ḥanẓala ibn Ṣafwān, who was deposed in 127/745, following the assassination in the east of the caliph al-Walīd II; a year later Abu 'l-Khaṭṭār al-Kalbī, the Umayyad governor of al-Andalus, was also overthrown by the army. Another coincidence is that the political vacuum was filled by members of the same family: in North Africa ʿAbd al-Raḥmān ibn Ḥabīb had been the leader of the coup that expelled Ḥanẓala, while in al-Andalus his cousin ʿAbd al-Raḥmān ibn Yūsuf al-Fihrī became governor with the support of the army. Both were descendants of the celebrated conqueror ʿUqba ibn Nāfiʿ, whose offspring had emerged as one of the most influential families in the region after his heroic death.[21] Both attempted to establish independent rule during the years of turmoil caused by the fall of the Umayyads in the east and the coming of the ʿAbbāsids. Both of them failed. In the case of the self-proclaimed governor of Ifrīqiya, family disputes prevented him from consolidating his dynasty as he was assassinated by his brothers in 137/755. Three years later (140/757) Qayrawān was plundered by the Berber tribe of the Warfajjūma, who had been summoned by one of the factions struggling for power.[22]

Meanwhile, the arrival in 137/755 of an Umayyad, ʿAbd al-Raḥmān ibn Muʿāwiya, frustrated the plans of Yūsuf al-Fihrī. His rule in al-Andalus was

21 P. Guichard, *al-Andalus: Estructura antropológica de una sociedad islámica en Occidente* (Barcelona, 1976; repr. Granada, 1998), pp. 526–45.

22 G. Marçais, *La berbérie musulmane et l'Orient au moyen âge* (Paris, 1946), pp. 43–53.

an extraordinary achievement. He was a grandson of caliph Hishām who had escaped the manslaughter of his family that was ordered by the ʿAbbāsids in the east. A young man in his twenties, when ʿAbd al-Raḥmān came ashore in al-Andalus he was met by an army whose leaders had never seen him before but who, nevertheless, were ready to fight for his cause. Many of these leaders were Umayyad clients (*mawālī*), who had arrived in al-Andalus in the ranks of the Syrian *jund*. Among the factions bidding for power in these years they displayed sufficient cohesion and political shrewdness to be able to convince other *jund* commanders to join their ranks in order to defeat Yūsuf al-Fihrī. The descendants of these *mawālī* became the backbone of the Umayyad administration for more than two centuries. Generations of the Banū Abī ʿAbda, the Banū Khālid or the Banū Bukht – to name just a few of these families – were appointed as viziers, generals or district governors, and all of them could boast that their ancestors had supported the claims of ʿAbd al-Raḥmān I when he arrived as a destitute fugitive.[23]

After his proclamation ʿAbd al-Raḥmān I (r. 138–72/756–88) had to curb a number of internal rebellions. Some were led by members of the Fihrid family or by ambitious leaders of the *jund*, and others were ill-fated attempts to extend ʿAbbāsid rule to this distant land. The most serious of these rebellions, however, affected the Berber tribes who had settled in central al-Andalus. It lasted several years (*c*. 151–60/768–77, the chronology is uncertain), until its leader, a certain Shaqyā al-Miknāsī, was killed by some of his supporters, perhaps fearing the authority he commanded among their fellow tribesmen. According to the cursory accounts of the sources, Shaqyā pretended to be a descendant of the Prophet because his mother was called Fāṭima, like the celebrated daughter of Muḥammad. It is difficult to draw any conclusive interpretation of what the preaching of Shaqyā stood for, but it seems that if it had any Islamic sectarian influence, it was Shīʿism that coloured it. In contrast, Khārijism seems to have lost momentum among the Berbers of al-Andalus. Even though the great rebellion of 122/740 is portrayed by some sources as inspired by Ṣufrism, later heterodox movements stirred by Khārijism were very few and unimportant.[24]

Quite the opposite happened in North Africa, where the political seeds of Khārijism took strong root among populations whose tribal structures were fertile ground for this movement. Sources depict two stages in the Islamisation

23 M. Méouak, *Pouvoir souverain, administration centrale et élites politiques dans l'Espagne umayyade (IIe–IVe/VIIIe–Xe siècles)* (Helsinki, 1999), pp. 74–7.

24 M. I. Fierro, *La heterodoxia en al-Andalus durante el período omeya* (Madrid, 1987), pp. 28–30, 39–41.

of the region. The first coincided with the Arab conquest, when some governors strove to extend the preaching of Islam among the Berbers with the help of numerous *tābiʿūn*, a name given to prestigious Muslims who had met Companions of the Prophet and could therefore boast a first-hand knowledge of his life and deeds. However, if we are to believe the accounts claiming that the great Berber rebellion of Maysara was inspired by Khārijism, these orthodox agents had been replaced by missionaries sent from Baṣra, the headquarters of the movement in the first decades of the second century AH.

The beginnings of the agitation by these missionaries are far from clear. Late sources describe the arrival in the west of a group of preachers with no weapon other than a message, which associated salvation with political action. The preference shown towards these missionaries in marginal regions allowed them to give up the practice of concealment (*taqiyya*), which caliphal repression had made obligatory in the east, and to turn their message into one that called for open rebellion, which found enthusiastic adherence among countless supporters. Oppressed audiences were receptive to an ideology that rejected the notion that Muslim authority had to be restricted to a single family, the Qurashite Umayyads, who, as holders of the caliphate, had been responsible for all the grievances suffered by North African populations. The loathing of tyranny and injustice was accompanied in Khārijite discourses by a historical interpretation, which deemed the unfair treatment of the Berbers to be the consequence of the wrongdoings of the caliphs who had ruled the *umma* since the first civil war (*fitna*).

The fading of caliphal administration in western North Africa allowed for the re-emergence of tribal leaders who, sources claim, profited from the ideological framework of Khārijism to consolidate their rule. Some narratives of the origins of these leaders explicitly link them with the rebellion of 122/740. This was the case of the Banū Midrār, who defined themselves as Khārijites and whose ancestor is said to have belonged to the tribe of Miknāsa and to have fought in the ranks of Maysara al-Madgharī. With a number of fellow tribesmen and believers he marched from Tangier southwards, to the region of Tafilalt, where he founded the city of Sijilmāsa in 140/757. In the following decades the city was surrounded by walls and endowed with a mosque. Its strategic location on the western route connecting the Maghrib with the rest of Africa stimulated its growth in the third and fourth (ninth–tenth) centuries as slave and gold trade with the Sudan and mining in the neighbouring regions attracted a mixed population of Arabs, Berbers, Jews and black Africans.

Sources also claim that a certain Ṣāliḥ ibn Ṭarif had fought in the army of Maysara, along with his father, who had taken part in the early conquest of al-Andalus. This Ṣāliḥ is credited with the foundation of the Bargawāṭa sect among the Maṣmūda and other tribes settled on the plain of Tamasna, south of the river Bou Regreg in modern Morocco. In this milieu he decided to present himself as a new prophet. He therefore produced a Qur'ān written in Berber and laid down a number of prescriptions on fasting, praying and dealings with unbelievers, which were kept secret until his grandson, Yūnus ibn Ilyās (227–71 / 842–84), decided that the time was ripe for preaching them in public.[25] Although this account is probably spurious, it reflects the perception of the Berber revolt as a reference for legitimacy which set the foundations of a dynasty that managed to rule on the Atlantic shores of Morocco until the time of the Almohads.

The Ibāḍī dynasty of Tāhert was the only Khārijite rule that fostered a doctrinal development in the Maghrib at this period. Its origins are associated with the arrival in Ifrīqiya of five 'bearers of learning' (*ḥamalat al-ʿilm*) around 139/757.[26] All of them came from Baṣra where they had received doctrinal training which stressed the need for active and communal adherence (*walā'*) to godly principles of justice, and rejection (*barā'a*) of the iniquities of Islamic rule as it had been exercised since the times of caliph ʿUthmān. Their success in getting Khārijite doctrines accepted by tribal chieftains earned them wide support, which soon became military strength. At the head of a tribal army one of these 'bearers of learning', Abu 'l-Khaṭṭāb al-Maʿāfirī, expelled the Warfajjūma from Qayrawān in 140/758. For a moment it seemed that a Khārijite imamate would be established in the Islamic capital of North Africa, but an army led by the ʿAbbāsid general Ibn al-Ashʿath expelled the Ibāḍīs and recovered Ifrīqiya for the caliphal administration in 144/761.

Despite this setback, one of the Ibāḍī missionaries, the Persian ʿAbd al-Raḥmān ibn Rustam, managed to recover the tribal following that the doctrine had attracted in previous years. Far away from the reach of ʿAbbāsid governors in Qayrawān, whose troops refused to get involved in campaigns beyond the Zab, he was acclaimed as imam in the recently founded city of Tāhert, near the ancient Roman settlement of Tiaret, in modern-day Algeria. Family and political links with some tribal groups, such as the Banū Ifran, who had retreated to the west in the face of ʿAbbāsid advance, allowed ʿAbd

25 M. Talbi, 'Hérésie, acculturation et nationalisme des Berbères Bargawāṭa', in *Actes du Premier Congrès d'Etudes des Cultures Mediterranéennes d'Influence Arabo-Berbère* (Algiers, 1973), pp. 217–33, repr. in M. Talbi, *Études d'histoire ifriqiyenne et de la civilisation musulmane médiévale* (Tunis, 1982), pp. 81–104.

26 W. Schwartz, *Die Anfänge der Ibaditen in Nordafrika: Der Beitrag einer islamischen Minderheit zur Ausbreitung des Islams* (Wiesbaden, 1983), pp. 105–18.

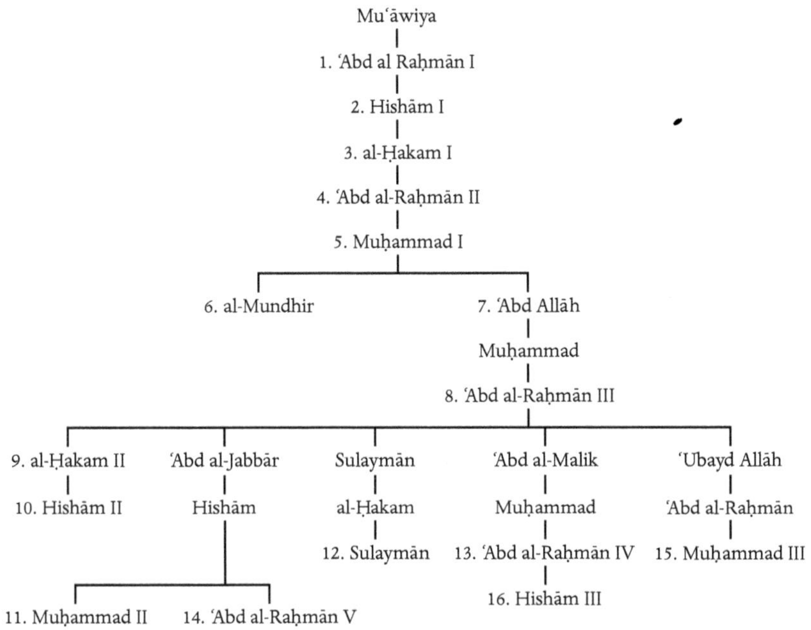

9. The Umayyads of Spain.
After P. M. Holt, A. V. S. Lambton and B. Lewis, *The Cambridge history of Islam*, vol. 1B, 1977, p. 736. Copyright Cambridge University Press, reproduced with permission.

al-Raḥmān ibn Rustam to proclaim himself imam in around 160/777. His rule was not so much territorial as based on the allegiance of a number of tribes whose leaders respected his authority and in turn were consulted on certain matters.

The Ibāḍī imamate had a seat, Tāhert, but no clear boundaries: it stretched loosely from the border with Tlemcen in the west to the Jabal Nafūsa in the east, occasionally also including Berbers from Tripolitania – as the *imām al-muslimīn* was only concerned with the rule of justice and the well-being of believers. The accessible and simple lifestyle, a genuine concern for the poor and the vastness of his wisdom lent ʿAbd al-Raḥmān ibn Rustam widespread recognition as the imam who fulfilled the Khārijite programme of moral rule. This programme had to be somewhat modified in 168/784 when ʿAbd al-Raḥmān died and his son, ʿAbd al-Wahhāb, succeeded him. Dynastic rule had replaced the choice of the believers, and controversy naturally arose. Those who claimed that the son of the best Muslim was the best Muslim himself allegedly gained the backing of Baṣran arbitrators, but some were not persuaded and abandoned their allegiance to ʿAbd al-Wahhāb, becoming the al-Nukkāriyya branch of Ibāḍism. This schism did not prevent Rustamid imams from continuing to transmit authority through the offspring of the dynasty for more than a century. However, the times of uprisings were also over and the rulers of Tāhert showed no apparent interest in further expansion in the neighbouring lands.

The map that emerged in western North Africa during the first decades of the second century was completed with the dynasty of the Idrīsids. Its origins are also linked to the arrival of an Eastern fugitive, called Idrīs ibn ʿAbd Allāh. He was a relative of al-Ḥusayn ibn ʿAlī, a descendant of ʿAlī ibn Abī Ṭālib, who had rebelled against the caliph al-Manṣūr under the banner of the greater claim of his family to rule the Muslim community and had been easily defeated near Mecca in 169/786. His cousin fled to the Maghrib, where he found refuge among the Awraba Berbers who lived around the ancient Roman city of Volubilis (Ar. Walīla).[27] The vexing question of how this Berber tribe came to acknowledge the superiority of Idrīs's lineage and be prepared to proclaim him imam in 172/789 is difficult to answer. Leaving aside the unclear ideas of the Andalusian heretic Shaqyā al-Miknāsī, this was the first time that the charisma associated with the descendants of ʿAlī ibn Abī Ṭālib was recognised in the Maghrib. At this stage Berbers were only familiar with the straightforward teachings of Khārijism, but late sources claim that the tribal chieftain who harboured Idrīs, the Awraba leader Isḥāq ibn Muḥammad ibn ʿAbd al-Ḥāmid, was a Muʿtazilite. It is doubtful whether at this early period this school of theological thought had reached this remote corner of the Muslim world, but it has been argued that Muʿtazilite beliefs were incorporated into Shīʿism very quickly, and that the proclamation of Idrīs as imam might reflect an early infiltration of Shīʿite missionaries seeking the overthrow of the ʿAbbāsids by turning the Maghrib into a new Khurāsān. But if this preaching actually took place, it only yielded the establishment of a dynasty, the Idrīsids, who notoriously lacked a strong Shīʿite doctrine. In contrast, a hundred years later a new movement preached in North Africa on behalf of ʿAlid claims – the one that led to the proclamation of the Fāṭimid caliphs – bore the sound ideological contents that characterised Shīʿism but which are conspicuously missing in the making of the Idrīsid dynasty.

27 A. Akerraz, 'Recherches sur les niveaux islamiques de Volubilis', in P. Cressier and M. García-Arenal (eds.), *Genèse de la ville islamique en al-Andalus et au Maghreb occidental* (Madrid, 1998), pp. 295–304.

The extraordinary career of Idrīs ibn ʿAbd Allāh culminated in the Maghrib with a short rule that was no less remarkable. He laid the foundations of Fez, near Volubilis, and also began territorial expansion to the south and east of his realm. When he was killed in 175/791, allegedly poisoned by an agent sent by the caliph Hārūn al-Rashīd, his Berber concubine, Kanza, was pregnant; several months later a child was born, and the supporters of the new dynasty were ready to endure a long minority which lasted eleven years until the child was proclaimed as Idrīs II in 187/803. The narrative of his rule suspiciously insists that he followed his father's footsteps by fostering the growth of Fez and undertaking an expansive policy towards the High Atlas, the Sūs al-Aqṣā and Tlemcen. When he died in 213/828 his domains were divided among his sons. Thus the Maghrib of the Idrīsids became a mosaic of petty principalities plagued by internal rivalries but with all of their rulers claiming descent from the prestigious ancestor, whose Sharīfian origins became a landmark in the process of Islamisation of the region.[28]

In the complex shaping of Islamic North Africa, Ifrīqiya remained a stronghold of caliphal rule. After having escaped the Khārijite tide, Qayrawān was firmly in the hands of ʿAbbāsid governors thanks to the victories of Ibn al-Ashʿath over the Ibāḍīs in 144/761. By then the province had become a de facto border against the potential rivals who had mushroomed in the Maghrib during the preceding decades. Instructions to fortify Qayrawān, the arrival of considerable numbers of troops and the appointment of experienced officials such as those from the family of the Muhallabids, who provided five governors between 155/772 and 178/794, show the importance of this frontier province for the early ʿAbbāsids.

Although these governors managed to keep the Khārijite threat in check, they were less successful in extending their rule beyond the limits of a territory that in broad terms coincided with the old Byzantine province. Their capacity for action was severely curtailed by an army that became increasingly restless during these years due to internecine conflicts. Open rebellions of the *jund* in 178/794 and, particularly, 183/799 convinced the caliph Hārūn al-Rashīd of the intractability of the province and the ineffectiveness of sending governors who either became frustrated with prevailing conditions or were expelled by rebels. In 184/800 he accepted a request by Ibrāhīm ibn Aghlab, a military leader whose father had already acted as governor of Ifrīqiya in 148–50/765–8, and appointed him *amīr*. Under the terms of this arrangement Ibrāhīm seems to have agreed to

28 H. L. Beck, *L'image d'Idris II, ses descendants de Fes et la politique sharifienne des sultans marinides (656–869/1258–1465)* (Leiden, 1989), pp. 28–48.

forward a fixed amount of 40,000 *dīnārs* to the caliphal treasury every year in exchange for making his rule hereditary. With the hallmark of ʿAbbāsid legitimacy – all the Ifrīqiyan *amīrs* seem to have received investiture from Baghdad – the Aghlabids managed to rule the westernmost territory in which the caliphs could claim recognition for more than a century.[29]

The creation of the new societies

The conquest of North Africa and al-Andalus took the Arabs to the western and southern shores of the Mediterranean basin. In a celebrated work published in 1937 the Belgian scholar H. Pirenne deemed this expansion the turning-point that gave the final blow to the legacy of the late Roman empire.[30] Networks of exchange and political bonds had survived the upheavals of the fifth and sixth centuries, but in Pirenne's view the coming of Islam disrupted the ancient unity of the Mediterranean and produced the landlocked landscape that was the hallmark of the European Middle Ages. As is always the case with visionary theses, Pirenne's has attracted a considerable amount of criticism since its inception, but has managed to survive, perhaps not as the grandiose explanation of long-term processes that its author had intended, but at least as an accurate perception of some symptoms prevailing in the Dark Ages which saw the emergence of the new societies that followed the Arab conquests.

One of these symptoms rightly singled out by Pirenne was the shrinking pattern of exchange throughout the Mediterranean in the seventh and eighth centuries. Contrary to what the Belgian scholar thought, this decline was not caused by the Arabs, as it clearly pre-dates their arrival, but, contrary to what some of his critics have claimed, the conquests did not produce a homogeneous realm where trade connections flourished all of a sudden.[31] From the seventh century onwards – or even earlier in some inland areas – archaeologists find growing evidence of a general withdrawal from trading circuits in the western Mediterranean. Pottery is a good indicator of this trend. In the Vandal and Byzantine periods industrial kilns located in modern-day Tunisia produced massive amounts of a pottery known as African red slip, which is

29 Talbi, *L'emirat aghlabide*, pp. 89–116. Talbi's remains the classic work on the history of the Aghlabid dynasty. Essential critical remarks on its contents and approach in J. Wansbrough, 'On recomposing the Islamic history of North Africa', *JRAS* (1969).

30 H. Pirenne, *Mahomet et Charlemagne* (Paris and Brussels, 1937).

31 D. C. Dennett, 'Pirenne and Muhammad', in A. Havighurst (ed.), *The Pirenne thesis: Analysis, criticism and revision* (Boston, 1958), pp. 84–101.

found throughout the whole Mediterranean basin. Suddenly these wares were replaced by local manufactures in urban and rural sites, reflecting a contraction of long-distance networks of exchange. In the early period following the conquests this trend did not change: kilns producing African red slip disappeared and the archaeological record dating from the second/eighth century, particularly in al-Andalus (North African data are more sketchy) provides no evidence of any substantial number of distinctive forms comparable to contemporary wares from the Near East.[32]

The conquerors therefore did not disrupt prevailing conditions in the territories they settled, but rather adjusted to emerging situations.[33] This adaptation allowed for a slow rearrangement of social and economic patterns, a transformation which ran so deep in the functioning of western Muslim societies that by the late third/ninth century the legacy of Late Antiquity was not easily recognisable in them. This process is fairly noticeable in the territorial configuration of the new conquests. In the western lands the collapse of sea routes had left coastal harbours as mere shadows of their former splendour. In contrast, inland sites experienced a demand which could benefit from local or regional trading circuits, as they were not so dependent on long-distance relations. The pattern is reflected in North Africa by the foundations of Qayrawān, Tāhert and Fez; in al-Andalus, where the Arabs took up the existing urban network rather than creating new cities from scratch, inland Cordoba soon became the residence of the governors, while Seville, Mérida, Toledo and Saragossa were the only cities worthy of the name. The decline of Carthage, Tangier, Tarragona or Valencia, to name just a few cases of formerly thriving cities whose importance diminished in the aftermath of the conquest, confirms the crisis of some coastal urban centres in the early stages of Arab rule.

This picture slowly changed during the second half of the third/ninth century when long-distance relations, unquestionably fostered by the slave trade, which in many cases was the same as naval piracy, favoured the growth of coastal cities. The case of Sousse, in Ifrīqiya, is paradigmatic. To its early *ribāṭ*, which was designed to defend the coast against attacks by the Byzantine navy, was added a great mosque in 236/850, thus reflecting the conversion of the garrison-city into a busy port where trade activities took the place of military ones. A similar

32 M. Mackensen, *Die Spätantiken Sigillata und Lampentöpfereien von El Mahrine (Nordtunesien)* (Munich, 1992), p. 492.

33 W. H. C. Frend, 'The end of Byzantine North Africa: Some evidence of transitions', *Bulletin Archéologique du Comité des Travaux Historiques et Scientifiques*, 19, 2 (1985).

conversion of a *ribāṭ* into a flourishing merchant town is seen in the case of Pechina in south-eastern al-Andalus from 271/884 onwards.[34]

During the early stages of Arab rule, however, inland cities were the main centres of demand. Some of them underwent rapid growth, boosted by having been selected as seats of power. The Umayyads changed the physiognomy of Cordoba by erecting new buildings and fostering its extraordinary expansion. An existing palace and the site of a nearby Christian church became respectively the *qaṣr* (Sp. *alcázar*), where the dynasty made its residence, and the mosque built by ʿAbd al-Raḥmān I in the final years of his life (*c.* 170/786). The two buildings faced each other, and were enlarged by ʿAbd al-Raḥmān's successors, who were well aware of their meaning as emblems of the dynasty. The *alcázar* was not only the main seat of Umayyad power, crowded with secretaries and officials of an administration that was becoming increasingly complex and inspired by eastern models at the time of ʿAbd al-Raḥmān II (r. 206–38/822–52), it was also a symbolic enclosure that housed the graves of the successive *amīrs*, who were buried within its walls. The nearby mosque also reflects this sense of dynastic continuity, as the original design consisting of double-arched naves was respected by all ʿAbd al-Raḥmān I's successors, who enlarged it during the following two centuries in order to meet the growing number of Cordoban Muslims. This conservatism went so far as to preserve the original orientation of the *qibla* in the full knowledge that it was totally misplaced and not properly aligned towards Mecca.

The expansion of Cordoba soon surpassed the limits of the Visigothic city.[35] Among the suburbs that sprang up outside the city walls was Shaqunda, which lay on the left bank of the Guadalquivir river opposite the *alcázar* and was connected to the city by a Roman bridge which had been restored in the aftermath of the conquest. The population of Shaqunda consisted of artisans and traders who were attracted by the growing demand from palatine officials and soldiers from the neighbouring *alcázar*. The relations between this emerging urban class and the Umayyad *amīr* al-Ḥakam

34 A. Lézine, *Deux villes d'Ifriqiya: Études d'archéologie, d'urbanisme de demographie. Sousse-Tunis* (Paris, 1971), pp. 17–32. Brett, 'The Arab conquests', pp. 551–2. M. Acién, F. Castillo and R. Martínez, 'Excavación de un barrio artesanal en Pechina', *Archéologie Islamique*, 1 (1990), pp. 147–68. On urban growth in the Maghrib al-aqṣā, see S. Ennahid, 'Beyond al-Basra: Settlement systems of medieval northern Morocco in archaeological and historical perspective', in N. L. Benco (ed.), *Anatomy of a medieval Islamic town: al-Basra, Morocco*, BAR Series 1234 (Oxford, 2004), pp. 79–91.

35 J. Murillo, M. T. Casal and E. Castro, 'Madinat Qurtuba: Aproximación al proceso de formación de la ciudad emiral y califal a partir de la información arqueológica', *Cuadernos de Madīnat al-Zahrā'*, 5 (2004), pp. 257–90.

I (180–206/796–822) became increasingly strained, due to the mounting tax demands decreed by this unpopular ruler. In 202/818 an incident between a craftsman and a soldier of the palatine guard sparked a fierce mutiny which led the inhabitants of Shaqunda to attack the *alcázar* with the aim of overthrowing al-Ḥakam and pillaging the palace. The uprising was defeated, brutal repression followed and al-Ḥakam ordered the destruction of Shaqunda, with strict orders that nothing was to be rebuilt there, a prohibition that apparently was duly respected by his successors.[36]

An unexpected outcome of the revolt of Shaqunda was that survivors were exiled, and some of them left al-Andalus for good. A group of outcasts crossed the Straits and settled in the Idrīsid city of Fez, on the riverbank opposite Idrīs I's original settlement. The arrival of these Andalusīs helped Idrīs II to consolidate the city his father had founded, which until then had been no more than a tribal agglomeration endowed with a mosque. This gave Fez its distinctive double-centred character with two quarters, the ʿIdwat al-Andalusiyyīn and what later became known as the ʿIdwat al-Qarawiyyīn.[37]

Fez was located at the crossroads of routes which linked the northern and southern regions of the extreme west (*Maghrib al-aqṣā*) and these with the rest of North Africa. The expansion of Idrīsid rule along these two axes shows that this choice was not accidental. The conquests led by Idrīs I and his son were aimed at controlling trade routes and natural resources, particularly the silver mines in the Atlas mountains, which allowed the early Idrīsids to coin *dirhams* in a number of mints scattered throughout their lands.[38] These coins were probably used to purchase the allegiance of tribal leaders, but also perhaps to assure the peaceful coexistence of the dynasty with the governors of Ifrīqiya. This may explain why Idrīsid coins show up alongside ʿAbbāsid pieces in hoards found in the Near East, the Caucasus and even Scandinavia – admittedly in small numbers, but nevertheless quite consistently. The lust for silver in the central lands of the caliphate during the early years of the third/ninth century was appeased with massive deliveries of *dirhams* which the governors of Ifrīqiya coined in their own province, but which they also received, perhaps as a tribute, from the Idrīsid lands. In contrast, Idrīsid *dirhams* are scarcely found in al-Andalus, and even less so in western Europe, a clear indication

36 New evidence for this episode in the recently uncovered Ibn Ḥayyān, *al-Sifr al-thānī min Kitāb al-muqtabis*, ed. M. A. Makki (Riyadh, 2003), pp. 140–74.

37 E. Lévi Provençal, 'La fondation de Fès', *Annales de l'Institut d'Études Orientales*, 4 (Algiers, 1938).

38 D. Eustache, *Corpus des dirhams idrīsites et contemporaines* (Rabat, 1970–1).

that ties between the two seaboards were virtually non-existent at this early period.[39]

The urban expansion of Fez has been described as the result of a conscious attempt to create a centre for Arabisation and Islamisation in the region with the help of immigrants from al-Andalus and Ifrīqiya. As such it may be compared to Tāhert, which under the aegis of the Rustamids seems to have kept a more distinctive Berber outlook. As described by Arab sources, the city lacked any central planning – it is unlikely that it was even walled – and was essentially an agglomeration of population clusters interspersed with mosques, whose inhabitants were of mixed origin who dealt with neighbouring Berber tribes. The main commodity traded at Tāhert was probably slaves from sub-Saharan Africa, and also raw materials such as gold.[40]

Founded at the early stages of the conquest, Qayrawān was a different sort of city. Although Arab sources describe ʿUqba ibn Nāfiʿ laying its foundations on a deserted spot frequented by wild animals, it is clear that a settlement had existed at least since Roman times. Its excellent strategic position dominated access to inland routes, making it a privileged garrisoned enclave for the early Arab expeditions. At the time of its foundation ʿUqba gave Qayrawān a mosque and a residence for governors (*dār al-imāra*), which were also built opposite each other. It is not clear whether Arab troops were accommodated in the city as in the *amṣār* of Kūfa and Baṣra, but the existence of several quarters bearing Arab tribal names points to a settlement of troops. Despite the internal turmoil of its early period, the city grew as markets were organised and impressive hydraulic works ensured the water supply. After demolishing and rebuilding the primitive mosque attributed to ʿUqba on several occasions, the Aghlabid ruler Ziyādat Allāh decided to rebuild it in 221/836, following a regular scheme that is still visible today in the present building.

It is telling that the Aghlabid rulers also faced revolts by the inhabitants of Qayrawān and that they decided to raze the walls that had surrounded the city during the decades of upheaval of the second/eighth century. Restless opposition within the city and the need to make their distinctive rule apparent led the Aghlabids to abandon Qayrawān and to take up residence at a palatine complex 3 miles to the south-east which was named al-ʿAbbāsiyya. Ibrāhīm I

39 B. Rosenberger, 'Les premières villes islamiques du Maroc: Géographie et fonctions', and E. Manzano Moreno, 'El desarrollo económico de las ciudades idrīsíes: La evidencia numismática', both in Cressier and M. García Arenal (eds.), *Genèse de la ville islamique*, pp. 229–55 and 353–75.

40 B. Zerouki, *L'imamat de Tahart: Premier état musulman du Maghreb (144–296 de l'hégire)* (Paris, 1987), pp. 20–4.

coined *dirhams* in this mint and recruited a personal guard of freed slaves who garrisoned its strong fortifications. Baths, markets and a Friday mosque gave shape to a self-sufficient city which was organised around its main palace called Ruṣāfa and was inspired by eastern models.[41] Several decades later, and soon after his accession in 263/876, the *amīr* Ibrāhīm II decided to move his residence to a new settlement, called al-Raqqāda, a few miles south of the former city, the townscape of which was dominated by a number of palaces (*quṣūr*).

Unlike the Ifrīqiyan *amīrs* the Umayyads of al-Andalus kept Cordoba as their seat for almost two hundred years. After the crushing of the revolt of Shaqunda their grasp on the capital seems to have been remarkably solid, as shown by the surviving tax receipts from the rural districts around the city or by the important role played by the *ṣāḥib al-madīna* in the Umayyad administration.[42] It was not until 325–9/936–40 that ʿAbd al-Raḥmān III al-Nāṣir, who had previously taken the title of caliph, decided to found the city of Madīnat al-Zahrāʾ a few miles west of Cordoba. The city, which covered 112 hectares, was also walled and possessed a Friday mosque and a mint. Its impressive remains, still visible today, bear witness to extraordinary urban planning which included roads, hydraulic infrastructures and the separation of residential, reception and administrative areas.[43]

Al-ʿAbbāsiyya, al-Raqqāda and Madīnat al-Zahrāʾ did not outlive their founding dynasties. They were abandoned once the Aghlabids had been replaced by the Fāṭimids and a destructive civil war brought the downfall of the Umayyads in al-Andalus. In contrast, both Qayrawān and Cordoba remained important urban centres even though the fall of these dynasties reduced their splendour. At least in part, this continuity was founded on the prestige that both cities had attained as centres of Islamisation in the west due to the number and influence of the *ʿulamāʾ* who lived and taught in them.

The growth in the study of religious disciplines in Qayrawān may have started at a very early date. If we are to believe *fiqh* (jurisprudential) and *ṭabaqāt* (biographical) literature, by the middle of the second century AH respected Muslim scholars were transmitting, teaching and writing about Qurʾānic exegesis and Islamic law in Qayrawān.[44] Apparently, a number of North African

41 A. Lézine, *Architecture de l'Ifriqiya: Recherches sur les monuments aghlabides* (Paris, 1966), pp. 137–8.

42 Al-ʿUdhrī, *Tarṣīʿ al-akhbār wa-tanwīʿ al-āthār wa l-bustān fī garāʾib al-buldān*, ed. A. al-Ahwani (Madrid, 1965), pp. 124–7.

43 A. Vallejo, *Madīnat al-Zahrāʾ: Guía oficial del yacimiento arqueológico* (Seville, 2004).

44 M. Muranyi, *Beiträge zur Geschichte der Ḥadīt und Rechtsgelehrsamkeit der Mālikiyya in Nordafrika bis zum 5. Jh. DH* (Wiesbaden, 1997), pp. 1–59.

students attended the teachings of Mālik ibn Anas (d. 179/796) in Medina and spread his legal views back in their native lands. How and when these interpretations became a coherent corpus of legal and doctrinal practices is a question that has given rise to considerable controversy in modern scholarship, but there remains little doubt that the Aghlabid period witnessed considerable activity among circles of scholars concerned with religious interpretation.[45] One of the most prominent figures of these circles was Saḥnūn ibn Saʿīd (d. 240/854), who gathered the teachings of Mālik ibn Anas in a compilation known as the *Mudawwana*, which became the main reference work for Mālikism in North Africa.

Saḥnūn left behind him a large number of disciples, many of whom had come from al-Andalus 'in pursuit of knowledge' (*fī ṭalab al-ʿilm*). Long journeys to North Africa, Egypt and the Near East were very common among the early generations of Andalusī religious scholars of the third century, many of whom were descendants of converts. The outcome of their endeavours was an imported Mālikism which spread mainly from Cordoba and was firmly endorsed by Umayyad rulers. An Andalusī contemporary of Saḥnūn was Yaḥyā ibn Yaḥyā al-Laythī (d. 234/848), whose Berber origins did not prevent him from becoming the most influential scholar of his time. He was a member of the council (*shūrā*) that advised the Umayyad *amīr* on legal matters and was famed for being responsible for the transmission of Mālik's legal work the *Muwaṭṭa'*, which gained wide recognition in the Maghrib.[46]

A comparison between the Islamic milieu in Ifrīqiya and al-Andalus at this early period shows a number of telling differences. Mālikism was not prevalent in North Africa, as Aghlabid rulers were prone to favour the Ḥanafī school of law. As a result of this, religious circles in Qayrawān became more heterogenous than those in Cordoba. The step taken by the Aghlabid ruler Ziyādat Allāh (201–23/817–38), of appointing both a Mālikī and a Ḥanafī judge in the capital was a measure of appeasement that would have been unthinkable in al-Andalus. The class of religious scholars that emerged in Cordoba under the shadow of Umayyad rule was always staunchly orthodox, and deviations from the dominant Mālikī doctrine were regarded with suspicion, if not with threats of accusation of heresy (*zandaqa*).

45 See, however, the controversial work by N. Calder, *Studies in early Muslim jurisprudence* (Oxford, 1993).

46 M. I. Fierro, 'El alfaquí bereber Yaḥyà ibn Yaḥyà al-Laythī (m. 234/848), el inteligente de al-Andalus', in M. L. Avila and M. Marín (eds.), *Biografías y género biográfico en el Occidente islámico*, Estudios Onomástico-Biográficos de al-Andalus 8 (Madrid, 1997), pp. 269–344.

Relations between rulers and religious scholars in Ifrīqiya and al-Andalus also contrasted. Rejection of the wrongdoings of political power and detachment from its mundane corruption (*inqibaḍ ʿan al-sulṭān*) were widespread *topoi* which contributed to shape the moral standing of the *ʿulamāʾ* all over the Muslim world. But beyond these generic ideals a close bond is easily discernible between the Umayyad rulers and the religious circles of Cordoba, which compares with the more strained relationships that the Aghlabids maintained with the Qayrawān *ʿulamāʾ*. At the height of the dangerous revolts against the North African *amīrs*, men of religion firmly refused to legitimise their fight against the rebels, emphasising instead the evils of their rule and their lack of arguments to claim authority over the Muslim community.[47] There are no records that the Umayyad dynasty suffered such strong condemnations. Even its most unpopular ruler, al-Ḥakam I, who did not hesitate to execute and crucify *ʿulamāʾ* opposing his rule, is portrayed in some accounts as a pious Muslim and conscious defender of the frontiers of the *dār al-islām*. In contrast to the defensive attitude of the Aghlabids vis-à-vis the religious establishment of Qayrawān, the Umayyads seem to have enjoyed almost uncontested support from Cordoban *ʿulamāʾ*. This ensured them a religious legitimacy, which was based on the idea that their deeds in the defence of orthodoxy justified the divine choice bestowed upon them to guide the *umma*.

It is not coincidental that by the fourth/tenth century, under the auspices of the Umayyad rulers, the names, origins and careers of these *ʿulamāʾ* began to be compiled in Cordoba in thick registers which included the stereotyped intellectual careers of literally hundreds of religious scholars. Recent work on these registers – also known as 'biographical dictionaries' – has uncovered the complex transmission of knowledge among this class of scholars and the orientation that religious learning took in a territory far away from the main centres of Islamic studies. These sources also provide an insight into the patterns and extension of Islam in al-Andalus because they usually mention the city or village where a given scholar came from. According to these data the main centres of Islamisation were the southern Peninsula, the Ebro valley and the central axis around Toledo, territories where the number of Muslims allowed for the emergence of a significant number of people who could engage in learning, teaching and enforcing the principles and commands of religion.[48]

47 M. Marín, 'Inqibaḍ ʿan al-sulṭān. ʿUlamāʾ and political power in al-Andalus', in *Saber religioso y poder político en el Islam: Simposio Internacional (Granada 15–18 de octubre 1991)* (Madrid, 1994), pp. 127–39. Talbi, *L'emirat aghlabide*, pp. 184–5, 243–4.

48 M. I. Fierro and M. Marín, 'La islamización de las ciudades andalusíes a través de sus ulemas (s.II / VIII–comienzos del siglo IV / X)', in P. Cressier and M. García Arenal (eds.), *Genèse de la ville islamique*, pp. 65–97.

Archaeology is also a good indicator of the unrelenting Islamisation of the Iberian Peninsula. There is evidence of Christian cemeteries containing graves where the corpse has been laid following the Muslim ritual. The practice – condemned in Qur'ān 9.85 – is possibly indicative of the conversion of indigenous people who still employed ancient burial sites but had adopted the new rites of the conquerors.[49] The decay of churches or their conversion into mosques also pinpoints the steady decline of Christianity in this period. In Tolmo de Minateda (Albacete), which was the same Madīnat Iyyih mentioned in the pact of Theodomir as one of the cities included in the domains of this aristocrat, a Visigothic seventh-century basilica became, within two centuries, a residential area with dwellings standing alongside kilns. Some fine examples of late Visigothic architecture – such as Melque (Toledo) or Santa María del Trampal (Cáceres) – have survived up to the present day, but excavations have revealed that by the fourth/tenth century they were no longer occupied.[50]

Arabic also spread rapidly. It not only affected the indigenous population, but also the Berbers who had arrived at the time of the conquest and maintained their original tongue, but quickly lost it in favour of Arabic. A very peculiar trait of Arabic words adopted in Spanish is the assimilation of the determinative article *al-* to the borrowed word – such as *algodón* (Ar. *(al-) quṭūn*: cf. Eng. *cotton*) or *alguacil* (Ar. *(al-)wazīr*.) This uncommon feature has been explained as deriving from the pidgin Arabic spoken by Berber populations who tended to incorporate a classifying prefix to commonly used words in the same way as they did in their original tongue.[51]

The decreasing use of Latin among the indigenous population was acutely felt by some Christians living under Muslim rule, usually called Mozarabs (a term that modern scholarship derives from *mustaʿrib*, meaning 'Arabised', and which is only mentioned in Latin documents, but never in Arab sources). In a celebrated text a Cordoban Mozarab called Alvarus complained that in his time only one among a thousand Christians was able to write a letter in Latin. Young Mozarabs in Cordoba preferred the beauty of Arabic poetry to the study of religious texts. Alvarus's complaints were bitter and accurate, but they made no impact on his co-religionists: by the fourth/tenth century

49 M. Almagro Basch, *La necrópolis hispano-visigoda de Segóbriga: Saelices (Cuenca)*, Excavaciones Arqueológicas en España 84 (Madrid, 1975). J. L. Serrano Peña and J. C. Castillo Armenteros, 'Las necrópolis medievales de Marroquíes Bajos (Jaén)', *Arqueología y Territorio Medieval*, 7 (2000), pp. 93–115.

50 L. Abad, S. Gutiérrez, and B. Gamo, 'La basílica y el baptisterio del Tolmo de Minateda (Hellín, Albacete)', *Archivo Español de Arqueología*, 73 (2000), pp. 193–221.

51 F. Corriente, *Diccionario de arabismos y voces afines en iberorromance* (Madrid, 1999), pp. 58–63.

Christian sacred books were being translated into Arabic in significant numbers, which bears witness that even among Christian populations that language was more widespread than Latin.[52]

Alvarus belonged to a group of militant Christians in Cordoba who were well aware of the decline of their religion and the growing supremacy of Islam a century after the conquest. They complained of the ruin of churches and the tax burdens, but their main concern was the increasing rate of conversion, a deep social change which was acutely resented by this group of well-to-do Cordobans. Feeling that they were facing a desperate situation, some of them decided to take desperate action: in the same way as early Christendom had prevailed thanks to the blood of the martyrs during the persecutions carried out by the Roman emperors, a similar response was necessary to meet the tough times they were living through. The voluntary martyrs thus presented themselves to the judge of Cordoba, hurling blasphemy and abuse against the Prophet and Islam in the full knowledge that this left the official no choice but to condemn them to death in application of the law. As a result almost fifty Christians were executed in Cordoba between 850 and 859. This movement of suicidal zealots gave rise to a considerable amount of apologetic and polemical literature. Apart from this, its only outcome was an increase of martyrs' relics in the monasteries around Cordoba. Their blood was shed in vain, as Umayyad authority remained unscathed. All these suicides did not justify the deep divisions they produced among the Christian community, and as a consequence the movement slowly disappeared.

The fate of North African Christendom was similar. In its heyday before the Arab conquest, Church councils would assemble more than two hundred bishops, but by the tenth century the list of episcopal seats had been reduced to about forty, many of which only existed in name. By the middle of the eleventh century only four or five bishoprics can be documented. This decline had begun shortly after the Arab conquest, when many clerics left North Africa for the northern shores of the Mediterranean. In the second half of the tenth century Christians from Carthage complained of the fortunes of their city: whereas it had once been a celebrated metropolis, now it was scarcely possible to find a priest in it. Although Christian communities survived even in cities founded by the Muslims, such as in Qayrawān and Tāhert, the only traces left of them are occasional inscriptions – such as those found in the cemetery of Ngila near Tripoli, which date from the second half of the tenth

52 Alvaro de Córdoba, *Indiculus Luminosus*, in *Corpus Scriptorum Muzarabicorum*, vol. I, p. 314.

century and the eleventh – or occasional statements by Arab geographers.[53] Contrary to what happened in al-Andalus, however, these communities do not seem to have produced literary or doctrinal works, or at least none of them has come down to us.

Internal and external enemies

The most serious rebellions against the rule of the Aghlabids in Ifrīqiya were led by members of the Arab army. Military leaders formed a hereditary aristocracy with extensive landholdings, cultivated in many cases by slaves.[54] Ibrāhīm I in 194/810 and, particularly, his son Ziyādat Allāh in 207/822 had to face this challenge as some of these leaders were able to gather sufficient support to dispute the authority of the *amīrs* in considerable parts of their domains. During the first uprising Ibrāhīm I was besieged by the rebels in al-ʿAbbāsiyya, whereas Ziyādat Allāh suffered several defeats which brought the dynasty to the brink of extinction. In both cases powerful army leaders seem to have resisted certain policies of the *amīrs* and to have contested the legitimacy of their rule over them. Failed appeals to the *ʿulamāʾ* in Qayrawān – who staunchly refused to take sides for any contender – to declare the Aghlabids unlawful show that the bid for power of this Arab aristocracy was based on the idea that this dynasty only deserved their loyalty as far as it was prepared to meet their demands. Allegedly, Ibrāhīm I only managed to put an end to the rebellion of 194/810 when fresh financial resources sent by the ʿAbbāsid caliph were distributed among the rebel army. During the second rebellion of the *jund* one of its leaders, Manṣūr al-Ṭunbudhī, minted coins in Qayrawān in 210/825, a clear sign that the aim of the insurgents was the overthrow of the Aghlabids. If they did not achieve their goal, it was only because internal divisions among the rebels permitted the military recovery of the forces that had remained loyal to the Aghlabid *amīr*.

It is significant that, once the danger posed by this rebellion was over, the triumphant Ziyādat Allāh embarked on an ambitious programme of holy war

53 M. Talbi, 'Le Christianisme magrébine de la conquête musulmane à sa disparation: Une tentative d'explication', in M. Gervers and R. J. Bikhazi (eds.), *Conversion and continuity: Indigenous Christian communities in Islamic lands, eighth to eighteenth centuries* (Toronto, 1990); J. Cuoq, *L'église d'Afrique du Nord du IIe au XIIe siècle* (Paris, 1984), pp. 105–51.

54 M. Talbi, 'Law and economy in Ifrīqiya (Tunisia) in the third islamic century: Agriculture and the role of slaves in the country's economy', in A. L. Udovitch (ed.), *The Islamic Middle East, 700–1900: Studies in economic and social history* (Princeton, 1981), pp. 209–49.

against the neighbouring island of Sicily, where Byzantine imperial administration was facing internal disarray. The expedition that left the port of Sousse in 212/827 was entrusted to Asad ibn al-Furāt, an old and respected religious scholar who had been an outspoken critic of some aspects of Aghlabid rule. As the first attempt of territorial expansion since the times of the great conquests, the invasion of Sicily was characterised by the alliance of militant Islam with a restless class of soldiers whose rebellions had provoked havoc and destruction in the previous decades. The timing was also propitious as sea-raiding expeditions by sailors from al-Andalus and North Africa had been attacking Christian shores for some decades in quest of slaves, unquestionably the most precious merchandise in the western Mediterranean. The same year as the departure of the Aghlabid expedition, Crete had been conquered by a band of Andalusī sailors coming from Alexandria, where they had earned a well-deserved reputation for violence and ruthless behaviour. Now it was the turn of the Aghlabids, a dynasty with a constant deficit of legitimacy, to profit from this situation with the support of the *jund* and the religious establishment of Qayrawān.

It was a long and difficult conquest, however. By the time Asad ibn al-Furāt died in 213/828 the conquerors had gained only a foothold in Mazara, after suffering several defeats and the devastating effects of plague. It was not until 216/831 that Palermo fell, allowing them to begin an expansion in the western part of the island. At the same time, intermingling of the complex politics of the Lombard ducate of Benevento and the cities of southern Italy led to a number of raids, which culminated in the sack of Rome in 231/846. During the following decades campaigns of attrition and conquests of strategic enclaves ensured the complete domination of Sicily, which was strengthened by the taking over of Syracuse in 264/878 and the creation of the emirate of Bari on the Italian Peninsula.[55]

Compared to the extraordinary achievements of the Aghlabids in Sicily, the outcome of Umayyad warfare in al-Andalus was far more modest. Although most Cordoban rulers regularly sent summer campaigns against the Christian kingdoms in the north, these never produced significant territorial gains. Their commanders seem to have been more interested in receiving the stipends from the Cordoban government they were entitled to for every military campaign, and in taking booty and captives, than in extending the

55 M. Amari, *Storia dei musulmani di Sicilia* (Catania, 1933–9) remains the classic work. But see also A. Ahmad, *A history of Islamic Sicily* (Edinburgh, 1975); or U. Rizzitano, *Storia e cultura della Sicilia musulmana* (Rome, 1995).

land under their rule. The defensive character of Umayyad *jihād* could not prevent some significant losses such as the conquest of Barcelona in 185/801 by the armies of Louis the Pious or the expansion of the kings of Asturias into the no-man's-land of the Duero valley during the ninth and tenth centuries. As a consequence, Christian kingdoms consolidated and, despite the supremacy of Andalusī armies throughout the whole period, by the time the Umayyad dynasty fell in 422/1031 northern kings and lords were more powerful than their forebears had been 300 years before.

For more than a century the Umayyads never faced widespread rebellion. Local revolts certainly disrupted some regions, but they were never a serious threat to their rule. Most of these revolts originated in the frontier regions (*thughūr*) and were led either by local aristocratic families such as the Banū Qasī or the Banū ʿAmrūs or, more intriguingly, by cities such as Toledo or Mérida, whose populations seem to have rejected the attempts of the Cordoban administration to impose certain taxes, a reason which may explain similar contemporary rebellions in Ifrīqiyan cities.[56] During the second half of the third/ninth century, though, these revolts extended to the whole of al-Andalus. Starting during the rule of *amīr* Muḥammad (238–83/852–86), local landlords severed their links with the Umayyads, erected fortresses (*ḥuṣūn*) and ceased forwarding taxes to Cordoba. By the time of *amīr* ʿAbd Allāh (275–300/888–912) minting of coins had practically ceased and Umayyad authority was barely recognised beyond the limits of the capital.

The major rebel of the period was a *muwallad*, a descendant of indigenous ancestors who had converted to Islam, called ʿUmar ibn Ḥafṣūn, who managed to build a considerable territorial domain extending from the fortress of Bobastro, set in the craggy mountains of Málaga, in south-eastern al-Andalus. ʿUmar ibn Ḥafṣūn was the main but not the only *muwallad* who rebelled during this period. Although sources point to the opposition of these *muwalladūn* to the Arabs as the main cause of the countless battles of these years, this explanation is belied by accounts from the same sources which show that ethnic divisions were not always followed by rebels in their alliances and political alignments. The bone of contention of these *muwalladūn* was more their loss of power within a rapidly changing social milieu. The undisputed authority, which the agreements of the time of the conquest had guaranteed them within their domains, was breaking up as the result of the

56 E. Manzano Moreno, *La frontera de al-Andalus en época de los Omeyas* (Madrid, 1991), pp. 314–83. Cf. Talbi, *L'emirat aghlabide*, p. 145.

increasing demands of the central administration and the flight of rural populations to the urban areas where Umayyad rule was more visible. Under these circumstances rebellion was the only alternative for this class, and the fact that during the first decades of the fourth/tenth century all these revolts were put down by the Umayyad ʿAbd al-Raḥmān III, who sometimes even received the support of the rebels' subjects, shows that at this period al-Andalus was rapidly becoming a more homogeneous social realm where the last remnants of the old Visigothic heritage were disappearing.[57]

The western caliphates

It is no coincidence that both Ifrīqiya and al-Andalus witnessed the proclamation of two rival caliphates in the early fourth/tenth century. Both societies had reached such a degree of Islamisation that the vast implications borne by the title 'Commander of the Faithful' were fully acknowledged by a considerable part of their populations. Religious authority of the caliphs entailed a political organisation, a legal system and an ideological framework which were shaped according to Islamic principles of government, law and legitimacy. In al-Andalus the principles upheld by the Umayyad orthodoxy faced no serious challenge, especially once the *muwallad* rebellions of the previous century had been defeated. By contrast, Ifrīqiya was again a much more complex social milieu, in which the definition of what exactly 'Islamic orthodoxy' stood for was not yet universally recognised.

It is likely that, by taking the unprecedented step of claiming spiritual rule over the whole Muslim community in 316/929, the Umayyad ʿAbd al-Raḥmān III al-Nāṣir was reacting to the defeat of the Aghlabid dynasty and the proclamation of the Fāṭimid caliph ʿAbd Allāh al-Mahdī in Ifrīqiya in 297/910. The consolidation of this militant rule in North Africa made a deep impact in the whole Islamic world. Fāṭimid partisans saw in the event the rising of the sun in the west, an image that was unashamedly plagiarised by Umayyad poets who also boasted that their masters' aim was to extend their authority to the east.[58]

The claims to legitimacy of the two caliphates were, however, different. The Umayyad *amīr*s of al-Andalus had always portrayed themselves as 'descendants of the caliphs'. But when al-Nāṣir took the title of *amīr al-*

57 M. Acién, *Entre el feudalismo y el Islam: ʿUmar ibn Ḥafṣūn en los historiadores, en las fuentes y en la historia*, 2nd edn (Jaén, 1997).

58 Cf. al-Qāḍī al-Nuʿmān, *Iftitāḥ al-daʿwa wa ibtidāʾ al-dawla*, ed. F. Dachraoui (Tunis, 1975), p. 65 and Ibn Ḥayyān, *al-Muqtabis fī ajbār bilād al-Andalus (al-Ḥakam II)*. ed. A. A. Hajji (Beirut, 1965), p. 163.

mu'minīn, it was not so much the genealogy linking him to the caliphs of Damascus that he stressed – perhaps because this argument could not explain why his predecessors had failed to assert their claim to the title – but rather the preference shown by God on account of his actions and good government.[59] In contrast, Fāṭimid claims were based on the lines of descent that connected this dynasty to ʿAlī ibn Abī Ṭālib and his wife Fāṭima, the daughter of the Prophet, through a succession of imams who had been appointed by God to preserve His faith.

It was not an undisputed claim. For the Shīʿa the genealogical line of imams had continued uninterrupted among the descendants of ʿAlī until the death in Sāmarrā' of the eleventh imam, al-Ḥasan al-ʿAskarī, in 260/874. Then, his infant son, known as Muḥammad al-Muntaẓar, had disappeared, becoming the hidden twelfth imam, who was expected to reappear at the end of time. While these ideas were followed by what was becoming the mainstream majority of Shīʿa, some were unpersuaded and claimed instead that upon the death in 148/765 of Jaʿfar al-Ṣādiq, great-grandson of al-Ḥusayn ibn ʿAlī, the imamate had passed to his second son Ismāʿīl, who had transmitted it to his own son Muḥammad.[60] As this Muḥammad ibn Ismāʿīl also went into hiding, for the next century the internal history of this group is made blurry by the genealogical arguments, allegations and counter-claims of its followers, dissidents and foes. These discussions were the product of the political and social circumstances of the end of the third century, when messianic expectations spread throughout many parts of the Muslim world. The generic idea that the period of hiding of the imam was over and that a new era was about to begin with the coming of the *mahdī*, a saviour sent by God to guide His community according to His principles of law and justice, was preached in a number of different ways by a number of different missionaries (*dāʿīs*). These travelled through different lands and found an encouraging response in places such as Yemen, Khurāsān or Baḥrayn.[61] A leadership located in the Syrian village of Salamiyya claimed ascendancy over this network of highly committed agitators, presenting itself as the proof (*ḥujja*) that endorsed the truthfulness of the whole movement. In 286/899 this cautious idea was abandoned and the leader

59 *Una Crónica Anónima de ʿAbd al-Raḥmān al-Nāṣir*, ed. and trans. E. Lévi Provençal and E. García Gómez (Madrid and Granada, 1950), pp. 78–9.

60 See, however, a contradictory account on this succession by the caliph al-Mahdī himself: A. Hamdani and F. de Blois, 'A re-examination of al-Mahdī's letter to the Yemenites on the genealogy of the Fāṭimid caliphs', *JRAS* (1983), pp. 173–207.

61 M. Brett, *The rise of the Fatimids: The world of the Mediterranean and the Middle East in the fourth century of the hijra, tenth century CE* (Leiden, 2001), p. 47.

of Salamiyya decided to present himself as the awaited imam, claiming lordship over the whole Muslim community. This bold decision was met with varying degrees of acceptance by the followers of the movement. Some of them were unimpressed by what seemed to them an allegation that was not clearly grounded.

One of the *dāʿīs* who maintained his allegiance to the general direction of the movement was a man called Abū ʿAbd Allāh, who had been recruited in Kūfa and later sent to Egypt and Yemen. In 279/892 while on a pilgrimage in Mecca he met a group of Berbers from the Kutāma tribe, an encounter which convinced him that the region of the Lesser Kabyilia (present-day Algeria) was a fertile ground for his activities. Abū ʿAbd Allāh spent the following nine years in that marginal area, making a place called Ikjān his particular *dār al-hijra* ('abode of emigration'), which mirrored the role played by Medina in the life of the Prophet Muḥammad, when he had to take residence in this city after escaping from Mecca. The *dāʿī* preached among the Kutāma a salvational message which stressed the idea that big things were about to happen when the *mahdī* finally arrived, provided the community of believers went back to its original roots. This message proved successful at a juncture in which Aghlabid rule was facing growing discontent due to the ruthless policies followed by Ibrāhīm II during his long government (261–89/875–902). The call of the *jihād* felt by this unpredictable *amīr* took him and his troops to Sicily and southern Italy, a circumstance from which Abū ʿAbd Allāh, who led the Kutāma to conquer Mila in 289/902, was to profit. Two years later the conquest of Sétif made his movement such a serious challenge that the *ʿulamāʾ* from Qayrawān issued a *fatwā* accusing the *dāʿī* of propagating heretical ideas. But by then the uprising was unstoppable: further conquests and the defeat of the Aghlabid army by Laribus in 296/909 forced the last Aghlabid *amīr*, Ziyādat Allāh II, to flee just before the *dāʿī* Abū ʿAbd Allāh made his triumphal entry into Qayrawān.

The road was open for the proclamation of the rule of the *mahdī*, who had fled from Salamiyya in 289/902 in the face of a mounting threat coming from both ʿAbbāsid armies and enraged co-religionists who did not recognise him as imam. His eventful escape had taken him to the west, but for some reason he had not joined his *dāʿī* in the territory of the Kutāma but had settled instead in Sijilmāsa in the *Maghrib al-aqṣā*. It was there that the victorious Abū ʿAbd Allāh went to rescue him. Soon afterwards the self-styled ʿAbd Allāh al-Mahdī (297–322/910–34) was sworn in as caliph in the Ifrīqiyan city of al-Raqqāda. Despite a number of mutinies and local revolts in Sicily and Tripoli, his government rapidly consolidated, and even endured the internal crisis caused by the suspicious attitude of both Abū ʿAbd Allāh and his brother Abu ʾl-ʿAbbās – the latter a key figure of the movement in previous years – who seem to have entertained some doubts about the authenticity of the *mahdī* and were killed in 298/911.

The Fāṭimids were not the first easterners who had arrived in North Africa and found support there for their claims; nor were they the last religious reformers to spread their message among marginal Berber tribes, who stood outside the main centres of Islamisation but would become the core of an expanding state, as the later cases of Almoravids and Almohads show. Their distinctiveness lay in the fact that their preaching had been bred in the east and that its *raison d'être* entailed universal rule, as the coming of the *mahdī* signalled the beginning of a new era. The conquest of Ifrīqiya was a first step towards this aim, and as a result of this the political map of North Africa, which for a century had remained almost unchanged, suffered a radical transformation.

The Rustamids of Tāhert were the first casualties of Fāṭimid expansionism. They were disposed of during the expedition led by Abū ʿAbd Allāh in search of the *mahdī*. A few years later, in 311/923, the Idrīsid ruler of Fez, Yaḥyā IV, was also deposed, whereas in Sijilmāsa the dynasty of the Midrārids was allowed to survive in exchange for recognition of the Ifrīqiyan caliph. It is telling, however, that the Fāṭimids never attempted to impose direct rule over territories west of Tāhert. They preferred to entrust the control of these regions to powerful tribal leaders such as the Miknāsa chieftain Masāla ibn Ḥabūs and his cousin Mūsā ibn Abi ʾl-Āfiya. This was an implicit recognition that tribalism held a supremacy in the *Maghrib al-aqṣā* that state administration could not challenge.

Tribal politics, however, were unstable, and they proved very unreliable as the Umayyad ʿAbd al-Raḥmān III began to show a deep interest in the situation in North Africa. Masāla ibn Ḥabūs was defeated and killed in 312/924 at the hands of the rival Maghrāwa chieftain, Muḥammad ibn Khazar, who became the main Umayyad ally in the region. Soon afterwards ʿAbd al-Raḥmān III ordered his navy to take the North African cities of Melilla and Ceuta in 317–19/929–31. With this bold move the self-proclaimed Cordoban caliph made clear his intention to stand up to Fāṭimid expansionism, which eventually could threaten his own lands.[62] In this situation tribal leaders such as Mūsā ibn Abi ʾl-Āfiya, the scions of the Idrīsid dynasty still active in

62 E. Lévi-Provençal, *Historia de la España Musulmana (711–1031)*, vol IV: *Historia de España dirigida por R. Menénedez Pidal* (Madrid, 1950), pp. 313–21, 385–97, 430–7 remains the most comprehensive account of Umayyad expansionism in the Maghrib.

the Maghrib or the rulers of Sijilmāsa could bargain for their loyalties with both caliphates. Fāṭimids and Umayyads engaged in a fierce competition to attract allies to their causes, converting the *Maghrib al-aqṣā* into a battlefield where these allies fought each other with the support of Umayyad armies deployed on the African coast and Fāṭimid governors established in the newly founded citadels of Msila and Ashīr, which commanded the route to Tāhert.

Therefore, despite the early support of the Kutāma, the revolutionary message of the Fāṭimids had failed to overcome the conditions that traditionally had made North Africa a distinctive region within the *dār al-islām*. This became clear to the caliph al-Qāʾim (r. 322–34/934–46), the successor of al-Mahdī, when a widespread rebellion of Berber tribes arose in the Hodna plains and the Aurès mountains in 322/944 under the leadership of Abū Yazīd Makhlad ibn Kaydad, a former schoolteacher who belonged to the Nukkārite branch of Khārijism. Rejection of the evil rule of the Fāṭimids, which had turned out to be as oppressive as any other, and the belief that the caliphate belonged to the best Muslim irrespective of his genealogy, led Berber tribes to conquer most of Ifrīqiya, including Qayrawān. In 333/945 al-Qāʾim found himself besieged by Abū Yazīd in al-Mahdiyya, a coastal city built by his predecessor as a symbol of the new order which now became the last stronghold of true faith against the attacks of the Dajjāl, the Muslim Antichrist, as Fāṭimid propaganda portrayed Abū Yazīd. His failure at the gates of the capital and his total defeat by al-Qāʾim's successor, al-Manṣūr (r. 334–41/946–53), earned the dynasty fresh justification for its divine mission.

The revolt of Abū Yazīd also affected the covert war between the Fāṭimids and the Umayyads. At the height of his power the rebel had pleaded his allegiance to ʿAbd al-Raḥmān III through a delegation composed of some Mālikī scholars from Qayrawān. Although the Andalusian navy arrived too late to be of any help to the rebels, the episode increased the enmity between the two dynasties. The caliph al-Muʿizz (r. 341–65/953–76) accused the Umayyad of being a usurper who belonged to an impious family and had adopted a title that his ancestors in al-Andalus had never dared to use.[63] In 347/958 he sent his general Jawhar on an expedition that took Tāhert, Fez and Sijilmāsa, and delayed retaliation for several decades of Umayyad supremacy.

63 M. Yalaoui, 'Controverse entre le Fatimide al-Muʿizz et l'Omeyyade al-Nasir d'après le Kitab al-Majalis w l-Musarayat du cadi Nuʿman', *Cahiers de Tunisie*, 26 (1978), suppl. pp. 7–33.

But the sights of the dynasty were no longer set on the west. Campaigns against Egypt had begun as early as 301/914.[64] Neither this nor subsequent expeditions in 307 and 323/919–35 proved to be successful, but they helped to increase military pressure which bore its fruits in 358/969 when Jawhar conquered Egypt almost without resistance. Four years later the departure of al-Muʿizz for al-Qāhira with the coffins of his ancestors showed that the intention of the Fāṭimids was to bring the new era to the east and to leave behind the land that had witnessed their early success, but had also failed to earn them widespread recognition. The government of North Africa was entrusted to a military man: Buluggīn ibn Zīrī, a tribal leader who belonged to the tribe of Ṣinhāja and whose father had earned a well-deserved reputation as a loyal supporter of the Fāṭimid cause in the wars in central Maghrib. As a deputy of the caliph, Buluggīn was expected to continue the fight on the western frontier, while the administration of Ifrīqiya was left in the hands of civil officials. The first task was accomplished by Buluggīn in the campaigns he led between 368/979 and 373/984, which disrupted the supremacy of the Umayyad allies in the *Maghrib al-aqṣā*. What had been left by the Fāṭimid caliphs as a subsidiary administration became the framework of an independent rule and this was the achievement of Buluggīn's successors, the Zīrid rulers of Ifrīqiya.

The wars in the Maghrib had far-reaching consequences for the Umayyads in al-Andalus. These struggles were not only caused by the rivalry with the Fāṭimids, but also by the need to control the trade routes of African gold. Soon after his self-proclamation as caliph al-Nāṣir began to strike *dīnārs*, the first time they had been minted in almost two centuries.[65] These *dīnārs* and the large amount of silver *dirhams* also minted by the caliphs bear witness to an economic expansion which is noticeable in both rural and urban areas. The extension of settlements, the introduction of agrarian techniques and crops imported from the east and the colonisation of marginal areas responded to a growing demand in urban areas.[66] Hitherto modest sites, such as Murcia,

64 H. Halm, *The empire of the Mahdi: The rise of the Fatimids*, trans. Michael Bonner (Leiden, 1996), pp. 196–213.

65 A. Canto, 'De la ceca de al-Andalus a la de Madīnat al-Zahrā'', *Cuadernos de Madīnat al-Zahrā'*, 3 (1991); M. Barceló, 'El hiato en las acuñaciones de oro en al-Andalus, 127–316/744(5)–936(7): Los datos fundamentales de un problema', *Moneda y Crédito. Revista de Economía*, 132 (1975), pp. 33–71.

66 New local examples based on the archaeological record in S. Gutiérrez, *La cora de Tudmīr de la Antigüdad tardía al mundo islámico: Poblamiento y cultura material* (Madrid and Alicante, 1996); and J. C. Castillo Armenteros, *La campiña de Jaén en época emiral* (Jaén, 1998).

Jaén, Almería or Badajoz, became thriving cities in an increasingly complex urban network, whose traditional main centres – Cordoba, Seville, Saragossa and Toledo – also underwent an extraordinary growth.[67]

All these cities made up the backbone of the provincial administration of the caliphate. Al-Andalus was divided into a series of provinces (*kūras*) whose governors were appointed and dismissed regularly. Each *kūra* comprised districts (*iqlīms*) which included rural settlements (*qaryas*) also serving as fiscal units liable to pay a sum in taxes which was fixed in advance. This organisation, which went back to the times of the settlement of the Syrian *junds*, seems to have worked very efficiently. The eastern traveller Ibn Ḥawqal, who visited al-Andalus in 337/948 and was probably an informant for the Fāṭimids, estimated that caliphal wealth amounted to 20 million *dīnārs*, a sum which is consistent with data indicating that the income from taxes for the whole of al-Andalus totalled 4 to 5 million *dīnārs* per year.[68]

The religious authority of the caliphs also depended on the territorial extension of Islamic institutions. Judges, mosque preachers, market supervisors and curators of charitable trusts (*awqāf*) were increasingly appointed not only for Cordoba but also for the main cities of al-Andalus. Most of these positions were filled by *ʿulamāʾ* who, despite their different geographical origins, had acquired their knowledge among the religious circles of the capital. The main corpus of doctrine that inspired the regulation of issues connected to ritual practices (*ʿibādat*) or civil affairs (*muʿāmalāt*) had already been fixed according to Mālikī principles, as shown by treatises such as the *Mukhtaṣar* by ʿAlī ibn ʿĪsā al-Ṭulayṭulī (d. after 297/910). Legal practice, which sprang from these principles, became increasingly complex. Opinions on difficult legal questions (*fatwās*) began to be compiled, as did the rulings of Cordoban judges. Other compilations, such as the *Kitāb al-wathāʾiq wa l-sijillāt* (Book of notary documents and records) by Ibn al-ʿAṭṭār (d. 399/1009), gathered models of notarial documents which were used for a variety of contracts (sales, share-cropping agreements, freeing of slaves, marriages, etc.) and whose contents bear witness to the high degree of sophistication that the practice of Islamic *fiqh* had attained in al-Andalus at this period.[69]

67 The standard work on Andalusian cities remains L. Torres Balbas, *Ciudades hispanomusulmanas* (Madrid, 1972).

68 Ibn Ḥawqal, *Kitāb ṣūrat al-arḍ*, ed. M. J. de Goeje, rev. J. H. Kramers, BGA 2 (Leiden, 1938), p. 112.

69 Alī b. ʿĪsā al-Ṭulayṭulī, *Mujtāṣar (Compendio)*, ed. and trans. M. J. Cervera (Madrid, 2000); Ibn al-ʿAṭṭār, *Kitāb al-wathāʾiq wa l-sijillāt*, ed. P. Chalmeta (Madrid, 1983), trans. P. Chalmeta and M. Marugán as *Formulario notarial y judicial andalusí*, estudio y traducción (Madrid, 2000).

There are some indications, however, of a mounting crisis in the Umayyad civil administration during the second half of the fourth/tenth century. Protests against the corruption and rapacity of some provincial governors grew worse during the caliphate of al-Naṣīr's son and successor, al-Ḥakam II (r. 350–66/961–76). Unlike his father, al-Ḥakam seems to have distrusted the powerful families of *mawālī* who had traditionally served in the main positions of the administration. His preference for the *ṣaqāliba* (eunuch slaves of northern European origin), or for obscure individuals who were notable for their meteoric careers, may have been a conscious policy dictated by a desire to get rid of the families that had become too powerful thanks to their control of the Umayyad administration.

It was in this context that the rapid promotion of the celebrated al-Manṣūr (Sp. Almanzor) took place. A scion of an Arab family whose ancestor had taken part in the early conquest and had settled in Algeciras, and which afterwards kept a very low profile, Muḥammad ibn Abī Āmir managed to set up a solid network of power relations which brought him from the humblest posts to the highest ranks of the caliphate. With other leading officials of the civil and military administration he profited from the situation created by the death of al-Ḥakam II in 366/976 and from the minority of his only son and successor, Hishām II, who was proclaimed caliph in spite of the rulings that explicitly forbade the title commander of the faithful being conferred upon a child. In subsequent years al-Manṣūr systematically eliminated all his rivals until he was appointed *ḥājib*. Once in full control of the administration he relegated Hishām II to the role of puppet-caliph, assuming for himself and his family all positions of power that the Umayyad administration had set up in the preceding decades.

Aggressive warfare against the Christian kingdoms, staunch religious orthodoxy and a firm grip on the apparatus of the caliphate were the means by which al-Manṣūr attempted to legitimise his rule. A crucial element in this scheme was the enrolment of Berber troops recruited in North Africa, whose ranks had been increasing since the time of al-Ḥakam II, but which now became the main body of the Umayyad army, replacing the old system of *junds*. Ibn Ḥawqal estimated their number at 5,000, but by the end of the fourth/tenth century they were at least 7,000, including tribal groups such as the Zanāta Banū Birzāl or the Ṣinhāja Zīrids, who were relatives of the ruler of Ifrīqiya but had deserted his ranks due to their frustration with the distribution of power in their native land. These troops received regular stipends and were garrisoned in Cordoba and in the new palatine city, Madīnat al-Zāhira, the construction of which the ambitious *ḥājib* ordered somewhere to the east of the capital.

Al-Manṣūr's aim was to create a dynasty. Upon his death in 392/1002 his son, ʿAbd al-Malik al-Muẓaffar, was also entrusted with the title of *ḥājib* by the weak Hishām II, and during the six years of his rule he followed the same policy as his father. His death in 399/1008 marked the beginning of the end of the Umayyad caliphate.[70] He was immediately replaced by his brother, ʿAbd al-Raḥmān – nicknamed Sanjūl because his mother was the daughter of King Sancho II of Navarra – who took the unprecedented step of forcing Hishām II to designate him as successor to the caliphate. Although the caliph had no offspring there were a number of descendants of al-Nāṣir, who were ready to oppose this extravagant move. A riot in the capital ended with the killing of Sanjūl but also sparked internal strife among members of the Umayyad kin. For more than two decades Cordoba was the scene of fierce fighting among these factions. Its population took an active role in these struggles, always siding with the party that opposed the Berber militias. The rejection of this army by the Cordobans enshrined their hostility to caliphal rule, which had become particularly oppressive in the preceding decades. The sacking of Madīnat al-Zāhira or the massacre of Berbers in 399/1009 were followed by the destruction of Madīnat al-Zahrāʾ and the pillage of Cordoba by the North African troops.

While these events were taking place in the capital, caliphal administration broke down in the rest of al-Andalus. Local elites severed their links with Cordoba throughout these years of turmoil, paving the way for the emergence of the *Ṭāʾifa* kingdoms. When in 422/1031 the last Umayyad caliph, al-Muʿtadd, was deposed in one of the frequent riots in the capital, he and his family were banned from Cordoba. As the former unity of the caliphate collapsed the new political map comprised a number of petty kingdoms, ruled by families of different origin: some were descendants of the early conquerors, such as the Berbers Banū Dhi ʾl-Nūn of central al-Andalus; some were Berbers of the caliphal armies who had left Cordoba and had settled in new territories, such as the Zīrids who founded the *Ṭāʾifa* of Granada; others were former members of the caliphal administration who managed to build up a territorial domain in some parts of eastern al-Andalus, as was the case of the *ṣaqāliba* who briefly ruled in Almería or Denia. All of them knew that the Umayyads had disappeared for good, but all maintained a fiction that the caliphate still existed and presented themselves as its self-appointed representatives. This was a recognition that political authority in al-Andalus could only be expressed in terms of Islamic legitimacy.

70 P. Scales, *The fall of the caliphate of Cordoba: Berbers and Andalusis in conflict* (Leiden, 1994), pp. 38–109.

PART IV

*

THE HISTORIOGRAPHY OF EARLY ISLAMIC HISTORY

15

Modern approaches to early Islamic history

FRED M. DONNER

Preliminary considerations

Western writing on Islam, including early Islamic history, has roots reaching back to the medieval period.[1] These earliest Western writings were almost without exception religious polemics – tracts intended to assert the theological claims of Christianity and to disprove or discredit those of Islam. They often pursued these goals by presenting grotesque misrepresentations of Islam and its history.[2] Polemicists devoted special attention to discrediting the Qurʾān and Muḥammad because this, they thought, would most effectively undermine Islam's faith-claims – that Muḥammad was a prophet, and that the Qurʾān was God's revealed word.

This polemical tradition cannot, of course, be considered scientific scholarship, the goal of which is to understand the subject of its study, not to discredit it; but it is important to remember that the Western tradition of anti-Islamic polemic formed the background against which more scholarly writings first developed, and thus in some ways inevitably helped shape the latter. Early Islamic history in particular, because it includes the story of the life of Muḥammad, the revelation of the Qurʾān and the early expansion of the Believers, was long closely entangled with polemic. Moreover, the polemical

1 'Modern' and 'Western' are obviously not exact equivalents, but the problem is too complex to be examined here. In the present chapter they will be used as rough equivalents, even though some examples of 'modern' writing have been produced by scholars who themselves hail from outside the 'West', and some Western authors write works that are not 'modern' in that they depart from widely accepted standards of modern scholarship.

2 On the polemical tradition see Norman Daniel, *Islam and the West: The making of an image*, 2nd edn (Oxford, 1993 [1960]); R. W. Southern, *Western views of Islam in the Middle Ages* (Cambridge, MA, 1962); Hugh Goddard, *A history of Christian–Muslim relations* (Edinburgh and Chicago, 2000); John Victor Tolan, *Saracens: Islam in the medieval European imagination* (New York, 2002). A deft summary of the origins of Western views of the 'Orient' is found in Zachary Lockman, *Contending visions of the Middle East: The history and politics of Orientalism* (Cambridge, 2004), pp. 8–65.

tradition never completely died out, but has survived right up to the present in a variety of guises. Besides straightforward tracts denouncing Islam as 'false religion', of which many continue to be published, particularly in the United States, there have occasionally been the more insidious works that adopt the externals of rigorous scholarship, but still adhere to the basic assumptions of the polemical tradition; the works of Sir William Muir (1819–1905), such as *The Life of Muhammad*,[3] are cases in point.[4] In another vein, there has emerged in recent years a secularised contemporary avatar of the medieval religious polemics against Islam that essentialises 'Islamic civilisation' as antagonist to the 'West' and which sometimes reaches back to the founding events of early Islamic history in an effort to find ammunition for its arguments.[5] In considering how scholars in the modern West have studied early Islamic history, then, it is important to be mindful of the many forms of the polemical tradition against Islam, even though that tradition cannot be considered scholarship in the proper sense of that word.

A few Western writers began to study Islamic history in a manner that was free of the assumptions of religious polemic as early as the seventeenth century,[6] but it was the Enlightenment of the eighteenth century, with its emphasis on the use of human reason to attain understanding of all subjects, that finally created the conditions under which some people in the West could leave polemics behind and begin to examine Islam and its history more open-mindedly. This process of looking at Islam and its history in a more sympathetic way was limited, however, by two factors. For one thing, not all people in the West were willing to abandon polemic and embrace rationalist principles. Moreover, the very rationalism of Enlightenment thinkers, which had caused them to reject the Church's polemical condemnations of Islam as 'false religion', also made them likely to view critically some religious dogmas of Islam as well, for human reason was seen as being of universal applicability in examining all traditional beliefs.

3 William Muir, *The life of Muhammad*, 1st edn (Edinburgh, 1861).
4 See Clinton Bennett, *Victorian images of Islam* (London, 1992), esp. pp. 176–7.
5 The historian Bernard Lewis's 'The roots of Muslim rage', *The Atlantic Monthly* (September 1990), and the political scientist Samuel P. Huntington's *The clash of civilizations and the remaking of the world order* (New York, 1996) seem to have served as the intellectual stimulus for this new kind of polemic. On this trend in modern writing, see Emran Qureshi and Michael A. Sells (eds.), *The new crusades: Constructing the Muslim enemy* (New York, 2003); Lockman, *Contending visions*, pp. 233–41. Maxime Rodinson, *La mystique de l'Islam* (Paris, 1980), trans. Roger Veinus as *Europe and the mystique of Islam* (Seattle, 1987), pp. 67, 104–5, seems to be warning against this trend towards essentialism and what he calls 'theologocentrism' – that is, a tendency to see 'Islam' as the root of all problems with modern Middle Eastern states.
6 On these pioneering writers see Daniel, *Islam and the West*, pp. 317–23.

Nonetheless, the Enlightenment greatly accelerated the study of Islam on a truly scholarly, rather than polemical, basis – that is, in a systematic way and with the goal of understanding Islam and its history, rather than of 'defeating' it intellectually. During this period, moreover, close first-hand observations of Muslim societies by Western sojourners became more numerous and provided Europeans with fuller information about Islamic societies than the polemical tradition had offered. Not all this information was accurate; it has been plausibly suggested that the bizarre stereotypes of 'the Oriental' that circulated in Europe and helped shape popular perceptions and colonial policy were probably the heritage not of scholars but of those increasing numbers of Europeans who had had direct contact with 'the Orient' but not with scholarship on it: sailors, merchants, colonial agents and others.[7] But some European contacts did yield accurate descriptions, which helped to counter the more grotesque misconceptions about Islam and Muslim societies that survived from the polemical tradition: noteworthy examples are the massive *Déscription de l'Égypte* (1809–29), prepared by the scholars who accompanied Napoleon's invasion of Egypt in 1798, and *An account of the manners and customs of the modern Egyptians* (1836) by E. W. Lane (1801–76).

As far as early Islamic history is concerned, Western scholars of the Enlightenment began to consult key texts of the Islamic tradition itself (often, of course, in manuscript) in search of information. This process was advanced not only by the establishment of chairs of Oriental languages at a number of European universities (notably Leiden, Paris and Oxford) – something that was already happening by the sixteenth century – but also by the demand in the courts of Vienna, Paris, London and elsewhere for diplomats and interpreters skilled in Oriental languages, some of whom, such as Joseph Freiherr von Hammer-Purgstall (1774–1856), published the fruits of their learning and experience. For the first time there emerged in the West a body of scholars who were competent to consult Islamic sources directly as they attempted to describe Islam's beliefs and historical development. In addition, some Oriental sources began to appear in translation into Latin, French and other European languages through the efforts of scholars such as Barthélemy d'Herbelot (1625–95), whose *Bibliothèque orientale* (1697) was reprinted several times (including a German translation) during the eighteenth century. This activity made some detailed information, drawn from Islamic sources, available to writers whose works commanded a large audience, but

7 William Montgomery Watt, *Muslim–Christian encounters: Perceptions and misperceptions* (London and New York, 1991), pp. 108–9.

who were not themselves trained in Oriental languages. Edward Gibbon's *Decline and fall of the Roman empire* (the first volume of which appeared in 1776), for example, contained a lengthy section on the rise of Islam, derived mainly from translations of late medieval Muslim authorities such as Abu 'l-Fidā' (d. 1331). Two generations later Thomas Carlyle (1795–1881) was inspired by translated sources to write a relatively sympathetic biography of Muḥammad in his *On heroes, hero-worship, and the heroic in history* (1841).

All of the activity briefly sketched above constitutes the background to the scientific study of early Islamic history in the modern West, which really only got under way in the middle of the nineteenth century. It was only at this time that the study of Islamic history began to be consistently disentangled from Islamic religious studies on a continuous basis by a (small) critical mass of scholars relatively free of the assumptions of the polemical tradition.[8]

In considering more closely the further evolution of Western scholarship on early Islamic history, it will be useful to discuss separately two aspects of it: first, the different approaches Western scholars have taken to the Muslim sources for early Islamic history, including the Qur'ān; and second, various problems of perception, conceptualisation and bias.

Approaches to the sources for early Islamic history

The general development of history as a scholarly discipline in the West following the Enlightenment – a process that encompassed, of course, much more than the study of the Islamic world and that was often closely tied to the early articulation of national identities in Europe – posited that the writing of history should rest as much as possible on the analysis of actual documents originating in the time and place under study. A major difficulty facing the historian who wishes to write about early Islamic history, however, is that for many chapters of this history truly documentary sources are either scarce or non-existent.[9] This is particularly true for the crucial earliest phases of Islam's history – the life of the Prophet Muḥammad, the expansion of the earliest community of Believers (often called the 'Islamic conquests' or the 'Arab conquests'), and the early caliphate and civil wars – for which almost no true documentation survives. Indeed, for most of what happened during at

8 On the nineteenth-century background in particular, see the illuminating comments of Albert H. Hourani, *Islam in European thought* (Cambridge, 1991).

9 A fuller discussion of the material presented in this section is found in Fred M. Donner, *Narratives of Islamic origins: The beginnings of Islamic historical writing* (Princeton, 1998), pp. 1–31.

least the first two centuries of the Islamic era (corresponding roughly to the seventh and eighth centuries CE) only a limited number of documents are extant, mostly from the later years of that time span.

The dearth of documentary evidence for much of early Islamic history forced Western historians to rely instead on the Muslim tradition's own narratives about Islam's origins, enshrined in a variety of Muslim chronicles, biographical dictionaries, geographical treatises, genealogical works, poetry collections and religious literature, particularly collections of *ḥadīths* or sayings attributed to the Prophet Muḥammad himself. (Works such as the *History* of al-Ṭabarī (d. 923), the biographical dictionary of Ibn Saʿd (d. 845), the *Futūḥ al-buldān* of al-Balādhurī (d. 892) and the *Muṣannaf* of ʿAbd al-Razzāq al-Ṣanʿānī (d. 827) may be mentioned as representative examples.) This body of narrative source material was voluminous in size and offered copious detail about many events, but even the earliest of these works are not documents, but rather literary compositions, compiled many years – sometimes several centuries – after the events they describe. While these texts were compiled from yet earlier (now lost) sources or informants, the transmission of this material and its reliability were often uncertain.

The first Western historians who wished to write about early Islamic history in the eighteenth and nineteenth centuries overestimated the documentary value of the Muslim literary sources and, wishing to move beyond the misrepresentation and bigotry of the earlier polemical tradition, understandably were drawn to the literary sources both by their rich detail and by the fact that, as Muslim sources, they were assumed to offer a less biased view of early Islam than did the overly fertile imaginations of polemicists. The Western scholarship that resulted can thus be said to have followed the Descriptive Approach: that is, it utilised Muslim sources in the first instance to describe Islam and its early history. The summary provided in Gibbon's *Decline and fall*, just mentioned, fits into this category, as did the works of the Orientalist Gustav Weil (1808–89), such as his *Muhammed der Prophet* (1843) and *Geschichte der Chalifen* (1846–51);[10] and, as we shall see, this approach is still widely followed, especially in survey texts.

Greater familiarity with the Islamic sources that provided the substance of what Western scholars said about early Islamic history soon brought an awareness of the limitations of these sources. It became clear, for example, that they contained many contradictory reports, such as the conflicting

10 On the latter, see D. M. Dunlop, 'Some remarks on Weil's History of the caliphs', in Bernard Lewis and P. M. Holt (eds.), *Historians of the Middle East* (London, 1962).

accounts of the early Islamic conquests or of the events of the first civil war. In the interest of establishing 'what actually happened' some scholars attempted to harmonise these reports by attributing their contradictions to different informants who had different agendas and degrees of reliability as reporters. Tracing earlier informants was possible in many cases because individual reports were introduced by a chain of narrators (called the *sanad* or *isnād*) that listed the putative originator of the report and those who had transmitted it. This scrutiny of earlier informants, which we can call the Source-Critical Approach, first came into general use in the second half of the nineteenth century, and yielded some astute analyses that shaped the contours of historical-critical scholarship on various aspects of early Islamic history for many years – and, indeed, still does. Julius Wellhausen's *Prolegomena zur ältesten Geschichte des Islams* (1899), for example, which followed on and further developed some of the insights of M.J. de Goeje's *Mémoire sur la conquête de la Syrie* (1864), led subsequent generations of Western scholars to dismiss, or at least to handle with great scepticism, the narrations – and especially the chronology – of the early Kūfan compiler Sayf ibn ʿUmar (*fl. c.* 800?), and to prefer the reports of Ibn Isḥāq (d. 767 or 768), al-Wāqidī (d. 823), al-Madāʾinī (d. *c.* 845) and others; only in the last decade of the twentieth century did some revision of Wellhausen's judgements of Sayf appear.[11] The massive compilations of Leone Caetani (1869–1935), particularly his *Annali dell'Islam* (1905–26), were based on the assumption that by tabulating all extant accounts for a given event, with their narrators, historians could successfully reconstruct early Islamic history by comparing all reports and setting aside those traceable to 'weak' informants and by identifying spurious later elaborations. The works of Tor Andrae (1885–1947) on the life of Muḥammad similarly assumed that one could sift earlier 'historical' from later 'legendary' material.[12] More recently, analogous assumptions underlie the works of W. Montgomery Watt (1909–2006) on Muḥammad and Wilferd Madelung (b. 1930) on the early caliphate.[13]

Another trend in Western scholarship on early Islam, also developing first in the late nineteenth century, challenged the assumption of the source-critics that the information in the traditional Islamic narratives represented copies of

11 Ella Landau-Tasseron, 'Sayf ibn ʿUmar in medieval and modern scholarship', *Der Islam*, 67 (1990).

12 Tor Andrae, *Die Person Muhammads in Lehre und Glauben seiner Gemeinde* (Stockholm, 1918); Tor Andrae, 'Die Legenden von der Berufung Muḥammeds', *Le monde oriental*, 6 (1912).

13 W. Montgomery Watt, *Muḥammad at Mecca* (Oxford, 1953); W. Montgomery Watt, *Muḥammad at Medina* (Oxford, 1956); Wilferd Madelung, *The succession to Muḥammad* (Cambridge, 1997).

early documents or the verbatim reports of actual eyewitnesses. Instead, these scholars, whom we may call advocates of the Tradition-Critical Approach, argued that the reports we find in the Islamic sources were in most cases merely the capture in written form of oral traditions about the past. These traditions had diverse – and often uncertain – origins, and had undergone a period of oral transmission of indeterminate duration; hence, they could be used to reconstruct events of the past only with great caution, because it is usually impossible to know what material may have been dropped, added or changed in the course of transmission. The pioneer in these studies was the Hungarian scholar Ignaz Goldziher (1850–1921), whose revolutionary *Muhammedanische Studien* (1889–90) presented insights many of which still seem essentially sound over a century later, such as the fact that many reports attributed to the Prophet (*ḥadīths*) seem to be stalking-horses for the claims of later partisan groups in the Islamic community.[14] A number of scholars subsequent to Goldziher built on his work; particularly noteworthy are Joseph Schacht (1902–69) in the field of Islamic law,[15] Erling Ladewig Petersen (b. 1929) on reports about the first civil war[16] and Albrecht Noth (1938–99) on the conquest narratives.[17] Since the last third of the twentieth century numerous scholars have offered detailed tradition-critical studies of particular problems, among which the works of M. J. Kister (b. 1914), U. Rubin (b. 1944), Michael Lecker (b. 1951), Klaus Klier and many others can be taken as representative.[18]

The problem of the instability of orally transmitted reports was exacerbated by the likelihood that many of the early written compilations from the second

14 See Ignaz Goldziher, *Muhammedanische Studien* (Halle, 1889–90), vol. II, pp. 88–130, trans. S. M. Stern and C. R. Barber as *Muslim studies*, 2 vols. (London, 1967–71), vol. II, pp. 89–125. The enduring value of Goldziher's work is apparent from the fact that, many decades after their first publication, some of his major works were still being translated, e.g. Stern and Barber's *Muslim studies* and his *Vorlesungen über den Islam* (Heidelberg, 1910) trans. Andras and Ruth Hamori as *Introduction to Islamic theology and law* (Princeton, 1981).

15 Especially Joseph Schacht, *The origins of Muhammadan jurisprudence* (Oxford, 1950).

16 Erling Ladewig Petersen, *ʿAlī and Muʿāwiya in early Arabic tradition: Studies on the genesis and growth of Islamic historical writing until the end of the ninth century*, 2nd edn (Odense, 1974 [Copenhagen, 1964]).

17 Albrecht Noth, *Quellenkritische Untersuchungen zu Themen, Formen, und Tendenzen frühislamischer Geschichtsüberlieferung* (Bonn, 1973) rev. edn (with Lawrence I. Conrad), trans. Michael Bonner as *The early Arabic historical tradition* (Princeton, 1994); Albrecht Noth, 'Iṣfahān-Nihāwand. Eine quellenkritische Studie zur frühislamischen Historiographie', *ZDMG*, 118 (1968).

18 E.g. M. J. Kister, *Studies in jāhiliyya and early Islam* (London, 1980); Uri Rubin, 'Morning and evening prayers in Islam', *JSAI*, 10 (1987); Michael Lecker, *The 'Constitution of Medina': Muḥammad's first legal document* (Princeton, 2004); Klaus Klier, *Hālid und ʿUmar: Quellenkritische Untersuchung zur Historiographie der frühislamischen Zeit* (Berlin, 1998).

and third centuries AH in which such reports are found were themselves transmitted orally; that is, compilers of early written works often transmitted their material to their students by lecturing. Hence many 'books' exist in two or more recensions traceable to the notebooks or other records made by different students of the work's compiler. F. Sezgin, R. Sellheim, S. Leder, N. Calder, G. Schöler and others have vigorously debated the question of the stability of the texts of the early 'books' of which we have knowledge, or even whether they originally existed in the form of books at all, rather than just as collections of notes.[19]

In recent years the complexities of the sources have led some to adopt what can be called the Sceptical Approach, which, building especially on the work of Schacht and the tradition-critics, rejects the historicity of almost all the traditionally conveyed material; noteworthy early contributions in this vein were Patricia Crone and Michael Cook's *Hagarism* (1977) and John Wansbrough's *The sectarian milieu* (1978).[20] The fundamental argument of scholars in this group is that the tradition may not, in fact, contain any 'kernel' of true material; and even if it does, it is impossible now to disentangle it from the many layers of distortion and fabrication built up over centuries of manipulation. Whatever 'true' memories about Islam's origins may have been retained by early generations and subsequently preserved by the Islamic community in written form, the sceptics argue, have been subjected to so many successive waves of compression, fragmentation, recombination and reinterpretation that we now have only what Crone terms 'debris of an obliterated past'.[21] The sceptical school has raised many pointed and valuable questions about the reliability of the sources for early Islamic history and, therefore, what the appropriate attitude of the historian towards these sources might be. These questions continue to be discussed, but the sceptics

19 See esp. Fuat Sezgin, *Geschichte des arabischen Schrifttums*, vol. I (Leiden, 1967); Rudolf Sellheim, 'Abū 'Alī al-Qālī: Zum Problem mündlicher und schriftlicher Überlieferung am Beispiel von Sprichwörtersammlungen', in H. R. Roemer and A. Noth (eds.), *Studien zur Geschichte und Kultur des vorderen Orients: Festschrift für Bertold Spuler* (Leiden, 1981); Stefan Leder, *Das Korpus al-Haitam ibn 'Adī (st. 207/822): Herkunft, Überlieferung, Gestalt früher Texte der ahbār-Literatur* (Frankfurt, 1991); Norman Calder, *Studies in early Muslim jurisprudence* (Oxford, 1993); Gregor Schoeler, 'Die Frage der schriftlichen oder mündlichen Überlieferung der Wissenschaften in frühen Islam', *Der Islam*, 62 (1985); Gregor Schoeler, *Écrire et transmettre dans les débuts de l'Islam* (Paris, 2002).

20 See also Patricia Crone, *Slaves on horses: The evolution of the Islamic polity* (Cambridge, 1980), pp. 3–17; Yehuda D. Nevo and Judith Koren, 'The origins of the Muslim descriptions of the Jāhilī Meccan sanctuary', *JNES*, 49 (1990); G. R. Hawting, *The idea of idolatry and the emergence of Islam: From polemic to history* (Cambridge, 1999).

21 Crone, *Slaves on horses*, p. 10.

have encountered some scepticism about their own approach, because some of their claims seem overstated – or even unfounded.[22] Moreover, their work has to date been almost entirely negative – that is, while they have tried to cast doubt on the received version of 'what happened' in early Islamic history by impugning the sources, they have not yet offered a convincing alternative reconstruction of what might have happened.[23]

These different approaches to the sources emerged at successive historical moments but, rather than supplanting its predecessors, each new approach simply coexisted beside them, and all approaches continue to be practised today in varying degrees. A descriptive approach still seems to provide the basis of most modern overviews of early Islamic history, which offer the externals of the Islamic tradition's own origins narratives, adjusted slightly in order to bracket out the miraculous and the assumptions of Islam's faith-claims (in particular, that Muḥammad was a prophet and that the Qurʾān is God's revelation). Such works rely so heavily on Muslim literary sources in formulating their own reconstructions, however, that they have recently been characterised, with much justice, as 'Muslim chronicles in modern languages and graced with modern titles'.[24] The descriptive approach's continuing popularity with authors of survey texts about early Islamic history, despite the misgivings of scholars about the sources, is probably attributable to the fact that it offers the kind of smooth, outwardly plausible narrative that other approaches have not yet been able to muster.

On the other hand, contemporary scholars who examine Islam's origins in depth mainly tend to follow the source-critical or tradition-critical school in their handling of the Islamic sources. This work should lead in time to a more historically grounded general presentation of early Islamic history, but

22 An overview of the criticisms of the sceptical approach is found in Donner, *Narratives of Islamic origins*, pp. 25–31.

23 John Wansbrough, *The sectarian milieu: Content and composition of Islamic salvation history* (Oxford, 1978), p. x, explicitly eschews the possibility that the history of early Islam can be reconstructed. The reconstruction in Patricia Crone and Michael Cook's *Hagarism: The making of the Islamic world* (Cambridge, 1977) is imaginative, but raises more questions than it resolves and has not been generally accepted. Gerald Hawting, 'The rise of Islam', in Youssef M. Choueiri (ed.), *A companion to the history of the Middle East* (Oxford, 2005), offers general revisionist perspectives on the traditional view of how Islam first arose, but not a coherent synthesis of what might have happened, and his survey of Umayyad history in *The first dynasty of Islam: The Umayyad caliphate, AD 661–750* (Beckenham and Carbondale, 1987) offers a view fully consonant in most respects with the traditional Muslim sources and with earlier studies such as Julius Wellhausen's *Das arabische Reich und sein Sturz* (Berlin, 1902), trans. Margaret Graham Weir as *The Arab kingdom and its fall* (Calcutta, 1927).

24 Crone, *Slaves on Horses*, p. 13.

progress towards this goal has been slow. For one thing, many contributions in the tradition-critical mould focus almost entirely on problems of textual criticism and leave it unclear how much can be said about 'what actually happened', at least for the origins period.[25] While a number of specific issues have been clarified in careful tradition-critical studies, these studies do not yet add up to a clear general picture.[26] Most alternative narratives based squarely on revisionist perspectives still seem too general or vague, and are often presented explicitly as a critique of the traditional narrative, knowledge of which on the part of the reader they therefore take for granted.[27] For these reasons, scholars have not yet had much success translating the insights of tradition-critical work into a clear narrative of Islam's origins suitable for non-specialists that stands independent of most aspects of the traditional narrative. At the same time, their tradition-critical work on the Islamic sources sometimes creates tensions between Western (or Western-trained) scholars and their counterparts in the Muslim world who still cling to the assumption that the traditional Islamic sources, including Prophetic *ḥadīth* and the *akhbār* (reports) of the chronicles and biographical dictionaries, are quasi-documentary in character, an assumption the tradition-critics cannot accept.

Finally, it is necessary to say a few words about use of the Qurʾān as a source for writing early Islamic history. The Qurʾān has occupied a special place among the sources for early Islamic history, and probably always will, if only because of its special stature as Islam's scripture. Western scholars, while usually distancing themselves from the idea that the Qurʾān is the actual word of God, nevertheless generally accepted it as a text contemporary with the Prophet Muḥammad and hence valuable as a source for his life (some flatly declared, or implied, that Muḥammad was the text's author or compiler, which is of course patent heresy to some Believers). Even the historian who accepts the idea that the Qurʾān is contemporary with Muḥammad, however,

25 E.g. Uri Rubin, *The eye of the beholder: The life of Muḥammad as viewed by the early Muslims. A textual analysis* (Princeton, 1995), who admits (p. 3) that in his work 'the effort to isolate the "historical" from the "fictional" in the early Islamic texts is given up entirely'.

26 E.g. the many articles by M. J. Kister, a selection of which can be seen in his *Studies in Jāhiliyya and early Islam*; but Kister nowhere offers his sense of the overall historical development of the early Islamic community.

27 Perhaps the most successful attempt is Albrecht Noth's chapter 'Früher Islam', in Ulrich Haarmann *et al.* (eds.), *Geschichte der arabischen Welt* (Munich, 1987). Other noteworthy recent efforts are Jacqueline Chabbi, *Le seigneur des tribus: L'Islam de Mahomet* (Paris, 1997), which focuses particularly on the Prophet's Arabian context, and Alfred-Louis de Prémare, *Les fondations de l'Islam: Entre écriture et histoire* (Paris, 2002), which tries to read through the formation of key texts to the historical realities that lay behind them.

has difficulty deriving much information about specific historical events from the Qur'ān, because its references to its own historical context are maddeningly vague: it rarely provides a specific name or time or event. Serious critical study of the Qur'ān in the West began with the pioneering *Geschichte des Qorāns* (first edn 1860) of Theodor Nöldeke (1836–1930), which accepted many of the Islamic tradition's own assumptions about how the Qur'ān text came to be, and long served as a point of departure for scholars in the West.[28] Since the 1970s, however, our assumptions about the historical context of the Qur'ān and its evolution as a text have been challenged fundamentally. John Wansbrough proposed in his *Qur'anic studies* (1977) that the Qur'ān text did not coalesce as a canon of scripture shortly after the Prophet's death, as maintained by Muslim tradition and long accepted by most modern scholars, but rather that it emerged as a canon only at the end of a process that took two centuries or more. John Burton (*The collection of the Qur'an*, 1977), on the other hand, proposed that the Qur'ān text as we have it was already fixed by the time of Muḥammad's death. Günter Lüling (*Über den ur-Qur'ān*, 1974) and Christoph Luxenberg (*Die syro-aramäische Lesart des Koran*, 2000) advanced hypotheses that, while quite different from one another, both implied that the Qur'ān may contain material that antedates the life of Muḥammad. All these hypotheses can be deeply unsettling to believing Muslims, and the circulation of such ideas in popular media[29] has attracted the attention, not always favourable, of more traditionally minded members of the Muslim community and sparked a debate over the text's authority and over who has the right to interpret it, and how. There is some danger that traditional believers may misinterpret critical studies of the Qur'ān by scholars as polemical efforts to undermine Islam's faith-claims,[30] and that popular pressure may deter scholars from pursuing this line of research. But these ideas are not much less unsettling for historians who were accustomed to

28 Theodor Nöldeke, *Geschichte des Qorāns* (Göttingen, 1860). The text was in later editions completely reworked and greatly expanded by Friedrich Schwally and Gotthelf Bergsträsser.

29 E.g. Toby Lester, 'What is the Koran?', *The Atlantic Monthly* (January 1999). Lester's article appeared before the publication of Christoph Luxenberg's *Die syro-aramäische Lesart des Koran: Ein Beitrag zur Entschlüsselung der Koransprache* (Berlin, 2000), which has reignited the discussion with, if anything, greater intensity; discussion of the debate it generated is surveyed in Christoph Burgmer (ed.), *Streit um den Koran: Die Luxenberg-Debatte: Standpunkte und Hintergründe* (n.p., 2004).

30 This danger is increased by some who are, in fact, anti-Islamic polemicists, who irresponsibly seize on the work of critical scholars to advance their own anti-religious agenda; for example, the pseudonymous 'Ibn Warraq', who has edited several collections of scholarly articles, such as *The quest for the historical Muhammad* (Amherst, NY, 2000).

resorting to the Qurʾān as a source for what the Islam of the time of the Prophet may have been. The debate on the nature and history of the Qurʾān text is still full-throated in the early twenty-first century, and will doubtless continue so for many years to come.[31]

One consequence of these disagreements over how to view, and consequently how to exploit, the sources for the period of Islam's origins is that there continue to be dramatic differences of opinion among active scholars on 'what actually happened' in early Islamic history. Differences over the Qurʾān have been noted above, and they are echoed for other aspects of Islam's origins. In the realm of *ḥadīth* studies, the view of Goldziher and Schacht – that most *ḥadīths* are spurious interpolations of later opinions that were put in the mouth of the Prophet, and that their *isnāds* 'grew backwards' – was developed more fully by Gautier Juynboll[32] and others, but it must be tempered by the work of Motzki,[33] who has shown that the transmission of *ḥadīths* as recorded in their *isnāds*, even back to the seventh century CE, may be more secure than hitherto believed. Regarding the conquest narratives, Noth emphasised their salvation-historical character and questioned whether the conquests had any centralised impetus or direction,[34] Sharon and others suggested they never occurred at all,[35] and Conrad has shown that some conquest accounts appear to have no secure factual basis;[36] on the other hand, Donner stressed the cogency of understanding the conquests as a unitary phenomenon[37] and Robinson demonstrated that some early, independent non-Muslim sources confirm certain Muslim conquest reports.[38]

31 A survey is found in Fred M. Donner, 'The Qurʾān in recent scholarship: Challenges and desiderata', in Gabriel Said Reynolds (ed.), *Towards a new reading of the Qurʾān* (Abingdon, 2008).

32 Gautier Juynboll, *Muslim tradition* (Cambridge, 1983).

33 Harald Motzki, *Die Anfänge der islamischen Jurisprudenz* (Stuttgart, 1991).

34 Noth, *Early Arabic historical tradition*.

35 Moshe Sharon, 'The birth of Islam in the Holy Land', in M. Sharon (ed.), *Pillars of smoke and fire: The Holy Land in history and thought* (Johannesburg, 1988); Yehuda D. Nevo and Judith Koren, *Crossroads to Islam: The origins of the Arab religion and the Arab state* (Amherst, NY, 2003). See also several essays in Karl-Heinz Ohlig and Gerd-Rüdiger Puin (eds.), *Die dunklen Anfänge: Neue Forschungen zur Entstehung und frühen Geschichte des Islam* (n.p., 2006).

36 Lawrence I. Conrad, 'The conquest of Arwād: A source-critical study in the historiography of the medieval Near East', in A. Cameron and L. Conrad (eds.), *The Byzantine and early Islamic Near East*, vol. I: *Problems in the literary source material*, Studies in Late Antiquity and Early Islam 1 (Princeton, 1993).

37 Fred M. Donner, 'Centralized authority and military autonomy in the early Islamic conquests', in A. Cameron (ed.), *The Byzantine and early Islamic Near East*, vol. III: *States, resources, and armies* (Princeton, 1995).

38 Chase F. Robinson, 'The conquest of Khūzistān: A historiographical reassessment', *BSOAS*, 67 (2004).

The examples offered above illustrate some of the vexations that have afflicted those who work on Islam's origins. For periods subsequent to the origins era (that is, after *c.* 750 CE) historians are blessed not only with somewhat more plentiful documentary sources, but also with a much larger corpus of textual materials that, while not documentary, passed through a shorter period of oral and literary transmission than the Islamic origins narratives before being fixed in their present forms. This makes them a somewhat more secure basis for reconstructing 'what actually happened', but even these sources were sometimes subjected to tendentious redaction and literary shaping, and must be used circumspectly.[39]

Practical and conceptual problems

Beyond the thorny problems posed by the heritage of the polemical tradition and by the deficiencies of the sources for early Islamic history, there exist other problems of perception and conceptualisation, as well as practical obstacles, that have affected Western approaches to early Islamic history.

Balance

The historian viewing the gradual crystallisation and elaboration of 'classical' Islamic civilisation would surely consider this to be a process that spanned four to five centuries, from the time of the Prophet Muḥammad in the late sixth century until at least the eleventh century. It took this long for the crucial questions of communal identity to be resolved and for the religious doctrines, legal and political institutions, and cultural and social practices that we consider typical of fully developed 'classical Islam' to emerge from the robust debates and disparate materials of the early Islamic centuries. For example, the institution of Muslim *qāḍīs* or judges, or the systematised law they administered, or the concepts of Prophetic *sunna* and scholarly consensus (*ijmāʿ*) that were among the fundamental principles of this law, were all things that emerged at the earliest only a century after the time of the Prophet.

39 See, for example, Tayeb El-Hibri, *Reinterpreting Islamic historiography: Hārūn al-Rashīd and the narrative of the ʿAbbāsid caliphate* (Cambridge, 1999), which explores how these sources were shaped to fit a political agenda; also Boaz Shoshan, *Poetics of Islamic historiography: Deconstructing Ṭabarī's* History (Leiden, 2004); Jacob Lassner, *Islamic revolution and historical memory. An inquiry into the art of ʿAbbāsid apologetics*, AOS Series 66 (New Haven, 1986); Antoine Borrut, 'Entre mémoire et pouvoir: L'espace syrien sous les derniers omeyyades et les premiers abbassides (v. 72–193/692–809)', Ph.D. thesis, Université de Paris I (2007).

Yet within this half-millennium of early Islamic history, Western scholarship has until very recently focused overwhelmingly on the very earliest episodes, while later periods, which must be seen as equally part of the long story of the formation of the classical Islamic paradigm, were relatively neglected. Thus, if one surveys the literature on the Islamic world written in the West before the mid-twentieth century one finds numerous contributions and some debate on the Prophet, the Qurʾān, the early Islamic conquests, early statecraft (including early taxation), the early civil wars and emergence of sectarian groups etc., but far less on the later Umayyads, the history of the ʿAbbāsid caliphate, and even less on such things as the Būyid emirate and Saljūq sultanate, the Fāṭimid caliphate, the Almoravids, the Ghaznavids, the history of Yemen etc.

There were probably several reasons for this imbalance. It may merely reflect a general tendency among historians to search for 'origins' on the assumption that they hold the key to later developments. It may also be that Western scholars inherited a bias against later periods from their Muslim sources, which viewed the age of the Prophet and Companions as the 'golden age' against which all others paled. But it also seems likely that this imbalance, or skewed focus, is an unintended echo of the many centuries of anti-Islamic polemic, which concentrated on the earliest chapters of Islamic history because it was there, the polemicists believed, that they could most easily score theological 'points' against Islam. This had the unintended consequence of bringing the historical problems of the beginnings of Islam into clearer focus and fuller debate, and in this way inadvertently set the historical agenda even for non-polemical scholars of a later age, who mostly ignored later episodes in early Islamic history (from Umayyad times to the eleventh century). There were a few exceptions, which revealed the preoccupations of late nineteenth- and twentieth-century Europe. The small subfield of Arabic-Islamic philosophy and science became relatively developed at an early stage because Western scholars of the nineteenth and early twentieth centuries, steeped since secondary school in Greek and in the classical philosophical tradition, were keen to help recover lost Greek works that survived in Arabic translation. They also became concerned with tracing the original contributions of Muslim philosophers such as al-Fārābī, al-Kindī and Ibn Rushd, who received serious scholarly attention by the nineteenth century.[40] The history of the Levant in the time of the European Crusades similarly piqued the curiosity of numerous scholars in

40 E.g. M. Steinschneider, *al-Farābī*, Mémoires de l'Academie Impériale de Sciences de Saint-Petersbourg 7, 8, 4, (St Petersburg, 1869); Ibn Rushd in particular has been the

the nineteenth century, as reflected in the compilation of the massive *Recueil des historiens des croisades* (1896–1906), containing excerpts of relevant texts, including Arabic and other Oriental texts, in the original and French translation; Claude Cahen's pioneering study of the principality of Antioch marked a watershed in such work.[41] But generally, studies of the historical, social and literary development of the Islamic world in the period after the Prophet and conquests were few and far between, at least until the 1960s, when the pace began to quicken. The Harvard historian Sir Hamilton Gibb (1895–1971) seems to have played some role in this process, as he encouraged many students to work in later periods, among them I. Lapidus, R. Bulliet and R. Mottahedeh.

Practical impediments

The problem of imbalance was partly also a consequence of the fact that the number of scholars actually engaging in research on early Islam was until recently very small, whereas the range of material they needed to cover was enormous. As late as the 1960s it was often the case that for a given major subfield (even something as vast as Islamic law) there was in each Western country (or even in several together) only one scholar who made that subfield his or her speciality and actively pursued research on it. The number of young scholars entering the field in each generation was sufficiently small that a new recruit was often encouraged to concentrate on something that was not 'already being done' by someone else. This contributed to an overly deferential attitude towards that one scholar, who was deemed a generation's real expert on a given subject because there was precious little by way of vigorous exchange of different views on it. (Thus, for two decades or more, Montgomery Watt was the dominant scholar in the British Isles who studied the Prophet Muḥammad, Joseph Schacht was almost the sole figure of renown in the United States who concentrated on Islamic law etc.)[42] There also seemed to be an exaggerated deference shown to traditional views, so that the work of scholars who challenged establish orthodoxies was neglected; the works of Henri Lammens

subject of a huge bibliography. A compact survey of this material is found in Franz Rosenthal, *Das Fortleben der Antike im Islam* (Zurich, 1965), trans. Emile and Jenny Marmorstein as *The classical heritage in Islam* (Berkeley, 1975).

41 *Recueil des historiens des croisades* (Paris, 1869–1906) included six large volumes devoted to 'historiens orientaux', including Arabic, Armenian, Greek and other sources. Claude Cahen, *La Syrie du Nord à l'époque des croisades et la principauté d'Antioche* (Paris, 1940) was among the first works to study closely the regions taken by the Crusaders, rather than just the movement itself and its Latin participants.

42 This also affected later historical periods: for example, David Ayalon was for roughly a quarter-century virtually the only Western scholar who specialised in the study of the Mamlūks of Egypt.

(1862–1937), criticised for their anti-Islamic tenor, or the study by Paul Casanova (1861–1926), *Mohamed et la fin du monde*, considered too radical for their day, come to mind.[43] This meant that these fields tended for long periods to be static, rather than involved in a dynamic scholarly discourse, and that in general the opening of new subfields was slow.

This problem was exacerbated by the fact that the teaching of Arabic and other languages relevant to early Islamic history (Persian, Syriac, Coptic, Pahlavi) was limited to a very few institutions in the West until the mid-twentieth century, and, as everyone knows, Arabic in particular is not an easy language to acquire. Moreover, these languages were often taught inadequately, and were in many cases never mastered sufficiently to enable a scholar to read the sources with facility. Most programmes of study before the mid-twentieth century provided little if any opportunity for students to polish their knowledge of living languages in parts of the Near East where they were actually spoken.

Furthermore, the heavily philological training that, while indispensable, should have been a necessary preliminary, often took so much time that it became virtually a scholar's complete scholarly formation, leaving little opportunity for strong training in historical method, literary analysis, intellectual history, social theory and the like.[44] Generations of Western scholars groomed above all to excel at close philological analysis of classical Arabic texts were usually neither trained nor temperamentally prepared to venture into synthetic considerations of a broader kind, and when they did so the results were often methodologically naive. In the field of history, moreover, the existence of voluminous Muslim chronicles seems to have sapped enthusiasm for undertaking the arduous labours of synthetic work in a field so understaffed; it was much easier to translate or paraphrase these chronicles to secure a basic historical story-line about 'what actually happened' in Islamic history[45] – a story that frequently accepted the interpretation embedded in the source either uncritically or with minimal critical scrutiny. When persuasive syntheses were prepared, moreover, they often remained the dominant paradigm for decades. For example, Wellhausen's *Das arabische Reich und sein Sturz*, first published in 1902, found its first real monographic alternative

43 E.g. Henri Lammens, *Fatima et les filles de Mahomet: Notes critiques pour l'étude de la Sîra* (Rome, 1912); Paul Casanova, *Mahomet et la fin du monde*, 3 vols. (Paris, 1911–24).

44 Rodinson, *Europe and the mystique of Islam*, pp. 88–9, 92–3; Richard Bulliet, 'Orientalism and medieval Islamic studies', in John Van Engen (ed.), *The past and future of medieval studies* (Notre Dame, 1994), esp. p. 98.

45 A case in point is Julius Wellhausen's *Muhammad in Medina, daß ist Vakidi's Kitāb al-Maghazi in verkürzter deutscher Wiedergabe herausgegeben* (Berlin, 1882).

only in the 1970s, and is still referred to regularly in the early twenty-first century.[46] The result was a fairly static picture of most of Islamic history, closely tied in its approach and emphases to the Muslim sources themselves (what we have above termed the descriptive approach).

Fortunately, since the middle of the twentieth century matters have improved markedly with regard to both balance and staffing. Partly due to funding provided by Western governments concerned with global diplomacy in the Cold War era, universities were in the 1960s able to devote more attention than before to training specialists in Middle Eastern languages, and many of these students also pursued Islamic studies generally, including early Islamic history.[47] Additional university positions were created, and more students drawn into the field. This process seems to have accelerated in the last years of the twentieth century with growing public awareness of the importance of Islam and the Middle East in the modern world. Language training underwent a transformation; the purely philological approach gave way to one that emphasised languages as living forms of expression, and language courses became both more widespread and more intense, and university programmes of study increasingly involved time spent in countries where the target languages were spoken.

As a result of these changes many fields that were hardly studied at all – including those in the later phases of the early Islamic period, such as Būyid or Fāṭimid history – or were the preserve of one or two specialists in a generation – such as Islamic law – are now actively pursued by numerous practitioners, and intellectual debate is often lively, sometimes carried out in an increasing array of specialised journals. Scholars of early Islamic history have shown increased interest in developing new approaches and methods, and in looking at such things as social history, gender relations, identity formation and economic history. Whole new disciplinary foci have begun to develop, such as the archaeology of the early Islamic period. At the same time, certain well-established but torpid subfields have been revitalised, often by the publication of revisionist works that have aroused controversy; the most notable example is the study of the Qurʾān and of Islam's origins, ignited by the near-simultaneous publication in 1977 of Wansbrough's *Qurʾanic studies* and Crone and Cook's *Hagarism*. In the early twenty-first century the study of early Islamic history seems finally to have shaken off its earlier stagnancy, inadequate linguistic training, methodological *naïveté* and conceptual conservatism, and to have matured as a field.

46 The alternative, inferior in some ways to Wellhausen's synthesis, was M. A. Shaban's *Islamic history: A new interpretation*, 2 vols. (Cambridge, 1971–6), vol. I: *AD 600–750 (AH 132)*.

47 Lockman, *Contending visions*, pp. 241–5.

Reductionism

The obvious parallels that any reader can note between some material in the Qurʾān and various passages in the Hebrew Bible or New Testament became a focus of early comparative research, often of a crassly reductionist kind: that is, it dismissively 'reduced' early Islam or the Qurʾān to being merely a deformed version of Judaic or Christian materials, which, it implied, were better because older. Such studies often proceeded on the simplistic assumption that the Qurʾān had borrowed material directly from the earlier scriptures, or at least was dependent on them in a way that, they implied, somehow undermined its truth-claims.[48] Sometimes one suspects that these works represent a thinly veiled (and perhaps partly subconscious) form of polemic, written by Western scholars who, despite their extensive scientific training, were deeply committed to their own faith (usually Christianity or Judaism). While a relationship of some kind between the Qurʾān and the earlier scriptures can hardly be doubted, these reductionist studies were marred by their failure to consider the possibility that the Qurʾān's contents might represent a truly original, creative reinterpretation of older materials, that the objectives of the Qurʾānic version of these materials might be utterly different from the objectives of the earlier scriptures, or that what was not 'borrowed' by the Qurʾān is just as important in assessing its spirit, intent and originality.[49]

Since the last quarter of the twentieth century Western scholarship (particularly on the Qurʾānic materials) has generally begun to move beyond a reductionist view of early Islam, and has emphasised the uniqueness and originality even of those Qurʾānic passages that find close parallels in earlier scriptural traditions. At the same time, some new works have appeared that argue for an even closer *textual* relationship between the Qurʾān and earlier scriptures than had hitherto been assumed – notably the studies of Lüling and Luxenberg, mentioned above. The debate on these issues continues.

Grip of traditional origins narrative

Another serious shortcoming of most Western studies of early Islam since the Enlightenment has been, until recently, a difficulty in constructing a

48 Noteworthy studies of this sort were Abraham Geiger's *Was hat Mohamed aus dem Judenthume aufgenommen* (Berlin, 1833); Richard Bell, *The origin of Islam in its Christian environment* (London, 1926); Charles Cutler Torrey, *The Jewish foundations of Islam* (New York, 1933).

49 A reaction to such reductionism is found in Marilyn Robinson Waldman, 'New approaches to "biblical" materials in the Qurʾān', *MW*, 75 (1985).

truly historical picture of Islam's origins due to an overdependence on the traditional origins narrative constructed long ago by early Muslim historians – what we have termed the 'descriptive approach'. The dearth of truly documentary sources and the apparent plausibility of the traditional origins narrative meant that it was not until the problem of the sources for early Islam was tackled more intensively that progress could be made on constructing a truly historical picture of early Islam. A series of revisionist works appearing since the mid-1970s have challenged some of the most familiar tenets of the older view. These include, to mention a few, the idea that the environment in which the Qur'ān crystallised was primarily one of paganism (challenged by Lüling (in 1974) and Hawting (in 1999)); that Mecca was a vibrant centre of international trade (Crone (1987)); that the Qur'ān text was a fixed textual canon from an early date, and even that it emerged in Arabia (Wansbrough (1977)); that anything recognisable as 'Islam' had crystallised during the time of the Prophet (Cook and Crone (1977)); that there occurred any military campaigns corresponding to the 'Islamic conquests' in the three decades after the death of the Prophet in 632 (Sharon (1988); Koren and Nevo (1991, 2003)); or that the earliest community of Believers was confessionally distinct from Christians, Jews and other monotheists (Donner (2002–3)). In general, there is a need to incorporate more fully a vision of early Islamic history as an organic continuation of trends in the history of the Late Antique Near East,[50] such as that articulated by Peter Brown's *The world of Late Antiquity* (1971) or Garth Fowden's *Empire to commonwealth* (1993). Such a perspective does not deny the importance of the Arabian context, but emphasises more fully the significance of Hellenistic–Roman and Sasanian–Iranian traditions in weaving the fabric of early Islamic history. These revisionist positions are still being vigorously debated, and the degree to which they will temper the vision of Islam's beginnings inherited from the Islamic origins narrative remains to be seen.

Secularising perspective

Another shortcoming of many Western studies of early Islamic history, particularly during the first two-thirds of the twentieth century, stemmed from the prevalence of a secular mentality among Western scholars. This

50 Cf. the remarks of Wilfred Cantwell Smith, 'The historical development in Islam of the concept of Islam as an historical development', in Lewis and Holt (eds.), *Historians of the Middle East*, pp. 484–502.

appears to have led many of them to discount the possibility that religious motivations may have been central to the spread of the Believers' movement: it was sometimes argued, in reductionist fashion, that the expansion was 'really' driven by economic interests, or a desire for social reform, or was a mere by-product of a process of state formation.[51] The fact that secular-minded historians do not themselves subscribe to the faith-claims of Islam, however, should not cause them to dismiss the efficacy of religious belief as a motivating factor in human societies. It seems more honest to acknowledge frankly the possibility that the early Believers' rapid expansion may indeed have been a consequence of religious inspiration and zeal for the faith. The fact that the early conquerors do not seem to have been particularly concerned with 'converting' the conquered populations to 'Islam' – sometimes offered as evidence against seeing the expansion process as fundamentally a religious movement – is hardly convincing; the Believers may have been concerned not to 'convert' individuals to their faith, but merely to sweep away what they viewed as the impious older regimes and replace them with a righteous public order, one that adhered more closely to what they understood as God's revealed law. In any case, the possibility that the early Believers' movement was not confessionally conceived – that is, that pious Jews and Christians may have formed an integral part of it – suggests that the whole question of 'conversion' is, for this early period, misleading and inappropriate, a retrojection of later conditions of confessional distinctness back into the origins period.

The dynamism ascribed to the early Believers during their rapid expansion from Arabia into Syria, Iraq, Egypt and Iran might be well explained by another kind of religious motivation, namely that the movement may have been inspired by apocalyptic speculations. Conviction that the Last Judgement was imminent is exactly the kind of idea that is sufficient to cause people to drop their normal way of life and join a cause in the interest of their own presumed salvation at the End-Time. The idea that Muḥammad and his followers may have been inspired by apocalyptic concerns, raised early in the twentieth century by Paul Casanova,[52] was long given a cool reception by most Western scholars, and is staunchly opposed by most devout Muslims. In recent years, however, the idea has

51 Among these are works by Grimme, Winkler, Caetani, Lammens, Becker, Hitti, von Grunebaum, Watt, Donner and Crone. See the discussion in Fred M. Donner, 'Orientalists and the rise of Islam', in Sami A. Khasawnih (ed.), *Conference on Orientalism: Dialogue of Cultures, 22–24 October 2002* (Amman, 2004), pp. 75–8.

52 Casanova, *Mahomet et la fin du monde*.

again gained some favour, particularly because evidence for apocalyptic concerns in the later seventh and eighth centuries CE has become more abundant,[53] so a final verdict on the question of apocalypticism as part of the original impetus of Islam remains for the future.

Nationalist conceptualisations

Yet another problem of perception that afflicts much modern scholarship on early Islam (in this case including both Western scholarship and that written in Islamic countries) is the projection of recent and modern nationalist identities into the distant past. Throughout the nineteenth and early twentieth centuries nationalism (and its foundations in racism) was the regnant ideology in Western historical studies, and was subsequently adopted by most non-Western societies, especially during the age of Western colonial domination. Nationalism, a manifestation of the Romantic reaction against Enlightenment concepts of rationalism, was one form of that philosophy that saw history as a kind of mysterious force moving towards certain ends through the agency of large collectivities such as nations or classes.[54] Nationalist ideology posited that humankind was 'naturally' divided into races or nations (such as 'Arabs', 'Turks', 'Jews' (as a national, rather than a religious, identity), 'Armenians' etc.), each of which exhibited a distinctive pattern of physical, mental and emotional or psychological characteristics; and much scholarship prior to the Second World War analysed history, including early Islamic history, as the product of the interaction (sometimes unconscious) of these supposed 'natural' national groups. So, for example, the ʿAbbāsid overthrow of the Umayyad regime in 750 was interpreted as a 'Persian national uprising' against 'Arab' domination,[55] and countless books and articles referred to the first expansion of the Believers following Muḥammad's death in 632 as the 'Arab conquest', implying (if not arguing outright) that the movement was at heart an expression of a kind of national solidarity among the

53 E.g. David Cook, *Studies in Muslim apocalyptic* (Princeton, 2002); M. J. Kister, '"A booth like the booth of Moses...": A study of an early *ḥadīth*', *BSOAS*, 25 (1962); Wilferd Madelung, 'Apocalyptic prophecies in Ḥimṣ in the Umayyad age', *JSS*, 31 (1986); Michael Cook, 'An early Islamic apocalyptic chronicle', *JNES*, 52 (1993); F. M. Donner, 'Piety and eschatology in early Khārijite poetry', in Ibrahim As-Saʿāfīn (ed.), *Fī miḥrāb al-maʿrifa: Festschrift for Iḥsān ʿAbbās* (Beirut, 1997).

54 Hourani, *Islam in European thought*, p. 44.

55 E.g. Theodor Nöldeke, *Orientalische Skizzen* (Berlin, 1892), p. 88: 'The victory of the Abbasids brought an end to the purely Arab, and therewith the purely Semitic, state; we see here for the most part a reaction of the Persian element and the restoration of the old Asiatic empires.'

'Arabs', the realisation of their 'natural' yearning for unity.[56] It is, however, highly questionable whether the peoples of Arabia in the seventh century, or those peoples who spoke some form of language that we today would categorise as Arabic, conceived of themselves as constituting a single 'people'.[57] Their operative identities were, rather, based on tribal and lineage categories, or on local (geographical) or religious conceptions. They would have thought of themselves as Tamīmīs or Qurashīs or Hāshimites, as Meccans or Yathribīs, or as Monophysite Christians or Jews or worshippers of Hubal; any ethnic or 'national' identity they felt would have been decidedly secondary and probably very weak.[58] The imposition of essentially modern national identities such as 'Arabs' onto a remote past when they were not yet operative thus distorts, sometimes grotesquely, the interpretation of what happened; at the very least it tends to mask other factors that may have been more important. So, for example, referring to the expansion of the early Believers as the 'Arab conquest' – a term that is still widely used – obscures its nature as a religious movement and converts it instead into an expression of a presumed 'national' solidarity. The damage caused by use of inappropriate 'national' conceptualisations has been increased by the translation of many of these Western works into Middle Eastern languages; this has reinforced these conceptualisations among Middle Eastern scholars, many of whom already embrace strongly nationalist ideas. 'National' conceptualisations remain deeply ingrained in much modern writing on early Islamic history, and eradicating them remains a challenge for the coming generations of historians.

Fragmentation

A final challenge that faces historians of early Islam is a consequence of the rapidly increasing pace of scholarship since the 1960s. As recently as the 1970s it was still possible for the determined fledgling scholar to read, within a few years, the majority of the important secondary literature in Western languages on medieval Islamic history from the rise of Islam up to the Mamlūks. The avalanche of new publications since that time means that

56 See J. Fück, 'Islam as an historical problem in European historiography since 1800', in Lewis and Holt (eds.), *Historians of the Middle East*. Even the great Goldziher could not completely escape the influence of such ideas: in his *Muhammedanische Studien* he frequently speaks of the 'national Arab character' of the Umayyad regime, etc.

57 See Jan Retsö, *The Arabs in Antiquity* (London and New York, 2003), esp. pp. 108–10.

58 See Saleh Said Agha and Tarif Khalidi, 'Poetry and identity in the Umayyad age', *al-Abhath*, 50–1 (2002–3); F. M. Donner, 'Modern nationalism and medieval Islamic history', *al-ʿUsur al-Wusta*, 13 (2001).

scholars now can only really keep up with developments in one or two corners of what used to be a more unified field of study. As noted earlier, whole new specialisations have emerged, the mastering of which is today virtually a full-time undertaking: Qur'ānic studies, *ḥadīth* studies, Islamic law, Islamic archaeology, the history of Islamic Spain and many others have developed a momentum of their own, and many long-recognised fields, such as Islamic art history and numismatics, have developed in depth and sophistication of method to the point that one cannot hope to control them without devoting one's full attention to them. The rich rewards brought by our advancing knowledge of early Islamic history are thus sometimes won at the cost of making it more difficult to encompass a broader view of things. This fragmentation caused by increased specialisation is, to be sure, a problem faced by all areas of knowledge, but historians of the early Islamic world will have to develop their own ways of handling the particular challenges it poses for them.

16

Numismatics

STEFAN HEIDEMANN

Islamic coins as a historical source

At least since Leopold von Ranke (1795–1886), the historical-critical approach to any study of history has demanded parallel independent proof in order to establish firmly a given historical fact. Historians of Islamic societies have almost no primary documents or archives for the period prior to the fifteenth century. In contrast to the scarce primary documents, the secondary sources – literary and historical accounts, especially from the ninth to the tenth centuries – are abundant.

This gross imbalance between the lack of primary documents, produced in the course of the events, and chronicles written much later has led scholars to depend greatly upon medieval but secondary authors. Since they typically wrote from the point of view of a city, a ruling house, a ruler or a religious community or school of law their accounts are necessarily biased. Without independent documents or material evidence the modern historian is often unable to corroborate or to refute these literary accounts; sometimes even important lacunae in our knowledge may remain unnoticed. After being widely neglected following the First World War the study and use of Islamic numismatic documents have again become a prospering academic subject, particularly in the 1990s.[1]

Islamic coins of the classical period can be characterised above all as bearers of texts of up to 150 words (fig. 16.35). The texts on coins struck during the first six-and-a-half centuries of Islam often mention up to five names, providing the entire hierarchy of power – from the local governor up to the caliph at the time and location of minting. They usually name the mint town, sometimes even the urban quarter, usually the year, and sometimes even the month and the day. Religious legends provide hints of the political orientation of the ruler

1 See the chapter bibliography below.

who commissioned the coin. The inclusion of the name onto the coin protocol (*sikka*) and in the Friday prayer (*khuṭba*) served in their time as proof of who the actual ruler was. Both had a similar political value. The reference to the hierarchy of rulers in the Friday prayer was purely verbal and therefore transient, whereas on coins the protocol can be found permanently stored on a metal object that was frequently reproduced, like a 'bulletin of state'. As what are normally precisely datable archaeological artefacts, they open a further dimension of information.[2]

Coins as source of economic and legal history

Money as a means of coordinating human decisions and economic exchange is a complex social invention. It must always adjust to the prevailing economic, political and juridical conditions. Seen from another angle, its design and evolution reveal much about the societies creating it. In the pre-modern world the supply of coins – the physical instruments for the exchange of goods and services – were usually scarce. However, in order to function as an 'absolute price' (*thaman muṭlaq*) or 'equivalent' (*thaman*) – that is, as money – at least one certain type of coin has to be available in sufficient quantities. Non-physical forms of money, bills of exchange (*ḥawāla*) and cheques (*suftaja*), were developed in the Middle East, but they were used only among small communities bound by ties of trust and kinship, such as, for example, in networks of long-distance merchants in major trade cities.

The value of coins was determined by market forces. It always exceeded the value of the same amount of metal as a mere commodity, although it was bound to the metal content, the difference being smaller for high-value coins than for petty coinage. If a coin-type was generally accepted and was in sufficient supply, it was maintained over a long period and remained stable in design and usually in metallic content.

Two separate currencies always existed side by side, serving distinct needs within different social classes: high-value money, usually gold or pure silver coins; and petty coinage, usually debased silver, billon or copper coins. Gold coins, and, to a certain extent, silver coins, constituted the principal currency for wholesale and long-distance merchants (*tujjār* and *jallābūn*) as well as for

2 S. Heidemann, 'Settlement patterns, economic development and archaeological coin finds in Bilād aš-Šām: The case of the Diyār Muḍar', in K. Bartl and A. Moaz (eds.), *Residences, castles, settlements: Transformation processes from Late Antiquity to early Islam in Bilad al-Sham. Proceedings of the International Conference held at Damascus, 5–9 November 2006*, Orient-Archäologie 24 (Rahden, 2009).

fiscal administration and state expenditure. It was also the money of high-ranking state officials and military, who needed it to store wealth, to transfer it conveniently over long distances and to make payments of large sums. High-value coins could be traded between regions, and stood in competition with other similar coins. Geographically well-defined borders of currency zones hardly existed. If they did exist, then it was for economic reasons and fiscal measures.

The second currency type fulfilled the needs for daily purchases. It was the money of small dealers, artisans, workers (*sūqa* and *bāʿa*) in the urban market (*sūq*) and, of course, of the rest of the urban population. The urban population was dependent for their livelihood on income that usually came from their activities within the boundaries of a city or town, and thus on purchases within the urban markets. The majority of the people in pre-modern societies – the rural population, peasants and nomads – relied mainly on subsistence. Only certain extra requirements and excess produce were bought and sold in the *sūq*.

The ratio in price between high-value and petty coinage was usually determined by supply and demand. The demand for small coins far exceeded their supply, as the central authorities usually neglected to provide a sufficient supply. This allowed a much higher profit for those who could provide these means of exchange – in other words, the local fiscal and political authorities or private money-changers. Petty coins could also be imported from other regions at a profit.

During the third/ninth century the legal prescriptions for money became fully developed, the most important among them being the theory of value and the prohibition of *ribā* (illegitimate profit according to the *sharīʿa*). Islamic law forbids two equal amounts of precious metal from being valued differently in one single transaction. This is the core of the prohibition of *ribā*. Islamic legal theory determined the value of money to be identical with the intrinsic value of the bullion. Only silver and gold were the commodities that could be legally used for any transaction as 'absolute price'. Muslim jurists of the fifth/eleventh century, however, were aware of the contradiction between observed empirical reality and the normative imperative of the revealed law. They recognised that the fluctuating value of coins was based on the interest of the public in it – that is, on the market forces. In order to facilitate a monetary economy in the period of regional currencies with different finenesses and weights the jurists invented several legal arguments to ensure that market exchanges were in accord with Islamic law.

The majority of the jurists did not regard copper coins – the generic term is *fals / fulūs* – as money or 'absolute price / equivalent'; if they regarded them at all, then they did so only as a substitute for money. Copper coins could serve in some, but not all, legal transactions, as did gold and silver.[3]

The development of the representation of a new universal religion and its empire: Zubayrid and Khārijite challenge and Umayyad reform

Coins and their imagery are our only contemporary continuous primary source for the genesis of the self-representation of the new religion and its empire in the seventh century. Our understanding on these early coins has grown quickly since the 1990s.[4]

The Islamic armies swiftly conquered three major zones of monetary circulation, and took over much of their fiscal organisation: the former Byzantine territories in the centre; the Sasanian empire in the east; and Germanic North Africa and Spain. In the Byzantine territories the workhorse of the fiscal cycle, of taxation and state expenditure, was the gold *solidus* or *nomisma* of about 4.55 grams (fig. 16.1). The money used for the daily

3 C. M. Cipolla, *Money, prices and civilization in the Mediterranean world* (Princeton, 1956), pp. 27–37; R. Brunschvig, 'Conceptions monétaires chez les juristes musulmanes (VIIIe–XIIIe siècles)', *Arabica*, 14 (1967); Avram L. Udovitch, *Partnership and profit in medieval Islam* (Princeton, 1970), pp. 55–6; S. Heidemann, *Die Renaissance der Städte in Nordsyrien und Nordmesopotamien: Städtische Entwicklung und wirtschaftliche Bedingungen in ar-Raqqa und Ḥarrān von der Zeit der beduinischen Vorherrschaft bis zu den Seldschuken*, Islamic History and Civilization, Studies and Texts 40 (Leiden, 2002), pp. 356–61, 367.

4 M. Bates, 'History, geography and numismatics in the first century of Islamic coinage', *Schweizerische Numismatische Rundschau*, 65 (1986); S. Heidemann, 'The merger of two currency zones in early Islam: The Byzantine and Sasanian impact on the circulation in former Byzantine Syria and northern Mesopotamia', *Iran*, 36 (1998); L. Treadwell, *The chronology of the pre-reform copper coinage of early Islamic Syria*, Supplement to Oriental Numismatic Society Newsletter 162 (London, 2000); S. Album and T. Goodwin, *The pre-reform coinage of the early Islamic Period*, Sylloge of Islamic Coins in the Ashmolean 1 (London, 2002); A. Oddy, 'Whither Arab-Byzantine numismatics? A review of fifty years' research', *Byzantine and Modern Greek Studies*, 28 (2004); T. Goodwin, *Arab-Byzantine coinage*, Study in the Khalili Collection 4 (London, 2005); C. Foss, *Arab-Byzantine coins: An introduction, with a catalogue of the Dumbarton Oaks Collection* (Cambridge, MA, 2009). For the economic and political history see esp. J. Johns, 'Archaeology and the history of early Islam: The first seventy years', *JESHO*, 46 (2003); M. G. Morony, 'Economic boundaries? Late Antiquity and early Islam', *JESHO*, 47 (2004). For the iconocgraphic development see S. Heidemann, 'The development of the representation of the early Islamic empire and its religion on coin imagery', in Angelika Neuwirth, Nicolai Sinai and Michael Marx (eds.), *The Qurʾan in context: Historical and literary investigations into the Qurʾanic milieu* (Leiden, forthcoming).

purchases, the copper *follis* (pl. *folles*) (fig. 16.2), was sold by the treasury as well. In 629/30 Heraclius (r. 610–41) had concentrated all minting in the imperial capital, Constantinople. During the Sasanian occupation between 606–7 and 628 irregular mints were established in Syria, supplementing the circulating stock of copper coins.[5] In the Sasanian empire the money of the fiscal cycle was the uniform silver *drahm* of about 4.2 grams, which was struck in the days of Khusrau II (r. 590/591–628) in about thirty-four mints (fig. 16.3). Almost nothing is known about late Sasanian copper coinage. Tiny coppers, which are now rare, probably circulated in the major urban centres. Their issues became especially rich in design under Arab rule, and constitute an excellent source for art history.[6] In Spain and North Africa monetary economy had receded since the Roman empire, since the fifth century. The third of the *solidus*, the *tremisses* (*c.* 1.5 g), was the main and only coin struck in Spain and the rest of western Europe (cf. fig. 16.4). In North Africa Carthage was the only mint to continue striking petty coinage.

In the first decades after the battle of Yarmūk in 636 CE and the establishment of the Taurus border zone, Byzantine coppers remained in circulation, and were with few interruptions almost continuously supplemented by new imports from Byzantium. In contrast, the influx of *nomismata* dropped considerably. The obverse of the *follis* shows the emperor – here (fig. 16.2) the standing figure of Constans II (r. 641–68) wearing a crown with cross, holding a globus cruciger in one hand and a long cross in the other. On the reverse the **m** indicates the Greek numeral 40, the mark of value of the Byzantine standard copper coin. According to archaeological finds, an end to the importing of these coins can be discerned in the late 650s.

The importing obviously disregarded political boundaries. The selling of coppers was profitable for the Byzantine treasury. Early Islam, outside the Ḥijāz, was the elite religion of a tribally organised military. During the period of conquest the Islamic religion possessed only a rudimentary theology, which was probably even more basic among military units. Contemporary Byzantium might have perceived the conquest as a menacing rebellion and – if they had noticed the religious dimension at all – an Arab heresy of Judaeo-Christian origin. This perception would not necessarily have challenged the universal claim of the all-embracing Roman empire, since the idea of Rome

5 H. Pottier, *Le monnayage de la Syrie sous l'occupation perse (610–630)*, Cahiers Ernest Babelon 9 (Paris, 2004).

6 R. Gyselen, *Arab-Sasanian copper coinage*, Österreichische Akademie der Wissenschaften, Philosophisch-Historische Klasse, Denkschriften 284, Veröffentlichungen der numismatischen Kommission 34 (Vienna, 2000).

was neutral to religion. In these early days the Umayyads in Damascus did not develop an imperial state ideology of their own. As leaders of the victorious Arab armies they were probably content with their de facto rule and modest fiscal exploitation. Numerous attempts to conquer Constantinople might be interpreted as the inheritance by the rising Islamic Arab power of the universal Roman claim.

The minting of the first copper coins in the former Byzantine territories commenced after 636 CE. These imitations supplemented the circulating stock and followed even weight reductions in Byzantium.[7] We do not know who the regulating authorities were, but it is possible that military authorities in the garrisons, local authorities in the cities, money changers or merchants were involved in their production. Beginning in the 660s with the Sufyānid reforms, some sort of coordination, if not central policy, can be assumed. In a study, Luke Treadwell focused his attention on the developments in the mints of the provincial capitals Damascus, Tiberias and Ḥimṣ. Although these 'imperial image' coppers still depict Byzantine emperors with cross insignias, they now have carefully prepared flans and carefully engraved dies. The mints were named on the coins, in Greek, Arabic or both. Validating expressions were included, such as KAΛON or *ṭayyib* (both meaning 'good'), or *jāʾiz* ('current') (figs. 16.5, 16.6). No attempt to represent the new state or religion was made; petty coinage first of all served as means of exchange. The Sufyānid government set up a 'very loose tributary state'.[8]

As a centralised state, the Sasanian empire fell while at its apogee – at least as far as its administration, its army, which was based on cash payments, and its monetary economy were concerned. Silver coins were the backbone of the fiscal cycle, and were available in enormous quantities. The typical late Sasanian *drahm* (fig. 16.3) of about 4.2 grams shows on the obverse the portrait of the *shāhānshāh* – either Khusrau II (r. 590–628) or Yazdegerd III (r. 632–51) – with an enormous winged crown as sign of their royalty. On the reverse, the fire altar served as the central symbol of the dualistic Iranian religion, Zoroastrianism. Priest attendants stand on either side, and beside them are abbreviations indicating the mint and the regnal year of the ruler. Dies were probably cut in a central workshop and then distributed to the provincial mints, a recurrent phenomenon in the later Islamic coinage. In his twentieth regnal year, 651, the last *shāhānshāh* Yazdegerd III was assassinated in Marw,

7 H. Pottier, I. Schulze and W. Schulze, 'Pseudo-Byzantine coinage in Syria under Arab rule (638-*c*.670): Classification and dating', *Revue numismatique belge*, 154 (2008).

8 C. F. Robinson, *Empire and elites after the Muslim conquest: The transformation of northern Mesopotamia*, Cambridge Studies in Islamic Civilization (Cambridge, 2000), p. 166.

the last eastern remnant of his empire. The coins in the conquered territories are almost indistinguishable from the coins under the authority of Yazdegerd III, except that mints lay outside his shrinking realm. For some time after 31/651 coins continued to be struck with the names and portraits of Khusrau II or Yazdegerd III and with the fire altar. Frequently – but not always – additional Arabic validating marks were set on the margin, such as *bism Allāh* ('in the name of God') or *jayyid* ('good'), as on Syrian copper coins. The resulting picture for the early decades seems to correspond to a situation in which the Sasanian administration remained operational, but broken down to a provincial level and now responsible to Arab governors.[9] Starting in about 40/661, with Muʿāwiya's regime, the names of Khusrau II and Yazdegerd III were replaced, first occasionally and then regularly with the names of the provincial governors in Pahlavi, placed in front of the traditional portrait of the *shāhānshāh*. In many mints, but not in all, the dating shifted to the *hijra* year (fig. 16.7)

The Zubayrid and Khārijite challenges between 681 and 697 – the period of the second *fitna* – mark the watershed towards the initial inclusion of Islamic symbols in the coin imagery and finally to a clear iconographic expression of religion and state. ʿAbd Allāh ibn al-Zubayr was a close, venerated and merited member of the family of the Prophet. He emphasised the religious–political character of his caliphate and demanded a state in accordance with the principles of Islam, whatever this meant at that time. After Muʿāwiya's death in 60/680 he strongly opposed the Sufyānid regime, and was supported in many parts of the empire. As early as 62/681f. his name was put on coins of Kirmān. The coins show in 64/684 that he assumed the caliphal title *'amīr* of the believers' (fig. 16.8). In 67/687 his brother Muṣʿab secured Baṣra, Iraq and the territories to the east as far as Sīstān. The Umayyads seemed to have lost their cause.

Between 66/685 and 69/688f., in the city of Bishāpūr, *Muḥammad rasūl Allāh* (Muḥammad is the messenger of God) was placed for the first time on coinage, on that of the Zubayrid governor of the east. The coin image itself remained as before, the portrait of the *shāhānshāh* and the fire altar. The Zubayrids thus propagated the new Islamic imperial rule with reference to the Prophet and putative founder of the state. Probably in 70/689f. the Zubayrid authorities created a coin with the name of Muḥammad in front of the portrait of the *shāhānshāh* and in the margin a reference to Muḥammad, for the first time including the profession of faith and the unity of God, the *shahāda*, in

9 S. Sears, 'A monetary history of Iraq and Iran, ca. CE 500 to 750', Ph.D. thesis, University of Chicago (1997).

Arabic: *lā ilāha illā Allāh waḥdahū.*[10] In 72/691f. the Zubayrid governor of the province of Sīstān, in south-eastern Iran, replaced the Zoroastrian fire altar with the profession of the new faith (*shahāda*). Iraj Mochiri read the Pahlavi script thus: 'Seventy-two / One God but He / another God does not exist / Muḥammad [is] the messenger of God / SK [mint abbreviation for Sīstān]' (fig. 16.9).[11] Clearly dated, the *shahāda* appears here on a contemporary document in Pahlavi script and in the Persian language. Together with the Prophetic mission of Muḥammad, it is the first symbol of the Islamic religion and its empire known. The Zubayrid governor had targeted the ideological–religious deficiencies of the Umayyad regime. In the same year the Marwānids re-conquered Iraq, and in 73/692 the caliphate of ʿAbd Allāh ibn al-Zubayr was brutally suppressed in Mecca.

The Marwānid activities that followed can be seen as aimed at integrating the defeated moderate Zubayrid movement in ideological terms, as well as a forceful reaction to the ongoing Khārijite menace. At this point in history at the latest, the idea was created of an Islamic universal empire in its own ideological right. In 72/691f. ʿAbd al-Malik built the present Dome of the Rock and the al-Aqṣā Mosque in Jerusalem as probably the first architectural manifestations of the new Islamic empire. The choice of Jerusalem placed the imperial religion in the tradition of Judaism and Christianity and in the centre of the medieval world.

Between 72/691f. and 77/696f. the Marwānid government experimented with new symbols as representations of religion and imperial power, not all of which are well understood today. Most famous is the image of the standing caliph on gold, silver and copper coins in Syria and northern Mesopotamia (figs. 16.10, 16.11). On the Syrian silver *drahms* and on some copper coins ʿAbd al-Malik asserted his claim to being *khalīfat Allāh* (the deputy of God), to enhance his politico-religious leadership (fig. 16.11).[12] However, the recurrent theme of all

10 L. Ilisch, 'The Muhammad-drachms and their relation to Umayyad Syria and northern Mesopotamia', *Supplement of the Journal of the Oriental Numismatic Society*, 193 (Autumn 2007).

11 M. I. Mochiri, 'A Pahlavi forerunner of the Umayyad reformed coinage', *JRAS*, (1981). Further discussion in S. Sears, 'A hybrid imitation of early Muslim coinage struck in Sijistan by Abū Bardhāʿa', *American Journal of Numismatics*, 1 (1989); and L. Ilisch, Review of *American Journal of Numismatics*, 1, *Der Islam*, 69 (1992).

12 For the iconographic interpretation see N. Jamil, 'Caliph and Quṭb: Poetry as a source for interpreting the transformation of the Byzantine cross on steps on Umayyad coinage', in Jeremy Johns (ed.), *Bayt al-Maqdis: Jerusalem and early Islam*, Oxford Studies in Islamic Art 9, part 2 (Oxford, 1999); L. Treadwell, 'The "orans" drachms of Bishr ibn Marwān and the figural coinage of the early Marwanid period', in Johns (ed.), *Bayt al-Maqdis: Jerusalem and early Islam*; L. Treadwell, '"Mihrab and ʿAnaza" or "sacrum and spear"? A reconsideration of an early Marwanid silver drachm', *Muqarnas*, 30 (2005).

experiments in coin design was the inclusion of the name of the founder of the religion and the putative founder of the empire, *Muḥammad rasūl Allāh*, sometimes together with the *shahāda*. This was the symbol of Islam comparable to cross, fire altar and menorah. The Zubayrid idea was firmly adopted.

Between 77/696 and 79/699, just after the final defeat of the Khārijite caliph Qaṭarī ibn al-Fujāʾa, the definitive symbolic representation of Islam and the Islamic empire on coinage was launched. In 77/696 new *dīnārs* were produced (fig. 16.12) – probably in Damascus – bearing the new religious symbols of the Islamic empire: the *shahāda*, encircled by the *risāla*, the Prophetic mission of Muḥammad (Q 9:33), and on the opposite side the word of God, the *sūrat ikhlāṣ* (Q 112) and the date of minting. Late in 78/697f. al-Ḥajjāj ibn Yūsuf, the governor of the east, ordered the reform of the *dirhams* in his realm, similar to the new *dīnārs*, but stating the mint name also, as on Sasanian *drahms*. The reform started in Kūfa, Azerbaijan, Armenia, Jayy and Shaqq al-Taymara in al-Jibāl, as far as we can currently tell. The following year saw the application of the new design in more than forty mints (fig. 16.13).[13]

Precious-metal coins remained anonymous until the time of the ʿAbbāsid al-Manṣūr (r. 136–58/754–75). The image and the name of the ruler were taken out of any representation of the empire. This constituted a historically unprecedented breach with a tradition of Hellenistic coin imagery going back about a millennium. The epigraphic image of the profession of faith and the words of God can be read as 'the sovereignty belongs to God', almost a concession to Khārijite thinking. Anonymity did not mean modesty, because the new Islamic universal emperor claimed nothing less than being *khalīfat Allāh*: the deputy of God.

Umayyad and early ʿAbbāsid coinage

The new currency system of the empire consisted of an almost pure gold *dīnār* regulated to the *mithqāl* weight (4.2 g), an almost pure silver *dirham* regulated to a *dirham* weight (2.8–2.9 g) and unregulated copper coins which had a token character. This became the standard model for currency in the emerging Islamic law. Although the Umayyad empire was far from a centralised state, the coinage does show a high degree of organisation and centralisation, owing

13 M. Klat, *Catalogue of the post-reform dirhams: The Umayyad dynasty* (London, 2002); L. Ilisch in *Dr. Busso Peus Nachf. Münzhandlung Frankfurt, Katalog 369* (31 October 2001), no. 1467, pp. 80–1.

to its Sasanian heritage.[14] It can be supposed that the gold coinage, which mentions no mint, would have been struck almost exclusively at the caliph's court, first in Damascus and later in Baghdad. Mints for *thulths* (*tremisses*), *niṣf* (*semissis*) and some *dīnārs* were set up in al-Andalus and Ifrīqiya (Qayrawān) (fig. 16.4). With ʿAbd al-Malik's reforms all old Byzantine gold coinage vanished immediately from circulation in Egypt, Syria and northern Mesopotamia, indicating a tight fiscal regime on the gold circulation in the former Byzantine territories. During the reign of Hārūn al-Rashīd (r. 170–93/786–809) the production of gold *dīnārs* in more than one mint became apparent, as indicated by the inclusion of the names of provincial governors and specific mint marks (fig. 16.14).

The organisation of silver coinage serving the fiscal authorities in the former Sasanian east was different. The new design soon spread to all mints in the east and the capital Damascus; in 97/715f. it was adopted in Ifrīqiya, and finally, in 100/718f., in al-Andalus. It was struck in about a hundred mints. After the foundation of Wāsiṭ in Iraq and the move of al-Ḥajjāj to his new capital in 83/703f., Wāsiṭ became the paramount silver mint of the empire until the ʿAbbāsid *coup d'état*. For a brief time between 84/703f. and 89/707f. Wāsiṭ was the only *dirham* mint except for Damascus; all others were closed down.[15]

Between 132/749f. and 147/765f. Baṣra and Kūfa became the principal silver mints of the empire. This paramount role then shifted in 146–7/765–7 to Madīnat al-Salām and to Rayy/al-Muḥammadiyya, the first after the foundation of the palace city in Baghdad – the mint was opened in 146/765f. – and the latter after the establishment of the heir apparent in Rayy in 145/762f.[16] The ʿAbbāsid takeover had little impact at first on the coin design; except that the *sūrat al-ikhlāṣ*, which was associated with the Umayyads, was replaced by *Muḥammad rasūl Allāh*, stressing the connection of the ʿAbbāsids to the family of the Prophet (fig. 16.15).

In Rayy in 145/762f., the year of the menacing ʿAlīd revolt and its repression, the heir apparent, Muḥammad (r. 158–69/775–86), began to insert the newly adopted honorific title (*laqab*) al-Mahdī and his name into the *dirham* coin protocol, abandoning the anonymity of precious metal coinage (fig. 16.16). Later he continued this as caliph.[17] From now on, until the coinage reform of

14 A. S. DeShazo and M. L. Bates, 'The Umayyad governors of al-ʿIrāq and the changing annulet patterns on their dirhams', *Numismatic Chronicle*, 14 (1974); M. Bates, 'The dirham mint of the northern provinces of the Umayyad caliphate', *Armenian Numismatic Journal*, 15 (1989).

15 R. Darley-Doran, 'Wāsiṭ, The mint', *EI2*, vol. XI, pp. 169–71.

16 T. S. Noonan, 'Early ʿAbbāsid mint output', *JESHO*, 29 (1986).

17 M. L. Bates, 'Khurāsānī revolutionaries and al-Mahdī's title', in F. Daftary and J. W. Meri (eds.), *Culture and memory in medieval Islam: Essays in honour of Wilferd Madelung* (London and New York, 2003).

al-Ma'mūn (r. 194–218/810–33), various names appear on the coinage – the caliph, the heir apparent, viziers, governors, officials – sometimes as many as four names, giving a kaleidoscope of the administrative structure of the empire, which is not yet fully understood (figs. 16.17, 16.22).[18]

The circulation of silver coins was far from uniform, unlike the new gold *dīnārs*. Umayyad and Sasanian *dirhams* still circulated until the early fourth/tenth century. Some regions maintained, along with the imperial coinage, a local one, usually debased silver of Sasanian appearance, notably in Ṭabaristān (an exception as they are of pure silver) (fig. 16.18), Sīstān and the oasis of Bukhārā (fig. 16.19).[19]

The copper coinage was of almost no concern to the central government; it was left for the regional or local Umayyad and ʿAbbāsid authorities to supply, and for some supplemental coinage even private commercial enterprises can be assumed. According to Islamic law copper coins did not constitute money that was legally valid in all transactions. Thus a huge variety of copper coins with many names of local *amīrs* and officials existed. Images were occasionally applied too. Thus the copper coins are an excellent source for local administration, history and art history (fig. 16.20).[20] This decentralised production resulted in temporary and regional shortages in petty coinage, frequently bridged by cast imitations (fig. 16.21) and importation from other regions. In the period of Hārūn al-Rashīd the growing demand in northern Mesopotamia exceeded by far the regular production of copper coinage. Coins were thus cast until their model was unrecognisable, and plain copper sheets were cut into mainly octagonal pieces.[21]

18 N. D. Nicol, 'Early ʿAbbāsid administration in the central and eastern provinces, 132–218 AH/750–833 AD, Ph.D. thesis, University of Washington (1979); N. Lowick and E. Savage, *Early ʿAbbāsid coinage: A type catalogue 132–218 H/AD 750–833. A posthumous work by Nicholas Lowick*, ed. Elisabeth Savage, distributed MS (London, 1996).

19 For Ṭabaristān: H. M. Malek, *The Dābūyid Ispahbads and early ʿAbbāsid governors of Ṭabaristān: History and numismatics*, Royal Numismatic Society Special Publication 39 (London, 2004). For Sīstān: S. Sears, 'The Sasanian style drachms of Sistan', *Yarmouk Numismatics*, 11 (1999).

20 H. Bone, 'The administration of Umayyad Syria: The evidence of the copper coins', Ph.D. thesis, Princeton University (2000); Lowick and Savage, *Early ʿAbbāsid coinage*; S. Shammā, *A catalogue of ʿAbbāsid copper coins: Thabat al-fulūs al-ʿabbāsiyya* (London, 1998). Single studies: see L. Ilisch, 'Die Kupferprägung Nordmesopotamiens unter Hārūn ar-Rashīd und seinen Söhnen (786–842 AD)', in International Association of Professional Numismatists (eds.), *Numismatics: Witness to history*, IAPN publication 8 (Basle, 1986); S. Heidemann, 'Die frühe Münzprägung von ar-Raqqa/ar-Rāfiqa als Dokumente zur Geschichte der Stadt', in S. Heidemann and A. Becker (eds.), *Raqqa*, vol. II: *Die islamische Stadt* (Mainz, 2003).

21 S. Heidemann, 'Der Kleingeldumlauf in der Ghazīra in früh-ʿabbāsidischer Zeit und die Münzemissionen aus al-Kūfa', in Heidemann and Becker (eds.), *Die islamische Stadt*.

a

b

Plate 16.1 (a, b, obverse and reverse)
Byzantium, Heraclius and Heraclius Constantine, *nomisma*, Constantinople, (*ca*. 616–25 AD)

a

b

Plate 16.2 (a, b, obverse and reverse)
Byzantium, Constans II, *follis*, Constantinople, regnal year 3 (643–4 CE).

a

b

Plate 16.3 (a, b, obverse and reverse)
Sāsānians, Khusrau II, *drahm*, ʾHM (Hamadhān), regnal year 29.

a

b

Plate 16.4 (a, b, obverse and reverse)
Umayyads, *tremisses/thulth dīnār*, Afrika (Qairawān).
Scale 1.5:1

a

b

Plate 16.5 (a, b, obverse and reverse)
Umayyads, *fals*, Emisis / Ḥimṣ, [*c*. 50s / 670s–74 / 692].

a

b

Plate 16.6 (a, b, obverse and reverse)
Umayyads, *fals*, Damaskos / Dimashq, [*c*. 50s / 670–74 / 692].

a

b

Plate 16.7 (a, b, obverse and reverse)
Umayyads, ʿAbd Allāh ibn ʿĀmir ibn Kurayz, *drahm*,
(Dārābjird), AH 43 (663–4 CE).

a b

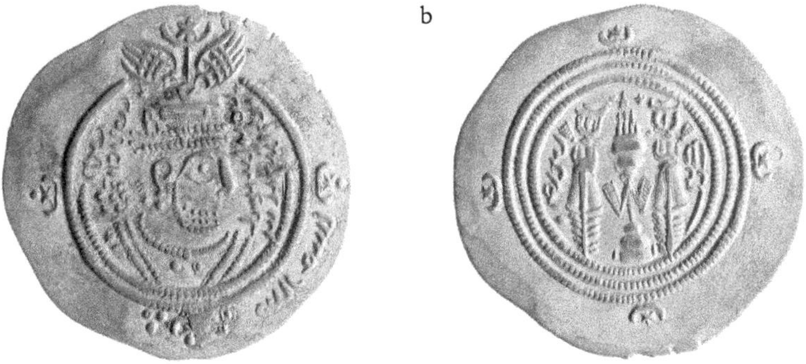

Plate 16.8 (a, b, obverse and reverse) Zubayrids, ʿAbd Allāh ibn al-Zubayr, *drahm*, (Dārābjird-Jahrum), Yazdegerd era 60 (72/692).

a b

Plate 16.9 (a, b, obverse and reverse)
Zubayrids, ʿAbd al-ʿAzīz ibn ʿAbd Allāh, *drahm*, (Sistān), year 72 AH (691–2 CE).

a b

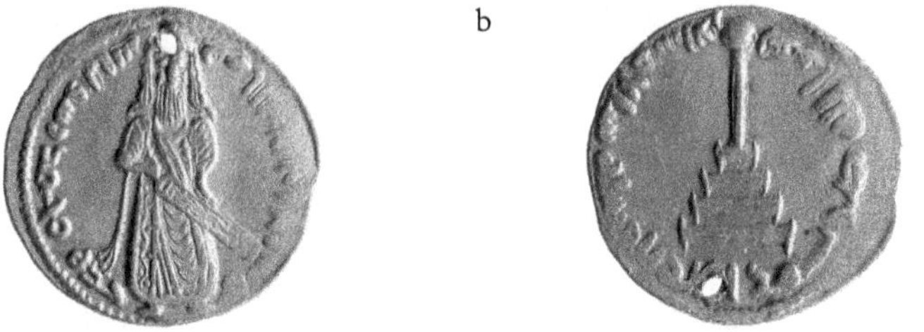

Plate 16.10 (a, b, obverse and reverse)
Umayyads, *dīnār*, [Damascus], year 77 AH (696 CE).

a b

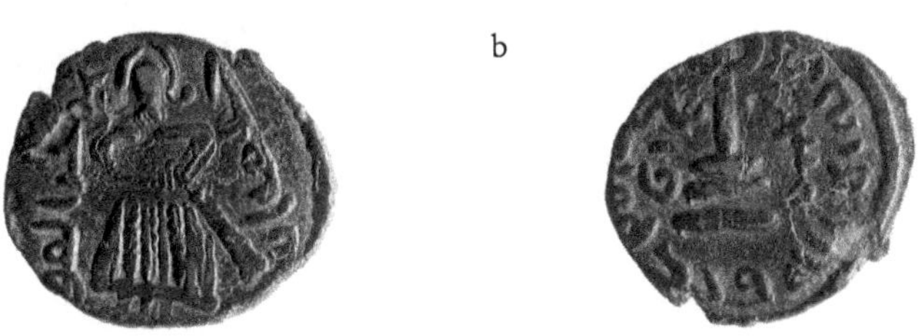

Plate 16.11 (a, b, obverse and reverse) Umayyads, *fals*, Manbij, [74–7/692–6].

a b

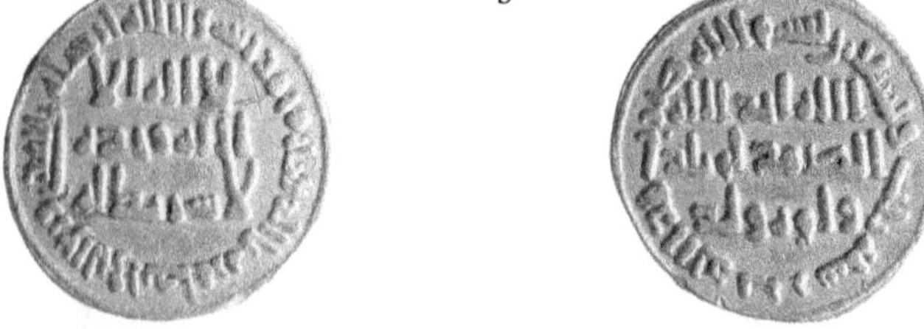

Plate 16.12 (a, b, obverse and reverse)
Umayyads, *dīnār*, [Damascus], year 93 AH (711–12 CE).

a b

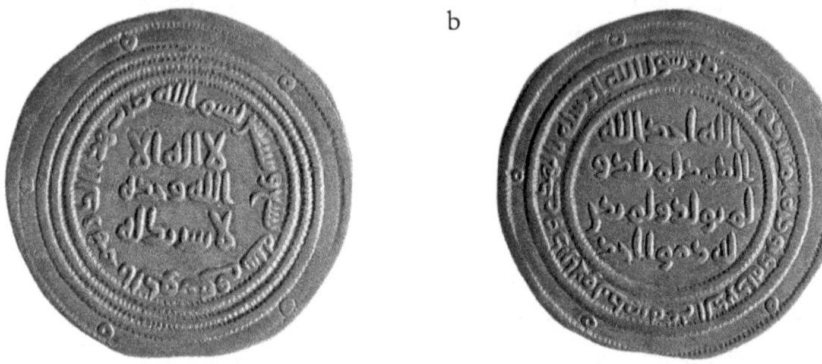

Plate 16.13 (a, b, obverse and reverse)
Umayyads, *dirham*, al-Kūfa, year 79 AH (698–9 CE).

a b

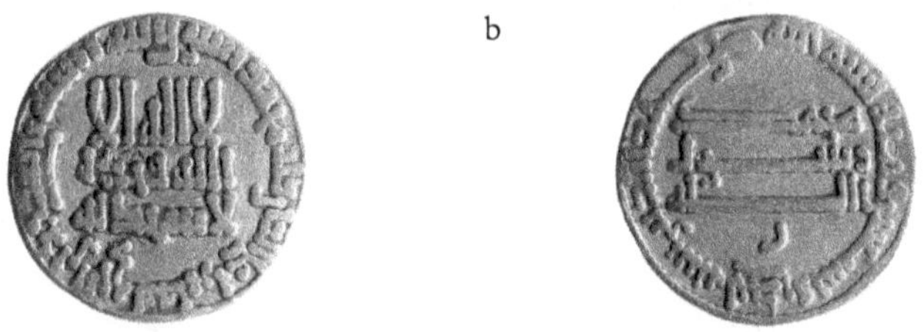

Plate 16.14 (a, b, obverse and reverse)
'Abbāsids, *dīnār*, [al-Rāfiqa], year 191 AH (806–7 CE).

a b

Plate 16.15 (a, b, obverse and reverse)
'Abbāsids, *dirham*, al-Kūfa, year 132 AH (749–50 CE).

a b

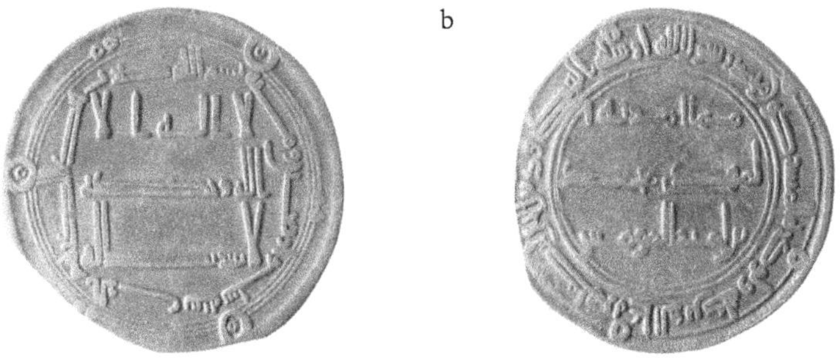

Plate 16.16 (a, b, obverse and reverse)
ʿAbbāsids, al-Mahdī, *dirham*, al-Rayy, year 146 AH (763–4 CE).

a b

Plate 16.17 (a, b, obverse and reverse)
ʿAbbāsids, al-Amīn, *dirham*, Armīniya (Dābil), year 190 AH (805–6 CE).

a b

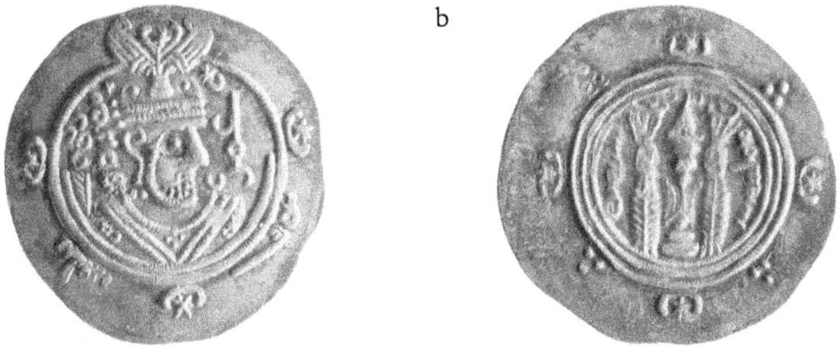

Plate 16.18 (a, b, obverse and reverse)
ʿAbbāsids, ʿUmar ibn al-ʿAlāʾ, *dirham*, Ṭabaristān, 123 post-Yazdegerd era (158/774–5).

a

b

Plate 16.19 (a, b, obverse and reverse)
ʿAbbāsids, al-Mahdī, *dirham*, [Bukhārā], [158–69/775–85].

a

b

Plate 16.20 (a, b, obverse and reverse)
ʿAbbāsids, al-Muʿtaṣim, *fals*, al-Rāfiqa, 226 AH (840–1 CE).

a

b

Plate 16.21 (a, b, obverse and reverse)
ʿAbbāsids, *fals*, (Syria), [*c.* 130–50/750–70], cast.

a

b

Plate 16.22 (a, b, obverse and reverse)
ʿAbbāsids, al-Maʿmūn, *dirham*, Iṣfahān, year 204 AH (819–20 CE).

a

b

Plate 16.23 (a, b, obverse and reverse)
ʿAbbāsids, *dirham*, Madīnat al-Salām, year 208 AH (823–4 CE).

a

b

Plate 16.24 (a, b, obverse and reverse)
ʿAbbāsids, al-Muʿtaṣim, *dirham*, Madīnat al-Salām, year 226 AH (840–1 CE).

a

b

Plate 16.25 (a, b, obverse and reverse)
Ṣaffārids, Yaʿqūb ibn al-Layth, *dirham*, Panjhīr, 261 AH (874–5 CE).

a

b

Plate 16.26 (a, b, obverse and reverse)
Dulafids, Aḥmad ibn ʿAbd al-ʿAzīz, *dīnār*, Māh al-Baṣra, year 273 AH (886–7 CE).

a

b

Plate 16.27 (a, b, obverse and reverse)
ʿAbbāsids, al-Muttaqī, *dirham*, Madīnat al-Salām, year 329 AH (940–1 CE).

a

b

Plate 16.28 (a, b, obverse and reverse)
Būyids, Qiwām al-Dīn, *dirham*, Shīrāz, year 400 AH (1009–10 CE).

a

b

Plate 16.29 (a, b, obverse and reverse)
ʿUqaylids, Janāḥ al-Dawla, *dirham*, Naṣībīn, year 385 AH (995–6 CE).

a

b

Plate 16.30 (a, b, obverse and reverse)
Sallārids, Jastān and Ibrāhīm, *dīnār*, Marāgha, year 347 AH (958–9 CE).

a b

Plate 16.31 (a, b, obverse and reverse)
Sāmānids, Ismāʿīl, *dirham*, al-Shāsh, year 292 AH (904–5 CE).

a b

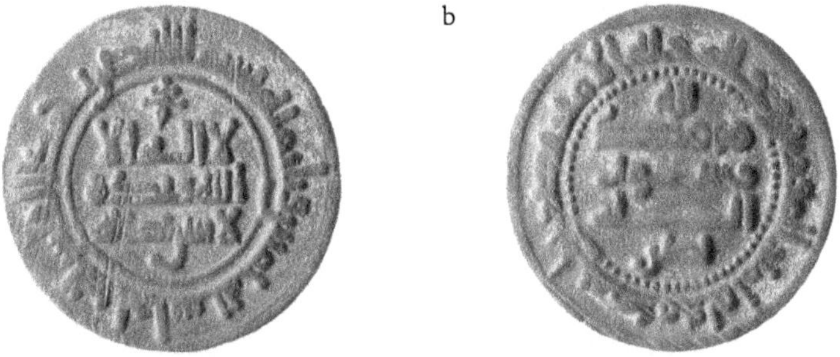

Plate 16.32 (a, b, obverse and reverse)
Sāmānids, Naṣr, *fals*, Bukhārā, year 305 AH (917–6 CE).

a b

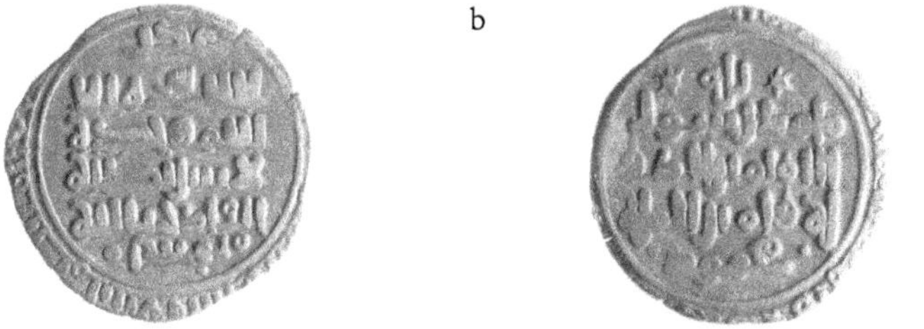

Plate 16.33 (a, b, obverse and reverse)
Ghaznavids, Maḥmūd, *dirham,* Ghazna, year 399 AH (1008–9 CE).

a

b

Plate 16.34 (a, b, obverse and reverse)
Saljūqs, Malikshāh, *dīnār*, Nīshāpūr, year 484 AH (1091–2 CE).

a

b

Plate 16.35 (a, b, obverse and reverse)
Saljūqs, Sanjar, *dīnār*, Walwālīj, Muḥarram 493 AH (1099 CE).

a

b

Plate 16.36 (a, b, obverse and reverse)
Fāṭimids, al-ʿAzīz, *dīnār*, Miṣr, year 368 AH (978–9 CE).

a

b

Plate 16.37 (a, b, obverse and reverse)
Fāṭimids, al-Muʿizz, *dirham*, al-Manṣūrīyya, year 358 AH (968–9 CE).

Plate 16.38 Fāṭimids, al-Mustanṣir, glass token.

a

b

Plate 16.39 (a, b, obverse and reverse)
Numayrids, Manīʿ (r. *c.* 440–54/1050–62), *dirham*.

a

b

Plate 16.40 (a, b, obverse and reverse)
Zangids, Nūr al-Dīn, *qirṭās*, Damascus, year 558 AH (1162–3 CE).

a

b

Plate 16.41 (a, b, obverse and reverse)
Zangids, al-Ṣāliḥ Ismāʿīl, *dirham*, Aleppo, year 571 AH (1175–6 CE).

The reforms of al-Maʾmūn and al-Muʿtaṣim billāh

The devastating war of succession between al-Amīn (r. 193–8/809–13) and al-Maʾmūn marked a turning-point. The latter initiated a reform in the design of the coinage, which went along with a reorganisation of coin production as a whole. The reform started with the first changes in design in 201/816f. (fig. 16.22) and found its definitive appearance in 206/821f. (fig. 16.23). The new style was consecutively adopted during the following years in almost all mints.[22]

First of all, gold and silver coins were given a standardised design based on the *dirham* without altering the weight standards. The most obvious change in the design was a second marginal obverse legend praising the victory of God (Q 30:4–5). This design continued with few alterations until the fifth/eleventh century. Whereas the old style preferred an angular Kūfic script, the new style exhibited a neat curvilinear calligraphy. The new-style coinage of al-Maʾmūn once again became anonymous. The number of mints was reduced to the major capitals of the empire. The production of silver and gold coinage dropped considerably, and even more under his successors.

Al-Muʿtaṣim billāh (r. 218–27/833–42) dismissed anonymity again, and added his name to the new design on the reverse in 219/834 (fig. 16.24). This became the rule. From 236/850 under al-Mutawakkil ʿalā Allāh (r. 231–47/847–61) the name of the heir apparent was also included. The production and distribution of dies was almost centralised. The extent of the new capital city of Sāmarrāʾ, built and provisioned entirely by tax money, is impressive proof of the high degree of the empire's centralisation at its peak.[23]

In the wake of the second devastating war of succession in 251–2/865–6 al-Muʿtazz billāh (r. 252–5/866–9) resumed the production of precious-metal coins on a large scale. Many mints were set up in the provinces. Weakened, the empire gradually lost its grip on its peripheral provinces. In Panjhīr/Transoxania in 259/872f. Yaʿqūb ibn al-Layth (r. 247–65/861–79)

22 T. El-Hibri, 'Coinage reform under the ʿAbbāsid caliph al-Maʾmūn', *JESHO*, 36 (1993); S. Shammā, *Aḥdāth ʿaṣr al-Maʾmūn kamā tarwīhā al-nuqūd* (Irbid, 1995).

23 M. Bates, *The expression of sovereignty in the Abbasid caliphate, 218–334 H/833–946 CE* (forthcoming); L. Ilisch, 'Stempelveränderungen an islamischen Münzen des Mittelalters als Quelle zur Münzstättenorganisation', in T. Hackens and R. Weiller (eds.), *Actes du 9ème congrès international de numismatique. Berne, Septembre 1979: Proceedings of the 9th International Congress of Numismatics, Berne, September 1979* (Louvain-la Neuve and Luxemburg 1982). Cf. L. Treadwell, 'Notes on the mint at Samarra', in C. Robinson (ed.), *A medieval Islamic city reconsidered: An interdisciplinary approach to Samarra*, Oxford Studies in Islamic Art 14 (Oxford, 2001).

was probably the first provincial ruler to add his name to the caliph's protocol on silver coins as proof of his autonomy (fig. 16.25). At least from 265/878f. on, with the rule of Aḥmad ibn Ṭūlūn in Egypt, the inclusion as an autonomous *amīr* into the coin protocol became a regular feature (fig. 16.26). His model was followed by the Sāmānids in Transoxania and many other ruling houses. *Sikka* and *khuṭba* in the name of the regional ruler became a sign of autonomy within the frame of the ʿAbbāsid empire until its end in 656/1258.

In the ʿAbbāsid core provinces the inclusion of the vizier's honorific title (*laqab*) in 291/903f. and in 320/932f. set precedents for the imperial government. In 324/936 the first *amīr al-umarāʾ*, Ibn Rāʾiq, had abolished the distinction between civil and military administration. The *amīr al-umarāʾ* Bajkam was the first to be included in the coin protocol in 329/940 (fig. 16.27). In 334/945 the caliph delegated his power to the Būyids (fig. 16.28) and following them to the Saljūqs (figs. 16.31, 16.32), and these always – with few exceptions – appear on the coinage with flourishing honorific titles (figs. 16.28, 16.32) until the sixth/twelfth century when the caliph freed himself from Saljūq political domination.[24] Autonomous rulers who depended on the Būyids, such as the ʿUqaylids in northern Mesopotamia (fig. 16.29), and the Ḥasanwayhids[25] in Kurdistān, among others, acknowledged the Būyids as overlords and added their names to the hierarchy of power listed in the coin protocol. Others at the periphery, such as the Ikhshīdids[26] in Egypt or the Sallārids[27] in Azerbaijan (fig. 16.30) acknowledged only the caliph. Sometimes further mint marks, names of die-engravers and dynastic emblems (*tamghās*) were added (figs. 16.34, 16.35). For the historian the *sikka* became an unrivalled tool for defining length of reigns, the extent of territories, especially for local dynasties, and shifting political–religious allegiance (cf. fig. 16.39), which are not in the focus of the main chronicles.

During the middle decades of the third/ninth century copper coinage vanished almost completely from the urban markets from Spain to Iran (fig. 16.20), remaining only in certain limited regions such as Sāmānid Transoxania (fig. 16.32). Fragmentation of the circulating precious-metal coins served the needs of small change in the rest of the Islamic empire.

24 L. Treadwell, *Buyid coinage: A die corpus (322–445 AH)* (Oxford, 2001).

25 ʿA. Qūchānī, 'The territory of Abū al-Nadjm Badr b. Ḥasanūyah based on his coins', *Iranian Journal of Archaeology and History*, 8, 2 (1994) (in Persian).

26 J. L. Bacharach, *Islamic history through coins: An analysis and catalogue of tenth-century Ikhshidid coinage* (Cairo, 2006).

27 R. Vasmer, 'Zur Chronologie der Gâstâniden und Sallāriden', *Islamica*, 3 (1927).

Coins were circulating more and more by weight expressed in standard *dirhams* and *dīnārs* instead of by tale or count.[28]

Starting slowly, probably in the time of al-Muqtadir billāh (r. 295–320/908–32), the fineness of the silver coinage dropped, varying from region to region, and the strict weight regulation was abandoned. After the political, economic and military collapse of the central lands of the ʿAbbāsid empire during the fourth/tenth century the silver *dirham* declined to a debased copperish coin with no regulated fineness or weight.[29] Now different kinds of *dirhams* were used, each current only within a limited region. Amounts of money were expressed in terms of monies of account.[30] Actual payments of coins were transacted by weighing the coins. In the fourth/tenth and fifth/eleventh centuries the number of coins being struck diminished dramatically in the central lands of the empire. In the narrative sources these coins are referred to as 'black *dirhams*' (sing. *dirham aswad*), because of their dark appearance (fig. 16.39). In Egypt they were then called *dirham wariq*,[31] the 'silver[ish] *dirham*'. Legal texts addressed them more appropriately as *darāhim maghshūsha*, 'debased *dirhams*'. The monetary sector of the urban economy in the core lands of the Islamic empire – northern Syria, northern Mesopotamia, Iraq and western Iran – shrank to a low that may not have been experienced since Hellenistic Antiquity.

This monetary situation caused frequent complaints by jurists and theologians. It was open to unintended violations of the *ribā* prohibition, the unequal market value of the same amount of precious metal: *dirham aswads* from different circulation zones might contain a different amount of silver alloy; the intrinsic amount of silver in foreign *dirhams* might be unknown (*majhūl*), or the coins might be valued differently in the market with no regard to the real content of precious metal. In order to avoid *ribā* and to facilitate commerce, jurists allowed transactions with *dirham aswads* only as long as they involved current *dirhams* circulating within a single zone (*rāʾij fī l-balad*).[32] In order to distinguish one issue of black *dirhams* from the other the issuing authorities gradually diverged from the classical coin design. To remedy this

28 L. Ilisch, 'Whole and fragmented dirhams in Near Eastern hoards', in K. Jonsson and B. Malmer (eds.), *Sigtuna Papers: Proceedings of the Sigtuna symposium on Viking-age coinage 1–4 June 1989, Stockholm*, Commentationes de nummis saeculorum in Suecia repertis. Nova Series 6 (London, 1990).

29 T. S. Noonan, 'The start of the silver crisis in Islam: A comparative study of Central Asia and the Iberian peninsula', M. Gomes Marques and D. M. Metcalf (eds.), *Problems of medieval coinage in the Iberian area*, vol. III (Santarém, 1988).

30 'Monies of account' are denominations not actually struck, or no longer struck, but used to determine legally amounts of money in transactions, contracts or debts.

31 M. Bates, 'Wariq', *EI2*, vol. IX, p. 147.

32 Heidemann, *Renaissance*, pp. 369–80.

unsatisfactory monetary situation, sporadic attempts at coinage reform were made in some regions, but were of no avail in the long run (fig. 16.28).

The eleventh century: the currency system at the brink of the reform

In the periphery, however, in Central Asia and in Egypt, a high level of monetary economy and an army based on cash payment remained. The Sāmānids had the advantage of rich silver mines in present-day Afghanistan, and the resulting huge volume of coinage fostered a trade with these coins which, via the Volga river, reached the countries around the Baltic Sea in the fourth/tenth century (fig. 16.31). Although by contrast the *dirhams* of the Ghaznavids (384–582/994–1186) with a high silver content in the late fourth/tenth and first half of the fifth/eleventh centuries were a regional coinage, they were nevertheless struck in abundant quantities. As early as the Sāmānid period the *dīnār* of Nīshāpūr gained fame for its purity and stability (fig. 16.34). It became one of the preferred trade coins circulating between Iraq, eastern northern Mesopotamia and Central Asia. It maintained its leading position into the Saljūq period while the *dīnārs* of the other eastern Iranian and Transoxanian mints, Ghazna, Herat, Marw, Balkh, Bukhārā and others debased, sometimes to such an extent that they consisted almost of pure silver and served only as regional standard currency (fig. 16.35).

The situation was different in Egypt. The Ismāʿīlī Shīʿite Fāṭimids challenged the ʿAbbāsid claim of universal rulership both ideologically and militarily, and thus their coinage named only the Fāṭimid caliph. After their conquest of Egypt their coins presented a visual distinction to the classical late ʿAbbāsid coinage, moving towards a design consisting mainly of rings of concentric inscriptions (figs. 16.36, 16.37). The Fāṭimids profited from the North African gold trade as well as from trade with the northern Italian mercantile republics. The Fāṭimid *dīnār* (fig. 16.36) of a regulated weight and an undisputed pure gold content became the preferred trade coinage for the Islamic Mediterranean, the Red Sea, the Persian Gulf and Iraq. On the level of the petty coinage the North African–Egyptian *dirham* suffered the same decline as it did in the entire Islamic world (fig. 16.37).[33] Copper coinage was also abandoned. A debate between Paul Balog and Michael Bates centring around the question whether the abundant glass tokens of the Egyptian

33 N. D. Nicol, *A corpus of Fāṭimid coins* (Trieste, 2006).

Fāṭimid and Ayyūbid period served the purposes of daily purchases has not yet been settled (fig. 16.38).[34]

Outlook: the reform

Islamic coinage of the middle Islamic period was quite different from the degenerated state of the classical coinage system. The renewal commenced slowly from the end of the fifth/eleventh century and ended at about the middle of the seventh/thirteenth. The 'black *dirham*' (fig. 16.39) disappeared mostly in the course of the sixth/twelfth century. In Syria Nūr al-Dīn Maḥmūd (r. 541–69/1150–74) issued it for the last time in 546/1151f. in Aleppo, although it continued to be struck in Mosul into the 650s/1250s and in Egypt into the Mamlūk period. In the last decades of the fifth/eleventh century copper coinage resumed in northern Syria, northern Mesopotamia and the Caucasus through the appearance of imported Byzantine *folles*, called in Arabic sources *qirṭās* or *qarṭīs* (pl. *qarāṭīs*). In the middle decades of the sixth/twelfth century a successful indigenous copper-coin production commenced, mainly in the Zangid and Artuqid realm (fig. 16.40). Regional copper coinages spread to the other western Saljūq successor states. In 571/1175f. – after almost 250 years – the Zangids in Aleppo and the Ayyūbids in Damascus reintroduced a *dirham* of almost pure silver with a regulated weight of about 2.8 grams (fig. 16.41). The success of the reform was achieved through the northern Italian trade of European silver. The reform spread from the Levant to the entire Middle East. Once again a currency system was established that conformed to the requirements of Islamic law.[35]

34 P. Balog, 'Fāṭimid glass jetons: Token currency or coin-weights?', *JESHO*, 24 (1981); M. L. Bates, 'The function of Fāṭimid and Ayyūbid glass weights', *JESHO*, 24 (1981).

35 S. Heidemann, 'Economic growth and currency in Ayyūbid Palestine', in R. Hillenbrand and S. Auld (eds.), *Ayyūbid Jerusalem: The Holy City in context* (London, 2009) pp. 1187–1250.

17

Archaeology and material culture

MARCUS MILWRIGHT

The last four decades have witnessed a massive expansion in the archaeology of the Islamic past in regions stretching from the Iberian Peninsula to Indonesia. While the coverage of research is far from complete – for instance, the first/seventh- and second/eighth-century occupation phases in key cities such as Baṣra, Damascus and Baghdad remain largely unexplored, and excavations are not permitted in the Holy Cities of Mecca and Medina – archaeology is now able to provide important insights into the study of the early Islamic period. Aside from its obvious role in the discovery and recording of artefacts, the discipline's most notable contribution to the study of early Islam is in the identification of economic, demographic and environmental processes that occur over the course of decades or centuries.

A recurrent concern in the archaeological study of early Islam is the degree to which the physical record exhibits significant continuity with the centuries prior to 1/622 (i.e. the Late Antique period). Conversely, the analysis of spatial and temporal patterns in the archaeological record from the first/seventh to the fourth/tenth centuries can reveal the emergence of new socio-cultural or economic phenomena. These competing dynamics are examined here with reference to four themes. The first part summarises the earliest evidence for a distinctive Muslim identity in the archaeological record. The second part assesses changes in the countryside with particular emphasis on the elite country residences (*qaṣr*, pl. *quṣūr*) of Greater Syria and the evolution of complex irrigation systems in different parts of the Islamic world. The third part discusses the changes in the urban environment from the Late Antique period to the creation of new cities in Syria and Iraq during the early ʿAbbāsid caliphate (132–279/750–892). The final part addresses changes in international trade from the Late Antique period to around 390/1000.

Muslim identity in the archaeological record

The Dome of the Rock in Jerusalem (dated by an inscription to 72/691f.) marks a watershed in Islamic material culture – not just in the fact of its remarkable preservation, but also in the evidence it gives about the new sense of artistic ambition among the Muslim elite. Leaving aside the Qurʾān pages in Ḥijāzī script and inscriptions dated on palaeographic grounds, we are left with a small group of artefacts from the period prior to the construction of the Dome of the Rock. Bilingual papyri (from 22/642) and Arab-Sasanian coins (*drachm/dirham*, from 31/651f.) bear the words *bism allāh* ('in the name of God') (see fig. 16.7). Longer inscriptions appear on the gravestone of one ʿAbd al-Raḥmān ibn Khayr in Egypt (31/652) and on graffiti in the Ḥijāz (from 40/660f.). Although these examples carry recognisably Muslim invocations, references to Muḥammad and his status as the prophet of Allāh are absent. Muʿāwiya ibn Abī Sufyān (r. 41–60/661–80) is the first caliph whose honorific, *amīr al-muʾminīn* ('commander of the faithful'), written in Arabic, or transcribed into Greek or Persian, appears on coins, papyri and monumental inscriptions.[1] Coins dating from 66/685f. until the minting of the first purely epigraphic issue of 77/696f. are notable for the inclusion of versions of the profession of faith (*shahāda*), as well as the name of Muḥammad (see chapter 16).[2]

In architecture the picture is even more sparse; prior to the Dome of the Rock we lack any buildings with inscriptions, and all dating is circumstantial. Recently it has been suggested that the first construction phase identified in Hamilton's survey of the Aqṣā Mosque in Jerusalem should be dated to the rule of Muʿāwiya in the 40s/660s.[3] Excavation of the *dār al-imāra* (governor's residence) in the garrison town (*miṣr*, pl. *amṣār*) of Kūfa revealed a large brick building surrounded by an *intervallum* and a fortified wall on the *qibla* side of the mosque (of which only one re-entrant corner was located). The *dār al-imāra* itself was constructed in three phases, the earliest of which may have

1 A graffito at Qāʿ al-Muʿtadil near al-Hijr in Saudi Arabia, dated 24/644, does contain a reference to the death of ʿUmar ibn al-Khaṭṭāb (r. 13–23/634–44), though without employing the title of caliph or the honorific *amīr al-muʾminīn*. See www.islamic-awareness.org/History/Islam/Inscriptions/kuficsaud.html.

2 Jeremy Johns, 'Archaeology and the history of early Islam: The first seventy years', *JESHO*, 46, 4 (2003), pp. 414–24; Robert Hoyland, 'New documentary texts and the early Islamic state', *BSOAS*, 69, 3 (2006); www.islamic-awareness.org/History/Islam/Inscriptions.

3 Jeremy Johns, 'The "House of the Prophet" and the concept of the mosque', in Jeremy Johns (ed.), *Bayt al-Maqdis: Jerusalem and Early Islam*, Oxford Studies in Islamic Art, 9, part 2 (Oxford, 1999), pp. 62–4.

been built by the governor, Ziyād ibn Abī Sufyān, in around 50/670 (fig. 17.1).[4] The earliest positive evidence for the dating of the *quṣūr* in Bilād al-Shām (Greater Syria) consists of a graffito carrying the date of 92/710 in Qaṣr al-Kharāna in Jordan (fig. 17.2), but recent archaeological research has provided plausible evidence for two earlier palatial structures. The first, Khirbat al-Karak in northern Israel, has been associated with Sinnabra/Sinnabris, a palace employed by both Muʿāwiya and ʿAbd al-Malik. The second is al-Bakhrāʾ, a Tetrarchic fort (293–305 CE) south of Palmyra, that was converted into a Muslim *qaṣr* through the construction, probably before 65/684, of an additional fortified zone to the north-east.[5]

This small body of data suggests that the period 1–72/622–91f. was one of rapid evolution for both the practices associated with the faith of Islam and the administrative framework of the nascent Islamic state. That so little that is recognisably 'Islamic' has been recovered is not, of course, due to a lack of archaeological activity; excavations and surveys have revealed considerable evidence of first/seventh-century occupation in the Middle East and North Africa. The overwhelming impression, however, is that the Arab conquests did not bring about radical and sudden change in the daily lives of the inhabitants of these regions. Continuity with the practices of Late Antiquity is evident in many aspects of the archaeological record into the second/eighth century and later.

The countryside

While knowledge of the urban palaces created by the Umayyad elite is limited,[6] the *quṣūr* (often misleadingly described as 'desert castles') survive in much larger numbers in diverse environments ranging from the Syrian desert to the plains of Jordan and the sub-tropical Jordan valley. Commonly adopting a square plan with a fortified outer wall and square or round towers at the corners, this building type derives ultimately from the Roman *castrum* (fig. 17.3). Recent research has highlighted the importance of fifth- and

4 K. Creswell, *A short account of early Muslim architecture*, rev. and suppl. James Allan (Aldershot, 1989), pp. 10–15; Johns, 'The first seventy years', p. 417.

5 For Khirbat al-Karak and al-Bakhrāʾ see Denis Genequand, 'Umayyad castles: The shift from Late Antique military architecture to early Islamic palatial building', in Hugh Kennedy (ed.), *Muslim military architecture in Greater Syria: From the coming of Islam to the Ottoman Period*, History of Warfare 35 (Leiden and Boston, 2006), pp. 10–12, figs. 2.5, 6.3.

6 See, however, Alastair Northedge, *Studies on Roman and Islamic ʿAmmān*, vol. I: *History, site and architecture*, British Academy Monographs in Archaeology 3 (Oxford and New York, 1992).

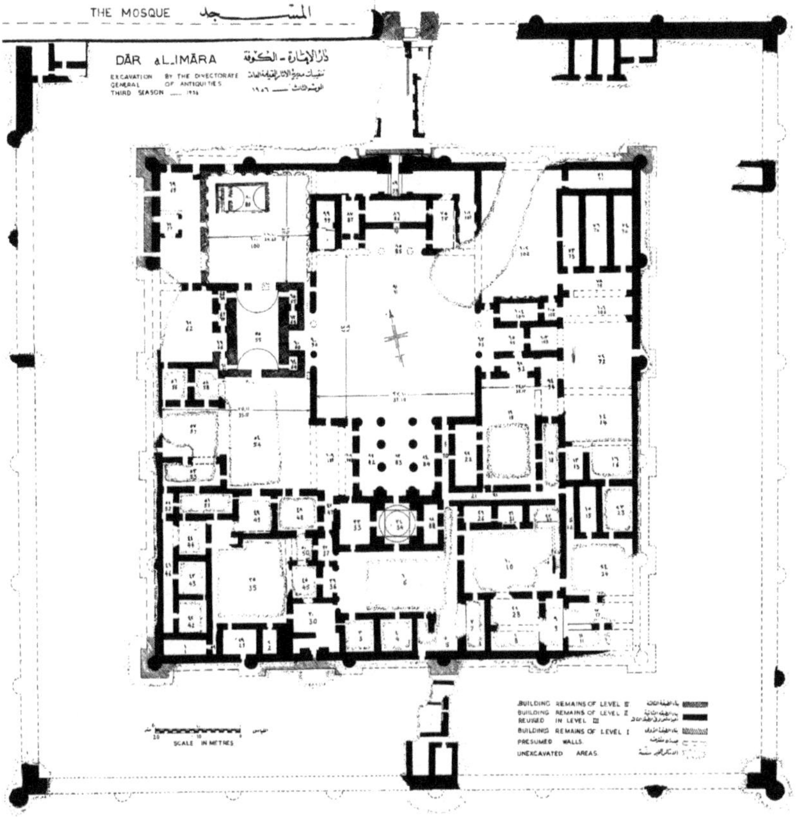

17.1 Plan of the *dār al-imāra* at Kūfa, Iraq, first/seventh century and later. After K. Creswell, *Early Muslim Architecture* (revised edition, 1969), volume I.1, fig. 18.

sixth-century Syrian fortified country residences of al-Andarīn, Isṭabl ʿAntar and probably Ḍumayr as intermediaries in the evolution of the specific characteristics of the second/eighth-century *quṣūr*.[7] While the opulent decoration encountered on sites such as Khirbat al-Mafjar and Quṣayr ʿAmra offers intriguing insights into the culture of Umayyad princely pleasure (known otherwise from textual sources), archaeological interpretations are increasingly focusing upon the roles played by the *quṣūr* in the cultivation of land and the maintenance of trade routes. For instance, an early Islamic perimeter wall enclosing an irrigated area of some 535 hectares has been

7 Genequand, 'Umayyad castles', pp. 20–4, figs. 6.2, 7.2, 7.4.

17.2 Exterior of Qaṣr al-Kharāna, Jordan (before 92/710). Photo: Marcus Milwright

17.3 Late Roman *castrum* known as Qaṣr al-Bashīr, Jordan (293–305). Photo: Marcus Milwright

identified at Maʿān in southern Jordan.[8] In the cases of Qaṣr al-Ḥayr al-Gharbī and Khirbat al-Mafjar the cultivation of surrounding land involved the renovation of Roman dams and aqueducts.[9]

Key considerations in the placement of many of the *quṣūr* were proximity to the ancient routes running north from the Ḥijāz into Syria, and the availability of water (map 7). For instance, the existence of a major route from the Arabian city of Taymā north via Wādī Sirḥān toward the plain of Balqāʾ in Jordan helps to account for the locations of Qaṣr al-Ṭūba, Qaṣr al-Kharāna (fig. 17.2) and Quṣayr ʿAmra. One of the northern routes from the Wādī Sirḥān passed around the eastern fringes of the basalt desert of southern Syria, and this makes sense of the otherwise remote Qaṣr al-Burqūʾ and Jabal Says (both of which were well provided with cisterns, and the latter also with a spring).[10] Several important Umayyad *quṣūr* can also be found along the Strata Diocletiana (established *c.* 297) linking Damascus to the Euphrates via Palmyra and Ruṣāfa. Another significant route that received extensive patronage in the second/eighth and early third/ninth centuries was the Darb Zubayda leading from Mecca to Kūfa. Reconnaissance along this road has revealed numerous fortified structures, as well as hundreds of wells, cisterns and rain catchment devices designed to provide a reliable water supply for the pilgrims, merchants and others passing through this arid region.[11]

Surveys in Iran and Iraq have demonstrated the extent to which the agricultural prosperity of the early Islamic period was reliant upon the engineering of the Sasanian period (*c.* 224–651), and earlier dynasties. Comprising large canals (such as the sixth-century Kāṭūl al-Kisrawī drawing water from the Tigris river and feeding the Diyālā plain in Iraq), underground channels (*qanāt*) and networks of smaller irrigation canals, these systems greatly enhanced the productivity of lands under Sasanian control. The most intensively studied of these is the ancient canal system of the Diyālā plain east of Baghdad. While both the methodology employed by Adams and his conclusions should be assessed in the light of criticisms made by economic historians and revisions made to his ceramic chronology, this study gives

8 Denis Genequand, 'Maʿān, an early Islamic settlement in southern Jordan: Preliminary report on the survey in 2002', *Annual of the Department of Antiquities of Jordan*, 47 (2003).

9 Creswell, *Short account*, pp. 135, 180.

10 Geoffrey King, 'The distribution of sites and routes in the Jordanian and Syrian deserts', *Proceedings of the Seminar for Arabian Studies*, 20 (1987).

11 Barbara Finster, 'Die Reiseroute Kufa–Saʿūdī-Arabien in frühislamische Zeit', *Baghdader Mitteilungen*, 9 (1978); J. Wilkinson, 'Darb Zubayda architectural documentation program. B. Darb Zubayda-1979: The water resources', *Atlal*, 4 (1980).

important insights into an agricultural region in the transition to Islamic rule. While there appears to have been a reduction in settlement levels and the number of active canals after the late Sasanian phase, the Diyālā plain remained relatively prosperous until the end of the third/ninth century. Political instability, overtaxation and lack of investment probably contributed to the deterioration of the agricultural infrastructure in subsequent centuries.[12]

In the Arabian Peninsula complex networks of open channels, *qanāt* and water mills have been identified inland from the Omanī port of Ṣuḥār. Allowing for the cultivation of 6,100 hectares, this system was probably constructed in the third/ninth and fourth/tenth centuries, when the area enjoyed considerable prosperity in international maritime trade.[13] The evidence from Spain suggests that, following the conquest in 92–100/711–20, the irrigation systems of the Islamic period synthesised aspects of the existing Roman–Visigothic infrastructure (which concentrated upon the provision of water to urban centres) with types of *qanāt* and rain-fed reservoirs introduced from the Middle East. These novel technologies in Islamic Spain were a necessary precursor to the introduction of new crops such as sugar cane, rice, mulberries, cotton and oranges.[14]

The urban environment

Important changes can be detected in the towns and cities of the Late Antique period. Excavations of urban centres report a broadly consistent pattern from the fourth century with urban institutions such as theatres, large public baths and pagan temples falling out of use, while church building proliferated.[15] These changes reflect both the increasing irrelevance of theatrical performance and other entertainment and the dominating role of the Church. Equally

12 Robert Adams, *Land behind Baghdad: A history of settlement on the Diyala plains* (Chicago and London, 1965), pp. 69–111. See also criticisms in Michael Morony, 'Land use and settlement patterns in late Sasanian and early Islamic Iraq', in Geoffrey King and Averil Cameron (eds.), *The Byzantine and early Islamic Near East*, vol. II: *Land use and settlement patterns*, Studies in Late Antiquity and Early Islam 1 (Princeton, 1994), pp. 221–9.

13 T. J. Wilkinson, 'Sohar ancient fields project: Interim report no. 1', *Journal of Oman Studies*, 1 (1975). See also 2 (1976), pp. 75–80; 3 (1977), pp. 13–16.

14 Thomas Glick, 'Hydraulic technology in al-Andalus', in S. Jayyusi (ed.), *The legacy of Muslim Spain* (Leiden, 1992); Andrew Watson, *Agricultural innovation in the early Islamic world: The diffusion of crops and farming techniques*, Cambridge Studies in Islamic Civilization (Cambridge, 1983), pp. 9–73, 103–11.

15 Hugh Kennedy, 'From *polis* to *madina*: Urban change in Late Antique and early Islamic Syria', *Past and Present*, 106 (February 1985).

important is the tendency for public spaces – fora and the wide colonnaded streets – to be encroached upon by private building. The abandonment of wheeled transport in favour of pack animals may have been a contributing factor, though the construction of shops, houses and industrial installations on public thoroughfares presumably also reflects the decreasing authority of municipal officials. This gradual evolution of the urban space through the Late Antique and early Islamic periods has been demonstrated on numerous excavations, of which the ancient Decapolis towns of Pella and Scythopolis (Bet Shean, Baysān) in the Jordan valley are well-published examples.[16] The discovery in Baysān of an impressive market ornamented with two inscriptions in blue-and-gold mosaic built in 120/737f. by the caliph Hishām (r. 105–25/724–43) demonstrates that the Umayyad elite did, at times, seek to invest in the improvement of the urban infrastructure.[17] The remarkable persistence of the idea of the 'classical' city is illustrated by the Islamic urban foundation of ʿAnjar (*c.* 92–6/711–15) in Lebanon (fig. 17.4). The unfinished city preserves its original rectangular plan with a *tetrapylon* marking the intersection of the colonnaded north–south and east–west streets (*cardo* and *decumanus* respectively).[18]

Similar dynamics can be detected in the towns and cities of Late Antique North Africa, though there are significant differences in the overall chronology. Excavations in Uchi Maius (now known as Henchir al-Douamis) in Tunisia revealed the intrusion after 364–75 of a cistern, an olive oil press, and later a kiln, into the Antique forum and surrounding areas. This radical change correlates well with archaeological evidence in other towns for increased agricultural productivity during Vandal rule.[19] A further shift away from the classical urban plan in Uchi Maius is signalled by the construction of a citadel in the late sixth century. A *miṣr* was established at Qayrawān in 50/670, and settlements such as Sétif and Rougga probably exhibit signs of continuous occupation into the first/seventh and second/eighth centuries, but more commonly the archaeological record indicates a hiatus in urban settlement from some time prior to the Islamic conquest until

16 Anthony McNicoll *et al.*, *Pella in Jordan*, 2 vols., Mediterranean Archaeology Supplements 2 (Sydney, 1992), vol. II, pp. 145–98; Yoram Tsafrir and Gideon Foerster, 'From Scythopolis to Baysān: changing concepts of urbanism', in King and Cameron (eds.), *Land use and settlement patterns*, pp. 95–115.

17 Elias Khamis, 'Two wall mosaic inscriptions from the Umayyad market place in Bet Shean/Baysān', *BSOAS*, 64 (2001).

18 Creswell, *Short account*, pp. 122–4.

19 Anna Leone, 'Late Antique North Africa: Production and changing use of buildings in urban areas', *al-Masāq*, 15, 1 (March 2003), pp. 25–7.

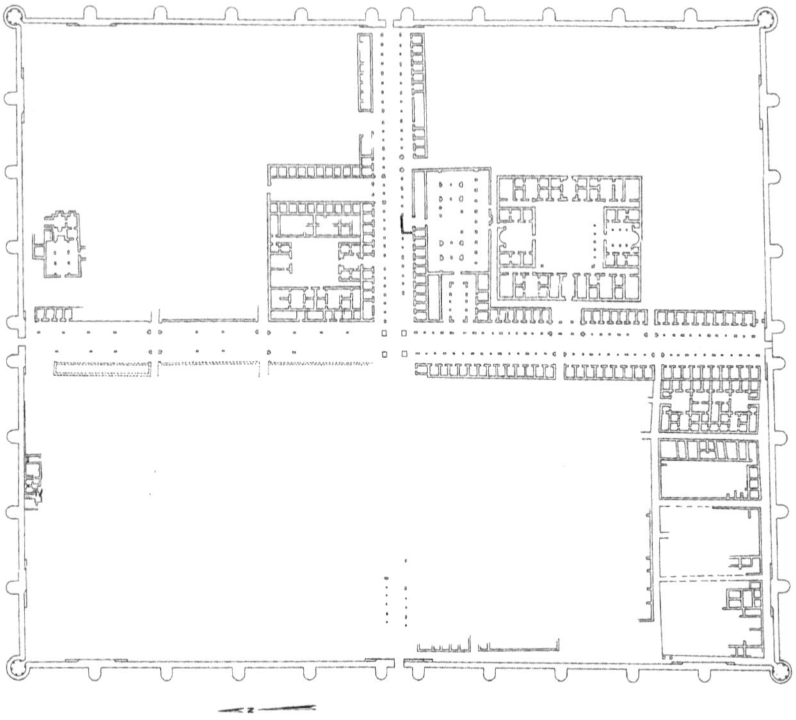

17.4 Plan of the town of ʿAnjar, Lebanon. After *Early Muslim Architecture* (revised edition, 1969), volume I.2, fig. 540.

the fourth/tenth or fifth/eleventh centuries. Like a number of other settlements in Islamic North Africa (Ifrīqiya), the re-urbanisation of Uchi Maius comprised a mosque and an area of closely packed courtyard houses within the citadel.[20]

Inscriptions on items as diverse as coins, seals, documents, road markers and buildings performed the task of announcing the religious and political values of the Muslim elite, but this was also achieved through the imposition of new architectural forms. As already noted, the conquests were often followed by the founding of *amṣār*, usually in the vicinity of established settlements. Of the first/seventh-century *amṣār*, only Kūfa, Fusṭāṭ (Egypt, 21/642)

20 Sauro Gelichi and Marco Milanese, 'Problems in the transition toward the Medieval in Ifriqiya: First results from the archaeological excavations at Uchi Maius (Teboursouk, Béja)', in M. Khanoussi, P. Ruggieri and C. Vismara (eds.), *L'Africa Romana: Atti del XII Convegno di Studio* (Sassari, 1998).

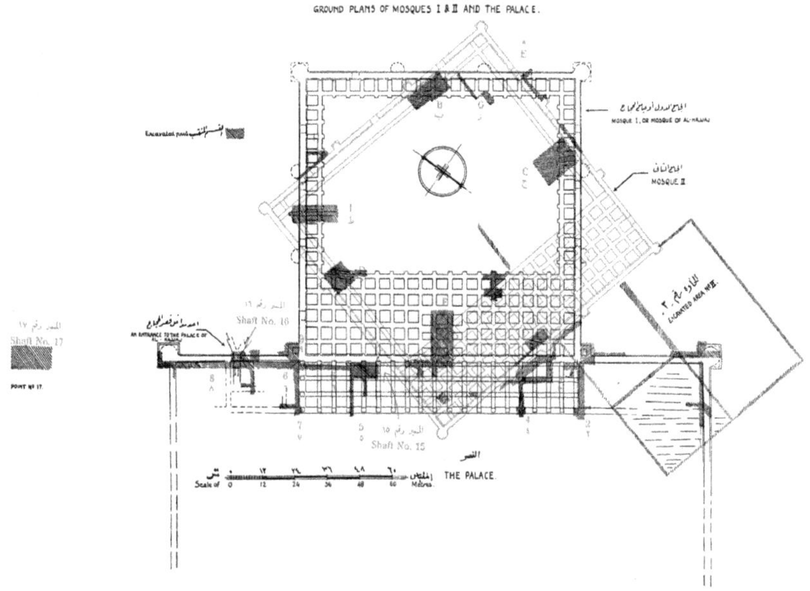

17.5 Plans of mosques I (possibly 84/703: marked in black) and II (marked in grey) in Wāsiṭ. After F. Safar, *Wâsiṭ, the sixth season's excavations* (1945), fig. 5.

and Ayla (Jordan, *c.* 30/650) have been excavated, and in each case little remains from the early decades of occupation.[21] Textual descriptions make clear the central role played by the congregational mosque (*masjid al-jāmiʿ*) and the governor's residence. The earliest mosque to preserve its original plan was excavated in the Iraqi *miṣr* of Wāsiṭ (dated on historical grounds to 84/703) (fig. 17.5).[22] Reviewing the archaeological data for the following decades, it becomes apparent how rapidly the concept of the courtyard mosque was adopted into the urban centres of the expanding Islamic empire. Early examples are known from widely dispersed locations including Banbhore and al-Manṣūra in Pakistan (before 108/727f. and second/eighth century respectively), Samarqand/Afrāsiyāb in Uzbekistan (*c.* 142–63/760–80), Sūsa in Iran

21 Roland-Pierre Gayraud, 'Fostat: Évolution d'une capitale arabe du VIIe au XIIe siècle d'après les fouilles d'Istabl ʿAntar', in Roland-Pierre Gayraud (ed.), *Colloque international d'archéologie islamique, IFAO, Le Caire, 3–7 février 1993*, Textes arabes et études islamiques 36 (Cairo, 1999); Donald Whitcomb, 'The *misr* of Ayla: Settlement at ʿAqaba in the early Islamic period', in King and Cameron (eds.), *Land use and settlement patterns*, pp. 155–70.

22 Fuad Safar, *Wâsiṭ: The sixth season's excavations* (Cairo, 1945), pp. 20, 24–7, fig. 11.

(second/eighth century), Ṣanʿāʾ in Yemen (92–6/711–16), Damascus in Syria (86–96/705–16), Ḥarrān in south-east Turkey (probably 127–32/744–50), the citadel and lower town of ʿAmmān in Jordan (*c.* 90–111/709–30 and before 133/750 respectively) and Cordoba in Spain (171–2/787–8).[23]

In archaeological terms what is of interest is the distribution of the mosques and their spatial relationship to other structures. Mosques were located in close proximity to the commercial centre within existing cities. At the Persian Gulf port of Sīrāf the mosque, constructed after 188/803f., occupied the site of the old Sasanian fort, but was also surrounded by the market (the lower storey of the south-eastern side of the mosque being made up of a series of shops).[24] At ʿAnjar the north wall of the mosque functions as the back wall of five shops that face onto the *decumanus* (fig. 17.4), while excavations in Ayla revealed that the expansion of the mosque necessitated the alteration of the route of the *cardo*. The close integration of the congregational mosque and governor's residence has been demonstrated in excavations at Kūfa, Wāsiṭ, ʿAnjar and al-Manṣūra. The extant urban plans of the second/eighth century reveal another important process: the spatial separation of the religious and palatial/administrative structures and the creation of a ceremonial route between them. This increased elaboration can be found in such cases as Hishām's palace and mosque in Sergiopolis/al-Ruṣāfa, the Aqṣā Mosque and the palaces to the south of the Ḥaram al-Sharīf in Jerusalem, and the citadels of ʿAmmān and Samarqand.[25]

The new cities of the early ʿAbbāsid period represent a break with the concept of the classical urban plan seen so powerfully at ʿAnjar. While the famous Round City of Baghdad constructed by the caliph al-Manṣūr (r. 136–58/754–75) is only known from written descriptions, two ʿAbbāsid urban foundations – al-Rāfiqa in Syria (after 155/771f.) and Sāmarrāʾ in Iraq (221–79/836–92) – have been subjected to archaeological study. The garrison city of al-Rāfiqa (lit. 'the Companion') was

23 F. Khan, *Banbhore: A preliminary report on the recent archaeological excavations at Banbhore*, 4th edn (Karachi, 1976); Abdul Aziz Farooq, 'Excavations at Mansurah (13th season)', *Pakistan Archaeology*, 10–12 (1974–86); Creswell, *Short account, passim*; Johns, 'Concept of the mosque', pp. 64–9; Yury Karev, 'Samarqand in the eighth century: The evidence of transformation', in Donald Whitcomb (ed.), *Changing social identity with the spread of Islam: Archaeological perspectives*, Oriental Institute Seminars 1 (Chicago, 2004).

24 David Whitehouse, *Siraf III: The congregational mosque and other mosques from the ninth to the twelfth centuries* (London, 1980), pp. 9–19.

25 On these structures see Dorothée Sack, *Resafa IV: Die Grosse Moschee von Resafa-Ruṣāfat Hisām* (Mainz, 1996); Creswell, *Short account*, pp. 94–6; Antonio Almagro and Pedro Jiménez, 'The Umayyad mosque on the citadel of Amman', *Annual of the Department of Antiquities of Jordan*, 44 (2000); Karev, 'Samarqand', pp. 53–60.

constructed on the north bank of the Euphrates river about 600 metres west of the existing settlement of al-Raqqa (ancient Kallinikos). Built largely of mud brick, and following a similar system to the fortifications of Baghdad, the double line of walls was punctuated with numerous major and minor entrances (fig. 17.6). To the north was an extensive complex of palaces and administrative structures, while to the west at Hiraqla is an unfinished structure surrounded by a circular wall that is believed to be a victory monument.[26] Another significant aspect of the plan was the creation of a large industrial zone. Excavations in the area known today as Tal Aswad, directly north of al-Raqqa, identified groups of ceramic kilns (operating until *c.* 210/825f.) producing a wide range of unglazed and glazed vessels, while further to the west a glass workshop was discovered constructed over the hypocaust of a bathhouse. Later industrial activity was largely focused in the land between al-Raqqa and al-Rāfiqa. Provided with its own defensive wall and a market, this industrial area was, by the late fourth/tenth century, understood as a distinct urban entity (*madīna*).[27]

Established by al-Muʿtaṣim (r. 218–27/833–42) in 221/836, and expanded by later caliphs, most notably al-Mutawakkil (r. 232–47/847–61), Sāmarrāʾ stretches more than 35 kilometres along the banks of the Tigris river. Like Baghdad, this ʿAbbāsid foundation made use of existing watercourses constructed in the Sasanian period. Comprising numerous palaces, two congregational mosques, barracks, a mausoleum, pavilions, racecourses, polo-grounds, highways and hunting reserves, Sāmarrāʾ is perhaps best considered as a series of linked urban units rather than a conventional city with a single administrative and economic centre. Indeed, the erection of a second congregational mosque of Abū Dulaf (245–7/859–61) lends the northern development of al-Mutawakkiliyya the status of city distinct from that of the remainder of Sāmarrāʾ (fig. 17.7). The palaces and other monumental structures of Sāmarrāʾ owe their scale partly to the cheap building materials – mud brick and pisé – employed in much of the construction. Baked brick and expensive decorative media were reserved for the two congregational mosques and the most important sectors of the palaces. While the palaces are evidently the focal points of each urban unit, they should not be seen in isolation; many are surrounded by 'cantonments' built in mud brick

26 Verena Daiber and Andrea Becker (eds.), *Raqqa III: Baudenkmäler und Paläste I* (Mainz am Rhein, 2004).

27 Julian Henderson *et al.*, 'Experiment and innovation: Early Islamic industry at al-Raqqa, Syria', *Antiquity*, 79 (2005); Stefan Heidemann, 'The history of the industrial and commercial area of ʿAbbāsid al-Raqqa, called *al-Raqqa al-Muḥtariqa*', *BSOAS*, 69, 1 (2006).

17.6 Corona satellite photograph of Raqqa, Syria, taken between 1960 and 1972. 1) Raqqa (Kallinikos); 2) walled city of Rāfiqa; 3) North gate; 4) 'Baghdad gate'; 5) Congregational Mosque; 6) Possible line of the wall enclosing al-Raqqa al-Muḥtariqa ('the burning Raqqa'); 7) site of an Abbasid-period glass workshop; 8) Tal Aswad.

17.7 Aerial view of Sāmarrāʾ with the mosque of Abū Dulaf (245–47/859–61). Creswell archive: EA.CA.271. Creswell Archive, courtesy of the Ashmolean Museum, University of Oxford.

that probably functioned as the housing blocks and markets of the Turkish troops.[28]

International trade

Two major spheres of Late Antique international mercantile activity – the Mediterranean and the Persian Gulf – are of particular relevance for the development of long-distance trading relationships in the early Islamic period (maps 2, 5, 7). In the fifth and sixth centuries volumes of trade in the Mediterranean declined considerably from the levels seen in earlier centuries. There is, however, textual and archaeological evidence for the continuity of established economic contacts. Furthermore, the supply to Europe of luxury goods from North Africa and the Middle East was not terminated by the Islamic conquests. For instance, papyrus from Egypt continued to be employed by the Merovingian chancery until the early second/eighth century, and the latest Papal papyrus carries the date of 1057.[29] Another interesting example of continuity with earlier Mediterranean trading practices can be seen in the occurrence of resin-coated ceramic amphorae, corresponding to a Late Roman type, in late second/eighth to early third/ninth-century excavated contexts in Iṣṭabl ʿAntar/Fusṭāṭ in Egypt. Comparable amphorae are reported from long-established wine-producing sites in Middle Egypt.[30] A similar continuity in amphora production may also have occurred in North Africa.[31]

The Persian Gulf presents a different picture. The phase from the second to the fourth or fifth centuries witnessed a decline in settlement levels in eastern Arabia, as well as the construction of fortified dwellings at sites such as Mheila and al-Dūr (similar structures in the Ḥijāz, including Qaryat al-Faw, also date to this phase). In spite of the evidence for reduced levels of sedentary occupation, mercantile activity remained vigorous, with the presence of South Asian ceramics being an indication of the long-distance commercial contacts. On the Persian coast the major port of Bushihr was established during the rule of the Sasanian shah Ardashīr (r. 224–40), while the fort at Sīrāf is attributed to Shāpūr II (r. 309–79). While many of the Arabian fortified buildings were abandoned between the fifth and the first/seventh-second/

28 Alastair Northedge, *The historical topography of Samarra*, Samarra Studies 1 (London, 2005).
29 Richard Hodges and David Whitehouse, *Mohammed, Charlemagne and the origins of Europe: Archaeology and the Pirenne thesis* (London, 1983).
30 C. Vogt *et al.*, 'Notes on some of the Abbasid amphorae of Istabl ʿAntar-Fustat (Egypt)', *BASOR*, 326 (2002).
31 Leone, 'Late Antique North Africa', pp. 21–4.

17.8 Earthenware bowl with tin glaze and cobalt (blue) and copper (green) painting, Iraq, third/ninth century. 1978.2141. Courtesy of the Ashmolean Museum, University of Oxford.

eighth centuries, sites such as Khatt, Ṣuḥār and Kush perhaps continued to trade into the early Islamic period.[32] Conversely, the decline in long-distance land trade via the Silk Route caused by Perso-Roman wars in 502–6, 527–61 and 602–29 may have invigorated Persian maritime activity. The presence of Sasanian *drachms* and bullae (perhaps used to seal packages destined for transport) in Oman, India, Sri Lanka and coastal sites in China illustrates the extent of Persian trading links.[33]

Archaeology has established that the greatest expansion in Persian Gulf commerce occurred in the early ʿAbbāsid period. The extent of this trade is well illustrated by the wide distribution of second/eighth- to fourth/tenth-century Iraqi glazed pottery (fig. 17.8) from ports such as Baṣra and Sīrāf; for

32 Derek Kennet, 'On the eve of Islam: Archaeological evidence from Eastern Arabia', *Antiquity*, 79 (2005); Derek Kennet, *Sasanian and Islamic pottery from Ras al-Khaimah. Classification, chronology and analysis of trade in the western Indian Ocean*, BAR International Series 1248 (Oxford, 2004), pp. 68–85.

33 Touraj Daryaee, 'The Persian Gulf trade in Late Antiquity', *Journal of World History*, 14, 1 (March 2003).

instance, tin-opacified wares and turquoise-glazed storage jars appear on sites as dispersed as Fusṭāṭ, Zabīd (Yemen), Mantai (Sri Lanka), Ko Kho Khao (Thailand), the East African coast and possibly Kwa Gandaganda (South Africa).[34] Finds of Islamic glass vessels in elite burials in China are another indication of the widespread demand for luxury commodities manufactured in the cities of the Islamic Middle East.[35] Although transport by sea was the most efficient mode of long-distance transport, reports of Iraqi ceramics at sites such as al-Raqqa–al-Rāfiqa, Sūsa and Samarqand demonstrate that there was also vigorous trade along the major land routes and rivers. Glazed ceramics, glass and metalwork found along the Darb Zubayda (most notably at the town of al-Rabadha) reveal that, in addition to the annual *ḥajj*, this major road was also employed by caravans bringing luxury merchandise from Iraq to the Ḥijāz.[36]

The excavations of the congregational mosque and other sites in Sīrāf provide evidence for the introduction of ceramics from South-East Asia. The imports of the late second / eighth and third / ninth centuries included stoneware storage jars ('Dusun ware'), two inscribed with Arabic names (probably those of merchants), as well as various types of Tang period (618–906) glazed stoneware bowls. Dusun ware has also been located at numerous sites in southern Iran (as far north as Sīrjān), on the island of Socotra, Banbhore in Pakistan, the East African coast and Sri Lanka.[37] Equally impressive is the distribution of the green glazed stoneware produced between the third / ninth and fifth / eleventh centuries in the area of Yuezhou, south of Shanghai. Finds of Yueh wares are concentrated in the Persian Gulf, Mesopotamia and Sind, but they also made their way along land routes as far as Nīshāpūr and Rayy.[38] Excavated contexts of the fourth

34 Robert Mason, *Shine like the sun: Lustre-painted and associated pottery from the medieval Middle East* (Toronto and Costa Mesa, 2004), pp. 23–60.

35 Numerous Islamic glass vessels were reported in the tomb of a Liao princess from Ch'en state, dated 1018. See Ts'ai Mei-fen, 'A discussion of Ting ware with unglazed rims and related twelfth-century official porcelain', in Maxwell Hearn and Judith Smith (eds.), *Arts of the Sung and Yüan* (New York, 1996), pp. 116–17.

36 Saʿd b. ʿAbd al-ʿAzīz al-Rashid, *al-Rabadhah: A portrait of early Islamic civilization in Saudi Arabia* (Harlow, 1986).

37 David Whitehouse, 'Chinese stoneware from Siraf: The earliest finds', in N. Hammond (ed.), *South Asian archaeology* (Park Ridge, NJ, 1973); Jessica Rawson, Michael Tite and M. Hughes, 'The export of Tang sancai wares: Some recent research', *Transactions of the Oriental Ceramics Society*, 52 (1987–8). On the criticisms of the Sīrāf ceramic chronology, see Kennet, *Sasanian and Islamic pottery*, pp. 83–4.

38 Andrew Williamson, 'Regional distribution of mediaeval Persian pottery in the light of recent investigations', in James Allan and Caroline Roberts (eds.), *Syria and Iran: Three studies in medieval ceramics*, Oxford Studies in Islamic Art 4 (Oxford, 1987), pp. 11–14.

or fifth to third / ninth centuries at Kush in Ras al-Khaimah are notable for the occurrence of significant quantities of Indian ceramics; Chinese wares only start to appear in the fifth / eleventh century.[39] Storage vessels for date syrup akin to types manufactured at Sīrāf in the fourth / tenth century have been located at sites including Manda, Shanga and Pate on the Lamu archipelago, while timbers employed in the buildings in Sīrāf were probably shipped from East Africa.[40]

Another dimension of the economic patterns from the late second / eighth to the fourth / tenth centuries is revealed by hoards found in Scandinavia, Denmark and the regions between the Black Sea and the Baltic. Of the huge number of coins from recovered hoards (more than 80,000 *dirhams* in Sweden, about 5,000 in Denmark and over seventy separate hoards of third / ninth-century coins are reported from European Russia) the vast majority are *dirhams* minted in the east of the Islamic world – particularly Madīnat al-Salām (Baghdad), al-Muḥammadiyya (Rayy), Balkh and Samarqand –about 164–390 / 780–1000 (see fig. 16.23). Umayyad, Sasanian and Byzantine coins are all very scarce, as are examples minted in North Africa or Spain (for a detailed consideration of early Islamic numismatics, see chapter 16). The northern flow of silver from the ʿAbbāsid caliphate and the lands controlled by the Sāmānid dynasty (204–395 / 819–1005) is an indicator of a vigorous period of mercantile activity conducted with the peoples living beyond the borders of the eastern Islamic world. Focused on slaves, furs, wax, honey and amber, this trade required the interaction of Muslim merchants, Bulghārs, Khazars and the group known in Arabic sources as the Rūs (probably Vikings as well as Slavs and Finns) at entrepôts along the Volga and as far north as Old Ladoga (Staraja) in north-western Russia. The rarity in Scandinavian hoards of coins minted after the 360s / 970s probably gives an approximate date for the decline of this long-distance trading network.[41]

39 Kennet, *Sasanian and Islamic pottery*, pp. 69–72.

40 David Whitehouse, 'East Africa and the maritime trade of the Indian Ocean, AD 800–1500', in B. Amoretti (ed.), *Islam in East Africa: New sources* (Rome, 2001).

41 Thomas Noonan, 'Ninth-century dirham hoards from European Russia: A preliminary analysis', in M. Blackburn and D. M. Metcalf (eds.), *Viking-age coinage in northern lands*, BAR International Series 122 (Oxford, 1981), pp. 47–117; Bengt Hovén, 'On Oriental coins in Scandinavia', in Blackburn and Metcalfe (eds.), *Viking-age coinage*, pp. 119–28; Anne Kromann and Else Roesdahl, 'The Vikings and the Islamic lands', in K. von Folsach *et al.* (eds.), *The Arabian journey: Danish connections with the Islamic world over a thousand years* (Aarhus, 1996).

Conclusion

Many areas of continuity can be detected between the early Islamic period and the patterns of Late Antiquity. This continuity is particularly apparent in the archaeological record of the first/seventh and much of the second/eighth centuries. At the same time, artefacts do provide indications of new directions. Arabic, though sometimes employed on monumental inscriptions prior to 1/622, becomes the pre-eminent vehicle for the expression of a new Muslim identity. The somewhat tentative experiments with religious formulae from 1/622 to 72/691f. give little indication, however, of the dominant place that the written word would have in later Islamic art and architecture. Other important developments of this first phase were the creation of the *amṣār* and the introduction of new institutions, the congregational mosque and the *dār al-imāra*, into the urban environment. It is evident that the orderly planning of the 'classical city' had started to erode from at least the fourth century, and that this process continued after 1/622, but it is perhaps the great ʿAbbāsid foundations of the later second/eighth and third/ninth centuries that mark the decisive shift in Islamic urbanism. Attracting skilled workers from other regions, these great cities provided a fertile environment for innovation in media such as glass, glazed pottery and metalwork. The fate of the irrigation networks of Iraq during the ʿAbbāsid period remains the subject of debate, but elsewhere the centuries after the Arab conquests brought renewed vitality to agriculture through the synthesis of existing technologies and the introduction of new crops. Likewise, the arrival of Islam does not appear to have radically altered the existing routes of international trade. What does change from the late second/eighth century onward is the volume of traffic. The presence of Far Eastern stonewares in the Middle East, *dirham* hoards in Scandinavia and Iraqi glazed ceramic bowls in locations as dispersed as Spain, East Africa, Sri Lanka and China attests to the vibrancy of commercial exchange in this new era.

Conclusion: From formative Islam to classical Islam

CHASE F. ROBINSON

The ancient and Late Antique history of Eurasia could be reasonably (if not generously) characterised as a series of experiments in assembling communities through two sometimes complementary, contradictory or overlapping processes. The first was unambiguously political: building states and empires through conquest and some combination of occupation, emigration, colonisation, administration and exploitation. The other was ambiguously ideological, intellectual, spiritual and cultural: creating religious and philosophical systems of thought and conduct through some combination of inspiration, revelation, reflection and systematic teaching. Some 1,500 years or so after the end of Late Antiquity some of the religious and philosophical systems have proven more durable than the necessarily fragile political ones, in large measure because they have ridden the back of those strong polities: from Hellenism through Christianity to Confucianism, the biggest success stories feature ruling elites that offered robust sanction and patronage. What would Near Eastern history be like had the Sasanian shah Wahrām I followed his predecessors in favouring, rather than imprisoning, Mani (d. 276)? The opposite scenario poses questions too. How would Chinese history appear had the Song failed to oversee the rise of Neo-Confucianism?

What is clearer is that only in the seventh- and eighth-century Near East did the two processes of community building fully synchronise and thereby inaugurate what was arguably one of the most creative stages of human history. This synchronicity – early Muslims were founders of both world empire and world religion, possessors of both power and truth[1] – is perhaps the most striking feature of Islamic history. As readers of this volume now know well, in the short space of a century the Arabs moved from the political and cultural margins of the Late Antique Fertile Crescent to the centre of Eurasia's political stage. Arguably the least promising environment for state

1 See P. Crone, *Medieval Islamic political thought* (Edinburgh, 2004), p. 16.

and empire building – the modest oasis settlements of western Arabia, which remained largely outside the influence of successive Byzantine, Sasanian and South Arabian imperialists who quite reasonably invested their moneys and armies elsewhere – produced Late Antiquity's most dynamic movement of organised expansion and rule.

It is difficult to exaggerate the scale and speed of the achievement or the role of exceptionally visionary and able leaders in realising it. We saw in chapter 5 how, in about a decade, Muḥammad extended his authority over most of the Arabian Peninsula, setting his polity on a policy of local expansion that his successors transformed into regional conquest. Given how quickly this happened, and also the divisions that appeared when the movements of conquest slowed, expansion seems to have been essential to the nascent polity's survival. For the most part, conquest destruction was restrained and, at least in some respects, discretionary: low- and mid-level bureaucratic functionaries were preserved so as to ensure fiscal continuity, and the material evidence shows continuities at other levels too. Having destroyed the Sasanian and dismembered the Byzantine empires in the middle of the seventh century, by the second decade of the eighth Muslim rulers shared continental hegemony with Eurasia's other great superpower, the Tang, whose armies they would defeat a generation later on the Talas river. Aside from inaccessible (and unattractive) pockets of mountainous and desert-filled regions, the Umayyad caliphs, necessarily relying on a variety of intermediaries, proxies and local elites, thus ruled territories that stretched all the way from the Atlantic to the Oxus. Stitched together by an increasingly uniform and centralising administration that took hold in the late seventh century, the lands formed in the first instance an enormous catchment area for agricultural revenues, since they conjoined the fertile soils of Byzantine Africa and Egypt with those of Sasanian Mesopotamia and Khurāsān. The tax bases of the two great powers of Late Antiquity were now funding the single state that succeeded them both. At the same time, the caliphate also functioned as a grid of interlocking networks of land-based and seaborne trade, which funnelled goods (especially through the Indian Ocean and across Central Asia), peoples, ideas and technologies into and through the cities of Iraq and Syria.

The revolutionaries who brought the ʿAbbāsids to power in 750 did so with a programme that called for the restoration of just rule by members of the Prophet's family, but the architects of that state worked with the ingredients they had to hand. They inherited Umayyad institutions and accelerated the Marwānids' move towards an increasingly complex, centralised and fully Arabic administration. The eastward move of the capital from Syria to

Baghdad also symbolised some changes to Umayyad practices of rule. Brought to power by eastern armies, and heirs to an easterly-oriented political tradition in Iraq, they broke from Umayyad tradition by building fixed and huge capital cities in the Iraqi heartland. They also greatly increased the recruitment of Central Asian retinues, eventually placing them at the very centre of the state's military establishment. Meanwhile, they were content to let the Mediterranean west rule itself under dynasties that respected, acknowledged or largely ignored their sovereignty, provided they did not directly and effectively challenge it; in any case, we saw in chapter 14 that Umayyad rule in al-Andalus appears to have been unprofitable. So instead of trying – presumably vainly – to reconstitute imperial power that had dissolved in al-Andalus and North Africa in the 740s, the ʿAbbāsids chose instead to concentrate their energies on consolidating and expanding in the east, thus challenging regions that had resisted Umayyad rule from within (such as Ṭabaristān) or had managed to remain outside it (such as much of Transoxania). Yet here too ʿAbbāsid rule did not necessarily mean direct rule, and although much of the symbolism and rhetoric of empire would have had its subjects believe otherwise, already at what is often considered to be the height of ʿAbbāsid absolutism (the reign of Hārūn al-Rashīd, 786–809), delegation to clients, especially on the empire's periphery, was a rule. But the lines between temporary delegation, structural devolution, alienation and usurpation were blurry, and the loyalty of these clients was more effectively retained when Baghdad could project power and authority than when it could not; given any slack by temporary instability in the capital, provincial elites were often inclined to wander towards self-reliance,[2] and by the end of the ninth century the two institutions originally designed for the task of enforcing centralised rule – the army and the office of the caliphate – were no longer fit for the purpose. Empire had been reconfigured as commonwealth, as chapters 8 and 9 have shown. From this perspective, one of the ʿAbbāsids' solutions to the logistical problem of ruling a huge empire emerged as one of the underlying causes of its dissolution in the tenth century.

Be this as it may, in both its late Umayyad and early ʿAbbāsid forms the caliphate was the most spectacular instalment of Mediterranean and Near Eastern empire building between the Achaemenids, about a millennium earlier, and the Ottomans, about half a millennium later. And all this, of course, the Arabs accomplished as Muslims, who, following in the footsteps of a

2 See H. Kennedy, 'Central government and provincial elites in the early ʿAbbāsid caliphate', *BSOAS*, 44 (1981).

visionary and reforming monotheist prophet, conquered and ruled for explicitly religious reasons. The caliphate was a political and military unit, but one that was assembled by believer-soldiers inspired to fight for God and His Prophet, and mustered and coordinated by men who had pledged their allegiance to a 'commander of the faithful' – the caliph, God's representative on earth. (The title is attested already in the reign of Muʿāwiya.) The Muslims' victories came quickly in part because their adversaries appear in at least some respects to have been weakened, and in part because their conviction to 'strive' for God – to make their belief manifest by carrying out *jihād* – was so strong: it seems to have been as intrinsic to belief as any other religious duty. Islam was made sovereign over all other religions, and non-Muslim monotheists (the category was interpreted generally so as to include Zoroastrians) were forced at least in theory to make open acknowledgement of their subordinate status as 'protected peoples'. They may have been second-class citizens in a theocracy designed to preserve Muḥammad's vision, but they were citizens with legally enforceable rights all the same, and the continuing vitality of non-Muslim communities within the multi-ethnic and religiously pluralist caliphate goes some way towards explaining its cultural creativity.[3]

So what made the state Islamic was not a majority population of Muslims, which would take some centuries to achieve; it was the state's purpose and design. Most important, the polity institutionalised in the caliphal office the Prophet's role as commander, leader and legislator – a strikingly concentrated portfolio of authority that owes its origins to the Late Antique Christian and Arabian tribal traditions out of which it emerged. As the state grew in size and complexity, successive caliphs naturally delegated their effective power to governors, tax-agents, commanders, judges and the like, all of whom wielded legitimate power only in so far as they served God's caliph on earth. In this way society was aligned with God's will as Muslims understood it through the Qur'ān and the cultural memory of the earliest community. Other transformations were at work too: as society grew more complex, especially through conversion and acculturation, the social and religious authority of late eighth- and ninth-century caliphs leached into its soil, producing in the short term legal authorities who rationalised and codified legal practice with reference to a past that they claimed to preserve and interpret. By the tenth century, with accounts of the failed *miḥna* of the 830s and 840s serving to

3 For one discussion of the traditional literature, see Y. Friedmann, *Tolerance and coercion in Islam: Interfaith relations in the Muslim tradition* (Cambridge, 2003).

underline the Traditionists' victory over the caliphs and their embrace of Ḥanafī rationalism,[4] it was the rare caliph who ventured into religious debates, which were taking place independently of state institutions. For all but those with revolutionary commitments (most significantly, Ismāʿīlī Shīʿa who, in the late ninth century, inherited the Khārijite mantle as the caliphs' most activist critics, rejecting ʿAbbāsid claims altogether), the caliphs now functioned as the symbolic centre of the 'abode of Islam', an unbroken dynasty of ruler-imams that linked the problematic present to the glorious and inspired first phase of the community's history. As such, the ʿAbbāsid caliphs legitimised, conventionally through increasingly archaic rituals and tokens of delegation, those who held de facto power in the provinces.

As much as it conditioned a social order, the caliphate also functioned as a greenhouse for cultivating the Islamic religious tradition. This was especially the case in the fast-growing towns and cities of Arabia and Iraq, where patronage was offered by the caliphs, their governors and their courts; meanwhile, non-state wealth deriving from landowning and mercantile activity promoted the accumulation, specialisation and professionalisation of knowledge more generally. By the early ʿAbbāsid period the means (including the wide availability of paper) were thus in place for an explosion of learning.[5] So, too, were the reasons. For as memories of the foundational periods of prophecy and conquest faded, and as Arab Muslims settled and mixed with non-Arabs in provinces that were at great geographical and cultural distances from Arabia, new bridges had to be built to a past that was at once increasingly remote from, and increasingly significant for, Arab and Muslim identity. Eighth-century Muslims disagreed about whether the Qurʾān fully preserved Muḥammad's revelations, about how it was transmitted or exactly what a given word or passage in the text might mean, but they all agreed that there *was* to be such a text, and, moreover, that it was now closed.[6] (This is a considerable achievement: in producing and then closing their scripture so quickly, Muslims telescoped into perhaps as few as five or six decades a process that Jews and Christians took centuries to accomplish.) Similarly, they disagreed about what had happened in 632 or 656 such that they even

4 For two accounts focusing on the Traditionist hero Aḥmad ibn Ḥanbal, see N. Hurvitz, *The formation of Ḥanbalism: Piety into power* (London, 2002); and C. Melchert, *Ahmad ibn Hanbal* (Oxford, 2006).

5 A summary account of paper's introduction into the Middle East can be found in H. Loveday, *Islamic paper: A study of the ancient craft* (London, 2001), ch. 2.

6 There is a great deal of literature, but, despite its title, an enormous amount of ground is covered in H. Modarressi, 'Early debates on the integrity of the Qurʾān: A brief survey', *SI*, 77 (1993).

took up arms, but they all agreed that a given set of events *was* important, and that the battles over the past should take place as much (or more) in books of history, exegesis and law as they should in the field. The conspicuous exception aside, Muslim historians very rarely suppressed embarrassing facts, generally choosing instead to discredit them or obscure them in mountains of alternatives.[7]

How things had been, and what they meant for the present and future, were thus both 'academic' and fiercely political concerns. Of course, the impulse to record, classify, interpret, elaborate and argue was not just driven by curiosity, professional ambition or intra-Muslim debate, although such 'internalist' factors can be adduced for fields of knowledge (such as theology) that one would usually assume to have roots outside the Islamic community itself.[8] Living in cities and towns that typically accommodated large non-Muslim populations, scholars often rubbed shoulders with transmitters of Classical and Late Antique traditions and techniques of learning that were much deeper and more richly developed than their own. As it happens, many learned men (and women) – fully a third, by one measure – were non-Arab converts to Islam.[9] Fuelled as they were by the confidence and enthusiasm that came with a newly revealed truth, along with the privilege and favour (both direct and indirect) that came with Islamic rule, Muslims argued with non-Muslim adversaries when they felt it necessary, appropriated of their tools what they needed, ignored what they did not, and so made up the cultural deficit by consistent industry and occasional brilliance. (Volume 4 of this series charts some of this very rich history.) The social context of learning, teaching and the transmission of ideas is as much as unrecoverable for nearly all of the first century of Islam, after which things improve unsteadily; in the late eighth and ninth centuries we have recognisable schools of thought in several disciplines (such as grammar, law, theology and history), some crystallising (or starting to crystallise) around master-eponyms who had taught, more or less formally or informally, in mosques and houses. Not surprisingly, Iraq in general, and Baghdad especially, were hugely

7 On the early historical tradition in general, see F. M. Donner, *Narratives of Islamic origins: The beginnings of Islamic historical writing* (Princeton, 1998); and C. F. Robinson, *Islamic historiography* (Cambridge, 2003).

8 The standard work is J. van Ess, *Theologie und Gesellschaft im 2. und 3. Jahrhundert Hidschra: Eine Geschichte des religiösen Denkens im frühen Islam*, 6 vols. (Berlin, 1991–7); for a review of the influences on theology, see S. Rissanen, *Theological encounter of Oriental Christians with Islam during early Abbasid rule* (Turku, 1993).

9 Thus J. Nawas, 'A profile of the *mawālī 'ulamā*'', in J. Nawas and M. Bernards (eds.), *Patronate and patronage in early and classical Islam* (Leiden, 2005); cf., however, H. Motzki, 'The role of non-Arab converts in the development of early Islamic law', *Islamic Law and Society*, 6 (1999).

productive of these teachers.[10] What is clearer is that a tidal wave of book-writing in a wide variety of disciplines and genres began to rise in the late eighth century, especially in the law, whose increasingly traditionalist character exercised much of the gravitational force: 'Individual teachers the traditionalists would not trust: what they wanted was an inspired textual basis for doctrine and practice.'[11] Late ninth-century Baghdad, along with Tang Chang-an, was becoming what must have been the most literate city in the world.[12]

That the Islamic religious tradition grew so explosively hardly means that it was fixed early on, despite the tradition's assumptions (and frequent assertions) that ideas, practices and institutions current in the ninth and tenth centuries were inspired or established by the Prophet, his contemporaries or immediate followers in the seventh. Instead, it took some time for the dust of this explosion to settle and for the ideas, practices and institutions to come on line; early Muslims were creatively faithful to the past, rather than dogmatically reverential towards it. To signify the very considerable differences between the earliest and subsequent phases of Islamic intellectual history, some Islamicists draw a distinction between the 'formative' and 'classical' periods. Periodisation is always imperfect, but the distinction is heuristically valuable because it reminds one that early Islam conforms to the broad patterns of religious history of Antiquity and Late Antiquity, when, far from being fully formed at birth, monotheist communities defined and organised themselves over time and in relation to other monotheist communities. Since these developments figure only marginally in the previous chapters, we might usefully outline – in only very schematic terms – the shape of these changes.

Here it is immensely important to see the tradition's assumptions and assertions for what they are. The very traditionalism that framed the experience of the first generation as necessarily paradigmatic for subsequent generations is itself a development of the mid- to late eighth century;[13] and only a century later did this development culminate, when accounts of the Prophet's conduct came to hold a virtual monopoly on the market of precedents, elbowing aside

10 Thus an entire volume (III) of van Ess's *Theologie und Gesellschaft* is devoted to Baghdad, about 850–950; see also D. Gutas, *Greek thought, Arabic culture: The Graeco-Arabic translation movement in Baghdad and early ʿAbbāsid society (2nd–4th/8th–10th centuries)* (London and New York, 1998).

11 C. Melchert, *The formation of the Sunni schools of law, 9th–10th centuries CE* (Leiden, 1997), p. 14.

12 For some sense of this culture, see S. Toorawa, *Ibn Abī Ṭāhir Ṭayfūr and Arabic writerly culture* (London and New York, 2005); and M. Cooperson and S. Toorawa (eds.), *Arabic literary culture, 500–925, Dictionary of Literary Biography*, vol. CCCXI (Detroit, 2005).

13 See, for example, G. H. A. Juynboll, 'Some new ideas on the development of *sunna* as a technical term in early Islam', *JSAI*, 10 (1987).

other authorities (especially his contemporaries, the 'Companions', their Followers and early ʿAbbāsid jurists). In this way, practices that owed their origins to extra-Arabian legal systems – especially varieties of Jewish and Roman law, no single tradition remaining uninfluenced by others – were naturalised into Islam and legitimised by Prophetic sanction.[14] (Such was the Sunnī formulation; the Imāmī Shīʿa endowed their imams with this paradigmatic authority.) This – the secondary emergence of the doctrine of Prophetic precedent (*sunna*) and its elevation to a governing principle of jurisprudence, along with the accompanying coining of traditions ascribed to the Prophet – is the single best documented case of the retrofitting of late Umayyad and ʿAbbāsid-era ideas onto seventh- and early eighth-century history. But there are many others. For example, closely related to the dogma of the Companions was the view, which came to be shared by the emerging Sunnī orthodoxy of the ninth century,[15] that there were four 'rightly guided caliphs' (Abū Bakr, ʿUmar, ʿUthmān and ʿAlī), all considered legitimate rulers, though some held that they were of declining merit. The formulation is nearly as ubiquitous in the secondary literature of early Islam as it is in the primary sources. Even so, it would have made little or no sense to these caliphs or their partisans, whose loyalties tended to be exclusive and whose polemics could be brutal, or indeed to most anyone else who actually lived during the seventh and eighth centuries.

The secondary appearance of this doctrine makes good sense because the political culture of early Islam was thoroughly adversarial. Above I emphasised the great speed of political and cultural change over the first three centuries, but I have understated just how deeply contentious and controversial things were to those experiencing that change. Despite the generally eirenic and triumphalist narratives that fill the surviving (and overwhelmingly Sunnī) sources of the late ninth and tenth centuries, a great deal of early Islamic history was made by men whose commitments and convictions were far too deep to allow them much room for negotiating consensus and unity. Although most agreed on the caliph's function, there were deep divisions about who was qualified to hold the office and what the necessary qualifications should be to hold it; and since obedience to the right imam was widely

14 The literature is enormous, but a clear statement can be found in P. Crone, *Roman, provincial and Islamic law: The origins of the patronate* (Cambridge, 1987); U. Mitter, 'Origin and development of the Islamic patronate', in Nawas and Bernards (eds.), *Patronate and patronage in early and classical Islam*; P. Crone, 'Jāhilī and Jewish law: The *qasāma*', *JSAI*, 4 (1984); M. Cook, 'Early Islamic dietary law', *JSAI*, 7 (1986); cf. N. Calder, *Studies in early Muslim jurisprudence* (Oxford, 1993), esp. pp. 209ff.

15 See, for example, Crone, *Medieval Islamic political thought*, pp. 134f.; cf. E. Kohlberg, 'Some Imāmī Shīʿī views on the *ṣaḥāba*', *JSAI*, 5 (1984).

regarded as salvific, the stakes could not have been higher.[16] We saw in chapter 5 that, by any reasonable reading of the evidence, Ibn al-Zubayr was as close as the Islamic community had to a caliph from 683 to 692, for all that the later tradition presents him as a heretic, rebel or 'counter-caliph'. Exclusive political and religious loyalties divided partisans of ʿAlī from those of ʿUthmān (and vice versa), Umayyads from ʿAbbāsids, Khārijites and so forth. Although it is perfectly true that some (such as the Murjiʾa) chose to 'suspend judgement' about the fate of the first two caliphs in the Hereafter, this hardly stopped them from taking active part in the political controversies of the day.[17]

Why was the political culture of early Islam so adversarial – indeed, so revolutionary? We began the volume with an account of Baghdad's founding and city plan, which put the all-powerful caliph at the symbolic centre, the 'Round City', of a world-bestriding empire, and gave physical expression to the early Islamic fusion of right belief and political power: authority was concentrated in salvific imams who occupied an office established by God in order to establish His rule the world over. One accordingly expects to find a political culture that was highly centripetal – and that is exactly what one finds. As we have seen, it is not merely that elite politics was conducted in Iraq, its capitals and courts, or that Iraq produced a disproportionate number of the most articulate spokesmen and critics and learned culture more generally, or even that the provinces' fates were invariably conditioned by political and military conditions prevailing in or around Baghdad. It is also that the radical model marrying belief and power fostered radical movements of opposition. Far more than secession, seclusion, much less indifferent individuality or Qumran-like withdrawal, it engendered organised rebellion for the purposes of reforming or replacing wayward caliphs who abused their power.

And all of this is just to mention the *explicitly* politico-religious issues that divided early Muslims. Other issues appear more narrowly intellectual or academic, and may appear to us now as only *implicitly* political; but this hardly made them any less contentious. I have already alluded to one such conflict among those specialising in the law, the *aṣḥāb al-ḥadīth* (the Traditionists) and

16 P. Crone and M. Hinds, *God's caliph: Religious authority in the first centuries of Islam* (Cambridge, 1986).

17 See, for examples, W. Madelung, 'The early Murjiʾa in Khurāsān and Transoxiana and the spread of Ḥanafism', *Der Islam*, 59 (1982); M. Cook, 'Activism and quietism in Islam: The case of the early Murjiʾa', in A. Cudsi and A. E. Dessouki (eds.), *Islam and power* (London, 1981); and S. S. Agha, 'A viewpoint on the Murjiʾa in the Umayyad period: Evolution through application', *Journal of Islamic Studies*, 8 (1997).

the *aṣḥāb al-raʾy* (the Rationalists). Since what was at stake here was nothing less than the authority to determine the law, the bitterness between the two parties is difficult to exaggerate. Of course holding scripture – that is, both the *sunna* and the Qurʾān – to be authoritative did not exhaust potential scripturalist positions: some held that the Qurʾān alone was authoritative.[18] In sum, what is characteristic of the 'formative' period of Islam is its very contentiousness, its controversies and unsettled questions: What constituted individual belief? How was one to know God's law? Where were the limits of community to be drawn? Who was to rule and by what qualifications? These and other questions were frequently asked, and although answers were given, they did not command broad agreement.

If the outstanding features of early Islam were the number and depth of some of its disagreements, those of the 'classical' period can be said to have been greater consensus – there is now a clearer sense of what constituted belief and membership in the community of Islam and its constituent sub-communities – as well as the (closely related) emergence of a traditionalist-based 'orthodoxy' itself. For in the end – that is, towards the end of the ninth century, which can reasonably mark the end of 'formative' Islam – it would be traditionalism that would dominate, imprinting its values not only on jurisprudence, but also on theology, historiography and other disciplines and fields as well.[19]

The 'four-caliph' theory is as good an example as any for the changes under way. By admitting ʿAlī and ʿUthmān respectively into the fold of legitimacy, partisans for ʿUthmān and for ʿAlī alike were burying the hatchet, exchanging exclusive partisanship for the unity of the community. In various forms, this accommodating narrative colonised historiography; the sources thus record not the story of competing communities, most holding the others misguided and un-saved, but that of a single community riven by civil war, rebellion and dissension. The emergence of another numbered doctrine, that of the 'five pillars' of Islam (witnessing faith, charity, prayer, pilgrimage and fasting) has a more complicated and less well-understood history. Still, in this pithy 'classical' form, which omits *jihād* and sets an inclusively low threshold for faith that turns principally on the discharge of ritual acts, it also reflects 'classical' concerns, which is why it too dates from no earlier than the late ninth

18 M. Cook, 'ʿAnan and Islam: The origins of Karaite scripturalism', *JSAI*, 9 (1987).

19 W. Graham, 'Traditionalism in Islam: An essay in interpretation', *Journal of Interdisciplinary History*, 23 (1993).

century.[20] Allegiance to a salvific imam has been eclipsed by adherence to the law that had been articulated in traditionalist terms by the scholars. In time the ascendance of Sunnī traditionalism would be institutionalised in the form of four schools of jurisprudence (Mālikī, Shāfiʿī, Ḥanbalī and Ḥanafī, each named after an eighth- or early ninth-century eponym), which, in offering mutual recognition to each other, contrast sharply with some of the bitter polemics associated with their purported founders.[21]

As faith and the law were being reconfigured, identity was too. In fact, the embrace of the 'four-caliph' doctrine was part of the process by which Sunnism emerged in its classical form, moving from a largely undefined set of implicit assumptions into a discrete body of beliefs and an increasingly sharply edged mode of communal identity that claimed the orthodox centre. The process extended into the tenth and eleventh centuries, when Sunnism became a rallying cry for weakened caliphs within Baghdad and powerful dynasts outside it, and it took place alongside, and in interaction with, the maturation of Imāmī Shīʿism. Compared to Sunnism, modalities of Shīʿite identity and thought are rooted more deeply in early Islam because, as opponents of the state, those who favoured ʿAlī's claims more clearly defined their views; some essential Imāmī ideas and institutions, for example, do seem to belong to the mid- to late eighth century.[22] But the fact remains that it took the occultation of the twelfth imam and its aftermath in the tenth and eleventh centuries to produce, under direct and indirect Būyid patronage, not only many institutions of Imāmī popular piety,[23] but also the full emergence of a scholarly elite that promoted its own brand of traditionism. As much as Būyid-era Sunnī jurists had to come to terms with a caliphate whose power had been usurped, Shīʿite jurists had to come to terms with the stubborn endurance of a Sunnī caliphate.

The solution that emerged was coexistence: the absence of the imam was taken to mean that the obligation to realise God's will politically (through revolution or secession) could instead be realised intellectually and socially, by putting in place institutions and hierarchies that framed and guided an Imāmī community within a non-Shīʿite state. Here, as in the Sunnī case, adherence to

20 For one discussion, see W. C. Smith, 'Arkān', in D. P. Little (ed.), *Essays on Islamic civilization presented to Niyazi Berkes* (Leiden, 1976).
21 For an overview, see Melchert, *The formation of the Sunni schools of law*.
22 See, for example, H. Modarressi, *Crisis and consolidation in the formative period of Shiʿite Islam: Abū Jaʿfar ibn Qiba al-Rāzī and his contribution to Imāmite Shiʿite thought* (Princeton, 1993); for an overview, Crone, *Medieval Islamic political thought*, pp. 111ff.
23 See chapter 9 above, and, more generally, H. Halm, *Shiʿism*, 2nd edn (Edinburgh, 2004), pp. 38ff.

the tradition and the law thus became the standard. It is true that some Shīʿa opted out of this co-optation and autonomy within the Sunnī state, stubbornly holding on to a revolutionary programme that the Imāmīs had abandoned in the ninth century by rationalising in quietist terms the disappearance and continued absence of the imam. The programme was now preached by those either propagandising for, or claiming to embody, the imams of the Ismāʿīlī line; as we have seen, they had some real success, particularly in North Africa and Arabia. But the imams' charisma could routinise fairly quickly (as it did in the Fāṭimid case), and when it did not, it could lead (as it did in the Nizārī case) to movements that were as futile as they were spectacular. Not only did the Ismāʿīlī experiments in revolutionary state building fail in the end, but the tenth century also witnessed the final disappearance of what was arguably the most potent opposition movement of early Islam, the Khārijites, who had receded to the peripheries (eastern Iran and the far west) during the ninth. The age of widespread revolutionary ideas seems to have closed – at least until the aftermath of the Mongol conquests and rule in the thirteenth and fourteenth centuries, which reordered the eastern lands of the Islamic world.

What explains these changes? As much as intellectual and cultural traditions can bear the signs of a centralising, imperial state, so too can they reflect the dis-integration or reconfiguration of such imperial states.[24] This volume's chronological survey ends with caliphs being held under something close to house arrest by Daylamī commanders, and with Baghdad in decline, now merely one of three capitals of the Būyids' confederated state, which was itself just one of several states that had replaced the empire. Baghdad and its centripetal political culture belonged to the past; belief was increasingly a matter of tradition-based law, and the production of high culture took place increasingly in what had been its provinces. Although some caliphs would exercise a measure of influence over the political life of the late ʿAbbāsid period, and forms of Shīʿism provided a language of state building in the short term, the future lay in a multiplicity of Sunnī states, capitals and ruling courts, all following trajectories that were largely independent of Baghdad. These could offer sporadic patronage to peripatetic scholars, authors and poets (such as Ḥamdānid Aleppo or Mosul), or the deeper soil in which new traditions of learning could flourish (such as Imāmī Qumm). At the same time, they produced rulers whose legitimacy derived not only from fictional devolution from weakened ʿAbbāsid caliphs, but also from practices and traditions that complemented or challenged the symbols of ʿAbbāsid sovereignty. Rulers in

24 Cf. D. McMullen, *State and society in T'ang China* (Cambridge, 1989).

Iran (such as the Būyids and Sāmānids) could tap into ancient Persian symbols of sovereignty, while rulers on the frontiers (such as the Ghaznavids or Marīnids) could prove their credentials by carrying out *jihād*. Meanwhile, Islamic societies in the west and east had become increasingly divergent in their politics (how they became so is described in volumes 2 and 3). Beneath all this diversity, however, a basic grammar of Islamic rule and belief was now in place. The Crusaders might have wished it otherwise, but Islam had taken irreversible hold on the Middle East.

Glossary

ʿabd	servant; slave; appears often in names, e.g. ʿAbd Allāh (lit. 'servant of God')
Abū	'father', appears often in construct in names, e.g. 'Abū Bakr' (lit. 'Father of Bakr')
Abnāʾ	'sons' (*abnāʾ*; sing. *ibn*), but in ʿAbbāsid political terminology, 'sons of the state (or dynasty)', that is, the soldiers and commanders who brought the ʿAbbāsids to power
ahl	people; family; *ahl al-bayt*, 'members of the (Prophet's) family'
ʿāmil	administrator; financial controller; governor
amīr	commander, governor, leader; thus *amīr al-muʾminīn* ('commander of the believers', caliphal title); *amīr al-umarāʾ* ('commander of commanders', title for military rulers of tenth and eleventh centuries)
amṣār	*see miṣr*
anṣār	'helpers' (of Muḥammad): the tribesmen of Medina who embraced Muḥammad
ashrāf	(sing. *sharīf*) tribal chiefs; descendants of Muḥammad
ʿaṭāʾ	military pay; stipend, gift or pension
banū	'sons of', used in construct with tribal names, e.g. Banū Taghlib (the 'Taghlib (tribe)')
caliph	(Ar. *khalīfa*) sovereign of the Islamic state; God's 'deputy' or 'representative'
dāʿī	'one who carries out the *daʿwa*' ('call', 'propaganda' and, by extension, the clandestine phase of revolution), thus 'missionary'

dār	residence, abode; thus *dār al-islām* ('the abode of Islam'), *dār al-imāra* (governor's residence)
dawla	dynasty; state; ('Abbāsid) revolution
dhimma	protection granted by treaty; thus *ahl al-dhimma* or *dhimmīs* or *dhimmiyūn* 'protected peoples' – those monotheists ('People of the Book') given protected status by Islamic states
dirham	silver coin; cf. *dīnār* (gold)
dīwān	register; administrative bureau; chancery; thus *dīwān al-jaysh* (Bureau of the Army); *dīwān al-dār* (Bureau of the Palace)
dihqān	village landlord; lower nobility; gentry
fiqh	(lit. 'understanding') Islamic jurisprudence; thus *faqīh* ('jurisprudent', 'jurist', pl. *fuqahā'*)
fitna	in early Islamic political terminology, 'civil war', 'strife'; said of the first (656–61), second (683–92), third (744–49) and fourth (809–13) civil wars
ghāzī	Muslim warrior, typically against non-Muslims on the frontier
ghulām	(pl. *ghilmān*) young man; slave; slave-soldier
ḥadīth	tradition, especially by or about Muḥammad
ḥājib	chamberlain
ḥajj	the Pilgrimage
hijra	emigration: thus *dār al-hijra* ('abode of emigration'); also sacred enclave
Ibāḍī	surviving branch of the Khārijites (*see below*)
Ibn	son; e.g. Muḥammad ibn 'Abd Allāh (Muḥammad, son of 'Abd Allāh); *see also* Abū
ijmā'	scholarly consensus
imam	religious (and Shī'ite political) leader; thus imamate (*imāma*, the office of religious leadership) and Imāmī (a Shī'ite of the Twelver persuasion)
imām	prayer leader
iqṭā'	(pl. *iqṭā'āt*) land grant; concession (of revenue)
jamā'a	community; communal practice
jihād	the 'struggle' on behalf of God; holy war

jizya	(poll-) tax levied on 'People of the Book' (*see above, dhimma*)
jund	(pl. *ajnād*) army; district
khāqān	(Tur.) leader; ruler
kharāj	(land-) tax
Khārijite	'one who goes out (or against)' in rebellion; member of a Khārijite sect
khuṭba	Friday sermon
kūra	(pl. *kuwar*) administrative district
mahdī	'rightly guided'; *al-mahdī* ('the rightly-guided one; the Saviour')
mawlā	(pl. *mawālī*) client; in Umayyad usage, usually non-Arab convert to Islam
miṣr	(pl. *amṣār*) military garrison; garrison-city
muhājirūn	'those who emigrated' (from Mecca to Medina with Muḥammad); *see also anṣār*
qāḍī	judge
qaṣr	(pl. *quṣūr*) palace; estate
qibla	prayer direction (towards Mecca)
ribāṭ	frontier fort or fortress
ridda wars	'wars of apostasy' that broke out upon Muḥammad's death
ṣāḥib	(pl. *aṣḥāb*) master; ruler; owner
Shīʿa	those who held that the imams were to be drawn from the Prophet's family, eventually organised into three branches: Imāmīs (Twelvers), Zaydīs and Ismāʿīlīs
sunna	(adj. *sunnī*, lit. 'path'); normative conduct as prescribed by Prophetic *ḥadīth*
Sunnī	Sunnite; majoritarian Muslim
ʿulamāʾ	(sing. *ʿālim*) those who possess *ʿilm* (religious knowledge); people of learning; religious scholars
umma	'community of believers', the Muslim community
ʿushr	tithe
wazīr	vizier; minister
zandaqa	heresy

Bibliography

Introduction

Acton, J. E. E. D. A. (Lord), *Lectures on modern history*, ed., J. N. Figgis and R. V. Laurence, London, 1906.

Becker, A. H., *Fear of God and the beginning of wisdom: The School of Nisibis and the development of scholastic culture in Late Antique Mesopotamia*, Philadelphia, 2006.

Bowersock, G. W., P. Brown and O. Grabar (eds.), *Late Antiquity: A guide to the post-classical world*, Cambridge, MA, 1999.

Brown, P., *The world of Late Antiquity*, London, 1971.

Bulliet, R., *Islam: The view from the edge*, New York, 1994.

The patricians of Nishapur: A study in medieval Islamic social history, Cambridge, MA, 1972.

Cameron, A., B. Ward-Perkins and M. Whitby (eds.), *The Cambridge ancient history*, vol. XIV: *Late Antiquity: Empire and successors, AD 425–600*, Cambridge, 2000.

Chalmeta, P., *Invasión e islamización: La sumisión de Hispania y la formación de al-Andalus*, Madrid, 1994.

Cobb, P., *White banners: Contention in ʿAbbasid Syria, 750–880*, Albany, 2001.

Crone, P., *Meccan trade and the rise of Islam*, Princeton, 1987; repr. Piscataway, NJ, 2004.

Slaves on horses: The evolution of the Islamic polity, Cambridge, 1980.

Crone, P., and M. Cook, *Hagarism: The making of the Islamic world*, Cambridge, 1977.

Daniel, E., *The political and social history of Khurasan under Abbasid rule, 747–820*, Minneapolis and Chicago, 1979.

Fowden, E. K., *The barbarian plain: Saint Sergius between Rome and Iran*, Berkeley and Los Angeles, 1999.

Fowden, G., *Empire to commonwealth: Consequences of monotheism in Late Antiquity*, Princeton, 1994.

Gil, M., *A history of Palestine, 634–1099*, Cambridge, 1992.

Goldziher, I., *Muhammedanische Studien*, Halle, 1889–90, trans. S. M. Stern and C. R. Barber as *Muslim Studies*, London, 1967–71.

Greatrex, G., *Rome and Persia at war, 502–535*, ARCA Classical and Medieval Texts, Papers and Monographs 37, Leeds, 1998.

Haldon, J. F., *Byzantium in the seventh century: The transformation of a culture*, rev. edn, Cambridge, 1997.

Harvey, S. A., *Asceticism and society in crisis: John of Ephesus and the* Lives of the Eastern Saints, Berkeley, 1990.

Heidemann, S., and A. Becker (eds.), *Raqqa II: Die islamische Stadt*, Mainz am Rhein, 2003.

Herrin, J., *The formation of Christendom*, Princeton, 1987.
Hoyland, R., *Seeing Islam as others saw it: A survey and evaluation of Christian, Jewish and Zoroastrian writings on early Islam*, Princeton, 1997.
Irwin, R., *For lust of knowing: The Orientalists and their enemies*, London, 2006; published in the USA as *Dangerous knowledge: Orientalism and its discontents*, Woodstock and New York, 2006.
Kennet, D., 'The decline of eastern Arabia in the Sasanian period', *Arabian Archaeology and Epigraphy*, 18 (2007), pp. 86–122.
Liebeschuetz, J. H. W. G., 'Late Antiquity and the concept of decline', *Nottingham Medieval Studies*, 45 (2001), pp. 1–11.
Macfie, A. L., *Orientalism: A reader*, New York, 2000.
Manzano Moreno, E., *Conquistadores, emires y califas: Los omeyas y la formación de al-Andalus*, Barcelona, 2006.
Martin, R., 'Qu'est-ce que l'antiquité tardive?' in R. Chevallier (ed.), *Aiôn: le temps chez les romains*, Paris, 1976, pp. 261–304.
Morony, M., *Iraq after the Muslim conquest*, Princeton, 1984.
Noth, A., *Quellenkritische Studien zu Themen, Formen und Tendenzen frühislamischer Geschichtsüberlieferung*, Bonn, 1973, trans., rev. and expanded by A. Noth and L. I. Conrad as *The early Arabic historical tradition: A source critical study*, Princeton, 1994.
Robinson, C. F., *Empire and elites after the Muslim conquest: The transformation of northern Mesopotamia*, Cambridge Studies in Islamic Civilization, Cambridge, 2000.
Said, E., *Orientalism*, New York, 1978.
al-Ṭabarī, Abū Jaʿfar Muḥammad ibn Jarīr, *Taʾrīkh al-rusul waʾl-mulūk*, ed. M. J. de Goeje *et al.*, 15 vols. in 3 series, Leiden, 1879–1901.
Walker, J., *The legend of Mar Qardagh: Narrative and Christian heroism in Late Antique Iraq*, Berkeley and Los Angeles, 2006.
Wansbrough, J., *Quranic studies: Sources and methods of scriptural interpretation*, Oxford, 1977.
The sectarian milieu: Content and composition of Islamic salvation history, Oxford, 1978.
Wendell, C., 'Baghdad: *Imago Mundi* and other foundation lore', *IJMES*, 2 (1971), 99–128.
Wickham, C., *Framing the early Middle Ages: Europe and the Mediterranean, 400–800*, Oxford, 2005.

Chapter 1: The resources of Late Antiquity

Practical suggestions for further reading

Belke, K., and F. Hild, J. Koder and P. Soustal (eds.), *Byzanz als Raum. Zu Methoden und Inhalten der historischen Geographie des östlichen Mittelmeerraumes*, Denkschriften der Österreichischen Akademie der Wissenschaften, philosophisch-historische Klasse 283, Vienna, 2000.
Cameron, A., and P. Garnsey (eds.), *The Cambridge ancient history*, vol. XIII: *The late empire, AD 337–425*, Cambridge, 1998.
Cameron, A., B. Ward-Perkins and M. Whitby (eds.), *The Cambridge ancient history*, vol. XIV: *Late Antiquity: Empire and successors, AD 425–600*, Cambridge, 2000.
Carter, F. W. (ed.), *An historical geography of the Balkans*, London, San Francisco and New York, 1977.

Chavarría, A., and T. Lewit, 'The Late Antique countryside: A bibliographic essay', in W. Bowden, L. Lavan and C. Machado (eds.), *Recent research on the Late Antique countryside*, Leiden, 2004, 3–51.

Christensen, P., *The decline of Iranshahr: Irrigation and environments in the history of the Middle East, 500 BC to AD 1500*, Copenhagen, 1993.

Fisher, W. B. (ed.), *The Cambridge history of Iran*, vol. I: *The land of Iran*, Cambridge, 1968.

Foss, C., 'The Near-Eastern countryside in Late Antiquity: A review article', in J. Humphrey (ed.), *The Roman and Byzantine Near East*, vol. II: *Some recent archaeological research*, JRA Supplementary Series 31, Portsmouth, 1995, 213–34.

Gyselen, R. (ed.), *Contributions à l'histoire et la géographie historique de l'empire sassanide*, Res Orientales 16, Bures-sur-Yvette, 2004.

Horden, P., and N. Purcell, *The corrupting sea: A study of Mediterranean history*, Oxford, 2000.

King, G. R. D., and A. Cameron (eds.), *The Byzantine and early Islamic Near East*, vol. II: *Land use and settlement patterns*, Princeton, 1994.

Kingsley, S., and M. Decker (eds.), *Economy and exchange in the east Mediterranean during Late Antiquity*, Oxford, 2001.

McCormick, M., *Origins of the European economy: Communications and commerce, AD 300–900*, Cambridge, 2001.

Morony, M. G., *Iraq after the Muslim conquest*, Princeton, 1984; repr. Piscataway, NJ, 2006.

Simpson, St J., 'From Tekrit to the Jaghjagh: Sasanian sites, settlement patterns and material culture', in K. Bartl and S. R. Hauser (eds.), *Continuity and change in northern Mesopotamia from the Hellenistic to the early Islamic period*, Berlin, 1996, 87–126.

Wagstaff, J. M., *The evolution of the Middle Eastern landscapes*, Canterbury, 1984.

Wickham, C. J. *Framing the early Middle Ages: Europe and the Mediterranean, 400–800*, Oxford, 2005.

Yarshater, E. (ed.), *The Cambridge history of Iran*, vol. III: *The Seleucid, Parthian and Sasanian periods*, Cambridge, 1983.

Secondary sources

Adams, R. M., *The land behind Baghdad: A history of settlement on the Diyala plains*, Chicago and London, 1965.

Alcock, S., *Graecia capta: The landscapes of Roman Greece*, Cambridge, 1993.

Avramea, A., *Le Péloponnèse du IVe au VIIIe siècle: Changements et persistances*, Paris, 1997.

Banaji, J., *Agrarian change in Late Antiquity: Gold, labour and aristocratic dominance*, Oxford, 2001.

Barthold, V., *Turkestan down to the Mongol invasion*, London, 1928.

Baruch, U., 'The late Holocene vegetation history of Lake Kinneret (Sea of Galilee)', *Palaeorient*, 12 (1986), 37–48.

Beaumont, P., G. H. Blake and M. Wagstaff, *The Middle East: A geographical study*, London, 1988.

Behnam, J., 'Population', in W. B. Fisher (ed.), *The Cambridge history of Iran*, vol. I: *The land of Iran*, Cambridge, 1968, 468–85.

Belke, K., 'Roads', in E. Jeffreys, J. F. Haldon and R. Cormack (eds.), *The Oxford handbook of Byzantine studies*, Oxford, forthcoming.

Blockley, R. C., *East Roman foreign policy: Formation and conduct from Diocletian to Anastasius*, Leeds, 1992.

Bobek, H., 'Vegetation', in W. B. Fisher (ed.), *The Cambridge history of Iran*, vol. I: *The land of Iran*, Cambridge, 1968, 280–93.

Bowden, W., L. Lavan and C. Machado (eds.), *Recent research on the late Antique countryside*, Leiden, 2004.

Bowen-Jones, H., 'Agriculture', in W. B. Fisher (ed.), *The Cambridge history of Iran*, vol. I: *The land of Iran*, Cambridge, 1968, 565–98.

Brandes, W., *Die Städte Kleinasiens im 7. und 8. Jahrhundert*, Berliner Byzantinistische Arbeiten 56, Berlin, 1989.

Brandes, W., and J. F. Haldon, 'Towns, tax and transformation: State, cities and their hinterlands in the East Roman world, ca. 500–800', in N. Gauthier (ed.), *Towns and their hinterlands between Late Antiquity and the early Middle Ages*, Leiden, 2000, 141–72.

Braudel, F., *The Mediterranean and the Mediterranean world in the age of Philip II*, 2 vols., London and New York, 1973.

Brogiolo, G.-P., N. Gauthier and N. Christie (eds.), *Towns and their territories between Late Antiquity and the early Middle Ages*, The Transformation of the Roman World 9, Leiden, 2000.

Brunner, C., 'Geographical and administrative divisions: Settlements and economy', in E. Yarshater (ed.), *The Cambridge history of Iran*, vol. III: *The Seleucid, Parthian and Sasanian periods*, Cambridge, 1983, 747–77.

Bulliet, R. W., *The camel and the wheel*, Cambridge, MA, 1975.

Canard, M., 'Le riz dans le Proche Orient aux premiers siècles d'Islam', *Arabica*, 6 (1959), 113–31.

Canivet, P., and J.-P. Rey-Coquais (eds.), *La Syrie de Byzance à l'Islam: VIIe–VIIe siècles*, Damascus, 1992.

Christensen, A., *L'Iran sous les Sassanides*, Copenhagen, 1944.

Conrad, L., 'Epidemic disease in central Syria in the late sixth century: Some new insights from the verse of Ḥassān ibn Thābit', *Byzantine and Modern Greek Studies*, 18 (1994), 12–58.

Curtis, P., S. Feierman, L. Thompson and J. Vansina, *African history: From earliest times to the present*, London and New York, 1995.

Dewdney, J. C., *Turkey*, London, 1971.

Donner, F., 'The role of nomads in the Near East in Late Antiquity (400–800 CE)', in F. Clover and R. S. Humphreys (eds.), *Tradition and innovation in Late Antiquity*, Madison, 1989, 73–85.

Durliat, J., *De la ville antique à la ville byzantine: Le problème des subsistances*, Rome, 1990.

Fisher, W. B., 'Physical geography', in W. B. Fisher (ed.), *The Cambridge history of Iran*, vol. I: *The land of Iran*, Cambridge, 1968, 3–110.

Friedmann, Y., 'A contribution to the early history of Islam in India', in M. Rosen-Ayalon (ed.), *Studies in memory of Gaston Wiet*, Jerusalem, 1977, 309–34.

Garnsey, P., and C. R. Whittaker, 'Trade, industry and the urban economy', in A. Cameron and P. Garnsey (eds.), *The Cambridge ancient history*, vol. XIII: *The late empire, AD 337–425*, Cambridge, 1998, 312–37.

Gatier, P.-L., 'Villages du Proche-Orient protobyzantin (4ème–7èmes.): Étude régionale', in G. R. D. King and A. Cameron (eds.), *The Byzantine and early Islamic Near East*, vol. II: *Land use and settlement patterns*, Princeton, 1994, 17–48.

Geyer, B., 'Physical factors in the evolution of the landscape and land use', in A. Laiou *et al.* (eds.), *The economic history of Byzantium from the seventh through the fifteenth century*, Washington, DC, 2002, 31–45.

Girgis, M. S., *Mediterranean Africa*, New York and London, 1987.

Haas, C., 'Alexandria and the Mareotis region', in T. S. Burns and J. W. Eadie (eds.), *Urban centres and rural contexts in Late Antiquity*, East Lansing, 2001, 47–62.

Haerinck, E., *Le céramique en Iran pendant le période parthe*, Ghent, 1983.

Haldon, J. F., *Byzantium in the seventh century: The transformation of a culture*, Cambridge, 1997.

'Some considerations on Byzantine society and economy in the seventh century', *Byzantinische Forschungen*, 10 (1985), 75–112 (1985).

Warfare, state and society in Byzantium, 565–1204, London, 1999.

Hassan, F. A., *Demographic archaeology*, London, 1981.

Hendy, M. F., *Studies in the Byzantine monetary economy, c. 300–1450*, Cambridge, 1985.

Horden, P., and N. Purcell, *The corrupting sea: A study of Mediterranean history*, Oxford, 2000.

Howard-Johnston, J., 'The two great powers in Late Antiquity: A comparison', in A. Cameron, (ed.), *The Byzantine and early Islamic Near East*, vol. III: *States, resources and armies*, Studies in Late Antiquity and Early Islam, 1, Princeton, 1995, 157–226.

Huff, D., 'Sasanian cities', in M. Y. Kiani (ed.), *A general study of urbanization and urban planning in Iran*, Tehran, 1986, 176–204.

Inalcïk, H. (ed.), *An economic and social history of the Ottoman Empire*, vol. I: *1300–1600*, Cambridge, 1994/1997.

Issar, A. S., *Climate changes during the Holocene and their impact on hydrological systems*, Cambridge, 2003.

Jones, A. H. M., 'The cities of the Roman empire: Political, administrative and judicial functions', *Recueils de la Société Jean Bodin*, 6 (1954), 135–73; repr. in P. A. Brunt (ed.), *The Roman economy: Studies in ancient economic and administrative history*, Oxford, 1974, 1–34.

The Greek city from Alexander to Justinian, Oxford, 1967.

Kaplan, M., *Les hommes et la terre à Byzance du VIe au XIe siècles*, Paris, 1992.

Karagiorgou, O., 'Urbanism and economy in Late Antique Thessaly (3rd–7th century AD): The archaeological evidence', D.Phil. thesis, Oxford University, 2001.

Kennedy, H., 'The last century of Byzantine Syria: A reinterpretation', *Byzantinische Forschungen*, 10 (1985), 141–83.

Kennet, D., *Sasanian and Islamic pottery from Ras al-Khaimah: Classification, chronology and analysis of trade in the western Indian Ocean*, BAR International Series 1248, Oxford, 2004.

'Sasanian pottery in southeastern Iran and eastern Arabia', *Iran*, 40 (2002), 153–62.

Koder, J., 'The urban character of the early Byzantine empire: Some reflections on a settlement geographical approach to the topic', in *17th International Byzantine Congress, Major Papers*, New Rochelle, NY, 1986, 155–87.

Krawczyk, J.-L., 'The relationship between pastoral nomadism and agriculture: Northern Syria and the Jazira in the eleventh century', *Jusur*, 1 (1985), 1–22.

Le Strange, G., *Lands of the eastern caliphate*, Cambridge, 1930.

Lev-Yadun, S., N. Lipschitz and Y. Waisel, 'Annual rings in trees as an index to climate changes intensity in our region in the past', *Rotem*, 22 (1987), 6–17 (Eng. summary p. 113).

Liebeschuetz, J. H. W. G., 'Administration and politics in the cities of the fifth to the mid-seventh century', in A. Cameron, B. Ward-Perkins and M. Whitby (eds.), *The Cambridge ancient history*, vol. XIV: *Late Antiquity: Empire and successors, AD 425–600*, Cambridge, 2000, 207–37.

The decline and fall of the Roman city, Oxford, 2001.

MacAdam, H., 'Settlements and settlement patterns in northern and central Transjordania, ca. 550–750', in G. R. D. King and A. Cameron (eds.), *The Byzantine and early Islamic Near East*, vol. II: *Land use and settlement patterns*, Princeton, 1994, 49–93.

Maier, A. M., 'Sassanica varia Palaestinensia: A Sassanian seal from T. Istaba, Israel, and other Sassanian objects from the southern Levant', *Iranica Antiqua*, 35 (2000), 159–83.

Mason, R. B., 'Early medieval Iraqi lustre-painted and associated wares: Typology in a multidisciplinary study', *Iraq*, 59 (1997), 15–61.

McCormick, M., *Origins of the European economy: Communications and commerce, AD 300–900*, Cambridge, 2001.

Mitchell, S., *Anatolia: Land, men and gods in Asia Minor*, vol. II: *The rise of the Church*, Oxford, 1993.

Morony, M. G., 'Economic boundaries? Late Antiquity and early Islam', *JESHO*, 47 (2004), 166–94.

'Land use and settlement patterns in late Sasanian and early Islamic Iraq', in G. R. D. King and A. Cameron (eds.), *The Byzantine and early Islamic Near East*, vol. II: *Land use and settlement patterns*, Princeton, 1994, 221–9.

'Trade and exchange: The Sasanian world to Islam', in L. Conrad (ed.), *Trade and exchange in the Late Antique and early Islamic Near East*, Studies in Late Antiquity and Early Islam 5, forthcoming.

Morrisson, C., and J.-P. Sodini, 'The sixth-century economy', in A. Laiou *et al.* (eds.), *The economic history of Byzantium from the seventh through the fifteenth century*, Washington, DC, 2002, 171–220.

Nandris, J., 'The perspective of long-term change in south-east Europe', in Carter (ed.), *An historical geography of the Balkans*, 25–57.

Neely, J. A., 'Sassanian and early Islamic water-control and irrigation systems on the Deh-Luran plain, Iran', in T. E. Downing and M. Gibson (eds.), *Irrigation's impact on society*, Tucson, 1974, 21–42.

Nicolle, D., *Historical atlas of the Islamic world*, New York, 2003.

Oates, D., *Studies in the ancient history of northern Iraq*, Oxford, 1968.

Philippson, A., *Das byzantinische Reich als geographische Erscheinung*, Leiden, 1939.

de Planhol, X., *Les fondements géographiques de l'histoire de l'Islam*, Paris, 1968.

'Geography of settlement', in W. B. Fisher (ed.), *The Cambridge history of Iran*, vol. I: *The land of Iran*, Cambridge, 1968, 409–67.

Priestman, S. M. N., 'The Williamson Collection project: Sasanian and Islamic survey ceramics from southern Iran, current research', *Iran*, 40 (2002), 265–7, 41 (2003), 345–8.

Puschnigg, G., 'A diachronic and stylistic assessment of the ceramic evidence from Sasanian Merv', Ph.D. thesis, University College London, 2000.

Reynolds, P., *Trade in the western Mediterranean AD 400–700: The ceramic evidence*, BAR International Series 604, Oxford, 1995.

Russell, J. C., *Late ancient and medieval population*, Philadelphia, 1958.

'Transformations in early Byzantine urban life: The contribution and limitations of archaeological evidence', in *Seventeenth International Byzantine Congress: Major Papers*, New York, 1986, 137–54.

Sajjadi, M., 'A class of Sassanian ceramics from southeastern Iran', *Rivista di Archeologia*, 13 (1989), 31–40.

Shoup, J., 'Middle Eastern sheep pastoralism and the hima system', in J. G. Galaty and D. L. Johnson (eds.), *The world of pastoralism: Herding systems in comparative perspective*, New York, 1990, 195–215.

Slicher van Bath, B. H., *An agrarian history of western Europe*, London, 1963.

Spieser, J.-M., 'L'Évolution de la ville byzantine de l'époque paléochrétienne à l'iconoclasme', in C. Morrisson *et al.* (eds.), *Hommes et richesses dans l'Empire byzantin, IVe–VIIe siècles*, Paris, 1989, 97–106.

Stathakopoulos, D., *Famine and pestilence in the late Roman and early Byzantine Empire: A systematic survey of subsistence crises and epidemics*, Birmingham Byzantine and Ottoman Monographs 9, Aldershot, 2004.

'The Justinianic plague revisited', *Byzantine and Modern Greek Studies*, 24 (2000), 256–76.

Tate, G., *Les campagnes de la Syrie du nord du IIe au VIIe siècle: Un exemple d'expansion démographique et économique dans les campagnes à la fin de l'Antiquité*, Paris, 1992.

Telelis, I. G., *Μετεωρολογικά Φαινόμενα και κλίμα στο Βυζάντιο*, 2 vols., Athens, 2003.

Tsafrir, Y., and G. Foerster, 'From Scythopolis to Baysân: changing concepts of urbanism', in G. R. D. King and A. Cameron (eds.), *The Byzantine and early Islamic Near East*, vol. II: *Land use and settlement patterns*, Princeton, 1994, 95–115.

Van der Veen, M., A. Grant and G. Barker, 'Romano-Libyan agriculture: Crops and animals', in G. Barker *et al.* (eds.), *Farming the desert: The UNESCO Libyan valley archaeological survey*, Tripoli, 1996, 227–63.

Wagstaff, J. M., *The evolution of the Middle Eastern landscapes*, Canterbury, 1984.

Ward-Perkins, B., 'The cities', in A. Cameron and P. Garnsey (eds.), *The Cambridge ancient history*, vol. XIII: *The late empire, AD 337–425*, Cambridge, 1998, 371–410.

'Land, labour and settlement', in A. Cameron, B. Ward-Perkins and M. Whitby (eds.), *The Cambridge ancient history*, vol. XIV: *Late Antiquity: Empire and successors, AD 425–600*, Cambridge, 2000, 315–45.

'Specialised production and exchange', in A. Cameron, B. Ward-Perkins and M. Whitby (eds.), *The Cambridge ancient history*, vol. XIV: *Late Antiquity: Empire and successors, AD 425–600*, Cambridge, 2000, 346–91.

Wenke, R. J., 'Imperial investments and agricultural development in Parthian and Sasanian Khūzistān: 150 BC to AD 640', *Mesopotamia*, 10–11 (1975/6), 31–221.

Wheatley, P., *The places where men pray together: Cities in Islamic lands, seventh through the tenth centuries*, Chicago, 2001.

Whitcomb, D., 'The "commercial crescent": Red Sea trade in Late Antiquity and early Islam', in L. Conrad (ed.), *Trade and exchange in the Late Antique and early Islamic Near East*, Studies in Late Antiquity and Early Islam 5, forthcoming.

Whittaker, C. R., 'Rural life in the later Roman empire', in A. Cameron and P. Garnsey (eds.), *The Cambridge ancient history*, vol. XIII: *The late empire, AD 337–425*, Cambridge, 1998, 277–311.

Whittow, M., 'Ruling the late Roman and early Byzantine city: A continuous history', *Past and Present*, 129 (1990), 3–29.

Wilkinson, T. J., *Archaeological landscapes of the Near East*, Tucson, 2003.
Williams, T., K. Kurbansakhatov *et al.*, 'The ancient Merv project, Turkmenistan: Preliminary report on the first season (2001)', *Iran*, 40 (2002), 15–41.

Chapter 2: The late Roman/early Byzantine Near East

Practical suggestions for further reading

Ball, W., *Rome in the East: The transformation of an empire*, London, 2000.
Bowman, A. K., P. Garnsey and A. Cameron (eds.), *The Cambridge ancient history*, vol. XII: *The crisis of empire, AD 193–337*, 2nd edn, Cambridge, 2005.
Butcher, K., *Roman Syria and the Near East*, London, 2003.
Cameron, A., and P. Garnsey (eds.), *The Cambridge ancient history*, vol. XIII: *The late empire, AD 337–425*, Cambridge, 1998.
Cameron, A., B. Ward-Perkins and M. Whitby (eds.), *The Cambridge ancient history, vol. XIV: Late Antiquity: empire and successors, AD 425–600*, Cambridge, 2000.
Fowden, G., *Empire to commonwealth: Consequences of monotheism in Late Antiquity*, Princeton, 1993.
Greatrex, G., *Rome and Persia at war, 502–532*, ARCA Classical and Medieval Texts, Papers and Monographs 37, Leeds, 1998.
Isaac, B., *The limits of empire*, Oxford, 1990.
Jones, A. H. M., *The later Roman empire, 284–602: A social, economic, and administrative study*, 3 vols., Oxford, 1964.
Matthews, J., *The Roman empire of Ammianus*, London, 1989.
Meier, M., *Justinian: Herrschaft, Reich und Religion*, Munich, 2004.
Millar, F., *The Roman Near East, 31 BC–AD 337*, Cambridge, MA, 1993.
Morrison, C. (ed.), *Le monde Byzantin I: L'Empire romain d'Orient (330–641)*, Paris, 2004.
Potter, D. S., *The Roman Empire at bay, AD 180–395*, London, 2004.
Sartre, M., *The Middle East under Rome*, trans. C. Porter and E. Rawlings, Cambridge, MA., 2005.
Tate, G., *Justinien: L'épopée de l'Empire d'Orient (527–565)*, Paris, 2004.
Whitby, M., *The Emperor Maurice and his historian: Theophylact Simocatta on Persian and Balkan Warfare*, Oxford, 1988.
Whittow, M., *The making of Orthodox Byzantium, 600–1025*, Basingstoke, 1996.

Primary sources

Ammianus Marcellinus, *Rerum gestarum libri*, ed. and trans. J. C. Rolfe, 3 vols., Cambridge, MA, 1935–9, rev. edn 1986.
Calvet, Y., and C. Robin, *Arabie heureuse Arabie déserte: Les antiquités arabiques du Musée du Louvre*, Notes et documents des musées de France 31, Paris, 1997.
Cameron, A., and J. Herrin (eds.), *Constantinople in the early eighth century*: The Parastaseis Syntomoi Chronikai, Leiden, 1984.
Chronicle of Pseudo-Joshua the Stylite, trans. with notes and introd. by F. R. Trombley and J. W. Watt, Translated Texts for Historians 32, Liverpool, 2000.
Codex Theodosianus, ed. T. Mommsen and P. M. Meyer as *Theodosiani libri XVI cum Constitutionibus Sirmondianis*, Berlin, 1905, trans. C. Pharr as *The Theodosian Code*, New York, 1952.

Diodorus Siculus, *Bibliotheca historica*, ed. and trans. C. H. Oldfather, C. L. Sherman, C. Bradford Welles, R. M. Geer and F. R. Walton, 12 vols., Cambridge, MA, 1933–67.
Dodgeon, M. H., and S. N. C. Lieu (eds.), *The Roman eastern frontier and the Persian wars*, part 1: *AD 226–363: A documentary history*, London, 1991.
Greatrex, G., and S. N. C. Lieu (eds.), *The Roman eastern frontier and the Persian wars*, part 2: *AD 363–630*, London and New York, 2002.
Herrmann, G., D. N. Mackenzie and R. Howell, *The Sasanian reliefs at Naqsh-i Rustam, Naqsh-i Rustam 6, The Triumph of Shapur I*, Iranische Denkmaler 13, Berlin, 1989.
John of Ephesus, *Ecclesiastical history*, ed. E. W. Brooks as *Iohannis Ephesini historiae ecclesiastica pars tertia*, CSCO, Scr Syr III.3, Louvain, 1935–6, trans. R. Payne Smith as *The third part of the ecclesiastical history of John, bishop of Ephesus*, Oxford, 1860.
Pliny, *Naturalis historia*, ed. and trans. H. Rackham, W. H. S. Jones and D. E. Eichholz, 10 vols., Cambridge, MA, 1917–32.
Procopius, *History of the wars*, ed. and trans. H. B. Dewing, 5 vols., Cambridge, MA, 1914–28.
Sebeos, *The Armenian history attributed to Sebeos*, trans. R. W. Thomson, with commentary by J. Howard-Johnston, Translated Texts for Historians 31, 2 vols., Liverpool, 1999.
Socrates, *Ecclesiastical history*, ed. G. C. Hansen, trans. P. Périchon and P. Maraval as *Histoire ecclésiastique*, vol. I, Paris, 2004.
Sozomen, *Ecclesiastical history*, ed. J. Bidez, trans. A.-J. Festugière as *Histoire ecclésiastique*, vol. I, Paris, 1983.
Strabo, *Geography*, ed. and trans. H. L. Jones, 8 vols., Cambridge, MA, 1917–32.
Theophanes, *Chronographia*, ed. C. de Boor as *Theophanis chronographia*, 2 vols., Leipzig, 1883–5, trans. C. Mango and R. Scott as *The chronicle of Theophanes Confessor*, Oxford, 1997.

Secondary sources

Ando, C., *Imperial ideology and provincial loyalty in the Roman Empire*, Berkeley and Los Angeles, 2000.
Banaji, J., *Agrarian change in Late Antiquity: Gold, labour, and aristocratic dominance*, Oxford, 2001.
Banning, E. B., 'De Bello Paceque: A reply to Parker', *BASOR*, 265 (1987), 52–4.
'Peasants, pastoralists and Pax Romana: Mutualism in the southern highlands of Jordan', *BASOR*, 261 (1986), 25–50.
Blachère, R., *Histoire de la littérature arabe des origines à la fin du xve siècle de J.-C.*, 3 vols., Paris, 1952–66.
Blockley, R. C., *East Roman foreign policy: Formation and conduct from Diocletian to Anastasius*, Leeds, 1992.
Christensen, A., *L'Iran sous les Sassanides*, 2nd edn, Copenhagen, 1944.
Dagron, G., *Naissance d'une capitale: Constantinople et ses institutions de 330 à 451*, Paris, 1974.
Dagron, G., and V. Déroche, 'Juifs et Chrétiens dans l'Orient du viie siècle', *Travaux et Mémoires*, 11 (1991), 17–273.
Elton, H., *Warfare in Roman Europe AD 350–425*, Oxford, 1996.
Equini Schneider, E., *Septimia Zenobia Sebaste*, Rome, 1993.
Foss, C., 'The Persian Near East (602–630 AD)', *JRAS*, 3rd series, 13 (2003), 149–70.
Genequand, D., 'Some thoughts on Qasr al-Hayr al-Gharbi, its dam, its monastery and the Ghassanids', *Levant*, 38 (2006), 63–83.

van Ginkel, J., 'John of Ephesus: A monophysite historian in sixth-century Byzantium', Ph.D. thesis, Groningen, 1995.

Golden, P. B., *An introduction to the history of the Turkic peoples: Ethnogenesis and state-formation in medieval and early modern Eurasia and the Middle East*, Wiesbaden, 1992.

Harris, W. V., *War and imperialism in republican Rome, 327–70 BC*, Oxford, 1979.

Hartmann, U., *Das palmyrenische Teilreiche*, Stuttgart, 2001.

Heather, P., *Goths and Romans 332–489*, Oxford, 1991.

'The Huns and the end of the Roman Empire in Western Europe', *English Historical Review*, 110 (1995), 4–41.

'The late Roman art of client management', in W. Pohl, I. Wood and H. Reimitz (eds.), *The transformation of frontiers: From Late Antiquity to the Carolingians*, Leiden, 2001, 36–56.

'New men for new Constantines? Creating an imperial elite in the eastern Mediterranean', in P. Magdalino (ed.), *New Constantines: The rhythm of imperial renewal in Byzantium, 4th–13th centuries*, Aldershot, 1994, 11–33.

Hendy, M., *Studies in the Byzantine monetary economy, c. 350–1450*, Cambridge, 1985.

Howard-Johnston, J., *East Rome, Sasanian Persia and the end of Antiquity: Historiographical and historical studies*, Aldershot, 2006.

'Heraclius' Persian campaigns and the revival of the East Roman Empire, 622–630', *War in History*, 6 (1999), 1–44.

'Pride and fall: Khusro II and his regime, 626–628', in *La Persia e Bisanzio*, Atti dei convegni Lincei 201, Roma, 14–18 ottobre 2002, Rome, 2004, 93–113.

'The two great powers in Late Antiquity: A comparison', in A. Cameron (ed.), *The Byzantine and early Islamic Near East*, vol. III: *States, resources and armies*, Studies in Late Antiquity and Early Islam 1, Princeton, 1995, 157–226.

Hoyland, R. G., *Arabia and the Arabs from the Bronze Age to the coming of Islam*, London and New York, 2001.

Jones, A. H. M., J. R. Martindale and J. Morris, *The prosopography of the later Roman Empire*, 3 vols., Cambridge, 1971–92.

Liebeschuetz, J. H. W. G., *The decline and fall of the Roman city*, Oxford, 2001.

Lightfoot, C. S., 'Trajan's Parthian war and the fourth-century perspective', *Journal of Roman Studies*, 80 (1990), 115–26.

Macdonald, M. C. A., 'Nomads and the Hawran in the late Hellenistic and Roman periods: A reassessment of the epigraphic evidence', *Syria*, 70 (1993), 303–413.

Mattern, S. P., *Rome and the enemy: Imperial strategy in the principate*, Berkeley and Los Angeles, 1999.

Moorhead, J., 'The Monophysite response to the Arab invasions', *Byzantion*, 51 (1981), 579–91.

Nicholson, R. A., *A literary history of the Arabs*, Cambridge, 1930.

Nöldeke, T., *Die Ghassānischen Fürsten aus dem Hause Gafna's*, Abhandlungen der königl. Akademie der Wissenschaften zu Berlin, Philosophisch-historische Klasse Abh. 1887, II, Berlin, 1887.

Parker, S. T., 'The defense of Palestine and Transjordan from Diocletian to Heraclius', in L. E. Stager, J. A. Greene and M. D. Coogan (eds.), *The archaeology of Jordan and beyond: Essays in honor of James A. Sauer*, Studies in the Archaeology and History of the Levant 1, Winona Lake, IN, 2000, pp. 367–88.

The Roman frontier in Central Jordan: Final report on the Limes Arabicus Project, 1980–1989, 2 vols., Dumbarton Oaks Studies 40, Washington, DC, 2006.
Pollard, N., *Soldiers, cities, and civilians in Roman Syria*, Ann Arbor, 2000.
Potter, D. S., *Prophecy and history in the crisis of the Roman Empire: A historical commentary on the Thirteenth Sibylline Oracle*, Oxford, 1990.
Price, S., *Rituals and power: The Roman imperial cult in Asia Minor*, Cambridge, 1984.
Retsö, J., *The Arabs in Antiquity: Their history from the Assyrians to the Umayyads*, London, 2003.
Rothstein, G., *Die Dynastie der Laḫmiden in al-Hīra: Ein Versuch zur arabisch-persischen Geschichte zur Zeit der Sasaniden*, Berlin, 1899.
Sartre, M., *Trois études sur l'Arabie romaine et byzantine*, Brussels, 1982.
Schippmann, K., *Grundzüge der Geschichte des Sasanidischen Reiches*, Darmstadt, 1990.
Shahid, I., *Byzantium and the Arabs in the fifth century*, Washington, DC, 1989.
Byzantium and the Arabs in the fourth century, Washington, DC, 1984.
Byzantium and the Arabs in the sixth century, vols. I–, Washington, DC, 1995–.
'Byzantium and the Arabs in the sixth century. *A propos* of a recent review', *Byzantinische Forschungen*, 26 (2000), 125–60.
Byzantium and the Semitic Orient before the rise of Islam, London, 1988.
Rome and the Arabs: A prolegomenon to the study of Byzantium and the Arabs, Washington, DC, 1984.
Whitby, M., 'Greek historical writing after Procopius: Variety and vitality', in A. Cameron and L. I. Conrad (eds.), *The Byzantine and early Islamic Near East*, vol. I: *Problems in the literary source material*, Princeton, 1992, 25–80.
'Recruitment in Roman armies from Justinian to Heraclius (ca. 565–615)', in A. Cameron (ed.), *The Byzantine and early Islamic Near East*, vol. III: *States, resources and armies*, Studies in Late Antiquity and Early Islam 1, Princeton, 1995, 61–124.
Whittow, M., 'Rome and the Jafnids: Writing the history of a 6th-c. tribal dynasty', in J. H. Humphrey (ed.), *The Roman and Byzantine Near East*, vol. II: *Some recent archaeological research*, JRA Supplementary series 31, Portsmouth, RI, 1999, 207–24.
Wickham, C., *Framing the early Middle Ages: Europe and the Mediterranean, 400–800*, Oxford, 2005.
Wolf, G., *Becoming Roman: The origins of provincial civilization in Gaul*, Cambridge, 1998.
Zwettler, M., 'Imra'alqays, Son of 'Amr: King of ...???', in M. Mir and J. E. Fossum (eds.), *Literary heritage of classical Islam: Arabic and Islamic studies in honor of James A. Bellamy*, Princeton, 1993, 3–37, pl. 1–5.

Chapter 3: The late Sasanian Near East

Practical suggestions for further reading

Börm, H., *Prokop und die Perser*, OrOcc 16, Stuttgart, 2007.
Cereti, C. G., *La letteratura pahlavi*, Milan, 2001.
Christensen, A., *L'Iran sous les Sassanides*, 2nd rev. edn, Copenhagen, 1944.
Demange, F., *et al.* (eds.), *Les Perses sassanides: Fastes d'un empire oublié (224–642): Musée Cernuschi, Musée des arts de l'Asie de la ville de Paris, 15 septembre–30 décembre 2006*, Paris, 2006.

Donner, F. M., 'The background to Islam', in M. Maas (ed.), *The Cambridge companion to the age of Justinian*, Cambridge, 2005, 510–33.

Greatrex, G., 'Byzantium and the east in the sixth century', in M. Maas (ed.), *The Cambridge companion to the age of Justinian*, Cambridge, 2005, 477–509.

Güterbock, K., *Byzanz und Persien in ihren diplomatisch-völkerrechtlichen Beziehungen im Zeitalter Justinians*, Berlin, 1906.

Gyselen, R., *La géographie administrative de l'empire sassanide: Les témoignages sigillographiques*, Paris, 1989.

Howard-Johnston, J., *East Rome, Sasanian Persia and the end of Antiquity: Historiographical and historical studies*, Ashgate, 2006.

Huyse, P., *La Perse antique*, Paris, 2005.

Reinink, G., and B. Stolte (eds.), *The reign of Heraclius (610–641): Crisis and confrontation*, Louvain, 2002.

Rubin, Z., 'Nobility, monarchy and legitimation under the later Sasanians', in J. Haldon and L. I. Conrad (eds.), *The Byzantine and early Islamic Near East*, vol. VI: *Elites old and new in the Byzantine and early Islamic Near East*, Princeton, 2004, 235–73.

'The reforms of Khusrō Anūshirwān', in A. Cameron (ed.), *The Byzantine and early Islamic Near East*, vol. III: *States, resources and armies*, Studies in Late Antiquity and Early Islam 1, Princeton, 1995, 227–96.

'The Sasanid monarchy', in A. Cameron, B. Ward-Perkins and M. Whitby (eds.), *The Cambridge ancient history*, vol. XIV: *Late Antiquity: Empire and successors, AD 425–600*, 2nd edn, Cambridge, 2000, 638–61.

Wiesehöfer, J., *Ancient Persia*, 2nd edn, London and New York, 2001.

'Chusro I. und das Sasanidenreich: Der König der Könige "mit der unsterblichen Seele"', in M. Meier (ed.), *Sie schufen Europa: Historische Portraits von Konstantin bis Karl dem Großen*, Munich, 2007, 195–215.

Wiesehöfer, J., and P. Huyse (eds.), *Ērān und Anērān: Studien zu den Beziehungen zwischen dem Sasanidenreich und der Mittelmeerwelt*, OrOcc 13, Stuttgart, 2006.

Yarshater, E., 'Iranian national history', in E. Yarshater (ed.), *The Cambridge history of Iran*, vol. III: *The Seleucid, Parthian and Sasanian periods*, Cambridge, 1983, part 1, 359–477.

Primary sources

Alram, M., and R. Gyselen, *Sylloge Nummorum Sasanidarum Paris – Berlin – Wien*, vol. I: *Ardashir I.–Shapur I.*, Vienna, 2003.

Assemani, S. E., *Acta Sanctorum Martyrum Orientalium et Occidentalium in duas partes distributa, Rome, 1748; repr.* 1970.

Back, M., *Die sassanidischen Staatsinschriften: Studien zur Orthographie und Phonologie des Mittelpersischen der Inschriften zusammen mit einem etymologischen Index des mittelpersischen Wortgutes und einem Textcorpus der behandelten Inschriften*, Acta Iranica 18, Leiden, 1978.

Bedjan, P., *Acta martyrum et sanctorum, 7 vols., Paris and Leipzig, 1890–7; repr.* 1968.

Bosworth, C. E. (ed.), *The history of al-Ṭabarī*, vol. V: *The Sāsānids, the Byzantines, the Lakmids, and Yemen*, Albany, 1999.

Braun, O., *Ausgewählte Akten persischer Märtyrer*, Kempten and Munich, 1915.

Brock, S. P., and S. Harvey (eds.), *Holy women of the Syrian Orient*, Berkeley, 1987.

Dodgeon, M. H., and S. N. C. Lieu (eds.), *The Roman eastern frontier and the Persian wars*, part 1: *AD 226–363: A documentary history*, London and New York, 1991.

Gardner, I., and S. N. C. Lieu (eds.), *Manichaean texts from the Roman empire*, Cambridge, 2004.

Gignoux, P., *Les quatre inscriptions du mage Kirdīr: Textes et concordances*, Paris, 1991.

Greatrex, G., and S. N. C. Lieu, *The Roman eastern frontier and the Persian wars*, part 2: *AD 363–630*, London and New York, 2002.

Grenet, F., *La geste d'Ardashir fils de Pâbag: Kārnāmag ī Ardaxšēr ī Pābagān*, Paris, 2001.

Hintze, A., *Der Zamyād-Yašt: Edition, Übersetzung, Kommentar*, Beiträge zur Iranistik 15, Wiesbaden, 1994.

Hoffmann, G., *Auszüge aus syrischen Akten persischer Märtyrer*, Leipzig, 1880.

Humbach, H., and P. O. Skjærvø, *The Sassanian inscription of Paikuli*, 3 parts, Wiesbaden, 1978–83.

Hutter, M., *Manis kosmogonische Šābuhragān-Texte: Edition, Kommentar und literargeschichtliche Einordnung der manichäisch-mittelpersischen Handschriften M 98/99 I und M 7980–7985*, Studies in Oriental Religion **21**, Wiesbaden, 1992.

Huyse, P., *Die dreisprachige Inschrift Šābuhrs I. an der Kaʿba-i Zardušt (ŠKZ)*, CII 3, vol. I, texts I, vols. **I**–II, London, 1999.

Kawerau, P., *Die Chronik von Arbela*, CSCO 467–8, 2 vols., Louvain, 1985.

Luther, A., *Die syrische Chronik des Josua Stylites*, Untersuchungen zur antiken Literatur und Geschichte 49, Berlin and New York, 1997.

MacKenzie, D. N., 'Kerdir's inscription: Synoptic text in transliteration, transcription and commentary', in G. Herrmann and D. N. MacKenzie (eds.), *The triumph of Shapur I (together with an account of the representation of Kerdir)*, Iranische Denkmäler, Lief. 13, Reihe II, Iranische Felsreliefs I: *The Sasanian rock reliefs at Naqsh-i Rustam. Naqsh-i Rustam 6*, Berlin, 1989, 35–72.

Nöldeke, T., *Geschichte der Perser und Araber zur Zeit der Sasaniden*, Leiden, 1878.

Die von Guidi herausgegebene syrische Chronik: Übersetzt und kommentiert, Sitzungsberichte der Akademie der Wissenschaften zu Wien, Philosophisch-Historische Klasse 128, Vienna, 1893, 1–48.

Panaino, A., *La novella degli scacchi e della tavola reale: Un'antica fonte orientale sui due giochi da tavoliere più diffusi nel mondo eurasiatico tra Tardoantico e Medioevo e sulla loro simbologia militare e astrale. Testo pahlavi, traduzione e commento al Wizārišn ī čatrang ud nihišn ī nēw-ardaxšīr*, Milan, 1999.

Schindel, N., *Sylloge Nummorum Sasanidarum Paris – Berlin – Wien*, vol. III, parts 1–2: *Shapur II.–Kawad I./2. Regierung*, Vienna, 2004.

Sebeos, *The Armenian history attributed to Sebeos*, trans. R. W. Thomson, with commentary by J. Howard-Johnston, Translated Texts for Historians 31, 2 vols., Liverpool, 1999.

Sundermann, W., *Mitteliranische manichäische Texte kirchengeschichtlichen Inhalts*, Schriften zur Geschichte und Kultur des Alten Orients, Berliner Turfantexte 11, Berlin, 1981.

al-Ṭabarī, Abū Jaʿfar Muḥammad ibn Jarīr, *Ta'rīkh al-rusul wa'l-mulūk*, ed. M. J. de Goeje *et al.*, 15 vols. in 3 series, Leiden, 1879–1901.

Trombley, F. R., and J. W. Watt (eds.), *The chronicle of Pseudo-Joshua the Stylite*, Translated Texts for Historians 32, Liverpool, 2000.

Unvala, J. M., *Der Pahlavi-Text 'Der König Husrav und sein Knabe'*, Heidelberg, 1917.

The Pahlavi text King Husrav and his boy: Published with its translation, transcription and copious notes, Paris, 1921.

Weber, D., *Berliner Papyri, Pergamente und Leinenfragmente in mittelpersischer Sprache*. CII III, 4–5, London, 2003.

Ostraca, Papyri und Pergamente: Textband, CII III, 4–5, London, 1992.

Winter, E., and B. Dignas, *Rom und das Perserreich: Zwei Weltmächte zwischen Konfrontation und Koexistenz*, Berlin, 2001.

Secondary sources

Abkaʿi-Khavari, M., *Das Bild des Königs in der Sasanidenzeit: Schriftliche Überlieferungen im Vergleich mit Antiquaria*, Texte und Studien zur Orientalistik 13, Hildesheim, 2000.

Altheim, F., *Geschichte der Hunnen*, vols. IV–V, Berlin, 1962.

Altheim, F., and R. Stiehl, *Ein asiatischer Staat*, Wiesbaden, 1954.

Finanzgeschichte der Spätantike, Frankfurt, 1957.

Altheim-Stiehl, R., 'Das früheste Datum der sasanidischen Geschichte, vermittelt durch die Zeitangabe der mittelpersisch-parthischen Inschrift aus Bīšāpūr', *Archäologische Mitteilungen aus Iran*, n.s. 11 (1978), 113–16.

'The Sasanians in Egypt: Some evidence of historical interest', *Bulletin de la Société d'Archéologie Copte*, 31 (1992), 87–96.

'Zur zeitlichen Bestimmung der sāsānidischen Eroberung Ägyptens', in O. Brehm and S. Klie (eds.), *Mousikos Aner: Festschrift für M. Wegner zum 90. Geburtstag*, Bonn, 1992, 5–8.

Arafa, M., J. Tubach and G. S. Vashalomidze (eds.), *Inkulturation des Christentums im Sasanidenreich*, Wiesbaden, 2007.

Aßfalg, J., and P. Krüger (eds.), *Kleines Wörterbuch des christlichen Orients*, Wiesbaden, 1975.

Baumstark, A., *Geschichte der syrischen Literatur mit Ausschluß der christlich-palästinensischen Texte*, Bonn, 1922; repr. 1968.

Bier, L., 'Notes on Mihr Narseh's bridge near Firuzabad', *Archäologische Mitteilungen aus Iran*, n.s. 19 (1986), 263–8.

'Sasanian palaces in perspective', *Archaeology*, 35, 1 (1982), pp. 29–36.

Bivar, A. D. H., 'Hephthalites', *EIr*, vol. XII, 198–201.

Blockley, R. C., 'The division of Armenia between the Romans and the Persians', *Historia*, 36 (1987), 222–34.

East Roman foreign policy: Formation and conduct from Diocletian to Anastasius, Leeds, 1992.

'The Romano-Persian peace treaties of AD 299 and 363', *Florilegium*, 6 (1984), 28–49.

'Subsidies and diplomacy: Rome and Persia in Late Antiquity', *Phoenix*, 39 (1985), 62–74.

de Blois, F., *Burzōy's voyage to India and the origin of the Book of Kalilah wa Dimna*, London, 1990.

Börm, H., 'Der Perserkönig im Imperium Romanum: Chosroes I. und der sasanidische Einfall in das Oströmische Reich 540 n.Chr.', *Chiron*, 36 (2006), 299–328.

Boyce, M., 'Gōsān', *EIr*, vol. XI, 161–70.

'Middle Persian literature', in *Iranistik II, Literatur I*, Handbuch der Orientalistik I.IV.2.1, Leiden, 1968, 31–66.

'The Parthian gōsān and Iranian minstrel tradition', *JRAS* (1957), 10–45.

Brock, S. P., *Brief outline of Syriac literature*, Kottayam, 1997.

Brockelmann, C., *Geschichte der arabischen Literatur*, 2nd edn, 2 vols., Leiden, 1943–9; suppl. 1–3, Leiden, 1937–42.

Bury, J. B., *A history of the later Roman empire*, vol. II, London, 1889.

Busse, H., 'Arabische Historiographie und Geographie', in H. Gätje (ed.), *Grundriß der arabischen Philologie*, vol. II, Wiesbaden, 1987, 264–97.

Cameron, A., 'Agathias on the Sassanians', *Dumbarton Oaks Papers*, 23–4 (1969–70), 1–150.

Procopius and the sixth century, London and New York, 1985.

Cereti, C. G., 'Primary sources for the history of inner and outer Iran in the Sasanian period', *Eurasiae Medii Aevi*, 9 (1997), 17–71.

Cribb, J., 'Numismatic evidence for Kushano-Sasanian chronology', *Studia Iranica*, 19 (1990), 151–93.

Curtis, V. S., 'Minstrels in ancient Iran', in V. S. Curtis, R. Hillenbrand and J. M. Rogers (eds.), *The art and archaeology of ancient Persia: New light on the Parthian and Sasanian empires*, London and New York, 1998, 182–7.

Daryaee, T., 'The construction of the past in Late Antique Persia', *Historia*, 55 (2006), 493–503.

'Memory and history: The reconstruction of the past in Late Antique Persia', *Nâme-ye Irân-e Bâstân*, 1, 2 (2001–2), 1–14.

'Mind, body, and the cosmos: Chess and backgammon in ancient Persia', *Iranian Studies*, 35 (2002), 281–312.

'National history or Keyanid history? The nature of Sasanid Zoroastrian historiography' *Iranian Studies*, 28 (1995), 129–41.

Döpp, S., and W. Geerlings (eds.), *Lexikon der antiken christlichen Literatur*, Freiburg, 1998.

Drijvers, J. W., 'Ammianus Marcellinus' image of Sasanian society', in J. Wiesehöfer and P. Huyse (eds.), *Ērān und Anērān: Studien zu den Beziehungen zwischen dem Sasanidenreich und der Mittelmeerwelt*, OrOcc 13, Stuttgart, 2006., 45–69.

Drijvers, J. W., and D. Hunt (eds.), *The late Roman world and its historian: Interpreting Ammianus Marcellinus*, London and New York, 1999.

Enderlein, V., and W. Sundermann (eds.), *Schāhnāme: Das persische Königsbuch: Miniaturen und Texte der Berliner Handschrift von 1605*, Leipzig and Weimar, 1988.

Felix, W., *Antike literarische Quellen zur Außenpolitik des Sāsānidenstaates*, vol. I: 224–309, Österreichische Akademie der Wissenschaften, philosophisch-historische Klasse, Sitzungsberichte 456 = Veröffentlichungen der Iranischen Kommission 18, Vienna, 1985.

Fiey, J. M., 'Review of P. Kawerau, *Die Chronik von Arbela*', *Revue d'Histoire Ecclésiastique*, 81 (1986), 544–8.

Fowden, E., *The barbarian plain: Saint Sergius between Rome and Iran*, Transformation of the Classical Heritage 28, Berkeley, 1999.

Frye, R. N., *The history of ancient Iran*, Handbuch der Altertumswissenschaft III, 7, Munich, 1984.

'The political history of Iran under the Sasanians', in E. Yarshater (ed.), *The Cambridge history of Iran*, vol. III: *The Seleucid, Parthian and Sasanian periods*, Cambridge, 1983, part 2, 116–80.

Fukai, S., *Persian glass*, New York, 1977.

von Gall, H., *Das Reiterkampfbild in der iranischen und iranisch beeinflußten Kunst parthischer und sasanidischer Zeit*, Teheraner Forschungen 6, Berlin, 1990.

Garsoian, N. G., 'Byzantium and the Sasanians', in E. Yarshater (ed.), *The Cambridge history of Iran*, vol. III: *The Seleucid, Parthian and Sasanian periods*, Cambridge, 1983, part 1, 568–92.

Gerland, E., 'Die persischen Feldzüge des Kaisers Herakleios', *Byzantinische Zeitschrift*, 3 (1894), 330–73.
Gerster, G., and D. Huff, 'Die Paläste des Königs Ardaschir', *Bild der Wissenschaft*, 11 (1977), 48–60.
Ghirshman, R., *Bichapour I–II*, Paris, 1956–71.
Gignoux, P., 'La chasse dans l'Iran sasanide', in G. Gnoli (ed.), *Essays and lectures*, vol. III: *Orientalia Romana*, Rome, 1983, 101–18.
'D'Abnūn à Māhān: Étude de deux inscriptions sassanides', *Studia Iranica*, 20 (1991), 9–17.
'Éléments de prosopographie de quelques mobads sasanides', *JA*, 270 (1982), 257–69.
'Une nouvelle collection de documents en pehlevi cursif du début du septième siècle de notre ère', *Comptes Rendus de l'Académie des Inscriptions et Belles-Lettres* (1991), 683–700.
'Pour une esquisse des fonctions religieuses sous les Sasanides', *JSAI*, 7 (1986), 93–108.
'Pour une évaluation de la contribution des sources arméniennes à l'histoire sassanide', *Acta Antiqua Academiae Scientiarum Hungaricae*, 31 (1985–8), 53–65.
'Pour une nouvelle histoire de l'Iran sasanide', in W. Skalmowski and A. van Tangerloo (eds.), *Middle Iranian studies*, Louvain, 1984, 253–62.
'Prolégomènes pour une histoire des idées de l'Iran sassanide: Convergences et divergences', in J. Wiesehöfer and P. Huyse (eds.), *Ērān und Anērān: Studien zu den Beziehungen zwischen dem Sasanidenreich und der Mittelmeerwelt*, OrOcc 13, Stuttgart, 2006, 71–81.
'Die religiöse Administration in sasanidischer Zeit: Ein Überblick', in H. Koch and D. N. MacKenzie (eds.), *Kunst, Kultur und Geschichte der Achämenidenzeit und ihr Fortleben*, Berlin, 1983, 253–66.
'Review of M. Back, Die sassanidischen Staatsinschriften', *Studia Iranica*, 13 (1984), 268– 73.
Gnoli, G., 'Farr(ah)', *EIr*, vol. IX, 312–19.
The idea of Iran: An essay on its origin, Serie Orientale Roma 62, Rome, 1989.
'L'inscription de Šābuhr à la Kaʿbe-ye Zardošt et la propagande sassanide', in P. Bernard and F. Grenet (eds.), *Histoire et cultes de l'Asie Centrale préislamique*, Paris, 1991, 57–63.
Iran als religiöser Begriff im Mazdaismus, Rheinisch-Westfälische Akademie der Wissenschaften, Vorträge G 320, Opladen, 1993.
'Nuovi studi sul Mazdakismo', in G. Gnoli and A. Panaino (eds.), *La Persia e Bisanzio*, Atti dei Convegni Lincei 201, Rome, 2004, 439–56.
Göbl, R., 'The Rabatak inscription and the date of Kanishka', in M. Alram and D. Klimburg-Salter (eds.), *Coins, art and chronology: Essays on the pre-Islamic history of the Indo-Iranian borderlands*, Österreichische Akademie der Wissenschaften, philosophisch-historische Klasse, Denkschriften 280, Vienna, 1999, 151–75.
Graf, G., *Geschichte der christlichen arabischen Literatur*, 4 vols., Vatican, 1944–53; repr. 1964–6.
Greatrex, G., 'Review of W. E. Kaegi, *Heraclius*', *The Medieval Review* (2004), available at http://quod.lib.umich.edu/cgi/t/text/text-idx?c=tmr;cc=tmr;q1=2004;rgn=main;view=text;idno=baj9928.0401.028.
Rome and Persia at war, 502–532, ARCA Classical and Medieval Texts, Papers and Monographs 37, Leeds, 1998.
Grignaschi, M., 'La riforma tributaria di Ḫosrō I e il feudalismo sassanide', in *La Persia nel medioevo*, Rome, 1971, 87–138.

Guidi, M., and M. Morony, 'Mazdak', *EI2*, vol. VI, 949–52.
Gyselen, R., *L'art sigillaire dans les collections de Leyde*, Leiden, 1997.
Collection générale, Paris, 1993, vol. I of *Catalogue des sceaux, camées et bulles sasanides de la Bibliothèque Nationale et du Musée du Louvre.*
The four generals of the Sasanian empire: Some sigillographic evidence, Rome, 2001.
Nouveaux matériaux pour la géographie historique de l'empire sassanide: Sceaux administratifs de la collection Ahmad Saeedi, Studia Iranica, Cahier 24, Paris, 2002.
'Sasanian glyptic: An example of cultural interaction between the Hellenistic world and the Iranian world', in M. Alram and D. Klimburg-Salter (eds.), *Coins, art and chronology: Essays on the pre-Islamic history of the Indo-Iranian borderlands*, Österreichische Akademie der Wissenschaften, philosophisch-historische Klasse, Denkschriften 280, Vienna, 1999, 293–301.
Sceaux magiques en Iran sassanide, Cahiers de Studia Iranica 17, Paris, 1995.
(ed.), *Charmes et sortilèges: Magie et magiciens*, Res Orientales 14, Bures-sur-Yvette, 2002.
(ed.), *Sceaux d'Orient et leur emploi*, Res Orientales 10, Bures-sur-Yvette, 1997.
(ed.), *La science des cieux: Sages, mages, astrologues*, Res Orientales 12, Bures-sur-Yvette, 1999.
Gyselen, R., *et al.*, 'Sylloge Nummorum Sasanidorum: Die Münzen der Sasaniden aus der Bibliothèque Nationale de France, dem Münzkabinett der Staatlichen Museen zu Berlin und dem Münzkabinett am Kunsthistorischen Museum in Wien (in Zusammenarbeit mit M. Alram u.a.)', *Anzeiger der philosophisch-historischen Klasse der Österreichischen Akademie der Wissenschaften*, 134 (1999), 15–41.
Haldon, J. F., *Byzantium in the seventh century: The transformation of a culture*, Cambridge, 1990.
Harper, P. O., 'Sasanian silver', in J. Boardman, I. E. S. Edwards, E. Sollberger and N. G. L. Hammond (eds.), *The Cambridge ancient history*, vol. III, part 2: *The Assyrian and Babylonian Empires and other states of the Near East, from the eighth to the sixth centuries BC*, Cambridge, 1983, 1113–29.
'Sasanian silver vessels: Recent developments', in V. S. Curtis, R. Hillenbrand and J. M. Rogers (eds.), *The art and archaeology of ancient Persia: New light on the Parthian and Sasanian empires*, London and New York, 1998, 67–73.
Silver vessels of the Sasanian period, vol. I: *Royal imagery*, New York, 1981.
'La vaisselle en métal', in *Splendeur des Sassanides: L'empire perse entre Rome et la Chine (224–642), 12 février au 25 avril 1993*, Brussels, 1993, 95–108.
Hartmann, U., 'Geist im Exil: Römische Philosophen am Hof der Sasaniden', in M. Schuol, U. Hartmann and A. Luther (eds.), *Grenzüberschreitungen: Formen des Kontakts zwischen Orient und Okzident im Altertum*, OrOcc 3, Stuttgart, 2002, 123–60.
Hinz, W., *Altiranische Funde und Forschungen*, Berlin, 1969.
Howard-Johnston, J., 'Heraclius' Persian campaigns and the revival of the east Roman empire, 622–630', *War in History*, 6 (1999), 1–44.
'The two great powers in Late Antiquity: A comparison', in A. Cameron (ed.), *The Byzantine and early Islamic Near East*, vol. III: *States, resources and armies*, Studies in Late Antiquity and Early Islam 1, Princeton, 1995, 157–226.
Huff, D., 'Architecture, III', *EIr*, vol. II, 329–34.
'Architecture sassanide', in *Splendeur des Sassanides: L'empire perse entre Rome et la Chine (224–642), 12 février au 25 avril 1993*, Brussels, 1993, 45–61.

'Recherches archéologiques à Takht-i Suleiman', *Comptes Rendus de l'Académie des Inscriptions et Belles-Lettres* (1978), 774–89.

'Sasanian cities', in M. Y. Kiani (ed.), *A general study of urbanization and urban planning in Iran*, Tehran, 1986, 176–204.

'Der Takht-e Suleiman: Sassanidisches Feuerheiligtum und mongolischer Palast', in T. Stöllner *et al.* (eds.), *Persiens antike Pracht*, vol. II, Bochum, 2004, 462–71.

Humbach, H., 'Herrscher, Gott und Gottessohn in Iran und in angrenzenden Ländern', in D. Zeller (ed.), *Menschwerdung Gottes: Vergöttlichung von Herrschern*, Fribourg and Göttingen, 1988, 89–114.

Huyse, P., 'Histoire orale et écrite en Iran ancien entre mémoire et oubli' (unpublished thesis).

'Kerdīr and the first Sasanians', in N. Sims-Williams (ed.), *Proceedings of the Third European Conference of Iranian Studies, held in Cambridge, 11th to 15th September 1995*, part 1, Wiesbaden, 1998, 109–20.

'Noch einmal zu Parallelen zwischen Achaimeniden- und Sāsānideninschriften', *Archäologische Mitteilungen aus Iran*, n.s. 23 (1990), 177–83.

'La revendication de territories achéménides par les Sassanides: Une réalité historique?' in P. Huyse (ed.), *Iran: Questions et connaissances: Actes du IVe congrès européen des études iraniennes organisé par la Societas Iranologica Europaea, t. 1: La période ancienne*, Studia Iranica 25, Paris, 2002, 297–311.

'Die sasanidische Königstitulatur: Eine Gegenüberstellung der Quellen', in J. Wiesehöfer and P. Huyse (eds.), *Ērān und Anērān: Studien zu den Beziehungen zwischen dem Sasanidenreich und der Mittelmeerwelt*, OrOcc 13, Stuttgart, 2006., 181–201.

'Vorbemerkungen zur Auswertung iranischen Sprachgutes in den Res Gestae des Ammianus Marcellinus', in W. Skalmowski and A. van Tongerloo (eds.), *Medioiranica*, Orientalia Lovaniensia Analecta 48, Leuven, 1993, 87–98.

Jeroussalimskaja, A., 'Soieries sassanides, A. Histoire culturelle', in *Splendeur des Sassanides: L'empire perse entre Rome et la Chine (224–642), 12 février au 25 avril 1993*, Brussels, 1993, 113–20.

de Jong, A., 'Sub Specie Maiestatis: Reflections on Sasanian court rituals', in M. Stausberg (ed.), *Zoroastrian ritual in context*, Leiden, 2004, 345–66.

de Jonghe, D., 'Soieries sassanides', in *Splendeur des Sassanides: L'empire perse entre Rome et la Chine (224–642), 12 février au 25 avril 1993*, Brussels, 1993, 121–2.

Jullien, C., and F. Jullien, *Apôtres des confins: Processus missionaires chrétiens dans l'Empire iranien*, Res Orientales 15, Bures-sur-Yvette, 2002.

Kaegi, W. E., *Heraclius: Emperor of Byzantium*, Cambridge, 2003.

Kaegi, W. E., and P. M. Cobb, 'Heraclius, Shahrbarāz, and al-Ṭabarī', in H. Kennedy (ed.), *al-Ṭabarī: A medieval Muslim historian and his work*, Princeton, 1999, 121–43.

Kaldellis, A., *Procopius of Caesarea: Tyranny, history, and philosophy at the end of Antiquity*, Philadelphia, 2004.

Kalmin, R. L., *Jewish Babylonia between Persia and Roman Palestine: Decoding the literary record*, Oxford, 2006.

Kawerau, P., 'Correspondance', *Revue d'Histoire Ecclésiastique*, 82 (1987), 338–40.

Keall, E. J., 'Ayvān (or Tāq)-e Kesrā', *EIr*, vol. III, 155–9.

Kellens, J., 'L'idéologie religieuse des inscriptions achéménides', *JA*, 290 (2002), 417–64.

Kettenhofen, E., 'Die Chronik von Arbela in der Sicht der Althistorie', in L. Criscuolo, G. Geraci and C. Salvaterra (eds.), *Simblos: Scritti di storia antica*, Bologna, 1995, 287–319.
'Deportations, II', *EIr*, vol. VII, 297–308.
'Die Einforderung der achaimenidischen Territorien durch die Sāsāniden: eine Bilanz', in S. Kurz (ed.), *Festschrift I. Khalifeh-Soltani zum 65. Geburtstag*, Aachen, 2002, 49–75.
'Einige Überlegungen zur sāsānidischen Politik gegenüber Rom im 3. Jh. n.Chr.', in E. Dabrowa (ed.), *The Roman and Byzantine army in the east: Proceedings of a colloquium held at the Jagiellonian University, Kraków in September 1992*, Crakow, 1994, 99–108.
'Review of E. Winter, Die sāsānidisch-römischen Friedensverträge des 3. Jahrhunderts n. Chr.', *Bibliotheca Orientalis*, 47 (1990), 163–78.
Die römisch-persischen Kriege des 3. Jahrhunderts n.Chr. nach der Inschrift Šāhpuhrs I. an der Ka'be-ye Zartošt, Beihefte zum Tübinger Atlas des Vorderen Orients, series B, no. **35**, Wiesbaden, 1982.
Tirdād und die Inschrift von Paikuli: Kritik der Quellen zur Geschichte Armeniens im späten 3. und frühen 4. Jh. n.Chr., Wiesbaden, 1995.
Kleiss, W., *Die Entwicklung von Palästen und palastartigen Wohnbauten in Iran*, Sitzungsberichte der Österreichischen Akademie der Wissenschaften, Philosophisch-historische Klasse 524, Vienna, 1989.
Kröger, J., 'From Ctesiphon to Nishapur: Studies in Sasanian and Islamic glass', in V. S. Curtis, R. Hillenbrand and J. M. Rogers (eds.), *The art and archaeology of ancient Persia: New light on the Parthian and Sasanian empires*, London and New York, 1998, 133–40.
Sasanidischer Stuckdekor, Mainz, 1982.
Lee, A. D., 'Close-kin marriage in Late Antique Mesopotamia', *Greek, Roman and Byzantine Studies*, 29 (1988), 403–13.
Information and frontiers: Roman foreign relations in Late Antiquity, Cambridge, 1993.
Lieu, S. N. C., *Manichaeism in Central Asia and China*, Leiden, 1998.
Manichaeism in Mesopotamia and the Roman east, 2nd edn, Leiden, 1999.
Manichaeism in the later Roman empire and medieval China, 2nd rev. edn, Tübingen, 1992.
Litvinsky, B. A., 'The Hephthalite empire', in B. A. Litvinsky (ed.), *History of civilizations of Central Asia*, vol. III: *The crossroads of civilization AD 250 to 750*, Paris, 1996, 135–62.
Livshits, V. A., and A. B. Nikitin, 'Some notes on the inscription from Nasrabad', *Bulletin of the Asia Institute*, 5 (1991), 41–3.
Luschey, H., 'Ardašīr I., II. Rock reliefs', *EIr*, vol. II, 329–34.
MacKenzie, D. N., 'The fire altar of Happy *Frayosh', *Bulletin of the Asia Institute*, 7 (1993), 105–9.
'Review of M. Back, Die sassanidischen Staatsinschriften', *Indogermanische Forschungen*, 87 (1982), 280–97.
Macuch, M., 'Barda and Bardadārī II', *EIr*, vol. II, 763–6.
'Charitable foundations, I', *EIr*, vol. V, 380–2.
'Inzest im vorislamischen Iran', *Archäologische Mitteilungen aus Iran*, 24 (1991), 141–54.
Rechtskasuistik und Gerichtspraxis zu Beginn des siebenten Jahrhunderts in Iran, Iranica 1, Wiesbaden, 1993.
'Die sasanidische Stiftung "für die Seele": Vorbild für den islamischen waqf?', in P. Vavroušek (ed.), *Iranian and Indo-European studies: Memorial volume of Otakar Klíma*, Prague, 1994, 163–80.

Malek, H. D., 'A survey of research on Sasanian numismatics', *Numismatic Chronicle*, 153 (1993), 227–69.

Mancini, M., 'Bilingui greco-iraniche in epoca sasanide: Il testo di Šāhpuhr alla Kaʿba-yi Zardušt', in E. Campanile, G. R. Cardona and R. Lazzeroni (eds.), *Bilinguismo e biculturalismo nel mondo antico: Atti del colloquio interdisciplinare tenuto a Pisa il 28 e 29 settembre 1987*, Pisa, 1988, 75–99.

Meisami, J. C., and P. Starkey (eds.), *Encyclopedia of Arabic literature*, 2 vols., London, 1998.

de Menasce, J., 'Zoroastrian Pahlavi writings', in E. Yarshater (ed.), *The Cambridge history of Iran*, vol. III: *The Seleucid, Parthian and Sasanian periods*, Cambridge, 1983, part 2, 1166–95.

Metzler, D., *Ziele und Formen königlicher Innenpolitik im vorislamischen Iran*, Münster, 1977.

Meyer, M., 'Die Felsbilder Shapurs I.', *Jahrbuch des Deutschen Archäologischen Instituts*, 105 (1990), 237–302.

Mikkelsen, G. B., *Bibliographia Manichaica: A comprehensive bibliography of Manichaeism through 1996*, Corpus Fontium Manichaeorum, Subsidia 1, Turnhout, 1997.

Millar, F. G. B., *The Roman Near East 31 BC–AD 337*, 2nd edn, Cambridge, MA, and London, 1994.

Morony, M., 'Bahār-e Kesrā', *EIr*, vol. III, 479.

Mosig-Walburg, K., *Die frühen sasanidischen Könige als Vertreter und Förderer der zarathustrischen Religion: Eine Untersuchung der zeitgenössischen Quellen*, Frankfurt and Bern, 1982.

Movassat, J. D., *The large vault at Taq-i Bustan: A study in late Sasanian royal art*, Lewiston, 2005.

Musche, B., *Vorderasiatischer Schmuck zur Zeit der Arsakiden und Sasaniden*, Handbuch der Orientalistik VII.I.2B.5, Leiden, 1988.

Naumann, R., *Die Ruinen von Tacht-e Suleiman und Zendan-e Suleiman*, Berlin, 1977.

Neusner, J., *A history of the Jews in Babylonia*, vols. II–V, Leiden, 1960–70.

Israel and Iran in Talmudic times, Lanham, 1986.

Israel's politics in Sasanian Iran, Lanham, 1986.

Nöldeke, T., *Das iranische Nationalepos*, Straßburg, 1896.

Oppenheimer, A., *Babylonia Judaica in the Talmudic period*, Beihefte zum Tübinger Atlas des Vorderen Orients, series B, no. 47, Wiesbaden, 1983.

Panaino, A., 'The bayān of the Fratarakas: Gods or "divine" kings?', in C. G. Cereti, M. Maggi and E. Provasi (eds.), *Religious themes and texts of pre-Islamic Iran and Central Asia: Studies in honour of Prof. Gherardo Gnoli on the occasion of his 65th birthday on 6th December 2002*, Beiträge zur Iranistik 24, Wiesbaden, 2003, 265–88.

'Greci e Iranici: Confronto e conflitti', in S. Settis (ed.), I Greci, vol. III: *I Greci oltre la Grecia*, Torino, 2001, 79–136.

'Women and kingship: Some remarks about the enthronisation of Queen Bōrān and her sister Āzarmīgduxt', in J. Wiesehöfer and P. Huyse (eds.), *Ērān und Anērān: Studien zu den Beziehungen zwischen dem Sasanidenreich und der Mittelmeerwelt*, OrOcc 13, Stuttgart, 2006, 221–40.

Peck, E. H., 'Clothing, IV', *EIr*, vol. V, 739–52.

Perikhanian, A., 'Iranian society and law', in E. Yarshater (ed.), *The Cambridge history of Iran*, vol. III: *The Seleucid, Parthian and Sasanian periods*, Cambridge, 1983, part 2, 627–80.

Pieler, P., 'L'aspect politique et juridique de l'adoption de Chosroes proposée par les Perses à Justin', *Revue Internationale des Droits de l'Antiquité*, 3 (1972), 399–433.

Potter, D. S., *Prophecy and history in the crisis of the Roman empire: A historical commentary on the Thirteenth Sibylline Oracle*, Oxford, 1990.

Potts, D. T., 'Gundeshapur and the Gondeisos', *Iranica Antiqua*, 24 (1989), 323–35.

Preißler, H., 'Arabien zwischen Byzanz und Persien', in L. Rathmann *et al.* (eds.), *Geschichte der Araber*, vol. I, 2nd edn, Berlin, 1975, 36–56.

Richter-Bernburg, L., 'Iran's contribution to medicine and veterinary science in Islam AH 100–900/AD 700–1500', in J. A. C. Greppin *et al.* (eds.), *The diffusion of Greco-Roman medicine into the Middle East and the Caucasus*, Delmar, 1999, 139–67.

'Mani's Dodecads and Sasanian chronology', *Zeitschrift für Papyrologie und Epigraphik*, 95 (1993), 71–80.

'Medicine, pharmacology and veterinary science in Islamic eastern Iran and Central Asia', in C. E. Bosworth and M. S. Asimov (eds.), *History of civilizations of Central Asia*, vol. IV: *The age of achievement: AD 750 to the end of the fifteenth century*, part 2: *The achievements*, Paris, 2000, 299–317.

'On the diffusion of medical knowledge in Persian court culture during the fourth and fifth centuries AH', in Z. Vezel *et al.* (eds.), *La science dans le monde iranien à l'époque islamique*, Tehran, 1998, 219–33.

Rothstein, G., *Die Dynastie der Laḫmiden in al-Ḥīra: Ein Versuch zur arabisch-persischen Geschichte zur Zeit der Sasaniden*, Berlin, 1899.

Rubin, B., *Das Zeitalter Iustinians*, vol. I, Berlin, 1960.

Rubin, Z., 'Diplomacy and war in the relations between Byzantium and the Sassanids in the fifth century AD', in P. W. Freeman and D. L. Kennedy (eds.), *The defence of the Roman and Byzantine east: Proceedings of a colloquium held at the University of Sheffield in April 1986*, BAR International Series 297, part 2, Oxford, 1986, 677–95.

'Ibn al-Muqaffaʿ and the account of Sasanian history in the Arabic Codex Sprenger 30', *JSAI*, 30 (2005), 52–93.

'Res Gestae Divi Saporis: Greek and Middle Iranian in a document of Sasanian anti-Roman propaganda', in J. N. Adams, M. Janse and S. Swain (eds.), *Bilingualism in ancient society: Language contact and the written text*, Oxford, 2002, 267–97.

'The Roman empire in the Res Gestae Divi Saporis: The Mediterranean world in Sāsānian propaganda', in E. Dabrowa (ed.), *Ancient Iran and the Mediterranean world*, Electrum **2**, Crakow, 1998, 177–85.

Sako, L., *Le rôle de la hiérarchie syriaque orientale dans les rapports diplomatiques entre la Perse et Byzance aux Ve–VIIe siècles*, Paris, 1986.

Schick, R., *The Christian communities of Palestine from Byzantine to Islamic rule: A historical and archaeological study*, Studies in Late Antiquity and Early Islam 2, Princeton, 1995.

Schippmann, K., *Grundzüge der Geschichte des sasanidischen Reiches*, Darmstadt, 1990.

Schneider, R. M., 'Orientalism in Late Antiquity: The Oriental other in imperial and Christian imagery', in J. Wiesehöfer and P. Huyse (eds.), *Ērān und Anērān: Studien zu den Beziehungen zwischen dem Sasanidenreich und der Mittelmeerwelt*, OrOcc 13, Stuttgart, 2006, 241–78.

Scholten, H., *Der Eunuch in Kaisernähe: Zur politischen und sozialen Bedeutung des praepositus sacri cubiculi im 4. und 5. Jahrhundert n.Chr.*, Prismata 5, Frankfurt, 1995.

Schwaigert, W., *Das Christentum in Ḫūzistān im Rahmen der frühen Kirchengeschichte Persiens*, Marburg, 1989.

Sezgin, F., *Geschichte des arabischen Schrifttums*, vol. I, Leiden, 1967.

Shahbazi, A. S., 'Army, I', *EIr*, vol. II, 489–99.

'Bahrām VI Čōbīn', *EIr* vol. III, 519–22.

'Early Sasanians' claim to Achaemenid heritage', *Nâme-ye Irân-e Bâstân*, 1, 1 (2001), 61–73.

'On the X^{w}adāy-nāmag', *Acta Iranica*, 30 (1990), 208–29.

Shahid, I., *Byzantium and the Arabs in the fifth century*, Washington, 1989.

Byzantium and the Arabs in the fourth century, Washington, 1984.

Byzantium and the Arabs in the sixth century, I.1–2, Washington, 1995.

'The Iranian factor in Byzantium during the reign of Heraclius', *Dumbarton Oaks Papers*, 26 (1971), 295–320.

Skjærvø, P. O., 'L'inscription d'Abnūn et l'imperfait moyen-perse, *Studia Iranica*, 21 (1992), 153–60.

'Thematic and linguistic parallels in the Achaemenian and Sasanian inscriptions', *Acta Iranica*, 25 (1985), 593–603.

Springberg-Hinsen, M., *Die Zeit vor dem Islam in arabischen Universalgeschichten des 9. bis 12. Jahrhunderts*, Würzburg and Altenberge, 1989.

Stausberg, M., *Die Religion Zarathushtras*, vol. I, Stuttgart, 2002.

Strobel, K., *Das Imperium Romanum im '3. Jahrhundert'*, Historia-Einzelschriften 75, Stuttgart, 1993.

Sundermann, W., 'The date of the Barm-e Delak inscription', *Bulletin of the Asia Institute*, n.s. 7 (1993), 203–5.

'*Kē čihr az yazdā*: Zur Titulatur der Sasanidenkönige', *Archiv Orientalni*, 56 (1988), 338–40.

'Mazdak und die mazdakitischen Volksaufstände', *Altertum*, 23 (1977), 245–9.

'Review of H. Humbach and P. O. Skjærvø, *The Sassanian inscription of Paikuli*', *Kratylos*, 28 (1983), 82–9.

'Shapur's coronation: The evidence of the Cologne Mani Codex reconsidered and compared with other texts', *Bulletin of the Asia Institute*, n.s. 4 (1990), 295–9.

'Studien zur kirchengeschichtlichen Literatur der iranischen Manichäer I/II', *Altorientalische Forschungen*, 13 (1986), 40–92, 239–317.

'Studien zur kirchengeschichtlichen Literatur der iranischen Manichäer III', *Altorientalische Forschungen*, 14 (1987), 41–107.

Tanabe, K., 'Iconography of the royal-hunt bas-reliefs at Taq-i Bustan', *Orient* (Tokyo), 19 (1983), 103–16.

Tavadia, J. C., *Die mittelpersische Sprache und Literatur der Zarathustrier*, Leipzig, 1956.

Tavoosi, M., and R. N. Frye, 'An inscribed capital dating from the time of Shapur I', *Bulletin of the Asia Institute*, n.s. 3 (1990), 25–38.

Teitler, H., '*Visa vel lecta?* Ammianus on Persia and the Persians', in J. W. Drijvers and D. Hunt (eds.), *The late Roman world and its historian*, London and New York, 1999, 216–23.

Trümpelmann, L., *Zwischen Persepolis und Firuzabad*, Mainz, 1991.

Tyler-Smith, S., 'Calendars and coronations: The literary and numismatic evidence for the accession of Khusrau II', *Byzantine and Modern Greek Studies*, 28 (2004), 33–65.

Ullmann, M., *Islamic medicine*, Edinburgh, 1978.

Weber, U., *Prosopographie des frühen Sasanidenreiches*, Kiel, 2004, available at www.uni-kiel.de/klassalt/projekte/sasaniden/index.html.

Whitby, M., *The emperor Maurice and his historian: Theophylact Simocatta on Persian and Balkan warfare*, Oxford, 1988.

'The Persian king at war', in E. Dabrowa (ed.), *The Roman and Byzantine army in the east: Proceedings of a colloquium held at the Jagiellonian University, Kraków, in September 1992*, Crakow, 1994, 227–63.

Whitehouse, D., 'La verrerie', in *Splendeur des Sassanides: L'empire perse entre Rome et la Chine (224–642), 12 février au 25 avril 1993*, Brussels, 1993, 109–11.

Widengren, G., 'Sources of Parthian and Sasanian history', in E. Yarshater (ed.), *The Cambridge history of Iran*, vol. III: *The Seleucid, Parthian and Sasanian periods*, Cambridge, 1983, part 2, 1261–83.

Wiesehöfer, J., 'Ardašīr I., I. History', *EIr*, vol. II, 371–6.

'From Achaemenid imperial order to Sasanian diplomacy: War, peace and reconciliation in pre-Islamic Iran', in K. Raaflaub (ed.), *War and peace in the ancient world*, Oxford, 2007, 121–40.

'Gebete für die "Urahnen" oder: Wann und wie verschwanden Kyros und Dareios aus der Tradition Irans?', in E. Dabrowa (ed.), *Tradition and innovation in the ancient world*, Electrum 6, Crakow, 2002, 111–17.

'Geteilte Loyalitäten: Religiöse Minderheiten des 3. und 4. Jahrhunderts n.Chr. im Spannungsfeld zwischen Rom und dem sāsānidischen Iran', *Klio*, 75 (1993), 362–82.

Iraniens, Grecs et Romains, Cahiers à Studia Iranica 32, Paris, 2005.

'Iranische Ansprüche an Rom auf ehemals achaimenidische Territorien', *Archäologische Mitteilungen aus Iran*, n.s. 19 (1986), 177–86.

'Narseh, Diokletian, Manichäer und Christen', in M. Arafa, J. Tubach and G. S. Vashalomidze (eds.), *Inkulturation des Christentums im Sasanidenreich*, Wiesbaden, 2007, 161–9.

'"Randkultur" oder "Nabel der Welt"? Das Sasanidenreich und der Westen: Anmerkungen eines Althistorikers', in J. Wiesehöfer and P. Huyse (eds.), *Ērān und Anērān: Studien zu den Beziehungen zwischen dem Sasanidenreich und der Mittelmeerwelt*, OrOcc 13, Stuttgart, 2006., 9–28.

'Rūm as enemy of Iran', in E. Gruen (ed.), *Cultural borrowings and ethnic appropriations in Antiquity*, OrOcc 8, Stuttgart, 2005, 105–20.

'Zeugnisse zur Geschichte und Kultur der Persis unter den Parthern', in J. Wiesehöfer (ed.), *Das Partherreich und seine Zeugnisse – The Arsacid empire: Sources and documentation. Beiträge des Internationalen Colloquiums, Eutin (27.–29. Juni 1996)*, Historia-Einzelschriften 122, Stuttgart, 1998, 338–40.

'Zum Nachleben von Achaimeniden und Alexander in Iran', in H. Sancisi-Weerdenburg, A. Kuhrt and M. C. Root (eds.), *Achaemenid history VIII: Continuity and change*, Leiden, 1994, 389–97.

Winter, E., 'Legitimität als Herrschaftsprinzip: Kaiser und "König der Könige" im wechselseitigen Verkehr', in H.-J. Drexhage and J. Sünskes (eds.), *Migratio et Commutatio: Studien zur Alten Geschichte und deren Nachleben. Th. Pekáry zum 60. Geburtstag am 13. September 1989 dargebracht von Freunden, Kollegen und Schülern*, St Katharinen, 1988, 72– 92.

'On the regulation of the eastern frontier of the Roman empire in 298', in D. H. French and C. S. Lightfoot (eds.), *The eastern frontier of the Roman empire: Proceedings of a colloquium held at Ankara in September 1988*, BAR International Series 553, part 1, Oxford, 1989, 555–71.

Die sāsānidisch-römischen Friedensverträge des 3. Jahrhunderts n.Chr.: Ein Beitrag zum Verständnis der außenpolitischen Beziehungen zwischen den beiden Großmächten, Europäische Hochschulschriften III, 350, Frankfurt, 1988.

Zeimal, E. V., 'The Kidarite kingdom in Central Asia', in B. A. Litvinsky (ed.), *History of civilizations of Central Asia*, vol. III: *The crossroads of civilization AD 250 to 750*, Paris, 1996, 119–33.

Chapter 4: Pre-Islamic Arabia

Practical suggestions for further reading

Hoyland, Robert G., *Arabia and the Arabs from the Bronze Age to the coming of Islam*, London and New York, 2001.

Kister, M. J., *Studies in jāhiliyya and early Islam*, London, 1980.

Peters, F. E. (ed.), *The Arabs and Arabia on the eve of Islam*, Aldershot, 1999.

Primary sources

Caskel, Werner, and Gert Strenziok, *Ǧamharat an-Nasab: Das genealogische Werk des Hišām ibn Muḥammad al-Kalbī*, 2 vols., Leiden, 1966.

al-Ḥillī, Abū l-Baqā' Hibat Allāh, *al-Manāqib al-mazyadiyya*, ed. Ṣāliḥ Mūsā Darādika and Muḥammad ʿAbd al-Qādir Khrīsāt, 2 vols., Amman, 1404/1984.

Ibn al-Kalbī, *al-Aṣnām*, ed. Aḥmad Zakī Bāshā, Cairo, 1343/1924.

Ibn Saʿīd al-Andalusī, *Nashwat al-ṭarab bi-ta'rīkh jāhiliyyat al-ʿarab*, ed. Naṣrat ʿAbd al-Raḥmān, 2 vols., Amman, 1982.

al-Marzūqī, Abū ʿAlī, *Kitāb al-azmina wa'l-amkina*, Hyderabad, 1332 {1913}; repr. Cairo, n.d.

al-Samhūdī, ʿAlī ibn Aḥmad, *Wafā' al-wafā*, ed. Qāsim al-Sāmarrā'ī, 5 vols., London and Jiddah, 1422/2001.

Secondary sources

Abdalla, Abdelgadir M., Sami al-Sakkar and Richard Mortel (eds.), *Pre-Islamic Arabia: Proceedings of the Second International Symposium on Studies in the History of Arabia, 1399/1979*, Riyadh, 1984.

Kister, M. J., 'Labbayka, allāhumma, Labbayka: On a monotheistic aspect of a Jāhiliyya practice', *JSAI*, 2 (1980), 33–57.

'Mecca and the tribes of Arabia', in M. Sharon (ed.), *Studies in Islamic history and civilization in honour of David Ayalon*, Jerusalem and Leiden, 1986, 33–57.

Levi della Vida, Giorgio, 'Pre-Islamic Arabia', in Nabih Amin Faris (ed.), *The Arab heritage*, Princeton, 1944, 25–57.

Maraqten, Mohammed, 'Writing materials in pre-Islamic Arabia', *JSS*, 43 (1998), 287–310.

Robin, Christian Julien, 'South Arabia, religions in pre-Islamic', *Encyclopaedia of the Qur'ān*.

'Yemen', *Encyclopaedia of the Qur'ān*.

Chapter 5: The rise of Islam, 600–705

Practical suggestions for further reading

Cook, M., *Muhammad*, Oxford, 1983.

Crone, P., *Meccan trade and the rise of Islam*, Princeton, 1987; repr. Piscataway, NJ, 2004.

Slaves on horses: The evolution of the Islamic polity, Cambridge, 1980.
Donner, F. M., *The early Islamic conquests*, Princeton, 1981.
Hawting, G. R., *The first dynasty of Islam: The Umayyad caliphate, AD 661–750*, 2nd edn, London and Sydney, 2000.
Hoyland, R., *Seeing Islam as others saw it: A survey and evaluation of Christian, Jewish and Zoroastrian writings on early Islam*, Princeton, 1997.
Humphreys, R. S., *Muʿawiya ibn Abi Sufyan: From Arabia to empire*, Oxford, 2006.
Ibn Warraq (ed.), *The quest for the historical Muhammad*, Amherst, NY, 2000.
Kennedy, H., *The great Arab conquests*, London, 2007.
The Prophet and the age of the caliphates, 2nd edn, London, 2004.
Madelung, W., *The succession to Muḥammad: A study of the early caliphate*, Cambridge, 1997.
Motzki, H. (ed.), *The biography of Muḥammad: The issue of the sources*, Leiden, 2000.
de Prémare, A. L., *Les fondations de l'islam: Entre écriture et histoire*, Paris, 2002.
Robinson, C. F., *ʿAbd al-Malik*, Oxford, 2005.
Rubin, U., *The eye of the beholder: The life of Muḥammad as viewed by the early Muslims*, Princeton, 1995.

Primary sources

Abū al-Fatḥ al-Sāmirī, *The continuatio of the Samaritan chronicle of Abū al-Fatḥ al-Sāmirī al-Danafī*, ed. and trans. M. Levy-Rubin, Princeton, 2002.
Ibn Hishām, al-Sīra al-nabawiyya, ed. M. al-Ṣaqqā *et al.*, 4 vols., Cairo, 1936; trans. A. Guillaume as *The Life of Muhammad*, Oxford, 1955.
John of Damascus, *Écrits sur l'Islam*, ed. and trans. R. Le Coz, Paris, 1992.
Sebeos, *The Armenian history attributed to Sebeos*, trans. R. W. Thomson with commentary by J. Howard-Johnston, Translated Texts for Historians 31, Liverpool, 1999.
al-Ṭabarī, Abū Jaʿfar Muḥammad ibn Jarīr, *Ta'rīkh al-rusul wa'l-mulūk*, ed. M. J. de Goeje *et al.*, 15 vols. in 3 series, Leiden, 1879–1901; sections trans. I. K. Poonawala as *The history of al-Ṭabarī*, vol. IX: *The last years of the Prophet*, Albany, 1990; trans. G. H. A. Juynboll as *The history of al-Ṭabarī*, vol. XIII: *The conquest of Iraq, southwestern Persia, and Egypt*, Albany, 1989.

Secondary sources

Agha, S., and T. Khalidi, 'Poetry and identity in the Umayyad age', *al-Abhath*, 50–1 (2002–3), 55–120.
Album, S., and T. Goodwin, *Sylloge of Islamic coins in the Ashmolean*, vol. I: *The pre-reform coinage of the early Islamic period*, London, 2002.
Andrae, T., 'Der Ursprung des Islams und das Christentum', *Kyrkohistorisk Årsskrift*, 23 (1923), 149–206.
Athamina, K., 'Abraham in Islamic perspective: Reflections on the development of monotheism in pre-Islamic Arabia', *Der Islam*, 81 (2004), 184–205.
'Arab settlement during the Umayyad period', *JSAI*, 8 (1986), 185–207.
Bamyeh, M., *The social origins of Islam: Mind, economy, discourse*, Minneapolis, 1999.
Bashear, S., 'ʿĀshūrā, an early Muslim fast', *ZDMG*, 141 (1991), 281–316; repr. in S. Bashear, *Studies in early Islamic tradition*, Jerusalem, 2004.

Bates, M., 'Byzantine coinage and its imitations, Arab coinage and its imitations: Arab-Byzantine coinage', *Aram*, 6 (1994), 381–403.

Beauchamp, J., F. Briquel-Chatonnet and C. Robin, 'La persécution des chrétiens de Nagran et la chronologie Himyarite', *Aram*, 11–12 (1999–2000), 15–83.

Beauchamp, J., and C. Robin, 'Le Christianisme dans le péninsule arabique dans l'épigraphie et l'archéologie', *Hommage à Paul Lemerle, Travaux et mémoires*, 8, Paris, 1981, 45–61.

Beeston, A., 'Himyarite monotheism', in A. M. Abdulla *et al.* (eds.), *Studies in the history of Arabia*, vol. II: *Pre-Islamic Arabia*, Riyadh, 1984, 149–54.

'Kingship in ancient South Arabia', *JESHO*, 15 (1972), 256–68.

Berg, H., 'Islamic origins reconsidered: John Wansbrough and the study of early Islam', *Method and Theory in the Study of Religion*, 9 (1997), 3–22.

Berthier, S. (ed.), *Peuplement rural et aménagements hydroagricôles dans la moyenne vallée de l'Euphrat, fin VIIe–XIXe siècle*, Damascus, 2001.

Bone, H., 'The administration of Umayyad Syria: The evidence of the copper coins', Ph.D. thesis, Princeton University, 2000.

Boyd, S., and M. Mango (eds.), *Ecclesiastical silver plate in sixth-century Byzantium*, Washington, DC, 1992.

Brock, S. P., 'North Mesopotamia in the late seventh century: Book xv of John Bar Penkāyē's *Rīš Mellē*', *JSAI*, 9 (1987), 51–75.

Busse, H., 'Omar b. al-Haṭṭāb in Jerusalem', *JSAI*, 5 (1984), 73–119.

Combe, E., J. Sauvaget and G. Wiet, *Répertoire chronologique d'épigraphie arabe I*, Cairo, 1931.

Conrad, L. I., 'Abraha and Muḥammad: Some observations apropos of chronology and literary topoi in the early Arabic historical tradition', *BSOAS*, 50 (1987), 225–40.

'The conquest of Arwād: A source-critical study in the historiography of the early medieval Near East', in A. Cameron and L. I. Conrad (eds.), *The Byzantine and early Islamic Near East*, vol. I: *Problems in the literary source material*, Princeton, 1992, 317–401.

Constantelos, D. J., 'The Moslem conquests of the Near East as revealed in the Greek sources of the seventh and eighth centuries', *Byzantion*, 42 (1972), 325–57.

Cook, M., ''Anan and Islam: The origins of Karaite scripturalism', *JSAI*, 9 (1987), 161–82.

'Magian cheese: An archaic problem in Islamic law', *BSOAS*, 47 (1984), 449–67.

'The opponents of the writing of tradition in early Islam', *Arabica*, 44 (1997), 437–530.

Crone, P., 'The first-century concept of *hiğra*', *Arabica*, 41 (1994), 352–87.

Medieval Islamic political thought, Edinburgh, 2004.

'Quraysh and the Roman army: Making sense of the Meccan leather trade', *BSOAS*, 70 (2007), 63–88.

'Were the Qays and Yemen of the Umayyad period political parties?', *Der Islam*, 71 (1994), 1–57.

Crone, P., and M. Cook, *Hagarism: The making of the Islamic world*, Cambridge, 1977.

Crone, P., and M. Hinds, *God's caliph: Religious authority in the first centuries of Islam*, Cambridge, 1986.

Crone, P., and F. Zimmermann, *The Epistle of Sālim ibn Dhakwān*, Oxford, 2001.

Dixon, A. A., *The Umayyad caliphate 65–86/684–705 (a political study)*, London, 1971.

Djait, H., *La grande discorde: Religion et politique dans l'Islam des origines*, Paris, 1989.

Donner, F. M., 'The formation of the Islamic state', *JAOS*, 106 (1986), 283–96.

'From believers to Muslims: Confessional self-identity in the early Islamic community', *al-Abhath*, 50–1 (2002–3), 9–53.
Elad, A., 'The southern Golan in the early Muslim period: The significance of two newly discovered milestones of 'Abd al-Malik', *Der Islam*, 76 (1999), 33–88.
Finster, B., *Frühe iranische Moscheen*, Berlin, 1994.
Flood, F. B., *The Great Mosque of Damascus: Studies on the makings of an Umayyad visual culture*, Leiden, 2001.
Foote, R. M., 'Commerce, industrial expansion, and orthogonal planning: Mutually compatible terms in settlements of Bilad al-Sham during the Umayyad period', *Mediterranean Archaeology*, 13 (2000), 25–38.
Foss, C., 'The coinage of Syria in the seventh century: The evidence of excavations', *Israel Numismatic Journal*, 13 (1994–9), 119–32.
'The Near Eastern countryside in Late Antiquity: A review article', *The Roman and Byzantine Near East: Journal of Roman Archaeology*, supplementary series 14 (1995), 213–34.
'The Persians in Asia Minor and the end of Antiquity', *The English Historical Review*, 90 (1975), 721–47.
'Syria in transition, AD 550–750: An archaeological approach', *Dumbarton Oaks Papers*, 51 (1997), 189–269.
'A Syrian coinage of Mu'awiya?', *Revue Numismatique*, 157 (2002), 353–65.
Gascou, J., 'De Byzance à l'Islam: Les impôts en Egypte après la conquête arabe', *JESHO*, 26 (1983), 97–109.
Gil, M., 'The creed of Abū 'Āmir', *Israel Oriental Studies*, 12 (1992), 9–57.
Gilliot, C., 'Le Coran, fruit d'un travail collectif?', in D. De Smet *et al.* (eds.), *al-Kitāb: La sacralité du texte dans le monde de l'Islam*, Brussels, 2004, 186–231.
Gran, P., 'Political economy as a paradigm for the study of Islamic history', *IJMES*, 11 (1980), 511–26.
Grierson, P., 'The monetary reforms of 'Abd al-Malik: Their metrological basis and their financial repercussions', *JESHO*, 3 (1960), 241–64.
Griffith, S. H., 'Disputes with Muslims in Syriac Christian texts: From Patriarch John (d. 648) to Bar Hebraeus (d. 1286)', in B. Lewis and R. Niewöhner (eds.), *Religionsgespräche in Mittelalter*, Wiesbaden, 1992, 251–73.
Grohmann, A., *Arabische Chronologie*, Leiden, 1966.
The world of Arabic papyri, Cairo, 1952.
Gyselen, R., and L. Kalus, *Deux trésors monétaires des premiers temps de l'islam*, Paris, 1983.
Halevi, L., 'The paradox of Islamization: Tombstone inscriptions, Qur'ānic recitations, and the problem of religious change', *History of Religions*, 44 (2004), 120–52.
Halm, H., *Shiism*, Edinburgh, 1991.
Hawting, G. R., *The idea of idolatry and the emergence of Islam: From polemic to history*, Cambridge, 1999.
'The significance of the slogan *lā ḥukma illā lillāh* and the references to the *ḥudūd* in the traditions about the *fitna* and the murder of 'Uthmān', *BSOAS*, 41 (1978), 453–63.
Healey, J. F., 'The Christians of Qatar in the 7th century AD', in I. R. Netton (ed.), *Studies in honour of Clifford Edmund Bosworth*, vol. I: *Hunter of the east: Arabic and Semitic studies*, Leiden, 2000, 222–37.
Heck, G. W., '"Arabia without spices": An alternate hypothesis', *JAOS*, 123 (2003), 547–76.

Heidemann, S., 'The merger of two currency zones in early Islam: The Byzantine and Sasanian impact on the circulation in former Byzantine Syria and northern Mesopotamia', *Iran*, 36 (1998), 95–112.

Hinds, M., 'The first Arab conquests of Fārs', *Iran*, 22 (1984), 39–53.

'Kūfan political alignments and their background in the mid-seventh century AD', *IJMES*, 2 (1971), 346–67.

Howard-Johnston, J., 'The official history of Heraclius' Persian campaigns', in E. Dabrowa (ed.), *The Roman and Byzantine army in the east: Proceedings of a colloquium held at the Jagiellonian University, Kraków, in September 1992*, Crakow, 1994, 57–87.

Hoyland, R., *Arabia and the Arabs from the Bronze Age to the coming of Islam*, London and New York, 2001.

'New documentary texts and the early Islamic state', *BSOAS*, 69, 3 (2006), 395–416.

'Writing the biography of the Prophet Muhammad: Problems and solutions', *History Compass*, 5 (2007), 581–602.

Humphreys, R. S., 'Qur'anic myth and narrative structure in early Islamic historiography', in F. M. Clover and R. S. Humphreys (eds.), *Tradition and innovation in Late Antiquity*, Madison, 1989, 271–90.

Ibrahim, A., *Der Herausbildungsprozeß des arabisch-islamischen Staates*, Berlin, 1994.

Ibrahim, M., *Merchant capital and Islam*, Austin, 1990.

Johns, J., 'Archaeology and the history of early Islam: The first seventy years', *JESHO*, 46 (2003), 411–36.

'The "House of the Prophet" and the concept of the mosque', in J. Johns (ed.), *Bayt al-Maqdis: Jerusalem and early Islam*, Oxford Studies in Islamic Art 9, part 2, Oxford, 1999, 59–112.

Jones, A., 'The language of the Qur'an', in K. Dévéni, T. Iványi and A. Shivtel (eds.), *Proceedings of the Colloquium on Arabic Lexicology and Lexicography*, Budapest, 1993, 29–48.

Kaplony, A., *Konstantinopel und Damaskus: Gesandtschaften und Verträge zwischen Kaisern und Kalifen 639–750*, Berlin, 1996.

Kennedy, H., 'From polis to madina: Urban change in Late Antique and early Islamic Syria', *Past and Present*, 106 (1985), 3–27.

Kennet, D., 'The decline of eastern Arabia in the Sasanian period', *Arabian Archaeology and Epigraphy*, 18 (2007), 86–122.

'On the eve of Islam: Archaeological evidence from eastern Arabia', *Antiquity*, 79 (2005), 107–18.

Kister, M. J., 'Ḥaddithū 'an banī isrā'īla wa-lā ḥaraja', *Israel Oriental Studies*, 2 (1972), 215–47.

'Labbayka, allāhuma, labbayka: On a monotheistic aspect of a jāhiliyya practice', *JSAI*, 2 (1980), 33–57.

'The massacre of the Banū Qurayẓa: A re-examination of a tradition', *JSAI*, 8 (1986), 61–96.

'On the papyrus of Wahb b. Munabbih', *BSOAS*, 37 (1974), 545–71.

'"Rajab is the month of God": A study in the persistence of an early tradition', *Israel Oriental Studies*, 1 (1971), 191–223.

Korotayev, A., V. Klimenko and D. Proussakov, 'Origins of Islam: Political-anthropological and environmental context', *Acta Orientalia Academiae Scientiarum Hungaricae*, 52 (1999), 243–76.

Landau-Tasseron, E., 'Features of the pre-conquest Muslim army in the time of Muḥammad', in A. Cameron (ed.), *The Byzantine and early Islamic Near East*, vol. III: *States, resources and armies*, Studies in Late Antiquity and Early Islam 1, Princeton, 1995, 299–336.

Lecker, M., *'The Constitution of Medina': Muḥammad's first legal document*, Princeton, 2004.

'The death of the Prophet Muḥammad: Did Wāqidī invent some of the evidence?', *ZDMG*, 145 (1995), 9–27.

'Did Muḥammad conclude treaties with the Jewish tribes Naḍīr, Qurayẓa and Qaynuqāʿ?', *Israel Oriental Studies*, 17 (1997), 29–36.

'Judaism among Kinda and the *ridda* of Kinda', *JAOS*, 115 (1995), 635–50.

Luxenberg, C., *Die syro-aramäische Lesart des Koran*, 2nd edn, Berlin, 2004; trans. as *The Syro-Aramaic reading of the Koran*, Berlin, 2007.

Magness, J., *The archaeology of the early Islamic settlement in Palestine*, Winona Lake, IN, 2003.

Morelli, F., *Documenti Greci per la fiscalità e la amministrazione dell'Egitto Arabo*, Vienna, 2001.

Morimoto, K., *The fiscal administration of Egypt in the early Islamic period*, Kyoto, 1981.

Morony, M., 'Economic boundaries? Late Antiquity and early Islam', *JESHO*, 47 (2004), 166–94.

'The effects of the Muslim conquest on the Persian population of Iraq', *Iran*, 14 (1976), 41–59.

Iraq after the Muslim conquest, Princeton, 1984.

Morrison, C., 'La monnaie en Syrie byzantine', in J. M. Dentzer and W. Orthmann (eds.), *Archéologie et histoire de la Syrie II*, Saarbrücken, 1989, 191–204.

'Monnayage omeyyade et l'histoire administrative et économique de la Syrie', in P. Canivet and J.-P. Rey-Coquais (eds.), *La Syrie de Byzance à l'Islam*, Damascus, 1992, 309–21.

Nevo, Y., and J. Koren, *Crossroads to Islam: The origins of the Arab religion and the Arab state*, Amherst, NY, 2003.

Nicolle, D., 'Arms of the Umayyad era: Military technology in a time of change', in Y. Lev (ed.), *War and society in the eastern Mediterranean, 7th–15th centuries*, Leiden, 1997, 9–100.

Olagüe, I., *Les arabes n'ont jamais envahi l'espagne*, Paris, 1969.

Palmer, A., S. Brock and R. Hoyland, *The seventh century in the West-Syrian chronicles*, Liverpool, 1993.

Pampus, K.-H., *Über die Rolle der Ḫāriǧīya im frühen Islam*, Wiesbaden, 1980.

Peters, F. E., 'The quest for the historical Muhammad', *IJMES*, 23 (1991), 291–315.

Petersen, E. L., *ʿAlī and Muʿāwiya in early Arabic tradition: Studies on the genesis and growth of Islamic historical writing until the end of the ninth century*, 2nd edn, Odense, 1974 [Copenhagen, 1964].

Potts, D., *The Arabian Gulf in Antiquity*, Oxford, 1990.

Puin, G., *Der Dīwān von ʿUmar ibn al-Ḫaṭṭāb: Ein Beitrag zur frühislamischen Verwaltungsgeschichte*, Bonn, 1970.

Rippin, A., 'RḤMNN and the Ḥanīfs', in W. B. Hallaq and D. P. Little (eds.), *Islamic studies presented to Charles J. Adams*, Leiden, 1991, 153–68.

Robin, C., 'Judaisme et christianisme en Arabie du sud d'après les sources épigraphiques et archéologiques', *Proceedings of the Seminar for Arabian Studies*, 10 (1980), 85–96.

'Le judaïsme de Himyar', *Arabia*, 1 (2003), 97–172.

'Du paganisme au monothéisme', in C. Robin (ed.), *L'Arabie antique de Karib'īl à Mahomet: Nouvelles données sur l'histoire des arabes grâces aux inscriptions*, Aix-en-Provence, 1991, 139–55.

Robinson, C. F., 'The conquest of Khūzistān: A historiographic reassessment', *BSOAS*, 67 (2004), 14–39.

Empire and elites after the Muslim conquest: The transformation of northern Mesopotamia, Cambridge Studies in Islamic Civilization, Cambridge, 2000.

'Neck-sealing in early Islam', *JESHO*, 48 (2005), 401–44.

'Reconstructing early Islam: Truth and consequences', in H. Berg (ed.), *Method and theory in the study of Islamic origins*, Leiden, 2003, 101–34.

Rotter, G., *Die Umayyaden und der zweite Bürgerkrieg (680–692)*, Wiesbaden, 1982.

Rubin, U., *Between Bible and Qur'ān: The Children of Israel and the Islamic self-image*, Princeton, 1999.

Sayed, R., *Die Revolte des Ibn al-Ashʿat und die Koranleser*, Freiburg, 1977.

Schick, R., *The Christian communities of Palestine from Byzantine to Islamic rule: A historical and archaeological study*, Princeton, 1995.

Schmucker, W., *Untersuchungen zu einigen wichtigen bodenrechtlichen Konsequenzen der islamischen Eroberungsbewegung*, Bonn, 1972.

Schoeler, G., *Charakter und Authentie der muslimischen Überlieferung über das Leben Mohammeds*, Berlin, 1996.

Sfar, M., *Le coran est-il authentique?*, Paris, 2000.

Shahid, I., *Byzantium and the Arabs in the fifth century*, Washington, DC, 1989.

Byzantium and the Arabs in the sixth century, vol. I, parts 1–2, Washington, DC, 1995 and 2002.

Shoshan, B., *Poetics of Islamic historiography: Deconstructing Ṭabarī's* History, Leiden, 2004.

Sijpesteijn, P., 'New rule over old structures: Egypt after the Muslim conquest', in H. Crawford (ed.), *Regime change in the ancient Near East and Egypt, from Sargon of Agade to Saddam Hussein*, Proceedings of the British Academy 136, London, 2007, 183–200.

Simonsen, J. B., *Studies in the genesis and early development of the caliphal taxation system*, Copenhagen, 1988.

Sims-Williams, N., *Bactrian documents from northern Afghanistan*, vol. I: *Legal and economic documents*, Oxford, 2000.

Smith, S., 'Events in Arabia in the 6th century AD', *BSOAS*, 16 (1954), 425–68.

Suermann, H., *Die geschichtstheologischen Reaktion auf die einfallenden muslime in der edessenischen Apokalyptik des 7. Jahrhunderts*, Frankfurt, 1985.

Trimingham, J. S., *Christianity among the Arabs in pre-Islamic times*, London, 1979.

Walmsley, A., *Early Islamic Syria: An archaeological assessment*, Bath, 2007.

'The social and economic regime at Fihl (Pella)', in P. Canivet and J.-P. Rey Coquais (eds.), *La Syrie de Byzance à l'Islam*, Damascus, 1992, 249–61.

Wansbrough, J., *The sectarian milieu: Content and composition of Islamic salvation history*, Oxford, 1978.

Ward-Perkins, B., *The fall of Rome and the end of civilization*, Oxford, 2005.

Watt, W. M., 'Belief in a "High God" in pre-Islamic Mecca', *JSS*, 16 (1971), 35–40.

Muhammad at Mecca, Oxford, 1953.

Muhammad at Medina, Oxford, 1956.

Whitby, C., 'Recruitment in Roman armies from Justinian to Heraclius (*ca.* 565–615)', in A. Cameron (ed.), *The Byzantine and early Islamic Near East*, vol. III: *States, resources and armies*, Princeton, 1995, pp. 61–124.

Whitehouse, D., and A. Williamson, 'Sasanian maritime trade', *Iran*, 11 (1973), 29–49.

Ye'or, B., *The decline of Eastern Christianity under Islam: From jihad to dhimmitude*, Cranbury, NJ, 1996.

Chapter 6: The empire in Syria, 705–763

Practical suggestions for further reading

Cobb, Paul M., *White banners: Contention in ʿAbbasid Syria, 750–880*, Albany, 2001.

Crone, Patricia, *Slaves on horses: The evolution of the Islamic polity*, Cambridge, 1980.

Hawting, G. R., *The first dynasty of Islam: The Umayyad caliphate, AD 661–750*, 2nd edn, London, 2000.

Kennedy, Hugh, *The Prophet and the age of the caliphates*, 2nd edn, London, 2004.

Primary sources

Agapius (Maḥbūb) of Manbij, *Kitāb al-ʿunwān*, part 2, ed. and trans. Alexandre Vasiliev as '*Kitāb al-ʿunvān* (histoire universelle)', *Patrologia Orientalis*, 8 (1911), 399–550.

Akhbār al-dawla al-ʿAbbāsiyya wa-fīhi akhbār al-ʿAbbās wa-wuldihi, ed. ʿAbd al-ʿAzīz al-Dūrī and ʿAbd al-Jabbār al-Muṭṭalibī, Beirut, 1971.

al-Azdī, Yazīd ibn Muḥammad, *Taʾrīkh al-Mawṣil*, ed. ʿAlī Ḥabība, Cairo, 1967.

al-Balādhurī, Aḥmad ibn Yaḥyā, *Ansāb al-ashrāf*, ed. M. al-ʿAẓm, Damascus, 1997.

Kitāb futūḥ al-buldān, ed. M. J. de Goeje, Leiden, 1866.

Chachnāmah, ed. N. A. Baloch, Islamabad, 1983.

al-Dīnawarī, Abū Ḥanīfa Aḥmad, *al-Akhbār al-ṭiwāl*, ed. V. Guirgass, Leiden, 1888.

Fragmenta historicorum arabicorum, ed. M. J. de Goeje, 2 vols., Leiden, 1869.

Ibn ʿAbd al-Ḥakam, Abū Muḥammad ʿAbd Allāh, *Sīrat ʿUmar ibn ʿAbd al-ʿAzīz*, ed. Aḥmad ʿUbayd, Cairo, 1983.

Ibn ʿAbd al-Ḥakam, Abū al-Qāsim ʿAbd al-Raḥmān, *Futūḥ Miṣr wa-akhbāruhā*, ed. C. C. Torrey, New Haven, 1922.

Ibn al-ʿAdīm, Kamāl al-Dīn ʿUmar, *Zubdat al-ḥalab min taʾrīkh Ḥalab*, ed. Sāmī Dahhān, 3 vols., Damascus, 1951–68.

Ibn ʿAsākir, Abū al-Qāsim ʿAlī, *Taʾrīkh madīnat Dimashq*, ed. ʿUmar al-ʿAmrāwī, 70 vols., Beirut, 1995–8.

Ibn Aʿtham al-Kūfī, Abū Muḥammad Aḥmad, *al-Futūḥ*, ed. Muḥammad ʿAbd al-Muʿīd Khān *et al.*, 8 vols., Hyderabad, 1968–75.

Ibn ʿIdhārī, Aḥmad ibn Muḥammad, *al-Bayān al-mughrib fī akhbār al-Andalus wa al-Maghrib*, ed. G. S. Colin and E. Lévi-Provençal, 4 vols., Leiden, 1948–51.

Ibn Khayyāṭ, Khalīfa, *al-Taʾrīkh*, ed. Akram al-ʿUmarī, 2 vols., Najaf, 1967.

Ibn al-Qūṭiyya, Abū Bakr ibn ʿUmar, *Taʾrīkh iftitāḥ al-Andalus*, ed. Ibrāhīm al-Abyārī, Cairo, 1982.

al-Iṣbahānī, Abū al-Faraj ʿAlī, *al-Aghānī*, 31 vols., Cairo, 1969–79.

Maqātil al-Ṭalibiyyīn, ed. Kāẓim al-Muẓaffar, Najaf, 1965.

al-Kindī, Abū ʿUmar Muḥammad ibn Yūsuf, *al-Wulāt wa-al-quḍāt*, ed. R. Guest, Leiden and London, 1912.

Lewond (Ghevond), *History of Lewond the eminent Vardapet of the Armenians*, trans. Zaven Arzoumanian, Wynnewood, PA, 1982.

al-Masʿūdī, ʿAlī ibn al-Ḥusayn, *Murūj al-dhahab wa-maʿādin al-jawhar*, ed. Charles Pellat, 7 vols., Beirut, 1965–79.

Michael the Syrian, *Chronique de Michel le Syrien*, ed. and trans. J.-B. Chabot, 4 vols., Paris, 1924.

al-Ṭabarī, Abū Jaʿfar Muḥammad ibn Jarīr, *Taʾrīkh al-rusul wa al-mulūk*, ed. M. J. de Goeje *et al.*, **15** vols. in 3 series, Leiden, 1879–1901.

Taʾrīkh al-Yaʿqūbī, ed. M. T. Houtsma, 2 vols., Leiden, 1883.

Taʾrīkh-i Sīstān, ed. Malik al-Shuʿarāʾ Bahār, Tehran, 1935.

Theophanes Confessor, *Theophanis chronographia*, ed. C. de Boor, Leipzig, 1883.

al-Yaʿqūbī, Aḥmad ibn Abī Yaʿqūb, *Kitāb al-buldān*, ed. M. J. de Goeje, Leiden, 1892.

Secondary sources

Abbott, Nabia, *The Ḳurrah papyri from Aphrodito in the Oriental Institute*, Chicago, 1930.

'A new papyrus and a review of the administration of ʿUbaid Allāh b. al-Ḥabḥāb', in G. Makdisi (ed.), *Arabic and Islamic studies in honor of Hamilton A. R. Gibb*, Cambridge, MA, 1965, 19–35.

Agha, Saleh Said, *The revolution which toppled the Umayyads: Neither Arab nor ʿAbbāsid*, Leiden, 2003.

ʿAthamina, Khalil, 'Arab settlement during the Umayyad caliphate', *JSAI*, 8 (1986), 185–207.

Bacharach, Jere L., 'Marwānid building activities: Speculations on patronage', *Muqarnas*, 13 (1996), 27–44.

Banaji, Jairus, *Agrarian change in Late Antiquity: Gold, labour, and aristocratic dominance*, Oxford, 2001.

Bates, Michael L., 'The coinage of Syria under the Umayyads, 692–750 AD', in M. A. Bakhit and R. Schick (eds.), *The history of Bilad al-Sham during the Umayyad period: Proceedings of the third symposium*, Amman, 1989, vol. II, 195–228.

'Coins and money in the Arabic papyri', in Y. Ragib (ed.), *Documents de l'Islam medieval: Nouvelles perspectives de recherche*, Cairo, 1991, 43–64.

'History, geography and numismatics in the first century of Islamic coinage', *Revue Suisse de Numismatique* 65 (1986), 231–61.

Becker, C. H., 'Studien zur Omajjadengeschichte. A) ʿOmar II', *Zeitschrift für Assyriologie*, 15 (1900), 1–36.

Bell, H. I., 'The administration of Egypt under the Umayyad khalifs', *Byzantinische Zeitschrift*, 28 (1928), 278–86.

Blankinship, Khalid Yahya, *The end of the jihād state: The reign of Hishām Ibn ʿAbd al-Malik and the collapse of the Umayyads*, Albany, 1994.

Bligh-Abramski, Irit, 'Evolution vs. revolution: Umayyad elements in the ʿAbbāsid regime 133/75–32–932', *Der Islam*, 65 (1988), 226–43.

Borrut, Antoine, 'Entre tradition et histoire: Genèse et diffusion de l'image de ʿUmar b. ʿAbd al-ʿAzīz', *Mélanges de l'Université Saint-Joseph*, 58 (2005), 329–78.

Bosworth, C. E., 'Rajāʾ b. Ḥaywa al-Kindī and the Umayyad caliphs', *Islamic Quarterly*, 15 (1971), 69–85.

Sīstān under the Arabs, from the Islamic conquest to the rise of the Ṣaffārids (30–250/651–864), Rome, 1968.

Brett, Michael, 'The Arab conquest and the rise of Islam in North Africa', in J. D. Fage and Roland Oliver (eds.), *The Cambridge history of Africa*, 8 vols., Cambridge, 1978, vol. II: *From c. 500 BC to AD 1050*, 490–555.

Brooks, E. W., 'The Arabs in Asia Minor 641–750, from Arabic sources', *Journal of Hellenic Studies*, 18 (1898), 182–208.

Brunschvig, Robert, 'Ibn Abd al-H'akam et la conquête de l'Afrique du Nord par les Arabes: Etude critique', *Annales de l'Institut des Études Orientales* (Algiers), 6 (1942–7), 108–55.

Canard, Marius, 'Les expéditions des Arabes contre Constantinople dans l'histoire et dans la légende', *JA*, 208 (1926), 61–121.

Chalmeta, Pedro, *Invasión e islamización: La sumisión de Hispania y la formación de al-Andalus*, Madrid, 1994.

Chavannes, Eduard, *Documents sur les Tou-Kiue (Turcs) occidentaux*, St Petersburg, 1903.

Collins, Roger, *The Arab conquest of Spain, 710–797*, Oxford, 1989.

Conrad, Gerhard, *Die Quḍāt Dimasq und der Madhab al-Auzāʿī: Materialen zur syrischen Rechtsgeschichte*, Beirut, 1994.

Conrad, Lawrence I., 'The quṣūr of medieval Islam: Some implications for the social history of the Near East', *al-Abḥāth*, 29 (1981), 7–23.

Crone, Patricia, *God's rule: Government and Islam: Six centuries of medieval Islamic political thought*, New York, 2004.

'On the meaning of the ʿAbbāsid call to al-Riḍā', in C. E. Bosworth *et al.* (eds.), *The Islamic world from classical to modern times: Essays in honor of Bernard Lewis*, Princeton, 1989, 95–111.

'Were the Qays and Yemen of the Umayyad period political parties?', *Der Islam*, 71 (1994), 1–57.

Daniel, Elton, 'The anonymous history of the Abbasid family and its place in Islamic historiography', *IJMES*, 14 (1982), 419–34.

Décobert, Christian, 'L'autorité religieuse aux premiers siècles de l'islam', *Archives de Sciences Sociales des Religions*, 125 (2004), 23–44.

Le mendiant et le combattant: L'institution de l'islam, Paris, 1991.

Derenk, Dieter, *Leben und Dichtung des Omaiyadenkalifen al-Walīd ibn Yazīd*, Freiburg im Breisgau, 1974.

Djaït, Hicham, 'Le Wilaya d'Ifriqiya au IIe/VIIIe siècle', SI, 27 (1967), 88–94.

Donner, Fred M., *Narratives of Islamic origins: The beginnings of Islamic historical writing*, Princeton, 1998.

Dunlop, D. M., *A history of the Jewish Khazars*, New York, 1954.

al-Dūrī, ʿAbd al-ʿAzīz, 'al-Fikra al-mahdiyya bayna al-daʿwa al-ʿabbāsiyya wa-al-ʿaṣr al-ʿabbāsī al-awwal', in W. al-Qāḍī (ed.), *Studia arabica et islamica: Festschrift for Iḥsān ʿAbbās*, Beirut, 1981, 123–32.

Eisener, Reinhard, *Zwischen Faktum und Fiktion: Eine Studie zum Umayyadenkalifen Sulaiman b. ʿAbdalmalik und seinem Bild in den Quellen*, Wiesbaden, 1987.

Elad, Amikam, 'Aspects of the transition from the Umayyad to the ʿAbbāsid caliphate', *JSAI*, 19 (1995), 89–132.

van Ess, Josef, 'Les Qadarites et la Gailaniyya de Yazīd III', *SI*, 31 (1970), 269–86.

Foote, Rebecca M., 'Commerce, industrial expansion, and orthogonal planning: Mutually compatible terms in settlements of Bilad al-Sham during the Umayyad period', *Mediterranean Archaeology*, 13 (2000), 25–38.

Fowden, Garth, *Quṣayr ʿAmra: Art and the Umayyad elite in Late Antique Syria*, Berkeley, 2004.

Frantz-Murphy, Gladys, *The agrarian administration of Egypt from the Arabs to the Ottomans*, Cairo, 1986.

Gabrieli, Francesco, *Il Califatto di Hishām: Studi di storia omayyade*, Mémoires de la Société Royale d'Archéologie d'Alexandrie 7, Alexandria, 1935.

'Muḥammad ibn Qāsim ath-Thaqafī and the Arab conquest of Sind', *East and West*, n.s., 15 (1964–5), 281–95.

'al-Walīd b. Yazīd, il califfo e il poeta', *RSO*, 15 (1935), 1–64.

Gaube, Heinz, 'Die syrischen Wüstenschlösser: Einige wirtschaftliche und politische Gesichtspunkte zu ehrer Entstehung', *Zeitschrift der Deutschen Palästina-Vereins*, 95 (1979), 182–209.

Genequand, Denis, 'Implantations umayyades de Syrie et de Jordanie', in *SLSA-Jahresbericht 2001*, Zürich, 2001, 131–61, and *SLSA-Jahresbericht 2002*, Zürich, 2003, 31–68.

'Rapport préliminaire de la campagne de fouille 2002 à Qasr al-Hayr al-Sharqi (Syrie)', in *SLSA-Jahresbericht 2002*, Zurich, 2003, 69–96.

'Rapport préliminaire de la campagne de fouille 2003 à Qasr al-Hayr al-Sharqi et al-Bakhrāʾ (Syrie)', in *SLSA-Jahresbericht 2003*, Zurich, 2004, 69–98.

Gibb, H. A. R., 'Arab–Byzantine relations under the Umayyad caliphate', *Dumbarton Oaks Papers*, 12 (1958), 219–33.

The Arab conquests in Central Asia, London and New York, 1923.

'Chinese records of the Arabs in Central Asia', *BSOAS*, 2 (1922), 613–22.

Golden, Peter B., *Khazar studies: An historico-philosophical inquiry into the origins of the Khazars*, 2 vols., Budapest, 1980.

Grabar, Oleg, R. Holod, J. Knustad and W. Trousdale, *City in the desert: Qasr al-Hayr East*, 2 vols., Cambridge, MA, 1978.

Griffith, Sidney H., 'Images, Islam and Christian icons', in Pierre Canivet and Jean-Paul Rey-Coquais (eds.), *La Syrie de Byzance à l'Islam, VIIe–VIIIe siècles*, Damascus, 1992, 121–38.

Grousset, René, *Histoire de l'Arménie des origins à 1071*, Paris, 1947.

Guichard, Pierre, 'Les Arabes ont bien envahi l'Espagne: Les structures sociales de l'Espagne musulmane', *Annales*, 29 (1974), 1483–513.

Guilland, Rodolphe, 'L'expédition de Maslama contre Constantinople (717–718)', *Revue des études byzantines*, 17 (1959), 109–33.

Hamilton, Robert, *Walid and his friends: An Umayyad tragedy*, Oxford Studies in Islamic Art 6, Oxford, 1988.

Hillenbrand, Robert, 'La dolce vita in early Islamic Syria: The evidence of later Umayyad palaces', *Art History*, 5 (1982), 1–35.

Humphreys, R. Stephen , *Islamic history: A framework for inquiry*, rev. edn, Princeton, 1991.

Judd, Steven C., 'Ghaylān al-Dimashqī: The isolation of a heretic in Islamic heresiography', *IJMES*, 31 (1999), 161–84.

'Narratives and character development: al-Ṭabarī and al-Balādhurī on late Umayyad history', in Sebastian Guenther (ed.), *Ideas, images, and methods of portrayal: Insights into classical Arabic literature and Islam*, Leiden, 2005, 209–27.

Jun-yan, Zhang, 'Relations between China and the Arabs in early times', *Journal of Oman Studies*, 6 (1983), 91–109.

Kennedy, Hugh, 'Byzantine–Arab diplomacy in the Near East from the Islamic conquests to the mid eleventh century', in J. Shepard and S. Franklin (eds.), *Papers from the Twenty-fourth Spring Symposium of Byzantine Studies*, Aldershot, 1992, 133–43.

The early Abbasid caliphate: A political history, London, 1981.

'Egypt as a province in the Islamic caliphate, 641–868', in C. F. Petry (ed.), *The Cambridge history of Egypt*, vol. I: *Islamic Egypt, 640–1517*, Cambridge, 1998, 62–85.

'Elite incomes in the early Islamic state', in John Haldon and L. I. Conrad (eds.), *The Byzantine and early Islamic Near East*, vol. VI: *Elites old and new in the Byzantine and early Islamic Near East*, Princeton, 2004, 13–28.

Muslim Spain and Portugal: A political history of al-Andalus, London, 1996.

King, G. R. D., 'The distribution of sites and routes in the Jordanian and Syrian deserts in the early Islamic period', *Proceedings of the Seminar for Arabian Studies*, 17 (1987), 91–105.

Lapidus, Ira M., 'Arab settlement and economic development of Iraq and Iran in the age of the Umayyad and early Abbasid caliphs', in A. L. Udovitch (ed.), *The Islamic Middle East, 700–1900: Studies in economic and social history*, Princeton, 1981, 177–208.

Lassner, Jacob, *Islamic revolution and historical memory: An inquiry into the art of ʿAbbāsid apologetics*, New Haven, 1986.

Laurent, Joseph, *L'Arménie entre Byzance et l'Islam depuis la conquête arabe jusqu'en 886*, rev. Marius Canard, Paris, 1980.

Lévi-Provençal, Evariste, *Histoire de l'Espagne musulmane*, 3 vols., Leiden, 1950–3.

Maclean, Derryl N., *Religion and society in Arab Sind*, Leiden, 1989.

Martin-Hisard, B., 'Les Arabes en Géorgie occidentale au VIIIe siècle: Étude sur l'idéologie politique Géorgienne', *Bedi Kartlisa*, 40 (1982), 105–38.

Morimoto, K., *The fiscal administration of Egypt in the early Islamic period*, Kyoto, 1981.

Morony, Michael G., 'Economic boundaries? Late Antiquity and early Islam', *JESHO*, 47 (2004), 166–94.

(ed.), *Manufacturing and labour*, Aldershot, 2003.

(ed.), *Production and the exploitation of resources*, The Formation of the Classical Islamic World 11, Princeton and Aldershot, 2002.

Nagel, Tilman, *Untersuchungen zur Entstehung des abbasidischen Kalifates*, Bonn, 1972.

Northedge, Alastair, 'Archaeology and new urban settlement patterns in early Islamic Syria and Iraq', in G. R. D. King and Averil Cameron (eds.), *The Byzantine and early Islamic Near East*, vol. II: *Land use and settlement patterns*, Princeton, 1994, 231–65.

de Prémare, Alfred-Louis. 'Wahb b. Munabbih, une figure singulière du premier islam', *Annales HSS* (2005), 531–49.

āl-Qāḍī, Wadād, 'The development of the term *ghulāt* in Muslim literature with special reference to the Kaysāniyya', in A. Dietrich (ed.), *Akten des VII. Kongresses für Arabistik und Islamwissenschaft*, Göttingen, 1976, 295–319.

'The religious foundation of late Umayyad ideology and practice', in *Saber religioso y poder político en el Islam: Actas del simposio internacional (Granada, 15–18 octubre 1991)*, Madrid, 1994, 231–73.

Qedar, Shraga, 'Copper coinage of Syria in the seventh and eighth century AD', *Israel Numismatic Journal*, 10 (1988–9), 27–39.

Ragib, Yusuf, 'Lettres nouvelles de Qurra ibn Šarīk', *JNES*, 49 (1981), 173–88.

Robinson, Chase F., *Empire and elites after the Muslim conquest: The transformation of northern Mesopotamia*, Cambridge Studies in Islamic Civilization, Cambridge, 2000.

Sauvaget, Jean, 'Châteaux umayyades de Syrie: Contribution à l'étude de la colonisation arabe aux Ier et IIe siècles de l'Hégire', *REI*, 35 (1967), 1–52.

Savage, Elizabeth, *A gateway to hell, a gateway to paradise: The North African response to the Arab conquest*, Princeton, 1997.

Sénac, Philippe, *Musulmans et Sarrazins dans le Sud de la Gaule du VIIIe au XIe siècle*, Paris, 1980.

Shaban, M. A., *The ʿAbbasid revolution*, Cambridge, 1970.

Islamic history: A new interpretation, 2 vols., Cambridge, 1971–6.

Sharon, Moshe, *Black banners from the east*, Jerusalem, 1983.

Revolt: The social and military aspects of the ʿAbbāsid revolution, Jerusalem, 1990.

Sijpesteijn, Petra M., 'Shaping a Muslim state: Papyri related to a mid-eighth-century Egyptian official', Ph.D. thesis, Princeton University, 2004.

'Travel and trade on the river', in P. Sijpesteijn and L. Sundelin (eds.), *Papyrology and the history of early Islamic Egypt*, Leiden, 2004, 115–52.

Spellberg, Denise A., 'The Umayyad north: Numismatic evidence for frontier administration', *American Numismatic Society Museum Notes*, 33 (1988), 119–27.

Suermann, H., 'Notes concernant l'apocalypse copte de Daniel et la chute des Omayyades', *Parole de l'Orient*, 11 (1983), 329–48.

Taha, ʿAbdulwahid Dhanun, *The Muslim conquest and settlement of North Africa and Spain*, London, 1989.

Tucker, William F., 'ʿAbd Allāh b. Muʿāwīya and the Janāḥiyya: Rebels and ideologues of the late Umayyad period', *SI*, 51 (1980), 39–57.

'Abū Manṣūr al-ʿIjlī and the Manṣūriyya: A study in medieval terrorism', *Der Islam*, 54 (1977), 66–76.

'Bayān ibn Samʿān and the Bayāniyya: Shīʿite extremists of Umayyad Iraq', *MW*, 65 (1975), 241–53.

'Rebels and gnostics: al-Mugīra Ibn Saʿīd and the Mugīriyya', *Arabica*, 22 (1975), 33–47.

Tūqān, Fawwāz, *al-Ḥāʾir: Baḥth fī al-quṣūr al-umawiyya fī al-bādiya*, Amman, 1979.

Vilá Hernández, Salvador, 'El nombramiento de los wālīes de al-Andalus', *al-Andalus*, 4 (1936–9), 215–20.

Walker, John, *A catalogue of the Muhammadan coins in the British Museum*, vol. I: *A catalogue of the Arab-Sassanian coins*, London, 1941; vol. II: *A catalogue of the Arab-Byzantine and post-reform Umaiyad coins*, London, 1956.

Walmsley, Alan, 'Production, exchange and regional trade in the Islamic east Mediterranean: Old structures, new systems?', in Inge Lyse Hansen and Chris Wickham (eds.), *The long eighth century*, Leiden, 2000, 265–344.

Wellhausen, Julius, *Das arabische Reich und sein Sturz*, Berlin, 1902; trans. M. G. Weir as *The Arab kingdom and its fall*, Calcutta, 1927.

Die religiös-politischen Oppositionsparteien im alten Islam, Berlin, 1901; trans. R. C. Ostle as *The religio-political factions in early Islam*, Amsterdam, 1975.

Wickham, Chris, *Framing the early Middle Ages: Europe and the Mediterranean, 400–800*, Oxford, 2005.

Chapter 7: The empire in Iraq, 763–861

Practical suggestions for further reading

Abbott, Nabia, *Two queens of Baghdad*, Chicago, 1946.

Abun-Nasr, Jamil, *A history of the Maghrib in the Islamic period*, Cambridge, 1987.

Collins, Roger, *Early Medieval Spain: Unity in diversity, 400–1000*, New York, 1983.

Daniel, E., *The political and social history of Khurasan under Abbasid rule, 747–820*, Minneapolis and Chicago, 1979.

Elad, A. 'Aspects of the transition from the Umayyad to the ʿAbbāsid caliphate', *JSAI*, 19 (1995), 89–128.

El-Hibri, Tayeb, *Reinterpreting Islamic historiography: Hārūn al-Rashīd and the narrative of the ʿAbbāsid caliphate*, Cambridge, 1999.

Kennedy, H., *The Prophet and the age of the caliphates*, London, 1986.

Lassner, J., *The shaping of ʿAbbāsid rule*, Princeton, 1980.

Le Strange, G., *The lands of the eastern caliphate: Mesopotamia, Persia, and Central Asia from the Moslem conquest to the time of Timur*, Cambridge, 1905.

Meinecke, Michael, 'al-Raḳḳa', *EI2*, vol. VIII, 410–14.

Nawas, John, 'A reexamination of three current explanations for al-Ma'mūn's introduction of the miḥna', *IJMES*, 26 (1994), 615–29.

Northedge, Alastair, 'The palaces of the ʿAbbāsids at Samarra', in C. F. Robinson (ed.), *A medieval Islamic city reconsidered: An interdisciplinary approach to Samarra*, Oxford Studies in Islamic Art 14, Oxford, 2001, 24–67.

Rogers, J. M., 'Samarra: A study in medieval town-planning', in A. Hourani and S. M. Stern (eds.), *The Islamic city: A colloquium*, Oxford, 1970, 119–55.

Watt, M., *The formative period of Islamic thought*, Edinburgh, 1973.

Wendell, C., 'Baghdad: *Imago Mundi* and other foundation-lore', *IJMES*, 2 (1971), 99–128.

Primary sources

al-Baghdādī, Abū Bakr Aḥmad ibn ʿAlī al-Khaṭīb, *Ta'rīkh Baghdād*, 14 vols., Cairo, 1931.

Balādhurī, Aḥmad ibn Yaḥyā, *Futūḥ al-buldān*, ed. S. al-Munajjid, 3 vols., Cairo, 1957.

Ibn ʿAbd Rabbihi, Abū ʿUmar Aḥmad ibn Muḥammad, *Kitāb al-ʿiqd al-farīd*, ed. Ahmad Amin *et al.*, 8 vols., Cairo, 1940–53.

Ibn Abī Ṭāhir Ṭayfūr, Abū'l-Faḍl Aḥmad ibn Ṭāhir, *Kitāb Baghdād*, Baghdad, 1968.

Ibn al-Athīr, ʿIzz al-Dīn ʿAlī ibn Aḥmad, *al-Kāmil fī'l-ta'rīkh*, 13 vols., Beirut, 1965–7.

Ibn al-Muqaffaʿ, *Athār Ibn al-Muqaffaʿ*, ed. ʿUmar Abu'l-Nasr, Beirut, 1966.

al-Jahshiyārī, Muḥammad ibn ʿAbdūs, *Kitāb al-wuzarā' wa'l-kuttāb*, ed. M. al-Saqqa *et al.*, Cairo, 1938.

al-Kindī, Muḥammad ibn Yūsuf, *Wulāt Miṣr*, ed. H. Nassar, Beirut, 1959.

al-Masʿūdī, ʿAlī ibn al-Ḥusayn, *Murūj al-dhahab*, ed. C. Pellat, Beirut, 1973 (the relevant sections for the early ʿAbbāsid caliphate are available in an English translation by P. Lunde and C. Stone, *Meadows of gold*, London, 1989).

al-Ṭabarī, Abū Jaʿfar Muḥammad ibn Jarīr, *Ta'rīkh al-rusul wa'l-mulūk*, ed. M. J. de Goeje, 15 vols. in 3 series, Leiden, 1879–1901 (al-Ṭabarī's work has been translated into English in a well-known multi-volume project entitled *The history of al-Ṭabarī*, Albany, 1985–99.

The relevant sections for ʿAbbāsid history for the period 763–861 are available in vols. XXVIII–XXXIV).
al-Yaʿqūbī, Aḥmad ibn Abī Yaʿqūb, *Kitāb al-buldān*, ed. M. J. de Goeje, Leiden 1892.
Ta'rīkh al-Yaʿqūbī, 2 vols., Beirut, 1960.

Secondary sources

Bakhit, M. A., and R. Schick (eds.), *Bilad al-Sham during the ʿAbbasid period, 132 AH/750 AD–451 AH/1059 AD: Proceedings of the Fifth International Conference on the history of Bilad al-Sham*, 2 vols., English and French section Amman, 1991; Arabic section Amman, 1992.
Beckwith, C. I., 'Aspects of the early history of the Central Asian guard corps in Islam', *Archivum Eurasiae Medii Aevi*, 4 (1984), 29–43.
Bligh-Abramski, I., 'Evolution vs. revolution: Umayyad elements in the ʿAbbāsid regime 133/75–32–932', *Der Islam*, 65 (1988), 226–43.
Bonner, Michael, 'Some observations concerning the early development of jihād on the Arab–Byzantine frontier', *SI*, 75 (1992), 5–31.
*Bosworth, C. E., 'The Ṭāhirids and Arabic culture', *JSS*, 14 (1969), pp. 45–79.
'The Ṭāhirids and Persian literature', *Iran*, 7 (1969), pp. 103–6.
Buckler, F. W., *Harunu'l-Rashid and Charles the Great*, Cambridge, MA, 1931.
Canfield, Robert (ed.), *Turko-Persia in historical perspective*, Cambridge, 1991.
Cooperson, Michael, *Classical Arabic biography: The heirs of the Prophet in the age of al-Ma'mūn*, Cambridge, 2000.
Crone, P., *Slaves on horses*, Cambridge, 1980.
al-Duri, ʿAbd al-ʿAziz, *al-ʿAṣr al-ʿAbbāsī al-awwal*, Baghdad, 1945.
El-Hibri, Tayeb, 'Coinage reform under the ʿAbbāsid caliph al-Ma'mūn', *JESHO*, 36 (1993), 58–83.
'Harun al-Rashid and the Mecca Protocol of 802: A plan for division or succession', *IJMES*, 24 (1992), 461–80.
Gordon, Matthew, *The breaking of a thousand swords: A history of the Turkish military community of Samarra (AH 200–275/815–889 CE)*, Albany, 2001.
Ismaʿil, O. S., 'Muʿtaṣim and the Turks', *BSOAS*, 29 (1966), 12–24.
Katibi, Ghayda, *al-Kharāj, mundhu al-fatḥ al-Islāmī ilā awāsiṭ al-qarn al-thālith al-hijrī*, Beirut, 1997.
Kennedy, H., *The early Abbasid caliphate: A political history*, London, 1981.
Kimber, R. A., 'The early ʿAbbāsid vizierate', *JSS*, 37 (1992), 65–85.
Lassner, J., *Islamic revolution and historical memory: An inquiry into the art of ʿAbbāsid apologetic*, American Oriental Society Series 66, New Haven, 1986.
The topography of Baghdad in the early Middle Ages, Detroit, 1970.
Le Strange, G., *Baghdad during the ʿAbbāsid caliphate from the contemporary Arabic and Persian sources*, Oxford, 1900.
Palestine under the Moslems: A description of Syria and the Holy Land from AD 650 to 1500, London, 1890.
Lewis, B., 'The regnal titles of the first ʿAbbāsid caliphs', in Tara Chand (ed.), *Dr Zakir Husain presentation volume*, New Delhi, 1968, 13–22.
Miah, S., *The reign of al-Mutawakkil*, Dacca, 1969.

Morony, Michael, 'Landholding and social change: Lower al-ʿIrāq in the early Islamic period', in Tarif Khalidi (ed.), *Land tenure and social transformation in the Middle East*, Beirut, 1984, 209–22.

Noonan, Thomas, 'The ʿAbbāsid mint output', *JESHO*, 29 (1986), 113–64.

Northedge, Alastair, 'Archaeology and new urban settlement patterns in early Islamic Syria and Iraq', in G. R. D. King and A. Cameron (eds.), *The Byzantine and early Islamic Near East*, vol. II: *Land use and settlement patterns*, Princeton, 1994, 231–65.

The historical topography of Samarra, Samarra Studies 1, British Academy Monographs in Archaeology / British School of Archaeology in Iraq, London, 2005.

Omar, F., *The ʿAbbāsid caliphate*, Baghdad, 1969.

Radtke, B., 'Toward a typology of ʿAbbāsid universal chronicles', *Occasional Papers of the School of ʿAbbāsid Studies*, 3 (1990), 1–18.

Sourdel, D., *Le vizirat abbaside de 749 à 936*, 2 vols., Damascus, 1959–60.

Talbi, Mohamed, *L'émirat aghlabide (184–296/800–909): Histoire politique*, Paris, 1966.

Yunus, Ahmad, *Taṭawwur anẓimat istithmār al-arāḍī al-zirāʿiyya fī'l-ʿaṣr al-ʿAbbāsī*, Beirut, 1986.

Zaman, Muhammad Q., *Religion and politics under the early ʿAbbāsids: The emergence of the proto-Sunnī elite*, Leiden, 1997.

Chapter 8: The waning of empire, 861–945

Practical suggestions for further reading

Bianquis, Thierry, 'Autonomous Egypt from Ibn Ṭūlūn to Kāfūr, 868–969', in Carl F. Petry (ed.), *The Cambridge history of Egypt*, vol. I: *Islamic Egypt, 640–1517*, Cambridge, 1998, 86–119.

Bosworth, C. E., *The history of the Ṣaffārids of Sīstān and the Maliks of Nimrūz (247/861 to 949/1542)*, Costa Mesa and New York, 1994.

Bowen, H., *The life and times of ʿAlī b. ʿĪsā, the 'Good Vizier'*, Cambridge, 1928.

Brett, Michael, *The rise of the Fatimids: The world of the Mediterranean and the Middle East in the fourth century of the hijra, tenth century CE*, Leiden, 2001.

Frye, Richard N., *The golden age of Persia: The Arabs in the east*, London, 1975.

'The Samanids', in R. N. Frye (ed.), *The Cambridge history of Iran*, vol. IV: *The period from the Arab invasion to the Saljuqs*, Cambridge, 1975, 136–61.

Gordon, Matthew, *The breaking of a thousand swords: A history of the Turkish military community of Samarra (AH 200–275 – 815–899 CE)*, Albany, 2001.

Halm, Heinz, *The empire of the Mahdi: The rise of the Fatimids*, trans. Michael Bonner, Leiden, 1996.

Madelung, W., 'The minor dynasties of northern Iran', in R. N. Frye (ed.), *The Cambridge history of Iran*, vol. IV: *The period from the Arab invasion to the Saljuqs*, Cambridge, 1975, 198–249.

Melchert, Christopher, 'Religious policies of the caliphs from al-Mutawakkil to al-Muqtadir, AH 232–295 / AD 847–908', *Islamic Law and Society*, 3 (1996), 316–42.

Mottahedeh, R. P., 'The ʿAbbāsid caliphate in Iran', in R. N. Frye (ed.), *The Cambridge history of Iran*, vol. IV: *The period from the Arab invasion to the Saljuqs*, Cambridge, 1975, 57–89.

Loyalty and leadership in an early Islamic society, Princeton, 1980; repr. 2001.
Paul, Jürgen, *The state and the military: The Samanid case*, Papers on Inner Asia 26, Bloomington, 1994.
Popovic, A., *The revolt of African slaves in the 3rd/9th century*, Princeton, 1998.
Tor, Deborah G., *Violent order: Religious warfare, chivalry, and the ʿAyyār phenomenon in the medieval Islamic world*, Istanbuler Texte und Studien 11, Würzburg, 2007.
Walker, Paul, 'The Ismāʿīlī daʿwa and the Fatimid caliphate', in Carl F. Petry (ed.), *The Cambridge history of Egypt*, vol. I: *Islamic Egypt, 640–1517*, Cambridge, 1998, 120–50.

Primary sources

Abū Bakr al-Mālikī, *Riyāḍ al-nufūs*, 3 vols., Beirut, 1981.
Anon., *Tārīkh-i Sīstān*, ed. Malik al-Shuʿarāʾ Bahār, Tehran, 1935; trans. Milton Gold as *Literary and historical texts from Iran*, vol. II, Rome, 1976.
ʿArīb ibn Saʿd al-Kātib al-Qurṭubī, *Ṣilat Taʾrīkh al-Ṭabarī*, Leiden, 1897.
al-Balawī, ʿAbdallāh ibn Muḥammad, *Sīrat Aḥmad ibn Ṭūlūn*, Damascus, 1939.
al-Hamadhānī, Muḥammad ibn ʿAbd al-Malik, *Takmilat Taʾrīkh al-Ṭabarī*, Leiden, 1897.
Hilāl ibn al-Muḥassin al-Ṣābī, *Rusūm dār al-khilāfa*, Beirut, 1964; repr. Beirut, 1986.
Tuḥfat al-umarāʾ fi taʾrīkh al-wuzarāʾ, Cairo, 1958.
Ibn al-Athīr, ʿIzz al-Dīn, *al-Kāmil fī l-taʾrīkh*, Beirut, 1418/1998.
Ibn Ḥawqal, *Ṣūrat al-arḍ*, Leiden, 1938.
Ibn Khurradādhbih, Abū l-Qasim ʿUbaydallāh, *al-Masālik wal-mamālik*, Leiden, 1889.
al-Iṣṭakhri, Abū Isḥāq Ibrāhīm, *Kitāb al-masālik wal-mamālik*, Leiden, 1870.
al-Khaṭīb al-Baghdādī, Abū Bakr Aḥmad, *Taʾrīkh Baghdād*, 14 vols., Cairo, 1931.
al-Maqrīzī, Aḥmad ibn ʿAlī, *Ittiʿāẓ al-ḥunafāʾ bi-akhbār al-aʾimma al-fāṭimiyyīn al-khulafāʾ*, Cairo, 1967.
al-Masʿūdī, ʿAlī ibn al-Ḥusayn, *Kitāb al-tanbīh wal-ishrāf*, Leiden, 1894.
Murūj al-dhahab wa-maʿādin al-jawhar, 5 vols., Beirut, 1966–74.
Miskawayh, Abū ʿAlī al-Rāzī, *Tajārib al-umam*, ed. A. Emami, Tehran, 2001; partial ed. and trans. H. F. Amedroz and D. S. Margoliouth in *The eclipse of the ʿAbbasid caliphate: Original chronicles of the fourth Islamic century*, vols. I–II, IV–V, London, 1921.
Nuʿaym ibn Ḥammād, *Kitāb al-fitan*, Beirut, 1993.
al-Qāḍī al-Nuʿmān, *Iftitāḥ al-dawla wa-ibtidāʾ al-daʿwa*, ed. W. al-Qāḍī, Beirut, 1970; ed. F. Dachraoui [Dashrāwī], Tunis, 1975.
al-Majālis wal-musāyarāt, Tunis, 1978.
Qudāma ibn Jaʿfar, *Kitāb al-kharāj wa-ṣināʿat al-kitāba*, ed. M. H. al-Zubaydi, Baghdad, 1981.
Sibt Ibn al-Jawzī, Mirʾāt al-zamān, British Museum, OR 4169.
al-Ṣūlī, Abū Bakr Muḥammad al-Shaṭranjī, *Akhbār al-Rāḍī wal-Muttaqī*, London, 1935, trans. Marius Canard as *Histoire de la dynastie abbaside de 322 à 333/933 à 944*, 2 vols., Algiers, 1950.
al-Ṭabarī, Abū Jaʿfar Muḥammad ibn Jarīr, *Taʾrīkh al-rusul wal-mulūk*, ed. M. J. de Goeje *et al.*, 15 vols. in 3 series, Leiden, 1879–1901; trans. as *The history of al-Ṭabarī*, 39 vols., Albany, 1985–99: see vol. XXXIV, trans. Joel L. Kraemer as *Incipient decline*, Albany, 1989; vol. XXXV, trans. George Saliba as *The crisis of the ʿAbbāsid caliphate*, Albany, 1985; vol. XXXVI, trans. David Waines as *The revolt of the Zanj*, Albany, 1992; vol. XXXVII, trans. Philip M. Fields as *The ʿAbbāsid recovery*, Albany, 1987; vol. XXXVIII, trans. Franz Rosenthal as *The return of the caliphate to Baghdad*, Albany, 1985.

al-Yaʿqūbī, Aḥmad ibn Abī Yaʿqūb ibn Wāḍiḥ, *Kitāb al-buldān*, Leiden, 1892.
Taʾrīkh, Leiden, 1883.

Secondary sources

Ali, Samer, 'Praise for murder? Two odes by al-Buḥturī surrounding an ʿAbbasid patricide', in Beatrice Gruendler and Louise Marlow (eds.), *Writers and rulers*, Wiesbaden, 2004, 1–38.

Bacharach, J., 'The career of Muḥammad ibn Ṭughj al-Ikhshīd', *Speculum*, 50 (1975), 586–612.

Bonner, Michael, *Jihad in Islamic history: Doctrines and practices*, Princeton, 2006.

'al-Khalīfa al-Marḍī: The accession of Hārūn al-Rashīd', *JAOS*, 109, 1 (1988), 79–91.

Bosworth, C. E., 'The armies of the Ṣaffārids', *BSOAS*, 31 (1968), 534–54.

The new Islamic dynasties: A chronological and genealogical manual, New York, 1996.

'Ṣanawbarī's elegy on the pilgrims slain in the Carmathian attack on Mecca (317/930): A literary-historical study', *Arabica*, 19, 3 (1972), 222–39.

'The Ṭāhirids and Arabic culture', *JSS*, 14 (1969), 45–79.

'The Ṭāhirids and Ṣaffārids', in R. N. Frye (ed.), *The Cambridge history of Iran*, vol. IV: *The period from the Arab invasion to the Saljuqs*, Cambridge, 1975, 90–135.

Bray, Julia, 'Samarra in ninth-century Arabic letters', in Chase F. Robinson (ed.), *A medieval Islamic city reconsidered: An interdisciplinary approach to Samarra*, Oxford Studies in Islamic Art 14, Oxford, 2001, 21–8.

Brett, Michael, 'The Mīm, the ʿAyn, and the making of Ismāʿīlism', *BSOAS*, 57 (1994), 24–39; repr. in Michael Brett, *Ibn Khaldūn and the medieval Maghrib*, Aldershot, 1999.

'The way of the peasant', *BSOAS*, 47, 1 (1984), 44–56.

Bulliett, Richard, *Conversion to Islam in the medieval period: An essay in quantitative history*, Cambridge, MA, 1979.

Busse, H., 'Das Hofbudget des Chalifen al-Muʿtaḍid billāh', *Islam*, 43 (1967), 11–36.

Cahen, C., 'L'évolution de l'*iqṭāʿ* du IXe au XIIIe siècle: Contribution à une histoire comparée des sociétés médiévales', in C. Cahen, *Les peuples musulmans dans l'histoire médiévale*, Damascus, 1977, 231–69; first published in *Annales, Economies-Sociétés-Civilisations*, 7 (1953), 25–52.

Mouvements populaires et autonomisme urbain dans l'Asie musulmane du moyen âge, Leiden, 1959.

Canard, M., *Histoire de la dynastie des H'amdanides de Jazira et de Syrie*, Paris, 1953.

Chabbi, Jacqueline, 'Remarques sur le développement historique des mouvements ascétiques et mystiques au Khurasan', *SI*, 46 (1977), 5–72.

Chamberlain, Michael, *Knowledge and social practice in medieval Damascus, 1190–1350*, Cambridge, 1994.

Cobb, Paul, 'al-Mutawakkil's Damascus: A new ʿAbbāsid capital?', *JNES*, 58 (1999), 241–57.

Crone, Patricia, *God's rule: Government and Islam*, New York, 2004.

Crone, Patricia, and Martin Hinds, *God's caliph: Religious authority in the first centuries of Islam*, Cambridge, 1986.

de la Puente, Cristina, 'El Ŷihād en el califato omeya de al-Andalus y su culminación bajo Hišām II', in Fernando Valdés Fernández (ed.), *Almanzor y los terrores del Milenio*, Aguilar de Campoo, 1999, 25–38.

Haarmann, Ulrich (ed.), *Geschichte der arabischen Welt*, Munich, 1987.

Halm, Heinz, *Die Traditionen über den Aufstand ʿAlī Ibn Muḥammads, des 'Herrn der Zanǧ': Eine quellenkritische Untersuchung*, Bonn, 1967.

Kennedy, Hugh, *Muslim Spain and Portugal: A political history of al-Andalus*, London and New York, 1996.

The Prophet and the age of the caliphates, 2nd edn, Harlow, 2004.

Kimber, Richard, 'The succession to the caliph Mūsā al-Hādī', *JAOS*, 121, 3 (2001), 428–48.

Kraemer, Joel L., *Humanism in the Renaissance of Islam: The cultural revival during the Buyid age*, Leiden, 1993.

Lewis, Bernard, *The Arabs in history*, London, 1958.

Massignon, Louis, *The Passion of al-Ḥallāj*, trans. Herbert Mason, 4 vols., Princeton, 1980.

Mez, A., *The renaissance of Islam*, trans. Khuda Bakhsh, London, 1937.

Miles, George, *The numismatic history of Rayy*, New York, 1938.

Minorsky, Vladimir, 'La domination des Dailamites', *Société des Etudes Iraniennes*, 3 (1932), 1–26.

Miquel, André, *La géographie humaine du monde musulman*, 4 vols., Paris and The Hague, 1967–.

Muth, Franz-Christoph, '"Entsetzte" Kalifen: Depositionsverfahren im mittelalterlichen Islam', *Der Islam*, 75 (1998), 104–23.

Paul, Jürgen, *Herrscher, Gemeinwesen, Vermittler: Ostiran und Transoxanien in vormongolischer Zeit*, Beirut and Stuttgart, 1996.

'The histories of Samarqand', *Studia Iranica*, 22 (1993), 69–92.

Robinson, Chase (ed.), *A medieval city reconsidered: An interdisciplinary approach to Samarra*, Oxford Studies in Islamic Art 14, Oxford, 2001.

Rosenthal, Franz, *A history of Muslim historiography*, Leiden, 1968.

Sabari, S., *Mouvements populaires à Bagdad à l'époque ʿAbbaside, IXe–XIe siècles*, Paris, 1981.

Sato, Tsugitaka, 'The iqṭāʿ system of Iraq under the Buwayhids', *Orient*, 18 (1982), 83–105.

State and society in medieval Islam: Sultans, muqṭaʿs and fallāḥūn, Leiden, 1997.

Savage, Elizabeth, *A gateway to hell, a gateway to paradise: The North African response to the Arab conquest*, Princeton, 1997.

Scott-Meisami, Julie, 'The palace-complex as emblem: Some Samarran *qasidas*', in Chase F. Robinson (ed.), *A medieval Islamic city reconsidered: An interdisciplinary approach to Samarra*, Oxford Studies in Islamic Art 14, Oxford, 2001, 69–78.

Sourdel, Dominique, *Le vizirat ʿabbaside de 749 à 936*, 2 vols., Damascus, 1959–60.

Stern, Samuel Miklos, 'Yaʿqūb the Coppersmith and Persian national sentiment', in C. E. Bosworth (ed.), *Iran and Islam, in memory of Vladimir Minorsky*, Edinburgh, 1971, 535–55.

Talbi, Mohamed, *L'émirat aghlabide (184–296/800–909): Histoire politique*, Paris, 1966.

Tor, Deborah G., 'A numismatic history of the first Ṣaffārid dynasty (AH 247–300/AD 861–911)', *Numismatic Chronicle*, 162 (2002), 293–314.

Treadwell, Luke, 'The political history of the Samanid state', D.Phil. thesis, Oxford University, 1991.

Vasiliev, A. A., and Marius Canard, *Byzance et les Arabes*, vol. II, part 1, Brussels, 1968.

Waines, D., 'The third-century internal crisis of the ʿAbbasids', *JESHO*, 20 (1977), 282–306.

Walker, Paul, *Exploring an Islamic empire: Fatimid history and its sources*, London and New York, 2002.

Wansbrough, John, *The sectarian milieu: Content and composition of Islamic salvation history*, Oxford, 1978.
Wittek, Paul, *The rise of the Ottoman empire*, London, 1938.

Chapter 9: The late ʿAbbāsid pattern, 945–1050

Practical suggestions for further reading

Bosworth, C. E., *The Ghaznavids: Their empire in Afghanistan and eastern Iran*, Edinburgh, 1963.
Donohue, John J., *The Buwayhid dynasty in Iraq 334H/945 to 403H/1012: Shaping institutions for the future*, Leiden, 2003.
Frye, R. N., *The golden age of Persia*, London, 1975.
Ibn Miskawayh, *Tajārib al-umam*, ed. and trans. H. Amedroz and D. S. Margoliouth in *The eclipse of the ʿAbbasid caliphate*, 7 vols., London, 1920–1.
Kennedy, Hugh, *The Prophet and the age of the caliphates*, 2nd edn, London, 2004.
Mottahedeh, R., *Loyalty and leadership in an early Islamic society*, 2nd edn, Princeton, 2001.
al-Muqaddasī, *Aḥsan al-taqāsīm*, trans. B. Collins as *The best divisions for the knowledge of the regions*, Reading, 2001.

Primary sources

Ibn al-Athīr, *al-Kāmil fī 'l-taʾrīkh*, ed. C. J. Tornberg, 14 vols., Leiden, 1851–76.
Ibn al-Azraq al-Fāriqī, *Taʾrīkh Mayyāfāriqīn*, ed. B. A. Awad, Cairo, 1959.
Ibn Ḥawqal, *Kitāb ṣūrat al-arḍ*, ed. J. Kraemer, Leiden, 1938.
al-Muqaddasī, *Aḥsan al-taqāsīm*, ed. M. J. de Goeje, Leiden, 1906.
Sibṭ Ibn al-Jawzī, *Mirʾat al-zamān*, ed. J. J. al-Hamawundī, Baghdad, 1990.

Secondary sources

Amedroz, H. F., 'The Marwanid dynasty of Mayyāfāriqīn', *JRAS* (1903), 123–54.
Berthier, S., *Peuplement rural et aménagements hydroagricoles dans la moyenne vallée de l'Euphrate, fin VIIe–XIX siècle*, Damascus, 2001.
Bosworth, C. E., 'Military organization under the Buyids of Persia and Iraq', *Oriens*, 18–19 (1965–6), 143–67.
Bowen, H., 'The last Buwayhids', *JRAS* (1929), 225–45.
Bürgel, J. C., *Die Hofkorrespondenz ʿAḍud ad-Daulas*, Wiesbaden, 1965.
Busse, H., *Chalif und Grosskonig: Die Buyiden im Iraq (945–1055)*, Beirut, 1969.
Cahen, C., 'L'évolution de l'*iqṭāʿ* du IX au XIII siècle: Contribution à une histoire comparée des sociétés médiévales', *Annales, Economies-Sociétés-Civilisations*, 7 (1953), 25–52.
'Mouvements populaires et autonomisme urban dans l'Asie musulmane du moyen âge', *Arabica*, 5 (1958), 225–50; 6 (1959), 25–56, 223–65.
Heidemann, S., *Die Renaissance der Städte in Nordsyrien und Nordmesopotamien: Städtische Entwicklung und wirtschaftliche Bedingungen in ar-Raqqa und Ḥarrān von der Zeit der beduinischen Vorherrschaft bis zu Seldschuken*, Islamic History and Civilization, Studies and Texts 40, Leiden, 2002.
Kennedy, Hugh, *The armies of the caliphs*, London, 2001.

'The decline and fall of the first Muslim empire', *Der Islam*, 81 (2004), 3–30; repr. in H. Kennedy, *The Byzantine and Islamic Near East*, Aldershot, 2006, XIV.

'The Uqaylids of Mosul: The origins and structure of a nomad dynasty', in *Actas del XII Congreso de la UEAI*, Madrid, 1986, 391–402; repr. in H. Kennedy, *The Byzantine and Islamic Near East*, Aldershot, 2006, XIII.

Kraemer, J. L., *Humanism in the renaissance of Islam: The cultural revival of the Buyid age*, Leiden, 1992.

Madelung, W., 'The assumption of the title shāhānshāh by the Būyids and "the reign of the Daylam (*dawlat al-Daylam*)"', *JNES*, 28, (1969), 168–83.

Makdisi, G., *Ibn ʿAqīl et la résurgence de l'Islam traditionaliste au XI siècle*, Damascus, 1962.

'Notes on Ḥilla and the Mazyadids in medieval Islam', *JAOS*, 74 (1954), 249–62.

Mez, A., *The renaissance of Islam*, trans. Khuda Bakhsh, London, 1937; repr. New York, 1975.

Minorsky, V., *La domination des dailamites*, Paris, 1927.

A history of Sharvān and Darband, Cambridge, 1958.

Studies in Caucasian history, London, 1953.

Mottahedeh, R., 'Administration in Būyid Qazwīn', in D. S. Richards (ed.), *Islamic civilisation 950–1150*, Oxford, 1975, 33–45.

Vanly, I. C. 'Le déplacement du pays kurde vers l'ouest', *RSO*, 50 (1976), 353–63.

Waines, D., 'The third century internal crisis of the ʿAbbāsids', *JESHO*, 20 (1977), 282–306.

Zakkar, S., *The emirate of Aleppo 1004–94*, Beirut, 1971.

Chapter 10: Arabia

Practical suggestions for further reading

Casey Vine, P. (ed.), *Oman in history*, London, 1995.

Dresch, P., *Tribes, government and history in Yemen*, Oxford, 1989.

Gochenour, D. T., 'The penetration of Zaydī Islam into early medieval Yemen', Ph.D. thesis, Harvard University, 1984.

al-Juhany, U. M., *Najd before the Salafī reform movement*, Reading and Riyadh, 2002.

al-Madʿaj, ʿAbd al-Muḥsin Madʿaj M., *The Yemen in early Islam 9–233/630–847: A political history*, London, 1988.

Motzki, H., *The origins of Islamic jurisprudence: Meccan fiqh before the classical schools*, Leiden, 2002.

Sayyid, Ayman Fu'ād, *Ta'rīkh al-madhāhib al-dīniyya fī bilād al-Yaman*, Cairo, 1988/1408.

Vidal, F. S., *The oasis of al-Ḥasā*, Dhahran, 1955.

Wilkinson, John C., *The imamate tradition of Oman*, Cambridge, 1987.

Primary sources

ʿAbd al-Razzāq al-Ṣanʿānī, *Muṣannaf ʿAbd al-Razzāq*, ed. Ḥ. al-Aʿẓamī, 11 vols., Beirut, 1403/1983.

Abū Nuʿaym al-Iṣbahānī, *Ḥilyat al-awliyā'*, 10 vols., Beirut, 1405/1985.

al-Ahdal, Ḥusayn ibn ʿAbd al-Raḥmān, *Tuḥfat al-zaman fī ta'rīkh al-Yaman*, ed. ʿA. M. al-Ḥibshī, Beirut, 1407/1986.

ʿAlī ibn Muḥammad ibn ʿUbaydallāh, *Sīrat al-Hādī Yaḥyā b. al-Ḥusayn*, ed. Suhayl Zakkār, Beirut, 1972.

Anonymous, *Ta'rīkh ahl ʿUmān*, ed. S. ʿA. ʿĀshūr, Oman, 1986.
al-Balādhurī, Aḥmad ibn Yaḥyā, *Ansāb al-ashrāf*, vol. V, ed. S. D. Goitein, Jerusalem, 1936.
Futūḥ al-buldān, ed. R. M. Riḍwān, Beirut, 1403/1983.
al-Bukhārī, Muḥammad ibn Ismāʿīl, *al-Ta'rīkh al-kabīr*, ed. H. al-Nadwī, 8 vols., Beirut, n.d.
al-Dhahabī, Muḥammad ibn Aḥmad, *Siyar aʿlām al-nubalā'*, ed. S. al-Arnā'ūṭ and M. N. al-ʿArqasūsī, 23 vols., Beirut, 1413/1993.
al-Fākihī, Muḥammad ibn Isḥāq, *Ta'rīkh Makka: see* Wüstenfeld, *Akhbār Makka*.
al-Fāsī, Muḥammad ibn Aḥmad, *al-ʿIqd al-thamīn fī ta'rīkh al-balad al-amīn*, ed. M. Ḥ. al-Faqī, F. Sayyid and M. M. al-Ṭanāḥī, 8 vols., Cairo, 1378–88/1958–69.
Shifā' al-gharām bi-akhbār al-balad al-ḥarām, vol. II, ed. ʿUmar ʿAbd al-Salām Tadmurī, Beirut, 1405/1985.
al-Zuhūr al-muqtaṭafa min ta'rīkh Makka al-musharrafa, ed. A. M. al-Ghazāwī, Beirut, 2000.
Francesca, E., 'Ṭālib al-Ḥaḳḳ', *EI2* (suppl.), vol. XII, 785.
al-Hamdānī, Ḥasan ibn Aḥmad, *Ṣifat jazīrat al-ʿArab*, ed. M. ibn ʿAlī al-Akwaʿ, Beirut and Ṣanʿā', 1403/1983.
al-Hamdānī, Muḥammad ibn ʿAbd al-Malik, *Takmilat ta'rīkh al-Ṭabarī*, ed. A. Y. Kanʿān, Beirut, 1957.
Ibn ʿAbd al-Barr al-Namarī al-Qurṭubī, Yūsuf ibn ʿAbd Allāh, *al-Istīʿāb fī maʿrifat al-aṣḥāb*, ed. ʿA. M. al-Bījāwī, 4 vols., Beirut, 1992/1412.
Ibn al-Athīr, ʿIzz al-Dīn, *al-Kāmil fī al-ta'rīkh*, 10 vols., Beirut, 1415/1995.
Ibn al-Daybaʿ, ʿAbd al-Raḥmān ibn ʿAlī, *Qurrat al-ʿuyūn bi-akhbār al-Yaman al-maymūn*, ed. M. ibn ʿAlī al-Akwaʿ al-Ḥiwālī, Cairo, n.d.
Ibn Fahd, ʿIzz al-Dīn ʿAbd al-ʿAzīz ibn ʿUmar, *Ghāyat al-murām bi-akhbār salṭanat al-balad al-ḥarām*, vol. I, ed. Fahīm Muḥammad Shaltūt, Mecca, 1406/1986.
Ibn Ḥajar al-ʿAsqalānī, Aḥmad ibn ʿAlī, *al-Iṣāba fī tamyīz al-ṣaḥāba*, ed. A. M. al-Bījāwī, 8 vols., Beirut, 1992/1412.
Ibn Ḥazm, ʿAlī ibn Aḥmad, *Jamharat ansāb al-ʿArab*, ed. ʿA. M. Hārūn, Cairo, 1382/1962.
Ibn al-ʿImād, ʿAbd al-Ḥayy ibn Aḥmad, *Shadharāt al-dhahab fī akhbār man dhahab*, 4 vols., Beirut, n.d.
Ibn Kathīr, Ismāʿīl ibn ʿUmar, *al-Bidāya wa-l-nihāya*, 14 vols., Beirut, n.d.
Ibn Manẓūr, Muḥammad ibn Mukram, *Lisān al-ʿArab*, 15 vols., Beirut, n.d.
Ibn al-Taghribirdī, Yūsuf, *al-Nujūm al-ẓāhira fī mulūk Miṣr wa-l-Qāhira*, 12 vols., Cairo, n.d.
Ibn Ẓahīra, Muḥammad ibn Amīn, *al-Jāmiʿ al-laṭīf fī faḍā'il Makka: see* Wüstenfeld, *Akhbār Makka*.
ʿImad al-Dīn, Idrīs, *ʿUyūn: see* Sayyid, Walker and Pomerantz, *The Fāṭimids and their successors*.
al-Iṣfahānī, Abū al-Faraj, *Maqātil al-Ṭālibiyyīn*, ed. Aḥmad Ṣaqr, Beirut, n.d.
al-Izkiwī, Sirḥān ibn Saʿīd ibn Sirḥān (attrib.), *Annals of Oman to 1728*, trans. and annot. E. C. Ross, Cambridge and New York, 1984.
(attrib.), *Kapitel XXXIII de anonym arabischen Chronik Kasf al-Ghumma al-Gami' li-Akhbār al-Umma*, ed. and trans. Hedwig Klein, Hamburg, 1938.
al-Juddī al-Ḥijāzī, ʿAbd al-Qādir ibn Muḥammad ibn Muḥammad ibn Faraj, *al-Silāḥ wa-l-ʿudda fī ta'rīkh Judda*, ed. M. al-Ḥudrī, Damascus, Beirut and Medina, 1988.
al-Kalāʿī, Sulaymān ibn Mūsā, *al-Iktifā' bi-mā taḍammanahu min maghāzī rasūl allāh wa-l-thalātha al-khulafā'*, ed. M. K. ʿAlī, 4 vols., Beirut, 1417/1997.
Khalīfa ibn Khayyāṭ al-ʿUṣfurī, *Ta'rīkh*, ed. A. Ḍ. al-ʿUmarī, 2 vols., Beirut and Damascus, 1397/1976.

al-Maqrīzī, Taqī al-Dīn Aḥmad ibn ʿAlī, *Ittiʿāẓ al-ḥunafāʾ bi-akhbār al-aʾimma al-Fāṭimiyyīn al-khulafāʾ*, ed. Jamāl al-Dīn al-Shayyāl, Cairo, 1368/1948.

al-Muqaddasī, Shams al-Dīn, *Aḥsan al-taqāsīm fī maʿrifat al-aqālīm*, ed. M. J. de Goeje, Leiden, 1906.

al-Muṭāʿ, A. ibn A., *Taʾrīkh al-Yaman al-Islāmī min sanat arbaʿ wa-miʾatayn ilā sanat alf wa-sitt*, ed. ʿA. M. al-Ḥibshī, Beirut, 1986/1407.

al-Nahrawālī, Quṭb al-Dīn, *al-Iʿlām bi-aʿlām bayt allāh al-ḥarām*: *see* Wüstenfeld, *Akhbār Makka*.

Nāṣer-e Khosraw, *Book of travels (Safarnāma)*, trans. W. M. Thackston Jr., Bibliotheca Persica, Albany, 1986.

al-Rāzī, Aḥmad ibn ʿAbd Allāh, *Taʾrīkh madīnat Ṣanʿāʾ*, ed. Ḥ. ibn ʿAbd Allāh al-ʿAmrī, Ṣanʿāʾ, 1401/1981.

al-Sakhāwī, Shams al-Dīn, *al-Tuḥfa al-laṭīfa fī taʾrīkh al-Madīna al-sharīfa*, 3 vols., Cairo, 1376/1957.

al-Sālimī, Nūr al-Dīn ʿAbd Allāh ibn Ḥumayd, *Tuḥfat al-aʿyān bi-sīrat ahl ʿUmān*, vol. I, Cairo, 1380/1961.

Sayyid, A. F., P. Walker and M. A. Pomerantz, *The Fāṭimids and their successors in Yaman: The history of an Islamic community*, Arabic edn and English summary of Idrīs ʿImād al-Dīn's *ʿUyūn al-akhbār*, vol. VII, London and New York, 2002.

al-Sinjārī, ʿAli ibn Tāj al-Dīn, *Manāʾiḥ al-karam fī akhbār Makka wa-l-bayt wa-wulāt al-ḥaram*, ed. J. ʿA. Muḥammad al-Miṣrī, 6 vols., Mecca, 1419/1998.

al-Ṭabarī, Abū Jaʿfar Muḥammad ibn Jarīr, *Taʾrīkh al-rusul wa-l-mulūk*, ed. M. A. Ibrāhīm, 10 vols., Cairo, 1960.

ʿUmāra al-Yamanī, *al-Mufīd fī akhbār Ṣanʿāʾ wa-Zabīd wa-shuʿarāʾ mulūkihā wa-aʿyānihā wa-udabāʾihā*, ed. Muḥammad b. ʿAli al-Akwaʿ, Ṣanʿāʾ, 1985.

Wüstenfeld, F., *Akhbār Makka al-musharrafa*, 3 vols., Göttingen, 1274/1857.

Yaḥyā ibn al-Ḥusayn, *Ghāyat al-amānī fī akhbār al-quṭr al-yamānī*, ed. S. ʿA. ʿĀshūr and M. M. Ziyāda, Cairo, 1388/1968.

al-Yaʿqūbī, Aḥmad ibn Abī Yaʿqūb, *Taʾrīkh*, 2 vols., Beirut, 1379/1960.

Yāqūt ibn ʿAbd Allāh, *Muʿjam al-buldān*, 5 vols., Beirut, n.d.

Zabāra al-Ḥasanī, Muḥammad ibn Muḥammad, *al-Inbāʾ ʿan dawlat Bilqīs wa-Sabaʾ*, Ṣanʿāʾ, 1404/1984.

Itḥāf al-muhtadīn bi-dhikr al-aʾimma al-mujaddidīn, Ṣanʿāʾ, 1343/1925.

Taʾrīkh al-Zaydiyya, ed. M. Zaynahm, Cairo, n.d.

al-Zubayrī, Muṣʿab ibn ʿAbd Allāh, *Nasab Quraysh*, ed. E. Lévi-Provençal, Cairo, n.d.

Secondary sources

ʿAbd al-Ghanī, ʿA., *Taʾrīkh umarāʾ Makka al-mukarrama*, Damascus, 1413/1992.

Umarā al-Madīna al-munawwara, Damascus, n.d.

al-ʿAlī, S. A., *al-Ḥijāz fī ṣadr al-Islām: dirāsāt fī aḥwālihi al-ʿumrāniyya wa-l-idāriyya*, Beirut, 1410/1990.

'Mulkiyyāt al-arḍ fī al-Ḥijāz fī al-qarn al-awwal al-hijrī', *al-ʿArab*, 3 (1969), 961–1005.

al-ʿĀnī, ʿA. ʿA., *Taʾrīkh ʿUmān fī al-ʿuṣūr al-Islāmiyya al-ūlā*, London, 1420/1999.

van Arendonck, C., *Les débuts de l'imamat zaidite du Yemen*, trans. J. Ryckmans, Leiden, 1960.

Bāshā, Ayyūb Ṣabrī, *Mirʾāt jazīrat al-ʿArab*, trans. A. F. Mutawallī and A. al-Mursī, Cairo, 1419/1999.
Bathurst, R. D., 'Maritime trade and imamate government: Two principal themes in the history of Oman to 1728', in D. Hopwood (ed.), *The Arabian Peninsula: Society and politics*, London, 1972, 89–106.
Bāwazīr, Saʿīd ʿAwaḍ, *Ṣafaḥāt min al-taʾrīkh al-ḥaḍramī*, Aden, n.d.
Canard, M., 'al-Ḥasan al-Aʿṣam',*EI2*, vol. III, 246.
Cook, Michael A., 'The historians of pre-Wahabī Najd', *SI*, 76 (1992), 163–76.
Crone, P., 'Muhallabids', *EI2*, vol. VII, 358.
Dietrich, A., 'al-Djār', *EI2*, vol. II, 454.
Drees, ʿA. ʿA., 'A critical edition of *Taʾrīkh al-Madīna* by al-Shaykh Quṭb al-Dīn', Ph.D. thesis, University of Edinburgh, 1985.
Elad, A., 'The rebellion of Muḥammad b. ʿAbdallāh b. al-Ḥasan (known as al-Nasf al-Zakiyya) in 145/762', in J. E. Montgomery (ed.), *ʿAbbasid studies: Occasional papers of the School of ʿAbbasid Studies, 6–10 July 2002*, Leuven, Paris and Dudley, MA, 2004, 147–98.
Grohman, A., 'Nadjd', *EI2*, vol. VII, 864.
al-Ḥāmid, Ṣāliḥ, *Taʾrīkh Ḥaḍramawt*, Jiddah, 1968.
al-Ḥarīrī, M. ʿI. *Dirāsāt wa-buḥūth fī taʾrīkh al-Yaman al-Islāmī*, Beirut, 1418/1998.
Hartmann, R., and Phebe Ann Marr, 'Djudda', *EI2*, vol. II, 571.
al-Hayla, Muḥammad al-Ḥabīb, *al-Taʾrīkh wa-l-muʾarrikhūn bi-Makka min al-qarn al-thālith al-hijrī ilā al-qarn al-thālith ʿashar*, Mecca, 1994.
al-Ḥibshī, ʿA. M., *Maṣādir al-fikr al-Islamī fī al-Yaman*, Beirut, 1408/1988.
Muʾallafāt ḥukkām al-Yaman, ed. Elke Niewoehner-Eberhard, Wiesbaden, 1979.
Hinds, M., 'An early Islamic family from Oman: al-ʿAwtabī's account of the Muhallabids', *JSS*, Monograph 17, Manchester, 1991.
Holes, C., 'ʿUmān', *EI2*, vol. X, 814.
Horovitz, J., *The earliest biographies of the Prophet and their authors*, ed. Lawrence Conrad, Princeton, 2002.
Hourani, G. F., *Arab seafaring in the Indian Ocean in ancient and medieval times*, Princeton, 1951.
al-Jāsir, Ḥamad, *Bilād Yanbuʿ*, Riyadh, n.d.
Fī shimāl gharb al-Jazīra, Riyadh, 1981.
'al-Ḥafṣī wa-kitābuhu ʿan al-Yamāma', *al-ʿArab*, 1 (1967), 673–91, 769–94.
Madīnat al-Riyāḍ ʿabra aṭwār al-taʾrīkh, Riyadh, 1386/1966.
'Muʾallafāt fī taʾrīkh al-Madīna', *al-ʿArab*, 4 (1969), 97–100, 262–7, 327–34, 385–8, 465–8.
'Muʾallafāt fī taʾrīkh Makka', *al-ʿArab*, 4 (1970), 949–58.
al-Muʿjam al-jughrāfī li-l-bilād al-ʿArabiyya al-Suʿūdiyya, Riyadh, 1399–1401/1979–81.
'al-Rabadha fī kutub al-mutaqaddimīn', *al-ʿArab*, 1 (1966), 418–27, 546–50, 625–31, 724–7.
'Wulāt al-Aḥsāʾ fī al-ʿahd al-Umawiyy', *al-ʿArab*, 1 (1966–7), 28–37.
al-Kāf, Saqqāf ʿAlī, *Ḥaḍramawt ʿabra arbaʿat ʿashar qarnan*, Beirut, 1410/1990.
Kister, M. J., 'The battle of the Ḥarra: Some socio-economic aspects', in M. Rosen-Ayalon (ed.), *Studies in memory of Gaston Wiet*, Jerusalem, 1977, 33–49.
'The struggle against Musaylima', *JSAI*, 27 (2002), 1–56.
Landau-Tasseron, E., 'Zaydī imams as restorers of religion: *Iḥyāʾ* and *tajdīd* in Zaydī literature', *JNES*, 49 (1990), 247–63.

Madelung, W., 'The Fāṭimids and the Qarmaṭīs of Baḥrayn', in F. Daftary (ed.), *Medieval Ismā'īlī history and thought*, Cambridge, 1996, 21–74.

'Ḳarmaṭī', *EI2*, vol. IV, 660.

'Manṣūr al-Yaman', *EI2*, vol. VI, 438.

'The origin of the Yemenite *hijra*', in A. Jones (ed.), *Arabicus Felix: Luminosus Britanicus, essays in honour of A. F. L. Beeston on his eightieth birthday*, Oxford, 1991, 25–44.

Mayy, Muḥammad al-Khalīfa, *Min Sawād al-Kūfa ilā al-Baḥrayn*, Beirut, 1999.

Muṣṭafā, S., *al-Ta'rīkh al-'arabī wa-l-mu'arrikhūn*, vol. I, Beirut, 1979.

al-Naboodah, Ḥasan M., 'Banū Nabhān in the Omani sources', in G. R. Smith, J. R. Smart and B. R. Pridham (eds.), *New Arabian Studies*, 4 (Exeter, 1997), 181–95.

von Oppenheim, M. F., *Die Beduinen*, vol. II, ed. E. Bräunlich and W. Caskel, Leipzig, 1943.

Die Beduinen, vol. III, ed. W. Caskel, Wiesbaden, 1952.

al-Rāshid, Sa'ad, *Darb Zubayda: The pilgrim road from Kūfa to Mecca*, Riyadh, 1980.

al-Rabadha: A portrait of early Islamic civilization in Saudi Arabia, Riyadh, 1986.

Rentz, G., 'Ḳaṭīf', *EI2*, vol. IV, 763.

Rotter, G., *Die Umayyaden und der zweite Bürgerkrieg (680–692)*, Wiesbaden, 1982.

al-Sayyābī, Sālim ibn Ḥamūd, *al-Ḥaqīqa wa-l-majāz fī ta'rīkh al-Ibāḍiyya bi-l-Yaman wa-l-Ḥijāz*, Muscat, 1400/1980.

Is'āf al-a'yān fī ansāb ahl 'Umān, Beirut, 1384.

Sayyid, Ayman Fu'ād, *Maṣādir ta'rīkh al-Yaman fī al-'aṣr al-Islāmī*, Cairo, 1974.

Schmucker, W., 'Die Christliche Minderheit von Najrān', *Studien zum Minderheitenproblem im Islam*, 1 (1973), 183–281.

Serjeant, R. B., 'Historians and historiography of Ḥaḍramawt', in R. B. Serjeant, *Studies in Arabian history and civilization*, Variorum Collected Studies, Aldershot and Brookfield, VT, 1981, X.

'The interplay between tribal affinities and religious (Zaydi) authority in the Yemen', *al-Abḥāth*, 30 (1982), 11–47.

'Materials for South Arabian history', *BSOAS*, 13 (1950), 281–307, 581–601.

'The sayyids of Ḥaḍramawt', in R. B. Serjeant, *Studies in Arabian history and civilization*, Variorum Collected Studies, Aldershot and Brookfield, VT, 1981, VIII.

'South Arabia', in R. B. Serjeant, *Studies in Arabian history and civilization*, Variorum Collected Studies, Aldershot and Brookfield, VT, 1981, IX.

Shalabī, Aḥmad, *Mawsū'at al-ta'rīkh al-Islāmī wa-l-ḥaḍāra al-Islāmiyya*, vol. VII, Cairo, 1982.

al-Shāmī, Aḥmad ibn Muḥammad, *Ta'rīkh al-Yaman al-fikrī fī al-'aṣr al-'Abbāsī*, 4 vols., Beirut, 1407/1987.

Shoufani, E., *al-Riddah and the Muslim conquest of Arabia*, Toronto and Beirut, 1975.

Smith, G. R., 'The political history of the Islamic Yemen down to the first Turkish invasion (1–945/622–1538)', in G. R. Smith, *Studies in the medieval history of the Yemen and Arabia Felix*, Variorum Collected Studies, Aldershot and Brookfield, VT, 1997, I.

'Yemenite history: Problems and misconceptions', in G. R. Smith, *Studies in the medieval history of the Yemen and Arabia Felix*, Variorum Collected Studies, Aldershot and Brookfield, VT, 1997, II.

Stookey, R. W., *Yemen: The politics of the Yemen Arab Republic*, Boulder, 1978.

Veccia Vaglieri, Laura, 'L'Imāmato Ibāḍita dell' Oman', *Annali* (Istituto Universitario Orientale, Napoli), n.s. 3 (1949), 245–82.

Wilkinson, J. C., 'Bibliographical background to the crisis period in the Ibāḍī imamate (end of the ninth to end of the fourteenth century)', *Arabian Studies*, 3 (1976), 137–64.
'The Julandā of Oman', *Journal of Oman Studies*, 1 (1975), 97–108.
Zakkār, Suhayl, *al-Jāmiʿ fī akhbār al-Qarāmiṭa fī al-Aḥsāʾ, al-Shām, al-ʿIrāq, al-Yaman*, Damascus, 1407/1987.
von Zambauer, Edward, *Muʿjam al-ansāb wa-l-usarāt al-ḥākima fī al-taʾrīkh al-Islāmī*, Beirut, 1980.

Chapter 11: The Islamic east

Practical suggestions for further reading

Bartold, W., *Turkestan down to the Mongol invasion*, 4th edn, London, 1977.
Bosworth, C. E., *The history of the Saffarids of Sistan and the Maliks of Nimruz*, Costa Mesa, 1994.
Sīstān under the Arabs, from the Islamic conquest to the rise of the Ṣaffārids (30–250/651–864), Rome, 1968.
Daniel, Elton, *The political and social history of Khurasan under Abbasid rule, 747–820*, Minneapolis and Chicago, 1979.
Frye, R. N., *Bukhārā: The medieval achievement*, Norman, OK, 1965.
The golden age of Persia, New York, 1963.
(ed.), *The Cambridge history of Iran*, vol. IV: *The period from the Arab invasion to the Saljuqs*, Cambridge, 1975.
Hovannisian, Richard G., and Georges Sabbagh (eds.), *The Persian presence in the Islamic world*, Cambridge, 1998.
Madelung, W., *Religious trends in early Islamic Iran*, New York, 1988.
Spuler, Bertold, *Iran in frühislamischer Zeit*, Wiesbaden, 1952.

Primary sources

Akhbār al-dawla al-ʿAbbāsiyya wa-fīhi akhbār al-ʿAbbās wa-wuldihi, ed. ʿAbd al-ʿAzīz al-Dūrī and ʿAbd al-Jabbār al-Muṭṭalibī, Beirut, 1971.
al-Baghdādī, ʿAbd al-Qāhir ibn Ṭāhir, *al-Farq bayna ʾl-firaq*, ed. M. ʿAbd al-Ḥamīd, Cairo, 1964.
al-Balādhurī, Aḥmad ibn Yaḥyā, *Ansāb al-ashrāf*, ed. M. al-ʿAzm, 25 sections to date, Damascus, 1996–2004.
Kitāb futūḥ al-buldān, ed. M. J. de Goeje, Leiden, 1866; trans. P. K. Hitti and F. C. Murgotten as *The origins of the Islamic state*, 2 vols., New York, 1916–24.
Balʿamī, Abu ʾl-Faḍl Muḥammad, *Tarjamah-yi Tārīkh-i Ṭabarī*, first part ed. M. Bahār as *Tārīkh-i Balʿamī*, 2 vols., Tehran, 1962; second part ed. M. Rawshan as *Tārīkh-nāmah-ye Ṭabarī*, 3 vols., Tehran, 1988; ed. and trans. H. Zotenberg as *Chronique de Abou-Djafar Mohammed ben Djarir ben-Yezid Tabari*, 4 vols., Paris, 1867–74.
Balkhī, ʿAbd Allah, *Faḍāʾil-i Balkh*, ed. ʿA. Ḥabībī, Tehran, 1350/1972.
Bayhaqī, Abu ʾl-Faḍl Muḥammad, *Tārīkh-i Bayhaqī*, ed. ʿAlī Fayyāḍ, Mashhad, 1350/1971.
Bīrūnī, Abu ʾl-Rayḥān, *Āthār al-bāqiya*, trans. C. Edward Sachau, London, 1879.
al-Dīnawarī, Abū Ḥanīfa Aḥmad, *al-Akhbār al-ṭiwāl*, ed. A. ʿĀmir, Cairo, 1960.
Fragmenta Historicorum Arabicorum, ed. M. J. de Goeje, 2 vols., Leiden, 1869.

Gardīzī, Abū Saʿīd, *Zayn al-akhbār*, ed. ʿA.-Ḥ. Ḥabībī, Tehran, 1347/1969.
Ḥamza al-Iṣfahānī, *Taʾrīkh sanī mulūk al-ard waʾl-anbiyāʾ*, ed. Y. al-Maskūnī, Beirut, 1961.
Ḥudūd al-ʿālam, trans. V. Minorsky, London, 1937.
Ibn ʿAbd Rabbihi, Abu ʿUmar Aḥmad ibn Muḥammad, *Kitāb al-ʿiqd al-farīd*, ed. A. Amīn *et al.*, 8 vols., Cairo, 1940–53.
Ibn Abī Ṭāhir Ṭayfūr, Abu ʾl-Faḍl Aḥmad ibn Ṭāhir, *Baghdād fī taʾrīkh al-khilāfa al-ʿabbāsiyya*, Baghdad, 1968.
Ibn Aʿtham al-Kūfī, Abū Muḥammad Aḥmad, *al-Futūḥ*, ed. Muḥammad ʿAbd al-Muʿīd Khān *et al.*, 8 vols., Hyderabad, 1968–75.
Ibn al-Athīr, ʿIzz al-Dīn ʿAlī ibn Aḥmad, *al-Kāmil fī ʾl-taʾrīkh*, 13 vols., Beirut, 1965–7.
Ibn al-Balkhī, *Fārs-nāmah*, ed. G. LeStrange and R. A. Nicholson, London, 1927.
Ibn al-Faqīh, Muḥammad ibn Isḥāq, *Kitāb al-buldān*, ed. M. J. de Goeje, Leiden, 1885.
Ibn Funduq Bayhaqī, Abu ʾl-Ḥasan, *Tārīkh-i Bayhaq*, ed. A. Bahmanyār, Tehran, 1317/1939.
Ibn Ḥazm, *al-Faṣl fīʾl-milal waʾl-ahwāʾ waʾl-niḥal*, ed. A. Khalīfa *et al.*, 5 vols., Cairo, 1317–21/1899–1903.
Ibn al-ʿImrānī, Muḥammad ibn ʿAlī, *al-Inbāʾ fī tāʾrīkh al-khulafāʾ*, ed. Q. al-Samarrāʾī, Leiden, 1973.
Ibn Isfandiyār, *Ṭārīkh-i Ṭabaristān*, ed. ʿAbbās Iqbāl, Tehran, 1944.
Ibn Khurradādhbih, Abu ʾl-Qāsim, *Kitāb al-masālik waʾl-mamālik*, ed. M. J. de Goeje, Leiden, 1889.
Ibn Miskawayh, Abū ʿAlī Aḥmad ibn Muḥammad, *Tajārib al-umam*, ed. M. J. de Goeje, Leiden, 1871.
Ibn al-Muqaffaʿ, *Āthār Ibn al-Muqaffaʿ*, ed. ʿU. Abu ʾl-Naṣr, Beirut, 1966.
Ibn al-Nadīm, *Kitāb al-fihrist*, ed. R. Tajaddud, Tehran, 1971; trans. Bayard Dodge as *The* Fihrist *of al-Nadīm*, 2 vols., New York, 1970.
Ibn Qutayba, Abū Muḥammad ʿAbd Allāh ibn Muslim, *Kitāb al-Maʿārif*, ed. T. ʿUkāsha, Cairo, 1969.
Kitāb ʿuyūn al-akhbār, 4 vols., Cairo, 1964.
Ibn Rustah, *Kitāb al-aʿlāq al-nafīsa*, ed. M. J. de Goeje, Leiden, 1892.
al-Iṣbahānī, Abū al-Faraj ʿAlī, *al-Aghānī*, 31 vols., Cairo, 1969–79.
Maqātil al-Ṭalibiyyīn, ed. Kāẓim al-Muẓaffar, Najaf, 1965.
al-Iṣṭakhrī, Abū Isḥāq, *al-Masālik waʾl-mamālik*, ed. M. J. de Goeje, Leiden, 1870.
al-Jahshiyārī, Muḥammad ibn ʿAbdūs, *Kitāb al-wuzarāʾ waʾl-kuttāb*, ed. M. al-Saqqa, Cairo, 1938.
Khalīfa ibn Khayyāṭ, *al-Taʾrīkh*, ed. Akram al-ʿUmarī, 2 vols., Najaf, 1967.
al-Khwārizmī, Abū ʿAbd Allāh, *Mafātiḥ al-ʿulūm*, ed. G. van Vloten, Leiden, 1895.
al-Maqdisī, Muṭahhar ibn Ṭāhir, *al-Badʾ waʾl-tāʾrīkh*, ed. and trans. C. Huart as *Le Livre de la création et de l'histoire*, 6 vols., Paris, 1899–1919.
al-Maqrizī, Abu ʾl-ʿAbbās, *al-Muqaffaʿ al-kabīr*, ed. M. al-Yaʿlāwī, 8 vols., Beirut, 1991.
al-Nizāʿ waʾl-takhaṣum fīmā bayna Banī Umayya wa Banī Hāshim, Cairo, 1947.
al-Masʿūdī, ʿAlī ibn al-Ḥusayn, *Mujmal al-tawārīkh waʾl-qiṣaṣ*, ed. M. Bahār, Tehran, 1940.
Murūj al-dhahab wa-maʿādin al-jawhar, ed. Charles Pellat, 7 vols., Beirut, 1965–79.
al-Muqaddasī [Maqdisī], Shams al-Dīn Muḥammad ibn Aḥmad, *Aḥsan al-taqāsim fī maʿrifat al-aqālim*, ed. M. J. de Goeje, Leiden, 1906.
Narshakhī, Abu Bakr Muḥammad, *Tārīkh-i Bukhārā*, ed. Mudarris Raḍavī, Tehran, 1972; ed. and trans. R. N. Frye as *The history of Bukhara*, Cambridge, MA, 1954.

al-Nawbakhtī, Ḥasan ibn Mūsā, *Firaq al-shīʿa*, Najaf, 1932; trans. Javad Mashkur as *Les sectes shiites*, Tehran, 1980.
Niẓām al-Mulk, *Nubdha min Kitāb al-taʾrīkh*, published as manuscript facsimile by P. A. Gryaznevich as *Arabskii anonim XI veka*, Moscow, 1960.
Siyāsatnāmah (Sīar al-mulūk), ed. J. Shiʿār, Tehran, 1969; trans. Hubert Darke as *The book of government: Or, rules for kings*, New Haven, 1960.
Qummī, Ḥasan ibn Muḥammad, *Kitāb-i tārīkh-i Qumm*, Tehran, 1353/1934.
Saʿd al-Qummī, *Kitāb al-maqalāt wa'l-firaq*, ed. M. J. Mashkūr, Tehran, 1963.
al-Samʿanī, ʿAbd al-Karīm, *Kitāb al-ansāb*, ed. ʿA. al-Yamānī, 13 vols., Hyderabad, 1962–82.
al-Shābushtī, Abu 'l-Ḥasan, *Kitāb al-diyārāt*, ed. Kūrkīs ʿAwwād, Baghdad, 1386/1966.
al-Ṭabarī, Abū Jaʿfar Muḥammad ibn Jarīr, *Taʾrīkh al-khulafāʾ*, published as manuscript facsimile by P. A. Gryaznevich, Moscow, 1967.
Taʾrīkh al-rusul wa'l-mulūk, ed. M. J. de Goeje *et al.*, 15 vols. in 3 series, Leiden, 1879–1901.
Tārīkh-i Sīstān, ed. Malik al-Shuʿarāʾ Bahār, Tehran, 1935, trans. Milton Gold as *The Tārikh-e Sistān*, Rome, 1976.
al-Thaʿālibī, ʿAbd al-Malik, *Ghurar akhbār mulūk al-furs*, ed. and trans. H. Zotenberg, Paris, 1900.
Thimār al-qulūb, ed. M. Ibrāhīm, 5 vols., Cairo, 1965.
al-ʿUtbī, Muḥammad ibn ʿAbd al-Jabbār, *al-Yamīnī*, ed. D. al-Thāmirī, Beirut, 2004.
al-ʿUyūn wa'l-hadāʾiq fī akhbār al-ḥaqāʾiq, ed. M. J. de Goeje, Leiden, 1869.
al-Yaʿqūbī, Aḥmad ibn Abī Yaʿqūb, *Kitāb al-buldān*, ed. M. J. de Goeje, Leiden, 1892.
Tāʾrīkh, ed. M. Houtsma as *Ibn Wādhih qui dicitur al-Jaʿqubī historiae*, 2 vols., Leiden, 1883.

Secondary sources

Agha, Saleh Said, ʿAbū Muslim's conquest of Khurāsān', *JAOS*, 120 (2000), 333–47.
'The Arab population in Ḫurāsān during the Umayyad period', *Arabica*, 46 (1999), 211–29.
The revolution which toppled the Umayyads: Neither Arab nor ʿAbbāsid, Leiden, 2003.
'A viewpoint on the Murjiʾa in the Umayyad period: Evolution through application', *Journal of Islamic Studies*, 8 (1997), 1–42.
al-ʿAlī, Ṣāliḥ, 'Istīṭān al-ʿarab fī Khurāsān', *Majallat kulliyat al-adab wa'l-ʿulūm fī Baghdād* (1958), 36–83.
Amabe, Fukuzo, *The emergence of the ʿAbbāsid autocracy: The ʿAbbāsid army, Khurāsān and Adharbayjān*, Kyoto, 1995.
Amoretti, B. S., 'Sects and heresies', in R. N. Frye (ed.), *Cambridge history of Iran*, vol. IV: *The period from the Arab invasion to the Saljuqs*, Cambridge, 1975, 481–519.
ʿAthamina, Khalil, 'Arab settlement during the Umayyad caliphate', *JSAI*, 8 (1986), 185–207.
'The early Murjiʾa: Some notes', *JSS*, 35 (1990), 109–30.
Azizi, Muhsen, *La Domination arabe et l'épanouissement du sentiment national en Iran*, Paris, 1938.
Bartold, W., *An historical geography of Iran*, trans. S. Soucek, Princeton, 1984.
Beckwith, C., 'Aspects of the early history of the Central Asian guard corps in Islam', *Archivum Eurasiae Medii Aevi*, 4 (1984), 29–43.
'The plan of the City of Peace: Central Asian Iranian factors in ʿAbbāsid design', *Acta Orientalia*, 38 (1984), 143–64.

'The revolt of 755 in Tibet', *Wiener Studien zur Tibetologie und Buddhismuskunde*, 10 (1983), 1–16.

The Tibetan empire in Central Asia, Princeton, 1987.

Blankinship, Khalid Yahya, *The end of the jihād state: The reign of Hishām Ibn ʿAbd al-Malik and the collapse of the Umayyads*, Albany, 1994.

'The tribal factor in the ʿAbbāsid revolution: The betrayal of the Imam Ibrāhīm b. Muḥammad', *JAOS*, 108 (1988), 589–603.

Bligh-Abramski, Irit, 'Evolution vs. revolution: Umayyad elements in the ʿAbbāsid regime 133/750–320/932', *Der Islam*, 65 (1988), 226–43.

Bosworth, C. E., 'The armies of the Ṣaffārids', *BSOAS*, 31 (1968), 534–54.

'Dailamīs in Central Iran: The Kākūyids of Jibāl and Yazd', *Iran*, 8 (1970), 73–95.

'The development of Persian culture under the early Ghaznavids', *Iran*, 6 (1968), 33–44.

'An early Arabic mirror for princes: Ṭāhir Dhū 'l-Yamīnain's epistle to his son ʿAbdallāh (206/821)', *JNES*, 29(1970), 25–41.

'The early Islamic history of Ghūr', *Central Asatic Journal*, 6 (1961), 116–33.

The Ghaznavids, 2nd edn, Beirut, 1973.

'The heritage of rulership in early Islamic Iran and the search for dynastic connections with the past', *Iran*, 11 (1973), 51–62.

'The interaction of Arabic and Persian literature and culture in the 10th and early 11th centuries', *al-Abhath*, 27 (1978–9), 59–75.

'Notes on the pre-Ghaznavid history of eastern Afghanistan', *Islamic Quarterly*, 9 (1965), 12–24.

'The rise of the Karāmiyya in Khurasan', *MW*, 50 (1960), 6–14.

'The rulers of Chaghāniyān in early Islamic times', *Iran*, 19 (1981), 1–20.

'The Tahirids and Arabic culture', *JSS*, 14 (1969), 45–79.

'The Ṭāhirids and Persian literature', *Iran*, 7 (1969), 103–6.

Bulliet, R. W., *Conversion to Islam in the medieval period: An essay in quantitative history*, Cambridge, MA, 1979.

Islam: The view from the edge, New York, 1994.

The patricians of Nishapur, Cambridge, MA, 1972.

Cahen, Claude, 'Points de vue sur la "Révolution abbaside"', *Revue Historique* (1963), 295–335.

Canfield, R. (ed.), *Turko-Persia in historical perspective*, Cambridge, 1991.

Cereti, C. G. 'Primary sources for the history of Inner and Outer Iran in the Sasanian period', *Archivum Eurasiae Medii Aevi*, 9 (1997), 17–71.

Chabbi, J., 'Remarques sur le développement historique des mouvements ascétiques et mystiques au Khurasan', *SI*, 46 (1977), 5–72.

Chavannes, Eduard, *Documents sur les Tou-Kiue (Turcs) Occidentaux*, St Petersburg, 1903.

Choksy, Jamsheed K., *Conflict and cooperation: Zoroastrian subalterns and Muslim elites in medieval Iranian society*, New York, 1997.

Chowdhry, S. R., *al-Ḥajjāj Ibn Yūsuf*, Delhi, 1972.

Christensen, A. E., *L'Iran sous les Sassanides*, 2nd edn, Copenhagen, 1944.

Christensen, Peter, *The decline of Iranshahr: Irrigation and environments in the history of the Middle East 500 BC to 1500 CE*, Copenhagen, 1993.

Cooperson, M., *Classical Arabic biography: The heirs of the Prophet in the age of al-Maʾmun*, Cambridge, 2000.

Crone, Patricia, 'The ʿAbbāsid Abnā' and Sāsānid cavalrymen', *JRAS*, ser. 3, 8 (1998), 1–19.

'On the meaning of the ʿAbbāsid call to al-Riḍā', in C. E. Bosworth *et al.* (eds.), *The Islamic world from classical to modern times: Essays in honor of Bernard Lewis*, Princeton, 1989, 95–111.

Slaves on horses: The evolution of the Islamic polity, Cambridge, 1980.

'Were the Qays and Yemen of the Umayyad period political parties?', *Der Islam*, 71 (1994), 1–57.

Crone, Patricia, and Martin Hinds, *God's caliph: Religious authority in the first centuries of Islam*, Cambridge, 1986.

Czegledy, K., 'Gardīzī on the history of Central Asia (746–780 AD)', *Acta Orientalia*, 27(1973), 257–67.

Daniel, Elton, 'The "Ahl al-Taqādum" and the problem of the constituency of the Abbasid revolution in the Merv Oasis', *Journal of Islamic Studies*, 7 (1996), 150–79.

'The anonymous history of the Abbasid family and its place in Islamic historiography', *IJMES*, 14 (1982), 419–34.

'Manuscripts and editions of Balʿamī's Tarjamah-yi Tārīkh-i Ṭabarī', *JRAS* (1990), 282–321.

'The Sāmānid "translations" of al-Ṭabarī', in Hugh Kennedy (ed.), *al-Ṭabarī: The life and works of a medieval Muslim historian* (forthcoming).

Daryaee, Touraj, 'Apocalypse now: Zoroastrian reflections on the early Islamic centuries', *Medieval Encounters*, 4 (1998), 188–202.

Dennett, Daniel C., *Conversion and the poll-tax in early Islam*, Cambridge, MA, 1950.

Dixon, A. A., *The Umayyad caliphate 65–86/684–705*, London, 1971.

Donner, F., *The early Islamic conquests*, Princeton, 1981.

Dunlop, D. M., 'Arab relations with Tibet in the 8th and early 9th centuries AD', *Islâm Tetkikleri Enstitüsü Dergisi*, 5 (1973), 301–18.

The history of the Jewish Khazars, Princeton, 1954.

'A new source of information on the battle of Talas or Aṭlakh', *Ural-Altaische Jaherbücher*, 36 (1964), 326–30.

al-Dūrī, ʿAbd al-ʿAzīz, *al-ʿAṣr al-ʿabbāsi al-awwal*, Baghdad, 1945.

'al-Fikra al-mahdiyya bayna al-daʿwa al-ʿabbāsiyya wa-al-ʿaṣr al-ʿabbāsī al-awwal', in W. al-Qāḍī (ed.), *Studia Arabica et Islamica: Festschrift for Iḥsān ʿAbbās*, Beirut, 1981, 123–32.

'Niẓām al-ḍarā'ib fī Khurāsān fī ṣadr al-islām', *Majallat al-majmaʿ al-ʿilmī al-ʿirāqī*, 11 (1964), 75–7.

Elad, Amikam, 'Aspects of the transition from the Umayyad to the ʿAbbāsid caliphate', *JSAI*, 19 (1995), 89–132.

'The ethnic composition of the ʿAbbāsid revolution: A reevaluation of some recent research', *JSAI*, 24 (2000), 246–326.

El-Hibri, T., 'The Mecca Protocol of 802: A plan for division or succession?' *IJMES*, 24 (1992), 461–80.

Reinterpreting Islamic historiography: Hārūn al-Rashīd and the narrative of the ʿAbbāsid caliphate, Cambridge, 1999.

Esin, Emel, 'Ṭarkhan Nīzak or Ṭarkhan Tīrek? An enquiry concerning the prince of Bādhghīs ...', *JAOS*, 97 (1977), 323–32.

Forstner, M., 'Yaʿqūb b. al-Laiṯ und der Zunbīl', *ZDMG*, 120 (1970), 69–83.

Fragner, B. G., *Die 'Persophonie': Regionalität, Identität und Sprachkontakt in der Geschichte Asiens*, Berlin, 1999.

Frye, R. N., 'The fate of Zoroastrians in eastern Iran', in R. Gyselen (ed.), *Au carrefour des religions: Mélanges offert à Philippe Gignoux*, Bures-sur-Yvette, 1995, 67–72.

'Feudalism in Sasanian and early Islamic Iran', *JSAI*, 9 (1987), 13–18.

Islamic Iran and Central Asia, London, 1979.

'The role of Abū Muslim in the 'Abbasid revolt', *MW*, 37 (1947), 28–38.

'The Samanids', in R. N. Frye (ed.), *The Cambridge history of Iran*, vol. IV: *The period from the Arab Invasion to the Saljuqs*, Cambridge, 1975, 136–61.

'Die Wiedergeburt Persiens um die Jahrtausandwande', *Der Islam*, 35 (1960), 42–51.

Gabrieli, Francesco, 'Muḥammad ibn Qāsim ath-Thaqafī and the Arab conquest of Sind', *East and West*, n.s. 15 (1964–5), 281–95.

'La successione di Hārūn al-Rashīd e la guerra fra al-Amīn e al-Ma'mūn', *RSO*, 11(1926–8), 341–97.

Ghirshman, R., *Les Chionites-Hephtalites*, Cairo, 1948.

Gibb, H. A. R., *The Arab conquests in Central Asia*, London and New York, 1923.

'Chinese records of the Arabs in Central Asia', *BSOAS*, 2 (1922), 613–22.

'The social significance of the Shu'ūbīya', in *Studia Orientalia Ioanni Pedersen septuagenario AD VII id. nov. anno MCMLIII a collegis discipulis amicis dicata*, Copenhagen, 1953, 105–14.

Golden, Peter B., *An introduction to the history of the Turkic peoples*, Wiesbaden, 1992.

'The Karakhanids and early Islam', in D. Sinor (ed.), *The Cambridge history of early Inner Asia*, Cambridge, 1990, 343–70.

Gordon, M., *The breaking of a thousand swords: A history of the Turkish military community of Samarra (AH 200–275/815–889 CE)*, Albany, 2001.

Grenet, F., *La geste d'Ardashir fils de Pâbag: Kārnāmag i Ardaxšēr ī Pābagān*, Paris, 2001.

Grignaschi, M., 'La riforma tributaria di Ḫosrō i e il feudalismo sassanide', *Atti del Convegno internazionale sul tema: La Persia nel medioevo (Roma, 31 marzo–5 aprile l970)*, Rome, 1971, 87–138.

Guest, R. 'A coin of Abū Muslim', *JRAS* (1932), 54–6.

Gyselen, R., *La géographie administrative de l'empire sassanide*, Paris, 1989.

Hasan, S., 'A survey of the expansion of Islam into Central Asia during the Umayyad caliphate', *Islamic Culture*, 48 (1974), 177–86.

Hawting, G. R., *The first dynasty of Islam: The Umayyad caliphate, AD 661–750*, London and Sydney, 1986.

Hill, D. R., *The termination of hostilities in the early Arab conquests, AD 634–656*, London, 1971.

Hinds, M., 'The first Arab conquests of Fārs', *Iran*, 22 (1984), 39–53.

'Kūfan political alignments and their background in the mid-seventh century AD', *IJMES*, 2 (1971), 346–67.

Housseini, A. M., 'The Umayyad policy in Khorāsān and its effect on the formulation of Muslim thought', *Journal of the University of Peshawar*, 4 (1955), 1–21.

Hoyland, R., *Seeing Islam as others saw it: A survey and evaluation of Christian, Jewish and Zoroastrian writings on early Islam*, Princeton, 1997.

Kaabi, Mongi, 'Les origines Ṭāhirides dans la da'wa 'abbāside', *Arabica*, 29 (1972), 145–64.

Les Ṭāhirides, Paris, 1983.

Karev, Yury, 'La politique d'Abū Muslim dans le Māwarā'annahr: Nouvelles données textuelles et archéologiques', *Der Islam*, 79 (2002), 1–46.

Kennedy, Hugh, *The armies of the caliphs: Military and society in the early Islamic state*, London and New York, 2001.

'The Barmakid revolution in Islamic government', in C. Melville (ed.), *Persian and Islamic studies in honor of P. W. Avery*, London, 1990, 89–98.

'Central government and provincial elites in the early 'Abbāsid caliphate', *BSOAS*, 44 (1981), 26–38.

The early Abbasid caliphate: A political history, London, 1981.

'Elite incomes in the early Islamic state', in John Haldon and L. I. Conrad (eds.), *The Byzantine and early Islamic Near East*, vol. VI: *Elites old and new in the Byzantine and early Islamic Near East*, Princeton, 2004, 13–28.

The Prophet and the age of the caliphate, London 1986.

Khanbaghi, Aptin, *The fire, the star and the cross: Minority religions in medieval and early modern Iran*, London, 2006.

Kimber, R. A., 'The early Abbasid vizierate', *JSS*, 37 (1992), 65–85.

'Hārūn al-Rashīd's Meccan settlement of AH 186/AD 802', *School of Abbasid Studies Occasional Papers*, 1 (1986), 55–79.

Klima, O., *Mazdak: Geschichte einer sozialen Bewegung im sassanidischen Persien*, Prague, 1957.

Lambton, Ann K. S., 'An account of the Tārīkhi Qumm', *BSOAS*, 12 (1948), 586–96.

Lapidus, Ira M., 'Arab settlement and economic development of Iraq and Iran in the age of the Umayyad and early Abbasid caliphs', in A. L. Udovitch (ed.), *The Islamic Middle East, 700–1900: Studies in economic and social history*, Princeton, 1981, 177–208.

Lassner, Jacob, 'Abu Muslim al-Khurāsānī: The emergence of a secret agent from Khurāsān, Iraq, or was it Isfahān?', *JAOS*, 104 (1984), 165–75.

'Abu Muslim, son of Salīṭ: A skeleton in the 'Abbāsid closet?', in M. Sharon (ed.), *Studies in Islamic history and civilization in honour of Professor David Ayalon*, Jerusalem and Leiden, 1986, 91–104.

Islamic revolution and historical memory: Abbasid apologetics and the art of historical writing, New Haven, 1986.

The shaping of Abbasid rule, Princeton, 1980.

Laurent, Joseph, *L'Arménie entre Byzance et l'Islam depuis la conquête arabe jusqu'en 886*, rev. edn, Paris, 1980.

Lazard, G., *La langue des plus anciens monuments de la prose persane*, Paris, 1963.

Les premiers poètes persans (IXe–Xe siècles), Paris and Tehran, 1964.

Le Strange, G., *The lands of the eastern caliphate*, London, 1905.

Lieu, S. N. C., *Manichaeism in Central Asia and China*, Leiden, 1998.

Litvinsky, B. A., 'The Hephthalite empire', in B. A. Litvinsky (ed.), *History of civilizations of Central Asia*, vol. III: *The crossroads of civilization AD 250 to 750*, Paris, 1996, 135–62.

Madelung, W., 'Abū Isḥāq al-Ṣabī on the Alids of Tabaristān and Gīlān', *JNES*, 26 (1967), 15–57.

'The early Murji'a in Khurāsān and Transoxiana and the spread of Ḥanafism', *Der Islam*, 59 (1982), 32–9.

Der Imam al-Qāsim ibn Ibrāhīm und die Glaubenslehre der Zaiditen, Berlin, 1965.

'The minor dynasties of northern Iran', in R. N. Frye (ed.), *The Cambridge history of Iran*, vol. IV: *The period from the Arab invasion to the Saljuqs*, Cambridge, 1975, 198–249.

'New documents concerning al-Ma'mūn, al-Faḍl b. Sahl and 'Alī al-Riḍā', in W. al-Qāḍī (ed.), *Studia Arabica et Islamica: Festschrift for Iḥsān 'Abbās on his sixtieth birthday*, Beirut, 1981, 333–46.

'The spread of Māturīdism and the Turks', in *Actas, IV Congresso de Estudios Árabes e Islâmicos, Coimbra-Lisboa, 1 a 8 de setembro de 1968*, Leiden, 1971, 109–68.

The succession to Muḥammad: A study of the early caliphate, Cambridge, 1997.
'The vigilante movement of Sahl b. Salāma al-Khurāsānī and the origins of Ḥanbalism reconsidered', *Journal of Turkish Studies*, 14 (1990), 331–7.
Marín-Guzmán, Roberto, 'The 'Abbasid revolution in Central Asia and Khurāsān', *Islamic Studies*, 33 (1994), 227–52.
Popular dimensions of the 'Abbasid revolution, Cambridge, MA, 1990.
Markwart, J. *A catalogue of the provincial capitals of Ērānshahr*, ed. G. Messina, Rome, 1931.
Mason, Herbert, 'The role of the Azdite Muhallibid family in Marw's anti-Umayyad power struggle', *Arabica*, 14 (1967), 191–207.
Mélikoff, Irène, *Abū Muslim: Le 'Porte-Hache' du Khorassan dans la tradition épique turco-iranienne*, Paris, 1962.
Miah, S., *The reign of al-Mutawakkil*, Dacca, 1969.
Miles, G. C., 'Some new light on the history of Kirman in the first century of the Hijrah', in J. Kritzeck and R. B. Winder (eds.), *The world of Islam: Studies in honour of Philip K. Hitti*, London, 1960, 85–98.
Minorsky, V., *Studies on Caucasian history*, London, 1953.
Morony, Michael G., 'Continuity and change in the administrative geography of late Sasanian and early Islamic al-'Irāq', *Iran*, 20 (1982), 1–49.
'The effects of the Muslim conquest on the Persian population of Iraq', *Iran*, 14 (1976), 41–59.
Iraq after the Muslim conquest, Princeton, 1984.
Moscati, S., 'La revolta di 'Abd al-Gabbār contro il califfo al-Manṣūr', *Rendiconti della Reale Accademia dei Lincei*, 8 (1947), 613–15.
'Studi su Abū Muslim', *Rendiconti della Reale Accademia dei Lincei*, 8 (1949–50), 323–35, 474–95, 8/5, 89–105.
Mottahedeh, Roy, 'Bureaucracy and the patrimonial state in early Islamic Iran and Iraq', *al-Abḥāth*, 29 (1981), 25–36.
Loyalty and leadership in an early Islamic society, Princeton, 1980.
'The Shu'ūbiyya controversy and the social history of early Islamic Iran', *IJMES*, 7(1976), 161–82.
'The transmission of learning: The role of the Islamic northeast', in N. Grandin and M. Gaborieau (eds.), *Madrasa: La transmission du savoir dans le monde musulman*, Paris, 1997, 63–72.
Nafīsī, Sa'īd, *Tārīkh-i khāndān-e ṭāhirī*, Tehran, 1956.
Nagel, Tilman, *Untersuchungen zur Entstehung des Abbasidischen Kalifates*, Bonn, 1972.
Nicol, N. D., 'Early 'Abbasid administration in the central and eastern provinces, AH 132–218/AD 750–833', Ph.D. thesis, University of Washington, 1979.
Nöldeke, T., *Geschichte der Perser und Araber zur Zeit der Sasaniden*, Leiden, 1878.
Sketches from eastern history, trans. J. S. Black, London, 1892; repr. Beirut, 1963.
Noth, Albrecht, 'Iṣfahān-Nihāwand: Eine quellenkritische Studie zur frühislamischen Historiographie', *ZDMG*, 118 (1968), 274–96.
Omar, Farouq, *The Abbasid caliphate*, Baghdad, 1969.
'The nature of the Iranian revolts in the early Islamic period', *Islamic Culture*, 48 (1974), 1–9.
Petrushevskii, I. P., *Islam in Iran*, trans. H. Evans, Albany, 1985.
Pourshariati, Parvaneh, *Decline and fall of the Sasanian empire*, London, forthcoming.

'Iranian tradition in Ṭūs and the Arab presence in Khurāsān', Ph.D. thesis, Columbia University, 1995.

'Khurasan and the crisis of legitimacy: A comparative historiographical approach', in N. Yavari *et al.* (eds.), *Views from the edge: Essays in honor of Richard W. Bulliet*, New York, 2004, 208–29.

'Local histories of Khurasan and the pattern of Arab settlement', *Studia Iranica*, 27 (1998), 41–81.

'Local historiography in medieval Iran and the Tarikh Bayhaq', *Journal of Iranian Studies*, 33 (2000), 133–64.

al-Qāḍī, Wadād, 'The development of the term *ghulāt* in Muslim literature with special reference to the Kaysāniyya', in A. Dietrich (ed.), *Akten des VII. Kongresses für Arabistik und Islamwissenschaft*, Göttingen, 1976, 295–319.

Rekaya, Mohamed, 'Le Hurram-Dīn et les mouvements Hurramites sous les ʿAbbāsides', *SI*, 60 (1984), 5–57.

'Māzyār: Résistance ou intégration d'une province iranienne au monde musulman au milieu du IXe siècle ap. JC', *Studia Iranica*, 2 (1973), 143–92.

'Mise au point sur Théophobe et l'alliance de Bâbek avec Théophile (833/34–839/40)', *Byzantion*, 44 (1974), 43–67.

'La place des provinces sud-caspiennes dans l'histoire de l'Iran de la conquête arabe à l'avènement des Zaydites (16–250 H/637–864 JC): Particularism régional ou rôle "national"?', *RSO*, 48 (1974), 117–52.

Richter-Bernburg, L., 'Iran's contribution to medicine and veterinary science in Islam AH 100–900/AD 700–1500', in J. Greppin *et al.* (eds.), *The diffusion of Greco-Roman medicine into the Middle East and the Caucasus*, Delmar, 1999, 139–67.

'Linguistic Shuʿūbīya and early Neo-Persian prose', *JAOS*, 94 (1974), 55–64.

Robinson, Chase F., 'The conquest of Khūzistān: A historiographic reassessment', *BSOAS*, 67 (2004), 14–39.

Empire and elites after the Muslim conquest: The transformation of northern Mesopotamia, Cambridge Studies in Islamic Civilization, Cambridge, 2000.

Sadighi, G. H., *Les mouvements religieux iraniens*, Paris, 1938.

Scarcia, G., 'Lo scambio di lettere fra Hārūn al-Rašīd e Hamza al-Ḫāriǧi secondo il "Ta'riḫ-i Sistān"', *Annali dell'Instituto Universitario Orientale di Napoli*, n.s. 14 (1964), 623–45.

Shaban, M. A., *The ʿAbbasid revolution*, Cambridge, 1970.

Islamic history: A new interpretation, 2 vols., Cambridge, 1971–6.

Shahbazi, A. S., 'On the X^{w}adāy-nāmag', *Acta Iranica*, 30 (1990), 208–29.

Sharon, Moshe, *Black banners from the east*, Jerusalem, 1983.

Revolt: The social and military aspects of the ʿAbbāsid revolution, Jerusalem, 1990.

Sims-Williams, N., *Bactrian documents from northern Afghanistan*, vol. I: *Legal and economic documents*, Oxford, 2000.

Skladanek, B., 'External policy and interdynastic relations under the Saffarids', *Rocznik Orientalistyczny*, 36 (1974), 133–50.

'The Kharijites in Iran', *Rocznik Orientalistyczny*, 44/1 (1985), 65–92, 44/2 (1985), 89–101.

'Khujistāni's uprising in Khurāsān (860–869): The anatomy of an unsuccessful rebellion', *Rocznik Orientalistyczny*, 46 (1989), 63–77.

'Settlements in Gharchistan during the early Islamic period', *Rocznik Orientalistyczny*, 34 (1971), 57–71.

Sourdel, D., 'Les circonstances de la mort de Ṭāhir Ier au Ḫurāsān en 207/828', *Arabica*, 5 (1958), 66–9.

Le vizirat Abbaside de 749 à 936, Damascus 1959.

Stern, S. M., 'The early missionaries in north-west Persia and in Khurāsān and Transoxania', *BSOAS*, 23 (1960), 56–90.

Studies in early Isma'ilism, Jerusalem, 1983.

'Ya'qūb the Coppersmith and Persian national sentiment', in C. E. Bosworth (ed.), *Iran and Islam*, Edinburgh, 1970, 535–55.

Sundermann, W., 'Mazdak und die mazdakitischen Volksaufstände', *Altertum*, 23 (1977), 245–49.

Treadwell, W. L., 'Ibn Ẓāfir al-Azdī's account of the murder of Aḥmad b. Ismā'īl al-Sāmānī and the succession of his son Naṣr', in Carol Hillenbrand (ed.), *Studies in honour of Clifford Edmund Bosworth*, vol. II, Leiden, 2000, 397–419.

'The political history of the Sāmānid state', D.Phil. thesis, Oxford, 1991.

Tucker, William F., ''Abd Allāh b. Mu'āwīya and the Janāḥiyya: Rebels and ideologues of the late Umayyad period', *SI*, 51 (1980), 39–57.

'Abū Manṣūr al-'Ijlī and the Manṣūriyya: A study in medieval terrorism', *Der Islam*, 54 (1977), 66–76.

'Bayān ibn Sam'ān and the Bayāniyya: Shī'ite extremists of Umayyad Iraq', *MW*, 65 (1975), 241–53.

'Rebels and gnostics: al-Mugīra Ibn Sa'īd and the Mugīriyya', *Arabica*, 22 (1975), 33–47.

van Vloten, G., *De Opkomst der Abbasiden in Chorasan*, Leiden, 1890.

Recherches sur la domination arabe, Amsterdam, 1894.

Watt, M., *The formative period of Islamic thought*, Edinburgh, 1973.

Wellhausen, Julius, *Das arabische Reich und sein Sturz*, Berlin, 1902, trans. M. G. Weir as *The Arab kingdom and its fall*, Calcutta, 1927.

Die religiös-politischen Oppositionsparteien im alten Islam, Berlin, 1901, trans. R. C. Ostle as *The religio-political factions in early Islam*, Amsterdam, 1975.

Wright, E. M., 'Bābak of Badhdh and al-Afshīn', *MW*, 38 (1948), 43–59, 124–131.

Yakubovskii, A. Y., 'Vosstanie Mukanny', *Sovetskoe Vostokovedenie*, 5 (1948), 35–54.

Zakeri, Mohsen, *Sāsānid soldiers in early Muslim society: The origins of 'Ayyārān and Futuwwa*, Wiesbaden, 1995.

Zaman, M. Q., *Religion and politics under the early 'Abbāsids*, Leiden 1997.

Zarrīnkub, 'Abd al-Ḥusayn, *Dū qarn sukūt*, Tehran, 1965.

Chapter 12: Syria

Practical suggestions for further reading

Cameron, A. (ed.), *The Byzantine and early Islamic Near East*, vol. III: *States, resources, and armies*, Princeton, 1995.

Cameron, A., and G. R. D. King (eds.), *The Byzantine and early Islamic Near East*, vol. II: *Land use and settlement patterns*, Princeton, 1994.

Canivet, P., and J. P. Rey-Coquais (eds.), *La Syrie de Byzance à l'Islam, VIIe–VIIIe siècles: Actes du colloque international, 11–15 septembre 1990*, Damascus, 1992.

Cobb, Paul M., *White banners: Contention in Abbasid Syria, 750–880*, Albany, 2001.

Donner, Fred M., *The early Islamic conquests*, Princeton, 1981.
Gil, Moshe, *A history of Palestine, 634–1099*, trans. Ethel Broido, Cambridge, 1992.
Grabar, Oleg, *The shape of the holy: Early Islamic Jerusalem*, Princeton, 1996.
Hawting, G. R., *The first dynasty of Islam: The Umayyad caliphate AD 661–750*, London and Sydney, 1986.
Hoyland, Robert G., *Seeing Islam as others saw it: A survey and evaluation of Christian, Jewish, and Zoroastrian writings on early Islam*, Princeton, 1997.
Humphreys, R. Stephen, *Muʿawiya ibn Abi Sufyan: From Arabia to empire*, Oxford, 2006.
Kennedy, Hugh, *The Byzantine and early Islamic Near East*, Aldershot, 2006.
Le Strange, Guy, *Palestine under the Moslems*, London, 1890.
Robinson, C. F., *ʿAbd al-Malik*, Oxford, 2005.
Sack, Dorothee, *Damaskus: Entwicklung und Struktur einer orientalisch-islamischen Stadt*, Mainz, 1989.
Sauvaget, Jean, *Alep: Essai sur le développement d'une grande ville syrienne des origines au milieu du XIXe siècle*, 2 vols., Paris, 1941.
Wellhausen, Julius, *Das arabische Reich und sein Sturz*, Berlin, 1902; trans. M. G. Weir as *The Arab kingdom and its fall*, Calcutta, 1927.
Wirth, Eugen, *Syrien: Eine geographische Landeskunde*, Darmstadt, 1971.

Primary sources

Abu Yūsuf, *Kitāb al-kharāj*, Bulaq, 1302/1184–5; trans. E. Fagnan as *Livre de l'impôt foncier*, Algiers, 1921.
Abū Zurʿa al-Dimashqī, Taʾrīkh, ed. S. A. al-Qujānī, 2 vols., Damascus, 1980.
Agapius of Manbij (Maḥbūb ibn Qusṭanṭīn), *Kitāb al-ʿunvān, histoire universelle*, ed. and trans. A. A. Vasiliev, part 2/2, Patrologia Orientalis 8 (Paris, 1912), 399–547.
Artsruni, Thomas, *History of the house of the Artsrunik*, trans. R. W. Thomson, Detroit, 1985.
al-Azdī, Yazīd ibn Muḥammad, *Taʾrīkh Mawṣil*, ed. ʿAlī Ḥabība, Cairo, 1967.
al-Azdī al-Baṣrī, *Taʾrīkh futūḥ al-Shām*, ed. W. Nassau Lees, Calcutta, 1854.
al-ʿAẓīmī, Muḥammad ibn ʿAlī, *Taʾrīkh Ḥalab*, ed. Ibrāhīm Zaʿrūr, Damascus, 1984.
al-Balādhurī, Aḥmad ibn Yaḥyā, *Ansāb al-ashrāf*, vol. III, ed. A. A. al-Dūrī, Wiesbaden and Beirut, 1978; vol. IV/1–2, ed. Iḥsān ʿAbbās, Wiesbaden and Beirut, 1979 (*see also* Levi della Vida and Pinto, (trans.), *Il Califfo Muʿāwiya*).
Futūḥ al-buldān, ed. M.J. de Goeje, Leiden, 1866; trans. Philip Hitti and Francis Murgotten as *The origins of the Islamic state*, 2 vols., New York, 1916–24.
Chronica minora (Maronite chronicle, Anon. chronicles of 724, 813, 846), ed. I. Guidi, E. W. Brooks and J.-B. Chabot, CSCO 1–6, Paris, 1903–5 (texts), 1903–7 (translations).
Chronicle of Zuqnin (=pseudo-Dionysius of Tell-Mahré), ed. J.-B. Chabot as *Incerti auctoris chronicon anonymum pseudo-Dionysianum dictum II*, CSCO 104, Paris, 1933; parts 3 and 4 trans. Amir Harrak, Toronto, 1999; part 4 trans. Robert Hespel, CSCO 507, Louvain, 1989.
Chronicon anonymum ad annum Christi 1234 pertinens, ed. and trans. J.-B. Chabot, CSCO 81–2, 109, Paris, 1916, 1920, 1937; trans. A. Abouna, CSCO 354, Louvain, 1974.
Elisséeff, Nikita, *La description de Damas d'Ibn ʿAsākir*, Damascus, 1959.
al-Harawī, Abū al-Ḥasan ʿAlī, *Kitāb al-ziyārāt*, ed. Janine Sourdel-Thomine, Damascus, 1953; trans. Janine Sourdel-Thomine as *Guide des lieux de pèlerinage*, Damascus, 1957.

Histoire nestorienne: Chronique de Séert, ed. and trans. Addai Scher, Patrologia Orientalis 4, 7, 13, Paris, 1907, 1911, 1919.

History of the patriarchs of the Coptic Church of Alexandria, ed. and trans. B. Evetts, Patrologia Orientalis 1, 5, 10, Paris, 1904, 1910, 1915.

Ibn al-ʿAdīm, Kamāl al-Dīn ʿUmar, *Bughyat al-ṭalab fī taʾrīkh Ḥalab*, ed. Suhayl Zakkār, 11 vols., Damascus, 1988.

Zubdat al-ḥalab min taʾrīkh Ḥalab, ed. Sāmī al-Dahhān, vol. I, Damascus, 1951.

Ibn ʿAsākir, *Taʾrīkh madīnat Dimashq*, ed. ʿAlī Shīrī, 70 vols., Beirut, 1995–8 (see also Elisséeff, *La description*).

Ibn al-Athīr, ʿIzz al-Dīn ʿAlī, *al-Kāmil fī taʾrīkh*, ed. C. J. Tornberg, rev. Iḥsān ʿAbbās, 13 vols., Beirut, 1965–7.

Ibn al-Faqīh al-Hamadhānī, *Kitāb al-Buldān*, ed. M. J. de Goeje, BGA 5, Leiden, 1885.

Ibn Ḥawqal, *Kitāb ṣūrat al-arḍ*, ed. M. J. de Goeje, rev. J. H. Kramers, BGA 2, Leiden, 1938; trans. J. H. Kramers and Gaston Wiet as *Configuration de la terre*, 2 vols., Paris, 1964.

Ibn Khallikān, Shams al-Dīn Aḥmad, *Wafayāt al-aʿyān wa-ʾ anbāʾ abnāʾ al-zamān*, ed. Iḥsān ʿAbbās, 8 vols., Beirut, 1972.

Ibn Manẓūr, Muḥammad ibn Mukarram, *Mukhtaṣar taʾrīkh Dimashq li-Ibn ʿAsākir*, ed. R. A.-H. Murād *et al.*, 31 vols., Damascus, 1984–96.

Ibn Shaddād, ʿIzz al-Dīn, *al-Aʿlāq al-khaṭīra fī dhikr umarāʾ al-shām wa-l-jazīra*: (a) *Taʾrīkh Ḥalab*, ed. D. Sourdel, Beirut 1953; (b) *Taʾrīkh Dimashq*, ed. Sāmī al-Dahhān, Damascus, 1956; (c) *Taʾrīkh Lubnān wa-l-Urdunn wa-Filasṭīn*, ed. Sāmī al-Dahhān, Damascus, 1963; (d) *Taʾrīkh al-Jazīra*, ed. Yaḥyā ʿAbbāra, 2 vols., Damascus, 1977–8; (e) 'Description de la Syrie du Nord', ed. and trans. Anne-Marie Eddé, Damascus, 1984; *Bulletin d'Études Orientales*, 32–3 (1980–1), 265–402 (Arabic text).

Ibn al-Shiḥna, Muḥibb al-Dīn, *al-Durr al-muntakhab fī taʾrīkh Ḥalab*, ed. Keiko Ohta, Tokyo, 1990; trans. Jean Sauvaget as *Les perles choisies d'Ibn ach-Chihna*, Beirut, 1933.

al-Iṣṭakhrī, Abu Isḥāq Ibrāhīm, *Kitāb al-masālik wa-l-mamālik*, ed. M. J. de Goeje, BGA 1, Leiden, 1870.

al-Jahshiyārī, Muḥammad ibn ʿAbdūs, *Kitāb al-wuzarāʾ wa al-kuttāb*, ed. Muṣṭafā al-Ṣaqqāʾ, Cairo, 1938.

Khalīfa ibn Khayyāṭ al-ʿUṣfurī, *Kitāb al-taʾrīkh*, ed. Akram Ḍiyāʾ al-ʿUmarī, 2 vols., Najaf, 1967.

Levi della Vida, G., and Olga Pinto (trans.), *Il Califfo Muʿāwiya i secondo il* Kitāb Ansāb al-Asrāf *di Aḥmad ibn Yaḥyā al-Balādhurī*, Rome, 1938.

Lewond (Ghevond), *History of Lewond the eminent Vardapet of the Armenians*, trans. Z. Arzoumanian, Wynnewood, PA, 1982.

al-Masʿūdī, *Kitāb al-tanbīh wa al-ishrāf*, ed. M. J. de Goeje, BGA 8, Leiden, 1894; trans. B. Carra de Vaux as *Livre de l'avertissement et de la révision*, Paris, 1896.

Murūj al-dhahab wa-maʿādin al-jawhar, 7 vols., Beirut, 1965–79; ed. and trans. Charles Pellat as *Les prairies d'or*, 5 vols., Paris, 1965–74.

Michael the Syrian, *Chronique de Michel le Syrien, patriarche jacobite d'Antioche (1166–1199)*, ed. and trans. J.-B. Chabot, 4 vols., Paris, 1899–1924.

Mingana, Alphonse, (ed. and trans.), 'The apology of Timothy the Patriarch before the caliph Mahdi', *Woodbrooke Studies*, 2 (Cambridge, 1928), 1–162.

al-Muqaddasī, Muḥammad ibn Aḥmad, *Aḥsan al-taqāsīm fī maʿrifat al-aqālīm*, ed. M. J. de Goeje, BGA 3, Leiden, 1906; trans. B. A. Collins as *The best divisions for knowledge of the*

regions, Reading, 1994; partial trans. André Miquel as *La meilleure répartition pour la connaissance des provinces*, Damascus, 1963.
Nau, François, 'Un colloque du patriarche Jean avec l'emir des Agaréens et faits divers des années 712 and 716 d'après le ms. du British Museum 17193', *JA*, 11, 5 (1915), 225–79.
al-Nuʿaymī, ʿAbd al-Qādir, *al-Dāris fī taʾrīkh al-madāris*, ed. Jaʿfar al-Ḥassānī, 2 vols., Damascus, 1948–51 (*see also* Sauvaire, *Description de Damas*).
Palmer, Andrew, S. Brock and R. Hoyland, *The seventh century in the West-Syrian chronicles*, Liverpool, 1993.
Reinink, G. J. (ed. and trans.), *Die syrische Apokalypse des Pseudo-Methodius*, CSCO 540–1 (syr. 220–1), Louvain, 1983.
al-Ṣafadī, Khalīl ibn Aybak, *Tuḥfat dhawī al-albāb fī-man ḥakama bi-Dimashq min al-khulafāʾ wa-l-mulūk wa-l-nuwwāb*, ed. Ihsān Khulūṣī and Zuhayr al-Ṣamṣām, 2 vols., Damascus, 1991–2.
Sauvaire, Henri, *Description de Damas*, 2 vols., Paris, 1895–6; originally published in *JA*, 3–7 (1879–87).
Sebeos, *The Armenian history attributed to Sebeos*, trans. R. W. Thomson, with commentary by J. Howard-Johnson, 2 vols., Translated Texts for Historians 31, Liverpool, 1999.
al-Shābushtī, ʿAlī ibn Muḥammad, *Kitāb al-Diyārāt*, ed. Girgis ʿAwwād, Baghdad, 1951.
al-Ṭabarī, Abū Jaʿfar Muḥammad ibn Jarīr, *Taʾrīkh al-rusul wa'l-mulūk*, ed. M. J. de Goeje *et al.*, 15 vols. in 3 series, Leiden, 1879–1901; trans. as *The history of al-Tabari*, gen. ed. Ehsan Yarshater, 39 vols., Albany, 1985–99.
Theophanes, *The chronicle of Theophanes Confessor*, trans. C. Mango and R. Scott, Oxford, 1997.
Wilkinson, John, (ed. and trans.), *Jerusalem pilgrims before the Crusades*, Warminster, 2002.
Wood. D., 'The 60 martyrs of Gaza and the martyrdom of Bishop Sophronius of Jerusalem', *Aram*, 15 (2003), 129–50.
al-Yaʿqūbī, Aḥmad ibn Abī Yaʿqūb, *Kitāb al-buldān*, ed. M. J. de Goeje, BGA 7, Leiden, 1892; trans. Gaston Wiet as *Les pays*, Cairo, 1937.
Yāqūt al-Rūmī, *Muʿjam al-buldān*, ed. F. Wüstenfeld with Latin trans. as *Jacut's Geographisches Wörterbuch*, 6 vols., Leipzig, 1866–73; ed. Anon., 5 vols., Beirut, 1955–7.

Secondary sources

ʿAbbās, Iḥsān, *Taʾrīkh bilād al-shām fī al-ʿaṣr al-ʿabbāsī, 132–255 H/750–870 M*, Amman, 1993.
Abbott, Nabia, 'Arabic papyri of the reign of Gaʿfar al-Mutawakkil ʿalā-llāh (AH 232–47/AD 847–61)', *ZDMG*, 92 (1938), 88–135.
Abiad, Malake, *Culture et education arabo-islamiques au Sam pendant les trois premiers siècles de l'Islam, d'après Taʾrīkh madīnat Dimasq d'Ibn ʿAsākir (499/1105–571/1176)*, Damascus, 1981.
ʿAthamina, Khalil, 'Arab settlement during the Umayyad caliphate', *JSAI*, 8 (1986), 185–207.
al-Bakhit, M. A., and I. Abbas (eds.), *Proceedings of the Second Symposium on the History of Bilād al-Shām during the Early Islamic Period up to 40 AH/660 AD*, Amman, 1987.
al-Bakhit, M. A., and R. Schick (eds.), *Bilād al-Shām during the Abbasid period: Proceedings of the Fifth International Congress on the History of Bilād al-Shām*, Amman, 1992.
Fourth International Congress on the History of Bilād al-Shām during the Umayyad Period, Amman, 1989.

Bates, Michael, 'History, geography and numismatics in the first century of Islamic coinage', *Revue Suisse de Numismatique*, 65 (1986), 231–61.

Bianquis, Thierry, 'Sayf al-Dawla', *EI2*, vol. IX, 103–10.

Blankinship, Khalid Y., *The end of the jihad state: The reign of Hishām ibn ʿAbd al-Malik and the collapse of the Umayyads*, Albany, 1994.

Bonner, Michel, *Aristocratic violence and holy war: Studies in the jihad and the Arab–Byzantine frontier*, New Haven, 1996.

Brock, S. P., 'North Mesopotamia in the late seventh century: Book xv of John Bar Penkāyē's *Rīš Mellē*', *JSAI*, 9 (1987), 51–75.

Brown, Peter, *Society and the holy in Late Antiquity*, Berkeley and Los Angeles, 1979.

Bulliet, Richard, *Conversion to Islam in the medieval period: An essay in quantitative history*, Cambridge, MA, 1979.

Cahen, Claude, 'Fiscalité, propriété, antagonismes sociaux en Haute-Mésopotamie au temps des premiers ʿAbbāsides, d'après Denys de Tell Mahré', *Arabica*, 1 (1954), 136–52.

'Le problème préjudiciel de l'adaptation entre les autochtones et l'Islam', in Claude Cahen, *Les peuples musulmans dans l'histoire médiévale*, Paris, 1977, 169–88.

Cameron, A., and L. I. Conrad (eds.), *The Byzantine and early Islamic Near East*, vol. I: *Problems in the literary source material*, Princeton, 1995.

Canard, Marius, *Histoire de la dynastie des H'amdanides de Djazira et de Syrie*, Algiers, 1951.

Sayf al-dawla, recueil de texts, Algiers, 1934.

Cobb, Paul M., 'al-Mutawakkil's Damascus: A new ʿAbbāsid capital?', *JNES*, 5 (1999), 241–57.

Conrad, Gerhard, *Die Quḍāt Dimasq und der madhab al-Auzāʿī: Materialen zur syrischen Rechtsgeschichte*, Beirut and Stuttgart, 1994.

Crone, Patricia, *Slaves on horses: The evolution of the early Islamic polity*, Cambridge, 1980.

'Were the Qays and Yemen of the Umayyad period political parties?', *Der Islam*, 71 (1994), 1–57.

Crone, Patricia, and Martin Hinds, *God's caliph: Religious authority in the first centuries of Islam*, Cambridge, 1986.

Dagron, Gilbert (ed.), *Travaux et mémoires*, 11, Paris, 1991.

Dennett, Daniel C., *Conversion and the poll-tax in early Islam*, Cambridge, MA, 1950.

Déroches, Vincent, 'Polémique anti-judaique et émergence de l'Islam (7e–8e siècles)', *Revue des études byzantines*, 57 (1999), 141–61.

Dussaud, René, *Topographie historique de la Syrie antique et médiévale*, Paris, 1927.

Elad, Amikam, 'Aspects of the transition from the Umayyad to the ʿAbbāsid caliphate', *JSAI*, 19 (1995), 89–132.

Medieval Jerusalem and Islamic worship, Leiden, 1995.

Fattal, Antoine, *Le statut légal des non-musulmans en pays d'Islam*, Beirut, 1958.

Foss, Clive, 'The coinage of the first century of Islam', *Journal of Roman Archaeology*, 16 (2003), 748–60.

'A Syrian coinage of Mu'awiya?', *Revue numismatique*, 158 (2002), 353–67.

Fowden, Elizabeth, *The barbarian plain: Saint Sergius between Rome and Iran*, Transformation of the Classical Heritage 28, Berkeley, 1999.

Fowden, Garth, *Qusayr ʿAmra: Art and the Umayyad elite in Late Antique Syria*, Berkeley, 2004.

Gènequand, Denis, 'The early Islamic settlement in the Syrian steppe: A new look at Umayyad and medieval Qasr al-Hayr al-Sharqi (Syria)', *al-'Usur al-Wusta*, 17 (2005), 21–7.

Gervers, M., and Ramzi Bikhazi (eds.), *Conversion and continuity: Indigenous Christian communities in Islamic lands, eighth to eighteenth centuries*, Toronto, 1990.
Grabar, Oleg, *The formation of Islamic art*, New Haven, 1973; 2nd rev. edn 1987.
Grabar, Oleg, R. Holod, J. Knustad and W. Trousdale, *City in the desert: Qasr al-Hayr East*, 2 vols., Cambridge, MA, 1978.
Griffith, S. H., *Arabic Christianity in the monasteries of ninth-century Palestine*, Aldershot, 1992.
'From Aramaic to Arabic: The languages of the monasteries of Palestine in the Byzantine and early Islamic periods', *Dumbarton Oaks Papers*, 52 (1997), 12–31.
Hage, W., *Die syrisch-jakobitische Kirche in frühislamischer Zeit*, Wiesbaden, 1966.
Haldon, John F., *Byzantium in the seventh century: The transformation of a culture*, Cambridge, 1990.
Hoyland, Robert, 'New documentary texts and the early Islamic state', *BSOAS*, 69, 3 (2006), 395–416.
Ḥusayn, Fāliḥ, *al-Ḥayāt al-zirāʿiyya fī bilād al-shām fī al-ʿaṣr al-umawī*, Amman, 1978.
Johns, Jeremy, 'Archaeology and the history of early Islam: The first seventy years', *JESHO*, 46 (2003), 411–36.
(ed.), *Bayt al-Maqdis: Jerusalem and early Islam*, Oxford Studies in Islamic Art 9, part 2, Oxford, 1999.
Johns, Jeremy, and J. Raby (eds.), *Bayt al-Maqdis: ʿAbd al-Malik's Jerusalem*, Oxford Studies in Islamic Art 9, part 1, Oxford, 1992.
Kaegi, Walter E., *Byzantium and the early Islamic conquests*, Cambridge, 1992.
Kennedy, Hugh, *The early Abbasid caliphate: A political history*, London and Sydney, 1981.
The Prophet and the age of the caliphate, London and New York, 1986; 2nd rev. edn 2004.
King, G. R. D., 'Islam, iconoclasm, and the declaration of doctrine', *BSOAS*, 48 (1985), 267–77.
Kraemer, Caspar J., *Excavations at Nessana*, vol. III: *Non-literary papyri*, Princeton, 1958.
Kurd ʿAlī, Muḥammad, *Khiṭaṭ al-shām*, 6 vols., Damascus, 1925.
Lammens, Henri, *Le califat de Yazid Ier*, Beirut, 1921.
La Syrie: Précis historique, 2 vols., Beirut, 1921.
Le Strange, Guy, *Lands of the eastern caliphate*, Cambridge, 1905.
Liebeschuetz, J. H. G., *The decline and fall of the Roman city*, Oxford, 2001.
Lindsay, J. E. (ed.), *Ibn ʿAsākir and early Islamic history*, Princeton, 2001.
Madelung, Wilferd, 'Fatimiden und Bahrainqarmaten', *Der Islam*, 34 (1959), 34–88.
'The Sufyani between tradition and history', *SI*, 63 (1984), 5–48.
Magness, Jodi, *The archaeology of the early Islamic settlement in Palestine*, Winona Lake, IN, 2003.
Moscati, Sabatino, 'Le massacre des Umayyades dans l'histoire at dans les fragments poétiques', *Archiv Orientalní*, 18 (1950), 88–115.
Répertoire chronologique d'épigraphie arabe, 17 vols., in progress, Cairo, 1931–.
Robinson, C. F., *Empire and elites after the Muslim conquest: The transformation of northern Mesopotamia*, Cambridge Studies in Islamic Civilization, Cambridge, 2000.
'Neck-sealing in early Islam', *JESHO*, 48 (2005), 401–41.
Rotter, Gerhard, *Die Umayyaden und der zweite Bürgerkrieg*, Wiesbaden, 1982.
Salibi, Kamal S., *Syria under Islam: Empire on trial, 634–1097*, Delmar, NY, 1977.
Sauvaget, Jean, 'Esquisse d'une histoire de la ville de Damas', *REI*, 8 (1934), 421–80.
Schick, Robert, *The Christian communities of Palestine from Byzantine to Islamic rule: A historical and archaeological study*, Studies in Late Antiquity and Early Islam 2, Princeton, 1995.

Sourdel, Dominique, 'La Syrie au temps des premiers califes abbassides (132/750–264/878)', *REI*, 48 (1980), 155–75.

Sourdel, D., and J. Sourdel-Thomine, 'Nouveaux documents sur l'histoire religieuse et sociale de Damas au moyen âge', *REI*, 32 (1964), 1–25.

'Trois actes de vente damascains du début du IVe/Xe siècle', *JESHO*, 8 (1965), 164–85.

Tate, Georges, *Les campagnes de la Syrie du Nord, du IIe au VIIe siècle: Un exemple d'expansion démographique et économique à la fin de l'Antiquité*, Paris, 1992.

Travaux et mémoires: *see* Dagron, Gilbert.

Von Sievers, Peter, 'Military, merchants and nomads: The social evolution of the Syrian cities and countryside during the classical period, 780–969/164–358', *Der Islam*, 56 (1979), 212–44.

Wellhausen, Julius, 'Arab wars with the Byzantines in the Umayyad period', in M. Bonner (ed.), *Arab–Byzantine relations in early Islamic times*, Burlington, VT, 2005, 31–64.

Wickham, Chris, *Framing the early Middle Ages: Europe and the Mediterranean, 400–800*, Oxford, 2005.

Witakowski, W., *The Syriac chronicle of Pseudo-Dionysius of Tell-Mahré: A study in the history of historiography*, Uppsala, 1987.

Wulzinger, K., and C. Watzinger, *Damaskus: Die islamische Stadt*, Berlin and Leipzig, 1924.

Yusuf, Muhsin D., *Economic survey of Syria during the tenth and eleventh centuries*, Berlin, 1985.

Chapter 13: Egypt

Practical suggestions for further reading

Brett, M., ''Abbasids, Fatimids and Seljuqs', in David Luscombe and Jonathan Riley-Smith (eds.), *The new Cambridge medieval history*, vol. IV, Cambridge, 2004, 675–720.

The rise of the Fatimids: The world of the Mediterranean and the Middle East in the fourth century of the hijra, tenth century CE, Leiden, 2001.

Goitein, S. D., *A Mediterranean society: The Jewish communities of the Arab world as portrayed in the documents of the Cairo Geniza*, 5 vols., Berkeley and Los Angeles, 1967–88, vol. I: *The economic foundations*.

Kennedy, H., *The Prophet and the age of the caliphates*, London and New York, 1986.

Lane-Poole, S., *A history of Egypt in the Middle Ages*, 4th edn, London, 1925.

The story of Cairo, London, 1902.

Petry C. F. (ed.), *The Cambridge history of Egypt*, vol. I: *Islamic Egypt, 640–1517*, Cambridge, 1998.

Raymond, A., *Le Caire*, Paris, 1993.

Sanders, P., *Ritual, politics and the city in Fatimid Cairo*, Albany, 1994.

Primary sources

(Abū Ṣāliḥ the Armenian), *Churches and monasteries of Egypt*, ed. and trans. B. T. A. Evetts, Oxford, 1895.

Grohmann, A. (ed. and trans.), *Arabic papyri in the Egyptian Library*, 6 vols., Cairo, 1934–62.

Ibn ʿAbd al-Ḥakam, *Kitāb futūḥ Miṣr wa ʾl-Maghrib*, ed. C. C. Torrey, New Haven, 1922.

Ibn Ḥawqal, *Ṣūrat al-arḍ*, ed. J. H. Kramers, 2 vols., Leiden, 1938–9; trans. G. Wiet as *Configuration de la terre*, 2 vols., Beirut and Paris, 1964.

Ibn Muyassar, *Choix de passages de la Chronique d'Egypte d'Ibn Muyassar*, ed. A. F. Sayyid, Cairo, 1981.

Ibn al-Ṣayrafī, *al-Ishāra ilā man nāla al-wizāra*, ed. A. Mukhlis, *Bulletin de l'Institut Français d'Archéologie Orientale du Caire*, 26 (1924).

John of Nikiou, *Chronique de Jean, Evêque de Nikiou*, ed. and trans. A. Zotenberg, Paris, 1883; trans. R. M. Charles as *The chronicle of John, bishop of Nikiu*, Oxford, 1916.

Karabacek, J., *Papyrus Erzherzog Rainer: Führer durch die Ausstellung*, Vienna, 1892.

al-Kindī, *Governors and judges of Egypt*, ed. R. Guest, Leiden and London, 1912.

al-Maqrīzī, *Itti'āẓ al-ḥunafā'*, ed. J. D. al-Shayyāl and M. H. M. Aḥmad, 3 vols., Cairo, 1967–73.

Kitāb al-mawā'iẓ wa 'l-i'tibār fī dhikr al-khiṭaṭ wa 'l-āthār (al-Khiṭṭaṭ), ed. G. Wiet (4 vols. only), Cairo, 1911; full text, Būlāq, 1853–4; autograph, ed. A. F. Sayyid, London, 1995.

al-Muqaffā, ed. M. Yalaoui, Beirut, 1991.

al-Muqaddasī, *Aḥsan al-taqāsim fī ma'rifat al-aqālīm*, Damascus, 1980.

Sa'īd ibn Baṭrīk [Eutychius], *Eutychii Patriarchae Alexandrini Annales*, ed. L. Cheikho, CSCO, Scriptores Arabici, 3rd series, vols. VI, VII, Beirut, Paris and Leipzig, 1906, 1909.

(Severus ibn al-Muqaffa'), *History of the patriarchs of the Coptic Church of Alexandria/the Egyptian Church*, ed. and trans. B. T. A. Evetts, Y. 'Abd al-Masih, O. H. E. Burmester and A. Khater, 3 vols., Paris, 1901; Cairo, 1943–59, 1968–70.

Yaḥyā al-Anṭākī, *Ta'rīkh*, ed. L. Cheikho, CSCO, Scriptores Arabici, 3rd series, vol. VII, Beirut, Paris and Leipzig, 1909; and J. Forsyth, *The Byzantine-Arab chronicle (938–1034) of Yaḥyā b. Sa'īd al-Anṭākī*, Ann Arbor, 1977.

Secondary sources

Ashtor, E., 'Migrations de l'Irak vers les pays méditerranéens', in E. Ashtor, *The medieval Near East: Social and economic history*, Variorum Series, London, 1978, IV.

Bianquis, T., 'al-H'âkim bi amr Allâh ou la folie de l'unité chez un souverain fât'imide', in C. A. Julien *et al.* (eds.), *Les Africains*, vol. XI, Paris, 1978, 105–33.

Brett, M., 'The Arab conquest and the rise of Islam in North Africa', in J. D. Fage and Roland Oliver (eds.), *The Cambridge history of Africa*, 8 vols., Cambridge, 1978, vol. II: *From c. 500 BC to AD 1050*, 490–555.

'The execution of al-Yāzūrī', in U. Vermeulen and D. De Smet (eds.), *Egypt and Syria in the Fatimid, Ayyubid and Mamluk Eras*, vol. II, Leuven, 1998, 15–27.

'al-Karāza al-Marqusiya: The Coptic Church in the Fatimid empire', in U. Vermeulen and J. Van Steenbergen (eds.), *Egypt and Syria in the Fatimid, Ayyubid and Mamluk eras*, vol. IV, Leuven, 2005, 33–60.

'The origins of the Mamluk military system in the Fatimid period', in U. Vermeulen and D. De Smet (eds.), *Egypt and Syria in the Fatimid, Ayyubid and Mamluk Periods*, vol. I, Leuven, 1995, 39–52.

'Population and conversion to Islam in the mediaeval period', in U. Vermeulen and J. Van Steenbergen (eds.), *Egypt and Syria in the Fatimid, Ayyubid and Mamluk eras*, vol. IV, Leuven, 2005, 1–32.

'The way of the peasant', *BSOAS*, 47 (1984), 44–56.

Brunschvig, R., 'Ibn 'Abdalh'akam et la conquête de l'Afrique du Nord par les Arabes', in R. Brunschvig, *Études sur l'Islam classique et l'Afrique du Nord*, ed. A.-M. Turki, Variorum Reprints, London, 1986, XI.

Butler, A. J., *The Arab conquest of Egypt and the last thirty years of the Roman dominion*, 2nd edn, with critical bibliography by P. M. Fraser, Oxford, 1978.
Canard, M., 'al-Ḥākim bi-Amri'llāh', *EI2*, vol. III, 76–82.
Chaudhuri, K. N., *Trade and civilisation in the Indian Ocean*, Cambridge, 1985.
Cortese, D., and S. Calderini, *Women and the Fatimids in the world of Islam*, Edinburgh, 2006.
Crone, P., and M. Cook, *Hagarism: The making of the Islamic world*, Cambridge, 1977.
Daftary, F., *The Ismāʿīlīs: Their history and doctrines*, Cambridge, 1990.
Décobert, C., 'Sur l'arabisation et l'islamisation de l'Egypte médiévale', in C. Décobert (ed.), *Itinéraires de l'Egypte: Mélanges offerts au père Maurice Martin, SJ*, Cairo, 1992, 273–300.
Dennett, D. C., *Conversion and the poll-tax in early Islam*, Cambridge, MA, 1950.
Forsyth, J., *The Byzantine-Arab chronicle (938–1034) of Yaḥyā b. Saʿīd al-Anṭākī*, Ann Arbor, 1977.
Geertz, C., *Islam observed: Religious development in Morocco and Indonesia*, Chicago and London, 1968.
Gellens, S. I., 'Egypt, Islamization of', in A. S. Atiya (gen. ed.), *The Coptic encyclopedia*, New York, 1991, vol. II, 609–11.
Goodchild, R. G., 'Byzantines, Berbers and Arabs in seventh-century Libya', *Antiquity*, 51 (1967), 115–24; repr. in R. G. Goodchild, *Libyan studies: Selected papers of the late* R. G. Goodchild, ed. J. Reynolds and Paul Elek, London, 1976, 255–67.
Halm, H., *The empire of the Mahdi*, trans. M. Bonner, Leiden, 1996.
Die Kalifen von Kairo: Die Fatimiden in Ägypten 973–1074, Munich, 2003.
Ḥasan, Y. F., *The Arabs and the Sudan*, Edinburgh, 1967.
Hurst, H. E., *The Nile*, London, 1952.
Issawi, C., 'The area and population of the Arab empire', in A. Udovitch (ed.), *The Islamic Middle East, 700–1900*, Princeton, 1981, 375–96.
Egypt: An economic and social analysis, London, New York and Toronto, 1948.
Johns, J., *Arabic administration in Norman Sicily: The royal* dīwān, Cambridge, 2002.
Kaegi, W. E., 'Egypt on the eve of the Muslim conquest', in C. F. Petry (ed.), *The Cambridge history of Egypt*, vol. I: *Islamic Egypt, 640–1517*, Cambridge, 1998, 34–61.
Kennedy, H., 'Egypt as a province of the Islamic caliphate, 641–868', in C. F. Petry (ed.), *The Cambridge history of Egypt*, vol. I: *Islamic Egypt, 640–1517*, Cambridge, 1998, 62–85.
Kubiak, W., *al-Fustat: Its foundation and early urban development*, Cairo, 1987.
Lapidus, I. M., 'The conversion of Egypt to Islam', *Israel Oriental Studies*, 2 (1972), 248–62.
Lev, Y., 'The Fatimid navy, Byzantium and the Mediterranean sea, 909–1036 CE', *Byzantion*, 54 (1984), 220–52.
State and society in Fatimid Egypt, Leiden, 1991.
'Tinnīs: An industrial medieval town', in M. Barrucand (ed.), *L'Egypte fatimide: Son art et son histoire*, Paris, 1999, 83–96.
Lombard, M., *The golden age of Islam*, Amsterdam, Oxford and New York, 1975.
Martin, M., 'La province d'Ashmunayn', *Annales Islamologiques*, 23 (1987), 1–29.
Miquel, A., 'L'Egypte vue par un géographe arabe du IVe / Xe siècle: al-Muqaddasī', *Annales Islamologiques*, 11 (1972), 109–39.
Morimoto, K., *The fiscal administration of Egypt in the early Islamic period*, Kyoto, 1981.
Rabie, H. H., 'Technical aspects of agriculture in medieval Egypt', in A. Udovitch (ed.), *The Islamic Middle East, 700–1900*, Princeton, 1981, 75–80.

Sanders, P., 'The Fāṭimid state, 969–1171', in C. F. Petry (ed.), *The Cambridge history of Egypt*, vol. I: *Islamic Egypt, 640–1517*, Cambridge, 1998, 151–74.
Sato, T., 'Irrigation in rural Egypt from the 12th to the 14th centuries', *Orient*, 8 (1972), 81–92.
Shaban, M. A., *Islamic history: A new interpretation*, 2 vols., Cambridge, 1971–6; vol. I: *AD 600–750 (AH 132)*, Cambridge, 1971.
Shinnie, P. L., '*Christian Nubia*', in J. D. Fage and Roland Oliver (eds.), *The Cambridge history of Africa*, 8 vols., Cambridge, 1978, vol. II: *From c. 500 BC to AD 1050*, 556–88.
Sijpesteijn, P. M., and L. Sundelin (eds.), *Papyrology and the history of early Islamic Egypt*, Leiden, 2004.
Turner, B. S., *Weber and Islam*, London, 1974.
Walters, C. C., *Monastic archaeology in Egypt*, Warminster, 1974.
Wilfong, T., 'The non-Muslim communities: Christian communities', in C. F. Petry (ed.), *The Cambridge history of Egypt*, vol. I: *Islamic Egypt, 640–1517*, Cambridge, 1998, 175–97.

Chapter 14: The Iberian Peninsula and North Africa

Practical suggestions for further reading

Abun-Nasr, J. M., *A history of the Maghrib in the Islamic period*, Cambridge, 1987.
Brett, M., and E. Fentress, *The Berbers*, Oxford, 1996.
Fierro, M. I., *ʿAbd al-Rahman III: The first Cordoban caliph*, Oxford, 2005.
Fierro, M. I., and J. Samsó (eds.), *The formation of al-Andalus*, vol. II: *Language, religion, culture and the sciences*, Aldershot and Brookfield, VT, 1998.
Guichard, P., *From the Arab conquest to the Reconquest: The splendour and fragility of al-Andalus*, Granada, 2006.
Jayyusi, S. K. (ed.), *The legacy of Muslim Spain*, Leiden, 1992.
Julien, C.-A, *History of North Africa from the Arab conquest to 1830*, London, 1970.
Kennedy, H., *Muslim Spain and Portugal: A political history of al-Andalus*, London, 1996.
Laroui, ʿA. A, *The history of the Magrib: An interpretative essay*, Princeton, 1977.
Lévi-Provençal, E., *Historia de la España Musulmana (711–1031)*, vol IV: *Historia de España dirigida por R. Menénedez Pidal*, Madrid, 1950.
Historia de la España Musulmana: Instituciones y vida social e intelectual, vol V: *Historia de España dirigida por R. Menénedez Pidal*, Madrid, 1957.
Marçais, G., *La berbérie musulmane et l'Orient au moyen âge*, Paris, 1946.
Marín, M. (ed.), *The formation of al-Andalus*, vol. I: *History and society*, Aldershot, 1998.
Norris, H. T., *The Berbers in Arabic literature*, London, 1982.
Sénac, P., *al-Mansūr: Le fléau de l'an mil*, Paris, 2006.
Terrasse, M., *Islam et Occident méditerranéen: De la conquête aux ottomans*, Paris, 2001.
Torres Balbas, L., *Ciudades hispanomusulmanas*, Madrid, 1972.
Vallejo, A., *Madīnat al-Zahrāʾ: Guía oficial del yacimiento arqueológico*, Seville, 2004.
Vernet, J., *Lo que Europa debe al Islam de España*, Barcelona, 1999.
Viguera, M. J., and C. Castillo (coords), *El Esplendor de los Omeyas Cordobeses: La civilización Musulmana de Europa Occidental*, Granada, 2001.

Primary sources

ʿAbd al-Malik ibn Ḥabīb, *Kitāb al-taʾrīkh*, ed. J. Aguadé, Madrid, 1991.

Abu l-ʿArab al-Tamimī, *Classes des savants de l'Ifriqiya*, trans. Muhammad ben Cheneb, Algiers, 1920.

Akhbār majmūʿa, ed. and trans. E. Lafuente Alcántara, Madrid, 1867.

ʿAlī ibn ʿĪsā al-Ṭulayṭulī, *Mujtāṣar (Compendio)*, ed. and trans. M. J. Cervera, Madrid, 2000.

al-Bakrī, *Kitāb al-masālik*, ed. M. J. de Goeje, Leiden, 1889; ed and trans. M. de Slane as *Description de l'Afrique Septentrionale*, rev. edn, Paris, 1965.

Corpus Scriptorum Muzarabicorum, 2 vols., ed. I. Gil, Madrid, 1973.

Crónica Mozárabe de 754, ed. J. E. López Pereira, Saragossa, 1980.

Crónica del Moro Rasis, ed. D. Catalán and M. S. de Andrés, Madrid, 1974.

Fatḥ al-Andalus, ed. L. Molina, Madrid, 1994; trans. M. Penellas as *La conquista de al-Andalus*, Madrid, 2002.

al-Ḥimyarī, *Kitāb al-Rawḍ al-Miʿṭār fī khabar al-aqṭār*, ed. I. ʿAbbās, Beirut, 1975; trans. E. Lévi-Provençal as *La peninsule ibérique au moyen âge d'après le Kitāb al-Rawḍ al-Miʿṭār*, Leiden, 1938.

Ibn ʿAbd al-Ḥakam, *Futūḥ Miṣr wa l-Magrib wa-l-Andalus*, ed. C. C. Torrey, New Haven, 1922.

Ibn al-Athīr, *al-Kāmil fī l-taʾrīkh*, ed. J. C. Tornberg, Beirut, 1979; partial trans. E. Fagnan as *Annals du Maghreb et de l'Espagne*, Argel, 1898.

Ibn al-ʿAṭṭār, *Kitāb al-wathāʾiq wa l-sijillāt*, ed. P. Chalmeta, Madrid, 1983, trans. P. Chalmeta and M. Marugán as *Formulario notarial y judicial andalusí*, Madrid, 2000.

Ibn Ḥawqal, *Kitāb ṣūrat al-arḍ*, ed. M. J. de Goeje, rev. J. H. Kramers, BGA 2, Leiden, 1938.

Ibn Ḥayyān, *al-Muqtabis V*, ed. P. Chalmeta, F. Corriente and M. Sobh, Madrid; 1979; trans. M. J. Viguera and F. Corriente as *Crónica del califa ʿAbdarraḥmān III an-Nāṣir entre los años 912 y 942*, Saragossa, 1981.

al-Muqtabis fī ajbār bilād al-Andalus (al-Ḥakam II), ed. A. A. Hajji, Beirut, 1965; trans. E. García Gómez as *El Califato de Córdoba en el Muqtabis de Ibn Ḥayyān*, Anales Palatinos del Califa de Córdoba al-Ḥakam II, Madrid, 1967.

al-Muqtabis min anbāʿ ahl al-Andalus, ed. M. A. Makki, Cairo, 1971.

al-Muqtabis fī taʾrīkh rijāl al-Andalus, ed. M. Antuña, Paris, 1937.

al-Sifr al-thānī min Kitāb al-Muqtabis, ed. M. A. Makki, Riyadh, 2003: trans. M. A. Makki and F. Corriente as *Crónica de los emires Alḥakam i y ʿAbdarraḥmān I entre los años 796 y 847*, Saragossa, 2001.

Ibn Ḥazm, *Jamharat ansāb al-ʿarab*, ed. A. S. M. Harun, Beirut, 1982.

Ibn ʿIdhārī, *Kitāb al-Bayān al-Mugrib*, vols. I–II, ed. G. S. Colin and E. Lévi-Provençal, Leiden, 1948–51; vol. III, ed. E. Lévi-Provençal, Paris, 1930, trans. E. Fagnan as *Histoire de l'Afrique et de l'Esppagne intitulée al-bayano l-Mogrib*, Algiers, 1901–4 and F. Maíllo as *La Caída del Califato de Córdoba y los Reyes de Taifas*, Salamanca, 1993.

Ibn Khaldūn, *Taʾrīkh ʿalāmat Ibn Khaldūn. Kitāb al-ʿIbar*, ed. Y. A. Dagir, vol. I, *Muqaddima*, Beirut, 1956; trans. F. Rosenthal as *The Muqaddimah: An introduction to history*, repr. London 1987; trans. M. de Slane as *Histoire des Berbères et des dynasties musulmanes de l'Afrique Septentrionale*, Paris, 1925.

Ibn al-Qūṭiya, *Taʾrīkh iftitāḥ al-Andalus*, ed. P. de Gayangos, E. Saavedra and F. Codera, Madrid, 1868.

Ibn Ṣagīr, 'La chronique d'Ibn Saghir sur les imams rustumides de Tahert', ed. and trans. A. C. Motylinski in *Actes du XIVe Congrès International des Orientalistes*, Algiers, 1905.

Ibn Sa'īd, *al-Mugrib fī hulā al-Magrib*, ed. Sawqi Dayf, Cairo, 1953.

Ibn Sallām, *Kitāb Ibn Sallām*, ed. W. Schwartz and Sālim ibn Ya'qūb, Wiesbaden, 1986.

'Iyāḍ, *Tartīb al-madārik wa taqrīb al-masālik li ma'rifat a'lām madhhab Mālik*, various eds., Rabat, 1980–7.

al-Khushanī, *Akhbār al-fuqahā' wa l-muḥaddithīn*, ed. L. Molina and M. L. Avila, Madrid, 1992.

Kitāb al-qudāt bi-Qurṭuba, ed. and trans. J. Ribera as *Historia de los Jueces de Córdoba por Aljoxani*, Madrid, 1914.

al-Maqqarī, *Nafḥ al-Ṭīb min guṣn al-Andalus al-raṭīb*, ed. I. 'Abbās, 8 vols., Beirut, 1968.

al-Qāḍī al-Nu'mān, *Iftitāḥ al-da'wa wa-ibtidā' al-dawla*, ed. F. Dachraoui, Tunis, 1975.

al-Raqīq, 'L'Occident musulman à l'avènement des Abbasides d'après le chroniqueur ziride al-Raqīq', trans. H. R. Idrīs, *REI*, 39 (1971), 209–91.

al-'Udhrī, *Tarṣī' al-akhbār wa-tanwī' al-āthār wa l-bustān fī garā'ib al-buldān*, ed. A. al-Ahwani, Madrid, 1965.

Una Crónica Anónima de 'Abd al-Raḥmān al-Nāṣir, ed. and trans. E. Lévi-Provençal and E. García Gómez, Madrid and Granada, 1950.

al-Ya'qūbī, *Kitāb al-buldān*, ed. and trans. G. Marçais as *Description du Maghreb*, Argel, 1962.

Secondary sources

Acién, M., *Entre el feudalismo y el Islam: 'Umar ibn Ḥafṣūn en los historiadores, en las fuentes y en la historia*, 2nd edn, Jaén, 1997.

'Poblamiento indígena en al-Andalus e indicios del primer poblamiento andalusí', *al-Qantara*, 20 (1999), 47–64.

'Sobre el papel de la ideología en la caracterización de las formaciones sociales: La formación social islámica', *Hispania*, 200 (1998), 915–68.

Akerraz, A., 'Note sur l'enceinte tardive de Volubilis', *Bulletin Archéologique du Comité des Travaux Historiques*, 19 (1985), 429–36.

Balaguer, A., *Las emisiones transicionales árabe-musulmanas de Hispania*, Barcelona, 1976.

Barceló, M., *El sol que salió por Occidente: Estudios sobre el estado Omeya en al-Andalus*, Jaén, 1997.

Bazzana, A., P. Cressier and P. Guichard, *Les châteaux ruraux d'al-Andalus: Histoire et archéologie des ḥuṣūn du sud est de l'Espagne*, Madrid, 1988.

Benco, N. L. (ed.), *Anatomy of a medieval Islamic town: al-Basra, Morocco*, BAR Series 1234, Oxford, 2004.

Berque, J., 'Qu'est-ce qu'une tribu nord-africaine', *Éventail de l'Histoire Vivante: Hommage à Lucien Febvre*, 2 vols., Paris, 1953, vol. I, 261–71.

Blachère, R., 'Fes chez les géographes arabes du moyen âge', *Hespéris*, 20 (1934), 90–113.

Brett, M., 'The Arab conquests and the rise of Islam in North Africa', in J. D. Fage and Roland Oliver (eds.), *The Cambridge history of Africa*, 8 vols., Cambridge, 1978, vol. II: *From c. 500 BC to AD 1050*, 490–555.

'Ibn Khaldūn and the Arabisation of North Africa', *Maghreb Review*, 4 (1979), 9–16.

The rise of the Fatimids: The world of the Mediterranean and the Middle East in the fourth century of the hijra, tenth century CE, Leiden, 2001.

Brunschvig, R., 'Ibn 'Abdalhakam et la conquête de l'Afrique du Nord par les Arabes', *Annales de l'Institut d'Etudes Orientales Université d'Alger*, 6 (1942–7), 108–55.

Caballero, L., and P. Mateos, *Visigodos y Omeyas: Un debate entre la Antigüedad y la Alta Edad Media, Anejos de Archivo Español de Arqueología, XXIII*, Mérida, 2000.

Caballero, L., P. Mateos and M. Retuerce (eds.), *Cerámicas tardorromanas y altomedievales en la Península Ibérica*, Madrid, 2003.

Camps, G., 'De Masuna à Koceila: Les destinées de la Maurétanie aux VIe et VIIe siècles', *Bulletin Archéologique du Comité des Travaux Historiques et Scientifiques*, 19 (1985), 307–24.

Canto, A., 'De la ceca de al-Andalus a la de Madīnat al-Zahrā'', *Cuadernos de Madīnat al-Zahrā'*, 3 (1991), 111–31.

Canto, A., and T. Ibrahim, *Moneda Andalusí: La colección de la Casa de la Moneda*, Madrid, 2004.

Chalmeta, P., *Invasión e islamización: La sumisión de Hispania y la formación de al-Andalus*, Madrid, 1994.

'Monnaie de compte, monnaie fiscale et monnaie réelle en al-Andalus', in Y.Raguib (ed.), *Documents de l'Islam mediéval: Nouvelles perspectives de recherche*, Cairo, 1991, 65–88.

Corriente, F., *Diccionario de arabismos y voces afines en iberorromance*, Madrid, 1999.

Cressier, P., and M. García-Arenal (eds.), *Genèse de la ville islamique en al-Andalus et au Maghreb occidental*, Madrid, 1998.

Cressier, P., M. I. Fierro and J. P. Van Staëvel (eds.), *L'urbanisme dans l'Occident musulman au moyen âge: Aspects juridiques*, Madrid, 2000.

Cuoq, J., *L'église d'Afrique du Nord du IIe au XIIe siècle*, Paris, 1984.

Dachraoui, F., *Le califat fatimide au Maghreb*, Tunis, 1981.

Djaït, H., 'La Wilāya d'Ifrīqiya au IIe/VIIIe siècle: Étude institutionnelle', *SI*, 27 (1967), 77–121.

Doménech Belda, C., *Dinares, dirhames y feluses: Circulación monetaria islámica en el País Valenciano*, Alicante, 2003

Estudios Onomásticos y Biográficos de al-Andalus, 14 vols., Madrid, 1988–2004.

Eustache, D., *Corpus de dirhams idrīsites et contemporaines*, Rabat, 1970–1.

de Felipe, H., *Identidad y onomástica de los bereberes de al-Andalus*, Madrid, 1997.

Fentress, E., 'The house of the Prophet: North African Islamic housing', *Archeologia Medievale*, 14 (1987), 47–68.

Fierro, M. I., *La heterodoxia en al-Andalus durante el periodo omeya*, Madrid, 1987.

Frend, W. H. C., 'The end of Byzantine North Africa: Some evidence of transitions', *Bulletin Archéologique du Comité des Travaux Historiques et Scientifiques*, 19, 2 (1985), 387–97.

García Arenal, M., *Messianism and puritanical reform: Mahdīs of the Muslim west*, Leiden, 2006.

García Arenal, M., and E. Manzano, 'Idrīssisme et villes idrīssides', *SI*, 82 (1995), 5–33.

García Sanjuán, A., *Till God inherits the earth: Islamic pious endowments in al-Andalus*, Leiden, 2007.

Gelichi, S., and M. Milanese, 'The transformation of the ancient towns in central Tunisia during the Islamic period: The example of Uchi Maius', *al-Masaq: Islam and the medieval Mediterranean*, 14 (2002), 33–45.

Gil, J., 'Judíos y cristianos en Hispania (siglos VIII y IX)', *Hispania Sacra*, 31 (1978–9), 9–80.

Guichard, P., *al-Andalus: Estructura antropológica de una sociedad islámica en Occidente*, Barcelona, 1976; repr. Granada, 1998.

Gutiérrez, S., *La cora de Tudmīr de la Antigüdad tardía al mundo islámico: Poblamiento y cultura material*, Madrid and Alicante, 1996.

Halm, H., *The empire of the Mahdi: The rise of the Fatimids*, trans. Michael Bonner, Leiden, 1996.

Hirschberg, H. Z., *A history of the Jews in North Africa*, Leiden, 1974.

Idrīs, H. R., 'Contribution à l'histoire de l'Ifrīqiya: Tableau de la vie intelectuelle et administrative à Kairouan sous les Aglabites et les Fatimites (4 premiers siècles de l'Hégire) d'après le *Riyād En Nufūs* de Abū Bakr al-Mālikī', *Revue d'Études Islamiques, Cahiers* (1935), 105–77.

Lévi-Provençal, E., 'La fondation de Fès', *Annales de l'Institut d'Études Orientales*, 4 (Algiers, 1938), 23–53.

'Un nouveau récit de la conquête de l'Afrique du nord par les Arabes', *Arabica*, 1 (1954), 17–43.

Lewicki, T., 'The Ibādi community at Basra in the seventh to ninth centuries and the origins of the Ibādite states in Arabia and North Africa', *Journal of World History*, 13 (1971), 51–130.

'Prophètes, devins et magiciens chez les Berbers médiévaux', *Folia Orientalia*, 7 (1965), 3–27.

Lirola Delgado, J., and J. M. Puerta Vílchez (eds.), *Biblioteca de al-Andalus*, vol. III: *De Ibn al-Dabbāg a Ibn Kurz*; vol IV: *De Ibn al-Labbāna a Ibn al-Ruŷulī*, Almería, 2004.

Madelung, W., 'Some notes on non Ismāʿīlī Shiism in the Maghrib', *SI*, 44 (1976), 87–97.

Makki, M. A., 'Egipto y los orígenes de la historiografía arábigo-española', *Revista del Instituto Egipcio de Estudios Islámicos*, 5 (1957), 157–248.

Malpica, A., 'Arqueología de los paisajes medievales granadinos: Medio físico y territorio en la costa de Granada', *Arqueología y Territorio Medieval*, 2 (1995), 25–62.

Manzano Moreno, E., *Conquistadores, emires y califas: Los Omeyas y la formación de al-Andalus*, Barcelona, 2006.

La frontera de al-Andalus en época de los Omeyas, Madrid, 1991.

Marín, M., 'Altos funcionarios para el Califa: Jueces y otros cargos de la administración de ʿAbd al-Raḥmān III', *Cuadernos de Madīnat al-Zahrāʾ*, 5 (2004), 91–105.

Mujeres en al-Andalus, Madrid, 2000.

'Ṣaḥāba et tābiʿūn dans al-Andalus: Histoire et légende', *SI*, 54 (1981), 5–49.

Martínez, M. A., 'Epígrafes a nombre de al-Ḥakam en Madīnat al-Zahrāʾ', *Cuadernos de Madīnat al-Zahrāʾ*, 4 (1999), 83–103.

Mattingly, D., 'Explanations: People as agency', in G. Barker (ed.), *Farming the desert: The UNESCO Libyan valleys archaeological survey*, Tripoli and London, 1996, 319–42.

Méouak, M., *Pouvoir souverain, administration centrale et élites politiques dans l'Espagne umayyade (IIe–IVe/VIIIe–Xe siècles)*, Helsinki, 1999.

Muranyi, M., *Beiträge zur Geschichte der Ḥadīṯ und Rechtsgelehrsamkeit der Mālikiyya in Nordafrika bis zum 5. Jh. DH*, Wiesbaden, 1997.

Ocaña Jiménez, M., 'Inscripciones árabes fundacionales de la mezquita catedral de Córdoba', *Cuadernos de Madīnat al-Zahrāʾ*, 2 (1988–1990), 9–28.

Picard, C., *Le Portugal musulman (VIIIe–XIIIe siècle): L'occident d'al-Andalus sous domination islamique*, Paris, 2000.

Ramírez del Río, J., *La orientalización de al-Andalus: Los días de los árabes en la Península Ibérica*, Seville, 2002.

Savage, E., *A gateway to hell, a gateway to paradise: The North African response to the Arab conquest*, Princeton, 1997.

Scales, P., *The fall of the caliphate of Cordoba: Berbers and Andalusis in conflict*, Leiden, 1994.

Schwartz, W., *Die Anfänge der Ibaditen in Nordafrika: Der Beitrag einer islamischen Minderheit zur Ausbreitung des Islams*, Wiesbaden, 1983.

Sénac, P., *La frontière et les hommes (VIIIe–XIIe siècle): Le peuplement musulman au nord de l'Èbre et les débuts de la reconquête aragonaise*, Paris, 2000.

Siraj, A., *L'image de la Tingitane: L'historiographie arabe médiévale et l'antiquité nord-africaine*, Rome, 1995.

Talbi, M., 'Le Christianisme maghrébine de la conquête musulmane à sa disparition: Une tentative d'explication', in M. Gervers and R. J. Bikazi (eds.), *Conversion and continuity: Indigenous Christian communities in Islamic lands, eight to eighteenth centuries*, Toronto, 1990, 313–51.

L'émirat aghlabide (184–296/800–909): Histoire politique, Paris, 1966.

Études d'histoire ifriqiyenne et de la civilisation musulmane médiévale, Tunis, 1982.

Vallejo, A., 'El proyecto urbanístico del estado califal: *Madīnat al-Zahrā'*', in R. López Guzmán (coord.), *La Arquitectura del Islam Occidental*, Madrid, 1995, 69–82.

Vallvé, J., *La división territorial de la España Musulmana*, Madrid, 1986.

Viguera, M. J., *Aragón Musulmán*, 2nd edn, Saragossa, 1988.

Wansbrough, J., 'On recomposing the Islamic history of North Africa', *JRAS* (1969), 161–70.

Wilkinson, J. C., 'The Ibāḍī imāma', *BSOAS*, 39, 3 (1976), 535–51.

Wolf, K. B., *Christian martyrs in Muslim Spain*, Cambridge, 1988.

Zerouki, B., *L'imamat de Tahart: Premier état Musulman du Maghreb (144–296 de l'hégire)*, Paris, 1987.

Chapter 15: Modern approaches to early Islamic history

Practical suggestions for further reading

Daniel, Norman, *Islam and the West: The making of an image*, Edinburgh, 1960; 2nd edn Oxford, 1993.

Donner, Fred M., *Narratives of Islamic origins: The beginnings of Islamic historical writing*, Princeton, 1998, introduction.

Goddard, Hugh, *A history of Muslim–Christian relations*, Edinburgh and Chicago, 2000.

Lockman, Zachary, *Contending visions of the Middle East: The history and politics of Orientalism*, Cambridge, 2004.

Said, Edward W., *Orientalism*, New York, 1978.

Southern, R. W., *Western views of Islam in the Middle Ages*, Cambridge, MA, 1962.

Tibawi, A. L., 'English-speaking Orientalists: A critique of their approach to Islam and Arab nationalism', *MW*, 53 (1963), 185–204, 298–313.

'On the Orientalists again', *MW*, 70 (1980), 56–61.

'Second critique of English-speaking Orientalists and their approach to Islam and the Arabs', *Islamic Quarterly*, 23 (1979), 3–54.

Tolan, John Victor, *Saracens: Islam in the medieval European imagination*, New York, 2002.

Waardenburg, Jacques, *Islam: Historical, social, and political perspectives*, Religion and Reason 40, Berlin and New York, 2002.

Islam and Christianity: Mutual perceptions since the mid-twentieth century, Leuven, 1998.

Watt, William Montgomery, *Muslim–Christian encounters: Perceptions and misperceptions*, London and New York, 1991.

Primary sources

Abū l-Fidā', Ismā'īl ibn 'Alī, *Mukhtaṣar ta'rīkh al-bashar*, trans. J. Reiske as *Annales Moslemici*, Leipzig, 1754.

al-Balādhurī, Aḥmad ibn Yaḥyā ibn Jābir, *Futūḥ al-buldān*, ed. M. J. de Goeje, Leiden, 1866.

Ibn Sa'd, Muḥammad, *al-Ṭabaqāt al-kabīr*, ed. E. Sachau *et al.*, 9 vols., Leiden, 1917–40.

al-Ṣan'ānī, 'Abd al-Razzāq ibn Hammām, *al-Muṣannaf*, ed. Ḥabīb al-Raḥmān al-A'ẓamī, 11 vols., n.p. and Beirut, 1970–2.

al-Ṭabarī, Abū Ja'far Muḥammad ibn Jarīr, *Kitāb al-rusul wa l-mulūk*, ed. M. J. de Goeje *et al.*, 15 vols. in 3 series, Leiden, 1879–1901; English translation: *The history of al-Ṭabarī*, 39 vols., Albany, 1985–99.

Secondary sources

Agha, Saleh Said, and Tarif Khalidi, '*Poetry and identity in the Umayyad age*', *al-Abhath*, 50–1 (2002–3), 55–120.

Andrae, Tor, 'Die Legenden von der Berufung Muḥammeds', *Le monde oriental*, 6 (1912), 5–18.

Die Person Muhammads in Lehre und Glauben seiner Gemeinde, Stockholm, 1918.

Becker, Carl Heinrich, 'The expansion of the Saracens', in H. M. Gwatkin *et al.* (eds.), *The Cambridge medieval history*, vol. II, Cambridge, 1913, chs. 11 and 12.

Bell, Richard, *The origin of Islam in its Christian environment*, London, 1926.

Bennett, Clinton, *Victorian images of Islam*, London, 1992.

Borrut, Antoine, 'Entre mémoire et pouvoir: L'espace syrien sous les derniers omeyyades et les premiers abbassides (v. 72–193/692–809)', Ph.D. thesis, Université de Paris I, 2007.

Bousquet, Georges Henri, 'Observations sur la nature et les causes de la conquête arabe', *SI*, 6 (1956), 37–52.

Brown, Peter, *The world of Late Antiquity, AD 150–750*, London, 1971.

Bulliet, Richard, 'Orientalism and medieval Islamic studies', in John Van Engen (ed.), *The past and future of medieval studies*, Notre Dame, 1994, 94–104.

Burgmer, Christoph (ed.), *Streit um den Koran: Die Luxenberg-Debatte: Standpünkte und Hintergründe*, n.p., 2004.

Caetani, Leone, *Studi di storia orientale*, 3 vols., Milan, 1911–14.

Cahen, Claude, *La Syrie du Nord à l'époque des croisades et la principauté d'Antioche*, Paris, 1940.

Calder, Norman, *Studies in early Muslim jurisprudence*, Oxford, 1993.

Cameron, Averil, and Lawrence I. Conrad (eds.), *The Byzantine and early Islamic Near East*, vol. I: *Problems in the literary source material*, Studies in Late Antiquity and Early Islam 1, Princeton, 1993.

Carlyle, Thomas, *On heroes, hero-worship, and the heroic in history*, London, 1841.

Casanova, Paul, *Mahomet et la fin du monde*, 3 vols., Paris, 1911–24.

Chabbi, Jacqueline, *Le seigneur des tribus: L'Islam de Mahomet*, Paris, 1997.

Conrad, Lawrence I., 'The conquest of Arwād: A source-critical study in the historiography of the medieval Near East', in A. Cameron and L. I. Conrad (eds.), *The Byzantine and early Islamic Near East*, vol. I: *Problems in the literary source material*, Studies in Late Antiquity and Early Islam 1, Princeton, 1993, 317–401.

Cook, David, *Studies in Muslim apocalyptic*, Princeton, 2002.

Cook, Michael, 'An early Islamic apocalyptic chronicle', *JNES*, 52 (1993), 25–9.

Crone, Patricia, *Meccan trade and the rise of Islam*, Princeton, 1987; repr. Piscataway, NJ, 2004.

Slaves on horses: The evolution of the Islamic polity, Cambridge, 1980.

Crone, Patricia, and Michael Cook, *Hagarism: The making of the Islamic world*, Cambridge, 1977.

Déscription de l'Égypte: Ou, recueil des observations et des recherches qui ont été faites en Égypte pendant l'expédition de l'armée française/publié par les ordres de Sa Majesté l'empereur Napoléon le Grand, 23 vols., Paris, 1809–29.

Donner, Fred M., 'Centralized authority and military autonomy in the early Islamic conquests', in A. Cameron (ed.), *The Byzantine and early Islamic Near East*, vol,.III: *States, resources, and armies*, Studies in Late Antiquity and Early Islam 1, Princeton, 1995, 337–60.

'From believers to Muslims: Confessional self-identity in the early Islamic community', *al-Abhath*, 50–1 (2002–3), 9–53.

'Modern nationalism and medieval Islamic history', *al-ʿUsur al-Wusta*, 13 (2001), 21–2.

Narratives of Islamic origins: The beginnings of Islamic historical writing, Princeton, 1998.

'Orientalists and the rise of Islam', in Sami A. Khasawnih (ed.), *Conference on Orientalism: Dialogue of Cultures, 22–24 October 2002*, Amman, 2004, 57–84.

'Piety and eschatology in early Khārijite poetry', in Ibrahim As-Saʿāfīn (ed.), *Fī miḥrāb al-maʿrifa: Festschrift for Iḥsān ʿAbbās*, Beirut, 1997, 13–19 (English section).

'The Qur'ān in recent scholarship: Challenges and desiderata', in Gabriel Said Reynolds (ed.), *Towards a new reading of the Qur'ān*, Abingdon, 2008, 29–50.

Dunlop, D. M., 'Some remarks on Weil's history of the caliphs', in Bernard Lewis and P. M. Holt (eds.), *Historians of the Middle East*, London, 1962, 315–29.

El-Hibri, Tayeb, *Reinterpreting Islamic historiography: Hārūn al-Rashīd and the narrative of the ʿAbbāsid caliphate*, Cambridge, 1999.

Fowden, Garth, *Empire to commonwealth: Consequences of monotheism in Antiquity*, Princeton, 1993.

Fück, J. W., 'Islam as an historical problem in European historiography since 1800', in B. Lewis and P. M. Holt (eds.), *Historians of the Middle East*, London, 1962, 303–14.

Geiger, Abraham, *Was hat Mohamed aus dem Judenthume aufgenommen*, Berlin, 1833.

Gibbon, Edward, *The history of the decline and fall of the Roman empire*, 6 vols., London, 1776–88.

de Goeje, Michael Jan, *Mémoire sur la conquête de la Syrie*, Mémoires d'histoire et de géographie orientales 2, 1st edn, Leiden, 1864.

Goldziher, Ignaz, *Muhammedanische Studien*, 2 vols., Halle, 1889–90; trans. S. M. Stern and C. R. Barber as *Muslim studies*, 2 vols., London, 1967–71.

Vorlesungen über den Islam, Heidelberg, 1910; trans. Andras and Ruth Hamori as *Introduction to Islamic theology and law*, Princeton, 1981.

Grimme, Hubert, *Mohamed*, 2 vols., Münster, 1892–5.

von Grunebaum, Gustave, 'The first expansion of Islam: Factors of thrust and containment', *Diogenes*, 54 (1966), 64–72.

Hawting, Gerald R., *The first dynasty of Islam: The Umayyad caliphate, AD 661–750*, Beckenham and Carbondale, 1987.

The idea of idolatry and the emergence of Islam: From polemic to history, Cambridge, 1999.

'The rise of Islam', in Youssef M. Choueiri (ed.), *A companion to the history of the Middle East*, Oxford, 2005, 9–27.

d'Herbelot, Barthélemy, *Bibliothèque orientale*, Paris, 1697.

Hitti, Philip, *The Arabs in history*, London, 1937.

Hourani, Albert H., *Islam in European thought*, Cambridge, 1991.

Huntington, Samuel P., *The clash of civilizations and the remaking of the world order*, New York, 1996.

Hurgronje, C. Snouck, *selected works*, ed. in French and English by G. H. Bousquet and J. Schacht, Leiden, 1957.

'Ibn Warraq' [pseud.] (ed.), *The quest for the historical Muhammad*, Amherst, NY, 2000.

Juynboll, Gautier, *Muslim tradition*, Cambridge, 1983.

Kister, M. J., '"A booth like the booth of Moses…": A study of an early *ḥadīth*', *BSOAS*, 25 (1962), 150–5.

Studies in jāhiliyya and early Islam, London, 1980.

Klier, Klaus, *Hālid und 'Umar: Quellenkritische Untersuchung zur Historiographie der frühislamischen Zeit*, Berlin, 1998.

Koren, Judith, and Yehuda Nevo, 'Methodological approaches to Islamic studies', *Der Islam*, 68 (1991), 87–107.

Lammens, Henri, *Fatima et les filles de Mahomet: Notes critiques pour l'étude de la Sîra*, Rome, 1912.

'La république marchande de la Mecque vers l'an 600 de notre ère', *Bulletin de l'Institute Égyptien*, 5, 4 (1910), 23–54.

Landau-Tasseron, Ella, 'Sayf ibn 'Umar in medieval and modern scholarship', *Der Islam*, 67 (1990), 1–26.

Lane, Edward W., *An account of the manners and customs of the modern Egyptians*, London, 1836.

Lassner, Jacob, *Islamic revolution and historical memory: An inquiry into the art of 'Abbāsid apologetics*, AOS Series 66, New Haven, 1986.

Lecker, Michael, *The 'Constitution of Medina': Muḥammad's first legal document*, Princeton, 2004.

Leder, Stefan, *Das Korpus al-Haitam ibn 'Adī (st. 207/822): Herkunft, Überlieferung, Gestalt früher Texte der ahbār-Literatur*, Frankfurt, 1991.

Lester, Toby, 'What is the Koran?', *The Atlantic Monthly* (January 1999), 43–56.

Lewis, Bernard, *The Arabs in history*, London, 1958.

'The roots of Muslim rage', *The Atlantic Monthly* (September 1990), 47–60.

Lewis, Bernard, and Peter M. Holt (eds.), *Historians of the Middle East*, London, 1962.

Lüling, Günter, *Über den Ur-Qur'ān: Ansätze zur Rekonstruktion vorislamischer christlicher Strophenlieder im Qur'ān*, Erlangen, 1974.

Luxenberg, Christoph [pseud.], *Die syro-aramäische Lesart des Koran: Ein Beitrag zur Entschlüsselung der Koransprache*, Berlin, 2000.

Madelung, Wilferd, 'Apocalyptic prophecies in Ḥimṣ in the Umayyad age', *JSS*, 31 (1986), 141–85.

The succession to Muḥammad: A study of the early caliphate, Cambridge, 1997.

Motzki, Harald, *Die Anfänge der islamischen Jurisprudenz*, Stuttgart, 1991.

Muir, Sir William, *The life of Muhammad*, Edinburgh, 1861.

Nevo, Yehuda D., and Judith Koren, *Crossroads to Islam: The origins of the Arab religion and the Arab state*, Amherst, NY, 2003.

'The origins of the Muslim descriptions of the jāhilī Meccan sanctuary', *JNES*, 49 (1990), 23–44.

Nöldeke, Theodor, *Geschichte des Qorāns*, Göttingen, 1860; 2nd rev. edn ed. F. Schwally and G. Bergsträsser, 3 vols., Leipzig, 1909–38.

Nöldeke, Theodor, *Orientalische Skizzen*, Berlin, 1892.

Noth, Albrecht, 'Früher Islam', in Ulrich Haarmann *et al.* (eds.), *Geschichte der arabischen Welt*, Munich, 1987, 11–101.

'Iṣfahān-Nihāwand: Eine quellenkritische Studie zur frühislamischen Historiographie', *ZDMG*, 118 (1968), 274–96.

Quellenkritische Untersuchungen zu Themen, Formen, und Tendenzen frühislamischer Geschichtsüberlieferung, Bonn, 1973; rev. edn (with Lawrence I. Conrad), trans. Michael Bonner as *The early Arabic historical tradition*, Princeton, 1994.

Petersen, Erling Ladewig, *ʿAlī and Muʿāwiya in early Arabic tradition: Studies on the genesis and growth of Islamic historical writing until the end of the ninth century*, 2nd edn, Odense, 1974 [Copenhagen, 1964].

de Prémare, Alfred-Louis, *Les fondations de l'Islam: Entre écriture et histoire*, Paris, 2002.

Qureshi, Emran, and Michael A. Sells (eds.), *The new Crusades: Constructing the Muslim enemy*, New York, 2003.

Recueil des historiens des croisades, Paris, 1869–1906.

Retsö, Jan, *The Arabs in Antiquity*, London and New York, 2003.

Robinson, Chase F., 'The conquest of Khūzistān: A historiographical reassessment', *BSOAS*, 67 (2004), 14–39.

Rodinson, Maxime, *La mystique de l'Islam*, Paris, 1980; trans. Roger Veinus as *Europe and the mystique of Islam*, Seattle, 1987.

Rosenthal, Franz, *Das Fortleben der Antike im Islam*, Zurich, 1965; trans. Emile and Jenny Marmorstein as *The classical heritage in Islam*, Berkeley, 1975.

Rubin, Uri, *The eye of the beholder: The life of Muḥammad as viewed by the early Muslims: A textual analysis*, Princeton, 1995.

'Morning and evening prayers in Islam', *JSAI*, 10 (1987), 40–64.

Schacht, Joseph, *The origins of Muhammadan jurisprudence*, Oxford, 1950.

Schoeler, Gregor, *Écrire et transmettre dans les débuts de l'Islam*, Paris, 2002.

'Die Frage der schriftlichen oder mündlichen Überlieferung der Wissenschaften in frühen Islam', *Der Islam*, 62 (1985), 201–30.

Sellheim, Rudolf, 'Abū ʿAlī al-Qālī: Zum Problem mündlicher und schriftlicher Überlieferung am Beispiel von Sprichwörtersammlungen', in H. R. Roemer and A. Noth (eds.), *Studien zur Geschichte und Kultur des vorderen Orients: Festschrift für Bertold Spuler*, Leiden, 1981, 362–74.

Sezgin, Fuat, *Geschichte des arabischen Schrifttums*, vol. I, Leiden, 1967.

Shaban, M. A., *Islamic history: A new interpretation*, 2 vols., Cambridge, 1971.

Sharon, Moshe, 'The birth of Islam in the Holy Land', in Moshe Sharon (ed.), *Pillars of smoke and fire: The Holy Land in history and thought*, Johannesburg, 1988, 225–35.
Shoshan, Boaz, *Poetics of Islamic historiography: Deconstructing Ṭabarī's* History, Leiden, 2004.
Steinschneider, M., *al-Farābī*, Mémoires de l'Academie Impériale de Sciences de Saint-Petersbourg 7, 8, 4, St Petersburg, 1869.
Torrey, Charles Cutler, *The Jewish foundations of Islam*, New York, 1933.
Waldman, Marilyn Robinson, 'New approaches to "biblical" materials in the Qur'ān', *MW*, 75 (1985), 1–16.
Wansbrough, John, *Qur'anic studies*, Oxford, 1977.
The sectarian milieu: Content and composition of Islamic salvation history, Oxford, 1978.
Watt, William Montgomery, *Muḥammad at Mecca*, Oxford, 1953.
Muḥammad at Medina, Oxford, 1956.
Muhammad, Prophet and statesman, Oxford, 1961.
Wellhausen, Julius, *Das arabische Reich und sein Sturz*, Berlin, 1902; trans. Margaret Graham Weir as *The Arab kingdom and its fall*, Calcutta, 1927.
Muhammad in Medina, daß ist Vakidi's Kitab al-Maghazi in verkürzter deutscher Wiedergabe herausgegeben, Berlin, 1882.
Prolegomena zur ältesten Geschichte des Islams, Skizzen und Vorarbeiten 6, Berlin, 1899.

Chapter 16: Numismatics

Practical suggestions for further reading

Bacharach, Jere L., *Islamic history through coins: An analysis and catalogue of tenth-century Ikhshidid coinage*, Cairo, 2006.
Broome, Michael, *A handbook of Islamic coins*, London, 1985.
Brunschvig, Robert, 'Conceptions monétaires chez les juristes musulmanes (VIIIe–XIIIe siècles)', *Arabica*, 14 (1967), 113–43.
Cipolla, Carlo M., *Money, prices and civilization in the Mediterranean world*, Princeton, 1956.
Heidemann, Stefan, 'Economic growth and currency in Ayyūbid Palestine', in Robert Hillenbrand (ed.), *Ayyūbid Jerusalem: The Holy City in context*, 1187–1250, London, 2009, 275–99.
'Settlement patterns, economic development and archaeological coin finds in Bilād aš-Šām: The case of the Diyār Muḍar', in K. Bartl and A. Moaz (eds.), *Residences, castles, settlements: Transformation processes from Late Antiquity to early Islam in Bilad al-Sham. Proceedings of the International Conference held at Damascus, 5–9 November 2006*, Orient-Archäologie 24, Rahden, 2009, 489–513.
(ed.), *Islamische Numismatik in Deutschland: Eine Bestandsaufnahme*, Jenaer Beiträge zum Vorderen Orient 2, Wiesbaden, 2000.
Johns, Jeremy, 'Archaeology and the history of early Islam: The first seventy years', *JESHO*, 46 (2003), 411–36.
Noonan, Thomas S., 'Early 'Abbāsid mint output', *JESHO*, 29, (1986), 113–75.
'The start of the silver crisis in Islam: A comparative study of Central Asia and the Iberian peninsula', in Mário Gomes Marques and D. Michael Metcalf (eds.), *Problems of medieval coinage in the Iberian area*, vol. III, Santarém, 1988, 119–44.

Phillips, Marcus, 'Currency in seventh-century Syria as a historical source', *Byzantine and Modern Greek Studies*, 28 (2004), 13–31.

Primary sources

Album, Stephen, *Arabia and East Africa*, Sylloge of Islamic coins in the Ashmolean 10, Oxford, 1999.

A checklist of Islamic coins, 2nd edn, Santa Rosa, 1998.

Iran after the Mongol invasion, Sylloge of Islamic coins in the Ashmolean 9, Oxford, 2001.

Album, Stephen, and Tony Goodwin, *The pre-reform coinage of the early Islamic period*, Sylloge of Islamic coins in the Ashmolean 1, London, 2002.

Bone, Harry, 'The administration of Umayyad Syria: The evidence of the copper coins', Ph.D. thesis, Princeton University, 2000.

Diler, Ömer, *Islamic mints*, 3 vols., Istanbul, 2009.

Djaparidze, Gotcha I., 'Nouvelles additions à l'ouvrage de Zambaur: Die Münzprägungen des Islams', *Bulletin d'Etudes Orientales*, 32–3 (1980–1), 89–97.

Goodwin, Tony, *Arab-Byzantine coinage*, Study in the Khalili Collection 4, London, 2005.

Gyselen, Rika, *Arab-Sasanian copper coinage*, Österreichische Akademie der Wissenschaften, Philosophisch-Historische Klasse, Denkschriften 284, Veröffentlichungen der numismatischen Kommission 34, Vienna, 2000.

Ilisch, Lutz, *Sylloge Numorum Arabicorum Tübingen: Palästina IVa Bilād aš-Šām*, Tübingen, 1993.

International Numismatic Commission, *A survey of numismatic research* 1972–1977, ed. Robert A. G. Carson *et al.*, Berne, 1979.

A survey of numismatic research 1978–1984, ed. Martin Price, London, 1986.

A survey of numismatic research 1985–1990, ed. Tony Hackens *et al.*, Brussels, 1991.

A survey of numismatic research 1990–1995, ed. Cécile Morrisson and Bernd Kluge, Berlin, 1997.

A survey of numismatic research 1996–2001, ed. Carmen Alfaro, Madrid, 2003.

Klat, Michel, *Catalogue of the post-reform dirhams: The Umayyad dynasty*, London, 2002.

Kochnev, Boris and Michael Fedorov, *Sylloge Numorum Arabicorum, Buḫārā*, Samarqand Mittelasien, 25a, Berlin, 2008.

Leimus, Ivar, *Sylloge of Islamic coins Estonian public collections*, Thesaurus historiae 2, Tallinn, 2007.

Lowick, Nicholas, and Elisabeth Savage, *Early 'Abbāsid coinage: A type catalogue 132–218 H/AD 750–833. A posthumous work by Nicholas Lowick*, ed. Elisabeth Savage, distributed manuscript, London, 1996.

Malek, Hodge Mehdi, *The Dābūyid Ispahbads and early 'Abbāsid governors of Ṭabaristān: History and numismatics*, Royal Numismatic Society Special Publication 39, London, 2004.

Mayer, Leo Ari, *The bibliography of Moslem numismatics India excepted*, Oriental Translation Fund 35, London, 1954.

Mayer, Tobias, *Sylloge der Münzen des Kaukasus und Osteuropas im Orientalischen Münzkabinett Jena*, Orientalisches Münzkabinett Jena 1, Wiesbaden, 2005.

Sylloge Numorum Arabicorum: Nord- und Ostzentralasien XVb, Mittelasien II, Tübingen, 1998.

Miles, Georges Carpenter, 'Additions to Zambaur's Münzprägungen des Islams', *American Numismatics Society Museum Notes*, 12 (1971), 229–33.
Nicol, Norman Douglas, *A corpus of Fāṭimid coins*, Trieste, 2006.
The Egyptian dynasties, Sylloge of Islamic coins in the Ashmolean 6, Oxford, 2007.
Schwarz, Florian, *Sylloge Numorum Arabicorum Tübingen: Balḫ und die Landschaften am obereren Oxus XIVc Ḫurāsān III*, Tübingen, 2002.
Sylloge Numorum Arabicorum Tübingen, Ġazna/Kābul XIV ad Ḫurāsān IV, Tübingen and Berlin, 1995.
Sears, Stuart, 'A monetary history of Iraq and Iran, ca. CE 500 to 750', Ph.D. thesis, University of Chicago, 1997.
Shammā, Samīr, *A catalogue of 'Abbāsid copper coins: Thabat al-fulūs al-'abbāsiyya*, London, 1998.
Treadwell, Luke, *Buyid coinage: A die corpus (322–445 AH)*, Oxford, 2001.
von Zambaur, Eduard, *Die Münzprägung des Islams*, ed. Peter Jaeckel, Wiesbaden, 1968.

Secondary sources

Balaguer Prunés, Anna M., *Las émisiones transicionales árabe-musulmanas de Hispania*, Barcelona, 1976.
Balog, Paul, 'Fāṭimid glass jetons: Token currency or coin-weights?', *JESHO*, 24 (1981), 93–109.
Bates, Michael L., 'The dirham mint of the northern provinces of the Umayyad caliphate', *Armenian Numismatic Journal*, 15 (1989), 89–111.
The expression of sovereignty in the Abbasid caliphate, 218–334 H/833–946 CE (forthcoming).
'The function of Fāṭimid and Ayyūbid glass weights', *JESHO*, 24 (1981), 63–92.
'History, geography and numismatics in the first century of Islamic coinage', *Schweizerische Numismatische Rundschau*, 65 (1986), 231–61.
'Khurāsānī revolutionaries and al-Mahdī's title', in Farhad Daftary and Josef W. Meri (eds.), *Culture and memory in medieval Islam: Essays in honour of Wilferd Madelung*, London and New York, 2003, 279–317.
DeShazo, Alan S., and Michael L. Bates, 'The Umayyad governors of al-'Irāq and the changing annulet patterns on their dirhams', *Numismatic Chronicle*, 14 (1974), 110–18.
El-Hibri, Tayyeb, 'Coinage reform under the 'Abbāsid caliph al-Ma'mūn', *JESHO*, 36 (1993), 58–83.
Foss, Clive, *Arab-Byzantine coins: An introduction, with a catalogue of the Dumbarton Oaks Collection*, Cambridge, MA, 2009.
Heidemann, Stefan, 'The development of the representation of the early Islamic empire and its religion on coin imagery', in Angelika Neuwirth, Nicolai Sinai and Michael Marx (eds.), *The Qur'an in context: Historical and literary investigations into the Qur'anic milieu*, Leiden, 2009, 149–95.
'Die Entwicklung der Methoden in der Islamischen Numismatik im 18. Jahrhundert: War Johann Jacob Reiske ihr Begründer?', in Hans-Georg Ebert and Thoralf Hanstein (eds.), *Johann Jacob Reiske, Persönlichkeit und Wirkung*, Beiträge zur Leipziger Universitäts- und Wissenschaftsgeschichte, series B, no. 6, Leipzig, 2006, 147–202.

'Die frühe Münzprägung von ar-Raqqa/ar-Rāfiqa als Dokumente zur Geschichte der Stadt', in Stefan Heidemann and Andrea Becker (eds.), *Raqqa, vol. II: Die islamische Stadt*, Mainz, 2003, 115–40.

'Der Kleingeldumlauf in der Ǧazīra in früh-ʿabbāsidischer Zeit und die Münzemissionen aus al-Kūfa', in Stefan Heidemann and Andrea Becker (eds.), *Raqqa, vol. II: Die islamische Stadt*, Mainz, 2003, 141–60.

'The merger of two currency zones in early Islam: The Byzantine and Sasanian impact on the circulation in former Byzantine Syria and northern Mesopotamia', *Iran*, 36 (1998), 95–112.

'Das Projekt, die Sylloge, der Bestand', in Tobias Mayer, *Sylloge der Münzen des Kaukasus und Osteuropas im Orientalischen Münzkabinett Jena*, Orientalisches Münzkabinett Jena, 1, Wiesbaden, 2005, xi–xxii.

Die Renaissance der Städte in Nordsyrien und Nordmesopotamien: Städtische Entwicklung und wirtschaftliche Bedingungen in ar-Raqqa und Ḥarrān von der Zeit der beduinischen Vorherrschaft bis zu den Seldschuken, Islamic History and Civilization, Studies and Texts 40, Leiden, 2002.

Ilisch, Lutz, 'Die Kupferprägung Nordmesopotamiens unter Hārūn ar-Rašīd und seinen Söhnen (786–842 AD)', in International Association of Professional Numismatists (eds.), *Numismatics: Witness to history*, IAPN publication 8, Basle, 1986, 101–21.

'The Muhammad-drachms and their relation to Umayyad Syria and northern Mesopotamia', *Supplement of the Journal of the Oriental Numismatic Society*, 193 (Autumn 2007), 17–24.

Review of *American Journal of Numismatics, 1, Der Islam*, 69 (1992), 381–2.

'Stempelveränderungen an islamischen Münzen des Mittelalters als Quelle zur Münzstättenorganisation', in Tony Hackens and Raymond Weiller (eds.), *Actes du 9ème congrès international de numismatique. Berne, Septembre 1979: Proceedings of the 9th International Congress of Numismatics, Berne, September 1979*, Louvain-la Neuve and Luxemburg, 1982, 777–83, pl. 93–4.

'Whole and fragmented dirhams in Near Eastern hoards', in Kenneth Jonsson and Britta Malmer (eds.), *Sigtuna Papers: Proceedings of the Sigtuna symposium on Viking-age coinage 1–4 June 1989, Stockholm*, Commentationes de nummis saeculorum in Suecia repertis, Nova Series 6, London, 1990, 121–8.

Jamil, Nadia, 'Caliph and Quṭb: Poetry as a source for interpreting the transformation of the Byzantine cross on steps on Umayyad coinage', in Jeremy Johns (ed.), *Bayt al-Maqdis: Jerusalem and Early Islam*, Oxford Studies in Islamic Art 9, part 2, Oxford, 1999, 11–57.

Mochiri, Malek Iraj, 'A Pahlavi forerunner of the Umayyad reformed coinage', *JRAS* (1981), 168–72.

Morony, Michael G., 'Economic boundaries? Late Antiquity and early Islam', *JESHO*, 47 (2004), 166–94.

Nicol, Norman Douglas, 'Early ʿAbbāsid administration in the central and eastern provinces, 132–218 AH/750–833 AD', Ph.D. thesis, University of Washington, 1979.

Oddy, Andrew, 'Whither Arab-Byzantine numismatics? A review of fifty years' research', *Byzantine and Modern Greek Studies*, 28 (2004), 121–52.

Pottier, Henri, *Le monnayage de la Syrie sous l'occupation perse (610–630)/Coinage in Syria under Persian rule (610–630)*, Cahiers Ernest Babelon 9, Paris, 2004.

Pottier, Henri, Ingrid Schulze and Wolfgang Schulze, 'Pseudo-Byzantine coinage in Syria under Arab rule (638–*c.* 670): Classification and dating', *Revue numismatique belge*, 154 (2008), 87–155.
Qūchānī, 'Abd Allāh, 'The territory of Abū al-Nadjm Badr b. Ḥasanūyah based on his coins', *Iranian Journal of Archaeology and History*, 8, 2 (1994), 46–65 (in Persian).
Robinson, Chase F., *Empire and elites after the Muslim conquest: The transformation of northern Mesopotamia*, Cambridge Studies in Islamic Civilization, Cambridge, 2000.
Sears, Stuart, 'A hybrid imitation of early Muslim coinage struck in Sijistan by Abū Bardhā'a', *American Journal of Numismatics*, 1 (1989), 137–69.
'A monetary history of Iraq and Iran, ca. CE 500 to 750', Ph.D. thesis, University of Chicago, 1997.
'The Sasanian style drachms of Sistan', *Yarmouk Numismatics*, 11 (1999), 18–28.
Shammā, Samīr, *Aḥdāth 'aṣr al-Ma'mūn kamā tarwīhā al-nuqūd*, Irbid, 1995.
Treadwell, W. Luke, *The chronology of the pre-reform copper coinage of early Islamic Syria*, Supplement to Oriental Numismatic Society Newsletter 162, London, 2000.
'"Mihrab and 'Anaza" or "sacrum and spear"? A reconsideration of an early Marwanid silver drachm', *Muqarnas*, 30 (2005), 1–28.
'Notes on the mint at Samarra', in Chase Robinson (ed.), *A medieval Islamic city reconsidered: An interdisciplinary approach to Samarra*, Oxford Studies in Islamic Art 14, Oxford, 2001, 141–56.
'The "orans" drachms of Bishr ibn Marwān and the figural coinage of the early Marwanid period', in Jeremy Johns (ed.), *Bayt al-Maqdis: Jerusalem and Early Islam*, Oxford Studies in Islamic Art 9, part 2, Oxford, 1999, 223–69.
Udovitch, Avram L., *Partnership and profit in medieval Islam*, Princeton, 1970.
Vasmer, Richard, 'Zur Chronologie der Gâstāniden und Sallāriden', *Islamica*, 3 (1927), 165–86, 482–5.

Chapter 17: Archaeology and material culture

Practical suggestions for further reading

Creswell, K., *A short account of early Muslim architecture*, rev. and suppl. James Allan, Aldershot, 1989.
Hodges, Richard, and David Whitehouse, *Mohammed, Charlemagne and the origins of Europe: Archaeology and the Pirenne thesis*, London, 1983.
Hoyland, Robert, 'New documentary texts and the early Islamic state', *BSOAS*, 69, 3 (2006), 395–416.
Johns, Jeremy, 'Archaeology and the history of early Islam: The first seventy years', *JESHO*, 46, 4 (2003), 411–36.
Kennedy, Hugh, 'From *polis* to *madina*: Urban change in Late Antique and early Islamic Syria', *Past and Present*, 106 (February 1985), 3–27.
Kennet, Derek, 'On the eve of Islam: Archaeological evidence from eastern Arabia', *Antiquity*, 79 (2005), 107–18.
King, Geoffrey, and Averil Cameron (eds.), *The Byzantine and early Islamic Near East*, vol. II: *Land use and settlement patterns*, Studies in Late Antiquity and Early Islam 1, Princeton, 1994.

Secondary sources

Adams, Robert, *Land behind Baghdad: A history of settlement on the Diyala plains*, Chicago and London, 1965.

Almagro, Antonio, and Pedro Jiménez, 'The Umayyad mosque on the citadel of Amman', *Annual of the Department of Antiquities of Jordan*, 44 (2000), 459–76.

Blackburn, M., and D. M. Metcalf (eds.), *Viking-age coinage in northern lands*, BAR International Series 122, Oxford, 1981.

Daiber, Verena, and Andrea Becker (eds.), *Raqqa III: Baudenkmäler und Paläste I*, Mainz am Rhein, 2004.

Daryaee, Touraj, 'The Persian Gulf trade in Late Antiquity', *Journal of World History*, 14, 1 (March 2003), 1–16.

Farooq, Abdul Aziz, 'Excavations at Mansurah (13th season)', *Pakistan Archaeology*, 10–12 (1974–86), 3–35.

Finster, Barbara, 'Die Reiseroute Kufa–Saʿūdī-Arabien in frühislamische Zeit', *Baghdader Mitteilungen*, 9 (1978), 53–91.

Gayraud, Roland-Pierre, 'Fostat: Évolution d'une capitale arabe du VIIe au XIIe siècle d'après les fouilles d'Istabl ʿAntar', in Roland-Pierre Gayraud (ed.), *Colloque international d'archéologie islamique, IFAO, Le Caire, 3–7 février 1993*, Textes arabes et études islamiques 36, Cairo, 1999, 435–60.

Gelichi, Sauro, and Marco Milanese, 'Problems in the transition toward the medieval in Ifriqiya: First results from the archaeological excavations at Uchi Maius (Teboursouk, Béja)', in M. Khanoussi, P. Ruggieri and C. Vismara (eds.), *L'Africa Romana: Atti del XII Convegno di Studio*, Sassari, 1998, 457–84.

Genequand, Denis, 'Maʿān, an early Islamic settlement in southern Jordan: Preliminary report on the survey in 2002', *Annual of the Department of Antiquities of Jordan*, 47 (2003), 25–35.

'Umayyad castles: The shift from Late Antique military architecture to early Islamic palatial building', in Hugh Kennedy (ed.), *Muslim military architecture in Greater Syria: From the coming of Islam to the Ottoman Period*, History of Warfare 35, Leiden and Boston, 2006, 3–25.

Glick, Thomas, 'Hydraulic technology in al-Andalus', in S. Jayyusi (ed.), *The legacy of Muslim Spain*, Leiden, 1992, 974–86.

Hearn, Maxwell, and Judith Smith (eds.), *Arts of the Sung and Yüan*, New York, 1996.

Heidemann, Stefan, 'The history of the industrial and commercial area of ʿAbbāsid al-Raqqa, called *al-Raqqa al-Muḥtariqa*', *BSOAS*, 69, 1 (2006), 33–52.

Henderson, Julian, *et al.*, 'Experiment and innovation: Early Islamic industry at al-Raqqa, Syria', *Antiquity*, 79 (2005), 130–45.

Johns, Jeremy, 'The "House of the Prophet" and the concept of the mosque', in Jeremy Johns (ed.), *Bayt al-Maqdis: Jerusalem and early Islam*, Oxford Studies in Islamic Art 9, part 2, Oxford, 1999, 59–112.

Karev, Yury, 'Samarqand in the eighth century: The evidence of transformation', in Donald Whitcomb (ed.), *Changing social identity with the spread of Islam: Archaeological perspectives*, Oriental Institute Seminars 1, Chicago, 2004, 51–66.

Kennet, Derek, *Sasanian and Islamic pottery from Ras al-Khaimah: Classification, chronology and analysis of trade in the western Indian Ocean*, BAR International Series 1248, Oxford, 2004.

Khamis, Elias, 'Two wall mosaic inscriptions from the Umayyad market place in Bet Shean/Baysān', *BSOAS*, 64 (2001), 159–76.

Khan, F., *Banbhore: A preliminary report on the recent archaeological excavations at Banbhore*, 4th edn, Karachi, 1976.

King, Geoffrey, 'The distribution of sites and routes in the Jordanian and Syrian deserts', *Proceedings of the Seminar for Arabian Studies*, 20 (1987), 91–105.

Kromann, Anne, and Else Roesdahl, 'The Vikings and the Islamic lands', in K. von Folsach *et al.* (eds.), *The Arabian journey: Danish connections with the Islamic world over a thousand years*, Aarhus, 1996, 9–17.

Leone, Anna, 'Late Antique North Africa: Production and changing use of buildings in urban areas', *al-Masāq*, 15, 1 (March, 2003), 21–33.

Mason, Robert, *Shine like the sun: Lustre-painted and associated pottery from the medieval Middle East*, Toronto and Costa Mesa, 2004.

McNicoll, Anthony, *et al.*, *Pella in Jordan*, 2 vols., Mediterranean Archaeology Supplements 2, Sydney, 1992.

Northedge, Alastair, *The historical topography of Samarra*, Samarra Studies 1, London, 2005.

Studies on Roman and Islamic ʿAmmān, vol. I: *History, site and architecture*, British Academy Monographs in Archaeology 3, Oxford and New York, 1992.

Rashid, Saʿd ibn ʿAbd al-ʿAzīz, *al-Rabadhah: A portrait of early Islamic civilization in Saudi Arabia*, Harlow, 1986.

Rawson, Jessica, Michael Tite and M. Hughes, 'The export of Tang sancai wares: Some recent research', *Transactions of the Oriental Ceramics Society*, 52 (1987–8), 39–61.

Sack, Dorothée, *Resafa IV: Die Grosse Moschee von Resafa-Ruṣāfat Hisām*, Mainz, 1996.

Safar, Fuad, *Wâsiṭ: The sixth season's excavations*, Cairo, 1945.

Vogt, C., *et al.*, 'Notes on some of the Abbasid amphorae of Istabl ʿAntar-Fustat (Egypt)', *BASOR*, 326 (2002), 65–80.

Watson, Andrew, *Agricultural innovation in the early Islamic world: The diffusion of crops and farming techniques*, Cambridge Studies in Islamic Civilization, Cambridge, 1983.

Whitehouse, David, 'Chinese stoneware from Siraf: The earliest finds', in N. Hammond (ed.), *South Asian archaeology*, Park Ridge, NJ, 1973, 241–55.

'East Africa and the maritime trade of the Indian Ocean, AD 800–1500', in B. Amoretti (ed.), *Islam in East Africa: New sources*, Rome, 2001, 411–24.

Siraf III: The congregational mosque and other mosques from the ninth to the twelfth centuries, London, 1980.

Wilkinson, J., 'Darb Zubayda architectural documentation program. B. Darb Zubayda-1979: The water resources', *Atlal*, 4 (1980), 51–68.

Wilkinson, T. J., 'Sohar ancient fields project: Interim report no. 1', *Journal of Oman Studies*, 1 (1975), 159–64.

Williamson, Andrew, 'Regional distribution of mediaeval Persian pottery in the light of recent investigations', in James Allan and Caroline Roberts (eds.), *Syria and Iran: Three studies in medieval ceramics*, Oxford Studies in Islamic Art 4, Oxford, 1987, 11– 22.

www.islamic-awareness.org/History/Islam/Inscriptions/, accessed 15 April 2007.

Conclusion: From formative Islam to classical Islam

Practical suggestions for further reading

Calder, N., *Studies in early Muslim jurisprudence*, Oxford, 1993.

Cooperson, M., and S. Toorawa (eds.), *Arabic literary culture, 500–925, Dictionary of Literary Biography*, vol. CCCXI, Detroit, 2005.

Crone, P., *Medieval Islamic political thought*, Edinburgh, 2004.

Crone, P., and M. Hinds, *God's caliph: Religious authority in the first centuries of Islam*, Cambridge, 1986.

Donner, F. M., *Narratives of Islamic origins: The beginnings of Islamic historical writing*, Princeton, 1998.

van Ess, J., *Theologie und Gesellschaft im 2. und 3. Jahrhundert Hidschra: Eine Geschichte des religiösen Denkens im frühen Islam*, 6 vols., Berlin, 1991–7.

Gutas, D., *Greek thought, Arabic culture: The Graeco-Arabic translation movement in Baghdad and early ʿAbbāsid society (2nd–4th/8th–10th centuries)*, London and New York, 1998.

Halm, H., *Shiʿism*, 2nd edn, Edinburgh, 2004.

Loveday, H., *Islamic paper: A study of the ancient craft*, London, 2001.

Melchert, C., *The formation of the Sunni schools of law, 9th–10th centuries CE*, Leiden, 1997.

Robinson, C. F., *Islamic historiography*, Cambridge, 2003.

Secondary sources

Agha, S. S., 'A viewpoint on the Murjiʾa in the Umayyad period: Evolution through application', *Journal of Islamic Studies*, 8 (1997), 1–42.

Cook, M., 'Activism and quietism in Islam: The case of the early Murjiʾa', in A. Cudsi and A. E. Dessouki (eds.), *Islam and power*, London, 1981, 15–23.

'ʿAnan and Islam: The origins of Karaite scripturalism', *JSAI*, 9 (1987), 169–82.

'Early Islamic dietary law', *JSAI*, 7 (1986), 217–77.

Crone, P., 'Jāhilī and Jewish law: The *qasāma*', *JSAI*, 4 (1984), 153–201.

Roman, provincial and Islamic law: The origins of the patronate, Cambridge, 1987.

Friedmann, Y., *Tolerance and coercion in Islam: Interfaith relations in the Muslim tradition*, Cambridge, 2003.

Graham, W., 'Traditionalism in Islam: An essay in interpretation', *Journal of Interdisciplinary History*, 23 (1993), 495–522.

Hurvitz, N., *The formation of Ḥanbalism: Piety into power*, London, 2002.

Juynboll, G. H. A., 'Some new ideas on the development of *sunna* as a technical term in early Islam', *JSAI*, 10 (1987), 97–118.

Kennedy, H., 'Central government and provincial elites in the early ʿAbbāsid caliphate', *BSOAS*, 44 (1981), 26–38.

Kohlberg, E., 'Some Imāmī Shīʿī views on the *ṣaḥāba*', *JSAI*, 5 (1984), 143–75.

Madelung, W., 'The early Murjiʾa in Khurāsān and Transoxiana and the spread of Ḥanafism', *Der Islam*, 59 (1982), 32–9.

McMullen, D., *State and society in T'ang China*, Cambridge, 1989.

Melchert, C., *Ahmad ibn Hanbal*, Oxford, 2006.

Mitter, U., 'Origin and development of the Islamic patronate', in J. Nawas and M. Bernards (eds.), *Patronate and patronage in early and classical Islam*, Leiden, 2005, 70–133.

Modarressi, H., *Crisis and consolidation in the formative period of Shīʿite Islam: Abū Jaʿfar ibn Qiba al-Rāzī and his contribution to Imāmite Shīʿite thought*, Princeton, 1993.
'Early debates on the integrity of the Qurʾān: A brief survey', *SI*, 77 (1993), 5–39.
Motzki, H., 'The role of non-Arab converts in the development of early Islamic law', *Islamic Law and Society*, 6 (1999), 293–317.
Nawas, J., 'A profile of the *mawālī* ʿ*ulamā*ʾ', in J. Nawas and M. Bernards (eds.), *Patronate and patronage in early and classical Islam*, Leiden, 2005, 454–80.
Rissanen, S., *Theological encounter of Oriental Christians with Islam during early Abbasid rule*, Turku, 1993.
Smith, W. C., 'Arkān', in D. P. Little (ed.), *Essays on Islamic civilization presented to Niyazi Berkes*, Leiden, 1976, 303–16.
Toorawa, S., *Ibn Abī Ṭāhir Ṭayfūr and Arabic writerly culture*, London and New York, 2005.

Index

NOTE. Locators in italics refer to the Figures.

Lightning Source UK Ltd.
Milton Keynes UK
UKHW021021160919
349768UK00013BA/189/P

9 780521 838238